Organizational Behaviour

From Andrzej
To Janet, Sophie and Gregory

From Dave
To Lesley, Andrew and Mairi

Pearson Education Limited
Edinburgh Gate
Harlow
Essex CM20 2JE
England

and Associated Companies throughout the world

Visit us on the World Wide Web at:
http://www.pearsoneduc.com

First published by Prentice Hall International (UK) Ltd, 1985
Second edition by Prentice Hall International (UK) Ltd, 1991
Third edition by Prentice Hall Europe, 1997
Fourth edition 2001

© Andrzej Huczynski and David Buchanan 2001

ISBN 0 273 65102 1

British Library Cataloguing-in-Publication Data
A catalogue record for this book is available from the British Library

Library of Congress Cataloging-in-Publication Data

Huczynski, Andrzej.
   Organizational behaviour: an introductory text/Andrzej Huczynski, David
   Buchanan.– 4th ed.
      p. cm.
   Buchanan's name appears first on the earlier edition.
   Includes bibliographical references and index.
   ISBN 0 273 65102 1
      1. Organizational behavior. I. Buchanan, David A. II. Title.

   HD58.7 .H83 2000
   302.3′5–dc21

                                        00–051660

10 9 8 7 6 5 4 3
06 05 04 03 02

Typeset by 3
Printed and bound by Rotolito Lombarda, Italy

Andrzej Huczynski

Department of Business and Management, University of Glasgow

David Buchanan

School of Business, De Montfort University, Leicester

Organizational Behaviour

An introductory text

Fourth Edition

FINANCIAL TIMES
Prentice Hall

An imprint of **Pearson Education**

Harlow, England · London · New York · Reading, Massachusetts · San Francisco
Toronto · Don Mills, Ontario · Sydney · Tokyo · Singapore · Hong Kong · Seoul
Taipei · Cape Town · Madrid · Mexico City · Amsterdam · Munich · Paris · Milan

Outline contents

Full contents

Acknowledgements

A large number of friends, colleagues and students have contributed their ideas, criticisms and advice to the development of this text. Our special thanks in this regard are therefore extended to Ian Beardwell, Phil Beaumont, Martin Beirne, Jos Benders, Bill Birrell, Carol Boyd, Alan Bryman, Sue Bryman, Lesley Buchanan, Andrew Burnett, Anthony Chung, David Collins, Roger Collins, Chris Dawson, Patrick Dawson, Frans van Eijnatten, Janie Ferguson, Moira Fischbacher, Mike Fitzpatrick, Amanda Grard, Tina Harness, Alan Harrison, Stuart Hay, Marielle Heijltjes, Janet Huczynska, Slawomir Magala, Rod Martin, Sue Marlow, Michael Mayer, Mike Noon, Sue Philips, David Preece, Stephen Procter, Max Tookey, Beverley Wagner, Fiona Wilson, James Wilson and Roy Wilson. While this work has benefited immeasurably from their comments, the gaps and flaws remain the sole responsibility of the authors.

We are grateful to the following for permission to reproduce copyright material:

Figure 2.3 from 'A brand new strategy' from *The Economist* 21.11.98, © The Economist Newspaper Ltd 1998, Chapter 2 extracts from 'As winter draws in' from *The Economist* 24.10.98 and Chapter 23 extracts from 'Negotiating by email' from *The Economist* 8.4.00, all rights reserved, reproduced by permission of The Economist Newspaper Ltd; Figure 2.4 from 'All abroad with takeover travel' from *The Times* 1.5.99, Chapter 2 extract from 'Big wheels don't drive Fiestas' by Celia Brayfield from *The Times* 18.3.99, Chapter 8 extracts from 'What's the worse job you've ever done?' from *The Times*, The World at the Millennium Supplement, 9.10.99 and Chapter 22 extract from 'To take a decision, first you have to be angry' from *The Sunday Times* 30.1.99, reproduced by permission of News International plc; Figure 4.3 from Pedler, M., Burgoyne, J. and Boydell, T. (1997) *The Learning Company: A Strategy for Sustainable Development, Second Edition* reproduced by permission of McGraw-Hill Publishing Company; Figure 5.5 from Robertson, I. T. (1994) 'Personality and personnel selection' in Cooper, C. L. and Rousseau, D. M. (eds) *Trends in Organizational Behaviour*, Vol. 1, Table 19.1 and Table 19.3 from Furnham, A. and Gunter, B. (1993) 'Corporate culture: definition, diagnosis and change' in Cooper, C. L. and Robertson, I. T. (eds) *International Review of Industrial and Organizational Psychology*, Vol. 8, reproduced by permission of John Wiley & Sons Ltd; Figure 8.4 from Hackman, J. R. *et al.* (1975) 'A new strategy for job enrichment' *California Management Review* Vol. 17, No. 4, copyright © 1975 by The Regents of the University of California, reprinted by permission of The Regents; Figure 9.3 and Figure 10.4 from Greenberg, J. and Baron, R. A. (1997) *Behaviour in Organizations, Sixth Edition* © 1997 Prentice-Hall, Inc., Upper Saddle River, NJ, Figure 14.5 from Robbins, S. P. (1990) *Organization Theory* © 1990 Prentice-Hall, Inc., Figure 21.3 from Hersey, P. and Blanchard, K. H. (1988) *Management of Organizational Behaviour: Utlizing Human Resources* © 1988 Prentice-Hall, Inc. and Table 14.2 from Gray, J. L. and Starke, F. A. (1984) from *Organizational Behaviour: Concepts and Applications, Third Edition* (pub Charles E. Merrill); Figure 9.6

and an extract from Likert, R. (1961) *New Patterns of Management* reproduced by permission of The McGraw-Hill Companies; Figure 10.3 from Shaw, M. E. (1978) 'Communication networks fourteen years later' in Berkowitz, L. (ed.) *Group Processes* and Chapter 10 extract from Helmreich, R. L. and Foushee, H. C. (1993) 'Why crew resource management? Empirical and theoretical issues in human factors training in aviation' in Weiner, E. L., Kanki, B. G. and Helmreich, R. L. (eds) *Cockpit Resource Management* reproduced by permission of Academic Press; Figure 10.5 from Bales, R. F. (1955) 'How people interact in conferences' *Scientific American* Vol. 192, reproduced with permission; Figure 10.7 from Belbin, R. M. (1996) *The Coming Shape of Organization* and Table 9.2 from Belbin, R. M. (2000) *Beyond the Team* reprinted by permission of Butterworth-Heinemann, a division of Reed Educational & Professional Publishing Ltd; Figure 11.1 from Aronson, E., Wilson, T. D. and Akert, R. M. (1994) *Social Psychology*, Figure 19.2 from Thomas, J, and Waterman, R. H. (1982) *In Search of Excellence*, Figure 24.1 from Pfeffer, J. (1981) *Power in Organizations*, Table 23.3 from Whetton, D., Cameron, K. and Woods, M. (1994) *Developing Management Skills, Second Edition* and Table 23.5 from Whetton, D., Cameron, K. and Woods, M. (1996) *Effective Conflict Management* reproduced by permission of HarperCollins Publishers; Figure 12.2 and Table 12.1 from 'Work teams' by E. Sundstrom, K. de Meuse and D. Futrell from *American Psychologist* February 1990; Figure 13.2 from Noon, M. and Blyton, P. (1997) *The Realites of Work*, Table 16.5 from Buttery, E., Fulop, L. and Buttery, A. (1999) 'Networks and inter-organizational relations' in Fulop, L. and Linstead, S. (eds) *Management: A Critical Text* and Chapter 16, Exercise 2, extract from Martin, J. M. (1994) *Critical Cases in Organizational Behaviour* reproduced by permission of Macmillan Press Ltd; Figure 15.2 from Morgan, G. (1989) *Creative Organization Theory* reprinted by permission of Sage Publications Ltd; Figure 15.3 from Woodward, J. (1958) *Management and Technology*, Crown copyright is reproduced with the permission of the Controller of Her Majesty's Stationery Office; Figure 17.1 from Blake, E. E. and McCanse, A. A. (1991) *Leadership Dilemmas: Grid Solutions* copyright © 1991, Gulf Publishing Company, Houston, Texas, 800-231-6275, all rights reserved, reprinted by permission of Gulf Publishing Company; Figure 18.5 from Dawson, P. (1996) *Technology and Quality: Change in the Workplace* reproduced by permission of Thomson Learning; Figure 20.3 from Fombrun, C. J., Tichy, N. M. and Devanna, M. A. (1984) *Strategic Human Resource Management* reproduced by permission of John Wiley & Sons, Inc; Figure 20.4 from Beer, M. *et al.* (1984) *Managing Human Assets* reproduced by permission of The Free Press, a division of Simon & Schuster; Figure 20.5 from Hendry, C. and Pettigrew, A. M. (1990) 'Human resource management: an agenda for the 1990s' *International Journal of Human Resource Management* 1 (1) reproduced by permission of Taylor and Francis Ltd, *http://www.tandf.co.uk/journals;* Figure 22.2 and Table 22.3 from Vroom, V. H. and Yetton, P. W. (1973) *Leadership and Decision-Making*, reproduced by permission of the University of Pittsburgh Press; Table 2.3 from Ansoff, I. (1997) 'Measuring and managing for environmental turbulence: the Ansoff Associates approach' in Hiam, A. W. (ed.) *The Portable Conference on Change Management* (pub HRD Press Inc) reproduced by permission of I. Ansoff; Table 9.1 from Cohen, A. R. *et al.* (1995) *Effective Behaviour in Organizations, Sixth Edition* reproduced by permission of The McGraw-Hill Companies; Table 11.3 and Table 22.7 from Gordon, J. R. (1993) *A Diagnostic Approach to Organizational Behaviour, Fourth Edition* and Table 24.8 from Taggart, W. M. and Sibley, V. (1986) *Informational Systems: People and Computers in Organizations* reproduced by permission of Allyn & Bacon; Table 12.4 from 'The art of building a car: The Swedish experience re-examined' by

Hammarstrom, O. and Lansbury, R. D. from *New Technology, Work and Employment* Vol. 6, No. 2, 1991, Table 16.1 from Grant, R. M. (1998) *Contemporary Strategy Analysis* and Table 20.6 from Sisson, K. (ed.) (1994) *Personnel Management* reproduced by permission of Blackwell Publishers Ltd; Table 15.6 from Litterer, J. A. (1973) *The Analysis of Organizations* reproduced by permission of John Wiley, Inc; Table 19.2 from Martin, J. (1992) *Cultures in Organizations: Three Perspectives*, copyright 1992 by Oxford University Press, Inc., used by permission of Oxford University Press, Inc; Table 20.8 and Table 20.9 from 'Linking competitive strategies with human resource management practices' by R. Schuler and S. Jackson *Academy of Management Executive* Vol. 9, No.3, 1987, Table 23.4 from 'Towards multidimensional values in teaching: The example of conflict behaviours' by K. W. Thomas from *Academy of Management Review* July 1997, Chapter 12 extacts from 'From chimneys to cross-functional teams: Developing and validating a diagnostic model' by D. Denison, S. Hart and J. Kahn from *Academy of Management Journal* Vol. 39, No. 4, 1996; Table 24.1 and Table 24.9 from Buchanan, D. and Badham, R. (1999) *Power, Politics and Organizational Change* reprinted by permission of Sage Publications Ltd and the authors; Prologue, Chapter 2, Chapter 4 and Chapter 6 *Calvin and Hobbes* cartoons © Watterson, reprinted with permission of Universal Press Syndicate. All rights reserved; Chapter 23 *cartoon by Cathy* © Cathy Guisewite, reprinted with permission of Universal Press Syndicate, all rights reserved; Chapter 2, Exercise 1 extract from article by D. Butcher and P. Harvey from *People Management* Vol. 5, No. 13, 30.6.99, Chapter 3 Table from 'Wired in the country' by Ursula Huws from *People Management* Vol. 5, No.23, 25.11.99 and Table from 'Ringing true' by Alastair Hatchett from *People Management* Vol. 6, No. 2, 20.1.00, reproduced by permission of Personnel Publications Ltd; Chapter 2 cartoon by Robert Mankoff, Chapter 4 cartoon by Tom Cheney, Chapter 11 cartoons by Robert Weber and Lee Lorenz, Chapter 15 cartoons by Dean Vietor and Leo Cullum, Chapter 17 cartoon by J. B. Handelsman, Chapter 22 cartoon by Henry Martin, all reproduced by permission of The Cartoon Bank, a division of The New Yorker Magazine; Chapter 3 extract from 'When men can't keep up with the machines of war' by Dave Griffiths *Business Week* 12.9.88, reproduced with permission; Chapter 3, Chapter 10, Chapter 12, Chapter 16, Chapter 19, Chapter 20 and Chapter 23 Dilbert cartoons, reproduced by permission of Knight Features; Chapter 4, Chapter 7, Chapter 10, Chapter 13, Chapter 16, Chapter 19 Alex cartoons, reproduced by permission of Andrew Mann Ltd; Chapter 5 The Far Side® cartoon, reproduced by permission of Creators Syndicate International; Chapter 5 and Chapter 8 Morris business cartoons reproduced by permission of Visual Humour; Chapter 5, Exercise 2 extract from Howard, P. J. *et al.* (1996) 'The big five locator: a quick assessment tool for consultants and trainers' *The 1996 Annual Handbook* (pub Pfeiffer and Company) copyright © 1996, reprinted by permission of Jossey-Bass, Inc., a subsidiary of John Wiley & Sons, Inc; Chapter 6 Figure from Pease (1985) *Body Language* reproduced by permission of Dorie Simmonds Literary Agency; Chapter 6 cartoon by Kevin Kallaugher reproduced by permission of Cartoonists and Writers Syndicate and the artist; Chapter 6 Table from 'When "no" means "yes"' by M. Kiely from *Marketing* October 1993 reproduced with permission of Haymarket Business Publications; Chapter 7 Real Life cartoon, reproduced by permission of Mirror Group Newspapers; Chapter 9 'Banana Time' extract from Ackroyd, S. and Thompson, P. (1999) *Organizational Misbehaviour* reprinted by permission of Sage Publications Ltd and S. Ackroyd; Chapter 9 Bristow cartoons reproduced by permission of Solo Syndication Ltd; Chapter 10, Exercise 1 extract from Pines, A. and Maslach, C. (1979) *Experiencing*

Social Psychology: Readings and Projects reproduced by permission of Alfred A. Knopf, Inc; Chapter 10 Figure from 'The Hellish Angels' Devilish Business' by A. E. Sewer from *Fortune* 30.11.92, reproduced with permission; Chapter 12 extract from Benders, J. *et al.* (1999) *Useful but Unused: Findings from the EPOC Survey, European Foundation for the Improvement of Living and Working Conditions*, Loughlinstown, Co. Dublin, used with permission; Chapter 14 'Hands on, chief executive' advertisement reproduced by permission of Ward Executive Ltd; Part 1, Introduction cartoon from *Harvard Business Review* Jan.-Feb. 2000, Chapter 3 cartoon from *Harvard Business Review* Nov.-Dec. 1999, Chapter 8 cartoon from *Harvard Business Review* Jan.-Feb. 1996, Chapter 9 cartoon from *Harvard Business Review* Nov.-Dec. 1999, Chapter 14 'Organigraphics' extract from 'Organigraphics: Drawing how companies really work' by H. Mintzberg and L. van der Heden from *Harvard Business Review*, Sept.-Oct. 1999, copyright © 1999 by the President and Fellows of Harvard College, all rights reserved, Chapter 18 cartoon from *Harvard Business Review* Sept.-Oct. 1997, and Figure 21.2 from 'How to choose a leadership pattern' by R. Tannenbaum ad W. H. Schmidt from *Harvard Business Review* Vol. 37, March-April, 1958, all reprinted by permission of Harvard Business Review, all rights reserved; Chapter 14 'L'organigramme' extract from Cadet, C. *et al.* (1990) *La Communication par Limage* (pub Nathan) reproduced by permission of Activites Internationales; Chapter 14 Moulson cartoon from *The Daily Telegraph* 30.3.00, reproduced with permission; Chapter 15 poem 'That's the way the wheel turns' by Leo Rosselson, reproduced by permission of the author; Chapter 18 cartoon by Ted Goff, reproduced by permission of Ted Goff; Chapter 18 advertisement from *Wired* March 2000, reproduced by permission of FreeAgent.com; Chapter 19 cartoon by John Thompson and extract 'German humour ready for take-off' by Denis Staunton *The Observer* 16.11.97; Chapter 20 Chandos cartoon, reproduced by permission of Bryan Reading; Chapter 21, Exercise 1 'Leadership style questionnaire and scoring key' from *Organizational Behaviour: Experiences and Cases, Third Edition* by Marcic, D. © 1992, reprinted with permission of South-Western College Publishing a division of Thomson Learning, Fax 800 730 2215; Chapter 21 cartoon by Tony Holland from *Punch* 5.6.74, reproduced by permission of Punch Ltd; Chapter 22 cartoon by Kew from *Personnel Today* reproduced with permission; Chapter 22 extract from Marshall Sashkin, M. and Morris, W. C. (1987) *Experiencing Management* reproduced by permission of Addison Wesley; Chapter 24 extracts from Griffin, R. W. and Head, T. C. (1987) *Practising Management, Second Edition* reproduced by permission of Houghton Mifflin Co; Chapter 24 cartoon by Tony Husband reproduced with permission;

We are grateful to the following for permission to reproduce photographs:

Academy of Management; Archives of the History of American Psychology, Photograph File – The University of Akron; C. Argyris; Mrs F. Asch; AT & T Archives; A. Bandura; W. Bennis; Bently Historical Library; Bethlehem Steel Corporation Collection; K. Blanchard; Brandeis University; Camera Press Ltd; Carnegie Mellon University; Cason Hall & Co; R. Cyert; T. Deal; Detroit Institute of Arts; Mary Evans Picture Library; F. Fiedler; Ford Motor Company; Harvard University; P. Hersey; F. Herzberg; Hewlett-Packard; G. Hofstede; Katz Pictures Ltd; E. E. Lawler; F. Luthens; J. G. March; The MIT Museum; D. C. McClelland; H. Mintzberg; Zerka Moreno, private collection; NASA; National Museum of American History; The Ohio State University; J. Pfeiffer; L. W. Porter; Carl Rogers Memorial Library; E. Schein; Sporting Pictures (UK) Ltd; K. Thomas; Time Magazine; UPI/Bettman Archive, Inc; University of Michigan; H. Mintzberg; University of Oklahoma; C. Perrow;

University of Pittsburgh; V. H. Vroom; Watertown Free Public Library; S. C. Williams Library, Stevens Institute of Technology; Yale University Archive; Professor P. G. Zimbardo

While every effort has been made to trace the owners of copyright material, in a few cases this has proved impossible and we take this opportunity to offer our apologies to any copyright holders whose rights we have unwittingly infringed.

A Companion Web Site
accompanies *Organisational Behaviour* 4/e,
by Huczynski and Buchanan

Visit the *Organisational Behaviour* Companion Web Site at *www.booksites. net/hucbuc* to find valuable teaching and learning material including:

For students:

- Study material designed to help you improve your results
- Multiple choice questions to test your learning
- An online glossary to explain those concepts

For lecturers:

- A secure, password protected site with teaching material
- A downloadable version of the full Instructor's Manual
- Downloadable PowerPoint slides directly related to the chapters in the book
- Extra FT articles
- Class exercise debriefs
- A 'users club' chat room – view comments about the book, recommendations on teaching methods, journal articles and other books etc., and give your own feedback .
- A syllabus manager that will build and host your very own course web page

Also: This regularly maintained site also has search functions.

Text aims and target readership

Key concepts

This book has four main aims:

1. To provide an *introduction* to the study of human behaviour in organizations for students with little or no previous social science education. The text is designed to serve both as a comprehensive introduction to the field and as a starting point for further and more advanced study. We seek to stimulate wider interest in the subject of organizational behaviour and an enthusiasm for more knowledge.

2. To enable readers to translate organizational behaviour theory, concepts and techniques into *practice* and to work more effectively with the organizations which they are likely to encounter. If one is going to work for, work with, develop, subvert or resist organizations, then one needs to know something of how and why they exist and function as they do.

3. To stimulate *debate* by encouraging readers to adopt a challenging, questioning perspective on organizational behaviour research and ideas. The 'correct' answers to organizational questions and the 'right' solutions to organizational problems can rarely be based on evidence and reason alone. Decisions and actions in organizational settings rely also on values, on judgement, on ideology. Our subject matter and its practical recommendations, however 'rigorous' the research and 'authoritative' the source, are not beyond challenge.

4. To make the subject matter of social science applied to organizations *interesting and intelligible* to students from a range of different educational and disciplinary backgrounds. Readers from other disciplines are often suspicious of what the social sciences can offer.

This book's target readership includes those who are new to the social sciences in general, and who are new to the study of organizational behaviour in particular. Organizational behaviour is now a core topic on business and management studies degree and diploma programmes, undergraduate and postgraduate. However, the subject is also taught on courses where the main subjects are not social sciences. Accountants, lawyers, doctors, nurses, engineers, teachers, architects, computer scientists, personnel managers, bankers, hoteliers and surveyors, for example, often have no previous background in social science subjects but find themselves studying organizational behaviour as a core element in their professional examination schemes.

This text is thus written from a multidisciplinary social science perspective. Our understanding of organizations derives from a number of disciplines. Other texts in this field adopt a managerial, a psychological or a sociological perspective. However, our readers are not all going to be managers, psychologists or sociologists, and many readers beyond those occupations require and can benefit from an understanding of organizational behaviour.

Individual chapters are self-contained. The understanding of one chapter does not rely on a prior reading of others, although in practice these topics are interrelated, and topic links to material covered in other chapters are indicated where appropriate. Ideas and theories build systematically, from the organizational context, to individual psychology, through social psychology, to organizational sociology, politics, and finally specific management topics. Each chapter introduces practical applications as well as theoretical background. Many issues are controversial, and each chapter aims to present competing views clearly. The aim is not, however, to identify 'correct answers' or 'best practices', which are often simplistic and misleading. The intention behind presenting the tensions and contradictions is to raise further questions, to trigger discussion and debate, to stimulate challenge and critical thinking.

The book has a consciously flexible design, appropriate for a two-semester programme or a traditional three-term course. Although this is an introductory text, a significant proportion of the material covered is more advanced, and 'springboard' sections in each chapter include references to further reading. The text may therefore be useful on second- and third-level courses. The subject matter of organizational behaviour overlaps with other topics, such as general and human resource management, and instructors and students are likely to find this text relevant to those other modules. The material does not have to be covered in the sequence in which it is presented here, leaving instructors the choice of what material to cover, in what sequence, and with what additional learning support.

The text incorporates material from a variety of cultural settings. Many organizational behaviour texts are written from the perspective of a single culture. Social science theories can be culture-bound, as laws, norms and traditions vary from country to country, sub-culture to sub-culture. It is important to stimulate awareness of the range of social and cultural factors that influence behaviour in organizations. While admitting a British bias in the authorship of this text, we—along with many colleagues—find ourselves typically working with multicultural student groups. It is increasingly important for students, and organization members, to understand and work effectively with cultural differences (see, for example, Adler, 1999).

Throughout the text, research summaries and *Stop and criticize* exercises provide opportunities for controversial and comparative issues to be explored. One way of bringing into relief the ways in which we behave in organizations is to compare our practice with that of others. Comparative studies have a long tradition in the social sciences. Each year, most of the readers of this book engage in some comparative study, in airlines, railways, buses, hotels, restaurants and hospitals, simply through exposure to different settings when on holiday.

The text uses a range of features to help and also to challenge readers:

- Each chapter is introduced by a list of the *Key concepts* to be covered and the *Learning objectives* to be achieved.

- Those key concepts can all be found in the *Glossary* at the end of the text.

- Readers are regularly invited to *Stop and Criticize*, to think through contradictory and controversial points and arguments, to apply ideas and arguments to their own experience, to challenge their own assumptions.

- *Applications* of concepts, theories and frameworks are discussed throughout, sometimes in boxed illustrations from practical organizational experience.

- Each chapter has *Recap* and *Revision* sections, which first summarize the chapter content in relation to the learning objectives and then offer a series of typical essay questions, which can be used either for personal study or as tutorial revision aids.

- Each chapter has a *Home viewing* section, which identifies a film (or films), and in some instances a television programme, which illustrates the issues and concepts in the chapter in a graphic and entertaining manner.

- Each chapter has an *OB in literature* section, which indicates illustrations of the concepts and other material covered in the text in novels and other creative writing.

- Each chapter offers a *Springboard* section, a short annotated guide to further and more advanced sources.

- At the end of each chapter are two *Chapter exercises*. One of these is designed for use with large classes and the other for small group tutorial and seminar settings.

- In addition, we have tried to make the book interesting and approachable by using novel, varied and unusual material where relevant. Examples, cartoons, illustrations, exercises and cases are used to change the pace, rhythm and appearance of the text, to make it more digestible, more engaging, more readable.

The style and content of this book thus reflect the participative teaching and learning strategies now commonly used across the business and management studies curriculum. This implies a more limited use of conventional lecturing input and more extensive use of a range of individual and group case and exercise work. Most instructors will, therefore, not teach *to* this text but teach *from* it, using it to introduce key ideas and theories as a platform for discussion, exercise, casework and further advanced study.

Challenge and debate

We have used a number of text features to encourage an active and questioning approach to the subject. We want to challenge readers by inviting them to confront real, practical and theoretical problems and issues for themselves. Readers are invited regularly to stop reading and to consider controversial points, individually or in group discussion. We want to alert readers to the significance of organizational behaviour in everyday life. The study of organizational behaviour should not be confined to the lecture theatre and library. Eating a pizza in a restaurant, joining a queue at a theme park, returning a faulty product to a store, arguing with a colleague at work, taking a holiday job in a factory, watching a movie or reading a novel—are all experiences that can be related to the material in this book.

A further aim of this text is to strike a balance between three characteristics:

Introductory: the text provides a comprehensive grounding in the subject, and its scope, concerns, research traditions, language and applications.

Practical: the content explores the practical organizational applications and consequences of theoretical perspectives, research findings and management techniques.

Challenging: the treatment encourages readers to question and debate rather than to accept as 'authoritative' received ideas, and to subject concepts, theories and their applications to challenge.

Some organizational behaviour texts offer a managerial perspective and give readers little or no encouragement to challenge the material presented, or to consider other lines of reasoning and practice. Some texts offer a critical perspective, encouraging debate, but without offering practical options. This text aims to strike a balance between these unsatisfactory extremes.

There are at least five grounds for developing a questioning approach to this subject:

1: Is the employment contract based on free choice?

The employment contract apparently relies on 'freedom of choice'. You choose whether to take that job, and the organization chooses to hire you or not. However, employers are rarely dependent on individual employees, but can pick and choose from the labour market. For an employee, the 'free choice' is between work and unemployment. Trade unions have not always been a solution to this power imbalance. The employment contract is unequal, operating in the employer's favour. Some commentators regard the employment contract in a capitalist economy as exploitative. One implication is that management techniques for improving quality of working life [**links**, chapter 8, motivation; chapter 12, teamworking] can be seen as cosmetic attempts to conceal the exploitative nature of the employment relationship.

2: Is organizational hierarchy inevitable?

Organizational hierarchy appears to be 'normal'. It seems that managers have superior ability, better information and well-developed powers of judgement, which is why they make the big decisions. Hierarchy, however, relies on power inequality and creates patterns of domination (by the elite) and subordination (of the weak). One trend during the 1990s was 'delayering', which simply means reducing the number of levels in the management hierarchy, producing 'flat' organization structures. However, even delayered organizations have hierarchies which perpetuate power inequalities and exclude large numbers of employees from positions of influence over management decisions. Why do organizations not employ the same democratic structures as the wider democratic society of which they are part? This argument has implications for organization structure [**link**, part 4, organization structures].

3: Is the state a neutral arbiter between employer and employee?

The state, that is the government, appears to be a neutral arbiter between competing interests in a pluralist society. Legislation upholds socially beneficial aims such as the maintenance of order and the deterrence of crime. This 'neutrality', however, is a fiction. Legislation strengthens rather than challenges the status quo, particularly with respect to the rights of trade unions and individuals to challenge management actions and decisions in the workplace. The state typically acts for, and not against, established interests and power bases. In part 1, we explore how the external environment of the organization, including political, economic, social, technological, legislative and environmental factors, affects organization structures [**link**, chapter 2, the world outside]. Different perspectives on conflict—unitary, pluralist and radical—are explored in chapter 23 [**link**, chapter 24, power and politics].

4: Is the technical language of organization and management neutral?

Are we really 'in control' of our thoughts, feelings, values and beliefs? Yes. We are presented with arguments and facts, we balance the evidence, we make up our own minds. However, the language in which we receive information is often biased. Take the statement, 'do a good job, and you will get promoted'. This assumes that 'a better worker is a better person'; you are deviant if you are not 'a good worker'. Better, then, to prove your worth by being a committed employee, offering ideas for improving efficiency in the interests of customer service. From a management perspective, this is an effective way of obtaining compliance from a potentially awkward workforce; the 'better worker' does not complain about conditions. The language of management (teamwork, flexibility, empowerment, discretion, job enrichment) sounds appealing and liberating. These techniques, however, can be seen as covert tools of manipulation and exploitation.

5: How new are 'new' theories and techniques?

Management theorists generate a constant stream of new ideas and techniques. Managers tend to be fashion-conscious and are always interested in the latest thinking, which can create competitive advantage. Students (and textbook authors) also need to keep up with this flood of innovation. Understanding the history of the subject, however, one can often see in 'new' thinking and methods aspects of familiar 'old' ideas. What appears to be new is often less a 'paradigm shift' in thinking and more of a 'packaging shift'. Is the technique of 'job sculpting', invented in the late 1990s, really 'new' or just a reworking of 'job enrichment' from the 1960s [**link**, chapter 8, motivation]? Is the 'McDonaldization' of work a contemporary trend or the continuing expression of early twentieth-century management thinking [**link**, chapter 13, traditional work design]?

These five apparently separate issues are linked by the common desire to challenge and to debate ideas which appear to be plausible, familiar, sensible, inevitable, traditional or orthodox and which may thus be accepted unquestioningly. Instead, we should question the notions that:

The contract between employer and employee is a fair one entered into freely; it is not.

Hierarchy is a natural model of organization, inevitable and beneficial; it is not.

The state plays a neutral role as arbiter in employment relations; it does not.

The terminology of organization and management is technical and neutral; it is not.

What is advertised as new is always new; it is not.

A perspective that encourages debate, challenge and criticism involves asking the following kinds of question when presented with a theory, with an argument, with evidence, or with recommendations for a line of action:

- Does this make sense, do I understand it, or is it confused and confusing?

- It the evidence compelling, or is it weak?

- Does a claim to 'novelty' withstand comparison with previous thinking?

- Is the argument logical and coherent, or do there seem to be gaps and flaws?

- What biases or prejudices are revealed in this line of argument?

- Is a claim to 'neutrality' realistic, or does it conceal a hidden agenda?

- Are the arguments and judgements based convincingly on the evidence?

- Whose interests are served by this argument, and whose are damaged?

- Is the language of this argument designed to make it more appealing than it is?

Where appropriate, chapters explore competing perspectives on the subject matter, from commentators who base their approaches on different values and assumptions. This approach is reinforced in the *Stop and criticize* exercises, and in the exercises at the end of each chapter. For a fuller treatment of a critical approach to understanding and researching organizational behaviour, see Mats Alvesson and Stanley Deetz (1999). For a text written exclusively from a critical stance, see Paul Thompson and David McHugh (1995).

Home viewing

In a direct challenge to orthodox thinking, John Hassard and Ruth Holliday (1998) unkindly observe that textbooks like ours offer a *sanitized* picture of organizational behaviour. Stephen Ackroyd and Paul Thompson (1999) similarly argue that orthodox texts overlook much evident *mis*behaviour—'soldiering', sabotage, pilfering and practical jokes. Gibson Burrell (1998, p.52) is particularly uncompromising in his view of what contemporary organization theory neglects: 'there is little mention of sex, yet organizations are redolent with it; little mention of violence, yet organizations are stinking with it; little mention of pain, yet organizations rely upon it; little mention of the will to power, yet organizations would not exist without it'.

Hassard and Holliday note that the medium of film and television, in contrast, 'plays out sex, violence, emotion, power struggle, the personal consequences of success and failure, and *dis*organization upon its stage'. Saturday evening. Dinner at home. A hospital drama on television. The usual mayhem and gore, stressed staff, shortage of resources, conflict between hospital administrators and doctors, tensions and secret relationships between doctors and nurses. Another portrayal of work and organization. Is this media view extreme and sensationalized, or is it realistic? To what extent do film, television and novels reflect popular perspectives and stereotypes of work, authority, power, status and organization structure?

The advertising for some controversial films suggests that popular stereotypes are being challenged; *Philadelphia* for its portrayal of AIDS, *Disclosure* for the portrayal of female rape and sexual harassment. Hassard and Holliday argue, however, that the media instead reinforce conservative values, reflecting social realities, albeit in a stylized manner, rather than presenting fundamental challenges. Read their text and you will never again watch police and hospital dramas on television without boring your companions with critical commentary on the traditional portrayal of hierarchy, group dynamics, sex role stereotyping, power relations, the role of authority figures, and dysfunctional bureaucratic rules. The same applies to movies, but your heated discussion usually has to wait until the end, unless you rent the video.

We seek to avoid this sanitization trap by including a *Home viewing* section at the end of each chapter, identifying films and occasionally television programmes that illustrate and reinforce the ideas, concepts, theories, techniques and applications explored in the text. This is a powerful way to bring textbook ideas to life, to help readers relate concepts and theories to actual (albeit fictional) settings. There is no need to stop with our recommendations. Readers are encouraged to identify other relevant film and TV illustrations in their own viewing.

OB in literature

Most of the topics and themes within the subject boundary of organizational behaviour are also addressed in powerful, insightful and entertaining ways in literature. To reinforce the aim of stimulating challenge and debate, considering and exploring ideas from unusual perspectives, each chapter identifies a relevant novel or other literature source.

Management courses based on novels have a long history. Novels can be deliberately written as didactic devices, illustrating points about, for example, quality management, as in *The Goal*, by Goldratt and Cox (1993). Fiction, however, can also be used for instructional purposes. For example, the allegorical novel *Watership Down* by Richard Adams (1973) provides a basis for discussing the management roles identified by Henry Mintzberg (1973). Sources dealing with this aspect of OB instruction include Thompson and McGivern (1996), Czarniawska-Joerges and de Monthoux (1994), Grottola (1994), Puffer (1991), and Knights and Willmott (1999).

Our literature selection has two limitations. First, it is inevitably idiosyncratic. Second, attention is focused on a specific aspect of the work (such as the different perceptual worlds of the characters in Louis de Bernière's *Captain Corelli's Mandolin*), which hardly does justice to the author's wider purpose. We hope that you will follow up these recommendations, and also that you will analyse your own wider reading in these terms.

The postmodern justification: beyond home entertainment

Films and novels potentially offer fresh and entertaining perspectives on organizational behaviour. However, there is another set of reasons why narrative fiction is worthy of analysis. Researchers, and film makers and writers, appear to have different purposes and use different methods and media. Researchers are concerned with scientific observation and the objective discovery of truth, resulting in peer-refereed journal papers. Film makers and novelists are concerned with creativity and entertainment, resulting in visually entertaining celluloid images and absorbing narratives in books. Do these groups have nothing in common?

The screen writer or novelist has to create an entertaining fiction—a narrative—and then decide how best to present it to their audience. This means choosing, within the broad conventions of novels and films, what will be revealed to the audience and what concealed, what will be shown or described in detail, the sequence in which information is presented, what is to be left unstated, and what will be revealed later in the narrative. This must also be a new story which the audience has not already seen or read.

The researcher has to create an academic paper—a narrative—and then decide how best to present it to their audience. This means choosing, within the broad conventions of academic journals, what will be revealed to the readership and what concealed, what will be shown or described in detail, the sequence in which information is presented, what is to be left unstated, and what will be revealed later in the narrative. This must also present new research findings with which the readership is not already familiar.

Film makers, novelists and academic researchers are, of course, constrained by the conventions of their respective media. Creative and inventive as well as entertaining, the James Bond movies produced by Albert (Cubby) Broccoli all follow a familiar formula. However ground-breaking, academic journal papers similarly follow a set of writing guidelines. Paradoxically, it is these constraints which turn the writing of both research papers and narrative fiction into creative acts. Authors must constantly make conscious choices so that their work will be meaningful, acceptable and plausible within these broader limits.

Surely the work of the social scientist is different in being concerned with offering a faithful representation of social and organizational life? Well, film makers and novelists are also concerned with remaining faithful to social experience, with presenting realistic accounts of the social world, and with the plausibility of their narratives and their characters. Even in science fiction, a genre which deliberately seeks to depart from 'reality', if the setting, plot and characters are not plausible, then the film or novel is likely to be a critical failure.

The postmodern perspective, explored in chapter 2, makes two observations relevant here:

1. All texts are social constructions, as authors are influenced by the language, interests, norms and expectations of the wider society. Even 'alternative'

writers, seeking to challenge and to shock, have to define their position, however radical, in relation to whatever passes for 'the established view' at the time they are writing.

2. There is no one 'correct' interpretation of what an author (of a book, a film or a research paper) has created. Different readers, from different backgrounds and perspectives, can have different interpretations. Postmodernism thus argues that any interpretation of a piece of work is 'correct', and that an author's meaning and intentions should not be given any special privilege.

It would be accurate to claim that research papers are regarded (sometimes at least) as having relatively high scientific value and low entertainment value. The opposing claim, that narrative fiction has high entertainment value and low scientific value, does not hold so true if we accept a postmodern account of the similarities between these domains. Films and novels can be seen just as entertaining examples of some of the ideas presented in a text such as this. In looking at the same issues from a completely different perspective, however, analysis of fiction is not only a teaching and learning device but can lead to quite different perspectives on and interpretations of the material. An example demonstrates the possibilities.

Joel Foreman and Tojo Thatchenkery (1996), offer an insightful analysis of the film *Rising Sun* (1993, director Philip Kaufman). *Rising Sun* concerns the murder of Cheryl, an American blonde, in the boardroom of the Nakamoto Corporation, a Japanese transplant in Los Angeles, during negotiations to acquire Microcon, an American defence company. John Connor (played by Sean Connery) and Web Smith (Wesley Snipes) are the detectives on the case. This entertaining thriller can be viewed from a number of different perspectives.

First, it can be seen as a study of a Japanese transplant in an alien culture, with the consequent clash of organizational behaviour styles. This culture clash is symbolized in the incongruous opening sequences. Portraying the male Japanese acquisition of American companies, technologies and women, the story also plays on American fears of Japanese world business domination.

Second, it can be viewed as instruction in cross-cultural communications. Connor has to teach his partner, Web, about doing business with the male Japanese, in terms of social norms and rituals, preserving 'face', conversation style and interpersonal relationships.

Third, it can be viewed as a study of organizational power politics, revealed in the symbolic use of architecture, the exploitation of friendships, the use of sophisticated surveillance technology, the importance of golfing relationships, and the links to national politics through the manipulation and blackmail of Senator John Morton (Ray Wise).

Fourth, it can be seen as a metaphor for the postmodern view of ambiguity, uncertainty, lack of 'closure' and the negotiable nature of reality. This is evident in the relationship between Eddie Sakamura (Cary-Hiroyuki Tagawa) and his girlfriend Cheryl Austin (Tatjana Patitz); it looks like it, but did he murder her? This is also evident in the closing scene with Web Smith and Jingo Asakuma (Tia Carrere), who reveals that she is (or was?) Connor's partner; she encourages him, but does Web get the girl? At the end, the plot returns to the opening theme of culture clash, initially between Japanese and American (seen in the relationship between Japanese Eddie and American Cheryl) and now between Afro-American Web and Japanese Jingo. Does the lack of closure in this narrative leave you feeling uncomfortable?

Beyond the entertainment, look out for the other perspectives illustrated in this film, and be alert to the fresh insights into aspects of organizational behaviour which this and other creative works can offer. We hope that you will follow up our film and novel recommendations in this spirit, identifying other more interesting and relevant examples from your own experience.

Instructors in particular may find the following summary of chapter features helpful:

Feature	Explanation
Engaging, entertaining layout and writing style	Introductory text, for undergraduate and postgraduate business and management studies, assumes no prior topic knowledge, mixed-ability student groups, some needing guidance and stimulation
Chapter independence	Each chapter stands alone but is linked to an overarching framework. Instructors are thus not 'locked in' but have the option to follow the text or to design their own course content
Chapter links	Topic links to material covered in other chapters are indicated where appropriate
Key concepts	Each chapter opens with a list of the main concepts defined, explained and illustrated in the chapter
Learning objectives	Each chapter opens with learning objectives
Integrating framework	Each part establishes how the topic relates to the integrating framework which opens the text and maps the OB territory
Practical interest	Each chapter opens by establishing the significance of the topic as addressing a set of practical issues and problems
Your call	Each part opens with a short case, inviting analysis and decision
Historical backdrop	Subject treatment provides definition of key concepts and classic research, key theories and authors, contrasting perspectives
Current thinking	Subject treatment emphasizes current research, theory and authors, cutting-edge thinking and issues, demonstrating modification of traditional thinking where appropriate, speculating about the future
Applications	Examples of how theory is translated into practice; recent management applications, broad range of organizational types used in illustrations, international examples
Controversy and debate	Examples of current controversies, theoretical and practical, encourage critical perspective, encourage debate and challenge
Stop and criticize	Stop sections throughout the text invite readers to pause and challenge ideas and theories, and their practical implications
Recap	A list of the key issues and arguments in the chapter, linked to learning objectives, for reminder and revision
Revision	Typical essay and examination questions, useful for personal revision or for tutorial discussion and revision purposes
Springboard	Annotated chapter bibliographies indicating 'classical' references and recent seminal and controversial contributions; useful for assignment or project work and for further advanced study
Home viewing	Films illustrating the wider relevance and application of ideas introduced in the chapter
OB in literature	Novels illustrating concepts and themes from the chapter
Lecture exercise	A short case, or questionnaire, for use in a lecture setting with large classes, to provoke critical analysis and discussion
Tutorial exercise	Longer case study and/or group exercise, for use in tutorial settings with smaller classes, to provoke critical analysis and debate

Chapter 1 Prologue

A field map of the organizational behaviour terrain

PESTLE: The **P**olitical, **E**conomic, **S**ocial, **T**echnological, **L**egal and **E**cological context

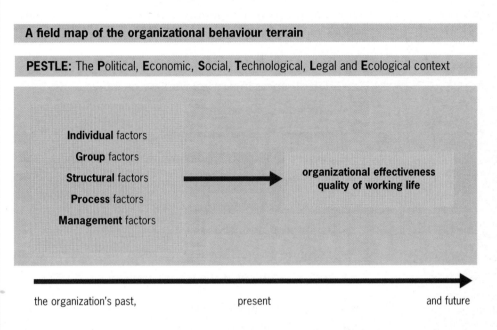

Key concepts

organizational behaviour	controlled performance
organization	the organizational dilemma
operational definition	behaviour
behaviourism	positivism
action	cognitive psychology
phenomenology	the social construction of reality

Learning objectives

When you have read this chapter, you should be able to define those key concepts in your own words, and you should also be able to:

1. Explain the significance of an understanding of organizational behaviour.

2. Explain and illustrate the central dilemma of organizational design.

3. Understand the need for explanations of behaviour in organizations that take account of relationships between factors at different levels of analysis.

4. Identify the features that differentiate the natural and social sciences, and the implications of this differentiation.

What is organizational behaviour?

Consider the last time you had a 'bad experience' in, say, a shop, a restaurant or a hotel. The person you dealt with was abrupt and unpleasant, and you left feeling angry, never to return.

What is the explanation? We can blame the 'wicked personality' of that shop assistant, waiter or receptionist. There are many other possibilities. Your experience could be due to:

- lack of training;
- staff absences increasing working pressure;
- long hours and fatigue;
- equipment not working properly;
- anxiety about anticipated organizational changes;
- domestic problems such as family disputes and ill health;
- low motivation due to low pay;
- an autocratic supervisor;
- a dispute with colleagues created an uncomfortable working atmosphere;
- and you came in at the wrong moment.

Your treatment could be explained by a range of individual, group, organizational and contextual factors arising in the workplace and beyond. The customer walks away from all this. As a member of that organization, these are the issues that you have to work with.

Organizational behaviour is now recognized as a significant field of investigation in its own right, although it draws from across the social sciences. Is this a dry, theoretical subject divorced from day-to-day practical concerns? No. Your 'bad experience' suggests that an understanding of organizational behaviour has many practical applications.

The definition of a field of study identifies its scope, and the themes, questions, issues and problems that it seeks to address and to explain. This is a controversial matter as different commentators have different ideas about the appropriate scope of the field, and of 'sub-fields'. This controversy is reflected in the range of similar titles to be found in the literature: organization theory, industrial sociology, organizational psychology, organizational analysis, organization studies. Organization theory and industrial sociology tend to concentrate on macro-level studies of groups and organizations. Organizational psychology tends to focus on micro-level studies of individual behaviour. Organizational analysis tends to adopt a more practical rather than a theoretical perspective, although analysis is, of course, dependent on theory. 'Organization studies' is a term which is increasingly used to reflect the proliferation of issues and perspectives that this field now embraces (Clegg, Hardy and Nord, 1996).

One influential definition of **organizational behaviour** comes from Derek Pugh (1971, p.9).

This definition covers macro-organizational and micro-individual concerns. Despite what other commentators suggest (Rollinson, Broadfield and Edwards, 1998), the scope of organizational behaviour has traditionally been specified in broad and inclusive terms. Indeed, the subject has more recently been defined in this 'inclusive' sense as:

Organizational behaviour is the study of the structure, functioning and performance of organizations, and the behaviour of groups and individuals within them.

the interdisciplinary body of knowledge and field of research, concerned with how formal organizations, behaviour of people within organizations, and salient features of their context and environment, evolve and take shape, why all these things happen the way they do, and what purposes they serve (Sorge and Warner, 1997, p.xii).

Organizational behaviour enjoys a controversial relationship with management practice. Our text is not alone in considering practical applications of theory, and most American and some British texts (e.g. Mullins, 1999) adopt a 'managerialist' perspective. However, this focus on management is regarded by some commentators as inappropriate, for at least four reasons, concerning power inequalities, the subject agenda, multiple stakeholders and fashion trends.

Power inequalities: Management is an elite occupational group, with access to information and resources beyond those available to mere employees. Organizations often display inequalities of power and reward. Why should a field of study support exclusively the affluent powerful at the expense of the powerless? Organizational behaviour used in this way becomes a 'servant of power'. A managerialist perspective on organizational behaviour encourages a non-critical approach to management practice.

Subject agenda: A managerialist perspective focuses on a narrow range of issues of perceived importance to managers, concerning management control and organizational performance. This pushes a range of other topics off the agenda, such as theoretical analyses that have limited practical application, topics significant to particular individuals and groups, and arguments that are critical of the managerial role. These topics can, however, be important to the wider community.

Multiple stakeholders: Management is only one social group with a stake in the behaviour of organizations and their members. An understanding of this subject is thus of value to employees, trade union members and representatives, customers, suppliers, investors, and also to members of the wider community in which an organization is embedded. Organizational behaviour is a subject of wide social and economic relevance.

Fashion victims: Management is prone to pursuing the latest in thinking and technique, in the interests of improving personal and organizational performance. A managerialist perspective on organizational behaviour, however, encourages a focus on current fashion trends. Some fashions survive, while others quickly fade. As some 'fads' turn out to be old ideas freshly packaged, it is necessary to consider these developments in the wider context of the history of the subject to reach an informed assessment.

This text adopts the 'multiple-stakeholders-broad-agenda' view of organizational behaviour, developing an eclectic social science perspective and avoiding a managerialist stance. This does not mean that practical applications are ignored. On the contrary, application of theories, concepts and frameworks are explored throughout. However, readers are encouraged to take a critical perspective, on research, theory and applications, rather than simply to accept a managerialist or a social scientific point of view.

Jack Wood (1995) notes that the term 'organizational behaviour' was first used by Fritz Roethlisberger in the late 1950s as it suggested a wider scope than the more fashionable term, 'human relations'. The term 'behavioural sciences' was first used to describe a Ford Foundation research programme at Harvard in 1950,

Management is an elite group?

Research in America shows that the average salary for a chief executive is US$7.8 million. This is 326 times the salary of the average factory worker. In the 1960s, that ratio was 44:1.

Based on 'Overworked and underpaid: the American manager', The Economist, 30 January 1999, p.69.

The chief executives of Britain's top 350 companies had average salaries in 1998 of £350,000 (excluding 'perks'). The average 'basic pay' of those running the top 100 companies was £497,000 in 1998, and bonuses increased this by over 20 per cent. The lowest paid executives in Europe are in Germany and Sweden where average basic salaries for chief executives were only £243,000 and £217,000 respectively. The chief executive of Barclays Bank appointed in 1999 had a remuneration package of £15 million over three years. The employer he left gave him a severance payment of £1.6 million. Manufacturing workers laid off in Britain in 1998 received only 23 per cent of their pay in compensation, the lowest of any developed country.

Based on Matthew Barbour, 'British fat cats take the cream', The Times, 29 March 1999, p.48.

The highest paid chief executive in Britain in 1999 was Paul Chisholm of Colt Telecom whose annual pay including bonuses and share options was over £50 million. The second most highly paid chief executive was Jan Leschly of Smithkline Beecham who earned only £29 million.

Based on John Waples and Adam Coffer, 'Which of Britain's bosses give best value for pay?' The Sunday Times, 31 October 1999,
pp.3.10–3.11.

Derek S. Pugh
(b. 1930)

Fritz Jules
Roethlisberger
(1898–1974)

and in 1957 the Human Relations Group at Harvard (previously the Mayo Group) became the Organizational Behaviour Group. Organizational behaviour was recognized as a subject at Harvard in 1962, with Roethlisberger as the first area head (Roethlisberger, 1977). The first British appointments to chairs in organizational behaviour went to Professor Derek Pugh at London Business School in 1970 and to Professor David Weir at Glasgow University Business School in Scotland in 1974.

Organizations, of course, do not 'behave'. Only people can be said to behave. The term 'organizational behaviour' is a verbal shorthand which refers to the activities and interactions of people in organizational settings such as hospitals, workshops, banks and police stations. Organizations pervade our social, cultural, political, economic and physical environment, offering jobs, providing goods and services, presenting us with substantial portions of our built environment, and in some cases contributing to the existence and fabric of whole communities. However, we tend to take organizations for granted precisely because they affect everything that we do. Such familiarity can lead to an underestimation of their impact.

The study of organizations is multidisciplinary, drawing from psychology, social psychology, sociology, economics and political science, and to a lesser extent from history, geography and anthropology. The study of organizational behaviour has become a distinct discipline, with its own research traditions, academic journals and international networks. This is an area where the contributions of the different social and behavioural sciences can be integrated. The extent of that integration, however, is still weak. 'Multidisciplinary' means drawing from a number of different subjects. 'Interdisciplinary' implies that different subjects collaborate. Full interdisciplinary collaboration is rare.

Organizational behaviour—a coherent subject area?

Management textbooks frequently state as fact that organizational behaviour is an inter-disciplinary field. It is not. It is in no way inter-disciplinary; multi-disciplinary perhaps, but not inter-disciplinary. OB is not a coherent field. It is a general area that encompasses thinking and research from numerous disciplines. It draws its material from psychology, sociology, anthropology, economics, the arts and humanities, law and medicine. Organizational behaviour is in reality a hodgepodge of various subjects; a collection of loosely related or even unrelated streams of scholarly and not-so-scholarly research. It is neither a discipline, nor is it a business function. And that makes it an anomalous area of management study.

From Jack Wood, 'Mastering management: organizational behaviour', *Financial Times* supplement, 3 November 1995, p.3.

At various points in this book, we will confront the issue of how terms are to be defined. This problem arises in a variety of contexts concerning, for example, what we mean by apparently straightforward terms like 'personality', or 'group', or 'conflict'. We must first address the problem of what we mean by the term **organization**.

Stop and criticize

Why should the term 'organization' be difficult to define? Consider the following list. Which of these would you call an organization and which not, identifying the reasons for your decision in each case?

- A chemicals processing company
- The Jamieson family, who live next door
- Leicester General Hospital
- A local street corner gang of boys
- Clan Buchanan

- The local squash club
- A baby-sitting circle
- A famine relief charity
- The Azande tribe
- A primary school

An **organization** is a social arrangement for achieving controlled performance in pursuit of collective goals.

Why are you uncomfortable about calling some of the items on this list organizations? Perhaps you considered size as a factor? Or the provision of goods and services for sale? Or the existence of paid employment? If we define the term too widely, it can become meaningless.

This definition should help to explain why you perhaps found it awkward to describe a street corner gang as an organization, but not a hospital, a company or a club. What about families, tribes, clans and baby-sitting circles? Let us examine this definition more closely.

Social arrangements

To say that organizations are social arrangements is simply to observe that they are groups of people who interact with each other as a consequence of their membership. However, all of the items on our list are social arrangements from this point of view, from the company to the club to the gang to the tribe. This, therefore, is neither a unique nor a distinguishing feature.

Collective goals

Common membership of an organization implies some shared objectives. Organizations are more likely to exist where individuals acting alone cannot achieve goals that are considered worthwhile pursuing. Once again, all of the items on our list are social arrangements for the pursuit of collective goals, so this is not a distinctive feature either.

Controlled performance

Controlled performance means setting performance standards, measuring actual performance, comparing actual with standard, and taking corrective action when necessary.

Organizations are concerned with performance in the pursuit of goals. The performance of an organization as a whole determines its survival. The performance of a department determines the amount of resources allocated to it. The performance of individuals determines pay and promotion prospects. Not any level of performance will do, however. We live in a world in which the resources available to us are not sufficient to meet all of our needs. We have to make the most efficient use of those scarce resources. Levels of performance of individuals, departments and organizations are therefore tied to standards which determine what counts as inadequate, satisfactory or good.

It is necessary to control performance to ensure either that it is good enough or that something is being done to improve it. An organization's members thus have to perform these control functions as well as the operating tasks required to fulfil the collective purpose of the organization. The need for controlled performance leads to a deliberate and ordered allocation of functions, or division of labour, between organizational members.

Admission to membership of organizations is controlled, usually with reference to standards of performance and behaviour; will the person be able to do the job? The price of failure to perform to standard is usually loss of membership. The need for controlled performance leads to the establishment of authority relationships. The controls only work where members comply with the orders of those responsible for performing the control functions.

To what extent are the Jamieson family, the Azande tribe or the street gang preoccupied with determining and monitoring performance standards and correcting deviations? To what extent does their existence depend on their ability to meet predetermined targets? To what extent do they allocate control functions to their members, programme their activities and control their relationships with other members? The way in which you answer these questions may explain your readiness or reluctance to label items on our list as organizations.

It is the preoccupation with performance and the need for control which distinguish organizations from other social arrangements.

Stop and criticize

In what ways could the Jamieson family be concerned with performance and control?

How is membership of a street gang determined? What do you have to do to become a member? What behaviours lead to exclusion from gang membership?

Are organizations different from other social arrangements in degree only, and not different in kind? Are *all* social groupings not concerned with setting, monitoring and correcting standards of behaviour and performance (defined in different ways)?

The way in which one defines a phenomenon determines ways of looking at and studying it. The study of organizational behaviour is characterized by the view that organizations should be studied from a range of different perspectives. In other words, it is pointless to dispute which is the 'correct' definition. The American management guru, Peter Drucker, presents another angle of view, arguing that organizations are like symphony orchestras. Information technology, he argues, reduces the need for manual and clerical skills and increases demand for 'knowledge workers'. Like musicians, Drucker sees knowledge workers exploring outlets for their creative talent, seeking interesting challenges, enjoying the stimulation of working with other specialists. There are implications in this perspective for individual careers, organization structures and management styles (Golzen, 1989).

One author who has popularized the 'multiple perspectives' view of organizations is the Canadian academic Gareth Morgan. In his book *Images of Organizations* (1997), he offers eight metaphors which invite us to see organizations through a series of different lenses, as:

- machines;
- biological organisms;
- human brains;
- cultures, or sub-cultures;
- political systems;
- psychic prisons;
- systems of change and transformation;
- instruments of domination.

Morgan presents these contrasting metaphors as ways of thinking about organizations, as approaches to what he describes as the 'diagnostic reading' and 'critical evaluation' of organizational phenomena. The 'organization as machine' metaphor suggests an analysis of its component elements and their interaction. The 'psychic prison' metaphor, in contrast, implies an analysis of how the organization constrains and shapes the thinking and intellectual growth of its members. He suggests how, 'By using different metaphors to understand the complex and paradoxical character of organizational life, we are able to manage and design organizations in ways that we may not have thought possible before' (Morgan, 1997, p.13).

It is necessary, therefore, to view critically our definition of the concept of organization. There is value in adopting other perspectives and ways of seeing.

Calvin and Hobbes

Why study organizational behaviour?

If we eventually destroy this planet, the cause will not lie with technology or weaponry. We will have destroyed it with ineffective organizations. The ultimate limitation on human aspirations lies not in intellect or in technology, but in our ability to work together. The cause of most major disasters (Bhopal, Chernobyl, the *Challenger* Shuttle) can be traced to organizational factors, as well as (if not contributing to) technical problems.

If we eventually destroy this planet

Why did Joseph Hazelwood, in 1999, agree to spen[...]ers collecting rubbish in Alaska? On 24 March 1989, the tanker *Exxon Valdez* hit a ree[...] Sound, leaking 11 million gallons of crude oil into the sea off Alaska. This was t[...] disaster in American history, fouling 1,300 miles of coastline and damagin[...] The owners and crew of the vessel attracted global condemnation. [...] he captain, Joseph Hazelwood; the *New York Times* headline re[...] d by journalists, received death threats, was fired by Ex[...] *me* magazine, however, argued that the evidence r[...] nizational factors (which also contributed to t[...]

1. There was no [...] n the ship ran aground. Although he ha[...]

2. Although Exxon [...] lcohol beer to tanker crewmen. Hazelwo[...] eve of the accident, which took place wh[...]

3. After the accident, Haz[...] against the reef, avoiding further spill and may[...] [...]

4. Exxon had cut the *Valdez* [...] ology made this possible, leaving fewer sailors working longer [...] uted to the disaster.

5. The second mate, who shou[...] ne vessel, was exhausted and asleep. The 'pilotage endorsement' of the th[...] control of the vessel in the sound, was disputed.

6. The acting helmsman had been pr[...] to able seaman one year earlier, from his job as room steward and waiter in the galley.

7. The coastguards failed to monitor the *Valdez* after it veered to avoid ice. They blamed this lapse on the weather, poor equipment and the 'change of shift preoccupations of a watchman'. The coastguards argued that they were not required to track ships as far as the reef which the *Valdez* struck; but the seamen said they depended on the coastguards.

Exxon paid $1 billion to the state of Alaska in 1991 and made compensation payments to 82 Eyak Indians in 1999. A sociological investigation in 1999 showed that local people remained depressed and traumatized, with high rates of alcoholism and other social ills, and were still catching deformed salmon. Hazelwood said: 'I feel terrible about the effects of the spill, but I'm just an ordinary fellow caught up in an extraordinary situation—a situation which I had little control over'. His rubbish collection was a form of personal penance.

Based on Richard Behar, 'Joe's bad trip', *Time*, 24 July 1989, pp.54–9;
'The Exxon Valdez: stains that remain', *The Economist*, 20 March 1999, p.63;
Giles Whittell, 'Exxon challenges payout a decade after Valdez spill', *The Times*, 25 March 1999, p.20.

Groups can achieve much more than individuals acting alone. We humans, like many other creatures on this planet, are social animals. We achieve psychological satisfaction and material gain from organized activity. Organizations, in their recruitment and other publicity materials, like you to think that they are 'one big happy family' working towards the same ends. Everyone is a team player, shooting towards the same goals. Organizations, of course, do not have goals. Only people can have goals. Collectively, the members of an organization may be making biscuits, curing patients, educating students—but individual members pursue a variety of goals of their own. Senior managers may decide on objectives and attempt to get others to agree with them by calling them an 'organizational mission' or 'corporate strategy'; but they are still the goals of the people who determined them in the first place.

Organizations can mean different things to those who use them and those who work in them, because they are significant personal and social sources of:

- money and physical resource;
- meaning, relevance and purpose;
- order and stability;
- security, support and protection;
- status, prestige, self-esteem and self-confidence;
- power, authority and control.

The goals pursued by individual members of an organization can be quite different from the collective purpose of their organized activity. This creates a central practical and theoretical problem in the design and study of organizations.

Forces of light, forces of darkness

From the beginning, the forces of light and the forces of darkness have polarized the field of organizational analysis, and the struggle has been protracted and inconclusive. The forces of darkness have been represented by the mechanical school of organizational theory—those who treat the organization as machine. This school characterizes organizations in terms of such things as: centralized authority, clear lines of authority, specialization and expertise, marked division of labour, rules and regulations, and clear separation of staff and line.

The forces of light, which by mid-20th century came to be characterized as the human relations school, emphasizes people rather than machines, accommodations rather than machine-like precision, and draws its inspiration from biological systems rather than engineering systems. It has emphasized such things as: delegation of authority, employee autonomy, trust and openness, concerns with the 'whole person', and interpersonal dynamics.

From Charles Perrow, 'The short and glorious history of organizational theory', *Organizational Dynamics*, Summer 1973.

The **organizational dilemma** concerns the perennial question of how to reconcile the potential inconsistency between individual needs and aspirations on the one hand, and the collective purpose of the organization on the other.

Organizations are social arrangements in which people strive to achieve control over resources in order to produce goods and services efficiently. However, organizations are also political systems in which individuals strive to achieve control over each other, to gain wealth, status and power. Power to define the collective purposes or goals of organizations is not evenly distributed. One of the main mechanisms of organizational control is hierarchy of authority. It is widely accepted (often with reluctance) that managers have the right to make the decisions, while lower-level employees are obliged to follow instructions. Those who have little influence on decision making typically must comply with directives, or leave.

A concern with performance leads to rules and procedures, and to jobs that are simple and monotonous. These features of job design simplify the tasks of planning, organizing and co-ordinating the efforts of large numbers of people. This efficiency drive, however, conflicts with the desire for freedom of expression, autonomy, creativity and self-development. It is difficult to design organizations that are efficient in using resources and also in developing human potential. Many of the 'human' problems of organizations arise from conflicts between individual needs and the constraints imposed in the interests of collective purpose. Attempts to control and co-ordinate human behaviour are thus often self-defeating.

That is a pessimistic view. Organizations are social arrangements, constructed by people who can also change them. Organizations can be repressive and stifling, but they can also be designed to provide opportunities for self-fulfilment and individual expression. The point is, the human consequences depend on how organizations are designed and run.

Happy cows give more milk

Clarence H. Eckles, in his book *Dairy Cattle and Milk Production* (Macmillan, New York, 1956, pp.332–3), identifies a number of methods for maximizing milk production:

1. Cows become accustomed to a regular routine; disturbing this routine disturbs them and causes a decrease in milk production.

2. Attendants should come into close contact with the cows, and it is important that the best of relations exist between the cows and keepers.

3. The cows should not be afraid of the attendants.

4. Cows should never be hurried.

5. Chasing cows with dogs or driving them on the run should never be allowed.

6. In the barn, attendants must work quietly; loud shouting or quick movements upset cows and cause them to restrict production.

Based on Jerry L. Gray and Frederick A. Starke, *Organizational Behaviour: Concepts and Applications*, Merrill Publishing, Columbus, third edition, 1984, p.14.

Stop and criticize

Suppose those dairy attendants are managers, and the cows are employees. To what extent can such methods be applied to employees in factories, hospitals, schools, shops and offices to resolve the organizational dilemma?

A field map of the organizational behaviour terrain

How can human behaviour in organizational settings be explained? To answer this question, we will develop a model of organizational behaviour to provide a guide to the content of the text. In other words, we will construct a 'field map' of the organizational behaviour terrain. A text has to cover individual topics one at a time. In practice, these discrete topics overlap. These interrelationships can be seen more clearly when we attempt to explain actual events.

Figure 1.1 shows an outline of our field map. Organizations do not operate in a vacuum but are influenced in various ways by their wider context, represented by the outer box on the map. One approach to understanding those influences is through 'PESTLE analysis', which explores the **p**olitical, **e**conomic, **s**ocial, **t**echnological, **l**egal and **e**cological forces impinging on the organization and its members. These are explored in chapters 2 and 3.

The map also shows that we want to explain two sets of factors. We want to be able to develop explanations for organizational effectiveness, and for the quality of working life, represented by the right-hand box on the map, which are considered throughout the text. There are five sets of factors which potentially provide those explanations. These concern individual, group, structural, process and management factors, which are explored in parts 2 to 6 of the text, and which are represented by the left-hand box on the map. Finally, we cannot consider organizations as static entities. Organizations and their members have plans for the future which influence actions today. Past events, achievements and disasters also

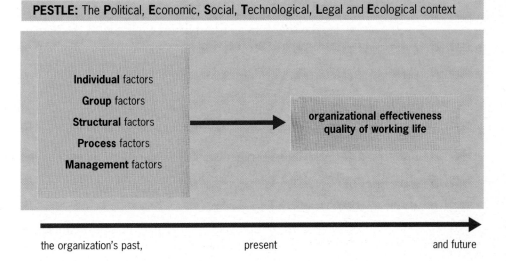

Figure 1.1: A field map of the organizational behaviour terrain

shape perceptions and actions, and it is often necessary to explain events and behaviours with reference to their location in time, represented by the arrow at the bottom of the map.

| **Stop and criticize** | The atmosphere just isn't the same any more, and the place is losing customers. Staff in the bar or restaurant that you frequent are less helpful and friendly than they used to be. The quality of service that you receive has declined sharply. Why? |

Use the field map in figure 1.1 as a source of possible explanations for this deterioration in performance. Can you blame context factors, new technology, particular individuals, aspects of teamworking, organization structure, recent changes to the culture or human resource management practices, or perhaps the management style? Maybe the cause of the problem lies with a combination of factors.

Let us return to the 'bad experience' you had earlier in the chapter. We now have a framework with which to develop explanations. Your treatment is a key dimension of organizational effectiveness—quality of customer service. Let us assume we are dealing with a shop assistant. The map allows us to suggest the following *possible* explanations.

Context factors

- Maybe the store is facing competition, sales have collapsed, the store is closing next month, and the loyal shop assistant is bitter about being made redundant (economic problems). Perhaps closure is threatened because the local population is declining, thus reducing sales (social problems). Perhaps the government faces European Union pressure for a new 'safe food tax' on retail outlets, making the cost structure of this store unviable (political problems). Maybe new 'point of sale' equipment has made staff anxious about the lack of training and their poor understanding of computers (technology problems).

Individual factors

- Maybe the shop assistant is not coping with the demands of the job because training has not been provided (learning problems). Maybe this shop assistant is not suited to the kind of work that involves interaction with a demanding public (personality problems). Perhaps your treatment resulted from a misunderstanding in communications between you and the shop assistant (communication problems). The shop assistant thought your complaint was minor, but you took it much more seriously (perception problems). Or perhaps the shop assistant finds the job boring and lacks challenge (motivation problems). Maybe the shop assistant is having personal, family or other domestic difficulties.

Group factors

- Maybe the employees in this part of the organization have not formed a cohesive working group (group formation problems). Maybe this shop assistant is excluded from the group for some reason (a newcomer, perhaps) and is unhappy (group structure problems). The informal norm for dealing with awkward customers like you is to be awkward in return, and this assistant is just 'playing by the rules' (group process problems). The organization may have introduced a new team approach without thinking through the training, supervision and pay issues (teamworking problems).

Structural factors

- Perhaps the organization structure is slow and bureaucratic, and the shop assistant is anxiously waiting for a longstanding issue to be resolved. Maybe there is concern about the way in which work is allocated. Perhaps the unit manager is unable to deal with problems without referring them to a regional manager, who doesn't understand local issues. Maybe the supervisor has too many responsibilities and is too distant from the shop assistants, or perhaps a 'working supervisor' gets in the way. Perhaps the organization structure was suitable when the store opened ten years ago, but not for today's pace of business change and more demanding customers (structural problems).

Process factors

- Perhaps the shop assistant is suffering from 'initiative fatigue' from the many changes introduced in recent years (change problems). Maybe communication problems and conflict with another unit have not been resolved (organization development problems). Perhaps the shop assistant is antagonistic towards many of this organization's taken-for-granted norms, processes and ways of working (organization culture problems). Maybe the shop assistant feels let down by the reward, training, promotion and career development systems (human resource management problems).

Management factors

- Maybe the shop assistant is annoyed at the autocratic behaviour of the unit manager (leadership style problems). Perhaps the shop assistant feels that management has made decisions without consulting employees who have useful information and ideas (management decision-making problems). Maybe management has inadvertently created conflict between members of staff and is not actively taking steps to address it (conflict problems). Perhaps managers and other staff have been playing 'power games' which have damaged the shop assistant in some way (politics problems).

This rehearsal of possible causes for your bad experience demonstrates a number of features of explanations of organizational behaviour.

1. It is always tempting to assume that the individual (our shop assistant) is to blame. However, it should be clear that this assumption will often be false. We need to look beyond such simple explanations and consider factors at different levels of analysis—individual, group, organization, management, the wider context.

2. It is also tempting to look for single or main causes of organizational behaviour. However, it should also be clear that behaviour is influenced by a wide range of factors which in combination contribute to organizational effectiveness and the experience of work.

3. While it is comparatively easy, and also helpful, to distinguish these factors and deal with them individually for the purposes of explanation and analysis, in practice they are interrelated. For example, in a crisis, or in a period of high uncertainty, some individuals may have a preference for a more directive style of management, particularly if that means fast and decisive action to restore order and predictability. So in this setting, we need to consider, at least, the relationships between context factors, individual factors and management factors. These relationships are not shown in figure 1.1 (because they would make it look untidy).

4. While this looks like a simple 'cause-and-effect' diagram, in practice the arrow between the two inside boxes also runs the other way. On the one hand, we might regard those individual, group, structural, process and managerial factors as *independent variables*, and organizational effectiveness and quality of working life as *dependent variables* (see glossary). But the opposite can also be the case. For example, it is reasonable to assume that high organizational effectiveness will have an impact on individual motivation, on group cohesiveness and performance, on organization structure and culture, and perhaps on management style. This and the previous point emphasize the need for *systemic thinking*: we need to be aware of the interrelationships between the factors that we are dealing with here.

Organizational effectiveness is a multidimensional concept defined differently by different stakeholders and stakeholder groups, using a wide range of quantitative and qualitative measures, and there is no common agreed definition of the term.

It is necessary to give some further consideration to the two factors, organizational effectiveness and quality of working life, which we want to explain. The term **organizational effectiveness** is controversial. The problem lies in the observation that an organization's many stakeholders have different definitions of what counts as 'effectiveness'. A *stakeholder* (see glossary) is anyone with an interest, or stake, in the actions of the organization and its members. We thus have to consider internal and external stakeholders.

Stop and criticize

Consider the institution in which you are currently studying. List the various internal and external stakeholders. Identify how you think each stakeholder would define 'organizational effectiveness' for this institution. Why the differences?

For commercial organizations, the obvious 'accounting' definition of effectiveness is 'profit'. But this is problematic for at least two reasons. First, timescale has to be considered, as actions to improve short-term profits may damage long-term profitability. Second, some organizations forgo profit, at least in the short to medium term, in the interests of gaining market share, which contributes to corporate survival, growth and stability of operations and employment. Shareholders want a return on investment, customers want quality products or services at reasonable prices, managers want high-flying careers and most employees want decent pay, good working conditions, development and promotion opportunities and job security. Environmental groups want the organization to spend money on conserving buildings and woodland, on reducing toxic emissions, on reducing traffic and noise levels, and so on. Organizational effectiveness, therefore, is a slippery concept, and it has been difficult to demonstrate clearly the links between organization and management practice on the one hand, and performance measures on the other.

The term 'organizational effectiveness' thus appears on our map as a 'shorthand' for a range of possible measures at different levels of analysis—individual, group, organizational and social.

One increasingly popular approach to this dilemma concerns the development of a **balanced scorecard** approach. This involves deciding on a range of quantitative and qualitative measures of the organization's performance, as a basis for evaluating management decisions and organizational effectiveness. The private utility company Anglian Water Services plc, for example, uses a balanced scorecard to guide executive board decisions and to evaluate organizational performance on four sets of criteria: shareholder value, internal efficiencies, employee development and environmental concerns.

The phrase *quality of working life* carries similar difficulties, particularly as we each have different needs and expectations from work. An additional difficulty with this concept is that it is intimately related both to organizational effectiveness and to most of the other factors on the left-hand side of our map. It is difficult to talk about quality of working life without considering motivation, teamwork, organizational design, organization development and change, human resource policies and practices, and management style.

What kind of model of organizational behaviour is this? The 'outputs' are difficult to separate from the 'inputs'. We began by suggesting that this could be read as a 'cause-and-effect' analysis. Manipulate the factors on the left of the model to change the values of organizational effectiveness and quality of working life on the right. That is an oversimplification. This is *one* way to view the terrain of organizational behaviour, but the 'simplifying assumptions' may cause us to overlook the interrelationships between the factors that we have separated out.

We need to be very cautious about using this model as a straightforward guide to 'cause and effect' in organizational behaviour. We would like to invite you instead to consider using this model as a guide to the text as a whole, as an 'organizing device', to locate each of the discrete chapters and parts in the wider context. We hope that this model will also serve as a reminder of the need for systemic thinking and analysis, recognizing the overlap and interrelationships between these factors.

The **balanced scorecard** approach to organizational effectiveness uses a predetermined range of quantitative and qualitative measures to guide management decision making and to assess organizational performance.

Natural and social sciences

Our field map of organizational behaviour highlights aspects of the debate surrounding the equivalence of natural and social science. There are two competing views on this issue. The *positivist* view claims that, as part of the natural world, human behaviour should be studied using methods comparable with those used to study the natural world.

Stop and criticize

We know that metals and gases expand when heated. This observation can be demonstrated and proved, repeatedly and reliably, by experiment.

Consider human behaviour in a busy night club. Why can our behaviour in such a setting *not* be studied using the same observational and experimental methods used to study what happens when metals are heated?

The interpretative or *phenomenological* view claims that we are *self-interpreting* beings; in other words, we attach meanings to what we do. The implication is that we cannot be studied using techniques that apply to natural objects and events. Chemical substances and rare metals, for example, do not attach meaning to their behaviour. They do not give interviews or fill in questionnaires. This division into competing camps obscures the fact that there are a number of different shades of positivism, and a variety of interpretative postures, a full examination of which is beyond the scope of our discussion (see Burrell and Morgan, 1979).

Is it possible to submit people to any kind of study that can be called 'scientific'? One major stumbling block seems to be that, when we know that we are being studied, we react by altering our behaviour—to appear more competent, more enthusiastic, more diligent, or just to help the researcher. As a result of these 'reactive effects', what the researcher observes and measures can be artificial, a false reflection of our 'true' selves and our behaviour (Bryman, 1988; 1989). Avoiding these reactive effects can be a methodological headache. Studying people without their knowledge is one solution, but this raises ethical problems. It seems that the standards of investigation used in natural science cannot easily be transferred to the study of people. For these reasons, some social scientists deny that they are scientists in the sense that biologists, physicists and astronomers are scientists.

The contribution of social and behavioural sciences to human knowledge is often regarded with scepticism and suspicion. It is a relatively simple matter to demonstrate the practical application of natural scientific endeavour. We can put people on the moon, deliver music, news and films to your computer down a phone line, genetically engineer disease-resistant crops, perform surgery using minimally invasive or 'keyhole' techniques, and so on. Natural science has also given us technologies with which we can do enormous damage, to each other and to the planet. Textbooks in electrical engineering, naval architecture, quantum mechanics and vascular surgery tell the reader how the world works, how to make things, and how to fix them. Students from these disciplines often find psychology and sociology texts disappointing because they do not offer practical guidance. Social science texts often raise more questions than they answer, and instead draw attention to debates, conflicts, ambiguities and paradoxes, which are then left unresolved. Science gives us *material technology*—mobile phones, personal transport, skyscrapers, antibiotics, video cameras, and so on—but social science has not given us a convincing *social engineering*, of the kind which, for example, would reduce car theft and eliminate football hooliganism.

Are we, and our organizations, really beyond the reach of scientific study? Surely not. We would like to encourage you to assess this issue for yourself. However, we would like to address the prejudice that can lead to a dismissal of anything that 'soft' social science may try to offer. We wish to encourage instead a critical approach to the social science enterprise in general, and to organizational research in particular, and to base that critical stance on an understanding of the issues that face all students of human behaviour.

The natural sciences—physics, astronomy, chemistry, biology, genetics—seem to be able to rely on direct observation, on consistent causal relationships between variables through time and space, on experimental methods to test

Table 1.1: Scientific goals and social science problems

Goals of science	Practical implications	Social science problems
description	measurement	invisible and ambiguous variables people change over time
explanation	identify the time order of events establish causal links between variables	timing of events not always clear cannot always see interactions
prediction	generalizing from one setting to another	uniqueness, complexity and lack of comparability between social settings
control	manipulation	ethical and legal constraints

hypotheses, and on mathematical reasoning. The study of human behaviour seems to founder on all of these issues. We cannot directly observe what is happening inside people's heads, different cultures and sub-cultures around the planet think and act differently, subjecting people to experimental methods is artificial and can be unethical, and many dimensions of behaviour are not amenable to quantification. The goals of science include description, explanation, prediction and control of events. These four goals represent increasing levels of sophistication. Table 1.1 summarizes the problems.

These 'problems' only become serious if we really expect social science to conform to natural science practice. However, if the study of people is a different kind of enterprise, then we need different procedures to advance our understanding, and different criteria will apply in evaluating success. Social science can thus be viewed as a different kind of science from the natural sciences. Social scientists are themselves divided on this issue.

Stop and criticize

Your instructor claims that the high turnover of supermarket checkout staff can be explained by the routine, repetitive and boring nature of the work.

How would you examine this claim using a positivist research approach? How would you examine this claim differently using a phenomenological approach?

Some social scientists argue that there is 'unity of method' in the study of natural and human phenomena. In other words, we should all use the same research perspective and techniques. The theoretical basis of this argument lies in the claim that human behaviour is governed by universal laws of the same kind that govern the behaviour of natural phenomena. These laws may just be complex and difficult to discern, and our social sciences may be relatively young.

One implication of the 'unity of method' perspective is a concern with refining social science methodology. Great care is taken to define terms precisely, to measure and quantify, to conduct controlled experiments, and to avoid or minimize the reactive effects generated by a researcher's presence. Social scientists, and organizational researchers, may just have to work harder on these issues. A second implication of this perspective is a concern with producing a social technology that can be used to predict and control human behaviour as effectively as we use material technologies to manipulate the natural order.

Stop and criticize

You discover that one of your instructors has a novel way of enhancing student performance on her module. She always gives students poor grades for their first assignment, regardless of their level of performance. This, she argues, stimulates higher levels of student performance in subsequent assignments.

This is an example of 'social engineering'. To what extent is this ethical?

Other social scientists argue that social and natural sciences are fundamentally different, and that the study of people cannot become more scientific by simply following more closely the procedures of quantum physicists and laboratory chemists. This distinction can be explored with respect to the four goals of description, explanation, prediction and control.

Description

There are three methods by which social scientists produce descriptions of the phenomena they study. These are observation, asking questions and studying documents. These methods can be applied in various different ways. The people studied may or may not know that they are research subjects. Questions can be asked in person by the researcher or through a self-report questionnaire. Documents of interest can include diaries, letters, company reports, committee minutes or published work. Physicists and chemists, for example, use only observation, albeit under specially designed and controlled conditions. Metals and chemicals, for example, do not respond to interrogation and do not publish autobiographies in the style that has become popular among senior organization executives.

Observation is useful in organizational research too. The researcher can listen to and watch informal discussion in a cafeteria, join a selection interview or follow participants through a training programme. However, in settings like these, it is often not possible to produce reliable measurements of terms that can be defined unambiguously. Suppose you want to measure aggression—a social phenomenon—at student dances through observation. How are you going to do this? A few moments thought should suggest that it is going to be difficult to decide what counts as 'aggressive' behaviour. Can you count as 'aggressive' the joking and

Jury science: a step towards social engineering?

To win a court case in America, litigants may soon need good behavioural scientists as well as good lawyers. Some companies are using them to help their lawyers distinguish friendly from unfriendly jurors and to assess how arguments in court are being received by the jury. University professors who are already boosting their earnings by providing such help occasionally must now reckon with Litigation Sciences, a firm based in California with 90 psychologists, sociologists, psychometrists and other professionals.

Its chairman, Dr Donald Vinson, holds a doctorate in marketing and sociology from the University of Colorado. He first got into the litigation business when, as an academic at the University of Southern California, his brains were picked by IBM in a $100 million anti-trust suit brought against it by California Computer Products. He recruited surrogate jurors who were as similar as possible to the real ones. Without disclosing which side had hired them, he asked his shadow jury to sit in court each day and quizzed them on their reaction to the arguments they had heard. His findings were passed on each night to IBM's lawyers to help them refine their strategy. IBM won the case.

From 'Jury science', *The Economist*, 8 July 1989, p.86.

friendly physical contact between people who know each other reasonably well? For research purposes, we must use terms like this precisely, and consistently, but this is not a straightforward matter.

The method that we use to decide what counts is known as an **operational definition** of the term in which we are interested.

Your operational definition of aggression could include raised and angry voices, physical contact, inflicting pain, and damage to property. You could count each event that you observe where at least one factor is evident. You could use this operational definition to construct a simple 'aggressiveness scale', with events where all four factors are evident rated as 'more aggressive'. Compare this with an operational definition of 'job satisfaction'. In practice, this can be measured by asking a single question, 'how satisfied are you with your job?' seeking answers on a five-point rating scale from very satisfied, through neutral, to very dissatisfied. However, we may feel that job satisfaction is affected by a range of factors such as management style, financial rewards, development opportunities, promotion chances, flexible working hours, and so on. Our operational definition could thus be a lengthy questionnaire with items relating to each of these factors.

We can overcome our inability to observe interesting factors. Consider the process of learning (chapter 4). As you read through this book, we would like to think that you are indeed learning something about organizational behaviour. However, if we could open your head as you read, we would have difficulty finding anything that could be meaningfully described as 'the learning process'. This is a convenient label for an invisible (or at least, invisible to a social scientist) activity whose existence we can assume or infer.

For research purposes, we must use terms precisely and consistently

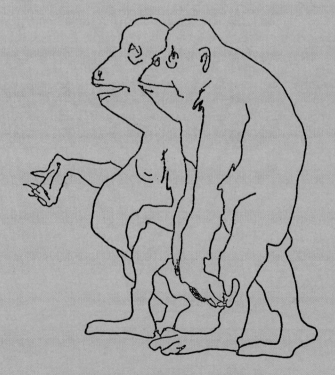

'... and then he raises the issue of, "how many angels can dance on the head of a pin?", and I say, you haven't operationalized the question sufficiently—are you talking about classical ballet, jazz, the two-step, country swing ...'

Some changes must take place inside your head if learning is to occur. Neurophysiology can help to track down the precise physical and biochemical events involved, but it is not clear how an improved understanding of the biochemistry of learning would help us to design better learning and training programmes.

The procedures for studying learning by inference are relatively straightforward. We can, for instance, examine your knowledge of organizational behaviour before you read this book and repeat the examination afterwards. We would expect the second set of results to be significantly better than the first. So we can confidently infer that learning has taken place. Your ability to perform a particular task has changed, and we can use that change to help us identify the factors that caused it. We can proceed in this manner to study the effects of varying inputs to the learning process, with respect to characteristics of the teachers, learners, abilities, and the time and resources devoted to the process. We can study variations in the delivery process, in terms of methods and materials. We can study the outputs from the process with respect to changes in the behaviour of our learners. In this way the relationships between the variables involved can be identified. Our understanding of the learning process can thus develop systematically, and from this knowledge we can suggest improvements.

Observation as a research method has many uses. Our understanding of what managers do, for example, is based largely on this method. But it has obvious limitations. What can we say about someone's motives merely by observing their behaviour? We could follow somebody—our target—around for a day or two and make guesses about their motives. But eventually we would probably want to engage them in conversation and ask some probing questions. The answers that we get are now our research data. The validity of those data, as an accurate reflection of the 'truth' of the situation, is questionable for at least three reasons.

1. Our target may lie. People who are planning a bank robbery, or who resent the intrusion of a researcher, may give misleading replies. There are ways in which we can check the accuracy of what people tell us, but this is not always possible or convenient.

2. Our target may not know. The mental processes related to our motives typically operate without conscious effort. Few of us make the effort to dig these processes out from our subconscious to examine them. Most of us struggle through life without the self-critical reflection that answers questions like, 'why am I here?' and 'what am I doing?' The researcher gets the answers of which the person is aware, or which seem to be appropriate, rational or 'correct' in the circumstances. The answers we get to some of our questions could be convenient inventions of the moment.

3. Our target may tell us what they think we want to hear. People rarely lie to researchers. They create problems by being helpful. Easier to give a simple answer than to relate a complex history of intrigue, heartbreak and family strife. The socially acceptable answer is better than no answer at all. People may tell researchers about their attitudes to, say, a controversial item of government legislation although they have never studied the details. A research interview is a peculiar form of social interaction. The participants in this interaction are usually strangers who quickly engage in a one-way exchange of (sometimes sensitive) information. The interview thus typically unfolds according to what the participants believe to be the unwritten social rules that guide such interactions. The researcher is expected to be curious, in control of the conversation, objective, friendly, non-threatening, and to respect confidentiality. The interviewee is expected to be open, honest and co-operative, and is allowed to be mildly curious about the researcher and

the aims of the study. Both parties thus want to appear competent and ethical, criteria which can be shown to influence both the questioning strategies that researchers use and the answers that respondents provide. This does *not* mean that the answers we get are wrong; rather, we need to be aware of the social context in which information is collected.

Explanation

It is often possible to infer that one event has caused another even when the variables are not observable. If your organizational behaviour test score is higher after reading this book than before, and if you have not been studying other materials, then we can infer that reading this book has caused your score to improve. The timing of events is not always easy to establish. Causes must happen before the effects they are said to explain. You are debating with someone who believes that women have a higher tolerance for repetitive work than men. Try arguing that the causal arrow points in the opposite direction. Women may learn to expect that the work available to them (in secretarial, clerical, retail, hotel, catering and manufacturing) will be boring and repetitive. In other words, the very notion of 'women's work' predates, or causes, the development of female 'acceptance'.

The rules or laws that govern human behaviour seem to be different from those that govern the behaviour of natural phenomena. The ways in which we understand causality in human affairs thus has to be different.

Consider, for instance, the meteorological law which states that 'clouds mean rain'. This law holds right around our planet. Now, a cloud cannot break that law, deliberately or by accident. The cloud does not have to be told, either as a youngster or when it approaches hills, about the business of raining. It has no choice in the matter. Compare this situation with the social law which states that 'red means stop'. A society can choose to change this law to one which says that blue means stop because some people are red–green colour blind (and thus cause hideous accidents). The human driver can get it wrong in two ways—by deliberately jumping the red light (in the early hours of a Sunday morning with no police in sight), or through lack of concentration and going through the red light accidentally. Clouds cannot vote to change the laws governing their behaviour; nor can they mischievously break these laws, or get them wrong by accident.

This has profound implications for social scientific research and understanding. The social scientist clearly cannot expect to discover laws that govern human behaviour consistently across time and place. Behaviour towards people over 40 years of age, as potential employees, changed markedly in the late 1990s compared with what has come to be known as an 'ageist' attitude common in the 1980s and early 1990s (to judge from the wording of job advertisements and the job-seeking experiences of those over 40). The employment of children is illegal in most of the planet's northern hemisphere but is still commonplace—and acceptable for social and economic reasons—in some developing countries.

We do not come into existence with pre-programmed behavioural guides. We have to learn the rules that apply in our particular society at a given time. There are strikingly different cultural rules concerning relatively trivial matters, such as how close people should stand to each other in different kinds of social setting. We have (mostly unwritten) rules about how and when to shake hands, about the styles of dress and address appropriate to different social occasions, about relationships between superior and subordinate, between men and women, between elderly and young. Even across the closely related cultures of Europe or of the Pacific Rim, there are striking differences in social rules, both between and within countries.

Social scientists concerned with explaining social or organizational behaviour have to start with the self-interpretations of their subjects. It is not enough to know *how* people do what they do; we also need to know *why*. People behave in accordance with their own theories and understanding of how the world works. These theories are not rigorously formulated or systematically tested. However, we share this understanding with other members of our society, and we are able to act competently without being objective and scientific about what we do. We know what behaviour is appropriate in particular settings, and what is not acceptable. We take our theories of how the world works for granted. We take our knowledge of how society, and its organizations, functions as common sense.

In addition, we live in a social and organizational world in which 'reality' means different things to different people. We live, therefore, in a world of multiple realities. The natural scientist does not have to confront this complication. Our individual views of reality depend on our unique social positions and are influenced in particular by our organizational positions. As customers who have done nothing obviously wrong, we have probably all met the unhelpful bus driver, the disgruntled waiter or the angry store manager—whose emotional response to us seems to have been triggered at least in part by a recent work experience.

Social science uses common words in unusual and special ways. This is not a unique stance. The medical profession also uses jargon. Your indigestion is dyspepsia to the doctor. This way of using language helps to ensure rigour and consistency in our thinking. The problem is that the 'technical' terms are often words that we use regularly in everyday conversation, and this can lead to confusion if we are not careful. A critical reading of the literature is necessary to identify and overcome these jargon problems.

It will be helpful to define some relatively common words in a more precise manner:

Some **behaviour** is readily observable. We see you walk, hear you talk, smell your perfume or aftershave, touch your hair and taste your cooking. There is a school of thought called **behaviourism** which argues that psychology should be confined to phenomena that can be directly observed, and which rejects the study of internal mental states, which can only be the subject of speculation.

The behaviourist stance has much in common with the positivist approach to social science. We cannot in this text address the range of perspectives and philosophical positions which claim the label of **positivism**. However, a brief definition will be helpful.

The behaviourist and positivist perspectives strike many commentators as incomplete and restrictive. In particular, behaviourism does not seem to fit comfortably with our self-understanding; we do have motives and attitudes, do we not? We seem to have thought processes and internally stored images of the world around us. These processes and images are certainly part of our daily, personal, conscious experience. As they appear to influence our behaviour, do they not deserve to be recognized as valuable objects of study, with the same research status as observable behaviour?

Various schools of thought have developed in response to the criticisms and limitations of behaviourism and positivism, in psychology and across the social sciences. In psychology and sociology, a research tradition has been established around the notion that, as people are self-interpreting, it makes sense to subject those self-interpretations to investigation through the study of what is often now called **action** rather than just behaviour.

The perspective that developed in response to behaviourism is known as **cognitive psychology**.

Cognitive psychology has much in common with the **phenomenological** approach to social scientific study mentioned earlier. Once again, we cannot address the range of perspectives and philosophical positions to which this broad term now apples (including, for example, hermeneutics, ethnomethodology, sym-

Cognitive psychology is a perspective which accepts as legitimate the study of internal mental states and processes, and which seeks to develop explanations of human behaviour based on the study of these factors, even though they are not directly observable.

Phenomenology is a broad social scientific perspective which claims that the social world has no external, objective, observable truth but instead that our reality is **socially constructed**; the social science task is not to gather facts and measurements but to study patterns of meanings and interpretations, to discover how experience is understood.

bolic interactionism, semiotics and interpretative sociology; see Denzin and Lincoln, 1994), but a brief definition will be helpful.

The claim that 'reality is socially constructed' (Berger and Luckmann, 1966) is not a straightforward one to grasp on first reading. A straightforward illustration might help.

We asked you earlier to consider how to measure the incidence of aggression at student functions by devising an operational definition of the term. If we now say that 'the reality of aggression at student functions is **socially constructed**', what do we mean? Suppose you observe one male student shout at and punch another male student on the upper arm. The second student responds by shouting back and pushing the first student away. A table is shaken, drinks are spilled, glasses are broken. This has all the trademarks of an aggressive encounter. However, on speaking to the parties involved, you find that they describe their behaviour in terms of friendship, fun and play. The other members of their group agree with this definition of the situation, which they too have observed. The socially defined version of events, for actors and for observers, does not concern aggression at all but strengthens an existing relationship. The researcher who only observes is in danger of reaching inaccurate conclusions. From this perspective, your operational definition is arbitrary. What matters is how those involved in this setting understand their own and each other's actions.

Positivism and phenomenology are now represented by many varying shades of opinion within and between these two extreme and oversimplified views. The main point which we want to establish here is that there are different standpoints from which people and organizations can be studied. There are, therefore, different approaches to producing explanations of human behaviour in social and organizational settings. While phenomenology and related perspectives seem to have become more influential, much published organizational research is still rooted in a positivist tradition. Even the relationship between these perspectives is controversial. Some commentators argue that these views are irreconcilable, while some researchers claim to draw from both perspectives in their work.

Stop and criticize

The social construction of reality is a perspective which, like **phenomenology**, argues that our social and organizational surroundings possess no ultimate truth or reality but are determined instead by the way in which we experience and understand those worlds which we construct and reconstruct for ourselves in interaction with others.

Hospital managers are concerned that some patients with medical emergencies wait for too long in the casualty department before they are diagnosed and treated.

The positivist wants to observe and record emergency patient numbers, waiting and treatment times, staffing levels, bed numbers and the availability of other resources.

The phenomenologist wants to talk to the doctors, nurses and ambulance crews to find out how they feel about working here and where they believe the problems lie.

Which approach is more likely to result in practical solutions, and why?

Prediction

Social science can often explain events without being able to make precise predictions (table 1.2). Social science predictions are often probabilistic rather than determinate. We may be able to predict the rate of suicide in a given society, or the incidence of stress-related disorders in an occupational group. However, we can rarely predict whether specific individuals will try to kill themselves, or suffer sleep and eating disorders. This limitation in our predictive ability is not necessarily critical. We are often more interested in the behaviour of groups of people than in individuals. We are often more interested in probabilities and tendencies than in individual predictions.

There is a more fundamental problem. Researchers often communicate their findings to those who have been studied. Suppose you have never given much thought to the ultimate reality of human nature. One day, you read about an American psychologist, Abraham Maslow, who claims that we have a fundamental need for 'self actualization', to develop our capabilities to their full potential. If this sounds like a good idea to you, and you act accordingly, then what he has said has become true, in your case. His prediction has fulfilled itself. This may be because he has given you a new perspective on human existence, or because he has given you a label to explain some aspect of your existing intellectual makeup.

Some predictions are thus self-fulfilling. The act of saying something will happen can either make that happen or increase the likelihood of it happening. Equally, some predictions are self-defeating, and intentionally so. Many of the disastrous predictions from economists, about exchange and interest rate movements for example, are designed to trigger action to prevent those prophecies from coming true. In an organizational setting, one could predict that a particular management style will lead to the resignation of a number of valuable employees, in the hope that this prediction will lead to a change in management style.

Table 1.2: We can explain—but we cannot predict	
we can explain staff turnover in a supermarket in terms of the repetitive and boring nature of the work	but we cannot predict which members of staff will leave, or when they will choose to do so
we can explain how different management styles encourage greater or lower levels of employee commitment and performance	but we cannot predict which managers will achieve the highest levels of performance in a given setting
we can explain the factors that contribute to group cohesiveness in an organization	but we cannot predict the level of cohesion and performance of particular groups
we can explain why some types of organization structure are more adaptable in the face of external change than others	but we cannot predict the performance improvements that will follow an organizational structure change

Organizational research can point to the options and demonstrate how those options can be evaluated. The researcher is often in a position to claim, say, that if a payment and appraisal system is designed in a particular way, the employee response is likely to be negative, and that an alternative approach would lead to more favourable responses. The prediction is thus made in the expectation that other options will be explored. The kinds of prediction that natural science makes cannot have such an effect on the phenomena studied.

Control

Social science findings induce social change; organizational research findings similarly induce change. The natural scientist does not study the natural order of things in order to be critical of that order, or to encourage that order to change and improve itself. It does not make much sense to argue whether nature could be better organized. It is hardly appropriate to evaluate, as good or bad, the observation that a gas expands when heated, or the number of components in a strand of DNA. Social scientists, on the other hand, are generally motivated by a desire to change society, or aspects of it, and its organizations. An understanding of how things currently work, and the strengths and weaknesses of current arrangements, is essential for that purpose. Such understanding, therefore, is not necessarily a useful end in itself. Social science can be deliberately critical of the social and organizational order that it uncovers, because that order is only one of many that we are capable of constructing.

Table 1.3: Interventions which attempt to control organizational behaviour

organizational intervention	attempts to control
staff training and development programmes (chapter 4)	employee knowledge and skills
psychometric assessments (chapter 5)	the types of people employed
employee communications (chapter 6)	employee understanding and compliance with management-inspired goals
job redesign (chapter 8)	employee motivation, commitment and performance
teambuilding (part 3)	levels of team cohesion and performance
reorganization—structure change (part 4)	levels of organizational response to external environmental turbulence
organizational change and development (chapters 17 and 18)	speed of change and reduction of conflict and resistance
organization culture change (chapter 19)	shared values, attitudes, beliefs and goals among management and employees

An agenda directed at inducing social and organizational change is not the same as controlling or manipulating human behaviour, which many people would regard as unethical. As already indicated, we do not have a social technology, comparable to material technology, that enables us to manipulate other people anyway. Perhaps we should be grateful for this. However, table 1.3 identifies interventions, explained in following chapters, designed to control various aspects of employee behaviour.

It is important to recognize that our judgements and our recommendations are based not only on evidence but also on values. Social science has been criticized as 'ideology in disguise'. However, if one studies organizations in order to change and improve them, then that 'criticism' is inescapable. Suppose we study repetitive clerical work in an insurance company, or unskilled packing work in biscuit-making. The people doing these jobs are bored and unhappy, and our research identifies work redesign options. Managers claim that their work system is a cost-effective way of producing the goods and services their customers, who have no complaints, want. The tension between these two positions cannot be resolved with reference only to empirical evidence.

Table 1.4 summarizes the two contrasting perspectives from which human behaviour in general and organizational behaviour in particular can be studied.

We must now revisit our field map of the organizational behaviour terrain and reinforce the caution raised earlier concerning its status and use.

Table 1.4: Positivism versus phenomenology

	Perspective	
	Positivist or behaviourist	**Phenomenological or cognitive**
Description	studies observable behaviour	studies internal mental states, meanings and interpretations
Explanation	seeks fixed universal laws governing behaviour	focuses on individuals' understanding and interpretation of the world to explain behaviour
Prediction	based on knowledge of consistent relationships between variables	based on shared understanding and awareness of multiple social and organizational realities
Control	aims to shape behaviour by manipulating external variables	aims at social and organizational change through stimulating critical awareness

Seen from a positivist perspective, that model prompts the search for causal links: this organization structure will improve flexibility, that approach to job design will enhance motivation, quality of working life and performance. The positivist is looking for method, for technique, for specific and codified universal solutions to organizational problems.

Seen from a phenomenological perspective, the model prompts a whole range of other questions: how do we define and understand the term 'organization', and what does the term 'organizational effectiveness' mean to different stakeholder groups? What kind of work experiences are different individuals looking for, and how do they respond to their experience, and why? The phenomenologist seeks to trigger organizational change by stimulating self-critical awareness.

This field map, or model, therefore, does not in any straightforward sense lay out causal links across the organizational behaviour terrain. It is simply one useful way of displaying a complex terrain quickly and simply. As indicated earlier, we hope that it serves as a reminder of the need for systemic thinking and analysis, and also as a reminder that there is no one 'correct' way to view this subject matter.

Recap

1. *Explain the significance of an understanding of organizational behaviour.*

   - Organizations influence almost every aspect of our daily lives in a multitude of ways.

   - If we eventually destroy this planet, the cause will not lie with technology or weaponry. We will have destroyed it with ineffective organizations.

2. *Explain and illustrate the central dilemma of organizational design.*

   - The organizational dilemma concerns the question of how to reconcile the inconsistency between individual needs and aspirations, and the collective purpose of the organization.

3. *Understand the need for explanations of behaviour in organizations that take account of relationships between factors at different levels of analysis.*

   - The study of organizational behaviour is multi-disciplinary, drawing in particular from psychology, social psychology, sociology, economics and political science.

   - Organizational behaviour involves the inclusive, multi-level study of the external environment, and internal structure, functioning and performance of organizations, and the behaviour of groups and individuals.

   - Organizational effectiveness and quality of working life are explained by a combination of contextual, individual, group, structural, process and managerial factors.

   - In considering explanations of organizational behaviour, systemic thinking is required, avoiding simple explanations based on single causes and considering a range of interrelated factors at different levels of analysis.

4. *Identify the features that differentiate the natural and social sciences, and the implications of this differentiation.*

- A positivist perspective assumes 'unity of method' with the natural sciences and attempts to use the same research methods and criteria.

- It is difficult to apply conventional scientific research methods to people, mainly because of the 'reactive effects' which come into play when people know they are being studied.

- A phenomenological or interpretativist perspective assumes that, as human beings are self-defining creatures who attach meanings to their behaviour, the social science enterprise is fundamentally different from natural science.

- The phenomenological or interpretativist perspective believes that reality is not 'out there' but is socially constructed.

- An interpretativist approach means abandoning scientific neutrality in the interests of seeking to stimulate social and organizational change through a combination of critical feedback and stimulating self-awareness.

Revision

1. How is organizational behaviour defined, what does the subject cover and what is its practical relevance?

2. What are the advantages and disadvantages of a managerialist perspective on organizational behaviour?

3. Organizations are an everyday feature of our lives. Why then is the concept of organization so difficult to define?

4. Describe an example of organizational *mis*behaviour where you as customer were treated badly. Explore systematically the possible explanations for your treatment. What does this reveal about the nature of explanations of organizational behaviour?

5. What, for the study of organizational behaviour, are the theoretical and practical distinctions between positivism and phenomenology?

Springboard

Bryman, A., 1989, *Research Methods and Organization Studies*, Routledge, London.

Offers a well-informed treatment of a range of social science methods to organizational research. Also explains methodological and epistemological debates.

Burrell, G. and Morgan, G., 1979, *Sociological Paradigms and Organizational Analysis*, Heinemann, London.

Seminal analysis of the competing paradigms from which organizations can be studied. Still widely referenced and used, and still generating debate.

Clegg, S.R., Hardy, C. and Nord, W.R., 1996, *Handbook of Organization Studies*, Sage, London.

An award-winning collection of essays displaying the breadth of empirical concern and theoretical perspective now characterizing the field of organization studies. A challenging text (also available in paperback part-works) but a difficult read.

Denzin, N.K. and Lincoln, Y.S. (eds), 1994, *Handbook of Qualitative Research*, Sage, Thousand Oaks, California.

Benchmark text on qualitative research methods, which confronts and explains the diversity of views and positions within the phenomenological or interpretative perspective. Another challenging text, and also a difficult read.

Harrison, M.I., 1994, *Diagnosing Organizations: Methods, Models and Processes*, Sage, Thousand Oaks, California.

A more focused treatment of organization research methods, demonstrating the similarities between research methods and management consulting techniques.

Morgan, G., 1997, *Images of Organization*, Sage, London (second edition).

Influential work popularizing the use of metaphors to develop different insights and perspectives on organizations.

Palmer, I. and Hardy, C., 2000, *Thinking About Management: Implications of Organizational Debates for Practice*, Sage, London.

Excellent counter to those who prefer 'the correct answer' and 'the one best way'. Explores clearly the relevance of contemporary debates in organization theory in an engaging style which is not typical of similar critical writing on management.

Home viewing

The Firm (1993, director Sydney Pollack), based on John Grisham's novel, powerfully demonstrates the use of a range of methods for 'cementing' the new employee Mitch McDeere (played by Tom Cruise) and his wife Abby (Jeanne Tripplehorn) into the structure, culture and goals of a large and successful American law practice. Note the techniques used to address the organizational dilemma. Consider how effective these methods are in encouraging hard work, commitment and compliance with company rules. The problem is, the firm is Mafia-controlled, and Mitch doesn't realize this until the FBI becomes involved.

OB in literature

Franz Kafka, *The Castle*, Penguin Books, Harmondsworth, 1926.

How is the organizational dilemma, in which the individual confronts a large, rigid, impersonal organization, illustrated in this novel? Here we see the individual's sense of autonomy and responsibility confronted with anonymous, impersonal and elusive organizational power. How well does this classic novel represent the relationships between employees and large bureaucratic organizations today?

Chapter exercises

1: Self-test

Objectives

1. To consider the nature of social science thinking and explanations.
2. To expose the limitations of common-sense explanations of human behaviour.

Briefing

We are all experts in the subject of human behaviour—or at least we like to think we are. There must be some truth in this belief, given the rich base of experiences from which we can draw. However, this thinking leads to the claim that psychology, social psychology and sociology, the subjects that underpin organizational behaviour, are merely common sense wrapped in jargon. It is therefore useful to confront this issue rather than to avoid it.

Your task is to indicate whether each of the following 20 statements is either true or false by writing a T or an F at the side. In some cases you will want to answer, 'it depends'. However, you are asked to take a stand and indicate whether you feel that, on the whole, in most circumstances, for most practical purposes, the statement is true or false.

Compare your responses with those of at least two other people. Share your thinking, and establish why you have disagreed. If time allows, share your reasoning on items where you were particularly unhappy about making a clear commitment.

Twenty statements self-test

1. Men are naturally better when it comes to decisive managerial decision making, compared with women.
2. People who are satisfied in their work are more productive than those who are not.
3. Resistance to new technology increases with age.
4. Alcohol in small amounts is a stimulant.
5. You can always 'read' a person's emotional state by watching their facial expressions closely.
6. The more challenging the goals you face, the more you are likely to accomplish.

7. Selection interviews, handled correctly, are effective ways to assess candidates' suitability for a job.

8. When asked to rank features of their work in order of personal importance, the vast majority of people put pay at the top of their list.

9. Punishment is an effective way of eliminating undesirable behaviour.

10. When you have to remain working for several hours, it is better to take a small number of long rest periods than a larger number of short breaks.

11. When people can share their thinking in groups, they can come up with more original ideas than individuals working on their own.

12. Most people, if they are being honest with themselves, can tell you what their motives are.

13. People have a natural resistance to organizational change, and managers always have to overcome this first.

14. Conflict in an organization is disruptive and should be avoided at all costs.

15. Some people are born leaders, and this is evident in their behaviour.

16. A reliable personality test is a good predictor of job performance.

17. People learn new tasks better when they are only told about their successes and their mistakes are overlooked.

18. It is not possible for individual managers to change their style, because this reflects an innate aspect of their personalities.

19. Organizations always become ineffective when people do not have clear job descriptions that set out their responsibilities and define their place in the organization structure.

20. Extroverts invariably make better salespersons.

2: This sporting life

Objectives

1. To illustrate the use of the field map of organizational behaviour as a diagnostic tool for understanding the factors contributing to organizational effectiveness.

2. To demonstrate the importance of systemic thinking, as opposed to looking for single causes, in developing explanations of organizational effectiveness.

Briefing

Why do some organizations succeed, while others fail? Why is an organization successful one year, and less successful the next? These simple questions can have complex answers. To understand more fully the factors contributing to organizational success, and also to appreciate the complex nature of the relationships between these factors, it is instructive to carry out your own analysis of an organization with which you are familiar. For the purposes of this analysis, it does not matter which organization you choose. If you are working in a group context, then it should be an organization with which most or all members of your group or syndicate are familiar.

However, why not choose a club from your favourite female or male team sport? This could, for example, be the British football club Manchester United (a male-dominated sport, but with many female followers). Why choose a sports club as the organization on which to base this analysis? Two reasons. First, sports clubs such as this are now significant commercial enterprises run in much the same way as any other profit-making business, generating revenue not only from ticket sales but also from advertising, sponsorship, television rights and 'cross selling' of club merchandise such as sports clothing. Second, and more important for the purposes of this analysis, the relative success of a sports club is usually attributed exclusively to the skills of the players. But are the players' skills the only factor to consider? The tools for analysing the organization's external environment are explained in chapter 2, so we will overlook this dimension for the purposes of this analysis. Your task is to identify, using the following table, the respective contributions, positive and negative, of individual, group, structural, process and management factors to club performance. If you are very familiar with the organization concerned, name names, point the finger, identify individuals where possible and appropriate.

Factors affecting sporting success

Factors	Examples	Positive and negative contributions
Individual factors	players' skills and abilities; personalities and egos; interpersonal communications; achievement motivation; perception of club status	
Group factors	group cohesion; status and leadership structure in the team; team behavioural norms; do the players like each other?	
Structural factors	club ownership; flexible structure or rigid bureaucratic approach; composition of the main board; financial health	
Process factors	plans for organization development; substance of organizational changes; how changes are implemented; the culture of the club; recruitment, retention, motivation and reward policies for players	
Management factors	leadership styles of team captain, coach and club chairman; power holders on the board; decision-making style; internal politics and conflicts	

When you have completed this analysis, consider in consultation with colleagues the following two questions:

1. How do these separate factors interact with and reinforce each other in contributing to and explaining organizational effectiveness?

2. Given the range of factors that can influence organizational effectiveness, how important are the players? Given their contribution following this analysis, to what extent do they deserve the high fees that leading clubs typically pay?

This analysis should demonstrate that there are many interrelated factors contributing to the success or failure of a sports club, whether in football, netball, basketball or hockey. The skill of an individual player is clearly important, but this is only one consideration among many, and the skills which players demonstrate on the pitch are themselves affected by other factors.

Part 1 The organizational context

A field map of the organizational behaviour terrain

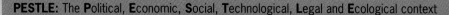

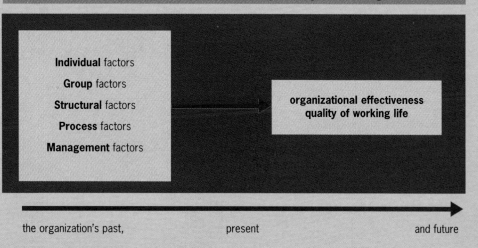

Introduction

Part 1, The organizational context, explores two topics:

- the relationships between internal organization structures and external environmental factors, in chapter 2;

- the influence of technology on jobs and organizations, in chapter 3.

The subject matter of organizational behaviour spans a number of levels of analysis—individual, group, organization and the wider environment, or context. Part 1 thus deals primarily with context. Technology can be regarded as one dimension of that context, but its implications are now so fundamental and widespread that it requires attention in its own right.

One of the recurring themes in this text concerns the design of jobs, and the organization and experience of work. The organization of work is subject to a number of shaping or influencing factors, operating at different levels of analysis. We explain how the experience and organization of work is influenced by:

- *contextual* factors, in chapter 2;
- *technological* factors, in chapter 3;
- *psychological* factors, in chapter 8;
- *social psychological* factors, in chapter 12;
- *historical* factors, in chapter 13;
- *managerial* factors, in chapter 20.

Our opening case study concerns recent organizational and technological trends concerning the increasingly popular use of call centres. However, the organization of work in call centres seems to create problems. If you were an external management consultant, how would you advise call centre managers on how to address and resolve these difficulties? It's your call.

"Telemarketing. And what do you do?"

YOUR CALL: (1): ENVIRONMENT AND TECHNOLOGY

The quantity–quality dilemma

A call centre is a business operation in which the employees' task is to handle incoming and outgoing telephone calls, assisted by computer access to customer or client information. Calls are processed and controlled by automatic call distribution (ACD). While the combination of telephone and computer technology is central to call centre functioning, their rapid growth in popularity is attributable to other business factors. These include the adoption, by some companies, of aggressive direct sales methods, and the apparently dramatic cost savings to be achieved by centralizing traditional 'back office' customer service functions.

The work of the call centre operator can be repetitive, emotionally draining and stressful. To establish consistency, some centres train operators to use 'interaction scripts', which specify what they can say and in what sequence. Some centres are operated 'round the clock', requiring staff to work twelve-hour shifts. Research has found that, in some centres, employees are given escalating performance targets and are pressured into increasing sales. The technologies on which call centres are founded create opportunities for detailed surveillance of staff activity. Employee behaviour and performance can easily be monitored by computer, and supervisors can 'listen in' and record conversations.

A survey revealed that the following monitoring measures were being used in call centres:

Form of monitoring	Percentage of call centres using this
politeness towards customers	85
length of calls	77
adherence to set procedures	73
call taping and review	69
adherence to script/form of words	65
content of calls	65
customer satisfaction measures	58
quality audit	54
time between calls	48

The fiercely competitive external environment, the demands of the call centre operator's work and labour market pressures have generated a number of management concerns. Call centres no longer handle simple enquiries but have developed a broad and sometimes complex range of 'value-added' customer services. The quality of the interaction between customer and operator is thus critical. However, given the pressures of the job, many call centres have high levels of staff turnover, which can reach 30 per cent a year.

Strict adherence to scripts can lead to operator fatigue and customer dissatisfaction, and some centres have switched to flexible scripting, or have discarded scripts. However, some centres found that this did not solve their problems and have reinstated scripts, arguing that technical and business considerations impose limitations on the discretion that can be given to staff. Some companies have discovered that, if operators are driven too hard with measurable output targets, the quality of customer service suffers. An emphasis on informality with relaxed targets and minimum surveillance may reduce the volume of business conducted.

From an external consultant's perspective, how would you advise call centre management to address and resolve these problems? It's your call.

This case is based on P. Taylor and P. Bain, 1999, 'An assembly line in the head: work and employee relations in the call centre', *Industrial Relations Journal*, vol.30, no.2, pp.101–17.

Chapter 2 The world outside

Key concepts

environment	PESTLE analysis	globalization
post-modern organization	postmodernism	environmental scanning
scenario building	environmental determinism	deconstruction
environmental complexity	environmental dynamism	consolidation

Learning objectives

When you have read this chapter, you should be able to define those key concepts in your own words, and you should also be able to:

1. Understand the mutual interdependence between the organization and its environment.

2. Appreciate the strengths and limitations of PESTLE analysis of organizational environments.

3. Explain the main contemporary organizational responses to environmental turbulence.

4. Describe the main features of the 'post-modern' organization.

5. Understand the main characteristics of a postmodern perspective on organizational behaviour, and the creative and critical dimensions of this approach.

Why study the world outside?

An organization, in order to function and to survive, has to interact constantly with the world outside, with its **environment**. Organizations do not operate in a vacuum. The operations of any organization—corner grocery, local high school, multinational motor car manufacturer—can be described in terms of its 'import–transformation–export' processes. The car plant 'imports' from its environment a range of resources such as component parts and manufacturing equipment, storage facilities, staff to run the factory, and energy to provide heating and lighting and run the machinery. The car plant then 'transforms' these resources into vehicles, which are 'exported' to a dealer network for sale to the public. The organization is involved in a constant series of exchanges with suppliers, customers, regulatory agencies and other 'stakeholders', such as share owners and trade unions.

The environment for a motor car plant in the early twenty-first century is complex. There is global overcapacity in car manufacturing. The industry consolidation of the late 1990s, in which smaller manufacturers (Saab, Rover, Jaguar,

The **environment** of an organization includes issues, trends, events and other factors which are outside the boundaries of the organization but which can influence decisions and behaviours inside the organization.

Volvo) were bought by larger companies (General Motors, Ford, BMW), continues. Cost competition encourages manufacturers to locate plants in low-wage countries (Hungary, Brazil, Romania), generating job losses and resentment in traditional car-manufacturing countries (Britain, America). In Japan, *gaiatsu*, or foreign pressure, justified major restructuring in Toyota, Honda and Nissan in the late 1990s. To reduce lead times and supply chain costs, motor manufacturers are increasingly bypassing dealers and selling direct to customers through the internet.

Cost competition has also encouraged the application of 'lean manufacturing' methods, based on Japanese experience, with consequences for working practices and the quality of working life. There is continuing concern over the environmental pollution generated by internal combustion engines which burn petrol and diesel fuel, encouraging product innovation to reduce toxic emissions and to develop 'cleaner' engines. Traffic congestion in many countries and cities around the world is driving governments to consider a range of road pricing and car and petrol taxation measures to encourage greater use of public transport, potentially reducing the demand for cars. These are just some of the factors in the external environment of a car plant forcing constant internal adjustments to ways of thinking about the business of making cars, the organization's strategy, a host of management decisions, and the organization structure, working practices and design of jobs.

Stop and criticize

What other factors, trends or developments in the external environment of a car plant have not been mentioned? How will these affect the company's behaviour?

What are the main factors in the external environment of a small grocery shop? What aspects of the behaviour of this business can you explain with reference to its external environment?

The argument of this chapter, that many aspects of organizational behaviour can be explained with reference to factors beyond the boundaries of the organization, is illustrated in figure 2.1. In other words, 'the world out there' influences 'the world in here'.

Social science texts often cause intense annoyance among readers from other disciplines by first introducing a model, explaining it in detail, then revealing that it is 'wrong'. As this is the strategy adopted in this chapter, an explanation is in order.

There are three reasons for using this 'build it up then knock it down' approach.

1. We have to start somewhere, so let us begin simple and work up to complex.

2. If we construct an argument using straightforward assumptions, then introduce more complex and realistic assumptions, the thinking behind the model and its interrelationships can be exposed more clearly.

Figure 2.1: The external environment–internal organization link

3. It is important to consider models like the one in figure 2.1 simply as singular perspectives, as 'one point of view', and not necessarily as 'correct' and beyond dispute. One of the other arguments of this chapter concerns the advantages of viewing organizations from many different standpoints. The search for 'the one best way' or 'the correct answer' is illusory.

An understanding of the dynamics of the environment is critical to organizational effectiveness, irrespective of organization size or sector. An organization which is 'out of fit' with its environment (still making stagecoaches now that railways have been invented) has to change, or go out of business. As the complexity and pace of environmental change seem to have increased, organizations that are able to adapt quickly to new pressures and opportunities are likely to be more effective than those which are slower to respond. One central concern for organizational behaviour, therefore, has been the search for 'fit' between the internal characteristics of the organization and features of the external environment.

Analysing the organizational environment

Identifying the factors 'out there' in the environment, now and into the future, which could potentially have an impact on the organization usually generates a long list. For our grocery store, this is likely to include, for example, the price of bananas at Tesco, on the one hand, and the preferences, values and shopping habits of an aging population, on the other. The first problem then is to identify all of those factors. The next difficulty, however, is to predict the impact of the factors identified. Will elderly shoppers maintain the habits of their youth, with a major weekly shop by car at an impersonal supermarket, or will they prefer convenient and friendly local service at higher prices?

The methods used to analyse the external environment of the organization are known as **environmental scanning** techniques.

Environmental scanning is a term for a number of techniques for identifying and predicting the potential impact of external trends and developments on the internal functioning of an organization.

Environmental scanning typically involves the collection of relevant information from a wide range of sources: government statistics, newspapers and magazines, internet sites, specialist research and consulting agencies, demographic analysis, and market research and focus groups, for example. Scanning can also be conducted at different levels of detail, from the broad and general to the highly specific. It appears that there are three major trends affecting just about all organizations. These are global competition, information technology, and social and demographic trends.

Global competition

Businesses in Europe and North America have been threatened, since the 1970s, from competition in the Pacific Rim region of the world, particularly from Japan, Taiwan, South Korea and Hong Kong. These countries were able to produce cars, motor bicycles and a range of consumer electronic and entertainment products with higher quality and lower prices, using shorter production times and new operating processes. European and American businesses in response have become significantly more cost- and quality-conscious, with an increased focus on continuous improvement and customer service. During the late 1990s, the economies of the Pacific Rim suffered through a combination of currency exchange rate collapses, banking system crises and cumbersome organization structures, but their earlier successes have made a lasting impression on European and American management practice.

The term given to these trends and developments (Giddens, 1990, p.64) is **globalization**.

> **Globalization** means the intensification of worldwide social relations which link distant localities in such a way that local happenings are shaped by events occurring many miles away and vice versa.

Globalization thus involves what has come to be called 'the death of distance' [**link**: chapter 3, technology], meaning simply that geographical separation, of countries and of individuals, has become insignificant. Globalization means that the fate of a Third World village, dependent on export sales revenues from a single crop, can be determined by price movements in exchanges in New York or Frankfurt. Globalization means that the actions of a financial markets trader in Singapore can cause the collapse of a London bank. Globalization means that decisions taken in Tokyo can influence employment in Derby in the English Midlands, where Toyota has a car manufacturing plant—at the time of writing. Globalization means that a dispute between Brussels and Washington over trade regulations can close knitwear factories in the Borders region of Scotland, as America threatens to block imports of European goods in retaliation for a European block on imports of American bananas.

Global communication, and the exchange of information and ideas, is now instantaneous, through a range of media including land-wired telephones, mobile telephones and satellite links, and the computer-based internet and e-mail. Such instant communication permits the creation of virtual organizations [**link**, chapter 16, organization strategy and design], whose members are scattered in various different locations rather than working in the same building. Globalization has also been assisted by the development of free trade through national and international deregulation, which has made it easier to move goods and money around the planet, and to relocate production facilities (for goods and services) in regions where labour and other costs are relatively low. For some commentators, this means that the role of the single nation-state in economic affairs is reduced, and we see the increasing importance of supranational bodies such as the European Union (EU), the Association of South East Asian Nations (ASEAN), the Organisation for Economic Co-operation and Development (OECD) and the North American Free Trade Agreement (NAFTA). Global access to advanced technology and weaponry also now means that local conflicts quickly attract global attention.

Consider your own experience of globalization. This is probably reflected in holiday plans, overseas job opportunities, the clothes that you wear and the food and drink that you consume, and the way in which you use the internet, phones and media technology. You are thus likely to have a range of direct and indirect encounters with other cultures almost on a daily basis, and this experience in turn is likely to change your understanding of the world. However, it is important to remember that many people around the planet do not have access to the goods and technologies that constitute the experience of globalization for affluent middle-class individuals in developed economies. Globalization is an uneven process from which many are excluded for geographic, political and economic reasons. Many societies and groups are also likely to reject the dislocation and disorientation of globalization.

We appear, however, to have entered an age of 'disorganized capitalism', complex and rapidly changing, in which the boundaries of large organizations in particular have become blurred, and in which the nature of work itself is in a constant state of flux. Figure 2.2, based on the work of John Kotter (1995), summarizes this argument. The arrows running down the figure set out a causal chain, from the technological, economic and geopolitical trends at the top of the figure to the organizational changes at the bottom. Kotter is arguing, with many others, that organizational changes in the direction of becoming faster, flatter and more flexible are being determined by a range of external environmental pressures, which are 'driving' globalization, introducing new threats and problems but also opening up new organizational and market opportunities. Organizational change seems, from this argument, to be inevitable. The message is 'adapt to survive'.

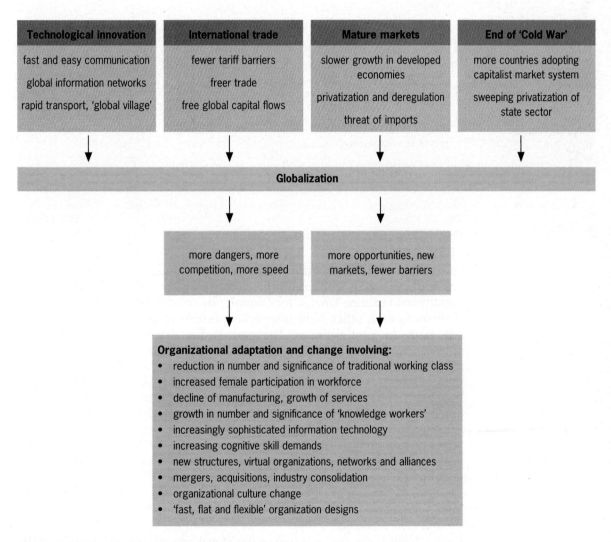

Figure 2.2: Globalization and organizational change

The 'adapt to survive' argument seems also to apply at the national level, and not just to organizations or sectors. For example, there is evidence to suggest that British organizations are less productive and less competitive than American, Japanese and German organizations because of specific national cultural characteristics that block innovation and change.

Why Britain is not competitive in global markets

British industry suffers from too little investment, poor management and a culture that looks down on technology. The causes of Britain's competitiveness gap include:

- The education system reinforces a cultural bias against industry.

- Top talent avoids industry for the City [of London] and other professions.

- An obsession with process, which stifles entrepreneurialism.

- The lack of competition, in service and manufacturing sectors, which generates productivity growth in other countries.

- Large companies are underrepresented in high-growth sectors relative to major American, Japanese and European competitors.

- Front-line managers are paid less than in Germany or America.

- A consultancy-dominated culture, which discourages the development of 'hands-on' management skills.

- Investment in information technology lags behind European and American rivals.

- Lack of innovation spending means that Britain is deficient in new product development.

- American companies have economies of scale, while French and German companies make higher-quality products which are more robust. Britain has neither of these strengths.

Based on Andrew Lorenz and David Smith, 'Britain fails to close the competitiveness gap', *The Sunday Times*, 11 October 1998, p.3.10–3.11.

Organizations traditionally have been regarded as independent entities, self-reliant and competing with each other. That perspective is no longer accurate. The traditional Japanese *keiretsu*, for example, are collections of companies which hold shares in each other, have interlocking boards of directors and are able to engage easily in joint ventures. The most widely known *keiretsu* is probably Mitsubishi. The Korean *chaebol* operate in a broadly similar manner but are more centralized and are often based on groups of managers who share a common background, such as family, educational institution or geographic region.

These kinds of intraorganizational arrangements and interdependencies are not confined to the Pacific Rim. McDonald's, Disney and Coca-Cola, for example, have a joint global marketing alliance, but they do not own shares in each other. At Animal World, a Disney theme park in Orlando, Florida, staff in the McDonald's restaurant wear uniforms depicting Disney characters, while an over-sized bottle in the middle of the restaurant serves coke. Coca-Cola has been the sole soft drinks supplier at Disney theme parks since 1955. When Disney released the film *Armageddon* in 1998, McDonald's sold cinema tickets and 'Astromeals' to promote it (*The Economist*, 1998).

Figure 2.3 illustrates the structure of the global entertainment business (at the end of 1998), showing the linkages between Asian, European, British and North American organizations in this sector. The percentages in figure 2.3 reflect ownership stakes. For example, Seagram owns 80 per cent of the shares in Universal Studios, which owns 75 per cent of PolyGram, which in turn owns 30 per cent of

How do Russian managers operate in a post-communist environment?

The constraints under which Russia's post-communist businesses work lead to some pernicious outcomes. Igor, the manager of the Izhevsk Radio Factory, has five rules for running a large organization in Russia:

- Sell some of your output to the federal government—ideally, about the level of your estimated federal taxes. You will not be paid for these sales, but you can use them to offset taxes.

- Export something to a hard currency market. You need some cash for your operations, mainly for urgently needed inputs. The exports need not be of your chief product.

- Set up some barter operations for the rest of your inputs, especially fuel, electricity and so on. It is best if you have some products that utilities need. Then they will pay you in *veskslya* [tradable promissory notes] that you can redeem for the inputs.

- Provide municipal services that you can offset against local taxes. Ideally, own a division that can repair school buildings.

- Finally, whatever you do, do not make much profit as the government will take the lot in taxes.

Playing by these rules, or variants of them, most of Russia's managers were engaged in a game that served customers only by chance, if at all. Productivity, competitiveness, cost control, and the quality of goods and services were all largely incidental.

The financial crisis of mid-August [1998] and its aftermath have served only to strengthen these perverse incentives. There is now even less need to worry about selling well-made products—foreign ones, if they are obtainable at all, have just become twice as expensive. Because of the payments crisis in the banking system, paying suppliers is now difficult, and barter looks more attractive. Equally, the pressure to pay taxes or wages has diminished. After all, companies can always blame chaos in the banking system. And with hyperinflation just around the corner, debts are likely to shrink.

Indeed, the best thing for a Russian businessman to do is nothing—which is largely the course Igor and his colleagues have been adopting.

From *The Economist* (abstracts), 'As winter draws in', 24 October 1998, pp.99–100.

Fingers in each other's pies

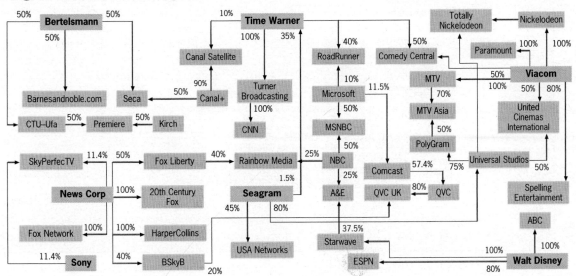

Figure 2.3: The interlocking ownership structure of the global entertainment industry
From *The Economist*, 'Technology and entertainment survey', 21 November 1998, p.11.

MTV Asia. Even the computer software company Microsoft has a small but significant number of stakes in this sector. This industry structure reflects the process of **consolidation**, which several sectors have experienced since the 1990s.

It has been predicted, for example, that the motor car industry will consolidate further during the first decade of the twenty-first century, leaving only six independent manufacturers, two in North America, two in Europe and two in Japan. As figure 2.3 illustrates, the entertainment sector is consolidated around half a dozen major international organizations. As figure 2.4 shows, if you bought a holiday in Britain in 1999, from one of dozens of travel agents and tour operators, you actually went on holiday with one of only four companies. The same process has also taken place globally in hotel and restaurant businesses. The next time you visit a city centre, identify how many of the restaurants ('quality' and 'fast food') you pass are independently owned and how many are part of national (or international) restaurant chains. National and global consolidation has affected the catering sector too.

> **Consolidation** is the process through which company ownership in a sector becomes concentrated in a smaller number of much larger and sometimes global enterprises.

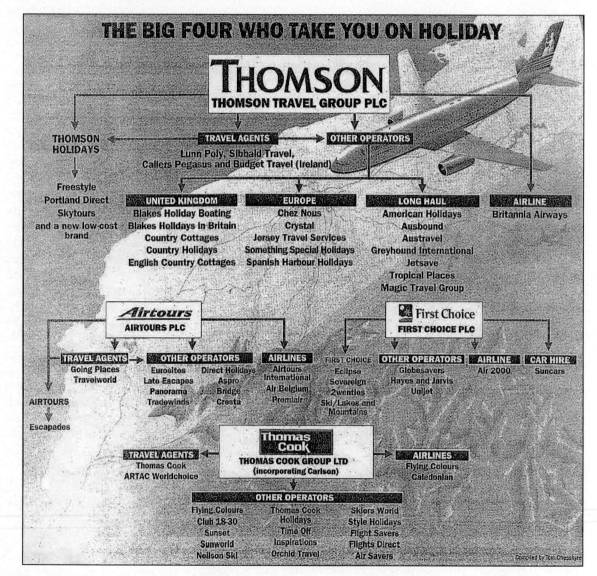

Figure 2.4: Consolidation in the holiday travel business
From Dominic Walsh and Phil Davies, 'All aboard with takeover travel', *The Times*, 1 May 1999, pp.30–1.

Information technology

New technology is probably the most visible and tangible aspect of contemporary environmental change. Applications of computing are now pervasive, affecting most aspects of social and organizational life, from entertainment to manufacturing methods to the provision of many services to modes of education. Developments in computing and communication have also led to an apparent increase in the number of 'knowledge workers' (a controversial term), whose value as employees depends more on what they know than on what they can do. Knowledge work such as computer software design is not dependent on physical location, and such activities are increasingly carried out in low-wage countries (such as India) rather than in Europe or America.

The preoccupation with computing can overlook technological developments in other fields, such as in new materials, for example, and in healthcare, where the pace of development of new drugs, treatment regimes and equipment seems to be almost as rapid as in computing. The relationships between technology and organizational behaviour, and particularly information technology, will be explored in more depth in chapter 3.

Social and demographic trends

There are several demographic trends relevant to organizational behaviour. The workforce in Western industrialized economies is *aging*. In other words, the proportion of the population who have retired from employment is growing in relation to the proportion of the population still in work. Organizations that discriminate against 'older' employees (which in some cases means over 30, or over 40 years of age) may find it difficult to recruit. An aging population may have different needs as consumers, opening up new markets for organizations smart enough to identify and meet those needs, and also putting pressure on healthcare services.

A range of factors, including civil wars and improvements in transport and communication, have contributed to a dispersion of the global workforce. This now means a higher ethnic, cultural and religious mix within a given workforce, putting a premium on the ability of the organization to manage that diversity of values, needs and preferences. Another demographic trend concerns what has been called the development of the 'bipolar workforce', split between educated and skilled professional knowledge workers, on the one hand, and poorly educated, untrained and poorly paid manual and clerical workers, on the other. Other developments under this heading include the increasing proportion of women in the workforce.

Lifestyles and values are changing, affecting the formation and composition of households, patterns of living and consumption, trends in leisure and education, and preferences in working patterns. Social values also change. High levels of ecological concern, which are expressed in punitive fines for organizations which create toxic waste and in a wide range of public protests (over the building of new roads and airports, for example) were relatively uncommon before the 1980s. Working patterns throughout the European Union (EU) have the following characteristics (Department of Trade and Industry, 1999, p.3):

- by 1996, 17 per cent of EU workers were part-time, from 4 per cent in Greece to 40 per cent in the Netherlands;

- around one-sixth of EU workers regularly do shift work, from 6 per cent in Portugal to 25 per cent in Sweden;

- one in seven workers in the EU works at night, regularly or occasionally;

- one in eight workers works from home, regularly or occasionally, including one in four in Britain;

- one in four workers in the EU sometimes works on Sundays.

The typical 40-hour working week, from Monday to Friday, is therefore becoming less common. This in turn has implications for how and when we buy and use a whole range of goods and services whose providers have to change their practices in turn. The internet now provides 24-hour shopping for some goods and services. Conventional outlets may need to provide similar levels of service in order to compete. There appears also to be a growing 'home management' industry, servicing in particular the needs of two-earner families where both work extended hours. Companies in this sector clean your house, tidy the garden, do the shopping, collect your car for servicing, and will even buy appropriate birthday presents.

Stop and criticize

In what three ways do your values differ from the values of your parents?

In what three ways do you expect your lifestyle to differ from that of your parents?

In what three ways do you expect that your experience of work will differ from that of your parents?

In what ways will your values and expectations as an employee make life easier or more difficult for the organizations that are likely to employ you?

Returning to figure 2.1, globalization, information technology and social demographic terms in combination make multiple demands, now and into the future, on the way organizations are structured and managed. The implications of these environmental trends can be felt at different levels, from long-term competitive strategy, through organization structure changes, to the provision of special facilities for particular ethnic or religious groups.

One popular and more detailed approach to environmental scanning is **PESTLE analysis**, which offers a method for reducing the complexity of the task by providing a simple structure.

PESTLE analysis involves identifying the political, economic, social, technological, legal and ecological factors affecting an organization.

Some commentators prefer to use the PEST acronym, rolling legal and ecological issues into the political category. Other commentators prefer PETS or STEPS, which sound more 'friendly' and positive. Figure 2.5 places the organization at the centre of a typical range of external trends and pressures based on the PESTLE headings. The detail under each of the six main headings is offered only as an illustration and is not comprehensive.

The best way to approach environmental scanning is to do an analysis yourself. This will almost certainly reveal that the neat categories in the model overlap in a rather untidy way in practice. Many legislative changes are politically motivated. Ecological concerns reflect changing social values and preferences. Some technological developments (electric cars) are encouraged by economic and ecological issues (the price and pollution of petrol). However, the point of the analysis is to identify the external environmental factors, their interrelationships and their impact. It is less important to get them into the 'correct' boxes.

Stop and criticize

Choose an interesting organization with which you are familiar: corner grocery, supermarket, university or college, the place you worked last summer.

Make a list of all the political, economic, social, technological, legislative and ecological factors and trends that you can think of affecting that organization.

Identify from this analysis the practical advice which you would feed back to the management of your chosen organization.

When you are finished, how would you rate the *value* of this exercise to the organization? Is this of practical significance, or was it just a theoretical exercise?

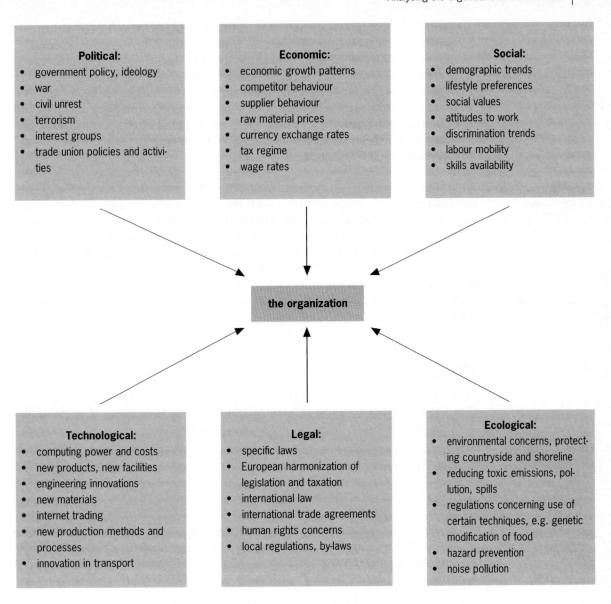

Figure 2.5: PESTLE factors affecting the organization

This analysis usually identifies a number of similar issues:

1. It is difficult to escape from the argument that the organization must pay attention to these PESTLE trends and developments in the external environment. The organization which ignores or fails to respond to those external factors will quickly run into difficulties. As indicated earlier, the implications of this analysis can affect all levels of the organization's functioning, including its strategy, structure, management style and working practices.

2. The list of external factors, even under these neat headings, can quickly become long and intimidating. The range of factors 'out there' is extremely wide. Identifying which are most significant, and predicting their impact, can be difficult.

3. A full understanding of those external factors can involve the collection and analysis of a substantial amount of information of different types, and this takes time. How about analysing demographic trends in south-central Scotland, for example, or pan-European regulations affecting the food and drink industry, or forthcoming information technology software innovations, or collating the results of consumer surveys on lifestyle changes and consumption patterns. The time spent on this kind of analysis has to be balanced against the need for a relatively rapid response to the trends and developments being analysed.

Environmental complexity makes prediction hazardous. We can predict demographic trends with some accuracy, with respect to mortality, and gender and age profiles. We can predict economic trends with some confidence in the short to medium term (up to three or five years), but not beyond. Trends in social values and lifestyles, in politics, in technological innovation, or in the impact of new technology, cannot be predicted with much confidence (an observation which does not stop journalists and others making the attempt). In other words, environmental scanning analysis requires a lot of informed guesswork and judgement.

The PESTLE environmental scanning approach thus has two strengths, and four weaknesses:

The *strengths* are:

1. The analysis encourages full consideration of the wide range of external factors affecting internal organizational arrangements.

2. The analysis is a convenient framework for ordering a complex and bewildering range of factors.

The *weaknesses* are:

1. Analysis of an organization's external environment can generate an infinite list of factors, not all of which may be significant. Striking a balance between identifying all relevant factors, and the factors which are particularly important, can be difficult.

2. It is difficult to anticipate 'defining events' such as, for example, war, new discoveries, economic collapse or major political upheavals which shift country boundaries or radically change government policies.

3. This analysis, if it is to be complete, can involve the time-consuming and expensive collection of very substantial amounts of data, some of which may be readily available and some of which may have to be researched specially. This can quickly become a major undertaking for the staff involved.

4. The time spent in information gathering and subsequent analysis may inhibit a rapid and effective response to the very trends and developments being analysed.

Scenario building involves the development of one or more likely pictures of the dimensions and characteristics of the future for the organization, based on environmental scanning, and with an attempt to identify the most probable future scenario as a basis for current planning and action.

Environmental analysis using PESTLE is often used for the purpose of **scenario building**.

In the field of corporate strategy, scenario building is used to explore 'best case, worst case' possibilities, and also to encourage 'out-of-the-box' or creative 'blue skies' thinking, as well as plotting probable futures. A typical scenario-building exercise for a small local grocery store is outlined in table 2.1.

Which of these scenarios is the most probable? The answer has fundamental

Table 2.1: The grocer's scenarios

Scenario	Main characteristics
1: Revival	Transport gridlock, increased cost of car ownership, ageing population, impersonal hypermarkets; local convenience and traditional 'face to face' service become increasingly popular.
2: Decline	Price wars between superstores reduce prices and improve in-store atmosphere as stores add services to retain customer loyalty; small local stores survive but with decreasing profits.
3: Obliteration	On-line banking and internet shopping combined with rapid delivery make traditional shopping trips almost redundant; large stores become warehousing and distribution centres instead.

implications for anyone planning to give up their day job and invest their life savings in a grocery store. Even if one believes that scenarios 2 and 3 are the most likely outcomes, there may still be innovations which the store owner could consider introducing to retain customers in the face of apparently overwhelming competition. It is instructive to consider what those innovations might be (in staffing, for example, or in organization design, service provision, interpersonal relationships with customers, technology-based purchasing, and so on). This is not merely a theoretical exercise. Scenario building can have a profound impact on organization strategy and planning, on management decision making, and on triggering a creative response to environmental trends and conditions.

We have, therefore, explored environmental scanning for two reasons—practical and theoretical. This is a useful predictive action planning tool, particularly when allied with scenario building, as a guide to creative organizational decision making. This is also a useful theoretical framework which exposes the range of external environmental influences on internal organizational behaviour and also highlights the relationships between those external factors. Environmental scanning has become a 'field' in its own right, with its own texts, tools and techniques. A fuller treatment of these and related issues can be found in the corporate strategy literature (Johnson and Scholes, 1999).

We are now in a position to 'update' the basic model introduced at the beginning of the chapter. Figure 2.6 shows the links between external environmental

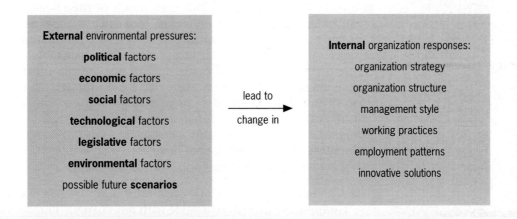

Figure 2.6: The external environment–internal organization link detailed

pressures, on the one hand, and internal organizational responses, on the other, in more detail.

This model relies on a number of basic assumptions, such as:

- It assumes that all the relevant data can indeed be identified, collected and analysed.

- It assumes that the analysis will lead to accurate forecasts of current and future trends, and to the construction of realistic future scenarios.

- It assumes that the analysis will be consistent and not pull the organization in different directions at the same time.

- It assumes that the kinds of internal organizational response indicated by the analysis can be implemented.

- It assumes that practical recommendations for internal organizational change can be implemented in time [**link**, chapter 18, organizational change].

In practice, therefore, this kind of analysis has to be used with care. Environmental scanning and scenario building can be more useful when carried out relatively quickly, relying on a combination of information, informed guesswork and judgement, rather than being driven by an insistence on fully comprehensive and verifiably accurate data. The results of a comprehensive and accurate analysis (and accuracy is difficult to judge anyway) may be available too late to be of any practical use to the organization.

The continuing search for 'fit'

Our concern in this argument is with the search for 'fit' between the internal characteristics of the organization and features of the external environment. One factor in particular stands out from the environmental scanning exercise for most organizations: **environmental uncertainty**.

Most managers today feel that the speed of events around them is increasing, and that they lack a sense of direction, a view of the way ahead, the nature of the terrain, obstacles, or even the final destination. This perception of change is often represented in the media, and in parts of the organizational behaviour literature, as a contemporary concern. However, much of the research into the design of organization structures and individual jobs since at least the mid-twentieth century has been, and continues to be, concerned with appropriate organizational responses to turbulent, rapidly changing and unpredictable environments.

One of the first systematic attempts to explore the implications of environmental uncertainty is in the work of Fred Emery and Eric Trist (1965). They developed a typology describing four broad kinds of organizational environment, from 'placid' at one extreme to 'turbulent' at the other. They also identified the kinds of organizational arrangements suitable for those different environmental circumstances. Their approach is summarized in table 2.2.

There are three main dimensions to this argument:

1. A hierarchical, bureaucratic organization can be effective when the external environment is relatively stable with few changes. Bureaucracy has had a bad press. Emery and Trist are suggesting that there are circumstances in which the rigid, hierarchical, stable bureaucracy can be effective.

Environmental uncertainty refers to the degree of unpredictable turbulence and change in the external political, economic, social, technological, legal and ecological context in which an organization operates; the more the dimensions of the external context are interrelated, the higher the environmental uncertainty.

Table 2.2: The Emery–Trist typology of organizational environments

Environment type	Characteristics	Organizational response
1: Placid, randomized	The simplest environment. Little uncertainty, stable, few changes.	Successful organizations have hierarchical, bureaucratic structures with standardized work processes.
2: Placid, clustered	Moderate uncertainty and a large number of variables to consider, somewhat predictable.	Planning becomes important, but some decentralization can be effective.
3: Disturbed, reactive	Increased levels of uncertainty and change, unstable environment confusing and difficult to predict.	Requires flexible, adaptable, decentralized structures to deal with change.
4: Turbulent field	Highly complex, rapidly changing environment, high interdependence between organizations and society, greatly increased uncertainty.	Requires very fluid organization structures, and flexible managers and staff at other levels.

Fred Edmund Emery

Eric Landsdowne Trist (1909–93)

Environmental complexity concerns the range of external factors—customers, suppliers, regulatory agencies, competitors—relevant to the activities of the organization; the more factors, the higher the complexity.
Environmental dynamism: the pace of change in relevant factors external to the organization; the greater the pace of change, the more dynamic the environment.

2. The greater the degree of environmental turbulence, the greater the degree of internal organizational flexibility required to deal with the unpredictability, the uncertainty and the consequent organizational change. We will meet this argument again in chapter 16 [**link**, chapter 16, organization strategy and design].

3. Emery and Trist argue that, for most organizations, environments tend to become increasingly turbulent over time. In the context of the argument of this chapter, it is interesting to note that, in the title of their paper, Emery and Trist (1965) refer to the 'causal texture' of the organizational environment. They felt that internal organizational arrangements could be explained, at least in part, by external environmental factors.

Robert Duncan (1972; 1973; 1974; 1979) defined uncertainty as the lack of adequate information to reach an unambiguous decision and argued that environmental uncertainty has two dimensions. One of these dimensions concerns degree of **simplicity** or **complexity**, and the other concerns the degree of **stability** or **dynamism**:

simple–complex	the number of different issues faced, the number of different factors to consider, the number of things to worry about
stable–dynamic	the extent to which those issues are changing or stable, and if they are subject to slow movement or to abrupt shifts

Duncan argued that the 'stable–dynamic' dimension is much more significant in determining environmental uncertainty. This is because complexity (which just

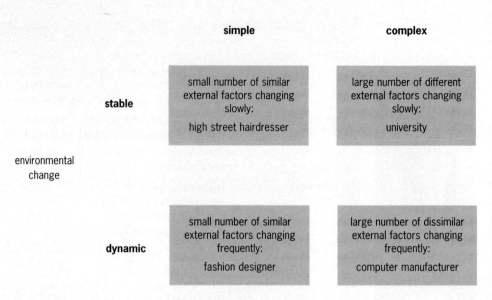

Figure 2.7: Duncan's typology of organizational environments

means an awful lot of variables to consider) is easier to manage than dynamism (which means you don't know what is going to happen next most of the time). Plotting these two dimensions against each other, Duncan produced the typology of organizational environments shown in figure 2.7. This typology is usually applied at the level of the organization. However, it can also be used to understand the environments of single units or departments within an organization. Duncan's typology appears to be similar to that of Emery and Trist. His argument is also the same: different environments require different organizational responses.

However, there is a major difference between these positions. Duncan argues that an organization's location in this typology is dependent on management perception and not on an objective observer's classification. In other words, if you don't perceive that your environment is turbulent, then you will probably not respond to it as such. As our perception can change, so the location of an organization's environment on this typology is unstable.

This is quite different from arguing that external environments determine internal structures and processes. Duncan's observation, that management decisions are based on perceptions of the external environment, is thus fundamental. The theory of perception [**link**, chapter 7, perception] shows that perception is selective, with some factors given prominence and others filtered out. The same environment may thus be perceived differently by different managers, and by different organizations, even in the same sector. It is management perceptions which affect decisions about organization strategy, structures and processes. In the language of Karl Weick (1979), managers enact rather than react to the external environment.

We thus have one perspective which claims that reality, the environment, is 'out there' waiting to be observed, studied, analysed, understood and reacted to in an appropriate manner. The second perspective claims that, on the contrary, 'the environment' is only what we perceive, understand and interpret it to be, and which therefore is enacted. This distinction between believing that 'the truth is out there', on the one hand, and believing that 'the truth is what we interpret it to be', on the other hand, will be explored later in this chapter. This second perspective reflects the social construction of reality argument, which was discussed in chapter 1. It is also a dimension of postmodern thinking to which we will turn shortly.

The work of Emery, Trist and Duncan dates from the 1960s and 1970s. What is the relevance of their analysis today? We can answer this question by examining the more recent work of Igor Ansoff (1997). Ansoff has developed that earlier work to some extent, but, as we will see, the basic arguments remain the same. Different external environments require different organizational and management responses. The greater the external turbulence, the higher the degree of required internal flexibility. Duncan's (1972) model is *descriptive*. In contrast, and like the model of Emery and Trist (1965), Ansoff's approach is *prescriptive*, offering specific organizational and managerial advice.

Stop and criticize

Can you apply Duncan's typology in practice? Where on this model would you position the following organizations?

- Oxfam charity organization

- The Leicester Royal Infirmary NHS Trust

- Burger King fast food chain

- Aldi high discount food retailer

- A Scotch whisky distillery in a remote Highland glen

- Hertz car rental company

- Marriott international hotels

- Oscar de la Renta perfume manufacturers

- BMW motor car company

Referring back to Duncan's typology, which type of organizational environment would *you* prefer to work in—stable/simple or dynamic/complex—and why? Share and explain your choice with a colleague. You will have to consider your answer to this question every time you seek employment.

Ansoff's argument is summarized in table 2.3. This is a difficult table to 'read' quickly, so let us work through it step by step. Ansoff first identifies five types of environment based on the type of turbulence or change being experienced, running from 'repetitive' at one extreme to 'surprising' at the other. This is similar to the 'placid–turbulent' scale of Emery and Trist, with different labels. The first two columns of the table have to be read *vertically*, taking you up and down this scale through 'repetitive', 'expanding', 'changing' and 'discontinuous' to 'surprising' levels of external environmental turbulence:

1. repetitive

2. expanding

3. changing

4. discontinuous

5. surprising

Table 2.3: Turbulence, strategy and attitude—Ansoff's typology of environments

	Environmental change	Organization strategy	Management attitude
1	*Repetitive* little or no change	*Stable* based on precedent	*Stability-seeking* rejects change
2	*Expanding* slow incremental change	*Reactive* incremental change based on experience	*Efficiency-driven* adapts to change
3	*Changing* fast incremental change	*Anticipatory* incremental change based on extrapolation	*Market-driven* seeks familiar change
4	*Discontinuous* discontinuous but predictable change	*Entrepreneurial* discontinuous new strategies based on observed opportunities	*Environment-driven* seeks new but related change
5	*Surprising* discontinuous and unpredictable change	*Creative* discontinuous new and creative strategies	*Environment-creating* seeks novel change

From I. Ansoff, 'Measuring and managing for environmental turbulence: the Ansoff Associates approach', in Alexander Watson Hiam (ed.), *The Portable Conference on Change Management*, HRD Press Inc., 1997, pp. 67–83.

Now turn to level 1, the repetitive environment, and read the table *across* the row. Ansoff argues that we can identify the most appropriate organization strategy and management attitude for that environment. In a stable environment, strategy should be based on precedent. What made the organization successful in the past will also work in the future. Also, in a stable environment, the appropriate management attitude is to reject change and seek stability. Innovation and change could ruin the business. In other words:

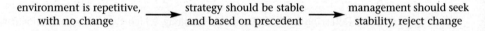

environment is repetitive, with no change ⟶ strategy should be stable and based on precedent ⟶ management should seek stability, reject change

Now jump down to level 5, to the surprising, discontinuous and unpredictable environment, and once again read across the row. As you might expect, the recommended organization strategy is creative, basing strategies not on what the organization has done in the past but on new and creative approaches. What worked in the past cannot work in the future. The management attitude to surprising change has to be novelty seeking, helping to shape, influence and create the environment in fresh ways. A failure to innovate by holding on to past precedents will in this context ruin the business. In other words:

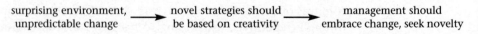

surprising environment, unpredictable change ⟶ novel strategies should be based on creativity ⟶ management should embrace change, seek novelty

Now read the other three intervening rows, again working *across* the table in each case, noting the strategy and management implications for each of the other levels of environmental change. Once that argument and the practical implications are clear, try reading the organization strategy column vertically. This can be read as an organization strategy scale, running from stability (precedent-driven) at one extreme to creativity (novelty-driven) at the other. The final column works in the same way. This offers a management attitude scale, from stability (rejecting change) at one extreme to creativity (embracing novelty) at the other.

In another departure from the typologies we have considered so far, Ansoff distinguishes between what he calls extrapolative and discontinuous environmental change, identified by the line on table 2.3 separating levels 3 and 4. Where environmental change is extrapolative, the future can be predicted, more or less, following (i.e. extrapolating from) current trends. When change is discontinuous, on the other hand, the ability to predict is much less clear. Ansoff (1997) claims that 80 per cent of managers say their organizations have level 4 or 5 environments.

Ansoff makes a number of cruel observations about managers who have been effective and successful in organizations with extrapolative environments. He claims that they are likely to lack the skills, knowledge, experience and attitudes required to deal with a discontinuous environment. Success in a discontinuous environment requires creative entrepreneurial vision, open to innovative opportunities and threats, anticipating change ahead of time. He comments bluntly that 'Managers incapable of developing an entrepreneurial mindset must be replaced' (Ansoff, 1997, p.76).

Stop and criticize	Does your educational institution face an extrapolative or a discontinuous change?

To what extent is the institution's strategy and management attitude appropriate to that level of change, according to Ansoff's model?

Apply this analysis to yourself. What level of environmental change are you personally subject to, and how does this influence your behaviour?

We are now in a position to 'update' yet again the basic model illustrated earlier in figures 2.1 and 2.6. The result is shown in figure 2.8 (including some organizational responses explored later in the text). This can now be presented as a 'stimulus–response' model, in which the stimulus of external change prompts organizational responses. The main argument of this model is that the scale, dynamism and complexity of environmental stimuli encourage the development of a new approach to organization, a new flexible and adaptive, environmentally responsive organizational 'paradigm'. This is sometimes referred to as the postmodern organization, a concept explored in the following section.

We promised earlier that, having built this model up, we would knock it down. This is an appropriate point at which to point out four of the flaws in the reasoning behind figure 2.8.

The first problem concerns the **environmental determinism** which the model implies. Duncan's argument, about the role of management perceptions, is a powerful challenge to this determinist perspective.

Environmental determinism is a perspective which claims that internal organizational responses are wholly or mainly shaped, influenced, or determined by external environmental factors.

We know that internal organizational arrangements reflect the influence of a range of factors: the dynamics of the senior management team, their approach to decision making, senior and middle management whims and preferences, plant-level trade union policy, employee suggestions, past experience. And we also know that, whatever the environmental reality 'out there', what really matters is how the environment is understood and interpreted 'in here'. This means that the environmental 'stimulus' is just one stimulus among many, and that this stimulus is not always guaranteed either a response, or the obvious expected response.

The second problem concerns the assumptions which the model makes about organizational boundaries. The argument up to this point has implied that the distinction between what is 'out there', in the environment, and what is 'in here', in the organization, is clear. That is not the case. The organization is involved in a constant process of exchange with the environment, importing staff and resources, exporting goods and services. Employees, however, are members of the

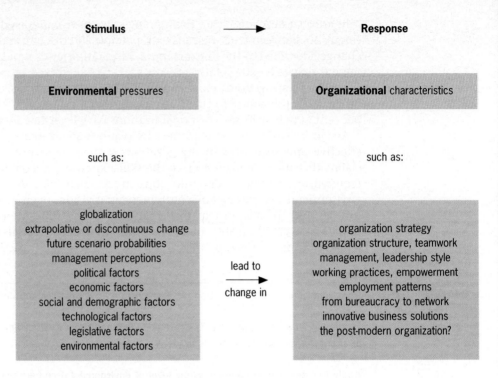

Figure 2.8: The search for environment–organization 'fit'

wider society, whose values and preferences are now 'inside' the organization as well as outside it. Many organizations now have special partnership arrangements with suppliers, who are linked by computer automatically to generate orders for stock items which are running low. Many organizations, such as some building societies, and roadside assistance organizations for motorists, regard their customers as 'members' who can respectively vote on changes to company rules, and receive free copies of their company magazine. Partnership arrangements now commonly occur between competitors, who find it profitable to share the costs, for example, of developing new materials, new processes and sometimes new products. In a previous section, the development of intraorganizational arrangements was mentioned. The boundaries between organizations, on the one hand, and between the organization and its environment, on the other, have become blurred.

The third problem is one of definition and interpretation. We are speaking of 'environment' and of 'organization' as separate domains. However, the organization chooses, shapes, influences and enacts its environment. The organization's environment is thus a matter of strategic choice (see Child, 1997). For example, the small grocery store on the corner changes its environment (its customers, its suppliers, its competitors) in strategic ways when the owner decides to stop selling fruit and vegetables, and starts hiring out domestic repair and garden maintenance equipment instead. In other words, the external environment of the organization is 'enacted': this simply means that the organization creates and to some extent even becomes its own environment, rather than being 'given' or 'presented with' that 'external' environment. The domains of external environment and internal organization overlap and are much less distinct than the language or our model presume.

The final problem concerns continuity. The model presents a picture of 'all change', and of rapid and radical change. However, we know that is not the case. Looking back over the past century, we can identify many continuities, environmental and organizational. The relationship between environment and organization is not exclusively about change.

The post-modern organization

"Sir, the following paradigm shifts occurred while you were out."

Table 2.4: From classical to modern to post-modern organization form

'Classical' organization 1800–1970 *industrial age*	'Modern' organization 1970–1990 *technological age*	'Post-modern' organization 1990– *information age*
organization as machine	organization as open system	organization as flexible tool
rigid, hierarchical	decentralized	action matters, not design
focus on internal process	focus on human relations	lean, efficient, innovative
mass production	customization	time to market
routine, repetitive work	teamworking	entrepreneurial units
full time employees	flexible working patterns	networks, sub-contractors
direct supervision	local problem solving	rules don't matter
emphasized control, predictability	emphasized quality, customer service	emphasizes change, flux, quick decisions
find the one best way	contingency approach	response-oriented
avoid uncertainty	manage uncertainty	exploit uncertainty

The **post-modern organization** (an idealized concept) is a networked, information-rich, delayered, downsized, lean, boundaryless, high commitment, organization employing highly skilled, well-paid autonomous knowledge workers.

Is there any substance in the claim that an increasingly turbulent external environment has encouraged the development of a new organizational paradigm? Does it make sense to talk about the **post-modern organization**?

It is fashionable to chart the development of organizational forms since the

Industrial Revolution in the eighteenth century, as in table 2.4 (based on Narayanan and Rath, 1993).

Stewart Clegg (1990, p.181) describes the post-modern organization in these terms:

> Where the modernist organization was rigid, post-modern organization is flexible. Where modernist consumption was premised on mass forms, post-modernist consumption is premised on niches. Where modernist organization was premised on technological determinism, post-modernist organization is premised on technological choices made possible through de-dedicated micro-electronic equipment. Where modernist organization and jobs were highly differentiated, demarcated and de-skilled, post-modernist organization and jobs are highly de-differentiated, de-demarcated and multiskilled. Employment relations as a fundamental relation of organization upon which has been constructed a whole discourse of the determinism of size as a contingency variable increasingly give way to more complex and fragmentary relational forms, such as subcontracting and networking.

Table 2.4 sets out one typical representation of current thinking. However, like our earlier model of environment–organization links, this one is also 'wrong'. For a start, those dates are arbitrary, giving only a very approximate indication of the timing of possible transitions in organization design. This kind of 'bad old days–good new days' picture suggests a logical, linear progression from 'then' until 'now' driven by external environmental imperatives. This suggests that rigid bureaucracy, macho managers and simple boring jobs are all in the past, replaced by flexible organizations with participative, supportive managers and interesting, multiskilled, empowered jobs. Change is not this logical or tidy.

The evidence is mixed. A report produced by the British Department for Education and Employment in 1997 (summarized in the 'organization and labour market trends' box) offers some support for the post-modern organization form. Employment in traditional manufacturing industry has declined as employment in services has increased. This study found increasing skill levels across the workforce and a movement away from traditional manufacturing methods and towards multiskilled, empowered teamworking. However, there is no evidence with respect to how widespread these organizational changes are.

Gallie *et al.* (1998), in their national survey of employment trends, found that the general response to technological change and competition in Britain had indeed involved job enrichment and devolved decision making. But manual workers had experienced more intense supervision and work pacing. Managerial and professional grades, on the other hand, appear to have enjoyed more discretion but are commonly subject to performance management systems based on target setting, appraisal and merit pay. The authors note that 'this survey's picture is one of extensive and expanding control systems'. The evidence for empowerment and job enrichment, on the one hand, thus has to be set against the evidence for tight—or tighter—management controls, on the other. We return to this theme in chapter 20, where trends in human resource management are explored.

Stop and criticize

McDonald's restaurants has one of the world's most widely recognized corporate logos—the big yellow 'M' that sits above each of its outlets. McDonald's is a successful business, with restaurants in most towns and cities around the world.

Go visit a McDonald's restaurant. Observe closely as many of the staff as you can see, preparing food, serving customers, clearing tables, restaurant supervisors.

Organization and labour market trends in Britain

- Primary and manufacturing sectors are expected to see further reductions in numbers employed, but future changes are likely to be smaller and more gradual than in the past. Between 1990 and 1996, employment declined in traditional manufacturing and expanded in the service sector. Employment grew in: real estate, renting and business activities, education (11%), health and social work (30%), and other community services (18%). Employment in mining and quarrying fell by 54%, by 44% in electricity, gas and water supply, by 15% in manufacturing, and 15% in construction. These changes in the balance of employment between manufacturing and services are expected to continue.

- New jobs are likely to arise in skill-intensive, knowledge-based occupations. Competitive pressures place a premium on communication skills, self-motivation, problem solving and flexibility. The 1996 Skill Needs In Britain Survey found that the skills most lacking included management skills, communication, computer literacy and personal skills. Around one in six members of the workforce have literacy or numeracy problems.

- The general skills content—level and range—of most jobs is increasing, due to new businesses and production systems, often based on new technology, and emphasizing increased quality and customer care. The 1996 Skill Needs Survey found that 74% of employers thought the need for skills in the average employee was increasing. Demand for manual workers is expected to continue to fall, in favour of non-manual occupations requiring high levels of qualification.

- The labour force is expected to increase by 1.6 million by 2006, and women will make up 1.3 million of this increase (total employment in 1997 was around 26 million). Women now form the majority—52 per cent—of employees in non-manual occupations. Despite office computerization, the role of the secretary—a female-dominated occupation—is increasingly important in flatter organization structures, with increased responsibility and autonomy, and with higher-level technical and social skills.

- Ethnic minorities in Britain make up 6 per cent of the population and are overrepresented in lower-paid jobs and underrepresented in higher-paid managerial positions.

- Under intense global competitive pressure, firms increasingly seek to concentrate on more customized products with shorter production runs, abandoning traditional production lines in favour of small, multiskilled manufacturing teams which have discretion in the organization of their own work. The life cycle of products, production and administrative systems is shortening, placing a premium on flexibility and on the ability to change.

Based on *A Plan for Objective 4 in Great Britain, 1998–1999*, Department for Education and Employment, November 1997.

Which organizational model—classical, modern, or post-modern—does McDonald's use, based on your observations?

How many organizations in your experience still display 'classical' features?

The single premise behind this apparent trend is that flexibility enhances organizational effectiveness and quality of working life. Is the post-modern form being forced on organizations as an inevitable consequence of environmental pressure? Will we see the pervasive spread of networked, information-rich, delayered, downsized, lean, boundaryless, high-commitment organizations with highly skilled, well-paid autonomous knowledge workers? As the final section of this chapter demonstrates, it is possible to interpret this post-modern trend in precisely the opposite direction, seeing stability, exploitation and domination where others see change, flexibility and empowerment.

Postmodernism: fresh perspectives on organizational behaviour

One of the factors which environmental scanning overlooks concerns changes in ways of thinking about social life in general, and organizations in particular. These changes lie within the domain of philosophy and epistemology. Chapter 1 explored the distinction between two broad epistemological perspectives within the social sciences. One of these is positivism, which relies on the natural science methods of testing hypotheses logically by deduction. The other has a range of labels, such as phenomenology and social constructivism. These perspectives are based on the premise that, as human beings are self-interpreting creatures which attach meaning to their behaviour, their study has to focus on those meanings and interpretations. This involves the use of a range of qualitative, ethnographic, inductive research methods quite different from the hypothetico-deductive methods of natural science.

One development not mentioned in chapter 1 concerns the influence of **post-modernism** in contemporary thought. Postmodernism represents a fundamental challenge to the ways in which we think about organizations, and about organizational behaviour. This is a potentially confusing issue, and one which is awkward to define and summarize clearly and briefly.

The concept of postmodernism has two connotations. One concerns a period in time. The period in which organizations develop the characteristics described in the previous section can be described as the post-modern period, although putting a precise date to the end of the 'modern' and the beginning of the 'post-modern' is problematic. The second use of the term concerns ways of thinking about and of theorizing society and organizations. Following Karen Legge (1995) among others, the hyphenated term **post-modern** is used in the former sense, and the unhyphenated term **postmodern** is used in the latter sense.

post-modern   a period in time, following the 'modern', a type of organization design appropriate for contemporary environmental conditions

postmodern   a philosophy, an epistemological perspective, a way of looking at, of thinking about, of developing theories, of criticizing organizations

Postmodernism is a mode of thinking, an epistemology, which focuses on the way in which language is used symbolically and selectively to construct versions of 'truth' and 'reality' to serve the interests of particular social groupings; postmodernism consequently rejects the positivistic approach which underlies modern science (natural and social) as a way of developing our understanding of the world.

Postmodernism represents a fundamental challenge to contemporary (or 'modern') science by rejecting the taken-for-granted notions of rationality, order, clarity, truth, realism and the idea of intellectual progress. Postmodernism draws attention instead to disorder, to contradictory interpretations, to ambiguity. Modernism is concerned with the development of appropriate methods and procedures for establishing 'the truth'. Postmodernism, however, uses the method of **deconstruction** to reveal the strategies that are used to represent 'truth claims'. This means exposing, for example, how an author establishes credibility, how language is used to disarm challenge to an argument, how data are selected and interpreted to support particular conclusions and proposals. Postmodernism is thus concerned with the use of language to support particular versions of 'the truth', by concealing uncertainties and by suppressing opposite meanings and contradictory viewpoints.

Deconstruction is the process of (1) identifying the assumptions underpinning arguments and claims about 'truth' and 'reality', (2) challenging and/or rejecting those assumptions, and (3) asking whose interests are served by representing 'the truth' in that manner in the first place.

The easiest way to understand this complex issue is to deconstruct a specific argument or 'truth claim'. The argument which we will deconstruct is this:

Contemporary organizations and their employees must respond to increasing environmental turbulence by becoming more flexible and adaptive.

1: *What are the assumptions underlying this argument?* These assumptions seem to be:

- the external environment is now more turbulent than ever before;

- organizations can change their internal arrangements more or less easily;

- flexibility and adaptability lead to employee empowerment, which is desirable;

- adaptation means organizational survival and job protection;

- failure to adapt will lead to organizational collapse and job loss;

- this is a natural, logical progress, replacing outdated 'classical' organizational forms.

2: *How can we challenge these assumptions?* The counter-arguments look like this:

- the environment is now just as turbulent as it was at the beginning of the twentieth century—we only think that the pace of change is accelerating (see Ogburn, 1922);

- major changes to organization structure and culture are stressful and slow and can take years to deliver benefits (see chapters 17 and 18);

- flexible, adaptable organization structures create uncertainty, instability and a lack of order, which many people find uncomfortable and stressful (see chapters 15 and 16);

- many organizations that have embarked on major restructuring have run into severe difficulties, sometimes with technology, but mainly with the human side of change;

- there are many highly successful organizations which have not adopted the characteristics of the 'post-modern organization'—McDonald's is one example;

- there is nothing 'progressive' about organizational arrangements which create pressure, stress and threat for many people.

When we set out to challenge and reject the original assumptions, it appears to be possible to produce an alternative set of counter-claims. If the assumptions that lie behind the original argument are shaky, what does this tell us about the argument itself?

3: *Whose interests are served by representing 'the truth' in this manner?* Major changes to organization structures invariably generate resistance and conflict, which can be reduced if those affected by change agree with it and accept it. What arguments persuade people that 'change is inevitable and good'? Well, arguments that are based on impersonal, external, overwhelming and inevitable pressures can be compelling. The argument that says 'we have to change because of an external threat' is likely to be more acceptable than 'we have to change because I think it's a jolly good idea'. An appeal to external environmental issues appears as more objective, convincing, powerful, imperative.

In other words, it looks as though management interests are served by representing 'the truth' in this way. Why? Because if this appeal to 'inevitable, impersonal, external pressures' is indeed compelling, then consent to management plans for change will be more readily forthcoming. This way of representing 'reality', therefore, is a way of ensuring compliance.

The deconstruction of our original 'truth claim' offers us a completely different perspective. What status does our argument about organizational responses to environmental pressures have now? The answer lies in a deeper consideration of the 'whose interests are served' question. We are now forced to consider what is not changing, given that we have rejected the assumptions behind the original argument. What is not changing includes:

- the ownership structure of the capitalist enterprise;

- the hierarchical nature of management–employee, superior–subordinate relationships;

- management–employee power inequalities;

- management–employee reward inequalities;

- differentials in physical working conditions;

- inequalities of development and career and opportunity.

Behind all this talk about organizational change thus lies considerable continuity. An argument which says 'adapt or die' is exposed as a potential fraud, as many features of work and organization are not changing. Here is an argument which, on the surface, is about 'radical change', but the argument is actually being used to perpetuate basic characteristics of organization structure and managerial prerogative. The nature of the management role, the employment relationship, and the ownership and control structures of capitalist organizations remain unscathed, intact. The postmodern perspective, by deconstructing this argument or 'truth claim', leads to a conclusion *precisely the opposite of the original argument*. This may seem to be a 'negative' outcome, particularly as postmodernism denies any firm or valid conclusions or truths. Postmodernism has indeed been attacked for its critical perspective, for its denial and rejection of 'modern' thinking, for its abstraction, scepticism and nihilism.

However, the postmodern perspective can be used positively and creatively. By exposing and challenging assumptions, unconsidered alternatives are exposed. We can return to our alternative assumptions and to the organizational features that are untouched, to trigger a debate about how to change those features. In the original argument or 'truth claim', those organizational features were not on the agenda, were not open for discussion. Now, they are.

Truth and language games

We commonly think of language as a neutral tool for communicating 'the facts'. From a postmodern point of view, however, language creates and imposes meaning. As our deconstruction example demonstrates, language is used for constructing versions of reality. The implication of this argument is that meaning is 'unstable'; it depends on how you 'read' or interpret it that counts. Postmodernism thus shifts attention away from the author of a text and concentrates instead on the reader, in the following way:

modernism asks   What does this text mean? What is the author really trying to say? What is the correct interpretation?

postmodernism asks   How do different readers interpret this text? What does it mean to them? One interpretation is as valid as another.

This means that our understanding of 'the truth' is always going to be fragmented, selective, biased and illusory. By injecting this sense of insecurity and indeterminacy into our thinking, postmodernism invites us to be sceptical and challenging when faced with arguments and claims which seek to tell us 'this is what it is really like, this is how it really is'.

Following the phenomenological, interpretative views introduced in chapter 1, postmodernism observes that 'the truth' is socially constructed. In other words, the claim that 'the truth is out there' is false. What we understand by 'reality' is actually a representation manufactured—manipulated—by the careful use of language and media image. Our contemporary understanding of, for example, war and famine is almost exclusively based on television imagery. Is that a problem? One aim of postmodern thinking is to make the commonplace problematic. While modern thinking will pursue 'the truth of the matter' and how to reach that understanding, the postmodern perspective is always asking, 'whose point of view is supported, whose interests are being served, by portraying issues and events in this way?'

Postmodernism thus removes our sense of certainty and order by removing fixed reference points, by demonstrating that what we thought was 'solid' or 'fixed' or 'real' is a socially constructed product. We are instead invited to see transience, fragmentation, ephemera.

You are what you consume

The focus on meaning, and how it is constructed or manufactured, applies not just to language but also to the use of symbolism. Capitalism, it appears, is less concerned with the production of goods and services and more with the production of signs, symbols and images. When we buy a product, we are invited to buy the image attributed to that product by advertising. The power of film and television images is such that it has become difficult to distinguish between what is representation and what is 'real'.

One of the central themes in postmodernist analysis concerns the notion of 'hypereality', when the image takes over and becomes perceived as more real, as more substantial, than the portrayal of reality. In many respects, what we assume to be 'the real world' appears mundane when compared with the hypereal world presented by the media. Form and substance merge; substance *is* form. History is simply a source of images to be worked and reworked by advertisers, the entertainment industry and politicians. The skills of the 'spin doctor', making sure that the message is constructed and articulated in the most acceptable, palatable, appealing way, are now key political attributes.

This means that our individual sense of personal identity is also manufactured by the images that we consume. In the past, when someone asked 'who are you?' we might answer with the name of our employing organization, or the title of our job. In other words, our sense of identity is defined by our role in relation to production (of goods or services). But from a postmodern perspective, we are defined not by our role in production but by our patterns of consumption. We consume images—we are invited by advertising to consume images—rather than the actual 'use value' of goods and services.

Stop and criticize

Apply the argument that 'you are what you consume' to yourself. Consider the clothes, shoes, aftershave or perfume, and accessories that you wear and carry, paying particular attention to the manufacturer's label or logo (which may be on display). How do these items reflect your identity, your self-image, the impression that you want to give to other people?

Consider the appearance of your friends and colleagues. How is their identity defined by their clothing—by the consumption of particular items for display to others?

Positivism is dead

Modernism relies on scientific and technological rationality, what in chapter 1 was identified as the positivist perspective. The modern project of natural science is to discover fundamental truths, universal laws. We take the notion of scientific and technological progress for granted. Modern organizations, in turn, rely on bureaucratic rationality, which seeks to establish organizational order through hierarchy, collective goals and controlled performance. This is reflected in the constant management pursuit of 'best practice'. This chapter has also presented an argument suggesting that there has been a rational development of organizational forms, from classical, to modern, to post-modern.

Postmodernism rejects the notion that 'the truth is out there' waiting to be discovered by rational, scientific, investigative or experimental procedures. There are no 'absolutes'. Understanding depends on the attribution of meaning. This is tied into earlier comments about language games. Postmodernism, as a way of think-

You are what you consume

Vehicles are the new class indicator, and *Brookside Nation*, a survey of suburban attitudes by the advertising agency Abbott Mead Vickers, proves it. The agency, desperate to map out some kind of mass market among our choice-crazed population, focused on the six million people living on new housing estates. With a statistical analysis backed up by focus groups spread over the South East, Midlands and North, they probed the tastes and values of estate dwellers and discovered that the car said it all. In the new Britain, you are what you drive.

The great thing about cars is that by adding and subtracting gadgets you can create a caste system more intricate than that of India. It is widely believed in the motor trade that models sold in Britain come in more variations than anywhere else in Europe, because of our desperate need to display our precise social status. The survey showed that Brooksiders were aware of every detail and nuance of car design—the letters after the model name on the boot conveyed as much social context as Jeeves could deduce from the buttons on a Saville Row suit. In the new neighbourhoods built American-style without fences or hedges, displaying the car is an essential ritual.

For maximum status a car's value must be displayed externally, but you can make only so many statements with alloy wheels and xenon headlamps. At BMW, where 65 to 70 per cent of business in Britain involves company cars, the letters SE, for special equipment, are used on the most sought-after models. This allows invisible extras such as air-conditioning to be advertised.

None of the folk in focus groups kept their cars in their garages; they kept them in their drives, where they were lovingly and regularly groomed. They definitely preferred to wash their cars by hand, and even washed them in the rain.

Washing the car was clearly a way of drawing the neighbours' attention to it. The consumption of car polish correlated to the value of the house—the richer the family, the more they polished their car. People who did not polish their cars were deemed nutters. White Van Man, lacking a driveway, compensates by turning on his radio to blast thundering hip-hop down the street while he's busy with the leather. One car per adult is required and wealthier families are twice as likely as other people to have three cars per household. Newness is all, and people who drive old vehicles are seen as morally unsound.

This class system is largely untouched by feminism. In *Brookside Nation*, the man of the house is the breadwinner and drives, or aspires to, a Rover 600, Mercedes, Range Rover or BMW, while his wife will fall behind in her career at the start of their family and is content to sling her gym bag into a frivolous 4 × 4, a Suzuki Vitara or Rav4. One of the agency's focus groups was fixated by a particular neighbour, judged a total slapper for having a Ford Fiesta and living with a man who drove a 5-series BMW. Who did she think she was? demanded the good wives of *Brookside Nation*.

From Celia Brayfield (abstracts), 'Big wheels don't drive Fiestas', *The Times*, 18 March 1999, p.22.

ing and theorizing, is therefore characterized by multiple perspectives. There is no single integrated perspective or theory. The search for 'the truth', for 'the one best way' or for 'the single most appropriate perspective' is itself a target of postmodern attack. Postmodernism argues instead for accepting a diversity of perspective, rejecting the notion that we should be dominated by single points of view. This also means rejecting what is called 'the progress myth', that scientific knowledge accumulates in a rational manner through time. On the contrary, the postmodern perspective demonstrates how those in power use 'progress' as a rationale for maintaining vested interests in the status quo, in maintaining their privileged positions.

The postmodern perspective demonstrates the limitations of the organizational behaviour field map from chapter 1. We can 'read' that map as a causal model, showing how organizational effectiveness and quality of working life are shaped and determined by a set of identifiable factors. This invites us to consider—if only we knew more about those factors and how they interact, we could 'engineer' better organizational performance and improve quality of working life. But that is only one way to 'read' and interpret the model.

Stop and criticize	Consider the field map of the organizational behaviour terrain in chapter 1.
	What are the assumptions underpinning that model?
	Can those assumptions be challenged, rejected, restated?
	Whose interests are served by presenting the field map in that way?

What is the wider value of the postmodern perspective to a practical understanding of organizational behaviour? Mary Jo Hatch (1997, p.45) argues that:

> Predictions are that the future will find us occupying smaller, more decentralized, informal, and flexible organizations that will be predominantly service- or information-oriented and will use automated production strategies and computer-based technology. As a result of these changes, we will experience organizations as more eclectic, participative, and loosely coupled than ever before; with the implication that members of organizations will confront more paradox, contradiction and ambiguity. These themes resonate with the philosophy of postmodernism suggesting that a postmodernist perspective will help us to adapt to changes already taking place, ironically, as a result of continuing applications of modernist science and technology.

Hatch asks how we should best prepare ourselves for a postmodern future and, in summary, offers the following advice:

- learn to take nothing for granted;
- deconstruct all claims to truth by exploring the assumptions behind them;
- keep asking whose point of view is benefited by this way of looking at things;
- focus on how language is used to construct reality and identity;
- focus on what is not said, on what is hidden by conventional expressions;
- avoid 'one right answer';
- dispute the categories into which we place people;
- forget the belief that everybody should think the same way that you do;

- be reflexive—challenge your own assumptions;
- maintain a critical distance between your idea of self, on the one hand, and socially and culturally defined ways of seeing the world, on the other;
- bring your own socially constructed understanding under conscious control and challenge;
- imagine alternatives to our 'taken for granted' understanding of organizational life;
- consider change 'as a form of thrill', 'as a state to be sought out as invigorating', as a welcome experience.

Postmodernism is thus a challenging perspective, offering positive and creative insights into personal identity, social relationships, and the structures and processes of organizations. This chapter has considered the effect of external environmental pressures on internal organizational arrangements. On the one hand, we can see organizational change as a predictable response to neutral, impersonal external forces. Organizational hierarchy is normal, natural, necessary. On the other hand, we can see organizational change as a vehicle for sustaining dominant social and organizational power positions, for maintaining management prerogatives and control. Resistance to control is disarmed by arguments about overwhelming external pressures which can be used to support the view that 'there is no choice' but to organize in this way. The postmodern perspective thus offers valuable fresh insights into ways of understanding organization and management.

Recap

1. *Understand the mutual interdependence between the organization and its environment.*
   - In order to survive, organizations have to adapt their internal structures, processes and behaviours to enable them to cope with complexity and the pace of external change.
   - External pressures on organizations come from the globalization of business, developments in information technology, and social and demographic trends.

2. *Appreciate the strengths and limitations of PESTLE analysis of organizational environments.*
   - PESTLE analysis for environmental scanning provides a coherent and comprehensive framework for the analysis of a diverse and complex range of factors.
   - PESTLE analysis generates vast amounts of information, creating a time-consuming analysis problem, and making predictions from this analysis can be difficult.

3. *Explain the main contemporary organizational responses to environmental turbulence.*
   - Emery, Trist and Ansoff argue that bureaucratic organizations are effective in stable environments, but that fluid structures are more effective in 'turbulent' environments.
   - Duncan and Weick argue that what counts is the

management perception of environmental uncertainty; perception determines the management response.

4. *Describe the main features of the 'post-modern' organization.*
   - The 'classical' bureaucratic organization is being replaced by the 'post-modern' organization, which is flexible, responsive and ignores hierarchy and rules. However, there are successful organizations which use traditional organizational designs.

5. *Understand the main characteristics of a postmodern perspective on organizational behaviour, and the creative and critical dimensions of this approach.*
   - Postmodernism does not regard language as a neutral tool for communicating 'facts' but as a way of creating and imposing meaning. As meaning depends on the interpretation of readers, meaning becomes unstable, transient and fragmentary.
   - Postmodernism uses deconstruction to explore the assumptions behind claims to 'the truth', exposing whose interests are served by expressing 'the truth' in that manner.
   - When deconstructed, the claim that 'organizations must adapt to survive' seems to rely on questionable assumptions, which disguise the

fact that many key features of organization structure and management control do not change at all.

- Postmodernism rejects attempts to find universal laws or truths, and encourages multiple and competing perspectives.

- Postmodernism encourages creativity by showing how we can be liberated from the trap of conventional assumptions and the domination of particular viewpoints.

Revision

1. What is 'postmodernism', and how can this perspective be of value to an understanding of organizational behaviour?

2. Explain the 'environment–organization fit' argument. What are the main assumptions behind this argument?

3. How can organizational environments be classified, and what are the implications of such categorization for organization structures, strategies and managers?

4. What is environmental scanning? Illustrate your explanation with an appropriate example, and assess the strengths and limitations of this technique.

5. Explain the technique of deconstruction, and apply this approach to the argument that 'organizations must become more adaptable and flexible to survive'.

Springboard

Appignanesi, R. and Garratt, C., 1995, *Postmodernism for Beginners*, Icon Books, Cambridge.

Difficult read, but with an informative introduction to the concept, made interesting with cartoons and drawings. Insightful on the postmodern perspective on the use of language, and on the way in which contemporary film mixes image and reality.

Bell, D., 1999, *The Coming of Post-Industrial Society*, Basic Books, New York.

First published in 1973, now with an updated introduction. Daniel Bell was among the first to analyse the role of technology in social change and the importance of theoretical knowledge, affecting occupational status and working patterns.

Buchanan, D. and Badham, R., 1999, *Power, Politics, and Organizational Change: Winning the Turf Game*, Sage, London.

Power is one key target for postmodern analysis, particularly in the work of Michel Foucault, whose examination of how managers and employees in organizations are caught in a web of 'disciplinary practices' is explored in chapter 8.

Burrell, G., 1998, *Pandemonium: Towards a Retro-Theory of Organization*, Sage, London.

Demonstrates how to write in a postmodern style, without using a modern linear rational approach. Don't expect to find a rational argument systematically developed here, however. The style is revealing, but not an easy book to read or to understand.

Hardy, C. and Palmer, I., 1999, 'Pedagogical practice and postmodernist ideas', *Journal of Management Education*, vol.23, no.4, pp.377–95.

An excellent and clear introduction to postmodern thinking, its relevance to and impact on organization and management, with innovative teaching ideas.

Hatch, M.J., 1997, *Organization Theory: Modern, Symbolic and Postmodern Perspectives*, Oxford University Press, Oxford.

An unconventional but clearly written and informative introduction to organizational behaviour, exploring issues from modernist (positivist), social constructivist and postmodern perspectives, demonstrating the contrasts in these three thinking styles.

Johnson, G. and Scholes, K., 1998, *Exploring Corporate Strategy*, Prentice Hall, Hemel Hempstead.

Many of the issues explored in this chapter—environmental scanning, PESTLE analysis, scenario building, organizational 'fit'—are also part of the subject matter of the discipline of corporate strategy. This is one of the leading strategy texts.

Sennett, R., 1998, *The Corrosion of Character: The Personal Consequences of Work in the New Capitalism*, W.W. Norton, New York.

A highly readable essay on the experience of work in the flexible post-modern organization, and the impact of change and insecurity on personal identity. Attacks the myths surrounding flexible multiskilled teamwork; not as much fun as it sounds.

Home viewing

The Matrix (1999, directors Andy and Larry Wachowski) is based on the assumption that what we think of as 'reality' is actually a façade. The computer hacker Neo (played by Keanu Reeves) discovers that human perception is artificially controlled by 'the Matrix' and that the world in which we think we live is manipulated by advanced artificial intelligence. Humans exist in an elaborate computer simulation, living in pods to provide energy to fuel the Matrix. Only when Neo is exposed to this alternative reality by the rebels Morpheus (Laurence Fishburne) and Trinity (Carrie Ann Moss) does he decide to fight back. How else does this film illustrate the postmodern argument that reality is what we perceive reality to be?

eXistenZ (1999, director David Cronenberg) portrays a future society addicted to computer games. Allegra Geller (played by Jennifer Jason Leigh) has developed an organic virtual reality game which plugs into the nervous system through a 'port' at the base of the spine. This allows players to experience the game as hyper-real. Allegra is threatened by 'reality terrorists', anti-game fanatics who pursue her into her own game, where she is accompanied by Ted Pikul (Jude Law). Note how the lines between reality and fantasy, between 'real' identities and game personae, intermingle, finally leaving characters and viewers uncertain about where the game stops and reality begins. What is image, which is reality?

OB in literature

Ian Banks, *The Business*, Little, Brown and Company, London, 1999.

Kate Telman is a technology specialist working for the Business, an organization with global reach: a Swiss headquarters, a ranch in America, a castle in Yorkshire, and a desire to buy a Himalayan principality to obtain a seat at the United Nations. A tale of organizational politics and world domination; is this what working life in the global corporation has become?

Michael Crichton, *Rising Sun*, Century Arrow, London, 1992.

Which elements of globalization affecting business practice are exposed in this murder story? This is the book of the film analysed briefly in the section titled 'Text aims and target readership', page xxiv.

Chapter exercises

1: Social responsibility

Objectives

1. To explore the environmental pressure on organizations to be socially responsible.
2. To expose the tensions between the goals of social responsibility and profitability.

Briefing

This chapter argues that organizations must be responsive to their environment. For example, organizations are expected to act in ways that demonstrate social responsibility with respect to the communities in which they operate, the physical environment and the people that they employ. However, social responsibility can be costly, and conflict with commercial goals. As a manager, how would you resolve these tensions?

This questionnaire is designed to help you explore your perceptions of the conflict between social responsibility and business performance. You are a senior manager with a major commercial organization. How would you respond to the following items? Tick the appropriate box on the scale on the right. Share your answers with colleagues and identify the reasons for any differences in your opinions.

Your instructor will then reveal how managers in Britain answered this questionnaire in 1999.

This exercise is based on David Butcher and Penny Harvey, 1999, 'Be upstanding', *People Management*, vol.5, no.13, pp.37–42.

Social responsibility survey

	strongly agree	agree	neutral	disagree	strongly disagree
the primary goal of any business should be to remain profitable over the long term in order to produce returns for shareholders	❐	❐	❐	❐	❐
the only social responsibility of business is wealth creation	❐	❐	❐	❐	❐
the social responsibility of business extends no further than behaving ethically in the pursuit of its business goal	❐	❐	❐	❐	❐
part of doing good business is taking responsibility for the impact of your activities on the natural environment	❐	❐	❐	❐	❐
business decision makers have a responsibility to take into account the impact of decisions on the communities in which they operate	❐	❐	❐	❐	❐
directors of a business should set an example as responsible and involved members of their communities	❐	❐	❐	❐	❐
since employment cannot be guaranteed, a socially responsible organization should support the employability of its staff through appropriate development	❐	❐	❐	❐	❐
organizations have a responsibility not only to conduct their affairs but also to develop their members as 'good citizens of society'	❐	❐	❐	❐	❐
in today's environment, businesses have to be seen to be socially responsible in order to remain competitive	❐	❐	❐	❐	❐
organizations can differentiate themselves in the marketplace by demonstrating social responsibility in the way they do business	❐	❐	❐	❐	❐
social responsibility needs to be balanced with pursuing economic interests	❐	❐	❐	❐	❐
business should seek to act in the interests of the wider society	❐	❐	❐	❐	❐
managers should see themselves as 'custodians of wealth', not only for shareholders but also for society as a whole	❐	❐	❐	❐	❐

2: The full impact of the environment

Choose an organization with which you are familiar. This could be an organization which you use as a consumer: supermarket, cinema, CD and video chain store, bar, restaurant, garage. Or this could be an organization which is currently in the news for some reason (probably concerned with the need to respond to environmental change). You are going to conduct an environmental scan for this organization. In other words, you are going to identify the issues, events, factors, development and trends, now and into the foreseeable future, which may have an impact, direct or indirect, on how this organization operates. You are also going to work this analysis through to a set of recommendations concerning organizational change; in other words, what are the practical implications of your analysis?

(a) Determine where on the Ansoff turbulence scale this organization is now operating:

1. repetitive
2. expanding
3. changing
4. discontinuous
5. surprising

(b) Use this template to record your analysis, taking turbulence level into account when framing your recommendations:

PESTLE factor	Trends and developments
Political	
Economic	
Social	
Technological	
Legal	
Ecological	

(c) Use your analysis to construct three possible future scenarios for this organization, identifying in each case the organization and management implications, and also identifying which scenario you think is the most probable, and why.

Scenario:	Organization and management implications and recommendations
1:	
2:	
3:	

Chapter 3 Technology

Key concepts

the death of distance

material technology

replacement mechanisms

autonomous work group

job rotation

system

socio-technical system

organizational choice

social technology

technological determinism

compensatory mechanisms

characteristics of mass production

job enlargement

open system

human-centred manufacturing

Learning objectives

When you have read this chapter, you should be able to define those key concepts in your own words, and you should also be able to:

1. Explain different uses of the term 'technology'.

2. Explain why predictions about technology and unemployment are exaggerated.

3. Demonstrate how the consequences of technological innovation depend on the organization of work and not simply on technical capabilities.

4. Define the characteristics of mass production and identify approaches to overcome them.

5. Apply the socio-technical system perspective to organizational analysis and design.

6. Contrast the Scandinavian and Japanese models of team-based work organization.

7. Explain how new technology is changing the nature of work for some people, through teleworking, call centres and increased surveillance.

Why study technology?

Technological innovation is one of the defining features of contemporary industrialized societies. The most significant innovations seem to be in computing and telecommunications, but engineering, materials and pharmaceuticals developments are also important. We are in an era of 'pervasive computing', with computer power built into everyday products, not confined to corporate systems and personal computers. These developments are influencing:

how we communicate with each other	e-mail, mobile phone, video telephone, video conferencing, digital video and still cameras
how we buy goods and services	smart cash cards, internet e-commerce, internet access to news, information services, and music
how we spend our leisure time	digital video disc, web surfing, interactive games, chat rooms, e-books, digital television

Technology is also influencing jobs and the organization of work. Numerous opportunities and threats are being created, for example, by the falling costs of communications, on the one hand, and increasing technological sophistication, on the other, leading to what has been called **the death of distance**. Communications with the far side of the planet, with e-mail and facsimile transmission, are now inexpensive and virtually instantaneous.

Unemployment, deskilling and the dehumanization of work are often blamed on technology. You might find it interesting to complete the short chapter exercise 1, 'technology test', before reading further, to explore your own understanding of the social and organizational impact of technology. In this chapter, we will develop three arguments that contradict the negative stereotype that is commonly found in popular and media accounts:

1. We will argue that the employment effects of technological innovation are indeterminate, and that new technology creates jobs.

2. We will demonstrate how technology has a skills upgrading effect rather than a deskilling one.

3. We will demonstrate that technology does not uniquely determine these outcomes, and that the implications are dependent on how work is organized.

The death of distance is the observation that geographical separation no longer determines the costs or difficulties of global person-to-person communication.

Where in the world?

Arguing that the implications will be as profound as the discovery of electricity, Frances Cairncross comments:

The death of distance will mean that any activity that relies on a screen or a telephone can be carried out anywhere in the world. Services as diverse as designing an engine, monitoring a security camera, selling insurance or running a secretarial paging service will become as easily exportable as car parts or refrigerators. ... India has built a flourishing computer-software industry around Bangalore. Its exports more than doubled between 1990 and 1993, to $270m. India is now attracting back-office work from airlines such as Swissair and British Airways. Some of Hong Kong's paging services are manned from China. In Perth, in Western Australia, EMS control systems monitor the air-conditioning, lighting, lifts and security in office blocks in Singapore, Malaysia, Sri Lanka, Indonesia and Taiwan. Telecom Ireland has been trying to build itself up as the main call centre for Europe, handling toll-free 0800 calls from all over the continent. Last April, it launched an intercontinental service to allow companies to link their European and American call centres and to take advantage of the time differences between them.

From Frances Cairncross, 'The death of distance: a survey of telecommunications', *The Economist*, 30 September 1995, special supplement, p.39.

In chapter 2, the concept of environmental determinism was challenged. In this chapter, the arguments behind technological determinism are given similar treatment.

When are you getting your implant?

Researchers at Reading University in England have been asked by a group of international companies to develop a microchip implant for workers, to monitor their timekeeping and location. Professor Kevin Warwick says that 'For a business the potential is obvious. You can tell when people clock into work and when they leave the building. You would know at all times exactly where they were and who they were with. It is pushing at the limits of what society will accept but it is not such a big deal. Many employees already carry swipecards. I think this is just a step on from that.' The telecommunications company AT&T already uses smart cards and smart badges which relay signals back to a central computer, to track staff movements around buildings so that their telephone calls can 'follow' them.

Based on Stephan Bevan, 'Companies seek chip implants to control staff', *The Sunday Times*, 9 May 1999, p.1.7.

Definitions and predictions

Most of the technology that we use today was unknown to, and barely imagined by, our parents. However, we need to be clear what we mean by the term 'technology'. Langdon Winner (1977) demonstrates how our use of the term changed as concern for 'technological implications' grew. The term was used in the eighteenth and nineteenth centuries simply to refer to machines, tools, factories, industry, craft and engineering. However, the term 'is now widely used in ordinary and academic speech to talk about an unbelievably diverse collection of phenomena—tools, instruments, machines, organizations, methods, techniques, systems, and the totality of all these things in our experience' (Winner, 1977, p.8).

Stop and criticize

Which technologies, in particular, shape your day-to-day experience?

Consider how you expect your life experiences to be different from those of your parents; what part does technology play in creating those differences?

Material technology is the technology—equipment—that can be seen, touched and heard.

Social technology is the technology which seeks to order the behaviour and relationships of people in systematic, purposive ways through structures of co-ordination, control, motivation and reward.

How has this confusion arisen? Rapid developments in technology leave the language behind. The word 'technology' is simply a convenient umbrella term. Ambiguity in the language reflects the pace of innovation, and the concern over technology and its consequences—individual, organizational and social. Winner also argues that this simplification of the language leads us to oversimplify and polarize the issues and arguments. Technology is either a good thing or a bad thing; you are either for it or against it.

The British sociologist Alan Fox (1974) distinguishes between **material technology** and **social technology**.

Social technology thus includes job definitions, payment systems, authority relationships, communications, control systems, disciplinary codes and 'all the many other rules and decision-making procedures which seek to govern what work is done, how it is done, and the relationships that prevail between those doing it' (Fox, 1974, p.1).

Considerable research effort has been devoted to identifying the effects of technology on organizations, jobs and society at large. Technology has often been

Figure 3.1: Technology as an independent variable

regarded as the *independent variable* (see glossary), the factor whose effects are to be studied. Economic growth, employment levels, organization structures, skill requirements and quality of working life become *dependent variables* (see glossary), variables that are expected to be affected by technology. This relationship is illustrated in figure 3.1.

However, as we have seen, some definitions of 'technology' go beyond the equipment itself and combine and overlap with notions of the independent and dependent variables. This makes it difficult to establish cause and effect.

Advances in technology, and developments in computing and information technology in particular, continue to attract widespread media predictions of disaster and doom. Does the evidence support these predictions?

Stop and criticize

Which of the following typical media representations of the impact of technology do you agree with, and with which do you disagree?

- Computers and robots will replace people in manufacturing; the 'unstaffed factory' is a reality.

- Office automation does away with clerical and administrative work; the 'paperless office' is here to stay.

- Nobody needs to work in an office any more because we can all work from our networked computers at home; the 'virtual organization' is here to stay.

- Where people are still required, work will be simple, routine, dehumanized.

- The days of craft skill and worker autonomy are gone.

Compare your views with those of colleagues. Have the media got it wrong, or not?

These predictions are all correct, in the sense that some jobs have been eliminated by machinery, some work has been dehumanized with technological change, much paperwork has been declared redundant, some people do work from a computer terminal at home, and some traditional crafts have disappeared.

The future of pervasive personal computing

Although personal computers (PCs) are sold in supermarkets as cheaply as television sets, new and specialist devices are replacing them: television set-top boxes which allow internet access, fixed-screen telephones, mobile phones with internet access and e-mail, palmtop computers, personal digital assistants (PDAs) and network computers (NCs; known as 'thin clients') which download software as required from the internet.

While the PC is a 'do everything' device, difficult to use and comparatively unreliable, these new devices are specialized, reliable and user-friendly. Your television set-top box, for example, provides access to digital broadcast signals, to the internet, to games and to home shopping. Your fixed-screen telephone provides ordinary calls, home banking, e-mail, e-commerce and internet access. Your mobile phone handles company sales and service information, for transferring data, for managing company supply chains. Your PDA and NC offer business applications—databases, other analytical tools, word processing. The networked computer in your car provides traffic information and speech-to-text e-mail.

In other words, the PC has lost its position as the single main 'one size fits all' computing solution. It is too complex, too unreliable—and always in the wrong room in your house. In most organizations, the spread of personal computers has meant the growth of a complex population of largely incompatible machines with different capabilities and software. These machines are switched on in the morning, switched off again at night. Organizations conducting business over the internet need their computers on line constantly.

The future lies with 'pervasive computing', based on a universal communications standard which allows appliances of different kinds to connect to web servers. The 'winners' in this evolution will be the appliance manufacturers: 3Com, Casio, Hitachi, Sony, Philips, Nokia, Ericsson, Motorola. The 'losers' are likely to be the traditional computer manufacturers, unless they develop competing applications.

Based on 'After the PC', *The Economist*, 12 September 1998, pp.93–5.

Replacement mechanisms are processes through which intelligent machines are used to substitute for people in work organizations, leading to unemployment.

The media image suggests that technology, particularly in the form of computing and information technology, will increase organizational productivity through what are known as **replacement mechanisms**, leaving many people unemployed as a result.

Claims about the unemployment consequences of technology rely on the assumption that, as machines do more, people do less. Job opportunities are reduced by replacement mechanisms. These unemployment fears date from the early nineteenth century, when Luddites destroyed the mechanical looms that were stealing their jobs. Why has subsequent technological change not confirmed those concerns? Why is technological unemployment not chronic?

Technological development is consistent with employment growth. Unemployment levels are not higher today than in earlier decades, and there is little proof of a technology-led fall in job opportunities. The overall effects of technological developments also depend on a number of **compensatory mechanisms**.

There are six main compensatory mechanisms.

Compensatory mechanisms are processes that delay or deflect replacement effects, and which can also lead to the creation of new products and services, new organizations, new sectors and new jobs through technological innovation.

1. *New products and services mean job creation*
Technological innovation has given us mobile phones, e-books, digital video discs, multimedia computers, the internet and e-mail, cybercafes, electronic engine management systems in cars, video conferencing, compact discs and their players, smart bankcards, personal organizers, portable text scanners, and so on. These developments create consumer demand, which leads to more investment in factories, offices and other infrastructure, thus creating jobs in manufacturing, distribution, sales and maintenance.

2. *Lower costs increase demand*

Technical innovation should improve productivity (same output, fewer resources) of existing operations. The consequent cost reduction leads to lower prices, and hence to increased demand. This also means that consumers have more money to spend on other goods and services, increasing demand and job creation elsewhere.

3. *Time lags can delay the implications*

It takes time to build new technology into existing systems, and into new products and services. Technical and organizational problems need to be overcome. This takes time and other resources. Organizations rarely adopt innovations as soon as they become available, and it is expensive to replace existing facilities quickly. Significant investments in factories and offices cannot be written off overnight. Despite the common complaint about the rapid pace of change, technological and organizational changes are often relatively slow.

4. *Hedging risk can delay the implications*

Most organizations turn to experimental and untested technologies slowly at first. The 'learning curve' with a new technology can be expensive, time-consuming and painful. One way to carry these risks is to introduce technological innovation gradually and cautiously.

5. *Expectations of demand*

An organization usually embarks on expensive innovations, with disruptive changes, only when the market for its goods and services is likely to expand. In that case, the organization has to retain, if not expand, the existing workforce. Organizations which expect demand for their output to fall or remain stable are unlikely to invest heavily in change, other than to reverse those expectations.

6. *Technical limitations*

New technologies do not always live up to the claims of those who sell them. They may, in fact, not be able to do everything that the 'old' technology was capable of doing. Existing jobs, skills and equipment may be found working alongside new devices for some time. It is still common to find 'old' land-wired telephones in households where family members have their own mobiles. It is still common to find 'old' machine tools in machine shops equipped with computer-controlled flexible manufacturing systems. The 'old' technology, combined with 'old' human skills, can often perform tasks more easily, faster and more effectively.

It is therefore unrealistic to assume that new technology will increase unemployment. It is equally plausible to argue that technological innovation will create as many jobs as it eliminates, and could create more. In other words, the effects of technology on employment are indeterminate, depending on the complex interrelationship between replacement and compensatory mechanisms, and their respective timing.

Determinism or choice?

Different technologies make different demands on whose who work with them. The technology of an organization appears to determine the nature of work there. When we compare a hospital with a biscuit factory, or a retail store with a coal mine, it seems reasonable to argue that the organization's technology determines the kinds of tasks that need to be done; the nature of individual jobs; the organization of work and the grouping of jobs; the hierarchy through which work is planned, co-ordinated and controlled; the knowledge and skills required to perform the work; and the values and attitudes of employees.

Does technology really determine these factors? Can we predict the shape of an organization, and the nature and content of jobs, from a knowledge of technology?

The determinist position assumes that work has to be organized to meet the requirements of the technology. Different technologies have different 'technological imperatives'. Turner and Lawrence (1965), for example, explained the background to their work on manufacturing jobs in the following terms: 'This research started with the concept that every industrial job contained certain technologically determined task attributes which would influence the workers' response. By "task attributes" we meant such characteristics of the job as the amount of variety, autonomy, responsibility, and interaction with others built into the design'.

It is now widely accepted that technological determinism is an oversimplified perspective. Technology suggests and enables; technology does not merely determine. There are at least three broad areas of choice in the technological change process.

> **Technological determinism** is the argument that technology can be used to explain the nature of jobs, work groupings, hierarchy, skills, values and attitudes in organizational settings.

1. There are choices in the design of tools, machinery, equipment and systems. One area of choice concerns the extent to which control is built into the machine or left to human intervention and discretion. There are many instances of automatic controls being removed from aircraft cockpits, ships' bridges and railway engine cabs following the discovery that pilots and drivers lost touch with the reality of their tasks when surrounded by sophisticated controls which functioned without their understanding or help.

2. There are choices in the goals that technology is used to achieve. David Preece (1995) demonstrates that competitive pressure for innovation is overriding. The needs to reduce costs, improve quality and customer service, and improve management information can be critical. Managers also promote innovation for personal and political reasons, to enhance power over resources and influence over decisions, to enhance status and prestige, and to exert closer surveillance and control over employees.

3. There are choices in the way work is organized around technology. As explored later, car assembly work can be designed in a number of different ways, and it is not clear which of these approaches may be 'correct' or 'best'.

These choices depend more on the assumptions we make about human capabilities and organizational characteristics. They depend less on the capabilities of items of equipment. These are called 'psychosocial assumptions' because they relate to beliefs about individuals and groups. To consider the 'impact' of a technology, therefore, is to consider the wrong question. Technological innovations trigger a decision-making and negotiation process which is driven by the perceptions and goals of those involved. The choices that form in that process determine the 'impact'. Technology has a limited effect on work independent of the purposes of those who would use it and the responses of those who have to work with it.

Figure 3.2 summarizes this argument claiming that the consequences of technological change depend on the interaction of technical capabilities, objectives and how work is organized.

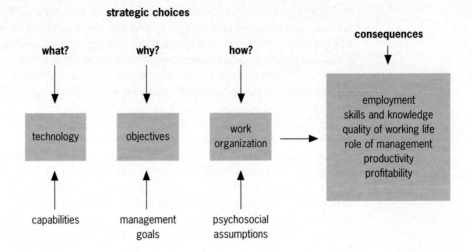

Figure 3.2: Technological indeterminism

Is this argument oversimplified? Surely technology must have *some* independent influence on the nature of work and organizations? Two prominent commentators who have challenged the 'organizational choice' argument, Ian

McLoughlin and Jon Clark (1994; McLouglin, 1999) claim that rejection of technological determinism 'results in the technology baby being thrown out with the determinist bathwater'. Instead, they argue that new computing and information technologies do create imperatives. These include:

- a reduction or elimination of the number of tasks that require manual skills;
- the creation of complex tasks that require interpretative and problem-solving skills;
- the ability to combine knowledge of new with old technology;
- a relationship between technology and user that relies on informed intervention based on an understanding of system interdependencies.

In other words, 'action-centred' abilities become less important, and cognitive skills become more valued. This is not to deny completely the significance of organizational choice, or the role of social shaping and negotiation, in affecting the outcomes for work experience that accompany particular technological innovations. Technology appears to have 'enabling' properties: the technology of motor car production enables task fragmentation and rigid supervisory control, but it also enables multiskilled, autonomous teamwork.

The politics of technology

Robert Merton argued in 1947 that technology had several social implications. He noted that technological change increased task specialization, took skill and identity from work, and increased discipline in the workplace. Merton's argument resurfaced in Harry Braverman's (1974) influential book *Labour and Monopoly Capital: The Degradation of Work in the Twentieth Century*. That work triggered a 'labour process debate' which continues to generate a controversial literature. The central argument of Braverman and his followers is that advances in technology give management progressive opportunities to reduce skill and discretion in work, and to tighten management surveillance and control over workers.

Humanization of work, or work intensification?

The problem as it presents itself to those managing industry, trade, and finance is very different from the problem as it appears in the academic or journalistic worlds. Management is habituated to carrying on labour processes in a setting of social antagonism and, in fact, has never known it to be otherwise. Corporate managers have neither the hope nor the expectation of altering this situation by a single stroke: rather, they are concerned to ameliorate it only when it interferes with the orderly functioning of their plants, offices, warehouses and stores.

For corporate management this is a problem in costs and controls, not in the 'humanization of work'. It compels their attention because it manifests itself in absenteeism, turnover, and productivity levels that do not conform to their calculations and expectations. The solutions they will accept are only those which provide improvements in their labour costs and in their competitive positions domestically and in the world market.

From Harry Braverman, *Labor and Monopoly Capital: The Degradation of Work in the Twentieth Century*, Monthly Review Press, New York, 1974, p.36.

This argument identifies technology as a political tool, as something which managers use to manipulate employees and conditions of work. This is a significant argument, because the technology of manufacturing and office activity is typically discussed as if it were politically neutral. However, if management can increase task specialization and reduce the level of skill required in a job, lower wages can be offered, and the organization's dependence on particular groups and individuals is weakened. If management can increase the discipline in work, improve surveillance of work activities and thus gain tighter control of employees, this can lead to reduced discretion and work intensification.

Managers can manipulate employees by appealing to the technological determinist argument: 'we have no choice but to do it this way because of the technology'. Technological determinism can thus be used to justify unpopular management decisions and to protect them from effective challenge; those who want to argue clearly don't understand the technology. Improved control can lead to lower costs and, in turn, to higher profits. Control maintains the role and status of management—the controllers. Some of the 'implications' of 'technology' may thus be viewed instead as the result of management strategies to improve control through appropriate forms of work organization. The consequences of technical change are not simply the inescapable outcomes of the rigid demands of technology.

Chapter 13 will explore scientific management, developed around the turn of the century but still applied today. Scientific management offers a rationale for task fragmentation and simplification, and thus for tighter control. Scientific

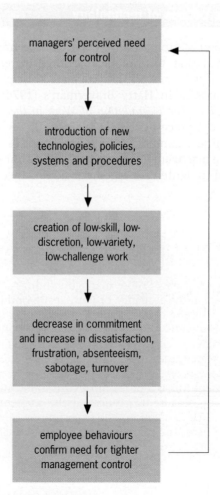

Figure 3.3: The vicious circle of control

management is thus self-perpetuating. How? The typical human response to specialized, repetitive work can confirm the management view that tight control of employees is necessary to maintain discipline, and to produce goods and services effectively. Scientific management can become self-justifying through the 'vicious circle of control' (Clegg and Dunkerley, 1980), illustrated in figure 3.3.

This vicious circle can only be broken by a change in management perceptions, starting with higher trust in, and higher discretion for, employees. Braverman and his followers argue that such a change is unlikely in a capitalist economy. Technological determinism is replaced in this perspective with a pessimistic and inevitable economic, political and technological logic—or rather, another form of gloomy determinism.

Technology and the nature of work

One of the first classic studies of the relationship between technology and the nature of work was carried out by Charles Walker and Robert Guest, whose book, *The Man on the Assembly Line*, was published in 1952. In it they argued, in a technological determinist mode, that some production technologies prevent the formation of work groups and frustrate the social needs of factory employees. Their attitude survey of 180 American automobile assembly workers identified six **characteristics of mass production** work.

The jobs of the car workers were scored on each of these mass production characteristics. Despite being content with pay and working conditions, employees in jobs with a high 'mass-production score' disliked those aspects of their work and had a higher rate of absenteeism than those in low-scoring jobs. These and similar findings prompted some managers to recognize that scientific management principles had taken task specialization too far. Morris Viteles (1950), for example, argued that the combination of increased mechanization with scientific management created routine, repetitive tasks. Monotony and boredom reduced work rate, output and morale and led to high levels of absenteeism and complaints. The 1950s solutions to boredom and monotony were **job rotation** and **job enlargement**.

The aim was to restore the variety that scientific management had eliminated. The first account of job enlargement came from Charles Walker (1950), at the Endicott plant of the American company IBM. In 1944, the jobs of machine operators were enlarged to include machine set-up and inspection of finished product, jobs previously done by other workers. There is nothing in the technology of machining to prevent machine operators from performing these additional tasks. The benefits from this simple change included improved product quality and a reduction in losses from scrap, less idle time for men and machines, and a 95 per cent reduction in set-up and inspection costs.

Although these methods reduce monotony and boredom and increase variety, they do this in a superficial way. However, job rotation and enlargement are still in use.

Work with mass-production characteristics can cause stress and illness, as well as boredom and monotony. Arthur Kornhauser's (1965) study of car assembly workers in Detroit showed that low-grade factory work could lead to job dissatisfaction and poor mental health. The workers that he studied had a long list of grievances, including:

low pay   simplicity of job operations

job insecurity   repetitiveness and boredom

The **characteristics of mass production** include mechanical pacing of work, no choice of tools or methods, repetitiveness, minute subdivision of product, minimum skill requirements and surface mental attention.

Job rotation is a work design method in which employees are switched from task to task at regular intervals.

Job enlargement is a work design method in which tasks are recombined to widen the scope of a job.

Job enlargement: the Linn Products experience

Linn Products was founded in 1973, near Glasgow, Scotland, manufacturing high-quality hi-fi equipment, including amplifiers, record decks, compact disc players and speakers. The company was nominated in 1990 by the British Institute of Management as one of the country's most advanced manufacturers. Linn first used a traditional assembly line. But as the business grew, problems arose over productivity, and delivery promises to customers were broken too often. The company's founder and managing director, Ivor Tiefenbrun, explains how they changed their methods, following a late night brainstorming session:

The next day I asked one of our assembly girls to go and get all the parts required to build a record player, build it and bring it into my office. Somewhat mystified, she did just that and returned about 17 minutes later. It took 27 minutes of labour to build the same item on our production line.

So we re-organized our factory. We eliminated 47 different main and buffer storage areas, went to a single store and a single-stage build where one responsible person builds the product from start to finish. To do this, we invested to create surplus capacity, so that we could pursue our objective of real-time manufacturing: to make what our customers want when they want it. Within six weeks we had made remarkable progress and three months later we were despatching the product the day the customer ordered it.

We now employ our home-grown principles of single-stage build and real-time manufacturing throughout our organization. This approach requires a higher skill level but is the route to a superior quality build. The actual output per employee on any specific product is irrelevant compared to the gain through improved labour flexibility.

The single-stage build method gives one person responsibility and control. Within the envelope of total time allocated to any particular task the individual has the freedom to take the time necessary over tasks which are difficult and to perform simpler tasks rapidly. No single component failure, instrument or plant failure or the non-appearance of any individual will necessarily have any impact on our ability to satisfy our customers' requirements. Pressure is removed from the manufacturing process and the person who builds, tests and packs his own product can take pride in his own workmanship and spot the connection between what he does, the way that product works and customer satisfaction.

Each employee on a conventional assembly line has to work at the same pace as the others, so that the whole line operates in a 'balanced' manner. Single-stage build, or job enlargement, overcomes this problem, and offers more meaningful and varied work at the same time.

From Ivor Tiefenbrun, 'Manufacturing in the future', *RSA Journal*, July, 1993, p.552.

poor working conditions

lack of control over the work

low status

non-use of abilities

restricted promotion opportunities

feelings of futility

the style of the supervisors

Workers in jobs with these characteristics had lower mental health, which meant that they:

were anxious and tense

were less satisfied with life

had negative self-concepts

were socially withdrawn

were hostile to others

suffered from isolation and despair

Kornhauser argued that work with mass-production characteristics produces this pattern of psychological reactions. In a later study, Karasek (1979) showed that the most stressful jobs were those which combined high workload with low discretion. Typical examples of such jobs included assembly workers, garment stitchers, goods and materials handlers, nursing aides and orderlies, and telephone operators. The main symptoms included exhaustion and depression (including nervousness, anxiety and sleeping difficulties).

Stop and criticize

What other jobs can you identify that combine a high workload with low discretion?

Do employees in those jobs display symptoms of fatigue or depression?

What advice could you give management to reduce workload and increase discretion in those jobs?

Swedish car makers were among the first to show that mass production characteristics can be avoided by creative work design. Saab–Scania began experimenting in 1970, when 40 workers in the chassis shop of a new truck factory were divided into production groups (Norstedt and Aguren, 1973). Group members were responsible for deciding how they would rotate between tasks, and also absorbed maintenance and quality-control functions. These changes eventually affected about 600 manual workers, with the following results:

- productivity increased and product quality improved;
- unplanned stoppages of production were significantly reduced;
- costs were reduced to 5 per cent below budget;
- labour turnover was cut from 70 to 20 per cent;
- absenteeism was not affected;
- co-operation between management and workforce improved.

Saab's best known experiment was at its engine factory at Södertälje. Here an oblong conveyor loop moved engine blocks to seven assembly groups, each with three members (Thomas, 1974). Each group had its own U-shaped guide track in the floor, to the side of the main conveyor. Engine blocks were taken from the main track, assembled by the group and then returned to the conveyor. The engines arrived with their cylinder heads, and the groups handled the fitting of carburettors, distributors, spark plugs, camshafts and other components.

Each assembly group decided for themselves how the work was allocated. The guide track for each group was not mechanically driven. The group simply had half an hour to build each engine, and the group decided how that time would be spent. Individual jobs on the conventional assembly track had cycle times of less than two minutes. In 1974, Saab–Scania estimated that it saved around 65,000 Swedish kronor a year on recruitment and training costs alone with this approach. This form of work organization is known as the **autonomous work group** (or self-regulating or self-managing group or team).

This is similar to the high-performance work system methods discussed in chapter 8 [**links**, chapter 8, motivation; and chapter 12, teamworking], and was also the approach used by Sweden's other car maker, Volvo, until the early 1990s. Volvo's plant at Kalmar pioneered the concept of 'dock assembly', in which teams completed whole stages of the final car assembly process in bays to one side of the main moving assembly track, in a specially designed factory layout.

An **autonomous work group** is a team of workers allocated to a significant segment of the workflow, with discretion concerning how the work will be carried out, and how tasks and responsibilities will be allocated, shared and rotated.

Technology and alienation

One classic study of the impact of technology is that of Robert Blauner, who analysed working conditions in the early 1960s in:

printing, dominated by craft work
cotton spinning, dominated by machine minding
car manufacture, dominated by mass production
chemicals manufacture, dominated by process production.

Blauner identified four components of alienation, concerning feelings of:

1. *Powerlessness*; loss of control over conditions of work, work processes, pace and methods.

2. *Meaninglessness*; loss of significance of work activities.

3. *Isolation*; loss of sense of community membership.

4. *Self-estrangement*; loss of personal identity, of sense of work as a central life interest.

Printing workers set their own pace, were free from management pressure, chose their own techniques and methods, had powerful unions, practised a complex skill, had good social contacts at work, had high status, identified closely with their work and were not alienated.

Textile workers performed simple, rapid and repetitive operations over which they had little control, worked under strict supervision and had little social contact at work. Alienation among textile workers, however, was low. Blauner argued that this was because they lived in close rural communities whose values and way of life overcame feelings of alienation arising at work.

Car assembly workers had little control over work methods, saw little meaning in the tasks they performed, were socially isolated and developed no meaningful skills.

Chemicals processing workers operated prosperous, technically advanced plants where manual work had been automated. They controlled their own work pace, and had freedom of movement, social contact and teamwork. They developed an understanding of the chemical reactions which they monitored, and also developed a sense of belonging, achievement and responsibility. In addition they had close contact with educated, modern management.

Blauner concluded that advanced technology would eliminate alienation.

Based on Robert Blauner, *Alienation and Freedom: The Factory Worker and His Job*, University of Chicago Press, Chicago, 1964.

Socio-technical systems analysis and design

> A **system** may be defined as something that functions by virtue of the interdependence of its component parts.

Swedish managers did not invent the autonomous work group. The idea came from the work of British researchers at the Tavistock Institute of Human Relations in London. The Tavistock group developed the concept of the organization as a **system**.

The term 'system' can be applied to a range of phenomena: solar system, nervous system, traffic management system, telecommunications system, waste disposal system. Any system is defined by its boundaries, which in turn depend on what one wants to study, and why. In an organizational context, we may wish to analyse a performance management system, a product distribution system, a raw materials purchasing system or a production system.

The human organism and the organization share one important property. They are each dependent on their ability to conduct an exchange with their environments. We breathe air, consume food and drink, and absorb sensory information.

An **open system** is a system that interacts, in a purposive way, with its external environment in order to survive.

Eric John Miller
(b. 1924)

Albert Kenneth Rice

A **socio-technical system** is a system which possesses both a material technology and a social organization (job specifications, management structure).

We convert these imports into energy and actions, disposing of waste products and expending energy in chosen behaviours. The organization, like the human body, is also an **open system**.

Open systems import resources, such as people, materials, equipment, information and money. They transform those inputs in organizations through producing services and goods. They then export those products back into the environment, as goods and satisfied customers. This treatment of organizational behaviour in terms of living organisms is known as the organic analogy (Rice, 1958; 1963; Miller and Rice, 1967).

Another property of open systems is their ability to reach a particular outcome from a variety of starting points and routes. The autonomous work group at Saab, for example, could assemble an engine in many different ways, but with the same end results. A chemical reaction, on the other hand, is a closed system in which the end result depends on the concentrations and quantities of the items used to begin with. This property is known as equifinality, and it has an interesting consequence for organizational design. Equifinality suggests that it is not necessary to specify in detail the organization structure and the duties of every member. If an organization can develop its own mode of operating, and change that as circumstances require, then it will only be necessary to detail the basic and most significant aspects. This approach to organizational design is called minimum critical specification.

Unlike closed systems, which maintain or move towards states of homogeneity, organizations become more elaborate, diverse and adaptable in structure in attempts to cope with their environment (Emery and Trist, 1960). This argument is consistent with demands for organizations to become even more flexible and responsive in an increasingly turbulent world [**link**, chapter 2, the world outside].

The Tavistock researchers developed systems thinking significantly beyond the ideas we have covered so far. Eric Trist introduced the idea that an organization can also be considered as an open **socio-technical system**.

The socio-technical system concept is illustrated in figure 3.4. The goal of socio-technical system design is to find the 'best fit' between the social and technical components. Trist argued that effective socio-technical system design could never satisfy the needs of both sub-systems. 'Sub-optimization' is, therefore, a necessary feature of good socio-technical design. A system designed to meet social needs, ignoring technical system needs, would quickly run into problems. Conversely, a system designed according to the demands of technology could be expected to generate social and organizational issues. What is required is a design approach

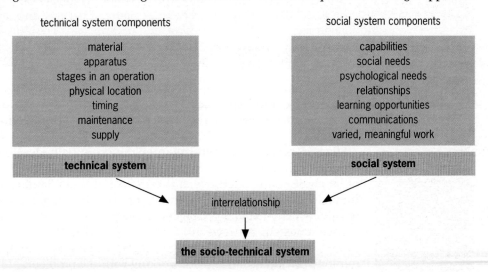

Figure 3.4: The organization as socio-technical system

aimed at joint optimization of the social and technical components and their requirements. The resultant socio-technical system design is thus a matter of choice.

A number of new concepts have been introduced in this section. These include:

system	anything that functions by virtue of the interdependence of its component parts
open system	a system that has to conduct regular exchanges with its environment in order to survive
the organic analogy	the organization as an open system has properties similar to a living organism
equifinality	the same end results can be achieved with different starting points and routes
minimum critical specification	it is not necessary to specify organization and task design in detail as open systems adapt themselves as necessary
socio-technical system	the organization combines a social system (people) with a technical system (plant and machinery)
joint optimization	the social and technical systems cannot effectively be designed in isolation; trade-offs are necessary to design for 'best fit' between the two sub-systems

Netherlands Car BV: contemporary socio-technical system design

NedCar is the only volume manufacturer of passenger cars in the Netherlands and is one of the most modern car plants in Europe. It is an international joint venture, owned by Mitsubishi Motors Corporation (Japan), Volvo Car Corporation (Sweden) and a bank on behalf of the Dutch state. Employing 4,400 people, annual production is 200,000 to 300,000 cars—750 to 800 cars a day. The Born plant makes equal numbers of the Volvo S40/V40 and the Mitsubishi Carisma, saloon and hatchback.

The Born plant is organized into four main units. In the Press Shop, body parts are made from coils of sheet steel. In the Body Shop, body parts are assembled to form complete bodyshells. In the Paint Shop, bodies are given their surface treatments. In Final Assembly, complete cars are made from the painted bodyshells. The Born complex also has a logistics centre, a delivery area, a parts warehouse, training centre and support facilities. The plant information pack explains The NedCar formula: $4 \times M$ = world class performance:

The socio-technical approach was developed in studies carried out by Tavistock researchers, who developed the concept of **organizational choice** with respect to technology.

Eric Trist and K.W. Bamforth (an ex-miner) initially developed the concept of the socio-technical system in their study of the social and psychological impact of longwall mining methods in the 1940s (Trist and Bamforth, 1951). Figure 3.5 summarizes the developments in technology, work organization and job characteristics which Trist and colleagues studied.

Their research, between 1955 and 1958 (Trist, Higgin, Murray and Pollock, 1963), contrasted the advantages of the traditional 'composite autonomous mining' method of single-place working with the problems of highly mechanized coal getting. During their study, however, they found that some pits had devel-

Organizational choice is the argument that work and organization design are not uniquely determined by technology, that the technical system does not determine the social system.

Men

- a well-trained workforce
- task groups have autonomous responsibility for quality and maintenance
- about 10 per cent have been trained in Japan, transferring skills to colleagues in Born
- continuous improvement is a priority

Machines

- only proven technology is used
- flexible automation with 430 robots (one-third of all robots in the Netherlands)
- equipment geared to maximum availability, minimum downtime
- maintenance is the responsibility of the production organization

Materials

- all parts supplied are certificated suitable for the manufacturing process
- only parts inspected and tested for quality are used
- most suppliers use just-in-time (JIT) delivery, directly to the assembly stations
- suppliers are involved at an early stage in new projects

Methods

- a common manufacturing process; two makes, one production line
- three 'islands' of automation in final assembly to eliminate heavy physical work
- close co-operation between product and process development
- computer-controlled ordering system
- production capacity of final assembly is one car every 68 seconds

Based on *NedCar in Perspective*, Netherlands Car BV, September 1996.

oped a form of 'shortwall' working, with methods similar to those of composite single-place working.

One case, called 'The Manley Innovation' after the name of the pit, describes how miners themselves developed a teamwork approach to shortwall mining, in response to underground conditions which made it dangerous to support and

technology	work organization	job characteristics
1: hand and pneumatic picks	single place	composite autonomous miner
2: mechanized coal cutters and belt conveyors	conventional cutting longwall	task fragmentation, mechanization, mass production features
3: electric coal cutters and belt conveyors	composite longwall	composite autonomous, self-regulating teams

Figure 3.5: From single place to composite longwall

The whole atmosphere on a composite longwall was different

The astonishing change in the physical appearance of the workplace, which would be the first thing to impress itself on a visitor, has come to be recognized as almost a hallmark of a composite group ... although the men were not responsible for equipment in the gates, they would use their lunch break to check and, if necessary, do repairs to the mothergate belt which leads to the face, anticipating and preventing possible disturbances of their work. No man was ever out of a job. If he finished hewing or pulling before others he would join and help them, or go on to some other job which was to follow. If work was stopped owing to breakdowns in the transport system on which the group was dependent for its supply of tubs, the men would go on to do maintenance work.

From P.G. Herbst, *Autonomous Group Functioning*, Tavistock, London, 1962, p.6.

work long coal faces. When management tried to restore conventional longwall working to reduce costs, the men resisted and negotiated an agreement to continue with their approach. This was based on composite, multiskilled, self-selecting groups, collectively responsible for the whole coal-getting cycle on any one shift. This contrasted sharply with conventional longwall working, in which each shift was restricted to one stage of the coal-getting cycle, and each miner was limited to one fragmented task, with limited opportunity for the development of other underground skills. The Manley groups had no supervisors but elected 'team captains' to liaise with pit management. They were paid on a common paynote, as all members were regarded as making equivalent contributions. The groups each comprised over 40 miners, who arranged their own work allocations, to develop and maintain their underground skills.

This research led to two main conclusions:

1. Work in groups is more likely to provide meaningful work, develop responsibility and satisfy human needs than work that is allocated to separately supervised individuals.

2. Work can be organized in this way regardless of the technology in use. Social system design is not uniquely determined by technical system characteristics and demands.

The work organization introduced when mechanical coal-getting methods replaced traditional techniques was not determined by the new technology. In other words, technical change is consistent with organizational choice, or with what John Bessant (1983) calls 'design space'.

Stop and criticize

Coal mining is hardly 'typical' manufacturing work. To what extent can the concept of organizational choice be applied to other kinds of work and organizations?

Although dating from the 1950s, socio-technical systems thinking remains influential, particularly in the Netherlands and Sweden. Under the influence of Swedish Ulbo de Sitter and Dutch colleagues (1994; de Sitter, den Hertog and Dankbaar, 1997), a more elaborate socio-technical system design methodology has been developed involving the following steps (Benders, Doorewaard and Poutsma, 2000):

1. an analysis of the external environment to establish the main organizational design criteria, such as market objectives, but also quality of working life and labour relations;

2. an analysis of the product flow pattern;

3. design of the production structure, first approximate and then in detail, based on semi-autonomous production units operated by 'whole-task groups';

4. design of the control structure, allocating control tasks to the lowest possible level, which can be an individual workstation or an autonomous group;

5. the creation of 'operational groups' which combine support and line functions (such as maintenance and quality control) and which assist a number of whole-task groups.

Contemporary examples of autonomous teamworking are explored in more detail in chapter 12 [**link**, chapter 12, teamworking].

Team versus lean: competing socio-technical paradigms

Until the early 1990s, the pioneering team-based plants of the Swedish car manufacturers Saab and Volvo were popular 'management tourist' attractions. Volvo's president, Pehr Gyllenhammar, explained his company's approach to making cars and organizing people in his 1977 book. The team-based approach remained popular in America into the 1990s, one study suggesting that over half of American manufacturing companies had scrapped their assembly lines in favour of 'cellular manufacturing' methods (*The Economist*, 1994).

Volvo built a new assembly plant at Uddevalla, on Sweden's west coast, in the late 1980s. Here, autonomous teams of eight to ten car builders were responsible for final assembly, on a static 'assembly dock', not on a paced assembly line. The plant had a central materials store from which parts and sub-assemblies were delivered to teams by automatically guided vehicles. Each team was responsible for its own training, maintenance, tooling, task planning and the selection of new members. Without supervisors, teams elected rotating spokespersons who handled planning, assigned work, led discussions, dealt with problems and were responsible for reporting to management.

However, in 1990 Saab was forced to sell its motor car business to the American company General Motors. In 1991, Saab closed its team-based plant at Malmo. In 1993, Volvo closed its plants at Kalmar and Uddevalla and concentrated production at its traditionally organized factory at Torslanda, outside Gothenburg. (The Volvo plant at Uddevalla was subsequently reopened to manufacture special vehicles.) In January 1999, Volvo Car Corporation was sold to the American Ford Motor Company.

These developments helped to tarnish the image of team-based manufacturing. As the Swedish car manufacturers were selling and closing their facilities, Japanese car manufacturers such as Toyota, Honda and Nissan were opening new plants in Europe and America, with much publicity and apparent success. What went wrong?

One explanation comes from the work of James Womack, Dan Jones and Daniel Roos. In their book, *The Machine That Changed The World* (1990), they compare the productivity of car manufacturers around the world and explain the wide variations in terms of production methods. One of their key measures was the number of hours of direct labour used to build, paint and finally assemble a car.

In summary, the main differences in 1989, between the best and the worst companies, on this measure of labour assembly hours, were as follows:

	Best	Worst
Japan	13.2	25.9
North America	18.6	30.7
Europe	22.8	55.7

These comparisons were damning, and pointed to significant advantages in Japanese manufacturing methods. At Uddevalla, the training time for team members was high, and the assembly time for each car was twice the European average. Despite the favourable working conditions, absenteeism and labour turnover also remained high (Wickens, 1993). Womack *et al.* argued that those productivity differences were caused, not by automation, but by the combination of production methods used. The Japanese advantage, they claimed, was due to their use of **lean production** methods (Oliver, Delbridge, Jones and Lowe, 1994).

Lean production, or lean organization, combines the following techniques and approaches:

Lean production is an approach to manufacturing which combines conventional machine pacing, standardized work methods, just-in-time materials flow, continuous improvement or *kaizen*, problem-solving teams, and powerful first-line supervision.

- Machine-paced assembly, with task specialization, placing responsibility on workers to improve the 'one best way' for each task.

- 'Just-in-time' delivery of materials to the point of assembly, replacing the need to hold costly inventories, and reducing the need for storage space.

- Continuous improvement or *kaizen*. When the worker identifies an improvement, this is agreed with supervision and engineering staff, and the work procedure sheet is revised.

- Aggressive problem solving with 'quality circles', a team approach to *kaizen* for addressing quality and manufacturing problems.

- A ruthless approach to reducing equipment adjustment and retooling times, and eliminating defects. In a Japanese plant, one worker can bring the plant to a halt if a problem arises. The plant is not restarted until the problem is fixed.

- Powerful first-line supervisors who monitor and encourage continuous improvement.

'Teamwork' in Japanese organizations, therefore, is not the same as 'teamwork' in most Scandinavian, European or American companies (MacDuffie, 1988; Buchanan, 1994; 2000). The assembler in a Japanese plant carries out a short-cycle repetitive task, under supervisory control, and is under pressure to improve productivity through adjustments to the job, or aspects of the manufacturing process. This is quite different from the experience of multiskilled autonomous team members, who decide how to allocate and rotate tasks, and how to solve problems, in collaboration with each other, at their own pace and discretion.

Is it safe to conclude that the Anglo-American-Scandinavian model of team-based manufacturing has been discredited, and that lean production is a more effective and productive socio-technical paradigm? This conclusion must be premature.

The evidence suggests that lean production is also 'mean' production. The pace and intensity, the demands of *kaizen,* supervisory regulation of methods, and lack of discretion are stressful. Parker and Slaughter (1988) studied a plant run jointly by Toyota and General Motors in California—New United Motors Manufacturing Incorporated (NUMMI). This was publicized as a lean 'industry standard' production approach, but Parker and Slaughter called it 'management by stress', with every worker motion and action timed meticulously to remove waste effort, reduce time and inventory, and streamline production continuously.

Hammarstrom and Lansbury (1991) point out that these workplace pressures are typically offset by high pay and job security, and that Japanese transplants are often located in areas of high unemployment and low trade union membership. They conclude that Japanese methods based on scientific management methods appear 'natural' and 'safe' to many managers.

Swedish researchers have been forceful in their defence of Scandinavian socio-technical methods. Christian Berggren, at the Swedish Institute for Work Life Research in Stockholm, has been scathing of the narrow range of measures used in the American research, which focused on final assembly hours and paid less attention to the way in which the overall supply chain, from design to customer, was organized (Berggren, Bjorkman and Hollander, 1991; Berggren, 1993; 1995). Berggren also argues that Volvo's decision to close the plants at Kalmar and Uddevalla was reached despite internal company analyses which revealed that these plants were at least as productive as the conventional, but much larger and older, plant at Torslanda. The company had excess production capacity in the early 1990s, and internal logistics and politics made it expedient to close the smaller and more experimental plants located some distance from the company's main facilities.

We are therefore faced with a dispute between two socio-technical paradigms, between two quite different ways of organizing people around production. A partial resolution to this debate began to emerge during the second half of the 1990s.

One dimension of this resolution concerns the extent to which it is possible to combine elements of the two approaches, to emphasize both concern for production and also maintain and improve quality of working life. Peter Wickens (1995), ex-personnel director for Nissan, Sunderland (UK), argues for the 'ascendant organization', which emphasizes both employee commitment and management control of manufacturing operations.

A second dimension relies on the observation that some cultures and groups more readily accept the 'high-pay, high-security, high-intensity' package of lean production, which is resisted in other countries, such as Sweden. The collection of papers by Ake Sandberg (1995) supports this view. Volvo has rarely used its Scandinavian model of manufacturing in its plants elsewhere in the world (in the Netherlands, Britain or Canada for example).

However, the 'team versus lean' debate is far from resolution. The arguments in motor car production are not resolved, and it is not clear how these issues can be applied to other manufacturing and service sector organizations. This debate is likely to run for some time.

Advanced technology and the nature of work

If technology does not create unemployment, then surely the jobs that remain will be deskilled at best and dehumanized at worst? The evidence again suggests that the 'technological implications' are not as one-dimensional as they are often portrayed. Technology can deskill, in some contexts, but it can also increase the demands on human skill and understanding.

Research has confirmed the view, previously expressed by Louis Davis and

James Taylor (1975; 1976), that technological innovation opens up new opportunities for work organization and increases the demands on cognitive and social skills. As Shoshana Zuboff (1988, pp.75–6) concludes, from studies of automated process control applications:

> As information technology restructures the work situation, it abstracts thought from action. Absorption, immediacy, and organic responsiveness are superseded by distance, coolness, and remoteness. Such distance brings an opportunity for reflection. There was little doubt in these workers' minds that the logic of their jobs had been fundamentally altered. As another worker from Tiger Creek summed it up, 'Sitting in this room and just thinking has become part of my job. It's the technology that lets me do these things.
>
> The thinking this operator refers to is of a different quality from the thinking that attended the display of action-centred skills. It combines abstraction, explicit inference, and procedural reasoning. Taken together, these elements make possible a new set of competences that I call *intellective skills*. As long as the new technology signals only deskilling—the diminished importance of action-centred skills—there will be little probability of developing critical judgement at the data interface. To rekindle such judgement, though on a new, more abstract footing, a reskilling process is required. Mastery in a computer-mediated environment depends on developing intellective skills.

Zuboff's conclusion about the importance of 'intellective' or problem-solving skills is supported by a considerable body of evidence. Many studies of manufacturing technology suggest that sophisticated, flexible, expensive equipment needs sophisticated, flexible, expensive people to operate it effectively. Richard Walton and Gerald Susman (1987) argue that advanced technology increases:

- interdependencies between organizational functions;

- skill requirements, and dependence on skilled people;

- capital investment per employee;

- the speed, scope and costs of mistakes;

- sensitivity of performance to changes in skill and attitudes.

Walton and Susman argue that the appropriate organizational response to these trends has four ingredients.

1. Develop a highly skilled, flexible, co-ordinated and committed workforce.

2. Develop a lean, flat, flexible and innovative management structure.

3. Retain experienced people.

4. Develop a strong partnership between management and trade unions.

Effective 'people policies', according to Walton and Susman, include:

- job enrichment;

- multiskilling;

- teamwork;

- 'pay for knowledge' reward systems;

- reconsideration of the organizational level at which decisions are taken;

- attention to selection and training, and to management development.

Too complex for mere mortals to comprehend

Instead of manning the bridge with helmet and heavy binoculars, the skipper of a $1 billion Aegis class cruiser exercises command from the hi-tech CIC, or Combat Information Center, a windowless room linked to the outside world through glowing computer and radar screens. Never before has a warship's captain had access to so much instant and accurate information. Even so, the skipper and his crew are not immune to confusion—the 'fog of war'. A horrified world learned precisely that in July [1988], when the *US Vincennes* shot down an Iranian airliner, killing 290 civilians.

The tragedy marked the first time an Aegis cruiser had fired its missiles in combat. And it should rekindle efforts to tame the complexity of weapons systems—especially with programmes such as Star Wars looming. Ever since the Aegis was designed in the late 1970s, critics have worried that its systems are too complex for mere mortals to comprehend. In its recently released investigative report, the Navy touched on the issue of breakdowns between man and machine. But the inquiry team found that the highly sophisticated computer and radar systems aboard the *Vincennes* had performed flawlessly.

The real lesson of the *Vincennes* is that electronic systems can produce far too much data for human beings to digest in the heat and strain of battle. Engineers who design such systems often forget this . . . A review board did recommend some changes in Aegis. One culprit: a hard-to-read computer display that doesn't show an aircraft's altitude beside its radar track. Investigators called for a redesigned screen and better training . . .

The loss of 290 innocent lives is too high a price for working out a new weapon system's bugs.

From Dave Griffiths, 'When man can't keep up with the machines of war', *Business Week*, 12 September 1988, p.28.

Supporting this argument, recent research shows that while computerization has reduced the labour content of industrial processes, it has triggered a trend away from low-wage blue-collar work towards higher-paid occupations (Bresnahan, 1999).

These considerations have led to the development of **human-centred manufacturing**.

Human-centred manufacturing faces two problems (McLoughlin and Clark, 1994). One concerns persuading organizations preoccupied with reducing costs to adopt such systems. A second concerns the problems of involving users in system design, given the complexity of the technology, and the location and membership of technical and academic research teams.

Research has also shown how technological advance encourages skills upgrading and teamwork in office settings. Word processing became, during the 1980s, the building block of the 'office of the future'. Many office 'typists' today work with a multimedia networked computer capable of performing a staggering range of tasks in comparison with the humble typewriter, including various data analysis and presentation operations, and national and international communications, through the internet and electronic mail. Several commentators have argued for a more human-centred approach to the design of office systems, in parallel with developments in human-centred manufacturing (Smith, 1987).

Technology is enabling three other changes in the nature of work:

1. Teleworking

2. Call centres

3. Employee surveillance

> **Human-centred manufacturing** is the design of production technologies in a way that complements human skills and abilities, rather than distance or replace them.

Distancing or complementarity: new technology options

David Buchanan and David Boddy (1983b) compared the consequences of computerization on two occupations—doughmen and ovensmen—in a Glasgow biscuit factory.

The company installed a new 'recipe desk', allowing changes to be made simply with thumb wheels. The doughman's job used to be done by master bakers. It was now unskilled and repetitive. Bored doughmen forgot to add sundry ingredients such as salt, and this was only discovered later. By replacing the doughman's craft skills, but still requiring human intervention at that stage of the process, computerization created a *distanced* role in which:

1. Operators had little understanding of the process and equipment, and they could not visualize the consequences of their actions.

2. Operators could not diagnose equipment faults, there were no backup systems for them to operate, and specialist maintenance staff were needed.

3. Operators became bored, apathetic and careless and rejected responsibility for errors.

4. Operators developed no skills to make them eligible for promotion.

These *distancing* features are typical of many jobs in 'nearly automated' systems.

The implications of computerization for ovensmen were different. They were responsible for baking biscuits with the correct bulk, weight, moisture content, colour, shape and taste. This was complex, as action to correct one feature affects the others. The training time for this job was three to four months.

At the end of the line, as each packet passed over a computerized weigh cell, the packet weight was recorded, and the computer displayed summary information at the ovensman's station. This information showed when something was wrong but could not indicate the cause of the problem, or what action to take. The ovensman had to consider the properties of the flour, and the dough that it made. He became a 'process supervisor', deciding how to deal with problems. The computerized weighing technology *complemented* the skill and knowledge of the ovensman, creating a role in which he:

1. Got rapid feedback on performance, and had discretion to control the process.

2. Had good understanding of the relationships between process stages.

3. Had a visible goal that could be influenced.

4. Felt that the job had more interest and challenge.

Equipment could have been designed to let doughmen see and hear the mixing process. Why not take the recipe desks out of the production office and let the doughmen adjust ingredient quantities themselves? Autonomous groups could have been organized, each responsible for a whole production line. The work experience of these two occupations was conditioned only in part by technological innovation and was influenced by work organization choices.

Based on David A. Buchanan and D. Boddy, 'Advanced technology and the quality of working life: the effects of computerized controls on biscuit-making operators', *Journal of Occupational Psychology*, 1983, vol.56, no.2, pp.109–19.

Teleworking

Teleworking, or telecommuting, means working from home (in your 'hoffice') with a personal computer, telephone and fax machine. Teleworkers are spared the daily trek to the office but have to turn part of their house into a workspace in return. The pace of change makes it difficult to give accurate figures about the number of people affected. One estimate says that there are over 2 million teleworkers in Britain, and 13 million worldwide (Stredwick and Ellis, 1998). This development has most relevance to service sector organizations and to office-based technical, administrative, clerical, financial, scientific and secretarial work. Manufacturing and other tasks that are tied to fixed locations are not so readily affected.

| **Stop and criticize** | Your employer gives you a computer with a modem and a fax machine and asks you to work at home. What are the advantages and disadvantages for the organization? For you? On the basis of this analysis, will you comply or resist? |

There are three types of teleworker:

home-based works mostly from home, technologically self-sufficient, may not come into the office at all, or makes periodic (weekly, monthly) visits

nomadic works 'on the road', from their car, travelling to customers or clients around a region or country, with portable computer and mobile phone

ad hoc office-based, but works at home occasionally, to meet deadlines, deal with domestic crises and transport strikes, illness, school holidays and so on

The time colonist

Kristin Hansen is a time colonist. She gets up at 6am in a suburb of Tokyo. After a quick breakfast, she takes the train into the financial district where she has an office in a building owned by a major Japanese bank. Ms Hansen doesn't work for the Japanese bank. She is senior vice president of a Danish trading firm with collateral relations to the bank. Her job is to watch over the flow of investments of her company as they move around the world in an endless cycle of cash transfers between Copenhagen, Karachi, Tokyo, San Francisco, Chicago, New York, London and Copenhagen again. She also manages a limited number of major trades on a personal basis. Many traders work with short-term investments. Hansen watches over long-term trading positions: she may hold some of her investments for as long as half an hour. As a senior vice president, however, Hansen's most important task is making an occasional urgent decision when her colleagues in Copenhagen and New York are asleep.

Hansen's business is located in time, rather than in space. Money moves around the world at the speed of light. The markets operate twenty-four hours a day. A second here or a minute there may represent immense gains or losses—millions of dollars, millions of kronor, billions of yen.

When evening comes, Hansen stops at a Tokyo restaurant for a meal. Then she returns home to her suburban apartment. She logs on to her computer to check a few last details of market action for the day. Then she makes a phone call to her boyfriend, a chef in Paris who has just finished the day's shopping for his restaurant. Finally, she settles into a chair with a glass of wine and a stack of books to work on her doctorate. This weekend, she'll be at school in Scandinavia. At any rate, her mind will. Her body will be in Tokyo while she interacts with students from Finland, Sweden, Denmark, England and Germany. Half of them are in Scandinavia. A few are in other countries. Some of them live in time colonies, as she does.

From Ken Friedman, 'Cities in the information age: a Scandinavian perspective', in M. Igbaria and M. Tan (eds), *The Virtual Workplace*, Idea Publishing, Hershey, 1998, pp.144–76.

Teleworking is not new. References first appeared in the 1970s. However, teleworking becomes a much more attractive option with the availability of low-cost, high-specification personal computers which can be connected easily to the internet, electronic mail and corporate databases. The growing popularity of teleworking, therefore, is technology-driven. Does this sound like 'technological determinism'? Well, there is no 'one best way' to do teleworking, and there are many non-technological reasons for and against this approach.

What technology is required? The typical teleworker needs the following:

- computer
- modem
- scanner
- software
- printer
- dedicated second phone line
- answerphone
- fax machine
- special office furniture
- space in house for all this equipment

Teleworking around Europe

Country	Number of teleworkers	Percentage of workforce
Finland	355,000	16.8
Sweden	5,944,000	15.2
Netherlands	1,044,000	14.5
Britain	2,027,000	7.6
Germany	2,132,000	6.0
Ireland	61,000	4.4
Italy	720,000	3.6
France	635,000	2.9
Spain	357,000	2.8

Estimated European total teleworkers in 1999: 9 million

From Ursula Huws, 'Wired in the country', *People Management*, vol.5, no.23, 25 November 1999, pp.46–7.

The British telecommunications company BT estimates that it can cost £17,000 (at 1998 prices) to equip a teleworker. In addition to the equipment, the employer may also have to pay for telephone bills, stationery, equipment insurance, technical support, and home rent and heating (all of which would be supplied at the office).

An IRS survey (1996) identified five main and five subsidiary reasons for introducing teleworking from the organization's perspective:

Main reasons:

1. in response to requests from employees (the most common reason cited);
2. to reduce costs;
3. to cope with maternity;
4. to help reduce office overcrowding;
5. following relocation of office to where some staff were unable to move.

Other reasons:

1. to cope with illness or disability;
2. 'fits the kind of work that we do';
3. because staff live some distance from the office;
4. allows more undisturbed working time;
5. database connections are faster out of main working hours.

There appear to be many advantages, for the organization and for the teleworker.

There is less need for expensive office space. There is no office 'chit chat' and other distractions. Reduced commuting means that more effective use is made of employee time. Many organizations using teleworkers report increased efficiency, productivity, work turnaround, accuracy, speed of response and morale. With jobs where location is not important (the 'death of distance' argument), an organization can use people who they might not otherwise be able to employ because of their respective locations. For the teleworker, commuting time, costs and frustrations are eliminated, there is no supervisor constantly checking, there is freedom to arrange the working day, and you become your own boss.

There are, however, a number of disadvantages, such as:

- the set-up costs can be expensive;
- staff are not able to share equipment and other facilities;
- lack of social interaction and sharing of ideas;
- no team spirit;
- staff lose touch with the organization culture;
- staff can be unaware of overall organizational goals;
- management cannot easily monitor and control staff activity;
- no access to office-based records and facilities;
- some customers expect to contact a 'conventional' office.

In spite of the disadvantages, teleworking is likely to increase in popularity as a flexible way of working for at least some jobs and organizations.

Telecommuting: a virtual disaster story

The claims about the changing nature of work are clearly exaggerated. Huge numbers of workers were mobile long before cellphones came along; on the other hand, some of the ties that tether people to their desks are much stronger than telephone wires. Five years ago TBWA Chiat/Day, an advertising agency, led the charge into the 'virtual workplace' when its offices in Venice, California, proved too small for a fast-expanding workforce. The company gave everyone a mobile phone, a laptop and a locker and told them to come into the office only when they needed to. The experiment proved a disaster: workers complained of isolation and lack of creative interaction. Last year the company traded virtual communication for the real thing, moving into large offices where everybody had their own desk, along with plenty of open spaces for informal meetings. TBWA Chiat/Day is only one of a huge number of companies to discover that people need to 'share the same air' as well as to 'share the airwaves'.

From Adrian Wooldridge, 'The world in your pocket: a survey of telecommunications', *The Economist*, 9 October 1999, pp.33–4.

Call centres

A call centre is a central facility for handling telephone enquiries and requests, usually from customers and clients. They are now particularly common in financial service sector organizations such as banks, building societies and insurance companies. Some call centres are extremely large. The bank First Direct, for example, has a call centre in Leeds in England employing 3,000 people; the Sky Television subscriber centre in Livingston in Scotland employs 2,000 people (Stredwick and Ellis, 1998). Air France announced in 1999 its intention to set up a multilingual call centre in London, with 200 staff advising customers in English, French, German, Spanish, Catalan and Italian.

One estimate put the number of people employed in call centres in Britain in 1998 at between 250,000 and 300,000, or around 1 per cent of the workforce (IPD, 1998). That was predicted to rise to one million employees by 2000, with half of all European call centre business being conducted in Britain. The average number of employees in a call centre is around 50, but with some, as just indicated, employing thousands.

There are two main types of call centre: help desks and interactive processing centres:

help desk   provides information, technical advice, flight and train times

interactive processing   provides a service, sells a product, handles transactions over the telephone, no paperwork

Like teleworking, the development of call centres is technology-driven. The person answering your call sits at a computer screen with access to the organization's database. Customer information can be called quickly onto the computer screen, transactions can be processed, questions can be answered. This is clearly beneficial from the customer's point of view. From the employee's perspective, however, there are advantages and drawbacks.

Most call centre employees are multiskilled. In a traditional insurance company, one department handles enquiries and new business, while a separate department handles claims. The customer who telephones with a question or a problem speaks first to a receptionist, who then has to transfer the call to the appropriate member of staff, who may in turn have to transfer the call again if the question or problem is complex, or if the customer has more than one question. Call centre staff, in contrast, are often trained to deal with a range of customer requests, questions and problems. This requires a much broader base of knowledge and skill, and can also involve considerable discretion in helping to resolve customers' difficulties.

Call centres have three main management advantages:

1. Location is not important, and call centres can operate in parts of the country where property and wage costs are low and staff are easier to recruit.

2. Call centre staff can deal with many more customers over the telephone than 'field' staff in branch offices or mobile sales staff contacting customers directly.

3. Staff work activities can be closely monitored by the automated call distribution system, which passes incoming calls to centre staff without the need for a conventional switchboard. Pay can be linked to number of calls handled.

The multiskilled call centre employee may thus be subjected to tight management

Factors affecting staff turnover in call centres

Factor	Percentage of call centres citing as important
Intensity of the call centre environment	42
Competition for staff from other call centres	40
Pay	34
Competitive local labour market	22
Working conditions	20
Other	30

From Alastair Hatchett, 'Ringing true', *People Management*, vol.6, no.2, 20 January 2000, pp.40–1.

control, and working conditions in some call centres can be unpleasant, as Stredwick and Ellis (1998, p.166) point out:

> There are call centres which resemble the industrial sweatshops of the past, involving very cramped conditions for staff who work on their computers throughout their shift under very tightly controlled conditions. Those on specialized sales areas even have a script written for them so that it is easy to believe that their individuality is being negated. In many ways this is identical to the assembly lines created by Ford engineers from the theories of Frederick Taylor and parodied by Charlie Chaplin in the film *Modern Times*.

Call centres thus tend to have high levels of absenteeism and staff turnover. Research suggests, however, that many centres are now attempting to shed their 'sweatshop' image by offering competitive pay, job security and trade union recognition. Some provide staff with swimming pools, saunas and subsidised restaurants. Conditions in some centres remain poor, and one study identified a new condition called 'repetitive brain injury', which leaves sufferers unable to speak after working in a high-pressure call centre (Incomes Data Services, 1999).

Employee surveillance

A survey of 900 large companies in 1997 by the American Management Association found that two-thirds admitted to some form of electronic surveillance of their workers (*The Economist*, 1999, p.105). As in call centres, technology provides numerous ways in which the activities of employees can be monitored. Computer usage is relatively easy to monitor where machines are connected to a main network. For example, the internet sites which employees explore can be logged, so that staff making 'recreational use' of this facility during working hours can be disciplined. E-mail traffic can be intercepted and monitored. Telephone conversations can be recorded, 'for training purposes', and the numbers and duration of calls can also be easily logged so that staff workloads can be compared. Some organizations are using closed-circuit television cameras covertly to monitor employee behaviour without their knowledge (Clarke, 1999). There currently appears to be no legal protection for employees against such uses of technology. See chapter exercise 2 for a real example.

Recap

1. *Explain different uses of the term 'technology'.*
   - Material technology means equipment, machines, apparatus. Social technology means organization structures and processes of co-ordination and control.

2. *Explain why predictions about technology and unemployment are exaggerated.*
   - The effects of technology on employment are indeterminate, because replacement mechanisms (through which jobs are lost) are offset by compensatory mechanisms (through which new jobs are created).

3. *Demonstrate how the consequences of technological innovation depend on the organization of work, and not simply on technical capabilities.*
   - The impact of technology on work depends on choices concerning equipment and system design, goals and objectives, and the organization of work.
   - New technology has, however, reduced the need for manual labour, creating instead jobs which demand high levels of interpretative and problem-solving skills.

4. *Define the characteristics of mass production and identify approaches to overcome them.*
   - Mass-production characteristics include mechanical pacing, no choice of method, repetition, task fragmentation, and minimum use of skills and mental attention.
   - Psychological reactions to work with mass-production characteristics include anxiety and tension, hostility, isolation and despair, and social withdrawal, which can be overcome to some extent by job enlargement and job rotation.

5. *Apply the socio-technical system perspective to organizational analysis and design.*
   - Socio-technical system design aims to find the best fit between social and technical sub-systems, to achieve joint optimization through minimal critical specification.

6. *Contrast the Scandinavian and Japanese models of team-based work organization.*
   - Scandinavian companies use autonomous work groups. Japanese companies use 'off-line' quality circles and problem-solving teams as part of a lean manufacturing approach, which has mass-production characteristics.

7. *Explain how new technology is changing the nature of work for some people, through teleworking, call centres and increased surveillance.*
   - Teleworkers escape direct management control but can become socially isolated.
   - Call centre workers may be highly skilled, but can suffer high workload and pressure.
   - Technology is increasingly used for covert employee surveillance, through computer monitoring, telephone call logging and closed-circuit television. These methods are legal but infringe individual privacy and generate resentment.

Revision

1. Why is 'technology' such an important aspect of organizational behaviour, and what in particular are the personal and organizational implications of 'the death of distance'?

2. Japanese and Scandinavian manufacturing companies use teams as part of their organizational design. What are the differences between the Japanese and Scandinavian approaches?

3. Your organization is considering the establishment of a central call-handling centre to deal with customer enquiries and problems. What are the main managerial benefits and drawbacks of this strategy, and what human resource benefits and problems is it likely to create?

4. What is 'technological determinism', and what are the criticisms of this perspective?

5. What are the characteristics of mass production, what problems do these characteristics generate, and how can these problems be addressed?

Springboard

Bredin, A., 1996, *The Virtual Office Survival Handbook: What Telecommuters and Entrepreneurs Need to Succeed in Today's Nontraditional Workplace*, John Wiley, New York.

Entertaining guide to the practical consequences of becoming a teleworker.

Dawson, P., 1996, *Technology and Quality: Change in the Workplace*, International Thomson, London.

Explores the role of technology in changing working conditions, demonstrating the shift to teamworking, computer-based covert controls and individual contracts.

Incomes Data Services, 1999, *Pay and Conditions in Call Centres 1999*, IDS, London.

Report based on a survey of 150 British call centres. While working conditions remain poor in some places, pay and working conditions are being improved to address recruitment and retention problems.

Jackson, P., 1999, *Virtual Working: Social and Organizational Dynamics*, Routledge, London.

Exploration of contemporary social, organizational and technological trends.

McLoughlin, I., 1999, *Creative Technological Change: The Shaping of Technology and Organizations*, Routledge, London.

Examines relationships between technology and organization from a metaphor-based postmodern perspective in which innovation is a 'configurational process'.

McLoughlin, I. and Harris, M. (eds), 1997, *Innovation,*

Organizational Change and Technology, International Thomson, London.

Explores the technology–organizational relationship from a range of perspectives. McLoughlin's entertaining chapter, 'Babies, bathwater, guns and roses', defends the technological determinist position against a constructivist interpretation.

Preece, D., 1995, *Organizations and Technical Change*, Routledge, London.

Analysis of managing new technology from a procesual perspective, with case studies, emphasizing the role of organizational choice and employee participation.

Ritzer, G., 1993, *The McDonaldization of Society: An Investigation into the Changing Character of Contemporary Social Life*, Pine Forge Press, Thousand Oaks/London.

Shows how the McDonald's philosophy of efficiency, calculability, predictability and control is spreading to other sectors. Suggests how this trend can be subverted.

Stredwick, J. and Ellis, S., 1998, *Flexible Working Practices: Techniques and Innovations*, IPD, London.

Comprehensive guide to trends in flexible working, including teleworking and call centres, with case studies and practical management advice.

Taylor, P. and Bain, P., 1999, 'An assembly line in the head: work and employee relations in the call centre', *Industrial Relations Journal*, vol.30, no.2, pp.191–217.

Contrasts the 'happy relaxed confident employees' image with the pressured reality.

Home viewing

In *The Net* (1995, director Irwin Winkler), Angela Bennett (played by Sandra Bullock) is a teleworker operating from her isolated, technologically cluttered and complex home office. Her job is to identify and fix bugs and viruses in the software which her employers send to her over the internet. One day, she accidentally sees files relating to a criminal syndicate, which consequently pursues her, using the internet in an attempt to erase her identity and existence. Angela thus uses her computing skill and knowledge not just to live but also to survive. Is the internet really a threat to privacy? If teleworking is the future of employment for many people, can this be regarded as a desirable future? How many different ways are computer networks used to intrude on the life of the individual in this film?

OB in literature

William Gibson, *Neuromancer*, Victor Gollancz, London, 1984.

How is new technology, and in particular the internet, affecting lifestyle, modes of thinking, interpersonal relationships, attitudes to work? As in the film *The Matrix* (see Home Viewing, chapter 1), the collective hallucination experienced by Gibson's characters is more real and engaging than 'normal' reality, and this is also a story of the lone individual battling the powerful corporation. A technological dream, or a technological nightmare? *Neuromancer* is reputedly the first *cyberspace* novel which takes place in *virtual reality*; Gibson claims to have invented these terms.

Chapter exercises

1: Technology test

Objective

1. To evaluate popular stereotypes of the impact of technology.

Rate your agreement or disagreement with each of the following ten statements about technology and work, ticking the appropriate box in the column on the right.

	definitely yes (1)	probably yes (2)	unsure (3)	probably no (4)	definitely no (5)
1. Once we know what a technology is capable of, we should be able to predict the work, organizational and social consequences	☐	☐	☐	☐	☐
2. The nature of jobs which rely on technology is determined by the technology	☐	☐	☐	☐	☐
3. Advances in technology are bound to increase unemployment	☐	☐	☐	☐	☐
4. Computers and robots are deskilling work for most people	☐	☐	☐	☐	☐

5. Japanese car manufacturing technology is superior to that used in America and Europe ☐ ☐ ☐ ☐ ☐

6. Boring repetitive jobs with 'mass-production characteristics' are a thing of the past ☐ ☐ ☐ ☐ ☐

7. Telecommuting, or working from home, will be the pattern of work for most of us in the future ☐ ☐ ☐ ☐ ☐

8. The success of Japanese car companies is based on teamwork ☐ ☐ ☐ ☐ ☐

9. Covert surveillance of employee behaviour at work is an invasion of privacy, which is illegal ☐ ☐ ☐ ☐ ☐

10. Computing power is replacing the need for people to think and to solve problems at work ☐ ☐ ☐ ☐ ☐

Calculate your score, between 10 and 50, and compare your score with colleagues.

- If you got a score of 20 or less, consider the extent to which your image of technology has been shaped by media accounts.

- If you got a score of 40 or more, consider why your views are inconsistent with contemporary media images of the role of technology.

2: Someone to watch over you

Objectives

1. To consider the possibilities, acceptability and limits of technological surveillance.

2. To assess the balance between an individual's right to privacy and an employer's right to monitor and control employee behaviour at work.

Read the following actual case account.

Last year, during a lunch break in the kitchen at Leeds Metropolitan University, cleaning supervisor Ros Johnstone was chatting to colleagues about the possibility of her husband and his friend bumping into her manager at a football match. The pair knew that Johnstone felt she had grievances against her boss and she was wondering aloud whether they would, in her words, 'kick the **** out of him'.

A few weeks later, back in the university's kitchen, Johnstone was again gossiping about how her husband would like to punch her boss. Soon after that, she was arrested by the police on suspicion of drug dealing. The university had received anonymous letters that she had been dealing drugs on campus and, to gather evidence, she had been covertly filmed and taped by management on a hidden microphone and a pinhole video camera secreted in a smoke detector.

Johnstone was not subsequently charged with drug offences, but in the process of gathering what proved to be non-existent evidence, she was arrested on suspicion of conspiracy to commit grievous bodily harm. There were tapes covering more than 1,000 hours of her break-time *tête-à-têtes*, but she was allowed access to a mere ten minutes of the 'damning' proof. The charges were later dropped, but she was suspended from work for six months pending a university hearing. The outcome? Johnstone was given a written warning from the university.

When you have read this account, prepare considered answers to the following questions:

1. To what extent was management in this case justified in the actions which it took covertly to monitor Ros Johnstone's behaviour at work?

2. To what extent have Johnstone's rights to privacy been infringed?

3. From a management perspective, what are the advantages and disadvantages of using technology for covert surveillance of employee behaviour at work, without their consent?

4. From the perspective of the individual employee, do you think that managers have a right to monitor your behaviour at work without your consent?

5. From an individual perspective, is surveillance acceptable if it is not covert, if employees are aware that they are being observed while they work?

This case account is from 'Someone is watching you—and it could be your boss', *The Times Magazine*, 6 November 1999, pp.26–30.

Part 2 Individuals in the organization

A field map of the organizational behaviour terrain

PESTLE: The **P**olitical, **E**conomic, **S**ocial, **T**echnological, **L**egal and **E**cological context

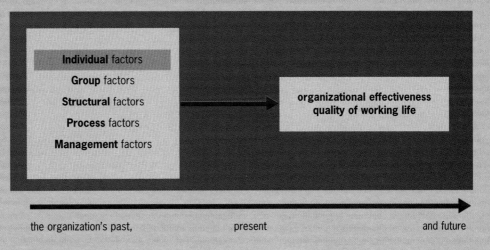

Individual factors
Group factors
Structural factors
Process factors
Management factors

organizational effectiveness
quality of working life

the organization's past,   present   and future

Introduction

Part 2, Individuals in the organization, explores the following five topics:

- Learning, in chapter 4
- Personality, in chapter 5
- Communication, in chapter 6
- Perception, in chapter 7
- Motivation, in chapter 8

These aspects of psychology are closely related. Each contributes in a different way to our understanding of behaviour in general, to our understanding of behaviour in organizations in particular, and to our analysis of performance at work and quality of working life.

Our opening case concerns a performance problem concerning a long-serving employee. If you were the manager, how would you address this problem? It's your call.

YOUR CALL (2): PEOPLE PROBLEMS

Let us be clear about the nature of 'people problems' in organizations. They can be frustrating, stressful, embarrassing and time-consuming. It is perhaps not surprising that many managers avoid these problems, and they can go unresolved.

Here is an account of a problem concerning the performance of a branch manager in a bank. The problem is a real one (disguised). If you were the regional manager, how would you address this problem?

As you read the case, first identify the *possible causes* or explanations for this problem. Could this concern the individual's learning, and the training they have received? Could this concern the individual's personality? How about communication with colleagues and management? Or the individual's perception of the job? Or the individual's motivation? Could the explanation lie with factors in the organizational context? Then identify *possible solutions* for each of these possible causes. Base your analysis on the case description, on personal experience, and on reasonable assumptions about what is happening here. Take a blank sheet, and make notes in this format:

possible causes	*possible solutions*

Harry's problem

Harry is in his early 40s and has been working for the Anytown Bank for over 20 years. He has been a branch manager for the last nine years and held a number of management posts in head office before that. It is now 1994, and Harry's regional manager has watched his performance deteriorate over the past 18 months. All banks saw their businesses change dramatically in the early 1990s, with increasing competition, new technology, and changes to organization structures and working practices.

The traditional paternalistic culture that characterized banking until the 1980s was transformed into a more dynamic customer-oriented culture by the early 1990s. The concept of 'selling financial products to customers', instead of providing professional services to clients, was reflected in new 'open plan' branch layouts.

In 1985, Harry became branch manager at Bridgford, a small suburban branch with an assistant manager, two supervisors, and twelve well-trained and efficient staff. The branch moved to larger premises in a more central location in the town in 1987, and the business grew. In 1988, the branch became a central site for handling some of the mortgage account administration of smaller branches in the region. A third supervisor was appointed and the staff rose to 17. In 1992, the branch was modernized with a new open plan layout, but the transfer of experienced personnel to a separate regional mortgage administration centre reduced

Harry's staff to 13, with only a customer service manager and a specialist sales-person to replace the assistant manager and supervisors.

The priorities of a branch manager were clear and included staff development, customer service, business results and use of resources. A manager's performance was judged against targets set in these four areas. From 1985 to 1992, Harry performed satisfactorily, demonstrating good leadership skills, but he did not excel. From 1992, his performance deteriorated. Business results were poor, new customer-oriented working practices were introduced, and Harry appeared not to be using and developing his branch team. In 1993, Harry's performance fell further, and branch staff morale and motivation collapsed.

The regional manager visited Harry's branch regularly to discuss the problems. Harry admitted that things had not been going well but blamed his inexperienced staff. He accepted advice but did not subsequently implement it. Harry appeared harassed in meetings, missed deadlines and was late with branch returns. He seemed to be easily side-tracked by small problems and did not focus on priority tasks. He did not plan adequately. Staff were not clear about their targets but found Harry sociable and friendly and always ready to listen sympathetically and help with personal problems. He carried out a lot of the administrative work of the branch himself without delegating it to staff. He did not spend much time with customers and was constantly in conflict with his customer service manager, who took a stricter line with the branch staff.

The regional manager also discovered that Harry had misled him about actions that were supposed to have been implemented, and that he had falsified staff development records. Harry had been able to persuade staff to support him in hiding the fact that these records had been falsified.

Chapter 4 Learning

Key concepts

learning
psychology
Pavlovian (classical or respondent) conditioning
intermittent reinforcement
behaviour modification
cognitive or information-processing psychology
intrinsic and extrinsic feedback
the learning organization
tacit knowledge
single-loop learning

behavioural self-management
behaviourist or stimulus–response
Skinnerian (instrumental or operant) conditioning
shaping
the cybernetic analogy
socialization
concurrent and delayed feedback
knowledge management
explicit knowledge
double-loop learning

Learning objectives

When you have read this chapter, you should be able to define those key concepts in your own words, and you should also be able to:

1. Explain the characteristics of the behaviourist and cognitive approaches to learning.
2. Explain and evaluate the technique of behaviour modification.
3. Explain the socialization process and assess the practical relevance of this concept.
4. Explain and evaluate the technique of behavioural self-management.
5. Describe the characteristics of the learning organization and explain why this concept has been popular since the 1990s.

Why study learning?

Learning is important to you personally. As a rule, the higher the level of your qualifications, the higher the salary you will be able to command. Our ability to learn is also important to organizations preoccupied with controlled performance. Employees have to know what they are to do, how they are to do it, how well they are expected to do it, and the consequences of achieving good or poor levels of performance. Learning theories have thus influenced a range of organizational practices, concerning:

- the induction of new recruits;
- the design and delivery of job training;
- the design of payment systems;
- how supervisors evaluate and provide feedback on employee performance;
- the design of forms of learning organization.

What is learning all about?

1. Learning is a part of work and work involves learning; these are not separate functions but intertwined; the separation we have made of them is artificial and often does not serve us well.

2. Learning is not only or even primarily about obtaining correct information or answers from knowledgeable others; it is fundamentally about making meaning out of the experience that we and others have in the world.

3. Organizational learning results from intentional and planned efforts to learn. Although it can and does occur accidentally, organizations cannot afford to rely on learning through chance.

4. As a collective we are capable of learning our way to the answers we need to address our difficult problems. It is ourselves we must rely on for these answers rather than experts, who can, at best, only provide us with answers that have worked in the past.

From Nancy M. Dixon, *The Organizational Learning Cycle: How We Can Learn Collectively*, Gower, Aldershot, second edition 1999, p.xiv.

Theories of learning thus have significant practical implications. However, this is one of the most fundamental and controversial topics in psychology. The extremes of the controversy are explained here, in the form of behaviourist and cognitive theories of learning.

The concept of the learning organization became popular during the 1990s. The learning organization is a configuration of structures and policies which encourage individual learning, with individual and organizational benefits. The organization itself can also be regarded as an entity which is capable of learning, independently of its members. Knowledge has thus become a more important asset for many organizations than materials and products.

Assets not on the balance sheet

The value of a business increasingly lurks not in physical and financial assets that are on the balance sheet, but in intangibles: brands, patents, franchises, software, research programmes, ideas, expertise. Few firms try to measure returns on these assets, let alone publish information on them. Yet they are often what underlines a firm's success. 'Our primary assets, which are our software and our software-development skills, do not show up on the balance sheet at all', says Microsoft's boss, Bill Gates.

From, 'A price on the priceless', *The Economist*, 12 June 1999, p.94.

Why is the concept of the learning organization now regarded as significant? Competitive advantage means knowing how to produce certain products, knowing how to innovate rapidly, knowing how to bring new products and services quickly to the marketplace, knowing how to meet changing customer needs. The capacity to develop new knowledge—the capacity to learn—has direct consequences for an organization's ability to develop and to survive as technologies, customer requirements, government policies and economic conditions change.

The learning process

How do we learn? How do we come to know what we know, and to do the things that we are able to do? These questions lie at the heart of psychology, and our understanding is in a constant state of development. It is, therefore, not surprising that the student of learning is confronted with different approaches to the topic. This variety helps to maintain controversy, excitement and interest in the subject, which in turn help to generate new ideas and methods.

Psychology is associated with the study of rats in mazes. Rats, and other animals, have contributed much to our understanding of human behaviour and have been widely used by psychologists concerned with the development of theories of learning. Rat biochemistry is similar to ours. We have to face the fact that we humans are animals in many respects, and that we can learn something of ourselves through studying other creatures.

The ability to learn is not unique to human beings. Animals also learn, as dog owners and circus fans can confirm. One feature that seems to distinguish us from animals is our ability to learn about, adapt to and manipulate our environment for purposes that we ourselves define. Animals can adapt to changes in their circumstances, but their ability to manipulate their environment is restricted, and they appear to have limited choice over their goals. In addition, animals have developed no science, technology or engineering.

"Oh, not bad. The light comes on, I press the bar, they write me a check.
How about you?"

The terms 'skill' and 'training' are used here in a broad sense. Skill to a psychologist covers a wide range of behaviours, from the trained ability to play tennis, to the routine ability to walk down the street. When the latter skill is analysed in detail, it turns out to be a complex and sophisticated performance. Training covers not just the acquisition of manual skills but also the learning of the 'correct' attitudes, values, beliefs and expectations.

We hope that when you have finished reading this book you should be able to say that you have learned something. The test of this hope concerns whether or not you will be able to do things that you could not do before. You should, for example, know what the study of organizational behaviour is concerned with, and you should be able to tell others what you know and think about it. You should be able to write essays and answer examination questions that previously you could not tackle.

We are concerned here with two related aspects of learning:

1. How we come to know things at all, through the process of learning.

2. The organization of our ideas, thoughts and knowledge, which constitutes the content of memory.

Learning is the process of acquiring knowledge through experience which leads to an enduring change in behaviour.

We refer to the process as **learning**, and to the result as knowledge.

Learning is defined in terms of enduring changes in behaviour through experience. It is important to note these limitations on what counts as learning. Behaviour can be changed temporarily, by many other factors, and in ways which we would not wish to call learning. These other factors include growing up or maturation (in children), aging (in adults), drugs, alcohol and fatigue (in the case of some academic staff, for example).

We cannot see what goes on inside your head as you learn. We can only infer that learning has taken place by examining changes in behaviour. If we assume that behaviour does not alter spontaneously, for no reason, then we can look for experiences that may be causes of behaviour change. These experiences may be derived from inside the body, or they may be sensory, arising outside. The task of inferring whether or not learning has taken place may be an obvious one, but observable behaviour may not always reveal learning.

It is helpful to distinguish between two types of learning. Procedural learning, or 'knowing how', concerns your ability to carry out particular skilled actions, such as riding a horse or painting a picture. Declarative learning, or 'knowing that', concerns your store of factual knowledge, such as an understanding of the history of our use of the horse, or of the contribution of the European Futurist movement to modern art.

Changes in behaviour can be quantified using a 'learning curve'. The graph in figure 4.1 represents the learning curve for a trainee word processor operator.

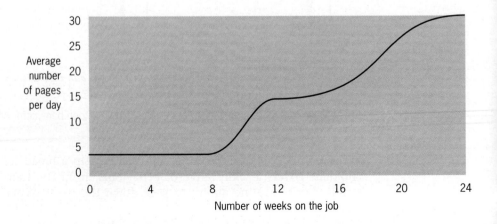

Figure 4.1: The typical word processing learning curve

A learning curve can be plotted for an individual, for a group of trainees, or even for a whole organization. This (fictitious) learning curve shows that:

1. It takes about six months for operators to become proficient, and for performance to 'level out' or peak at its maximum.

2. Top output is around 30 pages a day.

3. The trainee's ability develops slowly at first, rises sharply during the third month and hits a 'plateau' during the fourth month of training before starting to 'take off' again.

Most learning curves for manual skills suggest that trainees experience this plateau at some point. The shape of a learning curve depends, as one would expect, on the characteristics of the task and of the learner. It is often possible to measure learning in this way, to compare individuals with each other, and thus to establish what constitutes good performance. If we know what form a learning curve takes, and if we understand the factors influencing the shape of the curve, we may be able to develop fresh approaches to make learning more effective.

Stop and criticize

What is the shape of your learning curve for this course? Draw it.

Why is it that shape? Identify factors that you feel determine its form.

Should it be that shape—and what would be your ideal?

What could you do to change the shape of your learning curve?

The experiences that lead to changes in behaviour have a number of important features.

1. The human mind is not a passive recorder of information picked up through the senses [link, chapter 7, perception]. We can often recall the plot of a novel, for example, but remember very few of the author's actual words. This observation suggests that we do not record our experiences in memory in any simple, straightforward way.

2. We are usually able to recall events in which we have participated as if we were some other actor in the drama. We are able to reflect, to see ourselves 'from outside', as objects in our own experience. Now, at the time when we experienced the events, those cannot have been the sense impressions that we picked up. Reflection is a valuable capability.

3. New experiences do not always lead to behaviour change. Declarative learning, for example, may not be evident until we are asked the right questions. Our experiences must be processed in some way to become influential in determining future behaviours.

4. The way in which we express our innate drives is not merely inherited but also depends on experience [link, chapter 8, motivation]. We do have innate drives, but these are expressed in behaviour in many different ways. How they are expressed depends on many factors, including past experiences. Our innate makeup biases our behaviour in certain directions, but these biases can be overridden or modified by variations in experience.

Behaviourist or stimulus–response psychology is a perspective on the psychology of learning which argues that what we learn are chains of muscle movements. As brain or mental processes are not directly observable, they are not considered valid issues for study.
Cognitive or **information-processing psychology** is a perspective on the psychology of learning which argues that what we learn are mental structures, and that mental processes are both important and are amenable to study, even though they cannot be directly observed.

This chapter explains two current and influential approaches to learning, based on **behaviourist psychology** and **cognitive psychology**. These theoretical perspectives are in many respects contradictory, but they can also be viewed as complementary. These two perspectives have very different implications for organization and management practice.

These approaches are based on the same empirical data, but their interpretations of those data are radically different. These approaches are summarized in table 4.1.

Table 4.1: Behaviourist and cognitive perspectives on learning contrasted

Behaviourist, stimulus–response	Cognitive, information processing
studies only observable behaviour	also studies mental processes
behaviour is determined by learned sequences of muscle movements	behaviour is determined by memory, mental processes and expectations
we learn habits	we learn cognitive structures and alternative ways to achieve our goals
problem solving occurs by trial and error	problem solving also involves insight and understanding
dull, boring, but amenable to research?	rich, interesting, but complex, vague and unresearchable?

The behaviourist approach to learning

Positive reinforcement is the attempt to encourage desirable behaviours by introducing positive consequences when the desired behaviour occurs. The desired behaviour thus leads to positive consequences.
Negative reinforcement is the attempt to encourage desirable behaviours by withdrawing negative consequences when the desired

The oldest theory of learning states that ideas that are experienced together tend to be associated with each other. Behaviourist psychologists now speak of the association between stimulus and response.

Learning is a result of experience. We use knowledge of the results of past behaviour to change, modify and improve our behaviour in future. You learn to write better assignments and get higher examination grades by finding out how well or how badly you did last time and why. We cannot learn without appropriate feedback. Behaviourists and cognitive psychologists agree that experience affects behaviour but disagree over how this happens.

Feedback may be either rewarding or punishing. Common sense suggests that if a particular behaviour is rewarded, then it is more likely to be repeated. If it is punished or ignored, it is more likely to be avoided. This observation is encapsulated in the behaviourists' 'law of effect', which simply states that we learn to repeat behaviours that have favourable consequences and to avoid behaviours that lead to punishment or to other unfavourable or neutral consequences. Rats are thus trained to run through mazes at the whim of the psychologist using judicious applications of electric shocks and food pellets.

Behaviourism makes some subtle distinctions relating to reward and punishment. Table 4.2 illustrates these distinctions with examples.

behaviour occurs. The desired behaviour thus leads to the withdrawal of negative consequences. **Punishment** is the attempt to eliminate or to weaken undesirable behaviours through the application of negative consequences, or by withholding a positive consequence, following undesired behaviour. Punishment thus follows the undesired behaviour.

John Broadus Watson (1878–1958)

Extinction is the attempt to eliminate or to weaken undesirable behaviours by attaching no consequences, positive or negative. Indifference and silence thus follow the undesired behaviour.

Ivan Petrovich Pavlov (1849–1936)

Table 4.2: Reinforcement regimes illustrated

	behaviour	reinforcement	result	illustration
positive reinforcement	desired behaviour occurs	positive consequences are introduced	desired behaviour is repeated	If you confess, we will give you a shorter prison sentence
negative reinforcement	desired behaviour occurs	negative consequences are withdrawn	desired behaviour is repeated	If you confess, we will stop the torture
punishment	undesired behaviour occurs	punishment is introduced	undesired behaviour is not repeated	Fail to meet your quarterly target and we will fire you
extinction	undesired behaviour occurs	the behaviour is ignored	undesired behaviour is not repeated	Supervisor says nothing about poor timekeeping

The American psychologist John B. Watson introduced the term 'behaviourism' in 1913. He was critical of the technique of introspection, a popular psychological research method at that time, used to find out what went on inside people's minds. Subjects were simply asked to talk about their sensory experiences and thought processes, to look inside their minds, to introspect, and to tell the psychologist what they found there.

Watson wanted objective 'scientific' handles on human behaviour, its causes and its consequences. He could see no way in which introspection could ever produce this. This took him, and many other psychologists, away from the intangible and invisible contents of the mind to the study of the relationships between visible stimuli and visible responses. That is why behaviourist psychology is sometimes referred to as 'stimulus–response psychology'.

The behaviourist perspective assumes that what lies between the stimulus and the response is a mechanism that will be revealed as our knowledge of the biochemistry and neurophysiology of the brain improves. This biological mechanism must relate stimuli to responses in a way that governs behaviour. We can therefore continue to study how stimuli and responses are related without a detailed understanding of the nature of that mechanism.

In other words, behaviourists argue that nothing of psychological importance happens between the stimulus and the response. Cognitive theory, in contrast, argues that something of considerable psychological importance happens between stimulus and response.

The development of associations between stimuli and responses happens in two different ways, known as **Pavlovian conditioning** and **Skinnerian conditioning**.

Pavlovian conditioning is also known as **classical** and as **respondent** conditioning. The concept and related conditioning techniques were developed by the Russian physiologist Ivan Petrovich Pavlov.

Pavlov's work with dogs is well known. Dog owners are still trained today in the use of classical conditioning methods. If you show meat to a dog, it will produce saliva. The meat is the stimulus, the saliva is the response. The meat is an unconditioned stimulus, because the dog salivates naturally. Similarly, the saliva is an unconditioned response. The dog will produce saliva without any manipulation by a psychologist. Unconditioned responses are also called reflexes. Your lower leg jerks when you are struck just below the kneecap; your pupils contract when light

To punish or reward: the basis of behaviour modification

One well-established principle of behaviourist psychology is that reward is more effective than punishment in changing behaviour. This principle has been derived from extensive work with rodents and has also influenced practice with humans. The problem with punishment is that it creates fear, resentment and hostility in the punished person. Rewards for good behaviour are thus more likely to ensure compliance, now and in the future.

Charles O'Reilly and Barton Weitz studied how 141 supervisors in an American retail chain store used punishment to control the behaviour of their subordinates. Four sanctions were in use:

- informal spoken warnings
- loss of pay
- suspension from work
- dismissal

Supervisors used these sanctions to discourage undesirable behaviours such as:

- slack timekeeping
- low sales records
- sloppy appearance at work
- discourtesy to customers

Supervisors dealt with these undesirable behaviours in different ways. Some supervisors preferred to confront problems directly and quickly, gave subordinates frequent warnings and were quite prepared to fire those who did not behave correctly. One supervisor described his readiness to sack subordinates as 'an acquired taste'.

Other supervisors had difficulty in dealing with these problems, tried to avoid them and got depressed when they had to fire someone. They described their dealings with poor performers as 'traumatic'. These 'employee-oriented' supervisors were more sensitive to subordinates' needs and liked to give them time to put problems right.

The research showed that the departments run by the employee-oriented supervisors had poorer performance ratings than the departments run by the hard-line supervisors. Does this contradict the behaviourist position that punishment is not an effective way to influence or to modify behaviour?

We learn from others the behaviours and attitudes that are appropriate in particular circumstances. The employee who comes late to work regularly, or who does not work as hard as colleagues, violates socially established and accepted standards. The punishments used by supervisors can thus be effective where:

- they are perceived as maintaining the accepted social order; and

- they are perceived as legitimate by the 'victim'.

Based on Charles O'Reilly and Barton A. Weitz, 'Managing marginal employees: the use of warnings and dismissals', *Administrative Science Quarterly*, 1980, vol.25, no.3, pp.467–84.

Pavlovian conditioning, also known as **classical** and as **respondent conditioning**, is a technique for associating an established response (a dog salivating at the sight of food, for example) with a new stimulus (say, the sound of a bell).

is shone into your eyes. These are typical human reflexes. Humans also salivate naturally—another unconditioned response—at the sight and smell of food.

Suppose we now ring a bell when we show the meat to the dog. Do this often enough and the dog will associate the bell with the meat. Eventually the dog will start to salivate at the sound of the bell, without food being present. The bell is a conditioned stimulus, and the saliva is now a conditioned response. The dog has now learned, from that experience, to salivate at the sound of a bell as well as at the sight of food. It does not of course have to be a bell. All kinds of stimuli can be conditioned in this way. Pavlov in fact discovered this form of conditioning by accident. His research was initially concerned with salivation, but he observed that his dogs salivated at the sight and sound of his laboratory assistants, before they received their meat. He found this more interesting and switched the focus of the research.

Suppose we now stop giving the meat to the dog after the bell. The dog will con-

Skinnerian conditioning, also known as **instrumental** and as **operant conditioning**, is a technique for associating a response or a behaviour (a rat in a box nudges a lever) with its consequence (when the lever is nudged, food is delivered). If the consequence is desirable, the frequency of the behaviour is likely to increase.

tinue to salivate at the sound of the bell alone. But if we continue to do this, the amount of saliva produced falls and the association between the conditioned stimulus and conditioned response eventually suffers extinction.

The conditioned response may also be invoked by stimuli similar to the original conditioned stimulus, such as a bell with a different pitch. This phenomenon is called stimulus generalization. A complementary phenomenon, stimulus discrimination, can also be demonstrated by conditioning the dog to salivate at a bell of one pitch, but not at another.

Skinnerian conditioning is also known as **instrumental** and as **operant** conditioning. It is the discovery of the American psychologist Burrhus Frederic Skinner. Instrumental conditioning demonstrates how new behaviours or responses become established through association with particular stimuli.

Given a particular context, any behaviour that is rewarded or reinforced will tend to be repeated in that context. Skinner put a rat into a box (now known as a 'Skinner box') with a lever inside which, when pressed, gave the animal food. The rat was not taught to press the lever. However, in the process of wandering around the box, the rat eventually nudges the lever. It may sit on it, knock it with its head, or push it with a paw. That random behaviour is reinforced with food, and it is likely to happen again.

Classical conditioning has that name because it is the older of the two conditioning methods. Skinnerian conditioning is also called instrumental conditioning because it is related to behaviours that are instrumental in getting some material reward. Skinner's rat thus has to be under the influence of some drive before it can be conditioned in this way. His rats were hungry when they went into his box, and their behaviour led to a desired reward.

Where do the terms 'respondent' and 'operant' conditioning come from? Watson's stimulus–response psychology stated that there was no behaviour, or no response, without a stimulus to set it in motion. One could therefore condition a known response to a given stimulus. In other words, one could attach that response to another stimulus. Such responses are called respondents. Knee jerks, pupil contractions and salivation are well-known and clearly identified responses that are amenable to conditioning.

Shaping concerns the selective reinforcement of chosen behaviours in a manner that progressively establishes a desired behaviour or pattern of behaviours.

Skinner argued that this was inconsistent with known facts. Animals and humans do behave in the absence of specific stimuli. In fact, he argued, most human behaviour is of this kind. Behaviours emitted in the absence of identifiable stimuli are called operants. Operant conditioning explains how new patterns of behaviour become established. Respondent conditioning does not alter the animal's behaviour, only the behaviour's timing.

Skinner also introduced the concept of **shaping** behaviour by selectively reinforcing desired pieces of behaviour. In this way he was able to get pigeons to play ping pong and to walk in figures of eight—a famous demonstration of how random, aimless or spontaneous behaviour can be shaped by operant conditioning.

Intermittent reinforcement is the procedure whereby a reward is provided only occasionally following correct responses, and not for every correct response.

Skinner studied numerous variations on the operant conditioning theme. One important variation concerns the occasional reward of desired behaviour rather than delivering rewards in a continuous and regular manner. This mirrors real life more closely than the laboratory experiment. Why, for example, do gamblers keep playing when they lose? Why do anglers continue to fish when they catch nothing? Life is full of examples that demonstrate the power of **intermittent reinforcement**. In other words, desired behaviour can be maintained without regular and consistent reinforcement every time that it occurs.

A **schedule of reinforcement** establishes the pattern and frequency of rewards contingent on the display of desirable behaviour.

The pattern and timing of rewards for desired behaviour is known as the **schedule of reinforcement**. The possible variation in schedules of reinforcement is limitless, and Skinner investigated the effects of a number of these (Ferster and Skinner, 1957). However, there are two main classes of intermittent reinforce-

Table 4.3: Schedules of reinforcement

Schedule	Description	Implications
continuous	reinforcement after *every correct response*	can establish high performance, but can also lead to satiation; rapid extinction when reinforcement is withheld
fixed ratio	reinforcement after a *predetermined number* of correct responses	tends to generate high rates of desired responses
variable ratio	reinforcement after a *random number* of correct responses	can produce a high response rate that is resistant to extinction
fixed interval	reinforcement of a correct response after *a predetermined period*	can produce uneven response patterns, slow following reinforcement, vigorous immediately preceding reinforcement
variable interval	reinforcement of a correct response after *random periods*	can produce a high response rate that is resistant to extinction

Based on Fred Luthans and Robert Kreitner, *Organizational Behaviour Modification and Beyond*, Scott Foresman, Glenview, Ill., 1985.

ment, concerning interval schedules and ratio schedules, which are described in table 4.3, contrasted with continuous reinforcement.

Skinner claimed to be able to explain the development of complex patterns of behaviour with the theory of operant conditioning. This shows how our behaviour is shaped by our environment, by our experiences in that environment, and by the selective rewards and punishments that we receive. Thinking, problem solving and the acquisition of language, he argued, are dependent on these simple conditioning processes. Skinner rejected the use of 'mentalistic' concepts and 'inner psychic forces' in explanations of human behaviour because these were not observable, were not researchable, and were therefore not necessary to the science of human psychology. Why use complicated and unobservable concepts when simple and observable phenomena seem to provide adequate explanations?

Burrhus Frederic Skinner (1904–90)

Stop and criticize

In this Alex cartoon, is young Oliver's problem the result of respondent conditioning or of operant conditioning?

Skinner's ambitious project has been enormously influential. It has led to the widespread use of programmed learning, a technique of instruction designed to reinforce correct responses in the learner and to let people learn at their own pace. The behaviour modification techniques described later are also based on his ideas. As the behaviour of a conditioned animal is consistent and predictable, this can be used to test the effects of drugs for human use.

It is generally accepted that reinforcing desired behaviour is more effective than punishing undesirable behaviour. However, C.C. Walters and J.E. Grusek (1977), from a review of research, suggest that punishment can be effective if it meets the following conditions:

- the punishment should be quick and short;

- it should be administered immediately after the undesirable behaviour;

- it should be limited in its intensity;

- it should be specifically related to behaviour and not to character traits;

- it should be restricted to the context in which the undesirable behaviour occurs;

- it should not send 'mixed messages' about what is acceptable behaviour;

- penalties should take the form of withdrawal of rewards, not physical pain.

Stop and criticize

To what extent should the punishment criteria identified by Walters and Grusek be used by managers when disciplining employees in an organizational context?

The cognitive approach to learning

Why should we look only at observable stimuli and responses in the study of psychology? It is possible to study the internal workings of the mind in indirect ways, by inference. Behaviourism seems to be unnecessarily restrictive. It also seems to exclude those aspects that make us interesting, different and, above all, human.

How do we select from all the stimuli that bombard our senses those to which we are going to respond? Why are some outcomes seen as rewarding and others as punishments? This may appear obvious where the reward is survival or food and the punishment is pain or death. However, with intrinsic or symbolic rewards this is not always clear. To answer these questions, we have to consider states of mind concerning perception and motivation.

The rewards and punishments that behaviourists call reinforcement work in more complex ways than conditioning theories suggest. Reinforcement is always knowledge, or feedback, about the success of past behaviour. Feedback is information that can be used to modify or maintain previous behaviours. This information of course has to be perceived, interpreted, given meaning and used in decisions about future behaviours. The feedback has to be processed. Cognitive learning theories are thus also called information-processing theories.

This approach draws concepts from the field of cybernetics, which was established by the American mathematician Norbert Wiener. He defined cybernetics in 1947 as 'the science of communication in the animal and in the machine'. One central idea of cybernetics is the notion of the control of system performance through feedback. Information-processing theories of learning are based on what is called the **cybernetic analogy**.

The elements of a cybernetic feedback control system are outlined in figure 4.2.

The cybernetic analogy is a perspective which seeks to explain the learning process with reference to the components and operation of a feedback control system.

Norbert Wiener (1894–1964)

Feedback in the context of learning is information concerning the outcomes of our behaviour.

Intrinsic feedback is information which comes from within our bodies, from the muscles, joints, skin and other internal mechanisms such as that concerned with maintaining balance when walking (and is also called 'proprioception').

Extrinsic feedback is information which comes from our environment, such as the visual and aural information needed to drive a car.

Concurrent feedback is information which arrives during our behaviour and which can be used to control behaviour as it unfolds.

Delayed feedback is information which is received after a task is completed and which can be used to influence future performance.

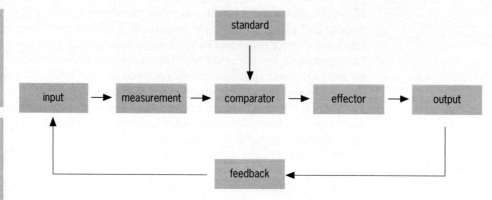

Figure 4.2: The elements of a cybernetic feedback control system

Consider a domestic heating control system. The temperature standard is set on a thermostat, and a heater (effector) starts to warm up the room. The output of the system is heated air. Changes in temperature are measured by a thermometer. The temperature of the room is continuously compared with the standard. When the room reaches the required temperature, the effector is switched off, and when the room cools, it is switched on again.

We will meet this concept later in our discussion of single-loop and double-loop learning. This example of cybernetic control illustrates single-loop learning. The cybernetic analogy claims that this control loop is a model of what goes on inside the mind. For standard, read motive, purpose, intent or goal. The output is behaviour. The senses are our measuring devices. Our perceptual process is the comparator which organizes and imposes meaning on the sensory data, thus controlling behaviour in pursuit of given objectives. We have in our minds some kind of 'internal representation' or 'schema' of ourselves and the environment in which we function. This internal representation is used in a purposive way to determine our behaviour. This internal representation is also called the image—also known as the individual's perceptual world [**link**, chapter 7, perception].

Our behaviour is purposive. We formulate plans for achieving our purposes. The plan is a set of mental instructions for guiding the required behaviour. Within the master plan (get a qualification) there are likely to be a number of sub-plans (submit essay on time; pass the organizational behaviour examination; make new friends). The organization of our behaviour is hierarchical—a concept which can be illustrated by comparison with a computer program, in which instructional routines and subroutines are typically 'nested' within each other.

However, unlike most computer programs, we can use information on how we are doing—feedback—to update our internal representation and to refine and adapt our plans. Feedback comes in different forms.

Stop and criticize

From your own experience, identify an example of each of the four varieties of feedback identified here. What changes in that feedback would be required for you to be able to improve your performance (on this course, at sport, whatever)?

When you submit an essay or assignment, **intrinsic feedback** is of limited value. **Extrinsic feedback** from your instructor is what matters, and feedback is typically **delayed** rather than **concurrent**. When you are attempting to throw rings over pegs at the funfair to win a soft toy, the concurrent visual feedback means that you know how well you are performing during the action. Instructors, of course, cannot provide concurrent feedback while you are writing an essay, but the longer the delay, the less effective the feedback is likely to be.

We need appropriate feedback

Appropriate feedback on work performance is necessary to ensure the learning and development of job skills. But do supervisors always tell their subordinates the truth? Daniel Ilgen and William Knowlton designed an experiment to answer this question.

The researchers asked 40 students each to supervise a group of three workers doing a routine clerical job for two hours. The supervisors were first shown the results of a test which was supposed to measure the abilities of their workers for such a task.

But each group had one worker, a confederate of the researchers, who performed much better or much worse than the others, working either enthusiastically or apathetically. The supervisors were led to believe that the level of performance of this exceptional group member was due to either high or low ability, or to their motivation.

After the work session, the supervisors rated the ability and motivation of all their subordinates on scales ranging from 'unsatisfactory' to 'outstanding'. They then completed a separate 'feedback report form', believing that they would have to discuss it with the exceptional (weak or strong) worker in person.

For the feedback, supervisors were asked to choose one of twelve statements which best described their evaluation of each worker, such as:

- 'You have done very well. I believe I would try to do even better next time if I were you.'

- 'Your performance is not good at all. You really need to put much more into it.'

The supervisors also had to recommend further action for the subordinate, to change either ability or motivation, such as:

- Attend a special training session.

- Concentrate more on the task.

- Try harder.

The supervisors were then told about the deception. There was no feedback session. The researchers wanted to find out how truthful the supervisors would have been with their feedback. As expected, ratings of ability and motivation were higher when supervisors believed that they would have to tell their subordinates this in person. Where low performance was attributed to low motivation, the feedback reflected this accurately. But where low performance was blamed on poor ability, supervisors recommended an inappropriate mix of feedback, directed at effort and skill.

The researchers conclude that supervisors systematically distort their assessments of subordinates and thus inhibit their learning.

Based on Daniel R. Ilgen and William A. Knowlton, 'Performance attributional effects on feedback from superiors', *Organizational Behaviour and Human Performance*, 1980, vol.25, no.3, pp.441–56.

Feedback, rewards and punishments, and knowledge of results, also have a motivating effect on behaviour, rather than simply a reinforcing effect. Several writers on motivation have argued that opportunities to learn new skills and knowledge, to understand more, to develop more effective ways of living and coping with our environment, are intrinsically motivating. The American psychologist Robert W. White (1959) suggests that we have a need to develop 'competence' in dealing with our environment and that this gives us satisfaction. As the section on the learning organization demonstrates later in this chapter, the 'urge towards discovery' and the 'will to understand' have triggered a search for novel organizational configurations in which individual and organizational learning are encouraged.

Applications: behaviour modification techniques in practice

Fred Luthans

Behaviour modification is a technique for encouraging desired behaviours and discouraging unwanted behaviours using operant conditioning.

Behaviourism has led to the development of the technique of **behaviour modification**. This was first used for the treatment of mental disorders, learning disorders and phobias, and for psychiatric rehabilitation and accident and trauma recovery. Applications have since been extended to organizational settings.

As developed by Fred Luthans (Luthans and Kreitner, 1985; Luthans *et al.*, 1998), organizational behaviour modification, or 'O.B.Mod.', has five mains steps:

1. *Identify* the critical, observable and measurable work performance-related behaviours to be encouraged.

2. *Measure* the current frequency of those behaviours, to provide a baseline against which to measure improvement.

3. *Establish* the triggers or antecedents for those behaviours, and also establish the consequences—positive, neutral and negative—that follow from those behaviours.

4. *Develop* an intervention strategy to strengthen desired behaviours and weaken dysfunctional behaviours through the use of positive reinforcement (money, recognition) and corrective feedback, noting that punishment may be necessary in some instances, for example to inhibit unsafe behaviour.

5. *Evaluate* systematically the effectiveness of the approach in changing behaviour and improving performance compared with the original baseline measurement.

Behaviour modification, as a means of changing employee behaviour, can appear particularly attractive to managers, who are typically in ideal positions from which to manipulate the reinforcement of different employee behaviours. Managers also tend to find this approach attractive because it argues that what has to be changed is behaviour, and that to achieve this one needs to know very little about the complex internal workings of the people concerned.

Desirable workplace behaviours could include, for example, working weekends to meet deadlines, attending training to develop new skills and being helpful to colleagues. Undesirable behaviours could include lateness, the production of poor-quality items and being rude to customers. Behaviour modification uses the principles of reinforcement to eliminate undesired behaviour and to increase the frequency of desired work behaviour. Suppose a manager wants more work assignments completed on time and fewer submitted beyond deadline. The behaviour modification options are summarized in table 4.4.

E. Scott Geller (1983) reports how the Radford Army Ammunition Plant in Virginia, America, used behaviour modification to encourage the wearing of seat belts among employees. The 'treatment' followed twelve days of unobtrusive observation at the three main entrances to the munitions complex, to establish a 'baseline' of seat belt wearing. 'Incentive fliers' were then distributed, encouraging seat belt use and offering opportunities to win prizes to those who did. The prizes included gift certificates and dinners at local restaurants, worth around $2 to $15. Only those wearing belts got a 'prize-winning' flier with a special symbol; those without belts got one which read, 'next time wear your seat belt and receive a chance to win a valuable prize'. This 'incentive condition' lasted for a month.

Seat belt use increased from an average of 20 per cent and 17 per cent in the mornings and afternoons respectively to 31 per cent and 55 per cent. After the programme was discontinued, seat belt use returned to baseline levels. Subsequent observation revealed that 'those individuals who showed the greatest response maintenance also evidenced the highest baseline rate of seatbelt usage' (which

Table 4.4: Behaviour modification options

Procedure	Operationalization	Behavioural effect
positive reinforcement	manager compliments employee each time work is completed on schedule	increases desired behaviour
negative reinforcement	unpaid overtime continues to be mandatory until work is completed on schedule, then overtime is rewarded	increases desired behaviour
punishment	manager asks employee to stay late when work is not handed in on schedule	eliminates or decreases undesired behaviour
extinction	manager ignores the employee when work is handed in late	eliminates or decreases undesired behaviour

implies that those who continued to use their belts were those who used them before anyway). Only nine prizes were claimed at a cost of $126, and four prizes had been donated by other local businesses, covering 40 per cent of the expense.

Fred Luthans and colleagues (1998) describe the application of organizational behaviour modification in a Russian textile mill. To improve worker productivity, two interventions were used. First, workers were offered extrinsic rewards for performance improvement, including valued American products such as adults' and children's clothing, jeans, T-shirts with popular logos, music tapes, and food that was difficult to get in Russia. Second, workers were given 'social rewards' for performing specific actions, such as checking looms, undertaking repairs, monitoring fabric quality and helping others. These social rewards involved attention, recognition and feedback from trained supervisors. The researchers note that this approach had a 'very positive impact' leading to 'highly significant increases in performance' (Luthans *et al.*, 1998, p.471).

In this case, a participative approach in which the factory workers were asked for ideas for improving performance did not work. The researchers argue that the cultural and political climate inhibited workers from making suggestions which could be regarded as criticizing existing methods and colleagues. On this evidence, they argue that the management technique of behaviour modification 'fits' Eastern European social and organizational cultures and is widely applicable.

From these examples, the typical features of organizational applications of 'O.B. Mod' are:

- It applies to clearly identifiable and observable behaviours, such as time-keeping, carrying out checks and repairs, and the use of particular work methods.

- Rewards are clearly and unambiguously contingent on the performance of the desirable behaviours.

- Positive reinforcement can take a number of forms, from the praise of a superior to cash prizes, to food, to clothing.

- Behaviour change and performance improvements can be dramatic.

- The desired modification in behaviour may be sustained only if positive reinforcement is continued (although this may be intermittent).

Stop and criticize

How would you feel about being given food, T-shirts and praise from your supervisor for working harder?

Do you regard this approach as realistic, or as demeaning—and why?

Applications: socialization and feedback

When people join an organization, of any kind, they give up some personal freedom of action. That is part of the price of membership. The individual thus concedes that the organization may make demands on their time and effort, as long as these demands are perceived to be legitimate. Other members of the organization have to teach new recruits what is expected of them. The process through which recruits are 'shown the ropes' is called **socialization**. Cognitive psychologists regard behaviour modification as simplistic and turn to more complex social explanations and methods for organizational behaviour change.

> **Socialization** is the process through which an individual's pattern of behaviour, and their values, attitudes and motives, are influenced to conform with those seen as desirable in a particular organization, society or sub-culture.

This perspective draws on social learning theory, which is based on assumptions about human psychology quite different from those behind behaviour modification techniques.

One of the most influential advocates of social learning theory has been Albert Bandura (1977; 1986). Bandura demonstrated that we learn new behaviours through observing and copying the behaviour of others, in the absence of any rewards or punishments. In this perspective, our capabilities for reflection and self-determination are central. We construct, through observation and experience, internal models of our environment and plan courses of action accordingly. The ways in which we 'model' ourselves on others are particularly apparent in children. However, this propensity to copy or imitate others continues into adulthood. In part 3, we will explore in more detail how those around us in an organization influence our perceptions, motivations and levels of performance.

Albert Bandura
(b. 1925)

The argument that we learn through social experience, through observation and modelling, does not deny the importance of reinforcement, which remains a factor in Bandura's social learning theory. Suppose, for example, that we choose to base some of our behaviours (how to handle a job interview; how to make new friends at parties) on a chosen model, presumably someone that appears particularly successful in those domains. Suppose that our new approach does not lead to the desired results (didn't get the job; failed to establish new relationships). We are likely to abandon our new behaviours in the absence of reinforcement.

How does social learning theory apply in an organizational setting? Organizations tend to encourage different standards concerning, for example:

- what counts as adequate and good work performance;
- familiarity in everyday social interactions at work;
- the appropriate amount of deference to show to superiors;
- dress and appearance;
- social activities after work;
- attitudes to work, colleagues, managers, unions, customers.

The newcomer has to learn these standards and the ways of behaving and related attitudes that they involve, to be a successful and accepted member of the organization. The individual does not have to believe that the organization's standards are appropriate. What matters is that individuals behave as if they believed in them.

The socialization process is often informal, rather than a planned programme of instruction. The newcomers learn the ropes simply by watching their new colleagues. Some organizations have formal induction programmes, but these are often brief and superficial, concentrating on mundane matters like the organization's structures and policies, and health and safety regulations, for example. Beyond formal programmes, we learn about an organization by just being there. Socialization is thus achieved without planned intervention, by giving rewards such as praise, encouragement, privilege and promotion for 'correct' behaviour. It is achieved by negative reinforcements and punishments, like being ignored, ridiculed or fined for behaviour that is 'out of line'. We quickly learn what attitudes to take, what style of language to use, what 'dress code' to obey, where to take lunch and with whom, and so on.

Stop and criticize	Most organizations plan the punishments and material rewards that members will get but leave the social and symbolic rewards to chance. From your knowledge of learning theory, what would you predict to be the consequences of such a policy?

Note that some of the 'rewards for good behaviour' offered by organizations are material rewards, in the form of money, and desirable working conditions (the bigger office and desk, the subsidized meals, access to free sports and leisure facilities, a space in the car park). Some of the available rewards, on the other hand, are symbolic and social rewards such as prestige, status, recognition and public praise. It is the symbolic and social rewards that address our 'higher-order' needs, according to Abraham Maslow [**link**, chapter 8, motivation].

Socialization—an alternative to behaviour modification

Social learning theory argues that we learn correct behaviours through experience and through the examples or 'role models' that other people provide.

Bruna Nota argues that this process now requires specific and proactive management attention and should not be left to chance, if the levels of commitment and competence required to compete in the 1990s and beyond are to be achieved. He describes a typical socialization programme based on experience in a number of 'new design plants'.

New recruits are first invited to a meeting where plant philosophy, operations, products and management style are explained, and they are invited to withdraw their job applications if they feel uncomfortable with this. Subsequent selection interviews are designed to find out whether applicants are 'team players', able to cope with uncertainty, take initiative, and if they are willing and able to learn new skills. They are also interviewed by a team supervisor, who probes their technical ability and 'overall fit' within the team. They are then interviewed by potential colleagues to ensure 'person fit'. Finally, they are interviewed by a senior manager, who looks 'for overall fit and appropriateness and ensures that the candidate is aware of the plant norms, mores, working and salary conditions, and so forth'.

People are hired in groups of five to ten and go through the same induction programme, after which they are placed in different departments. For their first week they each wear a badge which says, 'I am just starting', and they are met by department representatives, who act as 'godfathers'. The induction programme begins with the usual briefing on conditions, operations, safety, customer and quality issues, and the organization's philosophy.

The godfathers are colleagues with technical, social and administrative knowledge who act as counsellors, guides and role models for the recruits, helping them to learn the tasks assigned to them and also to become familiar with the culture of the plant. As recruits acquire this and take their full place in their teams, the role of the mentor is gradually phased out.

Once a month, families are invited to the plant to familiarize them with the activities and concerns of their spouse.

Nota admits that this is a complex process. However, turnover in one plant using these techniques had been under 6 per cent for its first three years of operation. Those hired are proud to have been selected in such a thorough process. Existing staff have a personal interest in those they are responsible for hiring and support them through difficulties, 'instead of automatically cursing the personnel office for "always sending us bums"'.

Based on Bruna Nota, 'The socialization process at high-commitment organizations', *Personnel*, 1988, vol.65, no.8, pp.20–3.

Behaviour modification versus socialization

Stop and criticize

Identify the main characteristics of, and contrasts between, behaviour modification and socialization as management techniques. Which more adequately deals with the realities of organizational life as you understand it—and why?

Is behaviour modification a generally applicable approach to employee learning and the development of appropriate behaviours? The evidence seems to suggest that the answer to this question is a heavily qualified 'yes'. There are two major qualifications.

1. Behaviour modification needs careful planning to identify specific behavioural goals and procedures for reinforcing the behaviours that will achieve those goals. The method can be effective when behaviour and reinforcement are clearly identified and linked; wear your seat belt and we'll give you cash. The method is less effective when this relationship is vague; demonstrate commitment and we'll consider you for promotion.

2. The 'rewards for good behaviour' method appears broadly consistent with American (and perhaps Eastern European) cultural values and aspirations. The transfer of this approach to other cultures is questionable. The most often cited practical examples are American.

Behaviour modification is overtly manipulative, potentially ignores internal needs and intrinsic rewards, and can be seen as a threat to individual dignity and autonomy. It can be viewed as a simplistic and transparent attempt at manipulation, invoking only a cynical rebuke as a 'new' behaviour. The technique is thus clearly limited in its application. However, behaviour modification requires the communication of goals and expectations to employees in unambiguous terms. Many would argue that this clarity is highly desirable.

Fred Luthans and Robert Kreitner (1985) summarize the problems with behaviour modification:

1. Appropriate reinforcers may not always be available, in limited and boring work settings, for example.

2. We do not all respond the same way to the same reinforcers; what one person finds rewarding may be of little consequence to someone else.

3. Once started, a behaviour modification programme has to be sustained.

4. There may not be enough extrinsic motivators (such as money and luncheon vouchers, for example) available.

They also argue, however, that the technique has made four significant contributions:

1. Behaviour modification techniques put the focus on observable employee behaviour and not on hypothetical internal states.

2. The method shows how performance is influenced by contingent consequences.

3. It supports the view that positive reinforcement is more effective in changing employee behaviour than punishment.

4. There are demonstrable causal effects on employee performance—a feature that is sometimes difficult to establish unequivocally with other behaviour change methods, such as job enrichment.

Behavioural self-management

Management attempts to modify the behaviour of others raise ethical questions. Self-improvement, however, is acceptable and fashionable. Fred Luthans and Tim Davis (1979) developed the technique of **behavioural self-management (BSM)** for individual use.

BSM combines the behavioural focus of 'O.B. Mod' with the cognitive processes central to social learning theory. It is not merely a form of self-imposed behaviour modification. Social learning theory argues that we actively process stimuli and consequences, in a self-monitoring fashion, whereas behaviourism sees our behaviour shaped by rewards and punishments.

The practice of BSM involves the following steps:

1. *Identify the undesirable behaviour* that you want to change, develop or improve.

2. *Manage the situational cues* which trigger desired behaviour. Avoid situations which trigger the target behaviour; seek situations which encourage desired behaviour instead. Use 'reminders and attention focusers' such as notes stuck in prominent places, and 'self-observation data' recording success and lapses. Set personal contracts, establish behavioural goals, post records of these in prominent places.

3. *Provide cognitive support* for the new behaviour. There are three ways to do this. First, through symbolic coding, using visual images and acronyms to support the desired behaviour (KISS, MBWA). Second, through mental rehearsal of the desired behaviour (a technique used by many successful sports people). Third, through self-talk, which is positive and supportive of the desired behaviour change.

4. *Develop self-reinforcement*, which is within your control, and which is delivered only on condition that the desired behaviour change is achieved. This can be strengthened by also arranging for positive reinforcement from supportive friends and colleagues.

This web of situational cues, cognitive support and self-reinforcement can be a powerful combination in helping to eliminate target behaviours and establish desired behaviours in their place. Using this technique, Rakos and Grodec (1984) report how American college students successfully modified behaviour problems concerning smoking, lack of assertiveness, poor study habits, overeating, sloppy housekeeping, lack of exercise and moodiness. Luthans and Davis (1979) describe how the technique was used to deal with management behaviour problems such as overdependence on the boss, ignoring paperwork, leaving the office without notifying anybody and failing to fill out expense reports.

Apply behavioural self-management to your own behaviour. Target a behaviour of current personal significance: drinking, smoking, overeating, excessive clubbing, inappropriate study habits. Establish a pattern of situational cues, cognitive support and self-reinforcement. Set a timescale, and use your experience to assess the power and relevance of this technique.

Based on Robert Kreitner, Angelo Kinicki and Marc Buelens, *Organizational Behaviour*, McGraw-Hill, London, 1999, pp.457–61.

Socialization has the advantage of flexibility. Social learning is dependent on the cultural context, and as a process rather than a specific technique, the general approach is not restricted to one culture. American induction and socialization procedures may be quite different from Swedish, Belgian, Nigerian, Malaysian or Spanish methods.

Socialization is a process that takes place anyway, planned or not. The issue concerns *appropriate* socialization, with respect to existing organization culture and behavioural preferences. Because it is a 'natural' process, with no clear financial or other material benefit from investing in its operation, it may be difficult to persuade management to give socialization the attention and resources that some commentators advocate. However, as the following section demonstrates, some organizations have started to introduce the apparatus of the learning organization. This approach can be regarded as an attempt to socialize an organization's members with respect to attitudes and behaviours related to the acquisition and development of new knowledge, creativity, innovation, flexibility and readiness for change.

Beyond supervisory appraisal: 360-degree feedback

Traditionally, it has been your immediate boss who conducts regular (usually annual) performance appraisals and gives you feedback on how well you are doing, and about what you need to do to improve. The limitations of this approach encouraged a number of organizations in the mid- to late 1990s to experiment with multi-source feedback at all levels, including management. The technique that became popular is known as *360-degree appraisal*. In 360-degree appraisal, you are appraised by, and given feedback from, your immediate boss, and your colleagues, and your subordinates, and perhaps other senior organizational members, and you may be invited to conduct a self-appraisal as well.

This also means that you get to appraise your manager, in a process called 'upward appraisal'.

Assuming that the feedback is honest and constructive, the individual receives a much wider set of comments, which can be used to reflect on and to change behaviour, and to improve work performance. However, as most appraisal schemes involve special forms for recording and monitoring, 360-degree appraisal generates a huge administrative workload.

Based on Mike Thatcher, 'Allowing everyone to have their say', *People Management*, 21 March 1996, pp.28–30.

Stop and criticize

What other advantages and disadvantages of 360-degree appraisal can you identify, for you as employee and also from a management perspective?

Table 4.5 summarizes one similarity and a number of contrasts between the techniques of behaviour modification and socialization.

Table 4.5: Behaviour modification versus socialization

Behaviour modification	Socialization
feedback needed in both approaches for behaviour to change	
planned procedure	naturally occurring, even if also planned
stimulus determines responses	individual needs determine responses
externally generated reinforcements	internally generated reinforcements
focuses on observable behaviour	focuses on unobservable internal mental states
focus on tangible rewards and punishments (money, other rewards)	focus on intangible rewards and punishments (social inclusion, material self-esteem)
clear links between desired behaviour and consequences	intangible links between desired behaviour and consequences
compliance required by external agent	conformity encouraged by social grouping

The learning organization

Chris Argyris
(b. 1923)

A **learning organization** is a form of organization that enables the learning of its members in such a way that it creates positively valued outcomes, such as innovation, efficiency, better alignment with the environment and competitive advantage.

The concept of the **learning organization** is derived from the work of Chris Argyris and Donald Schon (Argyris and Schon, 1974; 1978; Argyris, 1982) but became fashionable during the 1990s. Marleen Huysman (1999, p.61) offers the definition on the left.

A number of factors have stimulated interest in the learning organization concept:

- the production of goods and services increasingly involves sophisticated knowledge;
- knowledge is, therefore, as valuable a resource as raw material;
- many organizations lost knowledgeable staff through delayering in the 1990s;
- new information technologies are knowledge-intensive;
- knowledge can have a short life span, made obsolete by innovation;
- flexibility, creativity and responsiveness are now prized capabilities;
- knowledge can thus be a source of competitive advantage for an organization.

Ikujiro Nonaka and Hirotaka Takeuchi (1995) argue that the ability to create knowledge and solve new problems has become a 'core competence' for most organizations. In their view, everyone is a 'knowledge worker', not just those who work with books and computers. Anyone dealing with customers, for example the ticket clerk in a theatre run by the local council, is a valuable source of intelligence on customer perceptions of theatre facilities, productions, pricing and so on. These 'boundary workers' are typically employed in junior and poorly paid jobs (receptionists, porters, sales staff, secretaries), and their customer intelligence is often overlooked as their positions are distant, in terms of physical location as well as organization structure, from management decision makers.

There's no accounting for organizational knowledge

In an attempt to develop guidelines for the measurement of organizational knowledge, the trade ministry in Denmark asked 20 companies to produce 'intellectual capital reports' for three years. A Danish computer software company, Systematic, publishes information on customer satisfaction, education and average age of staff (83 per cent of whom are under 40) and the company's investment in innovation, which is over 10 per cent of annual turnover. These intellectual capital reports are published alongside traditional financial accounts.

Based on 'A price on the priceless', *The Economist*, 12 June 1999, pp.94 and 98.

The academic literature of this topic is preoccupied with refining the way in which learning, knowledge and the learning organization can be conceptualized. Karl Weick and Frances Westley (1996, p.440) point out that the concepts of 'organization' and 'learning' are contradictory. Organization implies structure, order, stability. Learning implies change, variety, disorganization. The practical management literature, on the other hand, is concerned with developing models of best practice and with management consulting tools. The management book by Senge *et al.* (1999) includes an 'owner registration form' at the back, to return after indicating in tick boxes your interest in speakers, seminars, further materials—or hiring the authors as consultants.

Stop and criticize

If we discount the inanimate buildings, equipment and furniture, organizations have no existence independent of their members. So what does it mean to claim that an organization can 'learn'?

Mike Pedler, John Burgoyne and Tom Boydell (1997) identify the eleven features of the 'learning company' in table 4.6. Why do they use the 'company' rather than organization?

> The original idea of eating bread together and of creating meaning through relationships, captures the conviviality of working together better than the more mechanical and lifeless 'organization'. As one of our oldest words for a group of people engaged in a joint enterprise, we continue to 'accompany' others and do things 'in company' (Pedler, Burgoyne and Boydell, 1997, p.5).

This usage assumes, of course, that an organization's members do indeed regard themselves as working 'convivially' towards shared outcomes.

This image of the learning organization is an ideal, something to which to aspire, rather than a description of any particular organization. These features 'cluster' under the five headings shown in figure 4.3. These clusters concern strategy, structure, looking in, looking out and learning opportunities. Pedler *et al.* (1997) provide a diagnostic questionnaire for evaluating an organization on these features, as a basis for developing them further.

Table 4.6: The features of the learning organization

Feature	Explanation
A learning approach to strategy	The use of trials and experiments to improve understanding and generate improvements, and to modify strategic direction as necessary
Participative policy making	All the organization's members are involved in strategy formation, influencing decisions and values and addressing conflict
Informating	Information technology is used to make information available to everyone and to enable front-line staff to act on their own initiative
Formative accounting and control	Accounting, budgeting and reporting systems are designed to help people understand the operations of organizational finance
Internal exchange	Sections and departments think of themselves as customers and suppliers, in an internal 'supply chain', learning from each other
Reward flexibility	A flexible and creative reward policy, with financial and non-financial rewards to meet individual needs and performance
Enabling structures	Organization charts, structures and procedures are seen as temporary and can be changed to meet task requirements
Boundary workers as environmental scanners	Everyone who has contact with customers, suppliers, clients and business partners is treated as a valuable information source
Inter-company learning	The organization learns from other organizations through joint ventures, alliances and other information exchanges
A learning climate	The manager's primary task is to facilitate experimentation and learning in others through questioning, feedback and support
Self-development opportunities for all	People are expected to take responsibility for their own learning, and facilities are made available, especially to 'front-line' staff

The learning organization concept was popularized by the work of Peter Senge, whose book, *The Fifth Discipline* (1990), became an international best-seller. Senge argues (1990, p.4) that work must become more 'learningful' at all organizational levels. He identifies five 'learning disciplines' for building the organization's learning capabilities. These disciplines are summarized in table 4.7.

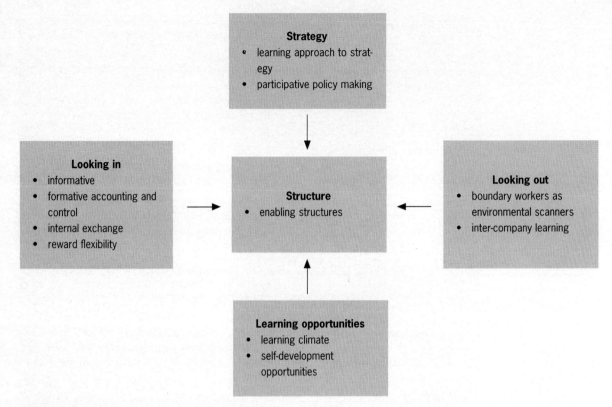

Figure 4.3: Clusters of learning organization features
From Mi, ke Pedler, John Burgoyne and Tom Boydell, *The Learning Company: A Strategy for Sustainable Development*, McGraw-Hill, London, second edition, 1997, p. 37.

Table 4.7: Peter Senge's five learning disciplines	
Learning discipline	**Explanation**
1. Personal mastery	A discipline of *aspiration*, concerning what you as an individual want to achieve
2. Mental models	A discipline of *reflection and enquiry*, concerning the constant refinement of thinking and development of awareness
3. Shared vision	A *collective* discipline, concerning commitment to a common sense of purpose and actions to achieve that purpose
4. Team learning	A discipline of *group interaction*, concerning collective thinking and action to achieve common goals
5. Systems thinking	A discipline which concerns *understanding interdependency and complexity* and the role of feedback in system development

A learning approach to strategy: the management challenge

Challenging your norms and assumptions is difficult. As the terms imply, these everyday structures of individual and corporate lives are taken for granted, not noticed. In effect, invisible to those who follow or hold them. They are much more obvious to others who follow different norms and assumptions who, while similarly blind to their own taken-for-granted norms and assumptions, can ask penetrating and provoking questions about those of others.

Royal Dutch Shell has tried to incorporate this potentially valuable process into its company operations with what it calls 'the management challenge'. Every three years, a senior executive from another plant, and usually another country, visits a given location to deliver a challenge to management. He or she spends a week or so at the site, wandering around, reading reports, talking to people before challenging the management team. The challenge itself involves presenting observations, impressions, making suggestions but, above all, asking 'naïve' questions that an insider would not ask because the answers are obvious. These questions are basically of the nature 'Why do you do such and such?' or 'How does this and that contribute to plant efficiency?' The local managers must publish the challenge and their response to it.

The management challenge is one way of ensuring that the 'hidden' fundamentals of 'how we do things around here' are questioned on a regular basis. Such questioning seems to be an essential component of 'double-loop learning' or the reframing essential to organizational transformation. You could institute your own management challenge and put in place this vital aspect of organizational learning by inviting different people in to question your operations. Why not start by inviting fellow managers from a sister plant? If you feel up to being more challenged than this you could invite a customer, a supplier or a stakeholder from the local community.

From Mike Pedler, John Burgoyne and Tom Boydell, *The Learning Company: A Strategy for Sustainable Development*, McGraw-Hill, London, second edition, 1997, pp.69-70.

Senge's argument is—have realistic goals, challenge your assumptions, commit to a shared vision, teamworking is good for you. The organizational application of these 'disciplines', however, is more problematic and can be related to our discussion of socialization, to encouraging the 'correct' attitudes, values and beliefs among employees at all levels. The most important of these learning disciplines (remember Senge's 1990 book title) is 'the fifth discipline', systems thinking, which means understanding how complex organizations function and how they can be changed to work more effectively. The theory is:

> The practice of organizational learning involves developing tangible activities: new governing ideas, innovations in infrastructure, and new management methods and tools for changing the way people conduct their work. Given the opportunity to take part in these new activities, people will develop an enduring capability for change. The process will pay back the organization with far greater levels of diversity, commitment, innovation and talent. (Senge *et al.*, 1999, p.33)

In other words, the manager who wants more commitment, flexibility and creativity from employees is advised to provide them with lots of learning opportunities.

Some commentators argue that a learning organization helps its members to learn. Others claim that the organization itself learns. How can this be? Silvia Gherardi (1997, p.542) treats the term 'learning organization' as a metaphor which regards an organization as a biological entity, as 'a subject which learns, which processes information, which reflects on experiences, which is endowed with a stock of knowledge, skills and expertise'.

Gherardi supports the view that organizations learn with experience, the proof lying with visible changes in an organization's behaviour. For example, it is recognized that, in the development of manufacturing processes, the staff hours required to produce a unit of output decrease with accumulated experience. Another example concerns the ways in which organizations evolve and adapt to 'fit' their environment, introducing internal structural changes in response to environmental opportunities and pressures.

Organizations also have available to them several different types of knowledge, not all of which are dependent on individual expertise (Gherardi, 1997, p.547). This includes learning from past experience through assessment and evaluation, and learning from the experience of other organizations. There is also knowledge 'built in' to equipment and even raw materials, with formulae, ingredients, recipes, known properties, and so on. Standard operating procedures can usually be found in instruction manuals, forms and job descriptions—all ways of codifying knowledge. Many organizations also possess patents and property rights.

Weick and Westley (1996) argue that organizational learning is best understood in terms of organization culture [**link**, chapter 19, organization culture]. Culture includes values, beliefs, feelings, artefacts, myths, symbols, metaphors and rituals—which taken together distinguish one organization or group from others. Organizations are thus 'repositories of knowledge' independent of their members (Schon, 1983, p.242). Organizations which accumulate stocks of codified, documented knowledge, independent of their members, can thus be said to learn.

The corporate university: a sign of the learning organization

There are around 1,600 corporate universities in America. Microsoft, Motorola and Disney all have one. The fast food chain McDonald's established its first 'hamburger university' in 1961, run by the company's own staff and managers, offering courses in human resource management, employment law, accounting and marketing. 'Burger U' today operates on six campuses, including one in London.

Although the idea has been around for some time, the development of corporate universities became more popular during the 1990s. In Britain, in 1996, Anglian Water Services established Aqua Universitas, or the University of Water, to run a mix of management, engineering and science courses for all its 4,000 staff, based at the Whitwell campus on Rutland Water. In 1999, British Telecommunications announced that it was establishing a university centre to offer degrees for its 125,000 employees. Other companies, including British Aerospace, General Electric, Unipart and Body Shop, have their own universities.

In order to compete effectively, these organizations require more highly educated and skilled workforces. This explains such a significant investment in learning, in developing the organization's intellectual capital.

Based on R. Dalton and M. Lynn, 'Companies lead university revolution', *The Sunday Times*, 7 February 1999, p.3.4.

Weick and Westley (1996) note how different organizational forms are better equipped for learning. The post-modern organization described in chapter 2 adapts to change in its external environment in an innovative, creative, responsive manner. This is an organizational form associated with creative thinking and rapid learning, and has also been described as *adhocracy* (see glossary and chapter 18). Bureaucracy, on the other hand, is concerned with efficiency, with division of labour, with rigid chain of command, with clear distinctions and rationality. Adhocracies explore, while bureaucracies exploit:

Single-loop learning concerns the ability to use feedback to make continuous adjustments and adaptations, to maintain performance (individual, group, organizational) at a predetermined standard.

Double-loop learning concerns the ability not only to maintain performance at a predetermined standard but also to challenge and redefine the assumptions underlying that standard to improve performance significantly.

Different forms of organizing create different problems for learning. Adhocracies explore, create and align with changes but, in embracing disorder with disorderly forms, they risk integrity, a loss of identity, and a loss of lessons learned from the past that undergird current efficiencies. Bureaucracies exploit lessons from the past as well as past identities. Adhocracies trade away retention for variation, bureaucracies trade away variation for retention. Adhocracies embody disorder, bureaucracies embody order. Only as each form adopts some of the other, or imitates the other, is it possible to achieve repunctuation [continuous learning] that persists (Weick and Westley, 1996, p.456).

How can 'organizational learning' best be understood? Argyris and Schon (1974) developed the distinction between **single-loop learning** and **double-loop learning**.

The concept of single-loop learning is borrowed from cybernetics, where control systems are considered in terms of norms, standards, procedures, routines and feedback; see figure 4.1. The classic example of cybernetic control is the domestic thermostat, which, by detecting temperature variations, takes action to correct deviations from a predetermined norm. In single-loop learning, the system maintains performance at that norm and is unable to 'learn' that the norm is too high or too low. In other words, it is unable to 'learn how to learn', to challenge and rethink its values and assumptions. The system just goes on doing what it has been asked to do. Limited to making small-scale changes and improvements, it can be argued that single-loop learning is not really learning at all.

Stop and criticize

Let us assume that you are learning through your organizational behaviour course. Is this single-loop learning or double-loop learning? Which of these two types of learning should you be engaged in during your college or university education?

Tacit knowledge is personal knowledge and understanding, specific to the individual, difficult to articulate or to communicate to others because it derives from accumulated experience and includes insights, intuition, hunches and judgements.

Explicit knowledge is knowledge and understanding which is codified, expressed and available to anyone.

Learning how to learn involves double-loop learning. This means challenging assumptions, beliefs, norms, routines and decisions, rather than accepting them and working within those limitations. In single-loop learning, the question is, how can we better achieve that standard of performance? With double-loop learning, in contrast, the question becomes, is that an appropriate target in the first place? Mary Jo Hatch (1997, p.372) observes that:

Double-loop learning, once strictly the domain of strategists and top managers, is increasingly being seen as taking place, or needing to take place, throughout organizations as they hire professionals and skilled technicians to help them adapt to the increasing rates of change they perceive as necessary to their survival. As double-loop learning diffuses, organizational stability is replaced by chaos and new organizational orders emerge from the internal dynamics of the organization rather than at the behest of top management.

When we learn, we acquire knowledge—of organizational behaviour, gardening, guitar playing, accountancy, electrical engineering, and so on. Knowledge, however, is a difficult term to define clearly. For Nonaka and Takeuchi (1995), there are two types of knowledge, **tacit** and **explicit**.

Tacit knowledge concerns the unarticulated mental models and skills possessed by the individual. Tacit knowledge tends to be personal, specific to particular contexts and difficult to communicate. For example, if you are able to drive a motor car with a manual gear shift, then you will know exactly where to position your

NUMMI Toyota–General Motors versus Volvo Uddevalla

Paul Adler and R. Cole (1993) compared work organization at the Toyota–GM joint venture at NUMMI in America with Volvo's innovative plant at Uddevalla in Sweden. Both plants manufactured motor cars but used radically different production methods.

At the NUMMI plant, teams of four or five employees performed well-documented work cycles, with each member carrying out tasks lasting around sixty seconds. This method 'is based on specialized work tasks supplemented by modest doses of job rotation and great discipline in the definition and implementation of detailed work procedures' (p.85).

At the Uddevalla plant, teams of ten people worked cycles which were not well documented but which lasted around two hours, representing 'a return to craftlike work forms that give teams substantial latitude in how they perform their tasks and authority over what have traditionally been higher-level management decisions' (p.85).

The researchers argue that differences in work cycle and in the documentation of working methods give the NUMMI plant a learning advantage. NUMMI is able to identify problems, define and implement improvements, and to share opportunities more readily. Employees have an explicit idea of what is required, which facilitates challenge and improvement. As work cycles are short, changes to correct problems are more easily identified.

Learning is more difficult at the Volvo plant, where individuals can improve their own skills without the need to make mutual adjustments to the work of others. Shared views and interdependencies are few. When problems arise, there are two hours' worth of activities to examine for the cause. So while NUMMI is an example of organizational learning, Volvo is an example of individual learning in an organizational context. The researchers conclude that 'without a well documented, standardized process, it is hard to imagine how these people could have spotted improvement opportunities or shared them across teams. You cannot sustain continued improvement in the production of products as standardized as automobiles without clear and detailed methods and standards' (p.89).

This example casts doubt on the 'shared vision, teamworking' image of the effective and competitive learning organization popularized by Peter Senge, and many others.

Based on P.S. Adler and R.E. Cole, 'Designed for learning: a tale of two plants', *Sloan Management Review*, 1993, vol.34, no.3, pp.85–94.

---

foot to 'slip the clutch' and prevent the car rolling backwards on a slope. You will be able to move your foot to that position, accurately and consistently, without much conscious thought. However, you can expect to run into difficulties when you try to explain this tacit skill to a learner driver.

Explicit knowledge on the other hand is articulated, codified, expressed, available to anyone. Nonaka and Takeuchi argue that the Japanese emphasize tacit knowledge, while Westerners emphasize formal, objective, codified explicit knowledge. In Western cultures, tacit knowledge is undervalued because it is intangible and difficult to measure. However, tacit and explicit knowledge are complementary. Nonaka and Takeuchi are thus concerned with 'knowledge conversion', in which tacit knowledge is made available to the organization, on the one hand, and organizational knowledge becomes the individual's tacit knowledge, on the other (Nonaka, Umemoto and Sasaki, 1999).

Some commentators thus distinguish between organizational learning and **knowledge management** (Rajan, Lank and Chapple, 1999).

Amin Rajan and colleagues (1999) describe how some organizations have developed 'intelligent search engines'. These are technology-based systems designed to facilitate access to expertise by creating a catalogue of specialists, each with their

Knowledge management concerns the conversion of tacit knowledge into explicit knowledge so that it can be shared with others and is about turning individual learning into organizational learning.

own web site in the company intranet, so that their knowledge can be accessed by e-mail or video conferencing. The number of times somebody's expertise is used can be monitored and used to influence pay and promotion decisions (Rajan, Lank and Chapple, 1999, p.6).

Knowledge management tends to be distinguished from the learning organization concept by the focus on information technology, on the development of databases accessed by internet. The supermarket chain Safeway, for example, gives its 2,500 suppliers for its 20,000 product lines access to its warehouse information over the internet. Company buyers and their suppliers have much better information and forecasts on which to base purchasing and delivery decisions. Zeneca Pharmaceuticals has developed a system called Concert to bring together information on new drug discoveries and licences in a highly competitive sector. Managers around the company are responsible for identifying relevant knowledge, and for putting it into the system (Coles, 1998). Harry Scarbrough (1999), however, is critical of the emphasis on technological solutions such as these, which tend to overlook the ways in which people develop, use and communicate knowledge as part of their working activity.

Table 4.8 summarizes the main positive and negative aspects of the learning organization, and its related concepts of intellectual capital and knowledge management.

The concept of the learning organization has remained fashionable for over a decade. This popularity has been reinforced by the growth of 'knowledge work', by the realization that ideas generate competitive advantage and by technological developments. However, there are organizational barriers to the implementation of this 'ideal', and it will be interesting to observe whether the learning organization remains fashionable in the twenty-first century.

Table 4.8: Learning organization positives and negatives

learning organization positives	learning organization negatives
a rich, multi-dimensional concept affecting many aspects of organizational behaviour	a complex and diffuse set of practices, difficult to implement systematically
an innovative approach to learning, to knowledge management and to investing in intellectual capital	an attempt to use dated concepts from change management and learning theory, repackaged as a management consulting project
a new set of challenging concepts focusing attention on the acquisition and development of individual and corporate knowledge	a new vocabulary for encouraging employee compliance with management directives in the guise of 'self-development'
an innovative approach to organization, management and employee development	an innovative approach for strengthening management control
innovative use of technology to manage organizational knowledge through databases and the internet or intranets	a technology-dependent approach which ignores how people actually develop and use knowledge in organizations

Recap

1. *Explain the characteristics of the behaviourist and cognitive approaches to learning.*

   - Behaviourism argues that we learn chains of muscle movements. As mental processes are not observable, they are not considered valid issues for study.

   - Cognitive psychology argues that we learn mental structures. Mental processes are important, and they are amenable to study although they cannot be observed.

   - In behaviourist theory, feedback contributes to learning by providing reinforcement; in cognitive theory, feedback provides information and is motivational.

2. *Explain and evaluate the technique of behaviour modification.*

   - Respondent (or Pavlovian, classical) conditioning is a method by which an established response (good work performance) is associated with a new stimulus (supervisory encouragement).

   - Operant (or Skinnerian, instrumental) conditioning is a method by which a behaviour (good work performance) is associated with a new consequence (bonus payment).

   - Positive reinforcement, negative reinforcement, punishment and extinction condition the target by manipulating the consequences of desirable and undesirable behaviours.

   - Behaviour modification works well when rewards are linked clearly to specific behaviours but does not work well when these links are ambiguous and vague; this manipulative approach may not be acceptable in some cultures.

3. *Explain the socialization process and assess the practical relevance of this concept.*

   - Social learning theory argues that we learn values, beliefs and behaviour patterns through experience, through observation and modelling.

   - Socialization can be informal—this happens anyway—or it can be formally organized with induction and training programmes, for example.

4. *Explain and evaluate the technique of behavioural self-management.*

   - Behavioural self-management involves identifying the behaviour you want to change, altering the situational cues which trigger that behaviour and establishing support and reinforcement for your new behaviour.

5. *Describe the characteristics of the learning organization and explain why this concept became popular during the 1990s.*

   - A learning organization is characterized by its approach to strategy, to environmental scanning, to the use of information, to the creation of learning opportunities, and to the creation of structures that are flexible and enable employee learning, in contrast to rigid bureaucratic organizations in which learning is the employee's responsibility.

   - The learning organization concept became popular as managers recognized the strategic need for more highly skilled and trained, flexible and creative workforces.

   - Knowledge management is a technology-based technique for making tacit knowledge available more widely in the learning organization, typically through individual and corporate databases which can be accessed through the organization's intranet.

Revision

1. Why is the psychology of learning a controversial topic, and what are the implications of this controversy for organization and management practice?

2. What are the main distinctions between behaviourist and cognitive perspectives on learning?

3. What is the difference between Pavlovian and Skinnerian conditioning? What relevance do these and their related laboratory-based concepts have in an organizational context?

4. Describe and illustrate the technique of organizational behaviour modification, and identify the advantages and disadvantages of this technique.

5. Why are positive and negative reinforcement usually more effective methods for encouraging behaviour change than punishment? In what circumstances can punishment be effective in encouraging behaviour change?

Springboard

Argyris, C., 1982, *Reasoning, Learning, and Action*, Jossey-Bass, San Francisco.

Classic text on the nature of individual and organizational learning.

Dixon, N.M., 1999, *The Organizational Learning Cycle: How We Can Learn Collectively*, Gower, Aldershot (second edition).

Theoretically informed and readable account of organizational learning in practice. Case illustrations include US Army, Bank of Montreal, Chaparral Steel, World Health Organization, Johnsonville Foods.

Dixon, N.M., 2000, *Common Knowledge: How Companies Thrive by Sharing What They Know*, Harvard Business School Press, Boston.

Argues that organizations deal with different types of knowledge, which have to be managed in different ways; the 'wrong' methods can block knowledge sharing.

Easterby-Smith, M., Burgoyne, J. and Araujo, L. (eds), 1999, *Organizational Learning and the Learning Organization: Developments in Theory and Practice*, Sage, London.

Academic critiques of the learning organization concept from different perspectives.

Miller, R. and Stewart, J., 1999, 'Opened university', *People Management*, vol.5, no.12, June, pp.42–6.

An account of how the motor components company Unipart developed a learning organization. Also describes Unipart U, the company university opened in 1993.

Pedler, M., Burgoyne, J. and Boydell, T., 1997, *The Learning Company: A Strategy for Sustainable Development*, McGraw-Hill, London (second edition).

Written for managers, this illustrates the dimensions of the learning organization and provides a diagnostic checklist against which to evaluate progress towards the ideal.

Scarbrough, H. and Swan, J., 1999, *Case Studies in Knowledge Management*, Institute of Personnel and Development, London.

Argues that a focus on technology will fail and that effective knowledge management requires supportive human resource management policies, concerning rewards and trust in particular. Knowledge is power; why should we share it?

Senge, P., 1990, *The Fifth Discipline: The Art and Practice of the Learning Organization*, Doubleday Currency, New York.

The best-seller which popularized the learning organization idea in the early 1990s.

Senge, P., Kleiner, A., Roberts, C., Ross, R., Roth, G. and Smith, B., 1999, *The Dance of Change: The Challenges of Sustaining Momentum in Learning Organizations*, Nicholas Brealey, London.

Presented as a set of ideas and resources for managers developing the learning organization in practice, very professionally produced, treads a thin line between theoretical framework and evidence, on the one hand, and an advertisement for management consultancy, on the other.

Home viewing

A *Clockwork Orange* (1971, director Stanley Kubrick) is based in a future totalitarian state in which the Droog (thug) Alex (played by Malcolm McDowell) is subjected to aversion therapy to cure him of his addiction to violence, rape, drugs and classical music. An extremely violent film for its time, Kubrick took it out of circulation in 1974 when it was accused of triggering 'copycat' crimes. The film was released again on the anniversary of Kubrick's death, in March 2000. The practical questions are, what kind of conditioning and reinforcement regime is Alex subjected to, and how effective is this in altering his behaviour? The moral question concerns society's right to interfere with individual behaviour in this way. Fiction? Aversion therapy was used to 'treat' homosexuals in the 1960s.

Full Metal Jacket (1987, directed by Stanley Kubrick) follows the experiences of an American photo-journalist, Private Joker (played by Mathew Modine), during the Vietnam War. The first 45 minutes is set in a Marine Corps training camp in Carolina and portrays the induction of new recruits. Their initiation is directed by Sergeant Hartman (R. Lee Ermey, a former marine drill instructor who was hired as a consultant to make sure the training scenes were realistic but who impressed Kubrick so much he was invited to play the role). Hartman uses a range of tactics to turn 'maggots into marines' who are 'ready to eat their own guts and ask for more', with 'killer instinct that is clear and strong'. Identify the behaviour modification and socialization techniques used and assess their effectiveness.

OB in literature

B. Frederic Skinner, *Walden II*, 1948, Macmillan, London.

Skinner's own novel is based on a fictional community which applies operant conditioning to establish desired humanitarian behaviours and to 'engineer' a better society (along the lines of *A Clockwork Orange*). What application does this vision have to contemporary society—in any culture? What would it be like to live in such a society?

Chapter exercises

1: The learning curve

Objectives

1. To identify factors affecting the process of learning.

2. To identify ways of improving the effectiveness of the learning process.

Learning can be measured in many ways. The learning of subject matter in an educational context is traditionally measured using examinations, essays, projects or assignments, and oral presentations. The learning process unfolds through time, and we establish whether learning has taken place by identifying changes in behaviour. Your ability to write a clear account of contemporary learning theory and practice, for example, should be higher towards the end of your organizational behaviour course than at the beginning (assuming this subject has not been encountered on other courses). This exercise asks you to assess your own learning process, to identify factors that inhibit your learning, and to identify what you, your colleagues and your instructor could do to improve the effectiveness of your learning.

Briefing

1. Using the example of a learning curve on page 110, construct a graph that will plot your learning on this organizational behaviour course. On the vertical axis, put percentage of course material read and understood, on a scale from 0 to 100 per cent. The horizontal axis represents number of weeks into the course.

2. Now consider your overall approach to this subject and to your personal studying methods and learning pattern. Draw a line on the graph that realistically portrays your learning curve. This will, of course, start at week one, and at 0 per cent. It may not, however, reach 100 per cent by the time the course is complete.

3. Compare your learning curve with those of colleagues sitting next to you. Note similarities and discuss differences.

4. Now consider an 'ideal' learning curve for you and for this particular course. Plot your ideal curve on the same graph, perhaps using a different pen or colour. Compare your ideal also with that of colleagues sitting next to you.

5. In buzz-groups of three people, compare your actual with your ideal learning and study patterns, and identify three things that you and fellow students could do to improve the effectiveness of your learning on this course:

    1: _____

    2: _____

    3: _____

6. Still in buzz-groups of three people, identify three things that your instructor could do to improve the effectiveness of your learning (be realistic):

    1: _____

    2: _____

    3: _____

2: Making modifications

Objectives

1. To demonstrate the practical dimensions of applying behaviour modification techniques.

2. To explore the benefits and limitations of behaviour modification techniques.

The theory and practice of behaviour modification appears to have significant potential in organizational settings. Organizations are concerned with eliciting 'appropriate behaviours' from employees. Managers typically occupy positions from which a range of rewards and punishments can be manipulated. The scope for changing working methods and practices through behaviour modification thus appears to be wide. In this exercise, you are invited to design and assess a behaviour modification approach that deals with specific problems of organizational behaviour—problems with which you may be familiar.

Briefing

1. Ensure that you are familiar with the behaviour modification approach explained in this chapter, including theoretical background and practical applications.

2. Read the 'Making modifications' brief below and, working on your own, make preliminary notes in answer to the questions that follow.

3. In syndicates with three to five members each, design a practical, realistic behaviour modification programme that addresses the issues in the brief. Think creatively with respect to appropriate reinforcement regimes.

4. When you have completed your design, make a realistic practical assessment. What are the three main strengths of your behaviour modification approach that give it a chance of working as intended? What are the three main weaknesses in your approach that might make it less effective? Don't forget to nominate a spokesperson to present your approach and assessment to the whole group.

5. Present solutions and assessments to the whole group. To avoid repetition, perhaps have only two groups present designs, with the third and fourth groups presenting their strengths and weaknesses, respectively, and with the audience each time commenting only on differences between their analysis and that presented.

Making modifications

Your organizational behaviour instructor, Lesley, has been experiencing some problems recently. She has asked you to design a behaviour modification programme to help her.

Lesley has become particularly concerned about the increase in undesirable behaviour in one of her large organizational behaviour student groups. There are around 250 students in this class, and organizational behaviour is one of the first courses they take as part of their qualification. The problem this year seems to be worse than in the past, but otherwise things are running much the same as they always have been. Lesley is not sure what is causing the increase in undesirable behaviour.

Many students are arriving late for lectures. This is disruptive, as Lesley has to stop for each noisy new bunch of arrivals. This also effectively cuts down the lecture duration, and some material has been covered more superficially than Lesley planned. There has also been an increase in students talking during lectures. This is not confined to the back rows, and there does not seem to be any acoustic problem; Lesley's voice can be heard clearly from all seats in the lecture theatre. The crosstalk is usually quiet, but it is loud enough to be distracting for Lesley and annoying for students listening to the lecture. The attitudes which students reveal in tutorial discussions, through their apparent lack of interest, lack of ideas and lack of willingness to get involved, are also disappointing. Lesley is accustomed to more positive attitudes; she regularly uses practical, interesting, stimulating tutorial exercises.

There are no explanations—or excuses—to be found in the conditions surrounding the course. Lecture rooms are all close to each other, so there is little delay in getting from one class to another. Lesley's sessions are not at awkward times (not first thing Monday, not last thing Friday), so students are not particularly tired or preoccupied in her sessions. In summary, we can assume that the undesirable behaviour is within the control of the students themselves and is thus amenable to behaviour modification.

Questions

1. What target behaviour(s) would it be realistic to consider modifying in this situation?

2. What reinforcement regime could be developed and applied to achieve the desired behaviour change(s)?

3. What behaviour changes would you hope to see?

Chapter 5 Personality

Key concepts

psychometrics

nomothetic

type

self-concept

thematic apperception test

neuroticism

openness

conscientiousness

Type A personality

need for achievement

personality

idiographic

trait

generalized other

projective test

emotionality

agreeableness

the big five

Type B personality

Learning objectives

When you have read this chapter, you should be able to define those key concepts in your own words, and you should also be able to:

1. Distinguish between type, trait and self-theories of personality.

2. Identify the strengths and limitations of formal approaches to personality assessment.

3. Explain the uses and limitations of objective questionnaires and projective tests as measures of personality.

4. Explain the relationship between personality and stress, and identify appropriate individual and organizational stress management strategies.

5. Evaluate the benefits and problems of psychometric assessment as a tool to assist management decision making, particularly in selection.

6. Assess realistically the main characteristics of your own personality.

Why study personality?

Who are you? How do you describe your characteristics? How do you differ from others? How can we define and measure those characteristics and differences? Psychologists answer these questions using the concept of *personality*. Many managers think that personality is related to job performance and career success, and personality assessment is a widely used selection tool. What are the foundations of these assessments, and what value are they?

Useful Latin terms

per sonare
to speak through

persona
an actor's mask; a character in a play

persona grata
an acceptable person

persona non grata
an unacceptable person

Quick personality check: are you a doormat or a bully?

- Do you dread being asked favours?
- Do you keep quiet when criticized unfairly?
- Would you quietly put up with lukewarm food in a restaurant rather than send it back?
- Do you find it hard to turn away canvassers and door-to-door salespeople?
- Do you tell white lies to avoid hurting friends' feelings?
- Do you sometimes agree to have sex with your partner when you don't feel like it?
- If you hailed a taxi, but someone else got into it, would you just slope off and look for another one?

If you got more than four 'yeses', you are veering towards doormat status. You need to practise being more assertive. One or nil suggests that, even if you think you are firm but fair, friends and colleagues may well regard you as a bit of a shit. Considering other people's needs could mean you get more done in the long run. If you scored two or three yeses, you've got the situation more or less sussed.

From Jerome Burne and Susan Aldridge, 'Who do you think you are?', *Focus Extra*, April 1996, p.6.

Psychometrics is an area of psychology concerned with the systematic testing, measurement and assessment of intelligence, aptitudes and personality.

The term **psychometrics** is now used to refer to the broad range of different types of assessments and measurements, of aptitude, intelligence and also of personality.

There are numerous tests for aptitudes related to particular occupations, such as the Computer Programmer Aptitude Battery. Tests are used to measure, for example, typing ability and arithmetic competence. When measuring aspects of aptitude or intelligence, we can use the term 'test' because a high score is usually better than a low score. When measuring aspects of personality, however, it is more appropriate to use the term 'assessment'. A 'high' score on a personality factor (extroversion, for example), cannot be said to be better or worse than a 'low' score. There are no right or wrong answers in a personality assessment. There are no correct or incorrect personality types or traits.

Psychometric assessment has a wide range of organizational applications in, for example:

- shortlisting and selecting candidates for jobs;
- assessment of suitability for promotion;
- assessment for redeployment purposes;
- evaluation of training potential;
- career counselling and development;
- graduate recruitment, for applicants with limited work experience;
- vocational guidance;
- redundancy counselling.

Psychometric assessments are used to complement less formal and more subjective methods to help managers reach more widely informed and objective judgements about people.

funny **Business**

by MORRIS

"What we are looking for is someone without an earstud."

We will focus here on personality assessment. The testing of intelligence and specific aptitudes are specialist topics beyond our scope. Two approaches are explained, with the awkward labels *nomothetic* and *idiographic*. Nomothetic approaches form the basis for most contemporary psychometrics. These are usually based on self-report questionnaires, which are easier to administer, to score and to interpret than idiographic methods. The latter use open-ended questioning strategies to capture the individual's unique characteristics. Nomothetic techniques appear to be more objective and quantitative than idiographic methods. However, idiographic techniques rely on radically different assumptions about human psychology. It is on the validity of these assumptions that our judgements of different methods should be based, and not simply on matters of operational convenience.

The definition problem

Personality refers to the psychological qualities that influence an individual's characteristic behaviour patterns, in a distinctive and consistent manner, across different situations and over time.

The concept of **personality** underpins psychology's attempt to identify the unique character of individuals and to measure and understand differences between individuals. The term describes those properties of behaviour which are striking and consistent. These properties concern the individual's typical ways of coping with life.

Personality is a broad, integrating concept. However, our definition of personality is restricted to properties which set us apart, and which are both *stable* and *distinctive*.

Stable

Personality theory deals with behaviour patterns that are consistent in different contexts and over time. We are not interested in properties that are occasional and transient. Mood swings and related behaviours caused by illness, or the consumption of drugs, are not stable and are thus not regarded as personality characteristics (unless they become permanent). However, there is a problem here. Personality appears to be flexible. The manager who is loud and autocratic in the office can be a caring and supporting parent at home. The 'stable' behaviours which we exhibit depend, in part, on social context. Some personality features (as with allergies) may appear only in specific social and physical conditions.

Distinctive

Personality theory is concerned with the pattern of dispositions and behaviours unique to the individual and is not so concerned with properties that all or most other people share. You may be aggressive towards waiters, friendly with librarians, deferential to professors and terrified of mice. You may share some of these dispositions with a friend who breeds mice.

The study of personality relies on two key propositions:

1. We have to accept that behaviour does have stable and distinctive features and does not change frequently. Most of us recognize consistency in our thought patterns, in our ways of relating to others, in meeting our needs, in solving problems, in our emotional responses, and in coping with stress and frustration. These regularities can be observed and studied.

2. We have to accept that the distinctive properties of individual personality can be measured and compared with the properties of others. Measurement does not necessarily imply quantification, but nomothetic methods do rely on sophisticated statistical analysis.

Some psychologists argue that personality is inherited, determined by genetics and the biochemistry of our brains. There is evidence to suggest that, because measures of job satisfaction are fairly stable over time and across different jobs, a predisposition to be content with or frustrated at work may have a genetic component. In this perspective, your personality is fixed at birth, if not before, and life's experiences do little or nothing to alter it.

Other psychologists argue that personality is shaped by environmental, cultural and social factors, that our feelings and behaviour patterns are learned. Social learning theory [link, chapter 4, learning] argues that we learn new behaviours through observing and imitating others. Motivation theory [link, chapter 8, motivation] demonstrates how job satisfaction can be influenced by changing job design and other factors such as supervisory style. Every society has distinctive ways of doing things. We cannot possibly be born with this local knowledge. In this perspective, your personality is flexible, changing with experience. It may be that psychological well-being depends on such adaptability.

The controversy over the relative effects of heredity and environment on personality is known as the 'nature–nurture' debate, but few psychologists, if any, now hold the extreme positions just set out here. Both genetic and situational factors influence behaviour patterns. Theorists disagree over the emphases to be given to these factors, how they should be measured, and how they interact. During the 1960s and 1970s, 'nurture' was the position in vogue. During the 1980s and 1990s, biological and genetic evidence moved thinking in the direction of 'nature'. For example, scientists in Israel and America claimed in 1999 to have isolated a dopamine receptor gene, nicknamed 'the novelty gene', which explains the personality trait of seeking excitement through the obsessive pursuit of innovation and change (Stuttaford, 1999).

This debate has profound consequences for organizational behaviour. If you believe that personality and behaviour are inherited, then organizational interventions, for example to redesign work to improve motivation and performance, are a waste of time. If, however, you believe that the expression of personality traits and behaviours is mediated by the social and organizational context, then those interventions begin to sound worthwhile.

Types and traits

Attempts to describe the components and structure of personality have focused on the concepts of type and trait. One of the most straightforward ways of describing and analysing personality concerns the categorization of people into personality **types**.

A **type** is a descriptive label for a distinct pattern of personality characteristics. Examples of personality types include extrovert, neurotic and open.

One of the first personality theorists was Hippocrates ('The father of medicine'), who lived in Greece around 400 BC. He claimed that personality type or 'temperament' was determined by bodily 'humours', generating different behaviour patterns as shown in table 5.1.

Table 5.1: Hippocrates' type theory of personality

body humour	temperament	behaviours
blood	sanguine	confident, cheerful, optimistic, hopeful, active
phlegm	phlegmatic	sluggish, apathetic
black bile	melancholic	depressed, sad, brooding, prone to ill-founded fears
yellow bile	choleric	aggressive, excitable, irritable

Hippocrates

These temperament labels are still in use today, with the same meanings. Hippocrates' theory, however, is unsound for two reasons. First, what we know about the relationships between body chemistry and behaviour fails to confirm the theory. Second, our personal experience reveals that there are more than four types of people in the world.

A more recent type theory was developed by William Sheldon (1898–1970), who argued that temperament was related to physique, or to what he called *somatotype* (Sheldon, 1942). In other words, your personality depends on your 'biological individuality', your size and shape:

The *ectomorph*, who is thin and delicate, is restrained, inhibited, cautious, introverted, artistic and intellectual.

The *mesomorph* is muscular, strong and rectangular, and is energetic, physical, adventurous and assertive.

The *endomorph*, who is fat, soft and round, is also sociable, relaxed and easygoing, and enjoys food.

This typology has intuitive appeal, but it is not a valid model for predicting behaviour. Can you think of an endomorph who is introverted and intellectual? Are you friendly with a mesomorph who is a relaxed gourmet—or with an ectomorph who is sociable and assertive?

The four basic personality types

The Ayurveda principle

The ancient Indian system of holistic medicine, Ayurveda, is founded on the principle that living matter is composed of earth, water, fire, air and ether, combining to give three basic personality types or *doshas*: *vata*, *pitta* and *kapha*:

Vata (air and ether): Slim, angular and restless. Creative and artistic, leaning towards athletics or dancing. Like to travel, can be flirtatious and emotionally insecure. Dry skin, prone to joint pains, rheumatism and depression.

Pitta (water and fire): Medium build with fair or red hair. Good leaders and executives who get things done. Articulate and impatient, can be irritable. Lunch is a very important meal. Skin is reddish. Prone to acne, rashes, ulcers and urinary infections.

Kapha (earth and water): Stocky, perhaps overweight. Loyal workers, not pushy. Patient, affectionate and forgiving. Smooth and oily skin. Prone to respiratory tract problems, asthma, bronchitis, colds and sinus problems, and to depression.

Each of us is a combination of all three *doshas*, the dominant one determining our physical and spiritual character. The key to health lies in balance, ensuring that one doshic personality is not too prominent. The similarities between Ayurveda and somatotyping are striking.

Based on Sally Morris, 'An Eastern art of healing that is heading West', *The Times*, 26 October 1999, p.47.

Carl Gustav Jung
(1875–1961)

Type theory owes a debt to the Swiss psychologist Carl Gustav Jung whose approach is based on psychological preferences for extroversion or introversion, for sensation or intuition, for thinking or feeling, and for judging or perceiving (Jung, 1953; 1971). At the heart of this complex theory lie four personality types, plotted across the sensation–intuition and thinking–feeling dimensions in figure 5.1 and described in more detail in table 5.2.

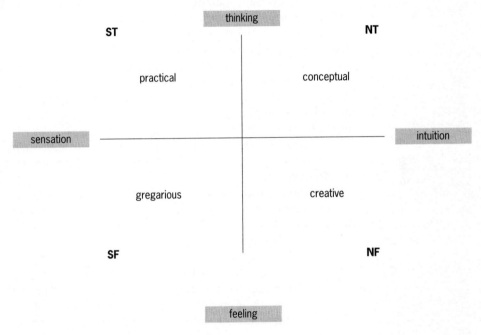

Figure 5.1: Jung's personality type matrix

Table 5.2: Jung's personality types described	
Sensation–Thinking (ST)	Practical, down to earth, impersonal, interested in facts, wants order, precision, no ambiguity, values efficiency and clear lines of authority in an organization.
Intuition–Thinking (NT)	Conceptual and inventive, sees future possibilities through analysis, is comfortable using flow charts and graphs, generates new ideas and change, sparks enthusiasm in others.
Sensation–Feeling (SF)	Gregarious and sociable, interested in facts about people, dislikes ambiguity, likes to establish settings in which people care for and support each other, has no time for reflection.
Intuition–Feeling (NF)	Creative, values imagination and warmth, is enthusiastic, has grandiose goals, dislikes rules, hierarchies and procedures, likes flexibility and open communication, is persistent and committed, can be seen as an idealistic dreamer.

From Jung's theory, the mother and daughter team of Katherine Briggs and Isabel Myers (Myers, 1962; 1976; Myers and McCaulley, 1985) developed the Myers–Briggs type indicator (MBTI), a widely used and still popular personality assessment. This assigns subjects to one side or other of all four of Jung's preference dimensions, establishing 16 personality types, each known by its letter code. Thus, if you are ENFP, you have been typed as extrovert, intuitive, feeling and perceiving. The MBTI has a number of practical applications. For example, problem-solving and decision-making groups need a complementary mix of personalities: intuitive types need sensing types, feeling types need thinking types. This echoes the theory of effective group composition developed by Meredith Belbin [**link**, chapter 10, group structure].

Type approaches fit people into categories possessing common behaviour patterns. A personality **trait**, on the other hand, is any enduring behaviour that occurs in a variety of settings. While individuals belong to types, traits belong to individuals. You *fit* a type, you *have* a trait. Traits are also defined in terms of predispositions to behave in a particular way.

The study of traits in personality research and assessment, and of how traits cluster to form personality types, is associated with the **nomothetic** approach in psychology.

Nomothetic means 'law setting' or 'law giving'. Psychologists who adopt this approach look for universal laws of behaviour. The nomothetic approach assumes that personality is inherited and that environmental factors have little effect. The nomothetic approach adopts the following procedures.

> A **trait** is a relatively stable quality or attribute of an individual's personality, influencing behaviour in a particular direction. Examples of traits include shyness, excitability, reliability, moodiness.

> The **nomothetic** approach to the study of personality emphasizes the identification of universal personality traits and looks for systematic relationships between different aspects of personality.

1. It is necessary to identify the main dimensions on which personality can vary. Trait approaches assume that there is a common set of dimensions on which we can be compared. Traits describe aspects of temperament and character, and reflect the individual's predisposition to behave in particular ways. This approach assumes that your unique personality can be measured and compared with others on the same dimensions.

2. The personalities of groups of people are assessed, usually through a self-report questionnaire. Popular magazines often use 'fun' versions of these questionnaires. The questions usually ask you to choose between a fixed number of answers. Responses may be confined, for example, to 'true' or 'false', to 'yes' or 'no', or to a rating scale that runs from 'strongly agree' to 'strongly disagree'. These are called 'forced choice' questions, and this procedure assumes that your answers reflect your behaviour.

3. Your personality profile is constructed across the traits measured. Your score on each dimension is compared with the average and the distribution of scores for the whole group. This enables the assessor to identify individuals around the norm and those with pronounced characteristics that deviate from the norm. Your personal score has little meaning outside the scores of the population with which you are being compared. You cannot have a 'high' or 'low' score; you can only have scores that are high or low when compared with others.

4. The group may be split into sub-groups, say by age, sex, or occupation. This produces other reference points, or norms, against which individual scores can be compared. Patterns of similarities and differences among and between sub-groups enable general laws about personality to be formulated. One may find, for example, that successful Scottish male managers tend to be introverted, or that women under the age of 30 employed in purchasing have unusually low scores on shyness. This approach is impersonal, and it is difficult to use the results to predict individual behaviour, even with 'extreme' scores. It may be possible, however, to make probabilistic predictions about groups, in terms of behaviour tendencies.

Personality types and sales maximization

Bluewater, a retail park in Kent in Britain, opened in March 1999. Research helped to design the 'customer-friendly' features of the centre: wide car park spaces, no shops in 'dead end' corridors, police station for security, natural materials on the floors, poetry on the walls, coffee shops at the entrances with welcoming aromas, and staff trained in positive body language [**link**, chapter 6, communication]. The research produced a breakdown of the centre's customers into seven personality types. This was used to determine the mix of shops, based on the percentage of each type in the area and expected sales to that category:

category	characteristics	Percentage of population	Percentage of sales
county classics	upmarket middle-aged women, house-proud and arty, shop at 'big name' stores	14.6	25.2
club executives	male equivalent of county classics, impatient, successful, status- and career-obsessed, like 'middle-of-the-road' stores	13.5	21.2
young fashionables	twentysomethings, vain and superficial fashion victims, like 'lifestyle' clothing stores and fashionable brand images	15.6	21.6
sporting 30s	middle-income men, casual, undomesticated, holding on to youth, fighting flab, want special-interest stores	13.4	12
young survivors	singles and couples with limited interests, abilities and ambitions—and limited incomes, seek budget stores	15.3	7.4
home comfortables	'cardigans and knitting' types, retired and more at home in the garden than a shopping mall, like 'traditional' stores	14.4	7.1
budget optimists	middle-aged and older women on low incomes, limited horizons, set routines, like 'traditional' clothing and food stores	13.2	5.4

Based on Paul Bray, 'Falling under the psychologist's spell', *The Sunday Times*, 'The Restless Customer' supplement, 13 June 1999, p.9.

It may seem odd that one approach to individual personality assessment relies on studies of large groups. However, through this method, one discovers what is normal or average for those groups and compares individuals with that. The terms 'normal' and 'average' are used in the statistical sense. Individuals who 'deviate from the norm' are not social outcasts. However, assessments based on this method are often used as a guide to the profile of individuals, especially in employment selection.

One of the most influential trait theories of personality is that of Hans Jürgen Eysenck (1970; 1990), who was born in Germany in 1916 and who worked in Britain until his death in 1997. Following Jung, his research explored the key dimensions on which personality varies, including the extroversion–introversion or 'E' dimension, and the neuroticism–stability or 'N' dimension. However, unlike Jung, Eysenck sought to identify trait clusters.

Eysenck's approach is nomothetic. His sympathies lie with behaviourist psychologists who seek a scientific, experimental, mathematical psychology. Behaviourists claim, however, that behaviour is shaped by environmental influences. Eysenck's explanations of personality, on the other hand, are based on genetics and biology.

Hans Jürgen Eysenck (1916–97)

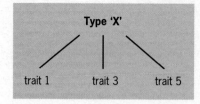
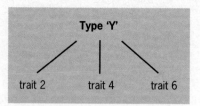

Figure 5.2: A hierarchical model of personality types and traits

Eysenck's model offers a way of linking types, traits and behaviour. He argues that personality structure is hierarchical. Each individual possesses more or less of a number of identifiable traits—trait 1, trait 2, trait 3, and so on. Research shows how individuals who have a particular trait, say trait 1, are more likely to possess another, say trait 3, than people who do not have trait 1. In other words, traits tend to 'cluster' in systematic patterns. These clusters identify a 'higher order' of personality description, which Eysenck refers to as personality types, as figure 5.2 illustrates.

This does not mean that every individual who has trait 1 has a type 'X' personality. It means that questionnaire analysis has shown that individuals with high scores on trait 1 are also more likely to have high scores on traits 3 and 5, putting them into the type 'X' category.

Eysenck presents statistical evidence from personality assessments to support the existence of personality trait clusters. However, individuals vary in a continuous distribution on trait scores. The result of an individual assessment using this approach is a personality profile across several traits rather than allocation to a single personality type.

The E dimension divides us into two broad categories of people—extroverts and introverts. American use of these terms refers to sociability and unsociability. European use emphasizes spontaneity and inhibition. Eysenck's account combines these notions. Most of us have a trait profile between these extremes on a continuum, and they are not exclusive categories.

Eysenck argues that seven pairs of personality traits cluster to generate the extrovert and introvert personality types. These traits are summarized in table 5.3.

Table 5.3: The trait clusters for Eysenck's extrovert and introvert types

extrovert	introvert
activity	inactivity
expressiveness	inhibition
impulsiveness	control
irresponsibility	responsibility
practicality	reflectiveness
risk taking	carefulness
sociability	unsociability

Extroverts are tough-minded individuals who need strong and varied external stimulation. They are sociable, like parties, are good at telling stories, enjoy practical jokes, have many friends, need people to talk to, do not enjoy studying and reading on their own, crave excitement, take risks, act impulsively, prefer change, are optimistic, carefree, active, aggressive and quick-tempered, display their emotions and are unreliable.

Introverts are tender-minded, experience strong emotions and do not need intense external stimuli. They are quiet, introspective, retiring, prefer books to people, are withdrawn and reserved, plan ahead, distrust impulse, appreciate order, lead careful sober lives, have little excitement, suppress emotions, are pessimistic, worry about moral standards, and are reliable.

The N dimension assesses personality on a continuum between neuroticism and stability. Neurotics are emotional, unstable and anxious, tend to have low opinions of themselves, feel that they are unattractive failures, tend to be disappointed with life, and are pessimistic and depressed. They worry about things that may never happen and are easily upset when things go wrong. They are obsessive, conscientious, finicky people who are highly disciplined and get annoyed by untidiness and disorder. Neurotics are not self-reliant and tend to submit to institutional power without question. They feel controlled by events, by others and by fate. They often imagine that they are ill and demand sympathy. They blame themselves excessively and are troubled by conscience.

Stable people are 'adjusted' and self-confident, they are optimistic, resist irrational fears, are easy-going and realistic, solve their own problems, have few health worries and have few regrets about their past.

The traits clusters for emotionally unstable and stable types are summarized in table 5.4. The questionnaire that Eysenck used to measure the E and N dimensions has 96 questions, 40 for each dimension, and 16 'lie detector' questions. The questions are mainly in the 'yes/no' format. The E and N dimensions are not correlated; if you are extroverted, you could be either stable or neurotic. If you are stable, you could be either extrovert or introvert.

Is one personality type more desirable than another? The extrovert may be sociable, friendly, cheerful, active and lively. However, extroverts are unreliable, fickle in friendships, and are easily bored with uninteresting or time-consuming tasks. There are positive and negative sides to the extrovert personality, as with the introvert. Those with extreme scores have what Eysenck calls an 'ambiguous gift'. If we are aware of such features, however, we may be able to act in ways to control and exploit them to our advantage. It is thus important to be aware of

Table 5.4: The trait clusters for Eysenck's emotionally unstable and stable types

emotionally unstable	emotionally stable
anxiety	calm
guilt	guilt freedom
hypochondriasis	sense of health
lack of autonomy	autonomy
low self-esteem	self-esteem
obsessiveness	casualness
unhappiness	happiness

your personality, and to be aware of the characteristics that might be seen by others as strengths and weaknesses. To understand other people, you must begin with an understanding of your own personality and emotions, and the effect that you have on others.

Surely a stable personality is more desirable than a neurotic one? Probably not. An open display of emotion is desirable in some settings and embarrassing in others. Emotions are a major source of motivation, and an inability to display or share feelings can be a handicap. Sharing feelings of frustration and anger can be as important in an organizational setting as showing positive feelings of, for example, praise, satisfaction and friendship. Emotional intelligence (see box and table 5.5), it has been argued, is a major factor explaining interpersonal and managerial effectiveness.

The management of feelings: an overlooked personality trait?

The concept of emotional intelligence was developed by Peter Salovey and John D. Mayer (1990), who argued that the concept of 'rational' intelligence ignores emotional competencies. This idea was popularized by Daniel Goleman (1995; 1998), who claims that emotional intelligence is more important to career success than technical skills or rational intelligence. Emotional intelligence is the ability to perceive, integrate, understand and reflectively manage one's own and other people's feelings. The five key dimensions are outlined in table 5.5.

Table 5.5: The five dimensions of emotional intelligence

	Dimension	Definition	Hallmarks
1	Self-awareness	the ability to recognize and understand your moods, emotions and drives as well as the effect you have on others	self-confidence, realistic self-assessment, self-deprecating sense of humour
2	Regulating feelings	the ability to control and to redirect your disruptive moods and impulses; the propensity to suspend judgement, to think before acting	trustworthiness and integrity, comfortable with ambiguity, openness to change
3	Motivation	a passion to work for reasons beyond status and money; a propensity to pursue goals with energy and persistence	high achievement need, optimism even in the face of failure, organizational commitment
4	Empathy	the ability to recognize and understand the emotional makeup of others; skill in dealing with the emotional responses of others	expertise in building and retaining talent; cross-cultural sensitivity; service to clients and customers
5	Social skills	effectiveness in managing relationships and building networks; ability to find common ground, to build rapport	effectiveness in leading change; persuasiveness; expertise in building and leading teams

Goleman argues that emotional intelligence gives anyone an advantage, at work or in day-to-day relationships, but that it is particularly important for success in senior management and leadership roles, where high intellect is taken for granted. At senior levels, high emotional intelligence is a mark of the 'star performer'. There are several assessments available for measuring emotional intelligence (sometimes confusingly called EQ), and some commentators, including Goleman (1998), are convinced that emotional intelligence is developed through experience and can be learned through training (Pickard, 1999).

The big five are broad trait clusters that appear from research consistently to capture the traits that we use to describe ourselves and other people; openness, conscientiousness, extroversion, agreeableness and neuroticism ('OCEAN').

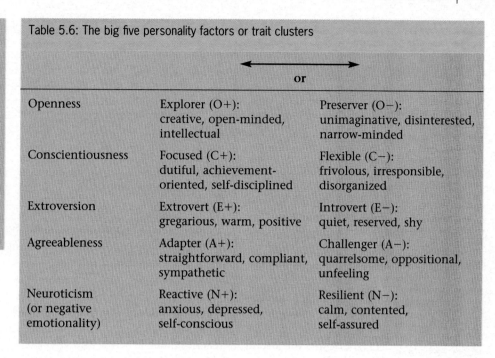

Table 5.6: The big five personality factors or trait clusters

	← or →	
Openness	Explorer (O+): creative, open-minded, intellectual	Preserver (O−): unimaginative, disinterested, narrow-minded
Conscientiousness	Focused (C+): dutiful, achievement-oriented, self-disciplined	Flexible (C−): frivolous, irresponsible, disorganized
Extroversion	Extrovert (E+): gregarious, warm, positive	Introvert (E−): quiet, reserved, shy
Agreeableness	Adapter (A+): straightforward, compliant, sympathetic	Challenger (A−): quarrelsome, oppositional, unfeeling
Neuroticism (or negative emotionality)	Reactive (N+): anxious, depressed, self-conscious	Resilient (N−): calm, contented, self-assured

The search for trait clusters has culminated in what are known as **the big five**. The most influential advocates of this approach are Paul Costa and Robert McRae (McRae, 1992). This approach has achieved broad acceptance as a common descriptive system. Research seems to reproduce these dimensions, in different settings, with different populations, with different forms of data collection, and in different languages. However, the labelling and interpretation of the factors and sub-traits remain controversial.

The big five are not personality types. These are sets of factors, 'super traits', which describe common elements among the 'sub-factors' identified as clustering together looking for a heading. Costa and McCrae identify six traits under each of the five headings, giving 30 traits in total. Table 5.6 summarizes the big five personality trait clusters, and one of the exercises at the end of this chapter invites you to profile your own personality using this approach.

The six traits relating to **openness** (fantasy, aesthetics, feelings, actions, ideas, values) run on a continuum from 'explorer', at one extreme, to 'preserver' at the other. Explorer (O+) traits are useful for entrepreneurs, architects, change agents, artists and theoretical scientists. Preserver (O−) traits are useful for finance managers, stage performers, project managers and applied scientists. Those in the middle of this spectrum (O) are labelled 'moderates' who are interested in novelty when necessity commands, but not for too long.

The traits relating to **conscientiousness** (competence, order, dutifulness, achievement striving, self-discipline, deliberation) run from 'focused' to 'flexible'. Focused (C+) traits are useful for leaders, senior executives and other high achievers. Flexible (C−) traits are useful for researchers, detectives and management consultants. Those in the middle (C) are 'balanced' and find it easy to move from focus to being flexible, from production to research.

The traits relating to **extroversion** (warmth, gregariousness, assertiveness, activity, excitement seeking, positive emotions) run from 'extrovert' to 'introvert' (surprise, surprise). Extrovert (E+) traits are useful in sales, politics and the arts. Introvert (E−) traits are useful for production management, and in the physical and natural sciences. Those in the middle of this spectrum (E) are 'ambiverts', who move easily from isolation to social settings.

The big five in action

Pierce and Jane Howard (1993) cite the case of Henry, a freelance television sports producer. Henry was rich and miserable, worn out by work and unable to sleep properly. He was a sports lover who was good at his job, but producing fast-paced live basketball games rattled his nerves and he took a long time to calm down afterwards. What was the problem? His big five personality profile was:

O–   C+   E+   A   N+

His scores for openness (preserver), conscientiousness (focused), extroversion (extrovert) and agreeableness (negotiator) were ideal for this job. The problem lay with his high N+ reactive, emotional score. A television producer has to be resilient and calm, monitoring the action and the camerawork, giving instructions to produce a smooth programme in a fast-moving and stressful environment with no margin for error. The solution? Henry moved to producing sports documentaries and took a degree in Eastern studies, planning to specialize in documentaries on Eastern culture (including sport).

The traits relating to **agreeableness** (trust, straightforwardness, altruism, compliance, modesty, tender-mindedness) run from 'adapter' to 'challenger'. Adapter (A+) traits are useful in teaching, social work and psychology. Challenger (A–) traits are useful in advertising, management and military leadership. Those in the middle of this spectrum (A) are 'negotiators', who move from leadership to followership as the situation demands.

The traits relating to **neuroticism**, called 'negative emotionality' in management settings so as not to offend (worry, anger, discouragement, self-consciousness, impulsiveness, vulnerability), run from 'reactive' to 'resilient'. Reactive (emotional) or 'N+' traits are useful for social scientists, academics and customer service professionals, but extreme reactivity interferes with intellectual performance. Resilient (unflappable) or 'N–' traits are useful for air traffic controllers, airline pilots, military snipers, finance managers and engineers. Those in the middle of this spectrum (N) are 'responsives', able to use levels of emotionality appropriate to the circumstances.

Personality Types A and B: propensity to suffer stress

A **Type A personality**, or behaviour syndrome, concerns a combination of emotions and behaviours characterized by ambition, hostility, impatience and a sense of constant time pressure. If you have a Type A personality, you are more likely to suffer stress-related disorders and heart disease.

Personality and health seem to be linked in a way particularly relevant to organizational behaviour. Meyer Friedman and Ray Rosenman (1974) identified two extreme 'behaviour syndromes' which explained differences in stress levels. In other words, they claim to have identified a 'stress-prone' personality. Much subsequent research has focused on what Friedman and Rosenman called the Type A behaviour syndrome and its opposite, Type B. Table 5.7 summarizes these two personality types.

Friedman and Rosenman found that Type A personalities were three times more likely to suffer heart disease than Type B personalities. The typical Type A thrives on long hours, large amounts of work and tight deadlines. These are socially and organizationally desirable characteristics, as are competitiveness and a high need for achievement. However, a Type A is seldom able to relax long enough to stand back from a complex organizational problem to make an effective and comprehensive analysis. They tend to lack the patience and relaxed style required of many management positions. A further problem lies in the fact that their impatience and hostility can increase the stress levels in those who have to work with them. Like the extrovert, although a Type A personality can appear to have many

A **Type B personality**, or behaviour syndrome, concerns a combination of emotions and behaviours characterized by relaxation, calm, lack of preoccupation with achievement and an ability to take time to enjoy leisure. If you have a Type B personality, you are less likely to suffer stress-related disorders and heart disease.

Table 5.7: Type A and Type B personality characteristics

Type A personality characteristics	Type B personality characteristics
competitive	able to take time out to enjoy leisure
high need for achievement	not preoccupied with achievement
aggressive	easy-going
works fast	works at a steady pace
impatient	seldom impatient
restless	not easily frustrated
extremely alert	relaxed
tense facial muscles	moves and speaks slowly
constant feeling of time pressure	seldom lacks enough time
more likely to suffer stress-related illness	less likely to suffer stress-related illness

admirable facets, this behaviour syndrome can be dysfunctional for the individual, and for others.

Stop and criticize

Are you a Type A or a Type B personality?

Do you suffer from any of these symptoms: alcohol abuse, excessive smoking, dizziness, upset stomach, headaches, fatigue, sweating, bad breath? If 'yes', these could be stress responses to your Type A behaviour pattern. Expect your first heart attack before you are 45.

If you don't suffer stress-related symptoms, perhaps you are a Type B. However, do you think that your dozy behaviour could damage your career prospects?

Whichever your response, what are you going to do about it?

Friedman and Rosenman argue that a Type A can change into a Type B, with awareness and the right training, and suggest a number of 're-engineering strategies':

- keep reminding yourself that life is always full of unfinished business;
- you only 'finish' when you die;
- learn how to delegate responsibility to others;
- limit your weekly working hours;
- schedule time for leisure and exercise;
- take a course in time management skills.

The problem, of course, is that the extreme Type A personality—the person most at risk—can never find enough time to implement these strategies effectively. Another problem lies with the question of whether you can 're-engineer' your personality this easily.

Stress management: individual and organizational methods

The work of Friedman and Rosenman is important in demonstrating a relationship between personality and health. Negative emotional states such as depression, hostility and anxiety appear to be linked to heart disease, respiratory disorders such as asthma, and headaches and ulcers. Health risks are greater where negative states are chronic, particularly when they are an aspect of personality. There are a number of other causes of stress that arise from individual factors: difficulty in coping with change, lack of confidence and assertiveness in relationships, poor time management, and poor stress management skills (Clarke, 1989).

Is stress really a problem?

- The Confederation of British Industry estimates that stress costs British industry around £7 billion a year, equivalent to 2–3 per cent of gross domestic product, or over £300 per employee per year.

- The Health and Safety Executive (HSE) estimates that 60 per cent of absenteeism from work is due to stress-related illness, a total of 40 million working days a year.

- The HSE also claims that one in five employees takes time off work due to work-related stress, and one in thirteen consults their doctors about stress problems.

- A survey in 1996 by the European Foundation for the Improvement of Living and Working Conditions found that 28 per cent of European workers consider their health to be affected by stress at work, that 'high-stress' working conditions are on the increase, and that women suffer to a greater degree than men.

Based on *Key Facts: Stress at Work*, Institute of Personnel and Development, London, October 1998, pp.2–3.

Stress has many causes other than personality. The pace of life, work and change in contemporary society generates stress by increasing the range and intensity of the demands on our time. A stressor is any condition that requires an adaptive response from the individual. Typical stressors that are likely to arise in an organizational context include:

- *inadequate physical working environment*: noise, bad lighting, inadequate ventilation, lack of privacy, extremes of heat and cold, old and unsuitable and unreliable equipment;

- *inappropriate job design*: poor co-ordination, inadequate training, inadequate information, rigid procedures, inadequate staffing, excessive workloads, no challenge, little use of skills, no responsibility or participation in decision making, role ambiguity;

- *poor management style*: inconsistent, competitive, crisis management, autocratic management, excessive time pressures placed on employees;

- *poor relationships*: with superiors, with colleagues, with particular individuals, lack of feedback, little social contact, racial and sexual harassment;

- *uncertain future*: job insecurity, fear of unemployment or redeployment, few promotion opportunities, low-status job;

- *divided loyalties*: conflicts between own aspirations and organization's requirements, conflict with family and social responsibilities.

Stress can also be arousing and exciting, and can enhance our sense of satisfaction

The organizational causes and costs of stress

In 1997, John Walker, a social worker, received an out-of-court settlement of £175,000 from Northumberland County Council, following two nervous breakdowns resulting from an excessive workload. In June 1999, a court awarded Beverley Lancaster, a housing officer with Birmingham City Council, damages of £67,000. The council allegedly failed to provide adequate training and support when she transferred jobs. Lancaster suffered serious physical injury as a result of work overload and was forced to retire on grounds of ill health. In September 1999, Muriel Benson, a teacher, reached an out-of-court settlement of £47,000 with Wirral Borough Council, which failed to act on complaints about her increasing workload, which caused her stress-related anxiety and depression and forced her into early retirement. In January 2000, Randy Ingram was awarded £203,000 damages for intense stress and depression caused by lack of management support at Hereford and Worcester Council for his difficult work in looking after residential sites for gypsies.

Stress is often regarded as a personal problem. These cases show that it is management's responsibility to monitor workloads and stress symptoms, and to respond effectively.

Based on Mark Whitehead, 'Watch your workloads', *People Management*, 15 July 1999, vol.5, no.14, pp.12–13; Russel Jenkins, '£47,000 for teacher made sick by stress', *The Times*, 1 October 1999, p.11; 'Council worker awarded £200,000 over stress claim', *The Times*, 11 January 2000, p.3.

and accomplishment and improve our performance. The term *eustress* is sometimes used to describe this positive aspect of stress. The prefix 'eu' is Greek for 'good'. This contrasts with *distress*, which means the unpleasant, debilitating and unhealthy side of stress.

Stress can be *episodic*. When dealing with life's many problems, we often get anxious, cope with the problem and then relax again. Some 'life changes' can be very stressful indeed, such as the death of a relative or friend, or a term in prison. Other life changes can also be stressful but can trigger a less extreme response, such as getting lower grades than expected in an exam, being fined for speeding or having an argument with a parent. Each of these episodes on its own is unlikely to cause lasting damage. Most of us overcome these problems quickly. However, when several of these episodes occur around the same time, in a manner beyond our control, the health risk is increased.

Stress can be *chronic*. This happens when we face constant stress, with no escape, and can lead to exhaustion and 'burnout'. This may be due to the coincidence of a number of unrelated stressful episodes. However, chronic stress also arises from the enduring features of our personal, social and organizational circumstances. If we are always under pressure, always facing multiple and unrealistic demands, always having difficulties with our work, our colleagues and our relationships, then the health risk from stress is likely to increase.

Stress can be a personal response to life's challenges. What you brush aside may be a debilitating problem for someone else. There seem to be three main factors moderating the impact of a stressor on an individual:

Condition: you are better able to cope with stress if you are in good health and full of energy to begin with.

Cognitive appraisal: if you believe that you are not going to cope with a particular event, this belief can become a 'self-fulfilling prophecy'. The opposite can also be true.

Hardiness: hardiness is an outlook on life characterized by a welcoming approach to change, commitment to purposeful activity and a sense of being in control. This combination of factors can increase resilience to stressful events.

Table 5.8: Typical stress symptoms

excessive alcohol intake	heavy cigarette smoking	dependence on tranquillizers
tiredness	low energy	dizziness
headaches	stomach upsets and ulcers	bad breath
high blood pressure	sleep problems	hyperventilation
temper tantrums	irritability	moodiness
loss of concentration	aggression	overeating
excessive worrying	anxiety	inability to relax
pounding heart	feelings of inadequacy	memory loss

Stress has many symptoms which, taken on their own, do not appear significant and are not particularly threatening if they are transient. An occasional headache is seldom cause for concern. Many of these symptoms have other causes, so they can be overlooked, and stress passes unrecognized and untreated. Table 5.8 identifies typical symptoms of stress.

Stress can thus have a number of emotional consequences for the individual—anxiety, fatigue, depression, frustration, nervousness, low self-esteem, and so on. At the (rare) extreme, stress can even contribute to mental breakdown and suicide. Stress also influences behaviour in many ways, from the so-called 'comfort tricks' involving alcohol and other drugs and excessive eating, to accident-proneness and emotional outbursts. Stress affects our thinking ability, interfering with concentration, decision making, attention span and reaction to criticism. There are a number of accompanying physiological responses too, such as increased heart rate and blood pressure, sweating, and 'hot and cold flushes'.

The organizational consequences of stress can, therefore, be highly damaging. The work performance of stressed employees can be poor. This is sometimes revealed in high levels of absenteeism, staff turnover, accidents and wilful sabotage. Stress can cause relationships to deteriorate (although poor relationships may cause stress in the first place), and commitment to work and to the organization are also likely to fall.

There are two broad strategies for reducing stress: problem-focused strategies and emotion-focused strategies.

Problem-focused strategies deal directly with the stressors and include:

- improved selection and training mechanisms;
- staff counselling programmes;
- improved organizational communications;
- job redesign and enrichment strategies;
- development of teamworking systems.

Emotion-focused strategies improve individual resilience and coping skills and include:

- consciousness raising to improve self-awareness;
- exercise and fitness programmes;
- self-help training, in biofeedback, meditation, relaxation, coping strategies;

- time management training;
- development of other social and job interests.

It is not always appropriate to 'blame' the individual for their experience of and response to stress, despite the known link to personality. Stress is also caused by organizational factors. While individual resilience can be improved, the need for organizational, or problem-focused, solutions is inescapable.

Figure 5.3 summarizes the argument of this section, with respect to the causes of stress, factors that moderate the experience of stress, stress symptoms and coping strategies.

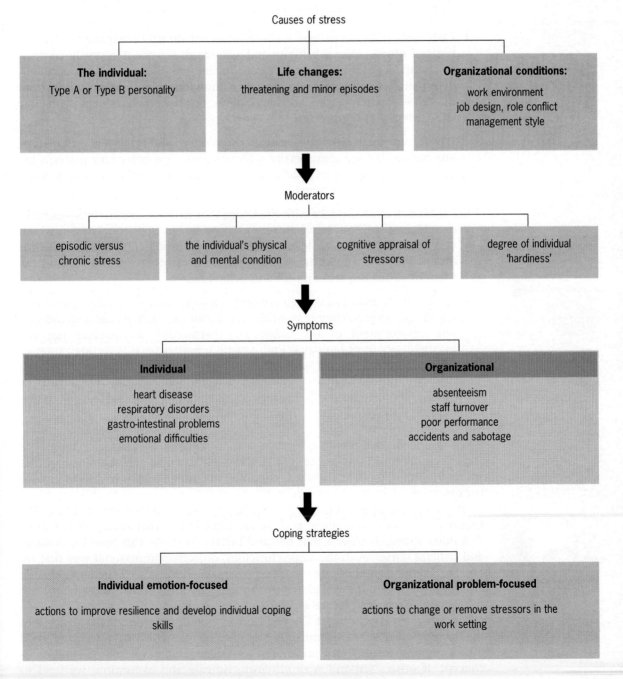

Figure 5.3: Stress causes, moderators, symptoms and coping strategies

The development of the self

The **idiographic** approach to the study of personality emphasizes the uniqueness of the individual, challenging the assumption that we can all be measured and compared on the same dimensions.

The nomothetic approach to the study of personality has been criticized by those who advocate an **idiographic** approach, which contrasts sharply in perspective and implications.

Idiographic means 'writing about individuals'. Psychologists who adopt this perspective begin with a detailed picture of one person. This approach aims to capture the uniqueness, richness and complexity of the individual. It is a valuable way of deepening our understanding but does not readily lead to the generation of universal laws of human behaviour, which is the aim of the nomothetic approach.

The idiographic approach makes the following assumptions.

1. Each individual has unique traits that are not directly comparable with the traits of others. Your sensitivity and aggression are not necessarily comparable with my sensitivity and aggression. Idiographic research produces in-depth studies of normal and abnormal individuals, with information from interviews, letters, diaries, and biographies. The data include what people say and write about themselves.

2. We are not just biological machines driven by heredity. This is only part of our nature. We are also socially self-conscious. Our behaviour patterns are influenced by experience, and by conscious reflection and reasoning, not just by instinct, habit and heredity.

Our **self-concept** is the way in which we view ourselves, the set of perceptions that we have about ourselves.

3. We behave in accordance with the image that we have of ourselves—our self, or **self-concept**. We derive this concept or image from the ways in which other people treat us. We learn about ourselves through our interactions with others. We take the attitudes and behaviours of others towards us and use them to adjust our self-concept and behaviour.

4. As the development of the self-concept is a social process, it follows that personality is open to change through new social interactions and experiences. The development of the individual's personality is therefore not the inevitable result of biological and genetic inheritance. It is through interaction with others that we learn to see and to understand ourselves as individuals. We cannot develop self-understanding without the (tacit) help of others. There is no such thing as 'human nature'. We derive our nature through social interactions and relationships.

Your self-understanding thus determines your behaviour. For example, confidence in your ability to do something is related to the successful demonstration of that ability. Ability combined with lack of confidence usually leads to failure or poor performance.

The mind's ability to reflect on its own functions is an important capability. We experience a world 'out there' and we are capable of experiencing ourselves in that outer world, as objects that live and behave in it. We can observe, evaluate and criticize ourselves in the same conscious, objective, impersonal way that we observe, evaluate and criticize other people and events and we experience shame, anxiety or pride in our own behaviour. Our capacity for reflective thought enables us to evaluate past and future actions and their consequences.

The American psychologist Charles Horton Cooley introduced the concept of the 'looking glass self'. Our mirror is the other people with whom we interact. If others respond warmly and favourably towards us, we develop a 'positive' self-concept. If others respond with criticism, ridicule and aggression, we tend to develop a 'negative' self-image. The personality of the individual is thus the result

Charles Horton Cooley (1864–1929)

of a process in which the individual learns to be the person they are. Most of us learn, accept and use most of the attitudes, values, beliefs and expectations of the society or part of society in which we are brought up.

In other words, we learn the stock of knowledge available in and peculiar to our society. Red means stop. Cars drive on the left-hand side of the road (in Australia and Britain). An extended hand is a symbol of respect and friendship, not of hostility or aggression. These examples, on their own, are trivial. Taken together, they comprise a vital and 'taken-for-granted' knowledge of how society works. Phenomenologists (see chapter 1 and glossary) call this 'recipe knowledge'. The 'rules' that govern our behaviour are created, recreated and reinforced through our continuing interactions with others based on shared definitions of our reality. We interact with each other competently because we share this broad understanding.

How could we develop such a shared understanding on our own in isolation from society? What we inherit from our parents cannot possibly tell us how to behave in a specific culture. We have to learn how to become *persona grata* through social interaction.

If we all share the same ideas and behaviours, we have a recipe for a society of conformists. This is, of course, not consistent with the available evidence, and the theory does not imply this. George Herbert Mead (1934) argued that the self has two components:

George Herbert
Mead (1863–1931)

The generalized other is what we understand other people expect of us in terms of our attitudes, values, beliefs and behaviour.

I The unique, individual, conscious and impulsive aspects of the individual

Me The norms and values of society that the individual learns and accepts, or 'internalizes'

Mead used the term **generalized other** to refer to the set of expectations one believes others have of one. 'Me' is the aspect of self where these generalized attitudes are organized. The 'Me' cannot be physically located. It refers rather to the mental process that enables us to reflect on our own conduct. The 'Me' is the self as an object to itself.

The 'I' is the active, impulsive component of the self. Other people encourage us to conform to current values and beliefs. Reflective individuals also adjust their part in the social process. We can initiate change by introducing new social values. Patterns of socially acceptable conduct are specified in broad and general ways. There is plenty of scope for flexibility, modification, originality, creativity, individuality, variety and significant change.

Stop and criticize

Make a list of the ten words or phrases that best describe the most important features of your individual identity.

These features could concern your social roles, physical characteristics, intellectual qualities, social style, beliefs and particular skills.

Then make a second list, putting what you regard as the most important feature at the top and ranking all ten items with the least important at the bottom.

Starting at the bottom of your list, imagine that these items are removed from your personality one by one. Visualize how you would be different without each personality feature. What difference does its absence make to you?

This is the start of the process of establishing your self-concept. How much more or less valid is this approach than one based on forced choice questionnaires—and why?

Carl Ransom
Rogers (1902–87)

Figure 5.4 illustrates what Carl Rogers called the 'two-sided self'.

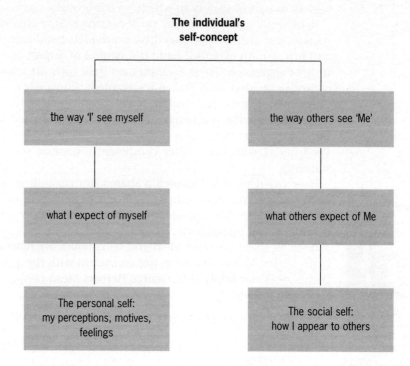

Figure 5.4: The two-sided self

Our self-concept gives us a sense of meaning and consistency. But as our perceptions and motives change through new experiences and learning, our self-concept and our behaviour change. Personality, therefore, is not stable, as the self-concept can be reorganized. We have perceptions of our qualities, abilities, attitudes, impulses, and so on. If these perceptions are accurate, conscious, organized and accepted, then we can regard our self-concept as successful in that it will lead to feelings of comfort, freedom from tension and psychological adjustment. Well-adjusted individuals thus have flexible images of themselves that are open to change through new experiences.

Personality disorders can be caused by a failure to bring together experiences, motives and feelings into a consistent self-concept. We usually behave in ways consistent with our self-images, and when we have new experiences or feelings that are inconsistent we either:

- recognize the inconsistency and try to integrate the two sets of understanding—the healthy response; or

- deny or distort one of the experiences, perhaps by putting the blame on someone or something else—an unhealthy defence mechanism.

'Maladjusted' individuals are those who perceive as threatening those experiences and feelings that are not consistent with their self-concept. They deny and distort their experiences in such a way that their self-image does not match their real feelings or the nature of their experience. This leads to a build-up of psychological tension as more defence mechanisms are required to keep the truth at a distance.

Rogers argued that the core of human personality is the desire to realize fully one's potential. To achieve this, however, the right social environment is required, one in which we are treated with what Rogers calls 'unconditional positive regard'. This means a setting in which one is accepted for whatever one is; in which one is valued, trusted and respected, even in the face of characteristics which others dislike. In this kind of environment, the individual is likely to become trusting, spontaneous, flexible, leading a rich and meaningful life with a harmonious self-concept. However, this is far from the type of social environment typical of most contemporary organizations. Most of us face highly conditional positive regard in which only a narrow range of thoughts and behaviours is accepted.

Compared with nomothetic techniques, the idiographic approach appears to be a complex, untidy view of personality and its development. It has been influential in phenomenological research but is conspicuous by its absence in contemporary psychometrics. How can the individual's self-understanding be studied? Questionnaires are not appropriate as the questions are determined by a researcher. You can always reject that wording as inappropriate to *your* self-concept.

We therefore need a route into the mind independent of the understanding and biases of the researcher. We can ask people to write about themselves and record them speaking about themselves. These and similar techniques are in common use, including free association, interpretation of dreams and the analysis of fantasies. Here the individual has complete freedom of expression, and responses are not tied to predetermined categories. The researcher's job is to identify in this material the themes that reveal the individual's preoccupations and interests— and personality. One successful technique for getting access to the content of someone's mind is the **thematic apperception test**, or TAT.

This breaks our rule about not describing personality assessments as 'tests'. However, we have to be consistent with the literature of the topic. You are unlikely to encounter discussion of a 'thematic apperception assessment'. This is how the TAT works.

First, you are told that you are about to take a test of your creative writing. Then you are shown photographs, typically including people, and asked to write an imaginative story suggested by what you see. The images do not suggest any particular story. These imaginative stories are then assessed in various ways. One of these concerns the assessment of **need for achievement**. This is not a test of your creative or imaginative writing at all.

The assessment procedure first involves determining whether any of the characters in your story has an achievement goal. In other words, does somebody in your story want to perform better? This could involve doing something better than someone else, meeting or exceeding some self-imposed standard of excellence, doing something unique, or being involved in doing something well or successfully. Points are scored for the presence of these features in the story. The more achievement imagery, the higher the score.

The TAT was invented by Henry Murray in 1938 and was subsequently developed by David McClelland (1961; McClelland *et al.*, 1976) as a means of measuring the strength of need for achievement. The TAT is also used to measure the needs for power and affiliation, using a similar scoring procedure but looking for different imagery. In a full assessment, you would be asked to write stories about between four and 20 pictures.

What can short, creative stories about ambiguous pictures tell us about your distinctive and stable personality characteristics? The thematic apperception test is a **projective** assessment.

The label 'projective' is used because subjects project their personalities into the stories they write. (The Rorschach test is a form of projective assessment which

A **thematic apperception test** is a type of 'projective' assessment in which the individual is shown ambiguous pictures and is invited to create stories of what may be happening in these pictures, projecting their own interests and preoccupations into their accounts, which are scored in terms of their achievement, affiliation or power imagery.

The **need for achievement** is a general concern with meeting standards of excellence, the desire to be successful in competition and the motivation to excel in an activity significant to the individual.

David Clarence McClelland (b. 1917)

Henry Alexander Murray (1893–1988)

A **projective test** or assessment is one based on abstract or ambiguous images, which the person being assessed is asked to interpret in a manner which reveals their inner feelings, preoccupations and motives, as these are 'projected' into their interpretations of the images presented.

uses random inkblots instead of pictures or photographs.) McClelland argues that it is reasonable to assume that the person with a strong concern with achievement is likely to write stories with lots of achievement imagery and themes. The evidence seems to support this view.

Need for achievement is important in an organizational context. People with low need for achievement are concerned more with security and status than with personal fulfilment, are preoccupied with their own ideas and feelings, worry more about their self-presentation than their performance, and prefer bright Scottish tartans. (The Buchanan tartan is bright red and yellow, and the author does not wear it.)

People with high need for achievement have the following characteristics:

- They prefer tasks in which they have to achieve a standard of excellence rather than simply carrying out routine activities.

- They prefer jobs in which they get frequent and clear feedback on how well they are doing to help them perform better.

- They prefer activities that involve moderate risks of failure; high-risk activities lead to failure, low-risk activities do not provide opportunities to demonstrate ability.

- They have a good memory for unfinished tasks and do not like to leave things incomplete.

- They can be unfriendly and unsociable when they do not want others to get in the way of their performance.

- They have a sense of urgency, appear to be in a hurry, to be working against time and have an inability to relax.

- They prefer sombre Scottish tartans with lots of blues and greens and dislike bright tartans with reds and yellows; unobtrusive backgrounds allow them to stand out better.

Organizations typically want to employ people with drive, ambition and self-motivation. Can the TAT be used to identify these people? It is not a good assessment for this purpose. Once you know what the 'test' is all about, it is easy to fake a 'good' score. The definition of achievement imagery is close to popular understanding, although the detailed scoring may not be obvious to the untrained. So we are left with the same problem here as with objective questionnaires. Personality assessment scores are not good predictors of job performance.

The TAT is up against other problems as an organizational selection tool. The output of the assessment is hard for the untrained eye to regard as 'objective data'. The scoring procedure involves some subjective interpretation. Expensive training is required in the full technical procedure to produce judges who can reach reliable assessments. Anyone with a scoring key can calculate accurately the results on an objective questionnaire.

McClelland argues that your achievement need can be increased by teaching you the scoring system and by helping you to write high-scoring stories. This increases need for achievement by encouraging you to see and understand daily life more vividly in achievement terms. This retraining in mental habits can thus be translated more readily into action.

Nomothetic versus idiographic?

The two approaches to the study of personality presented here are summarized in table 5.9. How should we choose between these perspectives? We can examine the logic of the arguments, consider how the evidence relates to and supports the theories and consider the comprehensiveness of the explanations. We can resort to practical considerations and assess the methods used to treat personality disorders, and to analyse and predict behaviour. However, these forms of judgement miss the point that these different approaches are based on widely conflicting views of human nature. The evidence is such as to leave us debating for a considerable time without satisfactory resolution. We thus have to resort to criteria that are in some respects unsatisfactory, such as:

- Which theory is more aesthetically pleasing?

- Which approach 'feels' right?

- How does each approach fit with my world view?

Another way to resolve this, however, is to regard these approaches as complementary. They offer two broad research strategies, each of which is capable of telling us about different aspects of human psychology. What each alone reveals is interesting, but partial. So perhaps we should use both approaches and not concentrate on one alone. However, contemporary employee selection methods ignore this advice and use nomothetic methods.

Table 5.9: Nomothetic versus idiographic

The nomothetic approach	The idiographic approach
Has a positivist bias	Has a phenomenological bias
Is generalizing; emphasizes the discovery of laws of human behaviour	Is individualizing; emphasizes the richness and complexity of the unique individual
Is based on statistical study of large groups	Is based on intensive study of individuals
Uses objective questionnaires	Uses projective assessments (tests) and other written and spoken materials
Describes personality in terms of the individual's possession of traits, and trait clusters or personality types	Describes personality in terms of the individual's own understanding and interpretation of their identity
Views personality as composed of discrete and identifiable elements	Believes that personality has to be understood as an indivisible, intelligible whole
Believes that personality is primarily determined by heredity, biology, genetics	Believes that personality is primarily determined by social and cultural processes
Believes that personality is given at birth and cannot be altered	Believes that personality is adaptable, open to change through experience

Selection methods

Choosing the right candidate for a job, or for promotion, is a critical decision. Wrong decisions lead to frustrated employees and poor performance. Selection procedures are costly and time-consuming, and it is expensive to repeat them to recover from errors.

A selection or a promotion decision is a prediction about the ability of a candidate to perform well in a particular job. Predictions are based on an understanding of the demands of the position to be filled, and on information about candidates. Traditionally, candidate information has come from application forms, from the testimony of referees and from face-to-face interviews. The application form provides background details, but is impersonal. Referees notoriously reveal only pleasant things about candidates. Research suggests that interviews can also be unreliable guides to future job performance.

Psychometric methods offer to strengthen the objectivity of selection and promotion decisions by systematically collecting information that has predictive power. Applications of psychometrics developed rapidly during the 1980s and 1990s. There are now over 5,000 such tests and assessments in use.

When choosing a psychometric assessment, for any purpose, a number of criteria are relevant, particularly those concerned with **reliability** and validity.

If the same group of people is given the same test or assessment on two or more occasions, and the results are the same or similar, then the assessment can be described as reliable. This method for establishing reliability is known as 'test–retest reliability'.

The validity of a test or assessment concerns the extent to which it actually measures what it sets out to measure. There are different types of validity, the main ones being face validity (does it look right), construct validity (does it relate to other similar measures) and **predictive validity**. In employee selection, predictive validity is critical.

The key question is, can we predict job performance from personality assessments? In principle, this question is easily answered, using the following method. First, assess a large applicant group. Second, hire them all regardless of their

Reliability refers to the degree to which an assessment or test produces consistent results when the assessment is repeated or when it is conducted in comparable ways.

Predictive validity concerns the extent to which scores on a test or assessment can accurately predict performance or behaviour on other measures.

Table 5.10: Predictive validity of different employee assessment methods

measure	predictive validity
astrology	0.0
graphology	0.0
references	0.13
unstructured interviews	0.31
personality assessments	0.38
biodata	0.40
assessment centres—performance	0.41
ability tests	0.54
work samples	0.55
structured interviews	0.62
assessment centres—promotion	0.68

Based on N. Anderson and V. Shackleton, *Successful Selection Interviewing*, Blackwell, Oxford, 1993.

scores. Third, wait for an appropriate period (say five years). Finally, assess their performance to see whether those with 'good' profiles are high performers, or not. If they are, then you have a valid test.

The evidence shows varying estimates for the predictive validity of personality assessments, but most suggest that it is low. If a test or assessment score predicts job performance accurately, the predictive validity coefficient would be 1.0. If there is no correlation, the coefficient is zero. Table 5.10 shows the estimates for different types of assessment.

There are two points to note from the figures in table 5.10. First, personality assessments have relatively low predictive validity. Second, any method which has a validity coefficient of less than 0.5 is going to be wrong more often than it is right.

Stop and criticize	The links between personality factors and job performance are difficult to establish. Why should this be the case? Explain your reasoning and share this with colleagues.

If you believe that psychometrics cannot make accurate predictions, then you belong to the two-thirds of job candidates who think the same way (Anderson, 1999).

Personality transplants?

In 1994, a merchant bank in London decided that, to compete in a rapidly changing context, it had to change its autocratic 'command and control' style of management and develop participative teamwork instead. One senior manager, 'Mr X', responsible for £500 million of profits a year, had problems shaking off his traditional style: 'he never opened a door with his hands, just kicked it in'. Other staff were afraid to approach or to challenge him. So the bank hired a consultant to address the problem:

- First, Mr X was ordered to see the consultant, who met him at 9.00pm, when Mr X finished work.

- Mr X completed a series of personality assessments, which showed him to be independent, single-minded, determined, forceful and tough on others.

- Ten colleagues of Mr X were asked to provide their assessment of him, pointing out that he was abrasive and insensitive, that he did not delegate to junior colleagues, and that he humiliated people in meetings.

- The consultant produced a 25-page report summarizing these assessments.

How did Mr X respond? He enjoyed the report and regarded the comments as 'a problem to solve'. To improve his interpersonal skills, the consultant asked Mr X to keep a diary of his exchanges with others, noting when and how he got into arguments. These incidents were then discussed with the consultant, to demonstrate how the same results could have been achieved by being less abrasive and impulsive. Part of his problem, apparently, was due to overwork. He worked twelve hours a day, six days a week, and took only one week's holiday a year. Mr X had problems delegating because he wished to protect a less than competent assistant and so did the work himself. He was eventually persuaded to 'let the assistant go'.

Did the 'personality transplant' work? The process lasted two years, at the end of which Mr X was less abrasive, worked as a team member, became more relaxed about work and delegation, and others found him more approachable. The consultant involved argues that the behavioural transformation is stable (implying a personality change) and that Mr X is an effective manager without his traditional aggressive style.

Based on Andrew Rogers, 'Personality transplant tames the boss', *The Sunday Times*, 13 June 1999, p.7.19.

The results of a personality assessment should never be used as the basis of a selection decision. While this may be a useful complement to other methods, personality assessments are poor predictors of performance because:

- people are flexible and multi-faceted, able to develop new skills and behaviours and to adapt to new circumstances; personality assessment captures a fragment of the whole;

- most jobs are multi-faceted in their demands on skill and knowledge, and traits which enhance competence in one task may not improve overall job performance;

- performance depends on many factors: ability, luck, training, payment systems, physical facilities, supervisory style, organization structure, company policies and procedures;

- most jobs change over time, so predictions based on current measures are unreliable;

- nomothetic methods work with populations and large samples, against which individual profiles can be compared; they are not designed to make predictions about individuals;

- in clinical and research settings, most people give honest answers about personality, but these assessments are relatively easy to falsify when job or career is at stake.

Situational interviewing is a form of structured interview with a relatively high predictive validity. Candidates are presented with a series of work-based problems and asked how they would respond. Situations and questions are based on job analysis which focuses on critical knowledge, skills and abilities. Neal Schmitt and David Chan (1998, p.31) give examples of situational interview questions used for selecting emergency telephone operators:

1. Imagine that you tried to help a stranger, for example, with traffic directions, or to get up after a fall, and that person blamed you for his misfortune or yelled at you. What would you do?

2. Suppose a friend calls you and is extremely upset. Apparently, her child has been injured. She begins to tell you, in a hysterical manner, all about her difficulty in getting her baby-sitters, what the child is wearing, what words the child can speak, and so on. What would you do?

3. How would you react if you were a sales clerk, waitress or petrol station attendant and a customer talked back to you, indicating that you should have known something you did not, or telling you that you were not waiting on him or her fast enough?

Candidates' responses are rated for communication skills, emotional control and judgement and can be compared against the actual behaviour of high-level performers in this occupation.

It is difficult for candidates to cheat or to practise their responses to a situational interview, not knowing what specific behaviours and replies are being sought by assessors. Companies using these methods report a high success rate (Maurer, Sue-Chan and Latham, 1999). The brewing company Tetley used situational interviewing long enough to allow it to compare the performance of 'new' managers with 'old' managers selected in a conventional manner (Lunn, 1988). The results are summarized in table 5.11.

Table 5.11: Tetley the brewer gains from situational interviewing

	new group (%)	old group (%)
sales up on last year	12	2
controllable expenses down	14	5
controllable profits up	25	5
house net profit up	17	8

Robert Sternberg (1988; 1999) has designed measures of successful intelligence, that is the ability to operate effectively in a given environment. Sternberg claims that successfully intelligent people have the three kinds of abilities shown in table 5.12. The techniques used to assess this concept in practice are similar to those used in situational interviewing. Sternberg (1999, p.31) reports this example:

> I have developed a test in which a candidate for a sales job would make a phone call and try to sell a product to an examiner. During the call, the candidate has to reply to standardized objections to the sale. Responses to test items are compared against the responses of designated experts in each field, and scoring is done by comparative profile analysis [comparing the profile of the candidate with that of the expert].

The most appropriate combination of techniques for employee assessment is through assessment centres, which were first used during the Second World War by the War Office selection boards. Groups of around six to ten candidates are brought together for one to three days. They are presented, individually and as a group, with a variety of exercises, tests of ability, personality assessments, interviews, work samples, team problem solving and written tasks. Their activities are observed and scored. This approach is useful for selection and promotion, staff development, talent spotting, and career guidance and counselling. The evidence suggests that this combination of techniques significantly improves the probability of selecting and promoting appropriate candidates.

Advocates of assessment centres argue that the information collected about candidates is comprehensive and comparable, and candidates have the opportunity to demonstrate capabilities unlikely to appear in an interview. The self-knowledge gained from the process can also be valuable to the candidate.

Critics point to the investment in time and money required to run assessment centres. There is a need for qualified assessors, and a lack of senior management commitment to the process can give both assessors and candidates inappropriate signals. The indiscriminate use of such methods cannot meet the needs of individual organizations, and the focus on observable and measurable aspects of behaviour overlooks less apparent and less easily assessed skills.

Table 5.12: Dimensions of successful intelligence

analytical	analysing, evaluating, making judgements on abstract data removed from day-to-day practicalities
creative	finding novel, high-quality solutions, going 'beyond the given', 'making do in a rapidly changing world'
practical	the solution of real problems, application of common sense, not dependent on educational qualifications

Does personality assessment have a future? The relationships between personality constructs and job performance are modelled by Ivan Robertson (1994), shown in figure 5.5.

Robertson argues that the link between personality and job performance and career success must be weak. There are too many factors to allow us to make realistic predictions. The model identifies the demands of the job and factors in the organizational context that can influence behaviour at work independently of (or in interaction with) personality. Robertson argues, however, that it is possible to relate personality measures to specific competences, such as judgement, resilience, sensitivity and energy. This argument has strong intuitive appeal. Robertson claims that the research evidence supports this view, and that this is where the future research agenda lies. He concludes that 'When the personality constructs involved are clear and thought is given to the expected link between these constructs and work behaviour, it is likely that worthwhile information may be derived from personality measurement' (Robertson, 1994, p.85).

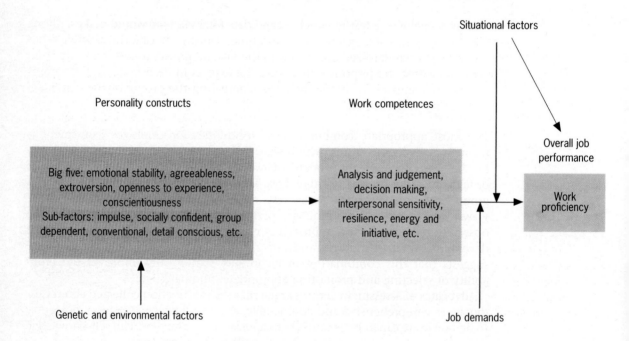

Figure 5.5: Personality and job performance
From I. T. Robertson 'Personality and personnel selection', in C. L. Cooper and D. M. Rousseau (eds), *Trends in Organizational Behaviour*, John Wiley, London, 1994, p. 8.

Recap

1. *Distinguish between type, trait and self theories of personality.*

   - Type theories use a range of perspectives (Hippocrates, Sheldon, Jung) to *classify* individuals using a limited number of personality categories.

   - Trait theories, based on a nomothetic perspective (Eysenck, Costa and McCrae), seek to *profile* the individual's personality across a number of different facets.

   - Self theories, based on an idiographic perspective (Cooley, Mead), seek to *describe* the unique personality of each individual.

2. *Identify the strengths and limitations of formal methods of personality assessment.*

   - Formal methods offer objective and comprehensive assessments of personality. But they are impersonal, based on group norms, don't capture individual uniqueness.

   - Formal methods provide further objective information about job candidates, but the links between personality assessment scores and job performance seem to be weak.

3. *Explain the uses and limitations of objective questionnaires and projective tests as measures of personality.*

   - Objective questionnaires are easy to score and offer quantitative rigour. But they can only be interpreted using group norms; individual scores are meaningless.

   - Projective tests capture the richness and uniqueness of the individual. But they have complex scoring, are subjective, and individual results cannot easily be compared.

4. *Explain the relationship between personality and stress, and identify appropriate individual and organizational stress management strategies.*

   - Type A personalities (competitive, impatient) are more stress-prone than Type B personalities (easy-going, relaxed).

   - Individuals can develop physical and psychological resilience and coping skills.

   - Management has to reduce or remove work-related stressors (job design, management style, adverse working conditions, excessive workload).

5. *Evaluate the benefits and problems of psychometric assessment as a tool to assist management decision making, particularly in selection.*

   - Psychometrics offers objective, systematic, comprehensive and quantitative information. They are also useful in career guidance, counselling and development.

   - Individual scores are meaningless unless interpreted against group norms.

   - It is difficult to predict job performance from a personality profile.

   - Personality assessment can identify strengths in specific areas of competence.

6. *Assess realistically the main characteristics of your own personality.*

   - Current thinking profiles personality on 'the big five' trait clusters of openness, conscientiousness, extroversion, agreeableness and neuroticism (OCEAN). Self theories argue that the self-concept is what is important, not your test scores.

Revision

1. What is 'psychometrics', and what are the main organizational applications? What are the benefits and drawbacks of psychometric assessment in organizational contexts?

2. We all seem to be good implicit personality theorists, but we also seem to be poor judges of personality. How can these two claims be reconciled?

3. What is 'personality', and why is this term difficult to define unambiguously and with precision?

4. What is the difference between 'type' and 'trait' theories of personality? Using at least one example of a trait theory, explain the benefits and problems associated with this approach to personality assessment.

5. Explain the distinction between nomothetic and idiographic perspectives on personality assessment. How do idiographic methods approach the assessment of personality, and what are the advantages and drawbacks of these methods?

Springboard

Cooper, C., Liukkonen, P. and Cartwright, S., 1996, *Stress Prevention in the Workplace: Assessing the Costs and Benefits to Organizations*, European Foundation for the Improvement of Living and Working Conditions, Dublin.

Authoritative text on the organizational causes of stress and effective stress management, exploring as the title suggests the advantages and costs involved.

Doherty, N. and Tyson, S., 1998, *Mental Well Being in the Workplace: A Resource Pack for Management Training and Development*, Health and Safety Executive, London.

Reinforces the argument that stress is an organizational problem, not a private individual issue, and that management needs to address it as such; also provides systematic practical management advice.

Goleman, D., 1995, *Emotional Intelligence: Why It Can Matter More Than IQ*, Bloomsbury, London.

The book which turned the concept of emotional intelligence into a management fad and turned Daniel Goleman into an international management guru. A deceptively easy read, but entertaining if you like this kind of style. One major problem with the argument is that if you are not committed to the organization, to teamworking and to high performance then you lack emotional intelligence. Is that a valid perspective?

Institute of Personnel and Development, 1997, *Key Facts: Psychological Testing*, IPD, London, August.

Uses the term 'testing' while pointing out that 'there are no right or wrong answers' in personality assessment. Offers practical advice on test selection and use, and sets out guidelines for establishing an organizational policy on test use. The IPD also publish a larger guide to psychological testing.

Maslach, C. and Leiter, M.P., 1999, *The Truth About Burnout*, Jossey-Bass, New York.

Argues that, while stress is an employee problem, 'burnout' is a problem particularly associated with management positions, caused by delayering, downsizing, work intensification, and demands for increased flexibility, customer retention and profitability. However, they also argue that this is an organizational management problem, not an individual one, requiring organizational solutions.

Sternberg, R., 1999, 'Survival of the fit test', *People Management*, vol.4, no.24, 10 December, pp.29–31.

Sternberg is critical of the lack of predictive power of psychometrics and of the lack of development in this field in this century. Proposes instead the development of tests of 'successful intelligence', defined loosely as the ability to function effectively in a given context (so the precise definition of this concept differs from one setting to another). Three management consultants who use conventional psychometrics are given the opportunity to respond to his criticisms (pp.31–3).

Zimbardo, P., McDermott, M., Jansz, J. and Metaal, N., 1995, *Psychology: A European Text*, HarperCollins, London.

A well-presented standard introductory text, chapter 12, pp.440–93, provides a more detailed and comprehensive treatment of the psychology of personality and individual differences than is possible in this text.

Home viewing

Glengarry Glen Ross (1992, director James Foley) is based in a Chicago real-estate office. To boost flagging sales, the 'downtown' manager Blake (played by Alec Baldwin) introduces a sales contest. First prize is a Cadillac Eldorado, second prize is a set of steak knives, third prize is dismissal. The sales staff include Ricky Roma (Al Pacino), Shelley Levene (Jack Lemmon), George Aaronow (Alan Arkin) and Dave Moss (Ed Harris). In the first ten minutes of the film, note how Blake in his 'motivational pep talk' conforms to the stereotype of the extrovert, competitive, 'macho' salesman. Observe the effects of his 'pep talk' on the behaviour of the sales team. Does Blake offer a stereotype which salespeople should copy? From a postmodern perspective, the film portrays the construction of individual identity through a 'performance' conditioned by the organizational context. This contrasts with the psychological view of identity determined by personality.

OB in literature

Bret Easton Ellis, *American Psycho*, Random House/Pan Books, New York/London, 1991.

How does the psychopath appear 'ordinary' to casual observers and fit effortlessly into society? What 'normal' personality traits has the author given his 'hero', Patrick Bateman? Here is a character with enormous intellect but lacking in what Daniel Goleman (1995; 1998) describes as 'emotional intelligence'.

David Ireland, *The Chosen*, Random House Australia, Sydney, 1997.

In drawing personality portraits of 52 diverse Australians in the town of Lost River, what aspects of their lives, appearance and behaviour does the novelist use? Note the personality traits and types described in each portrait. Are they Type A or Type B? Extrovert or introvert? Neurotic or stable? Can you give each character an OCEAN profile?

Chapter exercises

1: How stress-prone are you?

Objectives

1. To give you an opportunity to assess your personality in terms of propensity to suffer stress-related disease.

2. To assess critically this type of personality assessment method.

Briefing

This questionnaire is designed to identify whether you have a Type A or a Type B personality. Here are eight pairs of statements describing aspects of personality and behaviour. For each pair, decide which is more accurate as a description of you and circle the appropriate point on the seven-point rating scale. Be honest in your ratings. There are no 'right' or 'wrong' answers to this questionnaire.

I am casual about appointments	1 2 3 4 5 6 7	I am never late
I am not competitive	1 2 3 4 5 6 7	I am very competitive
I never feel rushed, even under pressure	1 2 3 4 5 6 7	I always feel short of time
I take things one at a time	1 2 3 4 5 6 7	I try to do too many things at once
I concentrate on finishing what I am doing right now	1 2 3 4 5 6 7	I am always thinking about what I am going to do next
I take my time, do things slowly	1 2 3 4 5 6 7	I do things, even walking and eating, fast
I like to express my feelings	1 2 3 4 5 6 7	I prefer to keep my feelings private
I have many interests	1 2 3 4 5 6 7	I have few interests outside work

When you are finished, calculate your score by totalling the numbers you have circled and multiplying that sum by three. Put your score in this box:

Interpretation

If your points total is:	Your personality type is:
less than 50	B
50 to 89	B+
90 to 119	A−
120 to 145	A
more than 145	A+

Discussion

tick the appropriate column

	low	medium	high
How would you rate the reliability of this assessment?			
How would you rate the face validity of this assessment?			
How would you rate the predictive validity of this assessment?			

2: The big five locator

Objectives

1. To assess your personality profile on 'the big five' personality trait clusters.
2. To assess the value of this kind of personality assessment in career counselling and employment selection.

Briefing

A 'big five' personality assessment involves either a short questionnaire (the NEO–FFI with 60 questions covering the five factors) or the 'full facet' version (the NEO–PI–R with 240 questions covering all thirty traits). These assessments can also be used for management development, in leadership and interpersonal skills, and for the assessment of conflict management and decision-making styles (Howard and Howard, 1993).

The big five locator, on the other hand, is an easy-to-use instrument for assessing an individual's personality profile. It can also be used to explore and resolve team conflict. It is presented here for demonstration and discussion and should be regarded as providing only an approximate measure of individual traits and individual differences.

Scoring

Calculate your **negative emotionality** score by adding the numbers you circled on the *first* row of each five-line grouping: row 1 + row 6 + row 11 + row 16 + row 21:
score = _____

Calculate your **extroversion** score by adding the numbers you circled on the *second* row of each five-line grouping: row 2 + row 7 + row 12 + row 17 + row 22: score = _____

Calculate your **openness** score by adding the numbers you circled on the *third* row of each five-line grouping: row 3 + row 8 + row 13 + row 18 + row 23: score = _____

Calculate your **agreeableness** score by adding the numbers you circled on the *fourth* row of each five-line grouping: row 4 + row 9 + row 14 + row 19 + row 24: score = _____

Calculate your **conscientiousness** score by adding the numbers you circled on the *last* row of each five-line grouping: row 5 + row 10 + row 15 + row 20 + row 25:
score = _____

Enter your five scores in this table, noting the different order (back to OCEAN).

trait	score
openness	_____
conscientiousness	_____
extroversion	_____
agreeableness	_____
negative emotionality	_____

On the centre scale, circle the point which most accurately describes you between each of the two terms presented. If the two terms are equally accurate in their description, then mark the middle point.

1	Eager	5	4	3	2	1	Calm
2	Prefer being with others	5	4	3	2	1	Prefer being alone
3	A dreamer	5	4	3	2	1	No-nonsense
4	Courteous	5	4	3	2	1	Abrupt
5	Neat	5	4	3	2	1	Messy
6	Cautious	5	4	3	2	1	Confident
7	Optimistic	5	4	3	2	1	Pessimistic
8	Theoretical	5	4	3	2	1	Practical
9	Generous	5	4	3	2	1	Selfish
10	Decisive	5	4	3	2	1	Open-ended
11	Discouraged	5	4	3	2	1	Upbeat
12	Exhibitionist	5	4	3	2	1	Private
13	Follow imagination	5	4	3	2	1	Follow authority
14	Warm	5	4	3	2	1	Cold
15	Stay focused	5	4	3	2	1	Easily distracted
16	Easily embarrassed	5	4	3	2	1	Don't give a damn
17	Outgoing	5	4	3	2	1	Cool
18	Seek novelty	5	4	3	2	1	Seek routine
19	Team player	5	4	3	2	1	Independent
20	A preference for order	5	4	3	2	1	Comfortable with chaos
21	Distractible	5	4	3	2	1	Unflappable
22	Conversational	5	4	3	2	1	Thoughtful
23	Comfortable with ambiguity	5	4	3	2	1	Prefer things clear-cut
24	Trusting	5	4	3	2	1	Sceptical
25	On time	5	4	3	2	1	Procrastinate

When you have calculated your five scores, transfer them to this interpretation sheet by putting a cross at the approximate point on each scale:

Big five locator score interpretation

low openness:	preserver	moderator	explorer	high openness:
practical, conservative, efficient, expert	10	15	20	curious, liberal, impractical, likes novelty
low conscientiousness:	flexible	balanced	focused	**high conscientiousness:**
spontaneous, fun-loving, experimental, unorganized	10	15	20	dependable, organized, disciplined, cautious, stubborn
low extroversion:	introvert	ambivert	extrovert	**high extroversion:**
private, independent, works alone, reserved	10	15	20	assertive, sociable, warm, optimistic
low agreeableness:	challenger	negotiator	adapter	**high agreeableness:**
sceptical, tough, aggressive, self-interest	10	15	20	trusting, humble, altruistic, team player
low negative emotionality:	resilient	responsive	reactive	**high negative emotionality:**
secure, unflappable, unresponsive, guilt-free	10	15	20	excitable, worrying, reactive, alert

Discussion

1. How accurate, in your view, is your personality profile as revealed by this assessment?

2. Does this assessment indicate that you have one or more 'dominant' traits?

3. Given your profile, what jobs or occupations would you not be suitable for?

4. How helpful is this personality assessment in enabling a manager to make predictions about a potential employee's future job performance?

5. How valuable is this personality assessment in enabling a careers guidance counsellor effectively to advise clients on suitable and unsuitable career options?

This exercise is based on:
Pierce J. Howard, Phyllis L. Medina and Jane Mitchell Howard, 'The big five locator: a quick assessment tool for consultants and trainers', *The 1996 Annual: Volume 1, Training*, Pfeiffer & Company, San Diego, 1996, pp.107–22.

Chapter 6 Communication

Key concepts

communication process   coding
decoding   feedback
non-verbal behaviour   impression management
high-context culture   low-context culture
noise   communication climate

Learning objectives

When you have read this chapter, you should be able to define those key concepts in your own words, and you should also be able to:

1. Explain the main components of the interpersonal communication process.
2. Identify the main barriers to effective interpersonal communication.
3. Understand the effective use of different questioning techniques, conversation controls and listening skills.
4. Explain the nature and significance of non-verbal behaviour.
5. Understand the nature and mechanisms of impression management skills and techniques.
6. Understand the ways in which corporate communication can be used to manipulate understanding and encourage compliance with management directions.

Why study communication?

There are at least five reasons why the study of communication is central to a theoretical and practical understanding of organizational behaviour:

1. The effectiveness of communication is central both to organizational performance and to individual promotion and career prospects.

2. Very few people work alone, and the job of most managers in particular involves interacting with other people—often for more than 90 per cent of their time.

3. Although the topic is relatively well understood, communication continues to be regarded as a major problem in many organizations.

4. In an increasingly diverse multicultural society, sensitivity to the norms and expectations of other cultures is vital to effective cross-cultural communication.

5. New communication technologies have brought about fundamental changes in the ways in which we communicate with each other, both in and out of work.

This chapter explores communication skills relevant to individual and organizational effectiveness. Most aspects of organizational behaviour involve communication. Responding to the job advertisement, attending the selection interview, meeting new colleagues, dealing with suppliers and customers, explaining problems to the boss, negotiating for a pay rise, liaising with other departments, attending meetings—all involve communication.

Despite wide variation in the work that managers do, it has long been recognized that most managers spend most of their time in meetings and in conversation, talking and listening, networking and influencing, gathering information and negotiating. The work of Henry Mintzberg (1973), for example, emphasized the monitoring, informational, decision-making and interpersonal aspects of the work of chief executives. From his study of general managers, John Kotter (1982; 1999) showed that most of their time was spent in conversation, often on topics not directly related to the business but nevertheless central to maintaining networks and relationships and to developing goals and action plans.

This chapter also explores the barriers to effective communication. Despite the importance of the topic, communication is still regarded as a major contemporary organizational problem. From their survey of managers' attitudes to trends in organization development and change, Buchanan, Claydon and Doyle (1999) report widespread concern about the quality and effectiveness of organizational communication, summarized in table 6.1.

Globalization [**link**, chapter 2, the world outside] and greater international mobility mean that we are now likely to find ourselves working alongside people from other countries and cultures. Understanding cultural diversity has become a key organizational communication skill. Different cultures have differing norms

Table 6.1: Management perceptions of organizational communication	
survey item	**percentage agreement**
Communication is too general a term. We need to plan more carefully the content, timing and targets of communication.	96
We need new and creative approaches to the problem of organizational communication.	85
We do try to communicate changes effectively, but people seem to be suffering 'information overload' in this area.	72
Changes in my organization are assessed on results, not on whether people feel happy or not about management communication.	67
I don't think that the senior management in my organization has a good understanding of the complexities of effective communication.	54

Communication between different occupational groups can sometimes be difficult. SQUAWKS, for example, are problems noted by United States Air Force pilots and left for maintenance crews to fix before their next flight. Here are some actual complaints logged by pilots and the replies from the maintenance crews (from *Focus*, May 1999, p.18):

pilot complaint	maintenance crew response
Test flight okay, except auto land very rough	Auto land not installed on this aircraft
DME volume unbelievably loud	Volume set to more believable level
Friction locks cause throttle levers to stick	That's what they're there for
Number three engine missing	Engine found on right wing after brief search
Target radar hums	Reprogrammed target radar with the words
Aircraft handles funny	Aircraft warned to straighten up and be serious
Dead bugs on windshield	Live bugs on order
Left inside main tyre almost needs replacement	Almost replaced left inside main tyre
Evidence of leak on right main landing gear	Evidence removed
IFF inoperative	IFF always inoperative in OFF mode
Something loose in cockpit.	Something tightened in cockpit

concerning the ways in which conversations should be handled, including appropriate greetings, the use of eye contact, suitable topics for discussion, the appropriate physical distance between speakers and the interpretation of gestures. Sensitivity to cultural differences in communication has thus become increasingly important.

One other factor shaping the conduct of organizational communication is the proliferation of new technologies, particularly video conferencing, e-mail, the internet and corporate intranets, and mobile telephony. These technologies make person-to-person communication faster, easier and less expensive, regardless of geographical distance. Do these technologies have implications for interpersonal communication different from those of the familiar telephone, which has been with us for some time?

A model of interpersonal communication: coding and decoding

Conversation: a competitive sport in which the first person to draw breath is declared the listener.

In most (not all) cultures, conversation is a social imperative in which silences are not allowed (Finland is different). Normally, as soon as one person stops talking, another takes their turn. The currency of conversation is information. We ask you the time. You tell us the time. Information has been transmitted. Interpersonal communication has been achieved. However, communication is more subtle and more interesting than this illustration suggests.

The **communication process** involves the transmission of information, and the exchange of meaning, between at least two people.

We will concentrate first on interpersonal communication, because of its significance in understanding organizational behaviour. A more detailed study would recognize the significance of other aspects of communication, including the use of different media and mass communication. The principles that we will explore, however, have wide application. For the moment, let us focus on 'one-on-one' communication, between two people, and let us examine more carefully our definition of the **communication process**.

Stop and criticize

We all have experience of ineffective communication. Either the other person misunderstood what you had to say, or you misunderstood what they were tying to tell you. Remember the last time this happened? What went wrong? Can you establish the cause or causes of that communication failure? Share your analysis with colleagues and establish whether there are common causes.

We do not passively 'receive' messages from other people. We process incoming messages, to interpret or to decode them. To the extent that we interpret communication from others in the manner they intended, and they in turn interpret our communication accurately, then we can claim that our communication is effective. However, interpersonal communication is an error-prone process.

Interpersonal communication typically involves more than the simple exchange or transmission of information. Pay close attention to the next person who asks you what time it is. You will almost always be able to tell something about how they are feeling, and about why they need to know. You will be able to tell, perhaps, if they are in a hurry, or if they are anxious or nervous, or bored with waiting for something or someone. In other words, their question has a purpose or a meaning. Although it is not always stated directly, we can usually work out what that purpose or meaning is from the context and from their behaviour.

The same considerations apply to your response. Your reply suggests, at least, a willingness to be helpful, may imply friendship, and may also indicate that you share the same concern as the person asking the question (we are going to be late; when will this film start?). However, your reply can also indicate frustration and annoyance: 'five minutes since the last time you asked me!' Communication, therefore, involves more than the transmission of information. Interpersonal communication is a process that involves the exchange of meaning.

This process of exchange is illustrated in figure 6.1, which identifies the principal elements in the interpersonal communication process. This model is based on the seminal work of Shannon and Weaver (1949), who were concerned with signal processing in electronic systems rather than with the organizational communication issues explored here.

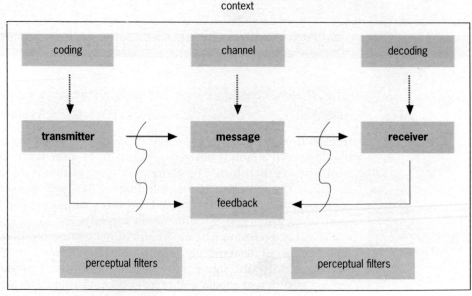

Figure 6.1: Exchanging meaning: a model of the communication process

Communication is an error-prone process

I rang the bell of a small bed-and-breakfast place, whereupon a lady appeared at an upstairs window. 'What do you want?' she asked. 'I want to stay here', I replied. 'Well, stay there then', she said and banged the window shut.

Chick Murray, Scottish comedian

Coding refers to the stage in the interpersonal communication process in which the transmitter chooses how to articulate and express that message for transmission to someone else.
Decoding refers to the stage in the interpersonal communication process in which the recipient interprets a message transmitted to them by someone else.

At the heart of this model, we have a transmitter sending a message to a receiver. We will assume that the channel is face-to-face, 'one-on-one' rather than over a telephone, or through a letter or memo, or a video conference, or electronic mail. It is useful to think of the way in which the transmitter phrases and expresses the message as a **coding** process; the transmitter chooses words and also chooses how the message will be expressed (loudly and with exasperation, or quietly and in a relaxed and friendly manner, for example). We can say that communication has been successful if the message is accurately **decoded** by the receiver; did they understand the language used, and appreciate the exasperation or friendship?

This is a particularly useful way of examining the communication process because it identifies many of the problems that can arise and also points to solutions. There are many ways in which the coding and decoding aspects of the process can go wrong. Some fairly common terms and expressions, for example, can be particularly awkward, such as:

term	popular use	dictionary definition
decimate	devastate	cut by ten per cent
exotic	colourful, glamorous	from another country
aggravate	to annoy, to irritate	to make worse
avid	keen, enthusiastic	greedy, desirous

The branch manager who receives from head office an instruction to 'decimate' his or her salesforce would thus be advised to check the original coding of the message before taking action. Using the dictionary definition of the word 'exotic' implies that Daewoo, Hyundai, Skoda and Lada are 'exotic' motor cars, in Britain. To be successful, therefore, both the transmitters and receivers in the communication process need to share a common 'codebook' and also need to use that 'codebook' consistently.

Language is also used to 'soften' or disguise unpleasant events. Employees being made redundant, for example, may be 'given the pink slip', 'downsized', 'rightsized', 'delayered', invited to 'take gardening leave', to 'spend more time with the family' or to 'put their careers on hold'. They may also be 'counselled on', 'repositioned', urged to 'develop their careers elsewhere' or to 'explore other opportunities for their talents', but they are rarely 'given the chop'.

Stop and criticize

From your experience, what other terms and expressions create coding and decoding problems?

Identify specific examples—which can sometimes be humorous (like the man who asked for wild duck in a restaurant. 'I don't have wild duck, sir', replied the waiter, 'But I can annoy one for you').

Perceptual filters are characteristics of the individual that interfere with the effective transmission and receipt of messages, such as predispositions to hear, or not to hear, particular types of information, or preoccupations which divert attention elsewhere.

The communication process is further complicated by the **perceptual filters** which affect what we say, and which in turn affect what we hear and how we hear it. When you asked what time it was, did you 'hear' the frustration or friendship in the response? Or did you simply focus on the time issue, because that was more important to you? How do perceptual filters affect communication [**link**, chapter 7, perception]? The transmitter of a message has motives, objectives, personality traits, values, biases and prejudices, which colour the content and expression of communication. We decide the information we wish to reveal, and we decide which information to withhold or conceal from others. We do not always perform this filtering consciously. Similarly, at the receiving end, perceptual filtering can affect what is heard, what is decoded, what is not decoded and the way in which the message is understood.

There is a further complicating factor—the physical, social and cultural context or setting. The casual remark by a colleague across a restaurant table ('we could all be redundant by Christmas') may be dismissed. The same casual remark by a colleague across an office desk can be a source of considerable alarm. An innocent gesture in one culture can cause offence in another. Status differences colour our communication. The style and content of conversation often depends on our relationships with others. We do not reveal to the boss what we reveal to colleagues. The style and content can change in a striking manner when organizational relationships are 'suspended', such as during an office party.

Noise concerns factors extraneous to the interpersonal communication process but which interfere with or distract attention from the transmission and reception of the intended meaning. Noise is 'anything that gets in the way'.

Electronics engineers use the term **noise** to refer to anything which interferes with a communication process.

Interpersonal communication suffers from noise, which covers more than the sound of machinery, telephones and other people talking in the background. Noise can be defined as anything that gets in the way. This includes coding and decoding difficulties and errors, perceptual filters, anything that interferes with the integrity of our chosen channel, and issues arising from our relationships with other people in the organization. Our motives, feelings and state of health can also constitute noise. For example, the effectiveness of our coding and decoding can deteriorate with anxiety, pressure, stress, enthusiasm or excitement.

Noise constitutes a barrier to effective communication. Our past experiences condition the way in which we see things today and lead us to filter what we transmit and what we receive. Communication stumbles when transmitter and receiver have different frames of reference and do not share experience and understanding, even where they share a common language. We make judgements about the honesty, integrity, trustworthiness and credibility of others, and decode their messages and act on them (or not) accordingly. People in an organizational setting may have time to reflect, or they may be under considerable time pressure, which will affect the care and attention devoted to communication. Some of us, from time to time, suffer from communication overload (or information overload), and our effectiveness can deteriorate for this reason also.

Feedback involves mechanisms through which the transmitter of a message in interpersonal communication can detect whether and how a message has been received and decoded.

There is a final aspect of our communication model which we have still to consider: **feedback** [**link**, chapter 4, learning].

When we communicate face to face, we can usually tell if the other person likes us, or if they agree with us, or if they are interested in what we have to say. We can usually tell if they don't understand what we are saying, if they disagree with us, or if they are simply bored and don't want to listen any longer. How do we know this? Well, they may simply say 'that's interesting', or 'I fundamentally disagree with your view', or 'I have to catch my bus now'. We can also tell from other cues, such as the tone of their replies, the expression on their face, the posture of their body or their limb gestures. We will explore the coding and decoding of non-verbal behaviour, or body language, later in the chapter.

When we communicate face to face, we get instant feedback in what others say and in how they say it. Our ability to exchange meaning effectively is greatly assisted by this rich feedback loop. Our communication can be awkward where feedback is delayed, or absent. Feedback allows us to check constantly the accuracy of the coding and decoding processes. We ask a question, see the other person look annoyed or puzzled, realize that we have not worded our question appropriately and 'recode' the message. Face to face, if we are paying attention, this can work well and work smoothly. We can do this to some extent over the telephone, decoding the tone of the other person's voice. With other more formal and more distant forms of communication, feedback can be slow or non-existent, and we need to take considerably more care over our coding, particularly with important messages.

Stop and criticize	Think of the people with whom you communicate regularly. What are the main barriers to effective communication in your experience? What would you have to do to improve the effectiveness of your communication?

We can be careless coders and lazy listeners. What might at first appear to be a simple process can be highly error-prone. Both sides of the exchange, coding and decoding, are subject to error. We cannot confidently assume that receivers will always decode our messages in a manner that leaves them with the meaning that we wanted to transmit. It is perhaps obvious to claim that communication processes are central to organizational effectiveness, and to the quality of working life, but this claim has major practical implications. We assume that organizations will function better if communication is open, if relationships are based on mutual understanding and trust, if relationships are co-operative rather than competitive, if people work together in teams, and if decisions are reached in a participative way. These features, however, are not widespread.

Some of the main barriers to communication concern:

power differences | research consistently shows that employees distort upward communication and that superiors often have a limited understanding of subordinates' roles, experiences and problems

gender differences | men and women use different conversational styles, which can lead to misunderstanding; men tend to talk more and give information, while women tend to listen and reflect more

physical surroundings | apart from noisy machinery, room size and layout also influence our ability to see others and our readiness to participate in conversations and discussions

language | even within a single country, variations in accent and dialect can make communication difficult; the English

| | spoken in London is not the same as the English spoken in Birmingham, Llandudno, Glasgow or Aberdeen |
| cultural diversity | different cultures have different norms and expectations concerning formal and informal conversations; lack of awareness of those norms creates misunderstanding |

What guidelines can we derive from this analysis to improve our communication? The following general advice applies in many specific contexts, such as selection interviewing, appraisal, counselling, joint problem solving or simply information gathering.

face to face	when we are able to speak with someone directly, we can use the feedback constantly to check the coding and decoding processes, and to correct mistakes and misunderstanding
reality checks	we should not assume that others will necessarily decode our messages in the way we intended, and we should instead check the way in which our messages have been interpreted
time and place	the right message delivered in the wrong place or at the wrong time is more likely to be decoded incorrectly, or even ignored, so choose the time and place with sensitivity and care
the 'you' attitude	put yourself in the other person's position, try to see things the way they see things, try to decode the message the way they might decode it, listen attentively to their feedback—adopt what Maureen Guirdham (1995) calls the 'you' attitude

Verbal communication: conversation control and listening skills

The word 'verbal' is one of those terms that can cause coding and decoding problems. 'Verbal' means 'in words'. However, words can be either spoken or written. The expressions 'verbal agreement' and 'verbal warning' can thus refer either to oral or to written arrangements. In this section we will concentrate on verbal communication. In the following section, we will shift our attention to non-verbal communication.

Most conversations involve an exchange of information—or more correctly, an exchange of meaning. How do we get the information we want? We achieve this by adopting a range of questioning techniques. The seven main types of question are shown in table 6.2. Here we are attaching labels to conversation control methods that we all use as a matter of routine, unconsciously. However, by using these labels, it becomes easier to analyse the conversation control methods of others, and it also becomes easier for us to make conscious choices about how to conduct our own side of a conversation more effectively.

The first basic distinction in question types is between *closed* and *open* questions. Closed questions are so-called because they invite a factual statement in reply, or a simple 'yes' or 'no' response. Open questions, in contrast, invite the person responding to reveal information. Predict the differences in response to these two questions, the first closed, the second open:

Will you have dinner with me this evening?
What are you doing this evening?

Table 6.2: Questioning techniques

question type	illustration	uses
closed	Did you enjoy the movie?	to get a 'yes' or 'no' answer; to obtain simple factual information; to establish early conversation control
open	What did you think of that movie?	to introduce a subject; to encourage further discussion; to keep the other person talking
probe	Can you tell me more about that?	to follow up an open question, to get more information, to demonstrate interest
reflective	You thought the acting was poor?	to demonstrate interest and concern, to encourage disclosure of feelings and emotions
multiple	What did you think of the movie, and wasn't the star excellent in that role, and did you think that the ending was rather sudden?	none: confuses the listener; gives them a choice of question to which to respond
leading	You didn't see anyone leaving the house then?	to get the answer that you expect to hear
hypothetical	What would happen if . . . ?	to encourage creative thinking in some circumstances

It seems as though closed questions are limited, while open questions are more effective. If the purpose is to get the other person to divulge information, then this assessment is correct. However, closed questions are especially useful in two settings. First, where all that is required is simple factual information: 'Are you coming to the meeting or not?' Open questions invite the discussion of irrelevant information, for which there may be no time.

Second, interviewers often begin with a short series of closed questions in order to establish the conversation pattern. We have all had experience of conversations where the other person took control, giving us information which we did not want. Closed questioning can avoid this. Consider the following questioning sequence used at the beginning of an interview:

What is your current job title?
How long have you been in your present position?
Have you worked for any other employers?
What was your previous position?

This can help to establish the conversation pattern by signalling to the other person, 'I ask the questions, you give the answers'. Usually, by the time the third or fourth closed question has been answered, the person being interviewed will wait in silence for the interviewer to ask their next question and will not begin talking about some other issue.

Probes are simply another type of open question. Probes indicate that the listener is interested in what the other person is saying. In most instances, that indication of interest encourages the disclosure of further information.

The *reflective* statement is a particularly powerful technique for maintaining rapport and for encouraging the disclosure of information, particularly concerning feelings and emotions. Simple in essence, all that you have to do is to mirror or reflect back to the person an emotion that they have 'given' to you. The feeling or emotion expressed can be spoken ('you said that you didn't enjoy your holiday') or it can reflect an unspoken, non-verbal expression ('you look particularly happy this morning'). As with probes, reflective statements signal interest and concern and usually encourage the other person to continue disclosing information.

Multiple questions and *leading* questions are rarely used by trained interviewers. Multiples are often heard on radio and television, particularly when politicians are being asked about their positions and views on topical subjects. Leading questions are particularly ineffective when fresh information is required. Watch a police drama on television and identify how many times witnesses and suspects are confronted with questions like these:

So you didn't see anyone else leave the house after five o'clock?
You can't think of anything else that would help us identify the murderer?
So these stolen televisions were put in your garage by somebody else?

Hypothetical questions can be useful in stimulating creative 'blue skies' thinking, but used in selection interviewing this only reveals how well the candidate can handle hypothetical questions and says little or nothing about their future job performance.

We also control our conversations through a range of conscious and unconscious verbal and non-verbal signals which tell the parties to a conversation, for example, when one has finished an utterance and when it is somebody else's turn to speak. These signals reveal agreement, friendship, dispute and dislike—emotions which in turn shape the further response of the listener. The four main conversation control signals are explained in table 6.3. Note that the uses and implications of pauses in conversation depend heavily on the context.

Table 6.3: Conversation control signals

signal	example	meaning
lubricators	'uh huh', 'mmm, mmm' and other grunts and groans	I'm listening, keep talking, I'm interested
inhibitors	'what!', 'really', 'oh!' and similar loud interjections	I'm surprised, I don't agree, I've heard enough of this
bridges	'I'd like to leave that and move on to ask you about . . .'	I'd like to make a clean link to the next conversation topic
pauses (1)	about two seconds silence	in normal conversation: same as lubricators
pauses (2)	silence of three seconds or longer	in a threat context: I'm going to wait until I get an answer
pauses (3)	silence of three seconds or longer	in a counselling context: I'll give you time to think

Stop and criticize

Record a television police drama, a magazine programme or a news broadcast. Watch somebody being interviewed; police interviewing suspect, host interviewing celebrity, news reader interviewing politician. Identify the questioning techniques used. Can you identify errors in technique? What advice would you give to the interviewer to help improve their questioning?

Replay the same interview with the sound off. Can you identify any communication barriers which made this exchange less effective than necessary, concerning, for example, physical layout, posture, timing, non-verbal behaviour? What further advice would you give to the interviewer to help them improve their technique?

When conversing normally, we use these signals unconsciously or habitually. However, an awareness of the methods being used can allow us quite easily to bring these under conscious control. Therapists and counsellors, for example, use a range of methods to shape conversations in ways that allow their clients to articulate their difficulties and to work towards identifying appropriate solutions. Managers holding employment selection, appraisal or promotion interviews need to understand conversation control techniques in order to handle these particular interactions effectively.

We can also use conversation controls to shape or steer the behaviour of others, to achieve our own preferred ends. Conscious command of these methods increases our ability to manipulate and control others. G.R. Walther (1993; see Huczynski, 1996, pp.35–41) offers a summary of 'high-power' and 'low-power' conversation tactics. Table 6.4 defines the seven main conversation control strategies used by powertalkers:

Table 6.4: Powertalking strategies	
Positive talk	Powertalkers respond positively, make genuine commitments, have high expectations, are optimistic, avoid conditional phrases, seek creative solutions, look for the benefits.
Give credit	Powertalkers either alter or ignore their shortcomings, describe their achievements positively, neither apologize nor justify, praise others for their success.
Learn from experience	Powertalkers say 'I learned' instead of 'I failed', seek the positive in the face of setbacks, think positive when feeling low, focus on options rather than on regrets.
Accept responsibility	Powertalkers admit their own feelings, accept responsibility for actions, control their use of time.
Persuade others	Powertalkers emphasize benefits, keep options open, seek ways to improve relationships, focus on positives, accept ideas of others.
Decisive speaking	Powertalkers commit to specific targets, extract detailed information, set realistic goals, decide what to say and then say it.
Tell the truth	Powertalkers avoid suspicious and misleading phrases, say 'no' when they mean 'no', avoid self-criticism, respect others with whom they interact—remembering and using others' names.

Table 6.5: Low-power indicators	
Hedges and qualifiers	'Maybe it has some strengths'
Irritators	'you know', 'sort of', 'kinda'
Intensifiers	'really', 'awfully', 'horrendously'
Tags	'aren't they?', 'didn't you?'
Hesitations	'um, er, ah, uhh, well'
Excessive questions	signal uncertainty and a need for attention

Table 6.5 summarizes conversation styles that signal uncertainty and lack of self-confidence and which also suggest that the speaker has low power (Huczynski, 1996).

As indicated earlier, gender differences can create barriers to effective communication. Deborah Tannen (1990; 1995) argues that boys and girls acquire different linguistic styles, and that these differences affect the career prospects of men and women at work. A linguistic style is a characteristic speaking pattern which includes factors such as tone of voice, speed of speech, loudness, directness or indirectness, pacing and pausing, choice of words, and the extent to which we use jokes, stories, figures of speech, questions and apologies. Tannen (1995, p.140) claims that 'Girls learn conversational rituals that focus on the rapport dimension of relationships whereas boys tend to learn rituals that focus on the status dimension'.

Boys as they grow up play in large groups, emphasize status and leadership, display their knowledge and abilities, challenge others, take 'centre stage' by telling jokes and stories, and try to acquire status in their group by giving orders to others. Girls focus on a small group of friends, sharing secrets with their best friend, emphasizing similarities and playing down ways in which someone could be better than others. Girls tend to be more modest, appear less self-assured and ostracize those who claim superiority.

These childhood differences affect adult behaviour in organizational settings. Men tend to think more in hierarchical terms and are concerned with status, power and with being 'one up'. Men strive to retain 'one up' by driving and by interrupting conversations. Men jockey for position by putting others down, appear competent by acting confidently and appear knowledgeable by asking fewer questions. Men tend to give negative feedback quickly and look for opportunities to criticize rather than pay others compliments.

Women are more likely to avoid putting others down and to act in ways that are face-saving for others. Women can appear to lack self-confidence by playing down their certainty and by expressing doubt more openly. Women also appear less self-assured and knowledgeable by asking more questions, tend to soften criticism by offering positive feedback first and pay others compliments more often than men do.

These linguistic differences are particularly important when speaking of achievements. Men tend to be more direct and use 'I' more often. Women tend to speak indirectly and speak of 'we' when talking about accomplishments. In summary, men tend to adopt linguistic styles and to behave in ways that are more likely to get them recognized and that are more likely to earn them attributions of effectiveness and competence. Women adopting a more 'masculine' linguistic style can be seen as too aggressive. Tannen advises us all to be more aware of these differences in linguistic styles, and to pay attention to the dynamics of our conversations.

Stop and criticize	Tannen was writing about women in America in the mid-1990s. To what extent does her analysis apply to linguistic and behavioural differences between men and women in your culture today?

Aboriginal culture and communication

Australian Aboriginal culture includes aspects of verbal and non-verbal behaviour which are quite different from most European and North American communication styles.

- Aborigines value brevity in verbal communication rather than detailed elaboration, and simple 'yes' and 'no' replies are common.
- There is no word for 'thank you' in Aboriginal languages. People do things for you as an obligation.
- In some Aboriginal tribes, it is unlawful to use the name of a dead person.
- The terms 'full-blood', 'half-caste', 'quarter-caste', 'native' and 'part-Aborigine' are regarded as offensive by Aborigines.
- Long silences in Aboriginal conversation are common and are not regarded as awkward.
- To some Aboriginal people, it is not acceptable to look another straight in the eye.
- Some Aboriginal groups do not allow men and women to mix freely.
- Aborigines do not feel that it is necessary to look at the person who is speaking to them.
- Aborigines do not feel that it is necessary to attend meetings (an interview, for example) at specific times.

How do these norms and preferences compare with the communication style of your culture?

Based on Richard Nelson-Jones, *Introduction to Counselling Skills*, Sage, London, 2000, p.54.

The significance of non-verbal communication

Which part of the human anatomy is capable of expanding up to ten times in size when we are emotionally aroused? The answer, of course, is the pupil of the eye. When we look at something we find interesting—an image, a scene, a person— our pupils dilate. When we lose interest, our pupils contract. There is, therefore, a physiological basis in non-verbal behaviour for the 'dark limpid pools' to which romantic novelists are apt to refer.

When we interact with others face to face, we are constantly sending and receiving messages through the signs, expressions, gestures, postures and vocal mannerisms that we seem to adopt unconsciously. In other words, **non-verbal communication** accompanies our verbal communication. As a general rule, we code and transmit factual information primarily through verbal behaviours. We code and transmit our feelings and emotions, and the strength of our feeling, through our non-verbal communication.

The term 'body language' has come into use in recent years as our knowledge of this fascinating side of behaviour has developed. We use the more cumbersome technical term here for two reasons. First, non-verbal behaviour is extremely rich and varied, and the term 'body language' is either partial or inaccurate if it is taken to imply a concern only with bodily movements and postures. Second, the

Non-verbal communication is the process of coding meaning through behaviours such as facial expressions, limb gestures and body postures, which do not involve the use of words.

Calvin and Hobbes

term 'body language' seems to suggest, and in the hands of some commentators does tend to imply, that particular gestures have particular meanings; in other words, we can produce a 'dictionary' of body language. That, as we will demonstrate, is rarely the case. The longer technical term has the advantage of including a range of behaviours, including bodily movements and postures, and also signals our concern with the way these behaviours are embedded in the communication process.

Allan Pease (1985; 1997), a popular writer and speaker on the subject of non-verbal communication, implies in the sub-title of his books that one can 'read' or decode somebody else's feelings, attitudes and emotions from this source. Does a knowledge of this aspect of human behaviour really give us the ability to read minds? Well, to some extent, maybe; if we are careful, sometimes. This 'mind reading' claim deserves some very cautious support. We are indeed able to exchange meaning with non-verbal codes, as long as we evaluate the verbal and non-verbal components together and also pay attention to the context.

Non-verbal hints for the job interview

When you sit down, lean forward slightly; this shows interest. Use open-handed gestures—palm upwards—to convey sincerity. Keep regular eye contact, but not for more than 60 per cent of the time, or you'll look mad. However, do it for less than 30 per cent of the time and you may seem shifty or bored.

Don't sit defensively—hands across the body, knees pressed together, hand over your mouth—it can look neurotic or unstable. Equally, don't fidget or play with your hair, or grin maniacally. Above all, don't slouch back in the chair, arms behind your head, with a challenging stare. It threatens the interviewer and makes you look arrogant and difficult.

From Jerome Burne and Susan Aldridge, 'Who do you think you are?', *Focus Extra*, April 1996, p.4.

Table 6.6: Dimensions of non-verbal behaviour

- eye behaviour (occulesics)
- facial expressions
- posture
- limb movements (kinesics)
- tone and pitch of voice (paralanguage)
- distance (proxemics)

Non-verbal behaviour is rich and varied. The main dimensions are summarized in table 6.6.

Maureen Guirdham (1995, p.165) lists 136 non-verbal behaviours, in nine categories. These include what we do with our mouths, eyebrows, eyelids and eyes, gaze, facial expressions, head movements, hands and arms, lower limbs and trunk movements.

The sub-heading 'mouth region' lists 40 behaviours, such as tongue out, open grin, yawn, wry smile, sneer, tight lips, lower lip tremble—and so on. The sub-heading 'hands and arms' lists a further 40 behaviours, such as scratch, sit on hands, hand flutter, digit suck, palms up, caress, hand on neck—and so on. The study of what we do with our eyes is known as 'occulesics'; the study of limb movements is known as 'kinesics'.

Non-verbal courtship

According to Allan Pease (1997), typical male courtship gestures involving non-verbal behaviour include preening (straightening his tie, smoothing hair), thumbs in belt (pointing towards genitals), turning his body to face a female, pointing his foot towards her, holding her gaze, hands on his hips, dilated pupils and the 'leg spread' (crotch display). Women, on the other hand, have a much richer repertoire of non-verbal courtship behaviour, which includes:

- preening gestures such as touching hair, smoothing clothing;
- one or both hands on hips;
- foot and body pointing towards the male;
- extended eye contact or 'intimate gaze';
- thumbs in belt, but often only one, or thumb protruding from pocket or handbag;
- pupil dilation;
- flushed appearance;
- the head toss, to flick hair away from face (used even by women with short hair);
- exposing the soft smooth skin on the wrists to the male;
- exposing the palms of the hands, easily done while smoking;
- the sideways glance with drooped eyelids ('you caught me looking at you');
- wet lips, mouth slightly open;
- fondling cylindrical objects (stem of wine glass, a finger);
- the knee point, one leg tucked under the other, pointing to the male, thighs exposed;
- the shoe fondle, pushing the foot in and out of a half-on, half-off shoe;
- crossing and uncrossing the legs slowly in front of the man;
- gently stroking the thighs (indicating a desire to be touched).

How many of these non-verbal courtship gestures, male and female, are illustrated in the sketch on page 192.

Another important aspect of non-verbal behaviour is 'paralanguage'. This concerns the rate of speech, and pitch and loudness of our voice, regardless of the words we are using. There are many different ways of saying the same sequence of words; it's not what you say but the way that you say it. Paralanguage demonstrates some of the overriding power of non-verbal behaviour. Consider the simple statement: 'That was a really great lecture'. Think of the many ways in

How many non-verbal courtship gestures can you spot?

which you can say this, the differences in gaze and posture as you say it, and particularly the differences in the tone and pitch of your voice. For some of these expressions, listeners will hear you say that you really *did* enjoy the lecture. However, there are a number of ways in which you can 'code' this statement, non-verbally, in such a way that listeners will be left in no doubt that you thought the lecture poor—even though the wording remains as it is written here. Where the verbal and non-verbal messages contradict each other, it is the non-verbal message which is 'heard' and believed, not the verbal message.

Yet another aspect of non-verbal behaviour concerns the way in which we use distance in interpersonal behaviour. The study of this aspect of behaviour is sometimes called 'proxemics'. British culture requires a 'social distance' of about half a metre or more between people in normal conversation. If you cross this invisible boundary and step into someone's 'personal space' they will usually move backwards to maintain the distance; a failure to 'retreat' implies intimacy. The comfortable distance in Arab and Latin (American and European) countries is smaller, and you are likely to be regarded as arrogant and distant by trying to maintain your personal space when interacting with members of those cultures.

It is possible to test the theory of personal space in many social situations. At a social gathering, a party perhaps, move gradually and tactfully into someone else's space, by pretending to reach for a drink, or by moving aside to let someone else past, or by leaning forward to be heard better, and so on. It is possible to move someone right across a room in this way. The same result can be achieved while seated, as long as the chairs are easy to move. However, if your chosen 'target' does not 'retreat' as predicted, and you are now in their 'intimate' space, you have a decoding problem, and the textbook can't help you.

When the verbal message is inconsistent with the non-verbal message, the non-verbal message is believed, and listeners discount the verbal component. However, when we are lying, we may unconsciously send non-verbal 'deceit cues', which include rapid shifts in gaze, fidgeting in our seats, long pauses and frequent speech corrections. To lie effectively, it is important to control the 'deceit cues' and ensure that our verbal and non-verbal messages are consistent. Similarly, when we want to emphasize the sincerity or strength of our feelings, it is important that the non-verbal signals we send are consistent with our verbal messages.

Maureen Guirdham (1995) calls non-verbal behaviour a 'relationship language'. This is how we communicate trust, boredom, submission, dislike and friendship

Lie detectors

Can we use non-verbal behaviour to detect when someone is lying? Adrian Furnham identifies several verbal and non-verbal 'lie detectors'. However, in other cultures, these cues may constitute *normal* interpersonal behaviour and may *not* signal deceit.

Verbal cues

• Response latency	The time between the end of a question and the start of a reply. Liars take longer, hesitate more.
• Linguistic distance	Not saying 'I' but talking in the abstract; for example, 'one might believe that . . .'
• Slow, uneven speech	As an individual tries to think through their lies. They might also suddenly talk quickly, attempting to make a sensitive subject appear less significant.
• Too eager to fill gaps in conversation	Liars keep talking when it is unnecessary, as if a silence signifies that the other person does not believe them.
• Too many pitch raises	Instead of the pitch dropping at the end of a reply, it is lifted in the same way as asking a question.

Non-verbal cues

• Too much squirming	Someone shifting around in their seat is signalling their desire not to be there.
• Too much eye contact, rather than too little	Liars tend to overcompensate.
• Micro-expressions	Flickers of surprise, hurt or anger that are difficult to detect. Sudden facial expressions of pain are often giveaways.
• An increase in comfort gestures	These often take the form of self-touching, particularly around the nose and mouth.
• An increase in stuttering and slurring	Including what are known as 'Freudian slips'.
• A loss of resonance in the voice	It tends to become flatter and more monotonous.

Based on Adrian Furnham, *The Psychology of Behaviour at Work*, Psychology Press/Taylor & Francis, Hove, Sussex, 1997, p.53.

without having to indicate these feelings openly or directly. When decoding non-verbal behaviour, it is important to pay attention to both the context of the behaviour and the pattern or cluster of verbal and non-verbal behaviours on display. For example, when someone wishes to indicate liking or friendship, they are likely to turn their body towards you, look you straight in the face, establish regular eye contact and look away infrequently, and to nod and smile a lot, keeping their hands and arms by their sides or in front of them. This cluster conveys openness, or positive non-verbal behaviour.

We can decode openness, liking, agreement and friendship in this non-verbal

It's the way that you say it: the power of paralanguage

Change your tone and you change your meaning:

Meaning 1	Why don't I take YOU to dinner tonight?	I was going to take someone else.
Meaning 2	Why don't **I** take you to dinner tonight?	Instead of the guy you were going with.
Meaning 3	Why DON'T I take you to dinner tonight?	I'm trying to find a reason why I shouldn't take you.
Meaning 4	WHY don't I take you to dinner tonight?	Do you have a problem with me?
Meaning 5	Why don't I TAKE you to dinner tonight?	Instead of going on your own.
Meaning 6	Why don't I take you to DINNER tonight?	Instead of lunch tomorrow.
Meaning 7	Why don't I take you to dinner TONIGHT?	Not tomorrow night.

From Michael Kiely, 'When "no" means "yes"', *Marketing*, October 1993, pp.7–9.

cluster. Similarly, we can often identify disagreement or dislike by negative non-verbal behaviour. This cluster includes a 'closed posture', which often involves turning the body away, folding the arms tightly and crossing the legs in such a manner that they point away from the other person. Negative non-verbal behaviours also include loss of eye contact, wandering gaze, looking at someone else or at the door (suggesting a desire to leave), and a lack of nods and non-verbal behaviour cluster even before they state their disagreement in words.

However, awareness of the context is critical to this decoding or 'mind reading'. People also engage in negative non-verbal behaviours when they are unwell, or when they are anxious about something, perhaps unrelated to your conversation and relationship. People 'close up' and fold their arms when they are cold as well as when they disagree.

Interpreting gesture clusters

cluster signals	indicating
flexible open posture, open hands, display of palms and wrists, removing jacket, moving closer to other person, leaning forward in chair, uncrossed arms and legs, smiling, nodding, eye contact	openness
rigid closed posture, arms and legs tightly crossed, eyes glancing sideways, minimal eye contact, frowning, no smiling, pursed lips, clenched fists, head down, flat tone of voice	defensiveness
drumming fingers, head cupped in palm of hand, foot swinging, brushing or picking lint from clothing, body pointing towards exit, repeatedly looking at watch, the exit, a book	boredom, impatience
small inward smile, erect body posture, hands open and arms extended outwards, eyes wide and alert, lively walk, expressive and well-modulated voice	enthusiasm
knitted forehead, deadpan expression, tentative nodding or smiling, one slightly raised eyebrow, strained voice, saying 'I understand' while looking away	lack of understanding
blank expression, phoney smile, tight posture, arms stiff at side, sudden eye shifts, nervous tapping, sudden mood shifts, speech toneless and soft or too loud and animated	stress

In a **high-context culture**, people tend to rely heavily on a range of social and non-verbal clues when communicating with others and interpreting their messages.

In a **low-context culture**, people tend to focus on the written and spoken word when communicating with others and interpreting their messages.

Our eye behaviour has also attracted much research. The dilation and contraction of our pupils is largely beyond our direct control, unlike, say, the movements of our hands, but this can convey significant non-verbal information. Our pupils dilate (expand) in low light and also when we see something or someone in which we have interest. This dilation conveys honesty, openness and sexual interest. However, our pupils also dilate when we are relaxed, and following the consumption of alcohol and other drugs. Once again, a knowledge of context is critical to accurate decoding. Pupils that are contracted can signify either low lighting conditions, or lack of interest, or distrust, or hatred, or hostility, or fatigue, or stress or sorrow, or perhaps even a hangover. It is only possible to decode the information provided by someone's pupil dilation or contraction with reference to other non-verbal clues and with knowledge of the context in which this behaviour appears (including, in some circumstances, what they were doing the previous evening).

The importance of cultural context in communication

The use and interpretation of non-verbal behaviours differ from culture to culture. In Japan, for example, smiling and nodding implies understanding but not necessarily agreement. In Australia, raising the pitch of your voice at the end of a sentence signifies openness to challenge or question, not a lie. In some Asian cultures, it is impolite to give superiors direct and prolonged eye contact; a bowed head thus signifies deference and not lack of self-confidence or defensiveness. People from northern European cultures prefer a lot of personal space and rarely touch each other. The French, Italians and Latin Americans, in contrast, stand closer together and touch more often to indicate agreement and friendship. The verbal and non-verbal 'lie detectors' described earlier are specific to British culture.

Simple gestures must also be used with care. Make a circle with your thumb and forefinger, extending the other three fingers. How will this be interpreted (DuBrin, 1994)? In America, it means, 'that's OK'. In Japan, it means money. In France, it means zero or nothing. In some Arab countries, it signifies a curse. But in Germany and Brazil it is obscene.

Edward Hall (1976; 1989) distinguished between **high-context** and **low-context** cultures.

high-context culture	low-context culture
establish relationship first	get down to business first
value personal relations and goodwill	value expertise and performance
agreement based on trust	agreement based on legal contract
slow and ritualistic negotiations	fast and efficient negotiations

China, Korea, Japan and Vietnam are high-context cultures, where people tend to take a greater interest in your position, your business card, your dress, material possessions, and other signs of status and relationships. Written and spoken communications are not ignored, but they are secondary. Agreements can be made on a handshake, on someone's word.

North America, Scandinavia, Switzerland and Germany are low-context cultures. Here people do pay attention to non-verbal messages. However, people in German organizations tend to be preoccupied with detailed written rules, and Americans like to have precise legal documents. Agreements are not made until the contract is in writing, signed.

These categorizations reflect tendencies and are not absolutes. Most countries have sub-cultures with very different norms. In addition, men tend to be more high-context than women, but clearly this observation does not apply to all men or to all women. Nevertheless, it is easy to understand how misunderstanding can arise when high- and low-context cultures meet, unless those communicating are sensitive to their respective differences.

Someone who is anxious usually indulges in non-verbal behaviour known as 'self-manipulation'. This includes playing with an ear lobe, stroking lips or chin, or playing with hair or a moustache. Anxiety can also be signalled by shifting direction of gaze. Friendship is conveyed, as we have indicated, by an open non-verbal behaviour cluster. There are a number of other friendship signals, and these can sometimes be amusing to use and to identify. When we meet someone to whom we are attracted, we typically use unconscious 'preening gestures': straightening our clothes, stroking our hair, straightening our posture. Observe a group of friends together and you will often see them standing, sitting and even holding cups or glasses in an almost identical manner. This is known as 'posture mirroring'. Sometimes you can identify the 'outsider' as the one not adopting the similar posture. Friendship groups also copy each others' gestures, known as 'gesture mirroring'.

Neuro-linguistic programming (NLP)

NLP is a technique for improving performance in interpersonal communication. Developed by Richard Bandler and John Grinder (1976; 1979), it is now widely used as a management development tool (Harris, 1992; Dimmick, 1995). The components of the somewhat clumsy name have the following sources:

neuro	the method is underpinned by an understanding of how the human nervous system processes incoming information
linguistic	the method in practice is based on the use of words, tone of voice, timing and gestures to improve the effectiveness of communication
programming	the aim of the method is to base interpersonal communication on systematic, and thus trainable, techniques

The conscious control of behaviour is fundamental to the practice of NLP, which advocates a form of objective detachment known as 'disassociation' from events going on around us. In a disassociated state, which can be achieved with practice, it is possible to observe and monitor one's behaviour during a 'live' conversation, consciously choosing a range of verbal and non-verbal behaviours and evaluating their impact. Feelings can also be directed consciously in a similar manner, by 'anchoring' the emotion of, for example, calmness to a specific event, which can be recalled to generate that emotion when required (for example, when called upon to make a presentation to a large audience). These examples of disassociation and anchoring help to explain the 'programming' element of the approach.

On the basis that effective communication is based on rapport, on establishing that 'we are very much alike', NLP advocates a series of techniques known as mirroring or 'matching'. These include, for example, matching the other person's body movements, the volume and rate of speech, breathing pattern, and mood or 'frame of mind'. Any aspect of the other person's behaviour can be matched in order to signal, 'see, I'm a lot like you', as long as it is done carefully and tactfully and not overdone.

Even the other person's preferred communication style can be matched. This style, according to NLP practitioners, is revealed by eye movements. When someone looks upwards frequently, this usually suggests a preference for *visual* imagery. Matching involves saying things like 'I can see that' or 'That looks right', and showing the person charts and diagrams. When someone looks frequently to the side, this usually suggests a preference for *auditory* signals. Matching involves using words like 'That sound right' or 'Listen to this' or 'That rings a bell'. Finally, when someone looks downwards frequently, this usually suggests a preference for *kinaesthetic* information, which is information received through actions or feelings. Matching involves using phrases like 'It doesn't feel right' or 'I can grasp that'. To clarify these distinctions, Sally Dimmick (1995) uses the example of 'splitting the bill' with a group of people at the end of a meal in a restaurant. Individuals with different communication style preferences need to be handled in different ways:

visual preference	they want to see the bill for themselves, to work out what each person has to contribute
auditory preference	they don't want to see the bill, they just want to be told the total and how much they have to pay
kinaesthetic preference	they will want to do the necessary calculation manually and will be the first to reach for a pen

To the extent that they are effective, NLP techniques are particularly useful to salespeople (trying to persuade customers to buy more of their product) and to negotiators (trying to gain concessions from their adversaries). The approach is thus open to the criticism that it is overtly manipulative and unethical. However, we all use the techniques of mirroring or 'matching' unconsciously anyway. The conscious, deliberate attempt to improve interpersonal communication is not necessarily devious or damaging. Or is it?

Impression management: form versus substance?

We usually send and receive non-verbal messages unconsciously. However, it is possible both to control most of the non-verbal signals we send and consciously to be aware of and read the cues that others are giving us. This level of conscious attention and control may be difficult for most of us to sustain, but this can be significant in organizational settings.

Impression management is the process whereby people seek to control the image others have of them.

The concept of **impression management** has its foundations in the work of Erving Goffman (1959). Our definition is taken from the more recent work of Paul Rosenfeld, Robert Giacalone and Catherine Riordan (1995, p.4), who add:

We impression manage in many different ways: what we do, how we do it, what we say, how we say it, the furnishings and arrangement of our offices, and our physical appearance—from the clothes and make-up we wear to non-verbal behaviours such as facial expressions or postures. All these behaviours in some way can help define who and what we are.

Effective impression management means being consciously aware of and in control of the cues that we send to others through verbal and non-verbal channels. This suggests that we consciously seek to manipulate the impression or perceptions that others have of us.

Stop and criticize

Is impression management simply a form of deceit? What in your view are the ethical problems raised by the advice that we consciously seek to manipulate the impression that others have of us through verbal and non-verbal behaviours? What are the practical problems? How long can you keep this up?

As with conversation controls, we can use impression management to manipulate the behaviour of others. We do this, for example, by 'giving off' the impression that we are friendly, submissive, apologetic, angry, defensive, confident, intimidating—and so on. The more effectively we manage our impression, the greater the control we can achieve in social interaction, and the greater our power to pursue our preferred outcomes over others.

Gardner (1992) speaks of impression management as 'organizational dramaturgy' and in terms of 'stagecraft': actors, audience, stage, script, performance and

Anita Roddick learns impression management

Anita Roddick started the Body Shop in 1976. At the end of 1999, her company was worth over £200 million and had 1,600 stores in 47 countries. She explains her initial problems:

The most difficult thing was raising money for the first shop. I knew I had a good idea and a reasonable business plan, and I thought naïvely that this was all that was important. I went to see my bank manager in my Bob Dylan T-shirt with my two small children in tow. I thought my enthusiasm and energy would convince the bank manager to believe in me. But he turned me down, which took me aback. Gordon, my husband, told me to have another go but this time to dress up like a bloke in pinstripes and leave the kids behind. He came, too. After taking this advice I was able to walk out of the same bank with a £4,000 loan.

From Rupert Steiner, 'Pinstripes put Roddick on the right scent', *The Sunday Times*, 24 October 1999, p.3.15.

Table 6.7: Creating a favourable self-image

Ingratiation	Use flattery, agree with the opinions of others, do favours to encourage people with power and influence to befriend you.
Intimidation	Convey the image of potential danger to those who could stand in the way of your advancement. Use veiled threats of exposure.
Self-promotion	Win respect and admiration of superiors through embellishing your accomplishments, overstating your abilities, displaying awards.
Exemplification	Create an impression of selfless dedication and self-sacrifice, so those in positions of influence will feel guilty and offer reward or promotion.
Accounting	Distance yourself from negative events, deny personal responsibility for problems, diminish the seriousness of difficulties.
Supplication	Get those in positions of influence to be sympathetic and nurturing, for example through requests for 'mentoring' and other support.

reviews. It is not surprising, therefore, that some people regard impression management as a form of acting. The problem with this view is that we 'manage' our impression all the time, whether we like this concept or not. It is hardly possible to avoid sending 'signals' to others through, for example, our style of dress, posture, facial expressions, gestures, tone and pitch of voice, and even location in a room. The only useful distinction here is between conscious (and by implication more effective—for the initiator) impression management and unconscious (and by implication less effective, or even misleading) impression management.

Conscious control of our impression management capability has many advantages. Social interactions run more smoothly when we provide the 'correct' signals to others, who in turn accurately 'decode' these signals of our attitudes and intents. Impression management is a critical skill in many organizational contexts, such as counselling, and in selection, appraisal and disciplinary interviewing.

Feldman and Klitch (1991) offer advice on how to manage your impression to enhance your career. They suggest six methods for creating a favourable self-image, summarized in table 6.7. They also argue that a contemporary 'careerist orientation' to work is based on six beliefs, which, incorporating much practical impression management advice, are that:

1. Merit alone is insufficient for advancement. Creating the appearance of being a winner, or looking 'promotable', is just as important.

2. To advance, it is critical to pursue social relationships with superiors and co-workers. On the surface, these relationships should appear to be social in nature, but in reality they are used instrumentally for job contacts and insider organizational information.

3. Looking like a 'team player' is central. However, you should still pursue self-interest at work through 'antagonistic co-operation'; that is, appearing co-operative and helpful while simultaneously seeking information about how to beat the competition.

4. In the long run, your career goals will be inconsistent with the interests of any

one organization. Therefore, in order to advance, you must appear to be loyal and committed to your current employer while 'keeping your options open'.

5. Dishonest or unethical behaviours are sometimes necessary in order to get promoted. Instead of advocating or even acknowledging the existence of such behaviour, you should become adept at inconsistency and develop the ability to hold public positions that are either mutually inconsistent or inconsistent with past public positions.

6. Much of the 'real work' of many jobs cannot be assessed; nor can relative success be easily validated. Thus it is important to construct the illusion of success through symbols such as dress and office design. These props include locks on file drawers, positioning visitors so the sun is in their eyes, and visitors' chairs lower than the occupant's desk.

Organizational communication: commitment and propaganda

Up to this point, we have focused on interpersonal communication, one-on-one. In this final section, the focus shifts to organizational communication, between management and employees. This raises a completely different perspective on the nature of communication in organizations. Although communication is widely recognized as central to both individual and organizational performance, many managers regard communication as a major problem (Buchanan, Claydon and Doyle, 1999), and many employees feel that they are not fully informed about management plans and organizational activities and goals. From a survey of communication concerning organizational restructuring, Katherine Burke (1999) concludes that many companies do not pay adequate attention to communication when planning and implementing change, resulting in absenteeism, turnover, low productivity and disputes.

The single main problem facing most organization managers lies with persuading employees to work effectively in the interests of the organization as a whole. However, the interests of individuals and organizations do not always coincide [link, chapter 1, prologue]. How can management channel employee behaviour in the desired directions? In a seminal contribution to organizational behaviour, March and Simon (1958) argued that management cannot change individual behaviour either directly or by attempting to alter people's personalities. It is far more effective and practical, they observed, to manipulate the premises on which people make their own decisions about how they will behave.

How can management 'manipulate the premises'—the underlying assumptions—which influence the day-to-day decisions of employees? This can be achieved in relatively straightforward ways, and mainly through the design of the organization's systems for reward and sanction. The basis on which pay is calculated, for example, can influence attendance, timekeeping and work rate (through piece rates and bonuses). The kinds of behaviour which are favoured, on the one hand, and which are not, on the other, can be indicated in the way in which annual appraisal is conducted and through the selective promotion of 'favoured' individuals. The rules in place, the way they are enforced and the vocabularies in use are also symbolic ways of 'signalling' or 'coding' desirable and undesirable behaviours [link, chapter 4, learning].

Stop and criticize

How does your educational institution use rewards and sanctions to influence the decisions you make about the nature and direction of your studies? What 'signals' are used to communicate teaching staff expectations of student behaviour?

To the extent that rewards, sanctions, appraisal and promotions policies, rules and vocabularies are within management control, then management can seek to influence the premises underlying the decisions of their employees. These 'signalling systems' are in effect saying, 'behave this way and you will be rewarded and/or promoted, but behave that way and you are likely to be overlooked for promotion—or fired'. These systems are often complemented by organization mission statements, vision statement and statements of corporate values. Peter Wickens (ex-human resources director for the Nissan Japanese car plant at Sunderland in the north-east of England) (1999), for example, argues that a clearly defined set of organizational values confers competitive advantage, and he offers a procedure for identifying what these values should be for an individual organization. In the following box, the 'vision and values' statement of a privatized English water utility is described.

Anglian Water Services plc, Huntingdon, England
Vision and Values Statement, November 1997

Vision

purpose	To sustain and enhance the lives of our customers through profitable management of water and waste water
vision and goals	The Anglian Group will be a winner in the competitive markets of the twenty-first century by becoming the customers' first choice
strategy	Our strategy to achieve this vision is to become the customers' first choice, to grow the business, to deliver superior shareholder returns, and to value and recognize employees, enabling them to achieve their full potential

Values

effective	do the right thing, get it right first time
competitive	be ready for competition, be open to change, be innovative, be efficient
responsible	fair to our customers and employees, contribute to the well-being of communities and sustainable development, operate the business as if we owned it ourselves
responsive	give the service we would expect ourselves, learn from ourselves and others, continuously improve the business
friendly	in our approach to customers, colleagues and others

Senior management at Anglian Water Services presented its vision and values statement to employees in a series of meetings held in late 1997 and early 1998. In response to a question concerning job security from the floor at one of these meeting, a senior manager replied:

> Vision and Values sets out clear guidelines for all employees to demonstrate the core values—to be effective, competitive, responsible, friendly and responsive in the day jobs. Those employees who really live these values will contribute to the growth of Anglian Water and be rewarded accordingly. By contrast, those people who do not take account of Vision and Values will be shown the door (*Anglian Water News*, April 1998, p.5).

Barbara Townley (1994) argues that British management has consistently neglected employee communication, although it is often advocated by management consultants as a cure for low morale, high absenteeism and labour turnover, labour unrest and conflict, low productivity and resistance to change. This advice is based on the theory that, if people know what is going on and understand why, then they will be more likely to agree to management requests, to follow management directions. In other words, a clearly articulated and logically reasoned case supported with evidence will result in consensus and compliance.

Organizations use a range of mechanisms for communicating with employees, such as:

- the management chain;
- regular meetings with senior and/or middle managers;
- in-house newspapers and magazines;
- notice boards;
- videos;
- conferences and seminars;
- employee reports (similar to but different from shareholder reports);
- team briefings, to cascade information through the structure;
- e-mail and intranets (for those with access to terminals).

Those tend to be one-way-downward modes of communication. Two-way exchanges of information are more effectively achieved through methods such as:

- 'speak out' programmes, in which problems are taken to counsellors;
- suggestion or 'bright ideas' schemes;
- open door policies;
- the appraisal system;
- quality circles;
- attitude surveys;
- interactive e-mail (where managers guarantee to reply).

Culture differences in organizational communication

In the 'North' [of Europe] the policy is that everyone knows. 'Southern' management discourages an open, critical attitude of younger and 'inexperienced' employees, whereas in the North such an attitude is welcomed. On the corporate information front, five years ago Unilever started 'Cascade', a system to acquaint all employees yearly with information about how the corporation was doing financially. For this, corporate HQ prepares a big packet full of information, complete with overhead sheets and even videos. All business groups receive the same information and are expected to pass it on to their companies and eventually to all employees. Random checks among employees after the Cascade exercise have shown that in Eastern Europe all employees are very interested in corporate information and that 'coverage' is near 100%; in Western Europe coverage is 'average', some 80%, but in Latin countries coverage is 'difficult', at around 65%, because local management seems to decide that not all information is 'necessary' or fit for their employees.

From C.V. Fourboul and F. Bournois, 'Strategic communication with employees in large European companies: a typology',
European Management Journal, 1999, vol.17, no.2, p.211.

What evidence is there concerning the ways in which organizational communication is practised? From a major national survey in Britain, of around 4,000 employees and 1,000 unemployed, in all occupational grades, Duncan Gallie and colleagues (1998) found that:

- mechanisms for informing the workforce about management decisions and organizational developments are widespread;

- it is more common for employers to distribute information (76%) than to hold meetings in which employees can express their opinions;

- the higher the skill level, the more likely that people will have good access to information;

- more than three-quarters of professional and managerial workers have meetings about organizational issues in which they can express their views;

- less than a half of all manual workers, skilled and non-skilled, have meetings in which they can express their views;

- involvement in communication is better in larger organizations;

- less than half of employees working in small businesses report any type of formal provision of company information at all;

- in larger establishments employing 500 people or more, 92% receive some type of information, 84% through meetings, and 71% are able to express their views.

Gallie *et al.* (1998, p.98) argue that larger organizations are more likely to have 'administrative sophistication', in the form of adequately resourced administrative or human resources departments, to implement communication policies systematically.

We will examine the concept of organization culture, or organization climate, in chapter 19 [**link**, chapter 19, organization culture]. However, it is appropriate here to examine briefly the related concept of **communication climate**, which was developed by Jack Gibb (1961).

Gibb argued that, in an *open* communication climate, people develop a sense of self-worth, feel that they can contribute freely without reprisal, know that their suggestions will be welcomed, that mistakes will be regarded as learning opportunities, and that they will feel trusted, secure and confident in their job and in the organization. In a *closed* communication climate, information tends to be withheld unless it is to the advantage of the sender, and the atmosphere of recrimination, secrecy and distrust can make working life very unpleasant. The distinction between open, supportive and closed, defensive communication climates is summarized in table 6.8. These extremes are not absolutes; most organizations are likely to have a communication climate which lies on the continuum between open and closed.

> The **communication climate** in an organization concerns the prevailing atmosphere in which ideas and information are exchanged; an open climate promotes collaborative working, which is discouraged by a closed communication climate.

Stop and criticize

How would you diagnose the communication climate of your educational institution? Of an organization where you have recently worked? Of your current employer?

One recurring theme in contemporary organizational communication concerns the need to improve effectiveness in increasingly turbulent and competitive markets—the 'adapt to survive' argument. Organizations thus require commitment from employees. Mere compliance or 'following the rules' is not enough. The need for commitment is often central to organizational communication programmes, is often accompanied by total quality management (TQM) or continuous quality improvement (CQI) methods and is an aspect of strategic human resource management (SHRM), explored in chapter 20 [**link**, chapter 20, human resource management]. The vocabulary of this argument revolves around 'survival', 'competitiveness', 'customer service', 'organizational effectiveness', and so on.

Table 6.8: Open and closed communication climates

Open, supportive communication climate	Closed, defensive communication climate
Descriptive: informative rather than evaluative communication	Judgemental: emphasis on apportioning blame, making people feel incompetent
Solution-oriented: focus on problem solving rather than on what is not possible	Controlling: conformity expected, inconsistency and change inhibited
Open and honest: no hidden messages	Deceptive: hidden meanings, insincerity, manipulative communication
Caring: emphasis on empathy and understanding	Non-caring: detached and impersonal, little concern for others
Egalitarian: everyone valued regardless of role or status	Superior: status and skill differences emphasized in communication
Forgiving: errors and mistakes recognized as inevitable, focus on minimizing	Dogmatic: little discussion, unwillingness to accept views of others or compromise
Feedback: positive, essential to maintaining performance and relationships	Hostile: needs of others given little importance

The theory that 'people will comply if they understand' suggests that organizational communication has an educational component. Employees who are better informed about 'economic realities' are more likely to have realistic expectations and make reasonable demands. However, as Townley (1994, p.611) notes, this argument equates communication with propaganda, which attempts to shape attitudes and behaviours in particular directions, to generate consensus on organizational issues and management decisions, 'giving the logic of managerial decision making a greater legitimacy'. With the widespread development of teamworking approaches to organizational design, management can bypass trade union representatives by working through team leaders instead.

Townley thus argues that communication in an organization is not 'neutral', merely providing information about some 'external reality'. Organizational communications are constructed from a management perspective, representing management interests. Organizational power inequalities require management to direct and dominate workforce behaviour. Information is not simply a commodity to be conveyed or transmitted. Organizational communication mechanisms are tools (not always effective) for manipulating workforce attitudes and behaviours. This argument reflects the postmodern perspective, which forces us to ask 'whose interests are served by this statement, by this way of presenting information, by this argument?' The 'context' indicated in our model of the communication process, in figure 6.1, must therefore consider not just the physical and interpersonal context but also the wider social and political context of organizational communication.

Not getting the message: employee responses to corporate communication

Alan Harrison explored employee attitudes to management communication in three British organizations; Royal Mail, GPT (now Marconi Communications) and BT (British Telecommunications). Focus groups of employees recruited through trade union contacts were conducted, in two cases following a union meeting and in one instance at an Indian restaurant before a meal. Each focus group was first invited to discuss management communication in general, then to discuss specific items of company communication, including articles from company magazines and a letter from a managing director about possible redundancies. The discussion revealed some common responses:

- The term 'bullshit' was used to describe management communication in every discussion.

- Most said that they threw away corporate magazines and letters without reading them.

- Team briefings were criticized for containing irrelevant material and for omitting important issues, due to management misunderstanding, or to conflict between managers.

- Management briefings in general were criticized for being late, inadequate and 'one way only', with no opportunity to provide feedback.

- Direct corporate communication to employees was seen as a way of bypassing trade unions; in GPT, for example, issues raised formally in union negotiation meetings were answered months later in the company magazine.

Scepticism about corporate communication was not related to trade union density or level of militancy, as had been expected. Harrison argues that employees have a sophisticated understanding of the management language used in corporate communication, and that they can decode the underlying messages effectively. Management, however, appears not to bring much sophistication to the coding of its corporate messages.

Based on Alan Harrison, 'Getting the message: resistance to corporate communication in three British organizations', paper presented to the Working Class Academics Conference, University of Arkansas, Little Rock, 1999.

Recap

1. *Explain the main components of the interpersonal communication process.*

   - Communication involves an exchange of meaning, achieved through the processes of coding, transmission, decoding and feedback.

   - Face-to-face communication allows instant feedback, and coding and decoding problems arise with other forms of communication where feedback is delayed or absent.

2. *Identify the main barriers to effective interpersonal communication.*

   - The main barriers to communication include power and gender differences, physical surroundings, language variations and cultural diversity.

   - Barriers can be overcome through face-to-face communication, by checking decoding, by paying attention to the context of communication, and by trying to see things the way the other person does.

3. *Understand the effective use of different questioning techniques, conversation controls and listening skills.*

   - Getting appropriate information from someone else involves the effective use of different questioning methods: open, closed, probe, hypothetical and reflective.

   - Effective communication involves the use of a range of simple conversation controls: lubricators, inhibitors, bridges and pauses.

   - Active listening involves a range of verbal and non-verbal skills.

   - Communication methods differ between high-context and low-context cultures.

4. *Explain the nature and significance of non-verbal behaviour.*

   - Non-verbal behaviour concerns communication through facial expressions, eye behaviour, gesture and posture, distance between ourselves and others, and paralanguage.

   - If the verbal and non-verbal messages which we

are sending are inconsistent, the verbal will be discounted and the non-verbal accepted.

- Lies can be detected in non-verbal behaviour, but many of the clues are culture-specific.

5. *Understand the nature and mechanisms of impression management skills and techniques.*

- We influence the image that others have of us through verbal and non-verbal signals.

- Impression management is used to create a favourable self-image through, for example, ingratiation, intimidation, self-promotion, exemplification, accounting and supplication.

- Impression management can be seen as natural

and unconscious, or as a deliberate attempt at deceit.

6. *Understand the ways in which corporate communication can be used to manipulate understanding and encourage compliance with management directions.*

- Organizations use a range of media for communicating with employees.

- The communication climate in an organization can be classed as open and supportive or closed and defensive.

- Organizational communication is not neutral but is constructed from a management perspective in an attempt to manipulate the attitudes and behaviour of recipients.

Revision

1. Explain with appropriate examples the various elements of the model of the interpersonal communication process, identifying why this apparently straightforward process is error-prone.

2. What are the main barriers to effective communication, and how can these barriers be overcome?

3. Explain with appropriate examples the questioning techniques which we use to get information from others, and the conversation control methods that we use to ensure that our interactions run smoothly and in our favour.

4. What is non-verbal communication, and what part does this play in human interaction in general and in organizational settings?

5. To what extent is it possible to tell if someone is lying when they are talking to you, and what is the role of contextual and cultural factors in making such an assessment?

Springboard

Guirdham, M., 1995, *Interpersonal Skills at Work*, Prentice Hall, Hemel Hempstead (second edition).

A comprehensive guide to the theory and practice of interpersonal skills, with many interesting and valuable self-assessment and group exercises.

Huczynski, A., 1996, *Influencing Within Organizations*, Prentice Hall, London.

A practical guide to the realities of influence in organizational life, arguing that job competence alone is usually not enough to ensure career advancement. Includes chapters on verbal and non-verbal influencing and on impression management.

McNeill, D., 2000, *The Face*, Penguin Books, London.

A fascinating guide to the 'uncanny semaphore' of the face, illustrating the richness of the signals that we send and that we can read in the facial expressions of others. You may never look at anyone else in quite the same way again.

Pease, A., 1997, *Body Language: How to Read Others' Thoughts by Their Gestures*, Sheldon Press, London (third edition).

Entertaining guide to the rich variety of non-verbal behaviour, also exploring gender differences, with illustrative line drawings. Essential reading for those with a deep interest in observing and decoding body language.

Rogers, C.R. and Roethlisberger, F.J., 1952, 'Barriers and gateways to communication', *Harvard Business Review*, July/August, pp.28–34.

Classic article on interpersonal communication problems, from the founder of non-directive therapy, Carl Rogers, and one of the founders of the human relations school of management, Fritz Roethlisberger. Some of the examples are dated, but the overall argument still rewards reading. Appears in many collections of readings.

Rosenfeld, P., Giacalone, R.A. and Riordan, C.A., 1995, *Impression Management in Organizations: Theory, Measurement, Practice*, Routledge, London.

Contemporary text on the nature and significance of impression management in organizational settings, demonstrating the progress made since Goffman.

Tannen, D., 1995, 'The power of talk: who gets heard and why', *Harvard Business Review*, vol.73, no.5, pp.138–48.

If you don't have time to read Deborah Tannen's book (1990), then read this article on the subject of male–female differences in approach to social interaction.

Walther, G.R., 1993, *Say What You Mean and Get What You Want*, Piatkus, London.

Walther argues that 'powertalking' skills can be taught, simply because it involves the conscious use of words and phrases that convey a positive and powerful impression of the speaker to the listener. American in style, Walther describes a number of powertalking techniques, some of which are summarized in this chapter.

Home viewing

You've Got Mail (1998, director Nora Ephron) is a romantic comedy about two bookshop owners who meet, anonymously, in an internet chatroom and establish an intimate relationship without ever meeting face to face. The problem is, Kathleen Kelly (played by Meg Ryan) owns a small bookshop, and Joe Fox (Tom Hanks) opens a book superstore just across the street, threatening to put her out of business. Inevitably they do meet as competing business managers, who don't realize that they already 'know' each other through their intimate e-mail exchanges. As you watch the first hour of the film, analyse their e-mail communication using the model (figure 6.1) in this chapter. Note how the development of their e-mail relationship is affected by their use of language (coding and decoding), their use of feedback and what they do *not* communicate. Does Joe put Kathleen out of business? Does he get the girl in the end? You'll have to watch the whole two hours to find out.

OB in literature

Louis de Bernières, *Captain Corelli's Mandolin*, Secker & Warburg/Vintage, London, 1994.

A love story set on a Greek island during the Second World War. Analyse the cross-cultural communication problems of (Greek) Pelagia and her (Italian) lover Captain Corelli, during and long after the hostilities, using the coding–decoding model of communication in figure 6.1 of this chapter. Note how their respective backgrounds and occupations (Correlli is an officer in the invading Italian army) affect their perceptions of each other and their communication.

Chapter exercises

1: Close encounters

Objectives
1. To explore the impact of non-verbal behaviour on interpersonal communication.
2. To expose the wide diversity of non-verbal cues that influence the quality and effectiveness of interpersonal communication.

Briefing
1. Imagine you are having a conversation with someone. They display the following non-verbal behaviours. Considering each in turn, do these behaviours make you feel **P**ositive or **N**egative about the other person, or does it leave you **U**naffected? Why?
2. Compare your responses with colleagues and identify and discuss any discrepancies.

3. What other non-verbal cues (including paralanguage) contribute to effective interpersonal communication?

4. In what ways, if any, do you think you need to change your own behaviour in order to communicate more effectively?

	behaviour	P/N/U	why?
1	picks nose		
2	calm manner		
3	leans far back		
4	head very close to yours		
5	tugs at ear		
6	looks towards you		
7	sits on the same level as you		
8	bounces a leg		
9	picks lint off clothes		
10	voice easy to hear		
11	stares at you		
12	facial expression matches what you feel		
13	relaxed seating position		
14	slouches		
15	raises eyebrows		
16	looks alert		
17	smiles when greeting you		
18	sits higher than you		
19	half closes eyes		
20	high-pitched voice		
21	leans slightly towards you		
22	looks clean		
23	comfortable speech rate		
24	monotonous voice		
25	open body posture		
26	flowery arm gestures		
27	has vacant look		
28	has warmth in voice		
29	pauses for you to continue		
30	whispers		

Based on Richard Nelson-Jones, 2000, *Introduction to Counselling Skills*, Sage, London, p.52.

2: How would you respond?

Here are three statements from employees, directed at you, their immediate supervisor. For each statement, four possible responses are suggested. In your role as supervisor:

- assess the effects of each response on the person concerned;

- select what you feel is the most effective response, and justify that choice;

- if you feel it appropriate, determine a response which is more effective than the four on offer, again justifying your wording.

Where appropriate, conduct your analysis yourself in the first instance, before sharing your conclusions with colleagues and deciding on a group response.

Assistant foreman, age 30, computer manufacturing plant

'Yes, I do have a problem. I'd like to know more about what happened with the promotions last month. Charlie got the foreman's job in motherboard assembly and I didn't even know he was interested. Why did you give the job to him? I would like to know more about what you think of my promotion prospects here. I've been doing this job for about three years now, and I've been with the company for almost five years. I haven't had any complaints about my work. Seems to me I've been doing a pretty good job, but I don't see any recognition for that. What do I have to do to get promoted round here?'

1. You'll make a great foreman, Charlie, but give it time. I'll do what I can to make your case. Don't be discouraged, OK? I'm sure you'll get there soon, you'll see.

2. So, you're not sure about how the company regards your work here, Charlie?

3. Charlie, I understand how you feel, but I have to admit it took me five years to make foreman myself. And I guess I must have felt much the same way you do today. But we just have to be patient. Things don't always happen when we'd like them to, do they?

4. Come on, you've been here long enough to know the answer to that one. Nobody got promoted just by waiting for it to happen. Get with it, you've got to put yourself forward, make people stand up and take notice of your capabilities.

Secretary, age 45, insurance company headquarters

'Can I ask you to do something about the calendars that Mr Johnson and Mr Hargreaves insist on displaying in their offices? They are degrading to women and I find them offensive. I know that some of the other secretaries who work on their floor feel exactly the same way as I do. I have to work with these men and I can't stay out of their offices. Don't we have a company policy or something? I'm surprised you've allowed it to go on this long as it is.'

1. You and some of the other secretaries find these calendars insulting?

2. Look, you're taking this all too seriously. Boys' toys, that's all it is, executive perks. Doesn't mean anything, and there's nothing personal behind it at all. You've no cause for concern.

3. You're right, I don't like that either, but we're talking about their own offices here, and I think that they have the right, within reason, to make their own decisions about what pictures to put on the walls, same as you and I do.

4. I'll see if I can't get a chance to have a quiet word with them some time next week, maybe try to persuade them to move their calendars out of sight, OK? I'm sure they don't mean anything by it.

Personnel officer, age 26, local authority

'I've just about had it. I can't put up with this kind of pressure for much longer. We just don't have the staff to service the level of requests that we're getting and still do a good job. And some of the people we have to deal with! If that old witch in administration calls me one more time about those files that went missing last week, she's going to get a real mouthful in return. How come you let your department get pushed around like this?'

1. You're not alone. Pressure is something that we've all had to endure at some time. I understand that, it comes with the territory. I think it's about developing the right skills and attitudes to cope.

2. You're right, this is a difficult patch, but I'm sure that it will pass. This can't go on for much longer, and I expect you'll see things start to come right at the end of the month.

3. Well, if you can't stand the heat, I suppose you just have to get out of the kitchen. And please don't refer to people who are senior to you in this organization in that manner.

4. Let me check—this is not about Mrs Smith in admin, you're saying the strain is such that you're thinking of leaving us?

Chapter 7 Perception

Key concepts

perception	habituation
selective attention	perceptual organization
perceptual set or perceptual expectation	perceptual world
halo effect	stereotyping
attribution	

Learning objectives

When you have read this chapter, you should be able to define those key concepts in your own words, and you should also be able to:

1. Identify the main features of the process of perception.

2. Distinguish between the bottom-up processing of sensory information and the top-down interpretation of that information.

3. Understand the nature and implications of selective attention (perceptual selectivity) and perceptual organization.

4. Give examples of how behaviour is influenced by our perceptions.

5. Explain and illustrate the main processes and problems in person perception, including false attributions, halo effects and stereotyping.

6. Explain some of less widely appreciated sources of discrimination at work, against men and women, arising from characteristics of the person perception and attribution processes.

Why study perception?

Of all the topics covered in this text, perception is perhaps the one which most directly sets social science apart from natural science. We humans seem to attach meanings, interpretations, values and aims to our actions. What we do in the world depends on how we understand our place in it, depends on how we perceive ourselves and our social and physical environment, depends on how we perceive our circumstances. We explain behaviour with terms like 'reason', 'motive', 'intention', 'purpose', 'desire', and so on. Physicists, chemists and engineers do not face this complication in coming to grips with their subject matter.

The issue is—we each perceive the world around us in different ways. It is our personal **perception** of that reality which shapes and directs our behaviour, and not some 'objective' understanding of external reality. If one person on a hillside perceives that it is cold, they will reach for their sweater. If the person standing next to them perceives that it is warm, they will remove their sweater. These contrasting behaviours can be witnessed happening at the same time, regardless of the actual ambient temperature as measured by a thermometer. Human behaviour is thus a function of the way in which we perceive the world around us, and how we perceive other people and events in that world.

Stop and criticize	Choose a film that you have seen recently and which you particularly enjoyed. This could, perhaps, be one of the 'home viewing' suggestions in this textbook. Now find a friend or colleague who has seen the same film and hated it.
	Share your views of that film. What factors (age, sex, background, education, interests, values and beliefs, political views, past experience) can you identify that explain the differences in perception between you and your friend or colleague?

We often find ourselves unable to understand other people's behaviour. People can say and do surprising things in settings where it is obvious to us that some other behaviour would be more appropriate. As just noted, we each perceive the world in different ways. If we are to understand why you behaved in that way in that context, we first need to discover how you perceive that context and your place in it. When we are able to 'see it the way you see it', to put ourselves in your position (what in chapter 6 is described as the 'you' attitude) [**link**, chapter 6, communication], then what initially took us by surprise is likely to become readily understandable. To understand each other's behaviour, we need to be able to understand each others' perceptions. We need to be able to understand why we perceive things differently in the first place.

Selectivity and organization in perception

We process and interpret the incoming raw data in the light of our past experiences, in terms of our current needs and interests, in terms of our knowledge, expectations, beliefs and motives. We do not passively register sense impressions picked up from the world around us. The main elements in the perceptual process are illustrated in figure 7.1.

From a psychological point of view, the processes of sensation, on the one hand, and perception, on the other, work together through what are respectively termed 'bottom-up' and 'top-down' processing.

The 'bottom-up' phase concerns the way in which we process the 'raw' data received by our sensory apparatus. One of the key characteristics of bottom-up processing concerns the need for selectivity. We are simply not able to process all

Perception is the dynamic psychological process responsible for attending to, organizing and interpreting sensory data.

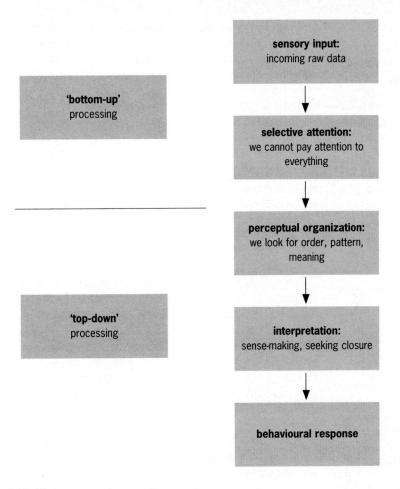

Figure 7.1: The process of perception

of the sensory information available to us at any given time. Bottom-up process-ing screens or filters out redundant and less relevant information so that we can focus on what is important.

The 'top-down' phase, in contrast, concerns the mental processing that allows us to order, interpret and make sense of the world around us. One of the key characteristics of top-down processing concerns our need to make sense of our environment and our search for meaning.

This distinction between sensation (bottom-up) and perception (top-down) can be illustrated in our ability to make sense of incomplete, or even incorrect, sen-sory information. The missing letter or comma, or the incorrectly spelled term, does not normally interfere with the comprehension of the human reader:

This sent nce us incorrect, bit yoo wull stell bi abl to udersta d it

Our top-down conceptual processing ability means that we are able to fill in the gaps and correct the mistakes, and thus make sense of 'imperfect' incoming raw data.

We each have a similar nervous system and share more or less common sensory equipment. However, we have different social and physical backgrounds, which give us different values, interests and expectations, and therefore different per-ceptions. We do not behave in, and in response to, the world 'as it really is'. This idea of the 'real world' is somewhat arbitrary. The 'real world' as a concept is not a useful starting point for developing an understanding of human behaviour in general, or organizational behaviour in particular. We behave in, and in response to, the world as we perceive it. We each live in our own **perceptual world**.

Successful interpersonal relationships depend on some overlap between our perceptual worlds, on some common perceptions, or we would never be able to understand each other. Our perceptual worlds, however, are in a detailed analysis unique, which makes life interesting but also gives us problems.

Our perceptual processing is normally carried out without much conscious deliberation or effort on our part. In fact, we often have no effective control over the process, and fortunately, such control is not always necessary. We can, however, control some aspects of the process simply by being consciously aware of what is happening. There are many settings where such control is desirable and can avoid dangerous and expensive errors. Understanding the characteristics of perception can be useful in a variety of organizational settings. For example, with the design of aircraft instrumentation and displays for pilots, in the conduct of selection interviews for new employees, in handling disputes and employee grievances.

Perception is a dynamic process because it involves ordering and attaching meaning to 'raw' sensory data. Our sensory apparatus is bombarded with vast amounts of information. Some of this information comes from inside the body, such as sensations of hunger, lust, pain and fatigue. Some of this information comes from people, objects and events in the world around us. We are not 'passive recorders' of this sensory data. We are constantly sifting and sorting this stream of information, making sense of it and interpreting it.

Perception, therefore, is an information-processing activity. This information processing is fairly well understood and concerns the phenomena of **selective attention** and perceptual organization.

Our senses—sight, hearing, touch, taste, smell, and the sensing of internal bodily signals or 'kinaesthesia'—each consist of specialist nerves that respond to specific forms of energy, such as light, sound, pressure, temperature changes, and so on. There are some forms of energy that our senses cannot detect unaided, such as radio waves, sounds of very low and very high pitch, and infrared radiation. Our sensory apparatus has built-in limitations that we cannot overcome without the aid of special equipment. We are unable to hear sound frequencies above 10,000 hertz, but many animals, including dogs and dolphins, have much better hearing. We are unable to hear sounds below 30 hertz, but whales can. Owls have much better eyesight than us.

The constraints imposed by our sensory apparatus can be modified in certain ways by experience. The boundary, or threshold, between what we can and cannot detect can be readily established by experiment. It is also a straightforward matter to explore individual differences in these thresholds across the various senses. These thresholds may be altered by experience, in the following manner. If there happens to be a clock ticking in the room where you study, you will almost certainly not be aware of the sound—until somebody mentions it, or the clock stops. Next time you use the library, close your eyes for a few seconds and listen carefully. Pay attention to the 'background' noise that you do not usually 'hear'. But surely, you must have heard it, as you must have heard the clock ticking, if your ears are working properly? Our sensory apparatus responds not simply to energy but rather to changes in energy levels. Having detected a stimulus, such as a clock, or the hum of air conditioning, the nerves concerned seem to become tired of transmitting the same information indefinitely and give up, until the stimulus changes. This explains our surprise, on some occasions, at the silence which follows when machinery stops suddenly.

Once stimuli become familiar, they stop being sensed. This phenomenon, in which the perceptual threshold is raised, is known as **habituation**.

Our sensory apparatus has design limitations which filter or screen out some

---

The individual's **perceptual world** is a personal internal image, map or picture of their social, physical and organizational environment.

Selective attention is the ability, often exercised unconsciously, to choose from the stream of sensory data, to concentrate on particular elements and to ignore others.

Habituation concerns the decrease in our perceptual response to stimuli once they have become familiar.

information, such as x-rays and dog whistles. Perception involves other filtering processes, as the phenomenon of habituation suggests. In particular, information that is familiar, non-threatening and unnecessary to the task in hand is 'screened out' of our conscious awareness. Just how this screening operates and what happens to the unwanted information is still the subject of controversy and research, but the implications are fairly clear.

Stand on the pavement of a busy street for a few minutes and pay attention to as much of the available information as you can; the noise and speed of the traffic and the makes and colours and condition of passing vehicles, the smell of rubber tyres and exhaust fumes, the pressure of the pavement on the soles of your feet, the breeze across your face, the smell of the perfume of a passing woman, the clothes of the man across the street and the type of dog he is walking, and so on. When you think you are taking it all in, start to cross the road. If you get across safely, you will find that your heightened awareness has lapsed, dramatically. You would be mown down fairly quickly if this were not the case. Selective attention allows us to concentrate on the important and significant and to ignore the insignificant and trivial.

Nancy Adler (1999) offers an excellent example of habituation in our use of language. Read the following sentence, and then very quickly count the number of Fs:

FINISHED FILES ARE THE RESULT OF YEARS OF SCIENTIFIC STUDY
COMBINED WITH THE EXPERIENCE OF YEARS

Most people who speak English as a second language see all six Fs. Native English speakers usually pick up only three or four because they tend to miss out the Fs in 'of'. Native English speakers have been conditioned—habituated—to skip the 'of' because it does not contribute to the meaning of the sentence.

Adler's explanation is that, once we stop seeing the 'ofs', we do not see them again, even as in this example when we are actually looking for them. There is simply too much information available at any one time for us to pay attention to all of it, so we screen out or filter that which is apparently of little or no value. The image of the world that we carry around inside our heads can only ever be a partial representation of what is 'really out there'. This leads to the conclusion that our behavioural choices are determined not by reality as such but by what we perceive that reality to be.

Perceptual filters are characteristics of the individual that interfere with the effective transmission and receipt of messages, such as predispositions to see, or not to see, particular types of information, or preoccupations which divert attention elsewhere.

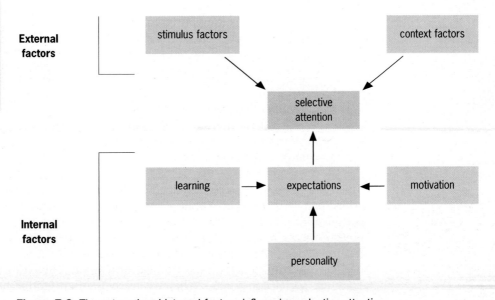

Figure 7.2: The external and internal factors influencing selective attention

The internal and external factors which affect selective attention are illustrated in figure 7.2.

The external factors affecting selective attention concern stimulus factors and context factors. With respect to the stimulus factors, our attention is drawn more readily to stimuli that are:

large		small
bright		dull
loud		quiet
strong	*rather than*	weak
unfamiliar		familiar
stand out from surroundings		blend with surroundings
moving		stationary
repeated (but not repetitive)		one-off

Note, however, that we do not merely respond to single features, as this list might imply; we respond to the pattern of stimuli available to us.

Stop and criticize

Identify examples of the ways in which advertisements creatively use stimulus factors to attract our attention, in newspapers and magazines, and on billboards and television.

Our attention is also influenced by context factors. The naval commander on the ship's bridge and the cook in the kitchen may both have occasion to shout 'fire', but these identical utterances will mean quite different things to those within earshot and will lead to radically different forms of behaviour (involving the taking and the saving of lives respectively). We do not need any help to make this crucial distinction, beyond our knowledge of the context.

The internal factors affecting perception include:

- *Learning*. You've heard that argument before, so are you going to listen carefully to it again? Our past experience leads to the development of perceptual expectations or perceptual sets, which give us predispositions to perceive and to pay attention to some stimuli and to ignore other information [**link**, chapter 4, learning].

- *Personality*. How come you (gregarious, sociable) saw the advertisement for the party, but your friend (reserved, shy) did not? Our personality traits predispose us to perceive the world in particular ways, to pay attention to some issues and events and human characteristics and not others [**link**, chapter 5, personality].

- *Motivation*. Do you get out of the shower to take a telephone call, perhaps expecting a party invitation or a job offer? We are more likely to perceive as important, and thus to respond to, stimuli that we find motivating [**link**, chapter 8, motivation].

Much of perception can be described as classification, or categorization. We categorize people as male or female, lazy or energetic, extrovert or shy. In fact our classification schemes are usually more sophisticated than that. We classify objects as cars, buildings, furniture, crockery, and so on, and we refine our classification schemes further under these headings. However, we are not born with a neat classification scheme 'wired in' with the brain. These categories are learned. They are social constructs. What we learn is often culture-bound, or culture-specific. An Indonesian visitor to one of our institutions once remarked, 'In your

Five ways the supermarket has you sussed

1. Different colours produce different reactions in shoppers. Cool blue, for example, is used at the fish counter to suggest freshness—and, of course, the sea.

2. The order in which a shopper looks over the goods is controlled by the order in which they are displayed. Goods at eye level are inspected first, then attention wanders to lower shelves.

3. Shelves of varying depth put more goods into view. This produces a sense of limitless stocks and encourages shoppers to notice less well-known products.

4. Strategic positioning of mirrors adds to the impression of abundance that the supermarket trades on ('you'll get everything here'). This is especially the case in the fruit and veg section.

5. Careful design of shelf units holds shoppers' attention. Curved shelving leads seamlessly from one aisle into the next. You probably won't even take your eyes off the displays as you progress through the store.

They say the trick when you are showing prospective buyers around your house is to brew fresh coffee and bake bread, as the smells produce a reassuring, homely atmosphere. Smell is a key tactic for supermarkets too. Coffee shops can create that same desirable smell, while bread smells can be pumped through air vents into the store, and in some cases into the car park so it hits you before you even enter the building. On trial in some American supermarkets is a process called micro-encapsulation, used at the point of sale. As the customer's hand brushes the surface of a pack of, say, coffee, or bread rolls, smell capsules that emit the smell of coffee or bread are broken. The capsules can also be triggered by heat, for instance by a neon sign above the display. Smell often affects us below the conscious level—we may not even know that we are responding to a supermarket's subtle manipulations.

From Gillian Drummond, 'Irresistible science of the super-sellers', *Focus*, November 1994, pp.24 and 26.

country, you feed the pigeons. In my country, the pigeons feed us'. The British revulsion at the thought of eating dog (classified as pet), the Hindu revulsion at the thought of eating beef (classified as sacred) and the Islamic aversion to alcohol (classified as proscribed by the Koran) are all culturally transmitted emotions based on learned values.

Problems arise when we and others act as if our culture had a monopoly on 'right thinking' on such issues. Different does not necessarily imply wrong. Different people within the same culture have different experiences and develop different expectations. The internal factors—our past experience and what we have learned our personalities, our motivations—contribute to the development of our expectations of the world around us, what we want from it, what will happen in it, and what should happen. We tend to select information that fits our expectations and pay less attention to information that does not.

Our categorization processes, and the search for meaning and pattern, are key characteristics of perception. This perceptual work is captured by the concept of **perceptual organization**.

The principles by which the process of perceptual organization operates were first identified by Max Wertheimer in 1923. The 'proximity principle' notes that we tend to group together or to classify stimuli that are physically close to each other and which thus appear to 'belong' together. Note how you 'see' three pairs rather than six blobs here:

Perceptual organization is the process through which incoming stimuli are organized or patterned in systematic and meaningful ways.

The 'similarity principle' notes that we classify or group together stimuli that resemble each other in appearance in some respect. Note how you 'see' four pairs here, not eight objects:

Max Wertheimer
(1880–1943)

The fact that we are able to make use of incomplete and ambiguous information, by 'filling in the gaps' from our own knowledge and past experience, is known as the 'principle of closure'. These principles of perceptual organization apply to simple visual stimuli. Of more interest here, however, is the way in which these principles apply to person perception. How often do we assume that people are similar just because they live in the same neighbourhood, or work in the same section of the factory or office building (proximity principle), or just because they wear the same clothes or have similar ethnic origins (similarity principle)? How often do we take incomplete information about someone (he's Scottish) and draw inferences from this (closure principle)? This can cause the spread of false rumours in organizations through what is sometimes called 'the grapevine'.

Perceptual sets and perceptual worlds

We have shown how the perceptual process selects incoming stimuli and organizes them into meaningful patterns. We have also argued that this processing is influenced by learning, motivation and personality—factors which give rise to expectations, which in turn make us more ready to respond to certain stimuli in certain ways and less ready to respond to others. This readiness to respond is called the individual's **perceptual set**.

A **perceptual set** is an individual's predisposition to respond to events in a particular manner. A perceptual set is also known as a **mental set**. As we tend to perceive what we expect to perceive, this can also be called our **perceptual expectations**.

The drawing on the following page was published by an international accounting firm in 1995. Some readers will recognize this as a variant on a drawing published in 1915 by the cartoonist W.H. Hill. What do you see here? An old woman, or a young woman? Your answer may be influenced by what you are predisposed to see at the time you are reading this. The reactions of different individuals will not be consistent, and it does not make sense to argue over which perception is 'correct'. We must accept that two people can observe the 'same' thing but perceive it in quite different ways. Failure to appreciate this feature of the perceptual process creates many organizational problems, and particularly communication problems. Hospital consultants, for instance, may perceive that junior doctors are overreacting to trivial issues and may dismiss their complaints lightly. The junior doctors, on the other hand, may perceive that their grievances are genuine, and that the consultants are simply not taking them seriously. It is not difficult to predict some of the outcomes in a situation like this. It makes little sense to ask whose perceptions are correct. The starting point for resolving issues such as this must lie with the recognition that different people hold different, but equally legitimate, views of the same set of circumstances.

The individual's **perceptual world** is their personal internal image, map or picture of their social, physical and organizational environment.

Chapter 1 identified two views of human behaviour [**link**, chapter 1, prologue]. The positivist perspective sets out to discover 'the world out there, as it really is'. The phenomenological perspective sets out to discover how our world is socially constructed, and how we experience and interpret that world. The argument in the last paragraph suggests that 'the world out there' is not a good starting point for developing an understanding of human behaviour. We each have a unique version of what is 'out there' and of our own place in it. In other words, we each live in our own **perceptual world**.

We each have a perceptual world that is selective and partial, and which concentrates on features of particular interest and importance to us. Through the processes of learning, motivation and personality development, we each have different expectations and different degrees of readiness to respond to objects, people and events in different ways. We impose meaning on received patterns of information; the meanings that we attach to objects, people and events are not

intrinsic to these things but are learned through social experience and are coloured by our current needs and objectives.

Our perceptions, that is the meanings that we attach to the information available to us, shape our actions. Behaviour in an organization context can usually be understood once we understand the way in which the individual perceives that context. Figure 7.3 (based on Dixon, 1999, p.30) illustrates the links between available information based on observation and experience, the perception based on that information, and outcomes in terms of decisions with respect to actions. This example explains why employees would ignore apparently reasonable management requests to become 'team players'.

Cultural factors pay a significant role in determining how we interpret available information and experience. You order a meal in a restaurant. Was the service fast or slow? Research into cultural differences in the perception of time suggest that your answer to this question depends to some extent on where in the world you come from. One well-known piece of research (Levine, 1990) compared the pace

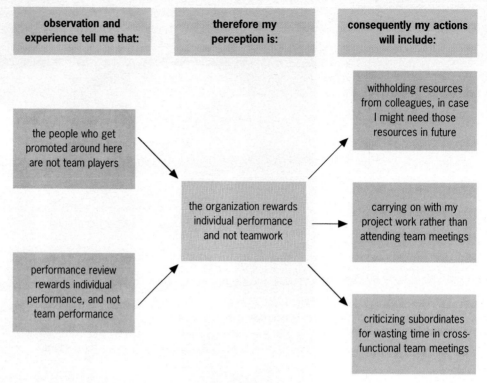

Figure 7.3: The information–perception–actions link

of life in six countries (Britain, Italy, Indonesia, Japan, Taiwan and the United States) by measuring:

- the accuracy of clocks in city bank branches;
- the speed at which city pedestrians walked;
- the length of time it took to buy a postage stamp.

The research revealed that Japanese cities had the most accurate clocks, the fastest pedestrians and the most efficient post office clerks. Indonesian cities, in contrast, had the least accurate clocks and the slowest pedestrians. Italy, however, had the slowest post office clerks. The overall results of this study were as follows:

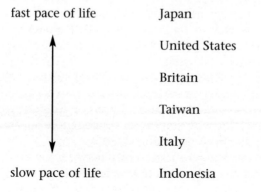

To understand an individual's behaviour, therefore, we need to know something of the elements in their perceptual world, and the pattern of information and other cultural influences that have shaped that world. To change an individual's behaviour, therefore, we first have to consider changing their perceptions, through the information and experiences available to them. In the example in figure 7.3, this would involve radical, visible and sustained changes in company performance review, and in promotion policies and practice.

Developing an understanding of one's own perceptual world is difficult because there are so many influences of which we are not fully aware. Information about the perceptual worlds of others is also elusive and, although this is by no means impossible, this does create a barrier to mutual understanding and to effective interpersonal communications. Unfortunately, we tend to forget that our own perceptual world is not the only possible or correct one.

Stop and criticize

Here is an anecdote from the history of the computer company IBM. How would an understanding of the concept of perceptual worlds have helped the manager, Reiswig?

The IBM programmers still found things heavy-handed at times, despite Reiswig's attempts to lighten up. For instance, Reiswig at one point made fifty-hour weeks mandatory. Some of the programmers, who had been working eighty- to ninety-hour weeks, took that as an insult. They said that if IBM wanted to play those sorts of penny-ante games, then they'd work exactly fifty hours a week. Progress on OS/2 actually *slowed* after extra hours became required. An apocryphal memo began circulating among the IBM programmers about a rowing race that had supposedly taken place between IBM and Microsoft. Microsoft had one coxswain shouting orders while eight people rowed, the memo said. IBM had eight coxswains shouting orders while one rowed. Microsoft won big. So IBM launched several task forces to do some coxswain/oarsman analyses and decided after several weeks that the problem was that the oarsman wasn't rowing hard enough. When the race was rerun and Microsoft won big again, the oarsman was fired.

After a month or so, though, Reiswig figured out what was going on and removed the requirement. Hours soared, and the OS/2 project became one of the most engaging in the history of IBM.

From Paul Carroll, *Big Blues: The Unmaking of IBM*, Orion Books, London, 1994, p.278.

Do we see to know or know to see?

Fortunately, we as individuals are not as isolated from each other as the argument so far seems to suggest. We do not live in a social and organizational world of constant misunderstanding and failed communication. A high proportion of our interactions are effective, or tolerably so. Why? We are, of course, not wholly unique as individuals, and our personal perceptual worlds overlap. We share the same, or similar, sensory apparatus. We share the same basic needs. We share much of the same background social environment. Within the same society, although there are vast differences in experience, we share some of the same problems and environmental features. All this common ground makes the tasks of mutual understanding and interpersonal communication possible.

We have defined the process of perception in terms of making sense of the information available to us. We are active processors of that information, not passive recipients. However, much of that information is already processed for us. We are bombarded with communication and information, from other people, from books and newspapers and magazines, from street advertising, from radio and television, from the internet, and from various internal organizational sources—annual reports, team briefings, newsletters.

In the contemporary organizational context, employees at all levels have experienced major upheavals in recent years as organizations have introduced initiatives to improve performance [**links**, chapter 2, the world outside; chapter 18, organizational change]. These changes, which have led to combinations of stress, burnout, initiative fatigue and work intensification as well as to improved organizational performance (Buchanan, Claydon and Doyle, 1999), have typically been communicated using arguments like this:

> In order to survive in a rapidly changing, turbulent and highly competitive environment, we need to become more efficient, more cost-conscious, more flexible and adaptable, and more customer-focused. Therefore, we need to implement the following radical changes to organization structures, procedures and jobs.

There are two ways to 'read' this 'turbulent world' argument:

1. This is an unexceptional and taken-for-granted expression of contemporary organizational reality. There is nothing unusual in this argument about the need for organizational flexibility to deal with external change. People have been saying that for years. It's obvious, isn't it? This is a widely accepted view.

2. This is an attempt to promote a particular perception of organizational reality, based on management values. After all, change is stressful and employees are likely to resist. However, if we can present a compelling argument that is beyond challenge, resistance can be avoided and the changes can go ahead more smoothly.

The key to this second reading lies with our use of language. One view of language is that we use it to communicate our observations and our understanding. An alternative view is that language, and in particular the concepts that we use, colours and shapes that understanding. You cannot 'see' twenty different types of snow until you know what they are called and can link those labels to different visual stimuli. In other words, one view of language simply says that we 'see in order to know'. The alternative view is that we need to know first, before we can 'see'. The implication of this second view of language, that 'we know to see', is that perceptions can potentially be influenced—that is, can be managed—through language.

Consider the 'turbulent world so we must change' argument. What language typically accompanies this exhortation? Looking through job advertisements and other forms of organizational literature, note how many times the following kinds of statement appear:

- we need to become more *customer-oriented*

- our mission is *excellence*

- we believe in employee *empowerment*

- our survival depends on *efficiency* and *cost-effectiveness*

- *initiative* and *creativity* are key competences

- *flexibility* is the key to competitive success

- we must strive for *continuous improvement*

- we are a *total quality* organization.

The 'turbulent world' argument is hard to challenge and criticize. Communications of this kind have the potential to lead employees to internalize management values as their own, without question. It is difficult to argue that 'there is so little change in the business environment that we should be developing a rigid bureaucracy', or that 'customers don't matter, let's pay attention to our own staff'. However, rapid change can be personally and socially damaging: factory and office closures and relocation, loss of jobs, loss of community. An organization that ignores the well-being of its staff may find that it loses customers who feel that they have been given inadequate or discourteous service.

Language promotes a particular set of perceptions related to a specific set of values. The 'turbulent world' language creates an impression of 'the way things are', of 'it makes sense doesn't it?', of 'that's obvious'. If you can get people to accept this language and these arguments, then language becomes a tool for manipulating perceptions. If we can manipulate perceptions, we can control behaviour because, as this chapter argues, our behaviour depends not on some 'external reality' but on our perception of reality.

This 'second reading' of the 'turbulent world' argument, viewing it as an attempt to manage perception, reflects an aspect of the postmodern perspective discussed in chapter 2 [**link**, chapter 2, the world outside]. This perspective argues that 'reality out there' is not simply waiting to be discovered but is created in social exchange through language. We don't go out and 'discover' reality. Multiple 'realities' are presented to us through our interactions. What matters is the version of 'reality' in which most people come to believe. The management of perception is thus a tool for 'keeping people in their place' by inhibiting challenge and criticism. You cannot readily challenge something that appears to be, and is widely accepted as, 'natural', 'obvious' or 'inevitable' without appearing deviant or eccentric.

Here we find, as chapter 2 argues, two strengths of the postmodern perspective: first, in pointing to the existence and value of differences in perception, of multiple perspectives, arguing that no single perspective should be given the privilege of being 'correct'; second, by inviting us to question the 'obvious' and the 'taken for granted'.

| **Stop and criticize** | The postmodernist argues that we are 'fed' information in language which reinforces the management definition of reality and justifies management decisions in order to make employees compliant. The manager can claim 'communication is part of my job'. The employee can claim 'I can tell when managers are trying to fool me'. Are our perceptions so readily manipulated by slick presentation and fancy jargon? |

Perceptual sets and assumptions

A **halo effect** is a judgement based on a single striking characteristic, such as an aspect of dress, speech, posture or nationality. Haloes can be positive or negative.

The concept of perceptual set, or perceptual expectation, applies to the ways in which we see other people, events and objects. To understand the nature of perception is to understand, at least in part, the sources and nature of many organizational problems. There are two related and prominent features of the process of people perception: the **halo effect** and **stereotyping**.

The term 'halo effect' was first used by the psychologist Edward Thorndike in 1920. Remember the concept of selective attention. This phenomenon applies to our perception of people. It is a natural human response, on meeting a stranger, to 'size them up', to make judgements about the kind of person they are and whether we will like them or not. We do this to others on a first encounter; they

Edward Lee
Thorndyke
(1874–1949)

Walter Lippmann
(1889–1974)

A **stereotype** is a
category or
personality type to
which we consign
people on the basis
of their membership
of some known
group [**link**, chapter
5, personality].

do this to us. It seems as if first impressions really do count, after all (and we don't get a second chance to make a first impression).

However, faced with so much new information about someone—the physical and social setting, their appearance, what they say, how they say it, their posture, their non-verbal behaviour, how they respond to us—we are forced to be selective with respect to the information to which we pay attention. In terms of the model of the perceptual process in figure 7.1, therefore, the halo effect is an error at the selective attention stage. Our judgements can thus rely on a single striking characteristic: the sound of their voice or a familiar accent, a perfume, their dress or tie, the car they drive or their hairstyle. If this judgement is favourable, we give the other person a positive halo, regardless of other information that, if we gave it due attention, might lead us to a different, more balanced, evaluation. If our judgement, on the other hand, is not favourable, we give the other person a negative halo. The halo effect can work in both directions.

The halo effect can thus act as an early screen that filters out later information which is not consistent with our earlier judgement. The problem, of course, is that what we notice first about another person is often not relevant to the judgement that we want to make. A confounding factor is that we tend to give more favourable judgements to people who have characteristics in common with us. However, since when did somebody's voice, hairstyle, deodorant or clothes enable us to predict, say, their ability to design bridges, or manage a department in a hotel? Some people feel that they can make such predictions from such limited evidence, based presumably on their own past experiences. The halo effect can apply to things as well as to people. How many examples can you think of where country of origin leads you automatically to believe that the product quality will be good or bad (Australian wine, Belgian chocolates, French perfume, German cars, Italian clothes, Scotch whisky)?

Remember the concept of perceptual organization? This phenomenon also applies to person perception. The term 'stereotyping' was first used by typographers to made-up blocks of type and was first used to describe bias in person perception by Walter Lippmann in 1922. The concept refers simply to the way in which we group together people who seem to us to share similar characteristics. Lippman saw stereotypes as 'pictures in the head', as simple mental images of groups and their behaviour. So when we meet, say, an accountant, a nurse, an engineer, a poet or a mechanical engineering student, we attribute certain personality traits to them because they are accountants, or students, or whatever. Everybody knows, for example, that Scots are mean and that blondes have more fun. In terms of the model of the perceptual process in figure 7.1, therefore, stereotyping is an error at the perceptual organization stage.

Stop and criticize

Explore your own stereotypes by completing each of the following sentences with three terms that you think describe most or all members of the category concerned:

university lecturers are . . .

artists are . . .

mechanical engineers are . . .

trainee nurses are . . .

airline pilots are . . .

You may find it interesting to share your stereotypes with those of colleagues, particularly if some of them have friends or close relatives who are pilots, nurses, mechanical engineers . . .

Why job applicants are not hired

A survey of 153 human resource managers in America identified the 20 most common errors made by applicants attending job interviews, listed here in order of importance:

1. Poor personal appearance.
2. Overaggressiveness.
3. Inability to express information clearly.
4. Lack of interest and enthusiasm.
5. Lack of career planning; no purpose and no goals.
6. Nervous, lack of confidence and poise.
7. Overemphasis on money.
8. Unwillingness to start at the bottom.
9. Makes excuses.
10. Lack of tact and courtesy.
11. Immaturity.
12. Condemns past employers.
13. No genuine interest in company or job.
14. Fails to look interviewer in the eye.
15. Sloppy application form.
16. Little sense of humour.
17. Arrives late at interview.
18. Fails to express appreciation for interviewer's time.
19. Fails to ask questions about the company and job.
20. Vague responses to questions.

Each of these behaviours can lead the interviewer to perceive the applicant in negative terms.

From Arthur G. Bedeian, *Management*, CBS International, 1986, p.376.

If we know, or assume, somebody's apparent group membership in this way, our instant categorization allows us to attribute a range of qualities to them. Stereotypes are overgeneralizations and are bound to be radically inaccurate on occasion. But they can be convenient. By adopting a stereotyped perspective, we may be able to shortcut our evaluation process and make quicker and more reliable predictions of behaviour. We can have problems, however, with those who fall into more than one category with conflicting stereotypes: the mechanical engineer who writes poetry, for instance.

Stereotyping also works at an international level. See if you can match these stereotyped (not necessarily accurate) images with the right countries:

	Culture		Stereotyped image
1	American	A	Demonstrative, talkative, emotional, romantic, bold, artistic
2	English	B	*Mañana* attitude, macho, music lovers, touchers
3	French	C	Inscrutable, intelligent, xenophobic, golfers, group-oriented, polite, soft-spoken
4	Italian	D	Conservative, reserved, polite, proper, formal
5	Latin American	E	Arrogant, loud, friendly, impatient, generous, hardworking, monolingual
6	Japanese	F	Arrogant, rude, chauvinistic, romantics, gourmets, cultural, artistic

Clearly, while some members of each of these cultures may possess some of the attributes of their stereotype, it would be false to claim that every member of a culture shared the same attributes to the same degree. Not all Asians are keen golfers; not all English people are reserved and polite; not all Americans are arrogant and hardworking.

Sex, appearance, attractiveness and discrimination

Fritz Heider
(1896–1988)

Attribution is the process by which we make sense of our environment through our perceptions of causality. An attribution, therefore, is a belief about the cause or causes of an event or an action.

We emphasized earlier in the chapter that the perceptual process is concerned with making sense of and explaining the world around us, and the people and events in it. Our need for explanation and understanding is reflected in the way in which we search for the causes of people's actions. Our perceptions of causality are known as **attributions**.

Attribution theory was developed during the 1950s and 1960s by Fritz Heider (1958) and Harold Kelley (1971). They argue that our understanding of our social world is based on our continual attempts at causal analysis based on how we interpret our experience. This understanding potentially allows us both to predict and to control certain future social events.

Why is that person so successful? Why did that project fail? Why are those people still arguing? If we understand the causes of success, failure and conflict, we may be able to adjust our behaviour and other factors accordingly. Attribution is simply the process of attaching or attributing causes or reasons to the actions and events we see. We tend to look for causes either in people's abilities and personalities or in aspects of the setting or circumstances in which they find themselves. This distinction is usually described in terms of internal causality and external causality. We may explain a particular individual's success, or promotion, with reference to their superior skills and knowledge (internal causality) on the one hand, or with reference to luck, 'friends in high places' and coincidence on the other hand (external causality).

Research has revealed patterns in our attributions. When we are explaining our personal achievements, we point to our capabilities, but when we are explaining our lack of success, we blame our circumstances. This is termed *projection*. We project blame onto factors beyond our control, to external causes. However, we tend to attribute the behaviour of others to their disposition, that is to aspects of their personality. In psychology, this tendency to exaggerate the influence of personality when explaining the behaviour of others, and to overlook the effect of contextual factors, is known as the fundamental attribution error.

Attribution theory may help to explain aspects of discrimination in organizational settings.

It has been demonstrated that sex and appearance influence the way in which we are perceived, paid and promoted. Two American researchers, Susan Averett and Sanders Korenman (1993), found that the hourly wage of overweight women, aged 23 to 31, was 20 per cent lower on average than that of women of average weight. They even found that underweight women also received underweight pay packets. However, the husbands of thin women earned on average 45 per cent more than those of fat ones (you might like to consider why this should be the case). Almost the reverse was found to be true for American men. Those who were underweight had the lowest earnings, with slightly overweight men earning as much as 26 per cent more than their lightweight colleagues. Daniel Hamermesh and Jeff Biddle (1993) found that attractive men and women earn about 5 per cent more than those with average appearance (based on interviewers' ratings of attractiveness). Plain women in their study were found to be earning 5 per cent less than those rated average, and plain men earned 10 per cent less.

The wrong attribution

June 1996   Sharon Wilson, 20, sales assistant at Jacket Racket and Destiny Clothing Company, Clydebank, dismissed for 'becoming too fat and ugly' when pregnant. Wins unfair dismissal claim of £1,049 against employer.

August 1998   Three teenage girls dismissed for being 'too ugly' at a nightclub in South Shields. Reported management wanted to bring in 'models' to hand out flyers.

October 1999   Patrick Carroll, offshore oil worker, dismissed for being 'too fat'. Wins £14,420 compensation after Aberdeen tribunal heard that the medical he underwent was incomplete.

October 1999   Disc jockey Steve Jackson, 40, sacked by Kiss FM after change of management, wins unfair dismissal claim. Claimed that both his race and age were a factor, but tribunal accepts only the latter allegation.

October 1999   Diana Holland, Transport and General Workers Union officer for women, race and equality, reports case of three young women who were dismissed from employment at a motorway services restaurant. A new manager told them they were 'not the sort of people we want to employ'. One wore thick glasses, one was 'too quiet' and the other was black.

From Jon Lamb, 'Face value gains credence in "unwritten" HR policies', *People Management*, vol.5, no.23, 25 November 1999, p.15.

Why should appearance have such an effect on career progression? Our attributions are related to the phenomenon of stereotyping. We seem to attribute explanations of, or causes for, people's behaviour to aspects of their appearance. Discrimination against particular groups and individuals on the basis of sex, sexual orientation, age or ethnic background is now widely recognized. Legislation seeks to address (with mixed results) sexual and racial discrimination, and social attitudes towards homosexuals and the elderly in organizational settings do seem, slowly, to be changing. However, attribution research suggests that discrimination, based on our perceptions of causal links between sex, appearance and job performance, are more subtle than this and considerably less public.

Leslie Martel and Henry Biller (1987) have demonstrated how the problems of sexism, ageism and racism also apply to 'heightism'. Their research showed how both men and women thought that short men, from 5 feet 2 inches to 5 feet 5 inches, were less mature, less positive, less successful, less capable, less confident, less outgoing, more inhibited, more timid and more passive. In other words, short men are judged negatively, as their behaviour—and competence—is attributed to size and related personality characteristics.

A summary of research in this field by the newspaper *The Economist* (1995) argued that the Western 'ideal' height for men is now 6 feet 2 inches, and rising. This summary argued that discrimination on grounds of height, or heightism, is now well established. In all but three American presidential elections this century, the taller man won. In 1980, over half the chief executives in America's largest 500 companies were six feet tall or higher, and only 3 per cent were 5 feet 7 inches or less. A recent British study suggested that for each four inches of height in adolescence, earnings rose by 2 per cent in early adulthood.

With respect to attractiveness, sex, height and weight, we are dealing with factors which cannot have any meaningful impact on performance for most jobs or occupations. The tall, attractive female computer programmer of average weight *may* be more effective in her job than the short, overweight male programmer with the unremarkable features. A moment's consideration, however, would probably lead us to reject height, weight and attractiveness as causal factors in th

equation and lead us to look for differences in education, experience and ability instead. The problem seems to be, however, that we make attribution errors by jumping quickly and unconsciously to judgements of this kind, particularly when we have little information about the other person on which to base a more careful assessment.

We can regard any aspect of our appearance as a form of non-verbal communication [**link**, chapter 6, communication]. We cannot control our age or height, for example, but these factors, combined with behaviour that is under our control, send signals that others decode in the light of their experiences (age is related to reliability), expectations (tall and handsome means self-confident and knowledgeable) and prejudices (short and overweight women will deter customers). This also applies to clothing, or style of dress. This is an aspect which is, of course, within our control. Dress style can be a significant indicator of organizational culture and can contribute significantly to the individual's impression management. The way in which we dress can tell others how we want to be seen (as formal, relaxed, creative, businesslike) rather than what we are really like. However, we may not always be aware how others perceive these attempts to manage our impression through our dress style.

Perceptions of personality based on voice quality

We seem to develop perceptions, or beliefs, about relationships between the physical characteristics of other people and their personalities and behaviour. In other words, we develop implicit personality theories. P.R. Hinton (1993) notes that we base these implicit theories, in part, on voice quality, such as:

voice quality high in	male voice	female voice
breathiness	young, artistic	feminine, pretty, petite, shallow
flatness	masculine, cold: same for both sexes	
nasality	having many socially undesirable features: same for both sexes	
tenseness	old, unyielding, cantankerous	young, emotional, highly strung

There is, however, no empirical basis for these judgements. A man with a tense voice is not necessarily old and cantankerous. A woman with a breathy voice is not necessarily petite and shallow. Think of a time when you first spoke to somebody on the telephone. Later, when you met them face to face, did they appear and behave as you expected?

Based on P.R. Hinton, *The Psychology of Interpersonal Perception*, Routledge, London, 1993, p.16.

Stop and criticize

Let us consider the styles of dress adopted by the instructors in your educational institution, across all the subjects you may be studying at the moment. (Let us not pick on organizational behaviour instructors in particular.) How does their style of dress influence your perceptions of their:

- approachability

- subject knowledge

- professionalism

- understanding of the world beyond the academic 'ivory tower'

How would you advise individual instructors to change their style of dress to improve the ways in which they are perceived by students on those criteria?

Is there a student 'dress code' in your institution—a code to which you adhere? What are you personally saying by sticking to this dress code? What messages would you send by deliberately breaking or ignoring this dress code?

Person perception: errors and avoidance

The main sources of errors in person perception seem to include:

1. Not collecting enough information about other people.

2. Basing our judgements on information that is irrelevant or insignificant.

3. Seeing what we expect to see and what we want to see, and not investigating further.

4. Allowing early information about someone to affect our judgement, despite later and contradictory information.

5. Allowing our own characteristics to affect what we see in others and how we judge them.

6. Accepting stereotypes uncritically.

7. Attempting to decode non-verbal behaviour outside the context in which it appears.

8. Basing attributions on flimsy and potentially irrelevant evidence.

The remedies, therefore, include:

1. Take more time and avoid instant or 'snap' judgements about others.

2. Collect and consciously use more information about other people.

3. Develop self-awareness, and an understanding of how our personal biases and preferences affect our perceptions and judgements of other people.

4. Check our attributions—the assumptions we make about the causes of behaviour, particularly the links we make between aspects of personality and appearance on the one hand and behaviour on the other.

If we are to improve our understanding of others, we must first have a well-devel oped knowledge of ourselves—our strengths, our preferences, our flaws and our biases. The development of self-knowledge can be an uncomfortable process. In organizational settings, we are often constrained in the expression of our feelings (positive and negative) about other people, due to social or cultural norms, and to the communication barriers erected by status and power differentials. This may in part explain the enduring appeal of training courses in social and interpersonal skills, self-awareness and personal growth designed to help us overcome these problems, to 'get in touch' with other people, and to 'get in touch with ourselves'. Training in interpersonal communication skills typically emphasizes openness and honesty in relationships, active listening skills, sensitivity to non-verbal behaviour, and how to give and receive both critical and non-evaluative feedback.

Adrian Furnham's unlucky thirteen

Adrian Furnham (1997) argues that the process of making evaluations, judgements or ratings of the performance of employees is subject to a number of systematic perception errors. This is particularly problematic in a performance appraisal context:

1. *Central tendency*: Appraising everyone at the middle of the rating scale.

2. *Contrast error*: Basing an appraisal on comparison with other employees (who may have received undeserved high or low ratings) rather than on established performance criteria.

3. *Different from me*: Giving a poor appraisal because the person has qualities or characteristics not possessed by the appraiser.

4. *Halo effect*: Appraising an employee undeservedly well on one quality (performance, for example) because they are perceived highly by the appraiser on another quality (attractiveness, perhaps).

5. *Horn effect*: The opposite of the halo effect. Giving someone a poor appraisal on one quality (attractiveness) influences poor rating on other qualities (performance).

6. *Initial impression*: Basing an appraisal on first impressions rather than on how the person has behaved throughout the period to which the appraisal relates.

7. *Latest behaviour*: Basing an appraisal on the person's recent behaviour, rather than on how they have behaved throughout the appraisal period.

8. *Lenient or generous rating*: Perhaps the most common error, being consistently generous in appraisal, mostly to avoid conflict.

9. *Performance dimension error*: Giving someone a similar appraisal on two distinct but similar qualities, because they happen to follow each other on the appraisal form.

10. *Same as me*: Giving a good appraisal because the person has qualities or characteristics possessed by the appraiser.

11. *Spillover effect*: Basing this appraisal, good or bad, on the results of the previous appraisal, rather than on how the person has behaved during the appraisal period.

12. *Status effect*: Giving those in higher-level positions consistently better appraisals than those in lower-level jobs.

13. *Strict rating*: Being consistently harsh in appraising performance.

Based on Adrian Furnham, *The Psychology of Behaviour at Work*, Psychology Press/Taylor & Francis, Hove, Sussex, 1997, pp.507–8.

Recap

1. *Identify the main features of the process of perception.*
   - People behave according to how they perceive the world, not in response to 'reality'.
   - The perceptual process involves the interpretation of sensory input in the light of past experience, and our store of knowledge, beliefs, expectations and motives.

2. *Distinguish between the bottom-up processing of sensory information and the top-down interpretation of that information.*
   - Sensation, or bottom-up processing, determines the data to which we pay attention.
   - Perception, or top-down processing, determines the way in which we organize and interpret perceived information in order to make behavioural choices.

3. *Understand the nature and implications of selective attention (perceptual selectivity) and perceptual organization.*
   - Perceptual selectivity is influenced by external factors relating to the stimulus and the context, and by internal factors such as learning, personality and motivation.
   - The way in which we organize and interpret sensory data in meaningful ways, even when it is incomplete or ambiguous, is known as perceptual organization.

4. *Give examples of how behaviour is influenced by our perceptions.*
   - We each have our own perceptual world, an internal mental image of our environment.
   - Supermarkets exploit an understanding of selective attention when designing store layout, when positioning goods, and in deciding which odours to use to entice customers.

   - Different cultures lead to differences in perception and consequently in behaviour.

5. *Explain and illustrate the main processes and problems in person perception, including false attributions, halo effects and stereotyping.*
   - An attribution is a belief about cause and effect. When speaking about ourselves, we tend to attribute success to personal factors and failure to external factors. When speaking about others, we tend to attribute success and failure to personality features.
   - Making an overall favourable judgement of someone on the basis of a single positive characteristic is known as the halo effect, which can be positive or negative.
   - Assuming that someone possesses a set of personality traits because they belong to a particular social group is known as stereotyping.
   - Errors in person perception can be overcome by taking more time, collecting more information, avoiding personal prejudices, and through increased self-awareness.

6. *Explain some of less widely appreciated sources of discrimination at work, against men and women, arising from characteristics of the person perception and attribution processes.*
   - Aspects of behaviour are attributed to appearance, leading to discrimination. You are likely to be paid less at work if you are an overweight or underweight female, a short man, a husband with an overweight wife, or are perceived to be unattractive.
   - The fundamental attribution error leads us to emphasize personality and ignore context.

Revision

1. You observe someone behaving in what you perceive to be a highly unusual manner at work, contrary as far as you can observe to 'common sense'. How would you proceed to understand and to make sense of their behaviour?

2. Explain the distinction between sensation and perception and also explain the significance of this distinction.

3. What is the individual's perceptual world, what factors influence this construct, and how does an understanding of someone's perceptual world help us to understand their behaviour?

4. What is the difference between selective attention and perceptual organization, and what factors influence the latter process?

5. What are the factors influencing selective attention, and how can a knowledge of these factors be exploited in commercial settings?

Springboard

Anderson, D. and Mullen, P., (eds), 1998, *Faking It: The Sentimentalization of Modern Society*, Penguin Books, London.

This is a controversial series of essays with a common and critical theme, that the media offer us a 'sentimentalized' view of contemporary events and problems including, for example, the death of Diana, Princess of Wales, illness and the hospital treatment of cancer, and school education. The authors argue that such media sentimentalization, which they demonstrate is widespread, distorts our perception of reality in ways that are dangerous because they lead us to overlook genuine social and organizational problems. Reading these accounts, consider the extent to which your perception of society and its organizations is influenced by the media.

Goldstein, E., 1998, *Sensation and Perception*, Brooks Cole, San Francisco.

A comprehensive student-focused introduction to the psychology and physiology of sensation and perception, offering a much more detailed treatment than is possible in an introductory organizational behaviour text. Describes how the senses function in tandem, exposing the complexity of perceptual processes. Also provides some fascinating illustrations and examples to reinforce the arguments.

Pinker, S., 1997, *How the Mind Works*, Penguin Books, London.

Pinker's explanation relies on two theoretical planks, evolutionary biology (a version of Darwinism) and the computational theory of mind. The computational theory, as might be expected, regards the mind as a kind of modular information processor of considerable complexity and sophistication. Pinker's investigation of the clues to how our information processor functions is insightful and entertaining. Pinker's writing style makes complex ideas accessible, and readers develop much more than an understanding of perception from his wide-ranging analysis.

Zalkind, S.S. and Costello, T.W., 1962, 'Perception: some recent research and implications for administration', *Administrative Science Quarterly*, vol.7, pp.218–35.

A popular and much quoted paper which has been often reproduced in collections of readings. Clearly written and still worth reading, Zalkind and Costello deal explicitly with the importance of an understanding of perception for management—which in those days was described as 'administration'. It is perhaps also interesting to note how perceptions of 'administrators' have changed, becoming today's professional business 'managers' who would reject that dated term.

Zimbardo, P., McDermott, M., Jansz, J. and Metaal, N., 1995, *Psychology: A European Text*, HarperCollins, London.

A typical introductory university or college text on psychology. Clearly written with many helpful learning features and illustrations. Chapter 6 offers a more detailed treatment of the psychology of perception than is possible in our text on organizational behaviour, but their treatment will be familiar if you have read our chapter first. There are a number of similar texts available where the treatment of perception (and other psychology topics) is similar, but the emphasis is conceptual and technical and does not focus on organizational applications.

Home viewing

The Sixth Sense (1999, director M. Night Shyamalan) concerns the attempts by a disillusioned child psychologist, Malcom Crowe (played by Bruce Willis), to cure a young boy, Cole (Haley Joel Osment), who is tormented because he sees dead people. Crowe's depression, and his eagerness to help Cole, are explained at the beginning, when he is attacked at home by an ex-patient who had the same problem but whom Crowe was unable to help. Crowe spends so much time with Cole that he ignores his wife Anna (Olivia Williams). However, this film cleverly manipulates the perceptions and assumptions of the audience. Once you have watched the film to the end, either reflect on the action or watch it again. Notice which clues you 'saw' but either ignored or misinterpreted the first time around. Notice how your interpretation of events relied on the assumptions that you made, or rather the assumptions that you were expected to make. It is only when you know the full plot of the film that you can begin to make 'correct' assumptions and interpretations, based on exactly the same evidence you were presented with the first time around. What does this reveal about the ease with which your perceptions, assumptions and understanding can be manipulated?

OB in literature

Aldous Huxley, *The Doors of Perception/Heaven and Hell*, Flamingo, 1994 (first published in 1954 by Chatto & Windus, London).

This is Huxley's account of his experiment, in 1953, with mescalin, a hallucinogenic drug with effects similar to those induced by LSD (and with echoes from the mystical Mexican writing of Carlos Castaneda). In *The Doors of Perception*, Huxley provides a fascinating account of how his perception of reality was altered by this experience, in effect opening up a whole new perceptual world. In *Heaven and Hell*, the sequel, he presents his later reflections on this experience. An interesting place to start questioning what we take to be 'real' with respect to the world around us and our perception and understanding of it.

Chapter exercises

1: Personality perception

Objectives

1. To explore how we make personality assessments based on perceptions of facial characteristics.

2. To consider the validity of these kinds of assessment.

When you meet someone for the first time, you immediately begin to assess what kind of person they are—friendly, hostile, shy, outgoing, warm, cold, helpful, reserved—and so on. Facial features and expressions are one of the main sources of clues for this assessment. It is particularly important for politicians to understand how these judgements are made, because they (presumably) want to appear open, honest and sincere and not to be perceived as uncaring, devious and manipulative. Television now plays a significant role in the promotion of political figures, and television typically concentrates attention on the face and voice. How do we make personality judgements based on facial features?

Briefing

First read these two descriptions of different people. As you read these descriptions, imagine what each person looks like, then rate their facial features on the following characteristics, placing an A at the appropriate point on the scale for the first person on each characteristic, and a B on the scale for the second person.

First person (A): This man is warmhearted and honest, has a good sense of humour, is intelligent, and is unbiased in his opinions. He is responsible and self-confident with an air of refinement.

Second person (B): This woman is ruthless and brutal. She is extremely hostile, quick-tempered and overbearing. She is known for her boorish and vulgar manner, and is a very domineering and unsympathetic person.

feature							
directness of gaze	direct gaze	☐	☐	☐	☐	☐	averted gaze
direction of gaze	upward gaze	☐	☐	☐	☐	☐	downward gaze
eyes	wide eyes	☐	☐	☐	☐	☐	narrow eyes
brow	smooth	☐	☐	☐	☐	☐	knitted
nostrils	relaxed	☐	☐	☐	☐	☐	distended
curve of mouth	corners up	☐	☐	☐	☐	☐	corners down

Now compare your ratings with colleagues, and consider the following questions:

1. Did you have difficulties in imagining what these two people could look like, leading you to hesitate in making judgements of their facial features on these characteristics?

2. Are there similarities between you and your colleagues with respect to expectations concerning the different facial characteristics of these two people? Or do you and colleagues have completely different expectations?

3. If you were making this judgement the other way around, inferring personality traits from your perception of facial features, how accurate do you think such personality judgements are likely to be?

2: Waiting for interview

Objectives

1. To examine how perception is influenced by knowledge and past experience.

2. To demonstrate how our individual perceptual worlds are shaped by these factors. You are about to go for a job interview, but you will be kept waiting in the interviewer's office for a time beforehand. During that time, you can observe clues about your interviewer and perhaps about the company. What clues do you consider to be significant and revealing? Can you identify your own personal experiences that affect how you observe and judge in this kind of setting? How does that past experience colour your perception today?

Briefing

This exercise can be completed in class time but may be more effective if steps 1 to 3 are completed beforehand. If the class lasts for only 50 to 60 minutes, time will be tight without some advance preparation.

Step 1 Read *The manager's room description* which follows to get a feel for the setting in which you find yourself.
Step 2 Complete the analysis sheet.

In the **data** column, record those observations that you find significant and revealing about the kind of person who occupies this room.

In the **experiences** column, record past incidents or events, recent or distant, that you think influence your observation.

In the **inferences** column, note the perceptions or conclusions that you reach from your data.

data I observe in the room	my past experiences	the inferences that I make

Step 3 Using that analysis, write a profile of your interviewer.
Step 4 Finally, record your answers to the following questions:

1 Would you work for this person?

2 What would you expect this person's management style to be like?

3 How confident are you of your analysis, your profile and your responses to the last two questions?

4 Explain how the analysis that you have just completed can be used to illustrate the concepts of selective attention, perceptual organization, perceptual world and stereotyping.

Step 5 Present your findings, according to your instructor's directions.

The manager's room description

You are now in the Acme Holdings company offices, top floor, for your job interview. It sounds like your ideal position. As personal assistant, you will be working for the managing director, who has asked to interview you. You have arrived on time, but the managing director's secretary apologizes and tells you there will be a delay. The managing director has been called to an important meeting, which will take up to fifteen minutes. The secretary tells you that you are welcome to wait in the managing director's private office and shows you in.

You know that you will be alone here for fifteen minutes. You look around the room, curious about the person with whom you may be working. The shallow pile carpet is a warm pink, with no pattern. You choose one of six high-backed chairs, upholstered in a darker fabric that matches well with the carpet and curtains, and with polished wooden arms. In the centre of the ring of chairs is a low glass-topped coffee table. On the table there is a large white ashtray, advertising a well-known national brand of beer. There is no sign of cigarettes, but the ashtray holds two books of matches, one from a hotel in Geneva and the other from a local restaurant. On the wall behind you is a large photograph of a vintage motor car, accompanied by its driver in leather helmet, goggles, scarf and long leather coat; you can't make out the driver's face. The window ledge holds four plants arranged equal distances apart; two look like small exotic ferns, and the others are a begonia and a geranium in flower.

On the other side of the room sits a large wooden executive desk with a black leather chair. A framed copy of the company's mission statement hangs on the wall behind the desk, and below that sits a closed black leather briefcase with brass combination locks. The plain grey waste paper basket by the wall beside the desk is full of papers. At the front of the desk sits a pen-stand with a letter opener. To the side is a 'state of the art' laptop computer and a desk lamp. In front of the lamp sits a metal photograph frame holding two pictures. One is of an attractive woman in her thirties with a young boy around eight years old. The other photograph is of a retriever dog in a field to the side of some farm buildings. In front of the frame is a stack of file folders. Immediately in front of the chair, on the desk, is a small pile of papers and a Mont Blanc pen with the Acme company logo stamped on the barrel.

On the other side of the desk is a delicate china mug. In front of it lies what looks like a leather-covered address book or perhaps a diary, and a pad of yellow paper. Beside the pad there is a pile of unopened mail with envelopes of differing sizes. On top of the mail and behind are some half-folded newspapers: *The Guardian*, *The Independent* and *The Financial Times*. You note that there is no telephone on the desk. Behind the desk is a small glass-fronted display case. There are some books lined up on top of the case: *The Pursuit of Wow*, *The Oxford Dictionary of New Words*, *Dealing with Difficult People*, *You Are What You Eat* and *Shattering the Glass Ceiling*. Also on top of the case sits a small bronze statue of a man sitting with his legs crossed in a yoga position. There is a cheese plant on the far side of the display case. Inside the case, you see company computing systems manuals and books and pamphlets on employment law, some of which deal with race and sex discrimination issues.

You decide to get up and look out the window. There is a three-seater settee under the window, covered in the same fabric as the armchairs with matching scatter cushions in the corners. From the window you can easily see people shopping and children playing in the nearby park. You turn to another table beside the settee. Several magazines sit in front of a burgundy ceramic lamp with a beige shade. There are two recent copies of *The Economist*, and a copy each of *Asia Today*, *Classic CD* and *Fortune*. As you head back to your chair, you notice that the papers on the desk in front of the chair are your application papers and *curriculum vitae*. Your first name, obviously indicating your sex, has been boldly circled with the Mont Blanc pen. As the managing director may return at any moment, you go back and sit in your chair to wait.

Chapter 8 Motivation

Key concepts

drives	job enrichment
expectancy	high-performance work systems
motivation	expectancy theory
equity theory	goal-setting theory
vertical loading factors	motive
empowerment	valence
intrinsic rewards	extrinsic rewards
content factors	hygiene factors
self-actualization	motivating potential score
job diagnostic survey	growth need strength

Learning objectives

When you have read this chapter, you should be able to define those key concepts in your own words, and you should also be able to:

1. Understand different ways in which the term 'motivation' is used.
2. Understand the nature of motives and motivation processes as influences on behaviour.
3. Use expectancy theory and job enrichment to diagnose organizational problems and to recommend solutions.
4. Explain the contemporary interest in this field with respect to the link between organization strategy and high-performance work systems.

Why study motivation?

We all have different reasons for getting out of bed in the morning. Why did Richard Branson want to fly around the world in a balloon? Why are you studying organizational behaviour? Our motives (from the Latin *movere*, to move) are major determinants of our behaviour. If we understand someone's motives (a desire for more leisure time, say), we can potentially influence their behaviour (take tomorrow off work if you finish that assignment).

Douglas Murray
McGregor
(1906–64)

Douglas McGregor (1960) set out two general sets of extreme propositions about human motivation, which he labelled 'Theory X' and 'Theory Y' respectively, and which are still part of the contemporary management vocabulary. To find out to which set of propositions you subscribe, complete the following questionnaire. Read each pair of statements and circle the number on the scale that best reflects your perception of people at work:

the average person inherently dislikes work	1	2	3	4	5	work is as natural as rest to people
people must be directed to work	1	2	3	4	5	people will exercise self-discretion and self-control
people wish to avoid responsibility	1	2	3	4	5	people enjoy real responsibility
people feel that achievement at work is irrelevant	1	2	3	4	5	achievement is highly valued by people
most people are dull and uncreative	1	2	3	4	5	most people have imagination and creativity
money is the only real reason for working	1	2	3	4	5	money is only one benefit from work
people lack the desire to improve their quality of life	1	2	3	4	5	people have needs to improve their quality of life
having an objective is a form of imprisonment	1	2	3	4	5	objectives are welcomed as an aid to effectiveness

If you scored 16 or less, then you subscribe to Theory X. If you scored 32 or more, then you subscribe to Theory Y. So what? One key question for many managers is—how can we motivate people to work harder, or smarter? One answer to this question lies with supervisory management style. The motivation theory to which you subscribe influences that style. David Buchanan and Diane Preston (1992, p.69) quote from their research a typical foreman in an engineering plant in England:

> People only come to work for money. You're not telling me that if you just left them they wouldn't go and have a chat or sit down and read the newspaper. If you're telling me that wouldn't happen, then one of us is kidding and it isn't me.

In this manufacturing unit, the machinists pinned up a notice: 'The floggings will stop when morale improves'. The foremen kept taking it down, but the machinists pinned it up again.

To which theory of motivation do these foremen adhere? How effective is this approach, in your judgement, in stimulating high performance at work?

What's the worst job you've ever done?

Erja Tikka, 46, diplomat, Helsinki, Finland
I was 17 years old and keen to improve both my money situation and my German, so I got a job packing eggs near Nienburg in Lower Saxony for two months. I was there with a friend, which certainly helped, but the real pain came from the 6am start and the subsequent ten-hour day, standing at a conveyor belt packing eggs into boxes of six or ten. Occasionally, when eggs were out of date or unsold, they were returned to the plant and I would get egg-breaking duty. This involved me standing next to a big metal industrial vat throwing in all these rotten eggs. The smell was quite extraordinary. I heard that they all went on to be whisked and then used to make biscuits, but this was a long time ago in 1971, so I'm sure they don't do that any more. I had done some agricultural work before, back when I was very little—picking out turnips which were too small to be sold. Packing eggs was much, much worse though, and for once I was grateful when I went back to school after the holidays.

Taro Saito, 39, data analyst, Tokyo, Japan
For two years I worked in the Tsukiji fish market in Tokyo. I was 18 when I opted out of going to college and started working as a cleaner or 'sanitary worker'. My job involved cleaning the area of the market where fish like tuna are cut up and auctioned each day. Generally this meant spraying surfaces with water from a hose pipe. Due to the nature of the job some of the water would end up on me and my clothes. To the outsider the market is an extremely interesting place because most of Tokyo's fish (and sushi) are obtained from here, but my memories of my time at Tsukiji are terrible. The smell of fish never seemed to leave my body. All my friends were also from the market and my social life was centred around the market area. The Japanese are generally tolerant people but my family decided that I smelt so bad that I would have to move to the back room in our house, which got very cold in winter time. Whilst I was there I met a girl who I loved and wanted to marry, but she could not bear the thought of being married to a fish market cleaner. After a while I found a job at the same place as a trainee fishmonger preparing fish for sushi chefs so things got better. I subsequently studied for a degree at night school and now work for a financial services company. Life is altogether better and I now have some prospects for a better future.

Hu Jin Feng, 22, waiter, Shanghai, China
Earlier this year I worked as a sales representative for a transportation company. My work started at 8.30am and I was expected to spend the whole day travelling around visiting different businesses trying to convince them to use our transportation services. The only problem was that I was very inexperienced and young and none of the representatives of the other companies knew who I was. Consequently I would spend whole days without getting any business. I did not relish returning to my office at the end of the day as the boss would give me a hard time. Like any boss he wants to make money and my failures made him pretty unhappy. He would make snide remarks about not being able to feed us if we did not improve our performance.

- What's the worst job you've ever done, and what kind of job would motivate you best?

From 'What's the worst job you've ever done?', *The Times*, The World at the Millennium supplement, 9 October 1999, pp.24–5.

Drives, motives and motivation

Motivation can be explored from three distinct but related perspectives:

1. What are the main motives for our behaviour? Wealth, status and power, for example, trigger behaviours directed towards their pursuit. This perspective views motivation in terms of desired goals. This question is addressed by content theories of motivation.

2. Why do we choose to pursue certain goals? Why do you study hard to earn distinctions while a friend has a full social life and gets pass grades? This perspective views motivation in terms of the cognitive decision-making pro-

cesses concerning the individual's choice of goals. This question is addressed by process theories of motivation.

3. How can we motivate you to work harder? Managers, for example, want to motivate employees to turn up on time and be helpful to customers. This perspective views motivation as a social influence process and is addressed by job enrichment theories.

Do we inherit the goals that we desire, or are they acquired through experience? If our motives are innate, then it would be pointless to attempt to change them. If they are acquired, then they can potentially be altered. Our behaviour is clearly influenced by our biological equipment. We appear to have an innate need for survival. Our needs for oxygen, water, food, shelter, warmth and sex can be overpowering. These needs are triggered by deprivation and are known as **drives**.

Drives are innate, biological determinants of behaviour, activated by deprivation.

The drives may not be restricted to basic biological needs. Some psychologists claim that we are active sensation seekers who have the innate cognitive drives listed in table 8.1.

Table 8.1: Innate cognitive drives

curiosity	the need to explore, to play, to learn more
sense making	the need to impose meaning and order on the world around us
order and meaning	the need for certainty, equity, consistency, predictability
effectance or competence	the need to exert mastery and control over the world around us
self-understanding	the need to know who and what we are

The drives come with the body. We do not have to learn to be cold, or thirsty, or hungry. However, we can override these drives. Some religious orders inflict celibacy on willing members. Altruism can overcome personal safety needs in extraordinary circumstances. The idea that our behaviour is pre-programmed is too simplistic. Psychologists once thought that human behaviour could be explained in terms of instincts, but the number of those instincts runs to thousands. Animal behaviour, in contrast, is triggered by instincts. Birds and squirrels cannot override their programming and remain locked into their niches in nature. The ways in which we, on the other hand, seek to satisfy our drives are innumerable and vary between individuals and across cultures. Consider the differences in eating habits around the world, and the range of things that individuals do to satisfy their sex drives.

Motives are socially acquired needs activated by a desire for their fulfilment.

Polygamy is a crime in most Western cultures but a sign of male achievement, wealth and status in parts of the Arab world. In some Muslim societies, the consumption of alcohol carries severe punishment, while gifts of alcohol are the norm in Western cultures. Our choice of goals and behaviours is influenced by the ways of thinking and behaving typical of our society. Those who choose not to conform are often shunned, ridiculed and sometimes even imprisoned.

The distinction between drives and **motives** is summarized in table 8.2.

Table 8.2: Drives versus motives

Drives	Motives
are innate	are learned
have a physiological basis	have a social basis
are activated by deprivation	are activated by environment
are aimed at satiation	are aimed at stimulation

However, this distinction between innate drives and acquired motives is an over-simplification. We seek to satisfy our biological drives in ways acceptable to our society. The potentially innate drives for competence, sense making and curiosity are socially prized in most cultures. The point is that human behaviour is purposive. We attach reasons to our goals and behaviours. To understand your motives and to influence your behaviour, we need to understand why you choose particular outcomes and how you decide to pursue them.

Motivation is the cognitive decision-making process through which goal-directed behaviour is initiated, energized and directed and maintained.

Motivation can thus be regarded as a broad concept which includes preferences for particular outcomes, strength of effort (half-hearted or enthusiastic), and persistence (in the face of barriers). These are the factors that we have to understand in order to explain your motivation and behaviour. These are the factors which a manager has to appreciate in order to motivate employees to behave in organizationally desirable ways.

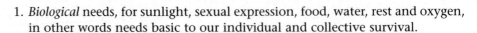

Content theories of motivation

Theories of motivation that focus on the goals to which we aspire are known as *content* theories, as they reveal the contents of the 'motives' compartment in our mental luggage.

Abraham Harold
Maslow (1908–70)

The motivation theory of Abraham Maslow aims to resolve the confusion between drives and motives. Maslow argues (1943; 1954; 1971) that we have nine innate needs or motives.

1. *Biological* needs, for sunlight, sexual expression, food, water, rest and oxygen, in other words needs basic to our individual and collective survival.

2. *Safety* needs, for security, comfort, tranquillity, freedom from fear and threat from the environment, shelter, order, predictability, and an organized world.

3. *Affiliation* needs, for attachment, belongingness, affection, love, relationships.

4. *Esteem* needs, for strength, confidence, achievement, self-esteem, independence, reputation, prestige, recognition, attention and appreciation—in other words, the need for a stable and high self-evaluation based on capability and the respect of others.

5. The need to *know and to understand*, to gain and to systematize knowledge, the need for curiosity, learning, philosophizing, experimenting and exploring.

6. *Aesthetic* needs, for order and beauty.

Self-actualization is the desire for personal fulfilment, to develop one's potential, 'to become everything that one is capable of becoming'.

7. The need for *transcendence*, a spiritual need, for 'cosmic identification', or 'to be at one with the universe'.

8. The need for *freedom of enquiry and expression*, an essential prerequisite for the satisfaction of the other needs.

9. *Self-actualization* needs, for the development of our full potential.

If our biological and safety needs are not satisfied, we die. If our needs for love and esteem are satisfied, we feel self-confident. If these needs are not satisfied, we feel inferior and helpless, emotional responses which can lead to mental disorder. Self-actualization and 'transcendence', Maslow argued, are the ultimate goals. In the organizational behaviour literature, the spiritual, metaphysical concept of transcendence has been largely ignored.

Maslow argued that self-actualized people were rare. He felt that establishing the conditions for people to develop their capabilities to this extent was a challenging task. The need for freedom of enquiry and expression is also often missing from accounts of Maslow's theory. However, this need can be significant, both in a wider cultural context (there are country variations with respect to such freedoms) and in organizational settings, where free enquiry and expression are frequently constrained by procedures, rules and social norms. Maslow argued that these nine needs are organized hierarchically, with biological and safety needs at the bottom and self-actualization and transcendence needs at the top, as in figure 8.1.

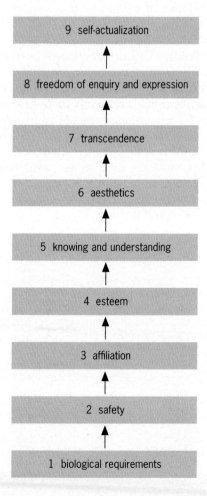

Figure 8.1: Abraham Maslow's needs hierarchy

This hierarchy, he argued, has the following properties.

1. A need is not an effective motivator until those lower in the hierarchy are more or less satisfied. You are unlikely to be concerned about the sharks (threat to safety), if you are drowning (biological deprivation).

2. A satisfied need is not a motivator. If you are well fed and safe, we would have difficulty energizing and directing your behaviour with offers of food and shelter.

3. Lack of need satisfaction can affect mental health. Consider the frustration, anxiety and depression that can arise from lack of self-esteem, loss of the respect of others, an inability to sustain relationships and an inability to develop one's capabilities.

4. We have an innate desire to 'work our way up' the hierarchy, pursuing the satisfaction of our 'higher-order' needs once our basic or 'lower-order' needs are more or less satisfied.

5. The experience of self-actualization stimulates desire for more. Maslow claimed that self-actualizers have 'peak experiences'. When you have had one of these, you want another. The need for self-actualization cannot be satisfied in the same way as the other needs.

Maslow did not intend this hierarchy to be regarded as a rigid description of the development of human motivation. He offered this as a typical picture of what might happen under ideal (and, therefore, rarely attained) social and organizational conditions.

Maslow's theory has attracted two main criticisms. First, it is vague and cannot readily predict behaviour. Second, it is more of a social philosophy reflecting white American middle-class values. Can his theory be dismissed as irrelevant to organizational behaviour in the twenty-first century? No. His thinking remains highly influential, particularly in the recognition that behaviour depends on a range of motives. His ideas continue to affect management practice in areas such as rewards policy, management style and job design. Many subsequent management fashions such as job enrichment, total quality management, business process re-engineering, self-managing teams, 'the new leadership' and employee empowerment, have incorporated his ideas in the search for practical motivational methods.

Is Maslow's theory 'culture-bound'?

Scandinavian cultures—Sweden, Norway, Finland, Denmark—place a higher value on quality of life and social needs. European and Anglo-American cultures place a higher value on productivity, efficiency and individual self-actualization. Chinese culture values collectivism and community activity higher than individualism. Maslow's theory may be 'culture-bound':

Maslow's hierarchy	The hierarchy of needs in China
self-actualization	safety and security (personal and national)
esteem	sense of belongingness and love
love and affiliation	esteem, family, tradition
safety and security	self-actualization through fitting in, non-individualistic
physiological	physiological

Based on E. Nevis, 1983, 'Using an American perspective in understanding another culture: toward a hierarchy of needs for the People's Republic of China, *Journal of Applied Behavioral Science*, vol.19, no.3, pp.249–64.

Clayton Alderfer (1972) argued that it was more realistic to consider three basic categories of needs, which he called existence, relatedness and growth, so this is known as the ERG theory of motivation. Table 8.3 illustrates how ERG and Maslow's theories relate.

Table 8.3: ERG theory	
Existence needs	physiological and safety needs
Relatedness needs	affiliation and esteem needs
Growth needs	self-actualization and self-esteem needs

ERG theory says that all three needs categories can be present at any one time, in contrast with Maslow's 'progression hypothesis', that we try to work our way up the hierarchy. Alderfer added a 'regression hypothesis', arguing that we drop to a lower category when attempts to satisfy higher needs are frustrated. Maslow was not initially concerned with work motivation, whereas Alderfer's theory is directed at organizational settings. Despite the differences between these theories, the practical managerial implications are similar.

Stop and criticize

Let us assume that you are not white, American, comfortably affluent, middle-class and living in the 1940s. From your own observations and experience (the primary research sources for Maslow's theory), devise a five-step needs hierarchy that you believe would apply to your own contemporary culture.

Would different needs hierarchies apply to particular sub-cultural groups (teenage job seekers, freelance management consultants, single-parent families)?

What are the main differences between your theory and that of Maslow?

Sheila Ritchie and Peter Martin (1999) argue that 'the task of the manager is to find out what it is that motivates people', to make them 'smile more and carp less' (p.xii). Observing that there has been little recent development in motivation theory, they aimed to devise a fresh approach and a practical tool. Their research identified twelve 'motivational drivers':

1. interest
2. achievement
3. recognition
4. self-development
5. variety and change
6. creativity
7. power and influence
8. social contact
9. money and tangible rewards
10. structure
11. relationships
12. physical conditions

Table 8.4: The motivation profile

Motivating factor	The high-needs individual	The low-needs individual
Interest	needs to feel that work is intrinsically interesting and useful	will do work regardless of its intrinsic interest or usefulness
Achievement	needs to set self-challenging goals; unhappy if nothing to achieve; requires constant stimulation	no motivation for achievement; world passes them by
Recognition	needs constant recognition and appreciation; can inhibit effectiveness	indifferent to other people's views about them; possibly insensitive to others
Self-development	needs to grow and develop; assesses work in terms of its contribution to personal growth	does what is required; does not assess in terms of contribution to personal development
Variety and change	needs constant variety, change and stimulation; high level of arousal and vigilance	happy to tolerate the mundane and boring
Creativity	explorative and open-minded; curious and thinks divergently	little need for creative thinking; lacks curiosity; can be closed-minded
Power and influence	strong impulse to influence others, competitive power drive dominates personality	no wish to attempt to exercise influence
Social contact	needs light social contact with a wide range of people	feels no compelling need for company but is able to work with others if necessary
Money and tangible rewards	needs high salary and tangible rewards; concentrates on monetary rewards	spends little energy thinking about reward; indifferent to money as a motivator
Structure	needs rules and structure, feedback and information; wants procedures	finds rules and structures restrictive; wants freedom; feels no need for compliance
Relationships	needs to form and sustain stable long-term relationships with a small number of people	feels no need to maintain deep relationships; is able to work with people if necessary
Physical conditions	needs good working conditions; constantly complains if not physically comfortable	largely indifferent to physical surroundings

The characteristics of 'high-needs' and 'low-needs' individuals are defined in table 8.4 (based on Ritchie and Martin, 1999, pp.11–12 and 245–6). They claim there is little correlation between scores on these factors, suggesting that they are independent of each other.

The twelve factors were derived from the literature and from their observations as management consultants. They developed a questionnaire which produces a motivational profile indicating the relative strength of each factor. This questionnaire was completed by 1,355 managers and other professionals, from several nationalities, mainly participants on the authors' management development programmes. The order in which the factors are listed is based on the questionnaire scores. In other words, this particular management group had relatively high levels of need for interest and achievement in their work, moderately high levels of need for creativity, power and influence, and lower levels of need for relationships and good physical working conditions. Money was rated ninth.

The composition of the sample allowed comparisons to be made between different professional and occupational groups and between different nationalities. Ritchie and Martin note, however, that differences in the motivational profiles between individuals are more significant than either international or occupational differences.

What are the practical implications of this perspective? The profile approach encourages sensitivity to individual differences, highlighting the need to use different motivational strategies for different employees and groups. Managers are advised to respond to the profile of the individual, regardless of the job they are doing, or of their country or culture of origin.

The motivation profile perspective seems to have a number of strengths:

- it is based on contemporary data drawn from managers and other professionals;

- it recognizes a range of individual differences;

- it offers a diagnostic tool for managers who are seeking to improve individual and group motivation, by indicating the factors on which to concentrate.

However, this perspective has a number of weaknesses:

- the derivation of the twelve factors seems arbitrary, relying on a combination of judgement and informed guesswork rather than on systematic research;

- the sample on which the perspective is based is atypical, comprising managers on training programmes run by the authors;

- it is difficult to identify motivating factors that are not already covered in Maslow's theory, and the originality of this work is not fully explored.

Ritchie and Martin appear to have developed a practical approach useful in a management training and development context, and also for guiding management action in response to employee motivation issues. As indicated earlier, although Maslow's content theory of motivation may be dated, his influence persists.

funny **Business**

— by MORRIS

"Ruston, you handled that boring thankless job so well I've decided to give you another one."

Process theories of motivation

J. Stacy Adams

Theories of motivation that focus on how we make choices with respect to desired goals are known as process theories. Unlike content theories, process theories give the individual a cognitive decision-making role in selecting goals and the means by which to pursue them.

Do we really come into the world with mental luggage labelled 'motives', containing goals that we are predestined to pursue? Individuals are motivated by different outcomes. Cultures encourage different patterns of motivation. We appear to have some choice of motives, and the means of achieving them. Content theories fail to recognize either individual choice or social influence. Maslow's is a universalist theory, which applies to everyone, and thus cannot readily explain differences between individuals and between cultures.

We will explore three process theories of work motivation: equity theory, expectancy theory and goal-setting theory.

Equity theory

Equity theory is a process theory of motivation which argues that the perception of unfairness in a social or organizational setting leads to tension, which in turn motivates the individual to act to resolve that unfairness.

Several theorists have argued that we seek what we perceive to be a just or equitable return for our efforts. The calculation of what is 'just or equitable' depends on the comparisons we make with others. **Equity theory** is thus based on our perceptions of 'fair treatment'. The most influential statement of this theory comes from the work of Stacy Adams (1963; 1965), who argued that we are motivated to act in situations which we perceive to be inequitable or unfair. Inequity occurs when you get either more or less than you think you deserve. The argument is based on perceptions of inequity but is traditionally called equity theory.

This theory bases explanations of behaviour on perceptions of social comparisons. Equity theory argues that the more intense the perceived inequity, the higher the tension and the stronger the motivation to act. Adams argues that we respond differently to 'over-reward' and 'under-reward'. We tend to perceive a modest amount of over-reward as 'good luck', and do nothing, while even a modest under-reward is not so readily tolerated.

How do you calculate inequity? Adams proposed that we compare our rewards (pay, recognition) and contributions (time, effort, ideas) with the outputs and inputs of others. Equity thus exists when these ratios are equal:

$$\frac{\text{my rewards (minus my costs)}}{\text{my effort and contribution}} = \frac{\text{your rewards (minus your costs)}}{\text{your effort and contribution}}$$

Table 8.5: Strategies for reducing inequity

strategy	example
1. alter your outcomes	I'll persuade the manager to increase my pay
2. adjust your inputs	I won't work as hard as Annika
3. alter the comparison person's outcomes	I'll persuade the manager to cut Annika's pay
4. alter the comparison person's inputs	I'll leave the difficult tasks to Annika
5. compare with someone else	Lars gets the same as I get
6. rationalize the inequity	Annika has worked here for much longer
7. leave	I'll get another job

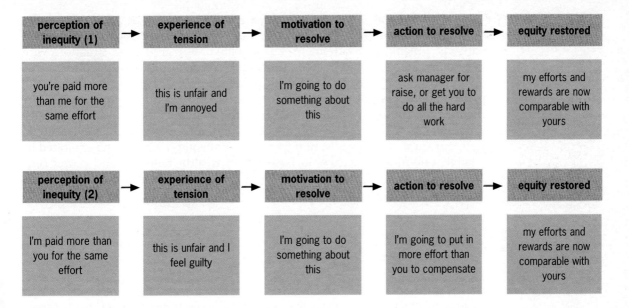

Figure 8.2: Equity theory—the causal chain

Outcomes can include a range of tangible and intangible factors including pay, status symbols, fringe benefits, promotion prospects, satisfaction and job security. Inputs similarly relate to any factor that you believe you bring to the situation, including age, experience, skill, education, effort, loyalty and commitment. The theory says nothing about the relative priority or weighting of these various factors. That depends on the individual's perception.

How do you resolve inequity? Let's imagine that you are working in a restaurant in Gamla Stan (the Old Town) in Stockholm and you discover that Annika is earning 12 Swedish kronor (about US$1.50) an hour more than you for the same work (about $50 a week more than you). Table 8.5 lists Adams's seven strategies for reducing this inequity.

Choice of strategy is a sensitive issue, and equity theory does not predict which strategy an individual will choose. Each option has different short-term and long-term consequences, which have to be taken into account. Arguing with your manager, reducing your input or making Annika do all the difficult tasks may reduce inequity in the short term but could have long-term consequences for your relationships and employment at this location.

The theory's causal chains for over-reward and under-reward are illustrated in figure 8.2.

Research evidence from laboratory studies in the 1960s supports the theory and also confirms that people who are overpaid reduce their perceived inequity by working harder. Further studies in real settings have continued to confirm, broadly, equity theory predictions. Interestingly from a management perspective, perceived equity seems to lead to greater job satisfaction and organizational commitment (Sweeney *et al.*, 1990).

Equity theory has some problems. A range of quantitative and qualitative variables have to be considered when calculating an equity ratio. These variables are dependent on individual perception and are difficult to weight or measure. Different people use different timescales when calculating fairness; the short-term calculation may be quite different from the long-term implications. There are individual differences in tolerance levels, and not everyone will respond in the same way to a particular level of inequity. The extent to which you believe that there is a valid explanation for the inequity will also moderate your response.

Equity theory, as a psychological perspective, ignores the wider social and organizational context in two ways. The first concerns the basis of our social comparisons, which can be extremely varied. Some of us compare our situations with our immediate colleagues, while others make comparisons with people in other organizations, other sectors and even other countries. There is no rationale for preferring one basis of comparison to another. The second way in which equity theory ignores social context concerns the systemic inequities in capitalist economies. You and I, close working colleagues, may receive the same treatment from our employing organization (perception of equity) while being exploited by relatively invisible characters in positions of wealth, influence and power (perception of inequity). However, the latter expression of 'inequity' is a 'normal' feature of capitalist society and is thus difficult to challenge.

Stop and criticize

What actions would you take if you were earning a little more than Annika in our earlier example from the Stockholm restaurant?

What actions would you take if you were earning much more than Annika?

To what extent do you think equity theory can make accurate predictions of your behaviour in 'inequitable' situations?

Edward Chace Tolman (1886–1961)

Victor Harold Vroom (b. 1932)

Expectancy theory is a process theory of motivation which argues that the strength or 'force' of an individual's motivation to perform well is expressed as the product of the *valence* of the outcome from that behaviour, the *expectancy* that effort will lead to good performance and the *instrumentality* of good performance in leading to valued outcomes.

Equity theory has significant implications for management practice. For example, it is important to recognize that employees compare pay (even in organizations that insist on 'pay secrecy'), and inequity quickly generates predictable resentment. Comparisons are often subjective and imprecise, particularly where information is lacking and employees rely on rumour. It is important for management to recognize that perceptions of inequity can generate tension, even where actual inequity is limited. The circulation of accurate information about rewards, and the links between effort and rewards, is thus crucial.

Expectancy theory

A motive is an outcome that has become desirable. The process through which outcomes become desirable is explained by the **expectancy theory** of motivation. This is a process theory which does not assume that we come complete with a package of predefined goals.

Cognitive theories in psychology assume that we are consciously purposive and aware of our goals and actions. Expectancy theory is a cognitive theory and was first developed by the American psychologist Edward C. Tolman in the 1930s as a challenge to the behaviourist views of his contemporaries. Tolman argued that behaviour is directed by the expectations that we have about our behaviour leading to the achievement of desired outcomes.

For high motivation, productive work has to be seen as a path to valued goals. If you expect to get more money for working hard, and you need more money, then we can predict that you will work hard. If you expect that hard work will only get you happy smiles from the boss, then we can predict that you will decide not to work hard unless you place a high value on happy smiles. The theory assumes that we behave in ways that are instrumental to the achievement of valued goals.

The American psychologist Victor H. Vroom (1964) developed the first expectancy theory of work motivation, based on three concepts: **valence**, **instrumentality** and **expectancy**. This is known as valence–instrumentality–expectancy theory—expectancy theory for short.

Valence concerns the perceived value or degree of preference that an individual has for a particular outcome. As one may either seek or avoid certain outcomes, or be ambivalent about them, valence can be positive, negative or neutral.

Instrumentality concerns the individual's perceived likelihood that good performance will lead to valued rewards. As a subjective probability, instrumentality can be measured on a scale from 0 (no chance) to 1 (certainty).

The 'force' (*F*) of your motivation to work hard is the result of the product (multiplication) of these three variables and not the sum (addition), because if one of the variables is zero, then, despite the value of the other two, the product, *F*, will be zero, and that is what we would expect. This cumbersome explanation is expressed in the expectancy equation:

$$F = V \times I \times E$$

What is the effect of a low '*V*' value? If you do not care what grade you get for your next essay or examination, then you will not be motivated to work hard for it.

What is the effect of a low '*E*' value? If you believe that long hours in the library will not lead to a high essay or examination grade, then you will not be motivated to work hard.

What is the effect of a low '*I*' value? If you believe that a good grade will not lead to a chosen qualification, job or career, then you will not be motivated to work hard.

Only when all three of the terms in the expectancy equation are positive will the motivating force be positive. However, behaviour typically has a number of outcomes. Working hard affects our work performance, levels of fatigue, social life, today's pay and tomorrow's promotion prospects. The expectancy equation thus has to be summed for all possible outcomes. The full expectancy equation is:

$$F = \Sigma \, (V \times I \times E)$$

The sign Σ is the Greek letter sigma, which means 'add up all the values of the calculation in the brackets'. Note that there will be only a single *E* value, concerning the probability that high effort will lead to high performance. However, there will be several different I values, one for each rated outcome, concerning the probability that these will be obtained.

Stop and criticize

Measure the force of your motivation to get a high grade in organizational behaviour:

What are your *V* values? Identify the range of possible outcomes from working hard for this subject. Rate the value of each of these to you, as 1 (positive), 0 (ambivalent) or −1 (negative).

What are your *I* values? For each possible outcome, estimate the subjective probability of that occurring (you could get a high grade, you will ruin your social life).

Expectancy concerns the individual's perceived likelihood that effort will result in good performance. As a subjective probability, expectancy can be measured on a scale from 0 (no chance) to 1 (certainty).

What is your *E* value? Estimate the probability, for you, that high effort will produce a high grade in this subject. This probability will be between 0 (little or no chance) and 1 (certainty of high grade).

Sum the calculation across all your outcomes and compare your score with colleagues. If the theory is correct, those with higher *F* scores are more highly motivated to get a good grade for the organizational behaviour course.

Consider the process through which you have just worked. To what extent is this a realistic picture of the cognitive decision-making process that we undertake when deciding on aspects of our behaviour?

Expectancy theory is more complex than content theories. Let us sum up what we have covered:

- Expectancy theory states that behaviour results from a conscious decision-making process based on the individual's subjective probability—the expectations that the individual has about the results of different behaviours leading to performance and to rewards.

- Expectancy theory helps to explain individual differences in motivation and behaviour, unlike Maslow's universal content theory of motivation.

- Expectancy theory provides a basis for measuring the strength or 'force' of the individual's motivation to behave in particular ways.

- Expectancy theory assumes that behaviour is rational, and that we are conscious of our motives. As we take into account the probable outcomes of our behaviour, and place values on these outcomes, expectancy theory attempts to predict individual behaviour.

Lyman W. Porter

Edward Emmett
Lawler III

Lyman Porter and Edward Lawler (1968; Lawler, 1973) developed Vroom's basic expectancy theory into a more comprehensive theory of work motivation. Their theory is illustrated in figure 8.3, which identifies the factors contributing to job performance (box 6).

The effort expended on a task (box 3) depends on the value of the rewards for performing well (box 1), and on the perceived expectation that those rewards follow (box 2) from performance (box 6). In this model, what Vroom called instrumentality becomes a feedback loop to effort through what is simply labelled the 'expectation' that performance will lead to rewards. What Vroom called expectancy, or the effort–performance link (will high effort lead to good per-

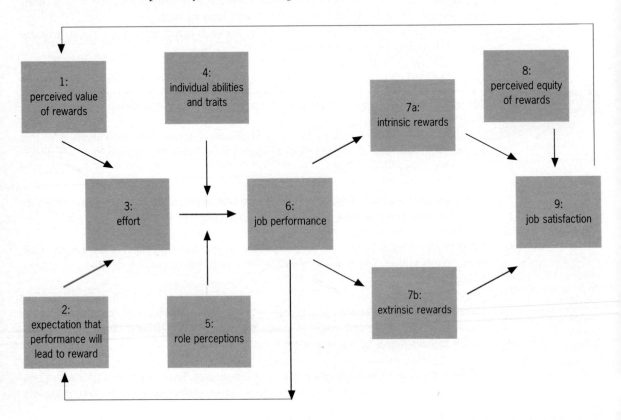

Figure 8.3: The Porter–Lawler model of work motivation (based on Porter and Lawler, 1968)

formance), is seen to depend not just on individual perceptions but also on abilities and traits (box 4) and on role perceptions (box 5), or the degree to which the individual feels that what they are required to do is consistent with their perception of their role. Your performance may suffer if you are asked to do something which you feel is not consistent with the job and your expertise.

This integrative approach takes into account job satisfaction (box 9), based on perceptions of intrinsic and extrinsic rewards (boxes 7a and 7b), and also incorporates equity theory (box 8). Satisfaction also influences the perceived value of rewards and thus has a feedback effect.

This model argues that performance affects satisfaction, and not the other way around. Why? Satisfaction depends on need fulfilment. Need fulfilment is in turn dependent on the range of intrinsic and extrinsic rewards which come from job performance. Job satisfaction may or may not be associated with good job performance. Job satisfaction is only one attitude, or set of related attitudes, potentially linked with performance. Good performance, however, appropriately rewarded, is likely to lead to job satisfaction.

This theory has intuitive appeal; it has face validity, it feels right. Research by the authors, and others, appears to support it. However, the theory faces a number of criticisms:

- the theory covers a range of interrelated variables and is complex;

- the assumption that we make decisions using such a detailed calculus is questionable;

- the impact of coercion and job insecurity on performance is overlooked;

- tests of the theory rely on being able to measure and correlate all those variables, using instruments and statistical methods of dubious validity.

The theory does, however, have several practical managerial consequences:

- the link between effort and performance must be supported by management, through the provision of adequate training, instruction and resources;

- the link between performance and rewards must be clear and visible if rewards are to have the desired motivational effect—the concept of 'pay secrecy' is a nonsense where pay is used to motivate high performance (as it is in most organizations);

- if employees are instructed to do one thing but rewarded for doing another, they will concentrate on the behaviours which are rewarded and ignore other instructions;

- money can be a motivator but is only one of a number of extrinsic rewards, and to be motivating it must be linked clearly to job performance and be perceived as equitable;

- performance standards must be clear and unambiguous, otherwise employees will not know how best to direct their efforts;

- there is no point in offering rewards which employees do not value, or which are not valued highly enough to influence behaviour;

- if different employees value different kinds of reward, it may be necessary to introduce a 'cafeteria benefits' or 'flexi benefits' scheme, with choices between fringe benefits such as medical insurance, health club memberships, car breakdown cover, bus passes, shopping vouchers, cinema tickets, bicycle allowances, financial planning advice and travel insurance, for example;

- the value of different rewards may change with time and has to be monitored;

- inconsistent or ambiguous performance ratings are a major potential source of inequity, and management must establish accurate and consistent ratings systems;

- the theory has been developed into a job-enrichment technique, examined shortly.

In other words, to ensure low motivation and poor performance:

1. keep performance goals vague and ambiguous;

2. provide inadequate advice and resources for goal achievement;

3. reward behaviour other than good job performance;

4. offer rewards which employees do not value;

5. concentrate on financial rewards and ignore other extrinsic and extrinsic rewards;

6. make sure performance ratings are subjective and inconsistent.

The theory has been tested mainly in situations where short-term targets can be expressed in clear and quantifiable terms. It is unclear if the theory applies to longer-term goals, say over a period of years, as targets are likely to be more qualitative and to change as circumstances alter. It is also unclear whether this applies where goals are difficult to measure, such as in most types of managerial work. Another problem is that the theory and its applications concentrate on individual goals and performance rather than on teamwork.

Goal-setting theory

Goal setting is now treated as a process theory of motivation. However, the main advocate of this approach, Edwin Locke (1968; Latham and Yukl, 1975), argues that 'goal-setting is more appropriately viewed as a motivational technique rather than a formal theory' (Locke, 1975, p.465). This 'technique' relies on a series of propositions which allow us to explain and to predict work behaviour, so it is entitled to the label of 'theory'.

Goal theory has established four main propositions, which are well supported by research:

1. *Challenging goals* lead to higher levels of performance than simple and unchallenging goals. Difficult goals are also called 'stretch' goals because they encourage us to try harder (unless the goal is beyond our level of ability).

2. *Specific goals* lead to higher levels of performance than vague goals such as 'try harder' or 'do your best'. It is easier for us to adjust our behaviour when we know precisely what is required of us, and goal specificity avoids confusion. One popular acronym states that goals should be SMART: specific, measurable, attainable, realistic and time-related.

3. *Participation* in goal setting, particularly when this is expected, can increase performance by increasing commitment to those goals, but managerially assigned goals that are adequately explained and justified can also lead to high performance.

4. *Knowledge of results* of past performance—feedback—is necessary for effective goal achievement. Feedback contains information and is also motivational.

Goal setting is both a process theory of motivation and a motivational technique, based on the argument that work performance can be explained with reference to characteristics of the objectives being pursued, such as goal difficulty, goal specificity and knowledge of results.

The main positive feature of goal-setting theory is the clarity of the practical management implications (Locke and Latham, 1990). These include:

Goal setting works with lumberjacks

Responding to criticism that goal setting had been tested mainly in laboratory settings, Locke (1975, pp.466–7) cited four studies in real organizational settings. In two separate studies of independent pulpwood producers, high productivity was maintained when a supervisor remained on the job with the men and set production goals for them.

In a third study of sawing crews, output per man was higher over a three-month period when specific and moderately difficult goals were assigned to the sawyers; this was not the case with other sawing crews, where no specific goals were assigned.

In a fourth study, loggers were given the goal of loading trucks to 94 per cent of the legal maximum; the old average was only 60 per cent. Performance improved immediately, and loading weights remained high, averaging 90 per cent, for the next 15 months, saving a quarter of a million US dollars, as the purchase of additional trucks was avoided.

Locke points out that, in all four cases, performance improvements were quickly obtained without the offer of financial rewards for goal attainment, or penalties for failure.

- *Goal difficulty*: set goals for work performance at levels which will stretch employees, but which are not beyond their ability levels.

- *Goal specificity*: express goals in clear and precise language, if possible in quantifiable terms, and avoid setting vague and ambiguous goals.

- *Participation*: allow employees to take part in the goal setting process to increase the acceptability of and their commitment to goals.

- *Acceptance*: if goals are set by management, ensure that they are adequately explained and justified so that those concerned understand and accept them.

- *Feedback*: provide information on the results of past performance to allow employees to adjust their behaviour, if necessary, to improve future performance.

Goal-setting theory thus has implications for the design and conduct of staff appraisal systems, and for 'management by objectives' methods which focus on the achievement of agreed or negotiated performance targets.

Stop and criticize

Yo! Sushi, a small Japanese restaurant chain, offers its staff financial bonuses of up to 20 per cent of annual salary every three months. To earn this bonus, staff have to meet restaurant targets, which include the number of customers, the average bill amount and profitability. Staff also have individual performance targets, which are documented and reviewed quarterly, and which affect the bonus. One of the chain's restaurant managers, Tony Pay, claims that the scheme is effective because bonuses are frequent (not annual), and targets are agreed upon by management and staff.

What are the strengths of this scheme from the perspective of goal-setting theory?

What potential problems does this approach have, for management, for employees, and perhaps also for customers?

How would you advise management to adapt and improve this scheme?

Based on Sally Patten, 'Incentives prove key method of keeping staff', *The Times,* 12 October 1999, p.38.

The social process of motivating others

This chapter first considered motivation in terms of the goals or outcomes towards which behaviour is directed. Second, we considered motivation as the cognitive decision-making process through which goals are selected and pursued. The third perspective explores motivation as a social process which involves influencing the behaviour of others.

A significant number of manual jobs in factories, and clerical jobs in offices, are still designed using methods advocated by an American engineer called Frederick Taylor. Taylor's scientific management approach to designing jobs is as follows [**link**, chapter 13, traditional work design]:

1. Decide on the optimum degree of *task fragmentation*, breaking down a complex job into a sequence of simple steps.

2. Decide the *one best way* to perform the work, through studies to discover the most effective method for doing each step, including workplace layout and design of tools.

3. *Train* employees to carry out these simple fragmented tasks in the manner specified.

4. *Reward* employees financially for meeting and exceeding specified performance targets.

Stop and criticize

You are employed on a job in which you repeat precisely the same simple task every fifteen seconds, perhaps wiring plugs for lamps, 9.00am until 5.30pm, every day (with a lunch break), five days a week. Maybe you have done work like this before?

Describe your emotional responses to work of this kind.

Do you think that it is inevitable that some jobs just have to be like this, given the nature of work and technology, and the need to keep quality high and costs low?

The advantages of task fragmentation include:

- employees do not need expensive and time-consuming training;
- specialization in one small task makes employees very proficient through repetition;
- lower pay can be given for such unskilled work; and
- some of the problems of achieving controlled performance are simplified.

The disadvantages, however, include:

- repetitive work can be extremely boring;
- the individual's contribution to the organization is meaningless and insignificant;
- monotony leads to apathy, dissatisfaction and carelessness; and
- the employee develops no skills that might lead to promotion.

Taylor's approach to job design appears logical and efficient, but it creates jobs that do not stimulate motivation and performance. Taylor had a simplified view

Job enrichment is a technique for broadening the experience of work to enhance employee need satisfaction and to improve work motivation and performance.

Motivator factors are aspects of work which lead to high levels of job satisfaction, motivation and performance, and include achievement, recognition, responsibility, advancement, growth and the work itself; also know as *content factors*.

Hygiene factors are aspects of work which remove job dissatisfaction but which do not contribute to motivation and performance, and include pay, company policy, supervision, status, security and working conditions; also known as *context factors*.

of human motivation, regarding 'lower-level' employees as 'coin-operated' and arguing that the rewards for working as instructed should be financial. Taylor's methods are more likely to encourage absenteeism and sabotage than commitment and flexibility. Managers are thus interested in theories of motivation as sources of alternative methods for encouraging motivation and high performance. During the 1960s and 1970s, these concerns created the quality of working life (QWL) movement, whose language and methods are still influential.

One popular QWL technique derived from work motivation theory as an antidote to Taylorism is **job enrichment**.

The concept of job enrichment was first developed by the American psychologist Frederick Herzberg (1966; 1968). To discover what factors influenced job satisfaction and dissatisfaction, 203 Pittsburgh engineers and accountants were interviewed and were asked two 'critical incident' questions. They were asked to recall events which had made them feel good about their work, and events which had made them feel bad about it.

Analysis of these 'critical incident' narratives revealed that the factors which led to satisfaction were different from those which led to job dissatisfaction. Herzberg called this a 'two-factor theory of motivation', the two sets of factors being **motivator** and **hygiene factors**, summarized in table 8.6.

The redesign of jobs to increase motivation and performance should thus focus on the motivators or content factors. Improvement in the hygiene or context factors, Herzberg (1968) argued, will remove dissatisfaction, but will not increase motivation and performance. He advocated the application of **vertical loading factors**, to achieve job enrichment.

Table 8.6: Motivator and hygiene factors

Motivator factors (content)	Hygiene factors (context)
achievement	pay
advancement	company policy
growth	supervisory style
recognition	status
responsibility	security
the work itself	working conditions

Is Herzberg's theory 'culture-bound'?

We noted earlier in this chapter that Maslow's 'universalist' theory of motivation may not apply beyond Western, capitalist, industrialized economies and cultures. Herzberg, however, makes a strong claim for the broad applicability of his theory, writing that:

> This is not a theory for American workers alone. Recent research by myself and others reveals that these principles hold up in diverse cultures. In other words, there are some common characteristics among workers throughout the world.

Herzberg's two-factor theory of motivation states that while dissatisfaction is caused by context or 'hygiene' factors, satisfaction is improved with content or 'motivator' factors.

This pattern was revealed in American studies. Herzberg claims that similar patterns have been identified in Finland, Hungary, Italy, Israel, Japan and Zambia. Studies in South Africa, on the other hand, produced different results. While managers and skilled workers—black and white—produced the expected results, unskilled workers' satisfaction appeared to be dependent on hygiene factors. Herzberg claims that 'the impoverished nature of the unskilled workers' jobs has not afforded these workers with motivators—thus the abnormal profile'.

Herzberg cites a comparable study of unskilled Indian workers, who were 'operating on a dependent hygiene continuum that leads to addiction to hygiene, or strikes and revolution'.

Based on Frederick Herzberg, 'Workers' needs the same around the world', *Industry Week*, 21 September 1987, pp.29–30, 32.

Frederick Herzberg
(b. 1923)

Vertical loading factors are methods for enriching work content and improving motivation through removing controls, increasing accountability, creating natural work units, providing direct feedback, introducing new tasks, allocating special assignments and granting additional authority.

Intrinsic rewards are valued outcomes or benefits which come from within the individual, such as feelings of satisfaction, competence, self-esteem and accomplishment.
Extrinsic rewards are valued outcomes or benefits provided by others, such as promotion, pay increases, a bigger office desk, praise and recognition.

The way in which a job is designed determines the rewards available and what the individual has to do to get those rewards. It is useful to distinguish **intrinsic** and **extrinsic rewards**.

Intrinsic rewards are valued outcomes within the control of the individual, such as feelings of satisfaction and accomplishment. For some of us, and for some actions, 'the outcome is its own (intrinsic) reward'. Mountaineers, poets, athletes, painters and musicians are usually familiar with the concept of intrinsic reward; few people ever get paid for climbing hills, and there are few wealthy poets on this planet. Extrinsic rewards are valued outcomes that are controlled by others, such as recognition, promotion and pay increases. The relationships between performance and intrinsic reward are usually more immediate and direct than those between performance and extrinsic reward. Edward Lawler (1973) thus argues that intrinsic rewards are more important influences on our motivation to work.

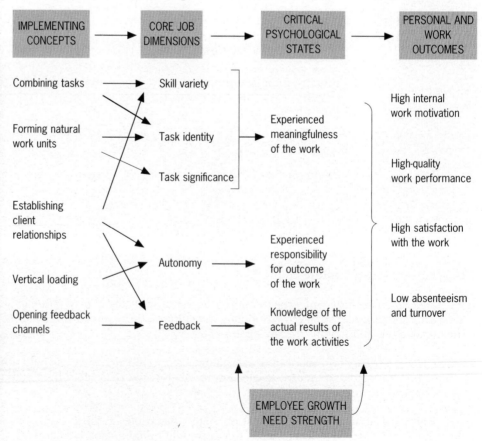

Figure 8.4: The job characteristics model
From J. R. Hackman, G. Oldham, R. Janson and K. Purdy, 'A new strategy for job enrichment', *California Review*, 1975, vol 17, no. 4, p 62.

Growth need strength is a measure of the readiness and capability of an individual to respond positively to job enrichment.

The *job characteristics model* is the basis of the job enrichment strategy of the expectancy theorists and is illustrated in figure 8.4.

The job characteristics model sets out the links between the features of jobs, the individual's experience and the outcomes in terms of motivation, satisfaction and performance. This model also takes into account individual differences in the desire for personal growth and development—**growth need strength** (similar to Maslow's self-actualization concept).

Growth need strength (GNS) is an indicator of your willingness to welcome job enrichment. The causal chain, from job design, through individual experience, to performance outcomes, depends on GNS. With employees whose GNS is low, enriched jobs will not lead to positive performance outcomes. This is a contingent model, not a universal one.

At the heart of this model is the proposition that jobs can be analysed in terms of five *core dimensions,* which are defined as follows:

1. *Skill variety*: the extent to which a job makes use of different skills and abilities.

2. *Task identity*: the extent to which a job involves a 'whole' and meaningful piece of work.

3. *Task significance*: the extent to which a job affects the work of others.

4. *Autonomy*: the extent to which a job provides independence and discretion.

5. *Feedback*: the extent to which performance information is relayed back to the individual.

Stop and criticize

Your manager offers to enrich your job. However, you see this as a way of getting you to take on more responsibility and work harder for no extra pay, and you turn down the offer. Familiar with the job characteristics model, your manager describes you as 'low in growth need strength'. How do you feel about this judgement?

Eat what you kill: do incentive schemes improve motivation and performance?

Performance-related payment schemes flourished in the 1990s as organizations tried to find new ways to motivate employees. These schemes link financial rewards to the achievement of performance targets. Alfie Kohn argues that these 'eat what you kill' incentive schemes are based on a false psychological assumption. People do not perform better when paid more and may even perform worse. His argument is based on six observations:

- Money helps us to meet many of our needs, but research reveals that money is not an overriding concern for most people.

- Pay that is dependent on performance ('If they have to bribe me to do this') is manipulative and heightens the perception of being controlled.

- Competition for rewards can disrupt relationships between individuals whose collective performance would be improved by co-operation and is damaged by rivalry.

- Dependence on financial incentives to improve productivity diverts attention from attempts to understand and solve the underlying problems facing an organization.

- Incentive schemes discourage risk taking, experiment and creative exploration by sending the signal 'do exactly what you are told'.

- Rewards that are contingent on particular levels of performance undermine interest in the job itself, whereas intrinsic motivation is usually the real basis of exceptional work.

Kohn concludes that performance-related pay schemes are based on a misunderstanding of the nature of extrinsic and intrinsic motivation. These two aspects of motivation cannot be 'added', and it is not simply a case of 'targeting' the behaviours that will attract additional bonuses. Extrinsic rewards buy compliance and do not encourage long-term commitment:

The more we experience being controlled, the more we will tend to lose interest in what we are doing. If we go to work thinking about the possibility of getting a bonus, we come to feel that our work is not self-directed. Rather it is the reward that drives our behaviour. [A]nything presented as a prerequisite for something else—that is, as a means toward another end—comes to be seen as less desirable (p.62).

Based on Alfie Kohn, 'Why incentive plans cannot work', *Harvard Business Review'*, 1993, vol.71, no.5, pp.54–63, and *The Economist*, 'Just deserts', January 1994, p.77.

The **Job Diagnostic Survey** is an opinion questionnaire designed to evaluate the motivating potential of jobs by measuring the five core job dimensions of skill variety, task identify, task significance, autonomy and feedback.

Jobs can be assessed on these core dimensions. Richard Hackman and Greg Oldham (1974; Hackman, Oldham and Purdy, 1975) developed an opinion questionnaire called the **Job Diagnostic Survey** (JDS) for this purpose. Skill variety and autonomy are measured in the JDS by questions such as:

How much variety is there in your job? That is, to what extent does the job require you to do many different things at work, using a variety of your skills and talents?

How much autonomy is there in your job? That is, to what extent does your job permit you to decide on your own how to go about doing the work?

The JDS provides *operational definitions* (see glossary) of the variables in the job characteristics model. The core job dimensions are *independent variables*, and critical psychological states and performance outcomes are *dependent variables* (see glossary). Growth need strength, which is also operationalized in the Job Diagnostic Survey, is a mediating variable in this causal chain. The JDS can be used to establish how motivating a job is by permitting the calculation of a *motivating potential score* (MPS), from answers across groups of employees on the same job, on those seven-point scales.

The **motivating potential score** is a measure of how motivating a job is likely to be for an individual, taking into account the core job dimensions of skill variety, task identity, task significance, autonomy and feedback.

The MPS is quantified using the following equation, where the values of the variables have been measured using the JDS:

$$\text{MPS} = \frac{(\text{skill variety} + \text{task identity} + \text{task significance})}{3} \times \text{autonomy} \times \text{feedback}$$

Autonomy and feedback are considered more important in their motivating influence than the other three core job dimensions. The equation is designed to reflect this by treating them as separate components and by treating as one component the arithmetic mean of the ratings for skill variety, task identity and task significance. If one of the three main components in this equation is low, then the motivating potential score will be low. A near-zero rating on either autonomy or feedback, for example, would pull the score down disproportionately (five plus zero equals five, but five times zero equals zero). A near-zero rating on variety, identity or significance would not have a significant effect on the overall score.

The five core dimensions stimulate three psychological states critical to high work motivation, job satisfaction and performance. These critical psychological states are:

1. *Experienced meaningfulness*: the extent to which the individual considers the work to be meaningful, valuable and worthwhile.

2. *Experienced responsibility*: the extent to which the individual feels accountable for the work output.

3. *Knowledge of results*: the extent to which individuals know and understand how well they are performing.

Jobs with high motivating potential scores are more likely to lead to the experience of critical psychological states than jobs with low scores. Expectancy theorists argue that all three critical states must be present if the personal and work outcomes on the right-hand side of the model are to be achieved. One or two is not good enough. It is important to recall that individuals who put a low value on personal growth and development (GNS) will not respond in the way suggested by the model. No point, then, in offering them enriched jobs (unless one believes that the experience of personal development can in itself stimulate growth need).

The model also shows how the motivating potential of jobs can be improved by applying five implementing concepts. These (including vertical loading, from Herzberg) are:

1. *Combining tasks*

   Give employees more than one part of the work to do. This increases the variety of the job and increases the contribution that the individual makes to the product or service. For example, all typists could handle short memos, letters and major reports instead of having separate groups of typists each specializing in one of these kinds of task.

2. *Forming natural work units*

   Abandon task fragmentation and give employees a meaningful pattern of work to perform. This increases individual contribution and task significance. For example, customer service staff for a mobile telephone company could be trained to handle all or most customer enquiries and problems, rather than being assigned to deal with single issues (I want a new handset, there is an error in my invoice, I need roaming facilities).

3. *Establishing client relationships*

   Give employees responsibility for personal contacts within and outside the organization. This increases variety, gives the person freedom in performing the work and also increases the opportunities for receiving feedback. For example, members of staff working in a hospital pharmacy can each be allocated to one or more specific wards in the hospital and deal directly with the doctors, nurses and patients on 'their' wards rather than making anonymous contact, with all task allocations by the pharmacy manager on a 'first come first served by whoever is free at the time' basis.

4. *Vertical loading*

   Give employees responsibilities normally allocated to supervisors. Such additional responsibilities include granting discretion for:

work scheduling	work methods	problem solving
quality checks	training others	cost control
work times and breaks	deciding priorities	recruitment decisions

   This gives individuals more autonomy and can be achieved by removing the supervisory role, or by redesigning it to involve activities other than direct supervision, such as training, coaching, and liaising with other departments. Vertical loading and other similar approaches to increasing employee discretion are also called *empowerment*.

5. *Opening feedback channels*

Give employees direct relationships with 'clients' and also to direct performance summaries. This improves opportunities for feedback of results. Performance feedback lets people know how well they are doing and thus provides a basis for performance improvement [**link**, chapter 4, learning].

A number of successful applications of job enrichment were reported during the 1960s and 1970s. In America, the best-publicized applications were at American Telephone & Telegraph, which conducted nineteen job enrichment projects between 1965 and 1969 affecting over 1,000 blue and white collar employees (Ford, 1969). The company was concerned mainly with the rising costs of employee dissatisfaction and labour turnover, which were attributed to monotonous, meaningless jobs. In Britain, the best-publicized applications of job enrichment were at ICI, a chemicals company. Paul and Robertson (1970) reported eight applications between 1967 and 1968, mainly with white collar groups, including sales representatives, design engineers, foremen and draughtsmen.

The popularity of job enrichment waned during the 1980s, as the economies of Europe and America were more preoccupied with unemployment. However, work enrichment enjoyed renewed popularity in the 1990s, based on teamworking approaches.

Can the theory and practice of job enrichment now be abandoned? On the contrary. The language and the method have become a taken-for-granted aspect of contemporary management practice. Applications of job enrichment no longer carry novelty value and thus pass unreported. The concept of job enrichment has been 're-invented' by Timothy Butler and James Waldroop (1999) under the label 'job sculpting'. However, practice in many organizations has gone beyond the enrichment of individuals jobs to encompass teamworking, organizational culture change and other forms of employee empowerment.

Job sculpting and staff retention

Timothy Butler and James Waldroop argue that well-educated high achievers are mobile because they can succeed in just about any job. They leave the organization when their work does not match their deeply embedded life interests. Life interests are a stable part of personality, not hobbies (skiing) or enthusiasms (Chinese history). Research with 650 'professionals' revealed eight main life interests:

Life interests	How to recognize them
application of technology	the person who is intrigued by the inner working of things; reads software manuals for fun
quantitative analysis	the 'quant jock' who excels at numbers; designs optimum production schedules for fun
theory development and conceptual thinking	the person who enjoys talking about abstract ideas, wants the 'helicopter' view; reads academic journals for fun
creative production	the imaginative thinker, good at inventing novel solutions; wears unconventional clothes for fun
counselling and mentoring	the person good at counselling, mentoring and guiding; gets satisfaction from feeling needed and helping others
managing relationships	the person interested in managing people for results; deals with others, face to face, for fun
enterprise control	the responsibility seeker and decision maker who wants to control things; runs projects and manages teams for fun
influence through ideas	the person who is fulfilled when writing or speaking; wants to persuade, negotiate or just communicate for fun

Butler and Waldroop argue that, to motivate people to perform well and to stay with the organization, managers have to use job sculpting. This involves:

- listening carefully to discover what really challenges, excites and motivates people;
- understanding the individual's embedded life interests;
- designing both the job and the individual's career path to match those interests;
- using assignments as opportunities to sculpt the job for the person;
- reviewing performance regularly to ensure that work and career interests are consistent.

A salesperson with an interest in quantitative analysis could be assigned to market research. An engineer with an interest in influence through ideas could help design sales support materials and manuals. A bank lending officer, good at customer services but with a life interest in theory development and conceptual thinking, was about to leave the company until it moved him to a role in competitive analysis and strategy formulation.

Based on Timothy Butler and James Waldroop, 'Job sculpting: the art of retaining your best people', *Harvard Business Review*, 1999, vol.77, no.5, pp.144–52.

Empowerment, commitment and high-performance systems

We are going to have to make some changes here

Throughout the 1960s, American Telephone & Telegraph (AT&T) suffered high labour turnover. One manager made the following comment when shown the figures:

We are going to have to make some changes in our thinking about the attitudes of young people today. We are told our potential employees are not motivated by fear of job security, for instance. We are going to have to appeal to them through having a reputation for providing jobs that allow a young person to make meaningful contributions in challenging work. Something is wrong, and we are going to have to look closely at our work, our measurements, our style of supervision.

From Robert N. Ford, *Motivation Through the Work Itself*, American Management Association, New York, 1969, p.15.

Empowerment is the term given to organizational arrangements that allow employees more autonomy, discretion and unsupervised decision-making responsibility.

Meaningful contribution? Challenging task? These were expectations of employees in the 1960s. Have expectations changed? During the 1990s, many organizations reconsidered job enrichment and other techniques for employee **empowerment** for some of the same reasons that triggered the AT&T applications. An educated, media-informed workforce, conscious of individual rights and social comparisons, is today less willing to tolerate oppressive management control and is more ready to challenge management decisions and actions.

Rapid economic and technological change, and increasing global competition, encouraged empowerment. It was common in the 1990s to argue that an organization with an empowered, committed, skilled and motivated workforce would be more able to adapt to change and better able to beat the competition. However, as chapter 2 argues, increases in employee discretion can be seen as cosmetic, typically leaving organization hierarchies, managerial prerogatives and power inequalities intact [**link**, chapter 2, the world outside].

Techniques for improving employee motivation and performance through empowerment fall into two categories: individual job enrichment and self-managing or autonomous teamwork. This chapter has concentrated on individual motivation and job redesign. Chapter 12 explores effective teamwork [**link**, chapter 12, teamworking]. These twin approaches converge in practice in what has come to be known as **high-performance work systems**.

A **high-performance work system** is a form of organization that operates at levels of excellence far beyond those of comparable systems.

The features of high-performance work systems were first explored by Peter Vaill (1982, p.25). Organizations, or sub-groups, qualify for the title 'high-performance system' if they:

1. Perform excellently against a known external standard.

2. Perform beyond what is assumed to be their potential best.

3. Perform excellently in relation to what they did before.

4. Are judged by observers to be substantially better than comparable groups.

5. Are achieving levels of performance with fewer resources than necessary.

6. Are seen to be exemplars, as a source of ideas and inspiration.

7. Are seen to achieve the ideals of the culture.

8. Are the only organizations that have been able to do what they do at all, even though it might seem that what they do is not that difficult or mysterious a thing.

Many organizations have developed high-performance systems, including Digital Equipment Corporation (Buchanan and McCalman, 1989). Empowered employees can also be found in the Body Shop, Unipart, Frizzell Financial Services, Ciba UK and Harvester Restaurants (Pickard, 1993). Garment makers in Hong Kong adopted empowered teamworking (Li, 1992). Many American companies have publicized their empowered teams, including Shenandoah Life Insurance, Harley-Davidson, Compaq, Cummins Engine Company, Procter and Gamble, and General Motors (Hoerr et al., 1986; Hoerr, 1989).

In most cases, the role of the first line supervisor was radically changed and was in some cases removed (Dumaine, 1990). Tom Peters (1987) argues that traditional supervision has to change and that the role, if it still exists, should have the following features:

- a span of control of 50 to 75;

- act as a coach not a policeman, a sounding board, co-ordinator, facilitator, trainer;

- do a lot of wandering around rather than watching people work;

- work across the organization, with other functions, to solve problems;

- help teams to develop and implement ideas to improve performance.

Team empowerment: a new means of organizing

Individual responsibility offers a much lower level of service than team responsibility. Individuals may argue about who exactly is responsible for what, whereas a team is responsible for the result. How any problem arising is best resolved then becomes an internal matter.

Team empowerment offers a new means of organizing work at a local level. The focus now shifts from the tasks to the output that is needed. It is up to the team to produce the results, which means that the members of the team have to divide the work in the most appropriate way between themselves. Team empowerment only works if the team is given the resources by management. Resources mean money, machines and people. How the three are best combined is up to the team.

It is difficult for team empowerment to work unless management relinquishes insistence on control over the process. That is why team empowerment fits so uncomfortably in a system of traditional hierarchy.

From Meredith Belbin, *The Coming Shape of Organization*, Butterworth Heinemann, London, 1996, p.51.

Empowerment thus implies changes to the role of management. Edward Lawler (1986; 1995) argues that, in what he calls 'new design plants', 'almost no aspect of the organization is left untouched'. New design plants are characterized by:

- common entrance and car parking, with no reserved top management slots;

- common eating and restaurant areas, with no executive dining room;

- salaried status for all staff, with no 'hourly paid' employees;

- self-managing teams performing 'whole' work processes with elected leaders;

- flat management hierarchy—no foremen;

- team responsibility for goals, task allocation, quality control and absenteeism;

- team responsibility for selecting and training new members;

- some support functions performed within teams;

- other support staff become consultants and trainers.

Lawler (1986) claims that because so many features are altered, new design plants are 'a new kind of organization'. This is a grand claim to make on behalf of methods aimed at relieving the monotony of jobs designed according to scientific management principles.

Are the claims for high-performance work systems justified? While work redesign methods have remained the same, and theories of motivation have seen little development since the 1970s, the organizational context to which these theories and techniques are applied has changed dramatically. The distinctions between the quality of working life (QWL) approach and the high-performance work systems (HPWS) approach are summarized in table 8.7.

Figure 8.5 offers an overview of the argument of this chapter. This begins with demands for involvement and autonomy in work, and with the meaning, challenge and personal development that we seem to desire. These needs seek fulfilment in contexts facing multiple socio-economic pressures. Addressing these needs and pressures involves individual job enrichment and self-managing teamworking. In theory, the increased emphasis on personal development and continuous improvement contributes to organizational adaptability, product quality and customer care—to organizational effectiveness, and to quality of working life.

Table 8.7: QWL versus HPWS

QWL in the 1970s	HPWS today
aimed to reduce costs of absenteeism and labour turnover and increase productivity	aims to improve organizational flexibility and product quality for competitive advantage
increased autonomy improved quality of work experience and job satisfaction	increased empowerment improves skill, decision making, adaptability and use of new technology
had little impact on management functions	involves redefinition of management function, particularly for supervision
'quick fix' applied to problematic groups	takes time to change the organizational culture, attitudes and behaviour
personnel administration technique	human resource management strategy

Stop and criticize

- Some commentators argue that empowerment, job enrichment, high-performance work systems and new design plants constitute a radical transformation in organization design and in management–employee relationships.

- Some commentators argue that these initiatives are purely cosmetic, having no effect on the power and reward inequalities and exploitation in contemporary organizations.

- What are arguments for and against these two extreme positions—and where do you stand on this debate?

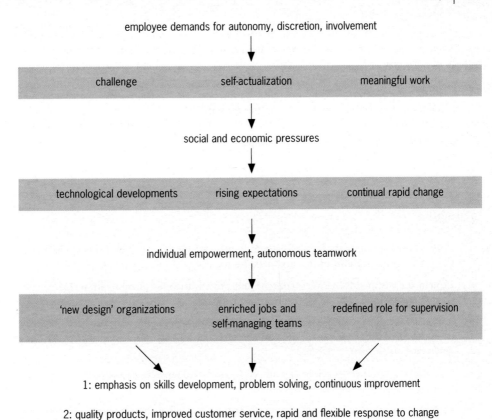

employee demands for autonomy, discretion, involvement

| challenge | self-actualization | meaningful work |

social and economic pressures

| technological developments | rising expectations | continual rapid change |

individual empowerment, autonomous teamwork

| 'new design' organizations | enriched jobs and self-managing teams | redefined role for supervision |

1: emphasis on skills development, problem solving, continuous improvement

2: quality products, improved customer service, rapid and flexible response to change

Figure 8.5: The case for the 'new design' organization

Recap

1. *Understand different ways in which the term 'motivation' is used.*

   - Motivation can refer to desired goals which we as individuals have or acquire.

   - Motivation can refer to the individual decision-making process through which goals are chosen.

   - Motivation can refer to social influence attempts to change the behaviour of others.

2. *Understand the nature of motives and motivation processes as influences on behaviour.*

   - Motives as desirable goals can be innate (drives) or acquired (socially learned).

   - Content theories of motivation explain behaviour in terms of innate drives and acquired motives.

   - Equity theory explains motivation in terms of perceived injustice or unfairness.

   - Expectancy theory explains motivation in terms of valued outcomes and the subjective probability of achieving those outcomes.

   - The Porter–Lawler model of work motivation combines expectancy theory with equity

   considerations in explaining job performance levels.

   - Goal-setting theory explains behaviour in terms of goal difficulty and goal specificity.

3. *Use expectancy theory and job enrichment to diagnose organizational problems and to recommend solutions.*

   - A job will only be motivating if it leads to rewards which the individual values.

   - Rewards motivate high performance when the link between effort and reward is clear.

   - Hygiene factors can overcome dissatisfaction but do not lead to motivation.

   - Content factors lead to job satisfaction, motivation and high performance.

   - Jobs can be enriched by applying vertical job loading factors.

   - The motivating potential of a job can be increased by improving skill variety, task identity, task significance, autonomy and feedback.

   - Job enrichment will not improve the performance of individuals with low growth need strength.

4. *Explain the renewed interest in this field in the 1990s, with respect to the evolving link between organization strategy and high-performance work systems.*

- Attitudes to work and employment have changed, and employees now expect more participation in management decisions and opportunities for self-development.

- In a rapidly changing competitive business environment, organizations want to motivate employees to be flexible, adaptable, committed and creative, not just to turn up on time and follow instructions.

- High-performance work systems are based on job enrichment and teamworking and a facilitative, coaching supervisory style.

Revision

1. Why is it difficult to make a clear distinction between innate drives and socially acquired motives, and what are the practical implications of this argument?

2. Explain the distinction between content and process theories of motivation. Explain an example of a content theory of motivation, its implications for organizational practice and its limitations.

3. Abraham Maslow meets Frederick Winslow Taylor; needs hierarchy meets scientific management. What criticisms would each of these gentlemen offer to the other, and how would they each defend their respective positions when faced with such criticisms?

4. How does equity theory seek to explain motivation and behaviour, and how can equity theory be used to diagnose and improve employee motivation?

5. Explain what is meant by the expectancy equation. How does this equation help to explain employee behaviour at work, and what criticisms can be levelled against this approach?

Springboard

Buchanan, D.A., 1994, 'Principles and practice in work design', in Keith Sisson (ed.), *Personnel Management*, Blackwell Publishers, Oxford, 1994, pp.85–116.

Reviews the literature on work design, from scientific management through autonomous groups and job enrichment, assessing developments and trends.

Lawler, E.E., 1996, *From the Ground Up: Six Principles for Building the New Logic Corporation*, Jossey-Bass, San Francisco.

Argues that single techniques for improving organizational effectiveness are not effective and argues that a range of methods have to be integrated to achieve success.

Lawler, E.E., Mohrman, S.A. and Ledford, G.E., 1998, *Strategies for High Performance Organizations*, Jossey-Bass, San Francisco.

Describes how Fortune 1000 companies use employee involvement, quality management and re-engineering to improve organizational effectiveness.

Locke, E.A. and Latham, G.P., 1990, *A Theory of Goal Setting and Task Performance*, Prentice Hall, New York.

Comprehensive overview of what appears to be one of the most robust motivational theories in work psychology—an important and influential treatment.

Maslow, A.H., 1943, 'A theory of human motivation', *Psychological Review*, vol.50, no.4, pp.370–96.

The original statement of Maslow's needs hierarchy theory, essential (and not too difficult) reading for all those who believe that his theory mentions only five needs.

Pfeffer, J., 1996, *Competitive Advantage Through People: Unleashing the Power of the Work Force*, Harvard Business School Press, Boston.

Attacks Taylor's scientific management and offers a range of techniques and management behaviours (which go beyond the more narrowly focused material on motivation in this chapter) for stimulating motivation and performance.

Pfeffer, J., 1998, *The Human Equation: Building Profits by Putting People First*, Harvard Business School Press, Boston.

Describes high-performance management methods to improve motivation and performance. Gives detailed evidence to persuade sceptical managers.

Porter, L.W. and Lawler, E.E., 1968, *Managerial Attitudes and Performance*, Irwin, Homewood, Illinois.

Clear explanation of the Porter–Lawler model, theoretical background, underpinning evidence and practical managerial implications. Seminal and still widely cited.

Ritchie, S. and Martin, P., 1999, *Motivation Management*, Gower, Aldershot.

A content theory of motivation, based on a motivational profile of the individual rather than a universalistic approach. Written for a practising management audience rather than a theoretical academic one. British, not American, in style.

Home viewing

Bringing out the Dead (1999, director Martin Scorsese) is based around three night shifts in the working life of a New York paramedic, Frank Pierce (played by Nicolas Cage). He is burned out and exhausted, alcoholic and insomniac, haunted by the memory of a girl he was unable to save and desperate to leave the job. He is unable to save many patients as they are either crazy, dead or dying by the time the ambulance reaches them. His supervisor won't accept his resignation, even when he turns up late, because they are short of ambulance drivers. On each night, Frank tours the city streets with a different partner. Larry (John Goodman) likes fast food. Marcus (Ving Rhames) preaches the gospel. Tom (Tom Sizemore) likes to beat up patients for excitement when the pace is slack. Identify which of the needs on Maslow's hierarchy Frank and his colleagues display in their behaviour. Can you identify Frank's motivational profile and the profiles of each of his partners? Use the Porter–Lawler model of work motivation to explain Frank's low job satisfaction. What advice would you give to management on improving the motivating potential of paramedic work?

American Beauty (1999, director Sam Mendes) is a story of 'the perfect family' falling apart. Lester Burnham (played by Kevin Spacey) quits his dead-end management job to work serving burgers in McDonald's, while his wife Carolyn (Annette Bening) has an affair with her main local competitor in the real estate business. The story displays the corrosive effects of dissatisfying, demotivating work on the family, personal identity, and relationships. Also of interest is the way in which the main characters define 'success' in life. What does this film reveal about the fate of those who decide not to comply with 'normal' social values?

OB in literature

David Ireland, *The Unknown Industrial Prisoner*, Angus & Robertson/Vintage, Sydney, Australia, 1971.

Classic, award-winning novel based on the 'Puroil Refining Termitary and Grinding Works' in Sydney, Australia. 'Termitary' because of the ant-like behaviour in the administration block. 'Grinding Works' because of what long-term employment does to those who work there. The opening chapter title, 'one day in a penal colony', sets the tone. The jobs are designed in the best traditions of scientific management. Dealing with autocratic managers and hazardous working conditions, note how employee motivation is systematically destroyed and how performance suffers. Note the employee strategies for coping with this environment, including practical jokes, sabotage, sex and alcohol. A poignant and hilarious account of factory life. Analyse the motivational profile and identify the embedded life interests of each of the plant employees as you read this.

John Grisham, *The Street Lawyer*, Century Random House, London, 1998.

Typical Grisham thriller about lawyers, but this plot has an unusual dimension. Which characters value intrinsic rewards and satisfaction with the work itself much more highly than they value extrinsic rewards? To what extent would you be prepared to sacrifice extrinsic reward in favour of intrinsic satisfaction, like these characters, in your own working life?

Chapter exercises

1: Growth need and job characteristics

Objectives

1. To identify your personal growth need strength and by implication your preference for enriched or empowered work.

2. To assess the motivating potential score of a particular job or jobs.

3. To determine which core job characteristics would need to change to improve the MPS of that job or those jobs.

Briefing

(a) Assessing personal growth need strength
We know that there are individual differences with respect to work preferences. Here are twelve pairs of statements of job characteristics. Taking each pair of characteristics, decide which kind of job you would prefer from the choice offered (these are not all opposing choices) by circling a number on the five-point rating scale.

a job that offers little or no challenge	1	2	3	4	5	a job that requires you to be completely isolated from co-workers
a job that pays very well	1	2	3	4	5	a job that allows considerable opportunity to be creative and innovative
a job that requires you to make important decisions	5	4	3	2	1	a job in which there are many pleasant people to work with
a job with little security in an unstable organization	5	4	3	2	1	a job in which you have limited opportunities to influence decisions affecting your work
a job in which greater responsibility is given to those who do the best work	5	4	3	2	1	a job in which greater responsibility is given to those who are loyal and have seniority
a job with a supervisor who is sometimes highly critical	5	4	3	2	1	a job that does not make too many demands on your abilities
a routine and undemanding job	1	2	3	4	5	a job in which your co-workers are not very friendly
a job with a supervisor who respects you and treats you fairly	1	2	3	4	5	a job that provides constant opportunities for learning
a job that gives you a chance to develop yourself personally	5	4	3	2	1	a job with excellent vacations and fringe benefits
a job in which there is a real chance you could be laid off	5	4	3	2	1	a job with very little chance to do challenging work
a job with little freedom and independence to do the work the way you think best	1	2	3	4	5	a job with poor working conditions
a job with very satisfying teamwork	1	2	3	4	5	a job that allows you to use your abilities to the fullest extent

To calculate your individual growth need strength, simply sum the numbers that you have circled and divide that total by 12.

A score of 3.5 or above suggests that you have high growth need strength and that you would respond positively to job enrichment, leading to the critical psychological states in the job characteristics model.

A score of 2.5 or less suggests that you would not find enriched jobs satisfying or motivating.

Scores between 2.5 and 3.5 suggest that you would find some job enrichment satisfying, but that you also welcome some structure and management control over your work.

(b) Applying the job characteristics model
To measure the motivating potential score (MPS) for a given job, researchers developed the Job Diagnostic Survey (JDS). The JDS is a lengthy questionnaire, which takes some considerable time to complete and analyse in full. However, here is a short version which still allows calculation of the MPS for a job. This in turn allows job design deficiencies to be identified and thus triggers ideas for job redesign and enrichment.

Complete this analysis for a job in which you are currently employed (full or part time), or for a job that you have performed recently. The JDS is designed for completion by the job holder and not by an observer. For each of the twelve items, indicate whether it is an accurate or an inaccurate description of the chosen job and give it a rating using this scale:

1 = very inaccurate
2 = mostly inaccurate
3 = somewhat inaccurate
4 = uncertain
5 = somewhat accurate
6 = mostly accurate
7 = very accurate

The job chosen for analysis is:

Item	Rating	
1	_____	supervisors often let me know how well they think I am performing
2	_____	the job requires me to use a number of complex high-level skills
3	_____	the job is arranged so that I have the chance to do a complete piece of work from beginning to end
4	_____	just doing the work required by the job provides many chances for me to work out how well I am doing
5	_____	the job is not simple and repetitive
6	_____	this job is one where a lot of other people can be affected by how well the work is done
7	_____	the job does not deny me the chance to use my personal initiative or judgement in carrying out the work
8	_____	the job gives me the chance to completely finish the pieces of work I begin
9	_____	the job itself provides plenty of clues about whether or not I am performing well
10	_____	the job gives me considerable opportunity for independence and freedom in how I do the work
11	_____	the job itself is very significant and important in the broader scheme of things
12	_____	the supervisors and co-workers on this job almost always give me feedback on how well I am doing in my work

Scoring
Work out the average of the two items that measure each job characteristic:

job characteristic	item numbers	average score
skill variety	2 and 5	_____
task identity	3 and 8	_____
task significance	6 and 11	_____
autonomy	7 and 10	_____
feedback from the job itself	4 and 9	_____
feedback from others	1 and 12	_____

You are almost ready to calculate the MPS for this job. First, add your scores for the two 'feedback' characteristics and divide by 2 to give the average score. Now put the scores into the MPS formula:

$$MPS = \frac{(\text{skill variety} + \text{task identity} + \text{task significance})}{3} \times \text{autonomy} \times \text{feedback}$$

If you have completed this analysis alone:

- assess the strengths and weaknesses of this job in terms of its motivating potential;
- identify recommendations for redesigning this job to improve the MPS;
- assess the difficulties in implementing these recommendations, given the nature of the work and the organizational context in which it is performed.

If you have completed this analysis alongside colleagues:

- share the results of your analysis with colleagues;
- pick the job in your group that has the lowest MPS;
- identify redesign options for improving the job's MPS (you will first need to ask the job holder for a detailed description of the job);
- assess the difficulties in implementing these recommendations, given the nature of the work and the organizational context in which it is performed.

2: The 'best place to work' blueprint

Objectives
1. To provide practice in applying motivation theory to a real-life organizational context.
2. To analyse critically the approach of one particular organization.
3. To reflect critically on one particular theoretical model of work motivation and job performance.

Briefing
First, familiarize yourself with the Porter–Lawler model of work motivation (figure 8.3) and the expectancy theory of work motivation from which this is derived. Then read the following (real) case, without discussion with colleagues, and turn to the case analysis.

After the merger – the best place to work?*

Commercial Union and General Accident merged in 1998 to become CGU, one of the largest insurance companies in Britain. As part of the process of creating a new company, a two-day conference was organized for 420 first-line managers and technical specialists, 80 managers, and union representatives. Conference participants were asked what would make CGU 'the best place to work'. Here is their blueprint:

Alignment

- I value knowing the big picture and having the support that enables me to 'own' it.

- I value knowing that our individual and team targets are clearly aligned to the key result areas (KRAs) and balanced business scorecard (BBS) objectives.

- I value knowing where I fit in terms of how my accountabilities and responsibilities help to achieve the KRAs and BBS objectives.

- It is important to me that I feel I belong to my team and to the organization.

Performance

- It is important to me to work for managers who acknowledge success and deal fairly and promptly with failure.

- I expect a fair reward that is aligned with my achievements and efforts.

- I value having the right skills, tools and authority to do my job.

- It is important for me to work for managers who are good at managing people and the business we are in, and who have the right level of technical knowledge.

- I value managers who consult me on issues that affect me but who are also prepared to take decisions quickly.

- I value working in a team that maintains a strong customer focus.

Support

- It is important for me to have leaders who inspire my confidence and trust.

- Give me structures, processes and practices that enable me to deliver.

- I value a stimulating, friendly, open working environment.

- I value company policies that enable me to balance my home life with work.

- I value focused and lively feedback about my work and the way I behave.

- I value responsibility, but within clear boundaries that stretch as I develop.

- I want to work for a company that has a long-term, structured approach to career planning, succession planning and personal development.

This 'blueprint' was based on employees' views and not on any theoretical framework.

Case analysis
Make notes for yourself in response to these five questions:

1. Compare this blueprint with the Porter–Lawler model of work motivation. If management at CGU is able to implement this blueprint, what would be your prediction? Will this motivate employees to high or low performance, or will it have no impact? And why?

2. What does the model, and expectancy theory, recommend that is missing from the blueprint? What advice would you give to the company based on this analysis?

3. What does the blueprint specify that is missing from the Porter–Lawler model? What advice would you give to Porter and Lawler based on this analysis?

4. What problems would you expect management to face in implementing this blueprint in a highly competitive and rapidly changing environment? How would you advise management in dealing with these issues?

5. Job enrichment—is this a genuine attempt to improve working conditions, employee skills development, career opportunities and the quality of working life, or is this just a cosmetic attempt to disguise the systemic power inequalities and exploitation in contemporary organizations?

When asked by your instructor, compare your answers with those of colleagues. Try to reach a consensus on each question and be prepared to present your answers to your group.

* This case is based on Tony Clarry, 'Premium bonding', *People Management*, vol.5, no.17, 2 September 1999, pp.34–9.

Part 3 Groups and teams in the organization

A field map of the organizational behaviour terrain

PESTLE: The **P**olitical, **E**conomic, **S**ocial, **T**echnological, **L**egal and **E**cological context

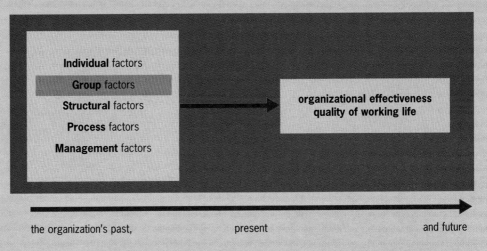

the organization's past,   present   and future

Introduction

Part 3, Groups and teams in the organization, explores the following four topics:

- Group formation, in chapter 9
- Group structure, in chapter 10
- Individuals in groups, in chapter 11
- Teamworking, in chapter 12

These four topics reflect the progress of collections of people over time within the organizational context. Thus, a number of individuals may informally develop into a group, or a team may be formally established by management and given a task. Each then develops its own internal structures to allow its members to work together. The group influences the attitudes and behaviours of its members, and the individual within it can affect the group as a whole. Meanwhile, management's ambition is to get individuals working together as a single, effective team. Groups and teams offer a separate but related level of analysis between the individual and the organization structure and its processes.

Our opening case study concerns a health service manager's problem with a group of domestic staff. The working arrangements of these employees (all women) were recently changed in order to improve efficiency and reduce costs. You are asked to consider the possible causes of this problem, and then to suggest possible solutions. This is based on a real case, although the context and the individuals have been disguised.

If you were the hospital manager, how would you analyse and resolve this group performance problem? It's your call.

YOUR CALL (3): MAKING THE WORK GROUP EFFECTIVE

The domestic service arrangements in a large hospital had, for many years, been based on the permanent allocation of domestic staff to specific wards. When staff shortages occurred (due to sickness or leave), these were made up from a reserve pool of staff, or by overtime working. Permanent allocation to a ward thus carried status among the domestic staff. New entrants to the hospital's domestic department would begin as 'reliefs' and would then be 'promoted' to a permanent ward position on completion of a satisfactory probationary period. Domestic supervisors also operated an unofficial sanction system whereby staff off sick frequently, or for long periods of time, were penalized for their absences by being 'demoted' to the reserve pool, only returning to the permanent ward position when their record of attendance proved to be satisfactory.

The domestic staff had a permanent placement within a particular ward or two adjacent wards. Over time, the staff working on the same ward got to know each other well. They had their tea and lunch breaks together, during which time they discussed the patients on 'their' ward. Working in the same wards, these domestic staff also got to know the regular nursing personnel who had been assigned to their ward. Getting the work done was achieved by group effort. Each domestic was expected to warn the others of the impending approach of a supervisor. Group members were required to support each other in the event of any 'harassment' by management. Bragging about the happenings on their ward was expected and acceptable. Different ward teams tried to outdo each other in terms of the dramas they had seen on their wards.

Following a recent re-organization, the hospital administrators called in management consultants to review the working practices of these domestic staff. The consultants conducted numerous time and motion studies and noted all the results. They recommended that efficiency could be increased, and overtime reduced, by changing work patterns and the type of equipment used. Following these recommendations, the hospital management purchased the new equipment. Meanwhile, the changes in work patterns resulted in the dissolution of the reserve pool and the allocation of staff to ward areas on a rotational basis. Each morning, domestic staff were allocated to different ward areas, to work alongside other staff. This was intended to increase flexibility in the transfer of staff on an *ad hoc* basis to any areas of shortage. These two changes resulted in the replacement of the old labour-intensive system, which depended on staff co-operation and co-ordination.

Much to the surprise of management, problems began to arise as soon as the revised system was put into operation. The levels of sickness and absenteeism among the domestic staff rose, their productivity and efficiency fell, and problems of liaison between domestic and nursing staff increased at ward level. Generally, a deterioration in working relationships between all concerned was observed.

You are the hospital manager. What's the problem? What's the solution? It's your call.

Chapter 9 Group formation

Key concepts

group relations
psychological group
aggregate
additive task
conjunctive task
disjunctive task
Hawthorne effect
informal organization

human relations approach
formal group
informal group
group self-organization
activities
interactions
norms
sentiments

Learning objectives

When you have read this chapter, you should be able to define those key concepts in your own words, and you should also be able to:

1. List the key characteristics of a psychological group.
2. Distinguish between different types of group tasks.
3. Name the four research phases of the Hawthorne studies.
3. Distinguish between a formal and an informal group.
4. Outline Homans' theory of group formation.
5. Enumerate the five stages of Tuckman and Jensen's model of group development.
6. Summarize Katzenbach and Smith's distinction between a group and a team.

Why study group formation?

Marion Hampton (1999, p.113) summarized both the symbolic and practical aspects of groups:

> Groups embody many important cultural values of Western society: team-work, co-operation, a collective that is greater than the sum of its parts, informality, egalitarianism and even the indispensability of the individual member. Groups are seen as having a motivating, inspiring influence on the individual, drawing the best out of him or her, enabling him or her to perform feats that would be beyond him or herself as a detached individual. Groups can have a healing effect on individuals, bolstering their self-esteem and filling their lives with meaning.

Groups play an important role in our lives. It has been estimated that the average person belongs to five or six different groups, and about 92 per cent of members are in groups of five people or less. These may include the quality control circle, the new product team, the local women's group and the sports team. Groups and teams are terms which are now used interchangeably, and readers are advised to read carefully to pick out the authors' definition. People join groups because of common needs, interests or goals, physical proximity or cultural similarity, or they may be assigned to them by management.

Much organizational work is performed in teams. Their performance thus affects the success of the organization as a whole. Being able to work productively with others is so important that companies place an emphasis on their recruits being good 'team players'. To ensure this, they invest in team development activities to develop their teamworking abilities. Hayes (1997, p.1) noted that 'To an ever-increasing extent, modern management has become focused on the idea of the team. Management consultants propose organizational restructuring to facilitate teamwork; directors make policy statements about the importance of the team to the organization; and senior managers exhort their junior staff to encourage team working in their departments'. Proctor and Mueller (2000, p.7) summarized the most recent statistics, which reveal the remorseless organizational trend towards group and teamworking all around the world, and in virtually all industries. Thus, since the chances of either working in a team or managing one are so high, it is prudent to know how they operate.

- In the USA, by 1990 almost half of the largest companies reported using self-managed work teams for at least some employees (Cohen *et al.*, 1996).

- In the UK, 40 per cent of personnel managers reported that their organization used some self-managed teams, about 65 per cent of which were no more than three years old (Industrial Society, 1995)

- A survey of manufacturing companies undertaken by the Institute of Work Psychology found that team-based working was used to some degree by 70 per cent of respondents (Waterson *et al.*, 1997).

- The fourth, authoritative Workplace Employee Relations Survey (WERS) found that 66 per cent of employers reported the use of team-based working for at least some employees (Cully *et al.*, 1998).

"I'll begin by reading the minutes from our last meeting: Higgins: 'If I don't get out of this room my head will explode.' Jenkins: 'I feel like I'm trapped in a Kafka-like nightmare.' Milbrook: 'This is two hours of my life I'll never get back'…"

Group relations refers to the interactions within and between groups, and to the stable arrangements that result from them.

Group and teamworking has been an aspect of organizational life for a long time yet remains controversial. The management literature promotes the benefits of group working and stresses the commonality of interests between individual workers, organised by management into teams, and the goals of the 'organization as a whole', that is, of senior management. Critics, in contrast, contend that the extent of group–management conflict has been misinterpreted, underplayed or simply ignored.

Stop and criticize

Suggest reasons why group working has become so popular in organizations.

What benefits does it offer to individual employees? To management?

Definitions of groups

Psychological group refers to two or more people, in face-to-face interaction, each aware of his or her membership in the group, each aware of the others who belong to the group, and each aware of their positive interdependence as they strive to achieve mutual goals.

Interpersonal behaviour builds up into group behaviour, which in turn sustains and structures future interpersonal relations. Groups develop particular characteristics, affecting not only the behaviour of the individuals within them but also their relation to other groups in the organization. Because of the importance of **group relations**, social psychologists have studied them extensively. The idea of a group is well known to most people who work, live and play in groups. Very often we may refer to persons standing at a bus stop or in a queue as a group. However, it has a more specialist and restricted meaning.

It is important to maintain a distinction between mere aggregates of individuals and what are called psychological groups. The latter are so-called because they exist not only through the (often visible) interactions of members but also in the (not observable) perceptions of their members. The term **psychological group** is thus reserved for people who consider themselves to be part of an identifiable unit, who relate to each other in a meaningful fashion and who share dispositions through their shared sense of collective identity. In the example below, only the football team would fulfil our criteria for a group. We can usefully adopt Johnson and Johnson's (1991) definition in order to distinguish it from an **aggregate**.

Stop and criticize

Why would only *one* of the following be considered to be a psychological group? In what circumstances could one of the other aggregates become a psychological group?

(a) People riding on a bus

(b) Blonde women between 20 and 30 years of age

(c) Members of a football team

(d) Audience in a theatre

(e) People sheltering in a shop doorway from the rain

Aggregate refers to a collection of unrelated people who happen to be in close physical proximity for a short period of time.

These definitions enable us to exclude aggregates of people who are simply individuals who happen to be collected together at any particular time. Like the bus travellers, theatre audience or rain shelterers, they do not relate to one another in any meaningful fashion or consider themselves a part of any identifiable unit, despite their temporary physical proximity. By the same token, the definition allows one to exclude classes of people who may be defined by physical attributes, geographical location, economic status or age. Even though a trade union in an organization may like to believe it is a group, it will fail to meet our definition if all of its members do not interact with each other, and if they are not aware of each other. This need for all members to interact has led to the suggestion that in practice, a psychological group is unlikely to exceed twelve or so persons. Beyond that number, the opportunity for frequent interaction between members, and hence group awareness, is considerably reduced.

It is possible for small aggregates of people to be transformed into a psychological group through outside circumstances. In fact, a whole series of 'disaster movies' in the cinema have been made in which people fight for their lives on board sinking ships, hijacked aeroplanes and burning skyscraper buildings. The story typically involves aggregates of people setting out at the start of the film. The danger causes them to interact with one another, and this increases their awareness of one another and leads them to see themselves as having common problems. By the end of the film. the survivors demonstrate all the characteristics of the psychological group as defined here. The disaster movie example helps us to understand some of the characteristics of a psychological group:

1. *A minimum membership of two people*: there is no 'official' size, and different authors discuss groups that range from two to 30 individuals; however, the more members a group has, the greater the number of possible relationships that can exist between members, the greater the level of communication that is required and the more complex the structure that is needed to operate the group successfully.

2. *A shared communication network*: members of a psychological group must be capable of communicating with every other member. In this communication process, the aims and purposes of the group are exchanged. The mere process of communication interaction satisfies some of our social needs and it is used to set and enforce standards of group behaviour.

3. *A shared sense of collective identity*: group members must identify with the other members of the group and not see themselves as individuals acting independently. They must all believe that they are both members of and participants in the group, which itself is distinct from other groups.

4. *Shared goals*: the goal concerned is therefore shared and is only achievable by the members working together and not as individuals. The goal may be the production of something (e.g. student group project, company marketing plan) or enjoying oneself (e.g. playing in a football team). While individuals may want to attain their own particular objective, they must perceive that the other members of the group should also share this same disposition. They must feel obliged to contribute to the attainment of the shared goal.

5. *Group structure*: individuals in the group will have different roles, e.g. initiator/ideas person, suggestion provider, compromiser. These roles, which tend to become fixed, indicate what members expect of each other. Norms or rules exist that indicate which behaviours are acceptable in the group and which are not (e.g. smoking, swearing, late coming).

Groups will differ in the degree to which they possess such characteristics. To the extent that they do have them, it will make the group more easily recognizable by others as a group, and this will give it more power with which to influence its members. The topic of influence and control in groups is dealt with in a later chapter. What will be said in the remainder of this chapter and this part of the book will refer only to psychological groups. For this reason, we shall use the shorthand label of 'group' to refer to a psychological group (Guzzo, 1996).

Stop and criticize	The groups to which you belong provide you with shared goals and a sense of identity and meet your social needs. However, they can also constrain your thinking, stifle your freedom of expression, limit your behaviour and restrict your freedom of expression? What is your opinion?

As the size and complexity of modern organizations has increased, the need to integrate the work of different individuals within groups, and groups within organizations, has also grown. Mohrman *et al.* (1995) list the benefits of group working:

- They allow organizations to develop and deliver products and services quickly and cost-effectively while maintaining quality.

- They enable organizations to learn, and retain that learning, more effectively.

- Cross-functional groups promote improved quality management.

- Cross-functional design groups can undertake effective process re-engineering.

- Production time can be reduced if tasks performed concurrently by individuals are performed concurrently by people in groups.

- Group-based organization promotes innovation because of the cross-fertilization of ideas.

- Organizations with flat structures can be monitored, co-ordinated and directed more effectively if the functional unit is the group rather than the individual.

- The rise in organizational information-processing requirements caused by increasing complexity can be better handled by groups than individuals.

Types of group task

The tasks that groups and teams are asked to perform vary greatly. Their nature is an important variable in their performance. Tasks can be divided in different ways. One simple dichotomy already cited is that of simple–complex. Research showed that that had an impact on the group's communication structure (see chapter 10) and affected an individual's performance in the presence of others as described in the discussion on social facilitation [**link**, chapter 11, individuals in groups]. Ivan Steiner (1972) classified group tasks on the basis of the type of interdependence that they required.

Additive task
With this type of task, all group members do basically the same job, and the final group product or outcome (group performance) is the sum of all their individual contributions. The final outcome is roughly proportional to the number of individuals contributing. There is low interdependency between these people. A group working together will normally perform better than the same number of individuals working alone, provided that all group members make

Additive task is a task whose accomplishment depends on the sum of all group members' efforts.
Conjunctive task is a task whose accomplishment depends on the performance of the group's least talented member.
Disjunctive task is a task whose accomplishment depends on the performance of the group's most talented member.

their contribution. Social loafing can, however, reduce performance on an additive task. Examples of additive tasks are tug-of-war contests and pedestrians giving a stalled car a push-start (Littlepage, 1991)

Conjunctive task

In this task, one member's performance depends on another's. There is high interdependency. Thus, a group's *least* capable member determines performance. A successful group project at university depends on one member finding the information, a second writing it up and a third presenting it. All three elements are required for success and hence co-ordination is essential in conjunctive tasks. Groups perform less well on conjunctive tasks than lone individuals. Examples of conjunctive tasks include climbing a mountain, running a relay race and playing chamber music (Steiner and Rajaratnam, 1961).

Disjunctive task

In this type of task, once again, one member's performance depends on another's. Again there is high interdependency. However, this time, the group's *most* capable member determines its performance. Groups perform better than their average member on disjunctive tasks, since even the best performer will not know all the answers, and working with others helps to improve overall group performance. Diagnostic and problem-solving activities performed by a group would come into this category. Co-ordination is important here as well, but in the sense of stopping the others impeding the top performers (Diehl and Stroebe, 1991). Examples of disjunctive task performers are quiz teams (*University Challenge*, pub quiz) and a maintenance team in a nuclear power-generating plant.

Groups will tend to outperform the same number of individuals working separately when working on disjunctive tasks than on additive or conjunctive tasks. This is provided that the most talented member can convince the others of the correctness of their answer. The attitudes, feelings and conflicts in a group setting might prevent this happening.

The Hawthorne studies

In the United States, during the 1920s and 1930s, the Hawthorne studies were to lead to the creation of the human relations movement and a highly influential school of academic and practical management thinking. In that period, factories used natural daylight or candles to illuminate the workspace of their workers. In an attempt to promote the sales of light bulbs in the early 1920s, the General Electric (GE) company paid for a series of experiments to demonstrate a positive correlation between the amount of light in a workplace and the productivity of workers. Proved to GE's satisfaction, it proceeded to advertise the results. Then, to counter some questions about the objectivity of such experiments conducted by a light bulb manufacturer, a series of more independent studies were initiated. It is for this reason that the original team of researchers operated under the aegis of the National Academy of Sciences' National Research Council, which included the Council on Industrial Lighting. They hoped to show that artificial lighting in a factory would reduce accidents, save the workers' sight and raise productivity by as much as 25 per cent. The original experiments therefore examined the effect of physical changes, originally illumination and later room temperature and humidity, on worker productivity (Gillespie, 1991).

The experiments were conducted at the Hawthorne plant of the Western Electric Company, the manufacturing subsidiary of the American Telephone &

Figure 9.1: The Hawthorne plant of the Western Electric Company, *c.* 1925
Source: AT&T Archives

George Elton Mayo
(1880–1949)

Fritz Jules
Roethlisberger
(1898–1974)

William J. Dickson
(1904–73)

Telegraph Company (AT&T), which supplied telephones to the entire Bell system. The factory was located in Cicero, Illinois. In November of 1924, the initial experiments began examining productivity improvements from a scientific management perspective assessing the effect of physical factors. By 1927, the initial results were so confusing that the company was preparing to abandon the work. Then, George Pennock, the Hawthorne plant's technical branch superintendent responsible for production methods, heard Professor George Elton Mayo speak at a meeting and invited him to bring an academic research team into the factory. Mayo was born in Australia in 1880. Initially a philosopher with psychoanalytical training, he came to the United States in 1922 and became a professor of industrial research at the Harvard Business School two years later.

The studies were among the most extensive social science research ever conducted. In addition to Mayo, the other members of the research team included Fritz Jules Roethlisberger (who later become the first professor of organizational behaviour (holding his post in the Harvard Business School)) and William J. Dickson. It was through their book *Management and the Worker* (1939) that the results of the Hawthorne studies were communicated to the world. These academics were assisted by a junior researcher, George Homans, who was to become famous later for this work in group dynamics, explained later in this chapter.

The Hawthorne studies revolutionized social science thinking. They were intended to have direct financial benefits for the company; that is, to appear as profits in company accounts rather than as papers in academic journals. Their investigation results demonstrated the overriding influence of social factors on workplace behaviour. Although many different studies were conducted, four in particular stand out. These were the illumination experiments; the relay assembly test room experiment; the interviewing programme; and the bank wiring observation room experiment.

Illumination experiments (1924–27)
The illumination studies explored the relationship of the quality and quantity of illumination to efficiency. Within a large assembly area, the intensity of the light

Figure 9.2: Relay Assembly Department, Hawthorne works, *c.* 1925
Source: AT&T Archives

was varied, but the results obtained were confusing. The researchers discovered that in no case was the production output obtained in proportion to the lighting provided. Production even increased when the light intensity was reduced. Two conclusions were reached. First, as far as employees' production output was concerned, lighting was only one of several factors involved, and apparently, a minor one. Second, a study of such a large number of workers prevented the identification and control of the effect of any single variable on output. A different research design and methods would be needed. The illumination experiments were abandoned.

Relay assembly test room experiments (1927–33)
Hawthorne's Relay Assembly Department assembled relays, which were electromagnetic switches used in telephones. Each relay consisted of about 35 parts and was assembled by hand. As figure 9.2 shows, the department contained hundreds of workers, contained many rows of benches, and had a regimented atmosphere that was characteristic of many of the other assembly areas within the plant.

The new research design involved a small group of female workers drawn from the regular workforce of the Relay Assembly Department. The research team selected two women who were friends. These two then selected the other four workers. The six women assemblers were placed in a separate room, where they could be observed more closely by the researchers. It was this room which gave its name to this phase of the research. The women had been working a 48-hour week including Saturdays with no tea breaks. The general physical environment and conditions of the room were similar to those of the larger assembly area.

The women were carefully and systematically studied by the researcher who was in the room with them. He kept a note of everything that happened; maintained a friendly atmosphere by listening to their complaints and by telling them what was going on. This phase of the research sought to answer questions about fatigue, rest pauses, length of working day, equipment change effects, and attitudes to their work and the company. A total of thirteen periods were studied during which changes were made to rest pauses, hours of work and breaks for refreshment.

Relay assembly test room	Selected results

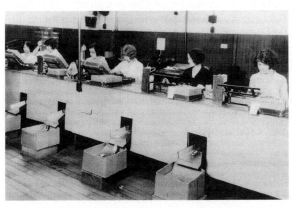

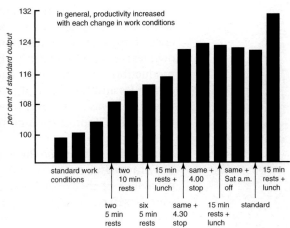

Figure 9.3: Relay assembly test room, *c.* 1929
Source: AT&T Archives

Based on data from Roethlisberger and Dickson, 1939. From J. Greenberg and R. A. Baron, *Behaviour in Organizations*, Prentice Hall, sixth edition, 1997, p.13.

As figure 9.3 shows, there was a nearly continuous increase in output. This increase began when employee benefits such as rest periods and early finishes were added but were maintained and continued even when these benefits were withdrawn and the women returned to a 48-hour week. The reasons offered for the increases in output included:

- the motivating effect of acquiring a special status through their selection for and involvement in the experiment;

- the effect of participation as the women were consulted and informed by the experimenter;

- the effect of observer friendliness, which improved their morale;

- a different and less intense form of supervision, which reduced their stress while increasing their productivity;

- the self-selected nature of the group creating higher levels of mutual dependence and support appropriate for group working.

One of these explanations has even established itself as a concept in social science research. This says that the changed behaviour of the women was just the result of being observed by the researchers, and that the manipulation of the aforementioned variables played no part. This is now referred to as the **Hawthorne effect**.

Hawthorne effect refers to the tendency of people being observed, as part of a research effort, to behave differently than they otherwise would.

The researchers were convinced that the women were motivated not solely by money or by improvements in their working conditions. Their attitudes towards and achievement of increased output seemed to be affected by the group to which they belonged. These results led management to study employee attitudes using an interviewing programme.

Interviewing programme (1928–30)

Management wanted to find out more about how employees felt about their supervisors and working conditions, and how these related to morale. The interviewing programme involved over 20,000 interviews. Initially, the interviewers asked employees highly structured questions about how they felt about their work. Later, this form of questioning gave way to non-directive, open-ended questions on non-work topics which the interviewees considered to be important. The sympathetic and non-judgemental approach of the interviewers led them, they claimed, to discover the true feelings and attitudes of the workforce. The information that was obtained went beyond issues of work conditions and supervision and extended to family and social issues. These interviews also revealed the existence of informal, gang-like groups within the formal working groups. Each had its own leaders and 'sidekicks', who built an elaborate structure of controls to ensure production was controlled. The discovery of this **informal organization** with its own rules and hierarchy of positions was one of the findings of this phase of the research. It was to discover how this worked in greater detail that the Bank Wiring Observation Room Experiment was established.

> **Informal organization** refers to the network of relationships that spontaneously establish themselves between members of an organization on the basis of their common interests and friendships.

Bank Wiring Observation Room experiments (1931–32)

The interviews revealed that groups exercised a great deal of control over the behaviour of their members. To test this and other hypotheses, a group of men were observed in another part of the company. The Bank Wiring Observation Room consisted of fourteen men who were formally organized into three subgroups, each of which contained three wirers and one supervisor (figure 9.4). In addition, two inspectors moved between the three groups. There were two major findings. First, the detailed observation of interactions between the men revealed the existence of two informal groups or 'cliques' within the three formal groups. The membership of these transgressed the formal group boundaries. These two cliques are shown in figure 9.5.

A second major finding of this phase of the research was that these cliques developed informal rules of behaviour or 'norms', as well as mechanisms with which to enforce these. Not only did the workmen control the work that that they

---

Bank wirers at work

Figure 9.4: Bank wiring observation room, *c.* 1932
Source: AT&T Archives

Norms and sanctions

Norms:
- Don't be a rate-buster, chiseler or squealer
  Don't act officiously

Sanctions:
- 'Binging' – tap on upper arm
- Ridicule
- Exclusion

The figure below shows the formal structure of the group as devised by the company's management. This consisted of three trios of workmen, each directed by their own supervisor. Two inspectors assessed the work of these three formal groups. The researchers noted which individuals interacted with whom, and who participated in whose work-time games. This revealed the friendship relations that existed between the men in the bank wiring room.

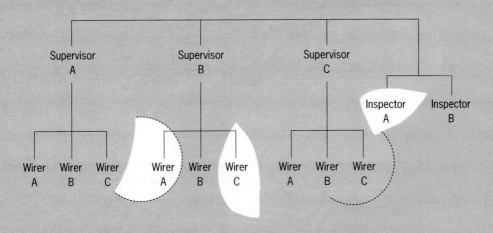

Figure 9.5: The informal as opposed to the formal organization of the groups in the bank wiring observation room

Within these three formal groups, the researchers identified two informal groups or 'cliques'. As the curving lines indicate the boundary of each informal group or clique. One clique consisted of a supervisor, his three wirers and a lone wirer from the adjacent group. The other clique consisted of a supervisor, two of his wirers (his third one was 'semi-detached'), and a different, lone wirer from the adjacent group. In addition, this clique included one of the inspectors. The three remaining individuals did not appear to be members of either clique.

Based on Fritz. J. Roethlisberger and William. J. Dickson, *Management and the Worker*, Harvard University Press, Cambridge, Mass., 1939, pp.501, 507 and 509.

physically produced, but individual members were also found to be giving incorrect reports to management on the output achieved. The total figure for the week would tally with the total week's output, but the daily reports showed a steady, level output regardless of actual daily production. The researchers decided that the group was operating well below its capability and that individual group members were not earning as much as they could. The norms under which the group operated were found to be the following (Roethlisberger and Dickson, 1939, p.522):

- You should not turn out too much work. If you do, you are a *rate-buster*.

- You should not turn out too little work. If you do, you are a *chiseler*.

- You should not tell a supervisor anything that might get a colleague into trouble. If you do, you are a *squealer*.

- You should not attempt to maintain social distance or act officiously. If you are an inspector, for example, you should not act like one.

The researchers discovered that members of the bank wiring observation room were afraid that if they significantly increased their output, the unit incentive rate would be cut and the daily output expected by management would increase. Lay-offs might occur and men could be reprimanded. To forestall such consequences, the group members agreed between themselves what was a fair day's output (neither too high nor too low). Having established such an output norm, they enforced it through a system of negative sanctions or punishments. These included

- ridicule, as when a group member was referred to as 'the slave' or 'speed king';

- 'binging' was used, in which a norm violator was tapped on the upper arm;

- total rejection or exclusion of the individual by the group as a whole.

Roethlisberger and Dickson concluded that 'The social organization of the bankwiremen performed a twofold function (1) to protect the group from internal indiscretions and (2) to protect it from outside interference ... nearly all the activities of this group can be looked upon as methods of controlling the behaviour of its members' (p.523–4).

These results showed that workers were more responsive to the social forces of their peer group than to the controls and incentives of management. A popular although oversimplified interpretation of the conclusions of the research was that employees' receptivity to management's goals depended on the extent to which the boss could meet employees' social needs, such as that for acceptance. In this sense, the **human relations approach** to management was born. The Hawthorne studies conclusions were that:

1. People at work are motivated by more than just pay and conditions.

2. Work is a group activity, and individuals should be seen as group members and not in isolation.

3. The need for recognition, security and a sense of belonging is more important in determining workers' morale and productivity than the physical conditions under which they work.

Human relations approach is a school of management thought based on the research findings of Elton Mayo, which emphasize the importance of social processes at work.

4. Through their unofficial norms and sanctions, informal groups exercise strong controls over the work habits and attitudes of individual group members. Hence, the ability of the informal group or clique to motivate an in individual at work should not be underestimated.

5. Supervisors need to be aware of both individuals' social needs and the power of the informal group in order to align these to achieve the formal (official) objectives.

A later chapter will examine the work of Frederick Winslow Taylor, whose major contributions came in the first decade of the twentieth century. His approach to organizational efficiency, known as scientific management, emphasized the detailed analysis of the work task to be performed; focused on the selection, training and supervision of the individual workers; and sought to motivate them through the use of financial rewards based on piecework [link, chapter 13, traditional work design]. Sheldrake (1995, p.114) observed that:

> just as the ideas of scientific management coalesced around the work and reputation of F. W. Taylor, so the notions of human relations and the social person took shape in relation to the work of Elton Mayo, in the process consummating a new era in management theory. Ironically, considering that Mayo's ideas are often placed somewhat artificially in opposition to those of Taylor by academic commentators, the two men were seeking much the same goals, namely industrial harmony and an end to antagonism between management and workers.

In the management textbooks, Taylor is stereotyped as focusing on the individual worker to the neglect of the work group. However, it has been argued that it was precisely the importance of groups in production that had concerned Taylor. His intention had been to destroy such groups, whereas Mayo sought to harness them towards management's goals.

Stop and criticize

How might the Hawthorne studies have been conducted differently if they had been:

- 'Pure academic' research, with Mayo a bearded sociologist in corduroy trousers, woolly cardigan and scruffy notebook, and band of graduate research students in tow?

- 'Pure management' research with Mayo as a management consultant with an expensive suit and tie, executive briefcase, and a team of smart associate consultants to support this work?

How might the findings and recommendations have differed from those actually obtained?

Group-oriented view of organizations

Elton Mayo went on to propose a social philosophy which placed groups at the centre of understanding human behaviour in organizations (Mayo, 1945). He stressed the importance of informal groups and encouraged managers to 'grow' them. He used the term *natural group* to refer to groups of three to six workers, which, through the normal interaction of its members, developed high levels of intimacy and cohesiveness. Unless such natural groups were nourished and supported, he felt, the normal processes of interaction would be impeded and the group would not develop.

A natural group, with a core of members who were held in high esteem by other workers, could be 'grown' into what Mayo called a family group of eight to 30 members. He estimated that this process would take between six and twelve months of continuous association. It would lead ultimately to the development of one large organized group, consisting of a plant-wide network of family groups, each with its natural groups. Mayo's vision was of a community organization, in which all or most employees were members of well-knit natural groups, which were linked together in common purpose. These were not the formal groups discussed earlier. Mayo invited managers to act somewhat like gardeners rather than engineers, and to use their skills, intelligence and experience to deliberately integrate individuals within groups.

To boldly go ... in groups

Again and again we have seen that *Star Trek* views [humankind] as the ultimate social animal, thriving in groups and utterly unable to exist alone or in isolation. Isolation in *Star Trek* is always the breeding ground for delusion, madness or megalomania. All the mad scientists in the series hatch their schemes in lonely corners of the galaxy. Entering human society and becoming a part of it is the sum and substance of the series' many fables of identity.

From Thomas Richards, *Star Trek in Myth and Legend*, Orion Books, London, 1997, pp.91–2.

Rensis Likert
(1903–81)

Another famous psychologist, Rensis Likert (1961), echoed the idea that organizations should be viewed and managed as a collection of groups rather than as individual entities. He felt that group forces were important, both in influencing the behaviour of individual work groups, with regard to productivity, waste, absence and turnover, and in affecting the performance of the entire organizations. In his book chapter entitled 'The principle of supportive relationships', Likert, like Mayo, attempted to derive a theory of organizational design with the group as the basic building block. He argued that:

1. Work groups are important sources of individuals' needs satisfaction.

2. Groups in organizations that fulfil this psychological function are also more productive.

3. Management's task is therefore to create effective work groups by developing 'supportive relationships'.

4. An effective organizational structure consists of democratic-participative work groups, each linked to the organization as a whole through overlapping memberships.

5. Co-ordination is achieved by individuals who carry out 'linking functions'.

Likert (1961) is also remembered for proposing the concept of the overlapping group membership structure. This he termed a 'linking pin' process. The overlapping works vertically by having the leaders of related subordinate groups as members of the next higher group, with their common superior as leader, and so on

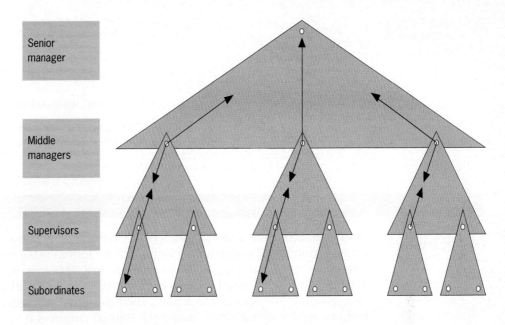

Senior manager

Middle managers

Supervisors

Subordinates

Figure 9.6: Rensis Likert's linking pin model
Based on Rensis Likert, *New Patterns of Management*, McGraw-Hill, New York, 1961, p.105.

up the hierarchy. The organization is therefore conceived as consisting of many overlapping groups. This is shown in figure 9.6. In his view, an organizational design based around groups rather than individuals improves communications, increases co-operation, provides more team member commitment and produces faster decision making.

While Likert's 'linking pin' concept focused on *vertical* co-ordination, today the stress is placed upon *horizontal* integration in the form of cross-functional teams [**link**, chapter 12, teamworking]. Nevertheless, most people in an organization are now members of several teams. This overlap of groups in organizations, due to matrix structures and cross-functional teamworking, means that an individual can be a member of a project team and a geographical group, all at the same time. This will hinder their ability to identify with any one distinct group.

Following Likert, a succession of well-known academics and consultants have followed Mayo in promoting the cause of organizations built around groups, rather than just including them. In the 1970s, Leavitt (1975) asked management to use small groups as the basic building blocks for an organization. Ouchi and Johnson (1978) echoed Mayo's thesis that people in society lacked social support and anchors which made life tolerable, and recommended that large organizations should be organized around 'clans' (similar to Mayo's natural groups), which could provide the associational ties and cohesion for their employees. In the 1980s, Tom Peters (1987, p.296) said that 'The modest-sized, task-oriented, semi-autonomous, mainly self-managing team should be the basic organization building block'. In the 1990s, Katzenbach and Smith (1993) proposed their own team-based organizational model, as has Jenkins (1994).

Your employer tells you that you will become 'part of the team', that you will be a 'member of one big happy family here'.

- How do you feel about the organization as your 'psychological home' in this respect?

- When managers say that they want you 'to belong', what do they *really* mean?

- From this analysis, can you explain why the concept of teamworking has been so consistently popular with managers interested in improving employee performance.

Formal and informal groups

Workplace behaviour can be considered as varying along a continuum from formally to informally organized. At one extreme, formal behaviour is organized to achieve the collective purpose of an organization. This may be to make washing machines, provide a repair service, earn £200,000 profit a year or achieve a 5 per cent return on investment. To achieve such collective purposes, the organization is structured in such a way as to use the limited resources it has at its disposal as efficiently and effectively as possible. It does this by creating what is called a formal organization. The overall collective purpose or aim is broken down into sub-goals and sub-tasks. These are assigned to different sub-units in the organization. The tasks may be grouped together and departments thus formed. Job requirements in terms of job descriptions may be written. The subdivision continues to take place until a small group of people is given one such sub-goal and divides it between its members. When this occurs, there exists the basis for forming the group along functional lines. This process of identifying the purpose, dividing up tasks and so on is referred to as the creation of the formal organization. The groups that are formed through this division of labour are labelled **formal groups**.

Managers make choices as to how technology and organization will be combined to create task-oriented (formal) groups. The purpose of the sub-groups in the production department may be to manufacture 100 cars a day, while that of the group in the design department may be to draw up a set of construction plans. Whatever type of formal group we are interested in, they all have certain common characteristics:

Formal group is one which one that has been consciously created to accomplish a defined part of an organization's collective purpose. The formal group's functions are the tasks which are assigned to it and for which it is officially held responsible.

- They are task-oriented.

- They tend to be permanent.

- They have a formal structure.

- They are consciously organized by management to achieve organizational goals.

- Their activities contribute directly to the organization's collective purpose.

Formal groups can be distinguished by the duration of their existence. There are permanent formal groups, such as a staff group providing specialist services (e.g. computer unit, training section). There are also likely to be temporary formal groups, for example a task group that is formally designed to work on a specific project. What makes a formal group permanent or temporary is not the actual time it exists but how it is defined by the company. Some temporary groups may last for years. What is important is whether or not the group's members feel that they are part of a group that might be disbanded at any time.

Alongside these formal groups, and consisting of the same employees, albeit arranged differently, will be a number of informal groups. These emerge in an organization and are neither anticipated nor intended by those who create the formal organization. They emerge from the informal interaction of the members of the formal organization. These unplanned-for groups share many of the characteristics of the small social leisure groups. These function alongside the formal groups. An **informal group** develops during the spontaneous interaction of persons in the group as they talk, joke and associate with one another.

Why do informal groups exist, and what purpose do they serve? Ackroyd and Thompson (1999) introduced the concept of group self-organization to help our understanding of the nature of formal and informal groups. Group self-organization refers to the tendency of groups to

Informal group is a collection of individuals who become a group when members develop interdependencies, influence one another's behaviour and contribute to mutual needs satisfaction.

- form interests,

- develop autonomy,

- establish identities.

In the case of the men in the bank wiring room in the Hawthorne studies, their interests centred around restricting their output. In so doing, they gained a degree of personal control, that is, they increased their autonomy *vis-à-vis* management. The two cliques that emerged developed their own, separate, identities. Self-interest and self-identity interact and reciprocate. These processes have implications for the behaviour of the groups concerned. This phenomenon is termed **group self-organization**.

First, using 'interests' in a broad sense, we can use it to encompass the human needs. In the chapter on motivation, we learned that people had a variety of different needs, among which were included those for love, esteem and safety. Love needs are concerned with belongingness and relationships; esteem needs focus on recognition, attention and appreciation; while safety needs concern security of employment. The failure to satisfy these needs may result in our inability to feel confident, capable, necessary or useful members of society. These needs concern our relationships with others, and while we may spend time outside of work with our wives, husbands, girlfriends, boyfriends, children or social club members, the time that we do spend at work remains considerable. In our relationships with work colleagues, therefore, we frequently seek to satisfy these needs. The difficulty is that the organizations in which we work are not primarily designed to allow individuals to meet such needs at work.

Group self-organization refers to the tendency of groups to form interests, develop autonomy and establish identities.

A formal organization is ostensibly designed on rational principles and is aimed at achieving the collective purpose of the organization. It thus limits employees' behaviour in order to be able to control and predict it. The individual brings their hopes, needs, desires and personal goals to their job. While the company may not be interested in these, the employee will, nevertheless, attempt to achieve his or her personal ambitions while at work by manipulating the situation in such a way as to fulfil unmet motivational needs. Most other staff will generally be seeking to do the same, so it will not be difficult to set up series of satisfying relationships. These relationships in turn will lead to the formation of informal groups. Because of our social nature, we have a tendency to form informal groups. The task-oriented formal groups rarely consider the social needs of their members. Indeed, these are frequently considered to be dispensable and counterproductive to the achievement of the formal purpose of the organization.

<table>
<tr><td>

Stop and criticize

</td><td>

Consider how your educational institution contributes to the satisfaction of your social needs while studying through your membership of social groups (class, tutorial groups, self-help and study groups, clubs and societies, sports teams). On the other hand:

</td></tr>
</table>

- How are other aspects of your institution's structure, rules, procedures and policies blocking your satisfaction?

- How could your institution meet your social needs and those of your fellow students, more effectively through different forms of group arrangement—and would these be consistent with good teaching and learning practice?

- How would instructors evaluate your recommendations? What would be their impact on your own academic performance?

Second, there is the issue of the group autonomy, that is, avoiding direct control by management or developing a group's economic interests. This can be seen as meeting members' safety needs. The group in the bank wiring observation room at the Hawthorne works sought to defend itself from outside interference. Many years later, Melville Dalton (1959) described how his research had revealed that many departments in the organization that he studied felt threatened by invasion from other work units and sections. They responded by aggressively maintaining their boundaries flexibly in the face of these offensive threats. They did it by creating a spy network to identify what other sections were planning to do and prepared defences against these. One of the strategies that they used was to create an informal, parallel organization whose purpose was to anticipate changes and

---

Banana time

The development of identity and control is present in even the most rudimentary groups. In a pioneering paper written in 1958, Donald Roy reports on a very small group of unskilled workers engaged in 'repetitive manual work'. He records the way in which the working day was divided by the group into a series of intervals demarcated by specific 'times'. Thus, 'peach time' marked one break from work followed by 'banana time', 'Coke time', 'fish time' and so on, the intervals being named after the kind of refreshment taken at each interval. Roy argued that these designated times broke up long periods of extremely tedious work, providing intervals of rest and diversion. They helped to 'kill the beast of monotony'. But this designation of 'times' is not simply a matter of marking the passage of time. The interludes are given meaning by their association with particular events. Clearly too, these meanings are intertwined with the creation and re-creatrion of group relationships. The 'banana time' which provides the title of Roy's paper is not simply a regular break time defined by members eating bananas. In fact, it is a relatively arbitrary time interval marked by the pilferage and consumption of a banana belonging to one worker by another.

According to Roy, each and every day, a worker called Ike would steal and consume a banana belonging to a co-worker called Sammy. 'Each morning, after making the snatch, Ike would call out "banana time!" and proceed to down his prize, while Sammy made futile protests and denunciations. George (the charge hand) would join in with mild remonstrations, sometimes scolding Sammy for making so much fuss. The banana Sammy had brought in for his own consumption at lunch time. He never did get to eat his banana but kept bringing one for his lunch. At first, the daily theft startled and amazed me. Then I grew to look forward to the daily seizure and the verbal interaction that followed' (Roy, 1958, p.159). The continued daily provision of the banana must have been to some extent a voluntary matter for Sammy. The banana must be regarded as some kind of quasi-voluntary tribute or gift, perpetually provided and perpetually 'stolen'. However, its summary but, after a few occasions, entirely predictable seizure clearly defined relative positions in the group, as well as providing entertainment and diversion ... Roy's report is interesting because he shows that, even in a very mundane work situation, subtle processes of self-regulation and group formation exist.

From Stephen Ackroyd and Paul Thompson, *Organizational Misbehaviour*, Sage, London, 1999, pp.65–6. Used with permission.

institute their own ones which were within the departmental tradition. This allowed the 'defending' department to maintain its control over its boundaries against any excessive demands which might be made by other sections. Thus the strategy used by the cliques in the bank wiring observation room was similar to that used by Dalton's line managers.

Third, there is the issue of identity and the group, and this has two aspects. First, there is each person's *individual identity,* which comes in part from his or her group membership. Second, there is group identity, which distinguishes one group from another. All groups develop informal hierarchies, which in turn become the basis for building both types of identity. They distinguish or differentiate themselves from other similar groups in the neighbourhood or organization. Street gangs in London and New York have their own, unique labels, as do company improvement teams. Groups use ritual 'fazing' techniques, initiation ceremonies and ongoing practical jokes (which management would define as 'misbehaviour') to socialize new members. Within the group, its members develop their own identities.

In any company, there will be numerous formal groups which interlink with each other, and also many informal groups which form a network. To distinguish these two different collectivities, they are referred to as the formal organization and the informal organization respectively. The two are not separate, since the composition, structure and operation of the different informal groups which make up the informal organization will be determined by the formal arrangements that exist in the company. These provide the context within which social relationships are established and within which social interaction can take place. Such formal contextual constraints can include plant layout, work shifts, numbers of staff employed and the type of technology used.

Commentators recommend that whenever possible, management should design groups in a way that informal and formal overlap. Even when this happens, the effect of the former on the latter can be considerable. In the end, however, when individuals have to choose between following the informal and the formal group, research has shown that they will tend to choose the former. To summarize therefore, one can say that the informal group can meet some of their higher-level needs in Maslow's hierarchy, while formal groups exist to meet organizational objectives and fulfil the individual worker's lower level needs.

Homans' theory of group formation

George Caspar
Homans

Of the many theories that have been put forward to explain the formation of groups, perhaps the most often cited is that of the sociologist George Caspar Homans. He had been a junior member of Elton Mayo's Department of Industrial Research at the Harvard Business School and had been involved as a researcher in the Hawthorne studies. Despite its popularity, Homans' theory of how a group comes to be formed is not the easiest to grasp if one is reading his book, *The Human Group* (Homans, 1951).

Part of the difficulty has to do with the subject itself—the processes involved in group formation are complex. However, Homans' own choice of language and mode of explanation exacerbate this problem. He uses the general term 'behaviours' to refer to concrete, observable phenomena such as the interactions between individuals and their activities. However, he also applies this label to abstract, unobservable concepts such as norms and sentiments.

The basic elements of Homans' theory will be presented here, and the terms that he used will be indicated. Homans argued that every group (he used the term 'social system') exists within an environment which affects the group. The group, in turn, seeks to influence the environment within which it exists. The mutual interactions between a group and its environment shape the characteristics of the group. Let us consider his model in more detail.

Background factors

These provide the context in which group activity takes place. Homans termed this the 'external system'. It can be seen as representing the 'stage' upon which group activity occurs and consists of five elements:

- *Physical context* refers to the spatial arrangement of physical objects and human activities, e.g. office architecture and furniture; assignment of workers to positions on an assembly line.

- *Cultural-personal context* refers to the aspects of the individuals themselves, specifically the norms, values and goals that make up their shared understanding within which the group will function.

- *Technological context* refers to the facilities that the group will have access to while pursuing its activities.

- *Organizational context* refers to company policies, practices and rules related to the way work is performed, e.g. bonus system, staff appraisal.

- *Socio-economic context* refers to economic situation as it affects the company, e.g. profitability, government legislation and so on.

Required and given behaviours

Activities, in Homans' theory, are physical movements, verbal or non-verbal behaviours engaged in by group members.

Interactions, in Homans' theory, are the two-way communications between group members.

Norms are expected modes of behaviour

Sentiments are the feelings, attitudes and beliefs held by group members.

These are behaviours which the managers in an organization require or expect of their employees. From the employees' perspective, they are given these. The organization requires individuals to perform certain **activities**; to have certain **interactions** with others; to adhere to certain **norms** or rules; and to hold certain **sentiments** or feelings towards their work. For example, all supermarket checkout operators are required to scan the customers' purchases (required activities). They are also given a checklist which specifies that they should greet the customer verbally before processing their purchases and again say 'goodbye' at the end (required interactions). They are also expected to appear positive and friendly towards customers and to hold positive attitudes about their employer (required sentiments). Homans referred to this collectively as the *external system*.

Emergent or actual behaviours

Emergent behaviours are those actions that members do in addition to, or in place of, the behaviours required by the organization. It consists of the activities, interactions and sentiments that can be observed, which emerge from the background factors and the required and given behaviours. It also includes the norms that develop from these. Thus, if the job is repetitive (technical context), operators might see how quickly they can perform it so as to give their work more challenge. If employees are in close proximity (physical context), they might relieve their boredom by talking to one another even though management rules prohibit this. They may come to view management control (organizational context) negatively and develop anti-management sentiments. The group will quickly develop informal norms (rules) and have an informal (unofficial) leader. Homans referred to this collectively as the *internal system*.

The concept of interaction, already introduced and defined, is at the heart of Homans' model. In his view, if circumstances permitted, the higher the frequency

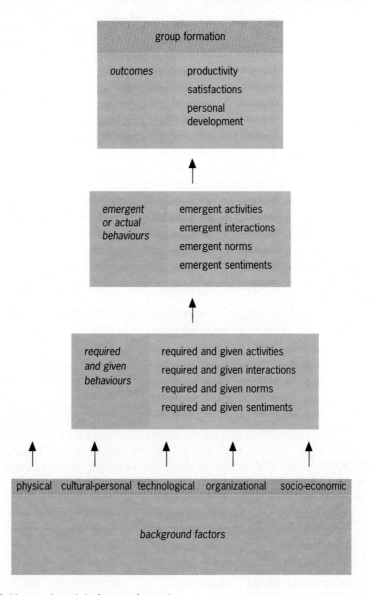

Figure 9.7: Homans' model of group formation

of interaction between individuals, the more positive the attitudes that individuals would have towards one another, and, as a consequence, the better the relations would be between them. The converse is also true, that is, the more positive the sentiments between individuals, the higher will be their rate of interaction. Both processes increase the likelihood that a group will be formed. The increased level of interaction develops sentiments (attitudes and emotions) which are not dictated by the external (organizational) system. Hence, the members come to share common norms and frames of reference. These in turn stimulate new behaviours. Finally, Homans stressed that:

- The internal and the external systems were interdependent. A change in one would produce a change in the other. For example, a change in an employee's perception of their job (internal) may increase the speed with which the work is performed (external). Similarly, if a task previously carried out by a supervisor was delegated to a group, it would create changes in the pattern of interactions between the group's members.

- Both the internal and the external systems were interdependent with the environment. Changes in the environment would produce changes in the formal and informal work organization. Thus, the activities and the norms of the internal system would eventually alter the physical, cultural and technological environment. The workers' informal method of solving problems might generate ideas for technological innovation, the redesign of work layout, or the development of new norms about the nature of the relationship between workers and management.

To summarize, Homans proposed that a group exists within an environment which consists of the background factors shown at the base of the model in figure 9.7. These interact with each other to produce what he termed the *required* behaviours of the group and, ultimately, also its *emergent* behaviours

Stop and criticize

Identify and explain the emergent behaviours in a work group that you are able to observe.

- How would group members explain and assess these emergent behaviours?
- How would management respond to these emergent behaviours?

Bull Dogs and Red Devils: a study of group formation

In 1949, Muzafer Sherif studied how a collection of individuals who had had no previous ties with each other formed themselves into a group. Sherif and his team of researchers used a field experiment research design to study the behaviour of 12-year-old boys who attended a summer camp in northern Connecticut in the summer of 1949. Unbeknown to the boys, all the camp staff—counsellors, leaders and handymen—were Sherif's collaborators. They created special test situations and observed and noted what occurred.

Twenty-four boys were carefully selected, and matched to be as similar as possible. so as to eliminate other possible bases for group formation (e.g. background, education. ethnicity, religion, friendship). Having arrived in camp, they were separated into two groups and directed to choose a bunkhouse, and then depart immediately on a hike. From then on, for five days, the two sets of boys were on separate schedules, sleeping in different bunkhouses and eating at different times.

Sherif considered that a common group goal was essential for group formation to occur. He predicted that, as members interacted to achieve this, the boys would produce a group organization with hierarchical status and role relationships, and develop common, unwritten rules (norms) of behaviour which would serve as the basis for individual members' attitudes. Hence, while the boys were allowed to choose their own activities—cooking, hiking, camping—all of these demanded co-operative behaviour. For example, food was supplied in bulk, and the boys had to cut it up, build a fire, and so on. Achieving the goals required discussion, planning and execution.

Sherif discovered that two groups formed over time. At the start, Sherif's researchers observed no consistent pattern of behaviour among the boys. Then, during swimming, one boy took the lead; when cooking, another took over, and so on. After a few day's interaction, the top and bottom status within the two groups became stabilized. The lower positions were established as it became obvious that some of the boys were not contributing to the task, were playing around, or lacked interest or skill. Over time, the boys jockeyed for positions, and ultimately the status structure of each of the two had fully stabilized. The early development of leadership showed that one person had begun to co-ordinate and initiate plans in a variety of different situations. Observational data revealed that certain boys were more popular than others and gained undisputed authority over others. As the structure formed within each group, their members' attitudes to their group became positive, and norms were established.

One of these was the naming of the groups—'Red Devils' and 'Bull Dogs'. Another was the conferment of nicknames on group members, 'Baby Face' and 'Lemon Head'. Each group came to prefer certain songs, developed its own jargon, special jokes, secrets and preferred places. Each group also had its special ways of performing tasks such as braiding lanyards and preparing meals, which was consistently followed by group members. Methods of praise and punishments (sanctions) were standardized in each group. Wayward members who failed to do the 'right' things or who did not contribute to the common effort found themselves receiving reprimands, ridicule, 'silent treatment' or even threats. In the Bull Dogs, the leader assigned any deviant to remove stones from the swimming pond.

The researchers concluded that when individuals who have no established relationships are brought together to interact in activities with common goals, they produce a group structure with hierarchical positions and roles within it. The interaction process produces common goals, which constitute the basis of individual members' attitudes in matters important to the group.

Based on Muzafer Sherif and Caroline W. Sherif, *Groups in Harmony and Tension*, Harper and Brothers, New York, 1953.

Stages of group development

Since we have been using the terms 'formal group' and 'informal group', it is important to relate these to our organizational definition of the psychological group. While an informal group is always also a psychological group, a formal group may not necessarily be a psychological group. Consider for a moment the staff in a company finance office. As a task-oriented formal group they have a responsibility for the control of the company finances, costing and control. Of the twenty individuals who compose it, half may have been there for over twenty years, while others will have joined the company when it merged. Consider also the definition of the psychological group. There is no reason why these staff should all necessarily interact with each other or perceive themselves to be a single group. The finance department as a formally established unit may consist of different informal groups. The question then arises as to how a collection of individuals becomes a psychological group.

Groups of whatever type do not come into existence fully formed. Bruce Tuckman and Mary Ann Jensen suggested that groups pass through five clearly defined stages of development, which they labelled forming, storming, norming, performing and adjourning (Tuckman, 1965; Tuckman and Jensen, 1977). Of course, not all groups develop through all the stages; some get stuck in the middle and remain inefficient and ineffective. Progress through the stages may be slow but appears to be necessary and inescapable.

Forming
This is the orientation stage, in which the set of individuals has not yet gelled. Everyone is busy finding out about each others' attitudes and backgrounds and establishing ground rules. Members are also keen to fix their personal identities in the group and make a personal impression on the others. In the personal relations area, members are *dependent* on some leader to provide them with structure in the form of ground rules and an agenda for action. Task-wise, they seek *orientation* as to what they are being asked to do, what the issues are and whether everyone understands the task.

Storming
This is a conflict stage in the group's life and can be an uncomfortable period. Members bargain with each other as they try to sort out what each of them individually, and as a group, want out of the group process. Individuals reveal their personal goals, and it is likely that interpersonal hostility is generated when differences in these goals are revealed. Members may resist the control of other group members and may show hostility. The early relationships established in the forming stage may be disrupted. The key personal relations issue in this stage is the management of *conflict,* while the task function question is *organization*—how best to organize to achieve the group objective.

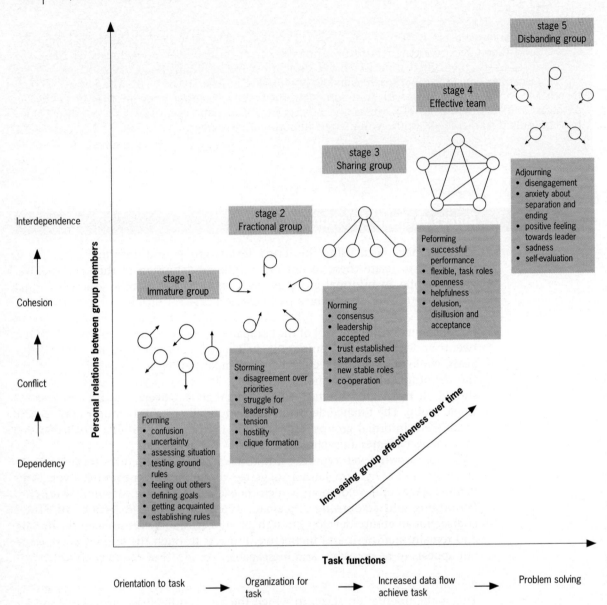

Figure 9.8: Stages of group development
Based on Tuckman (1965), Tuckman and Jensen (1977) and Jones (1973).

Norming

In this cohesion stage, the members of the group develop ways of working to develop closer relationships and camaraderie. The question of who will do what and how it will be done are addressed. Working rules are established in terms of norms of behaviour (do not smoke) and role allocation (Jill will be the spokesperson). A framework is therefore created in which each group member can relate to the others and the questions of agreeing expectations and dealing with a failure to meet members' expectations are addressed. The personal relations within the group stress *cohesion*. Members feel that they have overcome conflict, have 'gelled' and experience a sense of 'groupiness'. On the task side, there is an *increase in data flow* as members become more prepared to be more open about their goals.

Performing

By this stage, the group has developed an effective structure, and it is concerned with actually getting on with the job in hand and accomplishing objectives. The fully mature group has now been created which can get on with its work. Not all groups develop to this stage but may become bogged down in an earlier and less productive stage. In personal relations, interdependence becomes a feature. Members are equally happy working alone, in sub-groupings or as a single unit. Collaboration and functional competition occur between them. On the task side, there is a high commitment to the objective, jobs are well defined and problem-solving activity ensues.

Adjourning

In this final stage, the group may disband, either because the task has been achieved or because the members have left. Before they do so, they may reflect on their time together and ready themselves to go their own ways.

Stop and criticize

Identify a group to which you currently belong—sports club, drama society, tutorial group, project group, etc.

- Identify which stage of development it has reached.

- What advice would you give to this group based on your analysis of its development?

Tuckman and Jensen's model has been verified by research and, to complement it, Jones (1973) has described the personal relations issues that affect group members and the task functions that are addressed at each of its five stages. The combined framework is show in Figure 9.8. Its value is that it can help us to explain some of the problems of group working. A group may be operating at half power because it may have failed to work through some of the issues at the earlier stages. For example, the efficiency of a project team may be impaired because it has not resolved the issue of leadership. Alternatively, people may be pulling in different directions because the purpose of the group has not been clarified, nor its objectives agreed. Members might be using the group to achieve their personal and unstated aims (so-called hidden agendas). For all these reasons, effective group functioning may be hindered.

A group can be considered as a society in miniature. A college department or company sales team will have a hierarchy with leaders and followers. It will have rules, norms and traditions as well as goals to strive for and values to uphold. It will change and develop, and will also adapt to and create changes in the environment and its members. Like a society it may experience a period of difficulty and decline. It is in such mini-societies as the family and the work group that an individual learns about and is socialized into the wider society. It has been argued that small groups will reflect the social changes in the wider society. It is likely that the individual will most directly experience these through the small group. For example, as there are changes about the value and organization of work, these may be reflected in changes in job design and work group organization.

Groups influence the behaviour, beliefs and attitudes of their members. While we may all like to believe that we are free agents and would resent being told that we are influenced by others or conform to others' views, research shows that this is in fact the case. In varying degrees and under certain circumstances, we are all influenced by others when we are in a group. If it is any consolation, we can remember that we in turn play an important role ourselves in influencing and controlling other group members. This is the topic of a later chapter in this part of the book.

Table 9.1: Issues facing any work group

Issue	Questions
1. Atmosphere and relationships	What kinds of relationship should there be between members? How close and friendly, formal or informal?
2. Member participation	How much participation should be required of members? Some more than others? All equally? Are some members more needed than others?
3. Goal understanding and acceptance	How much do members need to understand group goals? How much do they need to accept to be committed to the goals? Everyone equally? Some more than others?
4. Listening and information sharing	How is information to be shared? Who needs to know what? Who should listen most to whom?
5. Handling disagreements and conflict	How should disagreements or conflicts be handled? To what extent should they be resolved? Brushed aside? Handled by dictate?
6. Decision making	How should decisions be made? Consensus? Voting? One-person rule? Secret ballot?
7. Evaluation of member performance	How is evaluation to be managed? Everyone appraises everyone else? A few take the responsibility? Is it to be avoided?
8. Expressing feelings	How should feelings be expressed? Only about the task? Openly and directly?
9. Division of labour	How are task assignments to be made? Voluntarily? By discussion? By leaders?
10. Leadership	Who should lead? How should leadership functions be exercised? Shared? Elected? Appointed from outside?
11. Attention to process	How should the group monitor and improve its own process? Ongoing feedback from members? Formal procedures? Avoiding direct discussion?

From Allan R. Cohen, Stephen L. Fink, Herman Gadon and Robin D. Willits, *Effective Behaviour in Organizations*, Irwin, Homewood, Ill., sixth edition, 1995, p.142.

Groups and teams

In the literature, the terms 'group' and 'team', are used interchangeably, with the personal preference of writers and tradition guiding the choice of word, rather than conceptual distinction. For example, the 'how-to-do-it' books aimed at a management audience tend to refer to teams in organizations, while, for historical reasons, discussions about shop floor working arrangements refer to autonomous work groups. Authors who are management consultants frequently use the term 'team' metaphorically, that is, they apply this label to a collection of employees to which it is imaginatively, but not literally, appropriate. Hayes (1997) noted that the idea of team must be one of the most widely used metaphors in organizational life. These same writers also use the term normatively, that is, to describe a collection of people as what they should be, or what they would prefer them to be, rather than as they actually are.

R. Meredith Belbin (2000) reported the results of an exercise that he ran asking participants to distinguish between groups and teams. He noted that many features that these people saw as typifying teams were also present, to some extent,

Table 9.2: Six differences between a team and a group

	Team	Group
1. Size	Limited	Medium or large
2. Selection	Crucial	Immaterial
3. Leadership	Shared or rotating	Solo
4. Perception	Mutual knowledge understanding	Focus on leader
5. Style	Role spread co-ordination	Convergence conformism
6. Spirit	Dynamic interaction	Togetherness, persecution of opponents

From R. Meredith Belbin, *Beyond the Team*, Butterworth Heinemann, Oxford, 2000, figure 3.

in groups. His list of reported differences is shown in table 9.2. He noted that few participants identified the first two features on that list, which, in his view, had the most radical effect on collective behaviour [**link**, chapter 10, group structure].

Most commonly, writers focus on the transformation of a group into a team. They see the difference between the two as being in terms of a group being 'stuck' in the forming, storming or norming stage of Tuckman and Jensen's model, while a team is a group that has successfully arrived at the performing stage. From the point of view of management, a team is a group which possesses extra, positive features. As a group comes to acquire these positive characteristics, it is seen as progressing towards the team end of the continuum. These positive 'team traits' include co-operation, co-ordination and cohesion. From this perspective, a group turns into a team once it has organized itself to fulfil a purpose. This implies a process of conscious self-management by the group's members during which they assign tasks, develop communication channels and establish decision-making processes. Thus, the transition from a group to a team is the result of a learning process.

One well-known example, which illustrates some of these points, is the book, *The Wisdom of Teams*. This was written by Jon Katzenbach and Douglas Smith, both partners in the consultancy firm McKinsey & Company. Its writing style indicates that it is targeted primarily at a management audience. The authors report that they examined 47 teams in 37 different organizations and spoke to 'hundreds of people in dozens of organizations, focusing on groups who were or might be teams' (Katzenbach and Smith, 1993a, p.1).

These writers use their own special definition of the concept of real teams, which appear to be groups attaining the performing stage of Tuckman and Jensen's model. They contrast these with work groups, which refer to people who may get on satisfactorily with one another, who do their jobs, but who do not necessarily share either common goals or who are not sufficiently co-ordinated. For Katzenbach and Smith, work groups are in an earlier phase of development. They distinctions between the two are summarized in table 9.3.

It is difficult to determine where Katzenbach and Smith's research findings end and where their prescriptive consultancy advice begins. On the basis of this definitional distinction, they identify some common features of what they have labelled 'real teams', which are presumably missing from those they refer to as 'non-teams'. They state that the 'essence of a team is common commitment. Without it, groups perform as individuals, with it, they become a powerful unit of collective performance' (Katzenbach and Smith, 1993b, p.113). They then list six key elements which both define and prescribe the characteristics of what they call a team:

Table 9.3: Contrast between Katzenbach and Smith's 'work group' and 'real team'

'Work group'		'Real team'
Strong, clearly focused leader	←*leadership*→	Shared leadership roles
Individual	←*accountability*→	Individual and mutual
Individual	←*work products*→	Collective
Individual contributions	←*performance depends on*→	Individual contributions and collective work products
Individual outcomes	←*accountability for outcomes rests on*→	Mutual outcomes
Common goals	←*members are interested in*→	Common goals and commitment to purpose
Demands of management	←*responsive to*→	Self-imposed demands

Based on Jon Katzenbach and Douglas Smith, *The Wisdom of Teams: Creating the High Performance Organization*, Harvard Business School Press, Boston, 1993.

Small number
This feature teams share with groups and is just the result of the fact that there is a limit to the number of people who can interact constructively.

Complementary skills
A team possesses the appropriate mix of three types of skill—technical or functional expertise; problem-solving and decision-making skills; interpersonal skills.

Truly meaningful purpose
Within this management-set boundary, there is sufficient flexibility to allow the team to establish common goals which are meaningful to members.

Collective product
A team produces an output for the organization which is unachievable by an individual, working alone, but which requires the involvement of other members, working together, making roughly equal contributions.

Clear working approach
Concerns how members work together to achieve their purpose, e.g. allocation of tasks; scheduling deadlines.

Sense of mutual accountability
Team members hold themselves accountable for the achievement of their goals, which underpins the commitment to and trust of one another.

Katzenbach and Smith went on to distinguish different levels of collective performance. It is a continuum, depicted as a rising curve, and attaching labels to those involved.

- *Working groups* are collections of individuals who work mainly on their own but who interact socially. Their performance is the sum of individual members' efforts who interact, sharing information and best practices.

- *Pseudo-teams* are collections of individuals who could perform more effectively but have shown no motivation in acquiring the skills or working methods that would allow them to do so.

- *Potential teams* consist of collections of individuals who recognize that they could be more effective and are taking steps to develop the methods and skills that they need.

- *Real teams* have members whose skills are complementary, and who have become committed to a common purpose and common working methods.

- *High-performance teams* have all the characteristics of real teams but, in addition, show commitment to the personal growth of their members and perform beyond the expectations of those around them.

Stop and criticize	Management has just told you that you are not a 'real team' and that you are certainly not a 'high-performance team'. How do you feel about that, and what are you doing to do about it?

Mayo's 'human relations approach' and Katzenbach and Smith's 'wisdom of teams' prescriptions are separated by over 70 years but have remarkable similarities. Both:

- are directed at managers who design jobs and structure organizations;

- promote the virtues of teams and groups over individuals;

- assume that teams and the individuals share common goals and interests;

- ignore or explain away areas of conflict or dissent;

- seek to use the power of the team to the management's interest.

The human relations approach to management developed from the Hawthorne studies and was based on the logic of the social individual and sentiment. It contrasted with the earlier, scientific approach to management of Frederick Winslow Taylor, which was based on the logic of economic man and efficiency [**link**, chapter 13, traditional work design]. While Taylor sought to break the power that work groups exercised, the human relations approach sought to harness it to management's goals. Sheldrake (1995, p.114) critically assesses Mayo's work thus:

> Central to Mayo's work was his antipathy to social conflict and possible social dislocation. His belief that industrial unrest sprang from personal problems, both physiological and psychological, strongly coloured his analysis of industrial society. It prompted him, for example, to construe industrial unrest as arising from the pessimistic reveries of individual workers rather than legitimate economic or sectional interests. Challenges to management were therefore depicted by Mayo as evidence of psychic disturbance rather than part of the normal rough and tumble of industrial life. Further, in his interpretation of the RATR [relay assembly test room] experiments, Mayo chose to wilfully disregard the significance of financial incentives on the behaviour of the participants, and to emphasize instead, the impact of group cohesiveness and benign supervision. Although Mayo's association with the Hawthorne experiments was, of necessity, pitched at the micro-level, his preferred focus was the macro-level of society and what he saw as the dire consequences of anomie. He was thus tempted to extrapolate from the apparent 'success' of the RATR experiments to the wider society, thereby allocating to industrial managers a significant role in the restoration and maintenance of social equilibrium.

Management's practical interest grew, and they became interested not just in observing groups but in designing and building effective teams. The general theme of making group behaviour contribute to management goals has been lately rediscovered at the level of the shop floor by the interest in Japanese-style teamworking [**link**, chapter 12, teamworking]. Writers have argued that the managerial belief that links all these contemporary writers with Elton Mayo back in the 1920s is the creation of a compliant and programmable workforce.

Recap

1. *List the key characteristics of a psychological group.*
   - The key characteristics are two or more people, in face-to-face interaction, each aware of his or her membership in the group, each aware of the others who belong to the group, and each aware of their positive interdependence as they strive to achieve mutual goals.

2. *Distinguish between different types of group task.*
   - Groups can be assigned many different tasks, many of which can be categorized under the headings of additive, conjunctive or disjunctive.

3. *Name the four research phases of the Hawthorne studies.*
   - The Hawthorne studies consisted of four major phases – illumination experiments, relay assembly test room experiments, interviewing programme and the bank wiring observation room experiments.

4. *Distinguish between a formal and an informal group.*
   - Formal groups can be distinguished from informal groups in terms of who creates them and the purposes that they serve.

5. *Outline Homans' theory of group formation.*
   - George Homans' theory of group formation uses the concepts of background factors, and required and emergent activities, interactions, sentiments, to explain how individuals come to form groups.

6. *Enumerate the five stages of Tuckman and Jensen's model of group development.*
   - Tuckman and Jensen distinguish five stages through which groups typically proceed, which they name forming, storming, norming, performing and adjourning.

7. *Summarize Katzenbach and Smith's distinction between a working group and a 'real team'.*
   - Katzenbach and Smith distinguish a working group from their concept of a 'real team', which they promote as being a necessary organizational design for successful companies.

Revision

1. Why have the Hawthorne studies remained so important? Of what value are they to working in and managing groups today?

2. In what ways does a group link an individual to the organization?

3. Think of two different groups that you joined in the past. In each case, identify what motivated you to join. To what extent have your needs been met or objectives realized?

4. Why do companies recruiting new graduates stress the importance of their being 'team players'?

5. 'Informal groups can be detrimental to management but beneficial to individual members'. Do you agree or disagree? Explain your view.

Springboard

Ackroyd, S. and Thompson, P., 1999, *Organizational Misbehaviour*, Sage, London.

A highly entertaining, academic study of organizational misbehaviour (time wasting, absence, sabotage, pilferage, fiddling, joking rituals, sex games) examined from a sociological perspective. It considers the part played by groups in initiating and sustaining such.

Gillespie, R., 1991, *Manufacturing Knowledge: A History of the Hawthorne Experiments*, Cambridge University Press, Cambridge.

At one level, this book provides a recent historical account of the Hawthorne studies, complete with photographs. At another level, it addresses the question of how knowledge is generated within the social sciences and explains how interpretations of data become official versions.

Katzenbach, J.R. and Smith, D.K., 1993, *The Wisdom of Teams: Creating the High Performance Organization*, Harvard Business School Press, Boston.

Probably the most influential book in recent years on teams; targeted at managers in organizations.

O'Connor, E., 1999, 'Minding the workers: The meaning of "human" and "human relations" of Elton Mayo', *Organization*, vol.6., no.2, pp. 223–46.

A consideration of Mayo's ideas from a contemporary perspective.

Roethlisberger, F.J., 1977, *The Elusive Phenomena*, Harvard University Press, Boston; and Homans, G.C., 1984, *Coming to My Senses*, Transaction Books, New Brunswick, NJ.

Two autobiographies of academics directly involved in the Hawthorne studies, the human relations movement and the development of organization behaviour as a distinct field of academic study.

Sonnenfeld, J., 1985, 'Shedding light on the Hawthorne Studies', *Journal of Occupational Behaviour*, vol.6, pp. 111–30.

A critiques of the Hawthorne studies which looks in depth at all six studies and reviews the contributions of those who have attacked and defended it.

West, M.A. (ed.), 1998, *Handbook of Work Group Psychology*, Wiley, Chichester.

Contains writings on group and team behaviour. Provides an overview of the field and current theoretical and research directions.

Wren, D.A., 1994, *The Evolution of Management Thought*, Wiley, New York.

Sets the Hawthorne studies and the human relations approach in its wider historical context. It demonstrates how the current popularity of teamworking of all kinds owes it debt to this research.

Homeviewing

The film *The Breakfast Club* (1984, director John Hughes) is set in the library of an American high school, where five students have been sent to spend a whole Saturday in detention under a teacher's less than watchful eye. Apart from the teacher and the school janitor, there are only five main characters in the film, representing different stereotypes:

Character	Stereotype	Played by
Andrew Clark	sports 'jock'	Emilio Estevez
Claire Standish	prom queen	Molly Ringwald
Allison Reynolds	weirdo	Ally Sheedy
Brian Johnson	nerd	Anthony Michael Hall
Judd Nelson	lout	John Bender

These five high school students have never met each other before, and each is being punished by this detention for a different act of organizational misbehaviour (see Ackroyd and Thompson, 1999). Shut in together in the school library for the day, they are forced to get to know each other. As the film unfolds, can you:

1. Identify the 'break points' in the action when the students move from forming, to storming, to norming, and finally, to performing as a group?
2. Identify examples of norming during the group forming stage?
3. Identify examples of performing during the group storming stage?
4. Establish where and why the leadership of this student group moves from one character to another?
5. Identify examples of organizational misbehaviour, not only among the five students, and also determine the purpose, objective or motive for that behaviour

Two classic disaster movies, *The Poseidon Adventure* (1972, directed by Ronald Neame) and *The Towering Inferno* (1972, directed by John Guillermin) both show aggregates of individuals becoming transformed into psychological groups. What circumstances in the movie turn the former into the latter? How is the interaction between the individuals changed?

OB in literature

Thomas Keneally, *Flying Hero Class*, Hodder & Stoughton, Sceptre, 1991.

Story of an airline hijack. How does the plot illustrate the distinction between mere aggregates of people and psychological groups? How does the 'aggregate' of people on an aeroplane become a 'psychological group'?

Graham Green, 'The Destructors' (short story written in 1954) in *Twenty-one Stories*, Penguin Books, Harmondsworth, Middlesex, 1975, pp. 7–23.

How does this short story demonstrate Homans' theory of group formation?

Chapter exercises

1: Group development phases questionnaire

Objectives

1. Introduce the Tuckman and Jensen model of group development.
2. Determine at which stage of development a given group is.

Briefing

1. Think of a group of which you are a member. This may be your university tutorial or syndicate group; a project team at work; or some other regularly meeting group such as a social club, sports club or society. This group should have some kind of objective to achieve.

2. Keeping the behaviour of this group in your mind as a focus, circle Y (Yes) or N (No) for each statement in relation to your group in the group development stages questionnaire.

3. Score the questionnaire as directed by your instructor.

Group development stages questionnaire

1. Members are unclear as to what the group's goals are.	Y N
2. At each meeting there is always a lot of talk about who is supposed to do what.	Y N
3. Members frequently look to the official chairperson or informal leader for guidance.	Y N
4. There is rarely, if ever, any discussion of how members feel about things.	Y N
5. When direction is provided by someone in the group, the others are reluctant to follow.	Y N
6. Members seems reluctant to tell others what they really think about things.	Y N

Total: F

7. People are discussing what part each will play in meeting the goal.	Y N
8. The group has developed a 'game plan' for achieving its priority objectives.	Y N
9. Measures are being produced to allow the checking of progress.	Y N
10. Group members look to others for direction as to what to do next.	Y N
11. Members argue a lot about what the group should be doing.	Y N
12. There are at least two people who want to be the group leader.	Y N

Total: S

13. Members comment intermittently on how well or badly the group is operating.	Y N
14. Relevant information is widely shared, and little is kept hidden by individuals.	Y N
15. Most people are working for the group, rather than for themselves.	Y N
16. There is a sense of 'togetherness' among the group.	Y N
17. Members trust and support each other.	Y N
18. Relationships between group members are for the most part amicable.	Y N

Total: N

19. The group is becoming good at identifying obstacles to achieving its goal.	Y N
20. We can diagnose problems in the way we work as a team and fix them.	Y N
21. We often develop creative solutions to achieve our objectives in different ways.	Y N
22. In this group, I feel able to risk expressing new ideas.	Y N
23. I can feel able to express my disagreement without others taking it personally.	Y N
24. Members take the lead as the situation requires it.	Y N

Total: P

2: Types of task

Objectives

1. Distinguish between the different types of task that a group may perform.

2. Recognise how type of task affects group process.

Briefing

1. Form into groups of four to five members.

2. You have 15–20 minutes to complete four tasks, which vary in their nature. Groups may consult references, etc. at their discretion.

3. The tasks are:

- Task 1—produce synonyms or antonyms for the fifteen words listed.

- Task 2—generate words that rhyme with the fifteen words listed.

- Task 3—arrive at the product of two matrices.

- Task 4—suggest the best route between here and the nearest coastal town or city.

4. Groups compare their answers and are provided with the correct solutions.

5. All the groups then

- identify the unique characteristics of each type of task they performed

- provide other examples of each type of task

- consider the effect of task type on their group decision-making processes

Task 1—Produce synonyms or antonyms for the fifteen words listed below:

celebrity	diminutive	traditional	moveable	sweet
fearful	crescendo	agitation	deliver	borrow
quietly	circuitous	paltry	foolish	indeterminate

Task 2—Generate words that rhyme with the fifteen words listed below:

feast	beard	battle	flowers	hissed
hurried	profit	world	orange	load
sorrow	song	accounting	great	smiles

Task 3—Solve the following equation:

Find x, y, z and w if $3 \begin{pmatrix} x & y \\ z & w \end{pmatrix} = \begin{pmatrix} x & 6 \\ -1 & 2w \end{pmatrix} + \begin{pmatrix} 4 & x+y \\ z+w & 3 \end{pmatrix}$

Task 4—Suggest the best route between here and the coastal town or city that is nearest to your educational establishment

From Diane Dodd-McCue, 'Led like sheep: An exercise for linking group decision making to different types of tasks', *Journal of Management Education*, 1991, vol.15, no.3, pp.335–9.

Chapter 10 Group structure

Key concepts

group structure
group process
power
reward power
coercive power
referent power
legitimate power
expert power
formal status
social status

sociometry
sociogram
communication network analysis
communigram
communication pattern analysis
interaction process analysis
social role
team role
group leadership

Learning objectives

When you have read this chapter, you should be able to define those key concepts in your own words, and you should also be able to:

1. List the six dimensions of group structure.
2. Identify the sources of power within the group.
3. Distinguish between two common uses of the concept of status.
4. Understand how emotional relationships within a group can be represented symbolically.
5. Distinguish between pattern network and IPA techniques for analysing communications between group members.
6. Distinguish between task, socio-emotional and individual roles within a group.
7. Distinguish Belbin's team roles.
8. Give examples of three leadership styles identified by White and Lippitt.
9. Distinguish between a task and a socio-emotional group leader.

Why study group structure?

Abraham Zaleznik (1993) has argued that:

> While Americans admire the 'hero', the individual who has the 'right stuff', they worry about his (*sic*) recklessness, his willingness to take risks that endanger others. Frequently the 'hero' is suppressed in favour of the team player who values the performance of the group over individual recognition. (p.180)

However, how the group as a whole performs depends very much on the behaviour and contribution of its individual members. Within organizations, a great deal of work is done by individuals working with others in groups and teams.

Because it is so important, management monitors how groups work in order to pinpoint any problems and rectify them so as to raise team effectiveness. When there is a problem with a motor car, it is taken into a garage and the mechanic drives it around, listens to the engine, feels the gear changes and attends to the smoothness of the ride. The individual parts of the car are then inspected, to ensure that all of them are performing their respective tasks and are working together satisfactorily in combination. Individual faulty or worn out parts are replaced. Linkages between the parts, which may have become loosened, are tightened. The mechanic checks that the vehicle is performing satisfactorily and can be returned to its owner.

This analogy is a useful way of introducing the concept of group structure from a management perspective. In this view, structure is an important aspect of 'engineering the group'. When a group or team is performing poorly, a consultant may be brought in to observe its operation and to evaluate its outputs. The consultant will focus on individual team members, assessing their performance of their roles and ensuring that everyone is working well together as a team. Individuals who are not contributing or who do not 'fit in' may be replaced by others. The consultant checks that communication between team members is timely and effective, and that leadership within the group is contributing towards the achievement of the goal.

Social scientists in general, and social psychologists in particular, are less directly concerned with improving team effectiveness and more concerned with understanding how the structure of a group develops; how it affects the individuals who comprise the groups; and how it impacts on group functioning.

Team problem

There were four team members named Everybody, Somebody, Anybody and Nobody.
There was an important job to do and Everybody was asked to do it.
Everybody was sure Somebody would do it.
Anybody could have done it, but Nobody did.
Everybody was angry about that, because it was Somebody's job.
Everybody thought Anybody could do it, but Nobody realized that Everybody wouldn't.
In the end, Everybody blamed Somebody when Nobody did what Anybody could have done.

Source unknown

Group structures

Group structure
refers to the relatively stable pattern of relationships between different group members. There is no single group structure and the concept can be expressed in several and overlapping ways.

A central idea in helping us to examine the nature and functioning of groups is that of structure. **Group structure** refers to the way in which members of a group relate to one another. The formation of group structure is one of the basic aspects of group development. When people come together and interact, differences between individuals begin to appear. Some talk, while others listen. These differences between group members serve as the basis for the establishment of group structure. As differentiation occurs, relations are established between members. Group structure is the label given to this patterning of relationships.

Group structure carries with it the connotation of something fixed and unchanging. While there is an element of permanency in terms of the relationships between members, these do continue to change and modify. Group members continually interact with each other, and in consequence their relationships are tested and transformed. As we describe the structure of any group, it is useful to view it as a snapshot photograph, correct at the time the shutter was pressed but acknowledging that things were different the moment before and after the photo was taken. Differences between the members of a group begin to occur as soon as it is formed. This differentiation within a group occurs along not one but several dimensions. The most important of these are:

- Power
- Status
- Liking
- Communication
- Role
- Leadership

There are as many structures in a group as there are dimensions along which a group can be differentiated. Although in common usage we talk about *the* structure of a group, in reality, a group will differentiate simultaneously along a number of dimensions. Group members will be accorded different amounts of status and hence a group will have a status hierarchy. They will be able to exert differing amounts of power and thus a power structure will emerge. In examining group functioning, social scientists have found it useful to consider differences between group members in terms of their liking for each other, status, power, role and leadership. While it is possible to examine each structural dimension of the group in turn, we need to remember that all are closely related and operate simultaneously in a group setting. Cartwright and Zander (1968) suggest that a group's structure is determined by:

1. the requirements for efficient group performance;

2. the abilities and motivations of group members;

3. the psychological and social environment of the group.

Why does a group have structure?

Why does a patterning of relationships between individuals in a group occur and what purpose does it serve? Robert Bales (1950a) offered a psychological explanation based on the individual's desire for stability, 'need for order' and 'low tolerance of ambiguity'. He argued that meeting and dealing with other people within a group can cause an individual stress. It is the potential uncertainty and unpredictability in the actions of others that causes this. If the behaviour between group members can be made predictable, this can reduce the tension for all concerned. This, he explained, is what group structure does.

A sociological explanation would point to structure as a manifestation of power, with structure 'imposed' on groups (as a natural aspect of efficient functioning, of course!) to maintain the power position of key players in the organization. All groups are overlaid with the power and cultural patterns of the organization within which they exist. This also raises gender issues concerning male domination.

Whether a group's structure results from its members' basic need for predictability or is imposed by powerful outsiders, the effect in either case is to create differences between the individuals within the group along several dimensions at the same time (e.g. status, role, power). One person will therefore simultaneously have high status and power, since each person stands at the intersection of several dimensions. The combination of all of these for each group member is referred to as their position in the group structure. A group's structure will be affected by **group process**. A group's process refers to the group activity which occurs over time, specifically to the verbal and non-verbal contributions of group members. Examples of a group's process include:

- Direction of communication   (who talks to whom)
- Quantity of communication   (number of times each group member speaks)
- Content of communication   (type of utterance made)
- Decision-making style   (how decisions are made in the group)
- Problem-solving style   (how problems are approached and solved)

The structure of a group can affect its process. For example, when an individual is appointed the leader of a formal group, they will tend to speak more often and will be listened to more closely. Being group leader will therefore determine the direction, frequency and content of their communication with others in the group. Conversely, group process can determine group structure. In an informal group, the individual who speaks most often to all fellow members may come to be liked the most. Their status will rise in the eyes of the other members and they may be given permission to take on a leadership role within the group.

When seeking to improve the performance of a group through the use of team-building activities [**link**, chapter 17, organization development], management consultants often focus on group processes, in order to locate problems in group functioning and to suggest solutions. They look at how a group does things and not on what it does. They may decide that a group is performing poorly because its members are not communicating with each other sufficiently; that there is an absence of goal clarity; that leadership within the group is poor; or that the way decisions are reached antagonizes members and fails to secure their commitment. Inevitably they will recommend that the group should become aware of its processes, and manage them better, in order to achieve improved outcomes.

Group process refers to the patterns of interactions between the members of a group.

Reward power is the ability of a leader to exert influence based on the belief of followers that the leader has access to valued rewards, which will be dispensed in return for compliance with instructions.

Coercive power is the ability of a leader to exert influence based on the belief of followers that the individual can administer penalties or sanctions that are considered to be unwelcome.

Referent power is the ability of a leader to exert influence based on the belief of followers that the individual possesses desirable abilities and personality traits that can and should be copied.

Power structure

Individual members of a group differ in terms of how much **power** they each possess, and hence in their ability to direct the behaviour of other members. For this reason, it becomes necessary for the group to have established control relations between members. By having a power structure, the group avoids continued power struggles, which can disrupt its functioning. It can also link goal achievement activities to a system of authority which is seen as legitimate.

Power is the capacity of individuals to overcome resistance on the part of others, to exert their will, and to produce results consistent with their interests and objectives.

Various writers have defined power in terms of influence. Power is an aspect not only in relationships between individuals within a group but also in leadership relations and political issues. We shall therefore revisit the work of these authors several times in a later chapter [**link**, chapter 24, power and politics]. For now, we can draw upon the classic work of John French and Bertram Raven (1958), who saw power as a property not of the individual but of the relationship. These authors distinguished five types of power, which are defined here.

Saying that power is a property of the relationship and not of the individual means that, for example, it is not having rewards to distribute or sanctions to exercise that matters, it's being perceived to be. So you have reward power when others think that you have rewards up your sleeve, even when you don't.

Stop and criticize

- Who gains from having a stable power structure in a group and why?
- Who loses, how and why?
- Make the argument for having an unstable power structure in a group.

Celebrity product endorsement syndrome

Would you buy something just because a famous person plugged it? 'It depends', says Bryony Gordon, 19, 'on the star and on the product'.

Referent (or personal or charismatic) power is defined as identification based on the personal characteristics of an individual. Marketing people are well aware of its impact and for this reason use well-known film and sports stars, TV personalities and top models to advertise their products and services. They hope consumers will identify with these people and buy their products. While teenagers are not duped by a star's face on a product, the star's power can get them to buy a product if it's done in the right way. There seem to be three conditions:

- A pop, film or sports star, and the product that they promote, have to go together, e.g. Madonna and Max Factor cosmetics, Bob Hoskins and BT telephone services, but not a footballer and fatty burgers.
- The star should not have endorsed many other products, e.g. for a period of time during the 1990s, the Spice Girls' faces appeared on many different products.
- When the audience clearly perceives that the outcome stated by the celebrity manifestly could not have been achieved by that person with the product alone.

Most people think that every time we buy something backed by a star, the fat cats in Armani suits are wielding more power over us, the consumer. But in actual fact, we're the ones with the power to make or break a trend. Can you think of an example where the referent (personal, charismatic) power of a TV, film, pop or sports star led you to make a purchase that you might not otherwise have made?

Based on 'Celebrity Endorsement', *Daily Telegraph*, 28 August 1999, T2, p.11.

Status structure

Formal status refers to a collection of rights and obligations associated with a position, as distinct from the person who may occupy that position.

Status is a prestige ranking within a group that is independent of formal status or position. It is closely related to leadership, since if an individual's higher status is accepted by others within the group, they can influence, control or command those around. Status ranking indicates the group's 'pecking order'. Some writers argue that status is important because it motivates people and has consequences for their behaviour. This is particularly the case when individuals perceive a disparity between their own perception of themselves and how others perceive them to be. Each position in a group has a value placed upon it. Within the organization, a value is ascribed to a position by the formal organization, e.g. chief executive officer, vice-president, supervisor, and can be labelled formal status. **Formal status** is best thought of as being synonymous with rank as in the police or the armed forces and reflects a person's position on the organizational ladder.

A second way in which value is placed on a position is the social honour or prestige that is accorded an individual in a group by the other group members. In this second sense, the word 'status' is prefixed by the word 'social', indicating the degree of informally established value accorded to that position as compared with other positions, as perceived by both the formal and the informal group. While one can view **social status** as a sort of badge of honour awarded for meritorious group conduct, it can also be viewed as a set of unwritten rules about the kind of conduct that people are expected to show one another. It can indicate the degree of respect, familiarity or reserve that is appropriate in a given situation.

One of the powers possessed by an informal group is its ability to confer status on those of its members who meet the expectations of the group. These members are looked up to by their peers, not because of any formal position they may hold in the organization but because of their position in the social group. Since many people actively seek status in order to fulfil their need for self-esteem, the granting of it by the group provides them with personal satisfaction. Similarly, the withholding of status can act as a group control mechanism to bring a deviant group member into line. The status accorded by the group to a member is immediate in terms of face-to-face feedback. The recognition and esteem given to group members reinforces their identification with the group and increases their dependence upon it.

Turning to consider a formal group or team, individual members will be accorded formal status within it based on hierarchical position and task ability. The organization is made up of a number of defined positions arranged in order of their increasing authority. The formal status hierarchy reflects the potential ability of the holder of the position to contribute to the overall goals of the organization. It differentiates the amount of respect deserved and simultaneously ranks them on a status scale. The outward symbols associated with formal status (e.g. size of office, quality of carpet) are there to inform other members in the organization of where exactly that person stands on the 'organizational ladder'. This topic leads ultimately to a consideration of organization structure, which will be considered later [**link**, chapter 14, elements of structure].

What effect does the status structure have on group behaviour? Research shows that, as one would expect, higher-status people in a group have more power and tend to be more influential than lower-status ones (Greenberg, 1976). Knowing this, individual members may take steps to enhance their status in the eyes of their colleagues and thereby be able to get the group to make the decisions that they want.

Legitimate power is the ability of a leader to exert influence based on the belief of followers that the individual has the authority to give instructions, which they in turn have an obligation to accept: referred as *positive power* as it depends on the leader's formal position in the organization.

Expert power is the ability of a leader to exert influence based on the belief of followers that the leader possesses superior knowledge relevant to the situation and the task in hand.

Social status is the relative ranking that a person holds and the value of that person as measured by a group.

Stop and criticize

Consider a group of which you are currently a member. What action could you take to change your status in this group, and what impact would this have on your relationships and friendships?

Interaction with others perceived as lower in status can be threatening because of the potential identification of the person with the group or individual being associated with. Status is abstract and ascribed through the perceptions of others. One's status is therefore always tenuous. It may be withdrawn or downgraded at any time. The reference group with which one identifies, and whose values and behaviour one adopts, plays an important part in establishing and maintaining one's status. To preserve that status, one cannot leave the reference group for a lower-status reference group.

Status and authority in an aeroplane cockpit

In aircraft, cockpit members comprise teams with a designated leader and clear lines of authority and responsibility. Status comes with position. The status ranking is captain, first officer and second officer. To fly safely, team members need to engage in the verbal behaviours of enquiry, advocacy and assertion. For example, *enquiring* why one member is taking certain actions; *advocating* alternative options; and *asserting* their views on matters. The accident literature is full of examples when this had not been done.

In a study of a major airline conducted by Harper *et al.*, captains feigned incapacitation at a predetermined point during final approach in simulator trials which involved landing in poor visibility. They discovered that 25 per cent of the flights 'hit the ground' because, for some reason, first officers did not take control even when they knew that their planes was well below glide slope. The authority status dynamic surrounding the role of the captain in a cockpit crew is extremely powerful and has a dramatic effect on overall group performance.

Based on C.R. Harper, G.J. Kidera and J.F. Cullen, 'Study of simulated airplane pilot incapacitation' Phase LL: Subtle or partial loss of function, *Aerospace Medicine*, 1971, vol.42, pp.946–8.

Status in *Animal Farm*

George Orwell's *Animal Farm* is a short and allegorical novel whose characters and events correspond to the Communist revolution in Russia at the start of the last century, and its aftermath. It describes the organization of the farm. In the story, the pigs, particularly Napoleon and Snowball, secure the highest status for themselves. This is reflected in the modification of one of the farm's seven commandments from 'All animals are equal' to 'Some animals are more equal than others'. The farm's status structure is summarized below:

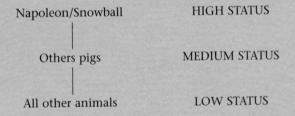

Orwell's novel not only provides us with a vivid description of the interrelatedness of the power, status, liking, role and leadership structures that exist within a group but also shows how these change over time. In the diagram above, the group structure is depicted as a static snapshot but should more accurately be considered as a moving film.

Based on George Orwell, *Animal Farm*, Penguin Books, Harmondsworth, 1946.

Hell's Angels' status structure

The Hell's Angels were first organized in San Bernadeno, California, in 1948 by Second World War veterans. They received national attention in the movies when Marlon Brando played an angst-ridden gang leader in the 1953 film, *The Wild One*. At the same time as cultivating their rebel image, they became more businesslike. They have 1,000 members worldwide organized into 70 local clubs called 'chapters'. There is a tight management structure, a communications system and paramilitary discipline. Each chapter has its own strict status structure as depicted here.

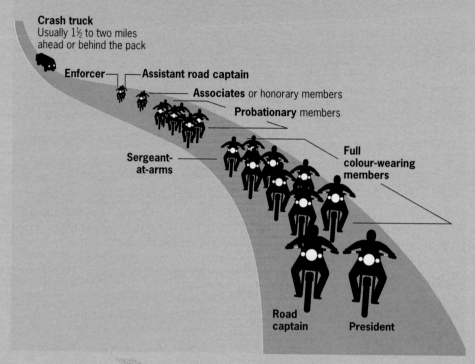

Crash truck
Usually 1½ to two miles
ahead or behind the pack

Enforcer — **Assistant road captain**

Associates or honorary members

Probationary members

Sergeant-at-arms

Full colour-wearing members

Road captain   **President**

The Hell's Angels therefore offer an example of an original, *informal group*, which replicated itself around the country and then around the world. These separate informal groups linked together to create an *informal organization*. Finally, as their objectives changed and management structures developed, they now represent a *formal organization* [link, chapter 14, elements of structure].

Based on Andrew E. Sewer, 'The Hellish Angels' Devilish Business', *Fortune*, 30 November 1992, pp. 84–90.

Liking structure

Sociometry is the study of interpersonal feelings and relationships within groups.

Within a group, individual members will like, dislike or be indifferent to other members, in varying degrees. Their combined feelings towards each other represent their group's liking structure. This can be studied using the technique of **sociometry**. The term derives from the Latin *socius* (companion) and the Greek *metron* (measure). Sociometry was devised by Jacob Moreno, who coined the term in his book *Who Shall Survive* (Moreno, 1953). Moreno and his colleagues originally used the technique in their research in the New York Training School for Girls in the 1930s. They mapped the friendship choices among girls in reformatory cottages.

Sociometry diagrammatically maps the emotional relationships between individual members in a group on the basis of their personal choices of selection and

Below are eight boxes.
- In the box marked 'Work With – Yes', write the name of two people in your class that you prefer to work with.
- In the box marked 'Work With – No', write the name of two people in your class that you prefer not to work with.

Repeat this with the remaining boxes marked 'Study With', 'Play With' and 'Live With'.

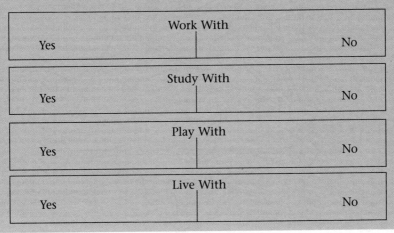

Figure 10.1: Sociometric assessment

Jacob Levy Moreno
(1889–1974)

Sociogram refers is a chart which shows the liking (social attraction) relationships between individual members of a group.

rejection of other group members using a few standard symbols. This network of a group's interpersonal feelings is exposed by the use of sociometric tests. These reveal the spontaneous feelings and choices that individuals in a group have and make towards each other. Moreno asked individuals to complete the test shown above. The spontaneous feelings within a person are divided into three classes— attraction (liking), rejection (disliking), and indifference (neutral feeling). A socio-metric assessment is most commonly set up as a group preference schedule such as the one depicted in figure 10.1.

After analysing the answers, Moreno calculated how many times an individual had been chosen as a comrade by the other members of the group for the activity in question. This feeling, the sociometric term for which is *tele*, may be one of attraction (positive tele) or repulsion (negative tele); alternatively there may merely be indifference. Group members' choices are depicted on a **sociogram**, which reveals the existence of any sub-groupings within the main group.

A sociometric assessment can reveal the 'stars', 'isolates', 'neglectees', 'rejectees' and 'mutual pairs' and 'mutual trios' in a group. These as defined as:

Star	recipient of a large number of choices, sometimes described as 'over-chosen'.
Isolate	person who makes no choices at all and receives none; i.e. a relationship of mutual indifference to the remainder of the group.
Neglectee	person who, although he or she makes choices, receives none at all.
Rejectee	person who is not chosen by anyone and who is rejected by one or more persons.
Mutual pair or mutual trio	individuals who choose one another.

Stop and criticize

Below is a sociogram. Identify a 'star', an 'isolate', a 'neglectee', a 'rejectee', a 'mutual pair' and a 'mutual trio' in a group.

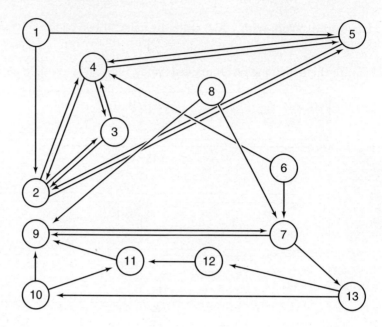

How might a researcher create a sociogram without having individuals complete a sociometric questionnaire? How reliable would such information be? For what purposes might sociograms be used in an organization?

How are sociometric assessments and sociograms used? Originally developed as a research method by sociologists, they were later used in industry (Jacobs, 1945). Sociometry continues to be applied in organizations today under the label 'social network analysis'. It can be used for:

Mapping the informal organization
Problems and opportunities in a company can be located in its informal organization. The company's formal organization structure is depicted in its organizational chart [**link**, chapter 14, elements of structure], but its informal organization is only revealed through a sociogram (see Krackhardt and Hanson, 1993, opposite).

Selecting group members
They have been used to determine the right mix of work team members to avoid personality clashes, raise group cohesion, and increase group performance [**link**, chapter 12, teamworking]. Sociograms have been used to design flight crews (Zeleny, 1947).

Revealing feelings
Sociograms can reveal people's feelings towards one another. Sociograms have been used in schools to reveal the existence of unhappy pupil isolates who have not adjusted to the class group, as well as isolate workers who have not adjusted to their work team.

Modifying the group structure
Sociograms of productive and unproductive teams can highlight areas where other aspects of group structure require modification.

Other

Sociograms have also been used in the selection and training of group leaders; to increase co-operation, productivity and morale among employees in a group; and to anticipate turnover and conflict problems.

Stop and criticize

Think of an organization that you are or have been a member of. Identify two individuals with whom you would *not* like to work in the group. List the reasons you would enter their names under 'Work With – No' category. Describe your feelings towards them.

Informal group structure

Informal organizations consist of networks of relationships that employees form across functions and divisions. Using a case study approach, David Krackhardt and Jeffrey Hanson studied how these operated in the banking industry. From a managerial viewpoint, such networks can be positive, cutting through reporting procedures, restarting stalled initiatives, and meeting ambitious deadlines; or negative, sabotaging their goals by blocking communications and fomenting opposition to change. The authors carried out a social network analysis, which consisted of a questionnaire which asked employees about who interacted with whom about what. The results obtained were cross-checked to ensure a consensus of the group, and then drawn onto a network map. This activity revealed three types of relationship:

- *advice* networks ('who depends on whom' to solve problems and provide information);
- *trust* networks (in which employees share potential information and back each other in a crisis); and
- *communication* networks (in which employees regularly talk to each other on work-related matters).

Such analyses can reveal the influence of the central figures in informal networks who wield the power, and how various coalitions of employees function. For example, one bank's 80 per cent staff turnover problem was not due to difficulties in its formal organization. Instead, the tellers had key informal relationships with others in the trust network, and when these people left the company, so did the tellers.

Krackhardt and Hanson argue that revealing the hidden aspects of the informal organization can address company problems such as turnover, poor communication and bad decision making; and also suggest solutions. For example, they analysed the functioning of a bank's task force team, which was failing to make progress. They found that while its leader held a central position in the advice network (many employees relying on him for technical advice), he had only one trust link with a colleague. Having understood the cause of the problem, senior management wanted to avoid labelling the team a failure or embarrassing a valued employee by dismissing him as team leader. Instead, it redesigned this task force to reflect the inherent strengths of the trust network by adding a person in the trust network to share responsibility for the group leadership role.

In a second example, the analysis of the informal communication structure of a bank branch showed that it had divided itself into two distinct cliques, with the tellers, loan officers and administrative staff distributing themselves between the two. Because of their different working times, the two clique cultures never clashed because they rarely interacted. In the end, it was customer complaints which stimulated the branch manager to unify the two groups and their cultures. He did this not by revamping the branch's formal structure but by expanding the informal organization to integrate both groups. He intentionally mixed members of the two cliques on training courses; temporarily changed their work schedules so that members of one would interact with the other; substituted a member from the other clique where there was a staff absence; and scheduled meetings so that all staff could attend. The level of customer satisfaction rose.

Krackhardt and Hanson recommend that managers should revamp their formal organizational structure to allow the informal one to thrive. By letting the formal organization complement the informal, the latter can be made to help solve problems, improve performance, and generally support the achievement of company goals.

Based on David Krackhardt and Jeffrey R. Hanson, 'Informal networks: the company behind the chart', *Harvard Business Review*, July–August 1993, pp.104–11.

Status and communication structure in an orchestra

In their study of two freelance orchestras, Kwiatkowski and Lawrence reported that status in an orchestra was denoted by geographical location on the concert hall stage. The further forward and closer to the outside one was (and therefore more easily seen), the higher was one's status. Considering the communication structure, they noted that if there was any technical disagreement within a section of the orchestra (e.g. brass), or if there was uncertainty about what the conductor wanted, this would be referred to the principal of that section for decision. If a musician asked the principal, and the principal was unsure, he or she would ask the conductor. The researchers observed that if any of the principals had to ask the conductor a question, they would do it in a deferential manner or else make it into a light-hearted joke.

Based on Richard Kwiatkowski and Susannah Lawrence, 'Orchestral metaphors and organizational reality: Or "Taylor rides again"', conference paper, 1996 British Psychological Society Conference, Occupational Psychology section.

Communication structure

To understand the communication structure of a group, it is necessary to know the pattern of positions, that is, the role and status of every member, and the duration and direction of communication from position to position. Each group member depends on information provided by others. Solving a problem, making a decision or reaching agreement all require information exchange between individuals. The members of a group may work closely together, interacting frequently and attending regular meetings. Alternatively, they may be physically dispersed within a building or located in different buildings, and therefore only able to come physically to attend a meeting occasionally. Increasingly, different members of the same group may be located in different countries (globally dispersed groups) and interact through video conferencing. Whatever the situation, there are different ways to determine a group's communication structure.

Communication pattern analysis

Communication pattern analysis is a technique that uses direct observation to determine the source, direction and quantity of verbal communication between congregated members of a group.

Communigram refers to a chart that indicates the source, direction and quantity of verbal communication between the congregated members of a group.

When group members come together physically and participate in a meeting around a table, a **communication pattern analysis** of the event can be conducted. The observer of the group makes a note of how often each group member speaks, and to whom they direct their comments. The outcome is the creation of a **communigram** (figure 10.2), which in some ways resembles the sociogram discussed earlier and which details the participation, quantity and direction of the verbal communication between the group's members. Essentially, it answers the question, who spoke to whom and how often.

Communication network analysis

When the members of a group are physically dispersed around the same building, around different buildings or are located in different countries, it is still possible to determine the source, frequency and direction of their communication with each other by using communication pattern analysis. Instead of observing the interactions between individuals, which is impossible, the researcher would note the initiation and direction of telephone conversations, memos, faxes and e-mails between the group's members.

For example, the information flow between the members of a group can take the form of a chain. A tells B, B tells C, and so on. In his classic study, William Foote Whyte (1948) described one such chain pattern in a restaurant in which

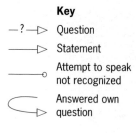

Key

—?—▷   Question

———▷   Statement

———o   Attempt to speak not recognized

⤶—▷   Answered own question

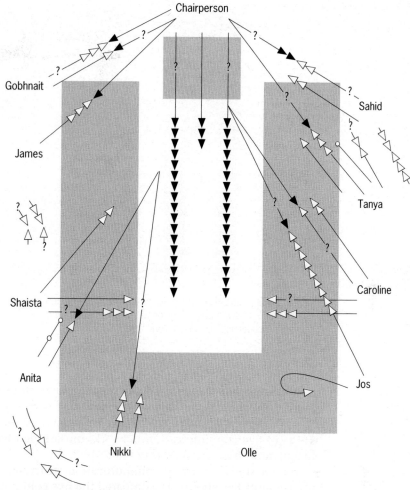

Figure 10.2: Communigram showing participation at a meeting

> **Communication network analysis** is a technique that uses analysis of documents, data and voice mail transmission, to determine the source, direction and quantity of verbal and written communication between the dispersed members of a group.
> **Communication network chart** indicates the source, direction and quantity of verbal and written communication between the dispersed members of a group.

customers gave their orders to a waitress, who passed it to a runner, who passed it to a pantry worker, before it was finally delivered to the cook. This communication network could produce a distortion in the message. When information arrived through this route, the cook was unable to check it, had no opportunity to negotiate with the customer and hence was unable to discuss any problems.

The aforementioned 'chain' is only one of several communication networks used by groups. To discover the full range, and the effectiveness of each, Marvin Shaw (1978) conducted a laboratory experiments to test if certain group com-

Table 10.1: Types of communication network

Criteria	Channel				
	Chain	'Y'	Wheel	Circle	All-channel
Speed	Moderate	Moderate	Fast	Slow	Fast
Accuracy	High	High	High	Low	Moderate
Leader emergence	Moderate	Moderate	High	None	None
Member satisfaction	Moderate	Moderate	Low	High	High

Based on Alex Bavelas and Dermott Barrett, 'An experimental approach to organizational communication', *Personnel*, March, 1951.

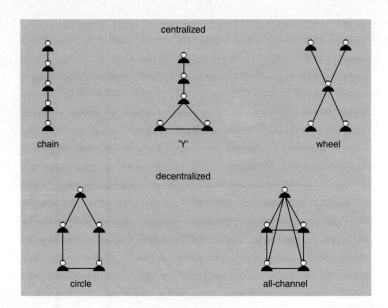

Figure 10.3: Centralized and decentralized communication networks in groups
From Marvin E. Shaw, 'Communication networks fourteen years later', in Leonard Berkowitz (ed.), *Group Processes*, Academic Press, New York, 1978, pp.351–61.

munication networks impeded or facilitated the performance of a task by its group. While all the communication networks studied were adequate for the group to do the task, he discovered that some were superior in terms of standing up to disruption and to encouraging emergence of leadership. Shaw studied the effects of five communication networks on task performance and member satisfaction, and these are shown in figure 10.3.

Another study on group communication structure, this time by Alex Bavelas and Dermott Barrett (1951), compared the five communication networks on four criteria, so as to highlight the differences between them (Bavelas, 1968). These are shown in table 10.1. The relationships between the form of the communication network and the emergence of leadership style and level of group member satisfaction are easy to see. Ralph White and Ronald Lippitt (1960) distinguished three styles of group leadership—autocratic, democratic and *laissez-faire* [**link**, chapter 21, leadership].

Autocratic leadership was accompanied by a wheel communication net and the democratic style by an all-channel network. The *laissez-faire* leadership style generated a somewhat fragmented communication pattern. Shaw noted that in centralized networks (chain, wheel and 'Y'), group members had to go through a person located at the centre of the network in order to communicate with others. This led to unequal access to information in the group, because the persons at the centre had more access to information than persons at the periphery. In decentralized networks (circle and all-channel), information could flow freely between members without having to go through a central person, thus equalizing access to information. The way in which different communication networks affect group functioning in terms of performance, structure and member satisfaction continues to be a subject of interest. Robert Baron and Jerald Greenberg (1990) studied the differences in performance between centralized and decentralized networks. The focus of their study was upon the type of task that a group was required to complete. The previous chapter distinguished between additive, conjunctive and disjunctive tasks [**link**, chapter 9, group formation]. Baron and Greenberg distinguished between 'simple' and 'complex' tasks. They concluded that centralized networks are superior on simple tasks (top half of figure 10.4),

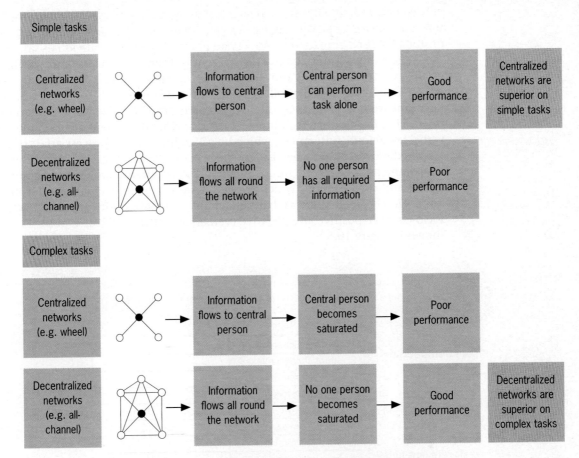

Figure 10.4: Task type and communication network performance
From Jerald Greenberg and Robert A. Baron, *Behaviour in Organizations*, sixth edition, Prentice Hall International, Upper Saddle, NJ, 1997, p.306.

and decentralized networks are superior on complex tasks (bottom half of figure 10.4). Managers in organizations are interested in ensuring that a group's communication network supports rather than impedes the achievement of its task. Hence, by first identifying the type of network used, and then assessing its effect, they can take steps to match the type of network with the type of group task.

Communication network research conducted in the 1950s by Robert Bales on all-male groups revealed a relationship between group size, seniority of status, and direction and quantity of communication. The most senior status individual ('top man') in groups larger than five members tended to speak more to the group as a whole than to specific individuals. Other members, in contrast, spoke more often to specific individuals, and particularly to the 'top man', rather than to the group as a whole. As group size increased, a larger percentage of the comments came to be addressed to the top man, and a smaller percentage to other members; and the top man increased the percentage of the remarks that he made to the whole group. The researchers concluded that as group size increased, the communication structure became centralized around the leader (Bales, 1953)

Interaction process analysis

The techniques of communication pattern analysis and communication network analysis provide information about the source, direction and quantity of verbal communication between members of congregated and dispersed teams respectively. However, neither of them consider the content of the communications

Robert Freed Bales

between the individuals involved. When we observe a congregated group in action, for example, rugby players discussing their strategy for the second half, or a group of students discussing their tutorial system, what we see are individuals saying certain things. If we want to study the content of their verbal behaviour within that group, we need a precise and reliable way of categorizing it. In the late 1940s, Robert Freed Bales and his colleagues at Harvard University's Laboratory of Social Relations went beyond their original research on who talked to whom and how often. They developed a technique for categorizing the content of group member's verbal behaviours (utterances) which he called **interaction process analysis** (IPA).

Bales discovered that when assigned a task such as solving a problem or making a recommendation, work groups inevitably encountered problems of communication and organization, which evoked a variety of individual member behaviours. He classified these verbal behaviours into task-positive (verbal) acts and socio-emotive positive and negative (verbal) acts (Bales, 1950a; 1950b). These are shown in figure 10.5.

Interaction process analysis refers to a technique used to categorize the content of speech.

The figure shows the twelve categories that Bales used to classify the verbal behaviours (utterances) of groups members that he observed. He grouped them into four general categories.

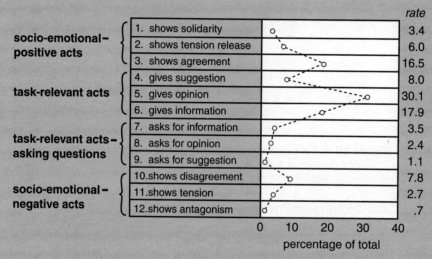

Figure 10.5: Bales's categories and summary of psychological events in small groups

The data are based on 71,838 observations of 24 groups in 96 different sessions. The behaviour profile shown here can be regarded as typical of many small groups. Of all the behaviours of these group members, 30.1 per cent are of the giving opinions type, while less that 1 per cent show overt antagonism.

Based on R.F. Bales, 'How people interact in conferences', *Scientific American*, 1955, vol.192, pp.31–5.

Bales distinguished twelve different categories into which one could classify or 'code' each person's verbal statements or utterances. For example, category 1 is 'shows solidarity, raises others' status, gives help, reward'. So, if one group member said, 'That's an excellent idea from Lucy', that would be an example of a category 1 utterance. In contrast, category 12 is 'shows antagonism, deflates others' status, defends or asserts self'. If another member said, 'Jill's report was pathetic! I could do one that was twice as good in half the time', that would be an example of a category 12 utterance. Bales felt that with his twelve categories one could classify most utterances that were likely to be made by individuals in a group when they engaged in verbal interaction. In his original experiments, his researchers acted as observers, watching groups from behind a two-way mirror.

Stop and criticize	Becoming a competent verbal interaction 'coder' takes a little time and practice. To develop your skill, videotape a 5-minute sequence from any television programme or film that involves four or five people together having a discussion. Rewind the tape to the start of the sequence and use the framework in figure 10.6 to categorize their speech utterances into the appropriate categories. Rewind the tape and repeat the procedure to check your accuracy, or ask a friend to do the same and then compare your results. Then analyse your data by totalling your observations.

After carrying out this exercise, assess the value of this information and of your analysis, to you as an observer of the group and to the group as a whole.

- If you were a group *member*, how would you use this information?
- If you were a group *consultant* or facilitator, how would you use this information?

Here is a simplified version of Bales' interaction process analysis (IPA) verbal behaviour classification scheme. It consists of six verbal behaviour categories, and each has an explanation alongside. Also provided is a chart for categorizing group members' verbal contributions. There is a space for their initials along the top row. Next time you are present at a group discussion, listen to what each individual says. Every time they speak, decide in which verbal category their utterance belongs and place a tick or dot beside that category, under their name. Continue to do this, building up a record of the whole discussion.

After you have finished observing your discussion, total up your ticks or dots in the columns (horizontally) and for each group member (vertically). Your horizontal score total gives you an indication of the behaviour of the group as a whole. For example, is this a group whose members are competing or co-operating with each other? Your vertical scores contrast the contributions of the individual group members and can provide a clue to the roles that they are playing in the group.

Verbal category	Explanation
Proposing	Any behaviour which puts forward a new suggestion, idea or course of action.
Building	Any behaviour which develops or extends an idea or suggestion made by someone else.
Supporting	Behaviour which declares agreement with or support for any individual or idea.
Disagreeing	Any behaviour which states a criticism of another person's statement.
Giving information	Any behaviour which gives facts, ideas or opinions or clarifies these.
Seeking Information	Any behaviour which asks for facts, ideas or opinions from others.

	Names (initials)				Totals
Verbal category					
Proposing					
Building					
Supporting					
Disagreeing					
Giving information					
Seeking Information					
Totals					

Figure 10.6: Analysing verbal interactions

Bales' IPA is the most refined and exhaustive (empirically usable) method yet developed which can be used to study the content of the verbal communication between individuals in groups. It has been extensively tested and has achieved an acceptably high level of agreement between different observer-coders. Bales' research, conducted in the 1940s and 1950s, provided the first rounded picture of what happens in face-to-face groups. He used the data gathered with this technique to develop a theory of group functioning. He argued that group behaviour could be explained by showing how groups dealt with certain recurring problems such as orientation, evaluation, control, decision making, tension management and integration (Bales, 1953). His theory of group functioning thus pre-dates the Tuckman and Jensen model discussed previously [**link**, chapter 9, group formation].

Crew resource management and IPA

Data from the Boeing Aircraft Company shows that between 1959 and 1989, the primary cause of aeroplane fuselage loss accidents in the worldwide commercial fleet (excluding military and sabotage) was flight crew error. Faults in the aeroplane itself took second place at about 15%. To overcome the problem of human error, the industry has designed and implemented numerous programmes of research, training and information, which are collectively referred to as Crew Resource Management (CRM). This is defined as the application of human factors in the aviation system. CRM programmes contain a training simulation which show that group communication patterns are a cause of many accidents, rather than either the plane itself, or the skills of the individual crew members.

Although not designed as a study of group processes, an experimental simulation sponsored by NASA and conducted by the late H. Patrick Ruffell Smith is a powerful demonstration of the operational significance of crew interactions. Eighteen airline crews flew a two-segment flight in a Boeing 747 simulator. The scenario consisted of a short flight from Washington, DC, to John F. Kennedy Airport in New York and a subsequent leg from New York to London. After departing from New York, the crew experienced an oil pressure problem that forced them to shut down an engine. Because the flight could not be completed with a failed engine, the crew had to decide where to land. This decision was complicated by the further failure of a hydraulic system, deteriorating weather at possible landing sites, complex instructions from air traffic control, and a cabin crew member who repeatedly requested information and assistance from the flight deck at times of high workload. The study showed a remarkable amount of variability in the effectiveness with which crews handled the situation. Some crews managed the problems very well, while others committed a large number of operationally serious errors, including one miscalculation of dumping more than 100,000 pounds of fuel. The primary conclusion drawn from the study was that most problems and errors were induced by breakdowns in crew co-ordination rather than by deficits in technical knowledge and skills. For example, many errors occurred when individuals performing a task were interrupted by demands from other crew members or were overloaded with a variety of tasks requiring immediate action. In other cases, poor leadership was evident, and resulted in a failure to exchange critical information in a timely manner.

This approach grew out of social psychological research into information flow within groups [Bales, 1950a; 1950b] and involved classifying each speech act as to type (i.e. observations regarding flight status, inquiries seeking information, etc.). The findings were clear: crews who communicated more overall tended to perform better and, in particular, those who exchanged more information about flight status committed fewer errors in the handling of engines and hydraulic and fuel systems and the reading and setting of instruments.

This methodology has been subsequently refined by Barbara Kanki and her colleagues at NASA-Ames Research Center and applied to communications records from additional experimental simulations. ... Communications sequences were contrasted between crews committing a large number of operational errors and those making few ... The primary finding of the study was the homogeneity of patterns characterizing the low-error crews. This was interpreted as the adoption of a more standard, hence more predictable form of communication. High-error crews., in contrast, showed a great diversity of speech patterns.

From Robert L. Helmreich and H. Clayton Foushee, 'Why crew resource management? Empirical and theoretical issues in human factors training in aviation', in E.L. Weiner, B.G. Kanki, and R.L. Helmreich, (eds), *Cockpit Resource Management*, Academic Press, New York, 1993, pp.5 and 17–18.

Role structure

It is a short step from identifying the main class of verbal contributions that an individual makes in their group to identifying their team member role. The occupants of every position in the group are expected to carry out certain functions when the members of the group interact with one another. The expected behaviours associated with a position within the group constitute the social role of the occupant of that position. **Social role** is the concept which relates the individual to the prescriptive dictates of the group. People's behaviour within the organization is structured and patterned in various ways. An understanding of role helps us to see and explain how this happens.

> **Social role** is the set of expectations that others hold of an occupant of a position.

Social role is the set of expectations that others hold of an occupant of a position in an organization structure, e.g. shop manager, bishop, head of the production department, etc. These expectations presume attitudes, relationships and behaviours. A role can be thought of rather like a script which actors are given. The same actor changes their roles, and can act out different parts in front of different audiences. The topic of role within the context of organizational structure will be discussed later [**link**, chapter 14, elements of structure]. Here, our concern is with the different roles that are played out by various members of a group or team.

Totalling vertically each individual's verbal contributions in figure 10.6 reveals that group members contributed in different ways to the discussion. Bales found that individuals played different roles (role differentiation) within their groups, and that this was a universal feature of face-to-face interaction in groups. As the group deals with its problems, individual members begin to 'specialize' in certain types of behaviour, taking on different 'roles' within the group. Bales also found that as roles become more differentiated, some of them contribute to the progress and welfare of the group, while others seemed to add little or nothing to either its happiness or success. The former set of roles come to be more highly regarded than the latter, and are generally referred to as leadership roles. The idea of leadership as a set of behavioural acts was considered by Edwin Fleishman and Ralph Stogdill at about the same period and will be examined later [**link**, chapter 21, leadership]

International Drinks plc

Each year, International Drinks plc recruits its graduate management from across Western and Eastern Europe. For one of its Europe-wide projects it creates a product development group of eight people drawn from its most recent graduate intake. As the group proceeds with its task, members notice that one of the members, Jos, concerns himself primarily with the personal problems of group members. His behaviour consists mainly of socio-emotional, positive acts. He may have few ideas about how to get the task done, but he is very knowledgeable about how to hold the group together, reduce anxiety and make everyone feel a worthwhile contributor. Anika, another group member, constantly pushes to get the group's task accomplished. She asks for suggestions—perhaps annoying some individuals. Hans does not contribute frequently, but when he does, it is to give information and to clarify the direction in which the group might move. Mariella frequently gives her opinion. Soon these individuals find that this is the way that they are expected to behave by the other group members.

Each of them now has a role in the group. This pattern of behaviour becomes more or less defined, not only in Jos', Anika's, Hans's and Mariella's own minds but also in the expectations of the other group members. This pressure constrains them from suddenly switching to different roles. It is in this way that role differentiation—the social 'division of labour' within a group—comes about. It should be mentioned that while 'role' concerns the expectations that others hold of an individual, the person in the role has their own understanding and expectations concerning what they are doing. This can give rise to role conflict where the expectations of the role holder, and the expectations of those others around the role holder, become inconsistent [**link**, chapter 14, elements of structure].

Table 10.2: Benne and Sheats' 27 roles commonly played by members in a group

	Group task roles
1. Initiator–contributor	Recommends new solutions to group problems.
2. Information seeker	Attempts to obtain necessary facts.
3. Opinion seeker	Asks for clarification of values related to the group task or to a suggestion made.
4. Information giver	Offers facts and generalizations.
5. Opinion giver	Shares own opinions with others.
6. Elaborator	Spells out suggestions in terms of examples.
7. Co-ordinator	Clarifies connections between various ideas; pulls them together; links activities of various members.
8. Orienter	Defines position of group with respect to their goals.
9. Evaluator–critic	Measures group achievements against standards.
10. Energizer	Stimulates group into action when interest sags.
11. Procedural technician	Does routine tasks for the group.
12. Recorder	Writes down suggestions.
	Group building and maintenance roles
13. Encourager	Praises and encourages others.
14. Harmonizer	Mediates in group conflicts.
15. Compromiser	Within a conflict situation, offers compromise by yielding status, admitting error.
16. Gatekeeper and expediter	Keeps communication channel open between members and suggests ways to help group operate more smoothly.
17. Standard setter	Expresses standards for the group to strive for, evaluates process using these.
18. Group observer and commentator	Keeps records of group process allowing group to evaluate its own procedures.
19. Follower	Goes along with the movement of the group passively, accepting the ideas of others and serving as their audience.
	Individual roles
20. Aggressor	Jokes aggressively, attacks group's problem.
21. Blocker	Acts stubbornly and resists group.
22. Recognition seeker	Tries to call attention to him/herself by boasting, etc.
23. Self-confessor	Uses audience to express personal feelings, insights or ideology.
24. Playboy	Displays lack of involvement through cynicism, nonchalance.
25. Dominator	Asserts authority or superiority by manipulating group or certain members of it.
26. Help seeker	Seeks sympathetic response by expressing insecurity, confusion or self-deprecation.
27. Special interest pleader	Cloaks own prejudices or biases in stereotype that best fits their need.

Based on Kenneth Benne and Paul Sheats, 'Functional roles of group members', *Journal of Social Issues*, 1948, vol.4, pp.41–9.

Group member roles

Within a group activity, such as a staff meeting or a tutorial discussion, some people will show a consistent preference for certain behaviours and not for others. The particular behaviour or set of behaviours that a person demonstrates in a group can lead them to be seen to be playing a particular role within the group. Bales showed that individuals adopted specific roles within their groups. Kenneth Benne and Paul Sheats, who distinguished the roles that were played by members of a group, developed Bales' work. They distinguished a total of 27 different group roles, which are shown in table 10.2.

Looking at that table, one sees that Benne and Sheats grouped their 27 roles under three main headings. The first of these was *group task roles,* which are principally directed towards achieving the group's task. The second heading, *group maintenance building and roles,* is concerned primarily with establishing and sustaining good relations between individual members so as to ensure the group as a whole can work together. Both of these categories of roles help the group to achieve its objective. In contrast, the third category, *individual roles,* impedes the group's efforts to achieve its aims. This distinction between behaviour that is oriented towards achieving the task and behaviour that is focused upon individuals was originally made in the 1940s and 1950s. It has become the foundation for many subsequent teamwork theories and training, and has also laid the foundation for many theories of leadership [**link**, chapter 21, leadership].

Following Benne and Sheats' list of 27 roles, many writers offered their own lists of team roles or team player roles, which vary in number from four to fifteen (Davis *et al.,* 1992; Margerison and McCann, 1990; Parker, 1990; Spencer and Pruss, 1992; and Woodcock, 1989). All proponents of the team role concept claim to have observed the behaviours typical of that role being manifested in a variety of teams in different organizations.

Belbin's team role theory

Team role refers to an individual's tendency to behave in particularly preferred ways which contribute to and interrelate with other members within a team.

A very popular and widely used framework for understanding roles within a group or team was developed by Meredith Belbin and his colleagues in the late 1970s (Belbin, 1981; 1993a; 1996). It was derived from observations that he conducted of general managers on training courses at the Administrative Staff College, Henley. These managers completed a number of personality assessments (e.g. 16PF personality inventory) before participating in a team simulation exercise. Belbin observed their behaviour during the exercise using Bales' IPA. From the information obtained, he produced a self-report questionnaire known as the Belbin Team Role Self-perception Inventory (team role questionnaire) and distinguished nine (originally eight) team roles. Each **team role** is listed and defined in figure 10.7.

Belbin argued that:

R. Meredith Belbin
(b. 1926)

1. Within an organization people are generally appointed to a functional role on the basis of their ability or experience, e.g. marketing. They are rarely selected for personal characteristics that would fit them to perform

roles and descriptions – team role contribution	allowable weaknesses
 **Plant** Creative, imaginative, unorthodox. Solves difficult problems.	Ignores details. Too preoccupied to communicate effectively.
 **Resource investigator** Extrovert, enthusiastic, communicative. Explores opportunities. Develops contacts.	Over-optimistic. Loses interest once initial enthusiasm has passed.
 **Co-ordinator** Mature, confident, a good chairperson. Clarifies goals, promotes decision making, delegates well.	Can be seen as manipulative. Delegates personal work.
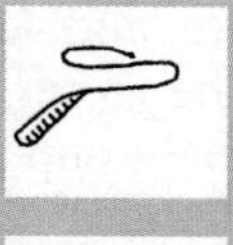 **Shaper** Challenging, dynamic, thrives on pressure. Has the drive and courage to overcome obstacles.	Can provoke others. Hurts people's feelings.
 **Monitor–evaluator** Sober, strategic and discerning. Sees all options. Judges accurately.	Lacks drive and ability to inspire others. Overly critical.
 **Teamworker** Co-operative, mild, perceptive and diplomatic. Listens, builds, averts friction, calms the waters.	Indecisive in crunch situations. Can be easily influenced.
 **Implementer** Disciplined, reliable, conservative and efficient. Turns ideas into practical actions.	Somewhat inflexible. Slow to respond to new possibilities.
 **Completer** Painstaking, conscientious, anxious. Searches out errors and omissions. Delivers on time.	Inclined to worry unduly. Reluctant to delegate. Can be a nit-picker.
 **Specialist** Single-minded, self-starting, dedicated. Provides knowledge and skills in rare supply.	Contributes on only a narrow front. Dwells on technicalities. Overlooks the 'big picture'.

Strength of contribution in any one of the roles is commonly associated with particular weaknesses. These are called allowable weaknesses. Executives are seldom strong in all nine team roles.

Figure 10.7: Belbin's nine team roles
From R. Meredith Belbin, *The Coming Shape of Organization*, Butterworth Heinemann, 1996, p.122.

additional tasks within a team. In an ideal world, a person's functional role and their team would coincide.

2. The personal characteristics of an individual fit them for some roles within a team while limiting the likelihood that they will be successful in other roles. For Belbin, therefore, team roles are individual preferences based on personality, and not the expectations of others as discussed earlier in this chapter with respect to social role.

3. Individuals tend to adopt one or two team roles fairly consistently.

4. Which roles individuals prefer or are naturally inclined towards can be predicted through personality assessments and the team role questionnaire, which identifies an individual's preferences.

5. In an ideal ('dream') team, all the necessary roles are represented, and the preferred roles of members complement each other, thereby avoiding 'gaps'.

This does not mean that every team has to consist of nine people. A single member can 'double up' and play several roles, thereby enabling the overall size of the team to be reduced.

6. The assessment, selection, placement and guidance of individual employees by management are the key tools for improving team effectiveness. Once management knows employees' team role preferences, it can use them to compose teams in which all the required role preferences are represented.

Stop and criticize

Many TV serials about the police, hospitals, people sharing a flat, etc., depict individuals operating as part of a group or team. Many children's novels also recount the ventures of a gang, e.g. *Famous Five*. Select a TV or book series and identify which character is most closely depicted as playing which of Belbin's team roles.

- How easy or difficult was it for you to determine their team role preferences through observing or reading about their behaviour?

- If you needed each of your characters to complete a Belbin team role questionnaire, to what extent could you trust the scores that you obtained from them? Why?

Critique of team role theory

Because of its widespread popularity and use, Belbin's theory has been extensively researched and continues to receive a great deal of critical assessment (Fisher *et al.*, 1996; 1997; 1998; Hayes, 1997; Senior, 1997; Manning, 1997; Broucek and Randell 1996; Dulewicz, 1995; Furnham *et al.*, 1993a; 1993b; Belbin, 1993b). The main criticisms of the theory are summarized below. Writers variously claim that:

- There is little empirical evidence to support his theory and that it is difficult to devise measures of team success that can be related objectively to team composition. It is difficult to say that a given team succeeded because it possessed all nine roles or failed because it lacked some of them.

- The questionnaire is based on respondents' self-reporting. Self-perceptions are a poor basis upon which to select team members. A more objective measure might be obtained through the use of peer ratings and an established personality assessment questionnaire.

- The questions are vague and inconsistent, and potentially open to creating misunderstandings. The more experience respondents have of working in diverse teams, the more unreliable the results are likely to be.

- The team role profiles derived from forced-choice personality and adjective checklists do not allow for a sufficiently detailed exploration of role-related issues. There is a difference between assessing an individual's potential to play various team roles and the actuality, which is influenced by their degree of autonomy in, and commitment to, those roles.

- How individuals see their team roles is influenced as much by the roles that they habitually play, especially in teams, and what is expected of them in such roles. Thus the questionnaire scores reflect not only an individual's personality traits but also their social learning of roles [**link**, chapter 4, learning: cognitive approach].

- The theory takes an excessively psychological perspective on role, neglecting the sociological dimension of the social position they habitually adopt, and on what is expected of them in such positions by others.

- The questions in the Belbin self-completion questionnaire describe vague situations. Some of them do not mention teams at all. Individuals behave differently in different circumstances and in different groups, e.g. project team at work, in the family at home, so specification of team context of behaviour is essential.

- The theory does not sufficiently take into account differences in the type of task that the team is being asked to perform. Additive, conjunctive and disjunctive tasks may require different combinations of team roles to achieve success [**link**, chapter 9, group formation].

- The theory underplays the impact of wider environmental factors. For example, team performance may be impeded by limited company resources.

- Performance is affected by a variety of different factors such as strategy and leadership, structure and management style and interpersonal skills. Focusing exclusively on team composition leads to ignoring these other critical factors.

- The concepts of team role and personality have become intertwined, being treated as interchangeable rather than as separate but interrelated. Team roles and individual personality differences have been insufficiently related.

Stop and criticize

You and your fellow team members have completed the Belbin Team Role Self-perception Inventory and been supplied with the results and analysis. You now know your individual role preferences, and your team knows which roles are over-represented and under-represented within it.

- How do you exploit the information about yourself?

- Can the team compensate by asking its members to switch to their second or third preferences. What might be the issues involved?

Leadership structure

There are many jobs to be done in a group if it is to be both productive and satisfying for its members. The emergence of a leader within any group is a function of its structure. Usually, a group makes a leader of the person who has some special capacity for coping with the group's particular problems. They may possess physical strength, shrewdness, or some other relevant attribute. The leader and the members all play roles in the group. Through them, a group atmosphere is created which enables communication, influence, and decision making to occur. In much of the management literature, leadership is considered exclusively as a management prerogative. Authors write about 'management style' rather than 'leadership style'. This material will be dealt with in a later chapter [**link**, chapter 21, leadership].

It has been found that the type of leadership exercised affects group performance and member satisfaction. Activities are performed and actions are taken by the leader. There has been an increasing interest in **group leadership** as opposed to individual leadership. One can distinguish between a leader and acts of leadership. If we accept Raymond Cattell's (1951) view that the leader is any group member who is capable of modifying the properties of the group by their presence, then we can acknowledge that any member of the group can perform acts of leadership, and not just a single, designated individual. The group leadership approach considers the characteristics of small groups, seeking to understand the organizational context in which they exist and the objectives that they seek to achieve. It seems more useful therefore to view leadership as a set of behaviours

Group leadership refers to the performance of those acts which help the group achieve its objectives.

that change their nature depending on circumstances, and which switch or rotate between group members as circumstances change, rather than a static status associated with a single individual.

The relationship between the group's leader, at a given point in time, and the followers may be thought of as one of social exchange. The leader provides rewards for the group by helping its members to achieve their own and the group's goals. They in turn reward the leader by giving the individual heightened status and increased influence. However, members can rescind that influence at any time if they feel that the leader is no longer worthy of their respect. Viewed as a social exchange process, leaders have power in terms of their ability to influence the behaviour of those around them. Nevertheless, it is the group members who give the leader the power to influence them.

Group atmosphere and leadership style

Task leaders in groups do not all perform their roles in exactly the same way. They use different approaches, which have different effects on group members' performance and satisfaction. One of the most famous of leadership studies was carried out by Kurt Lewin, Ralph White and Ronald Lippitt. Beginning in 1938, a series of studies designed to investigate group functioning under experimentally induced group atmospheres or social climates were carried out under the general direction of Lewin, and continued throughout the 1950s. One major study in the series was conducted at the Iowa Child Welfare Research Station by White and Lippitt.

Kurt Lewin
(1890–1947)

Ronald O. Lippitt
(1914–86)

It involved four groups of ten-year-old boys operating in a natural setting. Each group was a genuine hobby club that met after school and comprised five members. Each group's members had been matched on characteristics such as age, personality, IQ, and physical and socio-economic status, to be as similar as possible. Four adult leaders were trained to proficiency in the three leadership styles (see below), and shifted from club to club every six weeks. The clubs met in the same place and engaged in similar activities (arts and crafts, primarily the making of masks) with similar materials. The characteristics of each leadership style are as follows:

Authoritarian leadership: The primarily focus was upon achievement. The leader gave orders, praised or criticized the boys without giving reasons. He behaved in a distant and impersonal way, discouraging communication between the boys themselves.

Democratic leadership: The primary focus was on the boys' choice. When the leader made comments, he explained them. He used discussions to help the boys plan their projects; allowed them to choose their own work mates; and permitted them to communicate freely with each another. He also participated in the group activities himself.

Laissez-faire leadership: The primary emphasis was minimal involvement. The leader left the boys to themselves; only gave advice and help when directly asked; and provided no praise, blame or any other comments.

The researchers found that the autocratic leadership style led to high productivity, but only in the presence of the leader. It also created an aggressive but dependent atmosphere among the boys. The democratic leadership style led to relatively high productivity; to the boys liking of their leaders most; the creation of a friendly atmosphere; and the boys proceeding with their work, irrespective of the presence or absence of the leader. The *laissez-faire* leadership style led to low productivity, which only increased when the leader was present. It created a friendly but play-oriented atmosphere.

Based on Ralph White and Ronald Lippitt, *Autocracy and Democracy*, Harper & Row, New York, 1960.

One group, two leaders

When people think of leadership, they usually imagine a single person. Robert Bales and Philip Slater used a laboratory research design with which to study the patterns of leadership that emerged in small, unstructured groups. The subjects of the study were fourteen separate groups of Harvard University undergraduates, each consisting of between three and six men. They were selected so that they were strangers to each other, and were paid to spend one hour a day solving an administrative case study problem that they were supplied with. Their interactions were recorded and analysed in terms of Bales' twelve categories.

Source: Robert F. Bales

The researchers found that at the end of the first day, the group member whom the others rated as having the best ideas, that is, who was most helpful in moving the group towards a solution, was also rated as the most liked. However, after the first day, this person's equally high rating for best ideas *and* most liked dropped sharply.

From then on, two leaders seemed to emerge. One was the *task leader,* who specialized in making suggestions, giving information, expressing opinions and generally contributing most to helping the group achieve its objective. The second to emerge was the *socio-emotional leader,* who helped other group members to state their ideas, expressed positive feelings towards them, made jokes, and released tensions in the group. The socio-emotional leader generally acted to maintain the group as a functioning entity.

Bales and Slater thus discovered that leadership in a group split into two. Although there was some rivalry, the two group leaders, *task* and *socio-emotional,* typically co-operated and worked together well. Beyond the laboratory situation, such division of leadership can be seen in families when one parent assumes task leadership while the other deals with socio-emotional issues.

The researchers discovered that a split in leadership only occurred after the task leader had been identified and agreed upon. They argued that it was only after the group knew who would lead it to achieve its external goals that it could afford the luxury of a socio-emotional leader. Thus, the researchers did not view leadership as a single role but as applying to several roles within the group. A well-organized group, in which the leadership functions were being satisfactorily performed, would have both a task leader and a social-emotional leader.

Based on Robert F. Bales and Philip E. Slater, 'Role differentiation in small group decision-making groups', in T. Parsons, and R.F. Bales (eds), *Family, Socialization and Interaction*, Routledge, London, 1956, pp.259–306.

Structure and process in globally dispersed teams

The concept of the much discussed 'virtual organization' has been operationalized in the formation of globally distributed teams (GDTs) by multinational companies. The management of these does pose a challenge to the organization. GDTs consist of members located in different countries who have specific, short-duration project objectives to achieve. Moreover, they are prevented from travelling to meet face to face due to time and other resource pressures. Instead, they work separately and use electronic technology, including video conferencing, to hold meetings. Miller *et al.* (1996) considered four main issues with respect to GDT performance. These were objectives, technology, motivation and power.

Objectives

On the question of objectives, the authors stressed the importance of carefully balancing the content and process issues. These concepts were introduced and described at the start of this chapter. On the group content (task) side, they stressed the importance of negotiating and agreeing what is to be achieved by the team at the outset, since the process (interaction) issues, in this case technological ones, created unexpected problems. Distributed teams appeared to need to restate their unifying purpose at every opportunity, in order to avoid losing direction. This is a common problem in all teams but is exacerbated in GDTs.

Technology

With respect to technology, meeting through video conferencing rather than face to face changes the way in which group members interact. It emphasizes just how crucial the process dimension is for any form of successful team functioning. On the technological side, voice-activated cameras in video conferences focus on the person speaking the loudest. This causes problems when more than one person is speaking at a time. Interrupting the speaker, a common and easily managed feature of face-to-face interactions, causes a serious problem during such GDT meetings, as does passing data around, such as spreadsheets. While much effort was devoted to running the technological process of video conferencing, the researchers found little value-added output and suggested that e-mail, fax or telephone would achieve as much as less cost.

Motivation and performance

Turning next to the question of motivation and performance. Miller *et al.* found that as expected, managers had difficulty motivating people at a distance. Moreover, the chairperson found it difficult to assess the contribution of individual members at remote sites, who could more easily hide their limited input. This stresses the importance of establishing objectives, standards and deadlines at the start.

Power

The authors reported that the technology had an important impact on the exercise of power within the organization structure. Specifically, it hid the commonly observed sources of individual power within an organization and created a more organic and egalitarian form of company structure which appeared to change shape in response to the issues discussed, rather than being fixed by top management. This in turn had three consequences:

1. It made the transfer of responsibility between group members more of a problem.
2. It led to group members considering themselves as more equal. This could either encourage them to contribute more, unencumbered by group pressure, or it could reduce their need to participate and allow them to remain silent more easily.
3. It constantly changed the leadership role within the group, which moved not only between different group members but also from one geographical location to another. The cause of this was the absence of organizational indicators of individual group member's power, which, within face-to-face teams, constrains such changes in leader role taking. The researchers felt that such leadership switching could be dysfunctional for achieving the group task since it wasted time and encouraged 'power posturing'.

Physically dispersed and technologically integrated GDTs are likely to increase in number in the future. As yet, multinational companies have not discovered an effective way of managing them.

Based on P. Miller, J.M. Pons and P. Naude, 'Global teams', *Financial Times*, 14 June 1996, p.12.

Contemporary team structure

The original theoretical developments in the area of group structure and process occurred between the 1930s and 1950s. Many were conducted in non-organizational contexts and frequently involved children and university students. Their findings were then applied to companies. The more recent developments have been practical rather than theoretical. They have been accompanied by a linguistic change within the research and management literature, where the predominant term is now 'team' rather than 'group' [**link**, chapter 9, group formation: groups and teams]. While Western companies may have been reluctant formally to structure their organizations around groups, they have been prepared to train their managerial and technical staff to work more effectively in teams. Thus, team-building or team-development activities have established themselves as a major element in both management training and organization development (OD) activities [**link**, chapter 17, organization development].

illustration by Steven Appleby

Recap

1. *List the six dimensions of group structure.*
   - The six main dimensions along which the members of a group differ are power, status, liking, communication, role and leadership. A person may be placed high on one dimension and simultaneously low on another.
   - The group's structure acts to increase the predictability of behaviour between the group's members.

2. *Identify the sources of power within the group.*
   - There are five bases or types of power—reward, coercive, referent, legitimate and expert.

3. *Distinguish between two common uses of the concept of status.*
   - The status structure of a group is determined by how much status an individual member possesses. There is formal status and social status.

4. *Understand how emotional relationships within a group can be represented symbolically.*
   - The liking (emotional) structure of a group is revealed through the use of sociometry, a technique developed by Jacob Moreno.

5. *Distinguish between communication pattern analysis, communication network analysis and IPA analysis.*
   - Communication pattern analysis of a group maps the direction and quantity of verbal communication in a group. It is depicted on a communigram.
   - Communication network analysis analyses documents, data and voice mail transmission to determine the source, direction and quantity of both verbal and written communication between the dispersed members of a group. It is depicted as a 'chain', 'Y', 'wheel', 'circle' or 'all channel'.

- Interpersonal process analysis (IPA) classifies the content of verbal communications between group members. It was developed by Robert Bales.

6. *Distinguish between task, socio-emotional and individual classes of roles within a group.*
   - The role structure of a group can differentiate those members who perform task-focused roles, relations-oriented roles and self-oriented roles. This distinction was made by Benne and Sheats.

7. *Distinguish Belbin's team roles.*
   - Meredith Belbin's team role theory distinguishes the roles played by the members of a team. They are plant, resource investigator, co-ordinator, shaper, monitor–evaluator, teamworker, implementer, completer and specialist.

8. *Give examples of three leadership styles identified by White and Lippitt.*
   - White and Lippitt distinguished three leadership styles, which they labelled authoritarian, democratic and *laissez-faire*.

9. *Distinguish between a task and a socio-emotional group leader.*
   - Bales and Slater suggested that groups often have a task leader and a socio-emotional leader. The first drove the group towards task achievement; the second maintained the group as a co-operative working unit.

Revision

1. Group members may possess as much power as the group leader. Give examples of the kind of power possessed, and suggest how it can help or hinder group performance.

2. Select any two techniques for measuring some aspect of a group's structure (e.g. power, communication, liking, roles, leadership). List and define three criteria on which they could be compared. Then contrast your two chosen techniques using your three criteria.

3. Describe situations in which a (a) team role analysis and (b) a sociogram would be relevant to improving group functioning. How would you apply these two techniques? How would you use the results?

4. What are the strengths and weaknesses of Belbin's team role theory as a guide for the manager wishing to construct a team that will be effective?

5. What are some of the problems that a new leader of a group faces? How can they be overcome?

Springboard

Belbin, R.M., 1981, *Management Teams: Why They Succeed or Fail*, Heinemann, London.

This is the original work on team role theory, which explains each role in great depth.

Brotherton, C., 1999, *Social Psychology and Management*, Open University Press, Buckingham.

Written from a social psychological perspective, this text considers how the discipline can benefit from considering the contexts in which management is exercised.

Brown, R., 2000, *Group Processes*, Blackwell, Oxford.

Provides a recent review and assessment of the theory and research on group processes.

Furnham, A., Steele, H. and Pendleton, D., 1993, 'A psychometric assessment of Belbin's team role self-perception inventory', *Journal of Occupational and Organizational Psychology*, vol.66, pp.245–57.

Senior, B, 1997, 'Team roles and team performance: Is there "really" a link?' *Journal of Occupational and Organizational Psychology*, vol.70, pp.241–58.

Two empirical studies critically evaluating Belbin's team role theory.

Hayes, N., 1997, *Successful Team Management*, Thompson Business Press.

A book which blends past and present academic research and theory on groups and teams and offers practical recommendations for improving team performance.

Parkinson, M., 1999, *Using Psychology in Business*, Gower, Aldershot.

Taking a practical approach, this book considers what psychology has to offer business. It draws upon the theories and techniques that have been applied in a variety of organizational contexts.

Turniansky, B. and Hare, A.P., 1998, *Individuals and Groups in Organizations*, Sage, London.

Offers a range of approaches for looking at the way in which people interact with organizational life. It considers the individual in the group; the group in the organization; and the organization in the environment.

Wheelan, S.A., 1999, *Creating Effective Work Teams*, Sage, London.

Using a version of the Tuckman and Jensen framework, the author offers a range of strategies for building and supporting well-managed, high-performing teams. The book is more of a practical guide than a theoretical discourse.

Home viewing

The film *Aliens* (1986, director James Cameron) is a science fiction thriller set in the distant future on the planet LV-426. It is the sequel to the film *Alien*, in which the crew of the spaceship *Nostromo* is plagued by a creature which is described as a 'pure killing machine'. The lone survivor of this encounter, Ellen Ripley (Sigourney Weaver), spends 57 years in suspended animation drifting through space. After returning to Earth, she reluctantly agrees to return to LV-426 because contact has been lost with the colonists who settled there.

The first part of the film begins with Ripley's return to Earth and ends with the space marines' landing-craft crashing onto the planet's surface, leaving the investigation party marooned on the planet. The characters featured in this segment include Lieutenant Gorman, the senior officer of the space marines, Sergeant Apone and Corporal Hicks. Other individuals identified by name are Vasquez and Hudson. In addition to these military personnel, there is Burke, who represents the Weyland-Yutani Corporation (motto: 'Building Better Worlds'). This company built and owns the facilities on planet LV-426 and employs Ripley.

As you watch this first sequence of the film, use French and Raven's five power-base classification to decide which of the seven aforementioned characters possesses which types of power within the group. Also assess who gains and who loses what type of power? How does this happen? What does this tell us about the power in an organization in general, and the power structure of a group in particular?

OB in literature

William Golding, *Lord of the Flies*, Faber & Faber, London, 1954.

In this novel (also a film), a party of schoolboys is marooned following a plane crash. They form a society-in-microcosm. What group norms and sanctions develop? What aspects of group structure, group power and conflict are illustrated?

J.G. Ballard, *Cocaine Nights*, Flamingo/HarperCollins, London, 1996.

What social psychological theory of group cohesion is illustrated by the events and characters in this novel? Does your personal experience confirm this?

Chapter exercises

1: Tutorial pie

Objectives

1. To distinguish between different dimensions of group structure.
2. To analyse the structure of one group on a given dimension.

Background
Group structure can be a somewhat abstract concept, yet each person who is a member of a group, automatically and unconsciously rates the other members on the basis of some criteria. Having done so, they then interact with them accordingly. This rating or ranking of group members is at the heart of the concept of group structure. However, there is a misconception that a group can only have one structure. In reality, there are a number of different but simultaneous ranking systems operating within any group, and a person high on one ranking scale may be low on another.

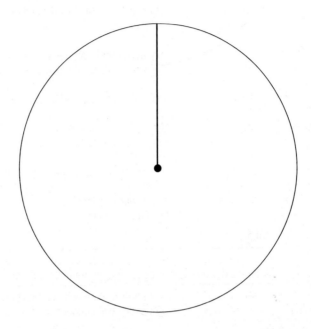

Briefing
Imagine that the circle below is a pie-chart which represents the members of your tutorial or syndicate group, and which accompanies this course. This group is scheduled to meet several times a semester or term, and you will have already participated in some of the group's discussions.

Divide the pie into slices—one for each of the member of your tutorial group. Be sure to include a slice for yourself, and for the group's tutor. The size of each slice should represent each person's contribution to the class. Label each slice by inserting the individual's name or initials. Having done this, form a pair with the person sitting next to you. Take turns to explain your division of your pie-chart to them. Your explanation should focus on the following four questions:

- What criteria did you use to decide on the size of each person's 'contribution slice' to the tutorial class?

- Describe the way in which you divided up the pie.

- Which three people did you give the largest slices to?

- How did you evaluate yourself in relation to the others in your tutorial group?

2: Belbin's team role questionnaire

Objectives
1. To introduce Belbin's team role theory.

2. To identify your preferred team roles.

Background
Before coming to class, complete the questionnaire below. For each section, distribute a total of <u>ten points</u> among the sentences which you think best describe your behaviour. The points may be distributed among several sentences: in extreme cases they might be spread among all the sentences or ten points may be given to a single sentence. Enter the points alongside each sentence in the space provided.

I What I believe I can contribute to a team:

(a)   I think I can quickly see and take advantage of opportunities.

(b)   I can work well with a very wide range of people.

(c)   I can usually sense what is realistic and likely to work.

(d)   My capacity to follow through has much to do with my personal effectiveness.

(e)   My ability rests on being able to draw people out whenever I detect they have something of value to contribute to group activities.

(f)   My technical knowledge and experience are usually my major asset.

(g)   I can offer a reasoned case for alternative courses of action without introducing bias or prejudice.

(h)   Producing ideas is one of my natural assets.

(i)   I am ready to face temporary unpopularity if it leads to worthwhile results in the end.

Total   10

II If I have a possible shortcoming in teamwork, it could be that:

(a)   I am not at ease unless meetings are well structured and controlled and generally well conducted.

(b)   My objective outlook makes it difficult for me to join in readily and enthusiastically with colleagues.

(c)   I find it difficult to lead from the front, perhaps because I am over-responsive to group atmosphere.

(d)   I am apt to get too caught up in ideas that occur to me and so lose track of what is happening.

(e)   My colleagues tend to see me as worrying unnecessarily over detail and the possibility that things may go wrong.

(f)   I am sometimes seen as forceful and authoritarian if there is a need to get something done.

(g)   I am inclined to be too generous towards others who have a valid viewpoint that has not been given a proper airing.

(h)   I am reluctant to contribute, unless the subject being discussed deals with an area I know well.

(i)   I have a tendency to talk too much once the group gets on to new ideas.

Total   10

III When involved in a project with other people:

(a)	I can be counted on to contribute something original.
(b)	My general vigilance prevents careless mistakes and omissions being made.
(c)	I have an aptitude for influencing people without pressuring them.
(d)	I am keen to look for the latest in new ideas and developments.
(e)	I try to maintain my sense of professionalism.
(f)	I believe that my capacity for judgements can help to bring about the right decisions.
(g)	I am always ready to back a good suggestion in the common interest.
(h)	I am ready to press for action to make sure that the meeting does not waste time or lose sight of the main objective.
(i)	I can be relied upon to see that all essential work is organized.

Total   10

IV My characteristic approach to group work is that:

(a)	I have a quiet interest in getting to know colleagues better.
(b)	While I am interested in all views, I have no hesitation in making up my mind once a decision has to be made.
(c)	I am not reluctant to challenge the views of others or to hold a minority view myself.
(d)	I think I have a talent for making things work once a plan has to be put into operation.
(e)	I have a tendency to avoid the obvious and come out with the unexpected.
(f)	I am ready to make use of contacts outside of the group itself.
(g)	I bring a touch of perfectionism to any job I undertake.
(h)	I can usually find a line of argument to refute unsound propositions.
(i)	I contribute where I know what I'm talking about.

Total   10

V I gain satisfaction in a job because:

(a)	I enjoy analysing situations and weighing up all the possible choices.
(b)	I feel that that I am using my special qualifications and training to advantage.
(c)	I like to find a field that stretches my imagination.
(d)	I feel in my element when I can give a task my full attention.
(e)	I am interested in finding practical solutions to problems.
(f)	I like to feel I am fostering good working relationships.
(g)	I can meet people who may have something new to offer.
(h)	I can get people to agree on a necessary course of action.
(i)	I can have a strong influence on decisions.

Total   10

VI If I am suddenly given a difficult task with limited time and unfamiliar people:

(a)	I tend to read up as much as I conveniently can on the subject.
(b)	I would retain a steadiness of purpose in spite of the pressures.
(c)	I would open up discussions with a view to stimulating new thoughts and getting something moving.
(d)	I believe that I would keep cool and maintain my capacity to think straight.
(e)	I would find some way of reducing the size of the task by establishing what different individuals might best contribute.
(f)	I would feel like retiring to a corner to devise a way out of the impasse before developing a line.
(g)	I would be prepared to take a positive lead if I felt the group was making no progress.
(h)	My natural sense of urgency would help ensure that we did not fall behind schedule.
(i)	I would be ready to work with the person who showed the most positive approach.

Total   10

VII With reference to the problems to which I am subject in working in groups:

(a)	I am apt to show my impatience with those who are obstructing progress.
(b)	I hesitate to get my points across when I run up against real opposition.
(c)	I am inclined to feel I am wasting my time and would do better on my own.
(d)	I am conscious of demanding from others the things I cannot do myself.
(e)	I tend to get bored rather easily and rely on one or two stimulating members to spark me off.
(f)	My desire to ensure that work is properly done can hold up proceedings.
(g)	Others may criticize me for being too analytical and insufficiently intuitive.
(h)	I find it difficult to get started unless the goals are clear.
(i)	I am sometimes poor at explaining and clarifying complex points that occur to me.

Total   10

Score the questionnaire by transferring your scores into the spaces below, and then summing up the totals for each of the nine columns.

Part	IM	CO	SH	PL	RI	ME	TW	CF	SP	Total
I	c	e	i	h	a	g	b	d	f	= 10
II	a	g	f	d	i	b	c	e	h	= 10
III	i	c	h	a	d	f	g	b	e	= 10
IV	d	b	c	e	f	h	a	g	i	= 10
V	e	h	i	c	g	a	f	d	b	= 10
VI	b	e	g	f	c	d	i	h	a	= 10
VII	h	d	a	i	e	g	b	f	c	= 10
Total										= 70
	Implementor	Co-ordinator	Shaper	Plant	Resource Investigator	Monitor–Evaluator	Team Worker	Completer	Specialist	

Briefing

Divide into groups of four to five.

1. Remind yourself of each of Belbin's nine team roles.

2. Compare and contrast your own team role scores with those of the other members of your group.

3. Reflect on your experiences of participation in teams in the past. How well do these scores reflect your preferred team roles?

4. Decide to what extent your preferred team roles are a reflection of your personality.

5. Identify which roles in this team are preferred and which are avoided, rejected or missing? If this was a real management or project team, what could be done to cover the avoided or rejected roles?

Decide whether certain roles are more important in certain phases of a team's operation? For example, which two team roles are likely to be crucial in the getting-started phase of a team's work; the generating-ideas phase; the developing-the-ideas phase; and the implementing-the-decision phase?

Chapter 11 Individuals in groups

Key concepts

self-concept
social identity
self-esteem
social representations
shared frame of reference
social influence
synergy
social facilitation
social loafing
conversion

group norm
pivotal norms
peripheral norms
group sanction
group cohesion
group socialization
organizational socialization
deindividuation
compliance

Learning objectives

When you have read this chapter, you should be able to define those key concepts in
your own words, and you should also be able to:

1. Explain the basic tenets of social identity theory and social representation theory.

2. Distinguish between social facilitation and social loafing.

3. Understand why groups develop norms and use sanctions to regulate the behaviour
   of their members.

4. Understand the process of group socialization of individuals.

5. Explain why individuals conform to the dictates of their group.

6. Distinguish between compliance and conversion.

Why study individuals in groups?

For the individual, group membership has benefits in the form of satisfaction of
some psychological needs. However, there are costs to the individual group
member in the form of their reduced freedom of action. William Foote Whyte
(1955, p.331) wrote that:

> The group is a jealous master. It encourages participation, indeed it demands it,
> but it demands one kind of participation—its own kind and the better inte-
> grated with it a member becomes the less free he is to express himself in other
> ways.

There are also costs in terms of possible negative mental consequences for the individual member, as Marion Hampton (1999, p.113) explains:

> Yet groups are also endowed with a darker side, one which is highlighted in mobs and crowds. They are seen as taking over the individual's mind, depressing intelligence, eliminating moral responsibility and forcing conformity. They can cause their members a great deal of suffering and despair and can perpetuate acts of great cruelty. If groups are capable of great deeds, they are also capable of great follies.

There is now extensive research evidence which demonstrates the power of groups to affect the behaviour of their individual members. This was originally revealed in the research conducted by Elton Mayo at the Hawthorne plant in the 1920s [link, chapter 9, group formation]. Since that time, managements have harnessed this power by creating groups and teams which police and discipline their own members, keeping their behaviour in line with organizational (management) objectives. The most developed form of such management-initiated group control is to be found in the Japanese teamworking which will be described in the next chapter [link, chapter 12, teamworking]. However, this chapter introduces the basic concepts of group norms, socialization and sanctions, and reports some research from an American multinational plant in Scotland.

The power of the group to affect the perceptions, performance and attitudes of its individual members is well established. However, since the 1980s, there has also been a growing body of research that shows how a lone individual can have an influence on a majority. The two concepts of conformity and conversion have generated a great deal of interest in this field.

Stop and criticize

Think of three things that you do alone that you would not do if someone else was with you at work.

• Why would you not do these things in the presence of others?

• What would be the consequences in each case if you did?

Is such self-control to the benefit of yourself, your employer or both? Explain how.

The individual and the group

Henri Tajfel and John Turner (1986) argue that as long as individuals see themselves as more important than the group, then the latter cannot function effectively. Their formulation takes Tuckman and Jensen's group development stages model a great step further [link, chapter 9, group formation]. Tuckman and Jensen proposed that a new group passed through the stages of *forming, storming* and *norming* before reaching the most productive phase of *performing*, before finally *adjourning*. Tajfel and Turner maintain that in order to achieve this, individuals have to stop seeing themselves as individuals and instead identify themselves as group members, treating the team's values as their own.

Such an individual attitudinal 'switch' and commitment facilitates the long-term existence and success of the group. This question of how much an individual should be part of the group (for their own well-being, for that of their group and organization) and how much separate from it (to remain creative, critical and for their own mental health) is a continuing debate in the literature.

Integration in the Borg

In the TV and film series *Star Trek*, the Federation comes up against its most powerful adversary, the Borg, a collective species with no distinct individuals. Part human and part machine, they seek to transform all other species into Borg, ending their will to resist by destroying their identities as individuals. In the story, Captain Picard and his crew realize that they are dealing not with an individual mind but with the collective minds of all the Borg. As a collective culture, the Borg have to continue consuming individuals in order to remain collective. The Borg threaten to multiply and spell the end of human individuality. Picard asks them what their objective is, to which they reply, 'We wish to improve ourselves'.

Based on Thomas Richards, *Star Trek in Myth and Legend*, Orion Books, London, 1997.

Let us first consider some theories which seek to explain the relation between the individual and their group. **Social identity** (or identification) theory was developed by Tajfel and focuses on those aspects of our identity which derive from our group membership (Tajfel and Turner, 1986). It holds that the groups or social categories to which people belong (e.g. student, manager, solicitor, parent or sports club secretary) are an integral part of their **self-concept [link**, chapter 5, personality].

That part of their self-concept which comes from their membership of a group is called social identity. Social identity fulfils two functions. First, it defines and evaluates a person (e.g. 'she's a member of the design team'). Such definition and evaluation is done both by others and by the person themselves. Second, it prescribes appropriate behaviour for them. They think and behave in characteristically 'design team' ways.

The way that this happens is based on social comparison. According to Tajfel, in order to evaluate their own opinions and abilities, individuals not only compare themselves with other individuals with whom they interact but also compare their own group with similar, but distinct, out-groups. The dimensions that are used to make these comparisons are called social categorizations. Categorization leads to assumptions of similarity among those who are categorized together. It minimizes the perceived differences between members of the in-group and maximizes the differences between the in-group and out-groups. The out-groups will tend to be stereotyped [**link**, chapter 7, perception]. When this happens, the individuals who are part of the in-group will have assumed social identity, and this represents the standpoint from which they will view other people.

We all see ourselves as members of various social groupings, which are distinguishable and hence different from other social groupings. The consequence is that by identifying with certain groupings but not others, we come to see the world in terms of 'us and them'. There are two benefits for us from this. First, our understanding of the world is enhanced by classifying everybody as either 'us' or 'them'. Second, our **self-esteem** can be maintained or even enhanced. Membership of a high-status group gives us prestige, which in turn raises our self-esteem. We are highly motivated to feel proud to belong to the group of which we are members. If we cannot achieve this feeling of pride, we will either try to

Self-concept refers to the way in which we view ourselves, and the set of perceptions that we have about ourselves.

Social identity refers to that part of the self-concept which comes from our membership of groups. It contributes to our self-esteem.

Self-esteem is the part of the self which is concerned with how we evaluate ourselves.

change the group's perceived status, or to detach ourselves from it. Although such social identification can potentially lead to conflict between different groups within an organization, it can also be effectively managed in a way that improves the performance of both groups.

Categorizing people into groups and identifying with some of these groups appears to be a fundamental human characteristic which derives from the fact that human beings are social animals. Because of these two basic needs for differentiating themselves from others and for belonging, individuals expose themselves to the control of others. Within the organizational context, we offer control to fellow group members who wish to direct our attitudes, thoughts and ideas in line with what the group considers appropriate; and also to managers who seek both to motivate and control us, through instituting various teamworking arrangements.

Stop and criticize

Which group memberships do you cite when you introduce yourself to others? From the 'us-and-them' perspective, who are 'us' and who are 'them', for you?

Has this helped your own group improve its performance? Has it raised your own self-esteem? Has the management in your organization used this distinction to motivate or control your group? How?

Group influences on individuals' perceptions

Social representations refer to the beliefs, ideas, values, objects, people and events that are constructed by current group members, and which are transmitted to its new members.

How does a group affect the perceptions of its individual members? One explanation is provided by social representations theory, which was formulated by Serge Moscovici (1984). This refers to the finding that when individuals join a new group, its members will construct and transmit complex and unfamiliar ideas to them in straightforward and familiar ways. This process creates what are termed **social representations**, which come to be accepted, in a modified form, by the new members of a group, and these help the new recruits to make sense of what is going on around them within the group and the organization. The explanation of some occurrence is simplified, distorted and ritualized by the group and becomes a 'common sense explanation', which is accepted as orthodoxy among its members and is then communicated to new members. Social representations are theories about how the world works and are used to justify actions.

At the start of the book, the social construction of reality perspective was introduced. This argued that our social and organizational surroundings possess no ultimate truth or reality but are determined instead by the way in which we experience and understand those worlds which we construct and reconstruct for ourselves, in interaction with others [link, chapter 1, prologue]. Among these important 'others' with whom we interact and with whom we experience and

In an exclusive ladies clothes shop in the centre of Glasgow, every day the sales staff had two meetings. The first of these followed their breakfast together. Before starting their shift, with managers present who brought a flipchart, sales staff met to discuss, as a group, their objectives for the day. The second meeting occurred at the end of the day when, once again as a group, they discussed what had happened and whether they had achieved their stated objectives.

Influencing perceptions – the Dutch admirals paradigm

Terrence Deal and Allen Kennedy defined a cabal as a group of two or more people who secretly joined together for mutual advantage, often to progress their careers within a company. The Dutch admirals paradigm holds that a cabal which establishes itself within a group can influence the perception of these people as to which members of the group members are high-fliers. The name comes from a story about two young officers from the Dutch Navy. They made a pact with each other that whenever one attended a naval social function, he would make a point of speaking in glowing terms about the merits of the other, and vice versa. This pact was revealed by them on the day they were both promoted to the rank of admiral and were the youngest naval personnel to achieve that position. Deal and Kennedy argued that their cabal had influenced the perceptions of senior naval and civil personnel who were influential in decisions concerning promotions. Thus, this was a case of 'believing was seeing' rather than of 'seeing was believing'. The message of the authors was that as long as one could positively influence the way that others perceived you (in relation to those around you), you would be able to rise in the organization hierarchy. The cabal was a crucial element in raising the estimation in which its members were held. This paradigm contradicts the well-known 'Peter principle' proposed by the late Laurence Peter, that people get promoted to their level of incompetence.

Based on Terrence E. Deal and Allen A. Kennedy, *Corporate Cultures*, Penguin Books, Harmondsworth, 1988, pp.95–6.

Shared frame of reference refers to a set of assumptions that are held in common by group members, which shape their thinking, decisions, actions and interactions, while being constantly defined and reinforced through those interactions.

understand the world, are the members of our psychological group. The prefix 'social' in both phrases reminds us about the collective way in which representations are created and accepted, and how they come to form a shared, manufactured reality.

As a new recruit, you discuss your role in the group with existing members. During these interactions, representations are presented, developed, adapted and negotiated before being incorporated into your own, existing, belief framework. This happens during the period of socialization, shortly after you join the group. It is not a matter of you, as a new recruit, being given and accepting a bundle of existing group assumptions, ideas, beliefs and opinions to absorb. Moscovici's theory emphasizes the interactive nature of the process between you as an individual, and the other group members. Once incorporated, the group representations are revealed in all members' speech and actions.

Through these social representations, group members gain a **shared frame of reference**. Over time, new joiners learn about the different assumptions, ideas, beliefs and opinions held by their fellow group members about their common work situation. Some agreement on perception and meaning is essential among the members of a group if they are to interact, communicate, agree on goals and generally act in concert on a common task. Such a shared view is essential for a group if it is to continue and develop. Moreover, as we work in groups we find that our views coalesce with those of other members of the group. A shared frame of reference and social representations suggest a group-level equivalent of the concept of organizational culture [link, chapter 19, organization culture]. Together, these determine the meaning that group members attach to events and other people's behaviour.

Group influences on individuals' performance

The presence of another person or a group of people changes our attitudes and behaviour. **Social influence** refers to the process where attitudes and behaviour are influenced by the real or implied presence of others. What type of student behaviour does the presence of a university invigilator in an examination hall

How the negotiators see it

A negotiating situation is therefore not merely one where two or more people discuss an issue. The people involved belong to groups (unions or management) and a conflict between individuals is always in addition a conflict between groups. Mr A does not just perceive himself as Mr A and perceive Mr B as Mr B, he perceives himself also as a union member and Mr B as a member of management—these groups as well as the individuals are in conflict. The ethos or culture of a management group is in many ways opposed to that of a shop-floor group. Management norms emphasize efficiency, rational efforts to increase productivity and profitability, the orderly conduct of affairs, and a general stress on individual self-advancement through promotion, social progress and approval from others. As people adopt the management reference group and spend their lives with other managers, they come to take this so much for granted that they often hardly notice the existence of the norms and the accompanying social pressures.

Similarly the manual worker may be unlikely to recognize how far his [sic] actions and feelings are socially determined and he will probably have only a limited conception of norms different from his own. The typical shop-floor culture is one which is also based upon approval from others (for we have seen that self-esteem through group membership is a basic ingredient of mental health), but here the approval goes to other kinds of behaviour than efficiency and striving for promotion. Efficiency can of course be valued as an individual sign of skill, and promotion can be desired, but prospects are in many cases severely limited. The norms of the manual worker's group are often likely to emphasize an interest in horse-racing or football, an ability to mend cars or television sets, skill at extracting loose piecework rates from management, being one of the lads who sticks up for his mates, and (in some areas) a concern for improving the lot of the working class. The worker, like the manager, aims for group respect or status, but his status is an informal one in the group whereas the manager's is more a formal placement in a hierarchy of positions. In both cases their status comes largely from conformity, but the norms to which they may conform are different ones.

From Peter Warr, *Psychology and Collective Bargaining*, Hutchinson, London, 1973, pp.15–16.

Multicultural perceptions

Increasing numbers of organizations create groups whose members are of different nationalities and ethnic backgrounds, in the hope of producing cross-cultural collaboration. These groups possess differences in language, culture and historical sensitivity. Kenwyn Smith and David Berg observed that every member of a newly formed multicultural group had their own understanding of how best to contribute to it so as to make it effective. These beliefs reflect the norms of their own culture. The authors found that expectations about how to contribute to the group's process varied along eight dimensions or 'polarities'. These are presented as questions to which individuals from different cultural backgrounds will have different answers:

1. *Confrontation v. conciliation*: When differences arise, do they confront each other, or do they overlook or discuss the aggravations that come from these differences?

2. *Individuality v. collectivity*: Is the individual paramount, with the work group providing the context for people to make their personal contribution to a common goal, or is the work group central with the individual merely a component of the collective?

3. *Participative v. autocratic*: Are individuals expected to express their views and thereby contribute to a quality decision, or are they expected to keep quiet, 'buy into' the vision of the 'legitimate authority' and be told how to implement it.

4. *Spontaneous v. orchestrated*: Does the group actually make a decision, or is it a sounding board or way of communicating already made decisions to which members have previously been exposed?

5. *Task v. process*: Is the group's primary focus on *what* it does, or on *how* it does it? Is productivity (task output) or the quality of the internal interactions (process) the key indicator of a group's value?

6. *Quality v. quantity*: Is the best indicator of the group's performance to be the quality or the quantity of the work it produces?

7. *Criticism v. diplomacy*: Will group members criticize each other directly in public, or will they seek more diplomatic, less overt ways of communicating their dissatisfaction?

8. *Productivity v. receptivity*: Is creativity recognized in terms of ideas implemented, problems solved or capabilities developed, or more abstractly in terms of light shedding, energy releasing or potential development?

Smith and Berg recommend that while single-culture group members can use what they have in common as the basis of their collective functioning; those in multicultural groups should use their differences as the basis for their shared actions. The latter might usefully begin their deliberations by sharing their own cultural assumptions about group process and outcomes with their colleagues. The object is to help individuals learn from each other in order to make the group function effectively.

Based on Kenwyn Smith and David Berg, 'Cross cultural groups at work', *European Management Journal*, 1997, vol.15, no.1, pp.8–15.

Social influence refers to the process where attitudes and behaviour are influenced by the real or implied presence of others.

seek to influence? For familiar, well-learned activities such as assembly line work and similar repetitive tasks, the presence of co-workers is likely to improve performance, and the presence of an observer such as a manager unlikely to hinder it unless it carries a message of distrust or punishment. In contrast, a person who is attempting to perform a complex, unfamiliar task will find that observation by others may cause them to make more mistakes, and their performance will decline. Hence the presence of others can improve or reduce an individual's performance. Elliott Aronson and his colleagues (Aronson *et al.*, 1994) suggested two alternative reactions by an individual to having one or more people present when performing a task (figure 11.1). One of these is *social facilitation*, and the other is *social loafing*. Their model stresses the importance of evaluation, arousal and task complexity.

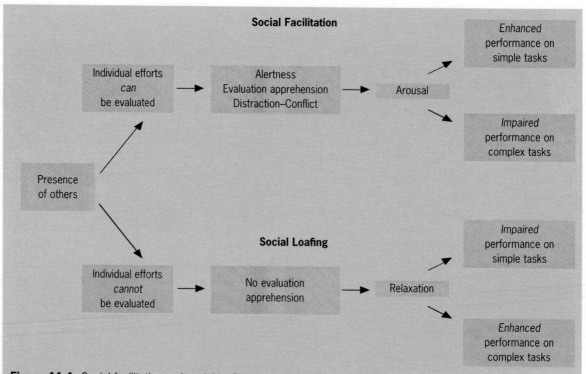

Figure 11.1: Social facilitation and social loafing
From Elliot Aronson, Timothy D.Wilson and Robin M. Akert, *Social Psychology*, HarperCollins, New York, 1994, p.332.

Synergy is the positive or negative result of the interaction of two or more components, producing an outcome that is different from the sum of the individual components.

Social facilitation refers to the strengthening of the dominant (prevalent or likely) responses due to the presence of others.

How might an individual's performance be improved by the presence of others? The biological concept of **synergy** helps us to do this. Strictly defined, synergy is the positive or negative result of the interaction of two or more components, producing an outcome that is different from the sum of the individual components. In the field of management and organization behaviour, 'individuals' have replaced 'substances', and the concept has been suitably amended. It is important to emphasize the word 'different' in the definition, because it indicates that the effect may be positive or negative.

Let us first consider positive synergy. Early research investigated individuals performing various physical tasks. Norman Triplett (1898) studied children winding fishing reels and cyclists racing. The children were found to turn the reels faster when other children were present, and the cyclists improved their performance by 20 per cent when accompanied by a pacemaker rather than when alone, even in a non-racing situation. He found that they performed better in the presence of another person (a co-actor). Later studies focused on non-physical tasks. Floyd Allport (1920) discovered that students completed mathematical calculations faster in the company of other students than when alone and coined the term **social facilitation** to indicate that the task was made easier, or was 'facilitated', by the presence of others.

This early work studied individuals who performed in the presence of others, but who were not necessarily part of a group. Nevertheless, the group situation remains one within which the social facilitation effect is the most likely to occur. The original definition of the concept of social facilitation was the tendency of people to perform simple, instinctive or well-learned tasks better when others were present. Later, researchers found that with more difficult tasks, when responses could easily be wrong, people performed more poorly in the presence of others. The view now is that, whatever you do well, you are likely to do it even better in front of an audience (especially a friendly one); whereas what you normally find difficult, you will find virtually impossible to do when others are watching. Hence the current definition of social facilitation stresses the strengthening of the dominant (prevalent or most likely) response, due to the presence of others (Myers, 1993, p.306).

Positive synergy is one of the fundamental concepts which underpins all kinds of group working in organizations. In particular, it supports the use of cross-functional teams [**link**, chapter 12, teamworking]. Positive synergy is the belief that the final output produced by a group of individuals working together, rather than separately, will equal more than the sum of the individual members' abilities and efforts. A popular shorthand term for this is 2 + 2 = 5. It has been argued that the designated purpose of group tasks should necessarily *require* more than its members are able to offer working as individuals, so as to benefit from the positive aspects of group dynamics. A number of theories of social facilitation have been offered:

- The mere physical presence of others instinctively causes arousal that motivates performance of habitual behaviour patterns. (Zajonc, 1965; 1980)

- The presence of co-actors or an audience raises an individual's awareness of the gap between their desires and their actual performance, which leads to their increasing their efforts. (Carver and Scheier, 1981)

- Individuals want to create the best impression in the presence of others and want to avoid embarrassment. (Bond, 1982)

Let us now consider negative synergy. Teamwork of all kinds is fraught with tensions, conflicts, obstacles and problems; so much so that, if it is not integrated and managed effectively, rather than surpassing the best member's capabilities, the total group output may actually equal *less* than the weakest members' efforts. This is caused by various 'process losses' which can hinder effective group functioning (Steiner, 1972). The mathematical equivalent would be 2 + 2 = 3. This challenges the idea that 'unity is strength'. If the aforementioned group process losses exceed group process gains, then one will have a situation of negative synergy. One example of this is the tendency for individuals to exert less effort when working as part of a group than when working alone.

Max Ringelmann, a French professor of agricultural engineering, conducted the original studies in the late 1920s on subjects pulling ropes (Kravitz and Martin, 1986). Research suggests that individual effort tends to decrease as the size of the group increases. Ringelmann found that three people pulling together achieved only two and a half times the average individual rate, while eight 'pullers' achieved less than four times the individual rate. Ingham *et al.* (1974) confirmed the original findings and reported an 18 per cent variation in effort when he later repeated these experiments. The 'Ringelmann effect' was renamed **social loafing** in the 1970s following the work of three Ohio University researchers, Bibb Latanae, Kipling Williams and Stephen Harkins (1979), who conducted their own investigations to confirm Ringlemann's original work.

Various explanations have been put forward for social loafing (Karau and Williams, 1993; Comer, 1995). These process losses in a group have been ascribed to many different causes:

Social loafing refers to the tendency for individuals to exert less effort when working as part of a group than when working alone.

- Equity of effort ('Others are not contributing, why should I?')

- Dispersion of responsibility ('I'm hidden in the crowd, no one will notice me')

- Negative effect of group reward ('Everyone will get the same, why should I work harder?')

- Problems of co-ordination ('People are getting in each others' way')

Laboratory studies have revealed key situational factors. Social loafing was found to occur most often when the:

- task was perceived as unimportant, simple or boring;

- group members thought their individual output was not identifiable;

- nature of each person's contribution was similar to that of the others;

- group members expected their colleagues to loaf.

Additionally, self-reliant individualists appeared to be more social loafers than group-oriented collectivists. This individual finding has a cultural equivalent. Studies have found that individualist societies which are dominated by self-interest (like the Americas, Britain, Australia) have more social loafing than collectivist societies, whose members are motivated by in-group goals. The Israelis and Chinese performed better in a group than working alone (Earley, 1989; 1993). The solutions offered to managers to overcome social loafing involve some degree of job redesign but mainly stress behaviour modification. For example, Greenberg and Baron (1997) suggest:

Make the work more involving:	Keeping people interested makes them perform at a high level.
Identify workers:	Pointing out each member's individual contribution prevents their getting away with a 'free ride'.

| Reward contributions to the group: | Rewarding members for helping others achieves the common goal, and not just for their individual contributions. |
| Threaten punishment: | Fear of punishment prevents loafing and gets members to 'pull their weight' in the group. |

How many pickles could a pickle packer pack if pickle packers were only paid for properly packed pickles?

What are the problems facing production line workers in a pickle factory? A key job is stuffing dill pickle halves into jars. Only dill halves of a certain length can be used. Those that are too long will not fit and those that are too short will float and dance inside and look cheap and crummy. The dill halves and jars are carried on a separate high-speed conveyor belt past the contingent of pickle stuffers. If the stuffers don't stuff quickly enough, the jars pile up at the workers' stations while they look for pickles of the appropriate length, so stuffers have a great temptation to stuff whichever pickles come to hand. The individual outputs of the stuffers are unidentifiable, since all jars go into a common hopper before they reach the quality control section. Responsibility for the output cannot be focused on one worker. This combination of factors leads to poor performance and improper packing. This research suggests making individual production identifiable and raises the question, 'How many pickles could a pickle packer pack if pickle packers were only paid for properly packed pickles?'

Based on Kipling Williams, Stephen Harkins and Bibb Latane, 'Identifiability and social loafing: Two cheering experiments', *Journal of Personality and Social Psychology*, 1981, vol.40, no.2, pp.303–11.

Stop and criticize

Are you a social loafer in an educational or work context? How is social loafing reducing or improving your studying or work performance? What advice would you give your instructor or manager on improving your performance and that of your colleagues, either through social facilitation or by encouraging social loafing in relation to particular tasks or activities?

Group influences on individuals' behaviour

Elton Mayo originally noted the existence of group norms, and their enforcement through sanctions, during the bank wiring observation room studies at the Hawthorne works [**link**, chapter 9, group formation]. The men there restricted their output to conform to a group-agreed norm or standard. In another study, which has now become a classic in experimental social psychology, Muzafer Sherif (1936) showed how group norms emerged. He demonstrated that the way an individual perceives motion can be affected by what others present at the time claim to see. Few of the subjects who took part in Sherif's experiments felt conscious that others had influenced their judgements.

Sherif's work showed that in a situation where doubt and uncertainty exist and where first-hand information is lacking, a person's viewpoint will shift to come into line with those of other group members. In essence this situation leads to the creation of a **group norm**. This occurs quickly among group members who have had little previous experience of the group's work, but it also occurs among those who have had experience, although somewhat more slowly. Sherif's work suggested that in order to organize and manage itself, every group developed a system of norms. Norms are behavioural expectations and they serve to define the

Muzafer Sherif
(1906–88)

Group norms are expected modes of behaviour and beliefs that are established either formally or informally by a group. Norms guide behaviour and facilitate interaction by specifying the kinds of reaction expected or acceptable in a particular situation.

nature of the group. They express the values of the members of the group and provide guidelines to help the group achieve its goals. A group may develop them consciously or unconsciously.

Not all group norms have equal importance. **Pivotal norms** guide behaviour which is central to the group, for example the level of output or the amount of work preparation done. In contrast, **peripheral norms** guide behaviour that is important but not essential, for example the choice of clothing or break time activities. Group members who violate pivotal norms can impede group objectives or endanger its survival. Therefore the consequences for such transgressing individuals are severe. In contrast, violation of peripheral norms, although frowned upon, has fewer negative consequences for the offender.

Why do norms develop within a group? David Feldman (1984) argued that their purpose was to:

- *Facilitate group task achievement or group survival*: Groups develop norms which increase their chances of being successful and protect themselves from outsiders.

Bloody beefers and hanging beef tongues

Over a nine-week period, William Thompson used the observational data collection method to study the day-to-day activities of assembly line workers in a beef-processing plant in the American Midwest. He reported that 'working in the beef plant is "dirty" work, not only in the literal sense of being drenched with perspiration and beef blood, but also in the figurative sense of performing a low-status, routine and demeaning job'. Thompson and his fellow workers had to hang, brand and bag between 1,350 and 1,500 beef tongues during an eight-hour shift. The work was both monotonous and routine.

Thompson described the camaraderie that existed among the 'beefers' as they called themselves. Because of the noise, the need for earplugs and the isolation of certain work areas, it was virtually impossible for the men on the assembly line to speak to each other. Instead, they communicated using an elaborate system of non- and paraverbal verbal symbols. These included exaggerated gestures, shrill whistles, 'thumbs up' and 'thumbs down', and the clanging of knives against stainless steel tables and tubs. Thompson observed that 'in a setting which apparently eliminated it, the workers' desire for social interaction won out and interaction flourished'.

To reduce the feeling of alienation and retain a sense of humanity, the beefers developed certain coping mechanisms. They replaced the formal, managerially imposed norms of the workplace with their own informal ones. At certain times, instead of working at a steady speed which matched the line speed, they would work at a frantic pace and get ahead of the line. While such behaviour added a few precious minutes to their scheduled break time, its importance was primarily symbolic in that it challenged the company's dictates concerning the speed of the line, and it gave them a small measure of control over the work process.

The informal group norms also encouraged certain types of rule breaking. Indeed, Thompson noted that the 'workers practically made a game out of doing forbidden things simply to see if they could get away with it'. For example, at Thompson's workstation, despite strict rules to the contrary, workers covered in beef blood washed their hands, arms and knives in a tub of water which was reserved for cleaning tongues. In addition, workers often cut out pieces of meat and threw them at other employees. If not noticed by the supervisor or inspector, the thrown meat chunks might be picked up off the floor and put back on the line—a blatant violation of hygiene rules. Thompson concluded that such 'artful sabotage served as a symbolic way in which workers could express a sense of individuality, and hence self-worth'.

Based on William E. Thompson, 'Hanging tongues: A sociological encounter with the assembly line', *Qualitative Sociology*, 1983, vol.6, Fall, pp.215–37.

Pivotal norms are socially defined standards relating to behaviour and beliefs which are central to a group's objective and survival.

Peripheral norms are socially defined standards relating to behaviour and beliefs which are important but not crucial to a group's objective and survival.

- *Increase the predictability of group members' behaviours*: Predictability means that internally, members can anticipate and prepare for the actions of colleagues, thereby smoothing social interaction. Externally, it allows them to relate appropriately to outsiders.

- *Reduce embarrassing interpersonal problems for group members*: knowing what to do and say in a group (and what not to) increases an individual member's comfort.

- *Express the group's core values and define their distinctiveness*: Norms allow members to gain a sense of the essence of the group.

Feldman (1984) also noted that group norms developed in four ways:

- *Explicit statement by a supervisor or co-worker*: This person may explicitly state certain expectations. The project leader may tell the newcomer that the group meetings starts promptly on the hour, when all members are expected to be present.

Discovering the norm

In a now classic study, Donald Roy, a researcher who acted as a participant observer in a factory, described the pressures that were placed on an individual to adhere to the group norm. Roy's earnings, and those of others, were based on a piecerate system The more he produced the more he earned.

> From my first to my last day at the plant I was subject to warnings and predictions concerning price cuts. Pressure was the heaviest from Joe Mucha, who shared my job repertoire and kept a close eye on my production. On November 14, the day after my first attained quota, Joe Mucha advised: Don't let it go over $1.25 an hour, or the time-study man will be right down here! And they don't waste time, either! They watch the records like a hawk! I got ahead, so I took it easy for a couple of hours. Joe told me that I had made $10.01 yesterday and warned me not to go over $1.25 an hour ... Jack Starkey spoke to me after Joe left. 'What's the matter? Are you trying to upset the applecart?' Jack explained in a friendly manner that $10.50 was too much to turn in, even on an old job. 'The turret-lathe men can turn in $1.35', said Jack, 'but their rate is 90 cents and ours is 85 cents.' Jack warned me that the Methods Department could lower their prices on any job, old or new, by changing the fixture slightly or changing the size of the drill. According to Jack, a couple of operators ... got to competing with each other to see how much they could turn in. They got up to $1.65 an hour, and the price was cut in half. And from then on they had to run that job themselves, as none of the other operators would accept that job. According to Jack, it would be all right for us to turn in $1.28 or $1.29 an hour, when it figured out that way, but it was not all right to turn in $1.30 an hour.

Well now I know where the maximum is – $1.29 an hour.

From Donald Roy, 'Banana time: job satisfaction and informal interaction', *Human Organization*, 1960, vol.18, pp.156–68.

- *Critical events in the group's history*: A shop-floor employee makes a suggestion for an improvement to his supervisor, who criticizes and ridicules him. Group members ensure that in the future, none of them offers any more suggestions.

- *Initial pattern of behaviour*: The first behaviour pattern that emerges in a group can establish group expectations. For example, if the first speaker shares his feelings and anxieties with the other group members, the discussion of emotions in a group can become a norm.

- *Transfer behaviours from past situations*: When individuals carry over behaviours from past situation, they can increase the predictability of group members' behaviours in new settings. For example, instructors and students transfer constant expectations from class to class.

Sherif's study of the emergence of group norms

If you place yourself in a room which is in complete darkness and look fixedly at a small point of light, the light will appear to move in an erratic manner, even though it is in fact stationary. You can test this out yourself if you have a completely dark room and one small pinpoint of light. The apparent movement is an optical illusion known as the 'autokinetic effect'. A person in the room who observes the light will be able to report estimates of the distances covered.

Muzafer Sherif placed a group of three subjects in such a darkened room and presented them with such a small spot of light. He then asked them to track the apparent movement of the spot and to say, aloud, each in turn, the direction in which they thought the light was moving. His subjects made three series of 100 estimates on successive days. Initially, there were quite wide individual differences in the response to this situation. Some subjects saw little movement, while others saw a lot. However, Sherif discovered that they started to agree on the amount of apparent movement quite quickly. Having exchanged information on their judgements, their behaviour changed. They began seeing the light moving in the same direction as those who had spoken earlier.

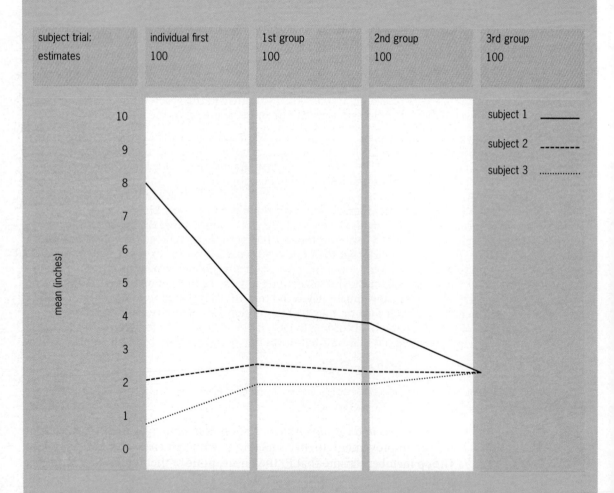

subject trial:	individual first	1st group	2nd group	3rd group
estimates	100	100	100	100

Gradually, all the members came to see the light as moving in the same direction at the same time. There was of course no 'real' movement of the light. Each individual began to see the light in the same way as the group saw it. The results Sherif obtained with two-person and three-person groups are shown in the diagram above. When a group norm emerged it was found that it became the basis for subsequent judgement when subjects were retested independently. The group norm therefore became a relatively permanent frame of reference for behaviour.

Based on Muzafer Sherif, *The Psychology of Social Norms*, Harper & Row, New York, 1936.

Elton Mayo, and the human relations approach to management that his research created, did propose that supervisors should attempt to modify the norms of work groups that they managed, so as to align them with organizational (management) goals [**link**, chapter 9, group formation]. However, it appears that once established, it seems that group norms are difficult to change. Since the group members originally created the norms, it is they who ultimately change them. Members will tend to resist any attempts by managers or any other outsiders to modify their group's norms. Once a group has established a set of norms, it will enforce them in order to:

- ensure its survival;

- help it achieve its task;

- clarify or simplify how members are to behave;

- avoid embarrassing situations between members;

- clarify its central values or unique identity .

Group sanction refers to both punishments and rewards given by members to others in the group in the process of enforcing group norms. Punishments are a negative sanction and rewards are a positive sanction.

Some examples of norms and the reasons for their enforcement are shown in table 11.1. To enforce its norms, a group develops a set of sanctions with which to police them. The term **group sanction** refers not only to punishments but also to rewards that are given by group members to others within their group, in the process of enforcing group norms.

The earliest examples of negative sanctions exercised in groups were revealed by the bank wiring observation room phase of the Hawthorne studies. The researchers discovered that persons who broke the group norm, for example producing either over or under the group norm, were 'binged'. This involved a group member flicking the ear of the norm, transgressor or tapping him on the upper part of their arm. Both actions were intended to indicate physically to the man

"Mother, I get enough pressure from my peer group without getting it from you."

Table 11.1: Norms and sanctions

Norm	Enforcement reason	Examples of sanctions to enforce the norm
Members attend all group meetings regularly and arrive on time.	Group survival	Absentees or latecomers are first teased or ridiculed, and then criticized.
All members are required to prepare written work before the group meetings to avoid delay at meeting.	Group task achievement	Group members compliment individuals whose preparation has been particularly thorough.
Members listen to each other's ideas without interrupting, allowing them to fully present their thoughts and opinions.	Clarification of behavioural expectations	A member who interrupts is taken aside after the meeting and asked, in future, to let the person finish speaking.
Members do not discuss their private lives with colleagues at work.	Avoidance of embarrassment	Members who insist on discussing such matters are ostracized until they stop doing so.

that his behaviour was unacceptable to the other group members. Other negative sanctions can also be used by the group and can be placed in ascending order of severity, as shown in figure 11.1. If negative sanctions represent the 'stick' to enforce group norm compliance, then the positive sanctions represent the 'carrot'. Such carrots for the conforming individual include accolades from other members, emotional support, increase in social status, and acceptance of their ideas by others.

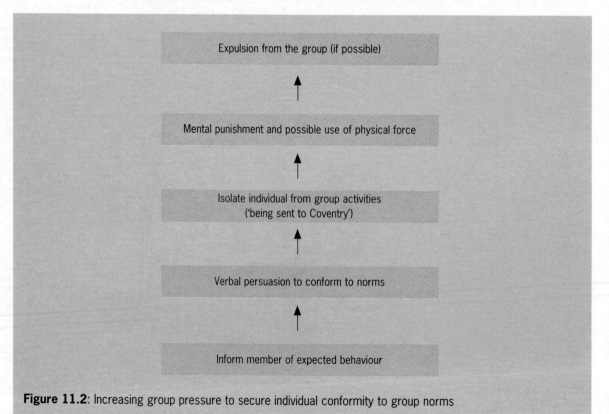

Figure 11.2: Increasing group pressure to secure individual conformity to group norms

Send to Coventry

Being 'sent to Coventry' means becoming a social outcast. Individuals in a group can be punished in this way by their colleagues, who ignore them, refuse to speak to them and isolate them from group activities. During the English Civil War (1642–51) fought between the Royalists and the Parliamentarians, the city of Coventry was a strong outpost of parliamentary support. Royalist prisoners who were captured in the Midlands were frequently sent to the city of Coventry, where the local population would have nothing to do with them.

Compliance with norms tends to increase under certain conditions. An increase in norm conformity is associated with a decrease in the size of the group; and also with an increase in the group's homogeneity, visibility and a stable experience. Diagnosing a team's norms and its members' compliance with them can help to explain group behaviour.

If you want to deviate from a group norm you have several options. You can try to persuade others of the force of your position, and thereby alter the group norm to accommodate what you want to do. Of course, the other members may respond by persuading you to conform to the existing norm. The higher your status, and hence your power in the group, the more likely you are to be success-

Controlling the deviants

The mechanisms by which internal control was exercised varied. Perhaps the most important were sarcasm, 'binging' and ridicule. Through such devices pressure was brought to bear upon those individuals who deviated too much from the group's norm of acceptable conduct. From this point of view, it will be seen that the great variety of activities normally labelled 'restriction of output' represent attempts at social control and discipline and as such are important integrating processes. In addition to overt methods, clique membership itself may be looked upon as an instrument of control. Those persons whose behaviour was most reprehensible to clique A, were excluded from it. They were in a sense, socially ostracized. This is one of the universal social processes by means of which a group chastises and brings pressure to bear upon those who transgress its codes ... It can be seen, therefore, that nearly all the activities of this group may be looked upon as methods of controlling the behaviour of its members. The men had elaborated, spontaneously and quite unconsciously, an intricate social organization around their collective beliefs and sentiments.

From Fritz J. Roethlisberger and William J. Dickson, *Management and the Worker*, John Wiley & Sons, New York, 1964, pp.523–4.

ful in changing the behaviours and beliefs of other members, and the less likely are they to change your own. If neither of these alternatives takes place, then something else will happen. If you are free to leave the group, and the group is of little importance to you, you may leave it. Conversely, if you are of little importance to the group, you may be faced with the choice of either conforming to its norms or else being rejected by its members. You may even be rejected by your act of deviance irrespective of whether or not you are willing to recant. If, however, you are of importance to your group because you are a high-status member possessing power, popularity or special skills, then the group may tolerate your deviant behaviour and beliefs in order to avoid the threat of losing a valued member. Hence, the power that a group has to influence its members towards conformity to its norms depends on three main factors:

- The positive and negative sanctions (rewards and punishments) that the group has at its disposal.

- The member's desire to avoid negative sanctions such as social and physical punishments or expulsion from the group.

- The degree to which individual members value their membership of the group and its accompanying rewards (e.g. recognition, status, prestige, financial inducements).

Group cohesion refers to the number and strength of mutual positive attitudes towards group members.

This last factor, the attraction that the group has for an individual, and the attraction that group members have for each another, is defined as **group cohesion**. It is the sum of all the forces that influence members to remain part of a group.

Table 11.2: Group cohesion—contributors and consequences

Contributors to group cohesion	Consequences of group cohesion
Small size	Group success
External threat	Member satisfaction
Stable membership	Productivity high or low
Past success of group	Greater conformity by members
Difficulty of entry to the group	Member's evaluations become distorted
Members sharing common goals	Co-operative behaviour between individuals
Opportunity to interact with others	Increased interaction between members
Members' agreement about their statuses	Increased group influence over members
Attractiveness of group to individuals	
Fairness of rewards between members	

Stop and criticize

Consider a group of which you are a member, and its norms and sanctions. Reflect on a situation in which a member (perhaps yourself) broke a norm and received a sanction.

Assess the positive and negative outcomes of this occurrence for the individual group member concerned and the group as a whole.

Group socialization is the process whereby members learn the values, symbols and expected behaviours of the groups to which they belong.

Having established a set of norms and the sanctions to enforce them, a group has to communicate these to new individuals who join the group. The new group member 'learns the ropes' and is shown how to get things done, how to interact with others and how to achieve a high social status within the group. An important aspect of achieving such status is to adhere to the group's rules or norms. Initial transgressions will be gently pointed out. However, the continued violation of norms by a group member puts at risk the cohesion of the group. When there is disagreement on a matter of importance to the group, the preservation of group effectiveness, harmony and cohesion requires a resolution of the conflict. Hence pressure is exerted on the deviating individual through persuasive communication to conform. The name given to this 'educational' process which the new member undergoes is **group socialization** and it occurs within most groups in all types of organization.

Organizational socialization is the process through which an individual's pattern of behaviour, and their values, attitudes and motives, are influenced to conform with those seen as desirable in a particular organization.

If new recruits are thoroughly socialized, they are less likely to transgress group norms and require sanctions to be administered. However, while such pressure to go along with the majority of other members may be beneficial in many respects for the group, it also carries costs. If conformity is allowed to dominate, and individuals are given little opportunity to present alternative and different views, there is the danger of the group collectively making errors of judgement, leading them to take unwise actions. A later chapter will consider the concept of groupthink, which, through internal conformity and external group pressure, leads individual members collectively to make poor decisions [**link**, chapter 22, decision making].

Table 11.3: Group development and organizational socialization compared

	Group development	Organizational socialization
Stage 1: Orientation	1. Forming • Establish interpersonal relationships. • Conform to organizational traditions and standards. • Boundary testing in relationships and task behaviours.	1. Getting in (anticipatory socialization) • Setting of realistic expectations. • Determining match with the newcomer.
Stage 2: Redefinition	2. Storming • Conflict arising because of interpersonal behaviours. • Resistance to group influence and task requirements.	2. Breaking in • Initiation to the job. • Establishing interpersonal relationships. • Congruence between self and organizational performance appraisal.
Stage 3: Co-ordination	3. Norming • Single leader emerges. • Group cohesion established. • New group standards and roles formed for members.	3. Setting in (role management) The degree of fit between one's life interests outside work and the demands of the organization. Resolution of conflicts at the workplace itself.
Stage 4: Formalization	4. Performing • Members perform tasks together. • Establishing role clarity. • Teamwork is the norm.	

From Judith R. Gordon, *A Diagnostic Approach to Organizational Behaviour*, Allyn & Bacon, 1993, p.184. Used with permission.

It is important to remember that while a work group will be attempting to get its new member to adopt its own values, symbols and expected behaviours, the organization which recruited the person will be endeavouring to do the same. Some companies, such as Disney and McDonald's, are famous for, and put much time, money and effort into, getting their new joiners to adopt the 'company way' of doing things. This equivalent process is called **organizational socialization**, and it too will be investigated in greater detail in a later chapter [**link**, chapter 19, organization culture].

Employees phone home!

Alan McKinley and Phil Taylor investigated the use of teamworking in the Scottish plant of an American electronics multinational which manufactured cellphones. The company's self-managing team members learned a variety of tasks and rotated between them. The work involved was neither skilled nor was it routine labour. The company produced sophisticated components using high-tech production lines. Moreover, 80 per cent of workers were male, which represented a 'masculinization of production' from the female-dominated assembly of the past.

The company had an ambitious objective based on a 'management-sanctioned team ideology' to produce 'a "socially individualized" pro-company workforce'. Management's ambition was to have individuals working together in groups or teams without their acquiring the characteristics of psychological groups. The research study revealed how teamwork was used by the organization for purposes of mutual control, self-surveillance, peer pressure and review [**link**, chapter 24, power and politics].

The authors described how teams took on the tasks of disciplining and policing norms through the use of what they termed 'peer review', which formed the basis of an intensive system of internal control. In this process, individual team members were required by management to rate each other on various attitudinal and production dimensions, and to assess the behaviour of their fellow members. In essence the company's management sought to harness the well-known power of groups to control and modify their members' behaviour (revealed in research by Mayo, Sherif, Asch and Janis) to achieve organizational goals.

McKinley and Taylor found that the company's work teams became increasingly variable and erratic. Not surprisingly, team members were initially distrustful of this process of peer review. Later, as the mutual scoring system became increasingly punitive, team members' dislike of it hardened, and the workers sought to 'trade' and equalize their scores. In this way, the processes of group policing of individual behaviour conceived and instigated by management was tamed.

Based on Alan McKinlay and Phil Taylor, *Inside the Factory of the Future: Work, Power and Authority in Microelectronics*, Routledge, London, 2000.

Group influences on individuals' attitudes

Why do members conform to group pressure? Group norms allow individual members to avoid chaos in their lives. They let them get on with their business by ensuring the survival of the group; focusing it on achieving its task; increasing the predictability of the behaviour of others; and avoiding individuals embarrassing each other. These might be termed 'external' for conformity to group norms. For example, speaking or dressing in a particular way. Observing norms is of such personal benefit to us that we are prepared to suppress any personal desires and are thus willing to limit our individual freedom and abide by them. Moreover, we punish those who violate the norms and reward those who do not. The earliest experimental studies into conformity to group norms were carried out by Solomon Asch. Alongside these external reasons, there are 'internal' reasons. One such internal reason is that we each have a desire for order and meaning in our lives, making attempts to 'make sense' of seemingly unconnected facts or events.

For many human beings uncertainty is disturbing and something that should be reduced to the absolute minimum. We like to know 'what's going on' and to be in control of the situations in which we find ourselves. Norms, and the adherence to norms, offer a contribution to the predictability which most human beings desire.

Asch's study of conformity to group norms

The experimenter and his study

In the early 1950s, Solomon E. Asch conducted a laboratory experiment into individual conformity in groups.

The subject

Only No. 6 was a real subject (second from the right). The remainder were Asch's paid accomplices.

The problem

In the experimental conditions, the accomplices had been instructed to lie about which line was correct. Under pressure, the subject (No. 6) shows signs of conflict, of whether to conform to the group judgement, or give the response he judges to be correct.

The situation

Seven men sat around a table supposedly to participate in a study on visual perception.

The task

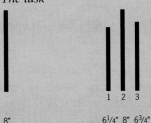

8"   6¼" 8" 6¾"

The task was an easy one. To judge which of three lines was equal in length to one they had seen earlier

The results

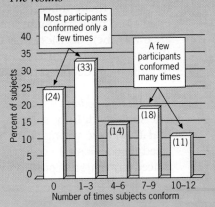

Most subjects conformed to group judgements at least once. However, most resisted group pressure most of the time. 58 per cent conformed three times or less on the twelve occasions when accomplices gave false answers.

The conclusion

Overall in twelve trials, involving 123 subjects, approximately 75 per cent of experimental subjects conformed at least once; 5 per cent conformed all the time; and 25 per cent never conformed; the average for conformers was 37 per cent. Later Asch found that three subjects were sufficient to create the effect. Large numbers did not increase conformity. A second dissenter cut the conformity rate by 25 per cent, even when the dissenter disagreed with the subject.

- Conformity increased if the group member was regarded as being of high status.
- Conformity decreased if subjects were not face to face.
- Conformity increased when the group members had to continue working together in the future.

The research indicates how difficult it can be for individuals to express their opinions when these are not in accord with those of other team members. It is interesting to consider the pressure that a group can exert on an individual if it can influence something as unambiguous and familiar as judging the length of lines. How much more powerful the influence if individuals have to make subjective and unfamiliar judgements. This may explain why groups are ineffective. The best decisions are not made because group members seek to fit in with the views of others rather than working for the best solution to the problem. Doms and Avermaet (1981) replicated Asch's studies and obtained results similar to Asch's original ones.

Based on Solomon E. Asch, 'Effects of group pressure upon the modification and distortion of judgements', in H. Guetzkow, (ed.), *Groups, Leadership and Men*, Carnegie Press, New York, 1951, pp.177–90.

Solomon Asch (1951; 1952; 1956) found that those subjects who yielded to group pressure did so for different reasons. He distinguished three types of yielding:

Distortion of perception
These subjects seem to have convinced themselves that they actually did see the lines the way the other group members stated their judgements. Yielding at the perceptual level was rare and occurred primarily among those who displayed a lack of trust in themselves. They were unaware that their estimates had been displaced or distorted by the majority.

Distortion of judgement
These subjects yielded either because they were unsure that they understood the task set for them or because they did not want to 'spoil the experiment'. They suffered from primary doubt and lack of confidence. The factor of greatest importance was their decision that their perceptions were inaccurate and that those of the majority were correct (akin to independence without confidence). Distortion of judgement occurred frequently.

Distortion of action
The subjects did not suffer a modification of perception, nor did they conclude that they were wrong. They yielded because they feared being excluded, ostracized or considered eccentric. These subjects suppressed their observations and voiced the majority position with a full awareness of what they were doing.

| **Stop and criticize** | Think of an occasion when you gave an opinion or supported a decision contrary to your own feelings and judgement, but consistent with those around you at the time. |

How can you live with yourself for acting in such a socially compliant and submissive manner? What is your pathetic excuse for having done so?

Milgram's 'electric shock' experiments

Stanley Milgram, experimenter
(1933–84)

Volunteer subject, accomplice 'learner' and
accomplice experimenter

A study by Stanley Milgram showed that a group can aid the individual to defy authority. Would you torture another person simply because you were told to do so by someone in authority? Of course not, you would probably reply with little hesitation. In a series of now famous and highly controversial experiments, Stanley Milgram examined people's level of obedience to authority. The research involved ordinary people of different ages, sexes, races and occupations. A group of psychiatrists, postgraduate students and social science lecturers were asked by Milgram to predict how many of the research subjects would actually obey the experimenter's order. There was a high agreement that virtually all subjects would refuse to obey. Only one in a hundred would do it, said the psychiatrists, and that person would be a psychopath.

Milgram's experiment involved volunteer subjects participating in a learning experiment. They were to act as teachers of people who were trying to learn a series of simple word pairs. As teachers they were told to punish the student when he failed to learn by giving him an electric shock. At the start the shocks were small in intensity but every time the learner made a mistake, the teacher was told to increase the size of the shock. In carrying out the experiments, Milgram found that two out of every three subjects tested administered the electric shocks up to a level which was clearly marked 'fatal' simply because an authority figure had told them to do so. In fact, no electric shocks were ever actually given, although the volunteer 'teachers' believed that the learners were really receiving the shocks they administered.

The main focus of this chapter is upon the processes of group influence. Asch's earlier experiment had shown that it only needed one other person to agree with a deviant for the conformity effect to be counteracted. In one variation of his experiment, Milgram placed two of his accomplices alongside the subject, so that the testing of the wired-up learner would be done by a group and not a single subject. This experimental situation is thus similar to Asch's.

The experiment began with one of the accomplices administering the shocks. He then refused to continue, argued with the experimenter and withdrew, sitting in the corner of the room. The second accomplice then took over, continued for a bit and then refused just as the previous one had done. The real subject now remained to administer the shocks himself. Milgram repeated this procedure 40 times, each with a different subject. In 30 of these 40 cases, he found that once the subjects had seen their group colleagues defy the experimenter, they also defied him. When group pressure (or support) for such defiance was lacking, only fourteen subjects defied the authority figure. Milgram concluded that peer rebellion is a very powerful force in undercutting the experimenter's authority.

Milgram offered seven explanations of why the group was effective in helping the individual to do this. The reasons are the same as those which explain the power the group has over the individual:

1. Peers instil in the subject the idea of defying the experimenter.

2. The lone subject has no way of knowing if defiance is a bizarre or common occurrence. Two examples confirm that it is a natural reaction.

3. The act of defiance by the accomplice defines the act of shocking as improper. It provides social confirmation for the subject's suspicion that it is wrong to punish a subject against his will, even in a psychological experiment.

4. By remaining in the room, the accomplices' presence carries with it a measure of social disapproval for the subject.

5. As long as the accomplices participated in the experiment, there was dispersion of responsibility among group members for the shocking. As they withdrew, the responsibility focused on the subject.

6. The subject witnessed two instances of disobedience and observed that the consequences of defying the experimenter were minimal.

7. Failing to keep the accomplices performing as required diminishes the experimenter's power.

Based on Stanley Milgram, *Obedience to Authority*, Tavistock, London, 1974.

Deindividuation

Deindividuation refers to an increased state of anonymity that loosens normal constraints on individuals' behaviour, reducing their sense of responsibility and leading to an increase in impulsive and antisocial acts.

Social facilitation explains how groups can arouse individuals, while social loafing shows that groups can diffuse and hence diminish individual responsibility. Together, arousal and diffused responsibility combine to decrease normal, social inhibitions and create deindividuation. **Deindividuation** refers to a person's loss of self-awareness and self-monitoring. It involves some loss of personal identity and greater identification with the group.

The writings of Gustave LeBon led to the theory of deindividuation, which was first proposed by Leon Festinger, Albert Pepitone and Theodore Newcombe (1952). However, Marion Hampton (1999, p.112) neatly captures the experience of deindividuation when she writes:

There are moments when we can observe ourselves behaving irrationally as members of crowds or audiences, yet we are swept by the emotion, unable to check it. In smaller groups too, like committees or teams, we may experience powerful feelings of loyalty, anxiety or anger. The moods and emotions of those around us seem to have an exaggerated effect on our own moods and emotions.

The influence of the crowd in history

Gustave LeBon stated that the crowd is 'always intellectually inferior to the isolated individual . . . mob man is fickle, credulous, and intolerant showing the violence and ferocity of primitive beings'. He observed events during a period of great upheaval in France, read accounts of crowd behaviour in the French Revolution of 1789, and in the Paris Commune of 1871. In his book *The Crowd*, originally published in 1895, he hypothesized that humans had a two-part personality. The upper half was conscious, unique to each individual and contained dignity and virtue. The lower half, in contrast, was unconscious, was shared with everyone else, and contained bad desires and instincts.

In normal circumstances the conscious part guided a person's behaviour, but in a group or a crowd situation, it somehow stopped functioning, and allowed the lower half to take over. LeBon attributed this primitive behaviour to three things:

Anonymity Individuals cannot be easily identified in a crowd.
Contagion Ideas and emotions spread rapidly and unpredictably.
Suggestibility The savagery that is just below the surface is released by suggestion.

Based on Gustave LeBon, 1908, *The Crowd: A Study of the Popular Mind*, Unwin, London (first published in 1895 by Ernest Benn).

Social information-processing theory tells us that individuals use information from their immediate environments to interpret events, develop appropriate attitudes and understand expectations about their behaviour and its consequences (Salancik and Pfeffer, 1977). Bandura's social learning theory [**link**, chapter 4, learning] reminds us that role models within that work situation can direct such non-inhibited behaviour in various ways within the organization (O'Leary-Kelly *et al.*, 1996). Edward Diener (1979) argued that when people were in a deindividualized state, they experienced:

- an inability to monitor or regulate their own behaviour;
- a reduction in the normal restraints against impulsive behaviour;
- a heightened sensitivity to emotional states and situational cues;
- a reduced concern with social approval of actions; and
- a reduction in the capacity for rational planning.

In his novel *Lord of the Flies*, William Golding describes how a group of boys marooned on a desert island, through their shouting, clapping and face painting, 'hype themselves up' and reduce their self-consciousness, turning themselves into a single organism within which the individual members lose their identity. The unrestrained behaviours are provoked by the power of the group. In certain kinds of group situation, attention is drawn away from the individual, their anonymity is increased, and they are more likely to abandon their normal restraints and to lose their sense of individual responsibility. Edward Diener (1979; 1980) extended the original work on deindividuation. He specified the conditions within groups in which individuals lose their personal identities and merge into it (figure 11.3).

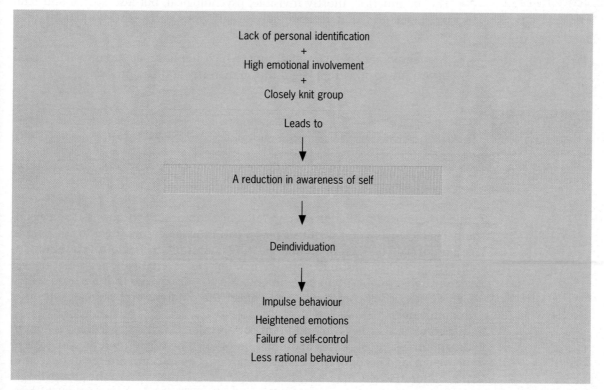

Figure 11.3: The process of deindividuation
From Tony Malim and Ann Birch, *Social Psychology*, Intertext Ltd, Bristol.

Studies have found that several factors encourage deindivituation:

Group size

Within a group, members consider themselves unidentifiable, and their own actions to be those of the group. As group size increases, the more its members lose self-awareness and the more they are willing to commit antisocial actions. In these circumstances, self-awareness and self-monitoring plummets.

Anonymity

Anonymity lessens inhibitions. It can lead to prosocial behaviour, for example, making people more intimate or playful, or antisocial behaviour, such as attacking a person as a mob. For example, warriors in a tribe painted their faces and wore masks; military personnel wear uniforms; and companies increasingly require staff to dress in standardized 'workware'. The positive aspect is that they associate with the company, but it can also increase anonymity.

All these writings make the point that an individual's mental processes are radically altered when they become part of a crowd. They come to share the emotional experience of others; and within the crowd, the forces of emotion and of the unconscious struggle against the forces of reason and the conscious. LeBon contributed to a number of core concepts in group theory, as suggested by Hampton (1999, pp.115–16):

- The group as a distinct level of analysis in a kind of nested hierarchy of human systems (the individual, the group, the organization, the society), each level requiring its own theories and means of analysis and not being reducible to its constituents.

- The 'boundaries', mostly invisible, psychological, but also spatial and temporal, features that differentiate groups from each other and from their environments.

- The temporary character of groups, which implies that these social systems have a life span, with a beginning, a maturity and an end.

Stop and criticize

What deindividuating tendencies can you identify in the organizations with which you are familiar? Are these being created consciously or unconsciously? What effect are they having on organizational employees and clients?

A great number of different factors influence conformity to norms. The personality characteristics of individuals play a part in predisposing them to conform to group norms. The kind of stimuli eliciting conformity behaviour is also important. That people conform to norms when they are uncertain about a situation was demonstrated by the Sherif experiments. He also discovered that a person with a high degree of self-confidence could affect the opinions and estimates of other group members.

Upbringing also plays an important part. A value which is particularly salient in Jordan, for example, is the subordination of one's personal interests and goals to the welfare and needs of one's family or group. Group-centredness can be seen in Arab cultures, where the individual is regarded as subservient to the group. Berger (1964) alluded to this trait when he wrote that 'Through most of their history, despite the recent introduction of Western political forms, Arab communities have been collections of groups rather than individuals. The family and the tribe have been the social units through which the individual has related himself to others and to governments' (p.33). The formal education can be considered as part of the process of upbringing and child socialization. In this context, Japan is particularly noted for the group orientation of its youngsters, although at the start of the twenty-first century, this is slowly beginning to change (*The Economist*, 2000) [**link**, chapter 19, organization culture].

The amount of conformity to a group standard generally corresponds strongly to the degree of ambiguity of the stimulus being responded to. Situational factors are also involved, The size of the group, the unanimity of the majority and its structure all have an effect. It has been found that conformity increased as the group size increased. It is also affected by a person's position in the communication structure of a group, with conformity being greater in a decentralized network than in a centralized one. Finally, there are the intra-group relationships referred to earlier. The kind of pressure exerted, the composition of the group,

Monkey see, monkey do

Sandra Robinson and Anne O'Leary-Kelly studied antisocial actions in organizations. These were defined as behaviours which could potentially harm the individual or organizational property. Such actions included sexual harassment, stealing, insubordination, sabotage, rumour spreading, withholding effort and absenteeism. The researchers studied 187 employees from 35 groups in 20 organizations. They examined the extent to which individual employees' antisocial actions were shaped by the group in which they worked.

They found that the antisocial behaviour exhibited by a work group was a significant predictor of an individual's antisocial behaviour at work. As the richness of the group experience increased, members became more likely to match their individual level of antisocial behaviour to that of the group in general. The stronger the group's antisocial behaviour climate, the greater was its ability to affect an individual's actions. Where individuals in the group had to rely on each other to complete a task, their behaviour was more strongly related to the level of antisocial behaviour exhibited by the group. Where an individual exhibited less antisocial behaviour than the group in general, he or she was less satisfied with their co-workers.

The effects of work groups on individual behaviour have been known since the time of the Hawthorne studies. Initially these were considered a problem for management, and later a solution. In practice, group effects can potentially be negative or positive. Groups can display high levels of either antisocial or prosocial behaviour, and can encourage similar behaviour from their members. The group provides a social context to an individual's interpretation of organization-level systems, and this context has a significant effect on the individual's antisocial behaviour in the organization.

Robinson and O'Leary-Kelly stress the organizational implications of their research, highlighting the need for managers to take strong actions quickly to nip the harmful behaviours in the bud so as to avoid the social influence effect. They point to the group-induced *contagion effect,* which can help to explain the spread or clustering of aggressive acts in a particular organization or industry. They conclude that antisocial groups encourage antisocial individual behaviour, and that isolating or ignoring them is unlikely to change them. They found that the likelihood of punishment was more effective than closeness of supervision in weakening the group–individual behaviour link.

Their conclusion was that antisocial behaviour was not solely an individual-level phenomenon, although individual characteristics such as personality, prior learning of aggressive behaviour, family background and upbringing all clearly play a part. The authors argued that the social context of the work group exerted a major influence on whether individuals behaved in an antisocial way at work. Managers, in turn, have both the ability and the responsibility to influence antisocial behaviour by shaping work group dynamics. In their view, antisocial behaviour at work is not only prevalent but also contagious.

Based on Sandra L. Robinson and Anne M. O'Leary-Kelly, 1998, 'Monkey see, monkey do: The influence of work groups on the antisocial behaviour of employees', *Academy of Management Journal*, vol.41, no.6, pp.658–72.

how successful it has been in the past and the degree to which the member identifies with the group are all examples of this.

Stop and criticize

Is such conformity by the individual within organizations a bad thing, and should it be eliminated? Or is it a good thing that should be encouraged?

Individual influences on group attitudes and behaviour

This chapter has concentrated on the way in which the group affects the attitudes, perceptions, motivations and behaviour of the individuals within it. This same direction of influence (group to individual) will also be considered in relation to decision making [**link**, chapter 22, decision making]. Does this mean that an individual can never influence their group? Clearly not, since history recounts numerous instances of individuals—revolutionaries, rebels, radical thinkers, religious zealots—who created minority groupings and as minorities successfully persuaded majorities. Indeed, leadership can be considered an example of minority influence [**link**, chapter 21, leadership].

The theoretical underpinning to the process of a minority's influence on a majority is provided by Serge Moscovici's (1980) social influence theory. He used the term **compliance** to describe what happens when a majority influences a minority through its possession of various kinds of power and its ability to implement positive and negative sanctions. He applied the term **conversion** to describe a minority's persuasion of a majority. The concept of conversion is illustrated every time an employee persuades their company to adopt a new product or create a new division. Well-known examples of this include the success of Art Fry in the 3M Corporation in producing Post-It® sticky notes.

Moscovici stressed the importance of consistency in the conversion process. The individual persuading the group had to stick unswervingly to his or her point of view. Moscovici's original work on conversion has stimulated much research, and we now possess a growing body of research and an understanding of how a minority can influence a majority (Nemeth, 1986). These different writings have been summarized by Huczynski (1996, p.192), who listed what a minority influencer of a majority has to do:

> **Compliance** refers to a majority's influence on a minority.
> **Conversion** refers to a minority's influence on a majority.

Become viable	Take a position that others are aware of, make yourself heard, get yourself noticed and generally overcome the illusion of unanimity.
Create tension	Motivate those in the majority to try to deal with your ideas.
Be consistent	Stick unswervingly to the same position. Do not take a variety of positions that disagree with the majority.
Be persistent	Restate your consistent position in the face of others' opposition to you.
Be unyielding	Being firm and unyielding involves digging your heels in and not compromising.
Be self-confident	This is conveyed by one's consistency and persistence. It raises self-doubts among the majority, leading it to reconsider its position.
Seek defectors	Defections from the majority increases the self-doubt of the remaining majority and frees its doubters, who may have self-censored themselves to speak out, perhaps encouraging more converts.

Before the 1980s, the idea that a minority could influence a majority was not a widely held view among social psychologists. However, through their research and publications, Moscovici and his colleagues presented an alternative view that possessed all the above characteristics. Minority influencing has now become an accepted and recognized phenomenon which regularly features in social psychology texts.

Recap

1. *Explain the basic tenets of social identity theory and social representation theory.*
   - Social identity theory holds that aspects of our identity derive from the membership of a group.
   - Groups construct social representations consisting of beliefs, ideas and values which they transmit to their new members.
   - Such representations, together with group socialization, lead to all members sharing a common frame of reference.

2. *Distinguish between social facilitation and social loafing.*
   - Individual behaviour is variously modified by the presence of others or by being a part of a group.
   - The concepts of social influence, social facilitation, synergy and social loafing distinguish the direction and nature of such modifications.

3. *Understand why groups develop norms and use sanctions to regulate the behaviour of their members.*
   - Social norms guide the behaviour of individuals in a group. They can be pivotal or peripheral.
   - Social norms are established in four ways—explicit statement. critical events, initial behaviour and transfer behaviour.
   - Sanctions are administered by members to those individuals who transgress or uphold the group's norms. Sanctions can therefore be negative (verbal abuse) or positive (praise). Groups possess an escalating hierarchy of ever-stronger negative sanctions.

4. *Understand the process of group socialization of individuals.*
   - Groups teach new members about their norms and incorporate them in their shared frame of reference through the process of group socialization.

5. *Explain why individuals conform to the dictates of their group.*
   - As individuals, we tend to conform to group norms because of benefits for us individually if others abide by the agreed rules; our desire for order and meaning in our lives; and a need to receive a satisfying response from others.
   - The 'cost' to the person who is a member of a group is the deindividuation that membership entails. Group membership brings with it anonymity and becoming 'lost in the crowd'. This can reduce our sense of individual responsibility, lower our social constraints and lead us to engage in impulsive, antisocial acts.

6. *Distinguish between conformity and conversion.*
   - Group orientation differs in depending on the culture in which an individual lives.
   - Research shows both that a majority influences an individual (called *conformity*), and that a minority can influence a majority (called *conversion*).

Revision

1. Consider the advantages and disadvantages at work of being (a) 'one of the gang' (b) a 'lone wolf'—loner (c) somewhere in between.

2. Your instructor is proposing to set a student group assignment as part of the continuous assessment for this course. However, you are concerned about the effect that social loafing might have on your group's overall performance, the likely contributions of your other group members, and the equitable award of marks among the individual group members. How would you respond to your instructor's proposal?

3. Is conformity by individuals within organizations a bad thing, and should it be eliminated? Or is it a good thing that should be encouraged?

4. Critically evaluate the empirical research on individual conformity to group pressure.

5. Suggest how an individual might go about persuading a majority.

Springboard

Diener, E., 1979, 'Deindividuation: Self-awareness and disinhibition', *Journal of Personality and Social Psychology*, vol. 37, pp. 1160–71.

Article describing the theory and research into deindividuation.

Doms, M. and van Avermaet, E., 1981, 'The conformity effect; A timeless phenomenon?' *Bulletin of the British Psychological Society*, vol.36, pp.180–8.

These authors replicated Solomon Asch's classic studies on individual conformity in groups and obtained similar results.

Hogg, M.A. and Vaughan, G.M., 1998, *Social Psychology*, Prentice Hall Europe, Hemel Hempstead.

An introductory textbook for social psychology. Chapter 7, entitled 'Basic group processes', provides more detailed, experimental description and discussion of the concepts briefly considered in this chapter.

Huczynski, A.A., 1996, *Influencing Within Organizations*, Prentice Hall, Hemel Hempstead.

This book discusses varied aspects of influencing. Chapter 12 concentrates on influencing a group, summarizing Moscovici's research findings and complementing them with other techniques to influence groups of people.

Latane, B., Williams, K. and Harkins, S., 1979, 'Many hands make light the work: The causes and consequences of social loafing', *Journal of Personality and Social Psychology*, vol.37. no.6, pp. 822–32.

This is a full account of the re-creation of Ringelmann's experiment which first revealed the existence of the phenomenon of social loafing.

McKinlay, A. and Taylor, P., 2000, *Inside the Factory of the Future*, Routledge, London.

Considers work, power and authority in a microelectronics plant, and highlights how group pressure is used to affect the performance of individual workers.

Home viewing

The film *I'm All Right, Jack* (1960, director John Boulting) is a satirical British tragi-comedy which looks at labour relations in the Britain of the 1950s. Stanley Windrush (played by Ian Carmichael) is the new, upper-class recruit to the company. He is torn between the demands of his work mates and the union shop steward, Kite (Peter Sellers), and his employer (played by Terry Thomas). He is keen to do well, but before he can be accepted by his fellow workers, he has to learn all the informal rules and practices that they have developed, and which they use against the management. Much of the first part of the film illustrates the concept of compliance. It deals with Windrush's socialization into the informal organization of the company. As you watch the film, answer the following three questions. What informal norms does he learn? How does he learn them? Where does he learn them?

In the film *Twelve Angry Men* (1957, directed by Sidney Lumet), a jury retires to deliberate and to decide on the guilt or innocence of a youth from a slum background. At the outset, eleven of the twelve jurors are convinced of the boy's guilt and are keen to find him guilty without further discussion. Only one member of the jury, played by Henry Fonda, has reservations and persuades the other members to take the time to review the evidence. Fonda manages to change the guilty votes of the other eleven jurors and persuades them to acquit the young defendant. The film illustrates the concept of *conversion*. Watch Fonda's behaviour carefully. At first sight it appears that it is random. But then, you'll see a pattern. What is that pattern? What influencing tactics does he use? Which types of power are possessed by which characters in the film?

OB in literature

Fred Voss, *Goodstone*, Bloodaxe Books, Newcastle upon Tyne, 1991.

Poems by a machinist who works on the shop floor of a US company which manufactures aircraft parts. The verses describe his experiences with groups of fellow workers and managers. Some informative, some cynical, but always thought-provoking.

Chapter exercises

1: The Ringelmann effect

Objectives

1. To introduce you to the concept of social loafing.
2. To recreate one of the experiments that identified it.

Briefing

1. Your instructor will ask some of you to come to the front and produce some shouts (raaaaaah!).
2. Shouters will be asked to make that sound for 5 seconds.
3. We are interested in how loudly each of you can sound.
4. You will be asked to produce these shouts in groups of one, two, four and six.
5. Although this is not a competition, you will not learn your scores until the end of the experiment.
6. Before each shout, put your hands over your ears.

2: Discovering the norms

Objectives

1. To raise your understanding of the effect of group norms on behaviour in a non-university and a university environment.
2. To demonstrate the link between behaviour in groups and the creation of group norms; and to enable you to identify group norm enforcement strategies.

Background

Often group norms are implicit rather than explicit, and are difficult to identify. Nevertheless, individuals' behaviour may be influenced by norms which they may not be fully conscious of. When people become aware of the norms that affect them, they are able to understand their own behaviour. This activity seeks to make group norms explicit.

Briefing

Step 1: Write down the THREE most salient norms that operate in your university class or tutorial group.

Step 2: For each of the three norms, respond to the three questions below:

- How was this group norm communicated to newcomers to the group, including yourself?
- What happens to people who violate this norm? How did the group 'police' itself? How does any individual feel who 'goes against' this group norm?
- Does the norm affect group performance positively or negatively? Explain how.

Step 3: In small groups, compare and discuss your answers to the questions about the operation of norms of your university group.

Step 4: If time permits, repeat this activity for a group of which you are a member *outside* the university (e.g. work team, sports team, church group, youth group).

Chapter 12 Teamworking

Key concepts

team autonomy	autonomous teamwork
advice team	total quality management
quality circle	just-in-time system
action team	external work team differentiation
project team	internal work team differentiation
cross-functional team	external work team integration
production team	team performance
empowerment	team viability
high-performance work system	

Learning objectives

When you have read this chapter, you should be able to define those key concepts in your own words, and you should also be able to:

1. Understand why 'team' is a contested concept in the organizational literature.

2. List the nine dimensions of team autonomy.

3. Differentiate between four major types of team and give an example of each.

4. Discuss the types of obstacle to effectiveness experienced by each type of team.

5. Contrast Western with Japanese concepts of teamworking.

6. Describe the four main variables in an ecological framework for analysing work team effectiveness.

7. Explain some of the problems of objectively assessing the costs and benefits of teamworking arrangements.

Why study teamworking?

Research shows that 70 per cent of air disasters are caused by failures in teamworking rather than by individual human errors or mechanical breakdown. If poor teamworking does not kill you, it can seriously reduce your work motivation and raise your level of job stress. Yet teamworking has been found to increase productivity and increase job satisfaction, to the benefit of both the organization and the employee. Managers want to know how they can obtain the benefits of teamworking without its costs.

The potential of teamworking to contribute to organizational (management) goals has been rediscovered at the level of the shop floor by the interest in Japanese teamworking, seen by many critics as a means of creating a compliant and programmable workforce. The research literature reveals a continuing, world-wide, organizational trend towards the introduction of teamworking. John Geary (1996) argued that senior management appeared to believe that teams were an effective way of

- identifying and solving work-related problems;
- increasing product quality;
- speeding up innovations;
- improving performance;
- achieving better industrial relations;
- increasing employee participation.

Indeed, some critics claim that teamworking is seen as a simple solution to virtually all organizational problems. Much management research, consultancy work and money has been, and continues to be, spent on making teams work well in companies. However, the research evidence on the effectiveness of teamworking remains ambiguous. There have been methodological problems of definitions and generalizability of results. The results of teamworking initiatives have been variable, and 'the jury is still out'. Despite research, our understanding of how to make teams effective remains incomplete. With the current popularity of teamworking in organizations, it is important to critically assess the suggestions, research and prescriptions on offer.

The T-word and team job design

Nicky Hayes saw teams as a sporting metaphor used frequently by managers and consultants. It stressed both inclusiveness and similarity—members sharing common values and co-operating to achieve common goals, while also emphasizing differences, as various individuals play distinct, albeit equally valuable, roles and have different responsibilities. She wrote that (Hayes 1997, p.27):

> The idea of 'team' at work must be one of the most widely used metaphors in organizational life. A group of workers or managers is generally described as a 'team', in much the same way that a company or department is so often described as 'one big family'. But often, the new employee receiving these assertions quickly discovers that what was described as a 'team' is actually anything but. The mental image of cohesion, co-ordination and common goals which was conjured up by the metaphor of the team, was entirely different from the everyday reality of working life.

Jos Benders and Geert Van Hootegem (1999; 2000) felt that after decades of experimentation, teams had finally achieved the status of 'good management practice' in Western organizations. Echoing Hayes' point, they wrote that 'team is a word for managers', that is, an appealing word used as a rhetorical strategy through which managers hope to achieve their goals. Academics and practitioners around the world had developed different notions of what was meant by teamworking [**link**, chapter 9, group formation]. Benders and Van Hootegem went on to distinguish three different meanings of the word 'team' as used by Japanese managers working in Western countries:

Team as collective spirit

The appealing label 'team work' is used to convey the necessity of the desired co-operative spirit when establishing Japanese transplants in Western countries (e.g. 'Team Toyota' in its plant in Kentucky, USA). Employees are socialized into an organization's cultural 'community of fate' [link, chapter 19, organization culture].

Teams as the hallmark of lean production

Based on the book *The Machine That Changed the World* (Womack *et al.*, 1990), teams are assigned a critical role in lean production's superior performance and are presented as a a break with European and American 'Fordist' production practices [link, chapter 13, traditional work design].

Teams as quality control circles

Groups of employees who meet to improve their work situation. These were widely adopted in Europe and America during the 1980s. However, their popularity was short-lived as they failed to deliver quick performance improvements. Although QC circles were, in theory, considered to be distinct from work units, in practice there was considerable overlap between the two.

Assigning a task to a team of people rather than to a single individual is a relatively recent practice. More is known about individual-based than team-based job design. J. Richard Hackman (1983; 1990), a major contemporary contributor to the theory and practice of work organization, is also an active promoter of team-working. Writing about job design in the context of teamworking, he argued that the job characteristics model recommendations were as valid at the team level as they were at the individual level (Hackman, 1987) [link, chapter 8, motivation]. Managers could expect a team to perform at a high level when:

- The team task required members to use a variety of relatively high-level skills.

- The team task was a whole, meaningful piece of work with a visible outcome.

- The task provided team members with substantial autonomy to decide how they would do the work.

- The outcomes of the team's work on the task possessed significant consequences for other people.

- Working on the task generated regular, trustworthy feedback about how well the team was performing.

Second, he felt that team composition was critical to successful teamworking. He recommended that managers should ensure that three conditions were met:

- Individual team members possessed the necessary task-relevant expertise and interpersonal skills to do their work.

- The team was large enough to perform the work.

- Membership was moderately diverse in terms of talents and perspectives.

Table 12.1: Types of teams and their outputs

Types and examples	Degree of differentiation from other work units	Degree of co-ordination with other work units	Degree of technical specialization	Work cycles/time frame	Typical outputs
Advice Committees Review panels and boards Quality control circles Employee involvement groups Advisory councils	Low	Low	Low	Work cycles can be brief or long; one cycle can be a team life span	Decisions Selections Suggestions Proposals Recommendations
Action Sports teams Entertainment groups Expeditions Negotiating teams Surgery teams Cockpit crews Military platoons and squads	High	High	High	Work cycles brief, repeated under new conditions	Competitive events Expeditions Contracts Lawsuits Concerts Surgical operations Flights Combat missions
Project Research groups Planning teams Architect teams Engineering teams Development teams Task forces	High	Low (for traditional units) or High (for cross-functional teams)	High	Work cycles typically differ for each new project; one cycle can be a team's life span	Plans Designs Investigations Presentations Prototypes Reports Findings
Production Assembly teams Manufacturing cells Mining teams Flight attendant crews Data-processing groups Maintenance crews	Low	High	High	Work cycles typically repeated or continuous process; cycles often briefer than team life span	Food Chemicals Components Assemblies Retail sales Customer service Equipment repairs

Based on Eric Sundstrom, Kenneth De Meuse and David Futrell, 'Work teams', *American Psychologist*, February 1990, pp.120–33: 125.

Types of team

Many different types of team operate within organizations. Eric Sundstrom, Kenneth De Meuse and David Futrell (1990) distinguished four types of team, based on their objective and type of output produced. These are summarized in table 12.1 and are labelled advice, action, project and production. Each team type is further differentiated along four dimensions:

- *Degree of technical specialization*: Are members required to apply special, technical skills acquired through higher education or extensive training (high differentiation); or do they draw upon their members' general experience and problem-solving ability (low differentiation)?

- *Degree of co-ordination*: Is its work closely related to and intertwined with that of other work units within the organization (high co-ordination); or does it operate relatively independently (low co-ordination).

- *Work cycles*: How much time does the team need to achieve its aims? Does it perform short, repetitive work cycles or a single, long one?

- *Typical outputs*: What does the team produce as its output?

Teams differ in terms of how much autonomy management grants them. Jan Gulowsen (1979), a Norwegian researcher, provided a framework which enabled more specific assessments to be made about **team autonomy** for comparative purposes (table 12.2). He distinguished nine 'task areas' or dimensions in a team's working which offered the potential for autonomy. Within each area, he specified four possible levels of team input. This allows teams to be distinguished in terms of the level of autonomy that they possess.

Team autonomy refers to the extent to which a team experiences freedom, independence and discretion in decisions related to the performance of its tasks.

Stop and criticize

An external management consultant has suggested giving greater autonomy to (choose a work team with which you are familiar) to improve its morale and performance. Looking at this as a manager, what are the advantages and disadvantages of giving this team high (level 4) autonomy on these nine task areas? Looking at it as a trade union representative? Looking at this as an employee in the team?

Table 12.2: Team task areas, levels of team input and team autonomy levels

Team task area / dimensions

1. Selection of the team leader
2. Acceptance of a new member into the team
3. Distribution of work
4. Time flexibility
5. Acceptance of additional work
6. Representation outside the team
7. Production methods (choice of)
8. Production goals (output determination)
9. Production goals (quality determination)

Team input levels

1. *None*: No team participation and total management control. Managers make all the decisions and teams implement them. Team members have no input into the decision-making process; there is no element of participation, not even in the form of suggestions or requests.

2. *Some*: Teams have some input into decisions concerned with their immediate working environment. They can make suggestions and requests and have discussions with management, who may adopt their ideas.

3. *Joint*: A situation of co-decision making, in which teams share decision-making power with management, having an equal role in the taking and implementing of decisions.

4. *Autonomy*: Teams are fully trusted by management; the teams are truly autonomous, reaching their decisions with no input from management whatsoever. They are accepted by management as full and equal partners.

Team autonomy level

low-autonomy teams	**moderate-autonomy teams**	**high-autonomy teams**
assembly line workers	quality circles	autonomous work groups
supermarket checkouts	semi-autonomous groups	high-performance teams
		self-directed teams
		self-designing teams

Based on Jan Gulowsen, 'A measure of work-group autonomy' in L.E. Davies and J.C. Taylor (eds), *Design of Jobs*, second edition, Goodyear, Santa Monica, 1979, pp.206–18.

How much team autonomy in automobile manufacture?

Thomas Murakami investigated the degree of autonomy possessed by different manufacturing teams in the car industry. Nineteen final assembly automobile plants were studied, owned by fourteen different car companies: Toyota and Nissan in Japan; Nissan, Ford (Engines), Rover, Vauxhall, Rolls-Royce and Peugeot in the UK; GM-Bochum, GM-Eisenach, GM Opel-Russelsheim; Mercedes-Benz-Bremen, Mercedes-Benz-Sindelfingen; VW-Wolfsberg, BMW-Bavaria, Ford-Cologne in Germany; GM in Vienna; and GM Saab in Usikapungi in Finland.

Murakami assessed the degree of autonomy given to teams by management to influence decisions within their immediate work areas. Unlike some similar studies which surveyed company managers asking them to state which traditional management functions their teams performed, Murakami interviewed team leaders and personnel managers in these car plants; used observation during personal visits; and cross-checked using secondary sources. Using Gulowsen's nine key 'task areas of decision making' and his four 'levels of autonomy' framework, Murakami calculated an 'arithmetic mean' level of team autonomy for each area.

1 = None—no team participation / pure management decision.
2 = Some—team participation / suggestion, request, discussion.
3 = Joint—co-decision making / equal power with management.
4 = Autonomy—a team decision / no management involved.

Team task area	Average score
1. Selection of the team leader	2.5
2. Acceptance of new member into the team	1.4
3. Distribution of work within team	2.7
4. Time flexibility	1.4
5. Acceptance of additional work	1.0
6. Representation outside the team	2.1
7. Methods of production (choice of)	2.0
8. Production goals (output)	1.6
9. Production goals (quality)	2.3

The figures indicate that few teams scored much above 2.0. Murakami ranked the work teams at GM-Eisenach (2.7) and at GM's Finnish Saab plant (2.6) as the most autonomous, but that just indicated the suggestion–request level of input. The other German work teams averaged 2.2, slightly ahead of the Japanese, who were on or just below 2.0. British work teams were the least autonomous, scoring only 1.6 on average.

In none of Gulowsen's nine task areas was the average work team granted full autonomy. However, in two aspects—self-organization (combination of dimension 1: team leader selection, plus dimension 6: representation outside the team); and in production (combination of dimension 3: distribution of work, plus dimension 9: production goals quality, and to a lesser extent, plus dimension 7: production methods choice), they had somewhat more autonomy.

Murakami's view was that while the work teams studied lacked any real autonomy, they could influence management decisions to some degree, and management had departed from sole decision-making responsibility in many areas. On the basis of this empirical study, he concluded that management's power in prime task areas of production remained unchallenged, despite the introduction of team-working.

Based on Thomas Murakami, 'The autonomy of teams in the car industry—a cross-national comparison', *Work, Employment and Society*, 1997, vol.11, no.4, pp.749–58.

Advice teams

Advice teams are created primarily to provide a flow of information to management for use in its own decision making. Depending on organization circumstances, an **advice team** may be given authority to implement solutions to the problems that it has identified. It requires little in the way of co-ordination with other work units in the company. Following a major accident or disaster, governments often set up committees of experts and eminent people to advise it on future action. The committee reviews the events that occurred, makes recommendations about improvements, and suggests changes in the law.

In organizations, the **quality circle** has been the best-known and most publicized advice team of recent times. The original concept was of a team of six to twelve employees from the shop floor of the same manufacturing department, meeting regularly to discuss quality problems, investigating their causes, and recommending solutions to management. In practice, a wide range of different arrangements were established under this label. Circles varied in terms of the number of members; were applied in service as well as manufacturing contexts; included supervisory staff; discussed non-quality issues; and some had authority to implement their suggestions. All these matters depended on the basis upon which the circle was established by management in the particular organization.

Quality circles are a Japanese export and have been used worldwide. They were introduced into the West during the 1980s in an effort to emulate Japanese successes. The first quality circle in the United States is claimed to have been at the Lockheed Missile and Space Company at Sunnyvale in California in 1974, the first one in Britain appeared at Rolls-Royce in Derby in 1978. Although originally used in manufacturing, quality circles have been applied extensively in the service industries, government agencies, voluntary sector, the British National Health Service and many other types of organization. Despite their differences, which were mentioned earlier, quality circles do possess some common features:

- Membership is voluntary, and members are drawn from a particular department.

- No financial rewards are given for team suggestions.

- Members receive training in problem solving, statistical quality control and team processes.

- Their problem-solving domain is defined by management (often, but not always quality, productivity and cost reduction).

- Meetings are held weekly, usually in company time, often with trained facil-

Advice team refers to a team created primarily to provide a flow of information to management to be used in its own decision making.

Quality circles consist of shop floor employees from the same department, who meet for a few hours each week to discuss ways of improving their work environment.

itators helping members with training issues and helping them to manage the meetings.

- The decision to install quality circles is made at the top of the organization, and the circles are created at the bottom.

- Management's objectives for introducing quality circles vary greatly. They include quality improvement, quality enhancement and employee involvement. Although an organization may claim to have introduced quality circles, even at the height of their popularity, only a small proportion of employees ever took part (Marchington, 1992).

- Circles were developed in a largely atheoretical manner, and whatever underpinning theory they have is either implicit or was developed *post hoc* by their promoters.

- Quality circles represent one of the largest experiments in the use of advice teams to improve organizational performance during the 1980s. During the 1990s quality circles began to be superseded by the 'total quality movement' (Hill, 1991).

How popular were quality circles in the late 1990s?

Companies experimenting with new forms of work organization seek to achieve higher performance by introducing various employee participation schemes. Using the British Workplace Industrial Relations Survey (WIRS3), Robert McNabb and Keith Whitfield identified the most popular schemes. Their survey showed that quality circles ranked seventh out of ten, being used by just under a third of the companies studied.

	%
1. Using the management hierarchy chain to communicate to employees	61
2. Briefing groups (regular meetings between management and workers)	46
3. Regular newsletters	41
4. Profit-related pay or bonuses	40
5. Regular meetings between senior managers and workers	40
6. Share ownership schemes	35
7. **Quality circles**	31
8. Suggestion schemes	28
9. Presence of a joint consultative committee	23
10. Surveys or ballots of employee views or opinions	19

Based on Robert McNabb and Keith Whitfield, 'The distribution of employee participation schemes at the workplace', *The International Journal of Human Resource Management*, 1999, vol.10, no.1, February, pp.122–36.

Action teams

Action team members are specialized in terms of the knowledge and skill that they possess and contribute to achieving their team's objective. The 'performance' of an **action team** is brief and is repeated under new conditions each time. Additionally, both the specialized inputs of the various team members and the need for individuals to co-ordinate with other team members is high.

If a football player sustains a serious injury, an action team consisting of an accident and emergency (A&E) unit in a hospital may deal with him. While there, he may be given surgery by another action team, in the operating theatre. Finally,

An action team executes brief performances which are repeated under new conditions. Its members are technically specialized, and the team has a high need to co-ordinate its output with that of other work units.

when recuperating, he may attend a theatre play or symphony concert performed by yet another action team. In all these situations, action team members have to exhibit peak performance on demand.

A example of an action team is a crew. This term is frequently used to refer to employees who work on aircraft, boats, spacecraft and film sets. A distinguishing feature of a crew is that that it is equipment- or technology-driven. If the technology is changed, then so too is the nature of the crew. A crew depends on its technology, which transforms difficult, cognitive tasks into easy ones. The crew's 'tools' affect the division of labour among its members; and crew members use various techniques to co-ordinate their activities (Hare, 1992; Hutchins, 1990).

Ginnett (1993) reported how, on a Boeing 727 aircraft, the crew members' roles were determined by the location of their seats in the cockpit. The captain sat in the left seat, from which he tested all the emergency warning devices. He was the only one who could taxi the aircraft, since the nose wheel steering gear was located on that side of the cockpit. The first officer, who started the engines and who communicated with the tower, occupied the right-hand seat. The flight engineer sat sideways, facing a panel that allowed him to monitor and control the various sub-systems in the aircraft. He was the only one able to reach the auxiliary power unit. In other transportation craft, the relationship of roles to equipment would be different.

Two crews can be considered as existing, those inside the cockpit—the cockpit crew (pilots, flight engineer), and those outside it—the cabin crew (flight attendants). Between 1959 and 1989, 70 per cent of all severe aircraft accidents were at least partly attributable to flight crew behaviour (Wiener *et al.*, 1993). Thus, it is a more common cause than either pilot error or mechanical failure. In recent years,

The 4.81-second tyre change

When the Grand Prix car flicks into the pits to collect fresh tyres, usually just before the half-way distance, it is time for the pit crew to take their brief place in the sun under the eyes of the packed grandstands and the TV cameras. These are the glamorous moments that compensate for the endless hard graft that goes into making a winning racing team. The dream tyre change is the result of constant practice. Every pit team has to work hard in order to achieve it. The rehearsals go on throughout the year. On one occasion, the Benneton Ford pit crew managed to change Michael Schumacher's tyres in 4.81 seconds. Other racing teams aim for under 6 seconds, and some teams achieve 4.3 seconds, although in non-race conditions. Chief mechanics agree that 'Pit stops are a critical time for the lads. The pressure is really on'. The crew knows well that a good tyre change can make all the difference between victory and defeat.

The quickness of pit crew practically defeats the eye. Have you seen a tyre change on a Formula I car? How many mechanics were involved? You're in for a surprise. The answer is fifteen. There are three men at each corner of the car; one with the wheel gun, another to remove the wheel and a third to put on the replacement. One mechanic operates the front jack, one the rear jack, and the last man holds the crash hoop steady behind the driver's head to steady the car while it is on the jacks. In fact, sixteen people are needed for a successful tyre change, since the driver, streaking down the pit lane, has to stop no more than 6 to 12 inches in front of where the mechanics are positioned. Moving equipment wastes valuable tenths of seconds.

Curiously it is not a situation the pit crew really relishes. It is fraught with the possibili-

ties of a slip-up: just one sticking wheel nut, just one man unable to fling arms up in the all-clear signal, and the race can be lost. To achieve such a level of team performance systematically requires a military operation with movement programmes carefully worked out well in advance. It is often not realized just how much effort and how many people are needed to get the top international racing drivers on to a Grand Prix grid.

Based on Brian Allen, 'Seconds out—The way of life in the fast pit lane', *Daily Telegraph*, 12 July 1986, p.14

crew resource management (CRM) has been introduced to address this problem. CRM is defined as using all available resources—information, equipment and people—to achieve safe and efficient flight operations. Investigations have revealed that despite their close working proximity, crew members' understanding of developing problem situations, and how these should be addressed, often differed widely.

Conflicting mental models among team members impaired communications and the management of the workload. CRM training focuses on the team rather than the individual. It addresses issues of effective team formation and maintenance, leadership, problem solving, decision making and the maintenance of situation awareness. The training is not performed with the intention of strengthening any one particular flight team, since its members are rarely together for long (unlike all other forms of team development). Instead, CRM has the goal of making the individuals more effective in whichever team or flight crew they happen to find themselves.

Exocentric teams

Paul Goodman and Jeanne Wilson describe the recent emergence of what they call exocentric teams. These are teams whose members' focus is primarily on external activities and relationships. The globalization of work has placed people in distributed environments; information technology has created new opportunities for bridging space and time; and refocusing upon customers, suppliers and other constituencies has created new external relationships.

Exocentric teams take many forms but differ from traditional teams on three dimensions: structure, membership and effectiveness. Traditional research has focused on teams with a stable membership, whose members work for the same organization and who are located in space and time, and have internally defined standards of effectiveness. In contrast, the members of exocentric teams are frequently, and continually, reconfiguring and take in external people (as in the case of project teams); may lack face-to-face interaction (as in the case of international product development teams); and it may not be possible to specify the criteria for their success.

One can consider the case of the recently created computer emergency response teams (CERTs) in the United States. These teams are composed of people from different functional backgrounds, who may have to co-operate across organizational boundaries to prevent or minimize attacks on the internet. The major role of a CERT is to identify when an attack is occurring and to advise users about what to do. The product of a CERT is an advisory e-mail that may be sent to hundreds of thousands of people. Once this advisory communication is despatched, the team disbands. The recipients of the e-mail are often unknown to the team, and there is rarely any feedback.

Goodman and Wilson's argument is that current models of team effectiveness may not be applicable to these new forms of work team. That is, the basic assumptions that are inherent in most current models are violated in exocentric teams. If they are, what are the implications for understanding and assessing new forms of team? Many of the predictors of group process and outcomes identified in the literature may not fit exocentric teams. It forces researchers to ask new questions. For example, if teams are continually reconfiguring, in what ways do they transfer knowledge from one group to another. If teams (e.g. software development) are distributed over space and time, how do they learn?

Paul Goodman and Jeanne Wilson, 'New forms of work groups: exocentric teams', conference paper presented at Negotiations and Change: From Workplace to Society, 30–31 October 1998, MIT.

Project teams

Project team refers to a collection of employees from different work areas in an organization brought together to accomplish a specific task within a finite time.

A **project team** consists of individuals who have been brought together for a limited period of time, from different parts of the organization, to contribute towards a management-specified task. Once this has been completed, the team is either disbanded or else its members are given new assignments. Project teams are created when:

- creative problem solving is required involving the application of different types of specialized knowledge;

- there is a need to closely co-ordinate the work on a specific project, e.g. design and development, production and testing of a new product.

Every university has hundreds of project teams who are conducting research. Most of their members are on 2–3-year contracts which span the period of the research project. Team members are recruited on the basis of their specialist knowledge, and their output is a research report and book and journal publications.

Within the organizational context, one of the best-known and most common types of project team is the **cross-functional team**. Jack Gordon (1992) reported the spread of work teams in the United States. His report showed that, across all sizes of organization (with more than 100 employees), 82 per cent stated that some employees were members of a working group identified as a team, and of these, 18 per cent of employees belonged to a cross-functional team. Another survey, this time by the Hay Group, revealed that approximately 25 per cent of US companies had implemented cross-functional teams, with variations across industries (Leshner and Brown, 1993, p.39).

Cross-functional team refers to a team composed of employees from about the same hierarchical level but from different work areas or functions in the organization, who are brought together to complete a particular task.

Traditionally, organizations have been divided into tall, functional 'boxes' or 'chimneys'. It has been argued that by forming teams consisting of people from these different boxes, organizations could break down the boundaries between their functions (e.g. accounting, marketing, research, product design, human resources), improve co-ordination and integration, release creative thought of their employees; and increase the speed and flexibility of their responses to customers. They are established with the objective of combining a wide range of expertise in order to reach a more informed and rounded outcome than would otherwise be possible.

Cross-functional teams comprise employees who traditionally work in different departments or work areas. Sometimes, they may also include customers, suppliers and external consultants. They are supported by their organization's structures, systems and skills, which enable teams to operate successfully as more independent units (less bound by functional ties) towards goals which transcend the abilities of individual members.

Proponents of cross-functional teams claim that they are beneficial to their customers, employees and the organization as a whole. Customers obtain more attractive and customized products, and have their needs met more rapidly. Team members benefit through having more challenging and rewarding jobs with broader responsibilities; greater opportunities for gaining visibility in front of senior management; increased understanding of entire processes across the organization; a 'fun' working environment; and closer relationships with colleagues. The organization gains through:

- increased productivity;

- improved co-ordination and integration;

- significantly reduced processing times;

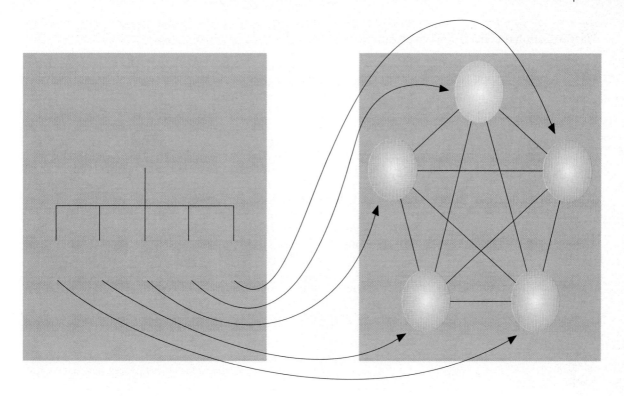

Figure 12.1: Cross-functional team

- improving market and customer focus;

- reducing the time needed to develop new products;

- improving communications by having boundaries between functions spanned.

In effect, therefore, the cross-functional team resembles a 'mini-company'. They most commonly take the form of teams which are located towards the bottom of the hierarchy. The project teams are overlaid upon the existing functional structure of the organization, and hence are an addition to it.

Cross-functional teams differ from other types of team in three important respects:

- *Representative*: They are representative in that their individual members usually retain their position back in their 'home' functional department.

- *Temporary*: They have a finite life, even if their end is years in the future.

- *Innovation*: They are established to solve non-conventional problems and meet challenging performance standards.

The most common application of cross-functional teams is in new product development, innovation or R&D. However, they have also been used whenever an organization requires an input of diverse, specialist skills and knowledge. For example, in manufacturing and production (e.g. Chrysler, Motorola); in IT development, automation and support, simultaneously developing the soft skills of technically oriented IT staff (e.g. Procter & Gamble); to implement quality, cost, speed improvements and process re-engineering initiatives (e.g. USAir, Hallmark

Organizational context and cross-functional teams

For cross-functional teams to exist within an organizational environment, they must first define their role in relation to upper management and resolve inherent conflicts between the functions that they represent. An example drawn from an interview in one product development team shows how difficult this can be:

> The total amount of electrical power in a vehicle is determined by the capacity of an alternator. This power must serve 20 subsystems, such as the stereo, the engine, the instrument panel, and so on. These subsystems are developed and controlled by separate 'chimney' organizations, and power allocations must be made for each system. The problem was, in this vehicle programme, when all the requirements of all the chimneys and teams were added up, they equalled 125 percent of the capacity of the alternator. Keith, who had recently taken over as head of this vehicle programme, which had made changes in direction and was behind schedule, called a meeting of the Programme Steering Team designed to resolve this conflict and reach a compromise. However, many of the chimney representatives who were the members of the team, came to this meeting with instructions from their bosses (who incidentally, did their performance appraisals ...) *not* to make any compromises, but to make certain that their chimney 'got what it needed' and 'didn't lose out'. After Keith presented the group with the problem and the need to reach a compromise solution, their response surprised him: 'It's not *our* problem', they replied, 'it's *your* problem'. Keith soon changed his job again. (p.1011)

From Daniel Denison, Stuart Hart and Joel Kahn, 'From chimneys to cross-functional teams: developing and validating a diagnostic model', *Academy of Management Journal*, 1996, vol.39, no.4, pp.1005–23

Cards); to implement customer service improvements (e.g. Unisys Client Server Systems Groups); to streamline purchasing and procurement; streamlining and optimization; for market research (e.g. Polaroid); for creativity and business improvement (e.g. Konica Imaging); or for benchmarking.

It has been argued by critics that cross-functional team members, since they are representatives, owe their true allegiance to their home functional department; that the chances of pressure and conflict are higher than in other teams; and that their temporary nature puts strain on members who have quickly to develop stable and effective working group processes. Cross-functional teams place great demands on the organizational support system and can have a negative effect on the individual team member. They suggest that organizations and managers need clearly to define cross-functional team assignments in order to maintain order and accountability.

Critics of cross-functional teams also acknowledge the restrictions on information flow, knowledge, and therefore on performance and the internal battles over intra-company territories that functional boundaries cause. They offer the example of sales managers who never see their impact on distribution costs when offering a service frequency promise to clinch sales. This view encapsulates the main tensions many researchers perceive in a shift to increased cross-functional team application. Nevertheless, in total, current literature projects at best a mixed, at worst a biased set of findings.

Stop and criticize

As a manager or graduate management trainee, you have just been assigned from your 'home' functional department (finance, marketing or production) to join a cross-functional team tasked with developing new company products. In six months time, your functional head of department will be appraising your performance and recommending promotions and pay increases. What concerns do you have about your membership of, and contribution to, the cross-functional team?

Team processes in a cross-functional team

The conflicting demands inherent in the organizational context place a premium on a team's internal processes. Team members need to be both representatives of their functional authority structures and creative problem solvers. Meeting both of these demands requires a broad and flexible team process. The following story, taken from a process improvement team, illustrates some of these dynamics:

> Our formalized approach to managing cross-functional teams can really get in the way. [For example] . . . our organization has several common practices that make an effective team process difficult. [First] . . . we always meet in large, horseshoe shaped conference rooms and take turns making presentations to each other. Very few of these meetings actually lead to creative problem solving. Sometimes, a representative from one of the chimneys will come in and 'drop the bomb' (deliver unexpected bad news) and then leave. [Second,] . . . the team is really a collection of sub teams that come and go during a meeting. The 'heavy breathers' (bosses) back in the functions will sometimes even send a delegate to our meetings with instructions to just watch and 'make sure nothing happens'. The result is that the team doesn't take collective responsibility, and that can be very de-motivating. [Third] . . . many teams are assigned 'content' leaders and 'process' leaders. The content leader is the technical expert—the 'real' boss—and the process leader helps run meetings and manage the team. The problem is that an effective team has to have flexible leadership— leadership and expertise need to change according to the issue and get passed around as needed.

This example illustrates the demands for both functional representation and creativity and the need to develop team identity and normative expectations if a team is to take collective responsibility for resolving a diverse set of demands. Leaders who facilitated flexible problem solving and team development seemed to have an advantage. (p.1012)

From D.R. Denison, S.L. Hart and J.A. Kahn, 'From chimneys to cross-functional teams: developing and validating a diagnostic model', *Academy of Management Journal*, 1996, vol.39, no.4, pp.1005–23. Used with permission.

Production teams

Production team refers to a stable number of individuals in a relationship involving shared and recognized production goals, with work status defined through a system of social roles and behavioural norms supported by a set of incentives and sanctions.

Typically, a **production team** consists of individuals who are responsible for performing day-to-day core operations. These may be product-oriented teams such as those assembling a computer on a factory floor; construction workers placing a bridge in position across a motorway; or teams assembling sound and light systems for a pop concert. The degree of technical specialization required of the team members varies from medium to low, depending on the nature of the duties performed. However, the degree of required co-ordination, both between the members of each team and between the team and other work units, is high. It is these other units that are either responsible for providing support activities such as quality control and maintenance or who provide the inputs to, or receive the outputs from, that team.

The modern concept of teamworking goes back to Eric Trist and Ken Bamforth (1951), who analysed the psychological and emotional responses to underground working by miners. The socio-technical paradigm was developed during the 1960s but became more widely known through applications in the late 1960s and 1970s. It was upon this basis that teamworking was established [**link**, chapter 3, technology].

Management's interest in production teams has always been in finding techniques for improving employee motivation and performance. The use of job enrichment and other individually based techniques for employee **empowerment** were considered earlier [**link**, chapter 8, motivation]. In this section, we examine empowerment from a team-based perspective, focusing upon self-

Suitable teamwork settings

There are different teams and many different types of work task and work setting. Some are suitable for teamworking, while others are not. Louis Davis and George Wacker cited situational factors which they believed facilitated autonomous group working:

1. When the work is not entirely unskilled.

2. When the work group can be identified as a meaningful unit of the organization, and when inputs and outputs are definable and clearly identifiable and the groups can be separated by stable buffer areas.

3. When turnover in the group can be kept to a minimum.

4. When there are definite criteria for performance evaluation of the group and group members.

5. When timely feedback is possible.

6. When the group has resources for measuring and controlling its own critical variances in workflow.

7. When the tasks are highly interdependent, so that group members must work together.

8. When cross-training is desired by management.

9. When jobs can be structured to balance group and individual tasks.

From Louis E. Davis and George J. Wacker, 'Job design', in G. Salvendy (ed.), *Handbook of Human Factors*, New York, Wiley, 1987.

managing or autonomous teamworking. The individual and the teamworking approaches have converged in practice in what has been become known as the **high performance work system**.

Alan Jenkins (1994) argued that management had become preoccupied with autonomous (or self-managed) teamworking, and that such teams had come to be seen as the basis for effective organizational designs. Other authors have noted some of the social and historical processes that have led to the emergence of **autonomous teamworking** as part of management's quest for better performance. Table 12.3 summarizes the two historical phases of interest in teams.

Empowerment is the term given to organizational arrangements that allow employees more autonomy, discretion and unsupervised decision-making responsibility.

High-performance work system refers to a form of organization that operates at levels of excellence far beyond those of comparable teams.

Autonomous teamworking refers to a process whereby management gives formal groups the right to make decisions on how their work is performed on a group basis without reference to management.

High-performance teams at Digital Equipment in Scotland

Digital Equipment Corporation (DEC) started to develop high-performance work systems around empowered teams at its manufacturing plant in Ayr, on the west coast of Scotland, in the early 1980s. These teams were responsible for the manufacture of the company's range of small business computers, and had the following features:

- autonomous teams of six to twelve employees were self-managing and self-organizing, functioning without first-line supervision;

- each team had full 'front to back' responsibility for a whole section of the manufacturing process, such as assembling a complete printed circuit board;

- teams negotiated their production targets with their product manager, based on available staff, materials and equipment;

- team members were expected to share their skills with each other, to become multiskilled, and had no job titles;

- team members were paid according to their skill level and not according to the particular job on which they were working at any one time;

- team members were involved in the performance appraisal of colleagues, and in the selection procedure for new recruits;

- the physical layout on the factory floor was open to facilitate communications, and technical support staff had their 'offices' and desks on the shop floor too.

This approach to work design improved productivity, reduced the time required to introduce new products, and led to more effective problem solving and decision making. Shop-floor personnel developed a range of analytic, problem-solving, interpersonal, process design and group management skills through this approach, leading in many instances to significant career opportunities and development.

Based on David Buchanan and James McCalman, *High Performance Work Systems: The Digital Experience,* Routledge, London, 1989.

Table 12.3: Historical changes in management's interest in autonomous teamworking

1970 to 1985	1985 to 1994
Focus on strategic organizational change	
• Break with negative consequences of assembly-line type (Taylorist) work design.	• More integrated organizational design.
• Aim to increase productivity, attendance, job satisfaction and quality of working life.	• High skill, responsible workers possess adaptability and flexibility.
• Other techniques include job enlargement, job rotation and, occasionally workplace democracy.	• They are capable of using IT to increase productivity and quality.
• Organizational designs *included* autonomous teams.	• Organizational designs *built around* autonomous groups.
Scale and scope of management involvement in team activities	
• Many time-limited autonomous group experiments, but only in specific and linked areas of operation.	• Teamworking initiatives part of an overall strategy of de-layering to create flatter, 'leaner' organization structures.

- 'Islands of autonomy' in a sea of orthodox, Taylorist theory and practice, lacking top management support.

- Neither extension of experiments nor equivalent changes in human resource areas like compensation, recruitment, training, etc.

- Initial concern that teamworking would destroy job demarcation, and replace a job focus with a task or team focus.

- Initial focus on shop-floor manufacturing and production teams. Often, greenfield sites of electronics and automotive sector companies.

- Recognition of the need to change managerial roles to fit these new structures.

- Greater recognition of the time and financial resources required to achieve such organizational re-design.

- Union acceptance of the need for greater job flexibility that team organization requires.

- Extension of autonomous groups to different types of organization and to different hierarchical levels. Contexts now include customer care, health care, prison service and technical support.

Implementing autonomous teamworking

AutoEuropa is an automobile manufacturing facility in Palmela, Portugal. It was established as a result of a $2.54 billion joint venture between the Ford Motor Company and Volkswagen AG. The state-of-the-art plant was inaugurated in April 1995. It produces a high-quality, multipurpose vehicle (MPV) using the most recent production processes and seeks to become best-in-class. Its 173 robots apply 60 per cent of the 4,600 welding spots automatically.

In addition to its lean manufacturing and leading-edge technology, the company has sought to involve employees and commit them to its success by allowing them to contribute to its long-term development. To achieve this, it planned to establish a form of autonomous teamworking involving *self-directed teams* (SDTs). The selection and recruitment of team members focused not just on their age and qualification but also on an appropriate regard and aptitude for teamworking. Those recruited were given not only technical training but also behavioural training, the latter to encourage co-operation, develop communication and foster a creative and satisfying teamwork spirit and environment of trust which encourages a commitment to personal and professional goals.

Each team of employees was considered to be an organizational unit responsible for a complete work process which delivered a product or service to an internal or external customer. Units were responsible for both their work functions and for their self-management. The team members would participate in setting their own goals; take responsibility for the quality of their products and services; co-ordinate their work with other teams and departments; plan, control and improve their own work processes;

participate in the hiring of new members and selection of the team leader; be responsible for planning their own work according to the needs identified; review their performance as a team; be empowered to share several management and leadership functions; and assume authority and responsibility for their work, becoming responsible for continuous improvement.

The move to autonomous teamworking was a planned progression. It began with an implementation phase, which lasted from 1992 to mid-1995. In this phase, three activities were found to be significant— defining the main criteria for teamworking; the empowerment process; and the continuous improvement system. The first of these concerned stating the conditions that needed to be in place if the project was to be a success. It involved detailing the team's goals, size, structure and format; selecting team leaders; planning and implementing job rotation and task enrichment; and arranging training. The second crucial activity was the empowerment process, during which the leadership style was defined. The objective was to change from a directive to an empowering style in which the leader played a facilitative role. Finally, the continuous improvement system operated to generate and reward new ideas and thereby commit employees to continually reassessing their working methods.

Following the implementation phase of the programme, the development phase was started. It involved specialists analysing each work team's problems, and suggesting appropriate team training or development activities. This assisted the team to progress through the four development stages, labelled 'getting started', 'going in circles', 'getting on course' and 'full speed ahead'. At each further stage, members participate more; are more able to set and follow their own ground rules; give and receive feedback; value individual differences; make use of each others' ideas; and suggest improvement in production processes and technology. During 1997, AutoEuropa launched its first autonomous work team (which it called a self-directed team).

Based on Joao Carlos Peixoto and Ulrich Schumacher, 'AutoEuropa: the team concept', *P1 European Participation Monitor*, 1997, Issue No.13, pp.20–5.

Total quality management refers to a philosophy of management that is driven by customer needs and expectations, and which is committed to continuous improvement.

Just-in time systems refer to managing inventory (stock) in which items are delivered when they are needed in the production process, instead of being stored by the manufacturer.

Japanese teamworking (also known as *Toyotaism*) refers a particular form of work organization that is based on the Japanese production model. It stresses lean production, the efficient use of factory labour and flexible work practices, and it incorporates **total quality management** (TQM) and **just-in-time systems** (JIT).

Japanese teamworking is not the same as the teamworking that came to prominence in most Scandinavian and American companies during the 1960s and 1970s (MacDuffee, 1998). The differences are summarized in table 12.4.

There has been confusion about the use of the concept of teamworking in different countries. Western teamworking emphasizes enhanced employee control and job satisfaction through participation, and represents an example of worker empowerment. Japanese teamworking, in contrast, operates at the other end of the autonomous teamwork continuum. It uses the scientific management principles of 'minimum manning, multi-tasking, multi-machine operation, pre-defined work operations, repetitive short cycle work, powerful first line supervisors, and a conventional managerial hierarchy' (Buchanan, 1994, p.219). Japanese work teams tend to be advice teams mistaken for production teams. They meet and function as teams 'off line' (outside the production context), in contrast to autonomous work groups, which function as teams 'on line' (in the production context).

Martin Parker and Jane Slaughter (1988) were critical of Japanese teamworking, describing it as part of an overall management package which they labelled 'management by stress'. In their view, what appears to be participation is in fact a new form of exploitation. Innovations like the 'team' concept increase the pace and pressure of work, despite the rhetoric of worker empowerment. The innovation expands management's control by getting workers to 'participate' in the intensification of their own exploitation. The outcome is a low-skill, repetitive ('lean and mean'), mass production system. Japanese teamworking contains the following elements (Parker and Slaughter, 1988, p.5, cited in Garrahan and Stewart, 1992, p.88):

> **Japanese teamworking** uses scientific management principles of minimum manning, multi-tasking, multi-machine operation, repetitive short-cycle work, powerful first-line supervisors and a conventional managerial hierarchy.

1. A rewritten contract announcing that a new relationship exists between the company and its workforce.

2. Interchangability, meaning that workers are required or induced (through pay for knowledge) to be capable of doing several jobs.

3. Drastic reduction of classifications, giving management increased control to assign workers as it sees fit.

4. Less meaning for seniority. In most cases seniority is explicitly undermined or modified. For example, if classifications are eliminated, opportunities to transfer to different classifications by seniority are also eliminated.

5. Detailed definition of every job step, increasing management control over the way jobs are done.

6. Workers' participation in increasing their own workload.

7. More worker responsibility, without more authority, for jobs previously performed by supervisors.

8. A management attempt to make workers aware of the interrelatedness of the plant's departments and the place of the individual in the whole; an attempt by union and management to get away from the 'I just come to work, do my job and mind my own business' outlook.

9. An ideological atmosphere that stresses competition between plants and workers' responsibility for winning work away from other plants.

10. A shift towards enterprise unionism, where the union sees itself as a partner of management.

Karen Legge (1995) asked why there in not more overt opposition from these production line workers, who were colluding in their own subjugation. She offered the first three explanations, to which Ruth Milkman (1998) adds a fourth.

1. *Careful selection of employees*: On greenfield sites, new staff are chosen on the basis of their behavioural traits (rather than relevant skills), and for having the 'right attitude' towards teamworking and flexibility.

2. *Team leader's role*: The role of the shop steward on the shop floor has been marginalized through developing the role of the team leader. This individual is responsible both for achieving production targets and for the social organization of the group.

3. *Innate appeal*: The appealing aspects of this teamworking approach—mutual support, limited participation, collective endeavour, emphasis on consensus—coupled with the company's 'family orientation', the potential to enhance job satisfaction and to save jobs, all make it appealing to recruits.

4. *Contrast with past*: Workers who have experienced both the traditional, authoritarian management system and the new participatory initiatives prefer the latter despite some criticism of them.

Several researchers have highlighted the contradictions between management desire for control and attempts to increase team autonomy. Anna Pollert (1996) studied the imposition of teamworking on a repetitive, low-skill assembly line manufacturing chocolate. She described how managers sought to gain employee

Table 12.4: A comparison of Japanese and Swedish approaches to the organization of production and work

Variables	Japan: Toyota	Sweden: Volvo
Production flow design	Trimmed lines JIT techniques	Socio-technical design Job enrichment
Relations between groups	High degree of sequential dependence. Elimination of buffers.	Group control of boundaries. Independence through buffers.
Supervision	High-density production. Emphasis on the authority and role of the supervisor.	Low-density production. Emphasis on planning and co-ordination by supervisors.
Administrative control	Leading hands appointed by management. Suggestions are encouraged but decisions are hierarchically determined to ensure standardization.	Leading hands appointed by the group. Job rotation.
Workload and performance	Intense peer and supervisory pressure for maximum job performance and low absenteeism.	Regulated by union–management agreements.
Role of unions	Management exclusively decides about work organization and wage systems. Weak union influence.	Job content and wage system regulated by agreement. Union involvement in production design and development.

From Olle Hammarstrom and Russell D. Lansbury, 'The art of building a car: the Swedish experience re-examined', *New Technology, Work and Employment*, 1991, vol.6, no.2, pp.85–90: 89.

commitment to the company in a situation in which work intensification and job rationalization engendered feelings of alienation, and where management values stressed cost control. Andrew Scott's (1994) study of a frozen food processing plant revealed how management conceded team autonomy provided that the shop-floor employees agreed to accept greater discipline and exert extra effort. Once employees had exercised this new autonomy by increasing their control over the work process, the management responded by re-establishing its own direct control.

Andy Danford also discussed the contradictions of applying this type of team-working to repetitive, low-skill, assembly line work. Teamworking espouses team participation and empowerment, but managers simultaneously seek to retain traditional control. His own case study research of a firm in South Wales which manufactured large pressed steel sub-assemblies such as car doors, subframes and dashboards for the auto industry (Danford, 1998) challenged the positive assessments of Japanese teamworking provided by earlier authors (Kenney and Florida, 1993; Womack *et al.*, 1990). He argued that management could exploit labour flexibility by using a form of teamworking which actually *disempowered* workers. He reported how temporary employee upskilling and team autonomy came to be replaced by a strengthening of management control. He pointed to the impact of external factors, specifically supplier–customer relations; management's wish to exert unfettered control over labour utilization; and its desire to have a co-operative and motivated workforce who were employed in an alienating, mass production environment. These inherent conflicts and contradictions appeared to be a feature of attempts to implement Japanese teamworking in lean production environments (Blyton and Bacon, 1997).

Teamwork and peer surveillance

The critical theorists would suggest that, apart from facilitating labour intensification, Japanese-style teamworking acts as a self-policing device through peer surveillance and control. At the same time, it provides a focus for collective solidaristic sentiment and 'manufactures consent' (Burawoy, 1979). At Nissan, peer surveillance takes the form of the 'neighbour check' system of quality control. In other words, workers in their roles as 'customers' of the previous production process, and within work teams, are encouraged to identify defects caused by other workers and to allocate responsibility for such errors. The objective is to bring peer pressure within the team not to 'let down' a fellow team member. In practice workers feel they have to pick up each other's faults as the same thing will happen to them. Similarly it encourages competition between teams. 'Faults' are also exposed in *kaizen* meetings where, as one worker put it:

If you'd done anything wrong you got put in the middle and shouted at—'You've done this wrong.' There are lads of 35 years old who would be shouted at by lads who are team leaders of 22 years old.

The 'Help Lamp' (or *jidoka*) at Nissan not only assists peer surveillance but self-regulation too. Theoretically workers have the power to stop the line to deal with process problems or product defects, before faulty work reaches another team ('customer') downstream. According to Garrahan and Stewart (1992, p.105) this generates its own stress as operators feel that if they regularly stop the line they will be identified as incompetent. As a result they will rectify minor faults created by others upstream because, if the line is stopped for a minor defect, the resultant check of all the work might also reveal defects of their own making.

Finally peer surveillance operates to control absenteeism. Under a JIT system there is no cover for absentees other than those team members present, hence there is a moral pressure not to 'let down' work mates. This is reinforced in some companies by prominently displaying a list of absentees, and their reasons for absence, along with messages of how fellow team members are 'hurt by absenteeism' (Parker and Slaughter, 1988, p.106).

From Karen Legge, *Human Resource Management: Rhetoric and Reality*, Routledge, London, 1995, pp.232–3.

Stop and criticize

What is your reaction to Nissan's 'neighbour check' scheme described by Legge (see box)?

Under what circumstances would you welcome it? Resent it?

To the management and the customer, the scheme appears a reasonable way of ensuring a reliable product. Make a case against it as an assembly line worker.

An ecological framework for analysing work team effectiveness

Historically, attempts to understand the factors influencing team performance have used an input–process–output model. Its advantage is that it is easy to understand since it looks at the team from within, and all of us have been team members. However, this 'inside-out' approach, although still influential (West *et al.*, 1998; Kretch *et al.*, 1962), underplays the interdependencies of teamworking.

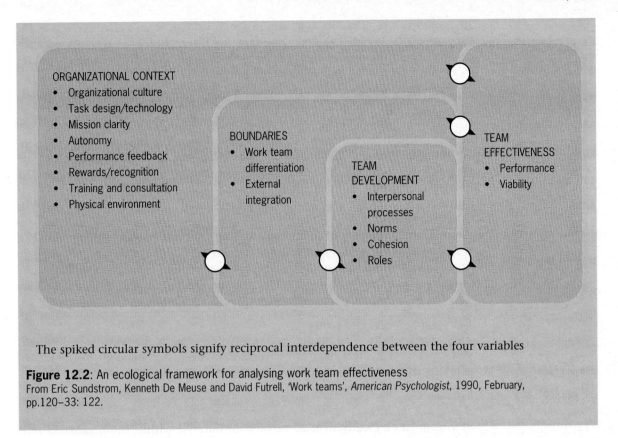

The spiked circular symbols signify reciprocal interdependence between the four variables

Figure 12.2: An ecological framework for analysing work team effectiveness
From Eric Sundstrom, Kenneth De Meuse and David Futrell, 'Work teams', *American Psychologist*, 1990, February, pp.120–33: 122.

In contrast, Eric Sundstrom, Kenneth De Meuse and David Futrell's (1990) ecological framework for analysing teamwork effectiveness provides an 'outside-in' perspective which looks at teams as embedded within their organization (see figure 12.2).

The framework emphasizes the interactions between a team and the different aspects of its environment. It also provides a reminder that the organization can facilitate or impede a team achieving effectiveness. It therefore offers a way to consider factors contributing to effectiveness. The framework holds that the effectiveness of any work team is best understood in terms of both its external surroundings and its internal processes, that is, in terms of factors that are external to the team itself but which exist within the organization. The framework is intentionally vague about causation and timing, seeing team effectiveness as more of an ongoing process than a fixed end-state. The framework also makes extensive use of the concept of boundary. Boundaries both separate and link the work team to its other work units and the organization as a whole. They act to:

- distinguish (differentiate) one work unit from another;

- present real or symbolic barriers to accessing or transferring information, goods or people;

- serve as points of external exchange with other teams, customers, peers, competitors or other entities;

- define what constitutes effectiveness for the team within its particular organizational context.

The framework suggests that, at any point in time, a team's effectiveness is the outcome of the reciprocal and simultaneous interactions between its organizational context, its boundaries and its level of development. Each of these four sets of variables will be described in turn.

Organizational context

The first major variable in Sundstrom *et al.*'s framework is the organizational context of the work team. This refers to those features of an organization which are external to the work team, but which are relevant to the way that it operates. The framework lists a total of eight such features.

1. *Organizational culture*
Every team operates within an organization that has its own culture and in a wider national cultural context [**link**, chapter 19, organization culture]. How do these values and beliefs impact on team effectiveness? Certain companies have a multi-stakeholder culture (e.g. Germany), where teamworking is more likely to succeed than in a shareholder culture (e.g. USA, Britain).

2. *Task design and task technology*
Every team works to complete its given task in a particular way. How do different types of task affect team effectiveness? Task technology refers to the way of working that is permitted or required. Technology may dictate a social organization of individual team roles.

3. *Mission clarity*
If a team has a clearly defined mission or purpose within the organization, it can assist those work units that are closely related to, or synchronized with, the team's work. How clear is the team's mission and how clearly has it been communicated to others?

4. *Autonomy*
Externally, management will determine a team's autonomy. Internally, it will depend on the role of the leader and how they delegate their authority within the team. Every effective team has to co-ordinate and integrate the contributions of its individual members. Which type of team leadership best achieves this?

5. *Performance feedback*
Does the team receive accurate, timely feedback on its performance from dependable measurement systems?

6. *Rewards and recognition*
These can be anything from financial rewards to verbal praise. Are the two sufficiently connected so that individual performance contributes to team effectiveness?

7. *Training and consultation*
Training and consultation in technical skills and interpersonal processes is seen as a key element in achieving team effectiveness. Cross-training in technical skills is very often a prerequisite for job rotation, which itself can be an aspect of autonomous group working.

8. *Physical environment*
The proximity of team members to each other affects both their ability to communicate and their level of team cohesion. Whether communicating across a table during a meeting or between workstations on a factory shop floor, territories can reinforce team boundaries and encourage or inhibit exchanges. Physical environments are therefore central to group boundaries (Sundstrom and Altman, 1989).

Organizational culture and teamworking

Teams failed to deliver results at Apple Computer in the 1980s because, in its early days in the previous decade, the company placed an emphasis on individualism. While individual creativity served it well in its initial phase, company growth heightened the need for communication between employees. Workers were assigned to cross-functional teams to set corporate strategy. The failure of the research and development, marketing, and manufacturing departments to work together undermined the corporation. 'When the dominant culture stresses the value of individual achievement and accountability rather than collective accomplishment, team structures won't be effective', wrote Michael Beer, a Harvard Business School professor.

Even companies that value collective efforts may undermine teams by basing salaries and promotion more on individual than on collective achievements. 'Unless a team's success is important to the employee's career, they probably won't pay much attention to it', said Jean Kahwajy, a management consultant with the Strategic Decision Group. Designing organization structures that achieve a balance between competition and co-operation, which combine team behaviours and individual motivation, is one of the hardest parts of building organizations. The more individualistic culture of the post-1980s makes this more difficult to achieve.

Based on Victoria Griffith, 'Teamwork's own goals', *Financial Times*, 18 July 1997.

Stop and criticize

Consider Denison *et al.*'s account of the alternator problem being addressed by the programme steering cross-functional team (see box, page 386). What does that description illustrate about the influence of the organizational context upon team effectiveness?

Work team boundaries

The second major variable in Sundstrom *et al.*'s framework is the set of work team boundaries. The boundary for a team is like the fence around a piece of property. It allows its members to know who is a member and who it not. It defines both physically and psychologically on whom group members can rely, and thereby indicates when it may be necessary for them to go beyond their own team for assistance and resources. For example, the boundary for an aircraft cockpit crew is physically defined by the design of the aircraft. A Boeing 727 has seats for three cockpit members and hence there is an expected boundary of three for the crew of that aeroplane.

Technological developments can change boundaries. On a C-141 aircraft, while there is space for a workstation and a seat for a navigator, the incorporation of inertial navigation has eliminated the need for a navigator (Ginnett, 1993). Thus, changes in technology, physical layout and member roles are constantly modifying team boundaries, thereby changing the interactions of members within and across them.

While working to complete an assigned task (e.g. improving a procedure; designing a new product; winning a match), a team has to meet the needs of the larger organization within which it is embedded (external integration). At the same time, it has to secure enough independence to allow it to get on with its own work (external differentiation). These two features define every team's boundary, and boundary management refers to the process by which teams manage their interactions with other parts of their organization. How successfully a team manages its boundaries will affect its performance.

External work team differentiation refers to the team as a whole in relation to the rest of the organization (team–organization focus). For example, a temporary team may be assembled by management and given resources to deal with a crisis. This team thus stands out, and hence differs from, other work units within the company by virtue of containing an identifiable collection of people (membership), working in a specific place (territory), over a set period of time (temporal scope), on a unique task.

These four features define the team's boundary, distinguishing it from other work units within the organization:

Team membership
The identity of the individuals treated as members by both the team and organization is crucial. Who decides the composition and size of a work team?

Team territory
A work team should have its 'own turf' to establish its identity and manage its external relations, especially in teams whose missions demand both external integration and differentiation.

Temporal scope
The longer a work team exists and the more time its members spend co-operating, the greater will be its temporal scope and differentiation as a work unit.

Team task
The task given to the team may be additive (accomplishment depends on the sum of all members' efforts); conjunctive (depends on the performance of the least talented member); or disjunctive (performance of the most talented member) [**link**, chapter 9, group formation].

Internal work team differentiation refers to the degree to which a team's members possess different skills and knowledge that contribute towards the achievement of the team's objective. A team may have high differentiation, with its members having special, perhaps unique, skills, such as the cockpit crew in an aircraft; or it may have low differentiation, when the knowledge and contributions of members tend to be similar, as in a quality circle team.

External work team integration refers to the fact that a work team has also, to some degree, to be linked to, that is integrated into, the larger organization of which it is a part. External integration refers to this team–organization fit. The degree to which a team's goals and activities need to be co-ordinated and synchronized with those of other work units will depend on the type of team and its task.

A systems perspective sees the team as receiving materials or information from outsiders; transforming or adding value to them in co-operation with others managers, peers and staff; and then delivering an output to its customers. These 'customers' may be internal (e.g. other work units or individuals within the same organization) or external (e.g. shoppers in the marketplace).

Team development

The third major variable in Sundstrom *et al.*'s framework concerns the internal development of the team. Four factors are relevant here—interpersonal processes, roles, norms and cohesion.

1. *Interpersonal processes*
A group of individuals moves through a series of stages before achieving effective performance at the performing stage. Tuckman and Jensen's (1977) model describes the characteristics of each stage—forming, storming, norming, performing and adjourning [**link**, chapter 9, group formation].

External work team differentiation
refers to the degree to which a work team stands out from its organizational context in terms of its membership, temporal scope and territory.

Internal work team differentiation
refers to the degree to which a team's members possess different skills and knowledge that contribute towards the achievement of the team's objective.

External work team integration
refers to the degree to which a work team is linked to the larger organization of which it is a part. It is measured in terms of how its goals and activities are co-ordinated and synchronized with those of other managers, peers, customers and suppliers.

Team boundary management

Deborah Ancona and D. Caldwell studied the boundary management activities of 45 new product teams in five high-technology companies. They found that team members engaged in four types of intergroup activity:

- *Ambassador*: representing the team to others. For example, protecting it from interference; 'talking it up' to obtain outside resources; reporting its progress to higher management; checking threats or opposition.
- *Co-ordinating*: communicating laterally to co-ordinate a team's effort on its task with other work units. For example, discussing problems; negotiating; obtaining feedback on team progress; and securing information on the progress of other teams.
- *Scouting*: scanning the team's immediate environment. For example, gaining information on what was going on elsewhere in the organization.
- *Guarding*: keeping information and resources within the group. For example, preventing another team or individual acquiring its resources.

The researchers also found that that the team's boundary management activities differed over the period of the product development cycle. In the first, *creation* phase, members were exploring issues, and hence ambassador, co-ordinating and scouting activities were high. In the second, *development* phase, members were exploiting the information and resources that they had acquired. Task co-ordinating remained high, while ambassador and scouting activities were reduced. In the third, *diffusion* phase, members were exporting the work that they had completed and convincing others to make their product a priority. External interaction levels were highest in this phase.

The third finding was that high-performing new product teams carried out more external activity than low-performing teams, even when controlling for the project cycle phase. They not only responded to but also initiated communications with other work units. While internal group operations to integrate information gained from outside are important, it is the organization and management of interactions with other groups that appears critical.

Based on Deborah Ancona and D. Caldwell, 'Improving the performance of new product teams', *Research Technology Management*, 1990, vol.33, no.2, March–April, pp.25–9.

2. *Roles*

Roles in general are a defining feature of a team, and the role of a leader is much studied. Are the required member roles being performed given the group's tasks, and are the task and interpersonal aspects of the leadership role being fulfilled? [**link**, chapter 10, group structure.]

3. *Norms*

Are the norms and rules of behaviour which are agreed by the team members supportive or in conflict with effective performance? Can organizational culture be used to modify team norms? [**links**, chapter 11, individuals in groups; chapter 19, organization culture.]

4. *Cohesion*

Team cohesion can engender mutual co-operation, generosity and helping behaviour, motivating team members to contribute fully. However, it can also stifle creative thinking as individuals seek to 'fit in' and not 'rock the boat'. Small group size, similar attitudes and physical proximity of workspaces have all been found to encourage cohesion. Does the level of cohesion aid or impede the team's effectiveness? [**link**, chapter 11, individuals in groups.]

Team effectiveness

The final dependent variable in the framework is the level of team effectiveness. Sundstrom *et al.* offer two criteria for measuring team effectiveness—

performance and viability. **Team performance** is externally focused and concerns meeting the needs and expectations of outsiders such as customers, company colleagues or fans. It is assessed using measures such as quantity, quality and time. Meanwhile, **team viability** is the social dimension, which is internally focused and concerns the enhancement of the group's capability to perform effectively in the future. Team viability indicators include degree of group cohesion, shared purpose and the level of member commitment. The two are closely related, since there is a possibility that a team may get a job done but self-destruct in the process.

Evaluating teamworking

Team performance refers to the acceptability of the team's output to the customers within or outside the organization who receive its products, services, information, decisions or performance events (such as presentations or competitions).

Team viability refers to the team members' satisfaction, participation and continued willingness to work together.

So why no neat summary? Why no big picture? When analysing any organizational innovation, whether quality circle or autonomous teamworking, a careful balance is needed because of both the complexities of the phenomena itself and the process of its diffusion between organizations. Paul Thompson and Chris Warhurst (1998, p.8), who reviewed workplace initiatives (including teamworking), concluded that:

> The banal but simple truth is that there is no simple or universal direction. Look in detail at case study research across companies and countries and we find the usual suspects of mediation by institutional factors; noticeably national industrial relations systems and labour markets, as well as strategic choices by firms themselves. This should be obvious, but runs counter to the investment in high theory and epochal breaks by those whose job description is to draw the 'big picture', resulting in too many commentators continuing to insist on a coherent transformation package.

Our knowledge, understanding and assessment of teamworking comes from three sources: management consultants, managers and academics. Each has its own preoccupations, perspectives and implications, which are summarized in table 12.5. The management authors may be consultants who are engaged by the company to work with their line managers to implement their teamworking initiative.

Teamworking is marketed by these management consultants as a 'liberating' approach to work design. They concentrate on employee skills development, autonomy and discretion. They combine these (in true organization development fashion) with the growth of individual well-being and career prospects; and with improved individual and team performance and organizational effectiveness [**link**, chapter 17, organization development]. Their writings take an upbeat and prescriptive stance on the merits and universal applicability of teamworking.

Managers separately report their companies' teamworking innovations in professional business magazines and management newspapers. Management readers of these business journals are not interested in what does not work but in what might. Thus journalists and editors are curious about the new and the apparently successful innovations. The managers themselves will tend to report successes based on their personal experiences. This makes it difficult to use the prescriptive managerialist literature to assess objectively what benefits there are for companies and their employees in investing in some form of teamworking.

Table 12.5 : Sources of teamworking literature

Authors	Source of data	Perspective	Offered as
Management consultants and consultancy firms	Intuition Theoretical rather than empirical data	Selling credible solutions to organizational problems	Description of implementation Recipes about implementation supported by 'successful', single-site case study teamworking innovations
Line managers (in association with consultants or business journalists)	Organizational and management practice	Short- to medium-term problem solving How to do it	
Business management academics	Empirical research from a managerial perspective, not questioning managerial roles or legitimacy	Objective detachment	Mainly single-site case studies; occasionally surveys
Critical academic theorists (e.g. labour process)	Empirical research from an employee perspective, challenging managerial roles and legitimacy	Employers' exploitation and manipulation of workers Drawing upon the work of Michel Foucault	Critical insights based on empirical, usually case, analysis Critical commentary which mostly eschews discussion of any practical applications

Stop and criticize

You are a middle or line manager in an organization with a history of 'downsizing' and 'delay-ering', which continues to be on the agenda. How do you respond to a proposed team empowerment initiative from senior management?

Does the academic literature provide any more useful insights about teamworking? Only to a degree. It seeks to be more objective and critical than the prescriptive, managerial writing. Undoubtedly, it contains less 'storytelling'; it is less anecdotal and speculative; it identifies obstacles; and it specifies the psychological and sociological conditions which help or hinder teamworking. It is more guarded and conditional in its conclusions. All this makes it a boring read for managers who are likely to implement teamworking. However, it too has its weaknesses:

- *Definitional*: Academics have problems in defining what they are evaluating. In one study, the authors, van Fleet and Griffin (1989), asked 'Just what is a quality circle?' This is due to companies introducing their own variants of teamworking. The concept of 'team' is 'infinitely flexible, malleable—or corruptible—' (Buchanan, 2000, p.34) Thus academics studying different teamworking innovations find that they are not comparing like with like.

- *Objectives*: What are management's objectives for introducing teamworking? Teamworking has been introduced variously: as a means of work enhancement; worker control; employee representation; organizing production in a novel way; and encouraging employee autonomy. However, managers may be reluctant to state their objectives explicitly to researchers for political reasons, or they may genuinely not clearly know them themselves. Teamworking may be introduced as an 'act of faith'.

- *Research design*: Limitations of time and money will often restrict academics to conducting a detailed, single-site case study over a limited period of time. The teamworking literature contains numerous such studies which use this research design [**link**, chapter 2, the world outside]. This approach limits the generalizability of results.

- *Organizational access*: Teamworking initiatives are organization-led, and academics need permission to enter companies to conduct their studies. Managers in those organizations can restrict access to the research site and may even seek to influence what is published.

Finally, the topic of teamworking attracts much interest and many publications from another group of academics who cluster under the banner of labour process theorists. These writers subscribe to the Braverman thesis and take a critical perspective. They look for the ever more innovative and sophisticated ways in which management seeks to establish tighter monitoring of, and exert control over, its employees (for control read manipulation and exploitation) through refinements in organization structure, and the way that it deploys technology and organizes work around it.

Far from seeing teamworking as liberating, labour process theorists attack it as just another insidious form of management control; insidious because 'control' is exercised by and on the team members themselves and not by some fat ogre of a first-line supervisor cracking a whip. From the labour process perspective, team members are not even aware of this management control, which operates 'at a distance' from the work of the team but which is still present in organizational rules and targets reinforced by the technological parameters. In short, while management consultants say teamworking is developmental, labour process theorists say that it is exploitative (Friedman, 1977a; 1977b; 1990). Does all this mean that there can be no objective evaluation of teamworking experiments? There are of course individual assessments in the academic literature. Probably the most useful insights into teamworking are to be found in studies which review collections of previous teamworking studies. However, even these have to be read cautiously.

Teamworking: useful but unused

Jos Benders, Fred Huijgem, Ulrich Pekruhl and Kevin O'Kelly conducted a survey on behalf of the European Foundation for the Improvement of Living and Working Conditions on 'group work'. This was defined as 'the process whereby management gives formal groups the right to make decisions on how their work is performed on a group basis without reference to management'. The EPOC (employee-direct participation in organizational change) survey received a response from 5,800 managers from manufacturing and services, and private and public sector organizations. Among the findings were the following:

- Direct participation involving groups is limited to only about 4 per cent of all organizations responding.
- There are significant economic benefits from introducing group work. The more intensively group work is practised, the greater the economic benefits.

- The motives for introducing group work are predominantly economic. Quality of working life is also mentioned frequently as a motive, but generally together with productivity/economic motives.
- Groups' decision-making rights are generally limited, with a clear hierarchy in the topics about which groups may take decisions.
- In the majority of cases, regardless of the intensity of the group work, the team leader is appointed by management. Joint decision making on this issue occurs in only a quarter of all cases. Management also decides the composition of the team in almost 40 per cent of workplaces, and in only 15 per cent of cases can the group members decide who are to become their colleagues.
- Training for group work occurs in about 25 per cent of organizations, and managers are trained slightly more than group members. There is a positive correlation between the intensity of group work and the intensity and duration of training.
- Payment systems change little with the introduction of group work.
- Contrary to expectations, manufacturing lags behind the non-profit sector in the intensive application of groups. However, in the less intensive forms of group work, manufacturing is ahead of the other business sectors.
- There are marked cross-national differences in the extent to which group work is used in the member states. Swedish and Dutch organizations are the most frequent users, whereas the use of group work lags behind in Spain, Portugal and Italy.
- A third of organizations report a reduction in employees following the introduction of group work. However, the reduction in managers is more significant as 44 per cent of organizations with intensive group work have fewer managers following its introduction compared with a 19 per cent reduction for organizations without any form of direct participation.

From Jos Benders, Fred Huijgem, Ulrich Pekruhl and Kevin O'Kelly, *Useful but Unused: Findings from the EPOC Survey*, European Foundation for the Improvement of Living and Working Conditions, Loughlinstown, Co. Dublin, 1999. Used with permission

Recap

1. *Understand why 'team' is a contested concept in the organizational literature.*

   - Teamworking is being increasingly adopted as a favoured form of work organization in different companies and industries around the world.
   - The different purposes and ways in which managers have introduced this innovation has meant that the term 'team' is used to describe a wide range of radically different working arrangements.

2. *List the nine dimensions of team autonomy.*

   - Gulowsen's nine dimensions of team autonomy are selection of the team leader; acceptance of a new member into the team; distribution of work; time flexibility; acceptance of additional work; representation outside the team; production methods (choice of); production goals (output determination); and production goals (quality determination).

3. *Differentiate between four major types of team and give an example of each.*

   - Teams in organizations can be classified as advice (quality circles); action (e.g. surgery team); project (cross-functional team); or production (autonomous work team).

4. *Discuss the types of obstacle to effectiveness experienced by each type of team.*

   - Advice teams frequently lack authority to implement their recommendations. Action teams can fail to integrate their members' contributions sufficiently closely. Project team members can suffer 'divided loyalties' between their team and their home department. Production teams may lack autonomy for job satisfaction.

5. *Contrast Western with Japanese concepts of teamworking.*

   - The Western concept is based upon principles of empowerment and on-line teamworking, while the Japanese concept is based upon management principles of individual working on-line and teams advising off-line.

6. *Describe the three main variables in an ecological framework for analysing work team effectiveness.*

   - Team development; work team boundaries and organizational context affect team effectiveness.

7. *Explain some of the problems of objectively assessing the costs and benefits of teamworking arrangements.*

   - The concept of 'team' is so vague that it is difficult to compare like with like.
   - In a complex organizational context, it is difficult

to judge the extent to which teamworking is a causal factor in company performance.

- Accounts of teamworking in the literature by managers and consultants tend to report only successes.

- Academic access to work teams is controlled by companies. Single-site case studies make generalizing difficult.

Revision

1. What is the relationship between a work team and the organization of which it is a part?

2. What impact can technology have on the behaviour and performance of teams? Discuss positive and negative effects, illustrating your answer with examples.

3. 'Autonomous team is a relative term'. Discuss the concept of team autonomy, explaining why similarly labelled teams may, in practice, operate very differently, and consider why management might have difficulty in increasing the autonomy that it gives to a team.

4. Highlight briefly the main differences between Western European and Japanese-style teamworking. Then, using references to the literature, consider the positive and negative aspects of both systems for EITHER shop-floor workers OR management.

5. Discuss the reasons why Japanese-style teamworking has become widely adopted around the world.

Springboard

Durand, J.-P., Stewart, P. and Castillo, J.J. (eds), 1999, *Teamwork in the Automobile Industry: Radical Change or Passing Fashion*, Macmillan Business, Basingstoke.

A collection of chapters which contrast four types of teamworking: traditional Fordist; Toyota-Japan; outside Japan; and Swedish–German.

Guzzo, R.A. and Dickson, M.W., 1998, 'Teams in organizations: Recent research on performance and effectiveness', in *Annual Review of Psychology*, Palo Alto, Calif., pp.307–38.

Reviews the recent research on groups and teams and seeks to identify those that influence the effectiveness of teams in organizations.

Hackman, J.R., 1990, *Groups That Work and Those That Don't*, Jossey-Bass, San Francisco.

A series of short case descriptions illustrating the creation and management of effective teams in many varied organizational situations.

Proctor, S. and Mueller, F. (eds), 2000, *Teamworking*, Macmillan, London.

The individual contributions consider teamworking from many different angles and perspectives, and different organizational contexts. Reporting research, theories and frameworks, it brings together current thinking on teamworking.

Sinclair, A., 1992, 'The tyranny of a team ideology', *Organization Studies*, vol.13, no.4, pp.611–26.

Jenkins, A., 1994, 'Teams: from "ideology" to analysis', *Organization Studies*, vol.15, no.6, pp.849–60.

Articles attacking and defending managers' obsession with teams.

Thompson, P. and Warhurst, C. (eds), 1998, *Workplaces of the Future*, Macmillan, Basingstoke.

A critical, empirically based review of a wide range of changes and trends taking place in the organization of work in Britain and around the world. It is particularly strong on contrasting the rhetoric with the reality.

Tjosvold, D., 1996, *Team Organization: An Enduring Competitive Advantage*, Wiley, Chichester.

A widely cited managerially oriented text on the topic of effective teamworking based on his research and theoretical work.

Wiener, E.L., Kanki, B.G. and Helmreich, R.L. (eds), 1993, *Cockpit Resource Management*, Jossey-Bass, San Francisco.

These collected readings examine all aspects of group and team formation, structure, process and effectiveness from the perspective of cockpit and aircrews.

Womack, J.P., Jones, D.T. and Roos, D., 1990, *The Machine that Changed the World: The Triumph of Lean Production*, Macmillan, New York.

The classic book that extolled the virtues of Japanese production arrangements and was influential in changing Western manufacturing practices. Commentators have criticized its pro-management bias.

Home viewing

The film *The Great Escape* (1963, director John Sturges) is a story of American and British airmen set in a German prisoner-of-war camp during the Second World War. It features Steve McQueen, James Garner, Charles Bronson, Richard Attenborough, James Coburn, David McCallum and Donald Pleasance. Apply Sundstrom *et al.*'s ecological framework to this work team. What represents team performance and team viability? Identify the eight aspects of the organizational context in which this team operates (culture, task design, task technology, etc.). Finally, use the same model to comment on the interpersonal processes within the team, its norms, role and level of cohesion. Use the concepts of external integration, external differentiation and internal differentiation to analyse the team within the context of the whole camp. What constituted its boundaries?

OB in literature

Tracy Kidders, *The Soul of a New Machine*, Random House, New York, 1997.

This is a true story which has been 'fictionalized'. It is based on how teams worked together to design and build a new computer. What aspects of effective teamworking and work team management does the story illustrate?

Chapter exercises

1: Team autonomy assessment

Objectives

1. To apply Gulowsen's autonomy framework to a team with which you are familiar.

2. Identify areas of a team's work where it would be beneficial to increase autonomy.

Briefing

1. Below are Gulowsen's task areas/dimensions of team autonomy. Select a team and rate it on each of the nine dimensions. Your chosen team can be:

   (a) a team of which you have been, or currently are, a member, or

   (b) a team that a relative or friend is a member of (interview the person), or

   (c) your tutorial group at university or college.

   Your team autonomy score will range between 9 (no autonomy) and 36 (high autonomy).

2. Discuss in which task areas/dimensions could that team's autonomy be increased? What benefits do you envisage from such a change?

Team (name/organization):

Team task area/dimensions	Level of team participation				
	None	Some	Joint	Autonomy	Total
1. Selection of the team leader	1	2	3	4	
2. Acceptance of a new member into the team	1	2	3	4	
3. Distribution of work	1	2	3	4	
4. Time flexibility	1	2	3	4	
5. Acceptance of additional work	1	2	3	4	
6. Representation outside the team	1	2	3	4	
7. Production methods (choice of)	1	2	3	4	
8. Production goals (output)	1	2	3	4	
9. Production goals (quality)	1	2	3	4	
Total team score					

2: Self-managing teams: costs and benefits

Objectives

1. To recognize the key aspects of the change to autonomous teamworking within an organization.

2. To evaluate the strengths and weaknesses of this teamworking innovation for the organization and for the employees involved.

Briefing

Divide into groups representing 'managers' and 'employees'. Read the case study below. From your allotted perspective, consider what are the strengths and the weaknesses of this team innovation.

Vesuvious Scotland

Vesuvious Scotland is located in Newmilns in Ayrshire. It is part of the British-owned Cookson Group, a large, diversified industrial conglomerate. It manufactures specialty ceramics and other components for the steel industry. As a manufacturing company, it sought to become 'as good as the rest and better than most'. To do this, it took steps to create an organizational culture in which all employees would take responsibility for improving company performance. It used self-managed teams to achieve this. 'The view was that if you gave people responsibility, they will be keen to grow themselves and the business, so it was a case of giving them the trust to go out and manage business processes', explained the human resources manager. To allow teamworking, new working practices were introduced:

- Over a three-year period, various wage rates traditionally paid for different production jobs were replaced with a single wage structure.

- Complete labour flexibility across all jobs and departments was agreed.

- Production workers were trained to enable them to do all the jobs within the team.

- Symbolically, the factory time clock was removed and clocking in and out was abandoned.

Teams were given responsibility for the tasks that they carried out, the materials that they used and the problems that they encountered. Regular two-way communication meetings between management and shop-floor employees were established. This created suspicion among Transport and General Workers' Union representatives. They were suspicious of teamworking, interpreting it as an attack on their traditional role and fearful that multiskilling might lead to job losses. The plant foremen, whose jobs would change radically, felt particularly vulnerable as their traditional duties became delegated to the teams. They were retrained to act as 'facilitators', focusing on safety, quality training and other people management issues. Once it was realized that no job losses would occur, people saw themselves as free to overcome their own work problems.

Having introduced self-managed teams throughout the production process, the company has now extended them to the whole business. All departments—human resources, purchasing, accounts and even senior management—operate as self-managing teams. Some Vesuvious Scotland employees work in customers' steel plants but remain team members and regularly attend their teams' meetings, which review performance and identify opportunities for improvement.

Assessing the outcomes of teamworking, senior management points to employee opinion survey results. They claim a more enthusiastic workforce. In the period 1993–96, overall satisfaction rose from 70 per cent to 89 per cent; satisfaction with health and safety rose from 53 per cent to 90 per cent; and scores of over 90 per cent were reported for quality, productivity, company image, employee involvement and career development. In the period 1993–98, the company's turnover rose from £37 million to £55 million. The company attributes this to the competitive edge gained by empowering its employees and giving them responsibility for quality. The number of customer complaints has decreased; its market share has grown; and the involvement of self-managing teams in business planning has secured cost savings of half a million pounds. Despite problems of establishing a causal connection, the company's operations director is convinced that these changes have contributed to improvement in performance.

Based on Anat Arkin, 'Peak Practice', *People Management*, 11 November 1999, vol.5, no.22, pp.57–9.

Part 4 Organization structures

A field map of the organizational behaviour terrain

PESTLE: The **P**olitical, **E**conomic, **S**ocial, **T**echnological, **L**egal and **E**cological context

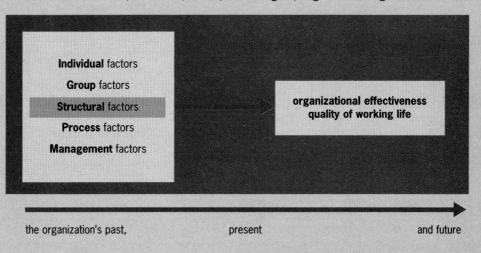

the organization's past,   present   and future

Introduction

Part 4, Organization structures, explores the following four topics:

- Traditional work design, in chapter 13

- Elements of structure, in chapter 14

- Early organization design, in chapter 15

- Organization strategy and design, in chapter 16

These four topics consider how the way in which work is designed for employees to perform, and how their roles are defined in the organization, affects their behaviour in organizations. Chapter 13 on traditional work design provides a historical foundation for the earlier chapter on technology [**link**, chapter 3]. It links technology to structure by highlighting how choices about the former have an impact on design decisions concerning the latter. Chapter 14 on elements of structure provides an introduction to the key concepts, theories, models and authors in the field. This 'vocabulary' is then applied to providing an understanding of early organization design, particularly the work of Weber, Fayol, Burns and Stalker, and Mintzberg. The final chapter explains how contemporary thinking about structures in the field of organization behaviour has merged with discussions about corporate strategy and strategic management. It also brings the consideration of structural forms up to date by discussing the networked virtual organization. The structural perspective offers a separate but related level of analysis after the individual and groups.

Our opening case study concerns a computer company's Europe-wide restructuring project, which is having major, unintended consequences. The board of directors is satisfied with the new structural arrangements and confirms that they will be retained. It is too late to implement the changes differently. However, the board is willing to modify elements of the new structure and address weaknesses as highlighted by their senior manager.

You are engaged as a consultant to help this senior manager with her review. What advice will you give her? What do you see as the main issues, and what would you change? It's your call.

YOUR CALL (4): SCAN GRAPHICA

It is January 1998. Scan Graphica is a British-based computer company with sales, marketing and distribution subsidiaries throughout Europe. Scan Graphica supplies graphics and image software and accessories such as scanners, digital cameras, customized circuit boards and printers. To improve customer service, reduce overheads and increase sales, the company is embarking on a major restructuring. The European operations need to be more integrated, more efficient and customer-facing with new systems and call centre technology.

A rapid improvement team is being formed under a senior German manager to design and implement a new business model by January 1999. Working with external consultants, the team is developing a set of 'best practice' proposals, which will be presented to the European board in May 1998. The proposals include:

- Each country subsidiary to focus exclusively on direct sales and marketing.

- All 'front office' functions (ordertaking, customer enquiries, product advice, returns) and all 'back office' functions (credit control, cash collection, payroll, accounting, purchasing) to be transferred to a central 'shared services' location.

- Standardized pan-European business processes and computer systems to be adopted.

- Central shared services to recruit young, multi-lingual graduates, organized by 'country cluster' and cross-trained to handle a wide range of front and back office service roles.

- Local warehouses to be consolidated into one central European distribution centre.

This is to be accompanied by continuous improvement on key performance metrics such as sales growth, profit ratios, order fill rates, customer satisfaction, inventory turns, cash collection rates and employee productivity. These proposals are endorsed by the board. However, in private, country managers are critical. They see the move to central control leading to erosion of their jobs, to a loss of expertise and to lowered morale. They are particularly concerned about the implications for relationships with customers. Nevertheless, Dublin is chosen as the site for central shared services and distribution, and implementation is completed on target by the end of 1998, which is viewed as an outstanding achievement.

It is now January 2000, and performance on virtually all key metrics has deteriorated. Key customers are moving to competitors due to poor service and communications, errors and unfilled orders, and a general loss of confidence in Scan Graphica. Staff in the new centre are stressed by customer complaints and criticisms from colleagues and management. In some countries, staff add to the problems of central services by continuing to deal directly with key customers. Some country managers also ignore the new procedures by making direct contact with the central 'country cluster' team leaders (with whom they share nationality). Many of the new central staff complain that their jobs are less interesting than promised and that there are no career prospects. Annual staff turnover around the company is 40 per cent.

The board appoints a senior manager to assess the situation and to recommend improvements. She is advised that the new model is sound and should be retained, but that constructive recommendations to modify elements or address weaknesses will be considered.

You are engaged as a consultant to help this manager with her review. What advice will you give her? What do you see as the main issues, and what would you change? It's your call.

Traditional work design

Key concepts

rationalism

scientific management

systematic soldiering

functional foremanship

mental revolution

job simplification

job specialization

time-and-motion studies

Fordism

systems

control

deskilling

McDonaldization

Learning objectives

When you have read this chapter, you should be able to define those key concepts in your own words, and you should also be able to:

1. Understand how scientific management met the needs of its historical context.

2. Describe the main features of the scientific approach.

3. Critically assess Taylorism.

4. Enumerate the contributions of the Gilbreths and Gantt to scientific management.

5. Understand how Fordism developed out of Taylorism.

6. Understand the deskilling debate, and the contribution of Braverman and Ritzer.

7. Critically assess the evidence for and against the deskilling thesis.

8. Provide examples of scientific management in contemporary society.

Why study traditional work design?

Only a handful of theories can claim to be truly revolutionary and to have had an enduring and worldwide impact on organizational thought and management practice. Frederick Winslow Taylor's scientific management is one of them. Many textbooks only mention this topic briefly, locating its place in history, before implying that his ideas are no longer relevant to our modern, high-tech, organizational lives. This chapter will argue the complete opposite. Specifically, it contends that scientific management is having a wider and more pervasive impact on society today than it did in Taylor's day.

Developments in information technology have increased rather than reduced its relevance. One needs only to look at the current interest in total quality management, ISO 9000 and the other management techniques for bringing greater discipline into manufacturing, clerical and professional work (including education) to realize that Taylorism is alive and well and thriving at the start of the twenty-first century (Jones, 1997; Wilson, 1995). For example, one current academic debate focuses on whether the virtual organization is a new organizational arrangement or a refinement of scientific management thinking [**link**, chapter 16, organization strategy and design]. Taylorism affects us all as students, employees, consumers and citizens. It is just that most do not realize this. By pointing out examples of it in contemporary life, we hope to raise readers' awareness.

Why is the topic of job design being considered in a part of the book which deals with organization structures? Buchanan argued that 'It has ... become increasingly unrealistic to distinguish between work design on the one hand and organization design on the other. The former now implies the latter' (Buchanan 1994, p.86). Work design and organization design are now interminably linked (Procter and Mueller, 2000). Taylor focused his attention on shop-floor workers, the design of the manual tasks which they performed, and on their motivation. Taylor's approach to prescribing the appropriate organization structure was 'bottom-up'. Beginning with the task, he established working practices for shop-floor workers before considering the question of appropriate supervision, and the implications of all this for senior management. He stands in contrast to other organization structure designers such as Max Weber and Henri Fayol, who were 'top-down' and looked at organization from the perspective of top management. Their contributions will be considered later [**link**, chapter 14, early organization design].

The birth of scientific management

Between 1880 and 1910, the United States underwent major and rapid industrialization, including the creation of the first large corporations. Complex forms of organization were emerging, with new technologies of production and large workforces. Many of today's well-known organizations, such as the Standard Oil Trust (Esso), United States Steel, General Motors and Ford, were created at that time. The workers in these new factories came from agricultural regions of America, or were immigrants from Europe. Directing the efforts of workers with little knowledge of the English language, few job skills and no experience of the disciplined work of a factory was a key organizational problem. Scientific management offered a solution and represented one of the first organizational practices capable of being applied to different companies.

Before the 1880s, work organization of the factory shop floor was based upon the authority of subcontractors and supervisors. Owners employed workers indirectly, and it was labour masters and gang bosses who recruited, paid and disciplined them. However, these informal, personal methods of control created inefficiencies. During this period of economic growth, scientific management ended such internal contracting, enabling owners to employ workers directly, and thereby introduced a formal system of industrial discipline. In this period most products were hand-made by skilled operators who handcrafted items using general-purpose machine tools such as lathes. It took these craftsmen years of training to acquire the necessary skills and experience. They could read a blueprint they visualize the final product, and they possessed a level of hand–eye co-ordination and gentleness of touch that allowed them to manufacture the required item (Littler, 1982). However, there were insufficient numbers of them to permit mass production.

Rationalism is the theory that reason is the foundation of certainty in knowledge.

It was against this background that Frederick Taylor and Henry Ford developed and implemented their ideas. They and their supporters all shared a belief in **rationalism**, which is the theory that reason is the foundation of certainty in knowledge. They believed that if one understands something, one should be able both to state it explicitly and to write a law or a rule for it. They held that the human mind could discover innate laws which governed the workings of the universe. The consequence of developing and applying rules, laws and procedures is to replace uncertainty with predictability, in both the human and non-human spheres [**link**, chapter 24, power and politics].

Taylor's approach is known by two names. **Scientific management** is the collective term for his ideas coined by his supporters. *Taylorism* is an eponym which, although applied by his supporters, was used mainly by his opponents, who regarded the other term as specious. In this chapter, the two terms are used interchangeably. Scientific management came to prominence during the hearings held by the US Interstate Commerce Commission in 1910. The railway companies had wanted to increase the charges for carrying freight. The lawyer who promoted the case of the shippers against the railways was Louis D. Brandeis. He argued that if the railways were managed more scientifically, greater efficiency would reduce costs and obviate the need to raise charges. Brandeis with some others agreed the term 'scientific management', publicized it widely and had it quickly accepted by engineers. Taylor himself only adopted it reluctantly, using it in his book, *The Principles of Scientific Management*, published in 1911.

> **Scientific management** is a form of job design theory and practice which stresses short, repetitive work cycles; detailed, prescribed task sequences; a separation of task conception from task execution; and motivation based on economic rewards.

In October [1910], Brandeis met at Gantt's apartment in New York with Frank Gilbreth, Jim Dodge and others. 'It seemed to me appropriate that all differences between the various advocates of efficiency should be eliminated', he recalled. For starters they needed something to call it. The Taylor system? Functional management? Shop management? Just plain efficiency? In the end, they adopted 'scientific management'. Taylor, among others, had used the term before; that his system was scientific was its central claim.

From Robert Kanigel, *The One Best Way: Frederick Winslow Taylor and the Enigma of Efficiency*, Little Brown and Company, London, 1997, pp.431–2.

Taylorism

Frederick Winslow Taylor (1856–1915)

> **Systematic soldiering** is the conscious and deliberate restriction of output by operators.

Taylor was born into a wealthy Philadelphia Quaker family in 1856. Philadelphia was the industrial heart of 1800s America. It contained many manufacturers who had ready access to the Pennsylvanian coal and iron mines. Taylor became an apprentice machinist in a firm of engineers before joining the Midvale Steel Company in 1878, where he developed his ideas. The company manufactured locomotive wheels and axles, and it was here that he rose to the position of shop superintendent by 1887. In this role, he observed that workers used different, and mostly inefficient, work methods. He also noticed that few machinists ever worked at the speed of which they were capable, a practice that he labelled **systematic soldiering**. Taylor attributed such soldiering to a number of factors:

- The view among the workers that an increase in output would result in redundancies.

- Poor management controls, which made it easy for them to work slowly in order to protect their own best interests.

- The choice of methods of work, which was left entirely to the discretion of the workers, who wasted a large part of their efforts using inefficient and untested rules of thumb.

Soldiering

Robert Kanigel (1997) explained that the word 'soldiering' had nautical roots. It related to soldiers who, when transported by ship, acted as privileged passengers. They were exempt from the work on board that the seamen had to perform. To the sailors, such work avoidance came to be known as 'soldiering'. Frederick Taylor distinguished, on the one hand, the tendency of workers to take it easy. This he labelled 'natural soldiering'. He considered it unfortunate, but almost excusable. On the other hand, and more insidious in his view, was 'systematic soldiering', which was the organized, collective behaviour of workers in the whole workshop, who restricted their production, prevented their employers knowing how fast they could work and thus allowed them to pursue their own narrow self-interest.

Appalled by what he regarded as the inefficiency of industrial practices, Taylor took steps to increase production by reducing the variety of work methods used by the workers, and he set out to show how management and workforce could both benefit from adopting his more efficient work methods. His objectives were to achieve:

- *Efficiency*, by increasing the output per worker and reducing deliberate 'underworking' by employees.

- *Predictability* of job performance—standarizing tasks by dividing them up into small and closely specified sub-tasks.

- *Control*, by establishing discipline through hierarchical authority and introducing a system whereby all management's policy decisions could be implemented.

Table 13.1: Frederick Taylor's five principles of scientific management

1. A clear division of tasks and responsibilities between management and workers.
2. Use of scientific methods to determine the best way of doing a job.
3. Scientific selection of the person to do the newly designed job.
4. The training of the selected worker to perform the job in the way specified.
5. Surveillance of workers through the use of hierarchies of authority and close supervision.

Taylor's approach involved studying each work task. He chose routine, repetitive tasks performed by numerous operatives where study could save time and increase production. A wide range of variables was measured, such as size of tools, height of workers and type of material worked. In his studies, he tried to answer the question, 'How long should it take to do any particular job in the machine shop?' He wanted to replace rules of thumb with scientifically designed working methods. Taylor experimented with different combinations of movement and method to discover the 'one best way' of performing any task.

His approach involved the use of analysis and synthesis. Analysis involved the job being divided up into its elementary motions; discarding non-essential motions; examining the remaining motions to determine the quickest and least wasteful means of job performance; and describing, recording and indexing these. Synthesis consisted of determining the proper sequence of motions; recombining

Table 13.2: Scientific approach to shovelling

1. Select suitable job for study which has sufficient variety without being complex, which employs enough men to be worthwhile and would provide an object lesson to all when installed.

2. Select two good steady workers.

3. Time their actions.

4. Get them to use large shovels on heavy material. Total amount within a set time period is weighed and recorded.

5. Shovel size reduced so that weight of shovel-load is decreased, but total amount shovelled per day rises.

6. Determine best weight per shovel-load and identify correct size of shovel for all other materials handled.

7. Study actual movements of arms and legs.

8. Produce 'science of shovelling', which shows correct method for each material and amount which should be shovelled per day by a first-class man.

Functional foremanship was an approach devised by Frederick Taylor in which the job of the general foreman was divided into its constituent parts. Each of the main parts was given to a different individual, who would oversee and be responsible for that aspect of a worker's job.

those motions in that sequence for optimal job performance; and presenting that information to the employees.

It was not only shop-floor workers who had their jobs fragmented. Taylor felt that every employee in an organization should be confined to a single function. He proposed a system called **functional foremanship**, which never became popular. The job of the general foreman was to be divided and distributed between eight separate individuals. Each of these would oversee a separate function of the work and would be called:

1. Inspector
2. Order of work and route clerk
3. Time and cost clerk
4. Shop disciplinarian
5. Gang boss
6. Speed boss
7. Repair boss
8. Instruction card clerk

Stop and criticize

You are a product line manager in a large factory in the English Midlands making chocolate biscuits. This guy Taylor, a management consultant, has told you that what you need in your factory to improve efficiency is functional foremanship. In replying 'I don't think so, Mr Taylor', give four reasons for rejecting his professional advice.

In 1898, Taylor was hired by the Bethlehem Iron Company (which later became part of the Bethlehem Steel Corporation) to improve work methods. For many years, the product of the company's blast furnaces had been handled by 75 pig iron handlers, who loaded an average of twelve and a half tons [tonnes] per man per day. Taylor estimated that a first-class pig iron handler ought to handle between 47 and 48 long tons [tonnes] per day. Taylor introduced his experimental changes, raised productivity by a factor of four and increased workers' wages by 60 per cent. The savings achieved with his improved work plan were between $75,000 and $80,000 per annum at 1911 prices. The cost of handling pig iron dropped substantially, and the employed men did the work previously done by many more. By the third year of working under his plan, the following results had been obtained at Bethlehem Steel (Taylor, 1911, p.71):

Machine Shop No. 2 at Bethlehem Steel Works in Bethlehem, Pennsylvania, USA

Pig iron handlers at the Bethlehem Steel Works. Courtesy of the Bethlehem Steel Corporation

	Old plan	**New plan**
Yard labourers	500	140
Tons [tonnes] per man per day (average)	16	59
Earnings per worker per day (average)	$1.15	$1.88
Cost of handling a ton [tonne] (average)	$0.072	$0.033

Initiative and incentive system refers to a form of job design practice in which workers are given a task to perform by management which also provides them with a financial incentive. Workers are then left to use their initiative as to how to complete the task and which tools to use.

Taylor's 'deal' with his workers was as follows: 'You do it my way, by my standards, at the speed I mandate, and in so going achieve a level of output I ordain, and I'll pay you handsomely for it, beyond anything you might have imagined. All you do is take orders, give up your way of doing the job for mine' (Kanigel, 1997, p.214). It was among the first attempts to align the goals of the workers with those of management.

Taylor's scientific management was a powerful and largely successful attempt to wrest the organization of production from the workers and place it under the control of management. Before Taylor, the use of the **initiative and incentive system** within the company involved management specifying production requirements; providing workers with incentives in the form of a piecerate bonus; and leaving them to decide how to organize their work. In Taylor's view, not only did this result in wasted effort but, more importantly, workers kept their craft secrets to themselves and worked at a collectively agreed rate that was below their ability. Taylor argued that management should exercise responsibility for the planning, co-ordinating and controlling of work, thereby leaving workers free to perform their tasks.

Taylor's view of workers, groups, unions and management

Taylor's views have often been misrepresented in numerous textbooks, yet they are clearly detailed in his own book, *The Principles of Scientific Management* (Taylor, 1911), and in his publications. As regards individual workers, Taylor sought to 'isolate' them, as far as possible, from their work mates. He neither ignored groups nor considered them as unimportant, as is sometimes claimed. On the contrary, his experience of systematic soldiering showed him exactly how individuals behaved when part of a group. His solution to the problem of output restriction was to eliminate collusion between workers and to introduce best practice. It is true, however, that his interest in securing a docile workforce led him to take a negative, one-dimensional view of groups in the workplace.

Taylor recommended 'not dealing with men in masses'. Instead, he stressed the importance of talking to, and dealing with, only one worker at a time, since each employee possessed their own special abilities and limitations. Again, contrary to popular myth, Taylor did not regard the workers as simply robots. Instead, he wanted workers to progress on the basis of their abilities. He sought to develop each individual to their highest state or rate of efficiency and prosperity. He felt that the objective of management should be to maximize the prosperity of both owners and employees, and he contended that the prosperity of the former should not be at the cost of the latter.

The popular misconception that Taylor considered workers to be machines may have been perpetuated in the term that scientific management is also known by, 'modern machine theory'. He has been criticized for his view of workers as 'coin-operated' beings, responding directly to financial incentives and guided in their actions by a pleasure–pain calculation that would lead them to exert effort in proportion to the rewards available. However, this criticism ignores the historical context of his work, which took place at a time in which a social welfare system was absent, and one in which workers focused more on economic issues than perhaps they do today.

Management–workers relations, in Taylor's eyes, should be co-operative rather than adversarial. He saw the two pulling together to produce as much product as possible for their mutual benefit. His techniques were meant to improve the efficiency and social harmony of industrial life, and they required, in his phrase, a 'mental revolution' by both parties. By this he meant the application of the principles of science to determine the best way to perform any given task and the acceptance of the results obtained thereby, by both workers and management.

Taylor's concern about the effects of groups on individual workers made him suspicious of unions. His individually oriented approach had no place for them. By their nature, unions emphasized group solidarity, common rules, and standardization of wages and conditions. This was contrary to his belief in individual assessment of workers, matching their abilities to job requirements, fulfilling their personal desires, and 'bettering themselves' in line with the Protestant work ethic. He also believed that his 'scientific' approach would end arbitrary management decisions. Management would plan and organize the work, and labour would execute it, all in accordance with the dictates of science. Once his methods had been introduced within a company, trade unions and collective bargaining would become redundant. Scientific assessment would eliminate all ambiguity and argument.

Workers were concerned that scientific management just meant 'work speed-up', that is, getting more work for less pay. Taylor was adamant that after the implementation of his methods, workers would be rewarded by large pay increases and managers would secure higher productivity and profits. Sometimes workers complained about the inequality of pay increases, as when a 300 per cent productivity increase resulted in a 30 per cent pay increase. Taylor argued that his

Symphonic engineering

Here is the way in which a literal-minded industrial engineer reported on a symphony concert.

For considerable periods the four oboe players had nothing to do. The number should be reduced and the work spread more evenly over the whole concert, thus eliminating peaks and valleys of activity. All the twelve violins were playing identical notes, this seems unnecessary duplication. The staff of this section should be drastically cut. If a larger volume of sound is required, it could be obtained by means of electronic apparatus. Much effort was absorbed in the playing of demi-semi-quavers; this seems to be an unnecessary refinement. It is recommended that all notes be rounded up to the nearest semi-quaver. If this were done, it would be possible to use trainees and lower grade operatives more extensively.

There seems to be too much repetition of some musical passages. Scores should be drastically pruned. No useful purpose is served by repeating on the horns something which has already been handled by the strings. It is estimated that if all redundant passages were eliminated the whole concert time of 2 hours could be reduced to 20 minutes and there would be no need for an intermission. In many cases the operators were using one hand for holding the instrument, whereas the introduction of a fixture would have rendered the idle hand available for other work. Also, it was noted that excessive effort was being used occasionally by the players of wind instruments, whereas one compressor could supply adequate air for all instruments under more accurately controlled conditions.

Finally, obsolescence of equipment is another matter into which it is suggested further investigation could be made, as it was reported in the programme that the leading violinist's instrument was already several hundred years old. If normal depreciation schedules had been applied, the value of this instrument would have been reduced to zero and purchase of more modern equipment could then have been considered.

From Robert M. Fulmer and Theodore T. Herbert, *Exploring the New Management*, Macmillan, New York, 1974, p.27.

approach enabled people to do more work in less time using less effort because of the more efficient physical movements. Since they were expending less effort, this had to be taken into account when calculating their wage increases. The efficiency savings also led to the requirement for fewer workers. Would existing workers be redeployed or made redundant? In later years the unions became reconciled with work study and accepted it, especially if financial benefits followed.

Taylor felt that managers who introduced his innovations deserved compensation for the costs of studying them, the purchase of special tools and the costs of reorganization. Nevertheless, his approach was resisted as much by managers (who resented the way that it diluted their prerogatives) as by workers, who were concerned about job intensification and redundancy. Taylor's approach was meant to be thorough, rigorous and systematic. However, 'scientific' implies an objectivity, a methodology and an impartiality [link, chapter 2, the world outside]. These had no place in his thinking and techniques. Thus Taylor's claim that his approach to work design was 'scientific' was challenged both by his opponents at the time and by succeeding generations of academics.

The savings achieved were considerable. However, the dramatic improvements in productivity were matched by the negative and often violent reactions to Taylor's techniques among workers, technicians, managers and government. The fragmented tasks designed by Taylor were boring, since workers required much lower levels of skill to perform them. Companies adopted scientific management selectively, and many took the opportunity to lower wages. One popular account exists of the application of Taylorism at the Watertown Arsenal in 1911.

The strike itself seems to have been more a result of managerial ineptitude than an example of worker resistance to scientific management methods. Nevertheless, the strike, together with the reaction of the American Federation of Labour to

Workers at the Watertown Arsenal

Taylor, which was both vocal and strident, resulted in the establishment of a Congressional committee to investigate Taylor's methods. The committee reported in 1912 and concluded that scientific management did indeed provide useful techniques. However, in 1914, an attitude survey of Arsenal workers was conducted, revealing their hostility and resentment to the approach. Concerned about industrial unrest in government arms factories in wartime, the American Congress banned Taylor's time study methods in its defence industry. The committee's chairman, William B. Wilson, felt that scientific management, improved methods and new technology would together reduce the worker's control over the labour process, thereby creating unemployment. This debate resurfaced in the 1970s, from the Marxist perspective, with Harry Braverman.

Scientific management was exported to other countries, In Britain, it was popularized by Lyndall Urwick and was first used in the J. Hopkinson works at Huddersfield in 1905. The Iron and Steel Institute evaluated the techniques and criticized them. In Germany, the director of the Borsig Works noted the hostility of his workmen to the methods. In France, Henri Le Chaterlier was its proponent. In 1912, the Renault motor car manufacturer introduced scientific management at its factory at Billancourt, and this led to violent conflict and strikes. The zealous application of time study in Renault had the following result: 'The workman had to adapt his human machine to the rate of the mechanical one; and workmen incapable of making all the necessary movements with their hands within the measured time aided themselves by using their heads as a third arm' (Friedmann, 1955, p.42). Taylorism was used extensively in the Soviet Union, though its effectiveness was questionable (Merkle, 1980). In 1918, the newspaper *Pravda* quoted Lenin as saying that every scientific suggestion of the Taylor system should be tried out. Perhaps most significantly, Taylor's book was translated into Japanese in 1912. Critics of Japanese teamworking argue that it contains more elements of Taylorism than of employee empowerment [**link**, chapter 12, teamworking].

Scientific management and eye surgery

The photograph shows one of twelve eye surgeries built in Russia in the late 1980s using assembly line principles. On an automated conveyor belt, eye surgery is carried out using a controversial five-stage assembly line operation. Up to fifteen patients an hour can pass through the specially designed operating theatre at the Moscow Research Institute of Eye Microsurgery. Each step of the operation is performed by a different surgeon, and each operation takes a maximum of 10 minutes. First the patient receives a local anaesthetic outside the theatre. Then, lying on one of the special tables shown in the photograph, they pass through the automatic doors into the operating room.

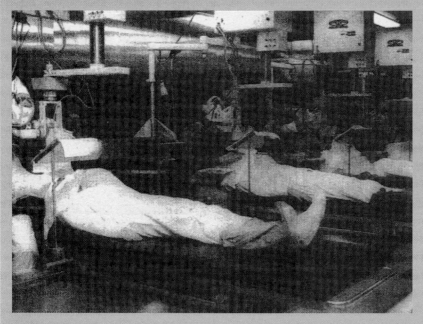

Russian eye surgery
Courtesy of Flakt AB, Stockholm, Sweden

Station 1:   The first surgeon marks exactly the depth and length of cuts to be made to the cornea, which have been calculated by a computer in advance.

Station 2:   The second surgeon makes between eight and sixteen cuts with a diamond scalpel.

Station 3:   The third surgeon adjusts the cuts to a micro-degree to ensure maximum eyesight gain.

Station 4:   The fourth surgeon cleans and dresses all the wounds.

Station 5:   A doctor administers the necessary antibiotics in case of infection. The patient then passes through another automatic door.

Run by Professor Sviatoslav Fiodorov, his 50-strong team can process 200 patients a day and treat 220,000 annually. His institute has become a $75 million a year business that is growing by 30 per cent per annum. Foreigners can buy an operation package holiday (operation included) for $2,000 for a two-week stay. Professor Fiodorov is planning to replace the surgeons on his assembly line with robots.

Based on Maggie Innes, 'Eye, Eye Comrade!', *News of the World Sunday Magazine*, 7 November 1987, pp.24–5; and Peter Pean, 'How to Get Rich Off Perestroika', *Fortune*, 8 May 1989, pp.95–6.

Criticisms of Taylorism

The following criticisms are commonly found in textbooks and historical accounts of Taylorism:

1. Assumed that the motivation of the employee was to secure the maximum earnings for the effort expended. It neglected the importance of other rewards from work (achievement, job satisfaction, recognition) which later research has found to be important.

2. Neglected the subjective side of work—the personal and interactional aspects of performance, the meanings that employees give to work and the significance to them of their social relationships at work.

3. Failed to appreciate the meanings that workers would put on new procedures and their reactions to being timed and closely supervised.

4. Had an inadequate understanding of the relation of the individual incentive to interaction with, and dependence on, the immediate work group, Taylor did attribute 'underworking' to group pressures but misunderstood the way in which these worked. He failed to see that these might just as easily keep production and morale up.

5. Ignored the psychological needs and capabilities of workers. The one best way of doing a job was chosen with the mechanistic criteria of speed and output. The imposition of a uniform manner of work can both destroy individuality and cause other psychological disturbances.

6. Had too simple an approach to the question of productivity and morale. It sought to keep both of these up exclusively by economic rewards and punishments. However, the fatigue studies of the Gilbreths during the 1920s did signal the beginnings of a wider appreciation of the relevant factors than had initially been recognized by Taylor. Incentive approaches under the scientific approach tended to focus on the worker as an individual and ignored his social context.

7. Functional foremanship was deemed to be too complex and unwieldy a mode of supervision.

Stop and criticize

You have travelled back through time and are able to meet Taylor. What three things would you congratulate him for, and what three things would you criticize him for?

Development of Taylorism: the Gilbreths and Gantt

Frank Bunker Gilbreth had participated in a meeting held in 1910 in Laurence Gantt's apartment, with Jim Dodge and Louis Brandies, when the group adopted the term 'scientific management'. His background resembled Taylor's in that both were practising engineers and managers. Gilbreth's experience was in the construction industry, and his most famous experiments involved bricklayers. His main contribution was to refine the techniques for measuring work. His wife Lillian was a trained psychologist, and her contribution was in the area of the human aspects of work.

Lillian Moller Gilbreth (1878–1972) and Frank Bunker Gilbreth (1868–1924)

- *Motion study*: This refers to the investigation and classification of the basic motions of the body, regardless of the particular and concrete form of labour in which those motions are used. Gilbreth develop motion study, including job simplification. Taylor had looked mainly at time and had not focused as closely on motions. Gilbreth sought to rectify this omission and to determine the fundamental units of work. His views were published in his book *Motion Study* in 1911.

- *Research techniques*: To implement motion study, Gilbreth devised techniques to study and improve workers' body movements. He used *stroboscopic pictures,* which involved keeping the camera lens open to show changing positions assumed by the worker. Small electric lamps were attached to workers' fingers, hands and arms, and their motions were photographed at slow shutter speeds. This method left paths of light, indicating acceleration and deceleration on the photographic plate as a series of dots. The outcome was a *chronocyclegraph,* which was a photograph of the workplace with motion paths superimposed. From these he made wire models, which allowed the work task to be analysed in detail and redesigned to be performed more efficiently. He also used *motion picture cameras* to record a worker's movements in the performance of a task. A clock, calibrated in hundredths of a minute, within the film frame, enabled the worker's motions, the time taken and the conditions surrounding the job to be recorded simultaneously.

- *Therbligs*: In motion and time study, the elementary movement was visualized as the building block of every work activity. He developed a comprehensive system of noting such elementary movements, as shown in the box opposite (Gilbreth's contribution), each with its own symbol and colour. They are called 'therbligs'—a variation of his name spelt backwards. Like dance, all the movements of the worker's body performing a particular task are noted down using the therbligs notation. In addition, Gilbreth developed a standard time for each job element, thereby combining time study with motion study. This was used for designing wage payment systems, whose universal application Gilbreth advocated. Process charts continue to be used in business process re-engineering. **Time-and-motion studies** are conducted to this day.

Time-and-motion studies are measurement and recording techniques which attempt to make operations more efficient.

Like Taylor, Gilbreth gave detailed rules on how to find out the best way of doing any job. He discovered that eighteen separate movements were made in laying each brick. By reorganizing the work pattern, he was able to reduce the movements to five and increase the bricklayers' productivity from 120 to 350 bricks an hour. Additionally, in order to control work carried out on building sites far from head office, he devised the 'field system'. This was a set of written rules and procedures intended to establish uniform practice on all work sites. It detailed how to mix concrete, transport materials, train apprentices, erect scaffolding, and so on.

Lillian Gilbreth's contribution came from psychology. Her book *The Psychology of Management* highlighted the importance of human factors in organizations and was published in 1916 (Gilbreth and Gilbreth, 1916). Her work complemented her husband's. The study of motions and the elimination of unnecessary and wasteful actions sought to reduce the fatigue experienced by workers. Since all work produced fatigue, for which the remedy was rest, the aim was to find the best mixture of work and rest to maximize productivity. The Gilbreths distin-

Gilbreth's contributions

Micro-motion studies and chronocyclegraphic models

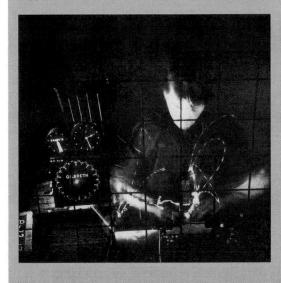

Therbligs symbols and colours

symbol	name	colour
	search	black
	find	grey
	select	light grey
	group	red
	hold	gold ochre
	transport loaded	green
	position	blue
	assemble	violet
	use	purple
	disassemble	light violet
	inspect	burnt ochre
	pre-position	pale blue
	release load	carmine red
	transport empty	olive green
	rest for overcoming fatigue	orange
	unavoidable delay	yellow
	avoidable delay	lemon yellow
	plan	brown

guished between necessary fatigue, which was a consequence of work that must be done to complete a task, and unnecessary fatigue, which resulted from effort that did not need to be expended at all. Through the use of motion study linked with the redesign of work, they sought to eliminate unnecessary fatigue and minimize necessary fatigue.

To do this, they focused on the total working environment and not just on selecting first-class workers, as Taylor had done. They shortened the working day, introduced rest periods and chairs, and instituted holidays with pay. They studied jobs to eliminate fatigue-producing elements. Changes were also made to heating, lighting and ventilation. The final ingredient was termed the 'betterment of work'. It included introducing rest rooms, canteens, entertainment and music into the factory. In the work of the Gilbreths we see the first realization that

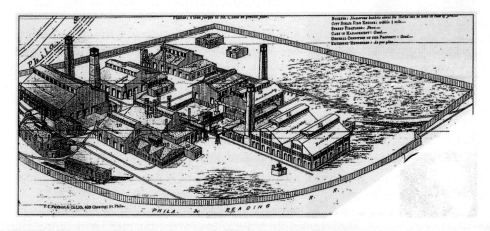

Midvale Steel Company

workers may have a variety of different needs. They thought that individual work performance depended on attitudes, needs and the physical environment as well as on correct work methods and suitable equipment. In 1916, the Gilbreths published their book *Fatigue Study*, which linked Frank's development of Taylor's scientific management ideas with Lillian's work in industrial psychology.

Midvale Steel Company

Henry Laurence
Gantt (1861–1924)

In 1887, Henry Laurence Gantt joined the Midvale Steel Company as an assistant in the Engineering Department. A year later, he became assistant to the company's chief engineer—F.W. Taylor. Gantt supported Taylor's approach, but he did much to humanize scientific management to make it more acceptable (Gantt, 1919). He tempered Taylor's work with greater insight into human psychology and stressed method over measurement. He believed that Taylor's use of incentives was too punitive and lacked sensitivity to the psychological needs of the workers. He believed in consideration for and fair dealings with employees. He felt that scientific management was being used as an oppressive instrument by the unscrupulous. He made three major contributions:

- *Best known way at present*: Gantt's system was based on detailed instruction cards in the best scientific management tradition. However, he replaced Taylor's 'one best way' with his own 'best known way at present'. This involved a much less detailed analysis of jobs than Taylor had suggested.

- *Task-and-bonus payment scheme*: He replaced Taylor's differential piecerate wage system with his own task-and-bonus scheme. Each worker was set a task, received a set day rate, and an additional 20–50 per cent bonus.

- *Gantt chart*: He developed a bar chart used for scheduling (i.e. planning) and co-ordinating the work of different departments or plants. His chart depicted quantities ordered, work progress and quantities issued from store. Although he never patented it, it is still in use today and bears his name

Fordism

Henry Ford
(1863–1947)

By 1920, the name of Henry Ford had became synonymous not only with his Model T motor car but also with his revolutionary techniques of mass production. Ford established his company in 1903. In the 1890s, it was skilled craftsmen who built motor cars. Ford claimed that there were not enough of them to meet the level of car production that he wanted, and that was why, in his view, deskilling of work was necessary. Others argue that deskilling made labour easier to control and replace. Ford's goal was 'continuous improvement' rather than the 'one best way'. Ford's objective was to increase his control by reducing or eliminating uncertainty (Ford and Crowther, 1924). Among his major innovations were:

- analysis of jobs using time-and-motion techniques;

- installation of single-purpose machine tools to manufacture standardized parts;

- introduction of the assembly line.

Analysing jobs

Ford applied the principles of scientific management to removing waste and inefficiency. Ford established a Motion Picture Department, which filmed work

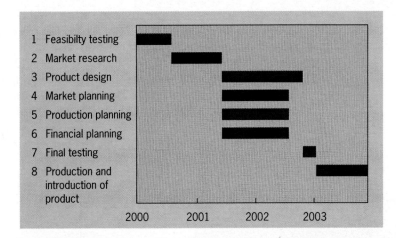

Figure 13.1: Gantt chart for new product development plan beginning 2000

methods in different industries so as to learn from them. He applied the principles of work rationalization, and employees were allocated simple tasks, all of which had been carefully designed to ensure maximum efficiency. Ford's approach was entirely experimental, very pragmatic and always open to improvements—try it, modify it, try it again, keep on until it's right. The Ford mechanic, originally a skilled craftsman, became an assembler who tended his machine, performing only low-grade tasks. For example, the wheelwright's job was divided into almost a hundred operations, each performed by a different man using specialized equipment.

Installation of single-purpose machine tools to produce standardized parts
Ford used rigid and heavy machine tools, carbon alloy tool steels and universal grinding machines. This ensured that each part was exactly like the next and hence interchangeable. This facilitated the division of labour and increased certainty. The single-purpose machines in his factory were called 'farmer machines' because farm boys, coming off the land, could be quickly trained to use them. Their operators did not have to be skilled, just quick. The skill was now incorporated within the machine. This eliminated the need for skilled mechanics, as the unskilled could now assemble an automobile.

Creation of the assembly line
Despite the aforementioned innovations, employees could still work at their own speed. In 1913, it still took 90 minutes to assemble a car. To overcome this problem, instead of moving the men past the car, the car was moved past the men. The assembly line imposed upon employees the working speed that Ford wanted. By 1914, the plant had installed a continuous automatic conveyor that met Ford's technical and philosophical objectives. The engineers arranged work in a logical order. The materials and semi-completed parts passed through the plant to where they were needed. The conveyor belt took radiator parts to assemblers, and then carried their work away to solderers, who finished off the product (Gartman, 1979).

After integrating other production processes, Ford's engineers produced a continuously moving line fed by overhead conveyors. Each worker was feeding, and being fed by, the assembly line. In 1908, when the Model T was introduced, production ran at 27 cars per day. By 1923, when the River Rouge plant had been completed, daily production had reached 2,000 cars. More than quantity of production, the assembly line involved, in Ford's words, 'the focusing upon a manufacturing process of the principles of power, accuracy, economy, system, continuity, speed and repetition'.

The credit for the introduction of the assembly line concept (manual and mechanically paced) is disputed. Some stories tell of Henry Ford getting the idea at an abattoir where beef carcasses, suspended from moving hooks, were being disassembled. Other accounts have him visiting a watch plant and seeing the staged assembly process of timepieces (Collier and Horowitz, 1987). Although Henry Ford claimed the authorship of the assembly line in the manufacturing plant at the Highland Park near Detroit, there is strong evidence to suggest that credit for it should be given to others (Heizer, 1998).

Early Ford assembly line

The photograph below shows men working on one of the early Ford assembly lines.

Many songs were written about Ford's assembly lines. One was sung to the tune of the *Battle Hymn of the Republic*. Its first verse and chorus ran:

Mine eyes hath seen the glories of the making of a Ford,
It's made under conditions that would offend the Almighty Lord,
With a most ungodly hurry, and amidst wild uproar,
The production rushes on.

Hurry, hurry, hurry, hurry,
Hurry, hurry , hurry, hurry,
Hurry, hurry, hurry, hurry,
Production rushes on.

Taylor's ambition had always been to wrest control of the production process from the workers and place it into the hands of management. Under Fordism, this was broadly achieved. Ford's objective was to allow unsophisticated workers to make a sophisticated product in volume. He sought to make his workforce as uniform and interchangeable as the parts that they handled. This created an authoritarian work regime with closely monitored, machine-paced, short-cycle, unremitting tasks. Ford made other, less publicized innovations, including the introduction of highly co-ordinated logistics systems; greater bureaucratic control through job classifications with uniform wage scales; and a limit on the prerogatives of supervisors and line managers.

The speed of the assembly line was increased, with Henry Ford being labelled the 'speed-up king'. This, plus the monotonous work, meant that in 1913, the company had an astronomical turnover rate. Newly hired workers stayed an average of only three months. Indeed, over 70 per cent of the men who left Ford were categorized as 'five-day men', i.e. they walked off the job without any formal notification and were simply presumed to have quit after missing five days work. Since it cost $100 to train each worker, this level of turnover was costing the company $3 million a year (Wilson, 1995).

Partly in response to this, Ford cut the working day from nine to eight hours and doubled the minimum wage from $2.50 to $5.00 a day. This was twice what was offered by any other motor car company. He believed that higher wages would lead to higher production and higher profits. As a result, turnover was reduced, absenteeism fell from 10 per cent to 0.5 per cent and Henry Ford became a hero overnight. The workers who had cursed him now wore their company identification badges as tie-pins on Sundays with pride. Ford knew that they could use the extra money to buy his cars. However, he was concerned that this wage increase could lead some workers to depravity. Hence, this wage increase was dependent on workers showing sobriety and industry. But who was to judge this?

The Ford Sociology Department (FSD) was established in 1914 as an early employment or personnel section and employed 100 investigators. The department met Henry Ford's interest in self-improvement. Ford's workforce was ethnically mixed, containing European immigrants and black employees. Shop-floor documents were printed in several languages. Ford clearly wished to Americanize them. The FSD's central role was to investigate, counsel and instruct workers to encourage their 'improvement'. FSD investigators visited workers in their homes, with translators, to check on how they lived. They checked on workers' drinking habits, cleanliness, debts and sexual relations. Employees had to produce their bank cheque books and marriage licences at the interviews. Where a Ford investigator considered a worker to be living in an amoral manner, the latter could receive a pay cut or suspension. The investigators persuaded single men to enrol in evening and correspondence courses. They also left them a leaflet entitled 'Rules of Living'. They encouraged employees to use plenty of soap and water, not to spit on the floor, avoid hire purchase and to go to Ford-operated schools if they needed to learn English. The wives of employees were counselled not to take in boarders in case a sexual relationship developed while the husband was out at work. The FSD was closed down in 1917.

Ford's legacy continues to dominate twentieth-century organization. He showed his successors how the world could be organized to solve problems using the closely related concepts of **system** and **control**. What Ford built was not just a factory but an entire production system. This system included the factory but went beyond its walls. What made that system so effective was the nature and the degree of control that he exerted upon it. It has been said that Ford was determined to gain complete control of all aspects of the manufacture and sale of his car. That he nearly succeeded testified to his genius (Zaleznik and Kets de Vries, 1975). His control over the manufacturing process was achieved through the log-

Systems concept refers to a management perspective which emphasizes the interdependence between the various parts of an organization, and also between the organization and its environment.

Control concept refers to the process of imposing a pattern on previously haphazard activities, such as the operation of machinery, the interaction of machinery with people, or the interactions between individuals.

Fordist model of work organization

1. Prescribed tasks and compulsory operational methods.

2. Timings based on time-and-motion method with little modification.

3. Centralized engineering department organizes the shop floor.

4. Unskilled operators relieved by 'multiskilled' workers.

5. Role of supervisors primarily disciplinary.

6. No motivation system; no local goals; respect for discipline.

7. System emphasizes discipline.

Based on Jean-Pierre Durand, Paul Stewart and Juan Jose Castillo (eds), *Teamwork in the Automobile Industry: Radical Change or Passing Fashion*, Macmillan Business, London, 1999, p.16.

ical organization of his plants. The output of one group of workers became the input of others. The production system was like a giant river fed by the tributaries that constantly flowed into it.

Control over the worker was exerted through task specialization and assembly line working. Such control was both invisible and non-confrontational. It was the system not the supervisor that told the employee to work faster. It de-personalized the authority relationship to such a degree that workers were no longer aware that they were being directed.

Control over the environment was achieved through purchase of vital raw materials. Ford experienced production hold-ups when his suppliers had strikes. To avoid this he sought to control all aspects of the production process. In the Brazilian rain forest, he carved out a rubber plantation the size of Connecticut, which was called 'Fordlandia'. He bought coal mines in Kentucky and iron mines in Michigan as well as shipping lines and railways. He was determined to control every element of the manufacturing process, both inside and outside his company.

The debate about Henry Ford's legacy continues to this day. On the positive side, there is agreement about his contribution to productivity. In 1913, before the assembly line, it took 12.5 hours to put together a Model T. In 1914, Ford's 13,000 workers produced 267,720 cars, while the other American motor companies, with a combined workforce at the time of 66,000, produced 287,770 cars. Further improvements were to occur. By 1920, one Ford car rolled off the line every minute, and by 1925, the figure was one every 10 seconds.

Ford's contribution to raising people's standard of living is also acknowledged. Having shown that something as complicated as a motor car could be built using the techniques of mass production, it was recognized that the manufacture of other, simpler, products was also possible. Mass production led to mass consumption and gave more people more access to more goods than ever in history. In the fifty years to 1970, the standard of living of Americans skyrocketed. Other countries which adopted Ford's system of manufacturing production also benefited.

Critics have argued that Ford destroyed craftsmanship and deskilled jobs. It did indeed change the work process by introducing greater amounts of rigidity and regulation, thereby affecting the skill content of jobs. Others argue that since there were insufficient numbers of skilled workers available to do the original jobs, Ford had to redesign the tasks so that the existing, pre-industrial labour force could cope with them. In their view, it was less a question of forcing a highly

Cathedral of Industry

In the 1930s, the Mexican artist Diego Rivera (1886–1957) was commissioned by the Detroit Institute of Art to paint frescoes devoted to the city's motor car industry. His panels feature Ford's River Rouge plant outside Detroit. In 1935, that plant spread over 1,096 acres, had 7.25 million square feet of floor space, possessed 235 acres of glass windows, had 90 miles of railway track, employed over 80,000 men, and built 2 million cars each year. Little wonder that it was called the Cathedral of Industry. Look at the panels below carefully. What do you see, and what does it tell you about Fordism?

Rivera was an independent artist with a Marxist perspective. He painted the factory workers and the machines that they used. The ethnic mix of the workforce is depicted. The panels show various stages in the production of the automobile. The men in the murals are depicted as sullen and angry, working amid the clamour and din of the machinery around them. The strength shown in their faces was perceived as intimidating by some observers, who accused Rivera of producing left-wing propaganda.

Detroit Industry (South Wall), Diego Rivera, 1932–33

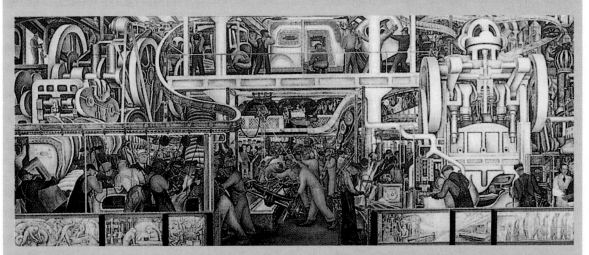

The machines themselves are shown as perfect designs, as part of a system that is so complicated and so intimidating that it dwarfs ordinary human beings. The murals exalt the sophistication of the production system, saying to the onlooker, 'Look at this incredible achievement'. They depict the triumph of rationality over nature's apparent disorganization; of new forms of manufacturing over old; and of the new order over the old. However, one obvious thing is missing from the pictures.

Look at the pictures again carefully. Can you see a completed car? The panels convey the awe-inspiring nature of Ford's technology, as something that helps human beings but which simultaneously dominates them.

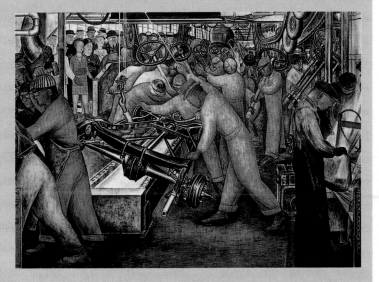

Source: Detroit Institute of Art

skilled, high-priced employee to accept a cheapened, dead-end job, and more an issue of identifying tasks appropriate for unskilled people to do who would otherwise have performed even less enjoyable, back-breaking work. The same critics also assert that short-cycle repetitive jobs have caused worker alienation and stress and have subjugated human beings to the machine. The assembly line is vilified for exerting an invidious, invisible control over the workers. The debate over the balance of costs and benefits of Fordism and its precursor, Taylorism, continue to this day, as the next section illustrates.

After Ford: the deskilling debate

The idea of fragmenting work tasks and simplifying jobs was begun by Taylor and developed by Ford. Since that time, has this process of deskilling work continued and been extended to other occupations and types of worker? Or, on the contrary, has work become more complicated, employees better trained and educated, and the jobs that they do more skilled? Taylor and Ford placed the issue of job skill at the centre of all subsequent discussions about work transformation and work organization. The deskilling debate provides a useful perspective from which to consider the plethora of theoretical, empirical and prescriptive writings produced by academics, managers and consultants during the twentieth century on the topics of work design.

Mike Noon and Paul Blyton (1997) provide a clear exposition of the deskilling debate, and this section draws heavily upon their explanatory structure. It also incorporates additional, more recent, contributions. However, it leaves untouched their basic contention that deskilling theory has failed to provide a satisfactory explanation of the diverse empirical evidence obtained by researchers. Instead, these authors offer an exploratory framework. We shall see how Noon and Blyton reached their conclusion; how recent studies confirm their assessment; and we shall apply their framework. Before proceeding, however, we need to go back briefly in time.

The last half of the twentieth century witnessed two seemingly contradictory trends in work design. From the 1950s, in both the United States and Europe, there was a reaction against Taylorism and a steady and consistent interest in more 'people-oriented' approaches. Labels like human relations, socio-technical systems, quality of working life, organization development and human-centred manufacturing reflected this inclination. Then, during the 1970s, Japanization, and in particular the success of Japanese 'lean production' manufacturing techniques and Japanese teamworking, became prominent. The contradiction was very apparent. On the one hand, lean production involved many features of Taylorist and Fordist work designs, while on the other, it appeared to incorporate numerous people-oriented features like teamworking. This paradox generated much research and debate [links, chapter 3, technology; chapter 12, teamworking].

At the same time, the gathering pace of information technology signalled the increasing importance of knowledge-based jobs, and of the need for so-called 'knowledge workers' to fill them. The necessity of having a well-educated and trained workforce to perform these more technically complex jobs was widely discussed. The question asked by many commentators was whether a fundamental change was taking place in the nature of work, and if so whether it was resulting in people being deskilled, and their work degraded, or upskilled, and their work and working lives enriched.

This then is the 'deskilling debate'. Although the deskilling and upskilling positions stand in opposition to one another, the deskilling one has, to date, generated the greater amount of research and literature. Indeed, it has created its own sub-field in sociology, that of labour process theory. Within this camp, debates have mostly occurred between the deskilling 'agnostics' and 'sympathizers'. In contrast, the upskilling position has been promoted primarily by business writers, management consultants and business school academics keen to identify abrupt and dramatic shifts and new trends in work, the workplace and the economy. There have been fewer inter-positional discussions between the 'deskillers' and 'upskillers' so far, but this may be changing.

The deskilling position

Crudely summarized, the deskilling of work thesis holds that the principles and practices of Taylorism and Fordism continue to be ever more widely applied in modern organizations. The thesis first appeared in 1974 in the book *Labour and Monopoly Capital: The Degradation of Work in the Twentieth Century.* The book was written by Harry Braverman (1920–74), an American theorist who had originally been trained as a craftsman coppersmith, and who had worked in naval ship-yards, railway repair shops and steel plants before becoming a journalist and sociologist. Braverman died shortly after his book was published, and he was not around to enjoy the reputation that his book brought, or to contribute to the debate—the labour process debate—that his work had triggered (Littler and Salaman, 1982).

The 'Braverman thesis', as it came to be known, has stimulated a wide-ranging debate among labour process theorists. It was based on Marxist economic theory and the crisis of capitalism in industrial societies. Braverman saw scientific management as the method used to control labour in growing capitalist enterprises, and being extended to clerical, administrative and other occupational (non-shop-floor) groups.

> **McDonaldization** is an approach to work organization based on efficiency, calculability, predictability and control, using sophisticated technology to enhance these objectives by limiting employee discretion and creativity.

Braverman sought to counter the popular view in social science and business literature that Taylorism has been superseded by human relations and other more sophisticated approaches, and that it no longer determined work design or management methods. On the contrary, he argued, far from being superseded, Taylorism was institutionalized and formed the basis of production control within organizations. Following this impetus, researchers rushed to study organizations to test the thesis. They conducted case studies to determine the existence and nature of deskilling in a wide range of different organizations in both production and service industries. The Braverman deskilling thesis was proposed in 1974 but by the 1990s was being discussed as the **McDonaldization** thesis. This followed the publication in 1993 of a book by George Ritzer, *The McDonaldization of Society* (1993)

In his book, Ritzer argued that the process of McDonaldization was affecting many areas of our social and organizational lives. He has no particular complaint against McDonald's hamburger restaurants; he merely used this fast food chain as

---

The Braverman deskilling thesis

There is a long-run tendency through fragmentation, rationalization and mechanization for workers and their jobs to become deskilled, both in an absolute sense (they lose craft and traditional abilities) and in a relative one (scientific knowledge progressively accumulates in the production process). Even when the individual worker retains certain traditional skills, the degraded job that he or she performs does not demand the exercise of these abilities. Thus, a worker, regardless of his or her personal talents, may be more easily and cheaply substituted in the production process.

From Andrew S. Zimbalist, *Case Studies on the Labour Process*, Monthly Review Press, London, 1979, p.xv.

an illustration of the wider process which was the real focus of his attention. For Ritzer, the new model of rationality, with its routinization and standardization of product and service, and represented by McDonald's, had replaced the bureaucratic structures of the past, as described by Max Weber [**link**, chapter 13, traditional work design]. Ritzer saw the McDonald's approach as possessing four key elements:

1. *Efficiency*: high speed of product manufacture or service provision.

2. *Calculability*: high value and minimum waste.

3. *Predictability*: of product or service irrespective of time or location.

4. *Control*: staff perform a limited range of tasks in a precisely detailed way.

Ritzer's argument is that the process of McDonaldization is spreading and that, while it yields a number of benefits, the associated costs and risks are, in his view, considerable. His own view is that this trend is undesirable. He looks at the issue primarily from the point of view of what the consumer, client or citizen is receiving—a uniform, standardized product or service, However, he recognizes that to achieve this, the jobs of producers have to be deskilled. In addition to the simplified jobs that McDonald's employees perform, their work is also limited by the sophisticated technology of fast food preparation, which gives them little or no discretion in how they prepare and deliver food to customers. Given our definition of action teams, it is perhaps appropriate that McDonald's restaurant employees are referred to by the company as 'crew members'. Crews are a form of action team which are equipment- or technology-driven, and if that technology changes, then so too does the nature of the crew [**link**, chapter 12, teamworking: action teams].

Hamburger grilling instructions are precise and detailed, covering the exact positioning of burgers on the grill, cooking times and the sequence in which burgers are to be turned. Drinks dispensers, french fries machines, programmed cash registers—all limit the time required to carry out a task and leave little or no room for discretion, creativity or innovation on the part of the employee. Such discretion and creativity would of course subvert the aims of efficiency, calculability, predictability and control. Fiona Wilson (1999) summarizes some of the other key features of McDonald's work design from the literature.

The McDonald's way

The McDonald's 'Counter Observation Checklist' is used to ensure that employees welcome customers in the prescribed way. For example. 'Greeting the customer': 1. There is a smile 2. Greeting is pleasant, audible and sincere 3. Looks customer in the eyes (quoted in Fineman, 1995). Similar checklists exist for other processes in the restaurants.

Stop and criticize

Robin Leidner's (1993) research revealed that McDonald's workers do not say that they are dissatisfied with their jobs. Do you find this disturbing or expected? Suggest an explanation for this finding.

The significance of this development is that much of current literature about the nature of work and workplace organization is discussed in terms of Ritzer and his McDonaldization thesis, rather than in terms of Braverman and his deskilling and work degradation thesis. The key point, however, is that both writers address broadly the same issues. Warhurst and Thompson (1998) reported that Ritzer acknowledged the links between his own work and that of Braverman, and between Max Weber's theory of rationalization and Karl Marx's theory of exploitation. There have been many criticisms of Braverman and his deskilling thesis. These include the following (Noon and Blyton, 1997; Fincham and Rhodes, 1998):

Ignores alternative management strategies
It ignores management's ability to choose between using Taylorism to deskill a job and empowering workers to create responsible autonomy [**link**, chapter 12, teamworking]. Leaving employees with some discretion can be to management's advantage. Thus, employee empowerment facilitates greater worker interchangeability, thereby allowing better assembly line balancing. These employees are not deskilled, but management nevertheless continues to control the labour process. This suggests that deskilling is neither inevitable nor necessarily always desirable.

Underestimates skill changes caused by technology
Technological developments are constantly creating new skills, specialists and entire occupations. If the economy and technology can create such new skills, there is no simple process of deskilling. There are many examples of both reskilling (the growth of wholly new skills) and of upskilling (the enhancement of existing skills).

Overstates management's objective of controlling labour
The thesis underestimates the diversity and complexity of management objectives and plurality of interests, many of which may be competing (Buchanan and Boddy, 1983a; 1983b; Child, 1985). Marketing, technological, financial and political considerations may have as much, if not more, impact on work organization. The cost of direct labour is, in many cases, only a small proportion of the total cost of a product, and its control today may not as significant a factor as it was in the past.

Treats workers as passive
The thesis treats workers as passive and compliant, yet there is evidence of collective, union and individual resistance to deskilling. The manifestations of such resistance have been extensively documented, although not widely discussed (Ackroyd and Thompson, 1999; Wilson, 1999). Historically, management's shift from direct Taylorist forms of control to technological, bureaucratic and now a cultural type of control is a testimony to the existence and effect of such resistance (Ray, 1986).

Underestimates the employee consent and accommodation
There is contrary evidence of workers welcoming rather than resisting the opportunity to 'Taylor their own jobs'. This phenomenon was originally proposed by Burawoy (1979) and has been observed by managers. 'They [workers] understood the technique because it had been done *to* them for years, and they liked the idea because now they had the chance to do it for themselves' (quoted in both Adler, 1993a, p.106 and Boje and Winsor, 1993, p.62).

Overlooks skill transfer possibilities
Deskilling in one area may be balanced by upskilling in another. The 'area' may be different national economies, different jobs within the same plant, or perhaps

even different aspects of one person's job. Observers of Japanese just-in-time (JIT) production systems note that one facet of a production worker's job can be upskilled (e.g. when they participate as a group in a job's design), while another aspect of it can be deskilled (e.g. when they have to perform the job that they themselves have 'Taylorized' (Conti and Warner, 1993).

Empirical research on the deskilling thesis

Researchers have studied organizations to determine whether new work initiatives have resulted in greater efficiency, calculability, predictability and control of the organization of work, and what effect they have had on the skill content of the job holders. They have considered jobs in manufacturing, service industries and those that involve 'emotional work and labour'. Brief examples of a range of recent empirical studies are given. It should be noted that these are often single occupational group, single site or single industry. This significance of this point will be discussed later.

Call centres in the UK

Taylor and Bain (1999) surveyed developments in the UK call centre sector, analysing its labour processes and employment relations. They view computer telephony developments as an extension of 'white collar Taylorism'. They involve the 'standardization in scripts' permitting certain predictable interactions to follow. They acknowledge that the (predominantly female) operator's work is demanding; that she knows that her work is measured and speech monitored; and that this often leaves her mentally, physically and emotionally exhausted. On the other hand, the control exercised by supervisors over operators is not as total as some exaggerated accounts would have one believe. Unions have successfully negotiating standard bargaining items for call centre staff, who themselves are resisting with widespread oppositional behaviour and practices. Taylor and Bain highlight management's dilemma of whether to prioritize quantitative output or the quality of service. Intense surveillance reduces staff motivation and commitment, yet monitoring is integral to call centre operations.

Domestic appliance manufacturing in North Wales

Jones (1997) reported the introduction of total quality management (TQM) at Hotpoint's home laundry factory (washing machines and tumble dryers) at Llandudno, North Wales. Jones conducted this practitioner-based research over fifteen years while he was an employee. It relies on *ex post* sources, including 'memory, diaries and informal exchanges with contemporaries', and investigates the links between TQM and Taylorism. Once General Electric (GE) had bought a major stake in the company, it sought to remove the 'boss element' by reducing the hierarchy from six levels to one and introducing JIT and TQM. Under TQM, the workers and not the work-study engineers applied the Tayloristic techniques. Operators were trained in the use of process charts, analysed their own jobs and were encouraged to increase efficiency by eliminating waste. Line balancing was also performed by the group, which shared out the work between its members. Jones concluded that the application of Taylorist techniques linked to TQM initiatives reduced employment levels and intensified work. Changes in the work organization at Hotpoint confirmed a negative view of TQM in which the flow of information from shop floor to management led to greater insecurity and tighter management control.

Grocery distribution in Australia

Wright and Lund (1996) looked at the introduction of a 'best practice' computerized time-and-motion system in one company of the grocery distribution sector in Sydney, Australia. They viewed management's adoption of this 'low trust' labour management system as a form of 'computerized Taylorism'. The adopted procedure allowed real-time measurement and monitoring of staff in a highly variable work process. In this case, the skill content of the warehouse workers' jobs did not change, but their ability to exert some control over their work pace was reduced. In contrast, management exerted greater control, which increased efficiency. Wright and Lund concluded that 'best practice' involved a search by employers for ways of intensifying work effort, reducing labour costs and centralizing control over the labour process.

The upskilling position

Noon and Blyton (1997) traced the genesis of the upskilling position to the 1960s with the economics of human capital theory (Becker, 1964; Fuchs, 1968). The theory held that 'human capital' (i.e. people) was more important than physical assets such as machinery or buildings in accumulating profits. Companies would invest in their workforce through the provision of education and training to help them cope with the greater complexity of work tasks. The upskilling position holds that the general tendency to greater technical sophistication of work requires higher levels of skill among employees, with flexible specialization being one such trend (Piore and Sabel, 1984).

This original view has now been developed and expanded by popular business and academic writers. It has been incorporated into what Warhurst and Thompson (1998, p.3) describe as 'claims of an emerging knowledge economy ... third waves, information societies and computopia'. Upskilling is now most commonly discussed in terms of whether or not there is a growth in 'knowledge workers'. Proponents of the upskilling thesis draw upon the features of the post-industrial economy (Bell, 1999) to support their claim that:

- success depends more on 'brains than brawn' (Barley, 1996);
- the information age has replaced the machine age (Hamel and Prahalad, 1996);
- locating vital information and using it to help understand what is happening in a turbulent environment has become a major determinant of organizational success (Quah, 1997);
- providing services is more important than making tangible products;
- a small group of core workers with steady jobs and fixed salaries will outnumber a growing number of 'portfolio workers' offering their skills to clients (Handy, 1984);
- the work of symbolic analysts who trade and manipulate symbols is too complex, domain-specific and esoteric to be subject to managerial control (Reich, 1993).

Noon and Blyton (1997) listed some of the criticisms of the upskilling thesis, saying that:

1. One cannot establish a causal relationship between technical change and rising skill levels.
2. Advanced technology does not always require increased skill levels.
3. The growth of the service sector does not necessarily lead to the creation of high-skill jobs.
4. Existing mass production methods are likely to continue supplying mass markets.
5. Because of multinationals, upskilling needs to be considered at global and national levels.

Stop and criticize

The obvious way to resolve the deskilling debate is to ask individual employees whether they think that their job now possesses a higher or lower level of skill requirement and responsibility compared to five years ago. Or, if they have a new job, whether that requires more skill to perform it than their previous job. Why is this approach unlikely to provide a reliable answer?

To determine whether or not Taylorist and Fordist practices are being introduced or replaced, one might give up the search for any general tendencies and look instead for specific trends in skill changes on the basis of survey data. This is what Gallie (1991) did on UK data obtained in the 1980s from the Social Change and Economic Life Initiative (SCELI). He found that:

- Within institutional classes, those who remained in the same job experienced less upskilling than those who moved.

- Within sectors, the general trend was towards upskilling rather than deskilling, with non-skilled workers in manufacturing experiencing more upskilling than those in the service sector.

- In every occupational class, work with advanced technology was associated with higher skill demands.

- Overall deskilling was rare, and the most common experience was upskilling.

- The evidence most strongly supports the argument that skills are being polarized, associated most closely with skill differentials, advanced technology and gender. (Noon and Blyton, 1997, p.115)

Chris Warhurst and Paul Thompson (1998) quote an OECD *Jobs Study* (1994), which showed that 'new professionals' like scientists, engineers and marketeers now form the largest occupational group in the UK. They refer to 'technicization', a situation in which theoretical knowledge now infuses previously tacit-knowledge-only jobs. However, this still leaves students without a way of critically evaluating the empirical evidence on work organizations, which predominantly comes not from surveys but from case studies of single occupational groups, single-site or single-industry case studies. What is needed is a conceptual framework with which to analyse and then map the case accounts that are available. Noon and Blyton (1997, pp.118–20) offer just such a conceptual framework which is capable of being developed into an analytical tool. These authors conceptualize the work performed by employees as varying along two dimensions— *work range* and *control over work*. These are shown in figure 13.2.

Range of work
The vertical work range dimension distinguishes at one extreme workers who repeatedly perform a single task, for example operators attaching a wheel on a car on an assembly line. Their work range would be low. At the other end of this dimension would be a person who performed a wide range of different tasks, for example a shop assistant serving staff, restocking shelves, stocktaking and changing window displays. Their work range would be high.

Control over work
The horizontal control over work dimension distinguishes at one extreme workers who, because of the specificity with which their work is defined, have little or no discretion as to how to perform it. For example, our assembly line operator who attaches a wheel on a car will follow a detailed, written specification of how he or she should perform their job. Their work control would be labelled low. At the other end of this dimension would be a person who had wide discretion as to how to perform their work, for example, a potter, a plumber or a doctor. Their control over their work would be high. Noon and Blyton's framework distinguishes four classes or types of work, which they label as follows:

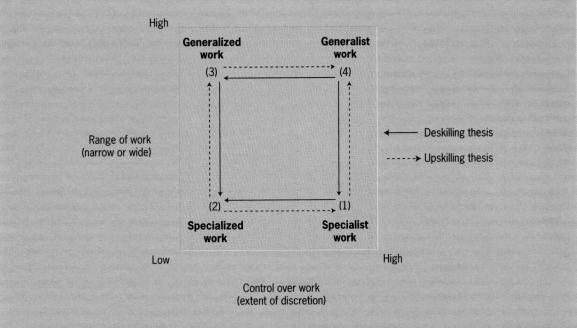

To assist clarity, the original labels *diffuse* and *specific* have been replaced by *high* and *low* respectively.

Figure 13.2: Types of work task and trends in work transformation
Based on Mike Noon and Paul Blyton, *The Realities of Work*, Macmillan Business, 1997, p.119.

1. *Specialist work*: high discretion over a narrow range of work.

2. *Specialized work*: a narrow range of prescribed tasks.

3. *Generalized work*: a wide range of prescribed tasks.

4. *Generalist work*: high discretion over a wide range of tasks.

Stop and criticize

Consider an organization with which you are familiar—a school, university, church, current employer. Give one of example of *specialist, specialized, generalized* and *generalist* work. What effect did it have on your satisfaction and motivation?

The framework can be used both to trace trends in skill changes, and also to compare different work organization initiatives described in empirical case studies. Noon and Blyton depict the deskilling trend with the solid arrows, from high to low on the range of work dimension, and from high to low control on the control over work dimension. Its most extreme position labelled is (2) Specialized work. The upskilling trend is shown with dotted arrows in the opposite direction with its extreme position labelled as (4) Generalist Work. Instead of looking for any general trends, Noon and Blyton's 'map' allows for the possibility of a single group, workplace, industry or industrial sector, to be represented.

Back to the future?

Just how alienating and demotivating is Taylorism? Paul Adler (1999) offers an interesting counter-argument to this established view, claiming that Taylorism

Intrinsic motivation refers to a form of motivation that stresses valued outcomes or benefits that come from within the individual, such as feelings of satisfaction, competence, self-esteem and accomplishment.
Extrinsic motivation refers to a form of motivation that stresses valued outcomes or benefits provided by others such as promotion, pay increases, a bigger office desk, praise and recognition.
Instrumental orientation to work refers to an attitude that sees work as an instrument to the fulfilment of other goals.

Introjection refers to a formerly external regulation or value that has been 'taken in' and is now enforced through internal pressures such as guilt, anxiety or related self-esteem dynamics.
Identification refers to the incorporation of thoughts, feelings and actions of others into one's self-esteem or reducing the threat from powerful others. Typically, it takes the form of 'I want'.

actually represents a fundamental emancipatory philosophy of job design. He reports that at the New United Motors Manufacturing Inc. (NUMMI) auto plant in Freemont, California, which uses a classical Taylorist approach, workers show relatively high levels of motivation and job commitment (Adler, 1993a; 1993b). How can this be? Adler's argument is that his research findings reveal two fundamental flaws in the standard view, which is based on two psychological assumptions. These are, first, that work is only truly motivating to the extent that it resembles free play; and, second, that workers have to have autonomy [**link**, chapter 12, teamworking].

Adler states that the standard critique of Taylorism just presents extrinsic and intrinsic motivation as polar opposites, and he holds that since Taylorized work lacks **intrinsic motivation** potential, it only leaves employees the possibility of obtaining **extrinsic motivation**. In so doing, it develops in them an **instrumental orientation to work** [**link**, chapter 8, motivation].

Adler draws upon the work of Richard Ryan and James Connell (1989) to argue that between the extrinsic and intrinsic polarities, there are two other intermediate positions—**introjection** and **identification**. These are presented in table 13.3.

Adler argues that job design at NUMMI taps into the identification motivation base. This focuses upon the internalization of company values, goals and the means by which these are absorbed and adopted. Instead of motivating through 'free play', NUMMI employees are motivated through:

- The desire for excellence, the instinct of craftsmanship, and a job well done.

- Their 'psychological maturity', which recognizes the reality of the competitive situation, and that they need to compete on quality and productivity with other autoworkers around the world.

- Respect and trust shown to them by management, which elicits reciprocal commitment.

Adler then considers the autonomy issue at the individual and team levels. Critics of Taylorism hold that the choice over work methods and pace of work is crucial for sustaining high levels of motivation and involvement. Adler argues that his research suggests it is not as important as claimed. NUMMI's use of the Japanese form of teamworking [**link**, chapter 12, teamworking] offered little in the way of team autonomy. The teams were organized by engineers, managers and workers; they were tightly coupled with other teams, both upstream and downstream, through just-in-time *kanban* systems; and with teams on other shifts. Yet workers endorsed such interdependence (low autonomy) as an effective way of managing. Adler (1999, p.12) quotes one worker:

The work teams at NUMMI aren't like the autonomous teams you read about in other plants. Here we're not autonomous, because we're all tied together really tightly. But it's not like we're getting squeezed to work harder, because it's us, the worker, that are making the whole thing work—we're the ones that make the standardized work and the kaizen suggestions. We run the plant—and if it's not running right, we stop it.

Adler argues that when workers establish a feeling of organization-wide responsibility for the effectiveness of their work, and they come to perceive their Taylorized jobs as an effective way of accomplishing the necessary interdependent tasks, then low individual and team autonomy can coexist with high morale.

Table 13. 3: Four bases of motivation

Extrinsic	Introjection	Identification	Intrinsic
• Following rules	• Self- and other approval	• Self-valued goal	• Enjoyment
• Avoidance of punishment	• Avoidance of disapproval	• Personal importance	• Fun
• Because I'll get into trouble if I don't	• Because I want the teacher to think I'm a good student	• Because I want to understand the subject	• Because it's fun
• Because that's what I'm supposed to do	• Because I'll feel bad about myself if I don't	• Because I want to learn new things	• Because I enjoy it
• So the teacher won't yell at me	• Because I'll feel ashamed of myself if I don't	• To find out if I'm right or wrong	
• Because that's the rule	• Because I want other students to think I'm smart	• Because I think it's important to	
	• Because if bothers me when I don't	• Because I wouldn't want to do that (negative behaviour)	
	• Because I want people to like me		

From Paul S. Adler, 'The emancipatory significance of Taylorism', in M.P.E. Cunha and C.A. Marques (eds), *Readings in Organization Science–Organizational Change in a Changing Context*, Instituto Superior de Psicologia, Lisbon, 1999, pp.7–14: 9.

Stop and criticize

Have the critics of Taylorist work organization 'got it wrong' after all these years, or has NUMMI management discovered something new?

Recap

1. *Understand how scientific management met the needs of its historical context.*

   • At the start of the twentieth century, European emigration to the United States and internal migration from rural to urban areas produced a large workforce with poor English language skills which lacked work discipline.

   • The same period saw the establishment of large corporations, and the development of technology that permitted, for the first time, mass manufacture of products. These factories required a large workforce.

2. *Describe the main objectives and principles of the scientific management approach.*

   • The objectives are efficiency, by increasing the output per worker and reducing deliberate 'underworking'; predictability of job performance—standarizing tasks by dividing them up into small and closely specified sub-tasks; and control by establishing discipline through hierarchical authority and introducing a system whereby all management's policy decisions could be implemented.

   • The principles are a clear division of tasks and responsibilities between management and workers; use of scientific methods to determine the best way of doing a job; scientific selection of employees; the training of the selected worker to perform the job in the way specified: and the surveillance of workers through the use of hierarchies of authority and close supervision.

3. *Critically assess Taylorism.*
   - It has been criticized for its assumptions about human motivation: neglecting the subjective side of work; ignoring the impact of the work group; disregarding the psychological needs and capabilities of workers; and taking too simple an approach to the question of productivity and morale.

4. *Enumerate the contributions of the Gilbreths and Gantt to scientific management.*
   - Frank Gilbreth's contributions were micro-motion study, the chronocyclegraph and the 'therbligs' notation system. Lillian Gilbreth contributed fatigue study based on physiological and psychological principles.
   - Laurence Gantt supplied the 'best known way at present' approach to job design, the task-and-bonus payment scheme and the 'Gantt chart'.

5. *Understand how Fordism developed out of Taylorism.*
   - Ford developed the analysis of jobs; installed single-purpose machine tools to produce standardized parts; and established the mechanically paced assembly line.

   - The twin concepts of system and control underpinned his approach.

6. *Understand the deskilling debate, and the contribution of Braverman and Ritzer.*
   - The 'Braverman thesis' holds that there is a long-run tendency for workers and their jobs to become deskilled through fragmentation, rationalization and mechanization.
   - Some argue for the deskilling thesis, while others reject it claiming that technological developments have upskilled both workers and jobs and created new, high-skill industries.
   - The deskilling debate is often discussed in the context of Ritzer's McDonaldization process, which refers to an approach to work design based on efficiency, calculability, predictability and control.

7. *Provide examples of scientific management in contemporary society.*
   - Apart from fast food restaurants, the process of granting credit through a credit card; semesterization and modularization of university courses; TV programmes; food packaging.

Revision

1. Taylorism has been much criticized. Which criticisms do you feel are valid and which are not? Give reasons for your assessment.

2. Have quality and flexibility requirements in modern organizations rendered Fordism redundant?

3. Discussions of Taylorism, Fordism and their successors have generated as much emotion as factual debate. Suggest why this has been so, and consider what effect this might have on achieving an objective assessment of this form of work organization.

4. Identify non-food examples of the McDonaldization process. Analyse them in terms of Ritzer's four central dimensions.

5. 'The very uncertainty that inevitably accompanies the human element, in itself often provided by relatively unqualified labour, drives management to *standardize* the encounter as a means of ensuring "quality" or at least consistency' (Warhurst and Thompson, 1998, p.5). Discuss the application of Taylorism in employee–customer, face-to-face work situations such as supermarket checkouts, hotels and call centres. Does this need for quality and consistency make the application of Taylorism more or less vital?

Springboard

Braverman, H., 1974, *Labor and Monopoly Capital; The Degradation of Work in the Twentieth Century*, Monthly Review Press, New York.

This book initiated the deskilling debate and the labour process school.

Durand, J.-P., Stewart, P. and Castillo, J.J. (eds), 1999, *Teamwork in the Automobile Industry: Radical Change or Passing Fashion*, Macmillan Business, London.

Wide-ranging critical assessments of the application of teamworking in automobile manufacturing in Europe, Japan and the United States.

Kanigel, R., 1997, *The One Best Way: Frederick Winslow Taylor and the Enigma of Efficiency*, Little, Brown & Company, London.

A biography of Frederick Taylor providing fascinating detail which links his personal and professional lives.

Leidner, R., 1993, *Fast Food, Fast Talk: Service Work and the Routinization of Everyday Life*, University of California Press, Berkeley.

Entertaining book which considers the effects of organizational efforts to control interactions between workers and customers.

Millman, R., 1997, *Farewell to the Factory: Autoworkers in the Late Twentieth Century*, University of California Press, Berkeley.

A critical assessment of automobile production plants which use the 'lean production' approach.

Noon, M. and Blyton, P., 1997, *The Realities of Work*, Macmillan Business, London, chapter 6.

Introduces the Braverman debate for those wishing to join in.

Parker, M. and Slaughter, J., 1988, *Choosing Sides: Unions and the Team Concept*, Labour Notes, Detroit.

Critiques the Taylorist principles and practices within 'lean production' manufacturing environments in the NUMMI plant in Freemont, California.

Ritzer, G., 1993, *The McDonaldization of Society*, Pine Forge, Thousand Oaks, Calif, 1993.

Ritzer, G., 1995, *Expressing America: A Critique of the Global Credit Card Society*, Pine Forge, Thousand Oaks, Calif.

Ritzer, G. (ed.), 1998, *The McDonaldization Thesis*, Sage, London.

Three books which build on Braverman's deskilling thesis and bring the debate up to the present day.

Thompson, P. and McHugh, D., 1995, *Work Organizations*, second edition, Macmillan, London.

A critical introduction to work organization.

Thompson, P. and Warhurst, C. (eds), 1998, *Workplaces of the Future*, Macmillan Business, London.

A set of chapters that challenge the currently accepted rhetoric about 'new' work organization by using empirical research to demonstrate just how much these are based on traditional Taylorist principles.

Home viewing

Modern Times (1936, director Charlie Chaplin) is a satire of the automated age. It stars Chaplin himself and Paulette Goddard. In the opening sequence, Chaplin is a comic victim of the assembly line in a huge manufacturing plant in the 1930s. Watch the first fifteen minutes of the film. Identify as many different aspects of Taylorism and Fordism as you can.

OB in literature

Aldous Huxley, *Brave New World*, Penguin Books, Harmondsworth, 1932.

Where in the plot are the techniques of Frederick Taylor and Henry Ford effectively deployed in the society which Huxley describes? This story also illustrates Pavlovian conditioning in action [**link**, chapter 4, learning]. Which aspects of Huxley's fictional account are found in some form in contemporary society?

Jacqueline Briskin, *The Onyx*, Grafton Books. London, 1983.

A story of the creation of the first mass-produced motor car in the world. It mixes fact with fiction, and business with romance.

Chapter exercises

1: Assembly line simulation

Objectives

1. To introduce you to the concept of assembly line production.

2. To highlight some of the key issues and debates about this form of work organization.

Briefing

1. While remaining in your lecture theatre seats, identify yourself as part of a group of six, counting off from the aisles. Your groups will consist of six people in a row, sitting next to each other. Each lecture theatre row will have a number of such sixes. However, a group may have one or more of its members in the row immediately in front of, or behind them.

2. Nominating the person nearest the aisle as A, assign letters B, C, D. E and F in order to the other members of your group who are sitting next to one another.

3. Your instructor will brief all the groups in the lecture theatre to perform the same assembly line task. He or she will 'train' you, explaining what each group member has to do.

4. After your training, you will have a practice production run, followed by one or more real production runs.

5. After your have completed the simulation, consider the following questions.

- What was the physical arrangement of group members. Did this help or hinder your task?

- In what direction did the work 'flow'? Did it affect left- or right-handed members?

- How many seconds did it take to complete your part of the task (cycle time)?

- How would you feel if you had to do this for eight hours every day?

2: McDonaldization

Objectives

1. To introduce you to the concept of McDonaldization.

2. To encourage you to recognize non-food examples of the McDonaldization process.

3. To allow you to critically evaluate the costs and benefits of McDonaldization.

Introduction

In his book *The McDonaldization of Society* (1993), George Ritzer argues that the process of McDonaldization *is* affecting many areas of our social and organizational lives, and that this trend is undesirable (see also Ritzer, 1997; Smart, 1999).

Ritzer has no particular complaint against McDonald's hamburger restaurants; he merely uses this fast food chain as an illustration of the wider process which is the real focus of his attention. The argument is that the process of McDonaldization is spreading and that, while it yields a number of benefits, the costs and risks are in Ritzer's view considerable. This exercise is based on what Ritzer identifies as the four central dimensions of McDonaldization. You are then invited to consider for yourself the benefits of this trend, and the associated costs and risks. Finally, using some of Ritzer's ideas as a basis, we will consider whether and how such an organizational trend can be subverted by individual action.

Everybody knows McDonald's, the fast food chain which has outlets in most towns and cities of any size on the planet. The large yellow McDonald's 'M' logo (golden arches) is one of the most widely recognized company symbols in the world (along with Holiday Inn and Coca Cola). Ritzer argues that the McDonald's approach has four central dimensions:

1. *Efficiency,* with respect to the speed with which you are transformed from being hungry to being fed, including the drive-through option.

2. *Calculability,* with respect to high-value meals for discounted prices—quarter pounders, Big Macs, large fries, all ordered, delivered and consumed with a minimum waste of time.

3. *Predictability,* as the Big Mac in New York is the same as the Big Mac in Helsinki is the same as the Big Mac in Singapore—no surprises, but nothing special either.

4. *Control,* as the staff who work in McDonald's are trained to perform a limited range of tasks in a precisely detailed way, and customers are similarly disciplined with queues, limited menu options, and by the clear expectation that they will eat and then leave.

In addition to the simplified jobs which McDonald's employees perform, their work is also limited by the sophisticated technology of fast food preparation. Their job specifications give them little or no discretion in how they prepare and deliver food to customers. Hamburger grilling instructions are precise and detailed, covering the exact positioning of burgers on the grill, cooking times, and the sequence in which burgers are to be turned. Drinks dispensers, french fries machines and programmed cash registers are all used to limit the time required to carry out tasks and leave little or no room for discretion, creativity or innovation on the part of the employee. Discretion and creativity would, of course, subvert the aims of efficiency, calculability, predictability and control.

Analysis questions

1. What are the benefits of this approach—to the company, to the customer, to society as a whole?

2. What are the disadvantages of this approach?

3. Identify examples of McDonaldization from sectors other than fast foods—work, travel, family, medical care and commerce.

4. To what extent is higher education susceptible to McDonaldization? Is your university currently being McDonaldized? Explain how.

5. Ritzer offers a number of suggestions for coping with McDonaldization: avoiding daily routine, using self-help rather than 'instant repair' chains, using small, local, independent traders and services rather than large companies, returning all 'junk mail', trying to establish meaningful communications with fast food counter staff, avoiding classes which are assessed using short answer examinations and computer-graded tests, and so on. Identify five other subversion strategies for yourself.

6. What is your realistic assessment of the impact of these subversion strategies? Can we really make a difference, individually or collectively? Is it worth the effort?

Chapter 14 Elements of structure

Key concepts

organization structure	functional relationship
job definition	formal organization
job description	informal organization
organization chart	departmentalization
hierarchy	matrix structure
span of control	role
authority	role set
responsibility	self-fulfilling prophecy
accountability	role conflict
chain of command	centralization
line employees	decentralization
staff employees	

Learning objectives

Once you have read this chapter, you should be able to define those key concepts in your own words, and you should be able to:

1. Explain how organization structure affects human behaviour in organizations.
2. List the main elements of organization structure.
3. Relate the concept of span of control to the shape of the organization hierarchy.
4. Identify line, staff and functional relationships on an organization chart.
5. Describe five different criteria on which jobs might be departmentalized.
6. Distinguish between the formal and the informal organization of a company.
7. Distinguish Mintzberg's five organizational parts, five types of organization structure and ten managerial roles.

Why study elements of structure?

Organizational social scientists are interested in studying three related questions. *What* are organizations trying to do? *How* are they trying to do it? *Why* are they trying to do it that way? Roy Payne (1996) explains that the 'what' question begins by classifying organizations according to their goals or purposes and leads to a consideration of why these goals are chosen and how. This is the area of corporate strategy or strategic management. The question of why organizations choose to pursue some goals in certain ways leads to a consideration of organization culture [**link**, chapter 19, organization culture]. The consideration of how organizations attempt to achieve their goals is the domain of organization structure. As Payne and many other authors point out, strategy, structure and culture are closely related, although rarely considered together.

Other social scientists, particularly sociologists, are interested in organization structure for another reason. They claim that people's attitudes and behaviour are shaped as much by the structure of the company in which they work as by the personalities that they possess. The constraints and demands of the job, imposed through the roles that they play, can dictate their behaviour and even change their personalities. For this reason, it is impossible to explain the behaviour of people in organizations solely in terms of individual or group characteristics. Alan Fox argued that, in seeking to make such explanations, the structural determinants of behaviour should be considered (Fox, 1966). He was critical of those who insisted on explaining human behaviour in organizations exclusively in terms of personalities, personal relationships and leadership. Such explanations were highly appealing to common sense, partly because such variables were clearly visible, while the effects of structure were hidden.

We now recognize that structure does affect the individual's behaviour in organizations. Transferring people from one part of a company to another involves moving them from one structural situation to another. Transferring a sales manager from headquarters to the regional office can change their behaviour. The changes can have more to do with the organization setting in which these people now operate than with the characteristics of the people themselves, for example in the work methods used, the types of communication system operated and the ways in which their performance is judged.

A consideration of organization structure is likely to be encountered by students in two ways. First, it will be considered on a corporate strategy course, as a vehicle for achieving organizational goals (Johnson and Scholes, 1999); second, on an organization behaviour course, in which the logical and rational elements of organizations are emphasized, while people's preferences or feelings are underplayed. The structural approach stands in contrast to the psychologistic approach, which holds that it is the internal (individual) factors that are the main determinants of human behaviour in organizations.

| **Stop and criticize** | Consider the behaviour of the instructor teaching this course. Identify aspects of their behaviour which you like and do not like. Decide if these positive and negative behaviours are influenced by that person's personality or by the organization structure within which they work? |

Organization structuring

Organization structure refers to the formal system of task and reporting relationships that controls, co-ordinates and motivates employees so that they work together to achieve organizational goals.

At the start of the book, organizations were defined as social arrangements for achieving controlled performance in pursuit of collective goals. One aspect of this 'arrangement' is the creation of a structure. The purpose of **organization structure** is, first, to divide up organizational activities and allocate them to subunits; and, second, to co-ordinate and control these activities so that they achieve the aims of the organization.

A popular way of depicting the structure of any large organizations is that of a pyramid or triangle, as in figure 14.1. This is only one of many possible shapes for a structure several others will be presented later in the chapter. For the time being, we can note that the pyramidal form shows that an organization has both a vertical and a horizontal dimension. Its broad base indicates that the vast majority of employees are located at the bottom and are responsible for manufacturing the product or providing the service (e.g. making refrigerators, selling insurance). Proponents of the formal system claim that the reporting relationships co-ordinate, motivate and control employees so that they work together to achieve organizational goals. Child (1984, p.8) identified the five main questions that any organization structure designer needed to answer:

1. *Specialization*: Should jobs be broken down into narrow areas of work and responsibility so as to secure the benefits of specialization? Or should the degree of specialization be kept to a minimum in order to simplify communication and to offer members of the organization greater scope and responsibility in their work? Another choice arising in the design of jobs concerns the extent to which the responsibilities and methods attaching to them should be precisely defined.

2. *Hierarchy*: Should the overall structure of an organization be 'tall' rather than 'flat' in terms of its levels of management and spans of control? What are the implications for communication, motivation and overhead costs of moving towards one of these alternatives rather than the other?

3. *Grouping*: Should jobs and departments be grouped together in a 'functional' way according to the specialist expertise and interests that they share? Or should they be grouped according to the different services and products which are being offered, or the different geographical areas being served, or according to yet another criterion?

4. *Integration*: Is it appropriate to aim for an intensive form of integration between the different segments of an organization or not? What kind of integrative mechanisms are there to choose from?

5. *Control*: How should management maintain control over work done? Should it centralize or delegate decisions, and all or only some of the decisions? Should a policy of extensive formalization be adopted in which standing orders and written records and rules are used for control purposes? Should work be subject to close supervision?

The answers to these questions will have a major impact on the nature of the jobs of all employees working within that structure. For example, a highly centralized structure, with little delegation, will mean that senior managers will spend more of their time making decisions, while junior staff may feel powerless and de-motivated. Choices about organization structure and the content of individual employees' jobs (both managers and non-managers) are intimately related.

In figure 14.1, each of the six successive levels above the workers represents a layer of management. On the left-hand side of the diagram, the managerial ranks are divided into three groupings: supervisory or first-line management; middle management; and senior or top management. The diagram's right-hand side lists the commonly used job titles of managers who are members of each grouping. The layers also represent differences in status. While most people will recognize an organization structure, they are less clear about its purpose. Robert Duncan (1979, p.59) said that:

> Organization structure is more than boxes on a chart; it is a pattern of interactions and co-ordination that links the technology, tasks and human components of the organization to ensure that the organization accomplishes its purpose.

For him, the purpose of a structure was two-fold. First, it facilitated the flow of information within the company in order to reduce the uncertainty in decision making which was caused by information deficiency. Second, a structure achieved

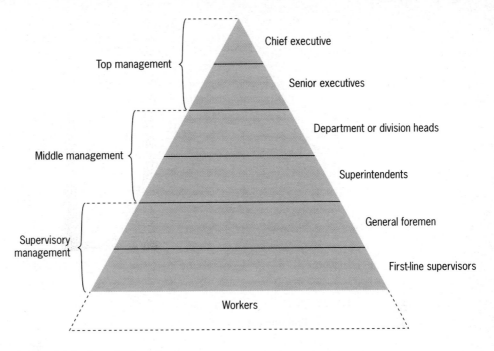

Figure 14.1: Organization structure

effective co-ordination–integration of the diverse activities occurring within the firm, integrating the actions of individuals, groups and departments, especially those which were interdependent, so that all became co-ordinated.

The structure of an organization signals the behaviour expected of its members (table 14.1).

Harold Leavitt has suggested that organizations can be viewed as complex systems which consist of four mutually interacting independent classes of variables: organizational objectives, company structure, technology used and people employed (figure 14.2). All of these were affected by the firm's environment, such as the economic, political or social situation. The differences in organization structure can be partly accounted for by the interactions of these elements.

Table 14.1: Elements of structure

Concerned with	Involves	Exemplified in
how the work of the organization is divided and assigned to individuals, groups and departments	• allocating tasks and responsibilities to individuals (e.g. how much choice they have about how they work)	• organization chart • job descriptions • establishing boards, committees and working parties
how the required co-ordination is achieved	• specifying and defining jobs • designing the formal reporting relationships • deciding on the number of levels in the hierarchy • deciding on the span of control of each supervisor and manager	• rules and policies • hierarchy • goal clarification • temporary task forces • permanent project teams • liaison roles • integrator roles

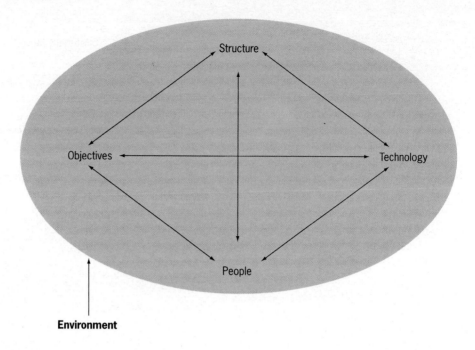

Figure 14.2: Leavitt diamond

Types of job

An important series of decisions on organization design relate to what types of job should be created. How narrow and specialized should these be? How should the work be divided, and what should be the appropriate content of each person's job? The detailed answer will of course depend on the type of job considered. Is it the job of a nurse, engineer, car assembly worker, teacher or politician that is being designed?

Specialization is a feature of knowledge, clerical and manual jobs. After their general medical training, some doctors become paediatricians, while on the assembly line, some workers fit car tyres while others fix on the doors. The choice concerning the extent and type of specialization depends on criteria used by the organization designer. These will be affected by their values, beliefs and preferences. It may be a case of trading off efficiency of production against job satisfaction. A value position might be to seek to maximize both elements. Too rigid specialization can lead to demarcation disputes. Once the elements of the job have been decided, it is possible to advertise the post.

How well defined ought a job to be? There is a school of management thought which argues that newly appointed staff should know exactly what their duties are in detail. They suggest that this high degree of **job definition** helps to motivate employees by letting them know exactly what is expected of them. Such detail can also assist in the appraising of their past performance.

Others commentators believe that, far from being motivating, a high level of job definition acts to control people's behaviour and set minimum performance standards. What is needed, they argue, is for the employee to create their own job. In practice, a detailed job definition is provided to those doing low-level manual and clerical jobs, while at more senior levels there is a greater degree of own job making. The physical manifestation of the choice about how much to define the

Job definition is determining the task requirements of each job in the organization. It is the first decision in the process of organizing.

HANDS ON CHIEF EXECUTIVE

To bring bags of presence and enormous energy to a unique global distribution operation

A package with bells on + sleigh   Far North

This intensely private operation, which has a brand that is recognised throughout the world, has carved a unique position in a highly seasonal business. Its President and owner, who has always maintained a close personal involvement in every aspect of the operation, has decided that it's time to hand over the reins. The opportunities and challenges presented by technological change, and the potential threat of imitators, are issues which call for fresh ideas, new perspectives and, candidly, younger eyes. Ideal candidates, probably entering their second century and quite possibly retired recruitment consultants, will have the maturity which goes with white hair, the vision to penetrate the darkest night, a lightness of touch, and the leadership to direct a diminutive yet dedicated team. Skills in more than one language and sensitivity to a wide range of cultures will be essential, and experience of working with quadrupeds, especially reindeer, will help. Above all, we will be looking for the humour to overcome the intense seasonal pressures and the ability to appear to be in several places simultaneously. Please post full career details, quoting reference WE2512, up the nearest chimney, and share the joy, mystery, and magic of this special time with those you value most—with best wishes to our readers, candidates and clients, Ward Executive Limited, 4–6 George Street, Richmond-upon-Thames, Surrey TW9 1JY.

WARD EXECUTIVE
LIMITED
Executive Search & Selection

Ward Executive Limited job advertisement, from *Daily Telegraph*, Appointments, 24 December 1998.

Job description (or post profile) is a summary statement of what an individual should do on the job.

job is the piece of paper on which is written the **job description**. Individuals who request more information about a job advertised in the newspaper are usually sent a job description and an application form. A job description will usually contain the following information:

- job title and the department in which it is located;

- job holder's position in the hierarchy;

- to whom the job holder is responsible;

- the objectives of the job;

- duties required of the job holder (regular, periodical and optional);

- liaison with other workers, staff, supervisors and managers;

- authority to carry out the task—the degree of freedom permitted to exercise own judgement in carrying out the job.

The specialization of work activities and the consequent division of labour is a feature of all large complex organizations. Once tasks have been broken down (or 'differentiated') into sub-tasks, these are allocated to individuals in the form of jobs. Persons carrying out the jobs occupy positions on the organization's hierarchy. Particular levels of responsibility and authority are allocated to these positions. The division of labour and the relationship of one position to another is reflected in the organization chart, which can act as a guide to explain how the work of different people in the organization is co-ordinated and integrated.

WINDWORTH UNIVERSITY BUSINESS SCHOOL
JOB DESCRIPTION

Post title	School Clerk
Position in the university	Reporting to School Registrar
Main purpose of the post	To provide an efficient and effective clerical/secretarial support for the wide-ranging activities of the Business School office

Main duties

- To provide clerical support to the various committees and sub-committees, including:
  - Preparation and circulation of agendas and minutes
  - Dealing with correspondence and related work falling within the scope of the School Office
  - Booking of accommodation and hospitality arrangements for committees and meetings
- To provide clerical support to the wide range of activities of the School Office, including:
  - Quality assurance processes and procedures
  - Research
  - Marketing
  - Programmes
  - Finance
- Maintenance of management information systems
- Maintenance of filing systems and records, both electronic and manual
- To carry out such duties as may be assigned from time to time by the Registrar or Dean

Profile of expected competencies

- Excellent communication skills both written and oral. Ability to liaise with colleagues at all levels within the university and with external contacts
- Excellent organizational skills, including:
  - Ability to work in a team and independently without supervision
  - Ability to carry out tasks efficiently and effectively
  - Motivated and enthusiastic team player
- Excellent IT skills, must be fully conversant with Microsoft Office including spreadsheets, databases and Microsoft mail
- HNC qualification is desirable
- Knowledge of university administration desirable, but not essential as training will be given

As a term of employment, staff may be required to undertake such other duties and/or hours of work at any Windworth University establishment as may be required to meet the needs and exigencies of the university.

SALARY SCALE: £11,898 – £12,405

The Job Description by Bertie Ramsbottom

I trod, where fools alone may tread,
To speak what's better left unsaid,
The day I asked my boss his view
On what I was supposed to do;
For, after two years in the task,
I thought it only right to ask,
In case I'd got it badly wrong,
Ad-hoc'ing as I went along.
He raised his desultory eyes,
And made no effort to disguise
That, what had caused my sudden whim,
Had equally occurred to him;
And thus did we embark upon
Our classic corporate contretemps,
To separate the fact from fiction,
Bedevilling my job description.
For first he asked me to construe
A list of things I really do;
While he – he promised – would prepare
A note of what he thought they were;
And, with the two, we'd take as well
The expert view from Personnel,
And thus eliminate the doubt
On what my job was all about.

But when the boss and I conflated
The tasks we'd separately stated,
The evidence became abundant
That one of us must be redundant;
For what I stated I was doing
He claimed himself to be pursuing,
While my role, on his definition,
Was way outside my recognition.
He called in Personnel to give,
A somewhat more definitive
Reply, but they, by way of answer,
produced some vague extravaganza,
Depicting in a web of charts,
Descriptive and prescriptive parts,
Of tasks, the boss and I agree,
Can't possibly refer to me.
So, hanging limply as I am,
In limbo on the diagram,
Suspended by a dotted line
From functions that I thought were mine,
I feel it's maybe for the best
I made my innocent request;
I hopefully await their view
On which job of the three I do!

From Ralph Windle, *The Poetry of Business Life: An Anthology*, Berrett-Koehler Publishers, San Francisco, 1994, pp.80–2.

Organization chart is a pictorial record which shows the formal relations which the company intends should prevail within it.

Once specified and defined, the jobs and the authority and responsibility relations between them are represented on an **organization chart**. Organization charts graphically depict an organization's formal structure and are a universal feature of organizational life. Only their form and contents differ in line with the company being represented. Alfred Chandler (1988) wrote that the first modern chart was constructed in 1854, when Daniel McCallum became the general foreman of the New York and Erie railway. At the time, it had 500 miles of track and was the world's largest. In order to co-ordinate the ever-increasing number of employees and equipment, McCallum needed a guide to indicate who reported to whom. The organization chart provided this information and had become a common feature of American companies by 1910. Possibly the earliest British chart was drawn up by Nobel Industries and was based on the DuPont model.

Let us consider the organization charts in figures 14.3a and 14.3b, since an examination of them can help to clarify some of the basic concepts associated with organization structure. **Hierarchy** refers to the number of levels of authority to be found in an organization. In a company which has a flat organization structure, such as that shown in figure 14.3a, only one level of hierarchy separates the managing director at the top from the employees at the bottom. In contrast, the organization structure depicted in figure 14.3b has four levels between the top and the employees at the bottom.

Hierarchy refers to the number of levels of authority to be found in an organization.

It is useful to distinguish between organizations which have many levels in their hierarchy, such as the armed forces, the police and the civil service (referred to as having a 'tall' hierarchy), and organizations which manage to operate with relatively few levels of hierarchy, such as small businesses and universities

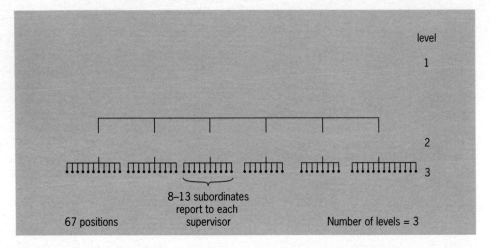

Figure 14.3a: Flat organization structure

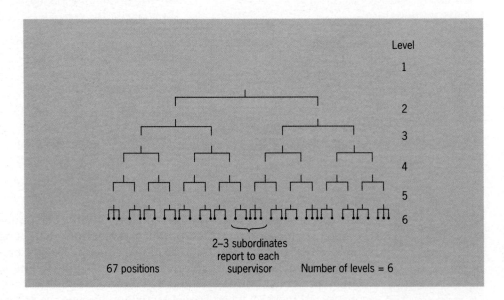

Figure 14.3b: Tall organization structure

(referred to as possessing a 'flat' hierarchy). The Catholic Church with its 800 million members, which has been in existence for over fifteen hundred years, operates with five hierarchical layers—parish priest, bishop, archbishop, cardinal and Pope.

Span of control refers to the number of subordinates who report to a single supervisor or manager and for whose work that person is responsible. Comparing the two organization charts in figure 14.3, it can be seen that in the one with a flat hierarchy, there are many employees reporting to each supervisor. Hence, that person has a broad span of control. In a tall organization structure, fewer employees report to each manager and hence the span of control of each of the managers is therefore narrow. The larger the number of subordinates reporting to one manager, the more difficult it is for her to supervise and co-ordinate them effectively. General Sir Iain Hamilton once said that 'No one brain can effectively control more than six or seven other brains'.

Harold Koontz (1966) wrote that if an organization with 4,000 employees

Span of control is the number of subordinates who report directly to a single manager or supervisor.

The five organization charts below show the same eleven positions (numbered 1, 21, 22, 23, etc.) in the same relationships to one another. They differ only in the way that they visually depict those relationships.

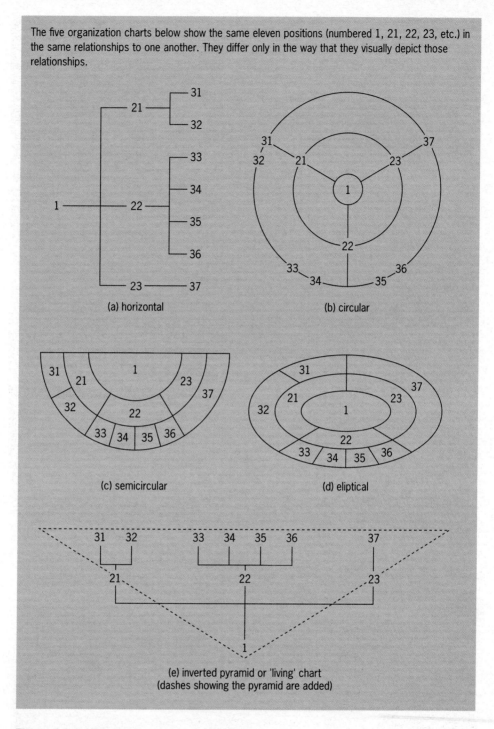

Figure 14.4: Variations in organization charting

broadened its span of control from 4-to-1 to 8-to-1, it could eliminate two hierarchical layers of management, which translates into nearly 800 managers. Stephen Robbins (1990) explained the simple arithmetic involved. Figure 14.5 shows an organization with 4,096 workers at level 7—the shop floor. All the levels above this represent managerial positions. With a narrow span of control of 4-to-1, 1,346 managers are needed (levels 1–6). However, with a broader 8-to-1 span of control, only 585 would be required (levels 1–4).

The army's span of control

The principle is to have a chain of command, so that each soldier knows to whom he or she is responsible, and there can be units of different managerial sizes for different purposes. For example, according to Xenophon counting on the fingers of two hands, the divisions of Cyrus's army were:

	Form	Under	
5 men	1 squad	corporal	5
2 squads	1 sergeant's squad	sergeant	10
5 sergeant's squads	1 platoon	lieutenant	50
2 platoons	1 company	captain	100
10 companies	1 regiment	colonel	1,000
10 regiments	1 brigade	general	10,000

With modifications in the numbers in different units, this is the principle on which armies have been organized. The general does not have to control 10,000 men directly; he controls the ten regimental colonels, and so on. In modern armies this would be considered an excessive span of control and two or three armies would form an army group, but the principle remains. Split the task up into manageable portions and do not have an excessive span of control so that real control is lost.

Based on Frank R. Jervis, *Bosses in British Business*, Routledge & Kegan Paul, London, 1974, p.87.

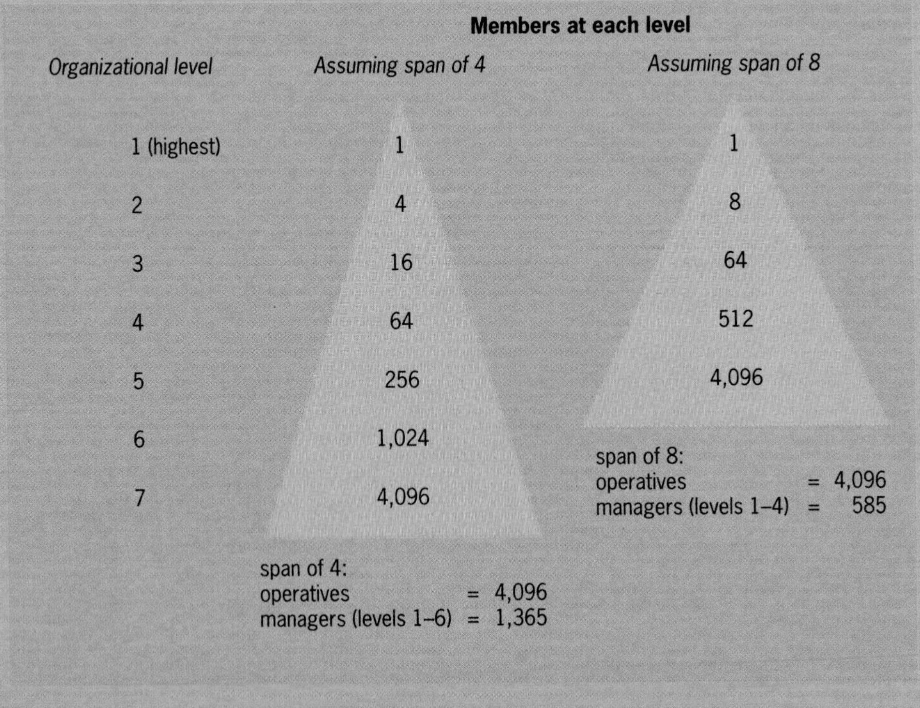

Members at each level

Organizational level	Assuming span of 4	Assuming span of 8
1 (highest)	1	1
2	4	8
3	16	64
4	64	512
5	256	4,096
6	1,024	
7	4,096	

span of 8:
operatives = 4,096
managers (levels 1–4) = 585

span of 4:
operatives = 4,096
managers (levels 1–6) = 1,365

Figure 14.5: Contrasting spans of control

From Stephen P. Robbins, *Organization Theory*, Prentice Hall, 1990, p.88.

The concepts of span of control and hierarchy are closely related. The broader the span of control, the fewer the number of levels in the hierarchy. At each level, the contact between the manager and each of those reporting to him will be reduced. A supervisor responsible for eight operatives will have less contact with each operative than a supervisor responsible for only four. This broad span of control with few levels of hierarchy produces a flatter organization structure with fewer promotion steps for employees to climb. However, it is likely that the communication between the levels will be improved as there are fewer of them for any message to pass through.

With a narrow span of control of one supervisor to four workers, the daily contact between the boss and her staff will be closer. This narrower span creates vertical differentiation and a taller hierarchy. Although it provides more steps in a career ladder for employees to rise through, communication tends to deteriorate as the message has to go through an ever-increasing number of layers both upwards and downwards. Because resources are always limited, they restrict the decision-making process.

Although flat hierarchies imply a broader span of control and fewer promotion opportunities, they also force managers to delegate their work effectively if they are not to be faced with an intolerable workload. Evidence suggests that individuals with high self-actualization needs prefer flat hierarchies, while those who emphasize security needs tend to gravitate towards organizations with tall hierarchies. Hierarchy is a co-ordinating and integrating device intended to bring together the activities of individuals, groups and departments which were previously separated by the division of labour and function.

Line, staff and functional relationships

Within any organization structure, individuals will have different relationships with one another. These can be line, staff and functional. The line relationship is a feature of every organization, irrespective of its size or simplicity. The staff and functional types are modifications of this basic line relationship which have become necessary because of the increased complexity of an organization's operations. The staff and the functional relationship usually exist in combination with the line relationship.

'Actually madam, I don't know how you managed it, but
you are talking to someone in authority'

To explain the differences between these types of relationship, it is first necessary to introduce and define the concepts of **authority**, **responsibility** and **accountability**. You cannot be held accountable for an action, unless you are first given the authority to do it. In a situation where your manager delegates authority to you, they remain responsible for your actions to senior management.

The line relationships in an organization are depicted vertically, and connect the positions at each level with those above and below it. It is this set of manager–subordinate relationships that are collectively referred to as the organization's chain of command. Using the analogy of a river, the line relationships are

> **Authority** is the right to guide or direct the actions of others and extract from them responses that are appropriate to the attainment of an organization's goals. **Responsibility** is an obligation placed on a person who occupies a certain position in the organization structure to perform a task, function or assignment. **Accountability** is the obligation of a subordinate to report back on their discharge of the responsibilities which they have undertaken.

the designated channels through which authority flows from its source at the top of the organizational pyramid, through the middle management ranks, down via the supervisors, to employees at the desk or on the factory floor. All non-managerial employees have some authority within their jobs, which may be based on custom and practice or formally defined in their job descriptions.

Every organization possesses **line relationships** if it has formally appointed leaders who have subordinates who report to them. All individuals in an organization report to a 'manager' from whom they receive instructions, help and approval. Managers have the authority to direct the activities of those in positions below them on the same line. Thus in the organization chart shown in figure 14.6, the operations manager (completions) has the authority to direct the activities of the four area managers. The operations manager (completions), in turn, can be directed by the director of production. All the aforementioned individuals are in the same line relationship. The line relationships in a company are found within departments and functions. Line managers are responsible for everything that happens within their particular department.

> **Line employees** are those workers who are directly responsible for manufacturing goods or providing a service.

> **Chain** (or **line**) **of command** refers to the unbroken line of authority that extends from the top of the organization to the bottom and clarifies who reports to whom.

Given the pyramidal nature of companies, managers located towards the top of an organization have more authority to control more resources than those below them. For this reason, lower-level managers are forced to integrate their actions with those above them by having to ask their bosses to approve some of their actions. In this way, managerial control is exercised down through the organization by the **chain of command**.

The line structure is the oldest and most basic framework for an organization, and all other forms are modifications of it. It is indispensable if the efforts of employees are to be co-ordinated. It provides channels for upward and downward communication and links different parts of the company together with the ultimate source of authority. As long as an organization is small and simple, and its managers can exercise effective direction and control, then an organization based exclusively on line relationships will be adequate. However, once a company becomes large and more complex, requiring perhaps an expert in human

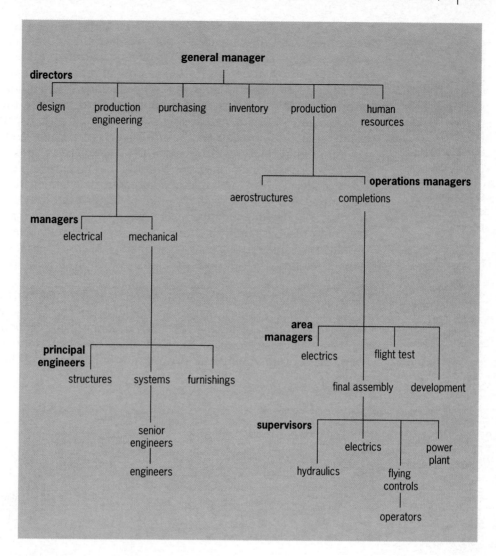

Figure 14.6: Line relationships

resources, in advertising or in buying, then some modifications to its existing structure will be required. These new activities support, but do not directly progress, the company's core task. In the way that an old man may lean on his walking stick or staff pole for support, so line managers can lean on their staff specialists for advice and guidance on technical matters.

One way to provide line managers with advice and support is to appoint an 'assistant to' an existing line manager. The line manager can delegate tasks and projects to their assistant. The assistant has no authority of their own but acts in the name of their line manager and with their authority. Because the assistant is not in a line relationship, they do not constitute a level in the hierarchy.

Another way of providing advisory support is to establish a separate department headed by staff specialists. This is a modification of the basic line structure and is referred to as a *line-and-staff structure*. These staff departments, such as market research, human resources, legal and training, exist to aid the line managers in achieving their departmental objectives. As with the 'assistant to' example, the staff department performs its tasks through the line structure, and not independently of it.

Staff employees are workers who are in advisory positions and who use their specialized expertise to support the efforts of line employees.

Functional relationship refers to a situation where staff department specialists have the authority to insist that line managers implement their instructions concerning a particular issue.

Staff departments can only plan for, recommend to, advise or assist other departments and their managers, but they lack the authority to insist that their advice is taken. Thus the human resources department cannot direct shop-floor workers, even when dealing with a personnel problem. It has to work with the line manager of the shop-floor workers concerned. Staff authority is usually subordinate to line authority, and its purpose is to facilitate the activities being directed and controlled by the line managers. Each staff department, like computing, legal or training, will of course have its own line relationships within it.

A **functional relationship** exists when a specialist is designated to provide a service which the line manager is compelled to accept. For example, the human resources department issues instructions concerning the length of time employees are allowed to work each week. The staff specialist's authority comes by delegation from a common superior. The general manger may decide that rather than have each piece of advice from the human resources department cleared personally, for onward transmission down to departmental heads, it is more efficient for the human resources specialist to issue an instruction directly to the departmental heads.

The functional specialists remain accountable to their functional manager, in whose name they issue instructions to line managers. If the general managers require functional assistance to be given to subordinates in an area such as training, they have to delegate some of their own authority to the functional specialist concerned, and the organization chart will look like that shown in figure 14.7.

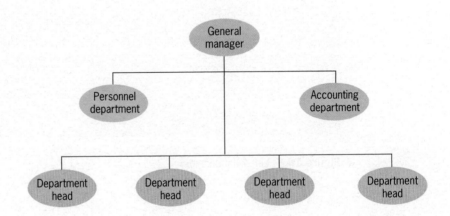

Figure 14.7: Functional relationship

The formal and the informal organization

Decisions about job descriptions, organization charts, types of authority and so on all relate to designing the formal organization. However, to understand and explain the behaviour of people in an organization, it is necessary to become familiar with the informal organization. There are two main problems with organization charts. First, they are static and do not show the ever-changing aspects of organizational life. Second, being depictions of how formal relations should prevail, they do not show the informal, social relations that actually do exist between company employees. The key differences between the **informal** and the **formal organization** are shown in table 14.2.

L'organigramme

Un organigramme représente sous forme de graphique l'organisation des responsabilités et des fonctions d'ine organisation.

La préparation de l'organigramme

On répertorie tous les organismes qui doivent figurer sur l'organigramme. Les différentes directions, les différents secteurs, les différents services...

On les désigne de manière cohérente en mentionnant trois informations:
--- le niveau de l'organisme (Division, Département, Secteur...);
--- la fonction de l'organisme (Production, Finances, Commercialisation...);
-- le nom du responsable de l'organisme.

Le dessin de l'organigramme

On visualise la nature et l'activité de l'organisme. La forme que l'on donne au cadre dans lequel on inscrit l'organisme (rond, rectangle, ovale...) doit permettre de différencier:
--l'organisme d'état-major: Comité de direction, Comité financier, Comité social...;
--l'organisme fonctionnel: Service finance, Service personnel, Service planification...;
--l'organisme opérationnel: Département achats, Département production...

La hierarchisation des composants

Verticalement, on détermine les niveaux de la structure. On visualise cette hiérarchie en diminuant la taille des cadres au fur et à mesure que leur nombre augmente.

Horizontalement, la place de l'organisme est située à son niveau hiérarchique. Elle est établie logiquement par le degré d'autonomie de l'organisme. On place côte à côte des organismes de même niveau qui entretiennent des relations dans le temps (le Service conditionnement se trouvera au côté du Service expédition).

Les types de relations entre les organismes

Relations operationnelles: des traits continus épais relient les cadres. Ils constituent la charpente de l'organigramme.
Relations fonctionnelles: elles sont etablies par des traits plus fins qui se greffent sur les relations operationnelles.
Relations informelles de collaboration ou de conseil: lorsqu'elles existent, ce qui n'est pas toujours le cas, elles sont souvent représentées en pointillés.

Le rôle de l'organigramme

Il est essentiellement destiné a donner une image de l'organisation d'un groupe. Il permet de situer précisément un service particulier dans ses relations avec les autres. C'est un moyen de savoir exactement qui est responsable de quoi.

Distinguer les différents types d'activites

Respecter les niveaux de la structure

Différencier les types de ralations

Direction Generale
Directions Fonctionnelles centrales
Branches
Départements
Secteurs

Exemple d'organigramme classique

Les niveaux de la structure sont presentes sur l'organigramme. Le plus important figure en haut de la pyramide. La hierarchie est marquee par la place dans la pyramide et par la grandeur du cadre.

Les différents types d'activites apparaissent dans la forme du cadre. Dans les rectangles sont inscrites les différentes branches d'activites. Dans les ovales figurent les directions. Dans le cercle, on trouve l'organisme de controle.

Les traits continus forts indiquent une relation de dependance entre differentes branches. Les traits fins marquent une relation de fonction. Les traits pointilles indiquent une collaboration occasionnelle entre les services.

Exemple d'organigramme classique

From Christiane Cadet, René Charles and Jean-Luc Galus, *La communication par limage*, Nathan, Paris, 1990, pp.66–7.

Formal organization refers to the collection of work groups that have been consciously designed by senior management to maximize efficiency and achieve organizational goals.
Informal organization refers to the network of relationships that spontaneously establish themselves between members of the organization on the basis of their common interests and friendships.

Table 14.2: The formal and the informal organization compared

	Formal organization	Informal organization
A structure		
(a) origin	planned	spontaneous
(b) rationale	rational	emotional
(c) characteristics	stable	dynamic
B position terminology	job	role
C goals	profitability or service to society	member satisfaction
D influence		
(a) base	position	personality
(b) type	authority	power
(c) flow	top down	bottom up
E control mechanism	threat of firing or demotion	physical or social sanction (norms)
F communication		
(a) channels	formal channels	grapevine
(b) networks	well defined, follow formal lines	poorly defined, cut across regular channels
G charting	organizational chart	sociogram
H miscellaneous		
(a) individuals included	all individuals in work group	only those 'acceptable'
(b) interpersonal relations	prescribed by job description	arise spontaneously
(c) leadership role	assigned by organization	result of membership
(d) basis for interaction	functional duties or position	personal characteristics status
(e) basis for attachment	loyalty	cohesiveness

Based on Jerry L. Gray and Frederick A. Starke, *Organizational Behaviour: Concepts and Applications*, third edition, Charles E. Merrill, Columbus, Ohio, 1984, p.412.

Design or evolution of structure

An organization can acquire a particular structure almost unconsciously. When a group of computer programmers hires an administrator and a secretary to 'deal with the paperwork' while they are doing their jobs, they are in fact designing structure. When a newly appointed chief executive of a multinational corporation centralizes the previously dispersed research and development activities into one location, they are consciously restructuring the company. Between these two extremes, incremental, *ad hoc* changes can be made. The point is that the structure of organizations evolves as often as it gets 'designed', and both can be messy processes.

There are many different types of organization—businesses, hospital trusts,

The two diagrams below show the *same* set of managers and workers. The top one identifies the positions and departments by name (e.g. president, personnel), while the lower one identifies them by numbers (e.g. 1 = president, 2 = head of accounting, etc.).

The top one depicts the formal relationships (the formal organization) as specified by senior management and as depicted in the organization chart. The lower diagram depicts the informal relationships (the informal organization). It shows how these same people actually interact on a day-to-day basis. To obtain this data, the researcher would either have to observe their interactions over a period of time or ask them to complete a sociometric questionnaire which asks with whom they prefer to lunch, car share, play cards, drink and share leisure time.

formal organization

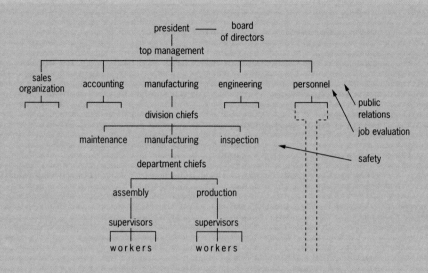

informal organization

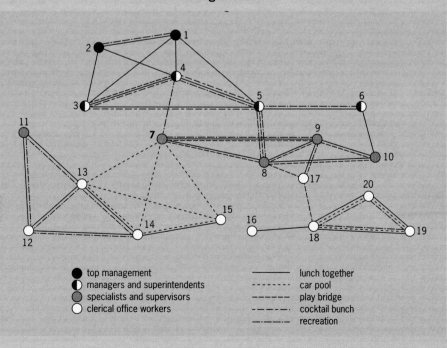

Figure 14.8 The formal and the informal organization

Departmentalization refers to the process of grouping together employees who share a common supervisor and resources, who are jointly responsible for performance, and who tend to identify and collaborate with each other.

schools, local authorities, football clubs and trade unions. All of these have a purpose and hence a policy. Those who design them, or change their design, can be seen as attempting to translate that policy into practices, duties and functions which are allocated as specific tasks to individuals and groups. Different organizations will have different structures. These differences partly represent divergences between goals and policies of the enterprises concerned. The organization structure that emerges results from the choices made about the division and grouping of tasks into functions, departments, sections and units.

Having decided on the degree of job specialization and job definition, there is the need to group the jobs into sections, place the sections into units, locate the units within departments and co-ordinate the departments. Thus job grouping or the **departmentalization** of jobs constitutes a second major area of organization design. Jobs can be grouped on several criteria, and usually an organization will use a mixture of such grouping criteria.

Function (e.g. marketing, engineering, production or finance)
Grouping of jobs based on the function which they perform. For example, the jobs in a manufacturing organization will be grouped according to production, marketing, sales, finance, and so on. In a hospital, grouping will be physiotherapy, nursing, medical physics.

Product or service (e.g. car insurance)
Traditionally, educational institutions are structured on the basis of the service. Thus all lecturers teaching management subjects in a university or college are located in its business school. Within that school, they are further divided into subject specialisms such as corporate strategy, quantitative methods, accounting.

Customer (e.g. retail, wholesale)
Separate groups organized for different types of customer. Thus, an educational publishing company may have separate divisions for schools, colleges, universities and general readers.

Geography or territory (e.g. northern England, Scotland)
Grouping on this basis is used where the service is most effectively or economically provided within a limited distance. Companies offering repair and maintenance services will be geographically divided to ensure that customer problems can be solved rapidly.

Time (e.g. shift, non-shift)
Hospitals and factories offering a 24-hour service or producing round the clock will have different groups for different shifts.

Technology or equipment used (e.g. small batch, mass production, process)
The type of technology employed can be a criterion, especially when several different types are used in a single plant. An organization chart shows which type of grouping has been adopted.

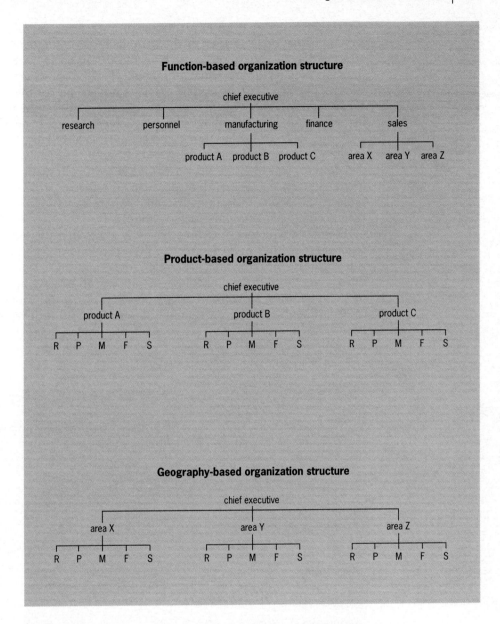

Figure 14.9: Function-, product- and geography-based organization structures

Matrix structure

The distinguishing feature of a matrix structure is that the employees within it report to two bosses rather than the traditional one. There is thus a dual, rather than a single, chain of command. This occurs because in a matrix, one type of structure has been superimposed upon another one. The matrix structure was developed in the late 1950s to cope with increasingly complex technological problems and rates of change. Some writers discuss the matrix structures alongside line, staff and functional ones, while others treat it as yet another form of departmentalization.

Simon Ramo, the co-founder of TRW Inc., is credited with introducing the first

Matrix structure is a type of organization design that combines two different, traditional types of structure, usually a functional structure and a project structure, which results in an employee being part of both a functional department and a project team, and in consequence having two reporting relationships.

matrix structure in 1957. As an aerospace company, TRW found that joint military–industrial projects, such as the manufacture of Minuteman, Atlas and Titan missile systems, could not be co-ordinated through the use of traditional functional or product departmental groupings. These projects were so complex that it was not possible to make a single manager responsible for their entire execution.

The most common type of matrix combination is departmentalization by product and by function simultaneously. Maybe your course is organized using such a structure. Table 14.3 shows a matrix structure in a university. In this example, the programmes or courses to be taught are listed horizontally, while the academic departments in which the instructors are based are shown vertically. In the case of the aerospace example quoted earlier, the matrix structure would combine projects or rockets to be manufactured (Titan, Delta) and company functions (engineering, marketing, research, testing).

The matrix structure chart in table 14.3 shows that the individual instructors report to two different bosses. One of these is responsible for the function, in this case the university academic department of accounting, economic or psychology. Their other 'boss' is the director of the product, in this example, the educational programme being provided—undergraduate, masters or doctoral. Both the heads of departments and the programme directors may in turn report to a common boss, who co-ordinates the activities of the academic functions and the educational programmes. This may be the dean of the faculty.

Table 14.3: Example of a matrix structure for university course teaching

	Products (*Educational programme*)		
	Director Undergraduate Programme	Director Masters Programme	Director Doctoral Programme
Subjects (*Academic departments*)			
Head: Accounting	A	B	C
Head: Economics	D	E	
Head: Psychology	F		

A: Department of Accounting lecturer teaching undergraduates.

B: Professor of accounting teaching on a postgraduate programme.

C: Senior lecturer from Economics Department teaching doctoral students.

D: Economics lecturer teaching undergraduate students.

E: Professor of economics teaching masters degree students.

F: Psychology lecturer teaching undergraduates.

One consequence of having a matrix structure is that employees simultaneously belong to two different groups. Instructor D is both a member of the Economics Department group (with colleague E and others), while at the same time, D is a member of the undergraduate programme teaching group (with colleagues A and F). Instructor D reports to two superiors. D's permanent functional boss is the head of the Economics Department, and D's temporary boss, as long as D contributes to undergraduate courses, is the director of the undergraduate programme. In industry, the latter is commonly referred to as the 'project manager'.

Thus, in every matrix, there are three sets of unique relationships. These exist between the top manager, who balances the dual chains of command; the directors of programmes and heads of functions, who share the subordinates; and the employees, who report simultaneously to their department head and to the programme director. Although the integration of product and function structures is the most common form of matrix organization, any two forms of departmentalization are capable of being combined, for example product and geography.

Companies use matrix structures when they have to be responsive to two sectors simultaneously (e.g. technology and markets); when they face uncertainties that require information to be quickly exchanged between all those involved; and when they are strongly constrained by financial or human resources). The aim of the matrix structure is to gain the benefits of the two previously separate structures (Davis and Lawrence, 1978). There are at least three advantages of the matrix structural arrangement in organizations:

- It avoids the duplication of overhead costs, since the same employees can contribute to different company projects or programmes.

- Being a member of a project team, employees from different departments and with different backgrounds can focus more directly on the project.

- It leaves heads of department free to develop and deploy their staff members, while programme directors become responsible for delivering the service to customers.

There are at least three disadvantages of the matrix structure:

- Occupying two roles can cause team members ambiguity and conflict, leading to stress.

- It may be difficult to demonstrate their individual contribution as they change from team to team.

- Their opportunities for promotion may be limited because movement is lateral.

Stop and criticize

Can you think of any *other* advantages and disadvantages of the matrix structure for (a) the individual team member (b) their organization?

Organigraphs

Henry Mintzberg and Ludo van der Heyden highlighted the deficiencies of traditional organization charts. To outsiders, such charts reveal little about a company's products, processes, customers or line of business—'using an organization chart to "view" a company is like using a list of municipal managers to find your way around a city'. To its employees, a chart does not tell them which parts connect to which; how people and processes should come together; or whose ideas should flow to where. To overcome these deficiencies, organigraphs have been developed. Although they do not totally eliminate little boxes, they do include 'sets', 'chains', 'hubs' and 'webs', which are forms that better reflect the way in which people organize themselves at work today.

Set	Chain	Hub	Web

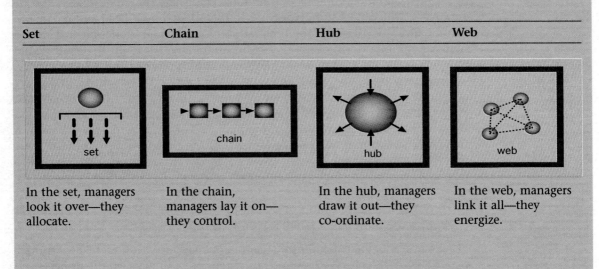

In the set, managers look it over—they allocate.	In the chain, managers lay it on—they control.	In the hub, managers draw it out—they co-ordinate.	In the web, managers link it all—they energize.

Newspaper organization chart

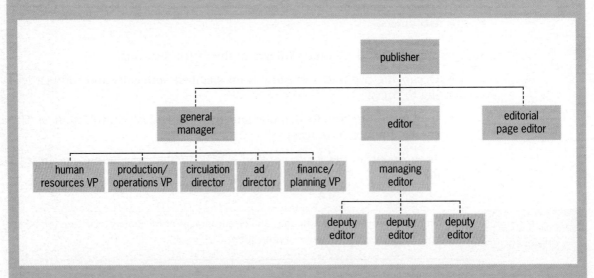

The organization chart treats everybody and everything as an independent box connected by a vertical chain—a chain of authority. In contrast, drawing an organigraph requires managers to create a customized picture of their company using sets, chains, hubs and webs and other meaningful symbols like 'funnels' (to depict transformations). Organigraphs have less to do with names, titles and formal authority and more to do with relationships and processes. The two diagrams above and opposite contrast an organization chart and an organigraph for the same newspaper.

Newspaper organigraph

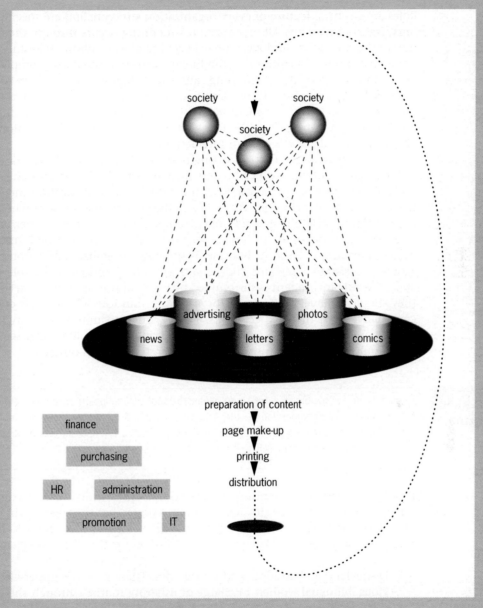

They show what a company is; why it exists; and what it does. They are not only pictures but also maps, providing an overview of the company's 'territory'—its mountains and rivers. They demonstrate *how* a place works by indicating the critical interactions between people, products and information. Their advocates claim that they show real businesses and their opportunities. Organigraphs have been used as an organization change and training tool by executives to stimulate discussions about how best to manage existing operations and to consider strategic change options.

Based on Henry Mintzberg and Ludo van der Heyden, 'Organigraphs: drawing how companies really work', *Harvard Business Review*, September–October 1999, pp.87–94.

Roles in organizations

Role is the pattern of behaviour expected by others from a person occupying a certain position in an organization hierarchy.

Roles are a central feature of every organization structure and are specified in the organization hierarchy. All organization structuring occurs through the specification of the roles that employees are expected to play. It follows that if individuals occupying different positions in the hierarchy have mutual and complementary expectations, then the patterning and predictability of their behaviour is increased. The formal positions identified on an organization chart of a company imply the expectation of certain behaviour by any person occupying that office. This becomes the person's **role**. Roles are thus associated with positions in the organization and are involved in interactions.

Role set refers to the collection of persons most immediately affected by the focal person's role performance, who depend upon the focal person for their own role performance, and who therefore have a stake in it.

A single office holder, such as an engineer, will have regular interactions with a limited number of other office holders such as workers, the department manager, trade union officials, and so on. Each individual in an organization therefore has their own particular **role set**. This refers to the collection of persons who are most immediately affected by how the role incumbent (the focal person) performs their role. They depend upon the focal person for their own role performance and therefore have a stake in it. Because of this, they mobilize instructions, encouragement, assistance, rewards and penalties to direct and elicit the role performance. The role incumbent is surrounded by expectations of their role set as to how they should behave. Their desire for approval from role set members encourages compliance with their expectations. Finally, one can note that a single person plays many different and sometimes conflicting roles in life, both sequentially and simultaneously (e.g. mother, team leader, trade union official).

Stop and criticize

It is common for people to refer to an organizational title or position (e.g. supervisor, scientist, manager) as the supervisor's role, scientist's role and manager's role, as though it were merely an established way of referring to these positions. What assumptions and problems does this use of the concept fail to appreciate?

People's roles in organizations are ranked by status. Individuals occupying the role of manager are generally accorded more status that those occupying the role of cleaner. In other companies, the ranking of roles is less obvious. John van Maanen (1991) described the rank ordering of occupations at Disneyland:

1. Disneyland ambassadors and tour guides. These were the upper-class, prestigious, bilingual women in charge of ushering tourists through the park.

2. Ride operators who either performed skilled work such as live narration or drove costly vehicles such as antique trains, horse drawn carriages or the monorail.

3. All the other ride operators.

4. Sweepers, who kept the concrete grounds clean, were designated as *proles*.

5. There was a still lower, fifth, category of *sub-prole* or peasant status.

6. The 'lowest of the low' included food and concession workers, pancake ladies, peanut pushers, coke blokes, suds drivers and soda jerks.

Organizations are, to a degree, co-operative arrangements that are characterized by give and take, mutual adjustment and negotiation. Their members get on with one another, often without explicit guidance, instruction or direction. The concept of role aids our understanding of this aspect of organizational life by stress-

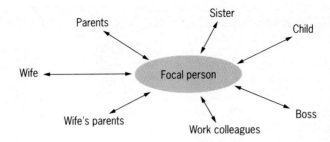

Figure 14.10: Role set

ing that employees monitor and direct their own work behaviour in the light of what they know is expected of them.

Many of the tasks involved in the job have been learned and assimilated so well that they become accepted as being part of the person. It raises the question of whether, in behaving in a certain way, we are ourselves or just conforming to what the organization (and society) expects of us. Role relationships are therefore the field within which behaviour occurs. People's behaviour at any given moment is the result of:

Philip Zimbardo
(b. 1933)

- their personalities;

- their perception and understanding of each other;

- their attitudes to the behavioural constraints imposed by the role relationship;

- the degree of their socialization with respect to constraints;

- their ability to inhibit and control their behaviours.

Prison experiment

To what extent do our attitudes, values and self-image affect the way we play roles in organizations such as student, lecturer, doctor, nurse or doorman. To what extent are our attitudes, values and self-image determined by the organizational roles we play?

Philip Zimbardo and two graduate student colleagues from the Department of Psychology at Stanford University in California created their own prison to examine the roles of prisoner and guard. Advertising in the Palo Alto city newspaper, they selected 21 young men from the 75 that they interviewed. These individuals were screened to ensure that each was a mature, emotionally stable, normal, intelligent North American male student from a middle-class home with no criminal record. Each volunteer was paid $15 a day to participate in a two-week study of prison life. A toss of a coin arbitrarily designated these recruits as either prisoners or guards. Hence, at the start of the study, there were no measurable differences between the two groups assigned to play the two roles (ten prisoners and eleven guards).

Those taking the role of guards had their individuality reduced by being required to wear uniforms, including silver reflector glasses, which prevented eye contact. They were to be referred to as Mr Correction Officer by the prisoners, and they were given symbols of their power, which included clubs, whistles, handcuffs and keys. They were given minimal instructions by the researchers, being required only to 'maintain law and order'. While physical violence was forbidden, they were told to make up and improvise their own formal rules to achieve the stated objective during their eight-hour, three-man shifts.

Those who were assigned the role of prisoners were unexpectedly picked up at their homes by a city policeman in a squad car. Each was searched, handcuffed, fingerprinted, booked in at the Palo Alto police station, blindfolded and then transferred to Zimbardo's 'Stanford County Prison', which was located in the basement of the university psychology building. Each prisoner's sense of uniqueness and prior identity was minimized. They were given smocks to wear and had nylon stocking caps on their heads to simulate baldness. Their personal effects were removed; they had to use their ID numbers; and they were housed in stark cells. All this made them appear similar to each other and indistinguishable to observers. Six days into the planned fourteen-day study the researchers had to abandon the experiment. Why?

In a matter of days, even hours, a strange relationship began to develop between the prisoners and their guards. Some of the boy guards began to treat the boy prisoners as if they were despicable animals and began to take pleasure in psychological cruelty. The prisoners in turn became servile, dehumanized robots who thought only of their individual survival, escape and mounting hatred of the guards. About a third of the guards became tyrannical in their arbitrary use of power, and became quite inventive in developing techniques to break the spirit of the prisoners and to make them feel worthless. Having crushed a prison rebellion, the guards escalated their aggression, and this increased the prisoners' sense of dependence, depression and helplessness.

Within 36 hours, the first 'prisoner' had to be released because of uncontrolled crying, fits of rage, disorganized thinking and severe depression. He was Doug Korpi (Prisoner No. 8612), who suffered a mental breakdown. 'I've never screamed so loud in my life. I've never been so upset', he said. Three more prisoners were released on consecutive days with the same symptoms. A fifth left with a psychosomatic rash. Others begged to be paroled, and nearly all were willing to forfeit their money if the guards agreed to release them.

Zimbardo and his colleagues were surprised by the changes in the behaviour and attitudes of their experimental subjects. The researchers attributed these changes to a number of causes. First, the creation of a new environment within which both groups were separated from the outside world. New attitudes were developed about this new 'mini-world', as well as what constituted appropriate behaviour in it.

A second explanation was that in this new 'mini-world' of the prison, the participants were unable to differentiate clearly between the role they were asked to play (prisoner or guard) and their real self. A week's experience of imprisonment (temporarily) appeared to undo a lifetime of learning. Human values and self-concepts were challenged, and the pathological side of human nature was allowed to surface. The prisoners became so programmed to think of themselves as prisoners that when their requests for parole were refused, they returned docilely to their cells instead of feeling capable of just withdrawing from an unpleasant psychological research experiment.

This study raises many different issues. Of particular interest is Zimbardo's conclusion that individual behaviour is largely under the control of social and environmental forces, rather than being the result of personality traits, character or willpower. In an organizational context such as a prison, the mere fact of assigning labels to people and putting them in situations where such labels acquire validity and meaning is sufficient to elicit a certain type of behaviour. The power of the prison environment was stronger than each individual's will to resist falling into his role. In the light of these research findings, what undesirable behaviours might be elicited by assigning the labels of student, lecturer, doctor, nurse or doorman to individuals?

Based on Craig Haney, Curtis Banks and Philip Zimbardo, 'A study of prisoners and guards in a simulated prison', *Naval Research Reviews*, Office of Naval Research, Department of the Navy, Washington, DC, September 1973; and P.G. Zimbardo *et al.*, 'A Pirandellian prison', *The New York Times Magazine*, 8 April 1973.

The roles that we play are part of our self-concept, and personality theory tells us that we come to know ourselves through our interactions with others [**link**, chapter 5, personality]. We play different roles throughout our lives, and these require us to use different abilities, thereby adding more aspects to our self-image. Which roles we play and how successfully we play them during our adulthood affects our level of self-esteem. Thus the roles that we play both inside and outside the organization affect our self-image and self-esteem.

Research by Philip Zimbardo showed that people possess mental concepts of different roles and conform to them when asked or required to do so (Zimbardo *et al.*, 1983). It also demonstrates the power of roles, not only to influence behaviour but also to affect a person's self-image. Robert Rosenthal's research demonstrates the concept known as the **self-fulfilling prophecy**. This is the observation that if you have certain expectations of people and treat them in a way that relates to these expectations, the people concerned will in turn respond to the way that you treat them. Their behaviour comes to fit your expectation of them—they behave as you thought they would.

Self-fulfilling prophecy is an expectation that leads to a certain pattern of behaviour whose consequences confirm the expectancy.

For example, a rumour (prophecy) that a bank is about to collapse leads people to withdraw their money from it all at the same time, and the bank then does indeed collapse. If a teacher expects children to work hard and do well at school, they will do so (Rosenthal and Jacobson, 1968). Interest in this study relates to whether supervisor behaviour may improve employee output through performance expectations. Rosenthal (1973) identified four factors which produced the effect:

Climate
The supervisor's expectations lead them to treat a worker differently. Such differences are manifested in their eye contact, smiling, nodding, posture and tone of voice. Their expectation is transmitted in this way.

Feedback
More detailed and accurate information is given to workers about their performance. The supervisor can say how they can improve, rather than just a general 'well done'.

Input
The supervisor gives the worker more demanding tasks to perform that stretch them.

Output
The supervisor gives the developing worker cues to respond to, for example, asking questions.

Psychologists have explained what must happen before the self-fulfilling prophecy can occur. This is shown in figure 14.11.

The woman who is both a manager and a mother may experience role conflict when the expectations in these two important roles pull her in opposite directions.

Stop and criticize	Identify any three roles that you currently occupy simultaneously in three different social contexts, e.g. work, home, leisure. Identify any two conflicts that you regularly experience as a result of such multiple role occupancy.

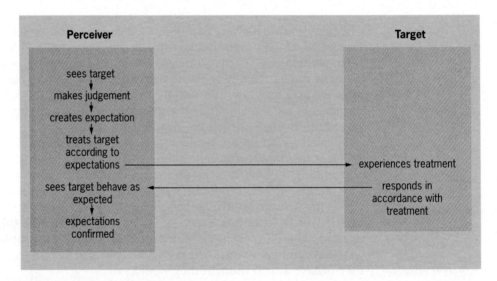

Figure 14.11: Self-fulfilling prophecy

Role conflict is the simultaneous existence of two or more sets of role expectations on a focal person in such a way that compliance with one makes it difficult to comply with the others.

Some senior company executives like to retain decision-making power in their hands and thus run highly centralized organizations. Others prefer to delegate their power and give more junior managers a greater responsibility to make decisions. Their organizations are more decentralized in their structure. The question of whether and how much to centralize has been one of the major topics discussed in organization structuring.

Arthur Bedeian and Raymond Zammuto argued that the balance between centralization and decentralization changes on an ongoing basis. It does so, in their view, in response to changes in company size, market opportunities, developments in new technology, and not least, the quality of existing decision making. On the one hand, it is possible to observe decentralization increasing as companies in new and developing markets such as Central and Eastern Europe and China leave decisions to their managers on the spot. On the other hand, developments in new technology have meant that banks and building societies have increased centralized decisions and shed thousands of staff in the process. Somewhat more cynically, Anthony Jay (1970) felt that whichever of the two is currently the more fashionable, it will be superseded by the other in due course. This may occur for no other reason than that the incoming chief executive wishes to make a highly visible impact on their managers, employees, shareholders and financial analysts. The advantages and disadvantages of each approach have been widely considered and are listed by Bedeian and Zammuto (1991, p.139):

Centralization refers to the concentration of authority and responsibility for decision making in the hands of managers at the top of an organization's hierarchy.
Decentralization refers to authority and responsibility for decision making being dispersed more widely downwards and given to the operating units, branches and lower-level managers.

Centralization

- A greater uniformity in decisions is possible.

- Top-level managers are more aware of an organization's future plans and are more likely to make decisions in its best interests.

- Fewer skilled (and highly paid) managers are required.

- Less extensive planning and reporting procedures are required.

Decentralization

- Lower-level decisions can be made more easily.

- Lower-level management problems can be dealt with on the spot.

- Lower-level managers have an opportunity to develop their decision-making skills.

- The motivation of lower-level managers is greater when they are entrusted to make decisions rather than always following orders issued at a higher level.

- An organization's workload is spread so as to allow top-level managers more time for strategic planning.

Organization structures and managerial roles

Henry Mintzberg, a Canadian business academic, has contributed widely to the field of management theory and research. In addition to being active in the field of strategic management, he has made major contribution to two topics in the field of organization behaviour. One of these relates to a consideration of different forms that an organization's structure can take. The other concerns the range of roles performed by managers. Both will be considered in this section.

Forms of organization structure

Henry Mintzberg
(b. 1939)

The concepts introduced so far provide a 'language' which can used to discuss the strengths and weaknesses of different structures of organizations. Mintzberg (1979; 1983a; 1989) provided a framework to help us engage in 'conversations' about them. He distinguished five basic parts of an organization, which he termed *strategic apex*, *middle line*, *operating core*, *technostructure* and *support staff*. He also suggested ways in which these parts could be co-ordinated. He used these five parts and five co-ordinating mechanisms to describe five different 'ideal' types of organization structure. This explains his book title, *Structure in Fives* (Mintzberg, 1983b).

Strategic apex contains those individuals who direct the organization. It consists of senior management, whether in the form of chief executive officers, archbishops or generals. It is here that policies are decided, plans made, resources allocated and instructions given. These individuals ensure that the organization meets its objectives, including the needs of stakeholders like shareholders, lenders, employees and congregation members. They also manage the boundary relations between the organization and the outside world.

Operating core refers to those who receive inputs and transform them into products or services. Functional core employees are located at the heart of every organization. This core may take raw materials and process them into motor cars, or ill patients and transform into well patients. Thus, in one company, the operators can be semi-skilled blue collar workers, while in another, they may be highly trained professionals like doctors and nurses.

Middle line employees and their departments are located between the strategic apex at the top and the operating core at the bottom. It consists of middle managers and supervisors who are responsible for carrying out orders and ensuring the policies are pursued. The middle line links the senior management to the operators, usually through a single line of authority or 'chain of command'. These managers pass information up and down the hierarchy, make decisions, deal with internal disturbances to smooth running and manage the relationships across the company boundary with suppliers, customers, media and other groups.

Technostructure consists of the technical support staff. The analysts and technical advisers comprising it serve those at all levels in the organization but are separate from them. The job of these technicians is to standardize the work throughout the entire organization. Technostructure activities include designing systems and procedures, redesigning work processes, providing information and library services, providing market information, and building financial systems.

Staff support refers to individuals who provide administrative and clerical support for the different levels. For example, by providing personnel and human resource management, security, catering, public relations, building maintenance, paying bills, delivering mail and other, similar, services.

To these five building blocks of organization design, Mintzberg added ideology or 'culture of the organization' [**link**, chapter 19, organization culture]. This refers to values, beliefs and taken-for-granted assumptions that underpin the way that parts and co-ordinated mechanisms could be configured. These are only possibilities, but not his recommendations:

Mutual adjustment: as people communicate with one another verbally and visually, they adjust to one another and to changing circumstances. An operating team in a hospital theatre or a basketball team on the court does this. For this co-ordinating device to be effective, individuals have to be committed to each other and the organization's goals, be personally competent and trust the others.

Direct supervision: as its name suggests, the supervisor will stand over or will frequently check what the employee has done. Such close monitoring will ensure that the task is being carried out as the manager desires and therefore fits in with what others are doing.

Standardize the input focuses on who gets things done. It ensures that the individuals who are selected either already possess, or are trained to have, the skills and knowledge necessary to achieve the standard of performance required. This co-ordination strategy is commonly used with professionals. They have to be trusted to provide the required service or product on time and to quality.

Standardize the work processes focuses on how things get done. Using technology in its broadest sense, work can be organized to incorporate rules and operating procedures that restrict employees' choice of behaviour and monitor their performances to ensure objectives are achieved. For this form of co-ordination to work, the operating and business processes have to have been well designed.

Standardize the output focuses on what gets done. This form of co-ordination

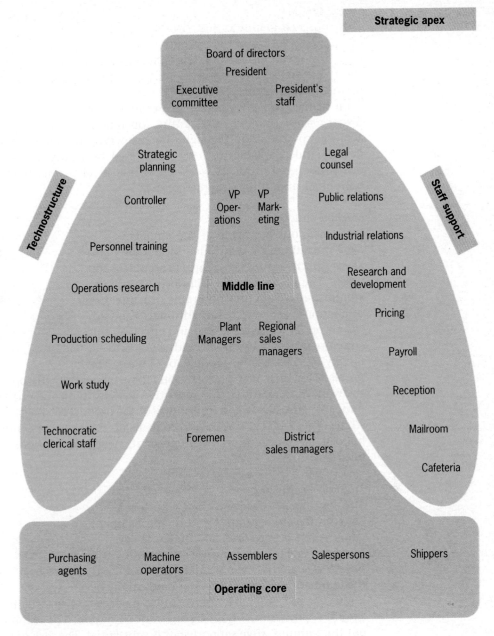

Figure 14.12: Mintzberg's five organizational parts
Based on Henry Mintzberg, *The Structure of Organizations*, Prentice Hall, Englewood Cliffs, NJ, 1979;
Henry Mintzberg, *Structure in Fives: Effective Organizations*, Prentice Hall, Englewood Cliffs, NJ, 1983;
and Roy Payne, 'The Characteristics of Organizations', in P. Warr (ed.), *Psychology at Work*, Penguin,
1996, pp.383–407.

involves the strategic apex specifying the quality, quantity and delivery of a product or service. Here, production standards and deadlines have to be clearly specified, together with sanctions for non-compliance.

Having distinguished five organization parts and five co-ordinating mechanisms, Mintzberg proposed five ideal or pure types of organization structure. The relative importance and size of each of the organization parts within each structure type differed. So too did the relationships between the parts. The five organization parts are shown in Figure 14.12.

Simple structure

This consisted mainly of just two of the parts—
the strategic apex and the operating core. It has
little or no technostructure, few support staff, a
short hierarchy and minimal differentiation
between departments. A garage owner and his
team of mechanics would be an example. The
owner, who can see the entire operation,

achieves co-ordination through direct supervision. Being simple, the structure is
flexible and adaptable. It is one possessed by nearly all new, entrepreneurial,
owner-managed firms. Its weakness is that it relies on one individual, who can
both block and initiate change, or die.

Machine structure

Most decisions are made at the strategic apex;
daily operations are controlled by middle managers directly, using standard procedures and
rules. There are many technostructure and
administrative support staff in this structure. Co-
ordination is achieved mainly through standard-
izing work processes. Efficient and effective, this
structure provides customers with a guaranteed,
unvarying, predictable product or service. The

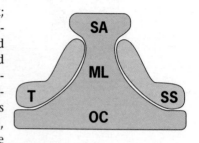

problem for their managers is motivating the staff in the operating core, where
the work is standardized and repetitive, yet creativity and challenge could undermine the consistency and uniformity of the product or service. A difficulty for the
strategic apex is that it receives problems up the chain of command for solution,
but being distanced from the situation, its suggested solutions may not meet local
needs.

Professional structure

This has a large operating core, with few levels
between the strategic apex and the professional
employees. Decentralized and therefore flat, it is
run by hierarchical authority but stresses the
power of expertise. Co-ordination is achieved
predominantly through the standardization of

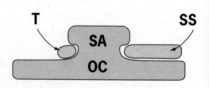

input. The professional employees (e.g. doctors, lawyers, engineers) have received
extensive professional training and indoctrination. The technostructure is small,
but the administrative support staff is substantial. The task of the latter is to serve
the professionals. By insulating their members from external interference, the
professional structure has problems of adapting to change and maintaining quality. Professional autonomy makes it difficult to implement changes and to deal
with professional incompetence.

Divisional structure

Quasi-autonomous divisions perform
the bulk of the work here. In consequence, the middle line and operating core are large, while the
technostructure and support structures are small. The internal structure
of these divisions can take any of the

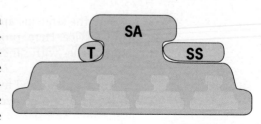

forms described in this section, but machine structures tend to be most common.
Each division serves its own market and houses its own functions. It enjoys a high

degree of autonomy but in return has to meet sales, profit and return-on-investment targets. Co-ordination is thus achieved predominantly through the standardization of outputs. While overall company rules and regulations exist, it is the managers in the middle line in each division that provide the direction and exert control. While offering potential for economies of scale and responsiveness, this structural form can experience a struggle for control between the operating core and the strategic apex.

Ad hoc structure

This is a loose, flexible, self-renewing organic form, which frequently includes experts from different backgrounds and disciplines. A small film or music company, advertising agency, 'think tank' or computer software firm may have this structure, as may any young, research-based company that needs to innovate in rapidly changing conditions. The most important parts are the support staff in research

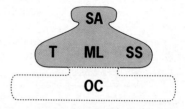

and development, as well experts in the operating core. It groups its highly trained specialists into mixed project teams in the hope of generating new ideas. Co-ordination is achieved through lateral communication and by members directly co-operating and mutually adjusting to each other. Its form is both organic and decentralized.

Managerial roles

Mintzberg's second major contribution was to conduct empirical research into how managers actually spend their time within these different organization structures. Although structures do not determine the roles that individuals play in an organization, they do greatly influence them. Mintzberg's work led to a reassessment of the nature of managerial work in organizations and a redefinition of the roles of the manager. It revealed a difference between what managers actually did and what they said they did. He showed that a manager's job was characterized by pace, interruptions, brevity and fragmentation of tasks. In addition, managers preferred to communicate verbally and spent a great deal of time in meetings or in making contacts with others outside meetings. Mintzberg (1977) distinguished ten managerial roles, which he classified under the three headings of *interpersonal*, *informational* and *decisional*.

Mintzberg argued that the ten roles that he identified could describe the nature of managerial work more accurately that other frameworks. The concept of role was introduced earlier in this chapter. One aspect of it is that any role holder can choose how to carry it out. In the case of a manager, he or she can decide how they wish to blend the ten listed roles, taking into account organizational constraints and opportunities. A consequence of this is that management becomes more of an art rather than a teachable science that can be reduced to a set of prescriptions which can be easily taught.

Table 14.4: Mintzberg's ten managerial roles

Role	Description
	Interpersonal
Figurehead	Symbolic head; obliged to perform routine duties of a legal or social nature.
Leader	Responsible for the motivation and activation of subordinates for staffing, training and associated duties.
Liaison	Maintains self-developed networks of outside contacts and informers who provide favours and information.
	Informational
Monitor	Seeks and receives wide variety of special information (much of it current) to develop thorough understanding of organization and environment; emerges as nerve centre of internal and external information of the organization.
Disseminator	Transmits information received from outsiders or from other subordinates to members of the organization; some information factual, some involving interpretation and integration of diverse value positions of organizational influences.
Spokesperson	Transmits information to outsiders on organization's plans, policies and actions, results, etc.; serves as expert on organization's industry.
	Decisional
Entrepreneur	Searches organization and its environment for opportunities and initiates 'improvement projects' to bring about change; supervises design of certain projects as well.
Disturbance handler	Responsible for corrective action when organization faces important unexpected disturbances.
Resource allocator	Responsible for the allocation of organizational resources of all kinds—in effect making or approving all significant organizational decisions.
Negotiator	Responsible for representing the organization at major negotiations.

From Henry Mintzberg, *The Nature of Managerial Work*, Addison Wesley, 1973.

Stop and criticize

What extra insights about management roles do Kotter's findings provide over Mintzberg's? What personal and professional advice would you give general managers on the basis of this work?

Patterns of general management behaviour

More recent research by John Kotter adds to our understanding of management roles. Like Henry Mintzberg, he studied management behaviour using various methods, including interviews, observation, questionnaires, inspecting relevant documents and interviews with colleagues. His analysis of the work of the general manager is as follows:

They spend most of their time with others	The average manager spends 25 per cent of his or her time alone; some spend 90 per cent with others
They spend time with many people in addition to their direct subordinates and their bosses	They regularly meet with people who appear to be unimportant outsiders
The breadth of topics in their discussions is extremely wide	Not limited to management concerns, managers discuss virtually anything
General managers ask a lot of questions	In a half-hour conversation, some managers ask literally hundreds of questions
During conversations, general managers rarely seem to make 'big' decisions	So why is 'decision making' considered such a key part of the manager's role?
Their discussions usually contain a fair amount of joking and often concern topics not related to work	Humour is often about others in the organization or sector; non-work discussions are usually about families
In more than a few of these encounters, the issue discussed is relatively unimportant to the business or organization	General managers regularly engage in activities even they regard as a waste of time
In these encounters, managers rarely give orders in a traditional sense	So why is 'giving direction' considered such a key part of the manager's role?
Nevertheless, general managers often attempt to influence others	Instead of telling people what to do, they ask, request, cajole, persuade, intimidate

Based on John P. Kotter, 'What effective general managers really do', *Harvard Business Review*, 1999, vol.77, no.2, pp.145–59.

This chapter has introduced the basic concepts and frameworks needed to understand the many debates about current and future organization structuring. For explanatory purposes, it has presented the process of designing an organization structure as a rational one performed by senior managers. In fact, organization structures are actively and socially created and recreated by a variety of organizational actors, who act upon and influence the behaviour of others. This chapter therefore provides only a starting point for analysing an organization's structure—telling readers something about formal structuring, division of roles, hierarchy, and so on.

However, to understand what really happens within an organization's structure and why, it is really necessary to get inside an organization and experience the structure, first-hand, for oneself. One example of this is noting how different individuals interpret the same role. This is most obvious when an individual takes up a position after a previous occupant has left it.

Armed with this vocabulary and structural concepts, readers can now assess whether the trend towards the so-called 'post-modern organization' is real or imagined, and how organization structures seem to be changing [**link**, chapter 2, the world outside]. Some of these issues were addressed in the context of team-working [**link**, chapter 12, teamworking], while others will be considered with respect to 'classical' and modern organizations [**link**, chapter 15, early organiz-ation design]. However, to evaluate the 'post-modern' organization of the infor-mation age, some additional concepts and terms will be needed, and these will be introduced later [**link**, chapter 16, organization strategy and design].

Recap

1. *Explain how organization structure affects human behaviour in organizations.*

   - The procedures employees are required to follow, and the rules by which they are required to abide, all control and direct their behaviour in specified directions.

   - The roles that people play, and the expectations that others have of role holders, all direct the behaviour of employees. Indeed, in the long term, these may even lead to a change in personality of the employee.

2. *List the main elements of organization structure.*

   - The main elements include chain of command, hierarchical levels, line employees, rules, staff employees, role expectations, span of control, departmentalization, authority and job description.

3. *Relate the concept of span of control to the shape of the organization hierarchy.*

   - The narrower the span of control, the taller the organization hierarchy (and vice versa) and the greater the consequences for employees of having one or the other.

4. *Identify line and staff relationships on an organization chart.*

   - Line relationships are depicted vertically on an organization chart, indicating that those above possess the authority to direct the behaviours of those below.

   - The former have responsibility for the work of the latter, while the latter are responsible for their work to the former.

   - Staff relationships are depicted horizontally on an organization chart, indicating that those who possess specific expertise, e.g. in personnel or computing matters, advise those in line positions.

5. *Describe five different criteria on which jobs might be departmentalized.*

   - Function (e.g. production, marketing, personnel); product or service (e.g. type of motor car); type of customer (e.g. health, computer, hospitality sector); geography (e.g. Europe, North America, Pacific); time (e.g. front shift, back shift); and technology used (e.g. small batch, mass production).

6. *Distinguish between the formal and the informal organization of a company.*

   - The formal organization refers to the collection of work groups that have been consciously designed by senior management to maximize efficiency and achieve organizational goals, while the informal organization refers to the network of relationships that spontaneously establish themselves between members of the organization on the basis of their common interests and friendships.

   - The two forms consist of the same people, albeit arranged in different ways.

7. *Distinguish Mintzberg's five organizational parts, five types of organization structure and his ten management roles.*

   - Mintzberg's five organizational parts consist of the strategic apex, middle line, operating core, technostructure and support staff.

   - His five types of organization structure are simple structure, machine structure, professional structure, divisional structure and *ad hoc* structure.

   - His ten managerial roles are figurehead, leader, liaison, monitor, disseminator, spokesperson, entrepreneur, disturbance handler, resource allocator and negotiator.

Revision

1. Is hierarchical control an inevitable part of organization design or a just a management convenience? Discuss.

2. The question of how many levels of hierarchy to have is one that has exercised managers and management writers for nearly a century. Why should it be so important?

3. How does the informal organization of a company contrast with the formal one? Can the informal organization ever be managed by senior company executives?

4. Distinguish the different bases upon which an organization can be departmentalized. Selecting TWO of these, compare the advantages and disadvantages of each and suggest the type of company or circumstances which would make it most appropriate.

5. Suggest how the relative importance of each of Mintzberg's ten managerial roles might be affected by the seniority of the post, type of organization or its size.

Springboard

Alvesson, M. and Willmott, H., 1996, *Making Sense of Management: A Critical Introduction*, Sage, London.

Takes a social scientific perspective and examines managing as a social process; often takes a critical perspective.

Groth, L., 1999, *Future Organizational Design*, Wiley, Chichester.

Treating co-ordination as the linchpin of organization, the author develops Mintzberg's five configurations, stressing the interplay between information technology and organization structure. Entertainingly written, historical examples of pre-computer technology are blended with discussions of contemporary and futuristic organizational forms.

Kotter, J.P., 1999, 'What effective general managers really do', *Harvard Business Review*, vol.77, no.2, pp.145–59.

Contemporary update on the tasks performed by and roles played by managers.

Linstead, S., Grafton Small, R. and Jeffcut, P. (eds), 1996, *Understanding Management*, Sage, London.

Takes a critical perspective on management topics and includes chapters on managing strategically and on networks and interorganizational relations.

Mintzberg, H., 1975, *The Nature of Managerial Work*, Harper & Row, New York.

Contains the research underpinning the ten managerial roles.

Mintzberg, H., 1983, *Structure in Fives: Effective Organizations*, Prentice Hall, Englewood Cliffs, NJ.

Mintzberg elaborates his ideas about the different parts of an organization and the different co-ordination mechanisms.

Reed, M., 1989, *The Sociology of Management*, Harvester Wheatsheaf, London.

A book on managers and managing which take a social scientific, often critical, perspective, in contrast to the usual descriptive managerialist stance.

Stewart, R., 1979, *Managers and their Jobs*, Macmillan, London.

Stewart, R., 1997, *The Reality of Management*, third edition, Butterworth Heinemann, Oxford.

Two books by Rosemary Stewart, a British academic who has also studied the content of managerial work. Usefully read alongside Mintzberg's and Kotter's studies.

Watson, T, 1994, *In Search of Management*, Routledge, London.

Looks at managing within the context of the organization.

Home viewing

Watership Down (1978, director Martin Rosen) is based on the book by Richard Adams. After a premonition of an impending disaster, one moonlit night, a group of ten rabbits leave the comfort and safety of their home warren on a long and dangerous journey. The hero rabbit of the story is Hazel. Remind yourself of Mintzberg's ten managerial roles and decide which of these roles are played by Hazel, and at which point in the film does he assume them. Does he play any roles not mentioned by Mintzberg? Which of Hazel's behaviours fall into several managerial role categories simultaneously? Which roles does Hazel *not* play, perhaps delegating them to others?

OB in literature

Kazuo Ishiguro, *The Remains of the Day*, Faber and Faber, 1989.

Stevens has spent the best part of his life as head butler to Lord Darlington. He narrates the story, set before, during and just after the Second World War. He discusses his career and his relationships with his master, with the housekeeper and then with his new (American) master. The main characters are 'trapped' in their respective hierarchical roles in the social and organization structure of their time. This is a story of how one's place in an organization structure and definition of role expectations shapes role relationships and individual attitudes and behaviour in quite stark and poignant ways.

What type of relationship does Stevens have (a) with the housekeeper and (b) with his own father?

How are these relationships affected by the respective positions of these characters in the organization structure of the household?

Chapter exercises

1: Invisible organization structure

Objectives

1. To make you aware of your existing experience of organization structures.

2. To allow you to consider how organization structures affects your behaviour.

Briefing

Organization structure is an abstract concept which has a pervading impact on our behaviour within organizations. Think about the job that you currently have, or have had in the past. If your work experience is limited, think about your 'job' as a pupil in school or a student at university. From this perspective, insert your answers to the questions below. If you are unsure, either guess the job title or insert the name of someone you know. If you get stuck, name a job title/character from an organization depicted in a TV programme. Leave the right-hand column blank.

Task	Insert answer	Concept

1. Write the job title of the 'manager' and the job title of the person to whom they report.

2. Write the job title of someone whose job it is to make things or to provide a service to others.

3. Write the job title of someone whose job it is to provide specialist advice or assistance to those people who make things or who provide a service to others.

4. If you share one boss with others, how many other people does this one person supervise?

5. Think of an instruction given to you by your boss, teacher or instructor, with which you complied.

6. About how many levels of hierarchy are there between your position in the organization and the most senior person?

7. Think of an organization rule that you have obeyed. What topic did it relate to?

8. Think of one thing that you did because of the position that you hold in your organization, rather than because of your natural inclinations.

9. At work or university, you are a member of a department. On what basis is your department organized?

10. Do you have a piece of paper that describes the tasks that you are required to perform in your job, and what decisions you can make on your own?

2: The Big Chip Electronics Company: function or product organization structure?

Objective

1. To give you the opportunity to compare the effects of function-based and product-based organization structures on company functioning.

Briefing

There are several different ways to organize work. Managers can often decide what form of organization structure they would like to have. However, each different form of structure has some advantages and disadvantages associated with it. In choosing a form of organization, a manager really is deciding which set of problems they want to live with. Read the description of the Big Chip Electronics Company. When you are finished answer the questions below. Base your answers on your own knowledge, guesses and common sense.

1. What is your choice of organization structure? Functional or product?

2. What are the reasons for your preference?

Big Chip Electronics (BCE)

Big Chip Electronics (BCE) manufactures and markets computers and peripheral electronic equipment for the UK and European markets. The company has been in business for the past 35 years and has established a major reputation in its industry. It has also been quite successful in marketing its products. Until now BCE has been a family business run by Alan Demerera, whose father and uncle started the business. He has had his son Clive working as his assistant since his own business was wound up. Basically there are three major sets of activities that must be accomplished to manufacture and market BCE's products. One group of workers and managers produces the computer systems using the latest technology to populate printed circuit boards, test systems and meet manufacturing schedules. Another group of workers and manager works in development research. This group is comprised largely of computer scientists, who attempt to improve the current products and introduce future additions to the BCE range of systems.

Marketing is handled by several sales personnel, who call on wholesalers and distributors in the UK and Europe. The sales staff is very large and has been, like all other employees, very effective. Alan and Clive have been managing BCE without many formal policies and procedures. The company has few set rules, procedures and job descriptions. Alan believes that once people know their job, they should and would do it well. However, BCE has grown fairly large and Alan and Clive believe that it is now necessary to develop a more formal organization structure. They have invited D.A. Buchan, a noted management consultant, to advise them. D.A. has told them that, basically, they have two choices. One is a functional organization structure and the second is a product-based organization structure. These two different forms are shown in the following diagram.

Big Chip Electronics Company: alternative organization structures

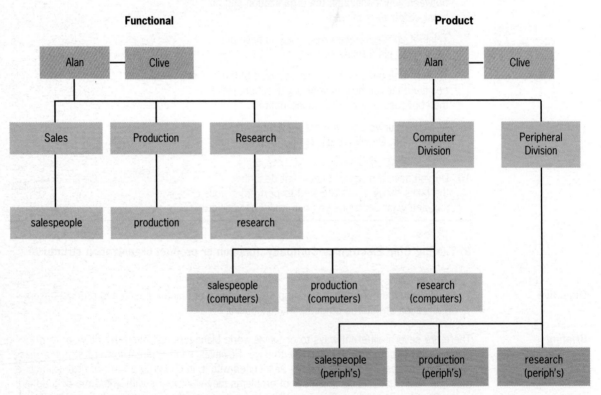

From H.L. Tosi and J.W. Young, *Management: Experiences and Demonstrations*, Irwin, London, 1982, pp. 75–8, using A. Filley, *The Complete Manager: What Works When*, Research Press, Champaign, Ill., 1978.

Chapter 15 Early organization design

Key concepts

traditional authority
charismatic authority
legitimate authority
bureaucracy
rules
formalization
machine bureaucracy
professional bureaucracy
time span of responsibility
contingency theory of organization structure
technological determinism
environmental determinism

technical complexity
technological interdependence
mediating technology
long-linked technology
intensive technology
task variety
task analysability
mechanistic structure
organic structure
differentiation
integration

Learning objectives

When you have read this chapter, you should be able to define those key concepts in your own words, and you should also be able to:

1. Distinguish between charismatic, traditional and legitimate forms of authority.

2. State the main characteristics of a bureaucratic organization structure as specified by Max Weber.

3. Summarize the approach and main principles of the classical management school.

4. Identify the writers who comprise the early contingency approach and state their main individual contributions.

5. Discuss the strengths and weaknesses of early ideas on the design of organization structure and the practice of management.

6. Identify the influence of early organization design ideas on contemporary organizations.

Why study early organization design?

Organization design refers to the process by which managers select and manage various dimensions and components of organization structure so that it achieves their goals. Organization design affects what they and others do, and how they spend their time. Many textbooks mention early twentieth-century writings on organization design only briefly before turning to explore team-based, network, virtual and similar contemporary developments in organization structure. This chapter will demonstrate that these early ideas, far from being either out of date or superseded, continue to exert a pervading influence on organizational life. In addition, their source and form exercise a similar, enduring influence on modern management and organizational thinking.

Max Weber's ideas on bureaucracy were developed at the start of the twentieth century and implemented from that time. Today, the vast majority of employees in industrial societies around the world continue to work in bureaucratic organizations whose structures Weber would easily recognize. Moreover, they will continue to work under these structural arrangements for the foreseeable future. Indeed, there is a 99 per cent chance that your own university is structured in this way. In contrast, at present, your chances of joining a so-called network or virtual organization are relatively slim. So we can note that the organization structure designs conceived in the past, which may have been updated, nevertheless continue to have a significant impact upon the present. This raises a number of questions:

- What are the benefits and costs of a bureaucratic organization structure?
- Why have the early structure arrangements remained so influential?
- In what ways has bureaucracy become modified?
- What does this imply for the nature of jobs?

A second significant feature of early management thought was its source and form. Little of it was based on systematic, empirical research. Max Weber was a historian and philosopher, while his contemporary, Henri Fayol, was a colliery manager. Fayol and his successors developed an approach to management knowledge which was based wholly on the experiences of, mainly successful, managers. Moreover, the form it took was of principles based on that experience. This trend continues to the present day. It is represented in the contrast between two bodies of management literature. On the one hand, there are the experience-based, prescriptive, often ghost or co-written books of the management gurus—typically retired or current chief executive officers (CEOs) of major world corporations, while on the other, there are the research-based, often critical, case studies and surveys produced by university academics from management and sociology departments (Huczynski, 1993; Collins, 2000; Furnsten, 1999).

Traditional authority is based on the belief that the ruler had a natural right to rule. This right was either God-given or by descent. The authority enjoyed by kings and queens would be of this type.

Charismatic authority is based on the belief that the ruler had some special, unique virtue, either religious or heroic. Religious prophets, charismatic politicians and pop and film stars all wield this type of power.

Max Weber and bureaucracy

Legitimate authority is based on formal, written rules which have the force of law. The authority of present-day presidents, chief executive officers and cardinals is based on the position that they hold.

The interesting aspects of bureaucracy are its widespread adoption as a form of organization and its continuing popularity. The literal meaning of bureaucracy is 'rule by office or by officials', and it is primarily with the German sociologist and philosopher Max Weber that one associates this concept. His work on the topic was carried out at the turn of the twentieth century and stemmed from his interest in power and authority. In this textbook, the term 'power' is used to refer to the capacity of individuals to overcome resistance on the part of others, to exert their will, and to produce results consist with their interests and objectives. Weber studied societies in history and distinguished three different types of authority. One of these types is **legitimate authority**, which carries with it position power.

Stop and criticize

Where does Shakespeare's Richard II believe that his power comes from when he says:

Not all the water in the rough rude sea
Can wash the balm off from an anointed king;
The breath of worldly men cannot depose
The deputy elected by the Lord.

From *Richard II*, Act 3, Scene 2, lines 54–57.

Max Weber
(1864–1920)

Bureaucracy
corresponds to the legal-rational type of authority. It is a form of organization structure that is characterized by a specialization of labour, a specific authority hierarchy, a formal set of rules, and rigid promotion and selection criteria.

Because of the process of rationalism in modern society (the belief that the human mind can discover innate laws which govern the workings of the universe), legitimate authority has predominated [**link**, chapter 13, traditional work design]. Within a **bureaucracy**, we do what managers, civil servants and university lecturers tell us, not because we think that they have a natural right to do so, or because they possess some divine power, but because we acknowledge that their exercise of power is legitimated and hence supported by two factors:

- The demonstrably logical relevance of their requests, directions and instructions to us. Their commands must seem rational by being justified through their relevance to the tasks of the bureaucracy and, ultimately, to its objectives.

- A shared belief in the norms and rules of the bureaucracy, which have been arrived at rationally (not based on tradition or personal whim) and which possess a law-like character.

Weber believed that an organization based on legitimate authority would be more efficient than one based on either **traditional** or **charismatic authority**. This was because its continuity was related to formal structure and positions within it rather than to a particular person, who might leave or die. Not every

---

Characteristics of Weberian bureaucracy

1. *Job specialization*: Jobs are broken down into simple, routine and well-defined tasks. Clear definitions of authority and responsibility are legitimated as official rules.

2. *Authority hierarchy*: Positions are in a hierarchy of authority, with each position under the authority of a higher one. There is a clear chain of command, and workers know clearly to whom they are responsible.

3. *Employment and career*: All personnel are selected and promoted on the basis of their technical qualifications and offered a full-time career.

4. *Recording*: Administrative acts and decisions are recorded in writing. Record keeping provides an organizational memory and continuity over time.

5. *Rules and procedures*: All employees are subject to rules and procedures that ensure reliable, predictable behaviour.

6. *Impersonality*: procedures and rules are impersonal and apply to managerial and non-managerial employees alike.

Based on Max Weber, *The Theory of Social and Economic Organizations*, translated and edited by A.M. Henderson and T. Parsons, Free Press, New York, 1947, pp.328–37.

formal organization will possess all the characteristics that Weber identified. However, the more of them that it has, the more closely it approximates to the 'ideal type' that he had in mind. Weber's description of bureaucracy is known as an 'ideal type'. It is not meant to describe any particular existing organization, but rather, it represents a model or a checklist against which to compare and assess real organizations.

Weber used the term 'bureaucracy' to describe a particular type of organization structure and was concerned with how work was divided, co-ordinated and controlled. It was a structure that was both impersonal and rational. Whereas in the past, authority had been based on nepotism, whim or fancy, in bureaucratic organizations it was based on rational principles. For this reason, it offered the possibility of being the most efficient ever, in comparison with what had preceded it. Bureaucracy for him was a form of organization which emphasized speed, precision, regulation, clarity, reliability and efficiency. This was achieved through creating a fixed division of tasks, imposing detailed rules, regulations and procedures, and monitoring through hierarchical supervision.

Many aspects of Weber's model reflected the organizational circumstances at the time in which he was writing. In the early twentieth century, establishing employment relationships on the basis of professional selection, and creating continuity of employment and career structures, was important when the methods commonly used at the time were amateur, personal and haphazard. Because they were adopted so widely, so long ago, it is difficult to believe that there was a time when organizations did not keep detailed written records.

Ford's pre-1979 bureaucracy

In their investigation of managers' experiences of working for Ford of Europe, Starkey and McKinlay vividly contrast that company's pre-1979 ideal-type bureaucratic organization with its post-1980 'after Japan' organization, which introduced employee involvement and participation. Historically, prior to 1979, Ford had been an archetypal 'machine bureaucracy', which was the classic, institutional form of twentieth-century big business. The design of its management structure mirrored its assembly lines: it was specialized, hierarchical and rigidly controlled. Following a 1945 reorganization modelled on General Motors, a managerial bureaucracy was created in which managers became the cogs in Ford's machine. Just like the specialized workers down on the assembly line, Ford's managers were operators of company procedures. A British systems manager reported:

> When I joined the company, it was full of empty boxes and you could put anybody with any intelligence at all in any one of those boxes, give him a statement of functions, the relevant procedure manuals, and he could read through these and do the job. The whole company was structured that way. There were a large number of people involved in writing policy manuals to make sure it was all up to date.

The same Ford structure, systems, philosophy and culture were so strong that managers could be rotated around Ford plants all over the world. The boxes on the organization chart not only provided certainty of task and responsibility but also meant it was possible to know exactly who to blame if there was a problem. It was a highly controlled environment in which the relationships between the functions, especially between sales and manufacturing, became aggressive and confrontational. The Fordist bureaucracy was developed by Robert McNamara and was designed to ensure that neither divisional nor functional managers had access to information or made decisions that could challenge the hegemony of the Detroit headquarters.

This pre-1979 ideal-type 'machine bureaucracy' was perfectly suited to a stable environment but represented a major handicap in a more dynamic market setting. What were earlier perceived as the cardinal virtues of Ford's managerial bureaucracy came later to be understood as its dysfunctions. One manager reported, 'The clarity of structure was terrific—the rigidity of it was terrible'. The exhaustive 'checks and balances' were redefined as counter-productive control mechanisms. A manager reported, 'there were so many rules and regulations that you spent half your time administering routines rather than managing. Innovation was pointless. Managers knew that bureaucracy would review the hell out of any initiative anyway'.

Ford's traditional bureaucracy came to be considered too slow and inflexible for a dynamic market environment over which the corporation had little control. The traditional Ford approach had been to manage *through* hierarchical levels and tasks. It changed to managing *across* levels and projects. It had to give up its enormous bureaucracy based on the fetish that it had to police everything.

Based on Ken Starkey and Alan McKinlay, 'Managing for Ford', *Sociology*, 1994, vol.28, no.4, pp.4, 975–90.

The strength of bureaucracy lay in its standardization. Employee behaviour was controlled and made predictable. In Weber's conception, this was achieved not through time-and-motion study but through the application of rules, regulations and procedures. Bureaucratic organizations have a reasonably consistant set of goals and preferences. They devote few resources to time-consuming information searches or the analysis of current activities to check if they are meeting stated goals. Instead, they rely on rules, tradition, precedent and standard operating procedures. Little time is spent on decision making, since decisions follow from the established routines, and few action alternatives are considered. The ideological emphasis is on stability, fairness and predictability (Pfeffer, 1981). Weber was struck by how the bureaucratic structure of a company routinized the processes of its administration, in a way similar to how a machine routinized production.

Although Weber's ideas developed independently, they neatly complement those of Taylor [**link**, chapter 13, traditional work design]. While Taylor focused on the worker on the shop floor, Weber's interest lay in a body of knowledge, administrative rules and organization hierarchy from the supervisor level upwards. The disciplining, rational conditioning and training of workers proposed by Taylor was known to and approved by Weber.

In modern usage, bureaucracy has acquired a pejorative meaning among the public and the media: for example, when they come up against red tape and obstructiveness in any aspect of organizational life. Weber's view was in direct opposition to this. For him, bureaucracy was the most efficient form of social organization precisely because it was so coldly logical and did not allow personal relations and feelings to get in the way of achieving goals. On the one hand, rules and other bureaucratic procedures provided a standard way of dealing with employees, avoiding favouritism and personal bias. Everyone knows what the rules are and receives equal treatment. On the other hand, there is frustration at having to follow what appear to be seemingly illogical rules, and thereby experience delays. This change in meaning has occurred because the principles of bureaucracy, originally designed to maximize efficiency, also resulted in inefficiencies. These negative aspects, costs or 'dysfunctions' of bureaucracy were the focus of debates in both organization behaviour and sociology during the 1950s and 1960s (Merton, 1940; Gouldner, 1954; Blau, 1966).

Research conducted during the 1960s and 1970s recognized that bureaucracy should be treated as a continuum. Thus the question changed from whether or not an organization was a bureaucracy to one that asked to what degree any given organization was 'bureaucratized'. For example, the Aston studies (Pugh and Hickson, 1976; Pugh and Hinings, 1976; Pugh and Payne, 1977; Hickson and McMillan, 1981) measured the bureaucracy of companies on a number of dimensions, as shown in table 15.1. Using these criteria, the Aston studies distinguished three types of structure:

- *Full bureaucracies,* which approximated to Weber's ideal type, and which tended to be rare and were found in central government.

Table 15. 1: Bureaucratic dimensions of an organization	
Specialization	To what degree are tasks subdivided into separate jobs?
Formalization	Are standard rules, standards and procedures laid down?
Standardization of practices	Are there standardized practices, e.g. employment, discipline?
Centralization	To what extent is the authority to make decisions located at the top of the management hierarchy?
Configuration	What is the 'shape' of the organization's structure measured in terms of managers' chain of command – long or short? managers' span of control – wide or narrow? number of specialized support staff – many or few?

- *Workflow bureaucracies,* which combined tight structuring of manufacturing with more decentralized authority.

- *Personnel bureaucracies,* which combined employment relationships which were bureaucratized with lower structuring of activities, allowing more personal forms of control. These were to be found in small branch plants and parts of local government.

Organization structures are rarely completely one type or another but tend to vary in degrees. Therefore, the idea of continua is one that features in many other discussions on organization structures. If will be met again in discussion of virtual organizations [**link**, chapter 16, organization strategy and design]

Weber was a sociologist and philosopher, not a manager or a management consultant. He neither advocated nor promoted bureaucracy. However, from his historical analysis, he did believe that bureaucracy was the most efficient form of organization design. Following Weber, many of the writers in the 1960s and 1970s

"I'd like to think of you as a person, David, but it's my job to think of you as personnel."

That's the Way the Wheel Turns

Fill in this application form in triplicate, and do,
  Supply the information, what and where, and how and who,
We want your registration number, age and height and weight,
  So that we can keep the nation, in a law and ordered state.

Chorus   Cause that's the way the wheels turn,
                       Round and round the wheels turn,
                       That's the way the wheels turn, round.

The forms are fumigated, then they're filed into files,
The files are stamped and dated, then piled into piles,
The piles are tabulated, then they're stored into rows,
The rows are consecrated, so the paper kingdom grows.

I am the man in uniform, the name without a name,
I'm the man who sees the rules are kept, the rules that others frame,
And if you want a question answered, there may be some delay,
Because it isn't my department, I'm not allowed to say.

I am a servant of the people, doing what I have to do,
I'm the man who turns the handles, and I'm turning them for you,
If you want to come and see me, join the queue and while you wait,
Fill in this form PC three-zero-FX-double eight.

From 'That's the Way the Wheel Turns', Leon Rosselson, *Songs About Life at Work*, Conference on Organizational Culture, University of British Columbia, Canada, April 1984.

Rules are procedures or obligations explicitly stated and written down in organization manuals.

Formalization refers to the degree to which formal procedures and rules exist and are used in an organization.

considered bureaucracy from a sociological perspective. As industrial sociologists, they were usually based in sociology departments and worked at the macro-level, examining the nature, determinants and variants of bureaucracy within society. Other writers, in contrast, looked at bureaucracy from a managerial perspective. They tended to be based in departments of management or in business schools, and they focused on the specific internal aspects of bureaucracy. Being practice-led rather than theory-led, the latter offered managers prescriptions about how best to maximize bureaucracy's benefits, eliminate its dysfunctions and generally create an efficient organization structure which would maximize productivity and profits.

A defining characteristic of every bureaucratic structure are its **rules**. From the 1930s, senior managements in large organizations increasingly adopted systems of bureaucratic (rule-governed) control. These complemented the control exercised through machinery and replaced those exercised through supervisor commands. Rules serve to regulate and control what individuals do and, to the extent that employees comply with company rules, they can ensure the predictability of human behaviour within organizations. Both parties benefited. For employees, rational and fair rules avoided managers' personal bias. This was true despite the fact that the rules were devised and policed by management, who could relax or ignore them at their discretion. Unions used rules to restrict the arbitrary power of employers, and demarcation rules protected jobs. Although rules can cause frustration to employees, they also reduce role ambiguity and offer them high organizational identification and low self-estrangement.

Management also benefits from rules. It uses formal rules and procedures to co-ordinate the activities of different employees and establish conformity among them. Bureaucratic structures created job hierarchies with numerous job titles,

A question of rule clarity

The parable of BT's [British Telecom] dress code deserves to be more widely told. After privatization, the company decided it was time to shake off the sloppy dress habits of the public sector. A directive went round telling senior employees that they should adopt suitable business dress. The directive caused some resentment. Those who opposed it demanded greater clarity and certainty. When they went to the wardrobe in the morning, how could they know what would represent suitable business dress. After advice from its legal and regulatory affairs department, the company agreed to promulgate a dress code. Senior male employees were expected to wear smart suits, shirts with collars, and ties. It was not long before someone came to the office in a red suit. When criticized, he pointed to the terms of the dress code. The suit was undeniably smart; but it was the smartness of a nightclub rather than a boardroom.

So the dress code had to specify a colour. Red was out, grey was in. But what of blue? Some blues were clearly acceptable. The chairman's favourite suit, in fact, was a fetching shade of navy. But bright blues could not be admitted. So how bright was bright? BT research came up with the answer. Brightness is determined by how much light a fabric reflects. A machine could measure this, and one was soon constructed and installed in the reception areas. But ties posed a more intractable problem. It was simply impossible to define which colours and motifs were acceptable. A clearance procedure seemed the best answer. Anyone who bought a new tie could submit it to the dress code department, which had 42 days to rule on whether or not it was suitable business dress. This was difficult, since the appropriateness of a tie might depend on its context—the suit and the shirt that went with it. So decisions were rather conservative. This raised the issue of an appeals mechanism.

Delegating discretion over approval of ties to the dress code department made it judge and jury in implementing regulations it had devised. But this violated natural justice. The company agreed that a small group of senior directors, with an independent fashion adviser, would hear complaints from employees who felt their ties had been unreasonably rejected. But there was the more general problem of changing fashion. After all, it was not so long ago that every gentleman had gone to work in a wing collar and frock coat. Not only were other forms of dress now acceptable, but wing collars had probably ceased to be acceptable. Not the image of a modern information company. A well-known fashion designer agreed to chair a standing working party to advise the company on fashion trends.

By this time, the dress code extended to 50 pages, largely impenetrable. No sensible employee read it, and when they were given a copy they were told that if they only behaved sensibly they would probably be all right. Knowledge of its contents was confined to the dress department, which by this time consisted of twenty people, mostly lawyers, the union representative who negotiated over it, and a few cranks who enjoyed pointing out inconsistencies and anomalies in the code.

Eventually a new management came in, determined to sweep the dress code department away. They quickly realized there were two alternatives. One was to supply a uniform to all employees. This was obviously an intolerable interference in personal affairs. The other was to sweep away the dress code and renew the instruction to everyone to wear suitable business dress. If anyone was in genuine doubt as to what constituted suitable dress—and not many people were—they were advised to have a word with the dress regulator. He had been given this role precisely because of his sound judgement and range of business experience. What the regulator said bound no one, but to ignore his advice was injudicious and might prejudice advancement in the company.

The demand for clarity and certainty in regulation has great superficial plausibility, and it is because it is difficult to argue against clarity and certainty that it is best to resort to parable. The world is rarely clear and certain, and if it seems so today, it will have ceased to be so tomorrow.

Based on John Kay, 'A question of clarity and certainty', *Financial Times*, 12 January 1996, p.10.

"I was just going to say "Well, I don't make the rules." But, of course, I do make the rules."

each with its own pay rate. Elaborate formal rules and apparently 'objective' criteria provided a basis for evaluating employee performance and determining rewards, allowing results to be traced back to the individual employee. This was all part of management's attempt to 'routinize' tasks, which, together with the use of forecasting, planning, creating buffer stocks, and so on, sought to remove the uncertainties involved in dealing with the environment. Provided that that environment was stable and unchanging, it was an effective strategy.

Stop and criticize

Think of some of the rules that you have encountered in organizations to which you currently belong, or used to belong. How effective are they in directing the behaviour of individuals? What problems do they cause, and what advantages do they offer, and for whom?

Strengths and weaknesses of bureaucratic organization structures

The writers who are critical of bureaucracy have argued that the challenge for management is to create work environments in which employees have the opportunity to grow and to mature as individuals. In their view, this means moving away from bureaucratic organization forms and towards some other type of organization design. They say that in the twenty-first century, the bureaucratic organization will be too expensive to maintain, will be incapable of responding sufficiently quickly to change and will not be using the innovative resources of its members. Failure to achieve profit targets will result in company collapse and large-scale redundancies. Their argument is that now that the slimming down has been completed in many companies, the new-look, leaner organizations are experimenting with radically different forms of structure which overcome the dysfunctions of bureaucracy (table 15.2).

Table 15.2: Positive and negative consequences of a bureaucracy

Characteristic	Positive consequence	Negative consequences	
		for the individual	for the organization
1. Job specialization	Produces efficient, repetitive working	Over-specialization of employees' skills and knowledge prevents them recognizing or caring about problems not in their domain	Inhibits rotation and hence flexible use of personnel, and thus can reduce overall productivity
2. Authority hierarchy	Clarifies who is in command	Prevents employees contributing to decisions	Allows errors to be hidden
3. Employment and career	Most appropriate person appointed to a position	Can restrict the psychological growth of the individual in their job	Individuals throughout the company are promoted to their level of incompetence
4. Recording	Creates an organization history that is not dependent on individual memory	Employees come to see record keeping as an end in itself rather than a means to an end	Recorded precedents stifle attempts at company innovation Inhibits flexibility, adaptability and responsiveness
5. Rules and procedures	Employees know what is expected of them	Introduces delays; stifles initiative and creativity	Leads to individual and sub-unit goals replacing organization objectives; rules define *minimum* levels of acceptable performance
6. Impersonality	Fosters efficiency, reduces bias	Dehumanizes those it purports to serve—officials prevented from responding to unique features of clients who are treated as standard cases	Creates a climate of alienation through the firm as employees come to see themselves as small cogs in a wheel

In contrast, there are other writers who are supportive of bureaucratic organiz-ation structures, in part or in whole. They note that most large organizations pos-sess many of the features of Weber's model; and that their longevity and continued existence confirm that they can achieve an acceptable level of efficiency. They cite examples of companies who have not adopted bureaucratic features and have failed. There is a prevailing view that organizations should be structured on the basis of rationality. This means that organization designers

Wot, *more* organization hierarchy?

Adrian Furnham commented on one aspect of the continuing trend to de-bureaucratization, that of re-organizing structures to reduce the number of levels in hierarchies, and thus create flatter organization structures. While supposedly aimed at securing the benefits of improved customer service, faster communication, better quality inspection and lower personnel costs, this strategy also resulted in many negative consequences for both the organization and its employees. This was particularly so when the organization concerned did not know the optimum number of hierarchical levels that it should have. Removing levels and making the managers within them redundant has a number of consequences.

First, the number of duties to be performed by each of the surviving managers is necessarily increased, as is their span of control. With more to do and an increased number of subordinates to manage, these managers communicate less with each one, and more slowly. Second, there is a particular problem in providing regular, two-way, manager–subordinate communication that is sufficiently specific, personalized and regular to allow the correction of errors and to motivate staff.

Furnham challenges the view that the percentage of managers grows in proportion to the increase in the size of the company. Indeed, by using standard procedures and systems that are relevant and supported by new technology, managers save themselves time and are able to supervise more people, while delegating more specialized work to support staff. In consequence, as organizations grow, their hierarchies actually become more efficient and flatter, he claims. A company of 800 may thus have the same number of personnel staff as one of 8,000.

Furnham says that there are limits to which technology can replace middle managers who have been made redundant. Technology deals well with routine, rule-based work but is inappropriate for tasks that have an innovative, strategic or political dimension. He stresses the difference between over-manning and optimal manning. In his view, a hierarchy is actually a good way to control work processes. This is because it defines who is responsible to whom for what. It encourages specialization throughout the entire organization, allowing those who possess the most knowledge and skill to perform the task. Top management level and shop-floor level decision making have very different time frames, needs and objectives and are unlikely to be performed well by a single individual. Ineffective decision making may be due more to poor selection of managers than to an inappropriate organization structure.

Furnham contends that the complexity and the size of an organization, and the complexity of the work performed in it, determine the number of levels in any hierarchy. Thus, if a company's work needs to be closely supervised and cannot be made routine, or if the employees performing it are physically distanced, then closer supervision, and hence a narrower span of control and a taller hierarchy, will be necessary (and vice versa). Many organizations which have made many of their middle managers redundant after business process re-engineering exercises have found that they have had to rehire many of them as consultants at twice their pay and half their responsibility.

Based on Adrian Furnham, 'Anti-hierarchy gurus fall flat on their faces',
Daily Telegraph Appointments, 1 April 1999, p.A3.

Machine bureaucracy is a type of organization which possesses all the bureaucratic characteristics. The important decisions are made at the top, while at the bottom, standardized procedures are used to exercise control.

should accept that a hierarchical structure is more likely to produce rational decisions and better control within the organization than any other structure of authority (for example, one based on teams).

'Post-industrial' does not necessarily mean 'post-bureaucratic'. Bureaucracy has adapted and survived. In the original **machine bureaucracy**, control was exercised through rules, technology and the supervisor's command. This made the behaviour of people in large, complex organizations highly predictable. Since that time, environmental conditions have changed, and authority has increasingly become based on knowledge. In response, **professional bureaucracy** has developed. Rational discipline has become internalized by professional employees like teachers, doctors, social workers, accountants and similar groups through a process of socialization, rather than being imposed externally. Thus, self-regulation through internalized professional standards has replaced external rules and controls or authority from above.

All over in a flash

The first thing the three technicians pouring the uranium oxide solution into a precipitation tank at Tokaimura on 30 September 1999 noticed was a blue flash. Then they began to experience waves of nausea and some difficulty in breathing. What they did not realize was that they had accidentally dumped in more than six times as much fissile uranium as they had meant to, and had therefore triggered a runaway chain reaction. . . . In one sense, they were lucky. They poured in 16kg of the solution. Had they poured in 40kg, they could have built themselves an amateur nuclear bomb.

Popular management and media writers consistently condemn the effects of bureaucracy, calling instead for employees to use they initiative, not be bound by rules, to look for the 'bigger picture', to avoid rigid, programmed behaviour, etc. However, the moment that an accident occurs, be it rail, road, aircraft, space or, as in this case, nuclear, the search is on for those who failed to adhere strictly to the rules and procedures that had been set down. A consideration of the main features of bureaucracy illustrates that it was precisely such occurrences that this form of organization structure sought to anticipate and avoid. In the case of the uranium-processing plant in Tokaimura, Japan, initial reports identified four causes of the accident:

1. The company had illegally compiled a manual that encouraged workers to cut corners in order to reduce costs. Instead of using the tower, they mixed the material by hand.

2. The workers making the fuel lacked the knowledge and experience to do it correctly and safety.

3. Because the workers were allowed to bypass the time-consuming mixing process in the tower, with its automatic controls to prevent such things happening, they were free to dump their material into a vessel that was not designed to take it. This further aggravated the problem.

4. The company procedure did not anticipate the possibility of such an accident occurring and hence lacked any containment facility.

Two of the three workers inside the plant received more than the lethal dose of 7 sieverts (a sievert is the unit that measures the intensity of radiation's impact on the body). One of them has since died. A further 46 employees were exposed to radiation as they sought to contain the problem. The International Atomic Energy Agency classified the accident in Tokaimura as level 4 on a seven-point scale, making it the world's most serious since the level 7 disaster at Chernobyl in the Ukraine in 1986.

Based on 'All over in a flash', *The Economist*, 9 October 1999, p.142; 'The land of disappointments', *The Economist*, 4 March 2000, p.115–17.

Professional bureaucracies modify the principle of centralized control and thus allow their staff greater autonomy. This is appropriate for working in relatively stable conditions in which tasks are relatively complicated. Universities and hospitals are examples of professional bureaucracies, whose staff possess key skills and abilities. Until recently in the UK, these occupational groups enjoyed a large degree of freedom and discretion in how they did their work. However, professional staff in both types of organization are being increasingly monitored and subjected to 'quality control and assurance' procedures. These have been instituted by government and have been implemented by senior managements.

Elliot Jaques and the time span of responsibility

Elliot Jaques (1990) is an uncompromising supporter of bureaucracy. Its essence is the hierarchically stratified employment system in which employees are accountable to their managers for the work that they do. He agrees with the need to release employee energy and improve morale in order to increase productivity. However, he rejects the fashionable team-based organization designs (e.g. autonomous work teams) as neither feasible nor necessary, and doomed to failure [**link**, chapter 12, teamworking]. He contends that bureaucracy is the only viable structural form for a large organization.

Elliot Jaques
(b. 1917)

Professional bureaucracy is a type of organization which possesses all the bureaucratic characteristics. In addition, there are few levels between the strategic apex and the operating staff, control of which is achieved through professional indoctrination.

Time span of responsibility refers to the time period for which an individual's decisions can commit an organization.

For him, the managerial hierarchy is 'the most efficient, hardiest, and in fact the most natural structure ever devised for large organizations' (Jaques, 1990, p.127). He contends that the admitted deficiencies of hierarchy, and the 'flight to groups', are not due to any inherent deficiency in the bureaucratic model itself but to the fact that it has been poorly understood and badly applied. That failure stems from a misunderstanding of how a managerial hierarchy functions; how it relates to the complexities of work; and how it can be used to encourage employee talent and stimulate their energy. Hierarchies in organizations should neither be tall nor flat, but requisite. He suggests that there is an optimum number of hierarchical levels for every organization (Jaques, 1989a).

To explain this thinking, he uses the concept of the **time span of responsibility**. This refers to the time period for which an individual's decisions can commit an organization. The assembly line operator who bolts on wheels commits the organization over a period of seconds or minutes; the supervisor drawing up rosters commits the organization for a period of days or weeks. Materials acquisition people potentially commit the organization to contracts lasting for months up to a year. A chief executive can commit an organization, for example a strategy, for five to ten years (Jaques, 1982; 1976). This can be related to the time interval in which supervisors check subordinates; middle managers check supervisors; senior management checks the material acquisitions department; and the board of directors checks the chief executive's performance. For Jaques, the key to making bureaucracy efficient was ensuring a match between a manager's responsibility and the time span for their position in the hierarchy.

Jaques found that efficient bureaucracies operated with seven basic steps or strata of increasing time spans. These corresponded to levels of thinking capability, from concrete thinking at the bottom to abstract thinking and envisioning at the top. The inefficiencies of bureaucracy (e.g. duplication) stemmed from the insertion of additional, unnecessary levels, for example for political purposes, to accommodate extra pay bands or to provide career ladder steps. The seven layers, with their associated time spans, are shown in figure 15.1.

The creative, motivational aspect of bureaucratic organization occurred when employees worked at a hierarchical level that corresponded to their current time span capacity, but which allowed them to progress to their maximum time-span capacity. Jaques extended his thinking on the seven-strata idea in two directions—assessing what employees should do (job evaluation), and how much they should be paid to do it (financial remuneration) (Jaques, 1956). He offers some-

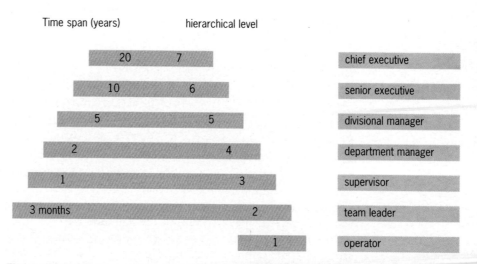

Figure 15.1: Elliot Jaques' time span of responsibility

thing unusual in organizational behaviour—a theory that links organizations and individuals. It has far-reaching implications for grading and payment systems; organization structuring; work organisation and programming, staff training and development, and decision making.

Stop and criticize

A company about to embark on a restructuring programme (possibly including the use of teamworking) has asked you to evaluate Jaques' ideas before it goes ahead with its changes. Assess the strengths and weaknesses of his ideas for senior management.

Henri Fayol and classical management theory

Henri Fayol
(1841–1925)

Classical management theory resembles bureaucracy even though it originated in France in the early twentieth century with the work of Henri Fayol. Fayol qualified as a mining engineer in 1860, after which he joined the Commentary-Fourchambault combine, a company in which he was to spend his entire working life. In 1866, he became manager of the Commentary collieries and, in 1888 at the age of 47, he was appointed to the general manager position at a time when the financial position of the company was critical. By the time he retired in 1918, he had established financial stability in the organization. Fayol's list of managerial activities provides a definition of management. Indeed, he is credited with 'inventing' management, that is, distinguishing it as a separate activity, and defining its constituent elements. Interestingly, the word *management* is not translatable into all languages, nor does the concept exist in all cultures. Managing of course occurs, but it is not always treated as anything special or separate.

It was in 1916, the year after Frederick Taylor died, that Fayol's book *General and Industrial Administration* was published. In it, Fayol put down in a systematic form the experience that he had gained while managing a large organization. He stressed methods rather than personalities, seeking to present the former in a coherent and relevant scheme. This formed his theory of organization. While Taylor focused on the worker on the shop floor—a bottom-up approach—Fayol began from the top of the hierarchy and moved downwards. However, like Taylor, he too believed that a manager's work could be reviewed objectively, analysed and treated as a technical process which was subject to certain definite principles which could be taught. Fayol's list of six management activities, originally developed some 80 years ago, remain broadly intact to this day (table 15.3). Only minor modifications have been made to the labels that he used.

Table 15.3: Fayol's six managerial activities

Forecasting	Predicting what will happen in the future
Planning	Devising a course of action to meet that expected demand
Organizing	Mobilizing materials and resources by allocating separate tasks to different departments, units and individuals
Commanding	Providing direction to employees, now more commonly referred to as *directing* or *motivating*
Co-ordinating	Making sure that activities and resources are working well together towards the common goal
Controlling	Monitoring progress to ensure that plans are being carried out properly

The six management activities are interrelated. For example, a company management team begins by *forecasting* the demand for its product, for example steel wire. It requires a sales forecast and will use market research to develop one. Once it is clear that there is a market for the product, the next activity, *planning*, will take place. For Fayol, planning involved 'making a programme of action to achieve an objective'. He collectively referred to the two activities, forecasting and planning, as *purveyance*. Because they are so closely related, some authors and books treat them as a single management activity.

Having made the plan, the third activity to be performed is *organizing*. This involves bringing together the money, materials and people needed to achieve the objective. It also involves breaking down the main task into smaller pieces and distributing them to different people. In a company structured along functional lines (accounting, production, marketing), the organizing of people may involve creating a special temporary project team consisting of members from the different functions. This is the matrix structure introduced in an earlier chapter.

Fayol used the word *commanding* to describe his fourth management activity. It has been defined as 'influencing others towards the accomplishment of organizational goals'. We would now refer to it as either *directing* or *motivating*. Whichever term is chosen, performing this activity involves the manager in ensuring that employees give of their best. To do this, managers must possess a knowledge of both the tasks to be done and the people who are to do them. This management activity is mainly, although not exclusively, performed in a face-to-face situation.

Earlier, organizing involved distributing task elements to various individuals. Now those separate elements have to be brought together. This represents the *co-ordinating* activity. Co-ordination can be achieved through memos, meetings and personal contacts between the people carrying out their unique activities. The sixth and final activity of managers is *controlling*. This involves monitoring how the objectives set out in the plan are being achieved, with respect to the limitations of time and budget that were imposed. Any deviations are identified and action taken to rectify them. It may be that the original plan will have to be amended. Although the six managerial activities have been presented as a sequence, in reality they occur simultaneously in a company. However, forecasting and planning tend to be primary. There are also loops when original plans have to be changed because certain resources are found to be unavailable (when organizing) or when cost overruns are discovered (through controlling).

Fayol's second major contribution was to identify fourteen 'principles of management' (table 15.4). These were not based on systematic research but on his personal reflections and his experience of management. The principles continue to be used today: they are referred to by chief executives and government ministers as 'best practice'. They contain rules and guidelines, but most are devoid of any research backing.

Fayol's ideas were complemented by those proposed by other contemporary writers, James Mooney, Edward Tregaskiss Elbourne and E.F.L. Brech. Later commentators like Lyndall Urwick and Luther Gulick developed and further disseminated his ideas. Their collective ideas, published in various forms over a long period of time, came to be known collectively as classical management theory (also dubbed scientific administration) Many felt that these mirrored, at the macro-organizational level, what scientific management offered at the micro-organizational level [**link**, chapter 13, traditional work design].

Classical management considered that there was one best organization structure which would suit all organizations, irrespective of their size, technology, environment or employees. This structure was based on the application of certain key principles which reflected the 'logic of efficiency', which stressed:

Table 15.4: Fayol's fourteen principles of management

1. Division of work	Efficiency will be maximized if employees specialized in certain tasks.
2. Authority	Authority is the right of managers to command and to be obeyed, and should match responsibility.
3. Discipline	Discipline is necessary to develop obedience, diligence, energy and respect within the limits fixed by an organization.
4. Unity of command	Each subordinate should report to only one boss.
5. Scalar principle	The line of authority (scalar chain) in an organization runs from the top of the hierarchy to the bottom, because of the unity of command. Communications usually go up and down this path, but employees at the same level should be able to communicate laterally.
6. Unity of direction	Each group of organized activities that have the same objective should have one manager using one plan to ensure consistency and responsibility.
7. Interest subordination	Organizational goals and interests should take precedence over individual ones.
8. Remuneration	Pay should be fair, sufficient to motivate to perform well but not unreasonably high.
9. Centralization	Over-centralization of authority and responsibility should be avoided; delegation encouraged; but with sufficient centralization to ensure accountability within the organization.
10. Order	People and materials should be in the right place at the right time.
11. Equity of treatment	Managers should be fair and kind to their subordinates.
12. Stability of employment	As employee turnover is inefficient, management should provide orderly personnel employment planning and ensure that replacements are available to fill vacancies.
13. Opportunity for initiative	Employees should be given the opportunity and freedom to originate and execute a plan, even if it sometimes fails.
14. *Esprit de corps*	Promoting team spirit will build harmony and unity within the organization.

Based on Henri Fayol, *General and Industrial Management*, translated from the French by C. Storrs, 1949, Sir Isaac Pitman and Sons, London, 1916.

- a functional division of work;

- hierarchical relationships;

- bureaucratic forms of control;

- narrow supervisory span; and

- closely prescribed roles.

Criticism of classical management

When considering classical management theory, it is important to locate it in its historical context. The managers of the period were dealing with larger, more complex organizations than had existed hitherto. At the beginning of the twentieth century many new companies developed. They employed vast numbers of people, had numerous plants and employed new technologies. All of this needed co-ordinating. With no model or experience to fall back on, those who managed these organizations had no choice but to develop their own principles and theories as to what to do to run them well. Inevitably these principles were grounded in their day-to-day experience of managing and owed much to the models offered by military, religious and governmental organizations. Over the years, various writers have criticized Fayol's principles (Thomas, 1993; Child, 1969; March and Simon, 1958; Peters and Waterman, 1982). Their criticisms include:

- Misleadingly proposed a single, standardized organizational model as the optimum one.

- Promoted a militaristic, mechanistic organization, which stressed discipline, command, order, subordinates and *esprit de corps.*

- Overlooked the negative consequences of tight control and narrow task specialization, which can demotivate employees and hinder efficiency.

- Over-emphasized an organization's formal structure while neglecting processes such as conflict management, decision making and communication.

- Underestimated the complexity of organizations.

- Were based on unreliable personal knowledge rather than systematic research evidence.

- Lacked a concern for the interaction between people.

- Underestimated the effects of conflict.

- Underestimated the capacity of individual workers to process information.

- Misunderstood how people thought.

- Were overrated, and that there was no one best way of organizing a company.

Stop and criticize

Identify one classical principle still being used in your organization and analyse its negative effects.

Gareth Morgan (1989) presents a continuum of different organization structural forms ranging from a bureaucratic one possessing classical features at one extreme to a flexible, organic network at the other (see figure 15.2). He stated that a bureaucracy could probably evolve from numbers 1 to 3, and perhaps even from number 4, but for an organization to move to 5 or 6 would require a major revolution. Such a transformation would require not only a structural change but also a cultural and a political one. If achieved, it would mean a loss of its bureaucratic features.

Why do the bureaucratic-classical structural features described in this chapter continue to be a feature of the majority of large companies to the present day? Stephen Robbins (1990) suggested seven reasons to account for their continued existence:

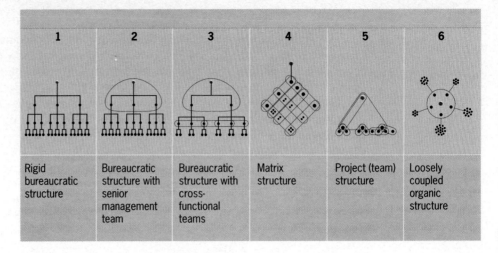

Figure 15.2: Types of organization structure

1. *Success*: For the most part, over the last 100 years, irrespective of technology, environment and people, and irrespective of whether it has been a manufacturing, medical, educational, commercial or military organization, it has worked.

2. *Large size*: Successful organizations survive and grow large, and the bureaucratic form is most efficient with large size.

3. *Natural selection favours bureaucracy*: Bureaucracy's natural features, the six identified at the start of this chapter, are inherently more efficient than any others and thus allow the organization to compete more effectively.

4. *Static social values*: The argument is that Western values favour order and regimentation, and bureaucracy is consistent with such values. People are goal-oriented and comfortable with authoritarian structures. For example, workers prefer clearly defined job responsibilities.

5. *Environmental turbulence is exaggerated*: The changes currently being experienced may be no more dynamic than those at other times in history. Management strategies can also reduce uncertainty in the environment.

6. *Emergence of professional bureaucracy*: Bureaucracy has shown its ability to adjust to the knowledge revolution by modifying itself. The goal of standardization has been achieved in a different way among professional employees.

7. *Bureaucracy maintains control*: Bureaucracy provides a high level of standardization, coupled with centralized power, which is desired by those in command. For this reason senior managers who control large organizations favour this organization design.

In modern organizations, power and authority continue to lie with those at the top. Robbins' seventh reason to explain the appeal of bureaucratic structures among senior management is that it centralizes power in their hands, which appeals to them. Those people at the bottom of the hierarchy are strictly controlled by those above them. In the end, the decision to replace bureaucracy may be a political one.

Rigid bureaucratic structure
This is Weber's classic bureaucratic structure. The organization operates in a very stable environment. Its structure is pyramid-shaped and under the control of a single chief executive. Since all important principles have been codified; and since every contingency is understood and has been anticipated, it is unnecessary for the executive to hold meetings.

Bureaucratic structure with senior management team
The environment is generating novel problems which cannot be anticipated, and for which responses cannot be codified. The chief executive creates a management team of departmental heads who meet regularly to deal with non-routine problems. Department heads have authority over their area of responsibility.

Bureaucratic structure with cross-functional teams
For problems requiring an interdepartmental view, a team is assembled consisting of lower-level staff from different departments. Members attend discussions as departmental representatives. They give the 'departmental view', report back on developments to their department head, delegate problems and information to that person, and receive decisions down. They operate as a less rigid bureaucracy.

Matrix structure
This is the matrix structure described in the previous chapter [**link**, chapter 14, elements of structure]. It attaches as much importance to functional departments, marketing and production as to projects or customer groups. It offers the benefits discussed earlier.

Project team structure
In this design, the majority of the organization's core activities are tackled through project teams. If functional departments do exist, they play a background role. The task consists of completing a series of projects, and the vehicle for task achievement is the team. These teams are given the freedom to manage themselves within the strategic parameters defined by senior management. The organization possesses more of the features of a network of interaction than of a bureaucratic structure.

Loosely coupled organic structure
A small core staff represents the organization and sets its strategic direction. It forms the organization's 'inside' centre and sustains a network which is coupled to others, located 'outside'. It uses contracting to get key operational activities performed. This network of firms is held together by its current product or service. The firm is really an open-ended system of firms, ideas and activities. It lacks a clear organization structure and a definable boundary, making it difficult to determine what or who is inside or outside at any given time.

Based on Gareth Morgan, *Creative Organization Theory*, Sage, London, 1989, pp 64–7.

Contingency approach

Contingency approach to organization structure: a perspective which argues that an organization, to be effective, must adjust its structure in a manner consistent with the type of environment in which it operates, the technology it uses and other contextual factors.

The contingency approach in organizational behaviour refers to the view that holds that the appropriate solution in any specific case depends, is *contingent*, upon the circumstances prevailing at the time. The approach has been influential in topics such as work design, leadership and, not least, organization structuring.

The approach was a reaction to management thinking in the first half of the twentieth century, which was dominated by the search for the 'one best way'. Despite their differing perspectives, Taylor, Weber, Mayo and Fayol all recommended single, universal solutions to management problems, often in the form of laws or principles. Subsequent contributions to the contingency school came from many different researchers, who studied such diverse topics as wage payment systems, leadership styles and job design. They sought to identify the kinds of situation in which particular organizational arrangements and management practices appeared to be most effective.

The approach derives from empirical research (Burns and Stalker, 1961; Woodward, 1965; Lawrence and Lorsch, 1967) which revealed that organizational success was not correlated with a single, simple set of factors but was contingent upon, depended upon, a number of factors. The most important contingency factors are held to be:

- the technology the organization uses;

- its environment, particularly its market;

- the size of the organization;

- the history of the organization;

- the expectations of its employees and customers.

The contingency approach holds that organizational success will be secured when a company achieves a match between its situation and its corporate strategy and organization structure. Thus, the bureaucratic structure described earlier in this chapter is said to be appropriate for (matches) a stable environment, while a turbulent environment require a more flexible or organic structure. A few other aspects of the contingency approach distinguish it from perspectives to be considered in the next chapter:

- It operates on a cause-and-effect basis (e.g. 'if your technology, environment, size, history or employees are like this, then your structure should be that').

- The causal connections are held to run in one direction (e.g. one type of environment will require a particular organization structure).

- It assumes that approximately the same cause will have approximately the same effect, e.g. it does not envisage a situation in which a small difference between two causes can escalate to cause radically different outcomes for a company.

- It assumes success to be the achievement of a state of equilibrium. Since successful firms are all held to be close to equilibrium, the future time paths of successful companies are held to be predictable.

Determinism versus strategic choice

The main debate within the contingency approach to organization structuring is between two of its sub-schools—the determinists and the strategic choice thinkers. The determinists assert that 'contextual' factors, like an organization's size, ownership, technology or environment, impose certain constraints on the choices that their managers can make about the type of structure to adopt. If the structure was not adapted to context, then opportunities would be lost, costs would rise and the organization's existence would be threatened. They view the aforementioned variables as determining organizational characteristics. Meanwhile, strategic writers contend that a company's structure is always the outcome of a choice made by those in positions of power within organizations. Linked to the question of the shape of the organization's structure is that of its performance and efficiency. Both sub-schools are interested in discovering if certain structural arrangements are more conducive to organizational success than others [**links**, chapter 2, the world outside; chapter 3, technology].

Technological determinism: the argument that technology can be used to explain the nature of jobs, work groupings, hierarchy skills, values and attitudes in organizational settings.
Environmental determinism: a perspective which claims that internal organizational responses are wholly or mainly shaped, influenced or determined by external environmental factors.

Contingency and technological determinism

Joan Woodward, James Thompson and Charles Perrow are the leading figures in the technological determinist school. While they all share the belief that technology determines an organization's structure, they differ both in the way in which they classify technologies and in how they conceive of the relationship between technology and organization structure.

Joan Woodward and technical complexity

Joan Woodward
(1916–71)

Joan Woodward was a British academic whose original research interest was not in technology at all but in productivity. She wanted to find out which organizational arrangements led to the highest levels of company economic performance (i.e. profitability). In the 1950s, classical management thinking was still dominant and promoted the 'one best way' to organize. However, since there were competing 'one best way' theories, Woodward sought to determine which of them was best. Her research is significant for at least three reasons. First, she created a typology for categorizing and describing different technologies, which gives us a 'language' with which to discuss them. Second, by discovering that no single organization structure was appropriate for all circumstances, she ended the supremacy of classical management theory and ushered in the modern contingency approach to the design of organization structures. Third, by recognizing the impact of technology on organization design, she began a research tradition that has enhanced our understanding of the relation of new technologies to organizational forms. All of her contributions continue to this day.

Technical complexity refers to the degree of predictability about, and control over the final product permitted by the technology used, and is usually related to the level of mechanization used in the production process.

In her initial attempts to discover the 'best' organization structure, Woodward studied 100 firms in south-east England. Having established their levels of performance, she correlated them with various aspects of organization structure which had been proposed by Weber, Fayol and other classical writers, for example with the number of hierarchical levels, with the span of control, the level of written communication, and so on. She had expected her analysis to reveal the relationship between some of these aspects of organization structure and the level of company performance, but it failed to do so.

In her search for an alternative explanation, she noted that her firms used different technologies. She classified their technologies according to the first date of their introduction; the interrelationship between the equipment used for these processes; and the amount of repetition of operations between one production cycle and the next. This produced a ten-step categorization based on three main types (unit, mass and process) and on increasing **technical complexity** (1 = least complex; 10 = most complex) as shown in figure 15.3.

In unit production, one person works on a product from beginning to end, for example a cabinet maker producing a piece of hand-built furniture. In mass production, the technology requires each worker to make an individual contribution to a larger whole, for example fitting a bumper on a car assembly line. In process production, workers do not touch the product but monitor machinery and the automated production processes, for example chemical plants and oil refineries.

Stop and criticize

Woodward's classification of technologies is based on the manufacture of products. How well does it fit the provision of services? Consider services such as having your windows cleaned, buying a lottery ticket; insuring your car; having a dental check-up, etc. What alternative classification system would you need for these?

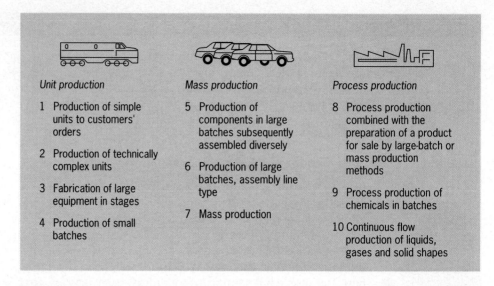

Figure 15.3: Woodward's classification of 100 British manufacturing firms according to their systems of production
From Joan Woodward, *Management and Technology*, HMSO, London, 1958, p.11. Crown copyright. Used with permission.

When she analysed the data in this way, she discovered that a firm's organization structure was indeed related to its performance, but through an important additional variable—technology. Thus, the 'best' or most appropriate organization structure, that is, the one associated with highest performance, depended (or was *contingent*) upon the type of technology employed by that firm. Table 15.5 shows differences in various aspects of organization structure between the firms, based on the type of technology they employed. Thus, it was Woodward (1965) who first introduced the notion of the technological imperative—the view that technology determines an organization's structure. Specifically, she held that it was the complexity of the technology used that determined the structure (table 15.5).

Woodward identified differences in the technical complexity of the process of production and examined the companies' organization structures. Following a statistical analysis, she related their technology to their structure. She found that as the technology became more complex (going from type 1 through to type 10), two main things occurred. First, the length of the chain of command increased, with the number of management levels rising from an average of three to six. The proportion of managers to the total employed workforce rose, as did the proportion of indirect to direct labour. Her second major finding was that the increasing complexity of technology meant that the chief executive's span of control increased, as did that of supervisors. The span of control of first-line supervisors was highest in mass production and lowest in process production. Span of control refers to the number of subordinates supervised by one manager and represents one of the ways of co-ordinating the activities of different employees.

Woodward argued that a relationship existed between a company's economic performance (i.e. profitability) and its organization structure. Having identified these statistical relationships, she went on to make observations about the effectiveness of performance of the companies. In her view, the companies which had an organization structure close to the norm for that category would be more commercially successful than those whose structures deviated from the pattern. This is summarized on the last line of table 15.5. Her conclusion was that 'there was a

Table 15.5: Dimensions of organization structure and type of technology used

Dimension of organization structure	Technology		
production	Unit production	Mass production	Continuous process
Levels of management	3	4	6
Span of control	23	48	15
Ratio of direct to indirect workers	9:1	4:1	1:1
Administrative ratio	low	medium	high
Formalization (written communications)	low	high	low
Centralization (of decision making)	low	high	low
Verbal communication	high	low	high
Skill level of workers	high	low	high
Overall structure type	organic	mechanistic	organic
Great success when possessed	• Narrow span of control • Few levels of management • Decentralized decision making	• Wide span of control • More levels of management • Centralized decision making	• Narrow span of control • Most levels of management • Decentralized decision making

Based on Joan Woodward, *Industrial Organization: Theory and Practice*, Oxford University Press, Oxford, 1965.

particular form of organization most appropriate to each technical situation' (Woodward, 1965, p.72). The reasoning underlying this conclusion is that the technology used to manufacture the product, or make available the service, places specific requirements on those who operate it. Such demands, for example in the need to control work or motivate staff, are likely to be reflected in the organization structure. The technology–structure link is complemented by the notion of effective performance, which holds that each type of production system calls for its own characteristic organization structure.

James David
Thompson
(1920–73)

James Thompson, technology and interdependence

The second contributor to the technological determinist perspective school was a sociologist, James Thompson (1967). He was not interested in the complexity of technologies (as was Woodward) but on the characteristic type of *relationship of interdependence* that each technology created (figure 15.4). His argument was that different types of technology create different types of interdependence between individuals, teams, departments and firms. These specified the appropriate type of co-ordination required which, in turn, determined the structure needed.

Technological interdependence refers to the extent to which the work tasks performed in an organization by one department or team member affects the task performance of other departments or team members. It can be high or low.

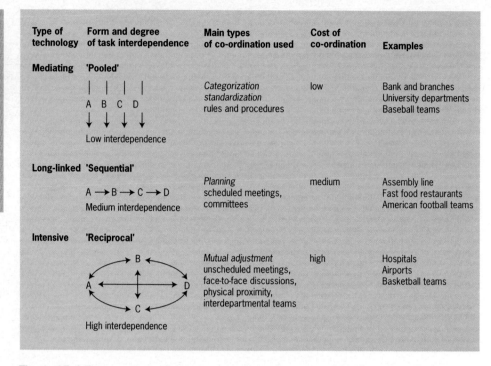

Figure 15.4 Thompson's typology of technology, interdependence and co-ordination

Mediating technology: creating pooled interdependence

Mediating technology: technology that links independent but standardized tasks.

This technology allows individuals, teams and departments to operate independently of each other. Pooled task interdependence results when each department or group member makes a separate and independent contribution to the company or team performance. The individual outputs are pooled. Lecturers running their own courses, secretaries in a firm, sales representatives on the road, insurance claims units and supermarket checkout operators: in each case, the individual contributor's performance can be easily identified and evaluated; and hence the potential for conflict between departments or individuals is low.

Thus, predetermined rules, common forms and written procedures all act to co-ordinate the independent contributions of different units and separate employees, while clearly defined task and role relationships integrate the functions. This produces a bureaucratic organization form in which the costs of co-ordination are relatively low.

Long-linked technology: creating sequential task interdependence

Long-linked technology: technology that is applied to a series of programmed tasks performed in a predetermined order.

Here, the technology requires specific work tasks to be performed in a predetermined order. Sequential task interdependence results when one department or individual group member must perform their task before the next can complete theirs. For example, in an organizational behaviour course taught by three lecturers, sequential task interdependence means that the first one has to complete their sessions on individual psychology before the second can teach group psychology, who is then followed by the third, who presents the material on organization structure. In a car factory, a car has to be assembled before it can be painted. Sequential task interdependence means that a department's or group member's performance cannot be easily identified or evaluated, as several individuals, groups or departments make a contribution to a single product or service.

At the company level, co-ordination is achieved through planning and scheduling, which integrates the work of different departments. At the group level, co-ordination is achieved by close supervision of workers, forming work teams consisting of employees of similar levels of skill, and motivating by rewarding group rather than individual performance. The relative cost of co-ordination with this type of technology is medium.

Intensive technology: creating reciprocal task interdependence

Intensive technology: technology that is applied to tasks that are performed in no predetermined order.

With reciprocal interdependence, all the activities of all the different company departments or all of the team members are fully dependent on one another. The work output of each serves as the input for another. For example, in an organizational behaviour course which uses the group project method, a group of students can call upon different lecturers to provide them with knowledge or skill inputs to enable them to solve the project problems. Each lecturer would notice what the other had done and contribute accordingly. For this reason, with reciprocal task interdependence, the sequence of required operations cannot be predetermined.

Thus, the mechanisms of co-ordination include unscheduled meetings, face-to-face contacts, project groups, task forces and cross-departmental teams. This in turn necessitates a close physical grouping of reciprocally interdependent units, so that mutual adjustment can be accomplished quickly. Where this is impossible, then mechanisms like daily meetings, e-mail and teleconferencing are needed to facilitate communication. The degree of co-ordination required through mutual adjustment goes far beyond what is necessary for the other technologies discussed and is thus the most expensive of the three.

Charles Perrow

Charles Perrow, technology and predictability

Task variety refers to the number of new and different demands that a task places on an individual or a function.
Task analysability refers to the degree to which standardized solutions are available to solve the problems that arise.

Charles Perrow is the third contributor to the technological determinist school. He saw technology's effect on organization structure as working through its impact on the predictability of providing the service or manufacturing a product. He considered two dimensions (figure 15.5). The first he labelled **task variety**, and this referred to the frequency with which unexpected events occurred in the transformation (inputs to outputs) process. Task variety would be high if many unexpected events occurred during a technological process. The second he termed **task analysability**. This term referred to the degree to which the unexpected problems could be solved using readily available, off-the-shelf solutions. Task analysability would be low if individuals or departments had to search around for a solution, and rely on experience, judgement, intuition and problem-solving skills (Perrow, 1970).

Types of technology

On the basis of these two dimensions, Perrow categorized technologies into four types, and discussed the effects of each one upon an organization's structure. He was particularly interested in co-ordination mechanisms, discretion, the relative power of supervisors and the middle managers who supervise them.

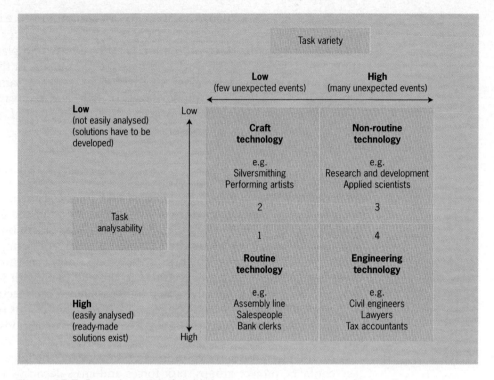

Figure 15.5: Perrow's model of technology
Based on Charles Perrow, *Organizational Analysis: A Sociological View*, Wadsworth, Belmont, Calif. 1970, p.78.

1. *Routine technology*

Located at one extreme in cell 1 are tasks which are simple and where variety is low (repetitive tasks). Task analysability is high (there are standard solutions available). Examples include supermarket checkout operations and fast food hamburger restaurants.

2. *Non-routine technology*

At the other extreme, in cell 3, are complex and non-routine tasks, where task variability is high (with many new or different problems encountered), and task analysability is low (finding a solution to the problem is difficult). The tasks performed by research chemists, advertising agencies, high-tech product designers and top management teams are all examples of non-routine technology.

3. *Craft technology*

Between the extremes, in cell 2, is craft technology, characterized by low task variety and low task analysability. The number of new problems encountered is small, but each requires some effort to find a solution. Examples include a plumber fitting a bath or shower an accountant preparing a tax return.

4. *Engineering technology*

Also located between the extremes, cell 4, is engineering technology, characterized by high task variety and low task analysability. Many new problems crop up, but each is relatively simple to solve. Civil engineering companies which build roads and bridges exemplify this type of technology, as well as motor manufacturers producing customized cars.

When an organization's tasks and technology are routine, its structure is likely to resemble that proposed by Weber and Fayol. With a tall hierarchy, channels of authority and formal, standardized operating procedures are used to integrate the activities of individuals, groups, units and departments. In contrast, when a firm's tasks and technology become complex and non-routine, an organization will tend to use a flatter hierarchy, more cross-functional teamworking, greater face-to-face contact to allow individuals, groups units and departments to observe and mutually adjust to each other, and engage in decision making and problem solving.

Summary of technology and structure

As technological determinists, Woodward, Thompson and Perrow all focused upon the way in which they believed that technology determined a company's structure. Following up on Woodward's original work, both Thompson and Perrow sought to explain some, although not all, of the relationships that she had discovered between the type of technology and the most appropriate organization structure for a company seeking to maximize its performance. Both their explanations focused on how different types of technology created uncertainties within organizations, and these needed to be managed by using co-ordination mechanisms. These, in their turn, produced the company's characteristic structural design (figure 15.6).

James Thompson's explanation of the technology–structure relationship was in terms of the type of interdependency (pooled, sequential or reciprocal) which was created by the type of technology used (mediating, long-linked or intensive). As uncertainty increased, so did the need for individual and departmental activities to be co-ordinated flexibly.

Charles Perrow's explanation of technology's effect on organization structure

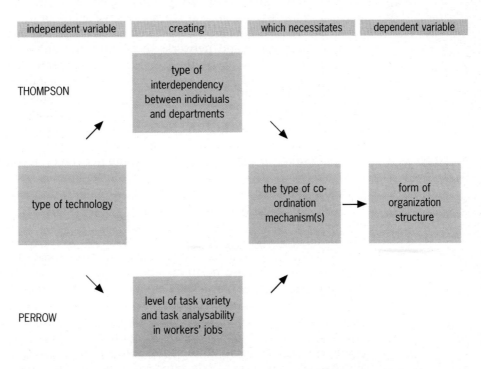

Figure 15.6: Comparison of Thompson's and Perrow's approaches to technology

was similar, but he emphasized its effect on the jobs of the workers, rather than the interdependencies created. He argued that a decline in the certainty with which a company could manufacture a product or provide a service (as measured by the number of unexpected problems it encountered and the degree of their analysability) meant that organizational co-ordination mechanisms such as rules, policies and procedures which were designed to anticipate problems and suggest solutions in a prescriptive and inflexible manner became less useful. In their place, more flexible ones which addressed the unexpected outcomes in a problem-solving manner were needed. For this reason, a prescriptive, rule-based organization structure would be very different from a flexible, problem-solving one.

Contingency and environmental determinism

The second strand of determinism in organization structuring has been environmental. Several researchers have had an interest in the relationship between a company's environment and its structure. Some of them argue that success depends on securing a proper 'fit' or alignment between itself and its environment. For these environmental determinists, environment dictates organization structure. One prominent environmental determinist, Paul Lawrence, even said, 'Tell me what your environment is and I shall tell you what your organization ought to be' (Argyris, 1972, p.88).

The environmental determinists see the organization as being in constant interaction with the environment within which it exists. That environment consists of 'actors' or 'networks' (e.g. competitors, investors, customers). It includes the general economic situation, the market, the competitive scene, and so on. Each organization has its own unique environment. The more actors or networks that are relevant to a given company, the more complex its environment is said to be (figure 15.7). Organizations vary in the relative degree of their *environmental complexity* (Duncan, 1972; 1973; 1974; 1979) [**link**, chapter 2, the world outside].

Those same actors and networks in an organization's environment can also change a great deal or remain the same. They thus differ in their degree of *environmental dynamism*. Different industries vary widely in their degree of dynamism. At one extreme of stability is the mainframe computer industry, where new players must confront the barriers of an entrenched set of standards and where the costs of switching are high. Here, the concepts of market segmentation, economies of scale and pre-emptive investment are all still important. Mainframe computers are not immune to change, as the mini-computer and PC revolutions showed, but there are periods of considerable stability. In the middle of the range, one finds that businesses like branded consumer goods. Substitution ranges from medium to high, and new entrants can replace established ones, but not overnight. Survival and success depend on capabilities and network relationships. Most industries are located in this middle ground. At the extreme of turbulence is a situation where customers can constantly and easily substitute. It consists of networks of players whose positions and prospects change suddenly and unpredictably. Many internet businesses are located at this end of the spectrum.

Environmental determinists argue that because a company is dependent on its environment for its sales, labour, raw materials, and so on, that environment constrains the kind of choices a organization can make about how it structures itself. As the environmental situation changes, the organization–environment relationship also changes. Hence, to be effective, a company has to structure and restructure constantly to maintain alignment. The environmental determinists use the key concepts of environmental uncertainty and complexity in their explanations. These will be considered later.

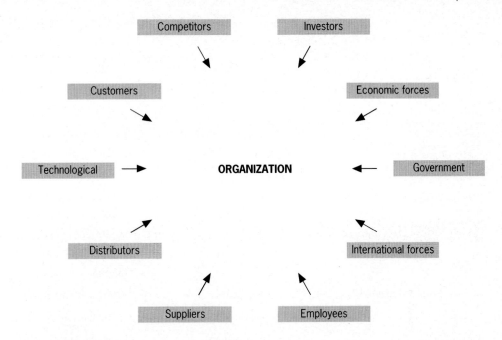

Figure 15.7: An organization depicted in its environment consisting of different 'actors' and 'networks'

Tom Burns, G.M. Stalker, mechanistic and organic organization structures

Mechanistic structure: a type of organization structure possessing a high degree of task specialization, many rules and tight specification of individual responsibility and authority, and one in which decision making is centralized.

Organic structure: a type of organization structure possessing little task specialization, few rules and a high degree of individual responsibility and authority, and one in which decision making is delegated.

In the late 1950s in Britain, Tom Burns and Graham M. Stalker studied the behaviour of people working in a rayon mill. Rayon is a yarn or fibre produced by forcing and drawing cellulose through minute holes. They found that this contented, economically successful company was run with a management style which, according to contemporary wisdom about 'best' management practice, should have led to worker discontent and inefficiency. Some time later, the same authors studied an electronics company. Again it was highly successful, but it used a management style completely different from that of the rayon mill studied earlier. This contradiction gave the authors the impetus to begin a large-scale investigation to examine the relationship between the management systems and the organizational tasks. They were particularly interested in the way management systems changed in response to changes in the commercial and technical tasks of the firm (Burns and Stalker, 1961).

The rayon mill had a highly stable, highly structured character which would have fitted well into Weber's bureaucratic organizational model. In contrast, the electronics firm violated many of the principles of classical management. It discouraged written communications, defined jobs as little as possible, and the interaction between employees was on a face-to-face basis. Indeed, staff even complained about this uncertainty. The authors gave the label 'mechanistic' to the first form of organization structure and 'organic' to the second. These represented ideal types at opposite ends of a continuum. Most firms would be located somewhere in between (table 15.6).

Burns and Stalker argued that neither form of organization structure was intrinsically efficient or inefficient, but rather that it all depended on the nature of the environment in which a firm operated. In their view, the key variables to be considered were the product market and the technology of the manufacturing

Table 15.6: Characteristics of mechanistic and organic organization structures

Characteristic	Rayon mill (Mechanistic)	Electronics (Organic)
Specialization	High—sharp differentiation	Low—no hard boundaries, relatively few different jobs
Standardization	High—methods spelled out	Low—individuals decide own methods
Orientation of members	Means	Goals
Conflict resolution	By superior	Interaction
Pattern of authority, control	Hierarchical—based on implied contractual relation	Wide net based upon common commitment and communication
Locus of superior competence	At top of organization	Wherever there is skill and competence
Interaction	Vertical	Lateral
Communication content	Directions, orders	Advice, information
Loyalty	To the organization	To project and group
Prestige	From the position	From personal contribution

Based on Joseph A. Litterer, *The Analysis of Organizations*, John Wiley, Chichester, 1973, p.339.

process. These needed to be studied when the structure of a firm's management system was being designed. Thus, a **mechanistic structure** may be appropriate for an organization which uses an unchanging technology and operates in relatively stable markets. An **organic structure** can be more suitable for a firm which has to cope with unpredictable new tasks.

Paul Lawrence, Jay Lorsch, organization design and environmental needs

Paul Roger
Lawrence (b.1922)

Jay William Lorsch
(b. 1932)

During the 1960s, Paul Lawrence and Jay Lorsch (1967) built on the work of Burns and Stalker, using the concepts of **differentiation** and **integration**. Differentiation refers to the process of a firm breaking itself up into sub-units, each of which concentrates on a particular part of the firm's environment. A university differentiates itself in terms of different faculties and departments. Such differentiation inevitably leads to the sub-units developing their own goals, values, norms, structures, time frames and interpersonal relations that reflect the job that they have to do and the uncertainties with which they have to cope.

Considering differentiation first, Lawrence and Lorsch found that effective organizations increased their level of differentiation as their environment became more uncertain. This was because it allowed staff to respond more effectively to their specific sub-environment for which they were responsible. On the other hand, the more differentiated the sub-units became, the more their goals would diverge, the more they would perceive the same things differently, and hence the more conflict there would be between them.

Turning next to integration, Lawrence and Lorsch use this term to refer to the process of achieving unity of effort among the previously differentiated sub-systems in order to accomplish the organization task. It is thus equivalent to co-ordination. Thus, having divided the university into faculties and departments, there is the need to ensure that all contribute to the goals of high-quality research, excellent teaching and income generation. The authors found that as environmental uncertainty increased, and thus the degree of differentiation increased, so

> **Differentiation** is the degree to which the tasks and the work of individuals, groups and units are divided up within an organization. **Integration** is the required level to which units in an organization are linked together, and their respective degree of independence. Integrative mechanisms include rules and procedures and direct managerial control.

organizations had to increase the level of their integration (co-ordination) between people in different departments if they were to work together effectively towards a common goal.

When environmental uncertainty is low, differentiation too is correspondingly low. The units share common goals and ways of achieving them, and the hierarchy of authority in a company and standard procedures are sufficient to integrate the activities of different units and individuals. However, as uncertainty increases, so too does the need for integration, and so too do the number of integrative devices used. Lawrence and Lorsch argued that the level of uncertainty in the environment that a firm has to cope with will determine the organization structure that is most appropriate for it.

> **Stop and criticize**
>
> How well are the activities performed by your educational institution differentiated and integrated? Identify the problems and recommend solutions that would improve organizational performance from the student perspective.

Recap

1. *Distinguish between charismatic, traditional and legitimate forms of authority.*
   - Traditional authority is based on the belief that the ruler has a natural right to rule.
   - Charismatic authority is based on the belief that the ruler has some special, unique virtue, either religious or heroic.
   - Legitimate authority is based on formal written rules, which have the force of law.

2. *State the main characteristics of a bureaucratic organization structure as specified by Max Weber.*
   - Job specialization; authority hierarchy; employment and career; recording and keeping of all administrative acts and decisions; rules and procedures to which all employees are subject; and impersonality of those procedures and rules, meaning that they apply to all equally.

3. *Summarize the approach and main principles of the classical management school.*
   - Based on the experience of managers and consultants rather than researchers.
   - Distinguished six managerial activities: forecasting, planning, organizing, commanding, co-ordinating and controlling.
   - Distinguished fourteen principles of management: division of work; authority; discipline; unity of command; scalar principle; unity of direction; interest subordination; remuneration; centralization; order; equity of treatment; stability

   of employment; opportunity for initiative; and *esprit de corps*.

4. *Identify the writers who comprise the contingency approach and state their main individual contributions.*
   - Contingency writers challenged Max Weber's and Henri Fayol's view that there was one best way to structure an organization.
   - They held that there was an optimum organization structure that would maximize company performance and profits, and that this structure would differ between firms.
   - Technological contingency theorists Joan Woodward, Charles Perrow and James Thompson saw technology determining appropriate organization structure.
   - Environmental contingency theorists Tom Burns and G.M. Stalker, Paul Lawrence and Jay Lorsch saw the environment determining appropriate organization structure.

5. *Discuss the strengths and weaknesses of early ideas on the design of organization structure and the practice of management.*
   - Provides a rationally designed organizational model that allows complex tasks to be performed efficiently. Persons who are best qualified to do it carry out the work. It provides safeguards against personal bias and individual favouritism.
   - It creates dysfunctional consequences of members

only interested in their own jobs, following rules obsessively and being slow to respond to changes. Bureaucracies perpetuate themselves.

6. *Identify the influence of early organization design ideas on contemporary organizations.*
   - Modern organizations continue to possess the features described by Weber and Fayol over a century ago.
   - Early design principles have been successful, have helped large organizations to survive, reflect the static social values of many nations and cultures, are capable of withstanding environmental turbulence and allow senior management to retain power.

Revision

1. Commentators argue that both too much and too little bureaucracy in an organization de-motivate employees and cause them stress. How can this be?

2. How does uncertainty affect the successful operation of rationally designed organization structures such as those proposed by Weber and Fayol.

3. Which of Fayol's principles of management emphasize human relations? Which emphasize production efficiency? Which emphasize the organizational or administrative aspects of management?

4. Define and distinguish differentiation from integration. Using an example from your experience or reading, illustrate these two processes in operation, and then highlight some of the problems that can be encountered.

5. Explain how technology and environment might influence the structure of an organization. Consider their effect on co-ordinating activities.

Springboard

Bauman, Z., 1991, *Modernity and the Holocaust*, Polity Press, Cambridge.

The Holocaust was unique among genocides in history because it involved the large-scale extermination of large numbers of people in death camps such as Auschwitz using bureaucratic means. Bauman argues that the organization structure of bureaucracy, with its emphasis on the division of labour, impersonality, rule following and abrogation of personal responsibility, made the Holocaust possible.

Burns, T. and Stalker, G.M. 1994, *The Management of Innovation*, Oxford University Press, Oxford.

This 1961 classic has been republished. It is one of the most influential books in organization theory and industrial sociology. Its central theme is the relationship between an organization and its environment, particularly technological and market innovations.

Du Guy, P., 2000, *In Praise of Bureaucracy*, Routledge, London.

Explores and analyses the positive and creative potential of bureaucracy in a time of complexity, uncertainty and disorder.

Jaques, E., 1990, 'In praise of hierarchy', *Harvard Business Review*, January–February, pp.127–33.

An article summarizing his thoughts on managerial accountability, hierarchy and the time span of discre-

tion for a managerial audience. A good starting point from which to move on to some of his more complex books.

Kanter, R.M., 1983, *The Change Masters: Corporate Entrepreneurs at Work*, George Allen & Unwin, London.

Her discussion about various organization structures introduces the terms 'integrative' and 'segmentalist', echoing similar distinctions from the past.

Kanter, R.M., 1989, *When Giants Learn to Dance*, Simon & Schuster, London.

Consideration of flexibility and speed of response possessed or lacked by large corporations. It includes a consideration of the types of organization structures.

Miller, E.J. (ed.), 1999, *Tavistock Institute Contribution to Job and Organizational Design* (2 vols), Ashgate, Aldershot.

Provides a historical overview and assessment of the theories, models and authors from the Tavistock Institute in London that contributed extensively to thinking about organization change and design.

Spear, S. and Bowen, H.K., 1999, 'Decoding the DNA of the Toyota production system', *Harvard Business Review*, September–October, pp. 97–106.

The Toyota system is well known. This article focuses on the unspoken rules that underpin the system and how they are taught to new employees.

Home viewing

Crimson Tide (1995, director Tony Scott) is the story of how a global emergency provokes a power play on a nuclear submarine between a pair of senior US naval officers on the *USS Alabama*, the battle-hardened Captain Frank Ramsay (played by Gene Hackman), who 'goes by the book', and his executive officer, Lt Commander Ron Hunter (Denzil Washington). When an order is issued, but is only half-received, concerning a nuclear strike, Hunter demands confirmation while Ramsay insists on unquestioning obedience to the rules.

List the different aspects of bureaucratic organization structure portrayed. Which of the two senior officers, Ramsay or Hunter, subscribes more to Weber's principles? Does adhering to bureaucratic principles 'save the day' or nearly cause disaster? Beyond the concern with bureaucracy, can you identify the formation of cliques? On what basis do they form? Are there examples of group pressure being exercised?

OB in literature

Joseph Heller, *Catch 22*, Jonathan Cape, London, 1955.

Set during the Second World War, it describes a world turned upside down where the supplies manager has more power than a general, and anyone seeking a discharge on the grounds of insanity is considered sane enough to keep on fighting. Which dysfunctional aspects of bureaucratic organization structures are illustrated in the book?

Chapter exercises

1: Personal orientation test

Objectives

1. To allow you to assess your preference for working within a bureaucratic organization structure.

2. To introduce you to the characteristics of Max Weber's bureaucracy.

Briefing

For each statement, tick the box that best represents your feelings:

Statement	Agree	Disagree
1. Job descriptions should be detailed and complete so everyone knows exactly what they are supposed to do.		
2. I like a predictable organization.		
3. Organization charts should be constructed so that everyone understands where they fit into the organization's structure.		
4. Relations with colleagues should be formal in nature.		
5. Rules, policies and procedures provide me with guidance, avoiding the danger of my making a mistake.		
6. Authority should be clearly related to position in each department so that higher-level positions have authority over lower-level ones.		
7. Senior managers should set objectives and communicate them down the hierarchy.		
8. Before accepting a job, I would like to see an exact job description.		
9. Work roles should be specialized with each person making their unique, expert contribution.		
10. Promotion should be based on demonstrated technical competence.		

2: Managerial activities quiz

Objective

1. To allow you to distinguish between Henri Fayol's six managerial activities.

Briefing

Indicate, by placing a tick under the appropriate heading, which one of Fayol's managerial activities is being described.

F: Forecasting: P: Planning O: Organizing
M: Motivating CD: Co-ordinating CN: Controlling

| | **Managerial activity** | | | | | |
	F	P	O	M	CD	CN
1. Government inspectors visit schools to assess their performance against a checklist and grade each one.						
2. The lecturer explains to students how working hard to get a good degree will help them to get a good job.						
3. The national census data will determine how many old people there are, and what residential care facilities will be needed.						
4. The government decides to increase the number of university students by 50% and considers how, and over what time period, to do this.						
5. The introductory course is divided between a number of staff, each of whom gives a number of lectures.						
6. Course team members meet periodically to ensure that their individual contributions complement each others' and that there are no gaps.						

3: Learning the rules

Objectives

1. To introduce you to the concepts of tacit knowledge and basic rules.

2. To illustrate how Socratic questioning and problem solving is used by Toyota to teach its workers that knowledge.

Briefing

1. Read the following case.

2. Divide into groups and apply the same approach to (a) tying a shoelace, (b) writing an essay.

How Toyota's workers learn the rules

If the rules of the Toyota production system aren't explicit, how are they transmitted? Toyota's managers don't tell workers and supervisors specifically how to do their work. Rather, they use a teaching and learning approach that allows their workers to discover the rules as a consequence of solving problems. For example, the supervisor teaching a person the principle of the first rule ['All work shall be highly specified as to content, sequence, timing and outcome'] will come to the work site and while the person is doing his or her job, ask a series of questions:

- How do you do this work?
- How do you know you are doing this work correctly?
- How do you know that the outcome is free of defects?
- What do you do if you have a problem?

This continuing process gives the person increasingly deeper insights into his or her own specific work. From many experiences of this sort, the person gradually learns to generalize how to design all activities according to the principles embodied in rule one. All the [four Toyota] rules are taught in a similar Socratic fashion of iterative questioning and problem solving. Although this method is particularly effective for teaching, it leads to knowledge that is implicit. Consequently, the Toyota production system has so far been transferred successfully only when managers have been able and willing to engage in a similar process of questioning to facilitate learning by doing.

From Steven Spear and H. Kent Bowen, 'Decoding the DNA of the Toyota production system', *Harvard Business Review*, September–October 1999, pp.97–106, p.99.

Chapter 16 Organization strategy and design

Key concepts

complementarities

strategic choice

enacted environment

managerial enactment

vertical integration

bounded instability

explosive instability

stable equilibrium

merger

acquisition

strategic alliance

joint venture

unilateral agreement

network organization

virtual organization

Learning objectives

When you have read this chapter, you should be able to define those key concepts in your own words, and you should also be able to:

1. Understand how contemporary perspectives on, and discussions of, organization structure differ from past ones.

2. Appreciate the reciprocal relationship between corporate strategy and organization structure.

3. Discuss theories that explain managerial changes in corporate strategy and organization structure with respect to the environment.

4. Distinguish between bounded instability and non-linearity, and state their implications for corporate strategy.

5. Define a 'transaction' and distinguish three major types of institutional arrangement for the conduct of transactions.

6. Differentiate between the main types of mutual inter-organizational arrangement.

7. Identify the distinguishing features of a virtual organization.

Saving the world from the indignities of the company picnic. One person at a time.

Working for yourself sounds like more fun. FreeAgent.com lets you choose from thousands of great projects at leading companies. We even offer things like health insurance and tax filing. It's like being part of a team. Without the potato salad.

FreeAgent.com for a brave new workforce.

Advertisement in the US edition of *Wired,* March 2000, pp.7–8.

Why study organization strategy and design?

After more than two decades of being in the shadow of more popular management topics such as leadership and teamwork, the subject of organization structure has re-emerged as the 'hot topic' at the turn of the millennium. Commentators are in agreement that some new form of organization is emerging which differs in most respects from its classical predecessors, and which has been dubbed 'post-bureaucratic'. Exactly what shape (or shapes) the new form will take is still not clear, but flexible, indirect, internalized controls exercised on the basis of cultural and ideological values are likely to be distinguishing features. Earlier in the book, we discussed this issue in relation to the environment [**link**, chapter 2, the world outside: the post-modern organization]. Here, the link is with strategy.

If the media rhetoric comes true, the quaint practice of travelling in to work, entering a building which contains 'your' office, deciding what your priorities are for the day and meeting colleagues for a discussion will all be things of the past. Instead, your work location will be where you are; your targets and tasks will be communicated to you by your boss through your cellphone and laptop; and if you are visiting headquarters, you will need to book a 'hot desk' before you arrive. Welcome to the world of the virtual organizations! For the manager, this arrangement offers reduced office overheads, but at the cost of less control over employees. For employees, it offers flexible working, but no real social contact with colleagues.

The centrality and importance of the new organization structures is reaffirmed every day in the world of business, technology, media and education. Whenever one reads about partnering relations, alliances, supply chains, networks, e-commerce, and just about anything with the prefix 'virtual' (as in organizations, teams, universities, markets, etc.), then one is considering organization structure. The new concept of organization sees them as 'a combination of both external circumstances and internal dynamics' (Adcroft and Willis, 2000). Gerry Johnson and Kevan Scholes observe that while a particular structure will not itself ensure the success of a company's corporate strategy, an inappropriate structure can impede its achievement (Johnson and Scholes, 1999, p.42):

> So the issue is how they [managers] might restructure the organization (internally) to reflect and exploit those developments, and how they might relate (externally) to other organizations within the value chain.

Andrew Pettigrew (1999, p.1) commented that:

> In describing new forms of organizing, the use of the active word 'organizing', instead of the passive term 'organization', is important. In the present competitive situation, few firms see organization change as a move from one static structure to another. Rather, innovations in organizing are seen as a strategic activity designed to improve flexibility, creativity and responsiveness of the company. The active term organizing thereby recognizes the dynamic and perpetual and simultaneous character of the process of changing. Organizing also entails a much more inclusive process with alterations in structural form being continuously shaped alongside movements in organization process and boundaries.

Discussing organization structures

The resurgence of interest in organization structures has created its own problems. Current debates about the topic differ in four significant ways from those of the past. They have become:

- less internal, more external focus;
- more strategy, less organizational behaviour;
- more new language, less old;
- less concrete, more abstract.

Less internal, more external focus

Early writings on organizations took a 'closed system' perspective and considered them to be insulated from their environments. Later contributions acknowledged the existence of historical and environmental variables on organizations (e.g. their origin, size, technology and market volatility) but still focused on the impact of these on the internal structural adjustments that the company made. When the environment was considered, it was seen as relatively unchanging—whether placid, volatile or somewhere in between. In contrast, modern theorists and researchers of structure integrate the external and internal perspectives. First, they focus beyond the boundaries of the individual organization, examining it in its environment, seeing how and why it links with other organizations in an ever more chaotic environment. Only then do they return to consider how such developments impact upon the organization's own internal structural arrangements.

More strategy, less organizational behaviour

One consequence of this change of emphasis has been that organization structure is increasingly being discussed in relation to strategy issues. John Kay (1999) defined the field of strategy as being concerned with the match between a company's internal capabilities and its external environment. From this perspective, organization structure becomes the vehicle for implementing any chosen strategy. Managers have always considered strategy and structure together, as have strategy lecturers in management and business schools. Organization behaviour academics have until recently avoided this field, but they may find it difficult to continue to do so.

More new language, less old

The language of discussion has changed in four ways:

- Corporate strategy concepts such as alliance, outsourcing, market segmentation, strategic advantage, core competences, critical mass and strategic innovation have become interwoven into discussions and explanations of organization structures.

- The language used to discuss organization structure has become more abstract and uses new models and paradigms. For example, the increased application of systems thinking invites consideration of abstract concepts such as bounded instability, stable equilibrium, negative feedback and nonlinearity.

- The language used to describe and contrast the emerging organizational forms is not precise. In the corporate strategy literature, the differences between the forms are neither explicit nor consistent (e.g. between a joint venture and an alliance).

- Some authors refer to a particular form (e.g. network organization) normatively, to describe what a company *should* become if it is to be competitive and survive; others use it as a metaphor; still others describe concrete examples of it. John Child and David Faulkner (1998) note that many of the terms used in current discussions of organization structures are 'destined to remain more indicative than precise' (p.113).

Less concrete, more abstract

Historically, organizations have been specific to a particular space, time and history, and their physical resources (management, personnel and equipment) have been their defining characteristics. However, due to the internet and the telecommunications revolution, many of the traditional barriers that have separated organizations are now disappearing. Never before could you have 'visited' a company like Amazon.com while seated at your own computer anywhere on the planet with a telephone socket or a modem and a mobile phone.

While many physical aspects of organizations continue to exist, albeit in a modified form, their perceptual aspects (e.g. what constitutes 'the organization') are now less clearly bounded and more abstract. Harrington (1991) referred to the distinction between perceptual organization and physical organization. Indeed, the distinctiveness and solidarity of organizations is becoming increasingly suspect as the boundaries that separate them from other organizations become ever more permeable due to outsourcing, alliances and networks. Cynthia Hardy and Ian Palmer (1999, p.389) stated that:

> Internally, organization structure is increasingly difficult to pin down because fluidity, flexibility and fast response break down the barriers between formally discrete levels and departments. Activities that would be centralized at corporate headquarters or divided into clear divisional or departmental responsibilities are, in modern organizations, distributed between an evolving, internal network of units.

Corporate strategy and organization structure

The terms 'corporate strategy', 'business strategy' and 'strategic management' are often wrongly used interchangeably. Although they are connected, they refer to different things.

Corporate strategy Addresses the question of 'what business are we in?' It is concerned with the determination of the future direction and scope of the entire organization and is performed by top management. In Virgin Ltd, Richard Branson and his senior management team decide this question.

Business strategy Relates to that part of the corporate strategy which is relevant to one of the company's divisions or business units. Thus Branson and his senior managers will set the corporate strategy of Virgin Ltd. Within that, Virgin Entertainment, Virgin Travel and the other Virgin business units that together make up the company will each have their own business strategies.

Strategic management Refers to the ongoing process performed by managers, which seeks to develop strategy while keeping the company matched to its environment. Virgin Ltd's executives are expected to manage strategically.

An organization's goals typically include growth, profitability and return on investment. Companies failing to achieve their goals will either go out of business or else become targets for takeovers. Historically, organizations have tended to pursue their strategic goals and manage their dependence on their environment unilaterally. The conventional wisdom held that strategic success criteria had to do with consistency, regularity and stability—the paradigm of the stable equilibrium organization. From this perspective, installing organization structures to implement the strategy to achieve goals involved designing hierarchical reporting, information and control systems, defining roles, allocating responsibilities, drawing up organization charts, etc. Such an 'internal' focus was the norm. Robert Grant (1998) summarized the evolution of corporate strategy during the second half of the twentieth century (table 16.1).

The first three rows of Grant's table—those to do with 'dominant theme', 'main issues' and 'principal concepts and techniques'—relate primarily to corporate strategy issues. The fourth row, the one that deals with organizational implications, concerns organization structure. The final, right-hand column summarizes the currently related concerns in these two fields. Reading across to those columns, from left to right, three contrasts are evident:

The lion's friendly approach

As the chairman of ING, one of Europe's biggest financial-services companies, Godfried van der Lugt likes clarity. He pulls out a slide, littered with colourful shapes, showing its activities around the world. The red circles, he explains, mark areas of market leadership while green squares signal the need for organic growth. And the blue triangles? 'That's where we're planning acquisitions', he replies, his eyes twinkling. 'You don't get strategy much clearer than that'.

From 'The lion's friendly approach', *The Economist,* 18 December 1999, pp.149–50, p.149.

Table 16.1: The evolution of corporate strategy

Period	1950s	1960s	1970s	Late 1970s to early 1980s	Late 1980s to early 1990s	Mid to late 1990s
Dominant theme	Budgetary planning and control	Corporate planning	Corporate strategy	Analysis of industry and competition	The quest for competitive advantage	Strategic innovation
Main issues	Financial control through operating budgets	Planning growth	Portfolio planning	Choice of industries, markets, and segments, and positioning within them	Sources of competitive advantage within the firm	Strategic and organizational advantage
Principal concepts and techniques	Financial budgeting Investment planning Project appraisal	Forecasting Investment planning models	Synergy SBUs Portfolio planning matrices Experience curves Returns to market share	Analysis of industry structure Competitor analysis PIMS analysis	Resource analysis Analysis of core competences	Dynamic sources of competitive advantage Control of standards Knowledge and learning
Organizational implications	Financial management the key	Rise of corporate planning departments and five-year formal plans	Diversification Multidivisional structures Quest for global market share	Greater industry and market selectivity Industry restructuring Active asset management	Corporate restructuring and business process re-engineering Refocusing and outsourcing	The virtual organization The knowledge-based firm Alliances and networks The quest for critical mass

From Robert M. Grant, *Contemporary Strategy Analysis*, Blackwell, Oxford, 1998, p.18.

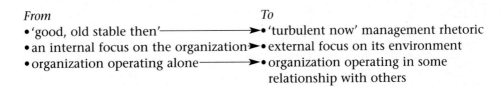

From   *To*
- 'good, old stable then'————————➤• 'turbulent now' management rhetoric
- an internal focus on the organization➤• external focus on its environment
- organization operating alone————————➤• organization operating in some relationship with others

Raymond Miles and Charles Snow (1986) conceived of more of a two-way influence between strategy and structure. Managers made strategic choices based on their perceptions of the environment and of their organization's capabilities. The success of these choices rested on how well their chosen competitive strategy matched the environmental conditions and management processes. They argued that, historically, strategy and structure have evolved together. Each advance in structural form was stimulated by the limitations of the previous form; and each new form built upon the previous form, highlighting its predecessor's strengths and weaknesses. Simultaneously, each development in structure permitted new competitive strategies to be pursued by the company. Innovative organization forms were thus developed to cope with new environmental conditions. They distinguished the most common generic strategies—prospectors, defenders and analysers (table 16.2). They argued that each strategic orientation also specified the major structural and managerial features needed by the company to support it.

Table 16.2: Strategy and structure

Corporate strategy	Organization structure
Prospector 'First-to-the-market', innovation-oriented, finding, developing and exploiting new opportunities; see their products as short-term ventures. They are better at developing prototypes than long-term, efficient production.	Flexible structure, which uses autonomous work groups or product divisions for planning and control; is highly decentralized. Permits market responsiveness but not at the expense of overall specialization and efficiency.
Defender Offers a limited, stable product line. They are cost-effective, maintain quality and use price competition to create barriers and defend their position against potential competitors.	Mechanistic structure, which relies on a functional form with centralized decision making and control, vertical integration, and high degrees of technical specialization.
Analyser Combines the strengths of defenders and prospectors. Pursues a 'second-in' strategy, imitating and improving on their competitors' product offerings, producing a range of high-quality products at lower cost.	Mixes functional and divisional structures to create a matrix where project or brand managers act as integrators between resource groups and project units. Internal differentiation allows some parts flexibility and change, while other parts remain traditional and stable.

Based on Raymond Miles and Charles Snow (1978; 1984; 1986)

Complementarities refer to the potential for mutually reinforcing effects when one or more business practices are operated in parallel or simultaneously.

Richard Whittington, Andrew Pettigrew and their colleagues (Whittington *et al.*, 1999a) developed Miles and Snow's 'equal partners' idea of strategy and structure, arguing that the new organizational 'fit' involves not only these two variables but also the other processes within an organization. In their view, these variables should not be interlocked in a static way but should be in a 'continuous co-evolution of a complex whole'. Their notion of the new fit is based on **complementarities**. These refer to the potential for mutually reinforcing effects when one or more business practices are joined together. Practices are said to be complementary when doing more of one increases the returns for doing more of another. Research suggests that within a company, there is a need to link strategy and structure to process. For example, the introduction of a just-in-time system needs to be complemented by appropriate manufacturing, information and human resource systems.

Strategic choice and environments

Strategic choice is the view that holds that the environments, markets and technology of an organization are the result of senior management decisions.

The debate about contemporary organization design involves consideration of the decisions that managers make about their organizations within their environments. Thus, strategic choice and environment are central concepts. Both Tom Burns and Graham Stalker (1961) and Paul Lawrence and Jay Lorsch (1967) stressed the importance of an organization's environment. Their original contributions were concerned primarily with market conditions and took a deterministic perspective [link, chapter 15, early organization design]. Their critics, however, pointed to the neglect of choice in decisions about organization structure. John Child (1972) rectified this omission, arguing that there was no one best organization structure and that companies could have different structures. However, he disagreed with the contention that those structures were determined by 'external, operational contingencies'. Instead, he stressed the part played by powerful

The INNFORM project

This research used an international survey to compare new forms of organizing in Europe between 1992 and 1996. A total of 450 large and medium-sized European companies responded. While finding no evidence of revolutionary change, the researchers discovered, as predicted by complementary theory, that 'whole system' change was required for success. To reap the benefits of organizational innovation, companies had to think and act holistically, making carefully aligned innovations in:

- *Structures:* delayering; decentralization of operations, although not strategic decisions; and greater use of project team structures to increase horizontal knowledge and resource sharing; and new human resource practices.

- *Processes:* investments in information technology and intranets to support internal networking to share knowledge horizontally and spread accountability vertically. Investments were also made in training and team and mission building.

- *Boundaries:* a focus on core competences, increasing use of outsourcing, joint ventures and alliances, but limited diversification.

Researchers concluded that high performance was obtained when change was implemented in many of the nine elements detailed in the figure below. Piecemeal changes (with the exception of IT) produced little performance benefit. Indeed, single innovations frequently produced loss of performance. Few European firms simultaneously changed their structures, processes and boundaries. However, the 5 per cent that did so in a complementary way gained an average performance premium of 60 per cent. The change element that singly produced the greatest benefit was investment in information technology.

New forms of organizing: the multiple indicators

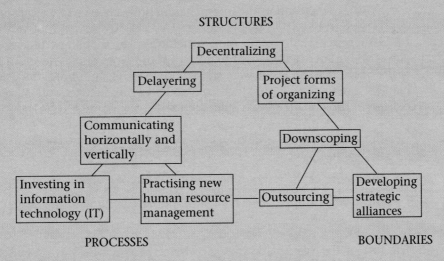

Source: Pettigrew (1999, p.1)

The authors noted that while many companies were moving towards flatter and more flexible ways of organizing, few were doing so coherently. They concluded that it was only those who innovated coherently that reaped the rewards. Piecemeal initiatives typically cost more than they were worth.

Based on Whittington *et al.*, 1999a; 1999b; Ruigrok *et al.*, 1999; Pettigrew, 1998; 1999; Pettigrew and Fenton, 2000.

leaders and groups, who exerted their influence to create organizational forms which suited their particular preferences.

Strategic choice holds that decisions about the number of hierarchical levels, the span of control, etc. are ultimately based on the personal beliefs and political manoeuvrings of those who make them. Strategic choice researchers continue to focus on companies' environments, but they became interested in how senior managers make the choices that link their firms' strategies to their organization structures. These commentators have criticized the deterministic writers on a number of issues:

1. *The idea that an organization should 'fit' its environment.* That is, while there are choices about organization structure design, these will be relatively limited. Thus, for two similar companies operating in a stable environment to succeed, each would make similar choices about the shape of their organization structures. However, there are examples of companies making very different structural choices in the same circumstances and both succeeding.

2. *The idea that cause and effect are linked in a simple (linear) manner.* This ignores the fact that organizations are part of a larger, complex environmental system consisting of other organizations with which they interact. Managers can create their own environments, and the idea that organizations merely adapt to their environment is too simple a view.

3. *The assumption that the choice of organization structure is an automatic reaction to the facts presented.* However, studies show that such decisions are made by managers on the basis of the interpretations that they have made about the nature of their environment. The same environment can be perceived in different ways by various managers, who might implement different structures, which can be equally successful.

4. *The view that choices of organization structure are not political.* Linked to the previous point, political factors will impinge on choices about structure as much as issues of perception and interpretation [**link**, chapter 24, power and politics].

Child suggested that organization structuring was a political process in which power and influence were used to decide on the types of jobs, levels of hierarchy, spans of control, etc. that were to be adopted and, by implication, also which markets to enter and with which companies to link up. His work stimulated discussion in three main areas (Child, 1997):

- the human agents (individuals or groups) who exercise choice in the design of organizations;

- the nature of the environment within which an organization exists;

- the relationships between organizational agents (e.g. managers) and that environment.

Enacted environment refers to those parts of the environment that an organization's managers perceive.
Managerial enactment is the active modification of a perceived and selected part of the organization's environment by managers.

The first of the two major strategic choice perspectives was presented by Karl Weick (1979), who argued that managers' perceptions of their organizations' environments provided the basis for their choices. Hence the focus should be on how they make such decisions. Perception theory tells us that while some environmental factors will be included, others will be filtered out and ignored [**link**, chapter 7, perception]. The latter will thus not be considered in their deliberations and choices. Hence exactly the same environment may be perceived differently by two organizations' managers. Their perceptions will be important in their decisions, not only about the most appropriate organization structure but also the firm's corporate strategy and management processes.

In Weick's view, managers *enact* rather than *react* to their environments. That is, they *create* their organization's environment, making it easier for them to understand and modify it. The term 'enactment' is used to indicate that the managers do not simply anticipate react or adapt to what they observe other organizations or other people doing in their environment. Instead, they take actions on the basis of their subjective perceptions of what is happening or might happen. They change their environment rather than being changed by it. This is different from the view of the environmental determinist school discussed in the previous chapter [**link**, chapter 15, early organization design]. However, the fact that managers make choices (based on their perceptions of their organization's environment) about their organization's strategy, processes, structures and relationships with other firms does not tell us *why* they should do so. Two other researchers offered the explanation for this.

The second major strategic choice perspective was presented by Jeffrey Pfeffer and Gerald Salancik (1978). Their theory sees every organization as being at the mercy of its environment, needing resources from it in the form of employees, equipment, raw materials, knowledge, capital and outlets for its products and services. The environment, which gives it power, also controls access to these resources. It makes the firm dependent on its environment. Hence the name of the theory. The environment (in the form of customers, suppliers, competitors, government and other stakeholders) uses its power to make demands upon the organization to provide not only desirable products and services at competitive prices but also efficient organization structures and processes.

Pfeffer and Salancik argue that although organizations are dependent on their environments, their managers can still achieve their chosen objectives. To do this, they need to identify the critical resources needed—defined as those without which the company cannot function. They then trace these back to their sources in their environment and identify the nature of their dependence. For practical reasons, only the most critical and scarce resources are focused on. While it is possible to distinguish and discuss a single dependency relation between an organization, in practice, a firm will be experiencing a complex set of dependencies between itself and the various elements in its environment.

For example, for McDonald's fast food restaurants, having beef, buns and cheese is critical having plastic customer seating is not. Scarcity refers to how widely available that resource is in the organization's environment. Control of resources that are most critical and scarce gives environmental elements the greatest power over a company. Pfeffer and Salancik state that the first step in applying the approach is to understand the organizational environment with respect to criticality and scarcity of resources. The second step is for managers to find ways of reducing that dependency, eliminating it altogether, or making the others dependent on their organization.

| **Vertical integration** refers to a situation where one company buys another in order to make the latter's output its own input, thereby securing that source of supply through ownership. |

One dependence-reduction strategy is to buy up all the resources that are critical to your company. In the case of a motor manufacturer, these would mean steel for car bodies, rubber for tyres, coal to fire factory furnaces, and ships and railways to transport this material. In order to secure access to the critical resources that he needed, we know that Henry Ford bought iron mines, coal mines, rubber plantations, shipping lines and railways [**link**, chapter 13, traditional work design]. This corporate strategy, which involves acquiring related businesses assimilated into the purchaser, is called **vertical integration**. Although a popular strategy, mergers and acquisitions are only one of many kinds of relationship that one company can have with another, as it seeks to reduce its dependency on its environment. Pfeffer and Salancik referred to their ideas collectively as the *resource dependence perspective theory*.

Stop and criticize

Select an organization that you have read about or have first-hand experience of. What is its strategy? How effective is it? What advice or recommendations would you make to its chief executive and the company board?

Bounded instability and non-linearity

Both Miles and Snow's and Pfeffer and Salancik's theories describe organizational environments that are unchanging enough to be understood by and acted upon by their managers. By about the mid-1990s, however, such thinking had changed. Commentators noted how organizations' environments, in both the private and public sectors, had become more complex, more prone to sudden unexpected changes, and would continue to be so in the future. Neil Glass (1996) summarized some of these features, which are shown in table 16.3.

Glass' assertion is one that is reinforced by the management rhetoric. It holds that the past was more predictable, and that such predictability has now disappeared. On the other hand, business historians who have studied the 'capitalist era', which began between the eighteenth and nineteenth centuries, challenge this view. Indeed, some of the management literature from the early twentieth century talks about 'an era of unprecedented social and technological change'. What we now refer to as the 'globalization' of trade was, in many instances, as widespread in 1990 as it is today. Hence, one cannot take it for granted that the past consisted of 'good old, stable days', whereas the organizations of today face increasingly turbulent environments (see Thompson and Davidson, 1995).

Stop and criticize	How does the rhetoric of 'turbulent environments' serve the interests of different groups? Consider this question from the point of view of managers, management consultants and the media.

Table 16.3: Organizations: past assumptions and current realities

Past assumptions	Current realities
Closed systems The organization is almost a simple 'closed system'. Generally, what it decides to do will take place without too much disruption from outside events.	*Open systems* Organizations are complex 'open systems' constantly, deeply influenced by and influencing their environments. Often, intended actions will be diverted off-course by external events or even by internal, political or cultural processes of the organization itself.
Stable environment The operating environment is stable enough for management to understand it sufficiently well to develop a relevant detailed strategy and for that strategy to be relevant by the time it comes to be implemented.	*Turbulent environment* The environment is changing so rapidly (continuously throwing up new opportunities and threats) that top management cannot expect to have sufficient sense of what is happening to formulate very detailed strategies. Moreover, by the time a strategy moves from concept to being operationalized, key aspects of the environment have often changed.
Predictable causality In an organization or an economy, there are a series of levers that you can apply to cause a known response (e.g. if you cut staff numbers, profitability should go up; if you increase interest rates, the value of your currency will rise).	*Unpredictable causality* The simple linear models of cause and effect have broken down and many actions can lead to quite unexpected (positive or negative) effects.

Based on Neil Glass, 'Chaos, non-linear systems and day-to-day management', *European Management Journal*, 1996, vol.14, no.1, pp.98–106, p.99.

Bounded instability is a state in which there is a mixture of order and disorder, many unpredictable events and changes, and in which an organization's behaviour has an irregular pattern.
Explosive instability is a state in which there is no order or pattern.
Stable equilibrium is a state in which the elements are always in, or quickly return to, a state of balance.

Bounded instability has a very specific scientific meaning. It refers to a state in which there is a mixture of order and disorder, but in which a basic pattern of the system's behaviour can be discerned. It can be contrasted with **explosive instability**, which is a state in which there is no order or pattern whatsoever. Glass (1996) argued that over the last 20 years, car markets had been affected by changes in oil prices, environmental pressure and consumer tastes. In 2000, the British government's Competition Commission's report into car prices; and reports into the selling of cars by the Consumers' Association and P&O Stenna Ferries, plus the start of internet car shopping in general, have increased industry uncertainty. In such a situation, motor manufacturers will tend to abandon long-term forecasts and instead will seek to identify and exploit general trends.

Historically, the concept of bounded instability is understood in relation to that of a **stable equilibrium**. The latter is a state whose elements are always in, or will quickly return to, a state of balance. Central heating systems with preset thermostats provide a domestic illustration of the concept. For many years, motor car and soap powder markets were in stable equilibrium. Product improvements and advertising affected sales of one company's product for a while, before the market shares of competitors returned to broadly the same percentages.

Commentators argue that, for many organizations, bounded instability has replaced stable equilibrium. Airlines have found that denationalization, followed by greater competition, dramatically changed their working environment (Colling, 1995). In Britain, banks were first challenged by legislation opening up competition from building societies; then by telephone banking; and shortly after, by internet banking. Competitors come from nowhere to dominate the market. For example, in 1999, Freeserve, the internet service provider (ISP) developed by Dixon's, the British high street electrical goods retailer, was floated on the stock exchange as a separate business. It has now been joined, and its future threatened, by other free or near-free ISPs.

A linear system is one in which a given action will cause a directly predictable outcome. Turn on a tap and water flows out. In non-linear systems, actions tend to have both expected and unexpected outcomes (both positive and negative) because changes or complex interactions of factors tend to amplify consequences. Hence, in complex, non-linear systems, small actions can very quickly create unforeseen consequences which are self-reinforcing. Actions can produce outcomes which are both unexpected and directly opposite to those intended.

New firms from nowhere

In fragmented, vertical markets, in which buyers and sellers have difficulty finding each other, there are consequent inefficiencies and high costs for everybody; there are no actors to push e-commerce forward. Chemdex is a business-to-business 'infomediary', and its founding chief executive is Mr David Perry. He is seeking to create a single market for life sciences research products in which everything can be sold, from monoclonal antibodies and restriction enzymes to beakers and Petrie dishes. The market for such products is currently worth $15 billion in America but is highly fragmented, with most of the 15,000 suppliers having sales of only $10 million or less. The largest company has a 15 per cent marker share. At the start of 1998, Chemdex had three suppliers offering 5,000 products; a year later, 40 suppliers were offering 125,000 products; at the end of 1999, 333 suppliers are selling more than a million products. Chemdex expects revenues of $129 million in 2000.

Based on 'Vertically challenged', *The Economist*, 6 November 1999, p.98.

Complexity and non-linearity in Cumbria

In February 2000, the British Nuclear Installations Inspectorate (NII) published a damning report into the falsification of safety data concerning MOX pellets destined for Japanese reactors, by staff at the Sellafield nuclear reprocessing plant in Cumbria in north-west England. Following this disclosure:

- John Taylor, the chief executive of BNFL, resigned.

- In March, equipment in the vitrification unit of the plant was sabotaged and detectives were interviewing employees.

- BNFL's biggest customer, Japan, insisted on returning the processed fuel rods that were accompanied by the false data. It warned that it would impose a permanent boycott of the company.

- Germany, Sweden and Switzerland instituted similar boycotts, and the USA planned to send a team of safety inspectors.

- The Irish and Danish governments then began discussing a bid to have BNFL shut down because of the environmental damage caused by its discharges into the North Sea.

- The British government was considering ending all nuclear reprocessing at Sellafield.

- Plans for the partial privatization of BNFL by the government were shelved.

The cause of the data falsification was that workers were said to have become bored by the repetitive process of measuring the uranium–plutonium oxide pellets. Their work was tedious, repetitive and not strictly necessary as computers had already performed the task. However, BNFL's Japanese customers insisted that it was done to ensure quality control. These employees simply copied the results of the previous tests to save themselves work. The full consequences of their actions are continuing to have an impact on the company.

Based on Cathy Cooper, 'Management blasted at nuclear plant', *People Management*, 2000, vol.6, no.6, 19 March, pp.16–17: 'Running scared', *The Economist*, 8 April 2000, p.37.

Structuring and managing endemic uncertainty

Complexity theory has been applied to business to understand the behaviour of large complex systems. The problem for managers is determining how all the different forces and elements interact to shape the overall system, especially in a situation where minor events can have enormous consequences because of the chain reaction that they trigger off. Chaos theorists argue that since radical uncertainty is now endemic, traditional, analytically driven strategies to shape the needs of the business are obsolete. The best management structures, they claim, do not adapt to their environment but emerge from it. The *survival* of the fittest has been replaced by the *arrival* of the fittest.

Sherman and Schultz wrote that the shift to a non-linear world means that the organization structure of any business works best when it is self-organized. Rather than imposing a given structure upon a company, senior management should allow the organization of effort and people to evolve in response to ongoing messages from customers. Being a complex system, the market reflects intricate, low-level interactions, and the best solutions to problems come from those who are constantly communicating with one another at ground level, rather than being issued with directives by those on high. The invisible hand of the market replaces the visible hand of the manager. The 'try something and see what happens' is the guiding principle.

Based on Thomas M. Hout, 'Are managers obsolete?' *Harvard Business Review*, March–April 1999, pp.161–8; Sherman, H. and Schultz, R., *Open Boundaries: Creating Business Innovation Through Complexity*, Perseus Books, Reading, Mass. 1998.

In an unpredictable environment, where it is difficult or impossible to plan, strategic intent replaces strategic planning. This involves setting a fairly clear direction, then continuously adapting the detail to cope with specific events, threats and opportunities. One needs entrepreneurial and creative people who are constantly on the lookout for small advantages. However insignificant these advantages may appear to be at the time, they can often be quickly amplified into self-reinforcing positive outcomes for the company. The stress is upon creating self-renewal, never-ending improvement and on rewarding change agents. In other words:

$$\text{contextual change} \rightarrow \text{organization strategy} \rightarrow \text{human resource requirements} \rightarrow \text{organization structure}$$

Market, hierarchy and interorganizational relationships

The environmental volatility discussed earlier has led many organizations to abandon isolation in preference to establishing interorganizational relationships. Discussions of organization structure have therefore increasingly focused on co-operative relationships between organizations, intended to develop new, joint strategies. Table 16.4 contrasts three 'ideal-type' organization forms. These do not describe any particular existing organization. Instead, each represents a model or provides a checklist against which to compare and assess real organizations.

On the far right of the table, the market portrays a particular 'perfect' market situation. Economists define this as a situation in which buyers and sellers possess full (perfect) knowledge of prices. On the left of the table is the hierarchical form, which is best represented by Max Weber's bureaucratic arrangements [**link**, chapter 15, early organization design]. In the centre are interorganizational relationships, characterized by various co-operative arrangements between organizations. Here it is important to identify those organizations that are networked (via technology or by some umbrella organization perhaps), and whose relationships typify the characteristics of the true network form, which emphasizes trust, common needs, etc. Not all examples of the interorganizational form—alliances, joint ventures or networks—will necessarily be governed or co-ordinated in a way that fits with the descriptors shown in table 16.4. In reality, a single organization will often exhibit all three types of arrangement because hierarchy, interorganizational forms and market are ideal-type concepts and in reality are not found in a pure form or in isolation.

Market

This perspective from market economics contrasts the relationship between the 'unplanned' nature of market relations between individuals, groups and organizations and the 'planned' nature of hierarchical organizational life. Institutional economists like Oliver Williamson (1975) and business historians like Alfred Chandler (Chandler, 1962; Chandler *et al.*, 1999) start from the perspective of a world without organizations and ask how and why they should arise. They then focus on the exchanges that take place between individuals, which they call 'transactions'. The selling of an item by one party and its purchase by another represents a 'transaction'. The authors consider how these can be achieved at the lowest cost to those involved.

In pursuing goods and services, individuals could obtain all they needed through the marketplace. The market will work to the benefit of all concerned, except when it 'fails', i.e. becomes inefficient. In these circumstances, they argue, transactions are removed from the marketplace and placed instead within organizations (which Williamson chooses to call 'hierarchies'). The interest of these writers was solely upon these two structural forms (markets and hierarchies), and focuses on the reasons why transactions occur in one or the other and why they move between them. The market is a central concept in economics, which is frequently encountered in strategy but is not one that is often discussed in organizational behaviour. The market model sees the co-ordination of social activity as being accomplished by private dealing between individuals, groups or organizations. Once a transaction is completed between the parties, it does not imply any repetition in the future. Markets are a way of bringing together buyers and sellers. A free-competition market has the following features (Colebatch and Lamour, 1993, pp.19–20):

- There are a large number of buyers and sellers.
- They know what they want.
- They are able to pay for it.
- They act independently of each other.
- They are free to enter and leave the market.
- Information about products and processes is free and accessible.
- There are no costs on making deals.

British National Health Service: from hierarchy to market?

In the early 1990s, under the Conservative government of Mrs Margaret Thatcher (now Lady Thatcher), the British National Health Service (NHS) was reorganized. At that time, it represented an example of a bureaucratic, hierarchical organization, and possessed all its advantages and disadvantages. In an effort to improve the efficiency of health care delivery, the government introduced the element of market discipline, thereby seeking to change its organizational form from hierarchy to that of the market.

Specifically, this meant that general practitioners (GPs) and health authorities were given funds to purchase certain health services from hospital and community providers. These were services which had previously been provided by the health authorities themselves. Hospitals were reorganized into nonprofit hospital trusts, thereby giving hospital and community health providers autonomous status. Separating the purchasing of services from their provision, and encouraging purchasers to respond to price signals, created a market.

Research into this political-economic innovation has revealed a variety of responses. In some situations, the NHS hospital trust's contract with the local health authority was an exceedingly detailed and formalized affair. In other situations, this was less so. Moira Fischbacher's case study conducted in the Glasgow area found that contracts were neither as detailed nor as specified as elsewhere. She argued that a network rather than a true market had developed. The purchasers and providers established long-term relationships (relational contracting) which were based on mutual trust, and they relied on social relationships rather than formal annual contracts to organize the activities and exchanges between themselves. She concluded that this case demonstrated the move from a hierarchy to a network, rather than to a market, as the Conservative government had wanted. In the late 1990s, the Labour government decided to modify the NHS structure once again and removed the purchasing function and contracting system from GPs and health boards, thereby returning the NHS to a more unified structure or hierarchical form.

Based on Moira Fischbacher and Arthur Francis, 'Purchaser provider relationships and innovation: A case study of GP purchasing in Glasgow', *Financial Accountability and Management*, 1998, vol.14, no.4, pp.281–98.

Table 16.4: Contrasting organization arrangements

	Hierarchy	Interorganizational relationships (includes *some* alliances, joint venture, consortia and network organizations, including virtual)	Market
Organizational boundaries	Single administrative authority	Blurred boundaries between firms	Distinct boundaries between firms
Flexibility	Low	Medium	High
Resource/asset management	Resources are managed within the organization.	Resources are complementary and may be jointly owned. Firms can influence the management of one another's resources.	Resources can be the basis of competition between firms and are used to gain competitive advantage.
Communication and co-ordination	Actors communicate within the framework of a formal bureaucracy in which activities are co-ordinated through a clear organizational hierarchy in which actors have degrees of authority. Communication is exercised through routines, rules and procedures.	Actors communicate on an open, often informal basis and activities are negotiated between parties. Communication may be face to face, articulated through contracts and/or electronically mediated. Activities are co-ordinated through mutual agreement and often interorganizational teams, which span individual firm boundaries.	Actors communicate on a formal basis and through contracts.
Information exchange	Information is widely shared within the organization in accordance with departmental and individual relationships depicted in the organization's structure chart/diagram.	Information is exchanged between parties on an ongoing basis. This is one of the key characteristics of network forms and is often a key motive for engaging in collaborative relations.	Information is exchanged largely through the price mechanism and relates to the product/service not to any internal aspects of the organization (e.g. the methods of production, costs, etc.).
Relationship between actors	The basis of actor relationships is the employment contract. There is a medium to high degree of trust between parties, and actors exhibit a high degree of dependency upon the employing organization.	Parties are interdependent. There is an expectation that the relationship between firms will endure for some time and that mutual trust will be developed over time.	Parties are independent of one another. The basis of their relationship is mainly competitive and does not advocate open exchange of information. There is no expectation of an enduring relationship.

Developed by Moira Fischbacher

Stop and criticize

To what extent is there a market in higher education at the present time? What are the costs and benefits for students and for the university if the former act as 'buyers' and latter behave as 'sellers'?

Hierarchy

This is the structural arrangement that most people think of when someone says 'organization'. In this context, the term 'hierarchy', is used in two different, albeit related, ways. First, following Williamson, it refers to a situation in which some transactions are removed from the marketplace and take place instead within the boundaries of a single organization, when, for example, a company decides to stop contracting out its catering and provides the service itself. Institutional economists would say that an organization hierarchy arises when the boundaries of a firm expand to bring within it the flow of transactions and resources that were previously conducted in the marketplace. A fully integrated corporation, in the traditional style, is then created in order to (Chandler, 1962; 1990):

- co-ordinate administrative activities;
- reduce risk and the cost of transactions; and
- take advantage of the economies of scale and scope.

Merger refers to a situation in which two companies voluntarily join together, pooling the ownership interests of the two sets of shareholders, who come to own the new combined entity.

Acquisition refers to a situation in which one firm buys the equity stake or assets of another. A major control acquisition is called a 'takeover' and may be friendly or hostile.

The second and more familiar usage of the term 'hierarchy', refers to the traditional structural arrangement whose various forms and typically mechanistic features were discussed earlier [**link**, chapter 14, elements of structure]. This is the most integrated and most formal arrangement. It is neither interorganizational nor co-operative. The organization is a single entity, although it may be divided into parts. The National Health Service in the UK is a single organization but consists of NHS trusts. Nevertheless, its members share many of the same values and norms, follow its practices and procedures, and exchange information about problems to be dealt with. The two concepts of hierarchy come together when, for example, having decided to end outsourcing its catering, a company establishes its own catering department and appoints a catering manager, who then appoints assistant managers, supervisors and restaurant staff. That is, a hierarchical structural arrangement is established to provide the service.

A single hierarchy arrangement can result from two companies merging, or of one company acquiring another. A corporate **merger** pools the ownership interests of shareholders of the previously separate companies, whereas in an **acquisition**, one firm buys the equity stake or the assets of another. Whichever form of combination is adopted, the assets of the two organizations are integrated and managed jointly, while their personnel are assigned positions within a single

Music direct?

Consider the changing marketplace for music at the start of the twenty-first century. Music buyers used to visit their local music stores in city centres to buy pre-packaged discs. How do they get their music now? In particular, what effect has the internet had on music purchase?

Consider the effect of the changes that you observe on the artists, recording companies, music publishing houses and music retailers. Are we close to reaching direct source-to-consumer selling in this retail sector, or is there still some way to go?

organization hierarchy. Mergers and acquisitions are most likely to occur when the assets of the two companies cannot easily be separated, where joint management is required, or where there is a high risk of assets being appropriated by one of the companies. The advisability of mergers (Haspeslagh, 1999) and of acquisitions (Anand, 1999) to form such a single hierarchical organization have been the focus of much debate in corporate strategy.

Contrasting markets with hierarchy, markets work best when the transactions between the parties:

- are straightforward;
- are non-repetitive;
- do not require specific investment in the transaction; and
- when all the necessary information is conveyed by price and is sufficient.

Hierarchies work best when the transactions between parties:

- are certain;
- occur frequently;
- require specific investments of time, money, energy, equipment and technology; and
- are not easily transferred out to the market.

Stop and criticize	You are the manufacturer of an internationally famous brand of alcoholic drink. A large part of your product's image and success is based on the packaging that surrounds your bottle and its contents. It is this that customers first see on the supermarket shelves. To obtain this, you are currently considering either establishing your own in-house printing–packaging department or tendering out your requirements to sub-contractors. List the advantages and disadvantages of each option.

Old-fashioned takeover?

In the first two weeks of 2000, America Online (AOL), the world's biggest internet service provider, agreed to take over Time Warner, the world's biggest traditional media company, giving the former control of the latter's content. The all-share deal is valued at £150 billion (twice the gross domestic product of Switzerland) and created one of the biggest half dozen companies in the world. Hailed by many as one of the 'new wave' mergers of the twenty-first century, it has been seen by others as an old-fashioned vertical integration. Such restructuring would be familiar to both Henry Ford and Alfred P. Sloan (head of General Motors in the early part of the century). Both engaged in similar practices. Ford bought up iron mines, rubber plantations and shipping and railway lines. Sloan, through acquisition and vertical integration, created a giant corporation that 'built a car for every purpose and purse'.

Critics argue that AOL is pursing a similar strategy of conglomeration in order to rule cyberspace, but at a time when access to greater resources, economies of scale and stability are not as important as in the past. Instead, flexibility, speed and agility are the crucial attributes. They feel that partnership arrangements, without the fixed costs, inventories and management headaches of pure ownership, are the antithesis of vertical integration. As one observer put it, 'there is no need to own content when you can partner for it'.

Based on John A. Byrne, 'Is this baby built for cyberspace?' *Business Week*, 24 January 2000, p.36.

Interorganizational relationships

Between hierarchy and markets, one finds intermediate examples of interorganizational relationships in which two or more organizations share resources and activities to pursue a common strategy. Walter Powell (1987, p.67) noted that 'By looking at the economic organization as a choice between markets and contractual relations on one side, and at conscious planning within a firm on the other, we fail to see the enormous variety that forms of co-operative arrangements can take'. He concluded that these non-market, non-bureaucratic organizational relationships were becoming highly significant features of the modern organizational landscape. Literature reviews have identified the internal and external triggers that lead organizations to form networks [link, chapter 18, organizational change]. The main ones are summarized in table 16.5.

Powell noted how many organizations had revamped their relationships with trading partners, suggesting a 'wholesale stampede into various alliance-type combinations'. His use of the phrase 'alliance-type' exposes the inconsistency and ambiguity of the existing terminology in the literature. The term 'interorganizational relationships' is used here to refer generically to the wide range of different co-operative relationships entered into between two or more organizations. The most common examples will be distinguished, defined and exemplified.

Strategic alliance refers to an arrangement in which two firms agree to co-operate to achieve specific commercial objectives.

One popular example of an interorganizational form is the **strategic alliance**. This is a tight, formalized, contractual relationship with a legal element, in which two firms co-operate to achieve certain commercial objectives for mutual advantage. An alliance may relate to supply or purchase agreements, to marketing or

---

Table 16.5: Triggers for interorganizational collaboration

Internal triggers

- Limited essential expertise
- Ensure the survival of the firm
- Increased profitability potential
- In foreign markets and cultures
- Limited finance for development
- Limited technological know-how
- Collecting information about a competitor
- Realization that market opportunities cannot be exploited solo
- Realization that a partner can produce a good more efficiently
- Limited management expertise / desire to buy in management talent
- Lack of resources for marketing products and services to best advantage
- Finding a means to replace the market mechanism (rather than trading in a market setting, the firm enters into a longer-term networking arrangement, which effectively supersedes the market)

External triggers

- Government encouragement (e.g. grants, allowances)
- Regional policy to 'lift the game' of a depressed region
- Spreading business risk by diversifying out of a single economy
- Overcoming pressure generated by customers in the marketplace
- Overcoming prejudice in a market by joining with an indigenous partner
- Generating national or global flexibility by being able to join and leave networks
- Taking advantage of a naturally occurring phenomenon, e.g. the opportunity to regenerate an area following a flood

From Ewa Buttery, Liz Fulop and Alan Buttery, 'Networks and inter-organizational relations', in Liz Fulop a nd Stephen Linstead (eds), *Management: A Critical Text*, Macmillan Business, London, 1999, pp.414–463: 416–17.

distribution agreements, or similar areas. Alliances tend to be established over a single specific initiative, although they may later be extended to cover other activities between the two companies. In a strategic alliance, companies merge a limited part of their domain with each other and attempt to achieve, with their existing respective value chains, the competitive advantage that might have individually eluded them.

One recent example of an alliance in the financial services industry took place between Standard Life and the Royal Bank of Scotland. The former, a life assurance company at the time, owned 30 per cent of the latter, a retail bank. The two undertook to cross-sell each other's products and services. When a customer indicates an interest in a mortgage, the Bank of Scotland branch will deal with all aspects of the mortgage up to the point where it needs to address the endowment. At this stage, the customer is referred to a financial consultant, an independently employed and regulated agent, who works with Standard Life on the endowment side of the mortgage. Another example is the Star Alliance in the airline industry, which involves code sharing. The airlines involved sell each other's connecting services on a single ticket. Alliances have been popular in uncertain industries such as biotechnology, as well as distant geographical markets (Reuer, 1999).

One reason that strategic alliances are created by companies is to bring about organizational learning. Rather than the partners being involved in skill substitution (one produces, while the other sells), they are interested in learning from each other, thereby strengthening the areas in which each is weakest. The primary reason for alliance creation is to secure specific competencies and resources to survive and succeed in globalizing markets, particularly those in which technologies are rapidly changing. Research shows, however, that often they end in disappointment for the organizations involved (Koza and Lewin, 1999).

Stop and criticize

For whom are strategic alliances more beneficial, the producer or the consumer? Consider the advantages and disadvantages for each group.

Joint venture refers to an arrangement in which two or more companies remain independent but establish a new organization that they jointly own and manage.

A second form of interorganizational relationship is the **joint venture** and the consortium. Here, two (joint venture) or more (consortium) companies remain independent but establish a new organization, which they jointly own and manage. The relationships between them are formalized, either through shareholding arrangements or by agreements specifying asset holding and profit distribution. For example, the Swiss company Nestlé, established a joint venture with America's General Mills in the specific field of breakfast cereals. Both parties' other businesses remained separate from this venture (Mitchell, 1999; Anand, 1999). During the early 1990s, Western European companies set these up with companies in the ex-Soviet bloc. They provided investment and expertise, while the latter supplied labour and entry to markets. The arrangement continues to be popular with Western companies operating in China.

Ford: strategy and structure

Jacques Nasser, president and chief executive of Ford, likes to test cars before he buys them. Earlier this year, Mr Nasser drove a tiny electric vehicle—built entirely of thermoplastic—from the carmaker's Michigan headquarters to Detroit airport. He liked it so much he bought the company and completed the deal last Friday by inaugurating Norway's first car plant, where the so-called 'Think' electric car will be built. As a guide to future car manufacturing, the plant is telling. All the components are bought in. Panels are colour-coded, avoiding the need for a paint shop. Assembly is simple and does not require a skilled workforce. Cars will be distributed and serviced by Hertz, Ford's rental subsidiary.

Mr Nasser is promising to make Ford the world's leading *consumer* company for automotive products and services. 'This industry is being transformed from a nuts and bolts industry into a consumer one, and from a transaction industry into a relationships business', he says. 'Ford Motor Company is essentially a design, engineering, manufacturing and distribution business—that part of it won't necessarily change. But gone are the days when we can rely on those basic disciplines'. So Mr Nasser has shaken up the entire group to be more consumer-oriented and more nimble in meeting customer demand.

Last month, he announced a management reorganization involving new geographic business units and consumer-defined divisions. That was followed by news of a joint venture with Oracle to exploit the internet in components purchasing and supply chain management. Since being appointed, Mr Nasser has signed a web-based alliance with Microsoft; acquired Volvo Cars of Sweden; formed a premier automotive group for luxury brands including Jaguar and Lincoln; and purchased Kwik-Fit, Europe's largest car repair business, while seeking to persuade its suppliers to sub-assemble more of its cars. It may eventually subcontract final assembly altogether.

Through these actions, Ford is seeking to extend its role from manufacturing to retaining a relationship with customers throughout the vehicle's lifetime. It means financing, servicing, insuring and ultimately recycling customers' Ford vehicles. The profit motive is clear. Margins in financial services and maintenance are more attractive than in manufacturing. Mr Nasser has also decided to de-merge or spin off Visteon, Ford's parts arm, which he hopes will improve flexibility and cut components purchasing costs. 'Compare our record results with anyone in the industry, and you will see how we are building Ford for the future', he said.

Based on Tim Burt, 'Ford chief takes a new direction', *Financial Times*, 15 November 1999, p.32; 'The revolution at Ford', *The Economist*, 7 August 1999, pp.61–2.

A third example of interorganizational relationship is *subcontracting* or outsourcing. This involves one organization selecting some of the tasks that it requires to be performed, to be done by outside companies. In many cases, such tasks might have previously been performed by the company itself, e.g. cleaning, transport logistics (delivering goods). The contracting organization is not likely to own its sub-contractor. In Britain, hospitals have outsourced their catering. In Powell's view, such contracting was 'blurring their [firms'] established boundaries and engaging in forms of collaboration that resemble neither the familiar "arm's length" market contract, nor the former, hierarchical, vertically integrated one. These include linking large, generalist firms with specialist, entrepreneurial start-ups, and large firms with other large firms into global strategic partnerships'.

Unilateral agreement refers to a co-operative arrangement in which one firm provides another with a service on a fairly intimate basis in exchange for money.

A fourth type of interorganizational relationship can be found in **unilateral agreements**. Here, one firm provides another with a service on a fairly intimate basis in exchange for money. Examples include provision of consultancy advice, training courses, marketing and technical transfer agreements and relational sub-contracting. A minority investment of a large company in a small one would also be an instance. Since the relationship is strictly financial, the service being provided for payment, the level of interdependence between the parties is very limited indeed. A company that ends a relationship with one supplier can establish a new one with another.

Outsourcing the HR function

BP Amoco signed a record £370 million, five-year deal to contract out the bulk of its human resources (HR) function to Exult, a US-based company. Exult beat PriceWaterhouseCoopers and two other 'Big Five' consulting firms. BP Amoco has 82,000 staff, and under the deal, the HR spend will be £90 per head per year. Exult will administer nearly all of BP Amoco's HR functions, including training, employee relations policy, recruitment and legal compliance. The core strategic HR function will remain in-house, and the vice-president of HR will stay with the oil giant. The 300–350 BP Amoco staff who will transfer to Exult will eventually be working on contracts for other firms.

A spokesman for the oil firm said that the deal would free in-house managers to concentrate on strategy and would mean their taking on greater amounts of higher-level HR work for BP Amoco. Other UK organizations which have signed similarly comprehensive outsourcing deals include the local government councils of Westminster (in London) and Lincolnshire (in eastern England). The human resource profession fears that if such outsourcing deals become widespread, the HR function will be fatally downgraded and its contribution marginalized.

Based on Jane Pickard, 'The truth is out there', *People Management*, 2000, vol.6., no.3, 3 February, pp.48–50.

Cisco-Atlantech unilateral agreement

Cisco Systems is the world's leading manufacturer of internet-based telecoms infrastructure. In 1999, it had a market capitalization of $220 billion, 24,000 employees and an annual revenue of $12.2 billion. In 1999, it bought a 10 per cent stake in Atlantech for £5 million. Atlantech was created in 1992 by David Sibbald on his return from the United States. It is based in Cumbernauld in Scotland and employs 110 staff. Its products ensure that different internet networks can communicate with each other. For example, its AccessVision software monitors that an internet service provider's infrastructure is working and ensures that transactions are secure.

Global sales through the internet are expected to exceed £155 billion in the next 18 months, and it is estimated that $360 billion of capital investment will be made by companies around the world in network systems. To take advantage of this, companies like Atlantech must not only have the right products but also possess established distribution channels. Prior to this development, Atlantech had been licensing its products and technology. Under the new arrangement, its branded products will be sold as Cisco's own by the latter's 4,000-strong sales force. As a result of this agreement Atlantech expects a 200 to 400 per cent increase in sales, which will raise turnover to £10 million. Sibbald has not ruled out a full take-over by Cisco, but he is happy with the present situation, 'They haven't imposed any direct rule and everything seems to be working in harmony', he said.

Based on Sharon Ward, 'Golden grin of the Cisco kid', *Sunday Herald*, Business, 14 November 1999, p.18.

Network organization refers to a collection of essentially equal agents or agencies which are in informal relationships with each other based on affiliation.

A fifth and increasingly popular form of interorganizational relationship is the **network organization**. The network of which these organizations are a part refers to a collection of essentially equal agents or agencies which are in informal relationships with each other, based on affiliation (Thompson *et al.*, 1991). The expectation is of a long-term relationship, openness of information, mutual dependency and long-term rather than short-term gains, all underpinned by mutual trust. In order to understand all the ramifications of a network, it must be viewed simultaneously from the perspective of its individual components and from the perspective of the whole (Ebers, 1999).

Various commentators have drawn upon the personal relationship analogy to describe an interorganization network. They see it as being more like a marriage than a one-night stand, but without a marriage licence. There is no common household, and no pooling of assets. Being neither a market transaction nor a hierarchical governance structure, it is a different mode of exchange which possesses its own logic. Within this arrangement, the network partners work in collaboration for their mutual advantage on the basis of trust rather than on the basis of a formalized contractual relationship.

In one sense, networks have been with us continuously from the moment that business people engaged in repeated transactions with their suppliers, distributors, employees and customers and decided whether to outsource any of their production (Child and Faulkner, 1998). Such early networks required verbal and written communication between their members and the development of trust in each other through experience and over time. In another sense networks, and the organizations which comprise them, represent a distinct structural form which has been discussed from the 1980s onwards (Miles and Snow, 1986; Snow *et al.*, 1992; Hinterhuber and Levin, 1994; Powell, 1990; Ebers, 1999).

Networks can range along a continuum from 'dominated' to 'equal-partner' (figure 16.1) (Child and Faulkner, 1998). The 'dominated' network has a single downsized, delayered, core competences-based, 'lean-and-mean' firm at its centre. This hub company relies on outsourcing its production functions, except those deemed to be strategically vital and close to its core competence, e.g. Marks & Spencer controls quality and supply. The distinguishing feature of a dominated network is the limited amount of communication that occurs *between* the smaller node companies. Instead, most of the communication is in the form of a series of one-to-one hub–node interactions. The relationship between Ford or General Motors and its suppliers would be an example of a dominated network.

At the other extreme of the continuum there is an equal-partner network, consisting of a collection of similarly sized companies. Its three distinguishing features are:

- no single partner has set up or controls the network's activities;

- partners have varying amounts of power, which change constantly;

- the network structure does not represent a substitute for the integrated (hierarchical) firm, which is retained.

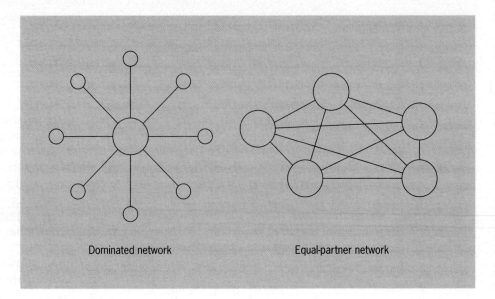

Dominated network   Equal-partner network

Figure 16.1: Dominated and equal-partner networks

The relationships between these component firms create a sub-structure that forms the basis for a co-operative, organizational entity, for example small firms developing computing and biotechnology in Silicon Valley in California. Nohria (1992) reports how these organizations have established a network of lateral and horizontal linkages within and between each other. They have sought to replace an arm's-length competitive relationship with a more collaborative one, through the use of a network. Whether dominant or equal-partner, all networks involve a collection of organizations loosely coupled together, each of which retains its autonomy and choice.

Child and Faulkner (1998) took the 'organic' concept from contingency theory, where it was applied to intraorganizational arrangements [**link**, chapter 15, early organization design], and extended it to interorganizational arrangements. They noted that in a turbulent and global economic world with fast-changing markets, companies have to adopt structural arrangements that emphasize strategic flexibility, involving simultaneous co-operation and competition. The formation of a network involves companies whose domains overlap in terms of products, markets, operating modes or territories, contacting one another and recognizing the benefits of co-operation:

- Network firms are linked to their suppliers, distributors and customers.

- The network is open flexible and dynamic, allowing members to enter and leave.

- Members are concerned with future rather than immediate benefits.

- Members seek to establish, maintain and strengthen the quality of the relationships between them.

Virtual organization

Virtual organization (1) refers to several conventional companies working very closely together (even fronting the market as one organization) with electronic channels or even common systems of communication.

Virtual organization (2) refers to an organization where a large number of the organization members use electronic channels as their main (or even only) medium of contact with each other, and with the rest of the organization.

Social scientists have used a wide variety of adaptive, electronic, futuristic and cybernetic terms to conceptualize emerging organizational forms, for example 'cyberspace corporation' (Pruitt and Barrett, 1991), 'learning organization' (Senge, 1990), 'modular corporation' (Clegg and Hardy, 1996) and 'Möbius strip' organization (Sabel, 1991); 'cyber-world' and 'info-institution' [**link**, chapter 2, the world outside]. However, the most popular analogy remains that of the **virtual organization** (Groth, 1999, pp.246–7).

Within the context of this chapter, the virtual organization can be considered as one example of a network. Many see it as a panacea for many of the current organizational problems. It has generated considerable discussion and debate among managers, management consultants and business commentators, although they disagree about its nature. Despite this, it is possible to describe an 'ideal-type' virtual organization or create a 'virtuality checklist' (table 16.6) on the basis of the 'flexible firm' concept, first popularized during the 1980s and 1990s (Atkinson, 1985), and on more recent descriptions (Carr, 1999; Handy, 1995).

The promise and appeal of the virtual organization is that by dispersing its operations through information technology, it can speedily adapt and reconfigure itself in response to the ever more common state of bounded instability. Specifically, it is able to adopt new information technologies, speed product development, raise quality, improve management–employee relations, and engender new collaborative links between suppliers, producers and customers. Some observers see this organizational form as being modelled on the internet itself, which, after all, was designed to sustain itself in the event of a nuclear strike on

Table 16.6: Features of a virtual organization

Feature	Description
1. Spontaneous association	Spontaneously created alliance of members, who come together to exploit a market opportunity.
2. Lack of physical structure	It is defined in terms of a network of members collaborating, rather than in terms of its physical space like its buildings.
3. Division of task	The total task is fragmented, given to separate individuals who perform it in geographical isolation from one another; the outputs are reintegrated in different ways.
4. Mobile working	Transfer of work from traditional office spaces to remote locations has increased the chances of its being performed in non-traditional ways.
5. Knowledge workers	Individuals are typically 'knowledge workers' (a controversial term), whose value as employees depends primarily on what they know.
6. Expertise	Members contribute their core competencies (those deemed essential to the company) to create a value-adding alliance.
7. Contracting out	Core competencies are retained (e.g. research, development, design), while non-essential ones are contracted out.
8. Electronically linked	Uses highly sophisticated information and communication technologies, allowing faster linking.
9. Reliance on communication technologies	People, assets and ideas are linked electronically much faster than ever before.
10. Switching	Ability of a firm to shift rapidly between suppliers.
11. Meta-management	A central management hub which co-ordinates these outsourced functions between the different suppliers, thereby creating supply chains.
12. Appearance of unity	Despite being individual network members, they act, in all appearances, as a single organizational unit.

Based on W. Davidow and M. Malone, *The Virtual Corporation*, HarperCollins, New York, 1992; A. Mowshowitz, 'Virtual organization: a vision of management in the information age', *The Information Society*, 1994, vol.10, pp.267–94; and N. Venkatraman and J.C. Henderson, 'Real strategies for virtual organizing', *Sloan Management Review*, vol.40, no.1, Fall 1998, pp.33–48.

the United States. All this is being implemented through processes of rationalizing, downsizing and the flattening of hierarchies (delayering). Increasingly one reads about company 'disembodiment' or 'hollowing out', which has been reflected in new configurations between work practices, employee relations and organization designs.

Just how revolutionary is the virtual organization as an organization design? Andrew Burnett (2000) noted that some evolutionists would argue that the concept goes back at least four decades to include 'organic' structure (Burns and Stalker, 1961); 'innovative adhocracy' (Mintzberg, 1983b) and the 'loosely coupled' network (Weick, 1977; Morgan, 1989). They would also see it as comparable with flexible specialization, lean production and business process engineering (Harris, 1998). In retrospect, the judgement that the structural forms used by companies like Benetton and Toyota were fledgling virtual organizations was

Amazon.com

Founded in July 1995 by Jeff Bezos, Amazon.com is currently the best-known virtual company in the world, 'existing only in the imagination'. It has 13 million customers, 2,100 employees, a valuation in excess of $30 billion, and 1999 sales expected to reach $1 billion. It originally sold books, then music and videos, and it remains the world's biggest bookstore. It is also the web's biggest retail store, because it has expanded into toys, home improvement products, consumer electronics and software. It has also taken an equity stake in start-up, web-based retailers of other products and services. Bezos' ambition is to make it the Earth's biggest store.

Amazon represents a 'benchmark' model of an e-commerce organization. It is a constellation of geographically dispersed individuals, groups, departments and entire plants, who are electronically linked. Most importantly, the company is linked to its *customers*, who no longer have to visit in person but 'visit' in cyberspace, wherever in the world they happen to be. It is this which makes the model potentially so powerful. Amazon is now less an American bookseller and more a global firm. It is yet to make a profit, however, and in 1999 was expected to lose $350 million. Nevertheless, it hopes to become profitable by the end of 2000. Its motto is 'Work hard, have fun, make history'. How does it work?

1. Visit the company's website (http://www.amazon.com) and make your purchases. A computer assigns your order to one of Amazon's seven US distribution centres, which collectively have 3 million square feet of floor space.

2. Your order is transmitted to the closest facility that has your product. Some of these stock up to a million different items. Rows of red lights indicate which products have been ordered, and workers retrieve the item from the shelf above and press a button to reset the light. Computers determine which workers go where.

3. Each item goes into a large green crate with that of other customers' orders, and the filled crates ride a series of conveyor belts that snake 10 miles at 2.9 feet per second. The bar code on each item is scanned 15 times by machine and by many of the 600 full-time staff, many of whom receive stock options.

4. All the crates arrive at a central point, and bar codes are matched with order numbers. Your items travel down one of thousands of 3-feet chutes and are placed in a cardboard box with a new bar code identifying your order.

5. An elite group of gift wrappers process 30 packages an hour, using 4.4 million yards of ribbon and 7.8 million square feet of wrapping paper.

6. The McDonough facility in Georgia, one of Amazon's seven, was designed to despatch 200,000 items per day. Of these, 60 per cent go by the US Postal Service and the remainder by United Parcel Service.

7. Between one and seven days later, your order arrives at your doorstep.

Based on Michael Krantz, 'Cruising inside Amazon', pp.48–51; Joe Zeff, 'From your mouse to your house', *Time*, 27 December 1999, vol.154, no.26, pp.52–3.

based solely on their focus on a dense network of suppliers rather than communications technology (Faulkner, 1996).

However, the virtual organization model of today would be inconceivable and impractical without increasingly sophisticated information technology. This has provided opportunity to fully automate work, disperse it across wide geographical areas, allow it to be performed in a non-synchronized, non-linear fashion while effectively integrating and controlling it. In this sense, the virtual organization does represent a revolutionary step beyond traditional, and also the network, organization design.

Some promoters consider that the virtual organization represents an epochal shift in the way we think about organizing work, and an example of the post-modern organization of the future, owing no debt to the technologically primitive past [**link**, chapter 2, the world outside]. Does it represent a post-modern model for the future? Others view it as a case of 'back to the future'. For them the virtual organization is a throwback to scientific work design of the past, and in particular to the scientific management of Frederick Taylor [**link**, chapter 13, traditional work design]. Andrew Burnett and Chris Warhurst (1999) argued that the virtual organization was a manifestation, and even perhaps the apotheosis, of scientific management. In their view, it is not just a technical practice but also a manifestation of the politics of production. The two opposing views are summarized in table 16.7.

Table 16.7: Contrasting views of the virtual organization

Postmodernist model of the future?	Scientific management model of the past?
Radical paradigm shift.	Provides old-style management control and work intensification in a new guise.
Offers flexibility and success for the company, and empowerment and job satisfaction for its employees.	The freedom and speed with which elements can be combined through 'switching' allows ever more fragmented production to be managed.
New developments in the technological and social arena allow managers to organize in distinct and novel ways.	Virtualization, with its emphasis on rational planning, control, and the achievement of economic advantage through cheaper production, represents a further and superior stage of Taylorization.
Allows the relaxation of geographical and organizational boundaries.	Isolates individuals, making them more dependent on organizational fiat.
Loosens the constraints upon co-operation, co-ordination and control on both managers and employees.	Stimulates the application of more sophisticated forms of monitoring and employee surveillance.
It thus provides the possibility for employees to take greater responsibility and control of their own work producing new multiskilled and therefore more intrinsically rewarding work.	Rationalistic, Theory X-oriented, managerial control device that continues the Taylorist/Fordist models of production rather than shifting to 'high-trust' organizational forms.
Offers efficiency and cost benefits on an unprecedented scale.	Offers efficiency and cost benefits on an unprecedented scale.

Stop and criticize What are the advantages and problems of working in a virtual organization? For you as an employee? As a manager?

The interest in post-Fordism, the flexible form, the virtual organization and all the other new social and organizational arrangements represents a major theme in the application of postmodernist thinking [**link**, chapter 2, the world outside]. Discussions of post-modern organizational forms feature increasingly in management magazines but have only just begun to be studied by academics. As Stewart Clegg (1990) noted, these organization designs offer the opportunity for the progressive development of industrial democracy and skill enhancement, or tight job specification and high levels of control. Since, so far, few of us have had first-hand experience of these 'new age' organizations, our ability to make a judgement about them is based on the information and views supplied to us by others. Whether employees or students, we need to be sceptical and questioning about the data provided by the commentators on this currently fashionable topic.

Stop and criticize William Gibson, the futuristic novelist, author of the book *Neuromancer* and creator of the term 'cyberspace', has described this medium as a 'consensual hallucination'.

In what way might the virtual organization be similarly conceived of as the consensual hallucination of organizational theorists, management journalists, practising managers and management gurus?

Recap

1. *Understand how contemporary perspectives on, and discussions of, organization structure differ from past ones.*
   - They focus on the relationships between organizations; include more concepts from the discipline of corporate strategy; use a new vocabulary (e.g. markets, non-linearity); and consider organizations more abstractly.

2. *Appreciate the reciprocal relationship between corporate strategy and organization structure.*
   - Structure can follow strategy (e.g. Miles and Snow's prospector, defender, analyser).
   - Structure complements process and boundaries (e.g. Whittington, Pettigrew).

3. *Discuss theories that explain managerial changes in corporate strategy and organization structure with respect to the environment.*
   - Strategic choice theory holds that all organization design choices are management decisions (Child).
   - Managers' perceptions of their organizations' environments provide the basis for their choices (Weick).
   - Organizations seek to reduce their dependency on aspects of their environment (Pfeffer and Salancik).

4. *Distinguish between bounded instability and non-linearity, and state their implications for corporate strategy.*
   - Bounded instability is a state mixing order and disorder, but one in which a basic pattern of the systems behaviour can be discerned. Non-linearity represents a state in which actions have both expected and unexpected outcomes and in which small actions can quickly escalate, producing unexpected consequences.
   - In such unpredictable environments, planning is less possible and is replaced by setting a fairly clear direction, then continuously adapting the detail to cope with specific events, threats and opportunities.

5. *Define a 'transaction' and distinguish three major types of institutional arrangement for the conduct of transactions.*
   - Any 'exchange' between actors (e.g. buying and selling; providing information and making a decision based upon it) is a transaction.

- Transactions can be conducted in a hierarchy, a market or in a mutual relationship.

6. *Differentiate between the main types of mutual inter-organizational arrangement.*
   - Strategic alliance, joint venture, unilateral agreement and network organization.

7. *Identify the distinguishing features of a virtual organization.*

- A virtual organization is one example of a network organization.
- A virtual organization possesses many of the following features: spontaneous association; lack of physical structure; division of task; mobile working; knowledge workers; expertise; contracting out; electronically linked; reliance on communication technologies; switching; meta-management; and appearance of unity.

Revision

1. Why might Max Weber and Henri Fayol be surprised by developments in contemporary organization design arrangements?

2. Why do organizational behaviour academics increasingly have to take corporate strategy into account in their considerations of the design of organization structures?

3. Select an organization with which you are familiar. Identify three significant environmental actors or agencies that are making demands on it at the present time. Suggest what type of power the latter have over the former. What is the nature of the dependency relationship between them. Suggest ways in which it could be reduced or eliminated.

4. How would organizing and managing a company which operated in a state of bounded instability differ from one that operated in a state of stable equilibrium?

5. Why are network and virtual structures preferred by managers seeking to encourage entrepreneurship and innovation?

Springboard

Chandler, A.D., Hagstrom, P. and Solvell, O. (eds), 1999, *The Dynamic Firm: The Role of Technology, Strategy, Organization and Regions*, Part 2: 'Strategy and Organizations', Oxford University Press, Oxford.

Contributions consider the relationship between corporate strategy and organization structure from a strategy perspective.

Child, J. and Faulkner, D., 1998, *Strategies of Co-operation*, Oxford University Press, Oxford.

Provides a contemporary discussion of organization structures which moves beyond the boundary of the firm to include a consideration of other agencies and actors.

Child, J., 1997, 'Strategic choice in the analysis of action, structure, organizations and environment: retrospective and prospective', *Organization Studies*, vol.18, no.1, pp.43–76.

An overview of the strategic choice debate which sets it within a contemporary context. A challenging read for those wishing to understand current thinking about organization structuring.

Ebers, M. (ed.), 1999, *The Formation of Inter-Organizational Networks*, Oxford University Press, Oxford.

Considers interorganizational perspective, how they form and what their strengths and weaknesses are.

Fulop, L. and Linstead, S. (eds), 1999, *Management: A Critical Text*, Macmillan Business, London.

Chapter 10 and 11 by Browne *et al.* and Buttery *et al.*, respectively, address the issues of strategy and inter-organizational relations from a critical organizational behaviour perspective.

Parker, M., 2000, 'Postmodernizing organizational behaviour: New organizations or new organization theory', in Barry, J., Chandler, J., Clark, H., Johnston, R. and Needle, D. (eds), 2000, *Organization and Management: A Critical Text*, Thomson Learning, London, pp.36–50.

Introduction to contemporary thinking about new forms of organization structuring.

Pettigrew, A. and Fenton, E. (eds.), 2000, *Process and Practice in New Forms of Organising*, Sage, London.

Reports the results of the INNFORM project, which investigated the importance of complementing strategic, structural and process changes.

Spector, R., 2000, *Amazon.com: Get Big Fast*, Random House Business, New York.

A clear and readable description of the origins and early growth of the company , as well as its founder's business philosophy and style.

Whipp, R., 1999, 'Creative deconstruction: strategy and organizations', in Clegg, S.R., Hardy, C. and Nord, W.R. (eds.), *Managing Organizations: Current Issues*, Sage, London, pp.11–25.

A book chapter which provides a brief historical background to the rising importance of corporate strategy to contemporary organization studies.

Home viewing

Other Peoples' Money (1991, director Norman Jewison) shows how the inability of a firm to react to an external threat leaves it vulnerable to a hostile takeover. It raises management and leadership issues related to corporate restructuring. New England Wire and Cable (NEWC) is an old-fashioned manufacturing company, paternalistically led for 26 years by Andrew Jorgenson (played by Gregory Peck), who values stability and predictability. He is unaware of the developing problems in one of his company's divisions, which requires urgent re-engineering and diversification. Meanwhile, Garfield Investment Corporation (GIC), headed by Lawrence Garfield (played by Danny DeVito), is using modern technology to scan the environment for firms that are ripe to be taken. GIC exemplifies the quintessential Wall Street firm, with its chrome, leather furniture, glass building and Manhattan location. Garfield expects to make a substantial profit by taking over and liquidating NEWC.

Once you have watched the entire film, consider:

1. What are some of the reasons why corporate restructurings take place?

2. How do Jorgenson's leadership and decision-making style leave his company vulnerable to a takeover?

3. What skills do you think are most useful for managers in the organizations of the future?

OB in literature

Mario Puzo, *The Godfather*, Arrow Books, London, 1998.

Originally published in 1969, this book (also a film) tells the story of Don Corleone and the New York Mafia. What are his 'Family's' (organization's) objectives, strategy and structure? It operates using both a hierarchy and interorganizational (network) relationships. Consider these within the context of trust, mutual respect, reciprocity and collaboration for mutual advantage between the individuals, groups and families involved. How did the leading Mafia families regulate the conflict of interests between them?

Dan Simmons, *Hyperion*, Headline Books, London, 1990.

Describes a world controlled by a pervasive web of artificial intelligence based on huge corporate and government databanks, worlds of instant information, of galactic networks all run neurally (so no keyboards or screens). Emphasis is on the speed at which decisions and actions can be precisely specified on the one hand, or are dependent on individual judgement, experience and trust on the other. In your view, does Simmons offer a view of the future which is closer to utopia or to a nightmare?

1: Career progression

Objective
    1. To introduce the differences between different organization designs.

Briefing
    You are a middle manager in a large organization and have been in the same job for three years. You are dissatisfied with your current position and want a more senior job that pays you more money.

- How do you go about getting a better job?
- What are the advantages and disadvantages of each option?

2. Take it away, maestro!

Objectives
    1. To identify the differences between past and future organization structures.

    2. To assess the degree of their newness.

Introduction
    The management guru Peter Drucker once claimed that the typical large business of the early twenty-first century would have an organization structure, management problems and concerns of a symphony orchestra. Recent writings on interorganizational co-operative relationships also stress the network form of organization.

Briefing
    Some if not many musicians in British symphony orchestras are self-employed. They work in a number of musical outfits, turning up for symphonic concerts as required. Some orchestras can have up to a third of their members 'bought in' in this way. The stability of membership has an impact on their sense of dynamics and timing.

1. Critically assess the different views expressed in this case.

2. What are the implications of this case for the management of interorganizational relationships.

3. Does leadership in a network necessarily entail an emotional or intellectual deskilling of followers?

The organization theorist: symphony orchestra

Not for the first time, the rehearsal ended in uproar. As on previous occasions, the musicians in the Organization Theorists' Symphony Orchestra were at loggerheads with their guest conductor. 'I'm not convinced we need a conductor at all', shouted Jim Hansard (trumpet). Turning to the person in question, he continued: 'Why on earth do you continue to conduct past the first few beats of the march we've been playing? The percussionists' rhythm combined with the tuba and the French horns provide a clear rhythmic core to the piece. Our orchestra has an inner pulse and rhythm and we don't need some idiot with a stick to remind us of it'.

'I suppose you would recommend applying organization theory to the question of conducting an orchestra', retorted Tim Peters the conductor, somewhat taken aback by the trumpeter's harsh words.

'I see no reason why not', exclaimed Hansard.

'Very well then', Peters conceded. 'According to conventional theory, a symphony orchestra of over 100 players should have several group vice-president conductors and perhaps a half-dozen divisional directors. In this orchestra we have a flat structure which many a business organization would envy'.

'With respect Tim, that shows how conventional your thinking is', suggested David Silver (violin). 'Each of us is a highly skilled specialist—you can't force us to play. Our motivation comes from a love of music and the thrill of playing with like-minded others. Not only that, the system of authority in an orchestra is more than a pattern of static roles and statuses. It's a network of interacting people each transmitting information to the other, sifting their transactions through an evaluative screen of standards and sanctioned ways of doing things. If anyone is conducting the orchestra, I suppose it is the composer of the score'.

'I believe that my role, at the very least, is to identify and correct errors and increase the scope of collaborative consensus', Peters replied.

Hilary Knights (tuba) could not agree: 'If that's so, why do you spend whole concerts standing on a rostrum waving a baton. We're experts and you should trust us to come in at the right time and in the right place. To be honest, I'm not sure why you attend concerts at all. Your role seems entirely superfluous after rehearsals are completed. To the "inner pulse" Jim referred to, one should add "inner autonomy". We can plot our own way through a complex musical composition, but the modern-day conductor insists on doing it him or (more uncommonly) herself by framing and defining the musical and social reality of the orchestral players'.

'I agree', interrupted Harry Jones (percussion). 'A deskilling process is evident here. Early conductors never assumed ensemble intonation as their responsibility. These conductors were usually the composer or sometimes a member of the orchestra. They would guide and facilitate the expertise of the ensemble. They didn't stand on a rostrum—they didn't control'.

'There is certainly an inherent danger in abdicating control to a power outside the self', opined Gareth Morton (harp). 'The presence of a well-defined leader will often decrease the ability of the group to experiment and consider alternative courses of action. Different musicians read the same musical score differently—so experimentation is possible in classical music. If (to distort Muktananada) "there is a great mirror in the conductors' eyes in which everything is reflected", then what Tim's eyes reflect is our sense of diminishing autonomy and learned helplessness'.

'These days the idea of a symphony orchestra without a conductor is inconceivable to most people', he continued. 'When I've told people about experiments with leaderless orchestras in the USSR in the late 1920s (and far more recently in the Netherlands), their usual reaction is disbelief and the question: how do the musicians know when to start?'

'You credit me with far too much power, Gareth', said Peters. 'My authority as conductor is not situationally approved (as this discussion proves!). It is socially created and maintained. As a collective body of musicians you have considerable expertise. I cannot play your instruments as well as you. You have an additional expertise in assessing my interpretative and communicative powers. And, if you so wish, you can remove me from the podium. I cannot make you play. But you can make me step down. Hence, you have power over me'.

'As for the conservatism of symphony orchestras', he continued, 'it is true that (conductorless) chamber orchestras can boast a far longer legacy of musical compositions. These ensembles improve and mature as they accept the problems and challenges of the old and the new. Many are active in commissioning new works. Chamber ensembles are open, receptive and accepting. Perhaps all these attributes must be incorporated into symphony orchestras. Successful musical (and conducting) techniques can and do transcend the boundaries between different ensembles'.

'You're missing the point, Tim', replied Gibson Cooper (double bass). 'The problem is not one of leadership style or technique, but one of a structural imbalance of power and the institutionalisation of alienation'.

'Well I'm glad it's not all my fault', the conductor confessed, flippantly. 'Same time next week, everyone?'

From J. Martin Corbett, *Critical Cases in Organizational Behaviour*, Macmillan, London, 1994, pp.80–2.

Part 5 Organization processes

A field map of the organizational behaviour terrain

PESTLE: The **P**olitical, **E**conomic, **S**ocial, **T**echnological, **L**egal and **E**cological context

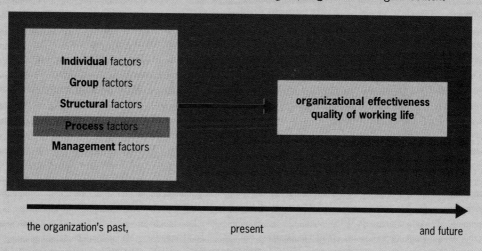

the organization's past,   present   and future

Introduction

Part 5, Organization processes, explores the following four topics:

- Organization development, in chapter 17

- Organizational change, in chapter 18

- Organization culture, in chapter 19

- Human resource management, in chapter 20

These are overlapping areas of organization process which contribute in different modes to the ways in which organizations change, develop and evolve. These processes also contribute in significant ways to organizational effectiveness and quality of working life.

Our opening case concerns Anglian Water Services plc, the largest privatized water utility company in England. Anglian Water embarked on a series of major organizational changes during the 1990s. You are invited to evaluate its approach, first from a management perspective and second from an employee perspective. You are invited to consider what advice you would give to management to develop the approach. It's your call.

YOUR CALL (5): Anglian Water's transformation strategy

This case is based on the following sources:

Previously a water treatment and supply utility under public control, Anglian was privatized, along with the other water authorities in England and Wales, in 1989. Anglian had an annual turnover of around £775 million (1997–98), served a population of around 5 million people over an area of 27,000 square kilometres, and employed over 4,000 people in 1998.

The 'old Anglian' had all the features of a public sector bureaucracy, with a safe and predictable environment. It was hierarchical, slow and risk-averse. There was a traditional autocratic 'command-and-control' management style. Employees were encouraged to follow rules and procedures, and were discouraged from taking initiative or developing creative solutions. There were good grounds for some rules, particularly with respect to actions that could affect water quality and public health. Unfortunately water is a product which, if it develops a fault, cannot be recalled by the supplier, so 'getting it right first time' is important.

The 'new Anglian' had to function as a private sector organization in a turbulent competitive environment. The main target became profitability, and staff had to think in commercial terms about costs, customers and shareholders. Between 1993 and 1995, management undertook a strategic systems review; hierarchical levels were reduced from eleven to five, and a third of white collar jobs were lost, saving £40 million per annum. However, these changes did not encourage the development of a more creative, entrepreneurial, customer-focused culture.

To change attitudes and behaviours, management launched a development programme called the Transformation Journey, which was open to all staff at all levels. Self-organizing groups of eight to ten employees were invited to form, not necessarily based on existing colleagues. The group's first task was to choose a project which could benefit the business, or the community. The group then recruited the help of a facilitator to help with group working and group problem-solving skills, and with project management capability. The group had to either generate the required resources or negotiate a budget. After that, how the project was progressed and delivered was up to the group, with no prescribed processes or outcomes.

Between 1995 and 1997, 3,000 people volunteered for the Journey, forming around 300 self-organizing project groups. The outcomes from these projects included improved teamwork, shared knowledge, environmental improvements, new systems, new business opportunities (domestic and international), community benefits, improved customer knowledge and public relations, and cost reductions. The approach was subsequently offered to other companies facing similar challenges. The Journey did not involve everyone in the organization, and many of the benefits were difficult to quantify precisely. However, the aim was to challenge the way people thought and worked, and to introduce the concepts of creativity, initiative and empowerment to employees accustomed to working in a public sector bureaucracy.

The Transformation Journey had three key features. First, the aim was to change the attitudes and behaviours of staff familiar with a mechanistic, bureaucratic style of working. Second, the programme sought to introduce all employees to the concept of empowerment—a radically new idea in a public sector context. Third, management invested in this programme as an act of faith, knowing that the 'returns' could not be quantified.

- From a management perspective, how would you assess this strategy?

- From an employee perspective, how would you assess this strategy?

- How would you advise management to develop this strategy?

It's your call.

Ciminero, S.M., 1997, 'Anglian Water: customer service transformation', Harvard Business School case N9–897–093, April.

Dean, A., Carlisle, Y. and Baden-Fuller, C., 1999, 'Punctuated and continuous change: the UK water industry', *British Journal of Management*, vol.10, special conference issue, pp.3–18.

Morton, C., 1998, *Beyond World Class*, Macmillan Business, Houndmills, Basingstoke.

Key concepts

organization development (OD)
force-field analysis
survey feedback
role negotiation

OD intervention
process consultation
sensitivity training
team building

grid OD
action research
intergroup development

Learning objectives

When you have read this chapter, you should be able to define those key concepts in your own words, and you should also be able to:

1. Explain the goals of OD.

2. Understand the values underpinning the OD movement.

3. Understand the main OD interventions, how they work, and what they aim to achieve.

4. Assess critically the difficulties in evaluating the effectiveness of OD interventions.

5. List the main skills and areas of knowledge required by an OD consultant.

Why study organization development?

Organization development (OD) offers a comprehensive, systematic and practical approach to improving individual and organizational effectiveness. Although this is an American perspective developed in the 1960s, it deserves study today for several reasons:

1. The perspective remains influential in practice, with senior management posts in OD still advertised, although published accounts are now rare as applications no longer have novelty value and attract less research attention.

2. The values which underpin OD and the techniques which it advocates make this approach distinct from the general field of organizational change management, which is explored in chapter 18 [link, chapter 18, organizational change].

3. Most other change implementation methodologies have been influenced by the values, concepts and frameworks of OD.

4. OD has also contributed to the organization culture change issues explored in chapter 19 [**link**, chapter 19, organization culture].

5. The OD values and techniques are similar to those advocated by the human resource management (HRM) movement in the 1990s [**link**, chapter 20, human resource management].

6. The perspective invites critical examination, as the quasi-religious values which underpin OD can be seen either as caring management or as an attempt to deny the reality of conflict in organizations [**link**, chapter 23, organizational conflict].

During the 1990s, many commentators became critical of the way in which management ideas and methods came into and went out of fashion, like clothing (Shapiro, 1996; Micklethwait and Wooldridge, 1996). Andrzej Huczynski (1993) identified the specific ingredients of management ideas which made them popular and turned their originators into wealthy management 'gurus'. Business process re-engineering (BPR) was one example. Brought to management attention in 1990, by 1995 critics were claiming that the approach had been discredited because it was not novel, not radical and not effective. In other words, it took only five years for this fashion to fade.

OD, in contrast, has endured for over half a century and continues to influence management thinking and practice. OD has been widely adopted and has many devotees among managers and management consultants. An understanding of the organizational change issues introduced in chapter 18 and the organization culture issues explored in chapter 19 is therefore not complete without an understanding of OD principles and methods.

The OD agenda: goals and processes

Chapter 1 introduced the concept of the organizational dilemma—the problem of meeting individual employee needs and aspirations while meeting the performance, survival and growth needs of the organization as a whole. The rapid developments in social science methodology and knowledge after the Second World War led to a growth in confidence in the practical application of that knowledge to organizational problems. During the 1960s, in America, this confidence generated a movement committed to the design and use of social science techniques for the development of organizational effectiveness and the development of an organization's members. In other words, the OD movement can be regarded as a long-running confrontation with the organizational dilemma.

OD dates back to the 1960s, when the term first began to find currency. OD practitioners believe that the conflicting interests of organizations and their members can be reconciled through appropriate interventions. We have the social science understanding, and we have the change techniques, through which problems can be diagnosed and resolved. OD also claims to develop the organization's independent capability to address and resolve its own problems, and thus to reduce dependence on OD 'experts' beyond an initial intervention. The field of OD has its own literature, with its own conceptual, theoretical and empirical bases, its own specialized courses, conferences and societies, and its own specialized higher degrees. It can, therefore, be seen as an organization studies discipline or sub-discipline in its own right, dealing with a specific set of issues, goals and problems.

OD also has some of the features of a religious movement, which may help to explain the durability of this perspective. In addition to the belief that conflict in organizations can be managed through appropriate intervention, the approach adheres to a broad set of underpinning social values, the pursuit of which may be regarded as valuable in its own right, independent of any implications for organizational productivity or financial performance.

It is not clear who first used the term **organization development**, but it was probably coined by Richard Beckhard while looking for a label for a consulting programme in which he was involved with Douglas McGregor in 1960. They did not want to describe their work as 'management development' because the whole organization was involved, and they wanted to avoid the term 'human relations training' because that was too narrow. The term 'organization development' was used instead. One of the other founders of the movement was Warren Bennis (1969), who defined OD as 'a response to change, a complex educational strategy intended to change the beliefs, attitudes, values and structure of organizations so that they can better adapt to new technologies, markets, and challenges, and the dizzying rate of change itself'.

More recently, Wendell French and Cecil Bell (1995, p.1) have defined OD as 'a planned, systematic process in which applied behavioural science principles and practices are introduced into ongoing organizations towards the goal of increasing individual and organizational effectiveness'. The organizational boundaries and focus of an OD intervention are a matter for judgement. The approach can be applied to one or more departments or sections of an organization. However, OD practitioners like to talk about 'getting the whole system in the room'. This implies an attempt to understand and to influence the entire organization, involving everyone about everything.

Although spread over three decades, these definitions are similar. The targets include individual development and organizational effectiveness. Interventions to achieve these goals are deliberate, planned and systematic. OD seeks to apply social and behavioural science knowledge and techniques in a manner that will enhance both organizational effectiveness and the quality of work experience for the organization's members. In pursuit of these twin objectives, OD has a clear and prescriptive value orientation. These values relate to the individual's experience of employment, and to the manner in which the organization treats and relates to its members.

> **Organization development** is an effort (1) planned, (2) organization-wide, and (3) managed from the top, to (4) increase organization development and health through (5) planned interventions in the organization's 'process', using behavioural science knowledge (Richard Beckhard, 1969, p.9).

Stop and criticize

Consider these definitions of OD from the perspective of the manager who wants a more compliant and committed workforce that will welcome and not resist organizational change. One route to achieving these outcomes involves reassuring employees that 'we all share common interests', that 'our conflicts and disagreements can be resolved', and that 'the changes we are about to make are in your interests because they will enhance the quality of working life'.

Now listen to these reassurances from the perspective of the employee who sees fundamental power inequalities and conflict between management and workforce.

To what extent can OD be used as a tool, not just to improve organizational effectiveness but also to exert management control over a workforce by appealing to human values—openness, trust, harmony—that are difficult to challenge?

Stephen Robbins (1998) outlines the values underpinning most OD efforts as follows:

- the individual should be treated with respect and dignity;
- the organization climate should be characterized by trust, openness and support;

- hierarchical authority and control are not regarded as effective mechanisms;

- problems and conflicts should be confronted, and not disguised or avoided;

- people affected by change should be involved in its implementation.

Some practitioners argue that this 'human-centred' agenda is worth pursuing in its own right, independent of attempts directly to enhance organizational functioning. Others argue that an organization cannot be productive, efficient and effective unless it adopts this human-centred agenda. The committed OD practitioner asks 'can an organization be effective without mutual trust and confidence, honesty, open communications, sensitivity to the feelings and emotions of others, shared goals, and a commitment to addressing and resolving conflict?'

Note that a definition of 'effective' in this context depends on who is using the term. Effectiveness can be considered in terms of profitability, in terms of the pursuit of organizational goals (at whatever cost), or in terms of quality of life for those involved. Some of the general characteristics of the 'effective' organization are set out in the table 17.1, from Dexter Dunphy. See how many of these you agree with.

Thomas Cummings and Christopher Worley (1993) claim that early practitioners in this field were more interested in projects which concerned the

Warren G. Bennis

Table 17.1: Characteristics of the effective and the ineffective organization

effective organization	ineffective organization
clearly defined goals	ill-defined or unknown goals
structure related to goals	no link between goals and structure
flexible forward planning	focus on immediately pressing problems
consistent, clear procedures which evolve purposefully	bureaucratic rigidity, or constant change without rationale
meaningful, varied work with learning opportunity	narrow, repetitive jobs with little learning opportunity
commitment to personal growth (planned skills development)	contempt for individuals and groups (the POPOs: 'pissed on, passed over')
power-recognizing mutual influence	politicking and defensive cliques
flexible, participative decisions	'what the boss says, goes'
information openness	secrecy, gossip, failure to listen
mutual trust, support, respect	the FUJIAR syndrome: 'fuck you Jack I'm all right'
accurate, timely performance feedback	unclear signals: 'what did the boss mean by that?'
just and equitable rewards	apparently arbitrary rewards
constant scanning of environment and appropriate adaptation	failure to perceive and act on critical environmental changes
initiative in external relations	reactive, selective responses
well-defined concept of social responsibility	'don't care' attitude to community values

Based on Dexter Dunphy, *Organizational Change by Choice*, McGraw-Hill, Sydney, 1981, reprinted 1993, pp.26–8.

Table 17.2. Bureaucratic diseases and OD cures

bureaucratic disease	symptoms	OD cures
rigid functional boundaries	conflict between sections, poor communications	team building, job rotation, change the structure
fixed hierarchies	frustration, boredom, narrow specialist thinking	training, job enrichment, career development
information only flows down	lack of innovation, minor problems escalate	process consultation, management development
routine jobs, tight control	boredom, absenteeism, conflict for supervisors	job enrichment, job rotation, supervisory training

'people problems', such as interpersonal relationships and group dynamics, and were less concerned with productivity issues. However, as French and Bell (1995) point out, the values and assumptions supported by the OD movement in the 1960s represented a radical departure for most organizations at that time. Managers in that era did not think in terms of involving their employees in decision making, or of inviting their ideas and contributions. Most managers did not recognize a link between interpersonal relationships, self-awareness and the exchange of emotions and feelings, on the one hand, and the performance of their businesses, on the other.

Since the 1960s the OD movement has been associated with the argument that 'bureaucracy is bad' and that the caring, sharing, empowering organization is not only a better place to work but is also financially and materially more effective. The 'bureaucracy-busting' agenda of OD relies on the diagnosis of problems and solutions summarized in table 17.2. Some of the terminology in table 17.2 will be explained later.

OD practitioners claim that the diseases of bureaucracy can be cured in commercial organizations but have also been concerned that the large public sector bureaucracies are resistant to such cures. Warner Burke (1980) for example claimed that the confrontation of OD and large organizations in national and local government or health care resembled the confrontation of 'David and Goliath' except, he argued, 'we are not as skilful as David'. Cummings and Worley (1993, p.647) claim, from personal experience, that 'OD still has limited application in large health systems' because of the special nature of their managerial and organizational problems. Moving into the twenty-first century, the large public sector bureaucracies are probably more in need of OD support and intervention than ever. Must OD settle for 'fine tuning' in such settings rather than seek radical change? Government policies and demographic trends in the early twenty-first century are pressing public bureaucracies to become even more commercial in outlook and in internal structure. Twenty years on, will Warner Burke's pessimism be overturned by a public sector revival of OD?

Stop and criticize

Use this as a checklist to assess the educational institution in which you are now studying. Use this checklist on another organization with which you are familiar. To what action recommendations does this analysis lead?

The OD matrix: levels and modes of intervention

The OD toolkit includes a large and expanding number of intervention techniques or strategies (Huczynski, 2001). In fact, many of the approaches to organizational improvement covered in earlier chapters—job enrichment, assessment centres, team building, participative management—can be regarded and have been used as **OD interventions**. The first step in any OD project, however, concerns diagnosis. Until one is clear about the nature of the problem and its roots, it is not possible effectively to select an appropriate strategy.

Problems in organizations can arise at different levels:

> An **OD intervention** is a specific methodology or technique used to effect change in the target organization or section of the organization, to improve organizational effectiveness (however defined).

- organizational level;
- intergroup level;
- group level;
- individual level.

An individual may be having difficulties at work: too difficult, not challenging, boring, no prospects. A group may not be functioning effectively: lack of leadership, poor relationships, personality clashes, team lacking cohesion. Two or more groups may find themselves in (intergroup) conflict for some reason: unwilling to co-operate or liaise, differences in outlook, physical distance, conflict of priorities. The whole organization may experience low morale, be out of touch with its environment, lack an effective structure, lack a clear strategy.

The first step in problem diagnosis thus concerns identifying the level at which the problem has arisen. In most complex organizations, as one might expect, problems are likely to be caused and reinforced by factors at more than one level. For example, those unhappy individuals may be concerned with their positions in the structure, and with a lack of understanding of the organization's strategic purpose, as well as with fellow section or group members and the lack of challenge in their own individual repetitive tasks. Problem diagnosis, therefore, is not always a straightforward step. The selection of an appropriate intervention strategy, or more often a solutions package, can thus be a complex choice.

To help with these issues of diagnosis and choice, Derek Pugh produced the OD matrix shown in table 17.3. This matrix first outlines problems that can arise at each of the four levels, with respect to behavioural factors, organization structural factors and wider contextual factors. Each cell in the matrix identifies, in italics, relevant OD interventions. If the problem lies with the individual, and the cause or causes are structural, then a job redesign approach may be relevant. If the problem lies at the organizational level, and the cause or causes are contextual, job enrichment is going to be of limited value, and a change of organization strategy or location may be necessary.

It is important to recognize that an intervention strategy, or package of strategies, cannot simply be 'read' mechanically from a matrix like this. This is simply a useful diagnostic and planning guide. A sound knowledge of the organizational context is also required. The approach that is both relevant, practical and acceptable is in part systematic diagnosis, part local context knowledge, part judgement.

The relationship between OD practitioner or consultant and the target or host organization has generated much discussion. Consultants, of course, work for clients. In an OD setting, defining 'the client' is not always straightforward. The person who invited the OD consultant into a preliminary discussion (the 'gatekeeper') may not be the person (the 'problem owner') who represents the section with the difficulty to be resolved. Someone else again (the 'paymaster') may eventually settle the consultant's invoice. The problem may actually lie, say, with

Table 17.3: The Pugh OD matrix for organizational diagnosis and choice of OD intervention

	behaviour what is happening?	structure what is the system?	context what is the setting?
organizational level	poor morale, pressure, anxiety, suspicion, weak response to environmental changes *survey feedback, organizational mirroring*	inappropriate and poorly defined goals, strategy unclear, inappropriate structure, inadequate environmental scanning *structure change*	geography, product market, labour market, technology, physical working conditions *change strategy, change location, change conditions, change culture*
intergroup level	sub-units not co-operating, conflict and competition, failure to confront differences, unresolved feelings *intergroup confrontation, role negotiation*	no common perspective on task, difficult to achieve required interaction *redefine responsibilities, change reporting relations, improve liaison mechanisms*	differences in sub-unit values and lifestyles, physical barriers *reduce psychological and physical distance, exchange roles, arrange cross-functional attachments*
group level	inappropriate working atmosphere, goals disputed, inappropriate leadership style, leader not trusted or respected, leader in conflict with peers and superiors *process consultation, team building*	task poorly defined, role relations not clear, leader overloaded, inappropriate reporting structures *redesign role relations, autonomous groups, socio-technical system redesign*	lack of resources, poor group composition, inadequate physical facilities, personality clashes *change the technology, change the layout, change group membership*
individual level	individual needs not met, frustration, resistance to change, few learning and development opportunities *counselling, role analysis, career planning*	poor job definition, task too easy, task too difficult *job restructuring or redesign, job enrichment, clear objectives*	poor individual–job 'fit', poor selection or promotion, inadequate training, inadequate recognition and reward *improve personnel procedures, improve training, align recognition and reward with objectives*

two groups of relatively low-status employees whose poor interaction is adversely affecting organizational performance. Can these groups be regarded as 'clients'? To make matters more complex, the consultant is also likely to become involved in the organization's political system. The people with the most status and influence in the organization (the 'power brokers') may not be the clients, gatekeepers, problem owners or paymasters.

We can examine this issue from a theoretical and from a practical perspective.

From a theoretical point of view, once engaged, the consultant quickly becomes involved in a complex and ongoing series of relationships within the host organization. It is useful, then, to consider the consultant interacting with, and intervening in, a 'client system', a term which captures the complexity and variety in the OD consultant's net of relationships in the host organization. Some parts of the client system will be critical, others less so. Some will collaborate willingly, while others will manifest resistance to creative interventions. Action that will affect one part of the client system may create 'knock on' or 'ripple effects' in other parts of the system.

In practice, however, the term 'client system' obscures and confuses a critical issue for the OD consultant as temporary employee of the host organization. In this respect, identifying clearly and without ambiguity the person or group responsible for settling invoices and writing cheques may be vital. But the simplicity of this mercenary stance has to be set against the need to recognize that the OD consultant may have many different clients, with different needs and expectations, within the one organization. It may be appropriate to identify the client differently for different activities and stages of the OD process.

Stop and criticize	As an OD consultant, you have been asked by the plant human resources director to conduct an attitude survey in a branch plant of a multinational electronics company in the Netherlands with over 200 employees on site. There seems to be a problem with morale, which may be affecting shop floor productivity. You are doing this through a combination of questionnaire and structured 'focus group' discussions with ten to twelve employees at a time. Individual employees are guaranteed anonymity, and management is happy with this approach. Four groups from one section of the site have independently asked you to represent their strong and critical views about supervisory and middle management style and behaviour to senior management on their behalf. They see this as the purpose of the attitude survey, and see this also as a legitimate aspect of your neutral OD consulting and advisory role. Other employee groups, however, have not made this special request. In this assignment, who is your client? How should you, as external OD consultant, handle the attempt to recruit you to a specific cause? (This account is based on a real case.)

How should an OD intervention take place? Kurt Lewin (1951) considered organizational change to have three main elements. These concerned *unfreezing* the current state of affairs (attitudes, beliefs, values), the *transition* to a new state, and *refreezing* or stabilizing the changes to make them permanent. OD interventions can be considered in terms of how they help with the unfreezing, transition and refreezing states of the OD process. Lewin also introduced, in 1947, a technique called **force-field analysis**. Lewin argued that the nature and pace of change depend on the balance of driving and restraining forces in relation to a particular change, or 'target situation'.

A typical force-field analysis could look like this:

Force-field analysis is a technique for assessing the factors that encourage and the factors that resist movement towards a desired target situation, thus allowing an assessment of the viability of the change, and suggesting action to alter the balance of forces, if necessary.

target situation: emigrate from Britain to Australia	
driving forces ———————→	←——————— **restraining forces**
friendly natives	family in Scotland
inexpensive lifestyle	high cost of moving
the wide open spaces	the long journey to anywhere
the beer, the wine	the mosquitoes, the spiders
clear skies, sunshine, beaches	sunburn, skin cancer, sharks

A force-field analysis involves identifying the forces supporting and impeding movement towards a given target situation. The forces can be weighted or scored, say from 1 (weak) to 10 (strong), to provide a rough guide to the balance of forces. If the driving forces are overwhelming, then the change can probably go ahead without any significant problems. If the resisting forces are overwhelming, then the change may have to be abandoned, or at least delayed until conditions have improved in some respect.

If the driving and restraining forces are more or less in balance, then the force-field analysis can be used to plan appropriate action. How can resisting forces be reduced or eliminated? How can the driving forces be strengthened? Are there any new driving forces that can be introduced? The weighting of forces and the adding of scores gives the technique a spurious air of scientific validity. Clearly, the extent to which the force field is balanced is a matter of judgement. Used in a group setting, the technique provides a valuable way to structure what can often be an untidy discussion covering a range of factors.

Stop and criticize

Your educational establishment plans dramatically to extend the use of objective testing of students in business and management studies. This will replace conventional essay-style assignments and exams with multiple choice tests, and one-word and other short-answer tests. Multiple choice tests, of course, can be scanned and marked electronically, avoiding the need for tedious essay marking.

Identify the forces driving this change, and the forces resisting; draw the force field.

Assess the balance of forces, and the ease or difficulty of introducing this change.

Construct a brief action plan for implementing this change.

Construct a brief action plan for blocking this change.

What does this exercise reveal about the strengths and limitations of force-field analysis as a diagnostic and action planning tool.

What approaches are used by OD to implement planned change? Thomas Cummings and Christopher Worley (1993) outline two main intervention models, the planning model and the action research model. The planning model summarized in table 17.4 assumes that change can be implemented in seven related stages.

Table 17.4: The planning model of OD intervention	
1: Scouting	consultant and client share information and ideas with respect to problems and the appropriate approach
2: Entry	a formal consulting or helping relationship is established
3: Diagnosis	information gathering to define the problem and identify causes
4: Planning	jointly establish the goals of intervention and the proposed approach
5: Action	intervention strategies are implemented
6: Stabilization	change is stabilized (refreezing) and outcomes are assessed
7: Termination	the consultant withdraws, or moves on to another OD project

In practice, change rarely unfolds in such a straightforward manner. The original plan is always subject to modification and refinement. The seven steps are not always followed in precisely this sequence. Some stages may be omitted or passed over quickly, or revisited several times during the change process. This does not invalidate the model, which remains a useful guide or route map for participants in the OD process.

The **action research** model differs from the traditional planning model in two respects. First, it is a cyclical or iterative process. This simply means that the results from an intervention are fed back in such a way that further changes and improvements can be implemented. Of course, this can happen with a planning model too, but in action research, this intention is designed into the approach from the beginning. Second, the 'research' in the label signals the aim of generating knowledge that can be applied in other organizational settings. This means that action research is a different kind of consulting model, and also a different kind of organizational research model.

Action research can also be defined as a model of organizational research in which generalizable knowledge is produced from attempts actively to change and improve organizational functioning, rather than from passive observation. Action research is sometimes seen as a contemporary approach which gained acceptance during the 1980s and 1990s. However, applications of this approach date from the mid-1940s.

Consistent with the overarching goals of OD, action research in practice is a collaborative method, involving consultant and organization members in joint planning, diagnosis, implementation, evaluation and further planning. The outline stages of an action research programme are, therefore, likely to include:

1. problem identification;
2. preliminary diagnosis;
3. data gathering from the client group;
4. data feedback to the client group;
5. joint evaluation of data;
6. joint action planning;
7. action, or implementation of proposals for change;
8. repeat the cycle—fresh data gathering and feedback of results of change.

As with the traditional planning model, action research is unlikely in practice always to unfold in such a tidy manner. Once again, the model is simply a useful guide. The main differences between the planning and action research models lie with their respective emphasis and goals. Action research emphasizes the cyclical nature of organization development and change, whereas the planning model presumes a 'one-off' intervention. The goals of the planning model are improved personal and organizational effectiveness. Action research adds the goal of generating new knowledge and insights for application elsewhere.

Action research is a model of OD consulting that involves the feedback of findings from interventions, or actions, to help in the design and implementation of further action and improvements to organizational effectiveness.

OD techniques: the toolkit

Designing a package of OD interventions is a creative assignment. The approach has to be tailored to fit the culture and problems of the client system. In any particular organization, some approaches are likely to be more appropriate, and perhaps more acceptable, than others. An examination of the OD toolkit has to bear this in mind. The main techniques are these:

Sensitivity training

> **Sensitivity training** is a technique for enhancing individual self-awareness and self–perceptions, and for changing behaviour, through unstructured group discussion.

If you join a **sensitivity training** programme, you will find yourself in a room with other participants, but without an agenda or discussion topic, or other obvious purpose. The aim is to allow participants to discuss themselves, to observe and discuss the ways in which they interact together, and to exchange feedback on each other and their interactions.

Probably the oldest OD intervention, sensitivity training is also known as laboratory training, T-groups (T stands for training or therapy) and encounter groups.

The sensitivity training group may have a facilitator, but sometimes participants are brought together without anyone 'in charge' and are left to create their own conversation. When a facilitator is present, he or she rejects any kind of leadership role, pushing any such requests and suggestions back to the group to discuss and resolve. Without an agenda beyond 'talk about yourselves', the sensitivity training group discussion can quickly turn to feelings and emotions. This may begin with the expression of how participants feel about being in such an unstructured setting. This can then turn into an emotionally charged discussion about how individuals feel about themselves, about other participants, and about the facilitators responsible for this awkward situation. The feelings and emotions exposed in this setting can be personal, confrontational and embarrassing.

Some participants in sensitivity training claim to develop from the experience profound insights about themselves and how they relate to others. Some participants, however, find the lack of structure and the open sharing of emotions uncomfortable, threatening and stressful. Critics have argued that the method can cause psychological damage (see Guest, 1984, pp.201–3, for a review of the evidence on this dimension).

The history of sensitivity training predates the founding of OD. The technique was invented, by accident, in the summer of 1946 when the Connecticut State Inter-Racial Commission asked Kurt Lewin at the Research Centre for Group Dynamics at Massachusetts Institute of Technology to run a training programme for community leaders. Lewin's team designed a programme of lectures, role plays and group discussions. During the evenings, the training team met to share their observations of the course and its participants, to assess how well the programme was progressing. However, some participants were staying in the training centre, and asked if they could observe these evening discussions. Lewin gave them permission to do this, although the other trainers were hesitant.

Kurt Lewin
(1890–1947)

One evening, one participant, listening to the training staff discussing her behaviour during the day, interrupted to challenge their interpretations and to describe what had happened from her perspective. Lewin immediately recognized the potential of this exchange, and an increasing number of participants started to join the evening discussions. Soon the evening sessions were proving as valuable in learning terms as the regular daytime sessions were supposed to be. In other words, participants became more sensitive to their own behaviour, to the effects they had on others, and to how others saw them and related to them.

This method was soon being applied in organizational settings to support change programmes. The first reported use was by the oil company Esso (today Exxon) in its refineries in Louisiana and Texas. Managers were given three-day training laboratories in order to help them develop and to change to a more participative management style

Change the structure

There are numerous ways in which the structure or design of an organization can be changed. Examples include the techniques of job rotation, job enlargement and job enrichment, which target individual jobs, and autonomous teamwork, which targets groups of employees. The techniques of socio-technical systems analysis and organizational design (including autonomous groups) have become part of the OD toolkit too. Business process re-engineering also leads to structural changes affecting organizational processes. It is possible to change the degree of centralization or decentralization in an organization, or to flatten or extend the organization structure, or to change the basis of the organization design from region to product, or vice versa. Rules and procedures can be relaxed or tightened up. These structural issues were discussed in Part 4 [**link**, part 4, organization structures].

Apparently simple structural changes can have profound implications. Structure has a significant influence over access to information and other resources, over work experience and career opportunities, and over the degree of autonomy an individual has. Structure also signifies which departments are marked for growth and which for decline, and structural changes can be used to signal changes in the organization's future direction and priorities.

Edgar Henry Schein (b. 1928)

Process consultation is an OD intervention in which an external consultant acts in a facilitating, supporting, advisory and catalytic capacity to enhance the diagnostic, conceptual and action-planning skills of managers in the organization.

Process consultation

Process consultation engages an external consultant in an advisory role, helping individuals to improve their understanding of organizational problems, and to identify problem-solving actions. One of the main advocates of this approach has been Edgar Schein (1969).

The role of the process consultant is to 'give the client insight', or rather to help clients to develop their own insights. This requires a great deal of skill, sensitivity and tact, and there are no standard procedures to follow. The process consultant may or may not be knowledgeable with respect to the problems facing the organization. The critical skills for a process consultant are in diagnosis, and in forming a supportive, helping relationship. The diagnostic and problem-solving activities of the process consultant are, by definition, joint activities, carried out with the client or clients and not for the client. The focus is on process, which explains the label. Process consultation contrasts with the conventional view of the consultant as an 'expert', where the client is buying specific knowledge and expertise to cover gaps in the organization and also to address and resolve a particular problem.

Survey feedback

Survey feedback is an OD intervention in which the results of an opinion survey are fed back to respondents in the organization in a manner that triggers problem solving with respect to the issues highlighted by the survey findings.

Survey feedback means just what the term implies. The results of an employee opinion survey are fed back (anonymously, protecting individual responses) to managers and employees to help in identifying action that will improve organizational effectiveness. A typical opinion survey includes questions on leadership and management style, aspects of organization culture such as communications, motivation and decision making, and member satisfaction with the organization, their job, their supervisor, their pay and their work group.

A survey can cover the whole organization, or just a department or section. Those responding may be invited to contribute to the initial design of the questionnaire, suggesting questions, highlighting significant issues. Opinion surveys typically reveal differences in perception around an organization, and usually highlight significant problem areas and issues. These findings are then used to trigger discussion about ways to resolve differences and solve organizational problems. The most popular approach for achieving this is through group discussions, in task forces, working parties or project teams, each working on a particular set of themes or issues, or directing their attention to a particular section of the organization.

Team building

Teamwork is fundamental to organizational functioning and is mentioned several times in this text [**link**, part 3, groups and teams in the organization]. The

Team building is an OD intervention which seeks to improve team performance by helping members to understand their own team roles more clearly, and to improve their interaction and collaboration.

performance of teams is central to organizational effectiveness. The issue has attracted a lot of attention from OD practitioners. The first application of **team building**, according to French and Bell (1995), was by Robert Tannenbaum in the early 1950s, at the Naval Ordnance Test Station in California.

There are many different approaches to team building. One popular team-building technique is based on the work of Meredith Belbin (1981; 1996), who argued that teams work most effectively when a number of interdependent roles are covered—Co-ordinator, Shaper, Plant, Evaluator, Teamworker, Completer, Implementer, Specialist, Resource-investigator [**link**, chapter 12, teamworking].

Belbin developed a diagnostic questionnaire to help you to identify your personal team role preference or preferences. Once you have identified your preferred role, you can play to that strength. Once the team has identified which roles are present and which are absent, action can perhaps be taken to compensate for any imbalance. One or more individuals, for example, may be invited to 'hold back' a preferred role if it is over-represented in the group. One or more individuals may be invited to 'cover' roles that are not among their strong preferences but which are missing from the group's overall profile.

Another popular team-building technique involves the simple process of group effectiveness rating. Team members rate their team on a number of criteria. These criteria may include, for example, clarity of goals, willingness to share ideas, time management, focus on achieving results, willingness to listen to others and ability to allow all team members to contribute. The rating questionnaire is first completed individually, and these scores are then shared and discussed in a team meeting. The combined data from the rating questionnaires can thus be used to identify and address differences in perception in the team, to highlight problems affecting teamwork, and to trigger a discussion of how the team is going to overcome those problems and improve performance.

Some training organizations offer team-building programmes based on 'outward bound' techniques. Participants are typically subjected to a series of outdoor challenges involving, for example, mountain walking (preferably in appalling weather), rock climbing, sailing and orienteering. The activities are designed to require teamwork, and to encourage the development of interpersonal trust, group decision making, communication skills and an awareness of leadership roles.

Intergroup development

It is common to find that sections, functions or departments in an organization develop their own unique perspectives and behaviours, which prevent effective interdepartmental communications and collaboration. The functional boundaries that exist between, say, the finance and personnel departments of a large retailing store, or between the inorganic chemistry and marketing departments in a university, can lead to dysfunctional conflict. Within a single unit or function, groups with different goals, backgrounds and working practices may find it difficult to work together when required. OD has, therefore, tried to find ways to improve intergroup relationships and working arrangements.

Intergroup development is an OD intervention which seeks to change the perceptions and attitudes that different groups in an organization hold with respect to each other, and to improve their interaction and collaboration. Variants of this technique are also known as **intergroup confrontation** and **peacemaking**.

How does one combine in harmony in an organization two groups (say, cost accountants and mechanical engineers) who have wholly negative stereotypes and perceptions of each other? One technique is the 'mutual expectations' approach. The two groups first meet separately. The members of each group are asked to note:

1. how they see themselves;

2. their expectations of the other group;

3. what they think the other group expects from them.

The groups then exchange these lists, and meet together to explore the similarities and differences in their perceptions and expectations. Such an exchange can be confrontational. If the meeting is deliberately designed as confrontational, special facilitation skills are required on the part of the OD consultant to keep the discussion under control and to achieve a positive outcome. Once the differences between conflicting groups are known, their causes can be explored, and action can be taken to reduce or remove barriers to effective integration and collaboration.

One variant on the intergroup development technique is known as 'organizational mirroring'. This involves the 'target group' seeking feedback from other groups in the organization on how it is seen and perceived. In this approach, several groups may be involved, and representatives from the other groups are only involved in providing information and ideas, rather than in full negotiation or confrontation with the target group members.

Role negotiation

Role negotiation is an OD intervention which seeks to change the perceptions and attitudes that different individuals in an organization hold with respect to each other, and to improve their interaction and collaboration.

Role negotiation can be a useful way to reconcile differences between two individuals whose working relationship is ineffective. The approach is similar to intergroup development.

The technique assumes that interpersonal friction is caused by a lack of mutual awareness and understanding. The aim in role negotiation, therefore, is to make individual perceptions and mutual expectations explicit so that differences can be identified and resolved.

Other approaches: change systems and procedures

Just about any tool, technique or approach for changing attitudes and behaviour and for improving organizational effectiveness can be regarded and used as an OD intervention. Beyond structural change and a number of specific tools, OD uses a range of other methods to change organizational culture, to encourage individual growth, to foster intergroup collaboration and to improve organizational effectiveness. For example, job definitions, work organization and group relationships can be significantly affected by technological innovation in both office and manufacturing settings. Goals, priorities and behaviours can be altered by making appropriate changes to the organization's payment system.

The whole range of human resource management policies and practices, including recruitment, selection, placement, training and development, promotion and career planning systems, can be used in attempts to influence attitudes and behaviour at work. The organization sends signals about what behaviour is valued through the design of its staff appraisal system, where individuals discuss their goals and their performance at least once a year with their manager. The effects of appraisal can be supported by planned career counselling and development systems designed to reinforce the same messages. Required changes in skills, knowledge, attitudes and behaviour can be encouraged through specially tailored training and development programmes. Communications and working relationships can be improved through a range of mechanisms, such as conferences, forums, workshops, discussion groups and project teams. These mechanisms can focus on particular groups, or can bring together staff from different sections and levels of the organization structure.

Grid organization development

Grid organization development, developed by Robert Blake and Jane Mouton (1964; 1968; 1969); is probably one of the most widely known OD interventions.

The evidence which they collected from around 200 American, British and Japanese companies suggested that the two main barriers to 'business excellence' were planning and communications. One of the main objectives of **Grid OD**, therefore, is to improve business planning by identifying the strategic organizational goals and policies that will guide decisions and actions. A second objective concerns the development of an effective supervisory management style.

Blake and Mouton developed the leadership grid shown in figure 17.1 to help managers to identify and if possible improve their interpersonal management style. The leadership grid assumes that management style has two critical dimensions. The first is *concern for production*, emphasizing task accomplishment. This can cover a wide range of factors, including efficiency and work load, units of output, number of units processed and number of creative ideas suggested. The second is *concern for people*, emphasizing the needs of employees. This can cover involvement, commitment, working conditions, concern for personal worth, job security, fair rewards and good social relationships at work.

The 'nine by nine' leadership grid is used to locate a manager's approach to interpersonal relationships in one of 81 possible variations. Blake and Mouton concentrate for simplicity on the four corner positions and on the style represented by the middle of the grid.

> **Grid OD** is an organization-wide, structured approach to organization development, based on a diagnostic approach to developing an effective management style and on a comprehensive six-phase organizational change model.

Style 1, 1: Impoverished management

This style is based on the belief that conflict should be avoided by avoiding people and by maintaining a neutral position in disputes. Combining a low concern for production with a low concern for people, managers using this style exert mini-

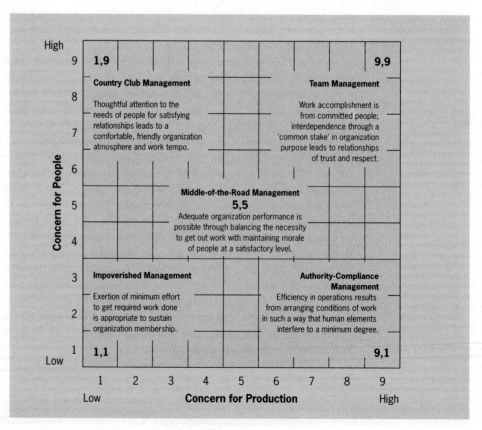

Figure 17.1: The Blake and Mouton leadership grid
From E.E. Blake and A.A. McCanse, *Leadership Dilemmas, Grid Solutions*, copyright © 1991, Gulf Publishing, Houston, 1991, p.29. Reproduced with permission. All rights reserved.

mum effort, keep out of trouble, avoid rocking the boat, focus on their own job security and can be described as defeatist, having abdicated management responsibility.

Style 9, 1: Authority-compliance management

This style is based on the belief that employees will perform well if they are supervised and controlled closely. Combining a high concern for production with low concern for people, managers using this style assume conflict between organizational and employee needs, and concentrate on maximizing output, ignoring employee attitudes, feelings, needs and ideas.

Style 1, 9: Country club management

This style is based on the belief that high work performance depends on treating employees in a friendly manner. Combining a high concern for people with low concern for production, managers using this style concentrate on employee needs, attitudes and feelings, seeking to provide secure and comfortable working conditions potentially at the expense of work output.

Style 9, 9: Team management

This style is based on the belief that organizational and employee needs are inherently compatible. Combining high levels of concern for both people and production, managers using this style share information and involve employees in management decisions. The '9, 9' manager aims to develop cohesive teamwork to achieve high productivity and high morale.

Style 5, 5: Middle-of-the-road management

This style is based on the belief that it is necessary to compromise when employee and organizational needs conflict with each other. Combining moderate levels of concern for both production and people, managers using this style seek workable compromises between employee and organizational needs, attempting to keep employees relatively satisfied while getting the job done to an adequate standard.

The five main styles identified in the leadership grid differ on one other major factor, and this concerns the underlying assumption concerning the nature of organizational conflict. The '9, 9' manager, according to Blake and Mouton, believes that there is no inherent conflict between employee and organizational needs, and that these can be integrated using an appropriate managerial style. Managers adopting the other four styles believe that such conflicts are inevitable, and their different approaches thus reflect different ways of dealing with those conflicts. The basic assumption of OD, of course, and therefore of the grid OD approach, is that conflict is unnecessary and undesirable, a result of poor management.

Blake and Mouton claim that the '9, 9 team management' style is the most effective. The '9, 9' manager gains support for organizational plans by involving employees and thus overcoming communication barriers by openly sharing information. Discussion and debate about decisions, it is assumed, lead to higher levels of commitment than requests for blind obedience. This participative approach to organizational change implementation is fundamental to most of the methodologies discussed in chapter 18 on organizational change.

Blake and Mouton advise that the grid OD approach is applied in a six-phase process, which can take from three to five years to complete, to overcome planning and communications barriers to organizational effectiveness. The six phases, in summary, are as follows:

Phase 1, the grid seminar: Over a full week, participants identify their management style from the leadership grid and learn about communication, problem-solving and teamworking methods from colleagues who have been through special 'pre-phase' training. The aim, of course, is to learn how to become a '9, 9' manager.

Phase 2, teamwork development: Participants develop further and perfect their teamwork with superiors and with subordinates, focusing on current organizational problems.

Phase 3, intergroup development: Groups in the organization who have to interact regularly, but who may have developed negative stereotypes of each other, share their perceptions of each other and meet to establish more effective working relationships by specifying the actions that each will in future take with respect to the other.

Phase 4, developing a strategic organizational model: Here the emphasis shifts to strategic planning. Top management develops clear definitions of financial goals, organizational activities, their customers and markets, the organization structure, decision-making policies, and a growth strategy. The aim is to describe what the organization would be like if its performance was truly excellent. This step alone can take up to one year to complete.

Phase 5, implementing the strategic model: By this stage, if the previous four steps have been effective, barriers to implementation have been removed and communications problems resolved. At this stage, planning teams responsible for implementing the model in detail are appointed for each business unit.

Phase 6, systematic critique: Progress towards the 'ideal' strategic model is reviewed, using a range of formal and informal measurements to assess the quantity and quality of progress, also identifying further organizational development needs and goals.

This is unlike any of the organization change methodologies discussed in the following chapter, for four reasons. First, this is designed as an organization-wide intervention, so it is time-consuming (and expensive) and can be difficult. It can be applied to individual units or departments, but the potential impact is reduced if planning and communication barriers persist in and with other departments.

"You know what I think, folks? Improving technology isn't important. Increased profits aren't important. What's important is to be warm, decent human beings."

Second, the approach recommends one universally effective style of management, not an approach that is contingent on the nature, scale or pace of the change in hand. The exploration of leadership styles in chapter 21 will suggest, in contrast, that the most effective style depends on the context. Third, this approach prescribes in great detail how each phase is to be carried out. Here we have given only a brief summary, but most change advice offers outline guidance only. Finally, the organization does not have to follow all six phases. Phases 1 through 3 deal mainly with communication barriers and can be used on their own, without 'follow-through' into the planning phases.

In presenting the work of Blake and Mouton, many organizational behaviour textbooks focus on their 'grid' model of leadership styles. Some readers will thus look for that model in our chapter on leadership. However, that is a misrepresentation of their contribution. The leadership grid is one tool in the systematic OD package which they advocate.

OD applications: the evidence

OD thus has two important features. First, it is potentially wide in its scope and implications for the organization and its members. Second, the design of an OD programme involves constructing an appropriate package of interventions, which will be different for each organization. Constructing the package requires judgement, creativity, and knowledge of the context. An appropriate package cannot be designed by reading off a matrix.

It is not difficult to see reflected in the OD toolkit the set of assumptions that underpin OD efforts. These assumptions were mentioned earlier but are perhaps now clearer:

- individual and organizational goals are compatible;

- conflict is caused by misunderstandings;

- conflict can be resolved by openly confronting differences in perception;

- the open display of emotions and feelings is valuable;

- people have the capacity and desire for personal growth;

- working relationships can be improved by enhancing self-awareness;

- collaboration and trust are better than conflict and secrecy.

This is why Warren Bennis described OD as a 'truth, trust, love and collaboration approach'. OD interventions rely on the free and open sharing of information and emotions. Where these values are compromised, the OD agenda may also be compromised. One of the other main criticisms of OD is that, although it claims to confront organizational conflict, the role of trade unions in representing employees and bargaining on their behalf for improved conditions is excluded from consideration.

Organization development in local government

Faced with the need to control costs, continue to deliver high-quality services and respond in a rapid and flexible way to change, South Somerset District Council embarked on a radical programme of organizational change in 1991. The main changes concerned a reduction in the number of departments and a flatter management structure. Unit managers in the flat structure had more autonomy to make decisions without having constantly to refer to more senior grades, as they had to do in the past.

To support and reinforce these changes in behaviours and values, the council also introduced an organization development programme. The OD programme had the following components, introduced between 1991 and 1993:

- *workshops* for potential unit managers, on the theme 'into the future';
- an *attitude survey* to discover the level of public satisfaction with the council's services and to identify potential further improvements;
- a *corporate forum*, for elected councillors and senior managers, meeting six times a year informally to discuss strategic issues;
- *service days*, during which teams providing a service meet once a year to explore barriers to improved performance and to plan improvements;
- *staff training*, to ensure that everyone has the skills, knowledge and attitudes to deliver the council's services;
- a *team leaders' programme*, for the hundred managers reporting to unit managers, to develop their skills as intermediaries between senior management and the 'front line';
- a *management skills programme*, based on a 'model manager checklist', to provide structured development for unit managers and others requiring similar skills;
- a *corporate network*, to maintain regular and informal communications between unit managers and others, to share ideas and experience;
- *development for elected councillors*, to equip them with appropriate skills and knowledge;
- *performance appraisal*, for all staff;
- *service reviews*, which regularly explore the need for and delivery of specific services in depth;
- *service agreements*, to ensure that sections providing internal services work to agreed quality standards;
- *upward feedback*, otherwise known as, 'telling your manager how you think they do something and how you might like them to do it differently'.

The aims of this programme were to support a change from a 'command-and-control' organization culture to one in which staff were empowered to make decisions and to make the organization more flexible and responsive to the needs of its local population.

Based on Bob Darbourne, *Lessons from Change at South Somerset District Council*, a South Somerset District Council publication, August 1993.

Stop and criticize

From a critical perspective, some commentators argue that OD is a powerful set of symbolic techniques for manipulating employee attitudes and behaviour. OD thus seeks to disguise the fundamental conflict of interests between the individual and the organization, between employees and management, in a false language of consensus, co-operation and conflict resolution. This is not a principled approach to humanistic management at all. OD from this perspective is highly devious and manipulative.

Where do you stand on this argument? OD as a cunning, underhand management plot, or OD as a sincere attempt to improve the quality of working life?

OD practitioners and their clients are preoccupied with the question 'does it work?' However, OD is a package of approaches to improving organizational effectiveness rather than a specific, well-specified technique: 'more of a process than a step-by-step procedure', as Warren Burke (1987, p.1) notes. The package is configured in different ways to suit differing organizational contexts. It is, therefore, difficult or impossible to conduct systematic research that allows comparisons to be made between interventions and across organizational settings.

The factors which OD seeks to change include a broad spectrum of attitudes and values as well as numerous quantitative indicators of organizational performance. The target of a typical OD programme may be the improvement of teamwork, or the enhancement of working relationships between groups or departments, or improvement of the performance of the organization as a whole, or target all of these levels. There may even be disagreement about which measures or indicators are most significant.

In rigorous research methodology terms (see glossary), the *independent variables* (OD interventions) are loosely defined and inconsistently applied, and the *dependent variables* (measures of organizational effectiveness) are similarly difficult to pin down and may be disputed. These problems are compounded when an action research model is used. Here the 'researcher' is both intimately involved with, and actually seeks to influence, the very interventions and consequences which are the focus of study. How can one adequately assess cause and effect when all the research rules about objectivity and rigour appear to be broken?

Providing any kind of systematic evaluation of the organization-wide approach taken by grid OD has proved to be especially difficult. There are a large number of individual, group, intergroup and organizational factors to consider, and the full process can take years to unfold and complete. Determining cause and effect unambiguously, therefore, is almost impossible. The mainstream OD texts (Cummings and Worley, 1993; French and Bell, 1995) are agnostic, claiming that the approach seems to work well in some settings and that further rigorous research is required to settle the matter.

Nevertheless, advocates of OD have sought to defend the approach with empirical evidence from across a range of applications, over a number of decades of experience. Don Warrick (1984), for example, listed ten potentially positive results from OD interventions:

1. improved organizational effectiveness, including better productivity and morale;

2. better management throughout the organization;

3. commitment to and involvement in making the organization successful;

4. improved teamwork;

5. better understanding of organizational strengths and weaknesses;

6. improved communications, problem solving and conflict resolution;

7. creativity, openness and opportunities for personal development;

8. decrease in dysfunctional behaviour—politicking, playing games;

9. increased ability to adapt to changing circumstances;

10. increased ability to attract and retain quality people.

French and Bell (1995) work through a 'review of reviews', presenting evidence from a broad range of studies and organizational settings. They claim that the literature of the field does indeed demonstrate that 'OD programs produce positive changes at the organizational and individual levels' (p.341). Much of the literature, of course, is produced by OD practitioners, who are in turn responsible for publishing the reviews of other reported OD interventions.

It is further interesting to note that French and Bell end their review by noting the faith that OD practitioners have in the power of OD intervention. Faith-plus-data would be reassuring, they point out, suggesting that, for many practitioners, faith alone is probably good enough. Is this an unsatisfactory conclusion? It was suggested earlier in the chapter that OD has some of the properties of a religious movement. The goals and values of OD concern, in part, the development of individuals through improving conditions of work across a number of dimensions. Improving quality of working life may be seen as a valuable outcome of OD interventions, even where the measurable performance of the organization from an accountant's point of view remains unaffected.

One of the short definitions of OD used at the beginning of the chapter was from Wendell French and Cecil Bell (1995). Here is their 'full' definition (from p.28):

> Organization development is a long-term effort, led and supported by top management, to improve an organization's visioning, empowerment, learning and problem-solving processes, through an ongoing, collaborative management of organization culture—with special emphasis on the culture of intact work teams and other team configurations—utilizing the consultant-facilitator role and the theory and technology of applied behavioural science, including action research.

The phrase 'long-term' implies that there is no 'quick fix' for organizational effectiveness. Change is usually difficult, and the active support of senior management is essential. OD assumes that people will work more effectively together if they share the same vision of the organization's future, and if they are able to develop skills and understanding through empowerment to make decisions and act on their own initiative. OD also assumes that people are capable of development through appropriate experience, hence the emphasis on problem solving and learning. As pointed out in earlier chapters, collaborative or participative management is generally believed to be more acceptable and effective than autocratic, directive management. Most commentators in the late 1990s regarded the team or group or unit as the basic building block of organizational design. Supporting teams and improving team and intergroup working have been longstanding goals of OD.

Stop and criticize	David Collins (1998) points out that, when considering how best to sell a product or service, organizations typically think in terms of market segmentation. In other words, it is usually necessary to tailor the product, or the service, or the marketing message differently for different segments of the potential market.

However, when 'selling' change, OD talks about the need for everyone in the organization to 'share the same vision'. Does this imply that an organization's members have common interests, values, perceptions and goals to a degree that surpasses the untidy differences among people outside the organization?

What does this observation suggest about the practicality of the OD perspective and the validity of the underpinning assumptions?

The OD consultant is a catalyst and a facilitator rather than an expert who is going to carry out the diagnosis and deliver the prescription single-handedly. OD consultants work with their clients as well as for them. OD has since its inception retained the goal of applying social or behavioural science knowledge in a more self-conscious and deliberate style than most management consultants, who may be excused a more pragmatic approach to their clients and their business. This approach is reinforced by the adoption of the action research model.

As the perceived pace of change increased through the 1990s, many commentators sought to challenge the 'no quick fix' assumption. Many organizations found that they needed to change more rapidly than OD seems to allow. OD appears to offer the somewhat elusive promise of improved effectiveness, in the long run, probably difficult to measure, following an extended and probably expensive programme of activities, which initially address intangible factors like beliefs, values and attitudes. This is not a compelling promise in a fast-moving, competitive world where even public sector organizations are required to deliver improvements within tight and non-negotiable timescales.

Robert Schaffer and Harvey Thomson (1992, p.80)—harsh critics—argue that:

The performance improvement efforts of many companies have as much impact on operational and financial results as a ceremonial rain dance has on the weather. While some companies constantly improve measurable performance, in many others, managers continue to dance round and round the campfire—exuding faith and dissipating energy.

This 'rain dance' is the ardent pursuit of activities that sound good, look good, and allow managers to feel good—but in fact contribute little or nothing to bottom-line performance. These activities, many of which parade under the banner of 'total quality' or 'continuous improvement', typically advance a managerial philosophy or style such as interfunctional collaboration, middle management empowerment, or employee involvement. ... Companies introduce these programs under the false assumption that if they carry out enough of the 'right' improvement activities actual performance improvements will inevitably materialize. At the heart of these programs, which we call 'activity-centred', is a fundamentally flawed logic that confuses ends with means, processes with outcomes.

Schaffer and Thomson argue for the advantages of what they call 'results-driven programs' compared with the 'activity-driven programs' of OD. Results-driven programmes aim to produce significant, short-term, measurable performance improvements, in areas where long-term benefits can also be achieved. In an educational context, a results-driven programme could pursue targets such as 95 per cent of student assignments will be marked and returned within four working days of submission; all members of staff who are active in research will publish three journal articles in each calendar year.

Results-driven programmes are built on ambition and impatience, on a desire to see tangible results, now. OD in contrast requires sustained commitment to the pursuit of intangible goals such as attitude change and new sets of values. This does not necessarily mean, however, that results-driven programmes and OD are incompatible. The teams or task forces searching for those rapid performance gains are going to encounter barriers. As they try to overcome those barriers, their actions may well parallel OD interventions to produce culture change. Schaffer and Thomson do not present their approach as 'fast-track' OD, but clearly the techniques of OD can be combined with a results-driven emphasis to generate such an approach.

If French and Bell are correct in their prediction that flatter, organic structures are replacing those based on the traditional paradigm of hierarchical, bureaucratic control, then OD will continue to play a central role in organizational change and improvement. The values and paradigms that OD advocates appear as relevant in the twenty-first century as they have been since the 1960s. As they also claim, the future for OD appears to be bright.

The future is flatter

It seems clear that in large part the old organizational paradigm is dying. It doesn't work well in this emerging environment. Top-down, autocratically directed, rigidly hierarchical, fear-generating organizations are giving way to something new. The new paradigm proclaims that the most innovative and successful organizations will be those that derive their strength and vitality from adaptable, committed team players at all levels and from all specialities, not from the omniscience of the hierarchy. Increasingly, organizations will be flatter, with smaller central staffs and with more real delegation to small groups and units. High-performance organizations focusing on the customer and continuous quality improvement and placing high value on human resources, diversity, and high performance teams will be the norm.

From Wendell French and Cecil Bell, *Organization Development: Behavioural Science Interventions for Organizational Improvement*, Prentice-Hall International, Englewood Cliffs, NJ, fifth edition, 1995, pp.349–50.

To be an OD consultant

What does it take to be an OD consultant? Wendell French and Cecil Bell conclude their text with these words (1995, p.357): 'What is OD all about? OD is really about people helping each other to unleash the human spirit and human capability in the workplace'. Warner Burke (1987, p.143) opens his discussion of this question as follows:

> To be seen as a consultant is to have status, and thus many people aspire to the label and the role. A consultant is one who provides help, counsel, advice, and support, which implies that such a person is wiser than most people.

Burke also lists the personal attributes that the effective OD consultant should possess:

- ability to tolerate ambiguity;
- influencing skill;
- ability to confront difficult issues;
- skills in supporting and nurturing others;
- ability rapidly to recognize one's own feelings and intuitions;
- conceptual skills;
- ability to mobilize self and others;
- ability to teach and to create learning opportunities;
- a sense of humour, to maintain perspective;
- self-confidence;
- a sense of mission about working as an OD consultant.

Stop and criticize

Could you be an effective OD consultant?

Assess yourself against Burke's list of personal attributes and identify your own strengths and weaknesses. Do you want to be a consultant in this field? To what extent do you think this specification is 'superhuman' and beyond the reach of one individual? And is there a place for humility in the consultant's toolkit?

French and Bell (1995) argue that the OD consultant's role is unique because it is based on a collaborative relationship with the client or client organization. The OD practitioner, in their view, is 'a facilitator, catalyst, problem solver, and educator'. This makes the OD consultant a peculiar kind of expert—expert on process, but not necessarily expert on the content of change. The OD consultant who diagnoses and then prescribes the solution is not helping the client organization to develop its own diagnostic and problem-solving capability. In brief, you do not help someone to learn simply by giving them the right answers all the time.

The traditional approach to management consultancy is based on a medical or 'doctor–patient' model. In this perspective, the consultant is the expert diagnostician who investigates and prescribes a cure. In contrast, the OD consultant works together with clients, designing interventions that help organization members to diagnose and resolve their own problems more effectively. The medical model is self-perpetuating. The next time you get sick, you still need to call the doctor. The OD model is self-developmental. If the intervention worked the last time, then you will be equipped to prescribe your own cure the next time you get sick.

OD consultants in particular, and management consultants in general, use a range of styles, distinguished by their reliance on their own skills and knowledge, or on their clients' skills and knowledge. The continuum of styles or approaches is illustrated in table 17.5.

Identifying the skills and knowledge of the effective OD practitioner, Cummings and Worley (1993) first identify four critical areas:

Intrapersonal skills
These may also be described as self-management capabilities. They include conceptual and analytical skills, integrity and moral judgement, being in touch with your own goals and values, learning skills, and stress management. Cummings and Worley recognize that the role can be extremely pressured and stressful. The OD consultant often faces ambiguity, time pressure, conflict and confrontation, emotional outburst, and uncertainty. Handling this kind of environment requires resilience, and an ability to manage one's own emotions and stress responses. The intrapersonal skills are not always visible, but they can be critical.

Interpersonal skills
These include general communication skills, listening, establishing trust and rapport, giving and receiving feedback, negotiation, counselling and coaching. This area also includes 'aptitude in speaking the client's language', which is essential in building rapport and credibility, and in maintaining effective helping relationships.

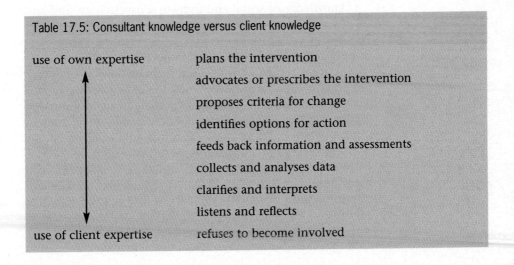

Table 17.5: Consultant knowledge versus client knowledge

use of own expertise

plans the intervention

advocates or prescribes the intervention

proposes criteria for change

identifies options for action

feeds back information and assessments

collects and analyses data

clarifies and interprets

listens and reflects

use of client expertise   refuses to become involved

General consultation skills
These include diagnostic capability, and skills in designing and implementing appropriate OD intervention packages. The latter involves action planning, customizing the package to fit the organization, and presenting ideas in a style that gains commitment and collaboration. Remember that this also involves understanding when and how effectively to involve the organization's members in collaborative diagnostic and implementation activities. This is a more subtle, complex and difficult skill than individual diagnosis and autocratic implementation would involve. The OD consultant should also be knowledgeable and skilled in the use of process consultation methods.

Organization development theory
The OD consultant should be familiar with OD theory and research, and have an understanding of planned change and the action research model. A knowledge of the range of interventions is useful, along with a knowledge of research findings concerning their application. A conceptual understanding of the role of the OD consultant is also valuable.

Cummings and Worley identify a number of other skills and areas of knowledge, including:

- entry and contracting;
- interviewing;
- reward systems;
- theories of learning;
- personality theory;
- cross-cultural theory;
- evaluation research;
- questionnaire design and use;
- participant observation methods;
- data collection and data analysis skills;
- presentation and training skills;
- line management experience;
- knowledge of social and industrial psychology, and anthropology.

This list of skills and knowledge areas could be applied to many organizational positions. They certainly apply to both internal and external consultants to an organization. Much of this list will, in addition, apply to members of internal project teams, working parties, task forces or steering groups. Even though we do not carry the job title 'consultant', many of us find ourselves from time to time involved in organizational data gathering, diagnosis, action planning and change implementation. These qualifications should not be seen as belonging exclusively to the 'professional' OD practitioner or consultant.

The OD consultant may not be 'expert' in a particular organizational area, function, system or problem. However, the range of relevant process expertise is extremely wide. It may be difficult to find many individuals skilled and knowledgeable in all of these areas. The role of the OD consultant does seem to be one with plenty of variety and challenge.

Recap

1. *Explain the goals of OD.*
   - OD aims to apply social science knowledge to solving organizational problems and improving individual well-being through a comprehensive approach to planned change.

2. *Understand the values underpinning the OD movement.*
   - OD is underpinned by a set of values, principles and beliefs concerning mutual respect, integrity, trust, honesty and support.
   - OD assumes that individual and organizational goals are compatible, that conflict is caused by misunderstandings, that the open display of emotions and feelings is valuable, that working relationships can be improved by enhancing self-awareness, and that collaboration and trust are better than conflict and secrecy.

3. *Understand the main OD interventions, how they work, and what they aim to achieve.*
   - OD interventions begin with diagnosis, to identify the level or levels at which the problem or problems arise—individual, group, intergroup or organizational.
   - Force-field analysis is used to assess the factors driving and resisting change so that these forces can be managed.
   - The OD planning model works through a logical, linear series of steps including scouting, entry, diagnosis, planning, action, evaluation and termination.
   - The OD action research model works through an iterative series of steps involving data collection and joint problem solving, which also generates new knowledge.
   - OD uses a range of intervention methods, including sensitivity training, structural change, process consultation, survey feedback, team building, intergroup development, role negotiation, and changes to other human resource management practices.

   - The most comprehensive intervention method is grid OD, an approach which aims to improve strategic planning, interpersonal and interdepartmental communications, and organizational effectiveness through a systematic six-phase model of change based on a leadership style emphasizing high levels of concern for both people and output.

4. *Assess critically the difficulties in evaluating the effectiveness of OD interventions.*
   - From a practical managerial perspective, critics have argued that organizations should target quick, ambitious, measurable performance improvements instead. OD interventions take too much time to deliver unquantifiable benefits.
   - From a critical theoretical perspective, OD can be regarded as a devious and manipulative plot to dupe employees into the belief that their interests are actually aligned with those of management and the organization, thus submerging power inequalities and genuine conflicts of interest. OD is thus a cunning management control mechanism.

5. *List the main skills and areas of knowledge required by an OD consultant.*
   - The OD practitioner requires a range of skills and knowledge, concerned mainly with the process rather than the substance of change, and particularly in social and interpersonal skills such as communicating, negotiating, influencing and conflict resolution.
   - OD practice varies in style. At one extreme is the 'medical' model, in which the consultant diagnoses and prescribes. At the other extreme, the role of the consultant as 'facilitator' is to help client organization members diagnose and resolve problems for themselves.

Revision

1. Organization development is an American-inspired management approach developed in the 1960s. Why is it still important today?

2. What is organization development, and why has it been described as a quasi-religious movement?

3. What skill, knowledge and attributes are required to be an effective organization development consultant?

4. Does organization development work as an approach to improving individual and organizational effectiveness? What does the evidence suggest?

5. What is the main reason for poor performance, from an organization development (OD) perspective, and how does OD address this problem?

Springboard

Beckhard, R., 1969, *Organization Development: Strategies and Models*, Addison-Wesley, Reading, Mass.

One of the first texts in the area, part of an influential Addison-Wesley series of OD books. Still worth reading as a source of the underlying values of OD as well as for specific intervention methods.

Bennis, W.G., 1969, *Organization Development: Its Nature, Origins, and Prospects*, Addison-Wesley, Reading, Mass.

Another seminal text from the Addison-Wesley series, from one of the 'founding fathers' of the OD movement.

Blake, R.R. and McCanse, A.A., 1991, *Leadership Dilemmas: Grid Solutions*, Gulf Publishing, Houston.

A full and up-to-date description of the grid OD approach, including intervention techniques and instruments, and assessing some of the evidence.

Cummings, T.G. and Worley, C.G., 1993, *Organization Development and Change*, West Publishing Company, Minneapolis/St Paul (fifth edition).

A comprehensive and contemporary American OD textbook, well informed and clearly written. An 'industry standard' treatment of the subject.

French, W.L. and Bell, C.H., 1995, *Organization Development: Behavioural Science Interventions for Organizational Improvement*, Prentice-Hall International, Englewood Cliffs, NJ (fifth edition).

A shorter and perhaps more accessible treatment than Cummings and Worley, but another American 'industry standard' OD reference text.

Oswick, C. and Grant, D. (eds), 1996, *Organization Development: Metaphorical Explorations*, Pitman, London.

This is a challenging, and at times entertaining, collection of fourteen chapters exploring contemporary aspects of OD through the lens of different metaphors. Organization development and change has often been described and analysed using the 'journey' metaphor, but these authors demonstrate the value of different metaphors and perspectives on organizational change.

Schaffer, R.H. and Thomson, H.A., 1992, 'Successful change programs begin with results', *Harvard Business Review*, January–February, pp. 80–9.

A critical but influential and much cited paper emphasizing the need to target rapid and measurable improvements in organizational performance instead of focusing on 'soft' and qualitative factors such as values and beliefs.

Schein, E.H., 1969, *Process Consultation: Its Role in Organizational Development*, Addison-Wesley, Reading, Mass.

Yet another text from the Addison-Wesley series, and a seminal treatment of process consultation from a key contributor both to the OD movement and to the subject of organizational behaviour in general.

Home viewing

Bob and Carol and Ted and Alice (1969, director Paul Mazursky) is a sex comedy about the values and inhibitions of two couples, and is a story of Californian wife swapping which appears to have little relevance to organization development. However, for the first fifteen minutes, Bob and Carol Sanders (played respectively by Robert Culp and Natalie Wood) join an encounter or therapy group as observers. This illustrates the classic OD technique of sensitivity training, with a group of around 20 participants in a room with no furniture. Their group has a facilitator who encourages participants to explore their inner feelings and to share their emotions. Bob and Carol are inexorably drawn out of their observing role and into the discussion, in which the emotions are raw and the feelings intense. How does this technique influence their self-awareness and self perception? How does this experience influence their relationship, and also their subsequent behaviour with respect to their friends Ted and Alice Henderson (Elliot Gould and Dyan Cannon)? How would you feel about participating in a therapy group? What are the strengths and weaknesses of this approach to conflict resolution from individual and from organizational perspectives?

Nine to Five (1980, director Colin Higgins) is a comedy about office workers dominated by an arrogant and sexist boss. One section of the film illustrates organization development practices. After years of working in an office with no pictures or plants, and with oppressive personnel policies, Judy Bernly, Violet Newstead and Doralee Rhodes (played by Jane Fonda, Lily Tomlin and Dolly Parton respectively) kidnap their boss, Franklin Hart (Dabney Coleman). They then write memos that dramatically change working conditions and which lead to a 20 per cent productivity increase. Note the organization development techniques used. In what way is each intended to improve working conditions? How do these initiatives contribute to organizational effectiveness?

OB in literature

Elliot Perlman, *Three Dollars*, Picador/Pan Macmillan, Sydney, 1998 (published in Britain by Faber & Faber).

Eddie Harnovey works for the Australian Federal Department of the Environment. He is asked to review plans for commercial smelting at Spenser's Gulf and to recommend pollution controls. Eddie discovers that the smelter will emit sulphurous acid, lead, zinc and arsenic, and recommends new regulations. However, his department manager asks him to delete all references to pollution and tells him that new legislation is unnecessary. Eddie then learns about a government agreement with the company, promising no new limits on heavy metal discharge. He sends his report direct to the minister, and when he receives no reply, he sends it to the newspapers. His line manager, Gerard, complains about Eddie's actions, and Eddie is made redundant in the next reorganization, discovering this through a computer-generated memo. Management in Eddie's department does not display the OD values of respect for the individual, trust, openness and support. What OD interventions could an external consultant have used to deal with the conflict between management and Eddie? How would you rate the success of such intervention in resolving conflicts of this kind?

Chapter exercises

1: What's the cause? What's the solution?

Objectives
1. To identify different perceptions of the causes of the same behavioural event.
2. To assess the range of causal explanations offered.
3. To highlight the importance of matching the solution to the cause of the problem.

Briefing
We know that people often perceive the same event or situation differently. In the case of an organizational problem, how we attribute cause determines, or at least influences, the choice of solution to the problem. In such settings, two reactions are common. First, people often jump to conclusions about causes without having first analysed the situation. Second, the conclusions to which they jump often tend to be narrow in scope.

Read the following 15-word incident report:

> **An elderly woman in a nursing home is found
> dead; she has apparently committed suicide.**

In the space provided, write four alternative hypotheses—possible explanations or causes—for this tragic event:

1: _____
2: _____
3: _____
4: _____

Be prepared to share your explanations with colleagues, and with your instructor.

Note: This activity was first developed by Professor Jack Denfield Wood, IMD, Lausanne, Switzerland. Used with permission.

2: What the chief executive wants—OD consultants in action

Objectives
1. To explore the tensions and dilemmas that can surface in practical OD consulting work.
2. To expose the ethical dimensions of OD consulting.

Briefing
As you read through the following incident report, based on a real (disguised) case, consider the following questions:

1. If you were a member of the consulting team, how would you have acted differently in these circumstances, and why?

2. On the evidence of this account, what advice would you give to this consulting team?

3. What advice would you give to the chief executive?

This incident was reported by a member of an external consulting team working for a local authority in Central Scotland. The OD assignment was to introduce structural and cultural change to an organization that had operated in much the same style since the early 1970s. A new chief executive had recently been appointed with this remit. The leader of the consulting team was a long standing personal friend of the new chief executive.

The annoying thing was, we got this assignment against stiff competition, because we didn't want to sell any one particular solution. They were impressed by our flexibility. Local council, they wanted a review of their twenty-year-old officer and member organization structures. In fact they wanted us to present options, maybe simple, maybe radical, from which they could choose, within the constraint of a no redundancy policy. We won the assignment in a presentation to [a policy and resources] sub-committee, mainly councillors, with a couple of senior officers present. The leader of our consulting team was an ex-colleague and friend of the council's new chief executive.

The following week, we were invited to a meeting with the chief executive, to launch the project, agree our liaison mechanisms, find a room to work in, and so on. We spent a couple of hours discussing the logistics, then he asked us if we would have some lunch, and sandwiches and stuff were trayed in. However, as we were hoovering this lot up, he produced a seven page document, and gave the four of us copies. He worked through this, line by line for about an hour. This set out what he wanted to see in our final report. Some of this had been in the original brief for the assignment, set out in general terms, and here it was again with some specific recommendations and markers for action, concerning parts of the organization structure and named individuals in specific posts, which were not expected to survive the review. We didn't have as much such flexibility as we had thought.

The project rolled out over that year, and our recommendations got firmed up as we collected more information. Basically, this was an autocratically managed, hierarchical, rigid, bureaucratic organization, with lots of time and money wasted on unnecessary procedures and rule-following, and with poor staff morale. So our recommendations were going to be about cutting hierarchy, empowering people, changing the management style, making procedures more flexible, getting decisions taken more quickly, and the chief executive was behind all this. The main client was the sub-committee to which we reported, about every quarter. But not before the chief executive had at his request seen an advance copy of the report, commented on it and suggested changes. Quite reasonable, as he would be directly affected by any recommendations about the structure, and also saw himself as a client for our services. This put us in an awkward position. We knew his thinking, and other managers would ask us about that, and we had to fudge answers like, 'that's one of the issues still under consideration'. This also meant we had to build his ideas into our reports, finding some rationale for supporting them, which was important because if questions came up in committee, we would have to explain and defend the point, although he might chip in and voice some agreement with and sympathy for our view from time to time.

Then we started getting bother from one of the councillors, saw himself as an expert in organization theory. He came up with a proposal for a matrix structure with multidisciplinary teamworking. The teamworking was our idea too, partly to address some communications problems. But the matrix wasn't going to fit their business. We got nowhere with the guy in the full committee, so two of us asked him if we could meet him the next day, maybe over lunch, to kick this around. Turned out his concern was not with a matrix at all, but with the way the new director roles would be specified, that they would be like the previous management group (which he didn't trust), just with new titles. So we built the teamworking ('great idea, thanks for that') and a revised role spec into the report, and he bought that.

The chief executive even sub-edited our final report, making changes to the recommendations which we then had to justify. What if we hadn't been able to roll with these pressures? We would have upset the chief executive, who saw our ability to incorporate his thinking as a reflection of our consulting expertise, and we would probably get no more work with this client. If we hadn't handled these individuals, and others, in this sort of way, the whole project could have been at risk, and the time and contributions of a lot of other staff would have been wasted.

From Dave Buchanan and Richard Badham, *Power, Politics and Organizational Change: Winning the Turf Game*, Sage Publications, London, 1999.

Chapter 18 Organizational change

Key concepts

adhocracy	future shock
triggers of change	resistance to change
the coping cycle	the Yerkes–Dodson law
business process re-engineering	change agent
strategic change	stakeholder
readiness for change	processual/contextual theory of change

Learning objectives

When you have read this chapter, you should be able to define those key concepts in your own words, and you should also be able to:

1. Understand the typical characteristics of human responses to change.

2. Identify the main external and internal triggers of organizational change.

3. Understand the nature of resistance to change and approaches to overcoming it.

4. Explain the advantages and limitations of participative methods of change management.

5. Explain the strengths and weaknesses of the processual/contextual perspective on change.

6. Outline the skill requirements of the effective change agent.

Why study organizational change?

Without question, the most desirable management skill for the nineties will be the ability to manage change. This is one of the rarest and most difficult skills to learn—for very good reasons. Management has always been about change, for it is uniquely the task of making more, or better, from less.

John Harvey-Jones' (1993, p.21) comment applies as much now as it did back in the 1990s. The organizational requirement to 'adapt or perish' remains just as powerful. Change is now one of the most pressing issues facing organizations, their managers and their employees. Organizations face an unrelenting stream of pressures from global competition, social and demographic trends, shifts in gov-

ernment policy, geo-political events, and a continuing stream of new technologies. The American management 'guru' Tom Peters claims that we should not be even talking about change any more, but that we need to think in terms of constant organizational revolution. Failure to adapt in an appropriate and timely manner implies organizational failure, with obvious consequences for individual jobs and careers.

The paradoxical nature of change

Stop and criticize

How would you respond to these three 'true or false' questions?

'People have a natural resistance to change.'   true or false?

'People get bored with routine and seek out new experiences.'   true or false?

'Older people are more resistant to change.'   true or false?

Did you want to answer 'true' to all three of these statements? A moment's reflection should suggest that these positive responses are inconsistent with each other and also contradict the evidence. For example, many people when they retire from work take up radically new activities and hobbies: painting, acting, community involvement, a musical instrument. We cannot have 'natural resistance' to change and be 'new experience seekers' at the same time, can we? Is there a paradox here? How can that paradox be resolved?

Change is a major and recurring theme throughout this text. In part 1, we explored the organizational context, noting how environmental and technological trends and pressures encourage particular kinds of organizational change. In part 2, we considered the possibilities of changing human learning, personality, communication skills, perception and motivation. In part 3, we examined how individual behaviour changes in group settings, and how group functioning can be changed to improve performance. In part 4, we explored changes and trends in organization design. In part 5, we explore four major organizational processes, including change, and in part 6 we consider how leaders can change employee behaviour, and also consider whether leaders themselves can and should change their styles.

The need for organizational change can be prompted or initiated by many different **triggers**.

External triggers for organizational change can include:

- developments in technology;
- developments in new materials;
- changes in customers' requirements and tastes;
- the activities and innovations of competitors;
- new legislation and government policies;
- changing domestic and global economic and trading conditions;
- shifts in local, national and international politics;
- changes in social and cultural values.

Internal triggers for organizational change can include:

- new product and service design innovations;
- low performance and morale, triggering job redesign;
- appointment of a new senior manager or top management team;
- inadequate skills and knowledge base, triggering training programmes;
- office and factory relocation, closer to suppliers and markets;
- recognition of problems, triggering reallocation of responsibilities;
- innovations in the manufacturing process;
- new ideas about how to deliver services to customers.

Listing triggers in this way makes organizational change sound like a reactive process. Clearly this is not always the case. In some instances, it will be appropriate to anticipate events and trends, and to be proactive in introducing appropriate organizational changes.

One of the best-known metaphors for organizational change is that developed by Kurt Lewin (1951), who argued for the need to unfreeze the current state of affairs, to move to the desired new state, then to refreeze and stabilize those changes. However, refreezing no longer seems to be an option. Constant transformation, it seems, is the norm. Permanent thaw is perhaps a more appropriate metaphor. Many organizations now face a 'high-velocity' environment

> A **trigger of change** is any 'disorganizing pressure' arising outside or inside the organization, indicating that current arrangements, systems, procedures, rules and other aspects of organization structure and process are no longer effective.

(Eisenhardt and Bourgeois, 1988) in which turbulent and rapidly changing external conditions are translated into a complex, multi-faceted, fluid and interlinked stream of initiatives affecting work and organization design, resource allocation, and systems and procedures in continuous attempts to improve performance. The environment for most organizations is likely to remain volatile, or become even more turbulent. Current trends do not lead to predictions of continuity and stability in the near future.

Organizational change problems will thus remain on the management agenda for some time. The study of change, however, is challenging and paradoxical for a number of reasons:

- As the triggers and consequences of organizational change are many and complex, establishing 'cause and effect' is problematic in most settings.

- Organizational change has to be studied at different levels of analysis—individual, group, organizational, social—which are interrelated in complex ways.

- Organizational change has to be studied as a process, in terms of a series of events unfolding through time, and not as a static or time-bounded event, raising questions concerning the appropriate time frame for analysis.

- Change that affects a large number of different stakeholders is difficult to evaluate as there may be no agreed common criteria on which to base judgements.

- Change can only be understood fully in relation to continuity, with respect to what has not changed.

This latter point, concerning continuity, is both fundamental and controversial. On the one hand, the rapid pace and wide scale of contemporary technological, organizational and social change appear to be obvious. Whole industries collapsed and almost disappeared (coal mining, steel making) in the twentieth century, while others mushroomed (computer software, mobile telephony). Many of the technologies that shape the nature of medicine, communications and home entertainment, for example, were not available even five years ago. And these technologies potentially affect the design of jobs, the experience of work, the progress of individual careers, and organization structures.

Change has never been so fast

That this is an age of change is an expression heard frequently today. Never before in the history of mankind have so many and so frequent changes occurred. These changes that we see taking place all about us are in that great cultural accumulation which is man's social heritage. It has already been shown that these cultural changes were in earlier times rather infrequent, but that in modern times they have been occurring faster and faster until today mankind is almost bewildered in his effort to keep adjusted to these ever increasing social changes. This rapidity of social change may be due to the increase in inventions, which in turn is made possible by the accumulative nature of material culture [i.e., technology].

From William Fielding Ogburn, *Social Change: With Respect to Culture and Original Nature*, B.W. Huebsch, New York, 1922, pp.199–200.

Table 18.1: Contemporary change management problems

per cent	agreed that
63	people are suffering from 'initiative fatigue'
67	there has been so much change, not all beneficial, that the main employee response is now cynicism
72	people are suffering from 'information overload'
78	fear of the unknown is a major cause of resistance to organizational change

Henry Mintzberg (1994) argues that our preoccupation with change is overstated. We are impressed by the contemporary sweep of technological marvels, the significance of which is typically exaggerated by enthusiastic journalists seeking apocalyptic predictions of things to come. Each new generation, Mintzberg argues, 'discovers' change anew, as something unique to them, which previous generations have not had to endure. The quotation from William Fielding Ogburn, writing in 1922, supports this view. This is not an argument which says 'nothing has really changed'. The point is that, when considering organizational change, we should be aware also of continuities, of what is not changing.

On the other hand, it is not difficult to list features of technology, jobs, organizations and society at the beginning of the twenty-first century that have barely changed since the beginning of the twentieth. For example, personal transport still relies on an internal combustion engine fuelled by petrol. Securing suitable employment remains a social norm and is central to most people's definition of personal identity. If you commit a serious crime in Britain, you will still be tried by a jury in a sombre courtroom with a judge wearing a funny wig. Some observers have pointed out, unkindly, that the British railways, in private ownership then as they are today, were more reliable and faster in the early twentieth century.

The paradoxical nature of change means that this area is still deeply problematic in practice. For example, a recent survey of management experiences of change (Buchanan, Claydon and Doyle, 1999) produced the results summarized in table 18.1. These findings suggest that organizational change can generate fear, fatigue and cynicism. Whatever our observations about continuity, these seem to be genuine and serious emotional responses. In this chapter, we will explore how these kinds of problem can be addressed by considering competing perspectives on organizational change and by exploring the advice on effective change implementation which can be found in the management literature. We will first consider the implications of change for individuals, then explore the nature of resistance to change and management techniques for overcoming that resistance. We will then explore contrasting theoretical and practical perspectives on the change process before finally considering John Harvey-Jones' challenge—what does it take to be an effective change agent?

Strategic change: the contemporary imperative

We need to be clear what kind of change we are discussing. Some changes are major, long-term, expensive and risky, while others are more straightforward. One way of distinguishing different types of change is to consider how deeply the change penetrates the organization. This approach, based on the work of Roger

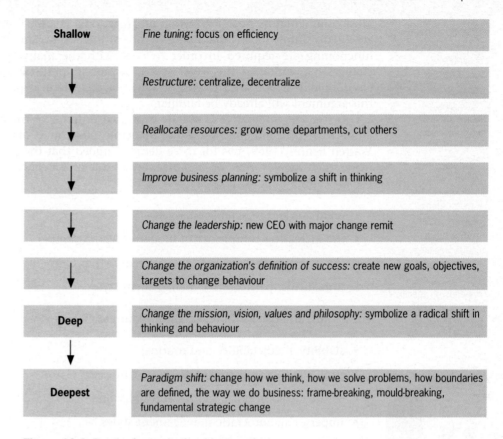

Figure 18.1: Depth of organizational intervention

Collins (personal communication), is illustrated in figure 18.1. The nature of the change management task shifts as one progresses down this classification. The job of managers engaged in fine tuning is more straightforward than the task of their colleagues implementing deep change.

What one finds in most organizations is a number of change initiatives being progressed simultaneously, at different levels. This classification does not lead to an argument that 'all change must be deep change'. Deep change is appropriate when dealing with 'deep problems', while 'fine tuning' is a more appropriate response to minor problems.

| **Stop and criticize** | If you aspire to a high-flying, fast-track management career, you are unlikely to get very far if you concentrate on the implementation of shallow changes. By definition, shallow changes do not contribute much to organizational performance and will not enhance your visibility and reputation in the eyes of more senior managers.

Identify representative examples of 'shallow' and 'deep' organizational change in your experience. Surely you would be better advised to be associated with major, deep changes, as long as they are seen to be successful?

To what extent does this argument lead to the cynical conclusion that major changes are often introduced in the interests of progressing individual careers?

Strategic change is a term used to describe organizational redesign or refocusing that is major, radical, 'frame-breaking' or 'mould-breaking' or 'paradigmatic' in its nature and implications. The term 'strategic' denotes scale, magnitude or depth. Deciding whether change is strategic or not depends on specific organizational circumstances.

Most commentators now accept that organizational change is a **strategic** imperative. This simply means that major or radical shifts in organizational design and functioning are required in order to cope with the many and unpredictable changes happening in the wider social, economic, political and technological environment. If you are studying strategic management as part of your course, this argument will already be familiar.

This strategic imperative is usually expressed in terms of the need for organizations to become more flexible, more adaptable, more 'fluid' and more responsive. Warren Bennis (1969) has for three decades argued that the pace of change has made traditional forms of organization obsolete. Bureaucratic structures, he claims, cannot cope with:

- rapid and unpredictable change;
- the increasing complexity of modern organization;
- the diversity of specialist expertise required in many organizations; and
- humanistic, participative management styles.

For Bennis, and others, bureaucratic structure may be appropriate to deal with:

- stability, predictability and routine;
- simple and orderly organization structures;
- standardized, routinized jobs and skills; and
- impersonal, autocratic management styles.

Alvin Toffler

Adhocracy is a type of organization design which is temporary, adaptive, creative, in contrast with bureaucracy, which tends to be permanent, rule-driven and inflexible. Adhocracy is similar to the concepts of **organic** and **integrative** organizational styles; while bureaucracy equates with **mechanistic** and **segmentalist** approaches.

Bennis spoke of 'adaptive structures'. Tom Burns and George Stalker (1961) distinguished between rigid, **mechanistic** management systems and fluid, **organic** systems. In 1970, Alvin Toffler used the term **adhocracy**. In 1983, Rosabeth Moss Kanter contrasted rigid **segmentalist** structures with innovative **integrative** approaches. The concept of the *post-modern organization* became fashionable in the 1990s. These commentators appear to have considered broadly the same issues and concepts, and to have adjusted the labels [**links**, chapter 2, the world outside; chapter 16, organization strategy and design].

Organization and management theorists have been remarkably consistent in their criticisms of traditional structures, and in their advocacy of flexible approaches to coping with change, uncertainty and turbulence. Cynics might point out that the main innovations in this research tradition have been in the names given to the 'old' and 'new' types of structure. One major problem that appears only recently to have been recognized concerns the need to create organizations that are flexible enough to adapt to pressures for change, and that are also stable enough to endure. The fluid, shifting organization may in theory seem to be an appropriate vehicle for dealing with external turbulence. However, this kind of organization can be an extremely uncomfortable and insecure place in which to work.

In summary, conventional wisdom claims that organizations must be able to respond rapidly to external changes if they are to survive, and that the necessary internal restructuring is likely to be strategic or 'mould-breaking'. The mould that needs to be broken is the rigid, autocratic, bureaucratic approach to organization and management. The new organizational framework required appears to be one that emphasizes flexibility, creativity and participation.

Out with the segmentalist, in with the integrative

Rosabeth Moss Kanter, in her book on organizational change in 1983, claimed that:

I found that the entrepreneurial spirit producing innovation is associated with a particular way of approaching problems that I call 'integrative': the willingness to move beyond received wisdom, to combine ideas from unconnected sources, to embrace change as an opportunity to test limits. To see problems integratively is to see them as wholes, related to larger wholes, and thus challenging established practices—rather than walling off a piece of experience and preventing it from being touched or affected by any new experiences. . . .

Such organizations reduce rancorous conflict and isolation between organizational units; create mechanisms for exchange of information and new ideas across organizational boundaries; ensure that multiple perspectives will be taken into account in decisions; and provide coherence and direction to the organization. In these team-oriented co-operative environments, innovation flourishes. . . .

The contrasting style of thought is anti-change-oriented and prevents innovation. I call it 'segmentalism' because it is concerned with compartmentalizing actions, events, and problems and keeping each piece isolated from the others. . . . Companies where segmentalist approaches dominate find it difficult to innovate or to handle change.

From Rosabeth Moss Kanter, *The Change Masters: Corporate Entrepreneurs at Work*, George Allen & Unwin, London, 1983, pp.27–8.

Change and the individual

Rapid change may be 'normal', but it can also have severe psychological consequences. Alvin Toffler (1970) argued that the rate of change was out of control, and that society was 'doomed to a massive adaptational breakdown'. Thirty years later, that massive breakdown does not appear to have happened. However, Toffler also believed that there is a limit to the amount of change that we as individuals can handle. He argued that 'the shattering stress and disorientation that we induce in individuals by subjecting them to too much change in too short a time' is unhealthy. He labelled this response **future shock**.

Stop and criticize

Think of the changes—technological, personal, social, organizational, political, economic— that you have seen and experienced over, say, the past two years. Do you feel disoriented and stressed as a result? How about family members and friends—are they displaying signs of stress and disorientation as a result of too much change? From your responses, do you think Toffler was right in his 'diagnosis'?

Future shock is the stress and disorientation suffered by people when they are subjected to excessive change. Toffler also called future shock 'the disease of change'.

Our response to change is neither as simple nor as predictable as Toffler suggested. One influential approach to understanding this comes from studies of the ways in which we cope with traumatic personal loss, such as the death of a close relative. Elizabeth Kubler-Ross (1969) argued that we deal with loss by moving through a series of stages, each characterized by a particular emotional response. This **coping cycle** has been used to understand responses to organizational change, which can sometimes be particularly traumatic and stressful.

The five typical stages in the Kubler-Ross response coping cycle are illustrated and defined in table 18.2. As with all such models, this 'universal sequence' disguises the fact of individual differences. We may not all experience the same five sets of responses. We may omit particular stages, 'revisit' some stages, or pass

The **coping cycle** is a human response to trauma and significant loss, suggesting that the individual typically (but not always) passes through a series of emotional stages, including denial, anger, bargaining, depression and acceptance.

Table 18.2: The coping cycle

stage	response
denial	unwillingness to confront the reality: 'this is not happening'; 'there is still hope that this will all go away'
anger	turn accusations on those apparently responsible: 'why is this happening to me?'; 'why are you doing this to me?'
bargaining	attempts to negotiate, to mitigate loss: 'what if I do it this way?'
depression	the reality of loss or transition is appreciated: 'it's hopeless, there's nothing I can do now'; 'I don't know which way to turn'
acceptance	coming to terms with and accepting the situation and its full implications: 'what are we going to do about this?'; 'how am I going to move forward?'

through them more or less quickly than others. From an organizational perspective, this can be a useful explanatory and diagnostic tool. If one is able to detect where in the response cycle a person may be, in the face of organizational change, one could be better placed to provide appropriate guidance, advice and support.

Just how much pressure can we take from organizational change? Psychology has long suggested that the relationship between arousal, or sensory stimulation, on the one hand, and human performance, on the other, varies systematically, in the form of an 'inverted U' function. This is sometimes known as the **Yerkes–Dodson law**, after the originators (Yerkes and Dodson, 1908), and is illustrated in figure 18.2.

The **Yerkes–Dodson law** states that task performance increases as our state of arousal increases, and that beyond some 'optimal' point, we become overwhelmed by the level of stimulation or pressure, and our performance starts to fall.

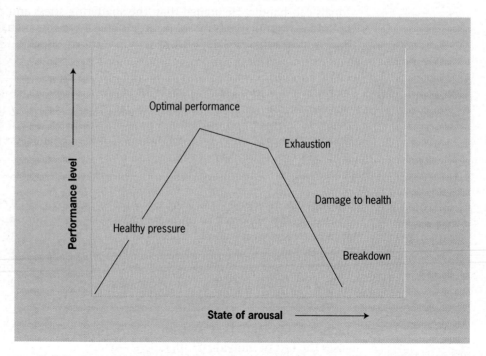

Figure 18.2: Pressure and performance—the inverted-U function

The 'optimum' point depends on the capacities of the individual. Applied to a work setting, this implies that performance is likely to be low if the level of arousal is low, perhaps because the task is repetitive and boring. Performance can sometimes be improved in such settings with background music, conversation, and by frequent job rotation. Now suppose that the job becomes more demanding, because it becomes more interesting and challenging, making more use of the individual's skills and knowledge. As the level of arousal and stimulation increases, performance is likely to increase. However, a point will eventually be reached where the level of arousal becomes so great that it is perceived not as stimulation but as overwhelming pressure. At this point fatigue sets in, leading eventually to ill-health and breakdown if the pressure continues to escalate.

Can organizational change induce such pressure, leading to poor performance? It is interesting to note that, in the survey cited earlier (Buchanan, Claydon and Doyle, 1999), 63 per cent of managers surveyed said that people in their organizations were suffering from 'initiative fatigue'. With each new change initiative, people have to spend time learning new tasks (and forgetting old ones), implementing new systems and procedures, developing new knowledge, using new skills and behaviours, and all of this, typically, under severe time pressure because the organization cannot stop functioning while this happens. Where change initiatives are frequent, as is now common, this can push people's arousal levels beyond their optimum performance point. In a subsequent survey, just under half of respondents claimed that the pace of change was causing middle management 'burnout'.

The Yerkes–Dodson law applied specifically to work settings is summarized in table 18.3, which plots typical changes in response, experience and performance for five escalating pressure levels. There are two qualifications to make to this explanation. First, determining the 'optimal' level of pressure can be hazardous, because this depends on the individual, and we are each capable of handling different levels of pressure. Second, appropriate levels of stimulation also depend on the difficulty of the task. The easier the task, the higher the level of appropriate stimulation. This explains why music can destroy our concentration during a

Table 18.3: The pressure–performance relationship explained

Pressure level	Response	Experience	Performance
very low	boredom	low levels of interest, challenge and motivation	low, acceptable
low to moderate	comfort	interest aroused, abilities used, satisfaction, motivation	moderate to high
moderate to high	stretch	challenge, learning, development, pushing the limits	high, above expectations
high to unrealistic	stress	overload, failure, poor health, dysfunctional coping behaviour	moderate to low
extreme	panic	confusion, threat, loss of self-confidence, withdrawal	low, unacceptable

Managers' emotional responses to change

Mike Broussine and Russ Vince (1996) asked 86 senior and middle managers in six public sector organizations (local government and health care) to 'draw a picture which expresses your feelings about change at work in your organization'. This use of visual imagery is novel in organizational research, and potentially allows respondents to reveal ideas and emotions that would be more difficult to express in language. The organizations from which these managers came had experienced considerable upheaval in the few years before this study.

Analysis of the managers' drawings displayed a range of emotions about change:

Emotional responses	Typical drawings
anxiety, fear, dread	organizational ship swamped by tidal wave, hospital being demolished
fear of personal catastrophe	gravestones, menacing clouds, unhappy faces, football team with three dead members
anger, violence, revenge	organization as decapitated maiden, castle blown apart by cannon
opportunity for personal development	ugly duckling becoming a swan, smiling face on strong body, flourishing tree
denial and rationalization	holiday scenes, oasis, idyllic surroundings
paradox, optimism and pessimism	angry politician pushing boulder uphill along with a ship sailing towards sunset and a gold cup for a prize, double-edged sword, *kamikaze* and astronaut
powerlessness and debility	piles of paperwork, long queues of people, computer spewing out information, very small tree in an empty landscape with a single acorn
destabilization, alienation	manager on a treadmill with sign reading 'business as usual during alterations'
a journey to endure	castles in the air, beach scenes, horse and cart in an ominous valley, vaulting barriers, boats tossed on shark-infested ocean close to tropical island

The researchers conclude that this approach reveals 'the paradoxical, sometimes contradictory and generally messy emotional reality that managers experience in a period of tremendous change' (p.65). The category with the smallest number of illustrative drawings was the one concerned with opportunity for personal development.

Based on Mike Broussine and Russ Vince, 'Working with metaphor towards organizational change', in Cliff Oswick and David Grant (eds), *Organization Development: Metaphorical Explorations*, Pitman, London, 1996, pp.57–72.

chess game (or perhaps while reading a complex chapter in an organizational behaviour textbook) but may be very enjoyable during a restaurant meal.

Many laboratory experiments have explored the pressure–performance relationship across a range of settings and factors. However, this theory has intuitive appeal as it can be applied to personal experience; if you are listening to the radio while reading this chapter, then clearly we made it too easy for you. But how can this theory be used in a practical organizational setting? How does management know what levels of pressure people are experiencing, or when people are getting 'close to the edge'? The obvious approach is to ask, but that may not always be appropriate or tactful. However, there are lots of useful 'proxy' measures which can indicate, among other things, that people are working under too much pressure. These proxy measures that can indicate people are suffering excessive work pressure include:

unexplained absences	high rates of sickness	labour turnover
more customer complaints	more employee grievances	accidents and mistakes

Physical appearance changes as people become stressed. Interpersonal relationships become strained. In other words, there are a number of observable signs which can indicate that people are suffering overload, prompting management action to reduce the pressure [**link**, chapter 5, personality].

Resistance to change: causes and management solutions

It is often possible to anticipate responses to organizational change, and to use that knowledge both to develop support for change and to address **resistance to change** at an early stage.

Change has both positive and negative aspects. On the one hand, change implies experiment and the creation of something new. On the other hand, it means discontinuity and the destruction of familiar structures and relationships. Despite the positive attributes, change can be resisted because it involves confrontation with the unknown and loss of the familiar.

It is widely assumed that resistance to change is a common and a natural phenomenon. Change can be threatening. Change presents those involved with new situations, new problems and challenges, and with ambiguity and uncertainty. Many people find change, or the thought of change, painful and frustrating.

Arthur Bedeian (1980) cites four common causes of resistance to organizational change:

Parochial self-interest
We understandably seek to protect a status quo with which we are content and regard as advantageous to us in some way. Change may threaten to move us out of our 'comfort zone', away from those things which we prefer and enjoy.

We develop vested interests in the perpetuation of organization structures and accompanying technologies. Change can mean loss of power, prestige, respect, approval, status and security. Change can also be personally inconvenient for many reasons. It may disturb relationships and other arrangements that have taken much time and effort to establish. It may force an unwelcome move in location. It may alter social opportunities. Perceived as well as actual threats to interests and values are thus likely to generate resistance. We may identify ourselves more closely with our specific functions and roles than with the organization as a whole. We then have a personal stake in our specialized knowledge and skills and in their creations, and may not be willing readily to see these made redundant or obsolete.

Misunderstanding and lack of trust
We are more likely to resist change when we do not understand the reasoning behind it, or its nature and possible consequences. Resistance can thus be reduced through improved understanding. If managers have little trust in their employees,

> **Resistance to change** can be defined as an inability, or an unwillingness, to discuss or to accept organizational changes that are perceived in some way damaging or threatening to the individual.

information about change may be withheld, or distorted. Incomplete and incorrect information creates uncertainty and rumour. This has the unfortunate result of increasing perceptions of threat, of increasing defensiveness, and reducing further effective communication about the change. The way in which change is introduced can thus be resisted, rather than the change itself.

Contradictory assessments

We each differ in the ways in which we perceive and evaluate the costs and benefits of change; a major disruptive threat for me can be a fresh and stimulating challenge for you. Our personal values ultimately determine which changes are welcomed, promoted and succeed, and which fail. Our contradictory assessments are more likely to arise when communication is inadequate, and where those concerned lack the relevant information. Bedeian points out that contradictory analyses of change can lead to constructive criticism and improved proposals. Resistance to change is not necessarily dysfunctional but can in some circumstances lead to more effective forms of change and change implementation.

Low tolerance for change

We differ in our ability to cope with change, to face the unknown, to deal with uncertainty. Change that requires people to think and behave in different ways can challenge the individual's self-concept. We each have ideas about our abilities and our competencies. One response to change may thus be self-doubt and self-questioning: 'can I handle this?' Some people have a low tolerance for ambiguity and uncertainty. The anxiety and apprehension that they suffer may lead them to oppose even potentially beneficial changes.

Are there only four reasons why people resist change? No. Bedeian summarized what he believed to be the main causes. In the previous section we identified 'initiative fatigue' as a possible source of resistance to change. Tony Eccles (1994), on the other hand, identifies thirteen possible sources of resistance:

- ignorance   a failure to understand the problem

- comparison   the solution is disliked because an alternative is preferred

- disbelief   a feeling that the proposed solution will not work

- loss   the change has unacceptable personal costs

- inadequacy   the rewards from change are not sufficient

- anxiety   the fear of being unable to cope with the new situation

- demolition   the change threatens to destroy existing social arrangements

- power cut   sources of influence and control will be eroded

- contamination   new values and practices are repellent

- inhibition   the willingness to change is low

- mistrust   management motives for change are considered suspicious

- alienation   other interests are more highly valued than new proposals

- frustration   the change will reduce power and career opportunities

There seems to be considerable overlap across these different headings; 'comparison' and 'contamination' sound as though they might mean much the same thing in practice, as do 'power cut' and 'frustration'. But this is not the main point, which concerns the observation that there are potentially as many differ-

Contemporary change barriers and success factors

Top ten barriers	%*	Top ten success factors	%
Competing resources	48	Ensuring top sponsorship	82
Functional boundaries	44	Treating people fairly	82
Change management skills	43	Involving employees	75
Middle management	38	Giving quality communications	70
Long IT lead times	35	Providing sufficient training	68
Communication	35	Using clear performance measures	65
Employee opposition	33	Building teams after change	62
HR issues (people, training)	33	Focusing on culture and skill change	62
Initiative fatigue	32	Rewarding success	60
Unrealistic timetables	31	Using internal champions	60

* Results from interviews with key managers associated with change processes over the previous three years in a global sample of 500 companies. With 70 questions, the survey covered 150 companies in Britain, 150 in America, 150 in Europe, and 50 in the Far East and Australia.

Based on PriceWaterhouseCoopers Consulting (PWC) and Market Opinion Research International (MORI), *Global Change Management Study*, 1997.

ent reasons for resisting change as there are individuals affected by the change in the first place. If we accept the 'adapt or perish' argument, which says that organizations must change to compete and survive, then the human aspects of change, in general, and the management of resistance, in particular, are critical.

How can resistance be managed in practice? One approach concerns *stakeholder analysis*. A second set of approaches concerns the use of a range of management techniques. One cannot expect everyone in an organization to respond in the same way to specific change proposals. Different individuals and groups are likely to be affected in different ways and are therefore likely to respond differently. Anticipating responses becomes possible when one understands the **stakeholders** concerned with a particular organizational change.

Stakeholder analysis is a useful first step in planning change. The process is:

1. Draw up a list of stakeholders affected by the changes proposed.

2. Establish what each will gain or lose if the change goes ahead.

3. Use the potential benefits to strengthen support for the proposals.

4. Find ways to address the concerns of those who feel they will lose out, by altering the nature of the changes proposed, perhaps, or offering to reduce losses in other ways.

Gerard Egan (1994) identifies nine types of stakeholder:

- Your *partners* are those who support your agenda.

- Your *allies* are those who will support you, given encouragement.

- Your *fellow travellers* are passive supporters, who may be committed to the agenda but not to you personally.

A **stakeholder** is anyone likely to be affected, directly or indirectly, by an organizational change or programme of changes.

- The *fencesitters* are those whose allegiances are not clear.

- *Loose cannons* are dangerous because they can vote against agendas in which they have no direct interest.

- Your *opponents* are players who oppose your agenda but not you personally.

- Your *adversaries* are players who oppose both you and your agenda.

- *Bedfellows* are those who support the agenda but may not know or trust you.

- *The voiceless* are stakeholders who will be affected by the agenda but have little power to promote or oppose and who lack advocates.

Egan argues that different stakeholders must be managed differently. Partners and allies need to be encouraged, to be 'kept on side'. Opponents need to be converted. Adversaries have to be discredited and marginalized. Egan suggests that the needs of 'the voiceless' should be addressed in case they are 'recruited' by adversaries and used against the change agenda.

John Kotter and Leo Schlesinger (1979) identify six methods for overcoming resistance:

1. *Education and commitment*

Managers should share their perceptions, knowledge and objectives with those affected by change. This can involve a major and expensive programme of training, face-to-face counselling, group meetings, and the publication of memos and reports. People may need to be informed about the nature of the problems necessitating change. Resistance may be based on misunderstanding and inaccurate information. It therefore helps to get the facts straight, and to identify and reconcile opposing views. Managers can use this approach only if they trust their employees, and if in return management appear credible to the employees.

2. *Participation and involvement*

Those who might resist change should be involved in planning and implementing it. Collaboration can have the effect of reducing opposition and encouraging commitment. This helps to reduce fears that individuals may have about the impact of changes on them and also makes use of individuals' skills and knowledge. Managers can use this approach only where participants have the knowledge and ability to contribute effectively, and are willing to do so.

3. *Facilitation and support*

Employees may need to be given counselling and therapy to help overcome fears and anxieties about change. It may be necessary to develop individual awareness of the need for change, as well as the self-awareness of feelings toward change and how these can be altered.

4. *Negotiation and agreement*

It may be necessary to reach a mutually agreeable compromise, through trading and exchange. The nature of a particular change may have to be adjusted to meet the needs and interest of potential and powerful resistors. Management may have to negotiate, rather than impose, change where there are individuals and groups who have enough power effectively to resist. The problem is, this creates a precedent for future changes—which may also have to be negotiated, although the circumstances surrounding them may be quite different.

5. *Manipulation and co-optation*

This involves covert attempts to sidestep potential resistance. Management puts

Readiness for change is a predisposition, perhaps even impatience, to welcome and embrace change. Where readiness is high, change may be straightforward. But when readiness is low, some 'groundwork' may be required to increase readiness among those affected.

Stop and criticize

forward proposals that deliberately appeal to the specific interests, sensitivities and emotions of the key groups or stakeholders involved. The information disseminated is selective, emphasizing the benefits to particular stakeholder groups and ignoring or playing down the disadvantages. Co-optation involves giving key resistors direct access to the decision-making process, perhaps giving them well-paid, high-status management positions.

6. Implicit and explicit coercion

Management here abandons any attempt to achieve consensus. This may be appropriate where there is profound disagreement between those concerned with the change, and where there is little or no change of anyone shifting their ground. This results in the use of force and threats. This need not involve violence. It may be sufficient to offer to fire, transfer or demote individuals, or to stifle their promotion and career prospects.

Egan advises that 'adversaries' should be discredited and marginalized. Kotter and Schlesinger suggest using manipulation and coercion. Other authors advocate the use of political tactics to neutralize resistance. Are there any circumstances in which such management behaviour can be considered professional, ethical, effective?

Kotter and Schlesinger point out that these six management methods can be used in combination. The choice in a given situation depends on the likely reactions of those involved, and on the long-term implications of solving the immediate

Are we ready for this?

From a practical change implementation perspective, it is usually useful to ask the question: are the conditions right, or do we have to do some preliminary work before we go ahead? One approach to 'preparing the ground' for change is based on the concept of **readiness**.

Tony Eccles (1994) identifies eight preconditions for successful change. These are:

1. Is there *pressure* for this change?
2. Is there a clear and shared *vision* of the goal and the direction?
3. Do we have effective *liaison and trust* between those concerned?
4. Is there the *will and power* to act?
5. Do we have enough *capable people* with sufficient resources?
6. Do we have suitable *rewards* and defined accountability for actions?
7. Have we identified actionable *first steps*?
8. Does the organization have a *capacity to learn* and to adapt?

Where the answers are 'yes', the organization's **readiness for change** is high, and resistance is likely to be localized and insignificant. Where the answers are 'no', readiness is low, and change is likely to be correspondingly more difficult to implement.

The concept of readiness draws attention to two practical issues. The first concerns *timing*. Some readiness factors may simply improve by waiting. The second concerns *action*, to manipulate readiness factors, to heighten the impatience for change, to strengthen a welcoming predisposition. In other words, these readiness factors can be managed.

problem in that way. Managers who try to impose change unilaterally, without participation, are usually responsible for less effective change implementation.

However, there may be circumstances in which manipulation and coercion are appropriate. For example, David Buchanan and Richard Badham (1999a and b) argue that the change agent who is not politically skilled in dealing with adversaries and opponents, and with supporters, will fail. Rosabeth Moss Kanter (1983) also argued that 'power skills' in influencing others are necessary attributes of the change agent. We will explore organizational power and politics in more detail in chapter 24.

The benefits and limitations of participative change management

The conventional approach to change implementation advocates a participative management style. This approach drew initially from the experiments of Lester Coch and John French (1948) at the Harwood Manufacturing Corporation in Marion, Virginia. The company made pyjamas, but employees complained about frequent changes in work methods through:

- complaints about pay rates;

- absenteeism, and leaving the company;

- low standards of efficiency;

- deliberate restriction of output;

- aggression towards management.

Managers were sensitive to the human relations and welfare needs of their employees, and they had used financial incentives to encourage employees to transfer to new jobs and methods. But the problems persisted, and Coch and French set out to discover why.

The company employed about 500 women and 100 men, with an average age of twenty-three, and most of them had no previous industrial experience. The company's time study experts set out standards for all the jobs in the factory. Each employee's output was calculated daily, and everyone's performance was made public in a daily list with the best producers at the top. High output led to more money and higher status. Most of the grievances concerned the fact that, as soon as they had learned a new job, and had started to earn bonuses, they were moved to another task. This meant that they lost the bonus and had to start learning all over again.

Coch and French designed an experiment with three production groups, each with a different level of participation in introducing the changes.

The non-participation group

A group of eighteen 'hand pressers' changed the way in which they stacked their finished work. The production department announced the change and the time study department announced the new standard work rate. The changes were explained to the pressers, but they were not allowed to participate in any of the decisions surrounding this change.

The group showed no improvement in efficiency. There was immediate resistance to the change. They argued with the time study engineer and were hostile to the supervisor. The group deliberately restricted their output, and some left. This group was eventually split up and allocated to other tasks around the factory.

The representation group

A group of thirteen pyjama folders had to fold trousers and jackets, having only done one of these tasks before. The group were given a demonstration of the need to reduce costs. The purpose of the meeting at which the demonstration was given was to get approval for a plan to improve work methods. Three representatives from the group were then given training in the new methods, and they subsequently trained the other folders. The representatives were interested and co-operative, and offered useful suggestions for further improvements.

This group adopted a co-operative attitude and their efficiency ratings rose rapidly. Nobody argued with the time study engineer or the supervisor, and nobody left the group.

The total participation group

Two groups of pyjama examiners altered their inspection routine. (One group had eight examiners, the other had seven.) They had a preliminary meeting, like that for the representation group, but everyone took part in the design of the new job and in the calculation of the new time standard. Coch and French remarked that 'It is interesting to observe that in the meetings with these two groups suggestions were immediately made in such quantity that the stenographer had great difficulty recording them'.

These groups recovered their efficiency ratings very rapidly, to a level much higher than before the change. Again, there was no conflict, and no resignations.

Two and a half months later, the remaining thirteen members of the initial non-participation group were brought together again for a new pressing job. This time, however, they followed the 'total participation' procedure, which resulted in a rapid increase in efficiency, with no aggression, and no resignations. This result confirmed that it was not the people involved but the way in which they were treated that affected resistance to or acceptance of change.

Since that study, employee involvement has been standard advice for managers seeking to overcome resistance and encourage a welcoming and creative approach to organizational change. Numerous books and articles are published every year, restating the same message. For example, Richard Pascale, Mark Millemann and Linda Gioja (1997) more recently urged managers to involve 'every last employee' in the interests of creative and effective change. However, participative methods have been challenged by the work of two Australian researchers, Dexter Dunphy and Doug Stace (1990; Stace, 1996). They first define the scale of change using four categories (echoing the 'depth' classification in figure 18.1):

- *Fine tuning* involves refining methods, policies and procedures, typically at the level of the division or department.

- *Incremental adjustment* involves distinct modifications to strategies, structures and management processes, but not radical enough to be described as strategic.

- *Modular transformation* involves the major realignment or restructuring of departments and divisions—which may be radical, but at the level of parts of the organization and not the whole.

- *Corporate transformation* (or strategic change) involves radical shifts in strategy, and revolutionary changes throughout the organization, to structures, systems and procedures, to mission and core values, and to the distribution of power.

Dunphy and Stace also identify four categories of change leadership style:

Style of change management	Scale of change			
	Fine tuning	Incremental adjustment	Modular transformation	Corporate transformation
Collaborative	Type 1		Type 2	
Consultative	Participative evolution		Charismatic transformation	
Directive	Type 3		Type 4	
Coercive	Forced evolution		Dictatorial transformation	

Figure 18.3: Scale of change and management style

- A *collaborative* style involves widespread employee participation in key decisions affecting their and the organization's future.

- A *consultative* style entails limited involvement in setting goals relevant to employees' areas of responsibility.

- A *directive* style involves the use of managerial authority in reaching decisions about change and the future and about how change will proceed.

- A *coercive* style means senior management forcing or imposing change on the organization.

Plotting scale of change against style of management produces the matrix in figure 18.3.

This matrix generates four ideal change strategies: participative evolution, charismatic transformation, forced evolution and dictatorial transformation.

	Incremental change strategies	Transformative change strategies
	Participative evolution	*Charismatic transformation*
Collaborative–consultative modes	Use when the organization needs minor adjustment to meet environmental conditions, where time is available, and where key interest groups favour change	Use when the organization needs major adjustments to meet environmental conditions, where there is little time for participation, and where there is support for radical change
	Forced evolution	*Dictatorial transformation*
Directive–coercive modes	Use when minor adjustments are required, where time is available, but where key interest groups oppose change	Use when major adjustments are necessary, where there is no time for participation, where there is no internal support for strategic change, but where this is necessary for survival

Figure 18.4: The Dunphy–Stace contingency approach to change implementation

Dunphy and Stace argue that incremental and consultative modes of change can be inappropriate. These strategies are time-consuming and generate conflicting views that are difficult to reconcile. Where rapid strategic change is necessary for the survival of the organization, transformative approaches carried out in directive and coercive modes can be effective. Dunphy and Stace thus propose the contingency approach to change implementation, summarized in figure 18.4.

Stop and criticize	Dictatorial transformation? Coercion to encourage organizational change? Surely this kind of approach is more likely to generate hostility and resistance to change, reducing organizational performance? What arguments would you use to support dictatorial transformation, on the one hand, and to criticize it, on the other?

The argument of Dunphy and Stace thus offers a significant challenge to the universal and oversimplified prescription of participative change management.

N-step recipes for change

The six phases of a project

1. enthusiasm
2. disillusionment
3. panic
4. search for the guilty
5. punishment of the innocent
6. praise and rewards for the non-participants

Although change is now a familiar feature of the organizational landscape, it does not appear to have become any easier to implement. However, much is known about the factors which contribute to effective change, and also about the barriers. That knowledge has been codified by numerous authors advising on 'best practice' on how to introduce change.

One popular, influential and conventional approach to change implementation draws on the methods of *project management*. This approach revolves around the concept of the phased project 'life cycle'. The typical project life cycle involves the following steps: identify problem, gather data, analyse data, generate solutions, select the best solution, plan the implementation, implement and test, monitor and evaluate. This makes the change process sound like a neat, tidy, rational, logical sequence of discrete and identifiable steps. One account (Hussey, 1998) uses the acronym 'EASIER' to argue that effective change involves just six steps: envisioning, activating, supporting, installing, ensuring and recognizing.

There are many such 'phase' models in the management literature. The American consultant and academic John Kotter (1995) outlines 'eight steps to transforming your organization':

1. establish a sense of urgency;

2. form a guiding coalition;

3. create a vision;

4. communicate the vision;

5. empower people to act on the vision;

6. create 'short-term wins';

7. consolidate improvements to produce further change;

8. institutionalize new approaches.

The British academic Tony Eccles (1994) identifies fourteen factors behind successful organizational change, in four main categories. These are:

purpose and initiative

1. *the pregnant executive*: there must be a champion who embodies and lives the new dream;

2. *the single goal*: there has to be a clear and sustained purpose to which people can commit;

3. *clarity of purpose*: there has to be a defensible, unambiguous reason for the change;

concordance and trust

4. *the illusion of unity*: don't expect everybody to back the change;

5. *how open to be*: tell people as much as practicable, taking some risks by being candid;

6. *communication*: effective communication is vital, and almost impossible to overdo;

leadership, capabilities and structure

7. *the rule of proportionate responsibility*: senior managers must take more responsibility;

8. *the limitations of empowerment*: even enterprising employees need to be led;

9. *teams and leaders*: good teams and leaders support each other;

10. *structure and culture*: use structure to change culture;

building on action and success

11. *creating winners*: personal success is a great motivation;

12. *fast change and initial acts*: early successes create productive momentum;

13. *caring for casualties*: caring for people is morally and organizationally commendable;

14. *minimizing unintended consequences*: you cannot avoid all the errors, but you can organize to anticipate some and to recover from others.

David Collins (1998) refers to these prescriptions as '*n*-step recipes', as different contributors compete to offer checklists of different lengths (with broadly similar content). There are many similar 'recipes' available and it is tedious to explore more of them. These models of change have one striking feature in common. They rely on the assumption that planned change unfolds in a planned, logical, step-by-step sequence. Solutions are not identified until the problem has been clearly defined. The 'best' solution is not chosen until the options have been compared and evaluated. Implementation does not begin until there is agreement on the solution. The key actors in the implementation process each have their clearly defined roles and responsibilities. Implementation is closely monitored and deviations from plan are detected and corrected. The implementation process is bounded in terms of resources (people, money, space) and time, with a clear project completion date.

This 'logical unfolding' property has earned project management accounts the label of 'rational linear' models of organizational change. These assumptions, concerning both rationality and linearity in organizational change, have attracted much criticism. In short, organizations seem rarely to operate in such a tidy and predictable manner, particularly with respect to strategic (major, messy, radical) change. In particular, Collins (1998) argues that these recipes fail on two counts. First, they do not capture the complex, untidy, politicized, iterative nature of organizational change. Second, they do not encourage a critical perspective with regard to the substance, the outcomes, the wider human implications or the process of change. In other words, in Collins' view, they are processually naïve, contextually naïve and politically naïve accounts of organizational change. Collins advises managers to adopt a more theoretically sophisticated approach to change, and urges academics to adopt a more critical perspective on change management.

This 'recipe' approach to 'best practice' in change implementation has two main advantages:

1. The approach codifies what research and practical experience suggest are the main factors contributing to effective change, even if many of the factors (established need for change, clear goals, communications) seem to be 'common sense'.

2. The recipe offers a framework, a checklist of required actions, for those involved in planning a change implementation, perhaps even more useful when accompanied by stakeholder analysis and readiness analysis.

The 'recipe' approach, however, has two major limitations:

1. The approach is theoretically weak and relies heavily on retrospective accounts and analyses of 'what went well' and 'what went wrong' in change. There is nothing intrinsically wrong with that approach, but such an analy-

"We decided to save the total screw up part for the end."

sis does not contribute to the development of our theoretical understanding of organizational change processes and of how these processes may themselves be changing.

2. While research and experience confirm that change is untidy, politicized, iterative and apparently irrational in terms of the way events unfold, the recipe approach assumes that change either is or should be a rational linear process. There is a presumption that, if change is messy, it must be because managers have 'failed to follow the recipe'. That may not be the case at all if change is intrinsically untidy.

Beyond the recipe: the process and context of change

Processual/ contextual theory argues that, to understand organizational change fully, it is necessary to consider how the substance, the context and the process of change interact with each other. In this perspective, the 'unit of analysis' that is to be understood is 'the process of change in context'.

The theoretical sophistication required by Collins (1998), among others, can be found in the **processual/contextual theory**, which dominated debate on organizational change in the 1990s.

The processual/contextual perspective is derived from the work of Andrew Pettigrew (1973; 1985; 1987; 1988), who is another critic of the atheoretical accounts of change offered in the prescriptive 'recipe' literature. He cautions against looking for single causes and simple explanations, pointing to the many related factors—individual, group, organizational, social—which influence the nature and outcomes of change. Pettigrew argues that change is a complex and 'untidy cocktail' of rational decision processes, mixed with competing individual perceptions, stimulated by visionary leadership, and spiced with 'power plays' and attempts to recruit support and build coalitions behind particular ideas.

Pettigrew argues that the unit of analysis should be 'the process of change in context'. This is a potentially confusing notion. However, this statement highlights two related aspects of change. First, this means paying attention to the flow of events, and not thinking of change as a static event or as neatly time-bounded. Second, this means paying attention to the wider context in which change takes place, and not thinking in terms of a particular location in time and geographical space (e.g. this new machine in this factory bay).

Pettigrew's concept of 'context' is unlike the notion of an organization's 'environment' (see chapter 2). It is a more elaborate notion, with three dimensions. The *internal context* includes the structure and culture of the organization, which influence patterns of behaviour and attitudes toward change initiatives. The *external context* lies beyond the organization and includes customer demands, competitor behaviour and economic conditions, all of which create opportunities and threats to be exploited and addressed. And past and current events also form part of the context, as previous experiences condition current thinking.

That last point, about the organization's 'history', is critical and relates to the earlier discussion of change and continuity, in two ways. First, with a narrow focus on current organizational changes, the nature and impact of which appear to be clearly visible, it is all too easy to forget how previous events and their outcomes have shaped current perceptions of and responses to change. Second, it is also easy to forget the continuities, to ignore those aspects of 'the past' which have not changed and which are still with us, and which again condition current thinking about specific change proposals.

Pettigrew argues that the change agent must be willing to intervene in the political system of the organization. He argues that the main management problem here is to legitimize change proposals in the face of competing ideas. The management of change is thus equated with 'the management of meaning', or with symbolic attempts to establish the credibility and legitimacy of particular definitions of problems and solutions, and to gain consent and compliance from other organization members. Part of the management task, therefore, is to do with 'the way you tell it'—or perhaps more accurately with 'the way you *sell* it' to other organization members. In other words, Pettigrew takes us back to our earlier argument about how manipulative, devious and coercive management should be in progressing change.

The processual/contextual perspective has been developed more recently by Patrick Dawson (1994; 1996) who argues that, to understand the process of change, we need to consider:

1. the past, present and future *context* in which the organization functions, including external and internal factors;

2. the *substance* of the change itself—new technology, new payment system, new structures and procedures—and its significance and timescale;

3. the *transition process*, tasks, activities, decisions, timing, sequencing;

4. *political activity*, both within and external to the organization;

5. the *interactions* between these factors.

Dawson's argument is illustrated in figure 18.5. This perspective follows Pettigrew by emphasizing the interaction of the context, substance and process of change, and also highlights the role of internal and external politics. Dawson identifies five specific aspects of the internal context: human resources, administrative structures, technology, product or service, and the organization's history and culture. He also identifies four key features of the substance of change: the scale, its 'defining characteristics', its perceived centrality, and the timeframe of change initiatives. The substance of change influences the scale of disruption to existing structures and jobs. The transition process may be slow and incremental, or rapid. In addition, managers can draw upon evidence from the context and substance of change to marshall support and to legitimate their own proposals through organizational political action. It is, therefore, the interaction between context, substance and political forces which shape the process of organizational change.

The processual/contextual theory of change seems to have three main strengths:

1. This approach recognizes the complexity of change, drawing attention to the many factors at different levels, and the interaction between these factors, that shape the nature, direction and consequences of change.

2. This approach recognizes change as a process with a past, a present and a future, rather than as a static or time-bounded event or discrete series of events.

3. This approach establishes clear recommendations for researchers studying organizational change, advocating longitudinal research across individual, group, organizational and social levels of analysis.

However, processual/contextual theory seems to have three limitations:

1. Change in this perspective is in danger of being presented as over-complex and overwhelmingly confusing, and thus as unmanageable.

2. The people involved in the change process (at least in Pettigrew's account, much less so in Dawson's) tend to be portrayed as minor characters on a wider tapestry of factors and events, relegated to the role of pawns moved around by wider social and organizational forces rather than being seen as proactive movers and shakers in the process.

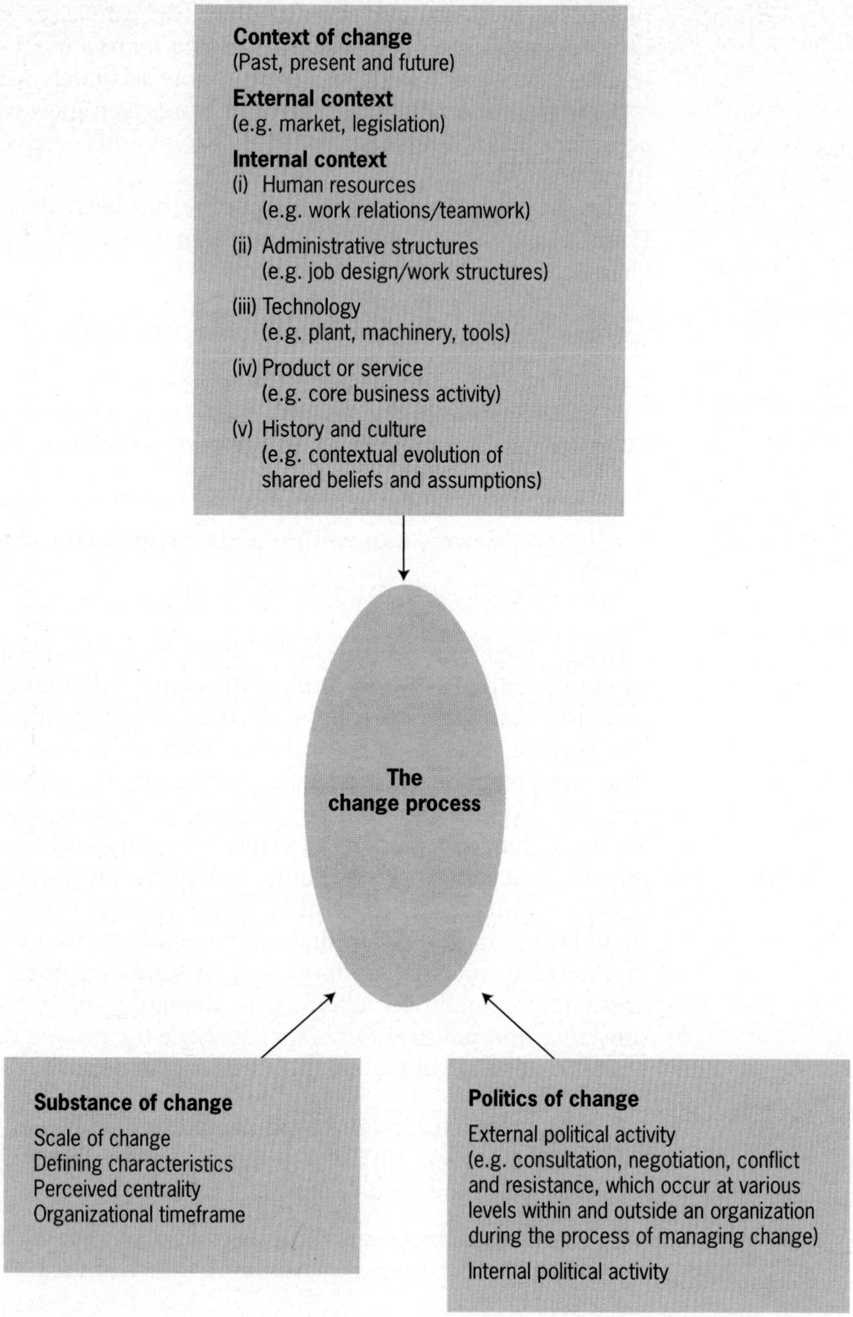

Context of change
(Past, present and future)

External context
(e.g. market, legislation)

Internal context
(i)   Human resources
      (e.g. work relations/teamwork)

(ii) Administrative structures
      (e.g. job design/work structures)

(iii) Technology
      (e.g. plant, machinery, tools)

(iv) Product or service
      (e.g. core business activity)

(v) History and culture
     (e.g. contextual evolution of
     shared beliefs and assumptions)

**The
change process**

Substance of change

Scale of change
Defining characteristics
Perceived centrality
Organizational timeframe

Politics of change

External political activity
(e.g. consultation, negotiation, conflict
and resistance, which occur at various
levels within and outside an organization
during the process of managing change)

Internal political activity

Figure 18.5: Determinants of organizational change (Dawson, 1996, p.27)

3. This perspective does not lend itself readily to the identification of practical recommendations for the more effective management of change, beyond generalized advice such as 'recognize complexity' and 'think processually'.

Processual/contextual theory thus seems to be a good guide to research and understanding but a relatively weak guide to management and organizational practice.

Business process re-engineering

One of the most controversial developments in the field of organizational change in the mid- to late-1990s concerned the methodology of **business process re-engineering** (BPR).

One key point to note about BPR is that is has no relationship whatsoever with the processual theory of change. On the contrary, these two perspectives could not be further apart in argument or prescription. Processual theory and BPR must not be confused.

BPR has polarized opinion. Some commentators argue that rapid and radical process improvement is essential to enable organizations to deal with increasing environmental turbulence. Some organizations have reported significant improvements in performance as a result of applying re-engineering methods. Other commentators dismiss the approach as a futile and irrelevant repackaging of traditional management methods. And research suggests that re-engineering has a high failure rate. In America, re-engineering quickly earned a 'slash-and-burn' reputation for the job loss or 'downsizing' that applications typically caused.

The 'inventors' of business process re-engineering include Michael Hammer and James Champy (1993), and Thomas Davenport (1993). Their approach has two main ingredients. First, they advocate a fresh start to organizational redesign. In other words, when considering organizational change, start with a blank sheet of paper and redesign from scratch. Second, they advocate a process orientation to the analysis and redesign of work.

The fresh start, blank sheet approach ignores past history and current practice in favour of considering how best to structure the organization and design work to meet the needs of today's business and today's customers. Clearly this conflicts with the advice of the processual/contextual theorists such as Dawson and Pettigrew. BPR is not a 'context-sensitive' approach, in the wider sense of context suggested by Andrew Pettigrew.

The process orientation also represents a departure from most traditional approaches to organizational analysis. A process is simply a set of activities that delivers a product or a service to a customer. The customer may be the eventual user of the product or service, or it could be an 'internal customer'—the person or section responsible for the next set of activities in the overall process. This is potentially radical because it requires a horizontal analysis of work along an activity chain. Most organizations are structured vertically, around functions such as purchasing, warehousing, production, finance, personnel and marketing.

A typical business process re-engineering project has four main stages:

process mapping	draw a flowchart of the work activity sequence
identify 'moments of truth'	decide which steps are critical, add value, introduce errors
generate redesign proposals	streamline the process, avoiding duplication and overlap
implementation	put the redesign into effect

The first step in BPR concerns defining and mapping an existing work process. For example, David Buchanan and Bob Wilson (1996a and b) map the activity chain, or 'patient trail', in a hospital, for patients undergoing elective surgery. The main stages in this process include outpatient appointment, outpatient clinic preparation, clinic attendance, adding patient to theatres waiting list, attendance at a pre-assessment clinic (for tests), admission to a ward, operating theatre procedure,

Business process re-engineering is the radical rethinking and redesign of organizational processes to achieve dramatic improvements in critical measures of performance, such as cost, quality, service and time.

Re-engineering at the Leicester Royal Infirmary NHS Trust

The Leicester Royal Infirmary NHS Trust (LRI) is a large acute hospital, with 1,100 beds and 4,200 staff. In a typical year, the hospital deals with 400,000 outpatient visits, 120,000 accident and emergency cases, and 103,000 inpatient and daycase episodes. As one of two National Health Service pilot projects, LRI launched a re-engineering programme in 1994. Around 140 projects were introduced, affecting the whole hospital, to make dramatic improvements to the delivery of patient care, and to provide a working environment in which staff could use their skills and abilities most effectively.

Patients typically move from one department to another, and process mapping showed that:

- 30 to 70 per cent of staff activity does not contribute directly to patient care;
- up to 50 per cent of process steps involve a 'handoff' to another member of staff, leading to errors, duplications and delays;
- individual jobs are narrow and fragmented;
- nobody is responsible for the patient's 'end-to-end' experience of treatment.

One typical example of a process re-engineered to follow the patient's needs and experience was the development of the outpatient testing service. As testing was fragmented across different locations in the hospital, patients could have a long and anxious wait for results, and clinic staff had problems with lost test results. Re-engineering streamlined the flow of work by bringing test services, staff and equipment, to one location. The results were:

	Before	After
average test turnaround	79 hours	5 hours
distance patient travels	650 paces	90 paces
times patient undresses	up to 3	1

Re-engineering improved quality of patient care in other ways:

- the numbers of patients in eye casualty seen within 5 minutes increased from 5 per cent to 97 per cent;
- time from referral to bed for emergency admissions reduced from 160 to 40 minutes;
- treatment waiting time for rectal bleeding cut from 4 weeks to 1 hour;
- diagnosis of hypertension reduced from 5 weeks to 3 hours.

Annual cost savings were around £900,000. Re-engineering also brought 'hidden' benefits, including team-based working and problem solving, improved teaching and research opportunities, improved working relationships, improved skills development, and more timely management decision making. Staff from all organization levels joined 're-engineering laboratories', developing new skills, responsibilities and career opportunities.

Re-engineering raised some problems. An attempt to analyse 'core processes', as in a commercial setting, was abandoned in favour of one based on the characteristics of different patient groups. The timescale was longer than anticipated, due to the degree of the changes to clinical practice, organization design and management style. The 're-engineers' in some cases found their roles stressful, and some lost friends in their 'home' occupational groups.

Based on *Re-engineering in Healthcare: The Leicester Royal Infirmary Experience*, The Leicester Royal Infirmary NHS Trust, September 1997.

recovery, and finally (if all went well) discharge. In this process, the patient may come into contact with anything from 50 to 150 different members of hospital staff, and will become temporarily the responsibility of most of the hospital's separate functional departments along the way.

Many of the problems in this situation arise from the fact that staff are concerned primarily with what happens at their own step on the trail and are not always aware either of what has gone before or of what will happen to the patient afterwards. This 'process fragmentation' leads to unnecessary duplication of some activities and the unwitting transmission of problems 'down the trail'. This lack of process orientation is typical for an organization structured vertically into distinct functions rather than horizontally around work processes.

These 'process fragmentation' features apply to commercial manufacturing concerns as well as to healthcare and educational organizations. What does re-engineering advocate in such situations? Hammer and Champy (1993) propose the following general principles:

- dismantle functional departments and create process teams;

- customers deal with a 'case manager' and don't get pushed around the structure;

- empower people, and give them enriched jobs with discretion;

- provide training and education to allow people to perform expanded roles;

- flatten the organization hierarchy;

- measure people on the results they achieve, not just on activity performed;

- promote people on the basis of ability;

- turn senior managers into leaders, not scorekeepers.

Stop and criticize

Flatten the hierarchy? Enrich jobs? Encourage teamwork? Empower people? Overcome functional barriers? Are these really radical recommendations? This advice is similar to that discussed in chapter 8, where we explored approaches to motivation through organization and work redesign.

These kinds of recommendation are similar to those made by the organization development movement since the 1960s [**link**, chapter 17, organization development]. One criticism of BPR has concerned its 'slash-and-burn' implications for job security. Another criticism is that it is not such a new technique after all. Many commentators have suggested that horizontal business process analysis is a conventional method, used by production and operations management specialists, and socio-technical systems analysts, for decades (Buchanan, 1996).

The expertise of the change agent

The new agents of change: athletes not cowboys

Our new heroic model should be the athlete who can manage the amazing feat of doing more with less, who can juggle the need to both conserve resources and pursue growth opportunities. This new kind of business hero avoids the excesses of both the corpocrat and the cowboy. Where the former rigidly conserves and protects, the latter relentlessly speculates and promotes. But the business athlete has the strength to balance somewhere in the middle, taking the best of the corpocrat's discipline and the cowboy's entrepreneurial zeal. Business athletes need to be intense, lean and limber, able to stretch, good at teamwork, and in shape all the time.

From Rosabeth Moss Kanter, *When Giants Learn to Dance: Mastering the Challenge of Strategy, Management and Careers in the 1990s*, Simon & Schuster, London, 1989, p.361.

What does it take to be an effective agent of organizational change? Two trends make this question more urgent. The first is that most managers now combine change responsibilities with their regular duties. Despite the use of project managers and external consultants, many functional managers are also key **change agents**. The second trend concerns the increased involvement of all levels of organizational membership in change teams. This 'dispersal' of change agency means that more people need to have the skills and knowledge required (Buchanan, Claydon and Doyle, 1999). A lot of the literature concentrates on external change agents, or management consultants. The role of internal change agents is equally important.

The change agent seems to require less technical expertise, and more interpersonal and managerial skill, in communication, presentation, negotiation, influencing and selling. Change agents are often chosen for their expertise in the substance of the change in hand; IT specialists, for example, are chosen to manage IT projects. However, expertise in managing the change process is usually more significant, and this implies capabilities in handling the human, organizational, managerial and political issues. It is interesting to note that this trend seems to be consistent with the way in which change is portrayed by processual/contextual theory: untidy, many factors, many players, politicized.

Rosabeth Moss Kanter (1989) identifies seven essential change agency skills:

> A **change agent** can be any member of an organization seeking to promote, further, support, sponsor, initiate, implement or deliver change. Change agents are not necessarily senior managers and do not necessarily hold formal 'change management' job titles and positions.

Rosabeth Moss
Kanter (b. 1943)

1. Ability to work independently, without management power, sanction and support.

2. An effective collaborator, able to compete in ways that enhance co-operation.

3. The ability to develop high-trust relationships, based on high ethical standards.

4. Self-confidence, tempered with humility.

5. Respect for the process of change as well as the content.

6. Able to work across business functions and units, 'multifaceted and ambidextrous'.

7. The willingness to stake reward on results and gain satisfaction from success.

Kanter's 'person specification' for the change agent seems to be consistent with what is known about flexible, organic organization structures, about participative management methods, and about the practice and implications of process re-engineering. Kanter speaks of this 'superhuman' change agent, in possession of such wide-ranging expertise, in terms of a 'business athlete'. Jon Katzenbach (see box opposite) makes a distinction between 'good managers', who analyse, organize, monitor and control, and 'real change leaders', who create, innovate, experiment and take risks.

Stop and criticize

Are you an athlete or a cowboy? Are you a good manager or a real change leader? Do you have the personal qualities required to make you an effective change agent? Match your expertise against Kanter's and Katzenbach's lists.

What further skills development do you think you need if you are to be effective in a change management role?

The effective change agent seems to be someone with an almost superhuman combination of skills and qualities. The change agent in a large organization can

Good managers (GMs) versus real change leaders (RCLs)

Key issues	GMs	RCLs
Basic mindset	*Analyse, leverage, optimize, delegate, organize and control it—I know best*	*Do it, fix it, try it, change it—and do it all over again; no one person knows best*
End-game assumptions	1. Earnings per share 2. Market share 3. Resource advantage 4. Personal promotions **Always make the numbers**	1. Value to customers, employees and owners 2. Customer loyalty 3. Core skills advantage 4. Personal growth **Satisfy customers and workers**
Leadership philosophy	1. Strategy-driven 2. Decide, delegate, monitor and review 3. Spend time on important matters 4. Leverages his/her time **A few good people will get it done for me**	1. Aspiration-driven 2. Do real work 3. Spend time on what matters to people 4. Expand leadership capacity **I must get the best out of all my people**
Sources of productivity and motivation	1. Investment turnover 2. Superior technology 3. Process control 4. Leverage people **People = exploitable resource**	1. Productivity 2. Superior people 3. Process innovation 4. Develop people **People = critical resource**
Accountability measures	1. Comprehensive measures across all areas 2. Clear individual accountability **I hold you accountable**	1. A few critical measures in the most critical areas 2. Individual and mutual accountability **We hold ourselves accountable**
Risk–reward trade-offs	1. Avoid failure and mistakes at all costs 2. Rely on proven approaches 3. Limit career risks 4. Analyse until sure **I cannot afford to fail, or leave**	1. Expect, learn from and build on 'failures' 2. Try whatever appears promising 3. Take career risks 4. If in doubt, try it and see **I can work here, or elsewhere**

Based on Jon R. Katzenbach, Frederick Beckett, Steven Dichter, Marc Feigen, Christopher Gagnon, Quentin Hope and Timothy Ling, *Real Change Leaders: How Do You Create Growth and High Performance at Your Company*, Nicholas Brealey, London, 1997.

thus be lonely and vulnerable. However, the personal and career rewards can be highly significant. The high-flying, fast-track management career is more readily built on contributions to strategic organizational change. Very few fast-track careers are likely to be made by introducing minor, slow, incremental organizational changes.

Table 18.4: Trends in organizational change

change in the late twentieth century	change in the twenty-first century
one organizational theme among many	an organizational preoccupation
importance of participation and involvement	significance of political motives and actions
rational-linear model of project management	messy, untidy cocktail of reason and motive
content skills are critical	process skills are critical
change as periodic adjustment	change as continuous upheaval
aimed at organizational effectiveness	aimed at competitive advantage and survival

There are a number of trends evident in this field. Change is set to remain a central theme. While participative management remains socially and ethically appropriate, there is a willingness to accept the use of directive methods. There is also increasing recognition of the role of organizational politics. The effective change agent must be sensitive to and skilled in appropriate modes of political intervention. There is also recognition of the need for rapid and continual adjustment to events and trends. In other words, change is no longer something which periodically disturbs the stable fabric; change is a feature of organizational life. The significance of a wide range of context factors in shaping the opportunities for and directions of organizational change is better understood and appreciated. And finally, while change may still be relevant to improving effectiveness, the ability to change rapidly is increasingly viewed as a factor contributing to competitive advantage and organizational survival.

These trends are summarized in table 18.4.

Recap

1. *Understand the typical characteristics of human responses to change.*
   - Individual emotional responses to traumatic changes differ, but the typical coping cycle passes through the stages of denial, anger, bargaining, depression and acceptance.
   - The Yerkes–Dodson law states that the initial response to pressure is improved performance, but that increasing pressure leads to fatigue and ultimately to breakdown.
   - The evidence suggests that continuous organizational changes do lead to work intensification, burnout and 'initiative fatigue'.

2. *Identify the main external and internal triggers of organizational change.*
   - Change can be triggered by a range of factors internal and external to the organization, and can also be proactive by anticipating trends and events.

   - Organizational changes vary in depth, or penetration, from shallow, fine tuning, to deep, paradigmatic or strategic change.
   - The broad direction of change in most organizations is towards becoming less mechanistic and bureaucratic, and more adaptive, responsive and organic.

3. *Understand the nature of resistance to change and approaches to overcoming it.*
   - Resistance to change has many sources, including self-interest, lack of trust and understanding, competing assessments of the outcomes, and low tolerance of change.
   - One technique for addressing possible resistance to change, as well as identifying and strengthening support, is stakeholder analysis.
   - The main prescribed approach for avoiding or dealing with resistance is participative management, in which those affected are involved in implementation.

- The use of manipulation and coercion to implement change are advocated by some commentators, but the 'political' role of management in change is controversial.

4. *Explain the advantages and limitations of participative methods of change management.*
   - Participative methods can generate creative thinking and increase employee commitment to change, but this process is time-consuming.
   - Some commentators argue that rapid and major corporate transformations are more successful when implemented using a dictatorial or coercive style.

5. *Explain the strengths and weaknesses of the processual/contextual perspective on change.*
   - Processual/contextual theory emphasizes the interaction of the substance, process, politics and context of change at individual, group, organizational and social levels of analysis, considering also how past events shape current and future thinking and actions.
   - Processual/contextual theory is analytically strong but is weak in practical terms.

6. *Outline the skill requirements of the effective change agent.*
   - The change agent has to be more skilled in managing the change process than knowledgeable with respect to the substance of the change in hand. This involves the 'soft' management skills of communication, presentation, selling, negotiating, influencing, and providing feedback and support.

Revision

1. What value do practical 'recipes' have for managers attempting to implement organizational change, and what are the limitations of this kind of advice?

2. What are the main sources of resistance to organizational change, and how can resistance be overcome?

3. Why has organizational change become a 'strategic imperative' and a management preoccupation?

4. The typical individual response to change is not necessarily negative. Why not, and how can individual responses to change be assessed and understood?

5. What are the benefits and limitations of a participative approach to the implementation of organizational change?

Springboard

Burnes, B., 2000, *Managing Change: A Strategic Approach to Organizational Dynamics*, Financial Times Prentice Hall, Harlow, Essex (third edition).

Comprehensive, well-informed and clearly written textbook on change which sets the topic in the wider context of organizational strategy, behaviour and management.

Collins, D., 1998, *Organizational Change: Sociological Perspectives*, Routledge, London.

Surveys current thinking and is critical of '*n*-step recipes' for change which lack theoretical underpinning. He is also critical of management for avoiding theory, and critical of academics for accepting managerial perspectives on change.

Dawson, P., 1994, *Organizational Change: A Processual Approach*, Paul Chapman Publishing, London.

An accessible account of processual theory, with case accounts of change which reveal the perspective in action.

Knights, D. and Willmott, H. (eds), 2000, *The Reengineering Revolution: Critical Studies of Corporate Change*, Sage Publications, London.

A collection of chapters assessing critically the impact of re-engineering on management thinking and practice, revealing that this 'fad' has not been abandoned.

Kotter, J.P., 1995, 'Leading change: why transformation efforts fail', *Harvard Business Review*, vol.73, no.2, pp.59–67.

An American example of an '*n*-step recipe' approach, Kotter lists eight steps for successful transformation. He has published a book with a similar title.

Leigh, A. and Walters, M., 1998, *Effective Change: Twenty*

Ways to Make it Happen, Institute of Personnel and Development, London.

A British example of a management guide to effective change implementation, full of tools, techniques, checklists and frameworks, with even a little theory up front.

McCalman, J. and Paton, R., 2000, *Change Management: A Guide to Effective Implementation*, Sage Publications, London (second edition).

Offers a theoretically informed and comprehensive practical framework for applying different perspectives on organizational change, clearly written with illustrative cases.

Preece, D., Steven, G. and Steven, V., 1999, *Work, Change and Competition: Managing for Bass*, Routledge, London.

Offers an entertaining and insightful 'insider' account of change in a pub retailing company, Bass, over five years from a processual/contextual perspective which covers the triggers for change, the management strategy and the messy politics.

Senior, B., 1997, *Organizational Change*, Pitman Publishing, London.

Another well-written text, which explores 'soft' and 'hard' approaches to understanding and managing change.

Home viewing

Lean on Me (1989, director John G. Avildsen) is a school drama, based on a true story. Joe Clark (played by Morgan Freeman) is an autocratic and controversial New Jersey high school principal who cleans up his school, East Side High. He institutes a programme of change which elicits various reactions from both the school staff and the students. Identify the trigger of change which prompts the Mayor to appoint Clark as principal. Using the Dunphy and Stace matrix, what is the scale of the change that Clark attempts to introduce? What change leadership style does Clark adopt? Which of Kanter's seven change agent skills does Clark demonstrate? Which change implementation methods are demonstrated? Draw a diagram showing the stakeholders affected by this change, inside and outside the school. Which of the techniques explained by Kotter and Schlesinger does Clark use to overcome resistance?

OB in literature

Jeff Torrington, *The Devil's Carousel*, Martin, Secker & Warburg/Minerva, London, 1996.

Set in the Main Assembly Division (MAD) of the Chimeford plant of the Centaur Car Company. Among the many colourful characters, the crimson-collared overalls of the senior foremen earn them the nickname Rednecks, while Greybacks are junior foremen wearing all-grey overalls to distinguish their lower rank. Senior managers are called Martians by the shop floor employees. Identify the symptoms and causes of resistance to change in Centaur cars. What factors explain the plant closure? What strategic changes could management have implemented to save the plant? In implementing those changes, would it have been more appropriate to use dictatorial transformation or participative evolution, and why?

Chapter exercises

1: Resistance is futile

Objectives

1. To examine the causes of individual resistance to change.

2. To explore the management problems in overcoming resistance to change.

Briefing

Your instructor will ask your class to engage in a short change experiment. When this is complete, consider your response to your instructor's requests using the following guide:

I resisted this change due to:

cause of resistance	applies to me (✓)
parochial self-interest: 'I don't want to be pushed out of my comfort zone'	
misunderstanding and lack of trust: 'why are you asking me to do this?'	
contradictory assessments: 'you might think this is good, but I don't'	
low tolerance of change: 'I can't cope with the uncertainty and the anxiety'	

Compare your responses with those of colleagues:

- What does this experiment reveal about you as a person?
- What does this experiment reveal about your colleagues?
- And what does this reveal about the problems that can be associated with even simple organizational changes?

2: Implementation planning

Objectives

1. To apply change implementation theory to a practical setting.
2. To assess the practical value of 'best practice' textbook advice on how to implement change effectively.

Briefing

Due to a combination of space constraints and financial issues, your department or school has been told by senior management to relocate to another building seven kilometres from the existing site within the next three months. Your management has in turn been asked to draw up a plan for managing the move, which will affect all staff (academic, technical, secretarial, administrative), all students (undergraduate, postgraduate), and all equipment (classroom aids, computing). The new building will provide more space and student facilities, but offices for academic staff are smaller, the building is on a different bus route, and car parking facilities are more limited. Senior management has reassured staff that e-mail will allow regular contact to be maintained with colleagues in other departments which are not being moved.

You have been asked to help management with its planning. Your brief is as follows:

1. Conduct a stakeholder analysis, identifying how each stakeholder or stakeholder group should be approached to ensure that this move goes ahead smoothly.
2. Conduct a readiness for change analysis, identifying any 'groundwork' that may have to be done to ensure the move goes ahead smoothly.
3. Determine a change implementation strategy. Is a participative approach appropriate, or is dictatorial transformation required? Justify your recommendation by pointing to the advantages and limitations of the various options you have explored.
4. Using one or more of the 'recipes' described in this chapter, draw up a creative and practical action plan for implementing this change effectively.

Prepare a short presentation of your results to colleagues.

In discussion, identify what this analysis reveals about the problems of turning organizational change theory and 'best practice' advice into practical management action.

Chapter 19 Organization culture

Key concepts

organization culture
surface manifestations of culture
organization values
basic assumptions
organizational socialization
pre-arrival stage of socialization
encounter stage of socialization
metamorphosis stage of socialization

integration (unitary) perspective
differentiation perspective
fragmentation (conflict) perspective
power distance
uncertainty avoidance
individualism–collectivism
masculinity–femininity
long-term–short-term orientation

Learning objectives

When you have read this chapter, you should be able to define those key concepts in your own words, and you should also be able to:

1. Account for the popularity of organization culture among managers, consultants and academics.
2. List, describe and exemplify Schein's three levels of culture.
3. Distinguish the stages of organizational socialization.
4. Contrast managerial and social science perspectives on organization culture.
5. Assess the link between organization culture and economic performance.
6. Distinguish different national culture dimensions and different culture clusters.

The new public sector management?

In September 1996, a recruitment advertisement appeared for Bath and North East Somerset District Council. It read:

> The new authority will be member-led, officer-driven, customer-focused; a team environment where the whole is greater than the sum of the parts; a flat management structure where employees and managers are fully empowered and decisions are devolved close to the customer: a culture of learning rather than blame; a clear sense of direction and purpose.

Why study organization culture?

When you walk into a hotel, a bank, a nightclub, a shop, a country pub, the office of a solicitor, what do you notice first? What do 'first impressions' tell you about the organization that you have just entered? How friendly will it be? How expensive will it be? What kind of behaviour is expected of you? How will the staff approach and deal with you? Now look more carefully at the physical surroundings. What positive and negative signs, symbols and signals do you get? How exactly are these being transmitted to you? These are all aspects of organization culture. The nature of that culture is thus significant, both for those who work there and for customers and clients. Culture seems to vary from organization to organization, and there is an argument that says that culture affects organizational performance, and hence managers must control and change the culture when necessary. Is culture that important? Can it be managed?

Culture derives from the idea of cultivation, mostly of land but also of gods. The concept evolved to conceptualize humankind's diversity. It asserts that we socially construct different understandings of nature and, hence, of the reality that surrounds us. An organization's culture focuses on the values, beliefs and meanings used by its members to grasp how its uniqueness originates, evolves and operates. It has often been considered within the context of corporate strategy and organization structure (Scholz, 1987). Organization culture has been a popular concept since the early 1980s. It quickly acquired a following among managers, for whom it possessed an intuitive appeal. It then attained the status of a management fad and was seized upon by many senior executives and management consultants as a quick-fix solution to virtually every organization problem. It was then adopted by academics both as an explanatory framework with which to understand behaviour in organizations and as a critical perspective (Morgan *et al.*, 1983; Meek, 1988).

Unlike many of the other popular management fads and fashions of the 1980s, the concept of organization culture has retained its place within business life and academic study. Managers have incorporated it into their everyday vocabulary. For example, following a train accident in London and a nuclear reprocessing error in north-west England, company executives and government ministers discussed the 'culture of safety' in the organizations involved. The publication of books on organization culture may have slowed, but it has not stopped (e.g. Parker, 2000; Yamashita, 1998; Sackmann, 1997). For many companies, interest in the topic has been sustained and indeed raised by increasing globalization, which has placed organization culture sharply into focus alongside national culture [**link**, chapter 2, the world outside]. The topic has also become linked with how leaders can use culture to implement change that would improve their company's financial performance [**links**, chapter 18, organizational change; chapter 21, leadership].

In a similar way, culture possesses an appeal for academics, who have researched and taught it for nearly two decades. In many organizational behaviour and management textbooks, the 'culture perspective' or the 'symbolic approach' now ranks alongside the rational and the human resource perspectives as an alternative way of understanding behaviour in organizations (Bolman and Deal, 1999; Alvesson, 1990). Finally, human resource practitioners, both managers and consultants, have used cultural change in organizations as the basis for new and reformed work practices.

Rise of the organization culture concept

The concept of organization culture, however, is not universally accepted. It remains controversial, and 'paradigm and definition wars' continue to rage. Some writers argue that just as one can talk about French culture, Arab culture or Asian culture, so too it was possible to discuss the organization culture of the British Civil Service, McDonald's, Microsoft or Disney. Others, in contrast, reject this notion completely. In his review of the organization culture literature, David Needle (2000, p.101) wrote that:

> The treatment of culture at the level of the firm varied considerably ranging across the banal, the simplistic, the misleading, the highly complex, the impenetrably academic and the highly critical.

One consequence of this is that although the numerous research articles, textbooks and managerial advice all draw upon a common body of work to varying degrees—the same authors, studies, frameworks, concepts and models—no two accounts will ever 'assemble' this material in exactly the same way. It is as if our knowledge about organization culture is contained on hundreds of separate children's plastic building bricks, and each time a model is constructed, a different collection of bricks is used. Depending on the chosen design, some 'bricks' will not fit, and are discarded, only to be integrated later when a different design is assembled.

This chapter begins with a general definition of the concept of organization culture, briefly charting its historical development. It then uses a popular culture model, describing and illustrating its main elements as most commonly discussed in the literature. Once these have been presented, the main controversies and debates surrounding the concept will be discussed. As many of the aforementioned organization culture 'bricks' will be incorporated as possible. However, readers should remember that this represents the authors' own particular 'model' or view of the topic of organization culture, and they should make their own assessment of the strengths and weaknesses of the concept as an explanatory device.

Organization culture is the collection of relatively uniform and enduring values, beliefs, customs, traditions and practices that are shared by an organization's members, learned by new recruits, and transmitted from one generation of employees to the next.

In Britain and within Europe, the concept is generally referred to as **organization culture**; in the USA, it is *organizational* culture; and the management literature prefers to use the term '*corporate* culture'. Its antecedents go back through anthropology, sociology, psychology and early management thought. In general, it is recognized that organizations have 'something' (a personality, philosophy, ideology or climate) which goes beyond economic rationality, and which gives each of them a unique identity. One writer referred to it as 'The way we do things around here' (Deal and Kennedy, 1982), while another saw it as 'the collective programming of the mind' that distinguished one group from another (Hofstede, 1984). Then, as now, there was no consensus about its definition. Competing definitions abound and do more to confuse than to clarify. Although a definition is offered here, readers are encouraged to devise their own on the basis of the discussion presented in this chapter and their own further reading.

Martin Parker (2000) argued that references to culture could be traced back to the work of human relations researcher Elton Mayo (1933; 1945) [**link**, chapter 9, group formation]. He and his associates were interested in the social engineering of 'sentiments', i.e. the non-logical rationalizations for actions. They argued that executives could manage better if they understood the irrationalities of ordinary employees. The cultural perspective therefore represents a break with the earlier rational-mechanistic view of organization, which saw employees as tools for achieving an organization's goals [**links**, chapter 13, traditional work design; chapter 14, elements of structure]. Many assumed that the hard 'scientific' management of companies could be replaced by a softer approach that relied on a more humane understanding of people's values, beliefs and feelings, which focused on the non-rational aspects. The perspective developed from an interest in the behaviour of people within informal organization structures, and examined the meanings individuals assigned to what they saw around them within their organizations, how this process occurred, and how those assigned meanings influenced their behaviour [**link**, chapter 1, prologue].

More recent references to culture in organizations go back half a century to the

Tom J. Peters

Robert H. Waterman

Terrance E. Deal

Allen A. Kennedy

work of Elliot Jaques and his book *The Changing Culture of a Factory* (Jaques, 1952). However, the current debates about culture are traceable to 1982, when two books catapulted the concept to the forefront of management attention. In their book, *In Search of Excellence*, two McKinsey consultants, Tom Peters and Robert Waterman (1982), studied the excellent American companies of the time. They claimed that what distinguished these from less successful rivals was the strength of their cultures. In the same year, Terrence Deal and Allen Kennedy (1982), an academic and a consultant, had their own book published, *Corporate Cultures*. In it, they suggested that a strong culture was a powerful lever for guiding behaviour, and that the culture of every company could be managed towards achieving greater effectiveness. They conceived of a company's culture as consisting of values and beliefs, myths, heroes and symbols that possessed meaning for all employees. In addition to the publication of the aforementioned books, four other factors stimulated an interest in organization culture at that time:

1. *Japanese success*: The economic success of Japanese organizations during the 1970s and 1980s, which appeared capable of establishing and maintaining co-operative, team-based organization cultures.

2. *Soft skills*: The view that more intangible (soft) factors such as values, beliefs and norms had as great an impact on company performance as financial (hard) ones.

3. *Strong cultures*: The belief that there was a correlation between strong organization cultures and organization performance, and that a company's culture was capable of being directed by managers.

4. *Union substitute*: The influence of the right-wing governments from the early 1980s (Thatcher and Reagan), which weakened union and employee rights, gave companies the opportunity to 'include' their employees within a new collectivity, which their managers controlled.

Although organization culture was originally introduced to managers by (predominantly) consultants, it was not long before academics started to take an interest in it as well. Some business school professors attempted to refine the concept, seeking to operationalize it for research purposes. Edgar Schein (1985) was among the first of these. His and competing definitions established the basis for later research in the concept. The role of academics has been to research the concept and develop it theoretically. Majken Schultz (1995, p.5) observed that:

Opposed to the study of both formal and informal organization behaviour, a cultural way of studying organizations is to study the meaning of organizational behaviour—or more specifically, the meanings and beliefs which members of organizations assign to organizational behaviour and how these assigned meanings influence the ways in which they behave themselves.

The culture concept, with its focus on myths, metaphors, rituals, stories, sagas, clans, heroes and heroines, ceremonies, artefacts, world views, ethos and aesthetics, has directed attention to new phenomena in the organization and expanded the field of study in at least two ways. First, the culture-symbolic perspective has reinterpreted well-known phenomena and questioned their significance. For example, organization structure is now considered in terms of dominant myths about effective organization. Strategic planning meetings are understood not only as decision-making occasions, but also as events for interpreting past events and signalling future directions. Similarly, the informal organization is no longer seen just as a behaviour pattern but is now also considered to be 'a cultural network where priests, spies, storytellers and "support clubs" translate and transmit the organization's key values' (Deal and Kennedy, 1982).

Second, Parker (2000) highlighted the increasing link between organization culture and postmodernism during the late 1980s [**link**, chapter 2, the world outside] has stimulated research, publication and conferences in organizational symbolism, myth and ritual, establishing it as a separate sub-field within organizational behaviour. The relationship is where postmodernist thinking attempts to understand modern organizations through an analysis of their corporate identity statements (lists of values). These are the images that companies seek to project through their self-marketing and the marketing of their products and services (Alvesson, 1990). Thus, after nearly twenty years of debate about organization culture, the concept remains as controversial as ever.

- Academic critics totally reject the idea that the concept of culture, which was taken from the anthropological tradition and developed for an analysis of tribes and societies, has any part to play in examining organizations.

- Academic supporters disagree both about the concept itself and about its importance as an explanatory tool. Attempts have been made to clarify the concept, there is still no accepted conceptual framework for analysing it, and several competing typologies exist.

- There are those who see the 'dark side' of the concept. They believe that it is manipulative and that it encourages managers to believe that they can use it successfully.

Before continuing with a discussion of the different perspectives on organization culture, and explaining why it remains such a controversial concept, it is necessary to first introduce, define and illustrate its major elements, as well as to relate them to each other. By doing so, the subsequent discussion can be made more understandable and meaningful.

Culture: surface manifestations, values and basic assumptions

Edgar Schein's model of culture is amongst the most widely discussed. It considers organization culture in terms of three levels, each distinguished by their visibility and accessibility to individuals (figure 19.1). Schein's (1985, p.14) view was that:

> Organization culture is the pattern of basic assumptions which a group has invented, discovered on developed in learning to cope with its problems of external adaption and integration, which have worked well enough to be considered valid, and therefore to be taught to new members as the correct way to perceive, think and feel in relation to problems ... culture is not the overt behaviour or visible artefacts that one might observe if one were to visit the company. It is not even the philosophy or value system which the founder may articulate or write down in various 'charters'. Rather it is the assumptions which lie behind the values and which determine the behaviour patterns and the visible artefacts such as architecture, office layout, dress codes and so on.

Edgar Henry Schein
(b. 1928)

Schein's fundamental view is that culture is the sharing of meanings and the sharing of 'basic' assumptions among organizational employees (level 3). He also implies that an organization's senior executives can manage these basic assumptions if they understand what culture is and how it operates.

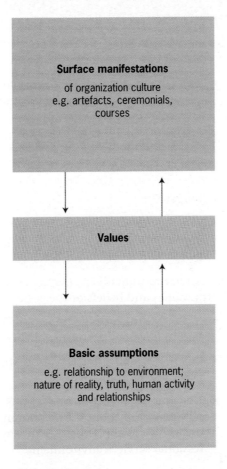

Figure 19.1: Schein's three levels of culture
Based on Edgar H. Schein, *Organizational Culture and Leadership*, Jossey-Bass, San Francisco, Calif., 1985, p.14.

Surface manifestation of culture are its most visible and most accessible forms, which are the visible and audible behaviour patterns and objects.

Schein's first level is the **surface manifestation of culture**. For him this is not the organization's culture itself but only its most visible, apparent and accessible aspect which can be perceived by people. Surface manifestations of culture include behaviour patterns that can be seen and heard, and which thus 'send a message' to an organization's visitors, customers and employees.

At this level, culture is manifested in company-specific objects, architecture, rituals and language. It has received a great deal of attention in the literature. Over the years our own students have enthusiastically participated in 'culture spotting' and have shared with us examples from those organizations with which they have been involved. Organization cultures naturally change, but here are a few past and present examples of surface manifestations:

Artefacts include tools, furniture, appliances and clothes ('work wear').

- Amazon's founder, Jeff Bezos, was short of money so, in order to minimize costs, he and his wife went to their local home improvement store, bought three wooden doors and angle brackets, and hammered together three desks at a cost of $60 each. That frugality continues at Amazon to this day, and every employee sits behind a door desk.

- NEXT (British retail clothing company) prides itself on its staff uniform, which employees chose from the new season's stock, so that they are smart and create a good image in front of customers.

Ceremonials involve a linked series of rites within a single event.

- Church of Scotland administrators all pray before commencing work and also pray for each other if anyone is sick or stressed.

- The Loyalty Group in Canada has an annual 'Funday' which all of its 700 employees attend, and which features a picnic, speeches, team games, dinner and an award ceremony.

Courses for induction, orientation and training are used to educate new members.

- McDonald's (US fast food restaurant chain) established its full-time training centre in 1961 called Hamburger University, which offers a 'degree' in 'hamburgerology'.

- Airlines have 4–5-week induction courses for cabin staff incorporating grooming, including how to apply make-up. The head of appearance & grooming carries out formal, random appraisals on individual crew members.

Heroes refer to individuals, living and dead, who established and/or who personify the values and beliefs of the culture and provide role models for emulation.

- In B&Q (British home improvements retailer), Mr Block and Mr Quale were said to have had a vision which is still being followed today.

- Bill Harley and John Davidson still embody the spirit of owning a Harley-Davidson motorbike.

- New joiners at Arthur Andersen & Co (international business audit and tax services) learn about the accountant Arthur Andersen, a Swedish émigré who, on arrival in the United States, worked assiduously to create a great professional services environment.

Language includes both specialist technical vocabulary related to the business (jargon) and general naming choices.

- A number of companies do not have 'employees'. Wal-mart and some divisions of BT have associates; McDonald's has crew members; Disney has cast members; Asda and Sainsbury's have colleagues; B&Q has team players; the John Lewis Partnership has partners; Brook Street Employment Agency has recruitment consultants; Debenhams has co-workers.

- Among staff and management, the McDonald's restaurant is known as the 'store', not restaurant. Thus, each has a 'store manager', not a restaurant manager.

- Asda (food supermarket) does not have shoppers, and many private train companies do not have passengers. Instead, both have customers.

Mottoes are maxims adopted as rules of conduct. Unlike slogans, mottoes are rarely, if ever, changed.

- John Lewis Partnership
  (British department store chain): 'Never knowingly undersold'

- Special Air Services (SAS)
  (British military): 'Who dares wins'

- Glasgow High
  School: 'Sursum semper' (Ever upwards)

Myths are universal explanations that lack a factual basis and hence are untestable.

- Safeway's (British food supermarket) story of a female employee who had typed in her own ABC (customer loyalty) card number instead of processing the customers', and making almost £1,000 in free shopping before being sacked.

- A staff member at Disneyland Paris dressed as Mickey Mouse was disciplined by the company after taking off his costume in front of tourists.

Norms are expected modes of behaviour based on an organization's values and beliefs that provide guidance for employee behaviour.

- Officer Training Corps (OTC) in universities have the norms of respecting authority, being both a leader and a team player, and persevering to see things through even in the face of opposition.

- Courage (brewing company) had a specified starting time of 9.00 am, but the norm was for employees to arrive at 8.30 am.

Physical layout concerns how an organization chooses to use its buildings, open spaces and office layouts.

- The headquarters at Nike (sportswear manufacturer) has a hall of fame of famous athletes who wore Nike equipment, down which all employees must pass each morning before arriving at their offices.

- PriceWaterhouseCoopers (international management consultants) operate a desk-booking system known as 'hotelling'. All employees have a 'preferred' area on a certain floor along with others in their 'group' but have no pre-designated desks. Instead, employees book their desks on a day-to-day basis.

Rites are planned, often dramatic activities, which are elaborately staged and which incorporate different expressions of culture into a single event (Trice and Beyer, 1984).

- The 'Wal-mart wiggle' and song are performed first thing in the morning by employees (US retailer).

- Every morning before moving into their sales territory, each Southwestern (book selling company) salesperson performs a dance to motivate themselves.

Rituals are a repetitive sequence of activities that express and reinforce the key values and beliefs of the organization. They are standardized techniques which help to manage employees' anxieties.

- Abbey National plc (British bank) designates the last Friday of every month as 'dress down day.'

- Asda (British food supermarket) staff have a 'huddle' each morning during which they are informed what is going on in the store on that day.

- When a new shift takes over in the Berlin Fire Brigade, all new shift members shake hands with those going off duty.

- Ben and Jerry's (US ice cream company) have a full-time employee to organize weekly theme days in which all staff have to participate, e.g. on 'Elvis Day' all staff have to appear dressed as Elvis or sing Elvis songs, or else pay a fine for charity, thereby contributing to the 'fun'.

Slogans are short, catchy phrases which are regularly changed. They are used both for customer advertising and to motivate employees.

• Nike	'Just do it'
• British Army	'Be the best'
• Ulster Bank	'The Friendly Bank'
• Audi (German auto manufacturer)	'Vorsprung durch Technik'
• GE (General Electric)	We bring good things to life'
• Bose Corporation (US hi-fi speakers manufacturer)	'Better sound through research'
• McDonald's	'Where would you be without McDonald's?'

Stories are usually based on true events but can include a mixture of both truth and fiction. They often contain a narrative about key decisions made by individuals that affect the company's future course (Feldman, 1991; Weick, 1995).

- Proctor & Gamble's story of an employee who noticed that the labels on a product at his local supermarket were mounted off-centre. He bought the whole stock assuming that P&G would reimburse him, which it did.

- NEXT's (British clothing retailer) staff handbook contains not only a mission statement and rules but also stories of how the company came to be as it is today after nearly collapsing, and how the staff helped to get it back on its feet.

- The story of when Henry Ford II was chairman of the Ford Motor Company he reminded executives who had become too arrogant, 'it's my name that's on the building', conveying the message that it was he who ran the company.

Symbols are signs that represent or recall something else (Barley, 1983).

- Coca-Cola and IBM logos, the Nike 'swoosh', *G* for Gucci and *x* for Coco Chanel, McDonald's 'Golden Arches'.

- Starbuck's (coffee shop chain) logo is intended to communicate the nautical spirit, pioneering drive and natural harmony at work. Its meaning is formally explained to newcomers during their induction training.

- The Red Cross symbol is a red cross on a white background, which is the reverse of the Swiss flag and means neutrality.

- Allied Irish Bank's (AIB) symbol/logo of a dove with an olive branch perched on an ark is intended to denote safety under any circumstances.

Organization values refer to those things that have personal or organizational worth or meaning to the founders or senior management. Values are typically based on moral, societal or religious precepts that are learned in childhood and modified through experience.

Schein's second level concerns **organization values** and beliefs. Again, in his view, this is not the organization's culture itself. These are located below the surface manifestations and underpin them. While values are not visible, individuals can be made aware of them. Many commentators agree that these values are the element that distinguishes the organization from other firms, since they affect the basic assumptions that Schein sees as truly being an organization's culture. Values are broad tendencies to prefer certain states of affairs over others. They are typically based on moral, societal or religious precepts that are learned in childhood and modified through experience.

Tom Peters and Robert Waterman's book (1982) proposed the 7-S framework to organizational success, whose variables are shown in figure 19.2. Values were positioned at the centre of that framework, holding the other elements together, and

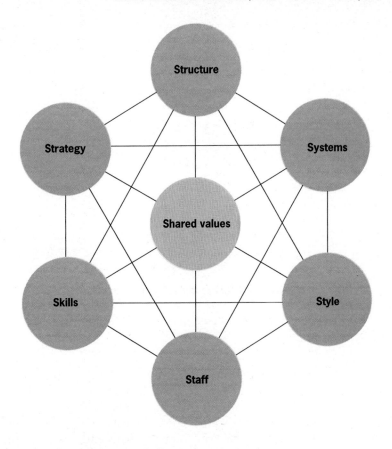

Figure 19.2: McKinsey 7-S framework ©
From Thomas J. and Robert H. Waterman, *In Search of Excellence*, Harper & Row, New York, 1982, p.10.

thus were considered to be a key element in achieving high organizational performance. Values are said to provide a common direction for all employees and guidelines for their behaviour: 'People way down the line know what they are supposed to do in most situations because the handful of guiding values is crystal clear' (Peters and Waterman, 1982, p.76).

Where do organization values come from? As indicated by Schein's earlier quotation, some authors see values representing organizational solutions to problems experienced in the past. Another source of values are the views of the original founder, as modified by the company's current senior management (Schein, 1983). Stephen Robbins described senior management as an organization's 'culture carriers'. Thus one can argue that organization values are the values of the current company elite (senior managers), rather like 'organization goals' represent the preferred aims of the same group. Values are operationalized into company practices and procedures, as detailed in the surface manifestations. Although senior management might like its employees to adopt the organization's (i.e. its) values, this is not only unlikely but also unnecessary. Employees only need to follow the specified, values-based practices and manifest expected responses. For example, they did not need to enjoy a company's 'Elvis Day', only participate enthusiastically in it and just act as if they were having a good time (figure 19.3).

In a sense, therefore, organization values are always backward looking, despite being developed to contribute to the future development of the company. For an organization culture to form, a fairly stable collection of people need to have

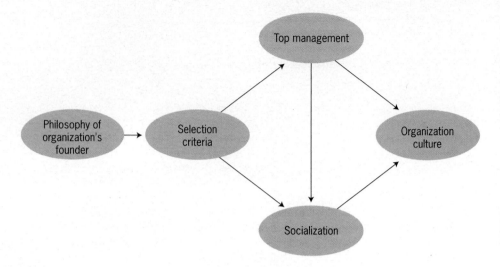

Figure 19.3: Where does organization culture come from?

shared a significant history, involving problems, which allowed a social learning process to take place. Organization which have such histories possess cultures that permeate most of their functions (Schein, 1985).

Company values come in lists. They are to be found printed in company reports, framed on company walls and published on organizational web sites. For example, Amazon's six core values are:

customer obsession	ownership	bias for action
frugality	high hiring bar	innovation

They have often been devised by teams of senior managers. Some cynics argue that organizational values are a passing fad and have little impact on what what employees actually think or do. However, there is some evidence that organizational values can be a source of controversy (Buono *et al.*, 1985). In November 1999, British Aerospace (BAe) and Marconi Electronics Systems merged to form BAE Systems, creating a single organization with 100,000 employees, operating from nearly 100 sites around the world. The merged company's values are:

customers our highest priority	innovation & technology partnership
people	performance

Controversy was aroused when it was reported that it would be BAe's company values, and not Marconi's, which would shape the newly formed organization. Marconi directors had been asked to take on BAe's values in the new organization when the merger was being discussed. Consultants warned that this would mean that BAe would dominate the new organization, and ex-Marconi employees would be disadvantaged. One consultant said, 'In my experience, one side is always the winner in these cases. You get the best of both companies by merging, so buying into one side's set-up is not necessarily the best way' (*Personnel Today*, 1999).

GE values

GE leaders ... Always with unyielding integrity ...

- Are passionately focused on driving customer success

- Live Six Sigma Quality ... ensure that the customer is always its first beneficiary ... and use it to accelerate growth

- Insist on excellence and are intolerant of bureaucracy

- Act in a boundaryless fashion ... always search for and apply the best ideas regardless of their source

- Prize global intellectual capital and the people that provide it ... build diverse teams to maximize it

- See change for the growth opportunities it brings ... i.e. 'e-Business'

- Create a clear simple, customer-centred vision ... and continually review and refresh its execution

- Create an environment of 'stretch', excitement, informality and trust ... reward improvements ... celebrate results

- Demonstrate ... always with infectious enthusiasm for the customer ... the '4-Es' of GE leadership: the personal Energy to welcome and deal with the speed of change ... the ability to create an atmosphere that Energises others ... the Edge to make difficult decisions ... and the ability to constantly Execute

Source: GE web site

Stop and criticize

Visit the web sites of some large European and American companies, for example Nokia, Body Shop, Hewlett-Packard, Amazon, Andersen Consulting, Eriksson, IBM, and locate their list of values. Also, look at some non-profit organizations like universities, local government councils, Greenpeace, Amnesty International, Red Cross and Medécins Sans Frontières. What purposes do these lists of values serve and for whom?

Basic assumptions refer to invisible, preconscious and 'taken-for-granted' understandings held by individuals with respect to aspects of human behaviour, the nature of reality and the organization's relationship to its environment.

Finally, **basic assumptions** are located at Schein's third level and are, in his view, the organization's culture. They include the assumptions that individuals hold about the organization and how it functions. They relate to aspects of human behaviour, the nature of reality and the organization's relationship to its environment. They are invisible, preconscious and 'taken for granted'. They are therefore difficult to access.

Organizational socialization

Organizational socialization is the process through which an individual's pattern of behaviour, and their values, attitudes and motives, are influenced to conform with those seen as desirable in a particular organization.

The ultimate strength of a company's culture depends on the homogeneity of group membership, and the length and intensity of their shared experiences in a group. One learns about a company's culture through the process of **organizational socialization**. It includes the careful selection of new company members, their instruction in appropriate ways of thinking and behaving, and the reinforcement of desired behaviours by senior managers (Pascale, 1985).

The concept of socialization has already been considered at the level of the individual and the group [**links**, chapter 4, learning; chapter 11, individuals in groups]. Socialization is important because, as John van Maanen and Edgar Schein (1979) argue, new organization recruits have to be taught to see the organizational world as their more experienced colleagues do if the tradition of the

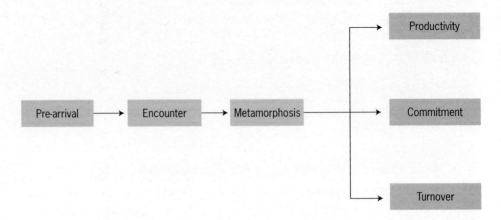

Figure 19.4: Organizational socialization

organization is to survive. Socialization involves newcomers absorbing the values and behaviours required to survive and prosper in an organization. It reduces variability of behaviour by imbuing employees with a sense of what is expected of them and how they should do things. By providing an internal sense of how they should behave, plus a shared frame of reference, socialization standardizes employee behaviour, making it predictable for the benefit of senior management. The socialization process is shown in figure 19.4.

The **pre-arrival stage of socialization** occurs before individuals are admitted to the organization and is targeted equally at both those who will be accepted and those rejected. Every individual comes to an organization already possessing a set of values, attitudes and expectations, which they will have acquired through their earlier socialization at school, university and in their previous employment.

The selection process is part of this socialization stage and has four objectives:

- Informs prospective employees about the organization.

- Ensures that the values and objectives of those recruited mesh with those of the firm, thereby ensuring homogeneity of the total membership (finding the 'right type' who 'fits in').

- Conveys to the minority ultimately admitted that they have surmounted a rigorous selection procedure, thereby making them feel that they were members of an elite, who have achieved a coveted and distinctive status.

Pre-arrival stage of socialization refers to the period of learning in the process that occurs before an applicant joins an organization.

Organizational clueing

Diane Preston and Cathy Hart studied new graduate management trainees at Taylor plc, a large retailing organization in the UK. They consider organizational socialization as involving the employer (through their human resources management department) leaving a trail of clues for new employees to discover which enable them to understand and to navigate their way through the organization. Such clues include job descriptions, appraisal guidelines, management competencies and promotion prerequisites. These denoted 'what it takes to get on' here. Clues were left at different stages in the employment cycle as employees progressed through the company. The authors suggest that different individuals might require different trails—each with a different number of clues with varying explicitness, depending on the person involved, and the stage of their career within the organization.

Based on Diane Preston and Cathy Hart, 'A trail of clues for graduate trainees', in C. Mabey, D. Skinner and T. Clark (eds), *Experiencing Human Resource Management*, Sage, London, 1998, chapter 12, pp.205–17.

Encounter stage of socialization refers to the period of learning in the process during which the new recruit learns about organizational expectations.

Metamorphosis stage of socialization refers to the period in which the new employee adjusts to their organization's values, attitudes, motives, norms and required behaviours.

- Reinforces the image the company wishes to project to its future applicants, as the accounts of the experiences of both successful and unsuccessful applicants will circulate through the grapevine.

Individuals joining an organization have expectations of what it will be like. During the **encounter stage of socialization**, they interact with their managers and colleagues, do their job and can judge the degree to which their expectations match the reality. Where there is a mismatch, the learning process detaches them from their previous assumptions and replaces them with another set of values, attitudes and motives that conform with those which the organization deems desirable. Many vivid accounts of this stage are contained in novels and films about new recruits joining the military and churches.

In the **metamorphosis stage of socialization**, the new employee adjusts to their organization's values, attitudes, motives, norms and required behaviours. Such adjustment may be real or fabricated. Where the gap between expectation and reality cannot be breached, the individual may leave their job by resigning.

Socialization is a process that is most intense when the employee enters the organization for the first time, but it continues throughout their stay. Senior man-

---

Disney-fication of new employees

Disney begins tugging on the heartstrings of employees even before they are hired. Think about the typical recruiting office in the hospitality industry—a windowless cubby-hole in the sub-basement between the laundry and the boiler room. Then walk into Disney's capacious 'casting centre', and you're in Wonderland. Well, not exactly, but the doorknobs on the entrance do replicate the ones Alice yanked during her adventures ... Ascend a gentle sloping hallway, whose walls are decorated with whimsical murals, and you're in a vast anteroom where the centrepiece is the original model of Snow White's castle.

Some 50,000 aspiring employees funnel through the Lake Buena Vista casting centre every year seeking jobs that start with pay as low as $5.95 per hour (Disney's other theme parks in California, Japan and France do their own hiring). What are Disney World's 40 interviewers—all of whom started as front line workers—most interested in? ... Says Duncan Dickson, director of casting: 'We're looking for personality. We can train for skills. We want people who are enthusiastic, who have pride in their work, who can take charge of a situation without supervision'.

... Disney has overhauled its approach to orientation, putting less emphasis on policies and procedures, and more on emotion. *Traditions*, the two-day initial training session attended by all new cast members, is part inculcation, part encounter group. Guided by two unfailingly upbeat cast members, neatly dressed neophytes seated at round tables in a small classroom discuss their earliest memories of Disney, their visions of great service, their understanding of teamwork.

Next comes the movie, a panegyric to Walt Disney himself. The film depicts the founder as a creative risk taker who overcame setbacks (his first character, destined for obscurity, was named Oswald the Lucky Rabbit), believed in teamwork (he and his brother Roy were partners), and preached the importance of exceeding expectations of his guests. Yes, Walt actually embraced that concept, now being peddled as a new management mantra, way back in 1955.

By encouraging ... spurts of spontaneity ... Disney World tries to instil verve in jobs that are otherwise tightly regimented. The 36-page cast members' appearance guide, for example, includes excruciatingly detailed ukases on length and style of hair, colour and quantity of cosmetics, and hues and textures of hosiery ... Disney World, where the average age of cast members is 37, loses only about 15 per cent of its front line employees to attrition each year, compared with a rate of 60 per cent for the hospitality industry as a whole. Wages are competitive ... but don't underestimate the power of sentiment. Listen to Rick Anderson, 20, a host in Tomorrowland: 'Sometimes, you get hot in your costume, you get fed up dealing with angry guests who are tired of waiting in line. But then a kid asks you a question, you answer it, and she breaks into a smile. You can make someone happy'.

From Ronald Henkoff, 'Finding and Keeping the Best Service Workers', *Fortune*, 3 October 1994, pp.52-8.

Ford culture

A Detroit-based human resources advisor described his socialization into the pre-1980s Ford culture. He reported that a partial list of the advice that he received from long-serving personnel went something like this:

- Don't disagree with the boss.
- Don't rock the boat.
- Look busy, even if you aren't.
- Don't smile, let alone laugh too much.
- Be obsessive about getting your numbers right; estimates won't do.
- If a colleague gets into trouble with the boss—don't help; be grateful it's not you.
- Observe the dress code.
- CYA (cover your ass).

From Ken Starkey and Alan McKinlay, 'Managing for Ford', *Sociology*, 1994, vol.28, no.4, pp.975–90 (p.979).

agers in the company may take the role of mentors or coaches. For example, two of the largest international management consultancy companies use this approach. They operate a formal counselling, mentoring and 'buddying' system. In one of them, upon appointment, all new staff members are allocated a counsellor who monitors their development and provides coaching. In the other firm, summer placement students are allocated to a team whose members they refer to as 'buddies' and whose role is to counsel and aid the student during the first few weeks in the company. In both cases, the responsibility of coaches, mentors and buddies is to guide and mould new members in line with organization expectations.

Performance-based appraisal systems and formal training programmes are also instituted by senior management to signal visibly which goals new joiners should be striving for and how. Finally, senior management's behaviour in promoting, censoring and dismissing employees also sends information to employees about company values, expectations about norms, risk taking, acceptability of delegation, appropriate dress, topics of discussion, and so on.

Perspectives on culture contrasted

The debate about organization culture takes place between two camps. On one side, there are the managerial writers and consultants who believe that there is a relationship between a strong culture and organizational performance. They hold that 'A well-developed and business-specific culture in which management and staff are thoroughly socialized ... can underpin stronger organizational commitment, higher morale, more efficient performance, and generally higher productivity' (Furnham and Gunter, 1993, p.232). Ranged against them are mainly academic social scientists, who believe that organization culture is a term that is, 'overused, over-inclusive but under-defined'. Although there are many debates taking place about organization culture at many different levels, we have chosen to contrast the managerial perspective with the social science one. We do this so as to enable readers to assess for themselves the discussions of culture in both American and British management-oriented textbooks and management 'self-improvement' books and compare these to the 'critical' contributions of mainly European academics.

The description of organization culture in the preceding pages is a managerial perspective. Its aim is to achieve managerial aims, seen by many to be enhancing organizational performance and controlling labour by integrating them within the organization. The perspective can be found in the British and American introductory management textbooks. It is based on the writings of managerially oriented authors (Peters and Waterman, 1982; Schein, 1985; Deal and Kennedy, 1982; Ouchi, 1981; Pascale and Athos, 1982). Its distinguishing feature is that it is both normative and prescriptive. As Needle (2000, p.101) explained:

It makes assumptions about employees that it does not explore and constitutes a set of beliefs and values that are deliberately created as part of a management strategy, and which are used to guide behaviour and processes within the organization.

It seems to be less concerned with explaining what the contemporary culture of any given organization actually is, accounting for its elements or assessing its significance. Instead, it takes a more pragmatic, even utopian approach, recommending what it should be, suggesting how it might be changed so as to encourage greater efficiency, and even encouraging managers to act as if that preferred culture already existed.

The social science perspective is that taken by those academics who understand organizational behaviour issues and seek to explain differences between organizations. It is an attempt to counter the euphoric and uncritical adoption of the concept. Managers around the world grasped cultural change as a 'turnaround strategy', while many management consultancies welcomed it as a 'killer application' which would boost their fees. Initially social science academics sought to operationalize key concepts and conduct meaningful research. Later, they adopted a more critical perspective questioning both the value of the organization culture and its very existence as a phenomenon [link, chapter 2, the world outside]. This group of social science writers includes Karl Weick (1979), Carol Axel Ray (1986), Debra Meyerson and Joanne Martin (1987), Martin (1985; 1992) and Hugh Willmott (1993). The managerial and social science debate about organization culture can be considered under five headings:

Managerial		*Social science*
Culture *has*	v	Culture *is*
Integration culture	v	Differentiation culture
Consensual culture	v	Fragmentation culture
Culture managed	v	Culture tolerated
Symbolic leadership	v	Management control

Culture 'has' versus culture 'is'

The 'has–is' debate is at the heart of the controversy and the debate on organization culture. The 'has' view holds that every organization possesses a culture, just as it has a strategy, structure, technology and employees. It sees organizations as culture-producing phenomena, with that culture being an attribute of the organization, manifested in its values and attitudes. That culture is then 'given' to its members from above, and they do not participate at all in its formation. From this perspective, culture is acquired by employees and is capable of being manipulated by senior management for its own ends (Smircich, 1983).

In contrast, the 'is' view holds that 'organizations *are* cultures', not possessing any objective, independent existence which imposes itself on employees. That culture is a product of the daily, routine interactions between organization members, who ongoingly produce and reproduce it. Hence organization culture exists only in, and through, their social (inter)action. It both shapes their actions and the outcome of the process of social creation and reproduction (Legge, 1995, p.186; Anthony, 1994). Companies are sources of social relationships and meanings for the members. If these individuals all suddenly vanished, so would the culture. However, this view does not totally reject the influence of leaders, since they are themselves involved in interactions and thus contribute to culture shaping.

The 'is' view of organization culture has been variously described in the literature as a 'social constructionist' perspective; as a 'root metaphor'; and as the perspective that 'sees organizations as a system of shared cognitions, of knowledge and beliefs, or as a system of shared symbols and meanings'. It therefore offers management fewer levers with which to shape it, or use as a tool of control. Several authors subscribe to the culture-as-metaphor perspective (Gregory, 1983; Smircich, 1983; Anthony 1994; Morgan *et al.*, 1983; Meek, 1988). For those who adopt the social science view, culture is deeper than its symbolic manifestations. Stories, rituals, material symbols and language within organizations may be a means of transmitting culture but are not the culture itself. Gareth Morgan (1986, p.133) wrote that:

> the slogans, evocative language, symbols, stories, myths, ceremonies, rituals and patterns of tribal behaviour that decorate the surface of organization life, merely give clues to the existence of a much deeper and all-pervasive system of meaning.

So what is the problem with organization culture? Roy Payne (1990) is one of several writers who have questioned whether organization culture, as a discrete variable separate from that of the concept of organization itself, has any meaning or value. The ability of an organization to anticipate and react to changing economic conditions has been seen as a more important variable than the nature of its culture [**link**, chapter 16, organization strategy and design]. This observation was

Semco culture: 'has' and 'is'

Semco is a Brazilian manufacturer of marine and food-service equipment. An innovative firm run on participative lines, it was forced to adopt even more radical measures in 1990 when the country's ministry of finance overnight reduced the country's money supply by 80 per cent. The company responded by encouraging its employees to form satellite enterprises that used company facilities. By 1994, these satellites were responsible for two-thirds of the products being launched.

The company is based on three fundamental values—employee participation, open information systems and profit sharing. Participation gives employees control of their work; profit sharing gives them a reason to do it better; and information tells them what is working and what is not. Semco does not have a single boss but an informal group of six top managers called 'associates'. Employees have total access to all financial information; receive training to help them to understand it; are consulted on major decisions; and receive a quarter of the profits each year.

Semco's practices include staff choosing when to work, no dress code, committees, open stockrooms, and employees designing their own working environment. Stories tell of employees agreeing to a pay cut in order to avoid lay-offs. Its symbols include Semco's organizational circle; and its language refers to councillors, partners and associates. Whether control has been internalized is unclear. Managers determine their own pay, and there are no job titles, security, reception or secretaries. Upward appraisal is used to appraise managers every six months, while flexible teams, which create their own sales and production quotas, also hire and evaluate their leaders. While formal control does not exist, informal contracts operate through peer pressure. Since such a large proportion of earnings are tied directly to company profits, peer pressure operates on employees not to abuse their freedoms.

Richardo Semler, the son of the founder, has sought to create a company free from fear and insecurity and characterized by freedom and trust. He describes the firm's management system as 'management by wandering about', which uses symbolic management to establish and communicate norms and values through emotional engagement. Semler and others are seen as heroes, internally and externally. Is its organization culture the result of the firm members' interactions or the owner's attempts to revolutionize its management system? At the start, Semler's values guided the changes, which were introduced by trial and error within specific departments, rather than the company as a whole. This suggests that culture is something that senior management has, and which is imposed on others. However, these changes became incorporated in the firm's daily life though existing employees' everyday interactions and the socialization of new staff. As participation is encouraged, strikes not punished, and conflict and change viewed as normal, employees both feel free and are motivated to contribute to the process of cultural formation. Semler sees the company as consisting of 'tribes' and the objective being to achieve co-existence rather than harmony.

Despite Semler's contention that what has occurred at Semco is 'more of a sociological experiment than a management technique', and despite his assertion that the ideas are not his own, but 'flow from the company's culture, there is still an aspect which sees these changes as an instrument to increase commitment, productivity and profitability. While the written accounts of this experiment produced by Semler himself and by journalists are interesting, they tell us little about the sources of his organization's culture. Thus his innovations might be more usefully analysed in terms of an organizational change framework [link, chapter 17, organization development] or a one of power and politics [link, chapter 24, power and politics].

Based on J. Bright, 'The man who drives Brazil nuts', *The Director*, September 1993, p.82; J. Pottinger, 'Brazil's maverick reveals his radical recipe for success', *Personnel Management*, September 1994, p.71; J. Quinn, 'The new mavericks', *Incentive*, October 1993, pp.18–24; M. Rigg, 'Vision and value: keys to initiating organization change, *Industrial Engineering*, June 1992, pp.12–13: R. Semler, 'Managing without managers', *Harvard Business Review*, September–October 1989, pp.76–84; R. Semler, 1993, *Maverick*, Century, London; and R. Semler, 'Why my former employees still work with me', *Harvard Business Review*, January–February 1994, pp.64–74.

made by several prominent culture authors (Peters, 1987; Willmott, 1993). Similarly, the ability of a company's culture to respond quickly to environmental circumstances (Kotter and Heskett, 1992) leaves one asking how, if it is able to do that, can it (by definition) be a culture?

Integration versus differentiation cultures

Integration (or unitary) perspective is a view which regards culture as monolithic, characterized by consistency, organization-wide consensus and clarity. It holds that these integrating features will lead to improved organization effectiveness through greater employee commitment and employee control, as measured by productivity and profitability.

The managerial approach to culture takes an **integration** or **unitary perspective** [**link**, chapter 23, conflict]. The controversial notion of a 'strong' culture is defined by three characteristics: first, that there exists a clear set of values, norms and beliefs; second, that the vast majority of members share them; and, third, that their behaviour is guided by these. The approach focuses on the consistencies and explores cultural consensus within organizations. It has dominated the managerial literature on organization culture and formed the basis of consultancy prescriptions and management development.

An important consequence of the managerial view that holds that an organization possesses a single, unified culture is that it is possible to create a typology, and assign different companies to it, on the basis of their cultural features. Adrian Furnham and Barrie Gunter (1993) listed four such typologies, all produced by different management consultants or managerially oriented academics (table 19.1). They commented on their similarity and simplicity, adding that that there was little evidence to demonstrate their veracity and described them as 'interesting intuitions which might or might not be validated'.

In contrast, the social science approach to organization culture tends to view it as differentiated or pluralistic [**link**, chapter 23, conflict: radical frame of reference]. It focuses on the variety of interests and opinions between different groups, and upon power in organizations. Organizations are seen as consisting of diverse interests which have different objectives (e.g. management v. labour; staff v. line; marketing v. production). The primary task from this view is to understand the lack of cultural consensus within organizations. These are seen as fluid and ever-changing, and interest is centred upon the way in which organization reality is constructed and reconstructed. Thus, the **differentiation perspective** sees 'cultural pluralism' as a fundamental aspect of all organizations; seeks to understand the complexity and the interaction between frequently conflicting sub-cultures; and therefore stands in direct contrast to the managerial unitary or integrationist perspective.

Differentiation perspective is a view which regards an organization as consisting of sub-cultures. Each represents a fenced-in island of localized consensus, beyond which ambiguity reigns.

This perspective pays particular attention to those cultural manifestations which are not consistent with each other, and this reduces the complexity of understanding culture to a series of dichotomies. A consequence of the differentiation perspective is the recognition of the existence and importance of sub-cultures within an organization. The managerialist view does not discount the possibility of sub-cultures (due to differences of function, hierarchical level, gender, and socio-economic and educational background) but considers these to be either unimportant or else capable of being managed. Leadership is seen as having the task of bringing sub-cultures into line with organizational (managerial) interests.

Culture is seen as the product of group experience and will be found wherever there is a definable group with significant shared history, values and beliefs. Given the existence of many different groups, one can expect there to be many different sub-cultures within a single organization. Schein acknowledged the existence of a managerial culture, various occupation-based cultures within functional units, and worker cultures based on shared hierarchical experiences. The social science perspective sees organizations as composed of nested and interacting sub-cultures, divided both laterally (e.g. marketing, accounting) and vertically (shop floor workers, supervisors, senior managers). More recently, Tony Watson (1994) distinguished between official and unofficial cultures existing in parallel.

Occupational sub-cultures are based around work, since different types of work require different sets of values. Alvin Gouldner (1957) was among the earliest researchers who distinguished two social identities, which he labelled *cosmopolitans* and *locals*. Cosmopolitans had low loyalty to their employing organization,

Table 19.1: Alternative organization culture typologies

Authors	Deal and Kennedy (1982)	Schein (1985)	Graves (1986)	Harrison (1972) Handy (1979) Williams *et al.* (1989)
Contrast between	Amount of risk (high/low)	Individualistic	Bureaucratic–anti-bureaucratic	Formalization (high/low)
	v.	v.	v.	v.
	Speed of feedback (slow/fast)	Collectivistic	Managerial–ego-driven	Centralization (high/low)
Culture labels • Culture feature	*Tough guy culture* • Risk-taking • Individualistic	*Power culture* • Entrepreneurial • Ability values	*Barbarian* • Ego-driven • Workaholic	*Power-oriented* • Competitive • Responsibility to person rather than expertise
	Work/play hard • Persistent • Sociable	*Achievement culture* • Personal • Intrinsic	*Presidential* • Democratic • Hierarchical	*People-oriented* • Consensual • Rejects management control
	Bet your company • Ponderous • Unpressurized	*Support culture* • Mutuality • Trust	*Monarchical* • Loyalty • Doggedness	*Task-oriented* • Competency • Dynamic
	Process culture • Bureaucratic • Protective	*Role culture* • Order • Dependable	*Pharaonic* • Ritualized • Changeless	*Role-oriented* • Legality • Legitimacy • Pure bureaucracy

Based on Adrian Furnham and Barrie Gunter, 'Corporate culture: definition, diagnosis and change', in C.L. Cooper, and I.T. Robertson (eds), *International Review of Industrial and Organizational Psychology*, 1993, vol.8, chapter 7, pp.233-61, p.247.

had a high commitment to their specialized role skills and were likely to use an extra-organization reference group. Locals, in contrast, were high on company loyalty, had low commitment to specialized role skills and were likely to use an in-company reference group.

Stop and criticize

You are an assistant bar manager in a fashionable city centre establishment. In terms of your orientation to work, would you describe yourself as a local or a cosmopolitan? With regard to the bar staff you manage, would you like them to be cosmopolitans or locals? If you were one of the bar staff, what would you be, a cosmopolitan or a local?

Charles Handy argued that because different departments within the same organization operated in different environments, they therefore developed, or needed to develop, their own unique sub-cultures. He distinguished four function-based cultures, each of which possessed their own type of structure (role, task or power). He distinguished four different sets of activities, which he labelled steady state, innovative/developmental, breakdown and policy (see figure 19.5). He suggested that 'if an appropriate culture prevails where a set of activities prevails, then that part of the organization will be more effective' (Handy, 1976, p.199).

Essentially, he was saying that within the same organization there needed to be

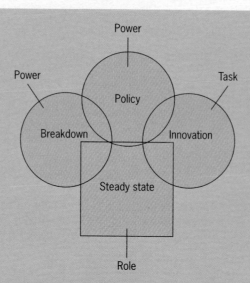

Figure 19.5: Handy's four types of organization activity

Steady state refers to departments whose activities can be programmed in some way and which are routine as opposed to non-routine. Examples would be accounting, secretarial or office systems.
Innovative/developmental activities relate to all activities which change the objectives of the organization, or the way that things are done within it. Examples would be research and development and marketing.
Breakdown/crises are dealt with by many departments, although some deal more often with the unexpected than others, and interact more frequently with the environment, for example marketing, customer care and top management.
Policy/direction activities concern allocating resources, establishing standards, setting priorities. Units within existing departments or senior managements might spend much of their time engaged in these.

From Handy, 1976, p.199.

different (sub-)cultures, based on the differentiation of activities. He implied that different sets of activities called for different values to prevail in those different departments, each based on its own particular time perspective, recognition system and recruitment standards, use of different equipment, etc. Thus functional sub-cultures would differ depending on the dominant type of activity performed in that division, department or section. What implications does Handy's view have for the idea of a single, strong organization culture?

Logically, if a number of different sub-cultures are held to exist within a single organization, be they based on occupation or function, then it is impossible to claim that all or most of the employees share a single, common organization culture. Thus, it is invalid to place an entire organization into one of the four cells in Deal and Kennedy's, or one of the other typologies shown in table 19.1.

Consensual versus fragmentation cultures

It is not surprising that, given its unitary view, the managerial view of culture emphasizes consensus. The possibility of conflict is acknowledged but seen as due to failures in communication [**link**, chapter 6, communication] and manageable through change interventions [**link**, chapter 17, organization development]. This approach assumes that senior management's articulation of its organization's culture is identical to the actual culture (assuming that only one culture exists). This places a focus on what the culture should be (in management's view), rather than explaining what the culture actually is and assessing its significance. Most problematically, it encourages managers to act as if their preferred culture (with its attributes) already existed, leading them to believe that acting out their cultural myth would create their desired organizational reality. The different perspectives are contrasted in table 19.2.

The social science view tends to see organizations as a collection of frequently opposed groupings (e.g. management v. labour; staff v. line; production department v. marketing department) which are rarely reconciled. It thus assumes the inevitability of conflict and focuses on the variety of interests and opinions between different groups and upon power in organizations. It is therefore is critical of managers and management consultants who underplay the differences that exist between individuals, groups and departments within a company. The **fragmentation** (or **conflict**) **perspective** sees organizations as being in constant flux, with reality constantly being constructed and reconstructed due to human interactions and environmental changes [**link**, chapter 23, conflict: radical frame of reference]. Ambiguity is an integral feature of organizational existence, with employees sharing some viewpoints, disagreeing on others, and being indifferent to yet others. What occurs is a mixture of consensus, disagreement and indifference, which prevents any ongoing agreement on values or basic assumptions ever being reached. This has two consequences. First, it suggests that conflict rather than consensus is the norm within organizations. Second, and perhaps more radical, such confusion makes it difficult to draw cultural or sub-cultural boundaries. In essence, it challenges the value of the concept of organization culture itself. It offers no comfort for either managers or academics who seek clarity (Becker, 1982).

Fragmentation (conflict) perspective of culture is a view which regards an organization as consisting of a loosely structured and incompletely shared system that emerges dynamically as cultural members experience each other, events and the organization's contextual features.

Table 19.2: Martin's contrasting perspectives on organization culture

| Features | Cultural perspective | | |
	Integration	Differentiation	Fragmentation
Orientation to consensus	Organization-wide consensus	Sub-cultural consensus	No consensus—multiplicity of views
Relations between different cultural elements	Consistent	Inconsistent	Complex
Orientation to ambiguity	Exclude it	Channel it outside sub-culture	Focus upon it

From Joanne Martin, *Cultures in Organizations: Three Perspectives*, Oxford University Press, Oxford, 1992, p.13.

Cultural perspective and hierarchical location

Joanne Martin argued that organization members acquired a particular frame (of reference) from which they experienced their organization's culture. A frame is a scheme of interpretation that makes it possible for individuals to interpret, organize and make sense of particular events and actions [**links**, chapter 7, perception; chapter 11, individuals in groups]. Frames therefore express the generally accepted norms of the social domain in which they are valid (e.g. group, occupational category, subject discipline, political allegiance). The same event may be interpreted differently by various individuals, each of whom uses a different frame. We all recognize a very large number of frames. Some are more or less universal, many are common to most people within a particular society, and many are local.

Emmanuel Ogbonna and Lloyd Harris applied this notion when studying organization culture in the retail grocery industry. They conducted three case studies of grocery multiples using interviewing, observation and document analysis of staff at head office, store manager and shop floor levels. Their radical conclusion was that 'culture was in the eye of the beholder' (perceptual). They found that an employee's position in the organization's hierarchy determined their perception of their organization's culture.

The authors reported that head office staff held an integration perspective, seeing themselves as self-appointed efficiency creators, understanding their role to be to achieve consistency and conformity in pursuit of improved performance. This led them to a view of organization culture from an integration perspective which was intolerant of individual or group conflict, and which favoured careful selection of staff so as to exclude potential 'non-conformers'.

Store managers, in contrast, held a differentiation view of their company's culture. They saw their objective as effectiveness creation and their role as being to reconcile the conflicting views of both head office personnel and shop floor employees. They saw their company as consisting of sub-components, and its culture as being divided into a series of dichotomous sub-cultures, each of which possessed different spheres of influence and dominance. Within these sub-cultures, store managers recognized consensus.

Finally, shop floor employees held a fragmentation view of their company's culture. They were confused as to what their company's values were, felt that the firm was changing at a speed faster than they were able to cope with, and described it as complex and unpredictable. The researchers stated that shop floor workers' jobs gave them a only a narrow understanding of their company's strategy, structure and systems. For them, hierarchical position and the nature of shop floor employment shaped the perspective which they held.

The authors make three recommendations. First, any change initiative based solely on head office values and perceptions was likely to fail. Instead, initiatives should incorporate the differentiation views of store managers and the fragmentation understandings of shop floor staff. Second, achieving an organization-wide consensus over values was difficult and unnecessary. Instead, policies needed to be pursued which recognized the sub-cultural differences resulting from hierarchical position and reconcile those which were most likely to have an impact on company performance. Finally, executives embarking on change programmes should be sensitive to their own biases and may require the assistance of a more objective outsider.

Based on Emmanuel Ogbonna and Lloyd C. Harris, 'Organization culture: It's not what you think', *Journal of General Management*, 1998, vol.23, no.3, pp.35–47.

Culture managed versus culture tolerated

Since the managerialist perspective sees culture as something that an organization *has* (along with its strategy, structure, people and technology), it further assumes that it is capable of being created and modified by organizational founders and corporate leaders. This has sparked three debates. First, it promotes a discussion between 'weak' and 'strong' cultures, considering how managers can turn their company's culture from the former into the latter. Second, it has stimulated a related discussion concerning 'inefficient' and 'efficient' cultures, which assesses the ability of an organization culture to innovate and to adjust rapidly and appropriately to changes in the strategic direction of the firm. Third, it assumes that leaders' visions make a distinctive contribution to cultures, and that they have a crucial role to play in 'culture management'.

- the unique and essential function of leadership is the manipulation of culture. (Schein, 1985, p.317)
- changing organization culture is an outcome of transformational leadership which impacts on followers' levels of effort and performance. (Bass, 1985a; Bass and Avolio, 1990)

The view that senior company executives can and should exercise cultural leadership brings together two of the most popular business concepts of the last twenty years [links, chapter 16, organization strategy and design; chapter 21, leadership]. The contingency approach stressed the importance of a company's structure, and indeed its culture, 'fitting' its strategy and environment, while the concept of strategic choice assigned the responsibility for achieving such a match to its senior management. Culture leadership is seen as having a *maintenance* and an *innovation* dimension (Trice and Beyer, 1990; 1993). Leaders may be required to maintain and reinforce the original culture established by a company's founder. Or they may be required to modify (and hence innovate) that culture, if it becomes a liability in changed environmental circumstances. Indeed, culture change has been a popular change strategy within companies during the 1980s and 1990s [link, chapter 18, organizational change].

In either case, their responsibility is to maintain a 'fit' between the organization's culture and its chosen strategy. This essentially involves leaders creating a culture that anticipates and responds to changes. Leaders either transmit the organization's culture (dispersing what is already there) or mould it (based on their own values), in both cases with a view to affecting how members are to think about the organization and their roles within it. Culture management is achieved through human resource management policies [link, chapter 20, human resource management], which use culture change programmes with organization development [links, chapter 17, organization development, chapter 18, organizational change], and complemented with a modified leadership style [link, chapter 21].

Since the 'is' writers treat culture as a mental state and a context, rather than a variable, they assume that every organization develops some sort of culture through the interactions of its members. However, they consider that it is inappropriate to designate organization cultures as 'weak' or 'strong' or 'inefficient–efficient', in the same way that individuals' personalities are not better or worse, just different. They also challenge the notion that, in the short term, culture can be managed by leaders and instead feel that it should be understood and tolerated. Over the medium to long term, however, they accept the possibility that managers, along with other organization members, can develop their company's culture in certain ways.

Symbolic leadership versus management control

Symbolic leadership is one way of encouraging employees to feel that they are working for something worthwhile, so that they will work harder and be more productive. It treats managers as heroes symbolizing the organization both internally to their employees and externally to customers, governments and others (Smircich and Morgan, 1982). These managers, said Carol Ray, 'possess direct ties to the values and goals of the dominant elites in order to activate the emotion and sentiment which may lead to devotion, loyalty and commitment to the company' (1986, p.362). The idea of the manager as inculcator of shared

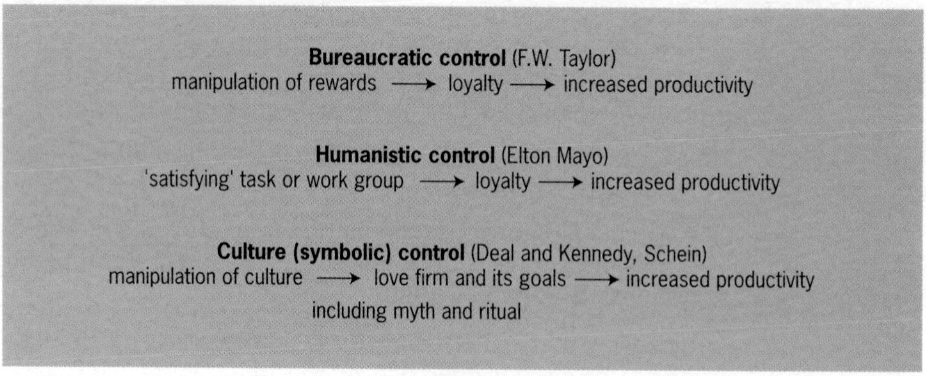

Bureaucratic control (F.W. Taylor)
manipulation of rewards ⟶ loyalty ⟶ increased productivity

Humanistic control (Elton Mayo)
'satisfying' task or work group ⟶ loyalty ⟶ increased productivity

Culture (symbolic) control (Deal and Kennedy, Schein)
manipulation of culture ⟶ love firm and its goals ⟶ increased productivity
including myth and ritual

Figure 19.6: Contrasting forms of organizational control
From Carol Axel Ray, 'Corporate culture; the last frontier of control?' *Journal of Management Studies*, 1986 vol.23, no.3, pp.287–97.

company values goes back to the 1930s, when Chester Barnard, one of the early classical theorists, wrote that 'the inculcation of belief in the real existence of a common purpose is an essential executive function ... [the manager] is primarily an expert in the promotion and protection of values' (Barnard, 1938, pp.28, 87–8). The managerialist view holds that employees can be helped to internalize organization values.

The social science perspective argues that symbolic leadership represents an attempt to internalize managerial control. Carol Ray (1986) distinguished different types of management control in history (figure 19.6). She noted the move away from bureaucratic control towards humanistic control. The former focuses on external, overt control of employees through rules, procedures, close supervision, appraisal and reward. Frederick Taylor, Henry Ford, Max Weber and Henri Fayol all recommended this rationalist approach to directing the behaviour of employees towards organization goals. It was expensive in terms of supervisory manpower required, frequently caused resentment and elicited grudging compliance from the workers. Humanistic control, in contrast, sought to satisfy employees needs' by providing a satisfying work task or a pleasant working group to promote internal control. Promoted by Mayo (1933; 1945), the hope was that individuals would willingly meet organization goals by meetings their individual ones (Van Maanen and Barley, 1984).

Ray suggested that by the end of the twentieth century, writers such as Deal and Kennedy and Schein saw the possibility of using a third, more effective, control tool—organization culture. The selective application of rites, ceremonials, myths, stories, symbols and legends by managers to directing the behaviour of employees is termed *symbolic management*. In the long term, this form of control could be cheaper, avoided resentment and built employee commitment to the company and its goals. This theme of 'internalized control' is at the heart of the work of Michel Foucault (1979), whose ideas will be considered in greater depth later [**link**, chapter 24, power and politics].

Paul Thompson and David McHugh (1990, pp.200–1) quote an American manager from a well-known high-tech company as saying, 'Power plays don't work. You can't make 'em do anything. They have to want to. So you have to work through the culture. The idea is to educate people without [their] knowing it. Have the religion, and not know how they got it'. Willmott (1993) saw this as an attempt to 'colonize the minds of organization members', to encourage employees to internalize desired company values and norms. External control is

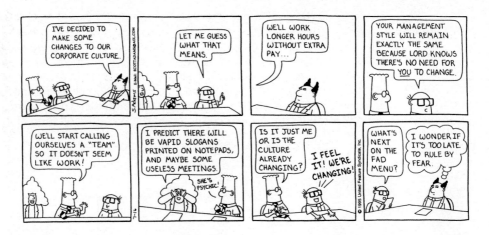

replaced by self-control, such as that used by professionals such as doctors, teachers, lawyers and priests. Colin Hales (1993, p.216) wrote that:

> the power of organization culture resides in the fact that it is not just another management 'technique' which can be applied at will, but is, rather, an influence upon behaviour which is not recognized as overt 'management'. The beliefs and values which shape employee behaviour are internalized, taken for granted and accepted as unobjectionable; therein lies their force. Culture can therefore exercise the most powerful and insidious form of control because it combines *de facto* compulsion with perceived freedom from coercion.

Organization culture and economic performance

The original writings on organization culture by Peters and Waterman and by Deal and Kennedy both promoted the merits of 'strong' organization cultures, defined as those in which key values were widely shared, intensely held, clearly ordered by employees, who were guided by them. Not all cultures are strong ones, but those that were, they claimed, produced improved economic performance. Strength refers to the degree to which employees share a commitment to a range of goals and values espoused by management, and have a high level of motivation to achieve them. The argument is that, with respect to employees, a strong culture:

- 'glues' them together;
- gives them a sense of purpose;
- provides them with a sense of identity;
- makes them feel better about what they do;
- increases their commitment to the company;
- makes their work more intrinsically rewarding;
- provides them with a sense of their own distinctiveness;
- helps them identify more closely with their fellow workers;
- supplies a set of informal rules which clearly signal how they are to behave;
- reduces ambiguity by enabling them to 'make sense' of different organization events.

The HP way: values and founders

Established in 1939 by William Hewlett and David Packard, two engineers from Stanford, California, Hewlett-Packard is a maker of high-technology electronic equipment. Headquartered in Palo Alto, California, it is one of the top twenty US companies, employing 102,000 people and earning annual revenues of $31 billion in the mid-1990s. It is often cited as the quintessential strong-culture company. Commentators tend to attribute the company's success to the strength and form of its organization culture.

Dave Packard

Bill Hewlett

Its booklet, *The HP Way*, contains information about the three main elements that together constitute its organization culture—company values, objectives and strategies and practices. In the wake of an economic downturn in 1992, the company faced difficult decisions on retrenchment. Senior management convinced employees about the emphasis on economic performance and management by objectives. By 1993, a combination of market changes, new product launches and cost-cutting measures (including voluntary severance) led the company to increase turnover by 43 per cent. McGovern and Hope-Hailey studied the aftermath of the crisis in 1994, and their conclusion was that the company weathered the crisis with most of its culture and traditions intact; the culture appears as healthy as ever and is still indispensable and conducive to its business, as the founders expected.

Based on P.G. McGovern and C. Hope-Hailey, *Inside Hewlett Packard: Corporate Culture and Bureaucratic Control*, Centre for Organizational Research, London Business School, UK, 1996.

However, there is no persuasive empirical evidence to suggest any relationship between the strength of a company's culture and its economic performance (Saffold, 1988). Nor has there been any real discussion of other market or environmental variables which could also contribute to company success. For example, IBM was included as one of Peters and Waterman's 'excellent' companies at the time. Its founder, Thomas Watson, asserted that the firm's success was based on a strong organization culture supported by strong common values. Yet IBM enjoyed a monopolistic and oligopolistic market position until the 1980s (Carroll, 1994). Then, when it was challenged by the introduction of the personal computer, its culture did not help it to rise to that challenge. Indeed, it has been argued that IBM's strong culture might have actually prevented it making the changes that were needed, for example by making it difficult for members to break out from old-established but now inappropriate ways of doing things (Thompson and McHugh: 1995; Pettigrew, 1985).

Strong culture—economic performance link?

Although managers tend to attest to the benefits of a strong company culture, academic researchers are less convinced. John Kotter and James Heskett (1992) researched the relationship between organization culture and economic performance. They empirically tested the cultural strength of 207 large firms from a variety of industries. Of these, Wal-mart, J.P. Morgan and Proctor & Gamble scored highest on strength of culture. They calculated a culture strength index for each firm and then correlated it with the firms' economic performance over an eleven-year period. The research showed a positive correlation, but it was weaker than most management theorists would have expected. Strong-culture firms seemed almost as likely to perform poorly as their weak-culture rivals. The authors concluded that the popular view that a strong organization culture led to economic success was 'just plain wrong'.

Another theory holds that only those organization cultures that help organizations adapt to environmental change are associated with excellent performance. Authors like Kilmann *et al.* (1986) and Kanter (1983) have argued that an adaptive culture can encourage confidence and risk taking among employees, and possesses a leadership that focuses on the changing needs of customers. To test this theory, Kotter and Heskett studied a sub-sample of 22 firms with adaptive and non-adaptive cultures. They found that what distinguished the successful from the unsuccessful was that the former did not let the short-term interests of the shareholders dominate over others, but they cared equally for all the company's stakeholders—customers, employees and shareholders. The main problem is that the right organization culture can take decades to evolve naturally. However, either appointing an unconventional boss from inside or choosing an outsider can speed up the process.

Based on John Kotter and James Heskett, *Organization Culture and Performance*, Free Press, New York, 1992.

National cultures

The controversy that surrounds the nature and impact of organization culture on individual employee behaviour and company performance is to some extent echoed in the discussions of the effect of national (societal) cultures on organization ones. National cultural stereotypes are well established: Scots are mean; Americans are brash; Germans are humourless; French are romantic; Japanese are inscrutable. However, researchers have studied how national cultures might affect organization cultures in specific country settings. They have been interested to see how attempts to establish a common organization culture in a multinational firm can be undermined by the strength of national cultures. Fombrun (1984) saw organization culture being partly the outcome of societal factors, while Laurent (1989) argued that the cultures of countries were more powerful and stable than those of organizations.

At both levels of the cultural debate, the organizational and the national, one sees not only attempts to identify specific traits but also attempts to classify organizations and countries into types. This creation of trait lists and typologies parallels work in personality discussed earlier [**link**, chapter 5, personality], and also leadership traits [**link**, chapter 21, leadership]. Not surprisingly, the most studied national culture is the economically most successful—that of the United States of America. Ferraro (1990) and Yamashita (1998) listed what they saw as the main traits or attributes of US culture:

1. Individualism.

2. Concept of precise time.

3. Value of work and performance.

4. Respect for diligence.

German humour ready for take-off

A German airline is turning its cabin crew into comedians in a desperate effort to cheer up sober-suited businessmen who fill most of its seats on internal flights. Deutsche BA, a subsidiary of British Airways, has hired a radio DJ to teach staff how to tell jokes and engage in running banter during short flights. 'We're not forcing them to be funny. But we have told them to be themselves and, if there's a good atmosphere on board, to be more relaxed and creative. It depends on the individuals, but some of them love doing it', said Anja Janke, communications executive at the airline's headquarters in Munich.

The idea of friendly, funny staff is almost revolutionary in Germany, where service usually comes with a scowl—if it comes at all. But passengers are lapping up the airborne comedy and one pair of stewardesses in Cologne has achieved cult status. Safety announcements are sacrosanct, but everything else is satirized, from the snacks served on board to the pilot's accent. One steward has introduced juggling into his act, and passengers now regularly applaud cabin crew and congratulate them on their performance when their plane lands. Deutsche BA is engaged in a cut-throat battle with Lufthansa on internal German flights and Janke admits that the comedy routine is just the latest move in this battle.

From Denis Staunton, *The Observer*, 16 November 1997, p.17.

5. Future-orientedness.

6. Youngness, newness.

7. Taking things easy.

8. Humankind controlling the natural world.

9. Competition.

10. Relative male–female equality.

11. Acceptance of immigrants.

Geert Hofstede
(b. 1928)

Interesting as this list may be, as with personality, it is the variations between national cultures that provides the greatest insight. Geert Hofstede (1984; 1986; 1991) carried out a cross-cultural study of 116,000 employees of the same multi-national company located in forty countries. His aim was to identify the basic dimensions of differences (predominant traits) between national cultures. He discovered four such dimensions—**power distance, uncertainty avoidance, individualism–collectivism** and **masculinity–femininity**. These were later extended

Power distance is the extent to which an unequal distribution of power is accepted by members of a society.
Uncertainty avoidance is the extent to which members of a society feel threatened by ambiguous situations and have created beliefs and institutions which try to avoid these.
Individualism–collectivism is the tendency to take care of oneself and one's family versus the tendency to work together for the collective good.
Masculinity–femininity is the extent to which highly assertive masculine values predominate (acquisition of money at the expense of others) versus showing sensitivity and concern for others' welfare and the quality of life.
Long-term–short-term orientation (confusion dynamism) is the ability to pursue long-term and general goals versus short-term gain and advantage.

to include a fifth, **long-term–short-term orientation** (Hofstede and Bond, 1988). Like personality assessment, each of the dimensions represents a different continuum, so that each country can be rated from high to low and placed somewhere along each one, and not just at the ends.

Using the original four culture dimensions or traits and a statistical technique known as cluster analysis, which forms clusters by placing together countries which are most alike while being as different as possible from others, Hofstede created an eight-category typology, into which he placed his forty countries (table 19.3).

Hofstede's work stressed the importance of organization cultural differences, which evolved from societal culture differences, and which impacted all aspects of organization behaviour. In his view, motivation, group behaviour, leadership style, conflict management, structure, predominant leadership style, training and HRM practices were all culturally relative. Trompnaars (1994) too explained why national cultures mattered in organizations. The argument of these others is pitched at two levels:

Airline safety and culture

Following the crash at Christmas time 1999 of a Korean Airlines (KAL) 747 cargo plane at Stanstead Airport outside London in which its four crew members died, the following account appeared in the press:

The rigid hierarchical culture of Korean Air is key to understanding why it has the worst recent safety record in international aviation. Airline analysts say the combination of an authoritarian management prone to put commercial considerations ahead of safety and a flight deck ethos where errors by the captain are rarely questioned goes a long way to explaining its five fatal crashes in 12 years. An audit of Korean Air's safety practices last year by Delta produced findings so alarming that the American carrier instantly cancelled a codeshare agreement.

It found that communication between KAL's management and pilots was very poor, and administrators often tried to overrule flight crews on vital safety issues such as the amount of fuel to be loaded or whether defunct warnings were significant enough to postpone take-off. Pilots were reluctant to complain as they felt it would damage career prospects. Morale was also low because many of the best paid jobs in the airline went to former military pilots, almost entirely on the basis of their air force status ... The pre-eminence given to military pilots reinforced the tendency for the captain's judgement never to be questioned by subordinates. This is the antithesis of Western airline practice, where a collaborative atmosphere on the flight deck and continual cross-checking of information is seen as critical to minimising human error.

The audit reported that Korean first officers (co-pilots) 'would *never* speak up if a Korean captain made a mistake, as it would certainly end his career due to causing loss of face'. In KAL cockpits, there was 'a volatile cocktail of complacency, arrogance, apathy and lack of self-discipline'. Crews were generally afraid to implement safety options such as landing 'go around' or diversion to another airport, because management might see these as a matter of 'embarrassment' to the company.

From Paul Marston, 'Rigid hierarchy where mistakes go unchallenged', *Daily Telegraph*, 24 December 1999, p.4.

- From an organizational behaviour perspective, the question is whether a manager from London, Amsterdam or Stockholm can be transferred to a position in Tokyo and still succeed. The focus is upon whether interpersonal skills acquired in one culture can be transferred to another. This question is reflected in the research and writings about expatriate and cross-cultural management.

- From a human resource management perspective, the question is whether it is possible to identify 'best practice' HR policies and initiatives in one culture and then transfer them across national borders to the company's plants in different countries.

Stop and criticize

To which of Geert Hofstede's culture clusters do you belong? How do you feel about being categorized in this way? Is his analysis accurate in your experience? How would you amend his diagnosis?

Although Hofstede saw national and organization cultures as phenomena at different levels, he felt that they were linked. Organization cultures are supported by employees' societal values, while national cultural differences reside in practices at organizational level. He argued that people's career behaviour was largely a reflection of societal cultural values, because careers were a trade-off between risk, security, success and family life. One could expect that societal power distance norms between countries would impact differently. Thus close supervision would generate more positive attitudes to the boss among Peruvian workers, while the reverse would be true for US workers. Hence US management systems advocate participation in the manager's decision by subordinates (Hofstede, 1994).

Stop and criticize

Prepare a list for overseas visitors intending to visit your country on business, listing what to do and what to avoid doing.

Table 19.3: Workplace manifestations of differences in national cultures

Power distance

Low (Australia, Israel, Denmark, Sweden)	High (Philippines, Mexico, Venezuela, India, Brazil)
• Less centralization	• Greater centralization
• Flatter organization pyramids	• Tall organization pyramids
• Structure in which manual and clerical work are equal jobs	• More supervisory personnel
• Subordinates expect to be consulted	• Structure in which white-collar jobs are more valued than blue-collar jobs
	• Subordinates expect to be told what to do
	• Ideal boss is benevolent autocrat

Femininity–masculinity

Low (Thailand, Finland, Denmark, Sweden, Yugoslavia)	High (Japan, Australia, Venezuela, Italy, Mexico)
• Gender roles are minimized	• Gender roles are clearly differentiated
• Organizations do not interfere with people's private lives	• Organizations may interfere to protect their interests
• More women in more qualified jobs	• Fewer women in more qualified jobs
• Soft, yielding, intuitive skills are rewarded	• Aggressiveness, competitiveness, decisiveness are rewarded
• Undersell yourself	• Oversell yourself
• Social rewards are valued	• Work is valued as a central life interest
• Assertiveness ridiculed	• Assertiveness appreciated
• Stress on life quality	• Stress on careers

Collectivism–individualism

Low (Venezuela, Columbia, Taiwan, Mexico, Greece)	High (USA, Australia, Britain, Canada, Netherlands)
• Organization as 'familiy'	• Organizations are more impersonal
• Organization defends employee interests	• Organizations defend their own self-interests
• Practices are based on loyalty, sense of duty and group participation	• Practices encourage individual initiative
• Relationships prevail over task	• Task prevails over relationships

Uncertainty avoidance

Low (Denmark, Sweden, Britain, USA, India)	High (Greece, Portugal, Japan, Peru, France)
• Less structuring of activities	• More structuring of activities
• Fewer written rules	• More written rules
• More generalists	• More specialists
• Greater variability	• More standardization
• Greater willingness to take risks	• Less willingness to take risks
• Less ritualistic behaviour	• More realistic ritualistic behaviour
• Tolerance of deviant persons and ideas	• Intolerance of deviant persons and ideas

From Adrian Furnham and B. Barrie Gunter, 'Corporate culture: definition, diagnosis and change', in C.L. Cooper and I.T. Robertson (eds), *International Review of Industrial and Organizational Psychology*, 1993, vol.8, chapter 7, pp.233–61, p. 245.

Adapting leadership style to culture

Models of leadership that deal with the concept of 'context' usually ignore the need to be able to manage in different cultures. An ethnocentric approach to leadership, which ignores the cultural context, is inadequate and impractical. The demand for expertise in working with different belief and value systems has grown rapidly, for several reasons:

- international recruitment to overcome domestic staff shortages;
- cross-border mergers, acquisitions and joint ventures;
- the opening up of new markets in Eastern Europe, South-east Asia and China;
- European social policy harmonization initiatives;
- developments in communications technology with global reach.

Michael Finney and Mary Ann Von Glinow argue that we need 'cognitively complex self-monitoring managers who have global perspectives and boundary spanning capabilities' with a geocentric value orientation. They also distinguish technical competence from contextual competence. Technical competence concerns industry knowledge and functional expertise. Contextual competence concerns the ability to understand home and host country values, speak the language, adapt behaviour to local conditions and customs, and act as a 'boundary-spanning interpreter' for home and host country personnel. They identify a 'superordinate value orientation and set of managerial strategies' for the international manager:

value orientation	description
cognitive	intuitive perceptual sensitivity to different cultures' thought and behaviour patterns
self-monitoring	personal flexibility, adjusting to social demands of different cultures
boundary-spanning	acting as interpreter between home and host countries across technical and socio-cultural issues
global orientation	understanding of interrelated and systemic nature of global community, and of role of home and host countries in global economy
geocentric	internalization of multiple world views and value orientations

Cognitive complexity is the ability to use 'multiple-solution models' rather than 'one best way' approaches to problem solving. High self-monitoring individuals are particularly sensitive to the thinking patterns and self-presentation—verbal and non-verbal—of others.

Based on Michael Finney and Mary Ann Von Glinow, 'Integrating academic and organizational approaches to developing the international manager', *Journal of Management Development*, 1990, vol.7, no.2, pp.16–27.

Recap

1. *Account for the popularity of organization culture among managers, consultants and academics.*

   - For managers, the concept offered the route to economic success to match that enjoyed by Japanese organizations of the time.
   - For consultants, the concept provided an appealing, easy-to-grasp, quick-fix solution to sell to managers wishing to improve their organization's performance.
   - For academics, it offered an alternative perspective with which to research and theorize about organizations and provided a new context within which to explore postmodernist ideas.

2. *List, describe and exemplify Schein's three levels of culture.*

- Schein distinguished surface manifestions of culture at level one (e.g. artefacts, rites, ceremonials); organizational values at level two (e.g. customer obsession); and basic assumptions at level three, which actually was the culture (e.g. nature of reality and truth).

3. *List the stages of organization socialization.*

- The stages of organization socialization are pre-arrival, encounter and metamorphosis.

4. *Contrast managerial and social science perspectives on organization culture.*

- Is organization culture something that a company has, or what a company is?
- Is an organization culture a single, integrated entity, or is it differentiated, consisting of multiple, different sub-cultures?
- Is there a consensus among organization members as to the company values, or do different groups possess their own?
- Can an organization's culture be managed by its leaders, or is it beyond their direct control and instead has to be tolerated by them?
- Does culture signal a new era of symbolic leadership which relies on internalized forms of employee direction, or is it old-style management control under a new guise?

5. *Assess the link between organization culture and economic performance.*

- Few research studies have been conducted which explicitly test a causal link between an organization's culture and its economic performance.
- Those that have been conducted do not illustrate any direct causal relationship between a 'strong' culture and high economic performance, suggesting, at a minimum, that other, more intermediate variables are more significant.
- There is anecdotal data as well as a logical argument to suggest that organizations possessing a strong culture at a time of required change may be less flexible, less able to change, and hence less likely to perform well economically.

6. *Distinguish different national culture dimensions and different culture clusters.*

- Hofstede suggested that national culture could be differentiated along four (later five) dimensions: power distance; uncertainty avoidance; individualism–collectivism; and masculinity–femininity (and later) short-term–long-term perspective.
- Hofstede grouped the countries in his study into eight different clusters.

Revision

1. 'A strong organization culture which can be used as a tool of management control helps to motivate staff, improves company performance and should therefore be encouraged'. Discuss.

2. 'As a way of understanding the behaviour of people in organizations, the concept of organization culture is more of a hindrance than a help'. Discuss.

3. What guidance does the theory and research into national culture offer managers working around the world for global, multinational corporations?

4. 'Managers and academics have totally different approaches to, and interests in, the concept of organization culture'. Discuss.

5. To what extent, and in what ways, might a national culture affect an organization's culture?

Springboard

Goldman, R. and Papson, S., 1998, *Nike Culture: The Sign of the Swoosh*, Sage, London.

Description of the organization culture of a leading sportswear company.

Hickson, D. and Pugh, D.S., 1995, *Management Worldwide: The Impact of Societal Culture on Organizations Around the Globe*, Penguin Books, Harmondsworth.

Builds on Hofstede's work on the impact of different societal cultures on organizational behaviour.

Hickson, D.J., 1997, *Exploring Management Across the World*, Penguin Books, Harmondsworth.

Provides a cross-cultural comparison of national factors that influence the practice of management in different cultures.

Kunda, G., 1992, *Engineering Culture: Control and Commitment in a High Tech Corporation*, Temple University Press, Philadelphia.

Research-based study of a high-tech organization's culture.

Linstead, S., 1999, 'Managing culture', in Fulop, L. and Linstead, S. (eds), *Management: A Critical Text*, Macmillan, London, pp. 82–121.

Provides a critical assessment of the concept of organization culture pitched at an introductory level and offers a comprehensive bibliography.

Needle, D., 2000, 'Culture at the level of the firm: organizational and corporate perspectives', in Barry, J. *et al.* (eds), *Organization and Management: A Critical Text*, Business Press Thompson Learning, London, pp. 101–18.

Another introductory, critical consideration of the organization culture concept.

Parker, M., 2000, *Organizational Culture and Identity*, Sage, London.

Considers organization culture from the critical symbolism perspective, focusing on how organizations shape their members' identities, and asks whether it is right for them to do so.

Rogers, M.F., 1998, *Barbie Culture*, Sage, London, 1998.

Description of the organization culture of a company manufacturing a well-known toy.

Sackmann, S.A. (ed.), 1997, *Cultural Complexity in Organizations*, Sage, London.

The different authors compare and contrast culture at the sub-organizational, organizational, regional, industry, national and greater regional levels.

Schultz, M., 1995, *On Studying Organizational Cultures: Diagnosis and Understanding*, De Gruyter, Berlin.

Considers how the theoretical concepts of organization culture can be applied to an analysis of organizations. It evaluates different frameworks for the understanding of culture so as to discover the strengths and weaknesses of each.

Home viewing

The film *Gung Ho* (1986, director Ron Howard) concerns the conflict of national cultures. A Japanese car manufacturer, Assan Motor, acquires an American motor car company. When the Japanese management team takes over, confrontations, conflicts and adjustments ensue. Hunt Stevenson (played by Michael Keaton), a working-class hero, is intent on salvaging Hadleyville, the struggling Rust Belt town where he lives. After acting as an emissary to bring the Japanese to the town, he is co-opted by the new management to be their spokesperson to the workers. The film uses a tongue-in-cheek approach to raise questions of perception and conflict. It uses outrageous stereotypes of both Japanese and American cultures, which it links to considerations of organization culture. Identify the key stereotypical elements that are presented. Consider how these can lead to similarities being overlooked, and racial bias displayed. In several places, the film strays seriously from reality. Can you find these? Finally, it considers individualistic versus group approaches to task performance and raises issues of leadership style, ethics and discipline.

OB in literature

John Grisham, *The Firm*, Arrow Books, 1993.

The plot describes in detail the recruitment of Mitchell Y. McDeere, a Harvard Law School graduate, by the Memphis legal firm of Bendini, Lambert and Locke. The first third of the book describes McDeer's socialization into the firm's culture. Identify which elements of the organization's culture he learns, and note how he learns them.

Chapter exercises

1: Learning the ropes

Objective

1. To highlight the process of organizational socialization

Briefing

Think of an organization that you recently joined, or one that you remember joining. This may be a new employer, a church, sports club, or even your university. In the space below, write down *two* examples of surface manifestations of culture from this organization. What purpose do those elements serve for the organization concerned?

Cultural surface manifestation	Example	Organizational purpose
Artefact		
Ceremonial		
Course		
Hero		
Language		
Motto		
Myth		
Norm		
Physical layout		
Rite		
Ritual		
Slogan		
Story		
Symbol		

2: National and organization cultures

Objective

1. To highlight the effect of the interaction of national culture and organization culture factors on company leadership and employee morale.

Briefing

Here is a recent factual account of the experience of a junior management trainee in Hong Kong. After you have read it, consider the following questions:

1. How can the management trainees act more effectively in this context, individually or collectively?

2. How would you advise the company, whose management trainee retention rate is less than 10 per cent?

After graduating with a master of business administration (MBA) degree from Glasgow University and being of Chinese origin, I accepted a post as a management trainee with a UK conglomerate based in Hong Kong. I was assigned to work in its airport division, which was entirely staffed by local Chinese. Having lived in the United Kingdom for over 10 years, I was extremely frustrated with the way things were done and how decisions were made. The managing director asked me to submit a monthly report recounting what I had learned from my assignments. I took this opportunity to provide constructive criticism as to how efficiencies could be improved. One day, a member of the personnel section from head office phoned me up to tell me that a number of people had complained that I did not 'give them face' in these reports, and one of these general managers even questioned my 'right' to submit such reports. I was then told by a head office manager to 'keep quiet' and get on with my work. It transpired that all the other management trainees had had a similar experience. I felt betrayed since, during all the career talks that I had received from the company, they had always emphasized their tradition to be critically aggressive, yet in reality, the complete opposite was true.

Feeling totally frustrated, I asked for a transfer to another division. I was given a job as an executive assistant to the division's director. Although this job involved greater responsibility and a much heavier workload, my salary remained the same! I thought this was another ploy to get me to resign, since they must have perceived me as a trouble-maker. I wondered why they did not just fire me. I later learned that the management trainee scheme was the brainchild and pet project of the company's chairman. For this reason, none of the managers would ever dare to fire any management trainees; instead they just did their best to give them such a hard time that they would resign, and leave of their own accord.

The atmosphere in this office was rather strange for a number of reasons. The head of my division was an Englishman who had lived in Japan for 16 years. He appeared to have inherited the Japanese 'master–slave' management style, particularly with respect to long office hours. He would often walk around the corridors at 7:30 p.m. to check who was not around. Within the division there were also many French nationals. They spoke French inside and outside the office, dined with each other, and ignored everyone else. In the building, everybody has their own rooms, and lateral communication was discouraged. The head believed that competition between employees improved overall performance, and he encouraged staff to criticize and score points off each other during meetings. Personally, I found such behaviour to be ethically dubious, and I avoided participating.

After some time, I became aware of the fact that the local (Hong Kong) management trainees, Chinese management trainees with British passports (like myself) and British management trainees were treated differently by the company. Despite having the same job title and experience, some trainees received a higher salary and could look forward to more rapid career progression than the others. Different 'classes' of management trainees, including myself, all worked in the same division. We became very angry about this arrangement. Whenever we met in a bar, we compared our salaries and how we were being treated. We Asian members were surprised and pleased that our European 'elite class' colleagues disagreed with the double-standard treatment. We considered reporting the company to the labour tribunal, but wondered what effect it would have on our careers. We needed them to write us good references. So in the end, no one spoke out; people resigned and the company's annual retention rate of management trainees was less than 10 per cent.

Since the company was so highly centralized, neither I nor any of the other managers in the division had the authority to make decisions. Instead we just carried out the instructions that we received from above. However, whenever a mistake occurred, it was we who were blamed by senior management. As a result, everyone disliked and felt unhappy working in that environment. When the time came for the annual performance appraisal, in order to save money, the head filled in the appraisal forms himself. He inserted both the employees' job objectives for the coming year and the end-of-year results, at the same time, and not separately, as was the usual practice. Thus, I was prevented from entering my achievements on the appraisal form, or receiving any recognition for my hard work.

Despite numerous complaints from staff, the central Human Resources Department failed to ensure that employees' 'job objectives' section of their appraisal forms was completed before the end of January, as was supposed to be the case. The reason I suppose was that within the company, the HR department was a cost-centre and not a profit-centre. It thus depended on goodwill, and was at the mercy of the company's senior managers for its continued survival. By his actions, the head saved all the bonuses for himself. This trick also made him 'irreplaceable' since it enabled him to give his capable staff a poor performance rating. I felt so demoralized working in such an environment that I resigned and left along with a number of other managers in the division.

Source: Anthony Chung, University of Hong Kong School of Business.

Chapter 20 Human resource management

Key concepts

personnel management	human resource management
hard HRM	soft HRM
employment cycle	psychological contract

Learning objectives

When you have read this chapter, you should be able to define those key concepts in your own words, and you should also be able to:

1. Explain why most medium-sized and large organizations have specialized personnel or human resource management functions.

2. Understand the distinction between personnel management and human resource management.

3. Explain the distinctions between different models of human resource management.

4. Explain the strategic contribution which the human resource function potentially makes to organizational effectiveness.

5. Identify the main criticisms levelled against human resource management, as a concept and as a management function.

Why study human resource management?

Human resource management has a direct personal impact on us as employees, in shaping, for example, the nature of our work, our pay and our career prospects. The reputation that an organization develops as a 'good employer' helps to attract and to retain quality employees. The 'people management' activities of an organization are usually handled by a specialized function. However, two labels are now in use; *personnel management* and *human resource management*. Is there a distinction, or are these simply different labels for the same thing?

Some commentators argue that human resource management is just a grander term for a mundane function, representing 'old wine in new bottles'. Others argue that human resource management reflects a fundamental shift in employment relations, made necessary by changes in the organizational environment. In this second view, personnel and human resource management are quite distinct in

perspective and in practice. Many organizations claim that 'employees are our most important asset'. Human resource management appears to represent a distinctive approach to managing that asset.

The debate about the distinction between personnel and human resource management is conceptually complex. It also has profound practical implications for the way in which the function, whatever it is called, is organized and operates. We will explore the terms and implications of this debate later in the chapter. In the meantime, we will use the term 'personnel management' in the first part of the chapter, explaining the nature and background of the function. The term 'human resource management' will be reserved for the second part of the chapter, where the distinction between these labels will be explored in more detail.

You cannot escape from the personnel management function. Figure 20.1 identifies the main stages of the **employment cycle**. Whatever the job, occupation or profession you are engaged in, you will encounter all or most of these steps at some point in your working life.

All organizations need to recruit, train, reward and motivate employees. It follows that all organizations have a personnel function responsible for the employment cycle. However, the way in which personnel policies are determined and applied varies from one organization to another and between different countries. In small organizations, without specialist personnel departments, line managers deal with people issues as they arise. Even in large organizations, line managers perform personnel functions, typically with the support of a central department.

The 'core' definition omits a range of other areas in which the function is involved. These include employee communication, collective bargaining, organizational change, health and safety, and a range of employee welfare services. The

The **employment cycle** is the sequence of stages through which all employees pass in each working position they hold, from recruitment and selection to termination; the stages of the employment cycle define the activities of the personnel function.

Personnel management is the specialist management function responsible for determining and implementing the policies and procedures which determine the stages of the employment cycle, in a manner that contributes to both the well-being and the quality of working life of employees and to organizational effectiveness.

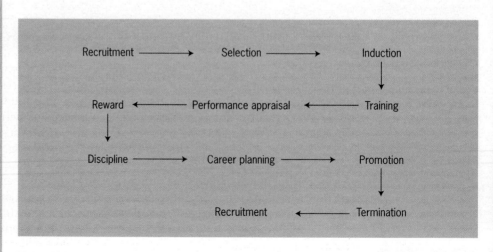

Figure 20.1: The employment cycle

employment contract is increasingly shaped by legal constraints. From a management viewpoint, a wrong decision, a failure to act or the insensitive handling of a situation can all lead to expensive litigation, damaging the organization's reputation and the career of the manager concerned. Employment law is a specialist subject beyond the scope of this text. However, the manager needs to know enough about employment law to recognize when to seek specialist legal advice.

Stop and criticize	Why should organizations incur the staff and overhead costs of maintaining a specialist personnel department when line managers can do most of this work themselves?

Some commentators argue that the personnel function should be devolved to line managers, saving the salary and office costs. The function's contribution, however, can be central. Technology, a product design or a service profile can be copied. The ways in which employees are managed, however, are difficult to copy and personnel policy can thus be a source of sustained competitive advantage. Personnel management is also fundamental to the quality and cost-effectiveness of public services. Most public services are labour-intensive. For example, payroll represents around 80 per cent of the annual cost of running a hospital.

What is the link between personnel management and organizational behaviour? Personnel management can be seen as 'organizational behaviour in practice', such that an appreciation of organizational behaviour is important if you want to become an effective personnel practitioner. However, while the two subjects are clearly related in this way, their agendas are different. Organizational behaviour is concerned with understanding a range of related micro- and macro-organizational phenomena, at individual, group, organizational and contextual levels of analysis. Personnel management has a more focused concern with theories and techniques which can develop the contribution of the personnel function and its practitioners to organizational effectiveness.

It is, however, possible to map organizational behaviour topics against personnel management functions, as table 20.1 illustrates.

The birth and growth of the personnel function

How did the personnel management function evolve? It is difficult to understand the nature of personnel management, or the significance of current debates about its role, without some knowledge of the history of the function. Personnel management has its roots in the industrialization of the latter half of the nineteenth century. The first personnel specialists were welfare workers employed to meet the paternalistic concerns of benevolent employers for their workforces. The bureaucratization of industry during the nineteenth century created some unpleasant working conditions. Factories concentrated large numbers of workers in a relatively small number of workplaces, so poor conditions were clearly visible to large numbers of people. Previously, workers had been dispersed, working mostly in their homes.

The British government appointed women factory inspectors in 1893, to monitor the implementation of regulations governing factory working conditions. The first (all female) industrial welfare workers, known as 'pioneers', were appointed by Rowntree and Company, in Britain, in 1896. Other concerned employers quickly followed that example, such as Boots of Nottingham, Jacobs of Dublin and Colmans of Norwich. The pioneers were mostly university graduates with

Table 20.1: Personnel management and organizational behaviour

personnel functions	issues and activities	OB topics
recruitment, selection, induction	getting the right employees into the right jobs; recruiting from an increasingly diverse population; sensitivity to employment of women, ethnic minorities, the disabled, the elderly	environmental turbulence; personality assessment; communication; person perception; learning; new organizational forms
training and development	tension between individual and organizational responsibility; development as a recruitment and retention tool; coping with new technology	technology and job design; new organizational forms; learning; the learning organization; motivation; organizational change
performance appraisal and reward	annual appraisal; pay policy; fringe benefits; need to attract and retain staff; impact of teamwork on individual pay	motivation; expectancy theory; equity theory; group influence on individual behaviour; teamworking
managing conduct and discipline	sexual harassment, racial abuse, drug abuse, alcohol abuse, health and safety; monitoring misconduct; using surveillance; formulation and communication of policies	surveillance technology; learning; socialization; behaviour modification; organization culture; managing conflict; management style
participation and commitment	involvement in decisions increases commitment; design of communications and participation mechanisms; managing organization culture; tap ideas, release talent, encourage loyalty	communication; motivation; organization structure; organization culture; new forms of flexible organization; organizational change; leadership style
organization development and change	the personnel/human resource management role in facilitating development and change; flexible working practices	organization development and change; motivation and job design; leadership style

degrees in social studies and they were concerned with issues of justice and social equity. They tended, therefore, to challenge management practices and ideologies, and many employers found them too critical. They were responsible for improving working conditions, for implementing government legislation affecting work and employment, for counselling, and for running company canteen and recreation facilities.

It was difficult for these welfare workers to be both management critics and agents of major organizational change while acting as personal counsellors and recreational amenities organizers. To make a more significant impact, welfare workers had to become fully integrated members of the organization management team. The strategy for gaining wider influence involved absorbing more expertise and responsibility, and in particular:

- becoming monitors of welfare legislation;
- taking over the selection role traditionally performed by foremen;

Pressures for a specialized personnel function

Although general and line managers perform personnel activities, there are several reasons why most organizations have specialized, dedicated personnel functions, including:

- Recruitment, selection, job grading and employee record keeping become critical with the growth in organizational size and complexity, and with increased task specialization among all employees, including management.

- The availability of advice and guidance on personnel issues become critical with state intervention in the form of employment law and regulations affecting, for example, working conditions, health and safety, discrimination, trade union rights and obligations, and management rights to discipline employees and to terminate employment contracts.

- Employee motivation and commitment become critical as the competitive climate intensifies the need for cost effectiveness, for increased productivity, and for improved product quality and quality of customer service.

- Negotiation and communication skills become critical with the development of industrial relations systems involving trade union recognition and collective bargaining.

- The public image of the personnel function, and the reputation of individual practitioners, is reinforced by the development of a professional body.

Based on Sarah Vickerstaff (ed.), *Human Resource Management in Europe: Text and Cases*, Chapman & Hall, London, 1992.

- looking after young employees, including apprentices;
- developing expertise in consulting and bargaining with trade unions;
- maintaining accurate employee records;
- performing timekeeping and employee payment operations.

Welfare workers thus evolved into employment officers and industrial relations officers, acting as the employee voice, on the one hand, and as management agents in negotiations and disputes, on the other. Their collective aspiration to gain professional status was reflected in the formation of an association of industrial welfare workers in 1913.

During the First World War (1914 to 1918), women were employed in manufacturing as many men were called up to fight. Women worked in munitions factories alongside men, for long hours, in remote locations to reduce the potential damage and injury from accidental explosions. The government of the day was particularly concerned about the implications of these arrangements for health and morality (men and women working nights together with minimum supervision). A study by the Health of Munitions Workers Committee in 1915 resulted in the appointment of many more (male and female) welfare workers to help maintain discipline and morale, supported by emergency training courses.

There was also a concern for the development of young employees at a time when public education opportunities were limited. Larger organizations established well-equipped apprentice schools, which offered an educational experience instead of just 'serving time' (the first learning organizations?). By the 1920s and 1930s, the range of industrial welfare activities carried out by welfare workers had broadened to include six main areas:

1. employment

2. education and training

3. health and safety

4. wages administration

5. employee consultation and negotiation

6. employee welfare services (e.g. canteen, savings schemes, pensions, legal and personal advice, social and recreational facilities).

Up until the Second World War (1939 to 1945), in many organizations with well-developed personnel functions, union negotiations and welfare work were performed in separate men's and women's employment offices. Anne Crichton (1968, p.23) notes an example of sexual discrimination—against men—during the inter-war period. This arose from the influx of men into welfare work, which had been exclusively female before the First World War:

> This was not very easy for the 'pioneer' women to accept, since they were anxious to maintain high standards of admission to their 'professional' group. These women were of two kinds. Many were graduates with a postgraduate social studies diploma. The others were upper-middle class women of good education; some had been known socially to the employers and invited to become their welfare officers. The men in industrial relations or employment officers' jobs were often clerks who had been promoted from the shop floor. It is not always easy to remember how high social-class barriers were in those days. (In 1919 the director responsible for welfare work in a biscuit factory was charming to his graduate welfare workers in the factory, but did not 'see' them in the street.) The graduate welfare workers were uncertain whether the ill-educated men's employment officers should be encouraged to join their association, although they could perceive the importance of bringing in all those employed in personnel specialist activities and raising general standards.

The Welfare Workers' Association became the Institute of Labour Management in 1929. The term 'personnel management' came into use during the Second World War. The Institute of Labour Management became the Institute of Personnel Management (IPM) in 1943. The IPM produced the first agreed definition of personnel management in 1945 (Crichton, 1968, p.26). This is a lengthy definition (subsequently revised), repeating and extending the definition offered earlier. It is worth considering in full, however, as a benchmark against which more recent debates about the distinctive role of human resource management can be assessed:

> Personnel management is that part of the management function which is concerned with human relationships within an organization. Its objective is the maintenance of those relationships on a basis which, by consideration of the well-being of the individual, enables all those engaged in the undertaking to make their maximum potential contribution to the effective working of that undertaking.
>
> In particular, personnel management is concerned with:
>
> Methods of recruitment, selection, training and education, and with the proper employment of personnel, terms of employment, methods and standards of remuneration, working conditions, amenities and employee services.
>
> The maintenance and effective use of facilities for joint consultation between employers and employees and between their representatives and of recognized procedures for the settlement of disputes.

As we shall see later, this definition from 1945 appears to capture many of the 'distinctive' features of the 'new' human resource management perspective of the 1990s.

During the Second World War there was total mobilization of all men of military age, and of women without children of school age. Full employment revealed several management inefficiencies and thus also exposed the need for assistance. The Essential Works Order of 1941 prevented employees from resigning, and also prevented management from dismissing employees in scheduled industries without the permission of the Ministry of Labour. Management and employees thus had to learn to work together with greater tolerance, and the demand for personnel specialists increased. First-line supervisors found that they now had to justify acts of discipline and punishment, and began to reconsider their management methods.

Engineering firms with government contracts to produce armaments were found to have very low productivity levels. Experienced welfare workers were seconded to Royal Ordnance factories to establish labour departments and train assistants. A Personnel Management Advisory Service was set up to raise the standard of first-line supervision. Joint consultation, involving employees in a range of issues other than wages, became popular as a means of 'achieving full citizenship in work' (Crichton, 1968, p.36).

After the Second World War, the emphasis on welfare work decreased for a number of reasons, mostly as a result of economic conditions and government policies concerning:

- commitment to full employment;

- introduction of the welfare state and National Health Service;

- commitment to equality of educational opportunity;

- improved social security with state legal aid and advice;

- growth of strong trade unions—blue and white collar;

- white collar benefits (paid holidays, pensions, sick pay) for manual workers.

The appalling working conditions which prompted the introduction of welfare workers had long since gone, and the combination of 'enlightened management' and a caring state reduced the need for such specialists. Organizations faced other problems, of productivity and economic growth, and even in those days had to be able to adapt quickly to technological developments. Despite the desire to contribute to the improvement of working conditions and organizational effectiveness, personnel management remained mainly an administrative activity. This was despite developments in social science theory and method during the 1940s and 1950s, which provided an underpinning for much personnel work. Peter Drucker, the American management guru, wrote in 1954 (quoted in Crichton, 1968, p.38):

> Is personnel management bankrupt? No, it is not bankrupt, its liabilities do not exceed its assets. But it is certainly insolvent, certainly unable to honour with the ready cash of performance the promises of managing workers and work it so liberally makes.

The IPM revised its definition in 1963, emphasizing the role of teams as well as individuals, noting that general management as well as specialists had personnel duties, and recognizing the function's role in dealing with organizational and economic change. However, personnel specialists in most organizations did not hold director posts and were rarely members of the senior management team. Tony Watson argued in 1977 that the personnel role was an ambiguous one, lacking in credibility (one sign of this being the inability to decide what to call yourself). Karen Legge argued in 1978 that personnel managers typically lacked the power and influence to implement their initiatives, and advocated the use of a range of strategies, including 'deviant innovation' to strengthen the status and contribution of the function. This picture began to change, slowly, during the 1980s.

Why is this historical background significant today? Three reasons:

1. *Because the administrative image survives*: Personnel management has not completely shed the traditional image of an administrative function working outside commercial imperatives. Clint Eastwood as Dirty Harry in the cult film *The Enforcer* (1976) says that 'personnel is for assholes'. Wickham Skinner (1981) describes personnel managers with the unkind phrase, 'big hat, no cattle'.

2. *Because we need to assess claims about 'novelty'*: As we shall see, human resource management tends to be defined in terms of how it differs from personnel management, and not just in its own terms. It is, therefore, hard to assess claims to what is distinctive about the 'new' human resource management perspective without an understanding of the way in which the personnel function has performed and developed previously.

3. *Because the function still seeks recognition*: A persistent theme in the history of the function is the pursuit of power, influence and professional status (Kamoche, 1994). This aspiration fuelled the human resource debate in the 1990s and triggered research to 'prove' the contribution of the function to organizational effectiveness. Accountants can quantify their contribution to cost reduction and profits; all large companies have a finance director, but only 30 per cent have a human resources director (Purcell, 1995). This aspiration culminated in July 2000 with the award of a Royal Charter to what is now the Institute for Personnel and Development, granting qualified members of the profession a status equivalent to that held by chartered accountants and engineers.

Table 20.2 summarizes the birth and growth of the personnel profession in Britain in the form of a timeline, from the appointment of factory inspectors and welfare workers in the late nineteenth century to the granting of a Royal Charter at the beginning of the twenty-first. By 2000, the Institute for Personnel and Development had more than 100,000 members. It also, as we shall see, had both a 'new' human resource perspective and empirical 'proof' of the contribution which the function makes to the organization's 'bottom line' or profitability.

Transformation: problems and solutions

Personnel management in Britain thus has four distinctive features:

- *The welfare factor*: It is rooted in a welfare tradition which was associated with industrial betterment at the turn of the twentieth century. Personnel management is the 'corporate conscience', representing the interest of workers to management.

- *The status factor*: The profession spent the twentieth century in pursuit of a clear identity; note the number of institutional name changes. Personnel management has also sought credibility and status as a function based on specialist knowledge and expertise. These aspirations culminate in 2000 with chartered status.

Table 20.2: The birth and growth of personnel management in Britain[*]

1893	The first women factory inspectors are appointed in Britain
1896	Rowntree and Co. appoint (female) industrial welfare workers, or 'pioneers'
1913	The Welfare Workers' Association (WWA) is founded
1915	Health of Munitions Workers Committee recruits and trains more welfare workers
1917	The WWA becomes the Central Association of Welfare Workers, with 400 members
1919	The Central Association becomes the Welfare Workers' Institute
1924	The Welfare Workers' Institute becomes the Institute of Industrial Welfare Workers
1931	Another name change, to Institute of Labour Management
1939	There are 760 practising personnel managers in Britain
1941	The first courses in the theory and practice of personnel and welfare work are run at the London School of Economics, with over 800 graduates in the first three years
1941	The Institute of Labour Management has 1,166 members; this more than doubles, to 2,881, by the end of the war in 1945
1946	Institute of Labour Management becomes Institute of Personnel Management (IPM)
1960	There are almost 3,000 practising personnel managers in Britain
1989	The Institute of Personnel Management has 35,000 members
1994	IPM merges with the Institute for Training and Development and becomes the Institute for Personnel and Development (IPD)
1999	IPD members vote overwhelmingly in favour of seeking a Royal Charter
2000	The IPD has over 100,000 members
2000	In July, the IPD is granted a Royal Charter

[*] Based on Crichton (1968), Child (1969), Kennedy (1989), Fowler (1994), and Institute of Personnel and Development sources.

- *The finance factor*: The boards of British organizations tend to be dominated by the finance and accounting function, which pushes 'soft' personnel voices aside, and which traditionally focuses on short-term organizational performance measures relating to share price movements, which directly influence top management rewards and careers.

- *The Cinderella factor*: The profession still has the stereotype of an administrative support function out of touch with commercial realities. It thus has 'Cinderella' status, reflected in its relatively low status and credibility, and by the fact that it is represented at board level in only a minority of organizations.

The pursuit of identity and status is clouded by at least three paradoxes surrounding the work of the function. First, how can the role of 'employee voice' be combined with management functions of controlling employee behaviour and performance? Second, how can a specialist role be maintained when it is acknowledged that general and line management also have personnel management responsibilities? Third, the claim to be a repository of expertise concerning the employment relationship is undermined by the dilution of the function with many other weakly related responsibilities. These paradoxes are summarized in table 20.3.

Table 20.3: Personnel management paradoxes

on the one hand	on the other hand
the personnel function is the voice of the employee, championing the employee cause with respect to working conditions, material rewards, health and safety, training and development and career progression	personnel is a management function, providing the right numbers of skilled employees, monitoring their performance and behaviour, ensuring compliance with management policies, rules and procedures
personnel is the specialist function responsible for the employment relationship, covering policy and practice affecting the stages of the employment cycle	all general and line managers perform personnel functions relating to, for example, recruitment, selection, training, performance appraisal, pay review, discipline, counselling
the personnel function is a repository of unique expertise, underpinned by social and behavioural science research, theory and method, requiring understanding of organization development, collective bargaining and employment legislation	the personnel function has been diluted with responsibility for pay systems, counselling, sports clubs, training programmes, company canteen, health and safety, leisure facilities, trade union negotiations, newsletters—more like a 'jack of all trades'

This pessimistic picture of the personnel profession was transformed during the 1990s as the ways in which people are managed, rewarded and motivated came to be recognized as fundamental to organizational survival and to competitive advantage. That decade witnessed a series of ongoing trends, particularly globalization, intensified competition and continuing technological innovation [**links**, chapters 2, the world outside; chapter 3, technology]. The resultant emphasis on product quality, and on the quality of customer service, in turn increased the emphasis on people management.

Administrative personnel work does not address these issues. The emphasis of the personnel role thus started to switch from employee administration to organization strategy. This is reflected in the more widespread use of the title human resource management (HRM), sometimes also called strategic human resource management (SHRM) to emphasize further the shift in the emphasis and contribution of the role. It is no longer adequate for the personnel function to operate as administrative tool and employee voice independently of commercial realities. The effectiveness of the human resource management function becomes central to the strategic and commercial success of the organization. The personnel manager may have sat in an isolated office. The human resources director sits on the organization's board of directors. Employees are not a cost, they are an asset.

The argument supporting these developments goes like this (based on Sisson, 1994):

- Management thinking has moved away from the traditional concepts of mass production, hierarchy, bureaucracy, task fragmentation and deskilling, as these methods are more suited to a world which changed slowly.

- Rapid change, domestic and international competition, fewer trade barriers, and competition from countries with low labour costs, organizational effectiveness relies on targeting niche markets, flat structures, flexible working and the development of skill and motivation through teamworking.

- Social trends are producing a better-educated workforce with higher levels of social awareness, with higher expectations of quality of working life, with a lack of loyalty or commitment to individual employers, and more willing and able to challenge management decisions.

- The provisions of the Social Charter (Holden, 1997, p.727) improve employee rights and harmonize employment legislation across the European Community.

- Technological developments have created an organizational world of near instant, low-cost communications and information flows encouraging new forms of organization, and also new ways of doing business (e-commerce).

- As the competition can copy product designs and service specifications, and acquire the same technology, the main source of competitive advantage lies with people, and with the policies and practices that develop and motivate employees to high levels of individual and organizational performance.

- Therefore, the ways in which people are recruited, selected, trained, organized, managed, appraised, rewarded, developed, disciplined and motivated are strategic issues, fundamental to organizational effectiveness.

- Therefore, human resource management policies and practices must be integrated with each other and aligned with organization strategy.

A related issue prompting a rethink of personnel management methods concerns changes in the **psychological contract** between employee and organization (Rousseau, 1990; 1995).

The **psychological contract** is an implicit set of obligations and expectations concerning what the individual and the organization expect to give to and receive from each other.

It is not possible to specify every aspect of the employment relationship in a detailed formal contract. The organization expects, for example, loyalty and commitment, while employees expect fair treatment, a degree of security and personal development. Much of our behaviour is thus based on tacit, unspoken beliefs. This concept was first developed by Chris Argyris (1960) but became a focus for research during the 1990s. Although the psychological contract is a personal construct, it is possible to suggest broad changes in its nature. For example, Philip Stiles and colleagues (1997) illustrate shifts in the nature of the psychological contract between 1990 and 1995 (table 20.4), indicating major changes over a short period.

Table 20.4: Changes in the psychological contract (based on Stiles *et al.* 1997, p.59)

	1990 expectations	1995 expectations
organization culture	paternalistic, authoritarian, hierarchical, bureaucratic	performance measures, continuous improvement
job security	high, no redundancy	low, contingent on performance
objectives	targets set by boss, aimed at financial goals	mutual targets linked to strategy, aimed at finance, quality and people goals
evaluation	limited feedback	ongoing appraisal
rewards	position and length of service	performance-related
personal development	organizational responsibility	individual responsibility
outcomes	compliance, dependence	adaptability, innovation

A psychological contract which is seen to be honoured in theory leads to employee satisfaction, commitment, motivation, a willing contribution and high performance. Problems arise when the contract is perceived to be broken. For example, Robinson and Rousseau (1994) found that 55 per cent of their management sample said their psychological contract had been broken by their employer. The consequences are damaging, leading to low job satisfaction, poor performance, high staff turnover, feelings of anger and betrayal, and the erosion of trust. The psychological contract is a relatively vague concept, but David Guest (1998) argues that it deserves further analysis. Managing the psychological contract seems to have become a key element of the 'new' human resource management role.

The prescription which follows from all these developments includes:

- Human resource management must be part of the strategic management of the organization, involved directly in major strategic decisions and not confined to administrative support functions.

- Integrated human resource policies must emphasize flexibility, teamwork, customer focus, total quality, empowerment, learning and skills development.

- Organization structures should be flat and decentralized, based on autonomous business units producing high-quality, high value-added goods and services for carefully defined niche markets.

- Management style must emphasize mutual trust, respect and autonomy, not rigid rules and procedures, with a leadership style which encourages flexibility, co-operation, commitment and high performance.

Why is employee selection a strategic issue?

If you wanted to work in the Millennium Dome, the giant exhibition in London which opened on 31 December 1999, you had to complete a rigorous selection process. The process was designed by Manpower, a national job agency, for the New Millennium Experience Company (NMEC), which managed the Dome. Employees included hosts ('meeters and greeters'), and visitor services managers, as well as drivers, IT specialists and clerical staff.

- The first step was a twenty-minute conversation at one of Manpower's 200 local offices, located around Britain, where the realities of working in the Dome were explained.

- Still at the local office, a formal interview then evaluated qualifications and experience, and candidates were given a 70-question computer-based assessment to determine their aptitude for a customer service role.

- The next stage (assuming the local office felt that you met the criteria) was a visit to the Dome itself, where a psychometric assessment followed another formal interview.

- Finally, candidates were put into small groups and given fictional problems to solve, such as being on a sinking ship or getting lost in a cave. Observers assessed candidates' initiative, teamworking and communication skills during this exercise.

In 1999, there were five applicants for every vacancy in the Dome, which employed around 5,000 people. Because 12 million visitors were expected during 2000, it was critical that staff had relevant skill and knowledge in customer services, the contents of the twelve exhibit zones, health and safety procedures, and first aid and evacuation procedures. NMEC wanted the workforce to reflect the diversity of visitors, and recruited people with varying ages (17 to 70) and backgrounds, including the previously unemployed, mothers returning to work, ethnic minorities (25 per cent of the workforce), and people from different parts of the country, including Northern Ireland. Most critically, the manager in charge of recruiting wanted staff who were 'effervescent, proactive and flexible'.

Based on David Littlefield, 'One in a millennium', *People Management*, vol.5, no.24, 16 December 1999, pp.38–9.

Table 20.5: Typical human resource policy and practice

HRM policy areas	high-commitment–high-performance practices
employee influence	wide participation and involvement in change and management decisions generally; extensive two-way communication; problem-solving groups
human resource flow	selection based on attitudes and values in addition to skills and experience; policies which deliver flexibility in *numbers* of employees, with a more stable core complemented as required by a flexible 'peripheral' workforce, and also flexibility in timing, with a range of part-time, annual hours and flexible hours practices
reward systems	open and participative appraisal with two-way feedback; performance-based pay; individual and group-based rewards; skills-based pay; profit sharing; share options; flexible 'cafeteria' benefits; lateral as well as upward promotions; equal opportunities
work systems	excellence, quality and continuous improvement are dominant values; emphasis on 'beyond contract' and 'can do'; visible, facilitating, inspirational leadership; flat decentralized structures; cross-functional project teams; autonomous teams with task flexibility

David Guest (1989; 1990) argues that the policy objectives of human resource management, in contrast with personnel management, are:

- high commitment;
- high quality;
- flexibility; and
- strategic integration.

He then argues that:

> Only when a coherent strategy, directed towards these four policy goals, fully integrated into business strategy and fully sponsored by line management at all levels is applied will the high productivity and related outcomes sought by industry be achieved. Such a strategy is only likely to exist where the 'cement' is in place in the form of supportive leadership from the top, reflected in the organization's culture and backed by an explicit strategy to utilize human resources.

Table 20.5 outlines typical 'high-commitment–high-performance' human resource management practices concerning employee influence, human resource flow, reward systems and work systems. These kinds of practices are said to lead to Guest's policy objectives. This illustrates the shift in emphasis from personnel to human resource management, and these four areas are the basis for one of the models considered in the following section.

The following sections answer three key questions. How can this new paradigm be defined? How well does it work in improving organizational performance? Is it really 'new'?

Stop and criticize

Human resource management practices seem to assume that employers and employees are equal partners with the same interests and goals.

Where in your view do these interests coincide? Where do they differ?

Why is employee training a strategic issue?

ISS is a successful Danish cleaning services company. The cleaning industry is characterized by low-skilled workers and high staff turnover. ISS is an exception, and it achieves high service quality and high employee loyalty through its approach to training.

Even in cleaning, customer satisfaction depends on the behaviour of front-line employees. Contracts are lost when cleaners do a poor job, irrespective of marketing and pricing strategies. ISS thus has a continuing stream of programmes to train employees and to encourage customer-friendly service.

Because ISS is a large international company, with an annual revenue in 1997 of US$1.8 billion, it can bid for large contracts with factories, offices and hospitals. Highly efficient cleaning staff are required to service these clients well and profitably. Efficiency means saving time and cleaning supplies, improving service quality, and avoiding accidents. In complex settings, such as hospitals and process plants, for example, the skills and equipment required are quite sophisticated. Cleaners also need to be able to identify and handle the different needs and expectations of different customers.

Here is the training programme for new recruits at the ISS small business services operation:

- recruits first undergo a six month training programme in cleaning techniques and safety;
- they are then trained to interpret contracts so they understand how profitable they are;
- after a year, trained staff are promoted to team leader posts;
- training is extended to customer handling, and coaching skills for developing new staff.

How are staff motivated and rewarded?

- staff are organized into two- or three-person 'hit squads' who work together regularly, even though many contracts could be handled by one person;
- cleaning shifts overlap half an hour with site employees, so they get to know each other;
- team leader performance targets include customer retention and profitability;
- the company pays above industry average wages to encourage retention.

The results? The company share price trebled between 1996 and 1998. In 1997, ISS won the contract to clean the hotel rooms at Disneyland Paris, a company famous for attention to detail. Company profits in 1998 were forecast to grow 15 per cent annually.

Based on 'Service with a smile', *The Economist*, 25 April 1998, pp.85–6.

Definitions and models of human resource management

Human resource management is a managerial perspective, with theoretical and prescriptive dimensions, which argues for the need to establish an integrated series of personnel policies consistent with organization strategy, thus ensuring quality of working life, high commitment and performance from employees, and organizational effectiveness and competitive advantage.

Commentators have struggled to articulate and agree a definition of **human resource management**. No single authoritative version has appeared. On the contrary, as Tom Keenoy (1990) points out, the label has a 'brilliant ambiguity' which enables its users to define it in the manner that best suits the purposes of the author and the occasion.

The definition of personnel management offered earlier was couched in structural terms; personnel management is an organizational function, a department. This definition of human resource management is different in defining it as a perspective. It is possible for an organization to adopt a human resource management perspective (however defined) without having a human resource management department. Indeed, many human resource management initiatives seem to have been initiated by general management (Storey, 1992).

John Storey (1989; 1992), one of the leading contributors to the human resource management debate in Britain, argues that the term is difficult to define for several reasons:

1. The term is used in different ways by different commentators. Some use it in a descriptive sense, reporting developments in practice. Others use it in a prescriptive manner, advocating a particular approach to employee relations. The term is also used in a theoretical sense, setting out causal links to aid understanding.

2. Some commentators use the term 'human resource management' in a loose or weak sense, as a modern-sounding label; others use it in a strong manner, to imply a specific set of management practices with a particular philosophical underpinning.

3. Storey argues for a distinction between **hard** and **soft** versions of human resource management, depending on the emphasis given to goals and their achievement.

Hard HRM is a human resource management perspective which emphasizes the full utilization of employees in a formal, calculating and dispassionate manner, to be treated in a manner similar to any other resources available to the organization.
Soft HRM is a human resource management perspective which emphasizes the need to develop the potential and resourcefulness of employees in order to encourage commitment and high performance in pursuit of shared organizational goals.

Thus, as Storey (1992, p.26) points out, the same term can be used to describe contradictory sets of beliefs and practices. Hard HRM can be viewed as instrumental and exploitative. Soft HRM can be viewed as woolly and inappropriate in a commercial context.

Hard HRM is quantitative and calculating, emphasizing the management of headcount and focusing on strategic issues. Hard HRM incorporates any practice that contributes to organization strategy, including task fragmentation, job insecurity and low pay. Soft HRM is people-oriented, rooted in human relations thinking, emphasizing motivation, communication and leadership. Soft HRM rules out practices that would deskill jobs and damage motivation.

This distinction is similar to the one explored in the chapter on leadership [**link**, chapter 21, leadership] between initiating structure (a task-oriented style) and consideration (a people-oriented style). Theory and evidence there suggest that the leaders who get the best performance from their people emphasize both structure and consideration. For effective leaders, therefore, this is not an 'either, or' choice.

Similarly, the human resource manager, to be effective, may have to find ways simultaneously to reduce labour costs and increase employee commitment, motivation and performance. The distinction between hard and soft HRM may thus be difficult to sustain in practice. Keith Sisson (1994, p.14) also notes that, 'there must be the danger that managers will be tempted to use the language of "the HRM organization" to cover the reality of what they are doing'. In other words, the language of soft HRM may be used to disguise a hard approach, to make it appear more legitimate, acceptable and palatable (see table 20.6).

Table 20.6: Soft rhetoric hiding hard reality in human resource management

Rhetoric	Reality
Customer first	Market forces supreme
Total quality management	Doing more with less
Lean production	Mean production
Flexibility	Management can do what it wants
Core and periphery	Reducing the organization's commitments
Devolution/delayering	Reducing the number of middle managers
Downsizing/right-sizing	Redundancy
New working patterns	Part-time instead of full-time jobs
Empowerment	Someone else taking risk and responsibility
Training and development	Manipulation
Employability	No employment security
Recognizing individual contributions	Undermining trade union bargaining
Teamworking	Reducing the individual's discretion

From Keith Sisson, 'Personnel management: paradigms, practice and prospects', in Keith Sisson (ed.), *Personnel Management in Britain*, Blackwell, Oxford, 1994, p.15.

Stop and criticize

How do you feel about being described as a 'human resource' or as a 'human asset'?

Does it matter? What are the practical advantages and disadvantages to you personally, as an employee, of being labelled in this way?

Human resources defined

A disturbingly distant phrase for 'people'. It is not necessarily innocent jargon: it may be that you can treat 'human resources' differently from the way you treat 'people'. If you talk about your requirement for human resources, it sounds as if a *rational* economic decision is being made, without moral or personal overtones. It may be easier for a manager to release human resources than it is to sack people. If you are the human resource in question, you will not be able to detect the difference. Human Resource Management (or HRM) is the phrase which turns this dehumanizing language into an academic subject, covering the areas previously known as personnel management and industrial relations.

From David Sims, Stephen Fineman and Yiannis Gabriel, *Organizing and Organizations: An Introduction*, Sage, London, 1993, p.256.

As indicated earlier, (new, radical) human resource management, particularly from a 'strong' perspective, is often defined in terms of the contrast with (old, traditional) personnel management. This is the approach which John Storey (1992) adopts, identifying twenty-seven points of distinction between the two perspectives. These are summarized in table 20.7, which can be read as a detailed definition of an 'ideal' approach to human resource management. Storey (1992, p.26) also identifies four main issues which 'express the essence of the concept' of human resource management, in contrast with personnel management:

- *people make the difference*: the belief that it is human resources, in terms of capability and commitment, which 'make the difference' in terms of organizational effectiveness;

- *people decisions are strategic decisions*: recognition that people management decisions, particularly those affecting investment in and development of human resources, are fundamental strategic decisions, and not background operational matters;

- *implementation by line managers*: acceptance that human resource policy has long-term organizational implications, and has to be implemented consistently and effectively by line management with central human resource management monitoring and support;

- *integrated policies*: appreciation that in practice, human resource policies must be integrated with each other in a systematic and mutually reinforcing manner, particularly recruitment and selection, communication of objectives, the organization of work, and performance appraisal and reward.

In other words, to find out if an organization is practising human resource management or not, first ask four questions:

1. Do you regard your employees as costs or as assets?

2. Does your personnel or human resource director sit on the organization's main board?

3. Are line managers skilled in and committed to implementing human resource policy?

4. Are human resource policies integrated and mutually supportive?

Second, turn to table 20.7 and identify which personnel or human resource practices the organization adopts. In practice, one would expect to find a mixed approach, but with a tendency or a bias, more or less powerful, towards one perspective or the other. It would be rare to find a 'perfect' personnel or an 'ideal' human resource approach in practice.

Can human resource management really improve organizational performance? To answer this question, it is first necessary to explore the models of human resource management developed during the 1980s and 1990s. We will consider four models, using the locations of their authors to label them (Sparrow and Hiltrop, 1994). It is useful to remember that these are simply four different ways of looking at the nature and contribution of the human resource management function. There is no consensus on these issues, no neat and agreed package.

1. The Michigan model.

2. The Harvard model.

3. The New York model.

4. The Warwick model.

Table 20.7: Personnel management versus human resource management *

dimensions of difference	traditional personnel management	the human resource management ideal
beliefs and assumptions	our role is to devise and monitor rules and procedures, to establish clear written contracts, to maintain custom and practice, and to handle conflict through established procedure	our role is to encourage people to go beyond contract, to put business needs before rules and precedent, to develop skills, and to reduce conflict by emphasizing common goals
approach to strategy	our contribution to corporate strategy is marginal; our focus is labour management; we implement incremental change; our decision making is slow	our contribution to corporate strategy is central; we focus on customers; we implement integrated change initiatives; our decision making is fast
relationship with line management	we communicate indirectly with line managers; we are prized for our negotiation skills; we emphasize standardization because 'parity' is a key issue; our management role is transactional	we communicate directly with line managers; we are prized for facilitation skills; we do not emphasize standardization because 'parity' is not an issue; our leadership role is transformational
key levers	we focus on personnel procedures such as selection, job grading and evaluation, and we control access to training courses; we deal with shop stewards and collective bargaining, and handle disputes through regular procedures; employee communications take place infrequently as required	we focus on culture change, to eliminate conflict and develop the learning organization; teamwork and performance-based pay have replaced task fragmentation and job grading; individual contracts reduce the trade union role; employee communication is constant

Based on John Storey, *Developments in the Management of Human Resources: An Analytical Review*, Blackwell Business, Oxford, 1992, p.35.

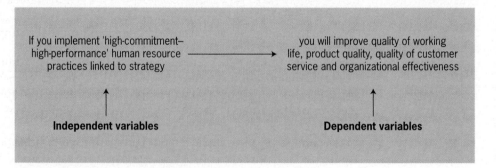

Figure 20.2: A basic model of HRM

These four models make the claim illustrated in figure 20.2. They argue that, if you design human resource policies in a particular way, then performance will improve (see Guest, 1989; 1997). Human resource policies are *independent variables* in this relationship, and quality of working life and organizational effectiveness are *dependent variables* (see glossary).

Students and practitioners of HRM are thus confronted with a number of competing models which explain these relationships in different ways, with different emphases.

The Michigan model—a 'matching' perspective

The Michigan model developed by Charles Fombrun, Noel Tichy and Mary Anne Devanna (1984) emphasizes the 'resource' element, arguing that people should be managed like any other resource, 'obtained cheaply, used sparingly and developed and exploited as fully as possible' (Sparrow and Hiltrop, 1994, p.7). They also argue that personnel policies, to be effective, must match, or be aligned, with the organization's strategy.

The Michigan model, figure 20.3, is based on the 'human resource cycle', emphasizing the contribution of selection, appraisal, rewards and development to employee performance. These issues reflect elements in the employment cycle, defined earlier. These factors must be linked to organization strategy, and they must also be consistent with each other in 'sending the same messages'. There would be no point in rewarding employees for following rules and procedures if the organization strategy involved change and innovation, and if selection and appraisal systems emphasized initiative and discretion.

One of the problems with this model concerns the narrow focus on these aspects of human resource management. This ignores the industrial relations context, the role and interests of trade unions, management and leadership style, and the organization of work, which could involve task fragmentation, deskilling, job enrichment or teamworking. For the model to work in practice, an organization's strategy has to be relatively stable and well understood. That is not always the case, particularly in today's rapidly changing competitive environment.

The Harvard model—a 'stakeholder' perspective

While the Michigan model emphasized 'resources', the Harvard model places more emphasis on the 'human' dimensions. The model developed by Michael Beer and his colleagues at Harvard (Beer *et al.*, 1984; 1985; Beer and Spector, 1985) is probably the best known and most widely cited of the models described here, and has been particularly influential in Britain and Europe (Sparrow and Hiltrop, 1994, p.12). Their 'map of the human resource management territory' is shown in figure 20.4. As with the Michigan model, this argues that human resource policy must be consistent with the organizational context and strategy. This considers a wider range of factors than the Michigan model. Critically, it demonstrates how policy choices are shaped and constrained by context factors, and by stakeholder groups whose interests have to be managed and reconciled through a series of 'trade-offs'.

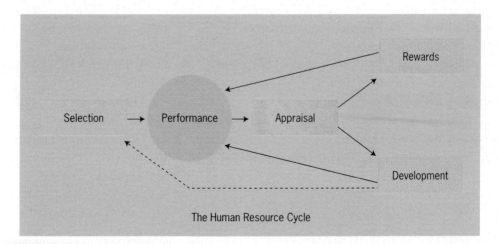

Figure 20.3: The Michigan model of human resource management.
Reproduced from C.J. Fombrun, N. Tichy and M.A. Devanna, *Strategic Human Resource Management*. Copyright © 1984. Reprinted with permission of John Wiley & Sons, Inc.

This is a *stakeholder* model (see glossary) presenting a causal chain linking the practice of human resource management with 'HR outcomes' and with organizational performance and quality of working life. There are four policy areas at the heart of the model:

- employee influence;

- human resource flow;

- reward systems;

- work systems.

These are the four policy areas used earlier in table 20.5 to illustrate a typical human resource management approach, leading in this model to high commitment, high competence, cost-effectiveness, and a high degree of congruence between individual and organizational goals. The precise nature of these causal links, however, remains woolly.

Mike Noon (1992) points out that the model was developed as a structure for the Harvard MBA syllabus in human resource management in 1981. It was a framework for organizing teaching and thinking and was not intended to be either an explanatory or a prescriptive model. However, it is not difficult to see how this model can treated either as a theory of how to manage human resources effectively or as a prescriptive guide to 'best practice'.

The New York model—a 'contingency' perspective
Randall Schuler and Susan Jackson (1987; 1996), from New York University, adopt an approach based on the 'needed role behaviours' to support different kinds of organization strategy. They first identify a series of twelve contrasting employee behaviours, arguing that some of these behaviours are appropriate for an organization strategy that involves cost reduction, while other behaviours are appropriate for a strategy that involves innovation. This argument is summarized in

Table 20.8: Organization strategy and employee behaviour

behaviours required for a cost-reduction strategy	behaviours required for an innovation strategy
highly repetitive, predictable behaviour	highly creative, innovative behaviour
very short-term focus	very long-term focus
highly co-operative, interdependent behaviour	highly independent, autonomous behaviour
very low concern for quality	very high concern for quality
very low concern for quantity	very high concern for quantity
very low risk taking	very high risk taking
very high concern for process	very high concern for results
high preference for avoiding responsibility	high preference for assuming responsibility
very inflexible to change	very flexible to change
very comfortable with stability	very tolerant of ambiguity and uncertainty
narrow skill application	broad skill application
low job involvement	high job involvement

From Randall Schuler and Susan Jackson, 'Linking competitive strategies with human resource management practices', *Academy of Management Executive*, 1987, vol.9, no.3, pp.207–19.

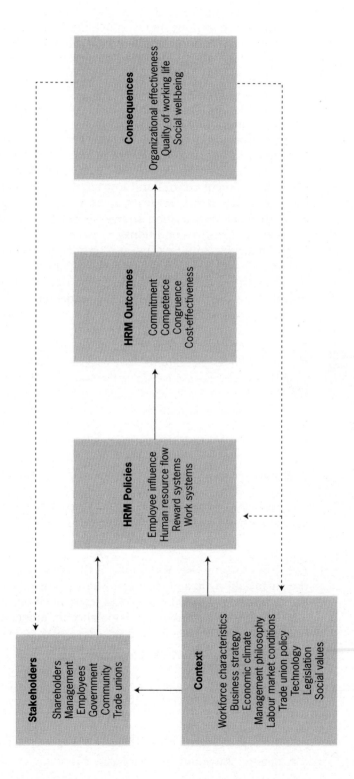

Figure 20.4: Map of the human resource management territory

From Michael Beer, Bert Spector, Paul R. Lawrence, D. Quinn Mills and Richard E. Walton, *Managing Human Assets*, Free Press, New York, 1984. Reproduced with permission.

table 20.8. Readers familiar with the work of Douglas McGregor (1960) will see his contrast between Theory X (people are lazy and avoid responsibility) and Theory Y (people are creative and independent) in the behaviours required for 'cost reduction' and 'innovation' respectively.

Once the organization strategy and required employee behaviours have been established, the obvious step is to determine human resource practices appropriate for encouraging those behaviours. The human resource manager is now offered the five practice 'menus' shown in table 20.9. The criterion of choice for each item rests on the degree of fit or alignment with organization strategy. Of course, the organization strategy has to be clearly articulated before the appropriate choices from the human resource 'menu' can be established. Should the organization strategy change, then it may be necessary to adjust some of the menu items.

This perspective does not exclusively advocate a 'high-commitment' approach. The choice of human resource policy and practice is contingent on the organization's strategy. An approach which encourages task fragmentation, deskilling, tight management control and low employee autonomy may be appropriate in some contexts, particularly with a cost-cutting strategy. It is also not possible to argue that one organization strategy is better than another as this depends on external, competitive conditions.

This model has intuitive appeal. Consider, for example, the choices concerning 'compensation', and how these choices might differ, say, for the management of casual part-time bartending staff, on the one hand, and for laboratory research scientists, on the other. However, the model tends to assume that the same policies apply to all staff.

Stop and criticize

You are human resource director for a company whose strategy involves innovation in new products and services, and enhancing the quality of customer care. Which human resource policies from the New York model in table 20.9 are more appropriate for this organization? Is it obvious, or difficult to choose?

However, due to a major shift in the competitive environment, the company strategy has changed. The focus now is on cost reduction. Which human resource policies from the New York model are more appropriate for these new conditions?

How easily and how quickly would you estimate you can change human resource policies as the model recommends? What problems would these changes create?

At the heart of the New York model is the concept of 'behavioural consistency'. If the organization has an innovation strategy, then it will be appropriate to encourage creativity, long-term focus, high levels of co-operation and interdependence, a high degree of risk taking and tolerance for ambiguity and uncertainty. Which human resource policies apply?

- job enrichment;
- multiple career ladders;
- high employee participation;
- many and flexible incentives;
- quality of working life emphasis.

This is a contingency model of human resource management. Policy and practice have to be tailored to organizational circumstances. There is no 'one best way' to

Table 20.9: The New York model of human resource management

Planning choices
Informal ... Formal
Short-term ... Long-term
Explicit job analysis ... Implicit job analysis
Job simplification ... Job enrichment
Low employee involvement ... High employee involvement

Staffing choices
Internal sources ... External sources
Narrow paths ... Broad paths
Single ladder ... Multiple ladders
Explicit criteria ... Implicit criteria
Limited socialization ... Extensive socialization
Closed procedures ... Open procedures

Appraising choices
Behavioural criteria ... Results criteria
Low employee participation ... High employee participation
Short-term criteria ... Long-term criteria
Individual criteria ... Group criteria

Compensating choices
Low base salaries ... High base salaries
Internal equity ... External equity
Few perks ... Many perks
Standard, fixed package ... Flexible package
Low participation ... High participation
No incentives ... Many incentives
Short-term incentives ... Long-term incentives
No employment security ... High employment security
Hierarchical ... High participatiion

Training and development choices
Short-term ... Long-term
Narrow application ... Broad application
Productivity emphasis ... Quality of work life emphasis
Spontaneous, unplanned ... Planned, systematic
Individual orientation ... Group orientation
Low participation ... High participation

Source: Schuler and Jackson (1987), reprinted with permission © Academy of Management Executives, 1993.

manage human resources. All this presumes that human resource managers are actually able to make the choices implied in the model, unconstrained by other organizational and contextual factors.

The Warwick model—a 'contextual' perspective
The models explored up to this point are American. From a European perspective, human resource management is an American import. These models reflect American cultural traditions, management styles, politics and industrial relations. The European tradition of collective bargaining, with trade unions, contrasts with a focus on the individual in American management practice in general and in human resource management in particular. Human resource management was thus regarded in Britain in the late 1980s as culturally inappropriate, and as simply a relabelling of familiar approaches.

Chris Hendry, Andrew Pettigrew and Paul Sparrow (1989; Hendry and Pettigrew, 1990), researchers at the Centre for Corporate Strategy at Warwick Business

School, extended the Harvard model to take into account the organizational context in which human resource policies are designed and implemented. The Warwick model is shown in figure 20.5.

This complex model has five elements. First, in 'HRM context', the model identifies the Harvard policy areas of human resource flows, work systems, reward systems and employee relations (see table 20.5 and figure 20.4). Second, the model identifies the external context of the organization (suggesting a PEST analysis of external political, economic, social and technical factors) [**link**, chapter 2, the world outside]. Third, the model recognizes how the external context influences the inner context of the organization, with respect to organization structure and culture, leadership, technology and business results. Fourth, the inner context both influences and is influenced by the 'HRM context', which concerns the way in which the organization defines the role and specifies the structure of the function and the outputs expected of it. Finally, as with the other models considered so far, human resource policies are seen also to depend on the business or organization strategy. The arrows in the model illustrate lines of mutual influence.

This model was used to analyse data from over twenty organizations in Britain in a study of how strategic change had affected human resource management.

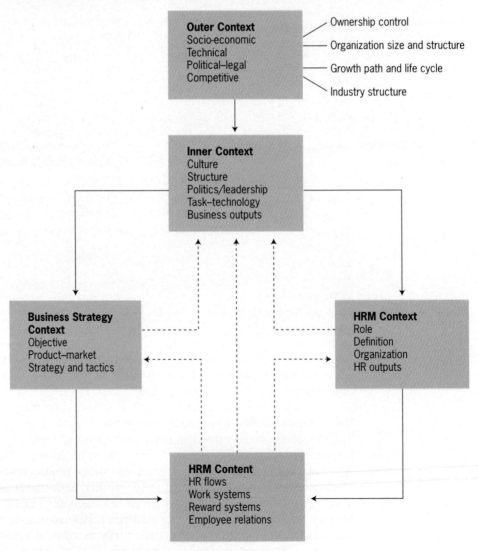

Figure 20.5: The Warwick model of strategic change and human resource management
From C. Hendry and A.M. Pettigrew, 'Human resource management practices', *International Journal of Human Resource Management* 1990, vol. 1, no. 1, pp. 17–43.

Table 20.10: Conceptual and process skills for implementing HRM

The Warwick research identified the following conceptual and process skills required to implement the human resource management approach effectively:

- A perception and understanding of the connections between business and HRM.

- Diagnostic skills to audit and take stock of existing skill bases in organizations in the light of anticipated business and technological changes.

- Ability to identify and advise on the business opportunities afforded by the existing skill base of the organization, creating a business case for why human resources are a perceived source of competitive advantage.

- Preparedness to initiate new styles and patterns of HRM activity in advance of business changes.

- Sufficient cultural understanding to be able to preserve what is valuable from previous missions and values, meet new task requirements and be sensitive to individual satisfaction and career needs.

- Development of the power base of the personnel management function by linking its activities to overarching information, commercial and financial policies.

- Sensitivity to the changing internal situation during major periods of change.

- Political skills to mobilize the internal and external forces of change, creating increasingly self-reinforcing patterns of HRM.

- Recognition of the wide range of pressure points within HRM that can be brought to bear in a strategic change.

- Ability to initiate timely adjustments in HRM agreements and practices.

From Paul Sparrow and Jean-M. Hiltrop, *European Human Resource Management in Transition*, Prentice Hall, Hemel Hempstead, 1994, p.18.

This approach highlights the influential role of the strategic change management process, often over a number of years (15 to 20), in developing different approaches to human resource management. The research also highlighted the conceptual and process skills required to implement the human resource management approach effectively (see table 20.10). This is a considerable development on welfare work, counselling, running sports and canteen facilities and administering employee payroll and personal records. This range of tasks and skills perhaps explains why HRM is sometimes referred to as strategic human resource management or SHRM.

This model is unique among those considered here in drawing explicit attention to the wider context (inner and outer) in which the human resource management function operates. Space prohibits a fuller consideration of how contextual factors impinge on the human resource function. However, it is important to recognize, first, that the human resource function does not operate free from contextual constraints and, second, that the topic should not be viewed merely as a contest between competing models.

These models all have various degrees of empirical research support, some convincing, and some less so. These models are all controversial. In the following section, we will explore some of the main criticisms of these perspectives and also consider the results of research which has specifically asked the question, 'does human resource management really contribute to organizational performance?'

The four models described here are not only controversial, they are also potentially confusing. Table 20.11 offers a summary of the main strengths and weaknesses of each.

Table 20.11: HRM models strengths and limitations summarized

Model	Strengths	Limitations
The Michigan matching model	• based on personnel policies affecting the employment cycle • emphasizes consistency of approach in supporting strategy	• focus on limited set of personnel policies • ignores context, organization design, industrial relations
The Harvard stakeholder model	• comprehensive, systematic and prescriptive causal map • recognizes the influence of a range of stakeholders	• not designed as prescriptive but regarded as such • nature of causal links unclear
The New York contingency model	• exposes a wide range of choices for personnel policy • advocates a clear link with organization strategy	• strategy has to be known before choices can be made • managers are not always free to make these choices
The Warwick contextual model	• recognizes that strategic change is a dynamic iterative process • takes into account the shaping role of many contextual factors over lengthy periods of time	• provides explanations for past events, and is complex and difficult to test • useful for researchers, limited guidance for practitioners

Criticisms

Human resource management has attracted much criticism. Two points have already been mentioned. One criticism concerns the definition of the term, which is ambiguous. It is used in 'strong' and 'loose' senses to describe 'hard' and 'soft' approaches to employee relations. A second related criticism concerns the potentially cynical use of the term to give a more modern 'up-beat' tone to the profession, to give the impression of change and progress. This image building is assisted by the addition of 'strategic' to the label 'human resource management', symbolizing even more clearly the shift away from personnel administration.

There are two other major substantive criticisms of the movement. These concern:

1. The *treatment of conflict*, which in American models tends to be overlooked.

2. The *treatment of strategy*, which tends to be treated as a 'given'.

Conflict
Human resource management relies on policies to encourage commitment, loyalty, a strong culture, shared goals and values (Guest, 1990). This is a *unitarist* perspective [**link**, chapter 23, conflict], which assumes that an organization's members are united behind a common purpose. This overlooks the potential inconsistency between an individual's needs and desires and the needs of the organization; this was explored in chapter 1 as the *organizational dilemma* (see glossary). This also ignores the view that employee interests and organizational needs are fundamentally irreconcilable, that industrial conflict is inevitable, and

that the trade union role is to provide a buffer protecting employee interests through collective representation and bargaining.

A 'high-commitment–high-performance' human resource management strategy is only likely to work where the industrial relations climate is sympathetic to notions of shared goals and values. In an adversarial climate (management propose, unions oppose), such a strategy is more likely to be seen as a cynical management attempt to disguise the realities of organizational conflict. North American management models do not 'travel' well, particularly to Europe, which has a more varied industrial relations history and context.

Strategy

The models that we have explored emphasize the argument that human resource management should be integrated, mutually supportive and reinforcing, and thus be closely linked to organization strategy. Personnel management historically operated in relative isolation from the strategy of the organization, beyond hiring more people when required and laying them off again when necessary. The strategy argument is thus central to the distinction between personnel and human resources.

Keith Sisson (1994) identifies a number of difficulties with this argument. First, organization strategy is rarely as systematic and ordered as these tidy models require. Strategy tends to be 'emergent', not rationally planned. This means that strategy tends to emerge over time from the various actions, successes and failures across the organization. HRM models assume that human resource management choices follow logically from formal organization strategy choices. HRM is thus placed in a reactive mode, not involved with helping to shape and develop strategy in the first place. However, developments in employee availability and skills, in organization culture and structure, or in other aspects of human resource management may shape the organization's strategic thinking and opportunities.

The problem remains: how is it possible to develop an integrated human resource management approach to support an emergent strategy which develops more or less slowly and which changes unpredictably? This point is highlighted by the Warwick model, which draws attention to the range of contextual factors which are likely to affect human resource management practice over extended periods of time.

Second, other senior managers may not accept that human resource management is strategically vital. Given today's aggressively hostile, competitive and volatile international markets, task fragmentation, deskilling, increased management control and cost reduction can also look like good human resource management strategies. Taylorism and Fordism look like easier and less risky options,

particularly where there is limited evidence to show a return on investment from a shift to human resource management.

Third, 'full-blown' human resource management can be expensive, in terms of set-up costs and support mechanisms (more specialist staff, more training for line managers). Consider the costs involved in implementing the shift from personnel to human resource management identified by John Storey (1992) and summarized in table 20.7. Consider the relative costs of the policy choices in the New York model of HRM from Schuler and Jackson (1987) in table 20.9. Even if these policy choices were considered appropriate, serious investment in human resource management may be beyond the financial capability of many organizations.

Does it work?

The question 'does it work?' has much more than theoretical interest. Proof that human resource management can indeed contribute to 'the bottom line', affecting an organization's costs and profitability, has fundamental implications for the identity, status and power of human resource practitioners. Practitioners and their professional institutes, therefore, have paid considerable interest to that research and to its findings.

As the previous section suggests, there are sound theoretical reasons why human resource management may not work as well in practice as it does in textbooks. However, several research findings during the 1990s suggested that the contribution of a human resource management approach to organizational effectiveness was positive and measurable. Here we will consider the work of Mark Huselid and of the University of Sheffield Group (Britain).

Mark Huselid

The contribution of Huselid (Rutgers University, New Jersey) to this debate has been to establish a quantifiable link between human resource management practices and an organization's financial performance. Huselid used a survey questionnaire to measure the extent to which the organizations studied used 'high-performance work practices' and the extent to which these were aligned with competitive strategy. The main hypothesis for the study was that high-performance work practices aligned with strategy would reduce labour turnover, increase productivity and increase financial performance.

Huselid's questionnaire, to which almost 3,500 replies were received, was sent to senior human resource professionals in a sample of American organizations with more than a hundred employees, from different sectors. A measure of the use of high-performance work practices was developed based on thirteen items in two categories, 'employee skills and organization structures', and 'employee motivation'. Huselid also obtained information on company performance from published accounts.

The main findings from this research were:

- Organizations using high-performance work practices had higher levels of productivity and corporate financial performance.

- Organizations using high-performance practices in the employee skills and organization structure category had lower employee turnover.

- A significant proportion of the impact of high-performance practices on financial performance is due to lower labour turnover or higher productivity, or both.

- High-performance practices contribute US$18,500 per employee in shareholder value, and almost $4,000 per employee in additional profits (1995 prices).

Investment in human resource management practice can thus bring a demonstrable financial return in the form of reduced employee turnover, improved productivity and profitability. What of the argument that such practices are only appropriate in some contexts? Huselid points to the substantial impact of high-performance practices independent of the internal and external contexts. The findings support the argument that high-performance work practices improve financial performance regardless of the organization's strategy.

At least five criticisms can be levelled at this work:

1. A survey provides only a snapshot in time, making it difficult to establish causality, and it lacks longitudinal data of the kind suggested, for example, by the Warwick model.

2. There are technical problems in subjecting straightforward survey questionnaire data to sophisticated (parametric, multivariate) statistical analysis.

3. The findings are based on commercial American firms, which may be different in their operations from companies in Europe, and public sector organizations in particular.

High-performance work practices

Mark Huselid designed a questionnaire which gave each organization he studied a score measuring the use of thirteen high-performance work practices in two categories.

Employee skills and organizational structures were measured on the following factors:

1. formal information-sharing programmes
2. formal job analysis
3. internal appointments for promoted posts
4. workforce attitude surveys
5. quality of work life programmes, quality circles and participative teams
6. company incentive and profit-sharing plans or gain-sharing plans
7. training hours per typical employee
8. formal grievance procedures and/or complaint resolution systems
9. employment testing for new recruits

Employee motivation was measured on the following factors:

10. performance appraisals used to determine financial reward
11. formal performance appraisals
12. promotion based on merit or performance rating, not seniority
13. the number of qualified applicants for the five most often recruited posts

These are the human resource policies which encourage the 'desired employee behaviours' identified in the New York model of HRM shown in table 20.8. They are also similar to the features of 'new design plants' identified by Edward Lawler (1986) [**link**, chapter 8, motivation].

Based on Mark Huselid, 'The impact of human resource management practices on turnover, productivity, and corporate financial performance', *Academy of Management Journal*, 1995, vol.38, no.3, pp.635–72.

The impact of people management policies

Jeffrey Pfeffer argues that human resource practices can raise an organization's stock market value by US$20,000 to $40,000 per employee. He claims that 'profits through people' are produced by seven people management policies:

1. emphasis on job security;

2. recruiting the right people in the first place;

3. decentralization and self-managed teamworking;

4. high wages linked to organizational performance;

5. high investment in employee training;

6. reducing status differentials;

7. sharing information across the organization.

Pfeffer's evidence, however, is anecdotal and fragmented.

Based on Jeffrey Pfeffer, *The Human Equation*, Harvard Business School Press, Boston, 1998.

4. Organizational performance is defined in terms of financial indicators, and individual and social well-being do not figure as relevant.

5. The definition of high-performance work practices omits other approaches and techniques, and does not permit the assessment of single methods or clusters of methods.

Nevertheless, Huselid's findings present a significant challenge to those who would dismiss human resource management as commercially irrelevant, and to those who seek to develop a more detailed understanding of the links between practice and organizational effectiveness.

The Sheffield Group

Malcolm Patterson, Michael West, Rebecca Lawthorn and Stephen Nickell (1997) at the Institute of Work Psychology at the University of Sheffield also explored the contribution of human resource management to organizational effectiveness, in a study commissioned by the Institute of Personnel and Development. The findings again reveal a measurable impact of human resource management on productivity and profitability. In a departure from Huselid's approach, this study also sought to establish the contribution to performance of other management strategies and tactics, none of which had the same positive impact on business performance as human resource management.

The findings are the result of a ten-year longitudinal study of management practice in over one hundred manufacturing organizations in Britain. Senior managers were interviewed every two years, and half the companies took part in a survey of employee attitudes to various aspects of company functioning, including job satisfaction and organizational commitment. Company performance data were collected from company and management accounts. This study also used thirteen 'human resource management variables', broadly comparable with those used by Huselid to define 'high-performance practices'. The adoption of these high-performance practices varied considerably, as did management attitudes, across this sample.

The findings revealed that two 'clusters' of 'high-performance' human resource management practices in particular are significantly related to organizational productivity and profitability. The labels are different, but these clusters are broadly similar to the two main factors in Huselid's list of thirteen high-performance practices:

1. *Skills development*: the acquisition and development of employee skills, through selection, induction, training and the use of performance appraisal systems.

2. *Job design*: the design of jobs, including skill flexibility, job responsibility, variety and the use of teams.

Some of the detailed findings include:

- High overall job satisfaction and organizational commitment are positively linked to high company profitability (but satisfaction is not clearly related to performance at an individual level).

- An organization culture that demonstrates concern for employee welfare is also linked to high company profitability.

- Skills development and job design practices are positively linked to increased productivity and profitability.

- Human resource management practice is a good predictor of performance: quality emphasis, corporate strategy, technological sophistication and investment in research and development contribute weakly to productivity and profitability.

Treat employees well, therefore, and profits will increase. This study is open to criticisms similar to those aimed at Huselid. In particular, the sample included only small to medium-sized manufacturing organizations (with up to 1,000 employees) and findings do not necessarily, therefore, apply to larger or to public sector organizations. However, the longitudinal data overcome the 'snap shot' problem with single surveys, and non-financial indicators (satisfaction, commitment and management attitudes) are considered.

Despite the criticisms of human resource management, the use of the label, its definition, its substance, and its treatment of particular issues, the Huselid and Sheffield studies provide positive, quantifiable evidence for its impact and value that is difficult to ignore. (Richardson and Thompson (1999) offer a critical overview of this and similar research.) Human resource management practitioners at last have hard data with which to justify their activity when confronted by the scepticism of colleagues in other functions.

Stop and criticize

The human resource management perspective based on high-performance work practices can be seen in two ways:

- These are enlightened management methods which empower, develop and emancipate employees leading to individual and organizational gains.

- These are sophisticated management controls which limit individual freedom by encouraging and rewarding 'good behaviour' to create a compliant workforce.

What are the arguments for and against these contrasting perspectives?

Is it new?

Some commentators argue that human resource management is facing a crisis of identity and that a 'new agenda' is called for (Sparrow, 1998; Ulrich, 1997; 1998). Dave Ulrich (1998) argues that the 'new' role for human resource management has four elements:

1. The function should work in partnership with line managers in strategy execution.

2. The function should deliver expertise in work organization to reduce costs and improve quality.

3. The function should be 'a champion for employees', representing concerns to management and working to increase employees' contribution.

4. The function should be 'an agent of continuous transformation', developing the organization's capacity for change.

The problem is that personnel managers have always worked with line managers, although the recent emphasis has certainly moved to strategy. Job design and work organization have been central facets of the personnel role, even from an administrative point of view (job classifications, job grading, more recently job enrichment and teamworking). The 'pioneer' welfare workers of the nineteenth century saw their role in part as being the 'employee voice'. The Institute of Personnel Management recognized in 1963 the profession's role in organizational change. Ulrich's radical 'new' agenda has very deep roots.

John Storey (1992) developed a classification of human resource management roles based on two considerations. Does the function perform a strategic or a tactical role? Is the function consultative or interventionist? The resulting four main roles are illustrated in figure 20.6.

Stop and criticize	Consider a personnel or human resource department or function with which you are familiar. Locate their current role on figure 20.6. Is that role appropriate and effective given the wider organizational context and circumstances? Should this function be adopting a different role, and why?

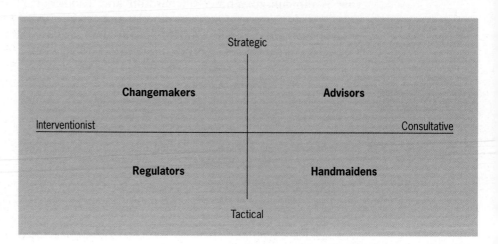

Figure 20.6: Four roles for human resource management

The first 'pioneer' welfare workers were handmaidens. Personnel management during and after the Second World War had a regulatory role. The aspiration of human resource managers combines strategic advisory and changemaking roles. In this respect, human resource management has indeed acquired a new emphasis and new responsibilities.

However, human resource management has been widely described as a new 'paradigm'—a new philosophy—of people management. How realistic is this claim? The evidence suggests that the adoption of high-performance work practices is not widespread (Storey, 1992; Bach and Sisson, 2000). Table 20.12 summarizes the findings of a major survey of workplaces in Britain in 1998. Only 2 per cent of workplaces reported using ten or more high-performance practices. However, the survey also found that organizations reporting the use of new practices were more likely to report high productivity (Cully *et al.* 1998, p.25).

In other words, these textbook 'best practices' are not as commonplace in practice as they are in textbooks. Why not? David Guest (1989) identifies five conditions for success:

1. There must be top management backing for human resource values.

2. There must be a shared management view that human resources are a key component of corporate strategy.

3. There must be no technological or production constraints to job redesign.

4. Employees must not have an instrumental approach to work, and the trade unions must not be adversarial.

5. Appropriate policies must be effectively advocated and implemented by human resource management specialists.

These preconditions are formidable and perhaps explain the relatively poor uptake.

There is further cause for concern, raised when claims for a 'new paradigm' are set against 'old' research, theory and organizational behaviour prescriptions. Here we will briefly consider the four sets of practices which are used to define the content of human resource management in the Harvard and Warwick models of HRM: employee influence, human resource flow, reward systems and work systems (see table 20.5).

Employee influence

Joint consultation gained widespread popularity in the 1940s. Participative management has its roots in research carried out during the 1940s. Employee communication and 'considerate' leadership were features of the human relations school and theories of leadership behaviour in the 1950s. Problem-solving groups became popular during the 1960s and 1970s through the development of 'quality circles' by Japanese organizations. Teamworking is a technique based on the work of socio-technical systems theorists in the 1960s.

Human resource flow

Managing the size of the workforce by using part-time and temporary employment contracts is a long-established tradition. In the nineteenth century, it was common practice in shipbuilding (on the River Clyde in Scotland, for example) for shipyard workers to be employed intensively while a ship was being built, for them to be laid off on the day the ship was launched, and to be hired again when another order was secured. 'Flexitime' as a formal management practice dates from the 1970s.

Table 20.12: Percentages of workplaces using high-performance practices

Appraisal and reward (non-managerial employees)	
performance appraisal	56
performance-related pay	11
share ownership	15
profit sharing	30
Involvement and participation	
joint consultative committee	28
regular meetings of workforce	37
problem-solving groups, such as quality circles	42
staff attitude surveys	45
team briefing	61
work teams	65
Training and development	
at least five days training per employee a year	12
supervisors trained in employee relations skills	27
Status and security	
no compulsory redundancy policy and guaranteed job security	14
single status between managerial and non-managerial employees	41
selection based partly on attitude tests	22

Reward systems

Frederick Taylor's scientific management, from the early twentieth century, was based on an individual pay for performance system; follow management instructions and meet and exceed targets and you got paid a high rate with bonus. The concept of tailoring rewards to individual needs and performance is an aspect of expectancy theory of motivation, developed during the 1960s. Profit- and gain-sharing schemes also date from the 1960s.

Work systems

The role of goal setting in improving performance, and in particular the concept of 'stretch goals', is another well-known motivational technique from the 1960s and 1970s. Interest in the personality traits of charismatic, inspirational leaders dates back to the turn of the century, and attracted renewed interest in the 1990s in the form of 'transformational leaders' and 'superleaders'. Alvin Toffler and Warren Bennis, among others, have argued since the late 1960s that tall, hierarchical, bureaucratic structures are ineffective in dealing with environmental change and that flat, flexible decentralized structures perform better. As already noted, the use of autonomous, self-managing teams is a work design technique which became popular and has been in use since the 1960s.

Personnel management has thus laid claim to a new title, human resource management, to the advocacy of 'best practice' in the form of 'high-performance work practices', and to a widened agenda that involves contributions to organization change and strategy. The label may be 'new'. The strategic role, broadened contribution, and increased credibility, status and influence of the profession may be 'new'. The practical, prescriptive dimension of the 'new' human resource management paradigm, however, repackages what organizational behaviour research has been advocating for most of the twentieth century.

Recap

1. *Explain why most medium-sized and large organizations have specialized personnel or human resource management functions.*

   - Increased organizational size and complexity, the growth in employment legislation, and the contributions of skilled, motivated and committed people to organizational effectiveness make this an area of specialist knowledge and expertise.
   - Wartime production pressures exposed general management weaknesses and heightened concern for employee welfare, strengthening the specialist role of the function.

2. *Understand the distinction between personnel management and human resource management.*

   - Personnel management is traditionally seen as a reactive background function, concerned with the administration of the employment cycle (hiring, training, paying, firing).
   - Human resource management is more concerned with the proactive design and implementation of integrated employment policies aligned to organizational strategy.

3. *Explain the distinctions between different models of human resource management.*

   - The Michigan model argues that the elements in the human resource cycle must be integrated and matched to organization strategy.
   - The Harvard model argues that human resource policies are shaped by stakeholders, and that effective policies lead to organizational, individual and social gains.
   - The New York model argues that there is a range of human resource policy choices which are contingent on the organization's competitive strategy.
   - The Warwick model argues that human resource policies are shaped over extended periods of time through a dynamic process influenced by a range of contextual factors.

4. *Explain the strategic contribution which the human resource function potentially makes to organizational effectiveness.*

   - High-performance work practices demonstrably increase organizational profitability by decreasing employee turnover and improving productivity.
   - Two 'clusters' of high-performance practices are significant, concerning the way in which skills are developed and the way in which jobs are designed.

5. *Identify the main criticisms levelled against human resource management, as a concept and as a management function.*

   - The definition of the concept is ambiguous, practitioners often suffer from a lack of commercial credibility, the 'new' high-performance work practices reflect well-known organizational behaviour thinking, and human resource 'best practice' is not in widespread use.

Revision

1. Why do most medium-sized and large organizations have specialist personnel or human resource management departments?

2. What factors contributed to the development of the personnel or human resource function as a distinct management profession during the twentieth century?

3. What factors in the second half of the twentieth century strengthened the argument that 'people are assets not costs' in an organizational context?

4. What is the distinction between personnel and human resource management? Why is this distinction important?

5. Many commentators argue that it is crucial to align human resource policies with the organization's strategy. Explain the strengths and difficulties of this argument, and show how it works in practice using one of the models of human resource management which take this approach.

Springboard

Bach, S. and Sisson, K. (eds), 2000, *Personnel Management: A Comprehensive Guide to Theory and Practice*, Blackwell Business, Oxford (third edition).

Authoritative overview with an academic emphasis, covering the context of personnel management, planning and resourcing, employee development, pay and performance, and work relations. Does not use 'human resource management' in the title.

Beardwell, I. and Holden, L. (eds), 1997, *Human Resource Management: A Contemporary Perspective*, Pitman Publishing, London (second edition).

A comprehensive introductory text which covers issues, trends and debates. Sections on the HRM context, resourcing, training and development, employee relations (contracts, rewards, involvement) and international human resource management. See in particular Len Holden's chapter on European issues and the Social Charter.

Legge, K., 1995, *Human Resource Management: Rhetorics and Realities*, Macmillan Business, Houndmills, Basingstoke.

A critical survey of contemporary debates from an author whose contributions in this field are seminal and always interesting. Challenging and clearly written.

Richardson, R. and Thompson, M., 1999, *The Impact of People Management Practices on Business Performance: A Literature Review*, Institute of Personnel and Development, London.

Clear, thorough and critical review of research into the contribution of high-performance work practices to organizational effectiveness. Also short at 78 pages. Companion publication to research findings in Patterson *et al.*, 1997.

Schuler, R.S. and Jackson, S.E. (eds), 1999, *Strategic Human Resource Management*, Blackwell Business, Oxford.

An excellent reference collection of 24 previously published papers exploring the human resource management debate of the 1990s. Wide-ranging in content, this is unusual in combining work from European and North American commentators.

Sparrow, P. and Hiltrop, J.-M., 1994, *European Human Resource Management in Transition*, Prentice Hall, Hemel Hempstead.

Explores different traditions across Europe based on national contexts and industrial relations systems. A good introduction to international strategic human resource management (ISHRM), with references to country-specific and comparative studies.

Storey, J. (ed.), 1995, *Human Resource Management: A Critical Text*, Routledge, London.

Definitive and authoritative collection of chapters on strategic issues, 'key practice areas' and international human resource management. Difficult but essential reading.

Torrington, D. and Hall, L., 1998, *Human Resource Management*, Prentice Hall, London (fourth edition).

Competition for Beardwell and Holden, more practitioner-oriented, covering contemporary debates and also exploring personnel techniques in some detail.

Home viewing

The Enforcer (1976, director James Fargo). Another 'Dirty Harry' movie in which the uncompromising San Francisco cop is played by Clint Eastwood. For his apparently indiscriminate slaughter of criminals (he is supposed to arrest some of them) Harry is disciplined by being transferred to the personnel department, where he is involved in the selection process for his next partner, who turns out to be—shock, horror—a woman, Kate Moore (played by Tyne Daly). Sadly, Kate doesn't survive the movie. In the scenes concerning Harry's transfer, what image of personnel work is being reinforced? What explicit and implicit criticisms of personnel management work are being exposed?

OB in literature

Floyd Kemske, *Human Resources: A Business Novel*, Nicholas Brealey Publishing, London, 1996.

A caricature of exploitative management, based on the methods of Pierce, the 'turn-around manager' hired to change the fortunes of Biomethods Inc., a struggling biotechnology company. Pierce, however, is a vampire; spot the symbolism. The company's human resource manager, Norman, survives Pierce's purge of top management because he has a skill that Pierce lacks—he 'affiliates'. Despite his title, Norman is a traditional administrator whose personnel procedures do not seem to fit with the faster and more flexible re-engineered style preferred by Pierce. Whose management methods are more effective?

Chapter exercises

1: Hard or soft?

Objectives

1. To identify individual differences in perceptions of the role of personnel or human resource management.

2. To examine the links between the concepts of 'hard' and 'soft' HRM and other theories of organizational behaviour.

Briefing

John Storey (1992) argues that the term 'human resource management' is used in a number of contradictory ways. What is your perception of the role of the function? Read each of the following ten statements, rating your agreement with them on the five-point scale on the right.

		strongly disagree	agree	neutral	disagree	strongly agree
1	human resource management must ensure that employees are treated like any other asset	☐	☐	☐	☐	☐
2	human resource management is about ensuring that all employees share the same goals	☐	☐	☐	☐	☐
3	one key human resource management job is to control headcount and payroll	☐	☐	☐	☐	☐
4	human resource management's task is to design policies that encourage commitment	☐	☐	☐	☐	☐
5	deskilling and task fragmentation are necessary steps to control labour costs	☐	☐	☐	☐	☐
6	employees should be encouraged to develop to their full potential	☐	☐	☐	☐	☐
7	human resource management must design work practices that fully exploit employees' potential	☐	☐	☐	☐	☐
8	the key aspect of human resource management concerns developing employee resourcefulness	☐	☐	☐	☐	☐
9	employees should be given performance targets and be expected to meet them	☐	☐	☐	☐	☐
10	human resource policies should be designed to encourage high individual performance	☐	☐	☐	☐	☐

Scoring

Use this scoring key:	Your 'hard' score:	Your 'soft' score:
strongly disagree = 1 disagree = 2 neutral = 3 agree = 4 strongly agree = 5	Add your scores for the odd-numbered items: Hard score: _____	Add your scores for the even-numbered items: Soft score: _____

2: To dismiss or not to dismiss

Objectives

1. To examine the circumstances in which it is legitimate to dismiss employees for misconduct of some kind, and when it is not legitimate to act in this way.

2. To consider the nature of human resource management expertise.

Briefing

As a professional human resource manager, you are frequently asked for advice on a number of matters. One of the most sensitive and difficult issues concerns employee misconduct, which can potentially lead to the dismissal of those concerned.

The following five cases of apparent employee misconduct are based on real examples. Consider, for each case, the following questions:

- As a human resource manager who believes in 'soft' HRM, what action would you recommend?

- As a human resource manager who believes in 'hard' HRM, what action would you recommend?

- In both cases, on what grounds (commercial, managerial, humanitarian, other) would you justify your decision?

1. You are the human resource manager for a fast food chain. One of your employees tells you that the manager of one of your outlets is often seen eating a rival brand of fried chicken.

2. You are the human resource manager for a major airline. You discover that one of your stewardesses is a member of a stripping and spanking service called Hot Sex.

3. You are the human resource manager for a small printing firm. You discover that the managing director's (male) chauffeur has a habit of flashing (and we don't mean his headlights) at motorists, and was found recently standing by the M40 wearing a bra, stockings and suspenders.

4. You are the human resource manager for a publishing company. You read in the local press that one of your advertising executives has been found guilty of using recreational drugs at home.

5. You are the human resource manager for a multinational toy company. You read in one of the 'sensationalist' Sunday papers that your chief executive has been having sex seven times a night with a woman from an escort service.

This exercise is based on Paul Simpson, 'Blurred boundaries', *Personnel Today*, 16 November 1999, p.31.

Part 6 Organization management

A field map of the organizational behaviour terrain

PESTLE: The **P**olitical, **E**conomic, **S**ocial, **T**echnological, **L**egal and **E**cological context

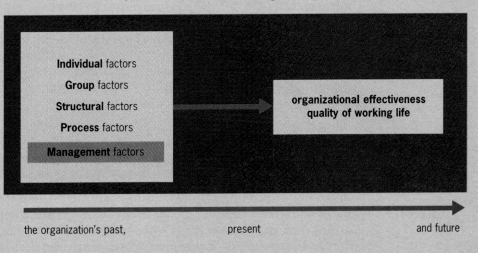

the organization's past,   present   and future

Introduction

Part 6, Organization management, explores the following four topics:

- Leadership, in chapter 21
- Decision making, in chapter 22
- Conflict, in chapter 23
- Power and politics, in chapter 24

Each of the four topics considered in this section has an enormous impact on how employees are managed within an organization, how they experience their work environment, and how successful their organization is in achieving the goals. All of them affect the process of 'managing' and involve both managers and non-managers. Thus, the most junior of employees may be called upon to exercise their leadership skills, become involved in group decision making and attempt to resolve a conflict between colleagues while engaging in political behaviour in order to increase their power.

Chapter 21 on leadership begins with a historical introduction to the topic which identifies the common themes in the different leadership theories, some of which were first considered within the context of the group [**link**, chapter 10]. It highlights contemporary debates about the nature of leadership, setting these in their wider context. Chapter 22 on decision making considers different models of decision making, different types of decision, different decision makers and different problems in decision making. It challenges the notion that most decisions are made logically for the benefit of the organization by managers who possess the necessary information and authority. Chapter 23 on conflict considers the topic from the point of view of contrasting perspectives on conflict and stresses how the way you perceive a situation influences what actions you take [**link**, chapter 7]. It examines how the way a company is organized itself engenders conflicts which, in turn, have to be managed through the incorporation of conflict resolution devices. Finally, Chapter 24 addresses the highly abstract but possibly the most crucial of all the concepts used to explain the behaviour of people in organizations—that of power and politics. The political perspective provides an alternative to the rational standpoint predominantly found in managerially oriented textbooks. It challenges readers to go back over earlier chapter topics to reassess their contents from this alternative viewpoint.

Our opening case study concerns a large British drinks company's acquisition of a small Italian firm and describes some of the problems that it experienced in managing its new purchase. Following a second, similar acquisition, you are engaged as a consultant to help its senior manager to avoid similar problems recurring. What advice would you give? It's your call.

YOUR CALL (6): AVOIDING FUTURE UPS AND DOWNS

In 1999, the British firm United Potable Spirits (UPS), one of 'the big three' international drinks companies, bought Minaro, an Italian company specializing in quality food and wines. Minaro, with strong customer relationships, was to be the European distributor for premium Scotch malt whiskies. Staff at Minaro were apprehensive as their small company became part of a global group, but they looked forward to exploiting UPS market research capabilities, to higher sales, and to learning about 'UPwardS and Onwards', a UPS employee motivation initiative. The bureaucracy at Minaro would be streamlined, with computerized information systems, a new Italian distribution centre, performance-related pay and more staff development opportunities. These were to be exciting, energizing, inspiring times.

UPS replaced Minaro managers with British expatriates, who were, on average, ten years younger and who did not speak Italian. In UPS, no excuse justified a failure to meet financial targets. Loyal and respected Minaro managers were asked to leave when they exceeded budgets and failed to meet sales targets. Sales managers who insisted on keeping close links with customers were replaced by MBA graduates with American and Australian experience. Customer communications and trust collapsed, along with sales. UPS sent a task force to Italy to solve the problems. A new matrix organization was established, and Minaro's managers were given more discretion over decision making. UPS management then decided to focus on a narrower product range, switching premium brand distribution to a company in Munich, leaving Minaro with only 'standard' products to distribute. Minaro brand managers and salespeople started to leave.

UPS introduced new job and performance evaluation systems, but Italian managers had no experience with objective setting, or with performance evaluations linked to pay. The job evaluations created inequities between new and existing staff. One month, Italian sales staff got salaries matching those of Minaro executives. UPS refused to recognize Italian trade union negotiation procedures and introduced a British salary planning method that led to strikes at two Italian distribution depots. The new headquarters staff did not understand European cultural norms and local feelings. They concentrated instead on their strategy of developing 'core' premium brands while dropping smaller brands despite country preferences. Pay-offs were cheaper than tackling cultural sensitivities. Headquarters staff also had little time for the mutually beneficial 'private deals' between salespeople and their customers, which were normal business practice in parts of Europe, but not in Britain.

The long-term UPS objectives for marketing and sales were not clearly explained. It was difficult for staff to accept that a 'more strategic' job with fewer subordinates was promotion. Italian managers with poor English saw their careers being damaged, and Minaro lost half of its managers in two years. The managing director in Italy, a British expatriate, spoke passionately about 'tough times', cut resources and tightened controls. Italian payroll administration is particularly complex. Administrative staff cuts created payroll errors.

A rumour spread that UPS intended to transfer all European distribution to Munich. More people resigned, including many top performers. The Italians were hurt by what they saw as ethnocentric and inconsistent British management. Changes in policy and new initiatives seemed to be related less to business needs and more to the personal careers of the young managers posted to the Italian operation from Britain. When the managing director was replaced by another British executive who could not speak Italian, nobody in Italy knew whether to feel reassured or uneasy. Sales continued to fall and more people left.

In 2000, UPS acquired another Italian company, Tuscallini, and Peter Allen was appointed as managing director. He has heard about the Minaro problems and wants to avoid them. As an external consultant, what advice would you give to Peter to prevent similar problems arising in his Tuscallini subsidiary? It's your call.

Chapter 21 Leadership

Key concepts

leadership	great man theory
power	reward power
coercive power	referent power
legitimate power	expert power
information power	affiliation power
group power	consideration
initiating structure	contingency theory of leadership
structured task	unstructured task
situational leadership	new leader
superleader	transactional leader
transformational leader	

Learning objectives

When you have read this chapter, you should be able to define those key concepts in your own words, and you should also be able to:

1. Explain the apparent difference between the concepts of leadership and management.

2. Understand why there is little relationship between personality traits and effective leadership.

3. Understand the bases of a leader's power in organizations and the role of followers in creating and supporting leaders.

4. Understand why effective leaders either adapt their style to fit the organizational and cultural context in which they operate or find contexts which fit their personal style.

5. Explain contemporary trends in this field concerning new leadership, on the one hand, and the dispersal of the leadership function, on the other.

Why study leadership?

Leadership appears to be a critical determinant of organizational effectiveness, whether we are discussing an army, an orchestra, a hockey team, a street gang, a political party, a group of mountaineers or a multinational corporation. It is not surprising to find, therefore, that leadership has been the subject of intense academic investigation and journalistic commentary throughout the twentieth century—but not the nineteenth; Frank Heller (1997, p.340) notes that in 1896, the

Leadership is the process of influencing the activities of an organized group in its efforts toward goal setting and goal achievement (Stogdill, 1950, p.3).

United States Library of Congress had not one book on the subject of leadership. The global literature on the subject is now vast and diverse.

Why, then, does the nature of leadership remain controversial? Part of the answer to this question lies with the observation that leadership is a subject with many paradoxes. We often hear the complaint that 'there are not enough leaders'. However, the organizational hierarchy and formal authority that appear to underpin leadership positions are increasingly challenged. We tend to equate leadership with positions of power, influence and status. However, acts of leadership can be observed across the organization structure. Leaders have job titles, responsibilities and working conditions which symbolize their power and influence. However, flat structures, team-based working, the growth of knowledge work, and 'virtual' and 'networked' organizational forms apparently weaken traditional **leadership** positions based on hierarchy and organizational symbolism.

Stop and criticize

Consider those who you would call leaders, including business and political figures, alive now or in recent decades.

What physical characteristics, skills and abilities, and personality traits do they have in common?

Which of these leaders, in your judgement, have had a *positive* impact on society and its organizations, and which have had a *negative* impact?

How can the *one label*, 'leader', apply to the *different* figures on your list?

Stogdill's definition has three key components. First, it defines leadership as an interpersonal process in which one individual seeks to shape and direct the behaviour of others. Second, it sets leadership in a social context, in which the members of the group to be influenced are subordinates or 'followers'. Third, it establishes a criterion for effective leadership in goal achievement, which is one practical objective of leadership theory and research. Most definitions share these processual, contextual and evaluative components.

Your list of 'familiar leaders' might include:

Megawati Sukarnoputri	Reverend Jim Jones	Anita Roddick
Richard Branson	Benazir Bhutto	Slobodan Milosovic
Mother Teresa	Robert Maxwell	Margaret Thatcher
Saddam Hussein	Aung San Suu Kyi	Bill Gates

As Frank Heller (1997) pointedly asks, how can the single term 'leadership' be applied to such a diverse set of personalities, behaviours and practical impacts on society? This chapter explores five approaches to the study of leadership:

1. *Trait spotting* attempts to identify the *personality traits* and other related attributes of the effective leader in order to facilitate the *selection* of leaders.

2. *Style counselling* attempts to characterize different leadership *behaviour patterns* to identify effective and ineffective leadership styles, in order to improve the *training and development* of leaders.

3. *Context fitting* *contingency theories* which argue that the effectiveness of particular leadership behaviours is dependent on the organizational and cultural setting, which can also facilitate leadership *awareness and training*.

4. *New leadership*   prescriptive approaches which identify 'new leaders', 'superleaders' and 'transformational leaders' as heroic and *inspirational visionaries* who give purpose and direction to others, with an emphasis on senior executives and politicians whose motivational role is said to be central to *organization strategy and effectiveness*.

5. *Dispersing the role*   a recent perspective which notes that leadership behaviour is not confined to those with formal leadership roles but can be observed *across the organization hierarchy*, and thus one aspect of the 'new superleadership' role is to *develop self-leadership skills in others*.

Alan Bryman (1996) notes that these perspectives have developed chronologically. Trait spotting was popular from the turn of the twentieth century until the 1940s, when inconsistent research findings led to disillusionment. Style counselling was then popular until the late 1960s but appeared oversimplified in the face of the contingency theories which dominated thinking until the early 1980s, at which point the 'new leadership' movement developed.

Towards the close of the century, recognition of the dispersed nature of leadership behaviour has attracted increasing theoretical and research attention. However, it would be incorrect to regard each shift in emphasis across these perspectives as having eliminated earlier accounts. On the contrary, much commentary about 'leadership in the twenty-first century' returns to trait spotting. Contemporary organization development methods [**link**, chapter 17, organization development] rely on leadership style-counselling theories and techniques. Contingency theories, arguing that the effective leadership style depends on the context, still offer useful prescriptive accounts of leadership behaviour for management development programmes. Much of the 'historical' material in this chapter, therefore, is 'current'.

Leadership versus management

We first have to deal with one crucial question: what is the difference between leadership and management? Some commentators argue that these terms are synonymous, as leadership is simply one facet of the management role. Other commentators argue that this distinction is significant. Leaders and managers play different roles and make different contributions: leaders have followers, managers have subordinates.

Those who make a clear distinction portray the leader as someone who develops visions and drives *new initiatives*, and portray the manager as someone who monitors progress towards objectives to achieve *order and reliability*. The leader is prophet, catalyst and mover-shaker, focused on strategy. The manager is operator, technician and problem solver, concerned 'with the here-and-now of goal attainment' (Bryman, 1986, p.6). The key distinguishing feature here is *orientation to change* (Zaleznik, 1977). As Warren Bennis and Burt Nanus (1985, p.21) observe, managers do things right, while leaders do the right thing.

John Kotter (1990) contrasts the functions of leaders and managers in the manner summarized in table 21.1. The leader establishes vision and direction, influences others to sign up to that vision, motivates and inspires them to overcome obstacles, and produces positive and sometimes radical change [**link**, chapter 19, organization culture]. The manager establishes plans and budgets, designs

Manager as leader as manager

Note how in this passage from his classic work on management, the American guru Peter Drucker equates management with leadership, defining one in terms of the other. The role of the *manager*, he argues, is to provide *leadership*:

The manager is the dynamic, life-giving element in every business. Without his [*sic*] leadership 'the resources of production' remain resources and never become production. In a competitive economy, above all the quality and performance of the managers determine the success of a business, indeed they determine its survival. For the quality and performance of its managers is the only effective advantage an enterprise in a competitive economy can have.

From Peter F. Drucker, *The Practice of Management*, Heinemann, London, 1955, p.13.

Peter F. Drucker
(b. 1909)

and staffs the organization structure, monitors and controls performance, and produces order, consistency and predictability.

Joseph Rost (1991) argues that this is a caricature of leadership and management in 'good guys, bad guys' terms (noting carefully that 'guys' is an American slang expression referring to both women and men). Kotter's terminology elevates leadership and denigrates management. Rost argues that management is a key ingredient of organizational effectiveness. If you really want to find out just how much people value the manager as 'routine administrator', Rost suggests the following strategies:

- deliver the payroll cheques late;

- cut off the supplies and services which people need to do their jobs;

- run the buses, trains and planes late and switch off traffic lights;

- deliver unworkable products to customers;

- base promotions and salary increases on arbitrary criteria.

Table 21.1: Leadership versus management

	Leadership functions	Management functions
Creating an agenda	Establishes direction: vision of the future, develops strategies for change to achieve goals	Plans and budgets: decides actions and timetables, allocates resources
Developing people	Aligning people: communicates vision and strategy, influences creation of teams which accept validity of goals	Organizing and staffing: decides structure and allocates staff, develops policies, procedures and monitoring
Execution	Motivating and inspiring: energizes people to overcome obstacles, satisfies human needs	Controlling, problem solving: monitors results against plan and takes corrective action
Outcomes	Produces positive and sometimes dramatic change	Produces order, consistency and predictability

Based on John P. Kotter, *A Force for Change: How Leadership Differs from Management*, Free Press, New York, 1990.

Henry Mintzberg
(b. 1939)

He concludes that 'Down with management and up with leadership is a bad idea'.

Many commentators ignore Rost's advice. Setting visions and strategies is much more fun than planning and budgeting. What is the value of order, predictability and consistency in today's turbulent, hostile organizational context in which innovation is at a premium?

If they are not leaders, what do managers do? From his observation of how managers spend their time, Henry Mintzberg (1977) distinguished ten roles under three main headings:

interpersonal roles   leader, figurehead, liaison

informational roles   monitor, disseminator, spokesperson

decisional roles   entrepreneur, disturbance handler, resource allocator, negotiator

Mintzberg's research suggested that, in practice, the distinction between leadership and management is blurred. The roles overlap. Leadership is one dimension of a multifaceted management role. The effective manager requires at least some leadership qualities. The neat conceptual distinction between leader and manager does not translate neatly into practice.

Leading by inspiring

If there is a clear distinction between the process of managing and the process of leading, it is in the distinction between getting others to do and getting others to want to do. Managers, we believe, get other people to do, but leaders get other people to want to do. Leaders do this by first of all being credible. They establish this credibility by their actions—by challenging, inspiring, enabling, modelling, and encouraging.

From James M. Kouzes and Barry Z. Posner, *The Leadership Challenge: How to Get Extraordinary Things Done in Organizations*, Jossey-Bass Publishers, San Francisco, 1987, p.27.

"Who put a middle-management chair at my top executive's desk?"

Trait spotting: the search for personality markers

Great man theory is a historical perspective based on the premise that the fate of societies, and organizations, is in the hands of key, powerful, idiosyncratic (male) individuals who by force of personality reach positions of influence from which they can direct and dominate the lives of others.

Ralf M. Stogdill
(1904–78)

For the first four decades of the twentieth century, researchers assumed that they could identify the personality traits of leaders [**link**, chapter 5, personality]. With the personality markers established, it would then be possible to select individuals who possessed those traits and to promote them into leadership positions.

This search for the qualities of good leaders was influenced by **great man theory**, which claims that (predominantly male) leaders are born as such, and emerge to take power, regardless of the social, organizational or historical context. Research thus focused on identifying the traits of these special people. Ralf Stogdill, for example, reviewed hundreds of trait studies (1948; 1974, p.81) and compiled for illustrative purposes this typical list of qualities:

- strong drive for responsibility;

- focus on completing the task;

- vigour and persistence in pursuit of goals;

- venturesomeness and originality in problem solving;

- drive to exercise initiative in social settings;

- self-confidence;

- sense of personal identity;

- willingness to accept consequences of decisions and actions;

- readiness to absorb interpersonal stress;

- willingness to tolerate frustration and delay;

- ability to influence the behaviour of others;

- capacity to structure social systems to the purpose in hand.

A profile of the superior chief executive

A study carried out by *Fortune* magazine on leading American executives revealed eight qualities that characterize 'the champs':

1. *Integrity, maturity and energy*. This is the foundation on which everything else is built.
2. *Business acumen*. Understanding the business and a strong profit incentive.
3. *People acumen*. Leading teams, coaching people, cutting losses when necessary.
4. *Organizational acumen*. Engendering trust, sharing information, decisive and incisive.
5. *Curiosity, intellectual capacity, global mindset*. External focus, hungry for knowledge.
6. *Superior judgement*.
7. *An insatiable appetite for accomplishment and results*.
8. *Powerful motivation to grow and convert learning into practice*.

Based on Ram Charm and Geoffrey Colvin, 'Why CEOs fail', *Fortune*, vol.139, no.12, 21 June 1999, pp.69–78.

Rosemary Stewart (1963) cites a study in which American executives were asked to identify indispensable leadership qualities. They came up with the following fifteen traits:

judgement	initiative	integrity
foresight	energy	drive
human relations skill	decisiveness	dependability
emotional stability	fairness	ambition
dedication	objectivity	co-operation

It is difficult to challenge the list of qualities cited by either Stogdill or Stewart. Can we say that effective leaders should lack judgement, be low in energy, be undependable, lack drive, ambition, creativity and integrity, and have little foresight? What happens when we compare Stewart with Stogdill? Both identify 'drive' as a key trait. However, Stogdill lists venturesomeness, self-confidence, stress tolerance and system structuring as traits which Stewart omits. Stewart identifies foresight, fairness, integrity, fairness and co-operation, which are missing from Stogdill's list.

Trait spotting presents several difficulties. First, there are more 'attributes' here than personality traits. Second, these attributes are vague. Willingness to tolerate delay? Capacity to structure social systems? Human relations skill? Ambition? Third, many of the items on these lists describe skills and behaviour patterns which have to be observed, rather than personality traits that can be assessed by questionnaire or interview: persistence in pursuit of goals, ability to influence others. It is difficult to see how trait spotting can be used effectively in a leadership selection context, as originally intended.

A further problem lies with the observation that one list of 'good leadership' qualities is as good as another. Stogdill's review revealed some overlap between research findings, but it also revealed disagreement and inconsistency. This line of research has been unable to establish a consistent set of leadership traits or attributes. Leadership is about power and influence, the chemistry of which is difficult to analyse in terms of personality traits.

Leaders are men with special qualities

Discussion of leadership is so often overloaded with vague but emotive ideas that one is hard put to it to nail the concept down. To cut through the panoply of such quasi-moral and unexceptionable associations as 'patriotism', 'play up and play the game', the 'never-asking-your-men-to-do-something-you-wouldn't-do-yourself' formula, 'not giving in (or up)', the 'square-jaw-frank-eyes-steadfast-gaze' formula, and the 'if . . . you'll be a man' recipe, one comes to the simple truth that *leadership is no more than exercising such an influence upon others that they tend to act in concert towards achieving a goal which they might not have achieved so readily had they been left to their own devices.*

The ingredients which bring about this agreeable state of affairs are many and varied. At the most superficial level they are believed to include such factors as voice, stature and appearance, an impression of omniscience, trustworthiness, sincerity and bravery. At a deeper and rather more important level, leadership depends upon a proper understanding of the needs and opinions of those one hopes to lead, and the context in which the leadership occurs. It also depends on good timing. Hitler, who was neither omniscient, trustworthy nor sincere, whose stature was unremarkable and whose appearance verged on the repellent, understood these rules and exploited them to full advantage. The same may be said of many good comedians.

From Norman F. Dixon, *On The Psychology of Military Incompetence*, Pimlico, London, 1994, pp.214–15 (emphasis added).

Despite these problems, the search for the personality markers of leaders has continued (see Leigh and Walters, 1998; Kamp, 1999). Contemporary interest in *the new leader*, explored later in this chapter, has shifted the focus of attention back to trait spotting.

Trait spotting entrepreneurs

Most leadership research is based on studies of large (typically American) organizations. However, in Britain in the 1990s, 96 per cent of employers had fewer than 20 employees, and firms with less than 100 employees accounted for 50 per cent of all employment. The evidence suggests that small firms are growing in number, and that they create more jobs than their large (often 'downsizing') cousins (Murphy, 1996, pp.3–4).

A small business has a number of distinguishing features:

1. The owner-manager, the entrepreneur, has an overwhelming influence, more than any single manager in a large organization.

2. The small firm is unlikely to be able to influence its market, and in particular the prices which it can charge and the range of services and products which it can provide, which makes the business risky.

3. The small firm is likely to be heavily dependent on a small number of customers, which heightens the vulnerability of the business and the risk for the entrepreneur.

4. Small firms often have problems raising capital, and this constrains strategy and growth.

So what are the personality traits of a successful entrepreneur, a different kind of leader from that found in a larger organization? Summarizing the research, Burns and Jewhurst (1996, pp.48–9) identify five psychological characteristics:

High need for achievement: This can mean, for example, making your first million, producing a work of art, or employing your hundredth person.

Internal locus of control: Entrepreneurs believe that events, or their 'destiny', are within their personal control. People with an external locus of control believe in 'fate' and are less likely to risk starting their own business.

Risk taking: Entrepreneurs are 'measured risk takers', rarely pursuing business opportunities which have a low chance of success, but prepared to put themselves in risky positions which will contribute to enterprise growth.

Independence: Entrepreneurs want to be their own boss, control their own destiny, fulfil their potential, and have difficulty working for anybody else (they make 'difficult employees').

Innovation: Entrepreneurs are more likely to do things that are slightly different, or to combine known business elements in new ways, rather than to base their businesses on truly innovative ideas.

Based on Paul Burns and Jim Jewhurst (eds), *Small Business and Entrepreneurship*, Macmillan Business, Houndmills, Basingstoke, second edition, 1996, pp.48–9.

Power: what is it, and how can I get more?

Power is the capacity of individuals to overcome resistance on the part of others, to exert their will, and to produce results consistent with their interests and objectives.
Reward power is the ability of a leader to exert influence based on the belief of followers that the leader has access to valued rewards which will be dispensed in return for compliance with instructions.
Coercive power is the ability of a leader to exert influence based on the belief of followers that the leader can administer penalties or sanctions that are considered to be unwelcome.
Referent power is the ability of a leader to exert influence based on the belief of followers that the leader has desirable abilities and personality traits that can and should be copied, also referred to as *charisma*.
Legitimate power is the ability of a leader to exert influence based on the belief of followers that the leader has authority to issue orders which they in turn have an obligation to accept, also referred to as position power as this depends on the leader's formal organizational position and title.
Expert power is the ability of a leader to exert influence based on the belief of followers that the leader has superior knowledge relevant to the situation and the task in hand.

Leadership is about influencing the behaviour of others. One cannot be a leader without followers. One key attribute of followers is that they must be willing to obey. Leadership is a property of the relationship between leader and follower. We need to know why people are willing to let themselves be influenced by some individuals and not by others. We thus need to understand the nature of compliance.

Power is a useful concept with which to explain the social process of interpersonal influence. Power is a critical dimension of leadership, and the two terms are often used with the same or similar meanings: a leader is someone with power,

Table 21.2: The effective use of power

Power base	Explanation	Perceived as
Reward	remuneration, awards, compliments, symbolic gestures of praise	P+
Coercion	physical or psychological injury, symbolic gestures of disdain, demotion, unwanted transfer, withholding resources	P−
Authority	management right to control, obligation of others to obey, playing 'the boss' and abusing authority	P−
	exercise of leadership in times of crisis or need	P+
Referent	identification based on personal characteristics, sometimes on perception of charisma; or reciprocal identification based on friendship, association, sharing information, common interests, values	
	and preferences	P+
Expert	possession of specialized knowledge valued by others, used to help others, given freely when solicited	P+
	unsolicited expertise creates barriers; expertise offered condescendingly is coercive; withholding expertise in times of need	P−
Information	access to information that is not public knowledge, because of position or connections; can exist at all organizational levels; secretaries and personal assistants to executives often have information power, and can control information flows	P−
Affiliation	'borrowed' from an authority source—executive secretaries and assistants act as surrogates for their superiors	P+
	acting on their own self-interest; using negative affiliation power by applying accounting and personnel policies rigidly	P−
Group	collective problem solving, conflict resolution, creative brainstorming; group resolution greater than the individual contribution	P+
	a few individual dominating the proceedings, 'groupthink'	P−

Based on Robert C. Benfari, Harry E. Wilkinson and Charles D. Orth, 'The effective use of power', *Business Horizons*, vol. 20, May–June 1986, pp. 12–16

Information power is the ability of a leader to exert influence based on the belief of followers that the leader has access to information that is not public knowledge.

Affiliation power is the ability of a leader to exert influence based on the belief of followers that the leader has close association with other powerful figures on whose authority they are able to act.

Group power is the ability of a leader to exert influence based on the belief of followers that the leader has collective support from a team or group.

powerful individuals are leaders. We can thus define power in much the same way that we have defined leadership—as the ability of an individual to control or to influence others, to get someone else to do something that they would perhaps not otherwise do (Astley and Sachdeva, 1984; Pettigrew and McNulty, 1995).

John French and Bertram Raven (1958) identified five main bases of power.

Table 21.2 summarizes the more recent contribution of Robert Benfari, Harry Wilkinson and Charles Orth (1986), who identify eight power bases, adding information, affiliation and group power.

Several points follow from these definitions, beyond the obvious comment that the leader has access to a wide range of power bases.

First, as indicated in the right-hand column of table 21.2, the exercise of power is not always perceived in negative terms (P−). Rewards are usually welcomed (P+). The exercise of authority or 'strong leadership' in a crisis is usually welcomed. Referent power is by definition positively perceived. When expertise is given freely, to help those in difficulties, it is perceived in positive terms but can be perceived negatively when it is used in a condescending or intrusive manner. The exercise of affiliation and group power can also be either positive or negative depending on how the leader uses them.

Second, these power bases depend on the beliefs of followers. A leader may be able to control rewards and penalties, have superior knowledge and so on, but if followers do not believe that the leader has these attributes then they may not be compliant. Similarly, leaders may be able to manipulate followers into the belief that they possess power which they in fact do not have. This observation reinforces the point made earlier, that power is a property of the relationship between leader and followers, not a property of the leader.

Third, these power bases are interrelated. The exercise of one power base may affect a leader's ability to use another. The leader who resorts to coercive power may, for example, lose referent power. The leader may be able to use legitimate power to enhance both referent and expert power.

Finally, a leader can operate from multiple bases of power, using different bases in different contexts and at different times. Few leaders may be able to rely on a single power base.

Stop and criticize

Which power base, or which combination of power bases, would you expect to be most effective for an organization leader? What is the power base, or what are the power bases, of your organizational behaviour instructor(s)? What countervailing power bases do you have as student (individually and collectively)?

Prestigious job titles no longer automatically confer legitimacy on the bosses' orders. Some employees have sources of power which they can use to subvert a leader's position. The 'prerogatives' or 'rights' of management are increasingly challenged, and employment does not guarantee loyalty or commitment to the organizational goals. Many employees are suspicious of managers and their motives and react cautiously to what managers say and do.

The most effective leadership style seems to be one in which the manager shares power with subordinates, as this increases their satisfaction and effectiveness. Managers who give discretion to subordinates can increase their referent power over those subordinates. Allowing discretion and access to information are forms of symbolic reward. Many managers feel that they must lose the influence they give to subordinates. The opposite can happen.

This section has presented a perspective which is particularly relevant to leadership, but this is only one approach to understanding the concept of power. Other perspectives are explored in chapter 24 [**link**, chapter 24, power and politics].

Building your referent power

Robert Benfari, Harry Wilkinson and Charles Orth argue that *referent power* is both important and under-utilized in organizational settings, observing that:

> Conflict is an everyday occurrence. The key to conflict resolution is the ability to negotiate workable psychological contracts with colleagues who have no formal reporting obligations. The use of threats (coercive power) or appeals to upper authority can lead to long-term conflict. The party under siege can, at some time in the future, make use of affiliation power to retaliate. Acquiring and using referent power effectively is important not only to managers in matrix organizations but to all managers at any level in any organization.

They offer suggestions for building your referent power:

- get to know the motives, preferences, values and interests of your colleagues;
- build relationships using shared motives, goals and interests;
- respect differences in interests and don't attack another person's style;
- give 'positive strokes', use reward power, confirm others' competence;
- invite reciprocal influence, show that you respect the opinions of others;
- share information, give your expertise, particularly where you stand to benefit;
- minimize concerns with status, put signs of office aside—people relate to equals;
- develop communication skills—people value clear and consistent messages;
- get to know how people react to stress and crisis;
- get to know the informal political structure of your organization.

Benfari and colleagues describe the use of 'positive strokes', for example, as a 'cheap and easy way to build a relationship', involving little time and no money.

Based on Robert C. Benfari, Harry E. Wilkinson and Charles D. Orth, 'The effective use of power', *Business Horizons*, vol.29, May–June 1986, p.16.

Jobs for the boys?

Leadership commentary, until the 1980s, assumed that leaders were *men* with special qualities. Women are thus poorly represented in the ranks of management and were largely ignored in leadership research until the 1990s. That position has changed markedly.

Rosabeth Moss Kanter (1977; 1979) argued that women are rendered 'structurally powerless' in being restricted to routine, low-profile jobs, as well as facing discrimination in promotion decisions. Deborah Tannen (1990; 1995) argued that women and men acquire different linguistic styles in childhood. Girls learn conversation rituals that focus on rapport, while boys focus on status. Men thus think in hierarchical terms, and of being 'one up', are more likely to jockey for position by putting others down, and appear confident and knowledgeable. Women are more likely to avoid putting others down, and in ways that are face-saving. Women can also appear to lack self-confidence by playing down their certainty and openly expressing doubt. Women adopting a 'masculine' linguistic style are regarded as aggressive.

Beating men at their own game

Several commentators predict that women will assume more leadership positions, because they score higher on *transformational* leadership, involving motivation and support. Men score higher on *transactional* leadership, involving traditional command-and-control. Shere Hite (2000) advocates a new 'emotional-psychological landscape', arguing that sexual politics prevents women reaching senior management positions. Her research shows that female managers are admired by male executives for:

- relative indifference to status symbols;
- not playing office politics;
- innovative ways of thinking;
- understanding of service industries;
- higher intellectual achievements;
- greater productivity;
- 'soft' skills such as communication and networking.

However, women still attract male criticism for taking time off work to have children, not fighting hard enough for power, not making themselves visible and disliking competition.

Val Singh at the Centre for Developing Women Business Leaders at Cranfield School of Management argues that women pursuing management careers should use these methods:

- ingratiation, building your relationships with superiors;
- window dressing, displaying your competence;
- taking credit for achievements beyond your contribution;
- keen, ready and attentive body language;
- adopt the style and mannerisms of the next management level up;
- 'good organization citizenship' behaviour such as conscientiousness and courtesy;
- actively repair damage to your image;
- volunteer for extra responsibility.

These are the *impression management* tactics [**link**, chapter 6, communication] that work for men, so why should women not use them too?

Cranfield research in 1999 also found that:

1. More than half of top and middle female managers use impression management methods.
2. More women (53 per cent) than men (38 per cent) admitted that they used impression management.
3. Women said that men used impression management more than women.
4. 25 per cent of women, compared with 10 per cent of men, said that they would not try to impress.

Based on Rebecca Johnson, 'Ascent of Woman', *People Management*, vol.6, no.1, January 2000, pp.26–32; and Shere Hite, *Sex and Business*, FT Prentice Hall, Harlow, 2000.

Tanya Arroba and Kim James (1988), in contrast, argue that women have innate attributes that can be exploited to their advantage. These include intuition, sensitivity, observation and a willingness to engage with feelings. Women, they argue, should put to one side their distaste for organizational politics and discomfort with the concept of power. Getting involved in the politics game, they note, is tough, but not getting involved means staying put.

Sandi Mann (1995) similarly argues that women are under-represented in leadership and management roles because they are less successful in acquiring power. Organizations which encourage long hours of work disadvantage women with family responsibilities. Failure to participate socially—the late drinks—can also lead to exclusion, exacerbated by inadequate child care facilities. Meetings are scheduled at times inaccessible for women, who are excluded from informal male meetings in inaccessible locations (the locker room at the gym). Male conversation is dominated by topics in which women do not share an interest. 'Passive strategies', she argues, are not as effective as self-promotion in terms of career progression.

Comparative data on women in management in different countries is difficult to obtain, but Susan Vinnicombe (2000, p.10) cites figures from an International Labour Organization study, summarized in table 21.3. This shows that while women account for just under half of the workforce in the six countries covered, they occupy only between one-fifth and one-third of administrative and managerial jobs.

Stop and criticize	What power bases can women exploit in order to strengthen their organizational positions and achieve promotion to more senior managerial positions?

Table 21.3: Women's share of administrative and managerial jobs (%)

country	administrative and managerial jobs	total employment
Austria	22	43
Finland	25	47
Israel	25	47
Norway	32	46
Switzerland	28	40
United Kingdom	33	45

The future for women in management

Peter York cites Yve Newbold, once company secretary for the conglomerate Hanson, as saying, 'I'll only be happy when there are as many mediocre women running organizations as there are mediocre men'. He studied a number of 'forty- and fifty-something' women who had broken through 'the glass ceiling' into top corporate and public sector jobs:

These women had got through the glass ceiling because they didn't believe it was there—or so they told us. They had a highly developed self-belief, often derived from supportive parents who'd told them anything was possible for girls. They didn't believe in role-playing—from kittens to nannies—any more than they believed in being an 'honorary man'. All those gambits were hopelessly outdated in their view. What they did concede was that there had been a need to network more intelligently, to make yourself useful and be assiduous in the early stages of your career.

York concludes that 'The future of management everywhere just has to be a lot more female'.

From Peter York, 'The gender agenda', *Management Today*, October 1999, pp.56–63.

Table 21.4: Changing beliefs about women in management

belief	agreement (%)
Women use their time more effectively than men	70
Women tend to praise their staff more frequently	70
I would trust a female boss not to take credit for my work	60
I would trust a male boss not to take credit for my work	40
Men make better bosses than women (whole sample)	40
Men make better bosses than women (women only)	30

Marilyn Davidson and Cary Cooper (1992) point out that women are not disqualified from management roles by ability, personality or aspiration. The single main beneficial change, they argue, to expand opportunities for women in management, would be in male attitudes. They also argue, however, that it is not necessarily effective for the ambitious woman to adopt a masculine style of behaviour. On the contrary, the solution they suggest is to adopt a flexible combination of masculine and feminine attributes. This combination, known as *androgyny*, means being decisive and emotionally expressive, independent and tender, aggressive and gentle, assertive and yielding. This involves flexible, adaptive behaviour and rejection of traditional, simple stereotypes—'typical female' or 'one of the boys'.

Davidson and Cooper argued in 1992 that the pace of change for women was slow. One more recent study, however, challenges this pessimism (York, 1999; MacDonald, 1999). The results from the 200 replies, half men and half women, are outlined in table 21.4.

Women saw male bosses as decisive and as team leaders, but also as insensitive. Men saw female bosses as considerate, open-minded and team players. Are men more likely to inspire confidence in staff? Overall, 60 per cent rejected this, and 72 per cent of women rejected it.

These findings suggest that women are now more likely to be promoted for their leadership and management attributes and skills and are less likely to be discriminated against on grounds of sex and so-called 'feminine' traits.

*"That's an excellent suggestion, Miss Triggs.
Perhaps one of the men here would like to make it."*

People prefer considerate leaders

As psychiatrists are too expensive, managers end up dealing with their employees' personal problems. Factory foremen, for example, do not just give orders to subordinates. They have to deal also with their personal problems. The style in which they carry out these extra responsibilities may influence their effectiveness as foremen.

Elizabeth Kaplan and Emory Cowen studied how American factory foremen felt about counselling—which is important as psychological well-being and productivity can be related. They asked 97 (male) foremen in twelve companies in New York about the kinds of problems that their subordinates brought to them, how much of their time this took up, how they went about solving these problems, and how they rated the importance of this part of their job.

The average foreman spent 7 per cent of his working time—about two-and-a-half hours a week—dealing with the personal problems of subordinates. The most difficult problems for the foremen to solve were those which concerned marriage, money and other employees.

The foremen's most popular counselling method was 'the sympathetic ear'. They encouraged subordinates to work out their own solutions and rarely suggested that they seek professional help. Most of the foremen were happy to have been approached for this kind of help, felt that this was an important issue, and felt satisfied when their advice had been successful.

The researchers argue that this informal counselling service is important to subordinates and to productivity and that supervisors who have to provide the service should be given formal training in listening and advisory skills.

Based on Elizabeth M. Kaplan and Emory L. Cowen, 'Interpersonal helping behaviour of industrial foremen', *Journal of Applied Psychology*, 1981, vol.66, no.5, pp.633–8.

Further evidence for this trend comes from the observation that some leading British companies have set up self-help groups and training programmes for male employees facing competition from women, in executive roles and in the workplace generally. Companies adopting this approach include NatWest and Midland Banks, Hampshire County Council and Mazda Cars. Women, seen as better at teamwork, communication, listening and handling relationships and people, are challenging men for promoted posts. The training now being offered to men covers assertiveness, listening techniques, recognizing feelings, stress management and understanding relationships—topics which used to belong on programmes to support women in the workplace (Laville, 1999).

Style counselling: the search for effective behaviour patterns

Disillusionment with the traits approach meant that leadership, management and supervisory style became a major focus for research. Attention switched from selecting leaders on personality traits to training and developing leaders in appropriate behaviour patterns. This research tradition argues that a considerate, participative, democratic and involving leadership style is more effective than an impersonal, autocratic and directive style.

Two projects, the Michigan and Ohio studies, underpinned the investigation of management style. The work of the Survey Research Center in Michigan in the 1940s and early 1950s (Katz, Maccoby and Morse, 1950), identified two dimensions of leadership behaviour:

1. *employee-centred behaviour*: focusing on relationships and employee needs;

2. *job-centred behaviour*: focusing on getting the job done.

This work ran concurrently with the influential studies of Edwin Fleishman and Ralf Stogdill at the Bureau of Business Research at Ohio State University (Fleishman, 1953a; 1953b; Fleishman and Harris, 1962; Stogdill, 1948; 1950; Stogdill and Coons, 1951). Foremen in the International Harvester Company, and employees in other organizations, were asked to rate the frequency with which their superiors behaved in the ways described in a leadership behaviour description questionnaire.

Consistent with the Michigan studies, the Ohio results identified two categories of leadership behaviour, **consideration** and **initiating structure**. The considerate leader is *needs- and relationships-oriented*. The leader who structures work for subordinates is *task-oriented*.

The considerate leader is interested in and listens to subordinates, allows participation in decision making, is friendly and approachable, helps subordinates with personal problems and is prepared to support them if necessary. The leader's behaviour indicates genuine trust, respect, warmth and rapport. This enhances subordinates' feelings of self-esteem and encourages the development of communications and relationships in a work group. The researchers first called this leadership dimension *social sensitivity*.

The leader initiating structure plans ahead, decides how things are going to get done, structures tasks and assigns work, makes expectations clear, emphasizes deadlines and achievement, and expects subordinates to follow instructions. The leader's behaviour stresses production and the achievement of organizational goals. This type of behaviour can stimulate enthusiasm to achieve objectives as well as encouraging and helping subordinates to get the work done. This is the kind of emphasis that the scientific management school encouraged, except that here it is recognized that task orientation can have a positive motivating aspect. The researchers first called this leadership dimension *production emphasis*.

The Michigan and Ohio studies developed the dichotomy between democratic and autocratic leadership. These dimensions have been found in numerous studies of the way in which leadership behaviour is perceived. This is the foundation for the *Grid Organization Development* perspective developed by Robert Blake and Jane Mouton (1964; 1968; 1969) [**link**, chapter 17, organization development], who argue that effective leaders and managers are those who combine what they call *concern for production* with *concern for people*.

Consideration and structure are independent behaviour patterns and do not represent the extremes of a continuum. A leader can emphasize one or both. Job satisfaction is likely to be higher and grievances and labour turnover lower where the leader emphasizes consideration. Task performance, on the other hand, is likely to be higher where the leader emphasizes the initiation of structure. Inconsiderate leaders typically have subordinates who complain and who are more likely to leave the organization, but can have comparatively productive work groups if they are high on initiating structure. This theory is summarized in figure 21.1.

The influential work of another University of Michigan researcher, Rensis Likert (1961), reinforced the benefits of considerate performance-oriented leadership. He interviewed 24 supervisors and 419 clerks in an American insurance company. He found that supervisors in highly productive sections were more likely to:

- receive general as opposed to close supervision from their superiors;

- give general as opposed to close supervision to their subordinates;

Consideration is a pattern of leadership behaviour that demonstrates sensitivity to relationships and to the social needs of employees.

Initiating structure is a pattern of leadership behaviour that emphasizes performance of the work in hand and the achievement of product and service goals.

Rensis Likert
(1903–81)

		Initiating Structure	
		High	**Low**
Consideration	**High**	High performance	Low performance
		Few grievances	Few grievances
		Low turnover	Low turnover
	Low	High performance	Low performance
		Many grievances	Many grievances
		High turnover	High turnover

Figure 21.1: The Ohio State leadership theory predictions

- enjoy their responsibility and authority;
- spend more time on supervision;
- be employee- rather than production-oriented.

Supervisors in sections where productivity was low were production-oriented and concentrated on keeping their subordinates busy and on achieving targets on time. The effective supervisors were not just concerned with employee needs. They were seen by subordinates as emphasizing high performance and had a 'contagious enthusiasm' for achieving goals. Likert and his team identified four main styles or systems of leadership:

System 1: *Exploitative autocratic*, in which the leader

- has no confidence and trust in subordinates;
- imposes decisions, never delegates;
- motivates by threat;
- has little communication and teamwork.

System 2: *Benevolent authoritative*, in which the leader

- has superficial, condescending trust in subordinates;
- imposes decisions, never delegates;
- motivates by reward;
- sometimes involves subordinates in solving problems.

System 3: *Participative*, in which the leader

- has some incomplete confidence and trust in subordinates;
- listens to subordinates but controls decision making;
- motivates by reward and some involvement;
- uses ideas and opinions of subordinates constructively.

System 4: *Democratic*, in which the leader

- has complete confidence and trust in subordinates;

- allows subordinates to make decisions for themselves;

- motivates by reward for achieving goals set by participation;

- shares ideas and opinions.

Likert's research showed that effective supervisors were those who adopted either System 3 or System 4 leadership, what Likert called an 'alternative organizational lifestyle'.

One of Rensis Likert's less effective supervisors

This interest-in-people approach is all right, but it's a luxury. I've got to keep pressure on for production, and when I get production up, then I can afford to take time to show an interest in my employees and their problems.

One of Rensis Likert's more effective supervisors

One way in which we accomplish a high level of production is by letting people do the job the way they want to so long as they accomplish the objectives. I believe in letting them take time out from the monotony. Make them feel that they are something special, not just the run of the mill. As a matter of fact, I tell them if you feel that job is getting you down get away from it for a few minutes . . . If you keep employees from feeling hounded, they are apt to put out the necessary effort to get the work done in the required time.

I never make any decisions myself. Oh, I guess I've made about two since I've been here. If people know their jobs I believe in letting them make decisions. I believe in delegating decision-making. Of course, if there's anything that affects the whole division, then the two assistant managers, the three section heads and sometimes the assistant section heads come in here and we discuss it. I don't believe in saying that this is the way it's going to be. After all, once supervision and management are in agreement there won't be any trouble selling the staff the idea.

My job is dealing with human beings rather than with the work. It doesn't matter if I have anything to do with the work or not. The chances are that people will do a better job if you are really taking an interest in them. Knowing the names is important and helps a lot, but it's not enough. You really have to know each individual well, know what his problems are. Most of the time I discuss matters with employees at their desks rather than in the office. Sometimes I sit on a waste paper basket or lean on the files. It's all very informal. People don't seem to like to come into the office to talk.

From Rensis Likert, *New Patterns of Management*, McGraw-Hill Book Company, New York, 1961, pp.7–8.

Context fitting: the development of contingency theories

The Michigan and Ohio perspectives offer leaders 'one best way' to handle followers, by adopting the 'high-consideration, high-structure' ideal. This advice is supported by the fact that most people like their leaders to be considerate, even when they are performance-oriented as well. The main criticism of this perspective lies with the observation that one leadership style may not be effective in all circumstances.

Departing from 'one best way', Robert Tannenbaum and Warren Schmidt (1958) presented the autocratic–democratic choice as a continuum, from 'boss-

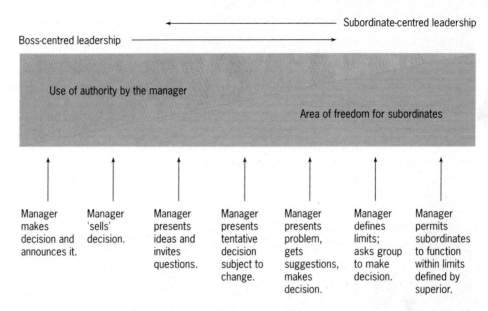

Figure 21.2: The Tannenbaum–Schmidt continuum of leadership behaviour

centred leadership' at one extreme to 'subordinate-centred leadership' at the other. This is illustrated in figure 21.2.

The steps in this continuum are presented as alternatives for the leader; their article was subtitled 'should a manager be democratic or autocratic—or something in between?' Tannenbaum and Schmidt argue that the answer depends on three sets of forces:

forces in the manager	personality, values, preferences, beliefs about employee participation, confidence in subordinates
forces in the subordinates	need for independence, tolerance of ambiguity, knowledge of the problem, expectations of involvement
forces in the situation	organizational norms, size and location of work groups, effectiveness of teamworking, nature of the problem

> The **contingency theory of leadership** is a perspective which argues that leaders, to be effective, must adjust their style in a manner consistent with aspects of the context, such as attributes of followers and the nature of the work being done.

Having concentrated on 'forces in the manager', and having challenged the notion of 'one best way' to lead, research now considered aspects of the context in which the leader was operating: the people being led, the nature of the work they were doing, and the wider organizational setting. This perspective suggests that leaders must be able to 'diagnose' the context and be able to decide what behaviour will 'fit'. As the best style is contingent on the situation, this approach is referred to as the **contingency theory of leadership**.

Stop and criticize

Leadership research and theory seems to be consistent in arguing that a considerate, employee-centred, participative and democratic style is more effective.

What factors in an organizational context would make an inconsiderate, goal-centred, impersonal and autocratic leadership style more effective?

The least preferred coworker score is an assessment of the kind of person with whom a leader feels they could not work effectively.

Frederick Edward Fiedler

The contingency theory of Fred Fiedler (1967; Fiedler and Chemers, 1974; 1984) provides a systematic approach to diagnosing contextual factors. Fiedler worked with groups whose leaders were clearly identified and whose performance was easy to measure, such as basketball teams and bomber crews. Fiedler first developed a new measure of a leader's basic approach to managing people—the leader's **least preferred coworker (LPC) score**.

This concept is best understood by completing the LPC assessment yourself. Think of somebody you have had problems working with, now or in the past. It does not matter whether you like this person. Rate them on the following scale (based on Fiedler and Chemers, 1984), and then identify whether your total score is consistent with the high and low LPC leader profiles summarized in table 21.5.

										score
pleasant	8	7	6	5	4	3	2	1	unpleasant	_____
friendly	8	7	6	5	4	3	2	1	unfriendly	_____
rejecting	1	2	3	4	5	6	7	8	accepting	_____
tense	1	2	3	4	5	6	7	8	relaxed	_____
distant	1	2	3	4	5	6	7	8	close	_____
cold	1	2	3	4	5	6	7	8	warm	_____
supportive	8	7	6	5	4	3	2	1	hostile	_____
boring	1	2	3	4	5	6	7	8	interesting	_____
quarrelsome	1	2	3	4	5	6	7	8	harmonious	_____
gloomy	1	2	3	4	5	6	7	8	cheerful	_____
open	8	7	6	5	4	3	2	1	guarded	_____
backbiting	1	2	3	4	5	6	7	8	loyal	_____
untrustworthy	1	2	3	4	5	6	7	8	trustworthy	_____
considerate	8	7	6	5	4	3	2	1	inconsiderate	_____
nasty	1	2	3	4	5	6	7	8	nice	_____
agreeable	8	7	6	5	4	3	2	1	disagreeable	_____
insincere	1	2	3	4	5	6	7	8	sincere	_____
kind	8	7	6	5	4	3	2	1	unkind	_____
									Total	_____

A score of 57 or less suggests that you are task-oriented or 'low LPC'. A score of 64 or higher suggests that you are 'high LPC' and that you are relationships-oriented.

Table 21.5: High- and low-LPC leaders

The low-LPC leader	The high-LPC leader
self-esteem based on task completion	self-esteem based on interpersonal relations
puts the task first	puts people first
is hard on those who fail	likes to please others
considers competence a key attribute	considers loyalty a key attribute
likes detail	is bored with detail

Fiedler appears to have found with the LPC score another way to uncover a manager's predispositions towards consideration and initiating structure. It should not be surprising, therefore, to find that Fiedler's attempts to correlate the LPC scores of leaders with the performance of their groups was not successful. This led Fiedler to the argument that effectiveness is influenced by three sets of factors:

1. The extent to which the task in hand is structured.

2. The leader's position power.

3. The nature of the relationships between the leader and followers.

Tasks vary in the extent to which they are **structured** or not.

Stop and criticize

Would you describe the task of writing an essay for your organizational behaviour instructor as structured or unstructured?

As a student, would you prefer this task to be more or less structured, and how would you advise you instructor to achieve this?

A **structured task** is a task with clear goals, few correct or satisfactory solutions and outcomes, few ways of performing it, and clear criteria of success.

An **unstructured task** is a task with ambiguous goals, many correct solutions and satisfactory outcomes, many ways of achieving acceptable outcomes, and vague criteria of success.

Fiedler identifies three typical sets of conditions under which a leader may have to work:

Condition 1

- The task is highly structured.

- The leader's position power is high.

- Subordinates feel that their relationships with the boss are good.

Task-oriented (low LPC score) leaders get good results in these favourable circumstances. The task-oriented leader in this situation detects that events are potentially under his or her control, sets targets, monitors progress and achieves good performance.

Relationships-oriented (high LPC score) leaders get poor results in these circumstances. They try to build and maintain good relationships with and among subordinates. However, when relationships are already good, and other conditions are favourable, the leader may take subordinates for granted and start to pursue other personal objectives.

Condition 2

- The task is unstructured.

- The leader's position power is low.

- Subordinates feel that their relationships with the boss are moderately good.

Relationship-oriented (high LPC) leaders get better results in these moderately favourable circumstances, where the maintenance of good relationships is important to the leader's ability to exert influence over subordinates and to getting the work done. The task-oriented (low LPC) leader ignores deteriorating relationships and, as the task lacks structure and the leader lacks position power, the results are likely to be poor.

Condition 3

- The task is unstructured.

- The leader's position power is low.

- Subordinates feel that their relationships with the boss are poor.

Task-oriented (low LPC) leaders get better results in these very unfavourable conditions. The relationships-oriented (high LPC) leader is unwilling to exert pressure on subordinates, avoids confrontations that might upset or anger them, gets involved in attempts to repair damaged relationships and ignores the task. The task-oriented leader gets impatient, tries to structure the situation, ignores resistance from subordinates, reduces the ambiguity surrounding the work and achieves good performance.

The research to support Fiedler's contingency theory is positive but weak. There seem to be four problems.

1. The key variables, task structure, power and relationships, are difficult to assess. The leader who wants to rely on this framework to determine the most effective style for a given situation has to rely more on intuition than on systematic analysis.

2. The concept of the least preferred coworker is an unusual one, and it is not clear just what this measures. It looks like another measure of employee-centred versus task-centred behaviour.

3. The framework does not take into account the needs of subordinates.

4. The need for a leader to have relevant technical competence is ignored.

This theory has two strengths. First, it demonstrates the importance of contextual factors in determining leader behaviour and effectiveness. It reinforces the view that there is no one ideal personality or best style that a leader must have to be successful. Second, it provides a systematic framework for developing the self-awareness of managers.

Most contingency theories argue that leaders should change their *style* to fit the context. However, Fiedler felt that most managers and supervisors have problems in changing their leadership style. To be effective, he argued, leaders have to change their *context*, choosing conditions in which their preferred style was most likely to be effective.

Another influential contingency theory of leadership was developed by Paul Hersey and Ken Blanchard (1988). With Fiedler, they argue that the effective leader 'must be a good diagnostician' and adapt style to meet the demands of the situation in which they operate. Unlike Fiedler, they believe that leaders can alter their style to fit the context.

Hersey and Blanchard call their approach **situational leadership**, summarized in figure 21.3, which describes leader behaviour on two dimensions.

The first dimension (horizontal axis) concerns 'task behaviour', or the amount of direction a leader gives to subordinates. This can vary from specific instructions, at one extreme, to complete delegation, at the other. Hersey and Blanchard identify two intermediate positions, where leaders either facilitate subordinates' decisions or take care to explain their own.

The second dimension (vertical axis) concerns 'supportive behaviour' and the

Paul Hersey

Kenneth H. Blanchard

Situational leadership is an approach to determining the most effective style of influencing, taking into account the amounts of direction and support the leader gives, and the readiness and maturity of followers to perform a particular task.

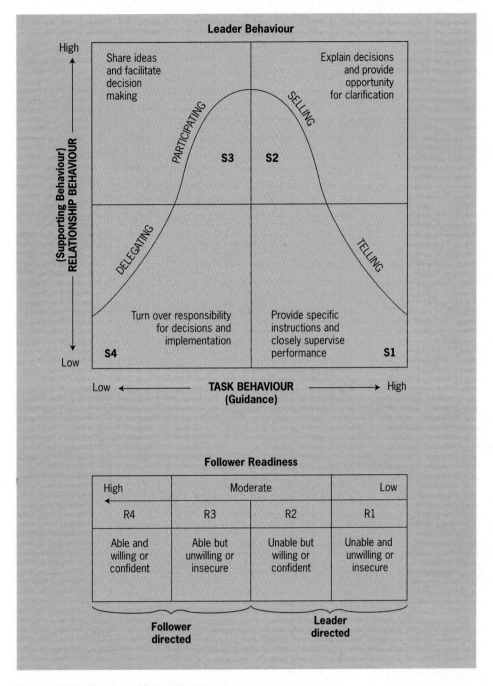

Figure 21.3: Situational leadership theory
From P. Hersey and K.H. Blanchard, *Management of Organizational Behaviour: Utilizing Human Resources*, Prentice Hall, Englewood Cliff, NJ, 1988.

amount of social backup a leader gives to subordinates. This can vary from limited communication, at one extreme, to considerable listening, facilitating and supporting at the other.

The model establishes four basic leadership styles, labelled S1 to S4:

S1 *Telling*: High amounts of task behaviour, telling subordinates what to do, when to do it and how to do it, but with little relationship behaviour.

S2 *Selling*: High amounts of both task behaviour and relationship behaviour.

S3 *Participating*: Lots of relationship behaviour and support, but little direction or task behaviour.

S4 *Delegating*: Not much task behaviour or relationship behaviour.

Hersey and Blanchard also argue that the readiness of followers to perform a particular task is a key factor. This is explained by the lower portion of the figure, in which follower readiness is drawn on a continuum, with insecure subordinates unwilling to act at one extreme to confident followers able and willing to perform at the other. Superimpose the readiness continuum on the top half of the model and you have a basis for selecting an effective leadership style. It is compelling, and consistent with other theories, to suggest that insecure subordinates need telling, while willing and confident groups can be left to do the job.

Alan Bryman (1986, p.149) points to the limitations of this model. There is no clear reason why S2 and S3 should be associated with R2 and R3 respectively. The S3 style could be appropriate for groups in a high state of 'psychological readiness' but without the depth of experience in the job that would enable them to perform effectively—that is with an R2 group. Bryman also points to the lack of evidence to support the model in practice.

As with Fiedler and House, however, the main strengths of this perspective lie with the emphasis on the need for flexibility in leadership behaviour, and in highlighting the importance of contextual factors.

Daniel Goleman (2000) reports research by the management consulting firm Hay McBer involving almost 4,000 executives in a worldwide sample. This work identified six leadership styles which have an impact on 'working atmosphere' and financial performance. The findings suggest that effective leaders use all of

Table 21.6: Goleman's six leadership styles

style	in practice	in a phrase	competencies	when to use
coercive	demands compliance	'Do what I tell you'	drive to achieve, self-control	in a crisis, with problem people
authoritative	mobilizes people	'Come with me'	self-confidence, change catalyst	when new vision and direction is needed
affiliative	creates harmony	'People come first'	empathy, communication	to heal wounds, to motivate people under stress
democratic	forges consensus	'What do you think?'	collaboration, team building	to build consensus, to get contributions
pacesetting	sets high standards	'Do as I do, now'	initiative, drive to achieve	to get fast results from a motivated team
coaching	develops people	'Try this'	empathy, self-awareness	to improve performance, to develop strengths

Based on Daniel Goleman, 'Leadership that gets results', *Harvard Business Review*, vol.78, no.2, March–April 2000, pp.78–90.

these styles, like an 'array of clubs in a golf pro's bag'. Each style relies on an aspect of *emotional intelligence* which concerns skill in managing your own emotions and in handling the emotions of others [**link**, chapter 5, personality]. Goleman's six styles are summarized in table 21.6.

While coercion and pacesetting have their uses, the research showed that these styles can damage 'working atmosphere', reducing flexibility and employee commitment. The other four styles have a consistently positive impact on climate and performance. The most effective leaders, Goleman concludes, are those who have mastered four or more styles, particularly the positive styles, and who are able to switch styles as the situation demands. This is not a 'mechanical' matching of behaviour to context, as other contingency theories imply, but a flexible, fluid, sensitive and seamless adjustment.

Contingency theories thus argue that the most effective leadership style depends on the context. Organizations, the skills of their managers, the characteristics of employees, the nature of their tasks and their structures, are unique. No one style of leadership appears universally better. There is, however, a good deal of research that indicates that a considerate, participative or democratic style of leadership is generally (if not always) more effective. There are two main reasons for this.

First, the development of participative management is part of a wider social and political trend which has raised expectations concerning personal freedom and the quality of working life. These social values encourage resistance to manipulation by impersonal bureaucracies and challenge the legitimacy of management decisions. Participation thus reflects evolving democratic social and political values.

Second, participative management has been encouraged by research, which has demonstrated that this style is generally more effective, although an autocratic style can be effective in some circumstances. A participative style can improve organizational effectiveness by tapping the ideas of people with knowledge and experience, and by involving them in a decision-making process to which they then become committed. This is reinforced by the growth in numbers of knowledge workers, who expect to be involved in decisions affecting their work, and whose knowledge makes them potentially valuable contributors in this regard.

People who are involved in setting standards or establishing methods are thus more likely to experience 'ownership' of such decision, and are more likely to:

- accept the legitimacy of decisions reached with their help;

- accept change based on those decisions;

- trust managers who ultimately ratify and implement decisions;

- volunteer new and creative ideas and solutions.

Autocratic management stifles creativity, ignores available expertise, and smothers motivation and commitment. Autocratic management can, however, be more effective:

- when time is short;

- when the leader is the most knowledgeable person;

- and where those who could participate will never all agree on a decision.

The contingency theories discussed here have met a number of criticisms. One concerns the questionable ability of leaders reliably to diagnose the context in which they are operating, given the relatively vague nature of the situational variables identified by the different theories. In addition, contingency theories typi-

Participative management leads to better decisions

Many managers reject the concept of participative management because they do not want to lose control over 'management' decisions. Employee participation thus depends on the attitudes of managers towards this aspect of their job.

William Pasmore and Frank Friedlander were asked to study work injuries which were reducing productivity in an American electronics company. About a third of the company's 335 employees complained about pains in their wrists, arms and shoulders, some had surgery to relieve their symptoms, and one woman had permanently lost the use of her right hand. A series of medical and technical investigations had failed to find the cause of the injuries.

Management had never thought of asking the employees themselves about the possible causes of their injuries. So the researchers suggested that a 'studies and communications group' be set up, drawing workers' representatives from each area of the factory. The group members discussed their own work experiences and injuries, designed a questionnaire, surveyed over 300 other employees, and produced sixty recommendations for solving the injury problem.

Management rejected the group's recommendations because management practices were identified as the main cause of the problem. The group found that injuries were related to:

- inadequate training;
- rapid, repetitive arm movements;
- badly adjusted machines;
- frustration at machine breakdowns;
- stress from supervisors' behaviour (such as favouritism);
- pressure from management for more output.

The first attempts by management to solve the problem had in fact made it worse. When workers were injured, production fell, management increased the pressure for more output, which increased stress, which in turn led to more injuries.

The researchers concluded that a permanent change in the relationships between workers and management was necessary to create a climate of effective participation. The managers in this company felt that they had lost control over the situation. But as the workers' recommendations were gradually implemented, the number of injuries fell and the overall performance of the factory rose.

Based on William Pasmore and Frank Friedlander, 'An action research programme to increase employee involvement in problem solving', *Administrative Science Quarterly*, 1982, vol.27. no.3, pp.343–62.

cally fail to consider a number of other key dimensions of the organizational context, such as the organizational culture, degree of change and levels of stress, working conditions, external economic factors, organizational design and technology. All of these factors potentially influence the leadership process in ways not addressed by these theoretical accounts (Hughes, Ginnett and Curphy, 1996).

Can leaders adapt their styles to fit the context in the ways in which theory advises?

Personality may not be flexible enough. Some theorists argue that personality is inherited, preventing the manager from being participative in some circumstances and dictatorial in others. The manager who is motivated by affiliation and who values the friendship of others may find it hard to treat employees in an impersonal and autocratic style.

Management styles vary around the world

André Laurent asked people from twelve countries whether they agreed with the statement, 'It is important for a manager to have at hand precise answers to most of the questions that his subordinates may raise about their work'. The percentages agreeing with this were:

Japan	78
Indonesia	73
Italy	66
France	53
Germany	46
Belgium	44
Switzerland	38
Britain	27
Denmark	23
United States	18
Holland	17
Sweden	10

Managers in France and Indonesia are seen as experts who are expected to have the answers. Managers in America and Holland are regarded as participative problem solvers. Differences like this explain some of the problems that, for instance, Japanese managers have when working in Denmark, or Swedish managers have in relationships with colleagues in Italy.

Based on André Laurent, 'The cultural diversity of Western conceptions of management', *International Studies of Management and Organization*, 1983, vol.13, no.1–2.

The expectations of other managers also determine what is 'acceptable' in the organization. There are advantages in honesty and consistency. People may not accept the fickle behaviour of the participative manager who adopts an autocratic style on some occasions. The leader who changes style from one situation to another may not inspire confidence and trust. However, leaders should be able to change style to suit the circumstances:

1. It is now broadly accepted that leaders and managers can learn with experience to adjust their behaviour according to circumstances.

2. Organizations are not rigid social arrangements with fixed tasks and structures. With the growth in demand for flexibility, adaptability, improved quality of working life and worker participation, leaders and managers who fail to respond will face problems.

3. The leader or manager who adapts in a flexible way to changes in circumstances may be seen as more competent than one who sticks rigidly to traditional routines.

There is, therefore, no simple recipe for the manager looking for the most effective leadership style. Leadership style probably can change, but only if management values change too. Any attempt to change deep-rooted values is ambitious, but this may be necessary in the interests of personal and organizational effectiveness.

Leadership in the twenty-first century

The **new leader** is an indispensable and inspirational visionary, a coach, a facilitator concerned with building a shared sense of purpose and mission, with creating a culture which ensures that everyone is aligned with the organization's goals and is skilled and empowered to go and achieve them.

The **superleader** is a leader who is able to develop leadership capacity in others, developing and empowering them, reducing their dependence on formal leaders, stimulating their motivation, commitment and creativity.

The **transactional leader** is a leader who treats relationships with followers in terms of an exchange, giving followers what they want in return for what the leader desires, following prescribed tasks to pursue established goals.

The **transformational leader** is a leader who treats relationships with followers in terms of motivation and commitment, influencing and inspiring followers to give more than mechanical compliance and to improve organizational performance.

Two related trends in leadership thinking are now evident:

1. recognition of the role of heroic, powerful, charismatic, *visionary leaders*;

2. recognition of the role of *informal leadership*, at all levels.

These trends appear to be contradictory. We have the **new leader**, who is an inspirational figure motivating followers to superlative levels of achievement. However, we also have the **superleader**, who is able to 'lead others to lead themselves' (Sims and Lorenzi, 1992, p.295). The superleader thus encourages, develops and co-exists with informal leadership dispersed throughout the organization hierarchy.

The new leadership (Bryman, 1996, p.280) originates from the work of James McGregor Burns (1978), who distinguished between **transactional** and **transformational leaders**.

Burns' work was based on political leaders, but his thinking has been translated into a business context. Transactional leaders see their relationships with followers in terms of trade, swaps or bargains. Transformational leaders are charismatic individuals who inspire and motivate others to go 'beyond contract', to perform at unexpected levels. Although Burns saw these as two types of leadership, it is easy to see why some commentators equate transactional with 'management' and transformational with 'leadership'.

Noel Tichy and Mary Anne Devanna (1986) argue that the transformational leader has three main roles: recognizing the need for revitalization, creating a new vision, and institutionalizing change. Bernard Bass and Bruce Avolio (Bass, 1985b; Bass and Avolio, 1994) similarly claim that transformational leadership occurs when leaders:

- stimulate others to see what they are doing from new perspectives;

- articulate the mission or vision of the organization;

- develop others to higher levels of ability; and

- motivate others to put organizational interests before self-interest.

They achieve this, according to Bass and Avolio, by using one or more of 'the four I's':

Idealized influence	act as role models, attract admiration, respect and trust, put needs of others before personal interests, take risks and demonstrate high standards of ethical conduct
Inspirational motivation	motivate and inspire by providing meaning and challenge, arouse team spirit, show enthusiasm and optimism, communicate expectations, demonstrate commitment
Intellectual stimulation	question assumptions, reframe problems, approach old issues in new ways, encourage innovation and creativity, avoid public criticism of mistakes
Individualized consideration	attend to individual needs for growth and achievement, act as coach or mentor, create new learning opportunities, accept individual differences, avoid close monitoring

It is tempting to regard the profusion of new terms and the shift in emphasis in leadership theory and research as a systematic development of earlier ideas. However, the identification of new, super, transformational leaders represents a simplification of the concept of leadership, returning to 'trait spotting' (hunt the visionary) and overlooks what is known about the influence of a range of contextual factors on leadership effectiveness.

| **Stop and criticize** | Considering senior business and political leaders with whom you are familiar, either directly or through the media, which come closest to these definitions of new leader, superleader and transformational leader?

The new, super, transformational leader looks like a 'one best way' approach. Does this vindicate trait spotting and discredit contingency perspectives? |

Strongman tactics versus visionary superleaders

Judith Scully and colleagues explored the relationship between leadership behaviour and company financial performance, collecting leader behaviour descriptions from the subordinates of chief executive officers in 56 high technology firms. They identified four dimensions of leader behaviour:

The strongman — Tells subordinates how to carry out their work; criticizes subordinates for reasons not directly related to performance.

The transactor — Establishes goals, expects good performance, offers rewards for success, recognizes good work, criticizes poor performance.

The visionary hero — Provides a sense of purpose and direction, motivates subordinates to perform beyond their perceived capacity.

The superleader — Leader encourages subordinates to be self-critical, to set their own goals, to solve their own problems, to judge their own performance.

Financial performance was poorer in firms with 'tough' CEOs than in firms with visionary or superleader CEOs. One explanation is that some leaders respond to poor performance with punishment and direction, which can cause performance to deteriorate further.

Based on Judith A. Scully, Henry P. Sims, Judy D. Olian, Eugene R. Schnell and Kenneth A. Smith, 'Tough times make tough bosses: a meso analysis of CEO leader behaviour', *Irish Business and Administrative Research*, 1996, vol.17, no.1, pp.71–102.

Alongside the focus on heroic and visionary superleaders sits recognition that leadership acts can be observed at all levels of the organization structure. Leadership is not the exclusive preserve of management in general, or of very senior organizational figures in particular. It is necessary to recognize that leadership is dispersed across the organization.

From a survey of middle and senior managers carried out in 1998, concerning experiences of organizational change, David Buchanan, Tim Claydon and Mike Doyle (1999) found that:

- Over 90 per cent of managers agree that change management knowledge and skills are relevant to people at all levels in the organization.

- Over 90 per cent agreed that all managers require a good understanding of change management principles and practice.

- Only 2 per cent agreed that 'change management is a specialized area of expertise which should be left to full-time professionals'.

In the distinction between leadership and management, orientation to change is a defining characteristic, a distinctive 'mark of the leader'. These results suggest, therefore, that leadership is a widespread phenomenon. Leadership behaviours are dispersed rather than concentrated in the hands of formally appointed managers. Leadership functions are best carried out by people who have the interest, knowledge, skills and motivation to perform them effectively. This observation is reinforced by the development of self-managing autonomous teams, which often have no leaders, or have 'coach–facilitators' whose role is to develop team skills. These 'coaching–facilitating' supervisors are superleaders [**link**, chapter 12, team-working].

Recognition of dispersed leadership does not imply a shift of focus away from formal, senior figures. It may be useful to separate notions of leadership from formal positions and prestige job titles. However, it is also necessary to recognize that senior figures with prestige titles continue to exercise leadership roles and functions as well.

This 'twin-track' approach, which combines recognition of visionary new leadership with the notion of a widely dispersed leadership decoupled from high office, is illustrated by Warren Bennis and Burt Nanus (1985). Their model of twenty-first century leadership (in which the new role of the leader is to be 'as leader of leaders') is summarized in table 21.7.

The 'new leader' is neither an autocratic dictator nor a wildly charismatic figure, nor is he necessarily male. The emphasis of the 'new leader' lies more with the 'soft' skills of enthusing and inspiring, of coaching and facilitating (see Hickman, 1998). While women faced systematic discrimination in the pursuit of senior management positions throughout the twentieth century, commentators were arguing as the century closed that, given the significance of interpersonal competencies (for economic, political and cultural reasons), women are better equipped than men for 'new leadership' roles.

Many commentators argue that the hostile, rapidly changing competitive cli-

---

Table 21.7: The Bennis–Nanus model of twenty-first century leadership

From	To
few top leaders, many managers	leaders at every level, few managers
leading by goal setting	leading by vision, new directions
downsizing, benchmarking, quality	create distinctive competencies
reactive, adaptive to change	creative, anticipate future change
design hierarchical organizations	design flat, collegial organizations
direct and supervise	empower, inspire, facilitate
information held by few decision makers	information shared with many
leader as boss, controlling	leader as coach, creating learning organization
leader as stabilizer, balancing conflicts	leader as change agent, balancing risks
leader develops good managers	leader develops future leaders

Based on Warren Bennis and Burt Nanus, *Leaders: The Strategies for Taking Charge*, HarperCollins, New York, 1985.

mate and consequently pressured conditions of work requires participative, visionary and inspirational styles of leadership [**link**, chapter 2, the world outside]. A traditional, autocratic, task-oriented style encourages little more than mechanical compliance with directions. The new, transformational superleader, in contrast, encourages commitment, initiative, flexibility and high performance. The style and behaviour of new leaders also seems more appropriate to the motivation of knowledge workers and the development of the learning organization [**link**, chapter 4, learning].

The new leadership concept can thus be used to draw together the three main strands of twentieth-century leadership thinking:

the theory	the new transformational superleader
trait spotting	must have the right personality, appearance, attributes, voice
style counselling	must be caring, inspirational and visionary, ethical, risk taker
context fitting	style is consistent with a hostile and rapidly changing environment, with the need to develop flexible organizational forms, with the need to motivate knowledge workers and develop a learning organization

Recap

1. *Explain the apparent difference between the concepts of leadership and management.*
   - Leaders are typically portrayed as inspiring, change-oriented visionaries.
   - Manager are typically portrayed as planners, organizers and controllers.
   - In practice, the roles overlap and can be difficult to distinguish.

2. *Understand why there is little relationship between personality traits and effective leadership.*
   - Many factors, besides personality traits, influence leadership effectiveness.
   - It has proved difficult to establish a consensus on specific traits.
   - The characteristics of the leader's role also influence behaviour and effectiveness.
   - Power and influence contribute to leader effectiveness, as well as personality.

3. *Understand the bases of a leader's power in organizations and the role of followers in creating and supporting leaders.*
   - A leader's power bases include reward, coercive, referent, legitimate, expert, information, affiliation and group.
   - Leaders have power only if followers perceive them to possess it.
   - Women are traditionally powerless by discrimination and exclusion by male behaviour.

   - Women are now widely recognized to have social and interpersonal leadership qualities, and are more likely to be promoted on merit than overlooked on account of sex.

4. *Understand why effective leaders either adapt their style to fit the organizational and cultural context in which they operate or find contexts which fit their personal style.*
   - Considerate behaviour reduces labour turnover and improves job satisfaction.
   - Initiating structure improves performance but reduces job satisfaction.
   - Effective leaders combine consideration with initiating structure.
   - Contingency theory argues that leaders are more or less effective depending on how structured the task is, how powerful the leader is and how good relationships are.
   - Situational leadership advises the manager to use telling, selling, participating and delegating styles depending on the task, relationships and employee readiness.
   - Some commentators argue that leaders cannot change their behaviour and that they have to move when less effective to a context more favourable to their style.
   - Most commentators argue that leaders can and should adapt their behaviour to fit the context and the culture in which they are operating.

5. *Explain contemporary trends in this field concerning new leadership, on the one hand, and the dispersal of the leadership function, on the other.*

- One trend recognizes the importance of charismatic, visionary, inspirational new leaders.

- New leadership, superleader and transformational leadership are approximate synonyms.

- One trend recognizes that leadership can be observed at all organizational levels.

- The new leader—visionary—is a superleader—helping others to lead themselves, and these two trends are consistent, not contradictory.

- The new leader has the right traits, and the right style, for the contemporary context, thus combining notions of trait spotting, style counselling and context fitting.

Revision

1. What is the difference between leadership and management, and why is it difficult to separate these concepts in practice?

2. Adolf Hitler meets Margaret Thatcher. They discuss the functions and traits of effective leaders, particularly in the context of implementing change. On what issues might they agree? Might they disagree? Alternative scenario: Mother Teresa meets Bill Gates.

3. Why is trait spotting such a popular theme in leadership research, what has trait spotting told us about the personality markers of successful leaders, and what are the problems with this perspective?

4. Leaders are, traditionally, men with special qualities. Why, at the beginning of the twenty-first century, are women now more likely to be considered effective leaders?

5. What is power, and how can the exercise of power be regarded in positive terms as well as negative? What has the leader's power got to do with his or her followers?

Springboard

Brown, M., 1998, *Richard Branson: The Authorized Biography*, Michael Joseph, London.

How close does Branson come to the ideal of the entrepreneur? The new leader? The superleader? The transformational leader?

Bryman, A., 1996, 'Leadership in organizations', in S.R. Clegg, C. Hardy and W.R. Nord (eds), *Handbook of Organization Studies*, Sage, London, pp.276–92.

A clear, concise and widely informed critical review of leadership research in the twentieth century. Demonstrates the links between leadership and organization culture, and explores methodological issues and trends in leadership research.

Davidson, M.J. and Burke, R.J. (eds), 2000, *Women in Management: Current Research Issues Volume II*, Sage, London.

A collection of 20 research papers exploring the problems facing women in management from an international comparative perspective.

Hickman, G.R. (ed.), 1998, *Leading Organizations: Perspectives for a New Era*, Sage, Thousand Oaks, Calif.

Reference work with 53 previously published 'big name' readings. Has an American bias and lacks a critical perspective, but this is comprehensive and up to date.

Kamp, D., 1999, *The 21st Century Manager: Future-Focused Skills for the Next Millennium*, Kogan Page, London.

Written for practising managers by a consultant. The section 'what are the skills and qualities of an effective manager' lists twelve: role model, self-aware, contextually aware, learner, delight in change, visionary, ethical, systemic thinker, positive thinker, good communicator, enthusiastic and realistic. This section ends with a comment on 'this checklist of the characteristics of the effective leader'.

Mandela, N., 1994, *The Long Road to Freedom*, Little, Brown, London.

Nelson Mandela's biography. Unfair to compare him with Richard Branson. However, it is interesting to consider the extent to which Mandela displays the attributes of the new leader, the superleader, the transformational leader.

Semler, R., 1993, *Maverick*, Century, London.

Ricardo Semler, highly successful Brazilian entrepreneur, explains his leadership and management approach. Does the so-called new, transformational leadership apply in other cultures? Seems so, from this popular account.

Zaleznik, A., 1977, 'Managers and leaders: are they different?' *Harvard Business Review*, vol.15, no.3, pp.67–84.

Classic article in the leadership versus management debate, arguing that the distinction revolves around personality and orientations to change. Reprinted in *HBR* in 1992 with author's commentary, arguing that the gap between leaders and managers has widened; 'leaders have much more in common with artists, scientists and other creative thinkers than they do with managers'.

Home viewing

Bandit Queen (Hindi, with subtitles, 1994, director Shekhar Kapur) is based on the true story of Phoolan Devi (played by Seema Biswas), a violently abused, exploited and eventually outlawed Indian woman persecuted and imprisoned in 1983 to 1984, but who achieved national celebrity status for the challenge to authority (particularly the Indian police) achieved through the actions of the group of bandits which she led.

Elizabeth (1998, director Shekhar Kapur) is based on the true story of the early years of Elizabeth I of England (played by Cate Blanchett), who succeeds to the throne following the premature death of her half-sister Queen Mary (Kathy Burke), who was being pressed to have her executed but who had refused to sign the warrant. In both films, Phoolan Devi and Elizabeth have to learn how to be effective in leadership roles and contexts which are initially unfamiliar to them. How do they each change their behaviours in order to improve their effectiveness? What part does ruthlessness play in effective leadership, and in what contexts? Would the leadership behaviours demonstrated as effective in these films be different if the characters were male?

OB in literature

Norman Augustine and Kenneth Adelman, *Shakespeare in Charge: The Bard's Guide to Leading and Succeeding on the Business Stage*, Hyperion Books, 1999.

Paul Corrigan, *Shakespeare on Management: Leadership Lessons for Today's Managers*, Kogan Page, London, 1999.

Fredrick Talbott (ed.), *Shakespeare on Leadership*, World Entertainment, 1996.

To save readers from having to turn to Shakespeare's originals, these texts painlessly extract the leadership and management insights in an entertaining manner from a range of plays. *Henry V* faces numerous leadership challenges. Is his position a legitimate one? How should he deal with those plotting against him? How should he influence his reluctant troops to follow him into battle against overwhelming odds at Agincourt? *Julius Ceasar* explores the positive and negative dimensions, and the ethical dilemmas, of organizational politics. *The Merchant of Venice* exposes male–female differences in perceptions of justice and mercy. *Hamlet* is a study of leadership in an uncertain world. *Macbeth* exposes the problems of the leader who is obsessed with power for its own sake. In partnership with the Globe Theatre in London, Cranfield University School of Management in Bedford in England runs executive programmes based on Shakespeare; 'Once more into the boardroom, dear friends, once more, or close the wall up with our English dread of the Bard' (Hamilton, 1999).

Chapter exercises

1: Leadership style preferences

Objectives

1. To assess your preferred leadership style.

2. To explore the diversity of style preferences across your group.

Briefing

This assessment is designed to help you assess your preferred leadership style. Answer this questionnaire, honestly, in relation to your behaviour and preferences, either with respect to your leadership behaviour or in relation to how you think you would like to behave in a leadership role. Put a tick in the appropriate response column on the right depending on how accurate you feel each statement describes your behavioural preferences, using this scale:

A   Always   B   Often   C   Sometimes   D   Seldom   E   Never

Employee-centred or consideration score

You get one point if you ticked either A or a B in response to these questions

2 _____   10 _____   22 _____

4 _____   12 _____   24 _____

6 _____   18 _____   28 _____

8 _____   20 _____

And you get one point if you ticked either D or E in response to these questions:

14 _____   16 _____   26 _____   30 _____

Total employee-centred score is: ☐

Job-centred or initiating structure score

You get one point if you ticked either A or B in response to these questions:

1 _____   13 _____   25 _____   34 _____

3 _____   15 _____   27 _____   35 _____

5 _____   17 _____   29 _____

7 _____   19 _____   31 _____

9 _____   21 _____   32 _____

11 _____   23 _____   33 _____

Total job-centred score is: ☐

Leader behaviours

		A	B	C	D	E
1	I would always act as the spokesperson for my group	☐	☐	☐	☐	☐
2	I would allow subordinates complete freedom in their work	☐	☐	☐	☐	☐
3	I would encourage overtime working	☐	☐	☐	☐	☐
4	I would let subordinates use their judgement to solve problems	☐	☐	☐	☐	☐
5	I would encourage the use of standard procedures	☐	☐	☐	☐	☐
6	I would needle members for greater effort	☐	☐	☐	☐	☐
7	I would stress being ahead of competing groups	☐	☐	☐	☐	☐
8	I would let subordinates work the way they thought best	☐	☐	☐	☐	☐
9	I would speak as representative for subordinates	☐	☐	☐	☐	☐
10	I would be able to tolerate postponement and uncertainty	☐	☐	☐	☐	☐
11	I would try out my ideas on subordinates	☐	☐	☐	☐	☐
12	I would turn subordinates loose on a job and let them go at it	☐	☐	☐	☐	☐
13	I would work hard for promotion	☐	☐	☐	☐	☐
14	I would get swamped by details	☐	☐	☐	☐	☐
15	I would speak for subordinates when visitors were around	☐	☐	☐	☐	☐
16	I would be reluctant to let subordinates have freedom of action	☐	☐	☐	☐	☐
17	I would keep the work pace moving rapidly	☐	☐	☐	☐	☐
18	I would give some subordinates authority that I should keep	☐	☐	☐	☐	☐
19	I would settle conflicts which occur between subordinates	☐	☐	☐	☐	☐
20	I would let subordinates have a high degree of initiative	☐	☐	☐	☐	☐
21	I would represent subordinates at external meetings	☐	☐	☐	☐	☐
22	I would be willing to make changes	☐	☐	☐	☐	☐
23	I would decide what will be done and how it will be done	☐	☐	☐	☐	☐
24	I would trust subordinates to exercise good judgement	☐	☐	☐	☐	☐
25	I would push for increased production	☐	☐	☐	☐	☐
26	I would refuse to explain my actions to subordinates	☐	☐	☐	☐	☐
27	Things usually turn out as I predict	☐	☐	☐	☐	☐
28	I would let subordinates set their own work pace	☐	☐	☐	☐	☐
29	I would assign subordinates to specific tasks	☐	☐	☐	☐	☐
30	I would be able to act without consulting subordinates	☐	☐	☐	☐	☐
31	I would ask subordinates to work harder	☐	☐	☐	☐	☐
32	I would schedule the work that had to be done	☐	☐	☐	☐	☐
33	I would persuade others that my ideas were to their advantage	☐	☐	☐	☐	☐
34	I would urge subordinates to beat their previous records	☐	☐	☐	☐	☐
35	I would expect subordinates to follow set rules and regulations	☐	☐	☐	☐	☐

Your two scores can be interpreted together as follows:

employee-centred score	job-centred score	your leadership style
0–7	0–10	you are not involved enough with either the work or with your employees
0–7	10–20	you are autocratic, a bit of a slave driver; you get the job done but at an emotional cost
8–15	0–10	people are happy in their work but sometimes at the expense of productivity
8–15	10–20	people enjoy working for you and are productive, naturally expending energy because they get positive reinforcement for good work

This exercise is based on the Leadership Style Inventory from Dorothy Marcic, *Organizational Behaviour: Experiences and Cases*, West Publishing, St Paul, Minn., third edition, 1992, pp.153–6.

2: Contemporary transformational icons

Objectives

1. To explore the nature of transformational leadership.

2. To explore the causal link between transformational leadership and organizational effectiveness.

Briefing

Individual (up to five minutes):
Remind yourself of the definition of the *new leader*, the *superleader*, the *transformational leader*. These labels each describe much the same package of leadership behaviours.

Syndicates of three to five (up to twenty minutes):
Identify someone who your group would all describe as a transformational leader. Each group should choose a different figure. This could be a leading politician, a business leader or a football club manager, for example. Nominate a spokesperson and prepare a ten-minute presentation to the whole class answering the following questions:

- What physical characteristics does this person have?

- What special knowledge, skills and abilities does this person have?

- What are this person's dominant personality traits?

- How would you describe this person's leadership behaviour?

- What are the causal links between this person's attributes and behaviour, on the one hand, and the effectiveness of their organization, on the other?

- Imagine someone else in this person's role, someone who does not have that package of attributes and behaviour. Predict what would happen to organizational effectiveness.

- Imagine your transformational leader in a different setting; put your football club manager in a computer company; put your computer company manager in charge of a hotel chain; give your politician a railway or a casino to run. How effective is your transformational leader likely to be in this different context?

Plenary (up to thirty minutes):
Present your findings to the group as a whole. Consider two main issues:

1. What characteristics do transformational leaders have in common, and in what ways do they differ from each other? Is there any 'common ground' here?

2. To what extent is their success context-specific? Would their unique combinations of physical, intellectual, personality and behavioural characteristics have been successful in other settings?

Chapter 22 Decision making

Key concepts

decision making
classical decision theory
rational economic model
rationality
rational decisions
prescriptive models of decision making
descriptive models of decision making
bounded rationality
behavioural theory of decision making
maximizing
satisficing
explanatory models of decision making
heuristics group
biases

representative heuristic
anchor-and-adjustment heuristic
availability heuristic
certainty
risk
uncertainty
routine decisions
adaptive decisions
innovative decisions
group polarization
risky shift phenomenon
groupthink
brainstorming

Learning objectives

When you have read this chapter, you should be able to define those key concepts in your own words, and you should also be able to:

1. Distinguish between prescriptive, descriptive and explanatory models of decision making and provide an example of each.

2. Distinguish different decision conditions on the basis of risk and programmability.

3. Consider the advantages and disadvantages of group decision making.

4. Identify the factors used to decide whether to adopt individual or group decision making.

5. Match organizational conditions with the decision-making processes that favour them.

Why study decision making?

Why are senior company executives paid such high salaries? One reason is that they are there to make crucial decisions. The consequences of their decisions may lead to increased company profits, raised market share, raised stock price and the chance to take over a competitor. Alternatively, those decisions might have the opposite consequences and the company itself might be taken over and its employees made redundant. Can you think of managers whose decisions have led their companies to success or failure?

However, decisions are made at all levels of the organization, not just at the top. Both managers and non-managers make them. Given the central role that decision making plays in the life of all organizations, and the effect that decision outcomes have on the lives of all organization members, it is not surprising that

Table 22.1: Levels of decision making

level of analysis	key issues	theoretical perspectives
individual	Limits to information processing Personal biases	Information-processing theory Cognitive psychology
group	Effects of group dynamics on individuals' perceptions, attitudes and behaviours	Groupthink, group polarization and group cohesiveness
organizational	Effects of conflicts, power and politics	Theories of organization conflict, power, politics and decision making

Decision making refers to the process of making choices from among several options.

it has attracted the attention of practising managers and consultants, management academics and social science researchers. Chester Barnard was one of the first people to put decision making at the centre of managerial work. Barnard was for many years the president of the New Jersey Bell Telephone Company and author of the book *The Functions of the Executive* (Barnard, 1938). He saw specialization, incentives, authority and **decision making** as the key elements of formal organizations.

Later writers, notably Herbert Simon (1957), an academic at Carnegie Mellon University, agreed that management theory should be based around the question of choice and decision making as the core of management. He argued that the art of getting things done, and of implementing those decisions that had been made, was indeed an aspect of management that could not be neglected. However, it logically followed from, and was subordinate to, the decision as to what had to be done—how, why, when and by whom? Henry Mintzberg (1989) felt that decision making was possibly the most important of all the managerial activities and represented one of the most common and crucial work tasks of managers. Decision making has been studied in order both to understand how decisions are actually made in practice and to advise managers how to make better decisions. It can be analysed at a number of different levels, as table 22.1 shows. Each level focuses on its own key issues and possesses its own theoretical perspectives. The levels are interrelated, however, with one influencing and being affected by the others.

Classical decision theory assumes that decision makers are objective, have complete information and consider all possible alternatives and their consequences before selecting the optimal solution.

Models of decision making

Rational economic model assumes that decision making is and should be a rational process consisting of a sequence of steps that enhance the probability of attaining a desired outcome.

The traditional approach to understanding individual decision making is based upon **classical decision theory** and the **rational economic model**. These were originally developed in economics, and they make certain assumptions about people and how they make decisions.

The rational economic model of decision making is described in figure 22.1. It is still popular among economics scholars in suggesting how decisions should be made. However, to understand its weaknesses, it is necessary to list its assumptions and demonstrate how they fail to match up to reality. These are shown in table 22.2.

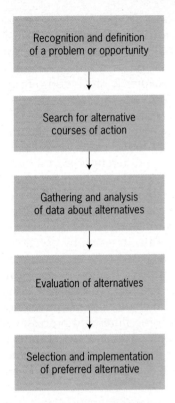

Figure 22.1: Rational economic model of decision making

Table 22.2: Rational economic model assumptions and reality

Assumption	Reality
All alternatives will be considered	• Rarely possible to consider all alternatives, since there are too many • Some alternatives will not have occurred to the decision maker
The consequences of each alternative will be considered	• Impractical to consider all consequences • Impractical to estimate many of the consequences considered
Accurate information about alternatives is available at no cost	• Estimation process involves time and effort • Information available is rarely accurate, often dated, and usually only partially relevant to the problem • Generated or purchased information has a cost • Decisions have to be made on incomplete, insufficient and only partly accurate information
Decision makers are rational beings	• Individuals lack the mental capacity to store and process all the information relevant to a decision • Frequently they lack the mental ability to perform the mental calculations required

Stop and criticize

Think of some personal or organizational decisions that you have made recently. How many of the steps and assumptions from the classical model were relevant in each situation?

Rationality refers to the use of scientific reasoning, empiricism and positivism, and to the use of decision criteria of evidence, logical argument and reasoning. **Rational decisions** refer to choices based on rationality, that is, on a rational mode of thinking.

The classical view of decision making has always employed the concepts of **rationality** and **rational decisions** in its discussions and prescriptions. Rationality is equated with scientific reasoning, empiricism and positivism, and with the use of decision criteria of evidence, logical argument and reasoning [**link**, chapter 2, the world outside]. Rational decisions are decisions which are based on rationality, that is, on a rational mode of thinking (Simon, 1986; Langley, 1989).

What term should be applied to decisions that are not based on the rational economic model of decision making? Irrational? Non-rational? These terms imply not only a different type of decision-making process but they also carry the connotation of something inferior. That is, they attach a negative value to the non-use of rationality. The classical view has now been accepted as not providing an accurate account of how people typically make decisions. Moreover, its prescriptions for making better decisions have often been incorrect. Instead, contemporary cognitive research by psychologists has revealed the ways in which decisions are made based on heuristic models, judgements and tacit knowledge.

Prescriptive models of decision making recommend how individuals should behave in order to achieve a desired outcome.

Prescriptive models of decision making recommend how individuals should behave in order to achieve a desired outcome. This makes the classical model, described above, a prescriptive one. Such models often also contain specific techniques, procedures and processes which their supporters claim will lead to more accurate and efficient decision making. Prescriptive decision models are thus similar to the principles of management described earlier, and they share their strengths and weaknesses [**link**, chapter 15, early organization design]. They are

Angry decision makers

A nurse in an intensive care unit for neonatal babies notices that there is something badly wrong with one of her patients. She can't explain what—and that is the point—but she is sure enough to persuade the doctor to start a course of antibiotics. A day later, conventional hospital tests show that the child is suffering from a potentially fatal condition that can spread too fast for antibiotics to have time to work. Early diagnosis is vital. The nurse's intervention occurred early enough to start the course, before there was any evidence. The treatment succeeded and the baby was saved.

This is a million miles away from a systematic and conscious review of alternatives. But the process is much more successful than the textbook model would be. Many business decisions are made this way. The chief executive and the team certainly analyse what to do. But when they decide, a key part of deciding well is to draw on tacit knowledge and experience, which cannot be made wholly conscious and cannot be mapped on a 'decision tree'. Their decisions are all the better for it. It seems that you don't have to be conscious of what you are doing to do it well.

Antonio Damasio (2000) argued that emotion, consciousness and reason have to work together, to achieve competent decisions. Emotional health matters. Your computer-like brain does not operate better without anger, love or sadness. On the contrary, it seems that the emotional part of our makeup is essential to making decisions. As with the example of the nurse, the rational model of decision-making leaves out a key part of the process. Rationality is not all bad, and jealousy, pain and fear do distort judgements. You can't just listen to your emotions. Sometimes it can be right to calm down and think it out logically.

But the point is this: when human beings make decisions—be they chief executives, prime ministers, nurses or firemen—they are acting as human beings, deciding as history and evolution has designed them to do. Understanding how we decide, and how we decide well, has to be about how all the components work together as a system in an organism which is the product of evolution. Every part matters. So the dominant idea—that deciding is about conscious, optimising analysis—may be a mistake, not only about how we actually operate, but also about how we can and should. Computers are different.

From Jeremy Hardie, 'To take a decision, first you have to be angry', *The Sunday Times*, 30 January 1999, News Review, p.5.

often based on observations of poor decision-making processes, where key steps might have been omitted or inadequately considered. They are developed and marketed by management consultants as a way of improving organization performance through improved decision making.

Many different prescriptive decision-making and problem-solving models can be found in management textbooks. Some are prescriptive in the sense that they specify how individuals should approach a problem, while others specify which decision-making styles should be effective in different situations. These models have labels such as decision trees, programme evaluation and review technique (PERT) and critical path method (CPM). Despite their differences, they typically possess certain common features, which include a list of steps, a logical framework and an emphasis on rationality.

One of the best-known prescriptive models of decision making was developed by Victor H. Vroom and Philip Yetton (1973), and was later expanded by Vroom and Arthur Jago (Vroom and Jago, 1988). Their model sought to help managers determine the degree to which they should involve subordinates in the decision-making process. It was based on the assumption that the effectiveness of managerial decisions was influenced by three situational factors, which were:

Quality   Does the decision achieve the aim? What does it cost to implement?

Acceptance How acceptable is the decision to others? Would they be committed to its implementation?

Time   How much time is available in which to reach a decision? How long does the decision take to implement?

Vroom and Yetton noted that leaders used different decision-making methods, and any of these could be effective, depending on the situation [links, chapter 10, group structure; chapter 21, leadership]. Leaders used these methods with either a group of subordinates or a single subordinate. They identified different decision-making methods, each represented by a letter: A for autocratic, C for consultative, G for group and D for delegation. The decision method choices, and their behavioural characteristics, for both group problems and for individual problems, are shown in table 22.3. In each case, the decision method options for the leader are as follows:

Group problem	AI	AII	CI	CII		GII
Individual problem	AI	AII	CI		GI	D

As one moves from left to right on the table:

- The leader discusses the problem or decision with more people.

- Such discussions change from leader–individual to leader–group interactions.

- Group input changes from merely providing information to recommending solutions.

- Group ownership and commitment to the solution increases.

- The time needed to arrive at a decision increases.

Vroom and Yetton argued that achieving effectiveness depended on the managers' ability to adjust their decision-making method to the requirements of the situation. To help managers achieve this match, they provided seven questions for them to ask in order. These are shown at the top of figure 22.2. Answers to these

Table 22.3: The Vroom–Yetton decision-making model

Style Label	Autocratic AI	Autocratic AII	Consultative CI	Consultative CII	Negotiation GI	Group GII	Delegation D
Participants	Leader	Leader and subordinate(s)	Leader and subordinate(s)	Leader and group	Leader and single subordinate	Leader and group	Leader and single subordinate
Information Suggestions/ ideas Alternatives	Leader uses information available at the time	Leader obtains necessary information from subordinate(s)	Leader obtains necessary suggestions and ideas from subordinate(s)	Leader obtains the collective ideas of subordinates	Leader obtains subordinate's ideas	Leader and subordinates together consider alternatives	Leader supplies subordinate with any information possessed
Role of subordinate(s)	None. Leader generates and evaluates solution alone	Consulted individually. Subordinate(s) provide only information	Consulted individually. Subordinate(s) provide ideas and suggestions	Consulted as a group. Subordinates provide ideas and suggestions	Joint problem solver	Joint problem solvers. Subordinates, collectively with leader, generate and evaluate alternatives to reach agreement (consensus) on a solution. Leader acts as a neutral chairperson	Sole problem solver. Leader may or may not request subordinate to inform him/her of the decision made
Leader explains problem to subordinate(s)?	No	Perhaps	Yes	Yes	Yes	Yes	Yes
Who makes decision/solves the problem	Leader alone	Leader alone	Leader alone	Leader alone (perhaps reflecting group inputs)	Leader and subordinate together arrive at a mutually agreeable solution	Leader accepts and implements any solution that has the support of the entire group	Leader delegates problem to subordinate

Based on Victor H. Vroom and Philip W. Yetton, *Leadership and Decision-Making*, University of Pittsburgh Press, Pittsburgh, PA., 1973; Victor H. Vroom, 'A new look at managerial decision-making', *Organizational Dynamics*, Spring 1973, pp.66–80, p.67.

questions lead along different routes, ultimately directing managers to the best decision-making method for that situation. For purposes of simplification, the problem situation depicted here is relevant to a group situation, and hence individual decision methods GI and D have been excluded. Moreover, in some books, Vroom and Yetton's model is shown as indicating that several decision methods are equally capable of generating an effective solution. In such a case, commentators recommend the method located furthest to the left of the decision-making model, on time and cost criteria. To avoid this complication, only the single, optimum decision method is shown in figure 22.2.

Figure 22.2 is called a 'decision tree' because it contains a series of choices which, like branches, lead to alternative end points. Obviously problems differ. Vroom and Jago (1988) went on to develop four different decision trees, each of which represents a generic type of problem encountered by managers in an organization. Their trees distinguish problems in terms of whether they are indi-

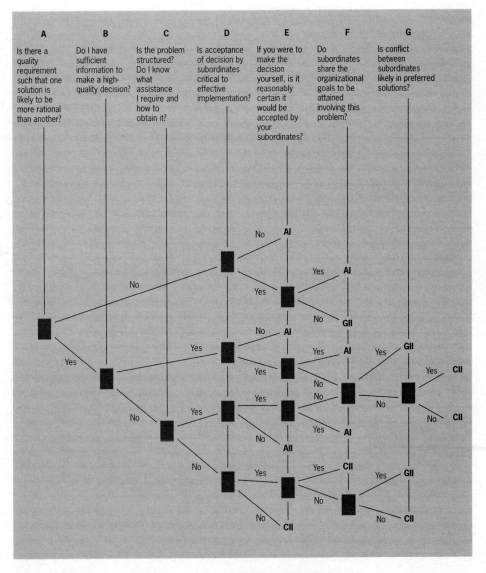

Figure 22.2: The Vroom–Yetton decision tree (group problem)
From Victor H. Vroom and Philip W. Yetton, *Leadership and Decision Making*, University of Pittsburgh Press, Pittsburgh, PA., 1973, pp.42–3.

vidual- or group-focused; whether or not the development of decision-making abilities is involved; and what the time constraints are. Their four decision trees are:

- Individual-level problems with time constraints.

- Individual-level problems in which a manager wants to develop an employee's decision-making abilities.

- Group-level problems in which the manager wants to develop employees' decision-making abilities.

- Group problems that are time-driven.

Stop and criticize

Read the following four cases and select which of Vroom and Yetton's decision-making methods (AI, AII, CI, CII or GII) you think will generate an effective decision.

1. *Shop redecoration*

As a city centre store manager, your staff have complained about the décor and the need to have the premises redecorated. You agreed to their request and received three tenders from three equally reliable decorating firms, all of which are equally capable of doing the job. Their quotations differ little in terms of cost or time to do the job. You asked staff about their suggestions about colour schemes, but there was considerable disagreement. Some staff wanted to retain a classic muted style of décor, while others argued for a more dynamic 'postmodern twenty-first century' appearance for the store. You now have to decide which tender to accept. Which decision method is the most appropriate for deciding on the décor?

2. *Foreign assignment*

You are a financial services manager in a firm of consultants. You have to select four of your financial advisors for a project team to work in a remote East European region whose economy began to develop rapidly in the late 1990s, and which is expected to grow steadily over the first decade of the twenty-first century. The project will involve collection of data, interviewing of clients, analysis of information, and preparation and presentation of a report. The assignment is in a remote part of Eastern Europe with poor facilities and an unstable political environment. Your advisors are all experienced, and each of them is capable of performing the task satisfactorily. Which decision method is the most appropriate for deciding who to send?

3. *Quality programme*

Based at company headquarters, you have been given the task of developing a more effective system for recording product quality in each of the company's six plants, which manufacture third-generation mobile telephony handsets. In the past, variations between the plants in the use of terminology and data recording have complicated the process and caused complaints. Although you have information on the terms in use, you have no information on local practices. Both headquarters and the plants would benefits from a standardized system which would provide more accurate data for quality control decisions. Implementing changes necessitates the co-operation and commitment of the quality control staff at each plant. While they will benefit from an improved system, they are likely to resent what they judge to be headquarters interference in plant procedures. Which decision method is the most appropriate for deciding on a recording system?

4. *Commissioning engineer*

You are the commissioning engineer responsible for building a new chemicals process plant. Your single main problem is to produce accurate estimates so as to avoid building delays.

You have to schedule the materials and the equipment required, estimating when each will be required. You have to ensure that materials are available when needed, or costs will be incurred by equipment arriving too early and lying around idle. Your team is committed to the plant being opened on time. Which decision method is the most appropriate for deciding the estimates?

1. Did the Vroom and Yetton model help you to make a better choice of decision method for dealing with each of the problems than your past experience or intuition?

2. Should managers be advised to think through this model and its practical implications before addressing decision-making problems such as these?

3. Do managers have time to work through this kind of prior analysis before approaching important decisions? Remember Vroom and Jago's four-tree version.

4. What are the main strengths of the Vroom–Yetton approach? What are its main weaknesses?

Conan, the Decision Maker

The British Inland Revenue (government tax collection department) sent the following reply to an inquirer:

Your letter has been received in Customer Services and I have passed this to the relevant section for the Decision Maker's attention. This is because I cannot deal with your request, it will be looked at by the Decision Maker, you should be contacted in due course.

From 'Taxing message behind IR jargon', *Personnel Today*, 18 April 2000, p.68.

Descriptive models of decision making focus on how individuals actually make decisions. Each decision made by an individual or group is affected by a number of factors. These include:

- individual personality
- group relationships
- organizational power relationships and political behaviour
- external environmental pressures
- organization strategic considerations
- information availability (or lack of)

The aim of these models is to examine which of these factors are the most important, and how they interrelate prior to a decision being made.

One of the earliest, and still among the most influential, descriptive models is the **behavioural theory of decision making**. It was developed by Richard Cyert, John March and Herbert Simon (Simon, 1960; Cyert and March, 1963; March, 1988). It is called 'behavioural' because it treats decision making as another aspect of individual behaviour. For example, if a research study interviewed brokers who bought and sold shares in the stock market to determine what factors influenced their decisions, it would be an example of a descriptive approach to decision making. It is also sometimes referred to as an 'administrative model', and it acknowledges that, in the real world, those who make decisions are restricted in their decision processes, and therefore have to settle for a less than an ideal solution. Behavioural theory holds that individuals make decisions while they are operating within the limits of **bounded rationality**. Bounded rationality recognizes that:

- The definition of a situation is likely to be incomplete.
- It is impossible to generate all alternatives.
- It is impossible to predict all the consequences of each alternative.
- Final decisions are often influenced by personal and political factors.

The effect of personal and situational limitations is that individuals make decisions that are 'good enough' rather than 'ideal'. That is, they 'satisfice', rather than 'maximize'. When **maximizing**, decision makers review the range of alternatives available, all at the same time, and attempt to select the very best one. However, when **satisficing**, they evaluate one option at a time in sequence, until they alight on the first one that is acceptable. That chosen option will meet all the minimum requirements for the solution but may not be the very best (optimal) choice in the situation. Once an option is found, decision makers will look no further.

Richard Michael Cyert (b. 1921)

James Gardiner March (b. 1928)

> **Descriptive models of decision making** investigate how individuals actually make decisions.

> **Bounded rationality** refers to individuals making decisions by constructing simplified models that extract the essential features from problems without capturing all their complexity.
> **Behavioural theory of decision making** recognizes that bounded rationality limits the making of optimal decisions.

Stop and criticize

When you chose your current partner—girlfriend, boyfriend, wife or husband—did you maximize or satisfice? Is this distinction a useful way of explaining the decision-making process?

Explanatory models of decision making look at what decisions were made and aim to provide an explanation of how they occurred. For example, there are studies of military fiascos which examine why generals took, or failed to take, certain actions. Often these explanations draw upon personality and leadership concepts and theories [**links**, chapters 5 and 21]. The poor decisions made by teams

Herbert Alexander Simon (b. 1916)

have also been studied using concepts from the group level of analysis such as groupthink and group polarization. These will be examined later in this chapter. Finally, decisions such as whether to acquire or merge with another company have drawn upon the theories of conflict, power and politics, and have been explained at the organizational level.

The **judgement heuristics and biases model** represents the current thinking in decision making (*The Economist*, 1999). Studies have highlighted the limits to rationality and introduced the concept of bounded rationality. What might affect the individual who makes a decision? Decision making involves choice, and choice requires both careful thought and much information. Excessive information can both overload and delay us. Many managers believe that making the right decision late is the same as making the wrong decision. Hence we speed up the process by relying on judgement shortcuts called **heuristics**.

Decision making using heuristics can be considered another model and represents a further step away from the classical model. The leading authors in this field have been Amos Tversky and Daniel Kahneman from the field of decision theory. Their work is contained in a series of articles (Tversky and Kahneman, 1971; 1973; 1974; 1981; 1983; 1992; Kahneman and Tversky, 1972; 1973; 1979; 1984), and a book by Robert Cialdini from the field of social psychology (Cialdini, 1988). Their work has revealed that heuristic-based decision making, although faster and simpler, exposes its users to **biases**, which are inherent in human intuition. Biases operate at the subconscious level, are virtually undetectable, and have a powerful and immediate impact on individuals' judgement. The representative, the anchor-and-adjustment and the availability are the three most common biases.

First, the **representative heuristic** refers to a situation in which people judge things on the basis of how well they represent, or match, particular prototypes. This heuristic uses the similarity of one object to another to infer that the first object acts like the second, and this can lead people to ignore other relevant information. For example:

- using price or packaging to infer the quality of a good or service;
- assessing the likelihood of an event's occurrence by the similarity of its occurrence to their stereotype of similar occurrences;
- predicting the success of a new product on the basis of its similarity to past successful and unsuccessful product types.

For example, a personnel manager may not offer jobs to graduates of a particular university because the last three that had been hired in previous years had all performed poorly.

The **anchor-and-adjustment heuristic** states that people find that starting from somewhere is easier than starting from nowhere. When individuals make estimates for values based on an initial value derived from past events (e.g. the cost of a building), they typically make insufficient adjustments, upwards or downwards, from that initial anchor, so as to reflect other significant factors when establishing a final figure (e.g. inflation, cost of materials). In all cases, the final figures are biased towards the initial figure, even if it is irrelevant. Different starting points therefore yield different answers. Companies ask job applicants their current salaries to find a value from which they can anchor an adjustment. When asking for a quotation for a job, you can suggest a 'figure that you are thinking of' which can anchor the bidder to give a much lower estimate than they might have provided independently. Alternatively, if asked what your fee is, select a high figure (Slovic and Lichtenstein, 1971).

Third, people use the **availability heuristic** to estimate the likelihood of an

Maximizing refers to a decision-making approach where all alternatives are compared and evaluated in order to find the best solution to a problem.
Satisficing refers to a decision-making approach where the first solution that is judged to be 'good enough' (i.e. satisfactory and sufficient) is selected, and the search is then ended.
Explanatory models of decision making seek to account for decisions made by individuals, groups and organizations.
Heuristics are simple and approximate rules, guiding procedures, shortcuts or strategies that are used to solve problems.
Biases refer to a prejudiced predisposition or a systematic distortion caused by the application of heuristics.
Representative heuristic: a predisposition of people to base their judgements of probability on the basis of things with which they are familiar.
Anchor-and-adjustment heuristic: refers to a predisposition to make a judgement by starting from an initial value or 'anchor' and then making adjustments from that point before making a final decision.

Availability heuristic: refers to the predisposition to base judgements of probability on the basis of information that is readily available.

event by assessing how readily instances of it come to mind. An event that is vivid, evokes emotions, is easily imagined and is specific will be more 'available' in your memory than one that is bland, stirs no emotions, is difficult to imagine and is vague. This is a useful heuristic, because more frequently occurring events are more easily revealed in our minds than less frequently occurring ones. However, the availability of information in our minds is determined equally by imagination and vividness, which are factors that are not related to the objective frequency of judged events.

Biases in decision making

Research suggests that decision making can be influenced by a number of different sources of bias:

Contrast bias
This bias of human perception affects the way that we see the difference between items that are presented one after another. If the second item is fairly different from the first, we will tend to see it as more different than it actually is. If you lift a light object first, and then a heavy object, the latter will appear heavier than it actually is.

Reciprocation bias
A basic norm in society is reciprocation, that is, one person must try to repay in kind in the future what another has provided them with in the past. We are socialized from childhood to abide by the reciprocation rule or suffer social disapproval and a feeling of personal guilt. Such reciprocation leads to concession making and allows different individuals' initial, incompatible demands to become compromised, so that they work together towards common goals.

Commitment and consistency bias
Commitment is a state of being in which individuals become bound to their actions, and through these, to their beliefs. Commitment sustains action in the face of difficulties. In these circumstances it is behaviour which is being committed. It represents a visible indicator of what we are and what we intend doing. After taking an initial decision, people will adjust their attitude to make it consistent with their action, and become committed to it.

Social proof bias
The social proof bias states that people decide what to believe or how to act in a situation by looking at what others believe and do. In situations of uncertainty and ambiguity, they observe and follow others, especially those they perceive to be most similar to themselves. Such similarity is defined in terms of status, social background, dress, manner or language. Market research suggests that 95 per cent of people are imitators, and only 5 per cent are initiators.

Liking bias
We enjoy doing things for people we like. That liking encourages us to comply with their requests. The liking bias is so powerful that the person concerned does not even have to be present for it to be activated. Often, just the mention of a friend's or mutual acquaintance's name will be sufficient.

Authority bias
Each of us has a deep-seated duty to authority and will tend to comply when requested by an authority figure. Since the opposite is anarchy, we are all trained from birth to believe that obedience to authority is right. The strength of this bias to obey legitimate authority figures comes from systematic socialization practices designed to instil in people the perception that such obedience constitutes correct conduct. Different societies vary its terms of this dimension.

Scarcity bias
We all know that things and opportunities that are difficult to obtain are more valued. We use information about an item's availability as a shortcut to decide quickly on its quality. Moreover, as things become less available, we lose freedoms. Since we hate this, we react against it and want these things more than before.

Based on Max H. Bazerman, *Judgement in Managerial Decision-making*, third edition, Wiley, New York, 1994; Robert B. Cialdini, *Influence: Science and Practice*, HarperCollins, London, 1988; Andrzej Huczynski, *Influencing Within Organizations*, Prentice Hall, Hemel Hempstead, 1996.

As individual decision makers, we all use judgement heuristics to reduce the information demands placed upon us. Considerable mental activity is saved by summarizing past experiences into the form of heuristics and using them to evaluate the present problems. In a similar way, managers in organizations substitute such simplifying strategies to save having to collect complex information and analyse it. While helpful in many situations, heuristics can lead to errors and systematically biased judgements. Although the three main biases have been discussed, many other errors, fallacies and biases exist. People have ideas about order, randomness, chance, and so on. Studies have shown how peoples' judgements become biased, and hence less rational.

Decision conditions: risk and programmability

Risks of decisions

An earlier chapter distinguished different types of environmental conditions faced by organizations and labelled these 'stable equilibrium', 'bounded instability' (or chaos) and 'explosive instability' [**link**, chapter 16, organization strategy and design]. The conditions under which a decision is made affect both how it is made and its outcome. Decisions differ in terms of the degree of risk involved and their programmability. Every decision is made under conditions of **certainty**, **risk** or **uncertainty**. We shall consider each in turn.

In circumstances of certainty, no element of chance comes between the alternative and its outcome, and all the outcomes are known in advance with 100 per cent certainty. In such circumstances, all that the individual has to do is to select the outcomes with the largest benefit. A situation of total certainty is so rare as to be virtually non-existent. Some writers, struggling to find an example, cite the example of government bonds, which guarantee a fixed rate of interest over a period of time and which will be paid barring the fall of the government. However, as the Russian government default in the late 1990s demonstrated, even government bonds carry an element of risk.

Perhaps the main reason for discussing a generally non-existent state is that it suggests one of the reasons why the most senior executives and managers of the world's leading companies are paid so much. As the trading conditions become more volatile, and technological changes such as the internet dramatically change established practices, the future becomes ever more difficult to predict. Those few individuals who have shown themselves capable of making what have turned out to be the correct decisions enter a seller's market for their skills. Or, to look at it another way, if decisions were made in conditions of certainty, managers would not be needed, and cheaper junior operatives supplied with a rulebook could replace them. Indeed, in conditions of certainty, a computer could quickly and accurately identify the consequences of the available options and select the outcomes with greatest benefits. Managers are paid to make those tricky 'judgement calls' in uncertain conditions.

Probably the most common real-life decisions are made under conditions of risk. When managers can assess the likelihood of various outcomes occurring on the basis of their past experience, research or other information, decision making can be said to take place under conditions of risk.

Decisions made under uncertainty are the most difficult, since the manager even lacks the information with which to estimate the likelihood of various outcomes and their associated probabilities and pay-offs (March and Simon, 1958, p.137). Conditions of uncertainty prevail in new markets, or those offering new technologies, or those aimed at new target customers. In all these cases there is no historical data from which to infer probabilities. In each case, the situation is so novel and complex that it is impossible to make comparative judgements.

Certainty: refers to a condition in which managers possess full knowledge of alternatives; a high probability of these being available; can calculate the costs and benefits of each alternative; and have high predictability of outcomes.

Risk refers to a condition in which managers have a high knowledge of alternatives; know the probability of these being available; can calculate the costs and know the benefits of each alternative; and have a medium predictability of outcomes.

Uncertainty: refers to a condition in which managers have a low knowledge of alternatives; a low knowledge of the probability of these being available; can to some degree calculate the costs and benefits of each alternative; but have no predictability of outcomes.

Table 22.4: Environmental and decision-making conditions

Environmental condition	Decision-making condition	Characteristics	Illustration
Stable equilibrium is a state in which the elements are always in, or quickly return to, a state of balance.	Certainty	Alternatives and outcomes known and fully predictable	Fixed interest rate savings accounts
Bounded instability (or *chaos*) is a state in which there is a mixture of order and disorder, many unpredictable events and changes, and in which an organization's behaviour has an irregular pattern.	Risk	Known alternatives with only probable outcomes predictable	Tomorrow's weather
Explosive instability is a state in which there is no order or pattern.	Uncertainty	Alternatives and outcomes poorly understood	Developing a new product

Without uncertainty as to what course of action to take, there would be be no decision to make. Hence, a decision-making manager would not be required. It is for this reason that so many writers over the years have emphasized the centrality of decision making in management. Having considered the various conditions under which decisions are made, let us investigate the greater complexity of each of the activities associated with the decision-making model presented earlier.

Stop and criticize

Identify three separate events in your university career or work life involving certainty, risk and uncertainty. Describe each situation and suggest how it could change, or has actually changed, from one condition to one of the other two, i.e.

Certainty

- from certainty to risk;
- from certainty to uncertainty.

Risk

- from risk to certainty;
- from risk to uncertainty.

Uncertainty

- from uncertainty to risk;
- from uncertainty to certainty.

From John T. Samaras, *Management Applications: Exercises, Cases and Readings*, Prentice Hall, Englewood Cliffs, NJ, 1989, p.51.

Programmability of decisions

Routine decisions are made according to established procedures and rules.

Organization members make many different decisions every day. Some decisions are routine, while others are not. **Routine decisions** are those which involve the use of pre-established organizational procedures or rules. Routine decision makers are given considerable guidance as to what to do and how to do it through a well-established process, clearly defined goals, and the provision of information sources and decision rules. Examples of routine decisions include the re-ordering of stock items which have fallen to a certain level, the efficient routing of delivery vans and the scheduling of equipment use. All these decisions tend to be repetitive and programmed, and are made by low-level employees on their own who rely on predetermined courses of action.

Adaptive decisions require human judgement based on clarified criteria and are made using basic quantitative decision tools.

Adaptive decisions typically require human judgement to be used. It is a form of judgement that no computer program, however complex, could produce. Once certain judgements are clarified, adaptive decisions can be made, using relatively basic quantitative decision tools such as break-even analysis, a pay-off matrix or a decision tree.

Innovative decisions address novel problems, lack pre-specified courses of action and are made by senior managers.

Finally, **innovative decisions** are made when a unique situation is confronted that has no precedent; when there are no off-the-shelf solutions; and when a novel answer has to be found. Innovative decisions are an outcome of problem solving; they frequently deal with areas of the unknown; and company professionals or top managers typically make them. Within the organizational context, such decisions tend to be rare: for example, the decision whether to acquire another company, to invest in a new technology or to adopt a new marketing approach. Many innovative decisions concern some aspect of company strategy, and hence are more likely to be made by groups than by an individual.

Stop and criticize

Think of three very different decisions that you have made recently. How well did they fit into this routine, adaptive, innovative decision framework presented? What additional decision-type categories would you add?

Table 22.5: Routine, adaptive and innovative decisions

Decision type	Routine ← Adaptive →	Innovative
Goals	Clear, specific	Vague
Level	Lower-level employees	Upper management
Problem	Well structured	Poorly structured
Process	Computational	Heuristic
Information	Readily available	Unavailable
Level of risk	Low	High
Involvement	Single decision maker	Group decision
Consequences	Minor	Major
Solution basis	Decision rules and procedures	Judgement, creativity
Decision speed	Fast	Slow
Time for solution	Short	Relatively long

Individual and group decision making

One of the main reasons why organizational activities are arranged around groups and teams is management's assumption that group decisions are better than individual decisions [**link**, chapter 12, teamworking]. The common sense belief is that with many members contributing their diverse skills, knowledge and experiences, they will make better decisions than individuals (Hill, 1982). These authors cite examples of situations in which groups make decisions that are better than the average quality of decisions made by individuals who are judged to be experts outside the group. However, experimental research data clearly show that while the average quality of a decision made by a group is higher than the average quality of a decision made by an individual, the quality of work group decisions is consistently below that made by their most capable individual members (Rogelberg *et al.*, 1992).

Stop and criticize	Suggest reasons why, despite the evidence of effectiveness, organizations continue to promote group-based decision making.

On the positive side, multiple individuals in a group can supply a greater range of knowledge and information to deal with the more complex questions. They can generate more alternatives, can have a better comprehension of the problem using multiple perspectives, and permit the specialization of labour, with individuals doing those tasks for which they are best suited. The effect of this is to improve the quality of group effort and facilitate wider decision acceptance, since more members will understand the decision better and have a feeling of ownership of it through participation. On the negative side, there are concerns that groups work more slowly, that the disagreements within them can create group conflict, and that group members may be intimidated by their group leader, creating only pseudo involvement in decision making.

Research has revealed that two main factors determine whether groups should be preferred to individuals. These are, first, how structured the task is, and, second, who the individuals are. If the task to be performed is structured (has a clear, correct solution), then groups are better, although they take longer (Weber, 1984). In the case of unstructured tasks (no single correct answer, and creativity required), individuals are better. Hence the counter-intuitive finding that the performance of brainstorming groups is inferior to that of individuals.

For a group to make a good decision, its members must possess the necessary knowledge and skills to pool. Two heads are better than one provided that they have something in them. The quality of the group's decision is partly determined by the ability of its members. Laughlin and Johnson (1966) found the superiority of the lone, high-ability individual compared with a low-ability pair. Pooling of ignorance does not help. Research suggests that for logical structured tasks, choose able people and put them into groups. For less well-structured problems, choose creative people, get them to work alone and pool the outcome of their separate deliberations.

Problems with group decision making

It is the very strengths of a group that are also its weaknesses. The diffusion of responsibility counters the advantage of getting contributions from supposedly independent minds and creates the phenomenon of *group polarization*. In addition, the pressure to conform fails to provide a safeguard against irrational and sometimes fatal wishful thinking fantasies of individuals and creates the phenomenon of groupthink.

Social psychologists have documented the situation in which individuals in a group begin by taking a moderate stance on an issue related to a common value and then, having discussed it, end up taking a more extreme stance. This tendency can lead to irrational and hence ineffective group performance. The groups involved may take a biased look at the problems they face and ignore important

Table 22.6: Advantages and disadvantages of group decision making

Advantages	Disadvantages
Greater pool of knowledge: A group can bring much more information and experience to bear on a decision or problem than can an individual alone.	*Personality factors*: Traits such as shyness can prevent some members offering their opinions and knowledge to the group.
Different perspectives: Individuals with varied experience and interests help the group see decision situations and problems from different angles.	*Social conformity*: Unwillingness to 'rock the boat' and pressure to conform may combine to stifle the creativity of individual contributors.
Greater comprehension: Those who personally experience the give and take of group discussion about alternative courses of action tend to understand the rationale behind the final decision.	*Diffusion of responsibility*: Members feel able to avoid responsibility for their actions, believing it can be shouldered by the others present.
Increased acceptance: Those who play an active role in group decision making and problem solving tend to view the outcomes as 'ours' rather than 'theirs'.	*Minority domination*: Sometimes the quality of group action is reduced when the group gives in to those who talk the loudest and longest.
Training ground: Less experienced participants in group action learn how to cope with group dynamics by actually being involved.	*Log rolling*: Political wheeling and dealing can displace sound thinking when an individual's pet project or vested interest is at stake.
	Goal displacement: Sometimes secondary considerations such as winning an argument, making a point or getting back at a rival displace the primary task of making a sound decision or solving a problem.
	Group brainstorming: Reduces rather than increases the quantity and quality of ideas compared with individual performance.
	'Groupthink': Sometimes cohesive 'in-groups' let the desire for unanimity override sound judgement when generating and evaluating alternative courses of action.
	Satisficing: Making decisions which are immediately acceptable to the group rather than the best ones.

Based on M.A. West, C.S. Borrill and K.L. Unsworth, 'Team effectiveness in organizations', in C.L. Cooper and I.T. Robertson (eds), *International Review of Industrial and Organizational Psychology 1998: Volume 13*, Wiley, Chichester, 1998 pp.1–48; Richard Kreitner, *Management*, Houghton Mifflin, Boston, fourth edition, 1989, p.238.

issues that conflict with its values. This phenomenon is referred to as the *risky shift*.

The psychological explanation is that when individuals in the group discover the position of their fellow members, they tend to move along the scale of opinion towards risk for two reasons. First, because of the *majority rule* influence, which says that the largest sub-group determines the group decision. Second, a process of *social comparison* takes place, where information about socially preferred ways of behaving leads to polarization. When we compare ourselves with and identify ourselves with those immediately around us in the group, we tend to move our position closer to the perceived average of the in-group rather than maintain our initial position (Hogg *et al.*, 1990; Myers and Lamm, 1976).

Table 22.7: Individual and group performance compared

Factor	Individuals when	Group when
Type of problem task	Creativity or efficiency is desired	Diverse skills and knowledge are required
Acceptance of decision	Acceptance is not important	Acceptance by group members is valued
Quality of the solution	'Best member' can be identified	Several group members can improve the solution
Characteristics of the individuals	Individuals cannot collaborate	Members have experience of working together
Decision-making climate	Climate is competitive	Climate is supportive of group problem solving
Time available	Relatively little time is available	Relatively more time is available

From Judith R. Gordon, *A Diagnostic Approach to Organizational Behaviour*, Allyn Bacon, Boston, 1993, p.253.

In the 1950s, the conventional wisdom was that the decisions that groups made were typically cautious and conservative. Jokes about management by committee abounded. James Stoner, at that time a graduate business student at the Massachusetts Institute of Technology (MIT), decided to test this assumption (Stoner, 1961). He carried out experiments to compare individual with group decisions which involved risk. The research questionnaire which Stoner used was devised by Wallach, Kogan and Bem (1962; 1964) and described twelve hypothetical risk situations. Two of these were:

- A man with a severe heart ailment must seriously curtail his customary way of life if he does not wish to undergo a delicate medical operation which might cure him completely or might prove fatal.

- An engaged couple must decide, in the face of recent arguments suggesting some sharp differences of opinion, whether or not to get married. Discussions with a marriage counsellor indicate that a happy marriage, while possible, would not be assured.

Risky shift phenomenon is the tendency of a group to make decisions that are riskier than those that the members of the group would have recommended individually.

Stoner's findings revealed that groups of management students were willing to make decisions involving greater risks than their individual preferences. This counter-intuitive finding was supported by researchers using populations other than management students. This tendency for individuals in groups to take greater risks than the average of the pre-discussion decisions became known as the **risky shift phenomenon**. A number of hypotheses have been put forward to account for this shift towards risk by the group:

- *Diffusion of responsibility hypothesis*: this was the earliest explanation given. When a person makes a decision in a group situation, the responsibility for any failure which might result is assumed to be shared among the group members. Since each individual feels less of a personal responsibility for failure, the group consensus moves towards greater risk taking.

- *Risk lovers dominate hypothesis*: this holds that risk-preferring individuals are dominant in any group and lead the other members to greater risk taking.

- *Cultural value hypothesis*: this states that in some cultures risk is valued and thus people in those cultures may hold boldness, courage and daring as things to be striven for. During a discussion in a risk-valuing culture, more arguments for risk taking are likely to be produced.

- *Social comparison hypothesis*: the questionnaire may be ambiguous, and respondents are unlikely to be comfortable with thinking in terms of numerical probabilities (e.g. 3 in 10). Being uncertain, they are pleased to have the chance to compare it with others. Seeing themselves as average, they compare their own score with another group member whom they also consider to be average. However, the group contains scores all along the range. On some items they will argue for risk, for others for caution. The high-risk takers and the low-risk takers will also seek out suitable comparisons.

Even the earliest studies revealed that group decisions tended to shift slightly, but consistently, in the cautious direction on one or two of the hypothetical dilemmas (Wallach, Kogan and Bem, 1962). It has now become clear that group discussion leads to decisions that are not necessarily more risky but which are more extreme than individual ones. So if group members are initially inclined to be risky on a particular issue, then the group as a whole will become more risky; if, in contrast, the group members are inclined to caution, the group as a whole will become more cautious. In consequence, the risky shift is now called **group polarization**, and over 300 studies of this effect exist (Myers and Lamm, 1976; Myers, 1990).

> **Group polarization** occurs when individuals in a group begin by taking a moderate stance on an issue related to a common value and, after having discussed it, end up taking a more extreme decision than the average of members' decisions. The extremes could be more risky or more safe.

There are two explanations for group polarization. The first is called *informational influence* and relates to the group members learning new information and hearing novel arguments that relate to a decision. The more arguments that are produced that favour a position, the more likely that the group will move to that position. The bias enters because group members will present points which support the action they initially favour, and the group will discuss these. Discussion will thus be biased in the direction of the group's initial position, counter-arguments will be absent, and the group will polarize as more of its members become convinced (Strasser and Titus, 1985).

The second explanation is labelled *normative influence* and takes place when group members compare their own views with the norms of their group. They learn that others have similar or more extreme views than their own. If they want to be seen positively by the group, they conform to the group's position, or even take a more extreme view. Normative influence goes beyond the group pressure discussed in an earlier chapter. The group provides its members with a frame of reference within which they can re-evaluate their initial positions. Both types of influence occur simultaneously in group discussions, with the informational effect being stronger than the normative (Isenberg, 1986).

One of the reasons why groups perform badly on complex, unstructured tasks is the dynamics of group interaction. Groups and teams can develop a high level of cohesiveness [**link**, chapter 11, individuals in groups]. This is generally a positive thing, but it also has negative consequences. Specifically, the desire not to disrupt the consensus can lead to a reluctance to challenge the group's thinking, which in turn results in bad decisions. Irving Janis studied a number of American foreign policy 'disasters' such as the failure to anticipate the Japanese attack on Pearl Harbour (1941); the Bay of Pigs fiasco (1961) when President John F. Kennedy's administration sought to overthrow the government of Fidel Castro; and the prosecution of the Vietnam War between 1964 and 1967 by President Lyndon Johnson. Janis concluded that it was the cohesive nature of these important committees which made these decisions and which prevented contradictory views being expressed. He named this process **groupthink**. He listed the symp-

Irving Lester Janis
(1918–90)

Table 22.8: Groupthink: symptoms and remedies

When groups become very cohesive, there is a danger that they will become victims of their own closeness.

Symptoms	Prevention steps
1. *Illusion of invulnerability*—members display excessive optimism that past successes will continue and will shield them, and hence they tend to take extreme risks.	(A) Leader encourages open expression of doubt by members
2. *Collective rationalization*—members collectively rationalize away data that disconfirm their assumptions and beliefs upon which they base their decisions.	(B) Leader accepts criticism of his/her opinions
3. *Illusion of morality*—members believe that, as moral individuals, they are unlikely to make bad decisions.	(C) Higher-status members offer opinions last
4. *Shared stereotypes*—members dismiss disconfirming evidence by discrediting its source (e.g. stereotyping other groups and their leaders as evil or weak).	(D) Get recommendations from a duplicate group
5. *Direct pressure*—imposition of verbal, non-verbal or other sanctions on individuals who explore deviant positions (e.g. those who express doubts or question the validity of group beliefs). Perhaps use of assertive language to force compliance.	(E) Periodically divide into sub-groups
6. *Self-censorship*—members keep silent about misgivings about the apparent group consensus and try to minimize their doubts.	(F) Members get reactions of trusted outsiders
7. *Illusion of unanimity*—members conclude that the group has reached a consensus because its most vocal members are in agreement.	(G) Invite trusted outsiders to join the discussion periodically
8. *Mind-guards*—members who take it upon themselves to screen out adverse, disconfirming information supplied by 'outsiders' which might endanger the group's complacency.	(H) Assign someone to the role of devil's advocate
	(I) Develop scenarios of rivals' possible actions

Based on Irving L. Janis, *Victims of Groupthink: A Psychological Study of Foreign Policy Decisions and Fiascos*, Houghton Mifflin, Boston, second edition, 1982.

Groupthink is a mode of thinking that people engage in when they are deeply involved in a cohesive in-group, when the members' strivings for unanimity override their motivation to appraise realistically the alternative courses of action.

toms of groupthink as well as how they could be remedied. These are outlined in table 22.8.

Groupthink led to a failure by the group to make the best decision. The group discussed a minimum number of alternatives; the courses of action favoured by the majority of the group were not re-examined from the view of hidden risks and other alternatives, nor were original, unsatisfactory courses. The group failed to use the expert opinion that it had, and when expert opinion was evaluated, it was done with a selective bias which ignored the facts and opinions which did not support the group view. The findings of Solomon Asch's experiments into group pressure and conformity, which were described in an earlier chapter, are relevant here.

In the groups studied by Janis, while individual doubt may have been sup-

"All those in favor say 'Aye.'"

"Aye."　　　　　"Aye."　　　　　"Aye."

"Aye."　　　　　"Aye."

pressed and the illusion of group unanimity and cohesiveness maintained, the group paid a high price in terms of its effectiveness. The factors affecting group cohesiveness are listed in table 22.9.

Thus, while group cohesion can make a positive contribution to group effectiveness, it may also have negative consequences on the process of group decision making. Group loyalty, instilled through cohesion, acts to stifle the questioning of controversial issues, which in turn leads to the making of poor decisions. At the heart of groupthink is the tendency for groups to seek concurrence and the illusion of unanimity. To prevent groupthink occurring, individuals who disagree with the group's evolving consensus must be willing to make their

---

Table 22.9: Factors affecting group cohesiveness

Size	Smaller groups are more cohesive than larger ones, partly because their members interact more frequently.
Duration	The longer members are together, they more opportunity they have to find out about one another.
Threats	An external threat can often (although not always) draw members together against a 'common enemy'.
Isolation	Leads a group to feel distinct and hence special.
Rewards	Group rewards can encourage co-operation to achieve the group goal.
Restricted entry	Difficulty of membership increases identification with the group.
Similarities	Where individuals share common goals and attitudes, they enjoy being in each others' company.

The space shuttle *Challenger* disaster—a case of groupthink?

On the 28th January 1986, seventy-three seconds after its launch from Cape Canaveral, Florida, the space shuttle *Challenger* exploded, killing all seven members of its crew, including a civilian school-teacher, Christa MacAuliffe. The evidence suggested that the physical cause of the explosion was an O-ring rubber seal that failed to do its job due to the freezing, overnight temperatures at the launch pad.

A presidential commission established to investigate the causes of the accident cited flawed decision making as one of the causes of the disaster. The subsequent analysis of documents and testimony by researchers has led some of them to argue that the negative symptoms of groupthink increased in the twenty-four hours prior to the launch in the group that consisted of Morton Thiokol, the builders of the rocket boosters, and NASA management personnel. Thiokol engineers argued for the cancellation of the launch because the O-rings would not withstand the pressure at the launch-time temperatures. The engineers were pressured by their bosses to stifle their dissent, and their opinions were devalued. The past record of success led to overconfidence, and various pieces of information were withheld from key individuals.

In consequence, the group failed to consider fully the alternatives; failed to evaluate the risks associated with its preferred course of action; used information that was biased when making its decision, and failed to work out a contingency plan. Although the physical cause of the disaster was an O-ring seal, many researchers claim that the actual cause was a flawed decision-making process which had been infected by groupthink.

Based on J.K. Esser and J.S. Lindoerfer, 'Groupthink and the Space Shuttle Challenger accident', *Journal of Behavioural Decision-making*, 1989, vol.2, pp.167–77; and G. Moorhead *et al.*, 'Group decision fiascos continue: Space Shuttle Challenger', *Human Relations*, 1991, vol.44, no.6, pp.539–50.

Brainstorming is a technique in which all group members are encouraged to propose ideas spontaneously, without critiquing or censoring others' ideas. The alternative ideas so generated are not evaluated until all have been listed.

voices heard. Research on groupthink suggests that the phenomenon is most likely to occur in groups where the leader is particularly dominant, and that, by comparison, group cohesiveness *per se* is not a crucial factor (McCauley, 1989).

One technique that seeks to improve group decision making is **brainstorming**. It asserts the superiority of a group's performance over than of an individual. Alexander F. Osborn, a principal of the New York advertising agency Batten, Barton, Durstine and Osborn, invented brainstorming in 1939. He coined the term to mean using the brain to storm a problem creatively. It is based on the belief that under given conditions, a group of people working together will solve a problem more creatively than if the same people worked separately as individuals. The presence of a group is said to permit members to 'bounce ideas off each other', or gives individuals the chance to throw out half-baked ideas which other group members might turn into more practical suggestions.

The purpose of the technique is to produce creative new ideas. Members of brainstorming groups are required to follow four main rules of procedure:

1. Avoid criticizing others' ideas.

2. Share even fanciful or bizarre suggestions.

3. Offer as many comments as possible.

4. Build on others' ideas to create their own.

The proponents of brainstorming argue that the flow of ideas in a group will trigger off further ideas, whereas the usual evaluative framework will tend to stifle the imagination. A brainstorming group may, on occasions, perform better than an individual who applies these rules to his own thought processes. However, if one has four individuals working alone, they can generally greatly outperform a group of four in terms of the number of ideas generated.

Research has consistently shown that group brainstorming actually inhibits creative thinking. Taylor, Berry and Bloch (1958) carried out one of the earliest studies and compared the performance of brainstorming groups with 'pseudo-groups' (constructed by the experimenter from individual scores). The authors found that the brainstorming groups produced more ideas than individuals, that they produced more unique ideas, and that the ideas were of better quality as judged by various criteria. However, when the brainstorming groups' performance was compared with that of the pseudo-groups, the pattern was reversed. The pseudo-groups were superior to the brainstorming groups on all criteria. The research demonstrated that the superiority of groups over individuals is simply the product of the greater number of person-hours that they take up. Even under brainstorming instructions, the presence of others seems to inhibit rather than enhance the creativity of these *ad hoc* groups. It may be that brainstorming is most effective with established or specially trained groups.

In nine out of the twelve studies that compared brainstorming groups with individuals working together independently under brainstorming instructions, the individuals produced more ideas (Lamm and Trommsdorf, 1973). Perhaps listening to others' ideas distracts group members, who fall into one-track thinking. Time limits have also been found to affect productivity. Groups that are allowed longer work periods usually produce more ideas under brainstorming instructions, continuing to produce up to the deadline, while individuals working for the equivalent time taper off towards the end (Shaw, 1971). Research by Bouchard *et al.* (1974) compared individual and brainstorming groups working on creative problems. The tasks were performed by groups of four to seven people and an equivalent number of individuals working alone. The individuals were far more productive than the groups. Brainstorming is based on two questionable assumptions. First, it assumes that people think most creatively when there are no obstacles to the stream of consciousness and that among this torrent of ideas (actually associations) there are bound to be some good ideas. Brainstorming presumes that solving problems is a matter of letting one's natural inclinations run free. Second, it associates the quantity of ideas with the quality of ideas.

This counter-intuitive finding is explained by the phenomenon of 'production blocking' (Diehl and Stroebe, 1987). When individuals are speaking in groups, the other members (temporarily) cannot put forward their ideas. Additionally, because they may be holding back their ideas, their ability to produce more is impaired by the competing verbal contributions of others (Sutton and Hargadon, 1996). The latest development has been to compare face-to-face brainstorming

How effective are brainstorming groups?

The inferiority of group brainstorming over individual thinking may be the result of group members being shy about offering unconventional ideas in the belief that, despite the rules, they will be evaluated anyway. Maginn and Harris conducted an experiment in which they studied 152 psychology students, who were split into groups of four and were asked to brainstorm answers to two problems. The first problem concerned 'the benefits and difficulties that would arise if people had found that they had suddenly grown extra thumbs'. The second asked for 'ideas that if put into practice would reduce people's consumption of gasoline'. Some groups were told that their ideas would be assessed for quality and originality by the judges either observing from behind a one-way mirror or listening to a tape recording. The other group were told that, although fellow students would be listening. their ideas would not be evaluated. The authors predicted that the groups facing evaluation would produce fewer ideas. The findings showed that the output of both sets of groups was similar. If groups brainstorm badly, therefore, it is not due to diffidence. Maginn and Harris concluded with the suggestion that individuals put less effort into a task when they share responsibility for the outcome with others. Unless this diminished responsibility effect can be overcome, individual brainstorming is best, if lonelier.

Based on Barbara K. Maginn and Richard J. Harris, 'Effects of anticipated evaluation on individual brainstorming performance', *Journal of Applied Psychology*, 1980, vol.65, no.2, pp.219–25.

groups with computer-mediated ones. Results suggest that electronic groups are superior or equal to the interacting ones. The explanation offered is that the use of the computer reduces the blockage on the production of new ideas, as members listen to others or await their turn to speak (Dennis and Valacich, 1993; Gallupe *et al.* 1992).

Organizational decision making

The making of decisions has been examined at the level of the individual and of the group. It now remains to consider it in the organizational context. The administration of any organization has two main tasks: first, to co-ordinate the work activities within the organization (e.g. ensure that jobs are divided between departments and performed); second, to adjust to circumstances outside the organization (e.g. regulate contracts with suppliers; adhere to government regulations; respond to customers). Individuals in the organization (mainly but not exclusively managers) have to deal with the fact that rules, procedures and precedents seldom determine what should be done in every particular case. Decisions which are 'unprogrammed' have to be made. This means that discretion has to be used, judgements have to be made and decisions promulgated. This ambiguity and uncertainty provides the political context within which decision making occurs in organizations.

Sociologists have studied how power and politics impact on the decision-making process and prevent the operation of the classical decision-making process described at the start of this chapter. Decisions in organizations involve power and conflict between individuals and groups in organizations. The more sources of uncertainty there are, the more possibility there is for individuals and groups to take up political positions. From this perspective, a particular decision is less an expression of the organization's goals and more a reflection of the ability of a particular individual or group to impose their view or 'definition of the situation' and solution on other groups [**link**, chapter 24, power and politics].

As noted earlier, Herbert Simon criticized the classical model of decision making,

| | | Consensus on goals or problem definition? | |
		agree	*disagree*
	certainty	I Computational strategy Rational model	III Compromise strategy Political model
Beliefs about cause- and-effect relationships	*uncertainty*	II Judgemental strategy Incremental model	IV Inspirational strategy Garbage can model

Figure 22.3: Conditions favouring different decision-making processes
Based on J. Thompson and A. Tuden, 'Strategies, structures and processes of organizational decisions', in J.D. Thompson, P.B. Hammond, R.W. Hawkes, B.H. Junker and A. Tuden, (eds), *Comparative Studies in Administration*, University of Pittsburgh Press, Pittsburgh, 1959, pp.195–216; J. Thompson, *Organizations in Action*, McGraw-Hill, New York, 1967.

saying that it ignored the internal politics of the organization system. He and his colleagues, Richard Cyert and James March, were influential in introducing politics into the consideration of decision-making in organizations. They linked the cognitive limits to rationality with political limits. The classical model had assumed that:

- Decision makers possessed a consistent order of preferences.

- There was agreement among the stakeholders about the goals of the organization.

- Decision rules were known and accepted by everyone.

In contrast to this, the bounded rationality view stressed that decision makers could not make the types of decision that the classical model recommended for two reasons. First, there was ambiguity over which direction to take on an issue. That is, people disagreed about which goals to pursue or which problems to solve. Second, there was the issue of uncertainty. This concerned the degree to which people felt certain that a given action would produce a given outcome (cause and effect).

The condition of uncertainty was examined earlier, and it was noted that extra information could reduce it. However, that same new information could also increase ambiguity, since it provided extra points over which different decision makers could disagree. James Thompson and Arthur Tuden used the dimensions of agreement or disagreement over goals and beliefs about cause-and-effect relations as a way of distinguishing four different situations faced by decision makers (Thompson and Tuden, 1959; Thompson, 1967). These are described in figure 22.3.

Any given choice situation can be mapped on these two continua: the degree of agreement that exists between parties on the goals to be pursued; and the level of certainty that a specified outcome can be achieved through the use of a given action. Each such situation can thus be defined as falling into one of the four quadrants in figure 22.3. The most likely form of decision-making model for each quadrant was specified.

I. Computational strategy—rational model

In this case, those concerned are clear and agreed on what outcome they desire (no ambiguity) and certain about the consequences of their actions (high certainty). For example, as demand for ice cream increases in the summer, the company introduces an extra shift. The rational model has already been considered and may be capable of being applied in this situation, since the management knows about the capabilities of its machines, the costs of extra manning and the income from extra sales. The company can therefore calculate the costs and returns using a computational strategy.

II. Judgemental strategy—incremental model

In this case, those concerned are clear and are agreed on what outcome they desire (no ambiguity) but are uncertain about the consequences of their actions (low certainty) because information is inadequate. In the case of the ice cream makers, new equipment may need to be purchased whose performance is unknown. In the case of NATO in 1999, the effect of aerial bombardment of Serbia was unknown. In these circumstances, computation cannot be performed, and hence a judgement strategy is required to assess the risk, which often involves trial and error.

Charles Lindblom (1959) described just such a situation. He built on Simon's notion of bounded rationality, saying that the limited search for and evaluation of alternatives meant that those which were offered differed only slightly (i.e. incrementally) from what already existed. Hence, current judgement choices were made on the basis of past decisions. Decision making in his view was thus remedial, concerned with 'fixing the past' by moving away from it, rather than oriented to achieving goals in the future. Decisions therefore were continually adjusted as they unfolded, and problems were continually attacked.

For Lindblom, policy formulation was thus not a single event but the outcome of countless small, separate, often disjointed decisions made individually by different individuals and groups over a period of years. By making many small decisions that avoided major consequences, incremental decision makers hoped to deal with uncertainty by being able to reverse a decision if required. Sometimes, these limited small decisions fitted together to provide a full solution (Mintzberg *et al.*, 1976). Lindblom referred to the process that he described as incrementalism or disjointed incrementalism, although it is more popularly referred to as the 'science of muddling through'.

III. Compromise strategy—political model

In this case, those concerned are unclear or divided as to what outcomes they desire (high ambiguity). Increasing production to manufacture a large number of extra low-profit products or a smaller volume of higher mark-up items might be equally appealing. The use of the technology provides certainty that either option can be achieved (high certainty). In this case, a compromise strategy is used.

These sorts of unprogrammed decisions are bound to be resolved, ultimately, by reasoning, judgement, influence and politics. When faced with a question such as how should we reformulate strategy for 2003, reasonable people will always disagree. Political behaviour is therefore an inevitable consequence of the prevalence of unprogrammed management decisions.

Many writers view an organization as a coalition of interests. Each department has its own goals, is interdependent with others and competes for scarce resources. The task of senior management is to balance these demands and resolve any ensuing conflicts. It does so by engaging in politics, in an effort to manage or manipulate the decision-making process, to 'cut a deal'. In such circumstances, a decision is not the result of the classical decision-making process but something that is the outcome of horse trading and acceptable to all those involved. From this perspective, individuals and groups unite their interests, propose alternatives, assess their power, join with others, negotiate and form coalitions. In conditions of high ambiguity, decision makers look for alternatives that can accommodate the interests of the parties involved. They are not greatly concerned with searching for information.

IV. Inspirational strategy—garbage can model

In this case, those concerned are unclear or are divided as to what outcomes they desire (high ambiguity). They are also uncertain about the consequences that their actions are likely to have (high uncertainty). When there is neither agreement on goals nor certainty about cause-and-effect relationships, ambiguity and uncertainty prevail, and decision making becomes random. If there is no preference between high-volume/low-profit ices and low-volume/high-profit ices, or certainty about what will happen if they do launch them, then the inspirational strategy is an inspired leap into the dark!

In such circumstances, said Cyert and March, decision-making processes become 'uncoupled' from the decisions actually made. That is, a link ceases to exist between the problems identified and the solutions proposed or implemented. The garbage can model was developed by James March and Johan Olsen and turned the classical model on its head. Whereas both the classical and the bounded rationality models treated decisions as the outcomes of a reasoned approach of information gathering and evaluation, the garbage can model contended that the elements that came to constitute decision problems were independent phenomena that came together in random ways (Cohen *et al.*, 1972; March and Olsen, 1976; Einsiedel, 1983). In their view, the various logical models of decision making had failed to recognize the amount of confusion that surrounded decision-making situations. Instead, they labelled these situations 'organized anarchies'. Within these, a decision 'occurred' rather than was consciously taken. Thus, decision making involved streams of activities which served to cope with uncertainty over time. It occurred when four separate but interdependent streams fortuitously met. The four streams were:

Choice opportunities	Every organization has a stream of 'occasions' at which there is an expectation of a decision, e.g. weekly staff meetings, product review meetings, government cabinet meetings.
Participants	A stream of people who have an opportunity to make a choice.
Problems	A stream of problems which represent matters of concern for individuals both inside and outside the organization, e.g. declining sales, need to recruit staff, increasing hospital waiting lists.
Solutions	The existence of a stream of solutions or answers, all seeking problems and questions, and all available from internal staff advisors or external consultants.

From this perspective, the choice opportunities act as the container (garbage can) for the mixture of problems, solutions and participants that are there at the time. Because of the disorder that characterizes managerial work, preferences are rarely well ordered, they often change, and the criteria for judging the relevance of information are vague. Thus the classical rational model, with its logic and order, does not describe what happens. For example, choices are made before problems are understood; solutions sometimes discover problems; and only rarely are problems resolved after choices are made. The actual decisions made are often irrelevant to the people concerned. For them, the priority may have been to blame others, pay off debts, store up favours, punish others or position themselves in a power struggle. March and Olsen (1976, p.52) felt that:

> choice situations are not simply occasions for making substantive decisions. They are also arenas in which important symbolic meanings are developed. People gain status and exhibit virtue. Problems are accorded significance. Novices are educated into the values of the society and organization. Participation rights are certification of social legitimacy; participation performances are critical presentations of self.

Recap

1. *Distinguish prescriptive, descriptive and explanatory models of decision making and provide an example of each.*

   - Prescriptive models of decision making recommend how individuals should behave in order to achieve a desired outcome. The original prescriptive model is the rational economic model, while a recent one was devised by Victor Vroom and Philip Yetton.

   - Descriptive models of decision making reveal how individuals actually make decisions. The behavioural theory of decision making is the earliest and most influential descriptive model and was developed by Herbert Simon, John March and Richard Cyert.

   - Explanatory models of decision making look at what decisions were made and aim to provide an explanation of how they occurred. The heuristics and biases model developed by Daniel Kahneman and Amos Tversky and Irving Janis' groupthink concept illustrate such explanations.

2. *Distinguish different decision conditions on the basis of risk and programmability.*

   - Decision conditions can be classified as those involving certainty, risk and uncertainty.

   - Decisions can be classified as routine, adaptive and innovative.

3. *Consider the advantages and disadvantages of group decision making.*

   - Groups offer the advantages of a greater pool of knowledge, different perspectives, greater problem comprehension and increased acceptance of decisions.

   - Disadvantages of groups can be considered under the headings of personality factors, social conformity, diffusion of responsibility, minority domination, log rolling, goal displacement, group brainstorming, groupthink and satisficing.

4. *Identify the factors used to decide whether to adopt individual or group decision making.*

   - Individual or group decision making has been made on the basis of the following factors: type of problem task; acceptance of decision; quality of the solution; characteristics of the individuals; and decision-making climate.

5. *Match organizational conditions with the decision-making processes that favour them.*

   - When there is certainty about cause and effects and there is consensus on goals or problem definition then a computational strategy involving the rational decision-making model is favoured.

   - When there is uncertainty about cause and effects, but there is consensus on goals or problem definition, then a judgemental strategy involving an incremental decision-making model is favoured.

   - When there is certainty about cause and effects but disagreement about goals or problem definition, then a compromise strategy involving a political decision-making model is favoured.

   - When there is neither certainty about cause and effects nor agreement about goals or problem definition, then an inspirational strategy involving the garbage can model of decision making is favoured.

Revision

1. How does a 'satisficing' decision differ from a 'maximizing' one? Provide examples of each from your own experience. In what circumstances would one be preferable to the other?

2. Identify three judgemental biases. How do they differ from each other? Give an example of each in an organizational context.

3. How does risk, certainty and uncertainty affect individuals when they make a decision?

4. Should decision making by groups be avoided or encouraged by organizations?

5. Suggest how political factors impact on the making of decisions by individuals and groups within the organization.

Springboard

Bazerman, M.H., 1994, *Judgement in Managerial Decision-making*, third edition, Wiley, New York.

A comprehensive, entertaining and interactive description of the judgement heuristics identified by the research of Daniel Kahneman and Amos Tversky.

Beach, L.R., 1997, *The Psychology of Decision-making*, Sage, London.

Examines the way that individuals make decisions both privately and in the context of organizations. Analyses the interplay of group and institutional dynamics on the decisions made.

Buchanan, D.A. and Badham, R., 1999, *Power, Politics and Organizational Change*, Sage, London.

The book focuses on theories and research dealing with power and politics in decision making within a context of organizational change. It has a practical approach which includes consideration of ethical issues.

Cialdini, R.B., 1988, *Influence: Science and Practice*, HarperCollins, London.

A comprehensive and entertaining summary of the social psychological research on judgement biases.

The Economist, 1999 'Rethinking thinking', 18 December, pp. 77–9.

Provides a 'quick tour' of the main biases and heuristics that psychological research is revealing that are challenging the rational economic view of decision making.

Harrison, E.F., 1999, *The Managerial Decision-making Process*, fifth edition, Houghton Mifflin, Chicago.

Focuses on middle and upper management decision making in organizations using a process model and drawing upon concepts from the social sciences.

Huczynski, A.A., 1996, *Influencing Within Organizations*, Prentice Hall, Hemel Hempstead.

A summary of the diverse research and theory on the process of decision-making organizations is contained in chapter 8.

Kahneman, D. and Tversky, A. (eds), 2000, *Choices, Values and Frames*, Cambridge University Press, London.

The book is edited by the leading researchers in the field of judgement biases and heuristics and is best read after the overview provided by the two earlier publications.

Home viewing

The film *Contact* (1997, director Robert Zemeckis) is based on a novel by the famous scientist Carl Sagan. It recounts humankind's first contact with alien life. The whole endeavour of searching for extraterrestrial life is fraught with personal, scientific, economic, political and ethical uncertainties. Throughout the film, individuals, groups, organizations (and indeed the aliens!) are making choices. Select any four of the major decision-making situations depicted in the film. For each one, answer the following questions:

- What is the problem or decision issue here?

- Who is involved—who is making the decision and who will be affected by it?

- On what basis is the actual decision made (facts, prejudice, hunch)?

- Which concepts, theories and frameworks presented in his chapter help to analyse and understand the decision-making process?

OB in literature

Michael Crichton, *Airframe*, Arrow Books, London, 1997.

A mid-air disaster aboard a commercial airliner leaves three people dead and 56 injured. The pilot lands the plane, and a frantic investigation begins by the aircraft's manufacturers to determine what occurred. The plot involves company managers seeking to determine the cause of the accident. Consider their approach to arriving at a decision. What factors affect both the decision-making process and its outcome?

Chapter exercises

1: It's your decision

Objective

1. To illustrate some of the biases in human decision making.

Briefing

Below are three situation descriptions, each of which requires a decision. Make that decision and, as you do so, be aware of and write down the basis on which you make it.

1. A large city hospital records births by gender in the order of their arrival. Here are some sequences of eight births. Which one of these three eight-birth sequences is likely to be most commonly recorded? (B = boy; G = girl)

    (a) BBBBBBBB

    (b) BBBBGGGG

    (c) BGBBGGGB

2. A recent university graduate with a degree in computing joins a software firm based in Manchester, UK. Estimate the starting salary for this employee. Your friend, who knows very little about the profession or the industry, guesses at an annual salary of £25,000 (€40,000; $38,000). What is your estimate?

3. In the English language, are there more words that begin with the letter 'r' or are there more words that have 'r' as their third letter?

2: Decision types

Objectives

1. To allow you to distinguish between different types of decision.

2. To make you aware of the requirements of each type of decision.

Briefing

The chapter defined and distinguished between routine, adaptive and innovative types of decision. This exercise gives you the opportunity to identify and deal with each of the three types.

1. Class divides into groups of four or five members. Each group represents the executive committee of a small manufacturing company which meets regularly to review and decide upon a list of problems. The list consists of items submitted by employees for decision. This week's list of issues is shown opposite.

2. Each group is to sort the items on the list into three decision categories—routine, adaptive or innovative.

3. Once all the items have been sorted into three piles, each group is to select one item from the routine pile and one item from the innovative pile and develop an action plan for each.

They should also select one adaptive decision issue and indicate what approach might be appropriate for working on that decision.

4. After 20–30 minutes, the executive committees/small groups reassemble in a class plenary session. Each group presents *one* of the decisions that it has worked on and describes its conclusions.

5. Class discusses:

- Was a routine or innovative decision harder to deal with? Why?

- Did group members and groups categorize the decision items in the same way?

- Over which items did group members disagree?

- How were disagreements over categorization dealt with by the group?

List of decision items

1. An assembly worker wants the committee to decide on a more equitable method for allocating scarce parking spaces.

2. A departmental manager wants a decision as to whether one of his programmers can be given a special bonus for developing a popular software item.

3. The facilities manager wants to know if part-time employees are eligible to join the company health club.

4. A division manager wants a decision on whether to open a new office in Paris, Berlin or Moscow.

5. The cafeteria manager has asked for a decision on how to choose between suppliers of foodstuffs.

6. The marketing manager wants a decision on a new product that will not compete with other manufacturers' products but will be popular because it fills an unmet need.

7. A supervisor has asked whether overtime should be given first to those who ask or to those who have the most seniority.

8. A decision has to be made whether to emphasize desktop or laptop computers during the next quarter in marketing.

9. The research department has developed an innovative and cheap memory chip which is capable of being incorporated into many devices. It has asked what direction your committee wants to take in developing applications for this chip.

10. The board of directors has told your committee to consider whether it would be better to open company-owned retail outlets in five major cities or to franchise the outlets.

From Marshall Sashkin and William C. Morris, 'Decision types', *Experiencing Management*, 1987, Addison-Wesley, pp.73–4.

Chapter 23 Conflict

Key concepts

conflict
unitarist frame of reference
pluralistic frame of reference
interactionist frame of reference
functional conflict
dysfunctional conflict
conflict resolution
distributive bargaining

integrative bargaining
mediation
arbitration
conflict stimulation
radical frame of reference
organizational misbehaviour
resistance

Learning objectives

When you have read this chapter, you should be able to define those key concepts in your own words, and you should also be able to:

1. Distinguish between the four major frames of reference on conflict.

2. Distinguish between functional and dysfunctional conflict.

3. Explain the relationship between organizing, co-ordinating and conflict.

4. List the causes of conflict in organizations.

5. Distinguish different organizational co-ordination devices.

6. Explain the conditions in which conflict is resolved and stimulated.

7. List Thomas' five conflict resolution approaches.

8. Distinguish between distributive and integrative bargaining.

Why study conflict?

Conflict is a fundamental force governing all aspects of life. Indeed, the word 'problem' itself is born of conflict. Because conflict provides such a useful starting point for studying complex situations and human behaviour, it has become one of the core concepts of social science and has been used by both historians and sociologists to explain changes in societies. Conflict specialists see the phenomenon as occurring both in various contexts (e.g. political, economic, social, psychological) and at a number of social levels (e.g. personal, domestic, organizational, communal, national and international). Despite these differences, they believe that it has sufficient common attributes to merit study as a distinct field.

Within organizational behaviour, conflict has the status of a 'crossroad' concept. That is, it links and relates to many other topics discussed in the field, both in a variety of ways and at a number of different levels. For example, within an organization, conflicts can occur between individuals, groups and departments; they can arise from the exercise of power and politics; emanate from particular leadership styles and decision-making processes; or arise from structural and cultural changes. At any time, conflicts may be occurring simultaneously, related to one or more of these.

One's job and perspective will determine one's interest in conflict. For the trade union member or official who takes a radical perspective, the question might be whether labour–management conflict, so prevalent in the 1970s, has now been replaced by consensual, co-operative relationships between employees and management. Did management finally eradicate resistance by the end of the twentieth century by making it ineffectual and secure the behavioural compliance of employees with managerial dictats? Is this the reason for the increasing number of 'workplace partnerships' being agreed between unions and companies? Or has the form of historical labour–management conflict changed, its location shifted to new areas and perhaps gone 'underground'?

Some commentators view the organizational landscape as consisting of just labour and management. For them, a company is composed of numerous 'tribes' or sub-groups, spread throughout the different levels and departments. Each one possesses its own interests and acts to promote it. When those interests clash, conflict ensues. From this perspective, the managers are the organizational politicians who 'wheel and deal', build alliances, secure commitments, and so on by using their skills of influencing, negotiation and meditation. From this perspective, the focus is on being able to anticipate clashes and to resolve them successfully.

Those who see conflict as a trigger of change would be concerned at both its absence and over-presence. They would be interested to know what the optimum level of conflict in an organization should be, and how it might be stimulated. There are managers who consider conflict to be a threat to co-operative, consensual relations and would seek to manage it so that either it does not arise or it is resolved rapidly and permanently. Managers taking this view are interested primarily in conflict resolution techniques.

In this chapter, the focus is upon conflict which emerges primarily from the formal interactions or job requirements of individuals operating in their roles within groups and departments inside an organization. It is seen as primarily the outcome of organizational politics, as individuals, groups, units and departments attempt to influence the decisions that affect their own interests, usually at the expense of others' interests. This perspective stresses the structural basis of conflict rather than the interpersonal. We are not dealing primarily with 'difficult people' from a personality perspective, although this may be an element in any conflict situation. Our perspective also implies a conflict management strategy that involves changing the situation rather than the people [**link**, chapter 24, power and politics].

Stop and criticize	Why does conflict get such a bad press? What are the benefits of conflict? In what circumstances could it be beneficial deliberately to stimulate conflict?

Context

Perhaps the most curious aspect of conflict, as a field of study, is the way in which key aspects of the topic have either been overlooked or else have been 'sanitized'. Roger Johnson (2000) noted that traditional organization behaviour textbooks consistently underplay or ignore certain organizational topics, many of which might be considered to be the causes of conflict within the workplace. Among these he listed pay, employee lay-offs, managerial delayering and unemployment. This chapter incorporates the work of those who see conflict in different ways and explains the theoretical and practical managerial implications of such contrasting perspectives.

To understand this traditional omission, one has to go back to the genesis of organizational behaviour as a separate discipline. Organizational behaviour is a relatively new subject. Fritz Roethlisberger was only appointed to his post in the late 1950s, and the Harvard Business School did not establish organizational behaviour as a recognized subject area until 1962 [link, chapter 1, prologue]. The subject is multidisciplinary, drawing upon much older social science disciplines like sociology, psychology, social psychology, anthropology, politics and economics. However, it can also be thought of as an artificial construction, in that it comprises only the parts of those disciplines which are pertinent to understanding human behaviour in organizations in general, and to managing it in particular.

Some critics complain that the contributions of industrial sociology, occupational psychology and group psychology have been sanitized to appeal to organizational behaviour and management classes. It is true that organizational behaviour was a topic designed to fit into a business management curriculum, typically a Masters in Business Administration (MBA) programme. Originally, the majority of MBA students were aspiring managers who attended business schools. This had some implications for the topic of conflict. The kind of conflicts that a line manager was most likely to encounter and had to handle were typically with a single individual or a small work group. Increasing numbers of MBA participants are now practising managers. This trend has reinforced the focus on interpersonal conflict skills and the management of conflict symptoms, to the relative neglect of the deeper causes of those symptoms. The reason for this is quite simply that MBA-trained managers are paid to do the former and have little control over the latter.

Such micro-management of workplace conflict can be contrasted with macro-management of organizational differences. Pay, lay-offs, strikes, lockouts, redundancies and unemployment have always been an aspect of organizational life, but rarely the direct responsibility of line managers in large organizations. Specialized staff based in human resource management departments who were versed in negotiation skills and labour law handled collective bargaining, restructuring and redundancy programmes. In periods of exceptionally fierce union–management conflict, sections of these departments were enlarged and spun off to form industrial relations departments. By 1970, under the initiative of John Dunlop, an American academic, institution-based conflict management became established as a distinct and separate field of academic study known as industrial relations. In Britain, universities appointed professors in this subject and created dedicated units to study it; some of those evolved into academic departments.

This historical summary explains why one does not find topics like pay, lay-offs, etc. in organizational behaviour textbooks. Either they are discussed in human resource management courses and textbooks or else they are not currently considered of sufficient importance for line managers and management students to find a place on an already crowded organizational behaviour curriculum. **Conflict** is a state of mind. It has to be perceived by the parties involved. If two or more parties are not aware of a conflict, then no conflict exists. This broad definition encompasses conflicts at different levels within an organization.

Typically, conflicts are based upon differences in interest and values, when the interests of one party come up against the different interest of another. Parties may include shareholders, managers, departments, professionals and groups; while conflict issues can include dividends, control and wage levels. Social relations are based on implicit or explicit values, which affect human interaction,

Conflict is a process which begins when one party perceives that another party has negatively affected, or is about to negatively affect, something the first party cares about.

judgement and normative behaviour. Organizations like hospitals, churches and Amnesty International have values that are very different from commercial organizations. However, within the latter there can be value conflicts with respect to issues such as environmental and employee diversity.

The aforementioned definition refers to 'parties' to the conflict process. Who exactly are these parties that are normally involved? Managerial prescriptions concerning conflict handing tend to assume that the conflict issue is between two individuals (dyad): either between a manager and her subordinate or between two individuals at the same hierarchical level (e.g. two supervisors or middle managers). Another popular focus is the conflict between the individual members of a team. This can be at any hierarchical level. Occasionally, inter-team or in-group conflict will be considered. Finally, and for reasons already given at the start of this chapter, institutional conflict between a trade or labour union on the one hand and the company's management on the other will rarely be the subject of organization behaviour studies. The significant point is that when assessing conflict research findings or prescriptions for managing conflict, it is important to ascertain where they came from and to whom they might apply.

Finally, writers on conflict differ. Some, like the radical theorists, see organizations as merely one of the 'theatres of war' in society where the class struggle continues to be waged. Within the company, there are a number of 'battle fronts' including wage negotiations, equal opportunities, health and safety, and employee involvement. Other writers, such as the pluralist academics, claim conflict within organizations is based on their own unique circumstances and should not be considered as part of a broader, society-wide picture. There is also a difference between those who distinguish the sources of conflict as subjective and those who view them as objective. The former see conflict as being 'inside a person's head' and perhaps not recognized by others. In contrast, the latter consider conflict 'outside in the world', as an observable reality which other people are able to recognize.

Frames of reference on conflict

The literature distinguishes four different frames of reference on conflict. They are labelled *unitarist, pluralist, interactionist* and *radical* (Fox, 1966; 1973). In this section, the first three will be introduced and contrasted, while the fourth, the radical, will be subjected to a more detailed analysis in its own section later. These frames are not 'right' or 'wrong', but different:

- *unitarist*: sees organizations as essentially harmonious and any conflict as bad;

- *pluralist*: sees organizations as a collection of groups, each with its own interests;

- *interactionist*: sees conflict as a positive, necessary force for effective performance;

- *radical*: sees conflict as an inevitable outcome of capitalism.

Earlier chapters have used the concept of frame of reference to refer to a particular position or set of assumptions which is acquired or possessed by organization members. A frame is a scheme of interpretation that makes it possible for individuals to explain, organize and make sense of particular events and actions. Frames therefore express the generally accepted norms of the social domain in which they are valid (e.g. a group, occupational category, subject discipline, pol-

Robert Reich described the 'pronoun test' that he used to evaluate the nature of the employment relationship in the companies that he visited as US Secretary of Labour during the first Clinton administration in the following way:

> I'd say, 'Tell me about the company'. If the person said 'we' or 'us', I knew people were strongly attached to the organization. If they said 'they' or 'them', I knew there was less of a sense of linkage. (cited in Rousseau, 1999)

itical allegiance, etc.). Within a single organization, various individuals, each of whom uses a different frame, may interpret the same event differently. Moreover, academics will also adopt one of these frames when they teach the topic to their students or research it. Neither organization employees nor academics will necessarily make their chosen frame explicit, and hence students need to ask or deduce which conflict frame of reference the person holds. The Marxist frame of reference on conflict sees it as the inevitable outcome of, or intrinsic characteristic of, capitalism.

Most of us are capable of bringing different frames of reference to bear on the situations that we face. If we analyse it this way, we reach these conclusions, but if we analyse it from another perspective, we reach different conclusions. Some people (students, academics, managers) may be wedded to a particular perspective. This becomes obvious in their conversations, actions or writings. Their chosen frame of reference on conflict will determine:

- what they will notice in their environment;

- how they will interpret those noticed events;

- how they expect others to behave;

- how they will behave themselves.

However, there is value in being able to view conflicts from a number of different standpoints, to 'switch between frames', in part so that we can understand the viewpoints of others.

The **unitarist frame of reference** on conflict views organizations as fundamentally harmonious, co-operative structures, consisting of committed, loyal, worker–management teams that promote harmony of purpose.

Stephen Ackroyd and Paul Thompson (1999) and Johnson (2000) identified the key features of the unitarist frame of reference:

Unitarist frame of reference is a perspective on conflict which regards management and employee interests as coincident and which thus regards (organizational) conflict as harmful and to be avoided.

1. Assumes a commonality of interests between an organization's workers and managers and, by implication, the company's owners (shareholders).

2. Accepts unquestioningly the political, economic and social framework within which management is performed, and adopts the language, assumptions and goals of management itself, which it supposedly seeks to study and understand.

3. De-politicizes the relationships between individuals, groups and classes within the workplace, treating conflicts and contradictions as peripheral.

4. Explains actual, observed instances of workplace conflict either in terms of a failure of co-ordination problems or in psychological terms (the personal malfunction or abnormal behaviour of deviant individuals).

5. Applies a liberal-humanistic, individually focused approach to conflict resol-

Unitarist frame of reference

To develop a close affinity with organizations which promote fellowship between workers, customers, members and employers.

(From the mission statement of The Co-operative Bank)

Safety is paramount. We all have a duty to take care of ourselves, colleagues and customers.

(From British Airways' Management Framework for Safety)

ution, which is rooted in the human relations movement and its developments [**links**, chapter 9, group formation; chapter 17, organization development].

6. Holds that managers are capable of permanently changing the behaviour of employees in a conflict situation in an organization through the application of conflict resolution techniques.

7. Claims that economic, technological and political developments had, by the 1990s, meant that management had virtually eliminated non-sanctioned employee behaviour within the organization.

8. Moves rapidly over the consideration causes of conflict within the workplace in order to focus on conflict resolution techniques.

9. When discussing the causes of workplace conflict, it focuses on communication failures between management and employees, and the interference of 'third party agitators', normally unions, in the relationship between the employer and the employee.

Pluralist frame of reference is a perspective which views organizations as consisting of different, natural interest groups, each with its own potentially constructive, legitimate interests, which makes conflict between them inevitable.

The **pluralist frame of reference** on conflict views organizations as a collection of many separate groups, each of which has its own legitimate interests, thereby making conflict between them inevitable as each attempts to pursue its own objectives. This frame of reference therefore rejects the view that individual employees have the same interests as the management, or that an organization is 'one big happy family' [**link**, chapter 19, organization culture].

The pluralist frame takes a political orientation in that it sees that some of the time, the interests of the different groups will coincide, while at other times, they will clash and so cause conflict between them. The outbreak of conflict provides a 'relationship regulation' mechanism between the different groups. That is, it provides a clear sign to both parties as to which issues they disagree fundamentally about, and thus provides a sort of 'early warning system' of possible impending breakdown which would be to the disadvantage of all concerned. The most common clashes may be between unions and management, but will also include differences between management functions (production versus marketing); levels of management (senior management versus middle management), and between individual managers.

These differences do not prevent an organization functioning, since all groups recognize that compromise and negotiation are essential if they are to achieve their goals even partially. Hence, from this perspective, the job of management becomes that of keeping the balance between potentially conflicting goals, and managing the differences between these different interest groups. This involves seeking a compromise between the different constituents, such as the employees, managers and shareholders, so that all these stakeholders, to varying degrees, can

Organizations as conflicting cliques

Melville Dalton described organizational structure as consisting of conflicting cliques which engaged in struggles in order to increase their power and thus obtain a greater share of the rewards which the organization had to offer. He found that individuals and groups were primarily interested in the pursuit of their own narrow interests. They tried to consolidate and improve their own position of power even if this was at the expense of the organization as a whole. He described how such political activity was skilfully and scrupulously camouflaged. As a result of this, the policies pursued appeared to be in harmony with the official ideology and the organizational handbook. His view of organizational life was one of swiftly changing and conflicting cliques cutting across departmental and other boundaries.

Based on Melville Dalton, *Men Who Manage*, Wiley, New York, 1959.

Interactionist frame of reference is a perspective on conflict which sees it as a positive and necessary force within organizations that is essential for their effective performance.

continue to pursue their aspirations. Underlying the pluralist view is the belief that conflict can be resolved through compromise to the benefit of all. However, it requires all parties to limit their claims to a level which is at least tolerable to the others, and which allows further collaboration to continue. A mutual survival strategy is agreed.

Acceptance of the pluralist frame implies that conflict is inevitable, indeed endemic. However, it does not see conflict as harmful and to be eliminated but believes that it must be evaluated in terms of its functions and dysfunctions. For while it may reinforce the status quo, it can also assist evolutionary rather than revolutionary change, acting as a safety valve and keeping the organization responsive to internal and external changes while retaining intact its essential elements, such as the organizational hierarchy and the power distribution. The inevitable conflict which results has to be managed so that organizational goals are reconciled with group interests for the benefit of mutual survival and prosperity. This ongoing internal struggle is seen as generally acting to maintain the vitality, responsiveness and efficiency of the organization.

The **interactionist frame of reference** on conflict views it as a positive and necessary force within organizations that is necessary for effective performance. It can be considered as part of the pluralist tradition and features extensively in American management textbooks. The pluralist frame accepts the inevitability of conflict and argues that, to be dealt with constructively, conflict has to be institutionalized within the organization through systems of collective bargaining. The interactionist frame not only accepts the inevitability of conflict but also contains the notion that there is an optimum level of it (not too little or too much), and that the way to achieve that level is through the intervention of the manager.

Functional conflict is a form of conflict which supports organization goals and improves performance.
Dysfunctional conflict is a form of conflict which does not support organization goals and hinders organizational performance.

The interactionist frame believes that conflict should be encouraged whenever its emerges, and stimulated if it is absent. It sees a group or a department that is too peaceful, harmonious and co-operative as potentially apathetic and unresponsive to changing needs. It fears that extreme group cohesion can lead to groupthink, as identified by Irving Janis (1982) and Coser and Schwenk (1990) [**link**, chapter 22, decision making]. This frame therefore encourages managers to maintain a minimum level of conflict within their organizations so as to encourage self-criticism, change and innovation and thereby counter apathy. However, that conflict has to be of the appropriate type. Thus, **functional conflict** supports organization goals and improves performance, but **dysfunctional conflict** hinders organizational performance.

The relationship between the two is depicted on a bell-shaped curve shown in figure 23.1. Insufficient conflict and the unit or group does not perform at its best;

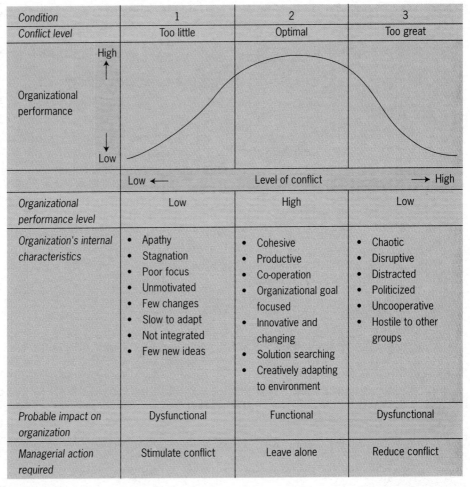

Condition	1	2	3
Conflict level	Too little	Optimal	Too great
Organizational performance level	Low	High	Low
Organization's internal characteristics	• Apathy • Stagnation • Poor focus • Unmotivated • Few changes • Slow to adapt • Not integrated • Few new ideas	• Cohesive • Productive • Co-operation • Organizational goal focused • Innovative and changing • Solution searching • Creatively adapting to environment	• Chaotic • Disruptive • Distracted • Politicized • Uncooperative • Hostile to other groups
Probable impact on organization	Dysfunctional	Functional	Dysfunctional
Managerial action required	Stimulate conflict	Leave alone	Reduce conflict

Figure 23.1: Types of conflict, internal organizational characteristics and required management actions
Based on Mary Jo Hatch, *Organisation Theory*, Oxford University Press, Oxford, 1997, p. 305; and Stephen P. Robbins, *Organisational Behaviour: Concepts, Controversies and Applications*, Prentice Hall, Englewood Cliffs, NJ, 1998, p.464.

too much conflict and its performance deteriorates. Performance improvements occur through conflict exposing weaknesses in organizational decision making and design, which prompts changes in the company.

Figure 23.1 is also sometimes referred to as the contingency model of conflict (Hatch, 1997) because it recommends that managers should increase or decrease the amount of conflict in their organizations depending on the situation. Thus, for example, in condition 1 there is too little conflict, and so they need to stimulate more. In contrast, in condition 3, there is too much conflict and they need to reduce it. In both cases they seem to achieve an optimum level of conflict, depicted in column 2. Taffinder (1998) felt that at optimal intensity (condition 2 in figure 23.1), conflict produced organizational benefits which managers rarely exploited and even suppressed by applying conflict resolution approaches too rapidly. Among the benefits of functional conflict that he listed were:

• motivating energy to deal with underlying problems;

• making underlying issues explicit;

- sharpening people's understanding of real goals and interests;
- enhancing mutual understanding between different groups of employees;
- stimulating a sense of urgency;
- discouraging engagement in avoidance behaviour;
- preventing premature and often dangerous resolution problems.

He believed that successful organizations created the conditions in which conflict over how tasks should be performed was increased, while conflict over values was eliminated. The latter was achieved by senior management building, managing and reinforcing a clear set of values that defused any value conflicts [**link**, chapter 19, organization culture]. He cited ABB, Levi Strauss and Microsoft as examples of companies which possessed deep-rooted cultural values that made them resilient and able to cope with change [**link**, chapter 18, organizational change]. ABB Calor Emag deliberately produced task-related conflict in its search for improvement, seeking to produce better decisions and excellent delivery times.

Differences can be fruitful

Conflict can improve rather than impede organizational decision making. When those who have opposing ideas try to agree, they develop a better understanding of each others' positions, bring their differences to the forefront, and reach a decision with which everyone is satisfied. Dean Tjosvold and Deborah Deemer reached this conclusion from the results of an experiment which they designed.

They asked sixty-six student volunteers to take the roles of shop floor employees and supervisors at an assembly plant in which conflict had arisen over the employees' job rotation schemes. The students were divided into three groups—two student–employee groups and one student–supervisor group. Both student–employee groups were given information about the benefits of the scheme (it gave more job satisfaction) and were asked to defend it. One of the two student–employee groups was told that the company had a good industrial relations record and that it tried, whenever possible, to avoid controversy. The other student–employee group was told that the company had a history of open, frank discussion of differences and that the norm was co-operative controversy, and that the group should try to win any arguments that arose. The 'student–supervisors' were told about the scheme's disadvantages (employees did not remain in their jobs long enough to develop expertise) and were asked to argue for its abolition. The students were offered lottery tickets for complying with these norms in the experiment.

The 'employees' and 'supervisors' then met in pairs for fifteen minutes to discuss and resolve the issue. They noted their decision and answered questions about their attitudes to their discussions. It was found that where controversy was avoided, the decisions were dominated by the views of the supervisors. Where controversy was competitive, the students were generally not able to reach any agreement and experienced feelings of hostility and suspicion towards their adversary. However, under conditions of co-operative controversy, decisions were reached that integrated the views of employees and supervisors. Feelings of curiosity, trust and openness were also found to be induced. Co-operative controversy may therefore be good for decision making. But how does one get real supervisors and real employees to comply with this apparently useful social or organizational norm?

Based on Dean Tjosvold and Deborah Deemer, 'Effects of controversy within a co-operative or competitive context on organizational decision making', *Journal of Applied Psychology*, 1980, vol.65, no.5, pp.590–5.

Co-ordination and conflict

The process of organizing by senior managers acts to differentiate activities, and an outbreak of conflict can thus be seen as a symptom of management's failure to adequately co-ordinate these same activities later on. The four-stage co-ordination–conflict model organizes the diverse theoretical discussions and research findings into a framework that explains how conflict in organizations arises and how it might be managed (figure 23.2). Such management may involve either the use of conflict resolution approaches (to reduce or eradicate conflict) or conflict stimulation approaches (to encourage and increase conflict).

Organizing

The first stage of the model consists of organizing. This concept was introduced earlier in the book, where it was defined as the process of breaking up a single task and dividing it between different departments, groups or individuals [**link**, chapter 15, early organization design]. For example, a car company allocates the work involved in building a new vehicle to its different sub-divisions (departments, groups and individuals)—personnel, accounting, production, sales and research. Such functional specialization is one of many bases on which to divide the total work involved. Specialization is rational because it concentrates specialists in proper departments, avoids duplication, allows performance goals to be established and specifies practices.

All forms of horizontal specialization result in each sub-unit becoming concerned with its own particular part of the total objective and work process. The degree of such separation of tasks can vary, but it creates the conditions in which conflict can potentially arise. It does so because, by definition, each department, group or individual receives a different part of the whole task to perform. This makes it distinct from the other departments in six different areas:

1. Goals orientation and evaluation.

2. Self-image and stereotypes.

3. Task interdependencies.

4. Time perspectives.

5. Overlapping authority.

6. Scarce resources.

Goals orientation and evaluation
Each department is given its own goal, and its members are evaluated on the extent to which they achieve it. Ideally, the goals of different departments, groups and individuals, although different, should be complementary, but in practice this may not be so. Moreover, the measurement process can reinforce differences. Each department's unique goals and evaluation methods lead it to have its own view about company priorities, and how these are best achieved.

Self-image and stereotypes
Employees in each department become socialized into a particular perception of themselves and seeing the other departments as different. A group may come to see itself as more vital to a company's operations than others, and come to believe that it has higher status or prestige. Such an evaluation can engender an 'us-and-them' attitude. The higher-status groups may cease to adapt their behaviours to accommodate the goals of other groups and, indeed, may try to achieve their

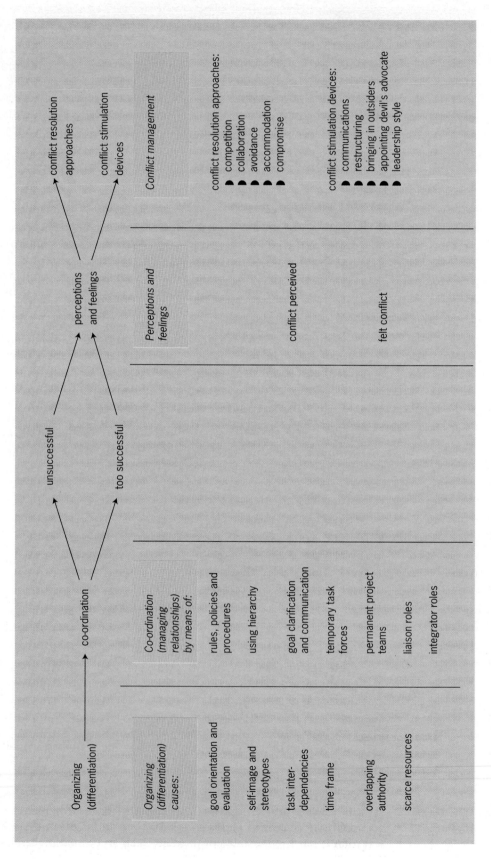

Figure 23.2: Co-ordination–conflict model

Areas of potential goal conflict between marketing and manufacturing departments

Goal conflict	*Marketing* versus	*Manufacturing*
	operating goal is customer satisfaction	**operating goal is production efficiency**
conflict area	*typical comment*	*typical comment*
1 Breadth of product line	'Our customers demand variety'	'The product line is too broad—all we get are short, uneconomical runs'
2 New product introduction	'New products are our lifeblood'	'Unnecessary design changes are prohibitively expensive'
3 Production scheduling	'We need faster response. Our lead times are too long'	'We need realistic customer commitments that don't change like a wind direction'
4 Physical distribution	'Why don't we ever have the right merchandise in inventory?'	'We can't afford to keep huge inventories'
5 Quality	'Why can't we have reasonable quality at low cost?'	'Why must we always offer options that are too expensive and offer little customer utility?'

Based on Benson S. Shapiro, 'Can marketing and manufacturing coexist?' *Harvard Business Review*, 55, September–October 1977, pp.104–14.

objectives at the cost of others, thus creating conflict. Whenever differences between groups and departments are emphasized, stereotypes are reinforced, relations deteriorate and conflict develops. Departments will often blame each other for problems and shortcomings.

Task interdependencies
The process of organizing which results in differentiation makes individuals, groups and departments dependent on one another to perform their own jobs satisfactorily and achieve their objectives. The degree of such interdependence

Source: CATTY copyright Cathy Guizewite, Reprinted with permission of Universal Press Syndicate. All rights reserved.

Table 23.1: Conditions for high and low conflict occurrence

Conflict will be	When task variety is	When analysability is	When information requirements are
Highest	high	low	high
Lowest	low	high	low

varies. An earlier chapter considered James Thompson's (1967) three types of interdependence—*pooled*, *sequential* and *reciprocal* [**link**, chapter 15, early organization design]. Groups in sequential interdependence, and even more, in reciprocal interdependence, required a high degree of co-ordination between their activities. If this was achieved, then each group would perform effectively and its members would experience satisfaction. When such co-ordination was absent, the result would be conflict between them. From this viewpoint, conflict results from a failure in co-ordination.

In addition, the types of task that individuals, groups and departments are allocated can cause difficulties. Such tasks can be either routine or non-routine. Charles Perrow's (1970) classification based on *task variety* and *task analysability* was also introduced in the same chapter [**link**, chapter 15, early organization design]. As table 23.1 summarizes, tasks which have high variety (possess many unexpected events) and low analysability (no ready-made solutions) require a great deal more information processing than those that do not. Groups performing such tasks have to interact more with other groups in order to obtain the volume and quality of information that they need to perform their tasks. This increases the chances of conflict between them. In contrast, tasks that have low variety (are predictable with few unexpected events) and possess high analysability (many ready-made solutions) require less information processing. The latter reduce or eliminate the need for individuals, groups or departments to obtain information from each other in order to do their job, and thereby reduce the chances of conflict occurring between them.

Time perspectives
Paul Lawrence and Jay Lorsch's (1967) study found that people's perceptions of the importance accorded to different items depended on the time frame that governed their work and their goal orientations. Groups with different perceptions would find it difficult to co-ordinate their activities, and this would result in greater intergroup conflict. This is partly because their time frames differ. These different goals are often incompatible, hindering communication, impeding co-ordination and encouraging conflict.

Overlapping authority
Demarcation disputes have always caused difficulties, and ambiguity over responsibility or authority is one example of this. Individuals or groups may be uncertain as to who is responsible for performing which tasks or duties; and who has the authority to direct whom. Each party may claim or reject responsibility, and the result can be conflict. This can occur particularly when a growing organization has not yet worked out the relationships between different groups, or after a takeover or merger, when new roles and responsibilities have yet to be clarified.

Groups may fight for the control of a resource, while individual managers may attempt to seize one another's authority.

Scarce resources
Once a task is allocated to an individual, group or department, it is also allocated resources to achieve it. Since resources are finite, conflict can arise with respect to how personnel, money, space or equipment are shared out. From a win–lose perspective, one party's gain is another's loss. For this reason, conflicts often arise at times of budget cuts, reduced promotion opportunities, and no increase in salaries or wages.

Staff–line conflict

In his classic study, Melville Dalton studied the conflict between line managers, those directly responsible for production, and staff managers, those not directly involved, but who performed a staff function, for example personnel managers who supplied line managers with advice on employment legislation. Dalton attributed the causes of the conflict between them both to the different roles that each occupied within the company and to differences in their personal characteristics. Conflicts between staff and line managers continue to this day and are based on similar concerns. The four main causes in this context include authority, personal differences, interdependence and differing loyalties.

Authority reduction: While line managers are afraid that staff specialists will intrude on their jobs and reduce their authority and power, staff specialists complain that line managers do not make good use of them or provide them with enough authority.

Social and physical differences: Line and staff personnel differ in terms of age, background and educational level. Dalton found that staff specialists had received more education and training, were appointed to their posts at relatively senior hierarchical levels, and tended to be members of professional associations. Line managers were generalists, had less professional training and had often worked their way up from the shop floor.

Line dependence on staff knowledge: Dalton also found that conflict could result because staff specialists considered their knowledge to be more relevant and up to date than the line manager's, while the latter felt that his experience was more relevant than 'book learning'. However, line managers are often dependent on staff personnel for current specialist knowledge, such as employment legislation. They have to visit staff personnel to fill the gap between their knowledge and authority. This caused conflict between them.

Different loyalties: Other sources of conflict included the staff member's loyalty to the company, in that they would pursue their professional career in different organizations, while the line manager was likely to remain with the same firm. When loyalties to a particular function or discipline are greater than to the overall company, conflict is likely. This is the 'cosmopolitan' versus 'local' distinction encountered earlier [**link**, chapter 19, organization culture]

Based on J.A. Balasco and J.A. Alutto, 'Line and staff conflicts: Some empirical insights', *Academy of Management Journal*, March 1969, pp.69–77; Melville Dalton, 'Conflict between staff and line managerial officers', *American Sociological Review*, June 1950, pp.342–51; and James E. Sorenson and Thomas L. Sorenson, 'The conflict of professionals in bureaucratic organizations', *Administrative Science Quarterly*, March 1974, pp.98–106.

Stop and criticize

How complete is this list of conflict causes—goal orientation, self-image, interdependencies, time frame, overlapping authority and scare resources?

Think of two conflict situations with which you have been involved in an organization. Do these causes satisfactorily account for your conflicts or would you wish to add other causes?

Table 23.2: Devices for co-ordinating relationships in organizations classified by class

Class of co-ordination	Description	Device
Formal direction	Written guidelines and adjudication	• Rules, policies and procedures by senior staff • Using hierarchy
Mutual adjustment	Members carrying out the work adjust to each other	• Goal clarification and communication. • Temporary task force • Permanent project team
Special liaison	Specially employed co-ordinators use consultation and communication	• Liaison roles • Integrator roles

Based on Colin Hales, *Managing Through Organization*, Routledge, 1993, p.55.

Co-ordinating

If organizing involved breaking up the task into bits, then co-ordinating is bringing the bits together again. Co-ordination involves ensuring that the previously divided tasks that were allocated between different departments, groups and individuals are brought together in the right way and at the right time. Co-ordination entails synchronizing the different aspects of the work process. The process of organizing creates the aforementioned differences but does not automatically result in conflict breaking out between parties. The three general classes of co-ordination devices are listed in table 23.2.

Provided that the relationships between the differentiated departments, units, groups or individuals are successfully co-ordinated, then conflict will not occur. By effectively using interparty co-ordination devices, a company can prevent conflict breaking out in the first place. The devices are designed to manage the relationships between the different individuals, groups, units and departments so that the reasons for conflict to arise are eliminated. It is only if and when these co-ordination devices fail, and conflict occurs, that conflict resolution techniques will be required. Organizations use seven devices with which to co-ordinate the activities of individuals, groups, units and departments:

1. Rules, policies and procedures.

2. Using hierarchy.

3. Goal clarification and communication.

4. Temporary task forces.

5. Permanent project teams.

6. Liaison roles.

7. Integrator roles.

Rules, policies and procedures
All of these specify how one party is to interact with another. For example, a standardized operating procedure will specify when additional staff can be recruited to a department. Rules and procedures reduce the need for both interaction and information flow between parties. They are most useful when interparty activities are known in advance, when they occur frequently enough to merit establishing rules and procedures to handle them, and when there is sufficient stability to make their relevant.

Using hierarchy
Co-ordination of different parties' activities is achieved by referring any problems to a superior located higher in the organizational hierarchy. The superior uses their legitimate authority, based on the position in the hierarchy, to resolve the conflict. For example, two managers unable to agree take the problem to their mutual boss. Resorting to hierarchy is only effective in the short term to provide solutions to specific, urgent problems.

Goal clarification and communication
By specifying and communicating its goals to the others in advance, each party knows what the other is attempting to do. At the individual level this may mean clear job descriptions, while at the departmental level, it could be statements of objectives. Parties can meet to ensure that they do not compete or interfere with the goals of others. Such discussions reduce the chances of each party misperceiving the other's intentions.

Temporary task force
Representatives of several different departments can come together on a temporary basis to form a task force. Once the specific problem they were created for is solved, the task force disbands and members return to their usual duties and departments. During their membership, individuals come to understand the goals, values, attitudes and problems of their fellow members. This helps to resolve their differences effectively, especially if more than two parties are involved.

Permanent project team
For complex tasks, a project team may be established consisting of cross-functional members (e.g. from engineering, marketing, finance). This creates a matrix structure, since each individual retains a responsibility to the permanent team leader and to their functional department. This solution allows co-ordination to occur at the team level, thus improving communication and decision making [**link**, chapter 12, teamworking].

Liaison roles
If differences remain unresolved by senior management, then a liaison role may be created. It would be used most by departments between whom the potential for conflict was highest. The occupant of this role has to be well informed about the needs and technology of the units involved, be seen to be unbiased and to be interpersonally skilled. By holding meetings, supplying units with information, liaison personnel keep the employees in different sections in touch with each other.

Integrator roles
An individual or department may be dedicated to integrating the activities of several highly conflicting departments, e.g. production, sales and research (figure 23.3). A scientist with financial and sales experience may be recruited to occupy an integrating role. By having a 'foot in each camp', this person can assist the departments to co-ordinate their activities. The integrator checks that the departments' objectives complement each other, and that the output of one becomes the timely input to the other.

Perceptions and emotions

The conditions described in the previous stage can exist without igniting a conflict. Perception plays an important part [**link**, chapter 7, perception]. It is only if one party, individual, group or department becomes aware of or is adversely affected by them, and cares about the situation, that latent conflict turns into perceived conflict. It occurs only when one party realizes that another is thwarting its goals. In this stage, the conflict issue becomes defined, and 'what it is all about' gets decided. Specifically, each party considers the origins of the conflict, why it

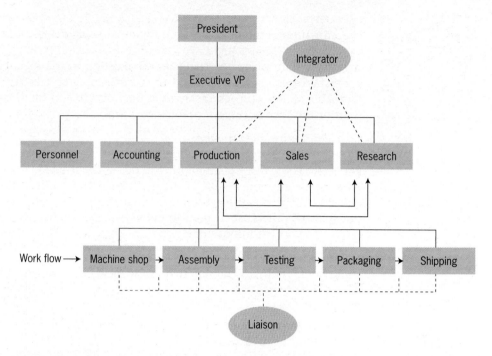

Figure 23.3: Co-ordinating using liaison and integrator roles

emerged, and how the problem is being experienced with the other party. The way that the conflict is defined at this stage will determine the type of outcome that the parties are willing to settle for in the later stages.

Not only must a party perceive a conflict but it must also feel it. That is, it must become emotionally involved in experiencing feelings of anxiety, tenseness, frustration and hostility towards the other party. The emotional dimension of conflict shapes perceptions. For example, negative emotions result in an oversimplification of issues, reductions in trust and negative interpretations of other parties' behaviour. Positive emotions, in contrast, increase the chances of the parties taking a broader view, seeing the issue as a problem to be solved and developing more creative solutions.

Managing conflict

Managers may judge the existing co-ordination devices to be inadequate, thereby causing conflict. They will therefore manage the situation by implementing conflict resolution approaches to reduce or eliminate the immediate conflict, before adjusting the co-ordination mechanism to prevent it occurring in the first place. Alternatively, they may consider that the co-ordination devices are working too well, thereby causing complacency and apathy. In this case, they may introduce conflict stimulation approaches to increase the level of conflict that exists within the company. Thus, within organizations, conflict can be managed through a combination of both conflict resolution and conflict stimulation approaches.

Kenneth Thomas (1976) distinguished five **conflict resolution** approaches, based upon the two dimensions of:

Conflict resolution refers to a process which has as its objective the ending of the conflict between the disagreeing parties.

- how assertive or unassertive each party is in pursuing its own concerns;
- how co-operative or uncooperative each is in satisfying the concerns of the other.

He labelled these *competing/forcing* (assertive and uncooperative); *avoiding* (unassertive and uncooperative); *compromising* (mid-range on both dimensions);

accommodating (unassertive and co-operative); and *collaborating* (assertive and co-operative). They are summarized in figure 23.4 and defined in table 23.3.

Thomas (1977) also identified the types of situation in which each conflict resolution orientation was to be preferred over another (table 23.4). Unless the manager was flexible and capable of switching between styles, their ability to resolve conflicts effectively would be limited. In practice, all individuals, whether managers or not, habitually use only a limited number of styles (perhaps just one) to resolve all the conflicts in which they are involved. It is not surprising that their success is limited.

Kenneth H. Thomas

Table 23.3: Conflict resolution approaches compared

approach	objective	your posture	supporting rationale	likely outcome
1 Competing/ forcing	Get your way	'I know what's right. Don't question my judgement or authority'	It is better to risk causing a few hard feelings than to abandon the issue	You feel vindicated, but the other party feels defeated and possibly humiliated
2 Avoiding	Avoid having to deal with conflict	'I'm neutral on that issue. Let me think about it. That's someone else's problem'	Disagreements are inherently bad because they create tension	Interpersonal problems don't get resolved, causing long-term frustration manifested in a variety of ways
3 Compromising	Reach an agreement quickly	'Let's search for a solution we can both live with so we can get on with our work'	Prolonged conflicts distract people from their work and cause bitter feelings	Participants go for the expedient rather than effective solutions
4 Accommodating	Don't upset the other person	'How can I help you feel good about this? My position isn't so important that it is worth risking bad feelings between us'	Maintaining harmonious relationships should be our top priority	The other person is likely to take advantage
5 Collaborating	Solve the problem together	'This is my position, what's yours? I'm committed to finding the best possible solution. What do the facts suggest?'	Each position is important though not necessarily equally valid. Emphasis should be placed on the quality of the outcome and the fairness of the decision-making process	The problem is most likely to be resolved. Also both parties are committed to the solution and satisfied that they have been treated fairly

From David Whetton, Kim Cameron and Mike Woods, *Developing Management Skills*, HarperCollins, second edition, 1994, p.384.

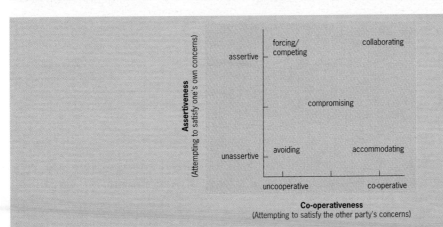

Figure 23.4: Conflict resolution approaches
From Thomas T. Ruble and Kenneth Thomas, 'Support for a two-dimensional model of conflict behaviour', *Organizational Behaviour and Human Performance*, 1976, vol.16, pp.143–55 (p.145).

Table 23.4: When to adopt which conflict resolution approach

Approach	Appropriate situations
1. Competing/forcing	1 When quick, decisive action is vital (e.g. in emergencies). 2 On important issues where unpopular actions need implementing (e.g. in cost-cutting, enforcing unpopular rules, discipline). 3 On issues vital to an organization's welfare when you know you're right. 4 Against people who take advantage of non-competitive behaviour.
2. Avoiding	1 When an issue is trivial, or more important issues are pressing. 2 When you perceive no chance of satisfying your concerns. 3 When potential disruption outweighs the benefits of resolution. 4 To let people cool down and regain perspective. 5 When gathering information supersedes immediate decision. 6 When others can resolve the conflict more effectively. 7 When issues seem tangential or symptomatic of other issues.
3. Compromising	1 When goals are important, but not worth the effort or potential disruption of more assertive modes. 2 When opponents with equal power are committed to mutually exclusive goals. 3 To achieve temporary settlements to complex issues. 4 To arrive at expedient solutions under time pressure. 5 As a backup when collaboration or competition is unsuccessful.
4. Accommodating	1 When you find you are wrong—to allow a better position to be heard, to learn, and to show your reasonableness. 2 When issues are more important to others than yourself—to satisfy others and maintain co-operation. 3 To build social credits for later issues. 4 To minimize loss when you are outmatched and losing. 5 When harmony and stability are especially important. 6 To allow subordinates to develop by learning from mistakes.
5. Collaborating	1 To find an integrative solution when both sets of concerns are too important to be compromised. 2 When your objective is to learn. 3 To merge insights from people with different perspectives. 4 To gain commitment by incorporating concerns into a consensus. 5 To work through feelings that have interfered with a relationship.

From Kenneth W. Thomas, 'Towards multidimensional values in teaching: the example of conflict behaviours', *Academy of Management Review*, July 1977, p.487.

Stop and criticize

Is it possible for us to switch our behaviour styles to deal with different types of conflict? Or are we trapped in a single style?

Distributive bargaining is a negotiating strategy in which a fixed sum of resources is divided up. It leads to a win–lose situation between the parties.

Richard Walton and Robert McKersie's (1965) research into negotiating behaviour distinguished **distributive bargaining** strategies from **integrative bargaining** strategies.

Distributive bargaining involves dividing a 'fixed pie'. It occurs if one party's gain is at another's expense. For example, within a hospital context, the redistri-

Constructive conflict in the Netherlands

Evert Van de Vliert and colleagues conducted interpersonal studies at a police management training centre; with university business students; and with managers, consultants and government administrators in the Netherlands. They focused on conflict between pairs in a simulated negotiation situation. The conflicting parties attempted to advance their own interests, their opponent's interests, or the interests of both.

The researchers treated problem-solving and competing/forcing conflict resolution approaches as complementary rather than as alternatives. Problem solving is reconciling both parties' basic interests, while forcing is furthering one's own interests by competing or battling with the opponent in a direct way. In the study, these two approaches were frequently combined, both simultaneously and sequentially. Conflict behaviour was judged to be personally effective only if an individual succeeded in realizing desired personal benefits. It was judged to be dyadically effective (or constructive) if the conflict resolution strategy achieved improved outcomes for both parties by resolving the conflict, improving the relationship between them, or both.

The study showed that the best outcomes for the organization were obtained when the problem-solving approach was followed by the forcing approach. This finding challenges the classic, 'one-best-way' school of conflict resolution and negotiating which favours the problem-solving approach as the most constructive approach (e.g. Fisher and Ury, 1981). It also takes a contingency perspective by suggesting that each of Thomas' five conflict resolution approaches can be appropriate under certain circumstances.

These authors' results question two other assumptions about conflict resolution. First that people adopt one pure resolution approach rather than another (e.g. either avoiding or forcing), and second, that this one, pure, chosen approach produces better outcomes than a combination of approaches. Instead, they argue that when reacting to a conflict issue, individuals tend to manifest multiple rather than single, behavioural responses (e.g. combining compromising, avoiding and accommodating). These responses are linked either simultaneously or sequentially. Moreover, they say, such linking tends to be the rule rather than the exception. Such combined usage affects the conflict outcome and the relationships between the parties.

The researchers reported other studies in which senior nurses in Dutch hospitals handled conflict more effectively when they combined problem-solving and forcing. Conflict issues might be so complex and multidimensional, that problem-solving may be appropriate for one aspect, while forcing can be suitable for another. Each of the five conflict approaches carries its own risks. For example, the value of a win–win outcome using problem-solving may not be commensurate with the time investment needed to achieve it. Combining two approaches can therefore reduce the risk associated with each—reducing the tendency of problem-solving approach to produce resolution stagnation, and the tendency of the forcing approach to produce conflict escalation. Overall, from their results, they concluded that 'conflict at work pays' in organizations.

Based on Evert Van de Vliert, Aukje Nauta, Ellen Giebels and Onne Janssen, 'Constrictive conflict at work', *Journal of Organizational Behaviour*, 1999, vol.20, pp.475–91.

Integrative bargaining is a negotiating strategy that seeks to increase the total amount of resources. It creates a win–win situation between the parties.

bution of beds or ward space between clinical services means that if medicine gets fifteen extra beds then surgery (or some other service) has to lose fifteen beds. Some conflicts in the workplace can only be resolved in this way. Appropriate bargaining tactics in this situation include asking initially for much more than you are ultimately willing to accept; persuading the opponent that their objective is unattainable or unrealistic; encouraging them to accept a figure nearer yours; getting the other party to feel emotionally generous towards you.

In contrast, integrative bargaining is built on the belief that there exist one or more settlements that can create positive outcomes for both parties. It involves finding ways to 'expand the pie'. As a strategy, integrative bargaining tends to be

Table 23.5: Comparison between negotiating strategies and conflict resolution approaches

Negotiating strategy:	Distributive bargaining	Integrative bargaining
Conflict resolution approaches:	Competing/forcing	
	Avoiding	
	Compromising	
	Accommodating	Collaborating

From David Whetton, Kim Cameron and Mike Woods, *Effective Conflict Management*, HarperCollins, 1996, p.20.

promoted as it is seen as preferable to distributive because it builds long-term relationships and facilitates a working together in the future. It bonds the parties, allowing each to believe that they have achieved a victory. Distributive bargaining creates animosities, deepens divisions among those who have to work together and leaves one party a loser. To operate integrative bargaining, both parties need to be open with their concerns, open in their communication, sensitive to the other's needs, trust each other and be willing to be flexible. These conditions are rarely present in an organization, and hence bargaining tends to be win at any cost.

Studies have revealed similarities between conflict management strategies and negotiating strategies (Savage *et al.*, 1989; Smith, 1987). Of the five conflict resolution strategies described earlier, four of them involve one or more of the parties sacrificing something. David Whetton and colleagues (1996) suggested that distributive strategies matched the natural inclination of those individuals to approach conflicts from a 'macho man', 'easy touch' or 'split the difference' viewpoint and they thereby engendered competition, exploitation or irresponsibility (table 23.5).

Over the last two decades, the major developers of the integrative bargaining concept have been Roger Fisher and William Ury (1981; 1987) from the Harvard Negotiating Project (table 23.6). Their scheme of 'principled negotiation' sets out guiding principles to apply when preparing and engaging in face-to-face negotiations. More recent work in this project has dealt with how negotiators should proceed if the other side does not 'play the game' (Ury, 1991; Ury and Patton, 1997).

Mediation is a process in which a neutral third party to the conflict assists in the achievement of a negotiated solution by using reason, persuasion and the presentation of alternatives.

Mediation involves bringing in a third party in order to resolve the dispute. In a negotiation situation, the behaviour and feelings of the parties can become sharply polarized, and each becomes isolated from the other. When this happens, a mediator can maintain contact and communication between the parties in dispute. In hostage-taking situations and local wars, independent third parties are often brought in to act as mediators. They do not control the agreement, but they influence the conflict resolution process. They guide the two parties to discover the solution to their problem.

Mediation techniques include asking each party to state the problem, to state the other's view of the problem and to confirm the accuracy of the other's repetition. Once the initial positions have been presented and understood, alternative solutions are generated using brainstorming. The use of recesses in the mediating process is valuable. These can help calm the parties after an emotional encounter; can be used to conduct private enquiries about interests; and can be used to de-escalate conflict.

Table 23.6: Bargaining strategies

Win–win strategy	Win–lose strategy
1 Define the conflict as a mutual problem	1 Define the conflict as a win–lose situation
2 Pursue joint outcomes	2 Pursue own group's outcomes
3 Find creative agreements that satisfy both groups	3 Force the other group into submission
4 Use open, honest, and accurate communication of group's needs, goals and proposals	4 Use deceitful, inaccurate and misleading communication of group's needs, goals and proposals
5 Avoid threats (to reduce the other's defensiveness)	5 Use threats (to force submission)
6 Communicate flexibility of position	6 Communicate high commitment (rigidity) regarding one's position

Based on David W. Johnson and Frank P. Johnson, *Joining Together: Group Theory and Group Skills*, Prentice Hall, Englewood Cliffs, NJ, 1975, pp.182–3.

Ten ways to fail as a mediator

1. After having listened to the argument for a short time, begin to non-verbally communicate your discomfort with the discussion (e.g. sit back, begin to fidget).

2. Take sides and communicate your agreement with one of the parties (e.g. through facial expressions, posture, chair position, reinforcing comments).

3. Say that you shouldn't be talking about this thing at work or where others can hear you.

4. Discourage the expression of emotion. Suggest that the discussion be held later after both parties have cooled off.

5. Suggest that both parties are wrong. Point out the problems with both points of view.

6. Suggest part way through the discussion that possibly you aren't the person who should be helping solve this problem.

7. See if you can get both parties to attack you.

8. Minimize the seriousness of the problem.

9. Change the subject (e.g. ask for advice to help you solve one of your problems).

10. Express displeasure that the two parties are experiencing conflict (e.g. imply that it might undermine the solidarity of the work group).

From David Whetton, Kim Cameron and Mike Woods, *Developing Management Skills for Europe*, HarperCollins, second edition, 1994, p.362.

Negotiating by e-mail

Who has not banged out any angry reply to an apparently brusque e-mail message, hit the send button—and then regretted it? Surely no technology has led to so many rifts and fractured friendships (not to mention subpoenas) as electronic mail. But nowhere is e-mail more perilous than in negotiations. Experiments by Michael Morris, an academic at Stanford Business School, have demonstrated that negotiations are more likely to go well if they are conducted, at least in part, face to face, rather than between strangers armed with keyboards and screens. Morris and his colleagues compared mock negotiations which used e-mail only with those that were preceded by a getting-to-know-you telephone call. The second type went more smoothly. Other experiments show that negotiations are easier when negotiators start by swapping photographs and personal details, or when they already know one another.

Why is e-mail such a snare? Heidi Roizen, who now works for Softbank Venture Capital, thinks that part of the problem is that most people don't think about the fact that an e-mail lasts for ever. She scrupulously follows two rules to avoid misunderstanding. 'Re-read each piece of mail before you send it from the point of view of the recipient; and when in doubt, leave it overnight.' As every Victorian letter-writer learnt, a night's sleep is the best filter to apply to a furious note. John Kay, a British economist, goes further. After having to calm a succession of weeping secretaries, he instituted a rule at London Economics, a consultancy that he founded, that e-mails should contain only information and never emotion.

Yet despite its pitfalls, e-mail is increasingly likely to be used for negotiations. Richard Hill, an IT manager and mediator with Hill & Associates in Geneva, worked with the University of Massachusetts on the establishment of an electronic mediation service called the Online Ombuds Office. He argues that mediation by telephone is genuinely simpler and faster: a three-minute telephone call contains more information than a typical brisk e-mail. But because online mediation can be done at a time that is convenient for the parties involved, it tends to be less costly. Just think a moment before you hit that send button, though.

From *The Economist*, 'Negotiating by e-mail', 8 April 2000, p.85.

Arbitration is a process in which a third party to a conflict has the authority to impose an agreement that is binding on the parties in conflict.

If mediation fails, disputes often go to **arbitration**. This may occur if negotiations between unions and management have reached an impasse: a grievance is presented and the arbiter listens to both sides. In this process, the dispute is referred to a third party, who is given the power to formulate a settlement that is binding on the other two. This is similar to a judge in a courtroom. Arbitration may be voluntary or compulsory. The former occurs when both parties involved have the choice of whether or not to have a decision imposed on them. Compulsory arbitration, perhaps due to government regulations, denies them that choice.

So far, it has been assumed that there are just two parties involved in a conflict. However, a manager's job also involves resolving conflicts between their subordinates. Managers dislike this task because they have to choose sides, and deal with the loser's frustrations. For this reason, managers avoid dealing with conflicts, smooth them over, or force the parties to work it out themselves. They may even punish subordinates who bring them problems by ensuring that no one ever wins, creating so-called 'lose–lose' situations.

Managers can however use these conciliation techniques with their subordinates in conflict by applying the principles of integrative bargaining. It may be possible to convert win–lose situations into win–win ones, and thus allow both parties to achieve their goals. A holiday allocation decision may be of this type. Two employees both want two weeks off in July, but there are not enough staff to cover. If one person gets their fortnight, the other does not (win–lose). Since one cannot have it, the other is similarly prevented from having theirs (lose–lose). If the manager investigates and finds that one of them wants it for a particular reason and the other for another reason, it may be possible to resolve the situation and create a win–win outcome for all concerned.

Alternatively, managers can choose to mediate between their subordinates. Both subordinates and their supervisor prefer this conflict resolution strategy. However, since staff have little experience of their boss guiding the conflict resolution process without making the final decision, they are rarely sure of how to respond. Some managers are more comfortable with arbitration. Playing the role of judge can be a fast and definitive conflict-resolving process, especially if one of the parties has obviously violated a rule or a policy. However, on the negative side, it rarely results in the parties being committed to a settlement that is imposed on them. Finally, the supervisor might use delegation, telling the parties so solve the conflict themselves. This may appeal to those who wish to smooth over conflicts, but it is often ineffective, because the parties lack the skills, information and impartiality to work through the conflict on their own.

Stop and criticize	Some individuals resolve conflict in one fixed way in different situations. Others change their approach to suit the circumstances. Think of a specific domestic, friendship or organizational context which involved conflict. How did you deal with it? Did you force, avoid, compromise, accommodate or collaborate?

Conflict stimulation refers to the process of engendering conflict between parties where none existed before, or escalating the current conflict level if it is too low.

Interactionists argue that there are conditions in organizations when what is needed is more and not less conflict, i.e. **conflict stimulation** (Robbins, 1997; Sternberg and Soriano, 1984; Robbins, 1974).

John Kotter (1996) discussed the dangers of complacency and the need to drive employees out of their comfort zones. Among the complacency-smashing and potentially conflict-stimulating techniques used by senior management were the following:

- Create a crisis by allowing a financial loss to occur or an error to blow up.
- Eliminate obvious examples of excess like corporate jet fleets and gourmet dining rooms.
- Set targets like income, productivity and cycle times so high that they can't be reached by doing business as usual.
- Share more information about customer satisfaction and financial performance with employees.
- Insist that people speak regularly to dissatisfied customers, unhappy suppliers and disgruntled shareholders.
- Put more honest discussions of the firm's problems in company newspapers and management speeches. Stop senior management's 'happy talk'.

Various techniques can be used to stimulate conflict where none existed before in order to encourage different opinions and engender new thinking and problem solving.

1. Communications
Managers can withhold information 'to keep them guessing' or send large amounts of inconsistent information ('we're expanding', 'we're going bust') to get people arguing. They might send ambiguous or threatening messages.

2. Restructuring a company
Realigning working groups and altering rules and regulations so as to increase or

create interdependence between previously independent units. This can easily stimulate conflict, particularly if the goals of the newly interdependent departments are made incompatible (one department's objective being to minimize costs, the other's to maximize market share).

3. Bringing in outsiders

Adding individuals to a group whose backgrounds, values, attitudes or management styles differ from those of existing members. For example, recruiting senior executives with a career experience in automobile manufacture to manage a health care organization.

4. Devil's advocate method

Named after a practice used in the Roman Catholic Church when a name is submitted to the College of Cardinals for elevation to sainthood. To ensure that the nominee has a spotless record, an individual is assigned the role of devil's advocate to uncover any possible objections to the person's canonization. Within the organizational context, a person is assigned the role of critic to stimulate critical thinking and reality testing. For example, in deciding to embark on an e-commerce strategy, one team member might be assigned the devil's advocate role to focus on its pitfalls and dangers.

5. Dialectic method

Plato and the dialectic school of philosophy in ancient Greece originated this approach. It explores opposite positions called 'thesis' and' antithesis'. The outcome of the debate between the two is the 'synthesis', which in turn becomes the new thesis to be opened up for debate. Before deciding on a takeover, a company may establish two or more teams, give them access to the same information and give them the task of arguing for and against the acquisition decision. The conflict of ideas throws up alternatives, which can be synthesized into a superior, final decision.

6. Leadership style

Organizations can appoint managers who encourage non-traditional viewpoints, rather than authoritarian ones who might be inclined to suppress opposing viewpoints. Leadership style has been found to be a key element in organization change programmes, and in particular those involving changes in organization culture [**links**, chapters 17, 19 and 21].

Radical frame of reference

Radical frame of reference is a perspective which views (organizational) conflict as an inevitable consequence of exploitative employment relations in a capitalist economy.

Sabotage at a nuclear facility (Cooper, 2000), racial harassment of ethnic minority staff in the British National Health Service (Rowe, 2000) and racism in the London Borough of Hackney (local government organization) (Hammond, 2000), as well as sexual harassment and bullying, are all examples of human behaviour in organizations. Yet the previous unitarist, pluralist and interactionist frames of reference on conflict have difficulty in explaining such actions. Indeed, it is only the radical frame of reference that draws attention to such behaviour in organizations. The other conflict perspectives either do not address such issues effectively or else simply ignore them.

The **radical frame of reference** on conflict sees the workplace as an arena of conflict between employees and managers (the agents of the owners). These controllers of the means of production exploit the employees. The logic of profit maximization involves managers relentlessly driving down the costs of production

Team fighting

'The absence of conflict is not harmony, it's apathy', asserts the first line of an article by Kathleen Eisenhardt and her colleagues. She and her fellow authors argue that management teams which challenge one another's thinking develop a more complete understanding of the choices, create a richer range of options, and ultimately make more effective decisions. As with others interactionist frame holders, they recognize that 'healthy conflict can quickly turn unproductive', and state that the challenge is to prevent conflict degenerating into dysfunctional interpersonal conflict and to encourage managers to argue without destroying their ability to work as a team.

Using interviewing and observation research methods, the authors studied twelve top management teams of between five and nine members in technology-based companies which competed in fast-changing competitive global markets. The teams made high-stakes decisions in situations of high uncertainty under pressure. Their study revealed how conflict was actually experienced and what part emotion played in decision making. They identified successful teams which were able to avoid interpersonal hostility and discord, vigorously debated issues while avoiding politicking and posturing, and separated substantive from personality issues. They distinguished these from the less successful, which fragmented into cliques and whose members openly displayed frustration, anger and intense animosity. How then can team members disagree on questions of strategic significance yet still get along with each other? The authors identified three strategies for successfully managing interpersonal conflict, each of which involved two tactics.

Tactic ——————————————————————————— *Strategy*

1. Base discussions on ample factual information

2. Develop multiple alternatives to enrich debate
   Focus on issues not personalities

3. Rally around agreed-upon goals
   Frame decisions as collaborations
4. Inject humour into the decision-making process
   aimed at achieving the best possible solution
   for the company

5. Maintain a balanced power structure
   Establish a sense of fairness
6. Resolve issues without forcing consensus
   and equity in the process

The authors conclude with a list of five approaches to help generate such constructive disagreements within a team:

- Meet as a team regularly and often.

- Manage any evolving conflict actively.

- Encourage the application of multiple minds.

- Create a heterogeneous team (diverse ages, genders, functions, industrial experience).

- Encourage assumption of roles beyond their obvious product, geographical or functional responsibilities.

Based on Kathleen M. Eisenhardt., Jean L. Kahwajy and L.J. Bourgeois, 'How management teams can have a good fight', *Harvard Business Review*, July–August 1997, pp.77–85.

and controlling the manufacturing process. This perspective argues that, as conflict is an endemic property of capitalist employment relations, it cannot be resolved by any 'techniques'.

The radical frame of reference on conflict is based on the Marxist critique of capital and capitalism, whose essential elements were summarized by Roger Johnston (2000, pp.16–35):

1. The fundamental aim of a capitalist enterprise is to expand its capital.

2. To do this, it needs to generate a profit (surplus) otherwise it will fail.

3. Marx's analysis involves two elements:
   (a) *Means of production*: this refers to the materials, artefacts, tools, machines and land which are required by the capitalist owner, and which are indirectly deployed.
   (b) *Organization of labour*: production of goods is socially organized in the sense that the capitalist owner uses labour to produce the goods. Workers are the direct producers.
       (i) Those available to do the work typically have no alternative means of subsistence, so there is an imbalance of power between capitalist-owners and workers.
       (ii) Employees contract their time to the capitalist-owner in return for payment. During their working hours, workers are directed by the capitalist-owners. This is a form of domination that eliminates worker freedom.
       (iii) A hierarchy of organization with specified duties, responsibilities and the authority (of the capitalist-owner) direct the activities of workers.

4. To succeed, the capitalist enterprise must sell its produced goods at a profit in the market.

5. The surplus (profit) generated through these sales is divided between the manager(s) who direct production (receiving salary and bonus) and the shareholders who financed the operation (receiving dividends). The workers do not share in this surplus, since labour is treated as a *cost*, not a beneficiary of success.

6. Companies compete with each other in the market on the basis of price, quality, quantity, availability or a combination of all. Given the problems with each of these competitive strategies, the tendency is for each firm to seek to reduce its costs (of production).

7. Lower costs can be achieved in various ways: by increasing output; reorganizing labour; paying labour less; replacing labour with technical improvements; or a combination of all.

8. It is argued that the inevitable outcome of cost reduction is that labour will earn less and will be worked more intensely. In consequence, it can be expected that this will generate a lack of consent, resistance or some form of political action, either individual or collective.

9. Management will be concerned and will have to deal with this tension by limiting the effects of worker resistance or overt conflict in order to secure at least compliance.

Labour process theory

This view is closely associated with labour process theory, whose Marxist analysis in the organizational literature is most widely discussed in terms of Braverman's 'degradation of work' thesis [link, chapter 13, traditional work design]. The main features of the radical frame of reference–labour process theory are that it:

1. Rejects the notion of a correspondence of interests. The organizational dilemma concerns the question of how to reconcile the potential inconsistency between individual needs and the aspirations of different organizational stakeholders on the one hand, and the collective purpose of the organization on the other [link, chapter 1, prologue]. The focus is upon vertical (manager–employee) conflict.

2. Challenges taken-for-granted assumptions by asking questions such as why do managers have to:

   - motivate employees (why are employees not already motivated)?

   - overcome employees' resistance to change (what do employees fear)?

   - create a 'strong' organization culture to gain employees' commitment (why are employees not already committed to their companies)?

   - manage conflict (what are employees resisting, and what is it that causes the conflict)?

3. Sees the workplace as a 'contested terrain' (Edwards, 1979) where employees, individually and collectively, seek to protect and extend their own interests in the production process, and resist management's attempts at control. Conflict is seen as a fundamental and central dynamic in organizational life.

4. Explains actual, observed instances of workplace conflict in sociological terms, stressing differences of interests, power, politics, domination, control, etc. and also in economic terms, focusing on capital maximization and profit distribution.

5. Holds that the degree to which managers can alter employee behaviour has been exaggerated. Ackroyd and Thompson (1999) distinguish between *tractability*, which refers to management's capacity to induce, through its actions, marginal, temporary changes in employee behaviour; and *corrigibility*, the permanent 'correction' of behaviour to conform with management expectations. They say that employee behaviour may be tractable, but that it is rarely corrigible.

6. Rejects the view that by the late 1990s management had successfully established control over employee behaviour, and asserts instead that the significant changes in organization structures have merely modified the form that employee resistance has taken (Thompson and Ackroyd, 1995).

7. Focuses primarily on causes of conflict within the workplace and tends to neglect conflict resolution techniques.

8. Focuses on internal contradictions (e.g. cost reduction strategies) more than external triggers (e.g. new technology) when discussing the causes of conflict.

Organizational misbehaviour
refers to anything that workers do in the workplace which they are not supposed to do.

Sabotage, racial and sexual harassment, and bullying are all examples of human behaviour in organizations that is rarely discussed. Stephen Ackroyd and Paul Thompson (1999) explained that management establishes a boundary that distinguishes employee behaviour that is and is not acceptable. Employee actions are then defined as falling on one or other side of that boundary. The authors use the term **organizational misbehaviour** to refer to 'anything you do at work which you are not supposed to do'.

Although much of the literature refers to 'conflict' in organizations, in reality, overt conflict is actually very rare. Thus, for Richard Edwards (1979) the struggle

Resistance refers to more or less covert behaviour which counteracts and restricts management attempts to exercise power and control in the workplace.

between capital and labour is the main dynamic which shapes the employment relationship. He refers to *structural antagonisms* rather than to conflict, and sees these as arising from the clash over the distribution of the surplus. A mixture of consent, co-operation and resistance characterizes daily interactions between managers and employees. Carter Goodrich (1975) wrote about the 'frontiers of control' and the notion of **resistance**. Management's attempt to exert control is met by employee resistance, and that produces clashes over interests. The notion of resistance carries with it the connotation of something intermittent (occurring regularly but not continually), changing (frontier being pushed forward and back), and occurring below the surface. This is in contrast to conflict, with its connotations of a single, visible, explosion.

The concept of resistance has an application at all levels of the organizational hierarchy, from shop floor employees resisting supervisory control, through professionals like engineers, academics or hospital doctors resisting management directions, right up to senior management resisting the control exercised by the board of directors. It also allows consideration of how that resistance moves to different areas within the organization and how the parties acquire and relinquish different types of power and gain and lose ascendancy over each other. Edwards (1979) noted that the perpetual struggle for control in organizations is not always constant, obvious or visible. Because employees' tactics of resistance are often covert, some knowledge of a particular organizational context is required for researchers (and indeed for managers) to become fully aware of what is going on. Resistance, as opposed to conflict, in the workplace is reflected in 'soldiering' (output restriction), pilferage, absenteeism, sabotage, vandalism, practical joking and sexual misconduct. Reviewing the managerial and academic literature on the presence and absence of such misbehaviour at work, Ackroyd and Thompson (1999) concluded that typically it:

- Provided sanitized accounts of employee behaviour that depicted employees as invariably constructive, conforming and dutiful.

- Saw employees' behaviour as being orderly, purposeful and directed towards the attainment of organizational (managerial) goals.

- Defined 'normal' employee behaviour as that which was programmed by management, and which complied with managerial norms and values, and treated employees' deviations from those (management-) expected standards of behaviour as misbehaviour.

- Assumed that when there was a lack of correspondence between management direction and the employees' response to it (i.e. occurrence of misbehaviour), what needed to change was the latter.

Stop and criticize

Ackroyd and Thompson define organizational misbehaviour in terms of employee behaviour within the workplace which management considers to be inappropriate, and they provide examples of this. However, they exclude any reference to managerial behaviour which managers or non-managers might consider inappropriate.

Define managerial misbehaviour? Provide examples to illustrate your definition.

Hard (emotional) labour

Steve Taylor reported how, at the Newcastle upon Tyne offices of 'Flightpath' (a major British airline), management electronically monitored the emotional labour of telephone sales agents (TSAs). Emotional labour refers to the management of human feelings during a social interaction while performing paid work (e.g. a supermarket checkout operator being required to smile at a customer even though she has no wish to do so, i.e. acting the emotion). The TSAs received and dealt with calls from people wanting to purchase or reserve a travel service provided by the company. The aim is to transform the calls into actual bookings. The telephone system allows supervisors to 'listen in' to any agent–customer interaction at any time. This can be done with (known) or without (remote) the agent being aware. Supervisors reported that they randomly and frequently monitored the agents, and sometimes taped the conversations for quality assurance purposes. These were then used in the weekly review and appraisal meetings between the agent and the supervisor.

Based on Steve Taylor, 'Emotional labour and the new workplace' in Thompson, P. and Warhurst, C. (eds), *Workplaces of the Future*, Macmillan Business, 1998, chapter 5, pp.84–103.

The rebirth of unitarism?

The radical frame of reference on conflict has rarely, if ever, featured in any American organizational behaviour textbooks. Indeed, after the 1980s, its general relevance was challenged in Britain and elsewhere in Europe. Some writers argued that employees had 'finally' come to realize that they shared common interests with management. A number of reasons have been suggested for this belief (Ackroyd and Thompson, 1999):

1. The start of that decade saw the publication of *In Search of Excellence*, a book that initiated the excellence movement within all types of organizations around the world.

2. The end of that decade saw the fall of the Soviet Union and the triumph of liberal capitalist democracy.

3. By the early 1990s, many authors felt that employees had been tamed and subdued by management.

4. Workplace changes in Britain during the 1980s and 1990s had produced structural changes in labour and capital markets, which coincided with a hostile political and legal climate. Among the changes one would point to the:
   - growth in non-standard employment;
   - individualization of the employment relationship between the employee and employer, causing the breakdown of collectivism (unionization);
   - decline in the size of manufacturing facilities;
   - shift from manufacturing to services;
   - shift from manual to white collar employment;
   - deregulation of labour markets;
   - injection of market rationality into public sector organizations;
   - legislative assaults on union organization, employment rights and collective bargaining.

Other commentators disagree, asserting that the radical frame of reference is more relevant that ever before. They cite the continuing need by organizations for 'cultural manipulation' and ever more sophisticated human management resource policies to maintain control over employees. If employees truly shared common interests with management, why are these necessary? [links, chapter 19, organiz-

Workplace partnerships: revolution or business as usual?

Has the radical frame of reference on conflict been supplanted by the unitarist? A recent trend in the British industrial relations scene has been the development of 'workplace or social partnership' deals between unions and employers. It involves joint consultation on company strategy and workplace issues, and a commitment to joint goals such as training. Workplace partnerships in the UK represent a watered-down version of the social partnership principle that operates in Germany, where employees have a clear say on company business and a right to information and dialogue.

Union supporters of workplace partnerships include the British Trades Union Congress (TUC) and the AEEU, the General and Municipal Workers Union (GMB) and the Transport and General Workers Union (TGWU), which argue that in some industries, it has been the salvation of several companies. Do these partnerships represent a real change in traditional, antagonistic union–management relations? Informed observers point to the underlying theory or aim of these arrangements as being to change collective bargaining from an adversarial (distributive) process to a joint problem-solving, mutual gains (integrative) approach.

The concept of 'partnership' itself is vague, elastic and possesses different meanings for different people. For example, Scottish Power, often quoted as one of the best examples of a company that has a union partnership deal, has cut thousands of jobs following its takeover of Manweb and Southern Water, yet managed to retain union support. The spread, and hence the importance, of partnership deals throughout the UK varies, with the number of deals yet to reach a hundred. They currently represent 'islands of innovation in a sea of unchanging relationships', as one observer put it. Media accounts typically recycle the same company names.

New Labour supporters, the TUC and some unions see workplace partnerships as offering some involvement in, and influence over, a company's human resource management process. However, it is significant that there has been limited tangible British government support for them. In contrast, left-wing opponents are critical of unions 'cosying up' to employers and claim these arrangements represent 'words without substance'.

In their turn, some employers see workplace partnerships as unwarranted union interference in company business, while others may view them as a bar to wider, German-type employee interference. Reports by the Involvement and Participation Association suggest that partnership is under threat because some managers are taking its benefits for granted and reverting to type, discarding the partnership after 'pocketing the benefits'. What is clear is that the limited number of workplace partnerships that have emerged have done so in special circumstances, for example in greenfield site developments, in privatized public utilities and in companies experiencing major financial difficulties where the company is standing on the 'edge of an abyss' and faces a 'reform or die' choice. The question of whether workplace partnerships will revolutionize traditional labour relations in Britain is still unanswered.

Based on *The Times*, 'Peace breaks out between UK workers and management', 21 May 1999, p.35; and *Personnel Today*, 2000, 'Manager commitment to partnership deals fading', 1 February, p.7.

ation culture; chapter 20, human resource management]. They also question the status of 'workplace or social partnership' deals between unions and employers, asking whether in Britain, these represent attempts to actually limit employee involvement in key organizational matters (Tailby and Winchester, 2000).

Some authors, however, have challenged this view. They claim that employees had neither become more acquiescent nor adopted the interests and values of management. Jermier *et al.* (1994) argued that there was a need to document the 'spirit of refusal' that was a feature of everyday resistance at work. Meanwhile, Farhad Analoui and Andrew Kalkabadse (1991) offered managers a guide on dealing with such resistance in their book entitled *Sabotage—How To Recognize and Manage Employee Defiance*.

Ackroyd and Thompson do not claim that in today's organizations, employee resistance, misbehaviour and conflict are present in the same force or form as in the past. Their own book draws upon empirical research conducted in the 1970s and 1980s rather than the 1990s. The exception to this is an account of 'Phoneco' in Scotland, which sought to create a 'socially individualized' pro-company workforce using a combination of selection, training, culture-change programme and a team approach (McKinlay and Taylor, 2000) [**link**, chapter 11, individuals in organizations]. This suggests reluctance among contemporary academics to apply the radical frame of reference on conflict to a consideration of non-traditional behaviour in organizations.

Thompson and Ackroyd called on their fellow industrial sociologists to reverse 'the virtual removal of labour as an active agency of resistance from their theories and research, and put labour back under the academic gaze' (Thompson and Ackroyd, 1995, p.629). They appealed to them to study 'unorganized conflict' since, in their view, the essential conditions for such behaviour continue to exist. Competition, increasing globalization, mergers and takeovers are contextual factors that have encouraged management to seek to reduce labour and others costs. They felt that academics could rectify this omission 'by doing theory and research in such a way that it is possible to "see" resistance and misbehaviour, and recognize that innovatory employee practices and informal organization will continue to subvert management regimes' (Thompson and Ackroyd, 1995, p.629).

The frontier of conflict and its negotiation has recently shifted. The previous focus was upon vertical conflict between manager and subordinate, or that between unions and management. Current interest is in lateral conflict and its resolution between peers, and between departments within an organization. There is relatively little experience and research into this type of conflict or how to manage it (Constantino and Merchant, 1996).

Stop and criticize

Why might managers prefer to ignore organizational misbehaviour? Why might academics?

Recap

1. *Distinguish between the four major frames of reference on conflict.*

   - The unitarist frame sees organizations as essentially harmonious and any conflict as bad.
   - The pluralist frame sees organizations as a collection of groups, each with its own interests.
   - The interactionist frame sees conflict as a positive, necessary force for effective performance.
   - The radical frame sees conflict as an inevitable outcome of capitalism.

2. *Distinguish between functional and dysfunctional conflict.*

   - Functional conflict is considered by management to support organizational goals and to improve organizational performance.

   - Dysfunctional conflict is considered to impede the achievement of organizational goals and to reduce company performance.

3. *Explain the relationship between organizing, co-ordinating and conflict.*

   - Organizing concerns dividing up a large task (e.g. designing, building and marketing of a car), into sub-tasks, and assigning them to groups (e.g. design department, production department, etc.). Co-ordination brings those previously divided sub-tasks together to ensure that all activities are directed towards organizational goals. In the process of sub-division, departments acquire their own subordinate goals and interests, which differ from organizational ones. Conflict ensues when these divergent interests and goals clash.

4. *List the causes of conflict in organizations.*
- Individual, groups, units and departments may be in conflict with each other due to the differences in their goal orientation and evaluations, self-image and stereotypes, task interdependencies and time perspectives, as well as overlapping authority and scarce resources.

5. *Distinguish the different organizational co-ordination devices.*
- Co-ordination devices include rules, policies and procedures; using hierarchy; goal clarification and communication; temporary task force; permanent project teams; liaison roles and integrator roles.

6. *Explain the conditions under which conflict is resolved and stimulated in organizations.*
- Some writers contend that conflict is dysfunctional, that is, does not achieve organizational goals, wastes time, de-motivates staff; wastes resources and generally lowers individual and hence organizational performance. In such cases it needs to be eliminated.
- Commentators argue that conflict stimulation is necessary if employees enter 'comfort zones', are reluctant to think in new ways and find it easier to maintain the status quo. In rapidly changing organizational environments such behaviour not only reduces organizational success but may endanger its very existence.

7. *List Thomas' five conflict resolution approaches.*
- Thomas' five conflict resolution approaches are avoidance, accommodation, compromise, collaborative and competition/forcing.

8. *Distinguish between distributive and integrative bargaining.*
- Distributive bargaining refers to a negotiation situation in which a fixed sum of resources is divided up. It leads to a win–lose situation between the parties.
- Integrative bargaining, seeks to increase the total amount of resources, and create a win–win situation between the parties.

Revision

1. Many commentators argue that conflict can serve a number of organizational purposes. What are the grounds for and against such an argument?

2. 'The unitarist frame of reference on conflict is the most dominant in the literature and practice'. Do you agree? Give reasons for your view and illustrate with examples.

3. 'Since every unit and department in an organization has its own goals and interests, destructive conflict will always be an aspect of organizational life'. Do you agree? Give reasons for your view and illustrate with examples.

4. 'Functional conflict is a contradiction is terms'. Discuss.

5. Kenneth Thomas distinguished five conflict resolution approaches. Suggest the difficulties for an individual seeking to switch between them.

Springboard

Ackroyd, S. and Thompson, P., 1999, *Organizational Misbehaviour*, Sage, London.

Adopting a radical frame of reference on conflict, the authors review the empirical and theoretical work on organizational misbehaviour, setting it within the context of employee resistance, conflict and social identity.

Barry, J., Chandler, J., Clark, H., Johnston, R. and Needle, D. (eds), 2000, *Organization and Management: A Critical Text*, Thomson Learning, London.

A set of critical chapters which consider resistance and conflict in organizations from a variety of different perspectives, themes and levels.

Carnevale, P.J. and Pruitt, D.G., 2000, *Negotiation in Social Conflict*, second edition, Open University Press, Buckingham.

A research-based analysis of negotiation focusing on the negotiator's role, conflict style, the way issues are framed, the relationship between the parties and the communication techniques used.

Dreu, C. and Van de Vliert, E. (eds), 1997, *Using Conflict in Organizations*, Sage, London.

A collection of readings taking an interactionist conflict frame, considering functional and dysfunctional conflict in organizations.

Fox, A., 1973, 'Industrial relations: A social critique of pluralist ideology', in Child, J. (ed.), *Man and Organization*, Allen & Unwin, London.

Alan Fox is credited with distinguishing the unitarist, pluralist and radical perspectives on conflict, which have formed the basis of all discussions of the topic.

Rius, 1999, *Introduction to Marx*, Icon Books, Duxford.

Uses a graphic approach to explain basic Marxist concepts and theories.

Thompson, P., 1983, *The Nature of Work: An Introduction to the Debates in the Labour Process*, Macmillan, London.

Labour process theory represents an important, if neglected, theme in contemporary organizational behaviour theory and research. Since the language used in these writings often creates obstacles to its wider dissemination, this book provides a useful introductory starting point.

Wilson, F.M., 1999, *Organizational Behaviour: A Critical Introduction*, Oxford University Press, Oxford.

Considers conflict using three major themes: the meaning of work; power, control and resistance; and changes in work organization.

Home viewing

The film *Dog Day Afternoon* (1975, director Sidney Lumet) is a crime drama based on a true event that occurred on a hot August day in 1972. Sony Wortzik (played by Al Pacino) and two accomplices enter a bank in Brooklyn, New York, and hold the staff up at gunpoint. However, the robbery goes wrong and the police surround the building. Sonny and his morose friend Sal (played by John Cazale) become trapped inside the bank with their hostages. As you watch the film, analyse the elements of the conflict situation, note which conflict resolution approaches are used and when, and what negotiating tactics are applied.

OB in literature

Lodge, D., *Nice Work*, Penguin Books, Harmondsworth, 1989.

The novel concerns Vic Wilcox, a middle-aged, male, managing director of a foundry, Midland Amalgamated, and Robyn Penrose, a committed feminist intellectual and member of a university English department on a short-term contract. She hopes that agreeing to participate in a 'manager shadowing' scheme will help her to renew her contract. Which frames of reference on conflict do Vic and Robyn hold respectively? How might they have come to adopt that frame? How does it affect their perception of events in the company?

Chapter exercises

1. What is your primary conflict resolution approach?

Objectives
1. To remind you of the different conflict resolution approaches available.
2. To allow you to identify which approach you typically use.

Briefing
For each of the fifteen statements, indicate how often you use that tactic to resolve a conflict by circling the appropriate number (1 = Rarely through to 5 = Always). After you have responded to all the items, insert your numbers into the scoring key that follows and add up the total for the five columns.

1. I try to show the other party the logic and benefits of my position. 1 – 2 – 3 – 4 – 5
2. I endeavour to satisfy all the needs that I and the other party have. 1 – 2 – 3 – 4 – 5

	Rarely Always
3. I give up some points in exchange for others.	1 – 2 – 3 – 4 – 5
4. I believe that some differences are not worth worrying about.	1 – 2 – 3 – 4 – 5
5. I avoid hurting the other's feelings.	1 – 2 – 3 – 4 – 5
6. I seek to convince the other person of the merits of my position.	1 – 2 – 3 – 4 – 5
7. I strive to get all concerns and issues out on the table, immediately.	1 – 2 – 3 – 4 – 5
8. I propose a middle ground between us.	1 – 2 – 3 – 4 – 5
9. I postpone a decision until I have had some time to think it over.	1 – 2 – 3 – 4 – 5
10. I sacrifice my own wishes for those of the other person.	1 – 2 – 3 – 4 – 5
11. I am determined when pursuing my goals.	1 – 2 – 3 – 4 – 5
12. I seek the other person's help in working out a solution.	1 – 2 – 3 – 4 – 5
13. I try to find a fair combination of gains and losses for both of us.	1 – 2 – 3 – 4 – 5
14. I refrain from taking positions which would create controversy.	1 – 2 – 3 – 4 – 5
15. I soothe the other person's feelings in order to preserve our relationship.	1 – 2 – 3 – 4 – 5

Scoring

Conflict resolution approaches

Competing/Forcing Item Score	Avoiding Item Score	Compromising Item Score	Accommodating Item Score	Collaborating Item Score
1.	4.	3.	5.	2.
6.	9.	8.	10.	7.
11.	14.	13.	15.	12.
Total =	Total =	Total =	Total =	Total =

Your primary conflict-resolving approach is _____ (the category with the highest number).

Your backup conflict-resolving approach is _____ (the category with the second highest number).

2: Different perspectives, resolving the conflict

Objectives

1. To introduce you to the different frames of reference on conflict.

2. To give you the opportunity to develop a conflict resolution strategy based on that perspective.

Briefing

1. Arrange yourself into groups of three–five members.

2. Read the announcement and response which follows as two positions.

3. Discuss the three questions that follow.

4. Each group prepares to make a contribution to the plenary discussion.

Performance-related pay for teachers

Announcement from the Minister of Education
The government has decided to introduce performance-related pay for teachers in high schools for 12–16-year-olds. In future, the better that a teacher performs, the higher the salary that they will receive. Its decision is based on the belief that employee reward systems in modern organizations, whether private or public, must recognize the differing contributions of individuals. The management of a teacher's performance using pay will identify and reward high-quality teaching and motivate poor performers to improve. This government initiative has the full support of parents, who are keen to ensure that the education of their children is of

the highest standard. The government is confident that it shares with professional teachers the desire to maintain and improve teaching quality in our schools, and this initiative is another major component of government policy designed to raise standards further.

Response of the United Union of Teachers
The UUT is appalled by the government's decision to introduce performance-related pay into high schools. It is a flawed system which 'measures the measurable and ignores the meaningful'. Children are not motor cars, and counting how many are produced by which teacher is not what education is about. Pupils' attainment depends as much on their social and family background as on what happens inside the classroom. The initiative will therefore reward and punish teachers on factors that are outside their direct control, and this is unfair, de-motivating and divisive. It will inevitably lead to a collapse in morale and in teaching standards. It will also damage relationships not only between teachers and pupils but also between staff members within schools and between teachers and parents. It is likely to increase stress for all concerned. The union is therefore considering strike action in protest against this government initiative.

1. How would a unitarist explain and seek to resolve this conflict?

2. How would a pluralist explain and seek to resolve this conflict?

3. How would someone holding a radical perspective explain and seek to resolve this conflict?

Chapter 24 Power and politics

Key concepts

power	need for power
strategic contingencies	personalized power
influencing	socialized power
rationalism	authority
rationality	Machiavellianism
rational model of organization	locus of control
political model of organization	risk-seeking propensity
politics	

Learning objectives

When you have read this chapter, you should be able to define those key concepts in your own words, and you should also be able to:

1. Appreciate the importance of power and politics in organizational life.

2. Compare and contrast different perspectives on power.

3. Distinguish different bases of power.

4. Identify organizational factors which enhance the power of departments.

5. Differentiate between power tactics and influencing strategies.

6. Distinguish between the rational and political models of organization.

7. Identify the characteristics of individuals most likely to engage in political behaviour.

8. Explain why politics is a feature of organizational life.

Why study power and politics?

Organizations have a political dimension as well as a social, technical, economic and cultural one. David Buchanan and Richard Badham (1999a, p.1) wrote:

> The relatively stable, ordered, bounded, predicable, rule-based hierarchical organization of today seems an anachronism. The so-called 'post-modern' organization is characterized by fluidity, uncertainty, ambiguity and discontinuity. Job security is replaced with 'employability security'. Organization boundaries are blurred with the development of partnerships and joint ventures, sub-contracting and peripheral workforces, and social and technology-based networks. Hierarchy is replaced by reliance on expert power; those with the best understanding of the problems take the decisions. In this stereotyped, 'post-modern context', individuals are stripped of the conventional resources of a relatively stable organizational position, and are deprived of a meaningful, predictable vision of their own future. This fluid and shifting context implies an

increased dependence on personal and interpersonal resources, and on political skills to advance personal and corporate agendas. There is clearly enhanced scope for political manoeuvring in a less well ordered and less disciplined organizational world. There is also clearly a greater need for a critical understanding of the shaping role of political behaviour in such a context.

Power and politics are inextricably entwined, affecting human behaviour in organizations. It has been said that power concerns the capacity of individuals to exert their will over others; while political behaviour is the practical domain of power in action, worked out through the use of techniques of influence and other (more or less extreme) tactics. Some writers believe that much management failure can be attributed to political incompetence, political naïveté and the inability or unwillingness to perform effectively the required political tasks in an organization (Kotter, 1985; Yates, 1985).

Politics is about overcoming the problem of resolving situations where different organization members bring different values to their work, and consequently do not share common goals or views yet have to continue to work with one another (Kakabadse, 1983). Even when they do share aims about company objectives, they may disagree about the means to those ends, and will fight (figuratively) for what they believe is the appropriate line of action. Ian Mangham (1979) felt that most significant organizational decisions were the outcome of social and political forces and were only partly influenced by evidence and rational argument—shaped by 'the pulling and hauling that is politics' (p.17). Henry Kissinger, an American diplomat, confirmed this view when he wrote:

> Before I served as a consultant to [President] Kennedy, I had believed, like most academics, that the process of decision-making was largely intellectual and all one had to do was to walk into the President's office and convince him of the correctness of one's view. This perspective, I soon realised, is as dangerously immature as it is widely held. (cited in Pfeffer, 1992a, p.31)

Lee Bolman and Terrence Deal (1991) summarized this political view of organization, seeing goals and decisions as emerging from bargaining, negotiation and jockeying for position by individuals and coalitions. These coalitions were composed of varied individuals and interest groups which possessed enduring differences of values, preferences, beliefs, information and perceptions of reality. Many observers feel that political behaviour plays a more significant role in organizational life than is commonly realized or admitted; and that the academic management literature does not adequately explore the shaping of political behaviour in organizational change.

Power in organizations

Power: the capacity of individuals to overcome resistance on the part of others, to exert their will and to produce results consistent with their interests and objectives.

Power is a controversial topic which is difficult to define and measure with precision. **Power** has been defined as the capacity of individuals to overcome resistance on the part of others, to exert their will and to produce results consistent with their interests and objectives. Although this is a definition from an individual perspective, power can be exerted not only by some individuals over others but also by some groups, sections, departments and organizations, and, indeed, by some nations over others.

Being abstract, power is also a difficult topic to conceptualize. For this reason, a number of different frameworks are offered. They share similarities and differences. Being able to view the complex and slippery notion of power from different angles enables readers to become aware of, and to draw on, the strengths and limitations of each viewpoint. The first, 'power-as-a-property' viewpoint, sees power as an attribute or characteristic and distinguishes three different perspectives. It is associated with writers such as Pfeiffer, and French and Raven. The second, 'face-of-power' viewpoint, considers it in terms of its visibility to outsiders. It is most closely associated with Steven Lukes. The third viewpoint focuses on disciplinary power and is associated with the work of Michel Foucault.

Power-as-a-property viewpoint

This viewpoint distinguishes three different perspectives on power that can be found in the literature. These perspectives are similar to 'frames of reference' on conflict considered earlier in the book [**link**, chapter 23, conflict]. The distinction is based upon the attribute or characteristic of power which the writer(s) consider to be crucial. The three perspectives are:

- Power as a property of individuals.
- Power as a property of relationships.
- Power as an embedded property of structures.

Power as a property of individuals
From this perspective, power is seen as being possessed by an individual who exercises it through a range of social and interpersonal skills. Proponents claim to 'know power when they see it'; can easily differentiate between those organization members who have and use power and those who do not; and can often even identify the source of the power being used by a particular individual. This perspective asks how much power an individual has, where it comes from and how more can be acquired. Table 24.1 lists the sources of individual power identified by Jeffrey Pfeffer (1992b). Notice how some of these come from the position

---

Table 24.1: Power as an individual property: sources

Structural sources of individual power include:
- Formal position and authority in the organization structure
- Ability to cultivate allies and supporters
- Access to and control over information and other resources
- Physical and social position in the organization's communication network
- The centrality of your own unit or section to the business
- Role in resolving critical problems, in reducing uncertainty
- Degree of unity of your section, lack of internal dissent
- Being irreplaceable
- The pervasiveness of one's activities in the organization

Personal sources of individual power include:
- Energy, endurance and physical stamina
- Ability to focus energy and avoid wasteful effort
- Sensitivity and ability to read and understand others
- Flexibility in selecting varied means to achieve goals
- Personal toughness: willingness to engage in conflict and confrontation
- Able to 'play the subordinate' and 'team member' to enlist the support of others

Based on Jeffrey Pfeffer, *Managing With Power: Power ad Influence in Organization*, Harvard Business School Press, Boston, 1992.

that the individual occupies within the organization hierarchy (structural sources) [**link**, chapter 14, elements of structure], while others relate to their personal attributes like personality, communication and motivation (individual sources) [**link**, part 2, individuals in the organization].

Stop and criticize

How would the 'power-as-individual-property' perspective explain why typically, accountants tend to be more powerful and influential in most organizations than, for example, personnel and training managers?

Power as a property of relationships

The second perspective on power to be found in the literature treats it as a property of a *relationship* between a power holder and others, rather than just a property of the individual alone. John French and Bertram Raven proposed this 'relational' view of power in which followers need to perceive that the leader has access to rewards, sanctions, expertise and so on (table 24.2). From this perspective, the exercise of power depends on the *beliefs*, *perceptions* and *desires* of the followers [**link**, chapter 21, leadership].

An individual may have access to rewards or possess expertise, but if his followers believe that he does not, they may be unwilling to comply. Similarly, a person may lack reward capacity or expertise but will gain compliance from others because she persuades them that she possesses these. An individual can manipulate followers' beliefs and perceptions to gain compliance. It is because two parties are involved that this view of power sees it as a relational construct and not just a property of the individual who accumulates it. David Knights and Hugh Willmott (1999) remind us that power can only be successful 'if those over whom power is exercised are tempted by the material rewards offered or have considerable respect for the knowledge surrounding the exercise of power' (p.166).

Second, the five power bases are both interrelated and dynamic. Using one of the power bases affects one's ability to use another. For example, using coercive

Table 24.2: Bases of power

Reward power	is the ability of a leader to exert influence based on the belief of followers that the leader has access to valued rewards which will be dispensed in return for compliance with instructions.
Coercive power	is the ability of a leader to exert influence based on the belief of followers that the leader can administer penalties or sanctions that are considered to be unwelcome.
Referent power	is the ability of a leader to exert influence based on the belief of followers that the leader has desirable abilities and personality traits that can and should be copied; referred to as *charisma*.
Legitimate power	is the ability of a leader to exert influence based on the belief of followers that the leader has authority to issue orders which they in turn have an obligation to accept, referred to as position power, as this depends on the leader's formal organizational position and title.
Expert power	is the ability of a leader to exert influence based on the belief of followers that the leader has superior knowledge relevant to the situation and the task in hand.

Based on John French and Bertram Raven, 'The bases of social power' in D. Cartwright (ed.), *Studies in Social Power*, Institute for Social Research, Ann Arbor, Mich., 1958.

power leaves the individual losing referent power, while an application of expert power may mean the individual gains referent power. Additionally, power is dynamic, changing in form and amount as the situation around the individual and followers changes. For example, a person's initial recommendation, based on their expertise, may initially be discounted by others. When proved to be correct by circumstances, followers' assessment of that person changes and their expert power may be enhanced. Note the continual relationship element in this example.

Third, individuals can operate from several bases of power, with the same person using different power bases in different combinations in different contexts at different times. The relationship issue here manifests itself in terms of the existence of different groups of followers and different issues being dealt with. In one relationship, certain power bases may be effective, whereas in a different relationship, others may be more appropriate. Similarly, situations change over time. In the past, leadership was based first on coercion, then on legitimate power; now it is based on expert power, and increasingly on referent power.

French and Raven listed five bases of power, since one's power base will depend on whatever resources are available and appropriate in the circumstances. Hence, the list of potential power bases is potentially infinite (Clegg and Hardy, 1996; Hardy, 1995). Buchanan and Badham added that 'Even being downtrodden, voiceless and marginalized is to possess a power source which can be exploited, if and when circumstances allow' (1999a, p.49).

Both the power-as-individual-property perspective and the power-as-relational perspective are also referred to as *episodic*. Current thinking about power distinguishes between 'episodic' and 'pervasive' perspectives. Episodic perspectives view power as something that one party uses every so often (episodically) to change the behaviour of another, while the *pervasive* perspective sees it as something that is diffused throughout an organization and which produces an ongoing effect on how employees behave. It is to a consideration of this view that we now turn.

Power as an embedded property of structures

The third perspective on power focuses on what factors give organization departments, and not individuals, power. It also considers how power is used to control the behaviour of individuals through less obvious means. It pays attention to the way in which power is 'designed into' the organization's fabric and embedded in such a way that makes it less visible and less detectable by those who are not sufficiently observant. The effect of this is to give certain privileged individuals

---

Richard III, power and relationships

In his analysis of Shakespeare's play *Richard III*, Corrigan explains that Richard is engaged in a 'joint venture' to secure the throne. Despite his individual talents, he is unable to achieve this goal alone, needing the services of others in his organization. He needs them to have commitment and to provide him with resources and information. The effective leader ensures that trust had been established with the crucial allies, but this is something Richard fails to do. His allies leave and he is left alone.

Corrigan concludes that whether one is a monarch or a manager, clear ambition and a will to act can overcome unfavourable odds. However, when you have threatened everybody, you are alone. Power cannot be used without there being other people who trust you. The ambitious need other people to help them to hold on to their power. Shakespeare stresses the consequences of failing to perform the time-consuming but vital task of building relationships [**link**, chapter 16, organization strategy and design].

Based on Paul Corrigan, *Shakespeare on Management*, Kogan Page, 1999, pp.102–3 and 106.

access to decision making, information sources and budgetary responsibility, while denying it to others. While this hidden or latent power may be less easily detected, analysed and challenged, it is not any less potent.

The embedded perspective sees power as so expertly woven into the fabric of the organization that we accept it, in a 'taken-for-granted' way, in the same way that we accept that offices have desks. We accept the social and organization structure of the company—our job description, the operating rules and policies, the budgets to which we work, the equipment which we are given to use, and how we will be rewarded. All of these we consider a perfectly 'natural' way of running the organization's systems and processes on a day-to-day basis. When power becomes so embedded, it becomes virtually invisible. Even when detected, it becomes difficult if not impossible to challenge. Clearly, it is in the best interests of those who possess power if its unequal distribution remains invisible and taken for granted and is accepted, and not challenged by those who are subject to it. Let us consider an example of embedded power.

> **Strategic contingencies** are events and activities, both inside and outside an organization, that are essential for it to attain its goals.

Strategic contingencies are events and activities which must occur, either inside or outside an organization, for it to attain its goals. This concept can explain the differences in the relative power of different departments (Hickson *et al.*, 1971; Salancik and Pfeffer, 1974; 1977). In the short term, a firm must manufacture a product and sell it to a customer at a profit to survive. Developing the next product or counting the money it has received is less important. In this short-term example, the sales department and production department provide greater strategic value to the company that do the R&D or the finance departments. Hence, individuals, groups or departments which are responsible for dealing with the key issues and dependencies in the company environment, which solve its pressing problems or which deal with a current crisis, will be more powerful than those that do not.

The power sources that indicate a department's ability to respond to strategic contingencies include dependency creation, financial resources, centrality of activities, non-substitutability and ability to decrease uncertainty. These five sources overlap, and the more of them a department possesses the greater the power that it will exert within its organization.

1. *Dependency creation*
A department is powerful if other units and departments depend on its products or services. These may include materials, information, resources and services which flow between departments. The receiving department is always in an inferior power position. The number and strength of the dependencies is also important.

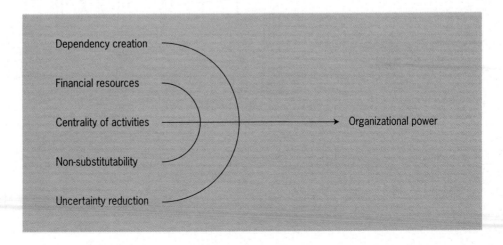

2. *Financial resources*

A department's ability to control financial resources gives it power. Money can be converted into many different resources that are required and valued by others. Because of the power-enhancing value of financial resources, departments in all organizations compete with others to grasp new projects or tasks which have new financial budgets attached to them.

3. *Centrality*

Centrality refers to the degree to which the department's activities are critical to producing the company's main product or service. It reflects the relative import-ance of the contribution made by one department in comparison with another, with respect to the organization's goal. The more central a department is, the more powerful. A good indicator of centrality is the likelihood of its work being sub-contracted. The least central functions are training, payroll management, computer management, personnel and advertising.

4. *Non-substitutability*

If what a department does cannot easily be done by another department, either inside or outside the organization, then it has great power. The more specialized its work, the greater the skill and knowledge required to do it, the more power that accrues to it.

5. *Uncertainty reduction*

Those who have the ability to reduce uncertainty can gain significant reputations and positions of significant influence by offering clear definitions of problems and by specifying solutions, thereby restoring otherwise confused situations. Three uncertainty-reduction techniques are *securing prior information*, e.g. fore-casting and market research; *prevention*, as when a negative event is predicted and its occurrence forestalled; and *absorption*, when a department acts after an event to reduce its negative consequences (Hickson *et al.*, 1971).

Stop and criticize	Do you think that the pursuit of power interferes with or contributes to improved organiz-ational performance?

"You're an evil bastard, Gilroy. I like that."

Dependency is power

During the late 1950s and early 1960s, Michel Crozier investigated a factory in the French nationalized tobacco industry. It was located outside Paris. At first glance, one would have expected that the production department which manufactured the product would be more powerful that its maintenance department. The cigarette production was automated and consisted of women whose job it was to operate the semi-automatic machines turning out the cigarettes. These production workers' jobs were routine, limited in scope, low skill, and remunerated on a piecework basis so as to encourage productivity.

All matters to do with finance, raw material acquisition, distribution and sales were controlled centrally from Paris. All the factory had to do was to produce cigarettes, without any other distraction. The only problems the factory manager had to deal with were machine stoppages due to equipment breakdowns. These were caused by variations in the tobacco leaf, which required constant adjustment of the machines. When the machines stopped, the work stopped, and the factory stopped producing what it was there for.

The maintenance department consisted of twelve male workers, who reported to the factory's technical engineer. Only they knew how to set and to repair the machines, and they did not explain what they did to anyone else. Their work was unpredictable, complex and required many years of experience to gain the craft skills needed. Moreover, the vital knowledge needed for machine repair was contained in the maintenance men's heads and not in any manuals.

The maintenance department was so powerful because it possessed three key characteristics. First, the production department was *dependent* on the maintenance department because of the unpredictable nature caused by the assembly line breakdowns. Second, the maintenance department had *centrality*, that is, it was critical to the final output of the organization. Third, it had *non-substitutability*. The production department could not effect the repairs itself, and the maintenance staff kept their knowledge to themselves. For these three reasons, the maintenance staff had gained control over a strategic contingency in this factory—the knowledge and ability to prevent or resolve work stoppages.

Based on Michel Crozier, *The Bureaucratic Phenomenon*, University of Chicago Press, Chicago, 1964.

Faces-of-power viewpoint

A second viewpoint on power was provided by Steven Lukes (1975). For him it ranged from power as clearly visible (overt) and self-evident to an observer, through to power being subtle, less visible (covert) and institutionalized, that is, embedded in the structure of the organization in which individuals work. He conceptualized it as having three 'faces' or dimensions:

Dimension 1   Power that is exercised to secure a decision in situations where there is some observable conflict or disagreement.

Dimension 2   Power that is exercised to keep issues on or off the decision-making agenda, so that potential conflicts or disagreements are precluded and therefore unobservable.

Dimension 3   Institutionalized power is used to define reality for its members. If norms and meanings that have been defined by senior management become internalized by workers, they will accept and act in accordance with them, even if it goes against their 'real' interests.

The first dimension is the most obvious and concerns a clash of interests between those making a decision. It focuses on the *observable behaviour* of individuals or groups that determines or influences the form or content of a decision. For example, in the army, a sergeant threatens to put a private on a charge unless he completes his assigned task before midnight. The sergeant's words (verbal and par-averbal behaviour) and manner (non-verbal) can both be observed by an onlooker who notices their effect on what the soldier decides to do (work more quickly).

The second dimension of power relates to the interest of certain groups being excluded from a particular bargaining or decision-making arena [**link**, chapter 22, decision making]. It concerns the *non-observable behaviour* that is involved in keeping issues on or off an agenda. This form of power can keep controversial issues from ever reaching the public domain to be either discussed or decided upon. Unlike in the first case, where individuals or groups, though they may be overruled are nevertheless involved in the decision-making process, here they are not admitted to the arena in the first place. Power is most commonly associated with someone doing something, such as making a decision or acting in a particular way. Yet *not* making a decision or doing nothing is often as powerful and significant as doing so (Wolfinger, 1971; Pettigrew, 1973). Peter Bachrach and Morton Baratz (1962) noted that by doing this, one could avoid resistance to, or overt conflict over, one's intentions completely. Stewart Clegg (1989, p.77) distinguished three forms of such non-decision making:

- The powerful deal with the grievances of the less powerful by ignoring them, dismissing them as minor, unsubstantiated or irrelevant, or subjecting them to endless inconclusive consideration by committees and enquiries.

- The less powerful expect their grievances or demands to be ignored or rejected, and hence fail to raise them in the first place.

- The powerful decide which matters are 'legitimate' and hence discussible, and how and where they are to be discussed, while stifling issues and demands judged as inappropriate.

The third dimension of power concerns the way that the 'powerful' define reality for the 'powerless' in the organization. They secure the support of those who are disadvantaged by the exercise of their power. The true interests and potential grievances of the 'powerless' are obscured or distorted, and they are distracted from them, becoming instead preoccupied by events that are more immediate and understandable to them, for example the use of induction programmes and company training [**link**, chapter 19, organization culture].

This radical dimension of power concerns itself with how power is exercised outside the usual and specific points of conflict or decision making. It is interested in *institutionalized* power—the way that it is used to prevent conflict by shaping people's perceptions and preferences so that they accept the existing order of things. What distinguishes institutionalized power is that it is difficult to associate it with the actions of any specific individual who may be influencing a decision (first dimension); or with backstage manoeuvring conducted by individuals and groups, who are seeking to prevent contentious issues being discussed (second dimension). Power holders, by defining reality for employees and getting them to internalize selected norms and meanings, cast a sort of 'spell' over them, whereby the powerless become unable to formulate consciously their real interests. Institutional power helps to sustain the dominance of senior management by reducing the ability of subordinates to dissent.

Disciplinary power viewpoint

A third viewpoint on power has been provided by Michel Foucault, a French philosopher and historian. He was interested in the rise of a distinctively modern form

Less obvious management controls

The six management control strategies described by Don Hellriegel and John Slocum exercise control over individuals on the basis of power that is not immediately obvious. Behind each control strategy a choice has been made. For example, controlling through organization structure involves deciding on the degree of formal authority to assign, and how much legitimate power to allocate. Choices involve what information the role holder will receive, what types of decision they will be allowed to make, and what budgetary responsibilities they will have, and so on.

Control through organization structure
Large organizations give their employees job descriptions which set out their tasks and responsibilities. These can be narrow, detailed and specific, or general, broad and vague. They also specify communication flows and the location of decision-making responsibility.

Control through policies and rules
Written policies and rules guide employees' actions, structure their relationships and aim to establish consistency of behaviour. Rules lay down standards, define acceptable behaviour and establish levels of required performance.

Control through recruitment and training
Companies wish to avoid having people who behave in unstable, variable, spontaneous, idiosyncratic and random ways. To achieve predictability, they select stable, reliable individuals, while consistency and reliability are achieved through training them.

Control through rewards and punishments
Employees receive extrinsic rewards in the form of material monetary incentives and associated fringe benefits like company cars and free meals. Intrinsic rewards include satisfying work, personal responsibility and autonomy. Offering to provide or withdraw these rewards gains employees' compliance.

Control through budgets
Individuals and sections in organizations are given financial and resource targets to guide their performance. These may relate to expenditure, level of cost incurred or sales volume to be achieved in a month. Production budgets include labour hours used and machine downtime.

Control through machinery
This form of control is a feature of assembly line production (Henry Ford) and is also popular in process industries, where chemicals are manufactured automatically. Developments in information and computer technology have increased the possibility of electronic surveillance of employees.

Based on Don Hellriegel and John W. Slocum, *Management: Contingency Approaches*, Addison-Wesley, 1978.

of disciplinary power. His work can be related to Lukes' third dimension of power, the institutional, which focuses on the way that management sustains its dominance by reducing subordinates' ability to dissent by creating their reality and managing meanings for them. Foucault considered how individuals and groups become 'socially inscribed' and 'normalized' through the routine aspects of organizations. He studied the 'rules of the game' which managements established, which both constrained and enabled the actions of those subject to those rules.

Foucault used the concept of *bio-power* in his arguments. This operated by establishing and defining what was normal or abnormal, acceptable or socially deviant. Bio-power is targeted at society in general; is achieved through talk, writing, debate and discussion; and controls us through getting us to consider what is 'normal'. At the level of the organization, once employees do this, they become self-disciplining and no longer require management to keep them under control. For Foucault, power was a set of tools which achieved their aims through *disciplinary practices* such as punishment, surveillance, coercion and assessment, and which acted to control and regiment individuals. Foucault's interpreters have identified examples of these (Hiley, 1987, p.351), including:

- the allocation of physical space in offices or factories, which establishes homogeneity and uniformity, individual and collective identity, ranks people according to status and fixes their position in the network of social relations;

- standardization of individual behaviour through timetables, regimentation, work standardization and repetitive activities;

- 'composition of forces', where individuals became parts of larger units such as cross-functional teams or assembly line workers;

- job ladders and career systems, which, through their future promises, encourage consent to organizational demands.

Foucault's practices are a feature of all organizations, and they shape our daily activities and interactions, controlling and regimenting us and guaranteeing our ready compliance with the social and organizational norms and expectations established by management. They tend to be 'micro-techniques'—so small and so embedded in the organization's structure that they are hardly noticed by employees. If employees do recognize them, the practices are difficult to argue against. They also contain a 'Catch 22' element. Resistance by employees to these disciplinary practices, said Foucault, merely demonstrates and reinforces the necessity for such discipline.

Where Foucault differs from Lukes is that, in his view, the drive to create these disciplinary practices does not necessarily come from the plans and intentions of specific individuals such as politicians or managers. For him, power is not equated with the domination of the powerful or the capitalist exploitation of the working class, even though it may be beneficial for both. He talks of people being trapped within a 'field of force relations', a sort of web of power which they help to create and which is constantly being recreated by them in an ongoing way. Individuals are both and simultaneously creators of that web and prisoners within it.

Within that web at the organizational level, specific disciplinary practices condition employees' thought processes, leading them to treat techniques like performance-based pay as being perfectly 'natural' and not to question it (Hardy and Clegg, 1996). The 'field of force relations' is neither stable nor inevitable. Instead, it changes as points of resistance are encountered; fissures open up, old coalitions break up and new ones are formed. It is a shifting network of alliances, not only in organizations but also in society in general (Clegg, 1989).

- Over the last few years in Britain, many lorries and trucks have had a panel attached to their rear doors with lettering large enough to be read by following drivers. The panel reads, 'Well driven? Call 0800–22 55 33'.

- Office stationery from a British bank (previously a building society) carries the following statement at the bottom of the page: 'To help us to improve our service we may record or monitor phone calls'.

Foucault uses the metaphor of the *panopticon* for his paradigm of disciplinary technology. The panopticon is a prison whose design allows all the inmates to be observed in their cells by one observer who remains unseen by them. The prisoners know that they cannot hide or escape from this surveillance, and that it is constant and regular, but they do not know exactly when they are being observed. The consequence is that they behave as if they are being watched. They 'self-survey' and become obedient and compliant by self-disciplining themselves.

Total quality management (TQM), a popular management technique of the 1990s, was launched as offering a multidisciplinary approach that empowered employees at all levels of the organization. Research by Sewell and Wilkinson

(1992) into its application in the manufacturing sector suggested that it had become a modern version of the 'panopticon gaze' (Foucault, 1979). Like Buchanan and Badham's 'embedded power' and Lukes' institutionalized power, Foucault's bio-power and panopticon structure provide an ongoing, pervasive exercise of power in which people's behaviour is constantly being controlled but is done so by the individuals themselves through their own self-monitoring. Employees are watched and they watch themselves. Put another way, Foucault argues that individuals are party to their own situation. Rules are not only devised and imposed by others but are also accepted by them. To become subject to rules implies an acceptance of them. For him, organizations are prisons, with their processes of decision making, information technology and human resource management only refining the process of 'capture'.

Stop and criticize

Foucault wrote about prisons, but his 'disciplinary practices' can be found in all organizations.

Suggest examples of Foucault's 'disciplinary gaze' from your experience. Explain how they control your behaviour, and why it is so difficult to argue or act against it.

Can people break free, get out and redesign this web?—Sadly not, Foucault argues. He used the single term 'power/knowledge' to indicate that the two are inextricably linked. One would expect that knowledge could set people free. However, argued Foucault, the way that knowledge is constructed and represented (about what is 'normal') is, itself, dependent on the exercise of power. Knowledge therefore is not an antidote to power; on the contrary, the generation of more knowledge only offers more power to be exercised by some in order to control and manipulate others. In Foucault's view, knowledge does not emancipate but merely perpetuates the changing web of power that subjugates people.

Buchanan and Badham (1999a, p.221) contrast the traditional concept of power with that offered by Foucault in table 24.3. They highlight three implications of Foucault's perspective for organizations in general, and for those managers seeking to implement change within them in particular:

1. Critically and sceptically look at so-called 'radical' changes. Are they real or cosmetic? Become aware of the continuities in organization structures and power relations (e.g. just how radical is the team empowerment programme?).

2. The manager is part of the field of force relations and not separate or outside it. He or she will both deploy their own power and be subject to the exercise of power. In seeking to implement change, they themselves will be changed.

3. Local points of resistance can be expected to emerge, and these can be exploited by the manager.

Power tactics and influencing strategies

How do individuals use their power and get others to do what they want? One definition of power is the ability 'to produce intended effects' in line with one's perceived interests (Pettigrew and McMulty, 1995). These effects can be produced in a way that those upon whom the power is being exercised are both aware of it and often resentful. Alternatively, those effects can be obtained in such a way that

Table 24.3: Foucault versus traditional concepts of power

Traditional concepts of power	Foucault's concepts of power
Power is possessed, is accumulated, is vested in the individual.	Power is pervasive, is a totality, is reflected in concrete practices.
Power is in the hands of social and organizational elites; resistance is futile.	Power is to be found in the micro-physics of social life; power depends on resistance.
We are subject to the domination of those who are more powerful than we are.	We construct our own web of power in accepting current definitions of normality.
Power is destructive, denies, represses, prevents, corrupts.	Power is productive, contributes to social order, which is flexible and shifting.
Power is episodic, is visible, is observable in action, is deployed intermittently, is absent except when exercised.	Power is present in its absence, discreet, operating through taken-for-granted daily routines and modes of living.
Knowledge of power sources and relationships is emancipatory, can help us overcome domination.	Knowledge maintains and extends the web of power, creating further opportunities for domination.

From David Buchanan and Richard Badham, *Power, Politics and Organizational Change*, Sage, London, 1999, p.221.

those being affected are unaware, only occasionally resentful, but more often actually grateful. We can thus distinguish two approaches—the 'power push' and the 'influencing pull'. Both see power as a property of the individual which is exercised in a relationship with other people, albeit in different ways.

Power push

Buchanan and Badham provide a typology of power-push tactics (table 24.4). Basing it on Gray and Starke's (1984) classification system, they add an additional category of more covert and ruthless ('dirty tricks') tactics. Their examples come from interviews and discussions with managers attending executive development programmes in Australia, Britain, Sweden and Finland. They were confident that these represent the taken-for-granted 'recipe knowledge' of many experienced managers around the world.

Influencing pull

Influencing is the ability to affect another's attitudes, beliefs or behaviours—seen only in its effect—without using coercion or formal position, and in a way that influencees believe they are acting in their own best interests.

This perspective also considers power as a property of the individual, which forms the basis for their **influencing**. Individuals in organizations are seen as possessing varying amounts of different types of power as discussed earlier. The more of each power type a person has, the greater the number of influencing strategies that they can use, and the greater the likelihood of achieving a desired outcome. Moreover, the amount of power possessed is not fixed. Organizational members both gain and lose power depending on what they do or fail to do, as well as on what those around them do.

Following his review of the influencing literature, Andrzej Huczynski (1996) defined influencing as one person's ability to affect another's attitudes, beliefs or behaviours. Its distinguishing feature is that generally it is seen only in its effect and is done without the use of either coercion or the use of formal position. If per-

Table 24.4: Power tactics

Power tactic	Definition and examples
Image building	Actions which enhance reputation and further career: appropriate dress; support for the 'right' causes; adherence to group norms; air of self-confidence. • 'You have got to be seen to be successful at all costs' • 'Seek to be associated with success; seek the spotlight'
Selective information	Withhold unfavourable information from superiors; keep useful information from your competition; offer only favourable interpretations; overwhelm others with complex technical data. • 'Exclude others as appropriate from your plans and activities' • 'Withhold information and dispense misinformation to maintain control'
Scapegoating	Make sure someone is blamed; avoid personal blame; take credit for success. • 'Blame a predecessor' • 'Pick your timing to discredit people'
Formal alliances	Agree actions with key people; create a coalition strong enough to enforce its will. • 'Gain access to key players and information' • 'Seek the support and affiliation of those in power'
Networking	Make lots of friends in influential positions. • 'Be mobile . . . out and about, talking networking' • 'Invite the "right" people to social events
Compromise	Give in on unimportant issues to create allies for subsequent, more important issues. • 'Be ready to change your opinions quickly' • 'Decide how much you are prepared to lose'
Rule manipulation	Refuse requests on the grounds of 'against company policy' but grant identical requests from allies on the grounds of 'special circumstances'. • 'Ask yourself . . . what can I get away with?' • 'Stay clean . . . never get caught playing the game'
Other tactics	These examples do not fit under Gray and Strake's headings and are more covert and ruthless, being concerned with political infighting. • 'When all else fails, do not be afraid to use coercion' • 'Undermine the expertise of others' • 'Play one person or group off against another' • 'Keep a "dirt file"' • 'Do it to them before they do it to you' • 'Undermine opponents through "whispers in the corridors"' • 'Use "subversives" to plant ideas with other managers' • 'Use other people to "fire the bullets"' • 'Trash the deal in the details; nit-picking can be an effective blocking tactic'

From David Buchanan and Richard Badham, *Power, Politics and Organizational Change*, Sage, London, 1999, pp.27–9.

formed successfully, the person being influenced, the influencee, will believe that they are acting in their own best interests. The ability to influence is not a mysterious gift or talent possessed only by those at the top of an organization with power. Anyone can have influence, at any level in the organization. The focus in this definition is upon behaviour and action. Changing another's attitudes, values or beliefs is only important to the extent that this affects what other people do and say. Research shows that changing a person's behaviour can lead them to change their original attitudes, values and beliefs. The arrow of causation thus points in both directions. Ultimately, influence is of course about getting one person to do what another wants.

Influencing is a process that will be unobservable to both the influencee and an observer. The first that influencees will know of it is when they have supported the influencer's proposal or suggestion, or have agreed to act as requested. Finally, influencing is seen as an alternative to the use of coercion or formal authority. Moreover, it is one which has long-term effects, avoids distrust and hostility and, if well executed, is not noticed. People will do things for others, without knowing exactly why, but will feel good about it. Their positive feelings come from their assessment that they are primarily acting in their own best interests, helping themselves to achieve their own personal goals rather than acting for the benefit of the influencer.

Influencing strategies

David Kipnis and his colleagues (Kipnis *et al.*, 1984) studied how managers influenced their own managers, co-workers and subordinates. They identified seven influencing strategies: reason, friendliness, coalition, bargaining, assertiveness, higher authority and sanctions (table 24.5).

They found that among the managers that they studied, the popularity of each strategy depended on the direction of their influence—upwards, downwards or lateral (table 24.6).

Table 24.5: Influencing strategies

Reason	Relies on the presentation of data and information as the basis for a logical argument that supports a request.
Friendliness	Depends on the influencee thinking well of the influencer.
Coalition	Mobilizing other people in the organization to support you, and thereby strengthening your request.
Bargaining	Negotiating and exchanging benefits based upon the social norms of obligation and reciprocity.
Sanctions	Positively sanctioning (rewarding) those who comply with requests, and negatively sanctioning (punishing) those who do not.
Assertiveness	Making strident verbal statements; regularly reminding the influencee of your request.
Higher authority	Uses the chain of command and outside sources of power to influence the target person, appealing to or threatening to appeal to higher authority to gain agreement.

From David Kipnis, S.M. Schmidt, C. Swaffin-Smith and L. Wilkinson, 'Patterns of managerial influence: shotgun managers, tacticians and bystanders, *Organizational Dynamics*, 1984, Winter, pp.58–67.

Table 24.6: Preferred order of use of influencing strategies

Influencing up (manager)	Influencing across (co-worker)	Influencing down (subordinate)
Reason	Friendliness	Reason
Coalition	Reason	Assertiveness
Friendliness	Bargaining	Friendliness
Bargaining	Assertiveness	Coalition
Assertiveness	Higher authority	Bargaining
Higher authority	Sanctions	Higher authority
(no sanctions)	Coalition	Sanctions

From D. Kipnis, S.M. Schmidt and L. Wilkinson, 'Intra-organizational Influence tactics: explorations in getting one's own way', *Journal of Applied Psychology*, 1980, vol.65, pp.440–52.

To boldly influence . . .

In the TV and film series *Star Trek*, contact and conflict between the Federation and other species typically follow three different scenarios. In the first, like explorers during the sixteenth- and seventeenth-century age of discovery on Earth, the Federation is considerably more powerful than those in the primitive societies that they encounter. The latter treat the former as gods. This is a feature of the first series and involves the *Enterprise*'s crew ritually playing out the 'death of a god' as part of some religious festival. In the second scenario, the Federation is roughly equally matched by the forces of the Klingon, Romulan and Cardassian empires. The second series specializes in interstellar tensions defused by the Federation's master diplomat-negotiator, Jean-Luc Picard. In the third scenario, the Federation is inferior and its very existence is threatened. The first contact with the Borg falls into this category. It is a scenario shared with H.G. Wells' *War of the Worlds*. The power relationship of the Federation and the *Enterprise* to the other party affects how the conflict is resolved and what influencing strategies are employed in the stories in each series.

Based on Thomas Richards, *Star Trek in Myth and Legend*, Orion Books, London, 1997, p.12.

Cohen and Bradford (1989; 1991), built on the work of Abraham Maslow [**link**, chapter 8, motivation] and identified a range of positive sanctions or rewards, which they termed organizational currencies. They showed how these could be used to influence others to comply with your requests:

Currencies	Examples
• Resources	Lending or giving money, personnel or space.
• Information	Sharing specific technical or company knowledge.
• Advancement	Providing a task that can assist in another's promotion.
• Recognition	Acknowledging another's effort or achievement.
• Network/contacts	Providing opportunities for linking with others.
• Personal support	Giving personal and emotional support.
• Assistance	Assisting with current projects or performing unpleasant tasks for others.
• Co-operation	Responding quickly to requests, approving a project or aiding implementation.

Stop and criticize

How would you go about increasing your own power bases (e.g. reward, coercive, referent, etc) within your organization?

What steps would you take to reduce the power bases of those around you?

Politics in organizations

The question of whether organizations are *rational* or *political* continues to be debated. The form and nature of the assessment of the role of power and politics within organizations depends on whether or not one considers organizations to be political entities. The rationalist frame or perspective is summarized on the

Table 24.7: Rational versus political models of organization

Rational model	Political model
The goals of an organization seem obvious. Commercial organizations seek to make a profit; trade unions protect their members' interests; schools educate their pupils; hospitals try to cure their patients; and so on.	An organizational goal can get distorted, as when technological leadership takes precedence over profitability. Union leaders can lose touch with their members; and schools can acquire latent functions like keeping youngsters off the labour market.
Within the company, the goals and preferences are consistent among different department, units and members.	The idea of a single, agreed organizational goal is a fiction. Different parties have their own set of interests and priorities which change, and which may be placed ahead of those of the company as a whole.
Even if an organization's goals get distorted, the means for achieving them remain clear and rational. The organizational structure provides a rational way of achieving ends. Most firms have an organizational chart showing who is responsible for what.	Max Weber's seemingly rational organization has many dysfunctions (e.g. goals are displaced; cliques develop; units compete with each other). The formal structure (chart and rules) only ever gives a partial guide to factors like leadership style, employee morale and informal group behaviour.
Information available in the company is extensive, systematic and accurate.	Ambiguous information has to be used, and is withheld strategically.
Even if both aims and means get distorted, employees behave rationally when dealing with work tasks and each other.	Corporations have cultures which can distort what goes on. Culture becomes unconsciously and uncritically adopted.
Even if corporate culture can distort reality, communication can overcome this by showing clearly what is really happening.	Good communication involves more than consulting or telling people. It comes from shared goals and values. Where consensus on these is absent, communication cannot fill the gap.
Improved top-down managerial decision making can overcome the problems listed by making choices that maximize benefits.	Perhaps the real problem is too much management control, producing low levels of employee involvement and commitment. Decisions can be the outcome of bargaining and interplays between competing interests.

Based on Michael Joseph, *Sociology for Business*, Basil Blackwell, Oxford, 1989, pp.108–9; and Jeffrey Pfeffer, *Power in Organizations*, HarperCollins, New York, 1981, p.31.

left-hand side of table 24.7, while the political is described in the right-hand column. These two frames or models have different implications for how people are understood to operate within organizations, and which interests they are held to give priority to.

The rational model of organization is based on **rationalism** and **rationality** and consists of four key elements:

1. *Reason*: A rational action is one undertaken on the basis of reason. If conduct is substantiated by one or more reasons, a person performing that action is judged to be acting rationally.

2. *Consistency*: A person adopts the same actions under the same circumstances and expresses logically consistent preferences.

3. *Empirical*: Choices are made on valid knowledge rather than on intuition, and thus knowledge is held to provide objectivity.

4. *Means–ends*: Rationality is identified when appropriate means are chosen to attain the stated ends.

Rationalism is the theory that reason is the foundation of certainty in knowledge. **Rationality** refers to the use of scientific reasoning, empiricism and positivism, and to the use of decision criteria of evidence, logical argument and reasoning.

In the organizational context, the beliefs of the **rational model of organization** are summarized in the left-hand column of table 24.7. They are contrasted with those held by the political model against eight key organizational characteristics. At the very heart of this perspective is the view that employees possess goals that conform to, and are compatible with, those around them. These individuals are considered to share a collective purpose that can even be called the organizational goal. All the remaining features of the model assume the existence of this goal.

The **rational model of organization** is a perspective that holds that behaviour within a firm is not random but that goals are clear, and choices are made on the basis of reason in a logical way. In making decisions, the objective is defined, alternatives are identified, and the option with the greatest chance of achieving the objective is selected.

For example, people's behaviour in organizations is not random or accidental, but their actions are held to be directed towards the achievement of this organizational goal. Next, rationalists argue that when making a choice, the decision maker is guided by the norm of optimization, that is, seeking the most favourable outcome for a particular end. In this process, the various available alternatives are uncovered, their likely consequences assessed and the risks of each considered. Finally, the course of action is selected which best meets the organizational goal, which, as mentioned earlier, is held to exist and to be shared by all.

Rationalists hold that this is the best way to make choices on issues such as the introduction of new technology, work organization, distribution of rewards and organization structure. However, rational writers are not only prescriptive, saying how, in their view, things should be done; they also claim to be descriptive, that is, they claim to be describing how decisions are actually made in real organizations.

| **Stop and criticize** | Suggest reasons that might account for the popularity of the rationalist view of organizations among managers, management consultants and management academics. |

In contrast, there is the **political model of organization**. Rationalism has not gone unchallenged. James March (1962) was among the earliest writers to highlight that the rationalist model failed to take into account the differences of interests and objectives that existed between individuals within organizations. Indeed, March described business firms as *political coalitions*. As mentioned above, the rational model is founded on the belief that an organizational goal exists and is accepted by those in the organization.

> **The political model of organization** is a perspective that holds that it is made up of groups that have separate interests, goals and values, and in which power and influence are needed in order to reach decisions.

Historically, the earliest attempts to engender a commonality of interests among employees was through the use of bureaucratic control devices such as standardized treatment for all, performance-based pay, career ladders, and rules and procedures. These were used in combination with organizational socialization processes, such as careful staff selection, induction programmes and company training courses. Together it was hoped that these would get employees to agree on a set of collective goals to which all would subscribe. In the process, the operation of individual self-interest would be eliminated. Writers such as Cyert and March (1963) argued that these attempts had failed [**link**, chapter 22, decision making].

The political model of organization holds that normally there is no overarching organizational goal to which all members subscribe; that the behaviour of individuals and cliques within organizations can be explained with reference to their attempts to achieve their own unique goals; and that those who possess the greatest amounts of power will be the most successful in furthering their interests and achieving their goals. The rational model, in contrast, asserts that individual and departmental goals typically fit into the main organizational objective.

Other researchers investigated how decisions were actually made in organizations. They discovered an absence of the use of reason, consistency, empirical data or means–ends sequencing, which were supposed to characterize rational organizational decision making. In the place of consensus they found conflict, and they discovered decisions being made on the basis of bargaining and compromise (Allison, 1971). In the place of an organization-wide consensus on the organizational goal, they found individuals, groups, units and departments which had their own objectives; which were in conflict with each other to attain their own parochial ends; and which resolved issues through negotiation and the use of power.

These studies have led another group of writers to promote the political model of organization (Baldridge, 1971). The key characteristics of organizations, as they see them, are summarized in the right-hand column of table 24.7. Their point of departure is the view that this is no overarching organizational goal to which all members subscribe, and even where there is a written company 'mission statement', decisions are rarely made which further its achievement. This is because people's goals are considered to be inconsistent with each other. For example, the differences between management's and workers' goals were examined with the concept of the *organizational dilemma* in chapter 1.

On the question of rules and norms, the political writers hold that optimization is impossible because people disagree about goals, and hence about what constitutes the most 'appropriate action' in any given situation. In the absence of rules and norms to guide behaviour, different individuals and groups in the company attempt to achieve their own unique goals, and those who possess the greatest amounts of power will be the most successful in furthering their interests, since power is used to overcome the resistance of others.

> **Stop and criticize**
>
> Suggest reasons that might account for the relative unpopularity of the political view of organizations among managers, management consultants and management academics.
>
> From your experience of organizations (school, club, church, company) does the rationalist or the political model better explain the behaviour of people within it?

Users of the political frame focus on who participates in the decision-making process; analyse what determines their position with respect to issues; where their power derives from; the process by which decisions are arrived at; and how the

Table 24.8: Contrasting rational and political decision cycles

Conventional (rational) system cycle	Real (political) development cycle
1. Feasibility study.	1. Wild enthusiasm.
2. Requirements analysis.	2. Disillusionment.
3. Systems analysis.	3. Total confusion.
4. Specification.	4. Search for the guilty.
5. Design and development.	5. Punishment of the innocent.
6. Implementation.	6. Promotion of non-participants.

From W.M. Taggert and V. Silbey, *Informational Systems: People and Computers in Organizations*, Allyn & Bacon, Boston, 1986.

Politics in organizations refers to those activities undertaken within an organization to acquire, develop and use power and other resources to obtain one's preferred outcomes in a situation in which there is uncertainty or an absence of consensus about choices.

preferences of different participants in the decision-making process are combined or resolved. Taggert and Silbey (1986) humorously contrasted the difference between the rational and the political model with respect to the implementation of computer systems within organizations. The rational cycle, shown on the left of table 24.8, stresses the logical, considered, step-by-step approach to decision making in a company. In contrast, the political cycle, depicted on the right-hand side of table 24.8, highlights the irrationality, chaos and power struggles used by those involved to gain advantage.

The rational and the political views of organization take a different view of the nature of organizations, and also of how the behaviour of people within them can be best explained. Rather like the *nature–nurture* debate on personality, the 'rationalists' and the 'politicals' each have their own supporters, each can provide theoretical and empirical evidence in their defence, and each is necessarily partial, not giving the full picture of what is happening [**link**, chapter 5, personality]. One view is neither better nor more realistic than the other. Perhaps it is best to treat the rational and political models as 'different ways of seeing' what goes on in organizations.

Political behaviour

The study of **politics**, whether inside or outside organizations, is the study of who gets what, when and how. Engaging in political behaviour or performing political acts involves individuals engaging in activities to acquire, develop, retain and use power in order to obtain their preferred outcomes in a situation where there is uncertainty or disagreement about choices. Political behaviour concerns the actions that individuals take to influence the distribution of advantages and disadvantages within their organizations (Allen *et al.*, 1979; Farrell and Petersen, 1982).

Stop and criticize

The main problem with political behaviour in organizations is that most people lack the skills necessary to engage in it effectively. Do you agree or disagree?

Why does political behaviour occur within organizations? Chanlat (1997) distinguishes three sets of characteristics—personal, decisional and structural—which account for such behaviour.

Personal characteristics

Organizations seek to recruit individuals who possess ambition, drive, creativity and ideas of their own. Thus organizational recruitment, appraisal and training and promotion policies directly encourage political behaviour. For example, staff selection methods seek to identify candidates who possess the personality traits that have been related to a willingness to use power and engage in political behaviour [**link**, chapter 5, personality]. These are the **need for power**, **Machiavellianism**, **locus of control**, and **risk-seeking propensity** (House, 1988).

Need for power

In the 1940s, David McClelland (1961) developed a theory that people culturally acquired, that is learned, three types of need. These were the need for power (*n*Power), for achievement (*n*Ach), and for affiliation (*n*Aff). In any single individual, the strength of these three needs varied. Some individuals had a strong desire or motive to influence and lead others, and thus were more likely to engage in political behaviour within organizations. Since a desire to control others and events, and thus to have an impact on what is going on, is often associated with effective management, it is not surprising that selectors look for this trait in candidates for managerial jobs (McClelland and Boyatzis, 1982).

McClelland and Burnham (1995) argued that an individual's strong power needs can take two forms: **personalized power** and **socialized power**.

Managers who desire personalized power:

- exercise power impulsively;
- are not good institution builders;
- seek to dominate those around them;
- seek advancement at the expense of others;
- want their subordinates to be loyal to them, not to the organization.

Managers who want socialized power:

- believe in the importance of centralized authority;
- have a keen sense of justice, rewarding hard work;
- enjoy the discipline of work and getting things done in an orderly way;
- feel responsible for developing the organizations to which they belong;
- seek to use it for the common good, on behalf of the organization as a whole;
- exercise this form of power to create a good working climate for those around them;
- help others to understand and perform their tasks, and commit them towards organizational goals.

Machiavellianism

A second trait possessed by those who tend to engage in the use of power and politics in companies is termed **Machiavellianism**. Niccolo Machiavelli was a sixteenth-century Florentine philosopher and statesman who wrote a set of guidelines for rulers to use in order to secure and hold governmental power. These were published in a book called *The Prince,* which suggested that the primary method for achieving power was the manipulation of others (Machiavelli, 1961). Since that time, Machiavelli's name has been turned into both an adjective and a noun

---

Need for power
(*n*Pow) is the desire to make an impact on others, change people or events, and make a difference in life.

Personalized power is that which is self-serving and used for personal gain, influence and advancement.
Socialized power is that used for the common good, on behalf of the whole organization.

US presidents' needs for power, achievement and affiliation

President	Power (*n*Pow)	Needs Achievement (*n*Ach)	Affiliation (*n*Aff)
Clinton, Bill	Moderate	High	High
Bush, George	Moderate	Moderate	Low
Reagan, Ronald	High	Moderate	Low
Kennedy, John F.	High	Low	High
Roosevelt, Frank D.	High	Moderate	Low
Lincoln, Abraham	Moderate	Low	Moderate
Washington, George	Low	Low	Moderate

Based on R.J. House, W.D. Spangler and J. Woycke, 'Personality and charisma in the U.S. president: A psychological study of leader effectiveness', *Administrative Science Quarterly*, 1992, vol.36, pp.395.

Niccolo Machiavelli (1469–1527)

Machiavellianism is a personality trait or style of behaviour towards others which is characterized by (1) the use of guile and deceit in interpersonal relations; (2) a cynical view of the nature of other people; and (3) a lack of concern with conventional morality.

Locus of control is an individual's generalized belief about internal (self-control) versus external control (control by the situation or by others).

and has come to be associated with the use of opportunism and deceit in interpersonal relations. Thus we speak about people's Machiavellian behaviour, or describe them as being Machiavellians. Christie and Geis (1970) discussed Machiavellian personality characteristics.

'High-Machs', those who score highly on pencil-and-paper tests to measure their level of Machevellianism, would agree to statements such as:

- The best way to deal with people is to tell them what they want to hear.
- It is simply asking for trouble to completely trust someone else.
- Never tell anyone the real reason you did something unless it is useful to do so.

In behaving in accordance with Machiavellian principles, they prefer being feared to being liked; effectively manipulate others using their persuasive skills, especially in face-to-face contacts; initiate and control interactions; use deceit in relationships; engage in ethically questionable behaviour; and believe that any means justify the desired ends. One might add here that a desire for revenge and retribution, especially if one has been on the receiving end of others' politicking, may be considered both acceptable and satisfying.

Locus of control

The third personality trait affecting the likelihood of an individual engaging in political behaviour is the locus of control. Some people believe that what happens to them in life is under their own control. These are said to have an internal locus of control. Others hold that their life situation is under the control of fate or other people. This group is classed as having an external locus of control (Rotter, 1966). It is 'internals', those who believe that they control what happens to them, who tend to be more political in their behaviour than 'externals', and are more likely to expect that their political tactics will be effective. Internals are also less likely to be influenced by others.

Risk-seeking propensity

The final personality trait that is likely to determine whether a person engages in political behaviour is their willingness to take risks. Engaging in political behaviour in companies is not risk-free, and there are negative as well as positive outcomes for those who do it. They could risk being demoted, passed over for

Risk-seeking propensity refers to the willingness of an individual to choose options which entail risks.

promotion, being given low performance assessments, and so on. Some people are natural risk avoiders, while others are risk seekers (Sitkin and Pablo, 1992; Madison *et al.*, 1980). Generally speaking, risk seekers are more willing to engage in political behaviour than risk avoiders. For the latter, the negative consequences of a failed influencing attempt outweigh the possible benefits of a successful outcome.

Possession of these personality traits is associated with a high desire for career advancement. Every organization will contain a proportion of ambitious people who compete with each other by arguing and lobbying for their personal ideas, innovations, projects and goals. However, traditional organizational structures are pyramidal or triangular in shape. That is, at each successive, higher level, there are fewer positions available. Hence, these ambitious people are in constant competition with each other to secure a scarce, desirable, more senior post within the company.

Decisional characteristics

The extent to which politicking enters the decision-making process depends on the type of decision that is being made and the context of the decision-making process. Decisions vary depending on whether they are structured or unstructured [**link**, chapter 22, decision making}. Structured decisions are programmable, that is, they can be resolved using decision rules. Routine, day-to-day decisions, such as how much stock to order, are of this type. In a standard situation, if a decision is structured or programmed, or if there is no opposition to what a manager wants to do, then it is unnecessary to use politics.

In general, however, the number of management decisions that can be reached unambiguously using information, analysis and logical reasoning tends to be small. Unstructured decisions are more common. These are unprogrammable and cannot be made in the way previously described, using the bureaucratic rules and procedures that Weber would have liked. Moreover, they have implications for inter-unit relationships, which is an aspect of organizational integration and is the most difficult to subject to routinization and techno-economic rationality so beloved by rationalists (Beeman and Sharkey, 1987). In these circumstances, the competition between individuals and groups is strong; managerial discretion is high; and decisions have widespread consequences, on both success and failure at work. Most of the significant decisions in organizations, and virtually all at senior management levels, tend to be unstructured. They cannot be based on reason and logic alone but involve in some way the values and preferences of key organizational members. Examples of unstructured senior management decisions include:

- Should we seek to maximize profitability now, or seek to extend our market share?

- Should we expand the internal training department, or close it down and outsource training from external suppliers?

- Should we develop our expertise in this sector, or take over a company that already possesses it?

Such unstructured decisions often have to be made in a period of change and uncertainty during which an organization is unlikely to have a single, unambiguous, clearly defined objective with which all its members agree. Such a context provides the greatest scope for political behaviour. It creates an opportunity for those who possess the appropriate political skill, knowledge and expertise to deploy them most effectively, because the usual rational arguments and empirical evidence surrounding each argument may be lacking, or because reason and 'facts' are not sufficiently compelling on their own. Who knows what the demand for the product will be in two years time? The costs of not entering the e-commerce market now are unknown.

In such circumstances, one can expect different managers, with their own unique past experiences, personal opinions, differing values and current preferences, to disagree. Since information, analysis and logical reasoning cannot resolve an unstructured decision, what strategy is left? In such circumstances, difficult choices will be made using political means (Drory, 1993; Schilt, 1986). The managers concerned will use various tactics to gain the support of the people around the table, while deflecting the resistance of others, in order to win the debate and have their preferred course of action endorsed by the decision-making meeting. To win the competition of ideas, players will do whatever they can, within the constraints imposed by the social norms, to ensure that their ideas prevail over others. The success or failure of rivals will have an impact on their individual position, reputation and career progression, and the status of their department, section or occupational group within the organization.

Thus, political behaviour is a direct consequence of the numerical superiority of unstructured over structured decisions, which explains why it predominates in the higher levels of organizations, where such decisions tend to be made most frequently. It also emanates from the tendency of informed and interested parties to disagree with each other, partly on the interpretation or information and analyses, and partly because they hold differing beliefs, values and preferences. Pfeffer (1992a, p.37) observed that:

> Power is more important in major decisions, such as those made at higher organizational levels, and those that involve crucial issues like reorganization and budget allocations; for domains in which performance is more difficult to assess such as staff rather than line production operations; and in instances in which there is likely to be uncertainty and disagreement.

Structural characteristics

Organization structuring creates roles and departments which compete with each other. Jeffrey Pfeffer (1981) described how such structuring produced the conditions within organizations in which power came to be exercised and politicking engaged in (see figure 24.1). Our starting point is the observation that in large organizations, tasks are divided between a number of departments. Differentiation (1) is the term used to refer to this specialization of both departments and employees' jobs in an organization by task. This division of labour enables an organization to achieve certain economies. However, it also has a number of divisive consequences. First, it creates differences in goals (2) and understandings about what the company does, or should do, because each department is assigned its unique goal as part of the differentiation process. Marketing's task may be to maximize sales, while Production's may be to minimize costs. Such objectives are frequently in conflict. Second, different departments receive different sets of information. Marketing receives data on sales, while Production receives data on costs. This causes parochialism, with each employee seeing the world through their own department's perspective.

Differentiation also causes the creation of differences in beliefs about how something should be done (3). Individuals can agree on a goal yet disagree on decisions and their outcomes. They can have different views as to what are the appropriate means to achieve the stated, and perhaps agreed, ends. Individuals are physically recruited into a department, not a company. For example, the research and development (R&D) department recruits scientists, while the human resources department hires personnel specialists. The differing personalities and backgrounds of the staff who compose the different company departments, their

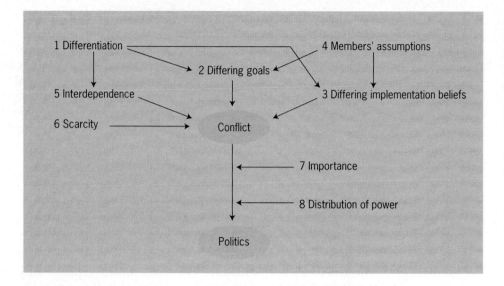

Figure 24.1: Structural conditions producing the use of power and politics in organizational decision making
From Jeffrey Pfeffer, *Power in Organizations*, HarperCollins, New York, 1981, p.69.

socialization, background, training and way of addressing business problems affects not only how they see their department's goals but also their beliefs and assumptions as to how these should be achieved (4).

Differentiation also creates interdependence between people and departments, where the actions of one affect the other (5). It thus ties groups and individuals together, making each concerned with what the other does and gets in terms of resources. Scarce resources are the most valuable. Labelling a resource as scarce produces a vigorous action to obtain it and greater dissatisfaction with its apparent unavailability (6). Gandz and Murray (1980) saw scarcity as existing in the following organizational areas: promotions and transfers, hiring, pay, budget allocation, facilities and equipment allocation, delegation of authority, interdepartmental co-ordination, personnel policies, disciplinary penalties, work appraisals, and grievances and complaints.

The combined existence of these factors can certainly lead to conflict between departments, groups and individuals, as was shown in the previous chapter. However, will these conditions inevitably result in the use of power and politicking? Pfeffer argues that they will if two further conditions are met. It depends partly on how important it is to those involved, and importance is relative (7). The exercise of power and engagement in political behaviour requires time and effort, so it will tend to be reserved for the more important issues. Finally, it depends on how widely power is distributed within an organization (8). Politicking, bargaining and coalition formation occur only when power is dispersed widely and not when it is centralized at the top. Political behaviour is thus an inevitable consequence of structural differentiation (Johnson and Gill, 1993).

Power and politics in the post-modern organization

Is there more political behaviour going on within organizations now than in the past? Following a review of the change management literature of the 1950s and

1960s, Buchanan and Badham (1999b) find that it presents a picture that is virtually politics-free. This stands in sharp contrast to the organizational research and consultancy produced in the closing decades of the twentieth century. They argue that a change in organizational context, whether actual or perceived, implies a change in the behaviours required by managers and others to operate effectively in that new context. The most obvious example of this is that if an organization context becomes more turbulent, then political skills will be required to a greater degree than if it is placid. This in turn encourages particular character types and associated behaviour to emerge and prosper, e.g. Machiavellian.

However, there is another argument which they offer. This is that the political dimension of organizations has always been a perennial feature of organizations encountered by all managers and others, even though it may not have previously featured extensively in theoretical frameworks, research papers or management handbooks. Hence, whether or not there has been a shift in substance, what has altered, in Buchanan and Badham's view, has been management's increased emphasis on and thinking about power and politics in organizations. Several factors in recent times may have contributed to this:

1. Widened scope of organizational change strategies
There has been a shift away from a relatively narrow concern with work design towards organization design and the development of all-embracing strategies, sometimes labelled 'organizational renewal'. This shift, combined with a frantic search for novel techniques to implement the changes, has increased the number of different individuals, groups and departments ('constituencies') affected by the proposed changes. This in turn has necessitated greater political skills when dealing with these multiple constituencies.

2. Increased organizational uncertainty
The effect of radical organization redesign is often to increase uncertainty, and the prevalence and significance of unstructured decisions. Organization structures become more differentiated, fragmented and fluid. Different constituencies and stakeholders come to the fore and engage in political activities to support or oppose the measures.

3. Increased competitive nature of managerial careers
Each new technique or 'management fad' (e.g. teamworking, quality circles) can act as a vehicle for a manager to gain both visibility and promotion within their company or to another one. Technique 'champions' compete with each other to have their preferred approaches adopted by the company, and they use political tactics to build coalitions to secure support.

4. Increased job insecurity and mobility
Threats to job security, caused partly by internal factors (e.g. delayering, downsizing) and partly by external changes (e.g. privatization), can generate defensive responses by employees at all hierarchical levels. Individuals also come to depend on their own resources and interpersonal skills. They create networks and interdependencies, and acquire power resources, to defend their positions. The traditional notion of career has became replaced by a company commitment to employability. In such circumstances, employees change their jobs, occupations and organizations more frequently, and in the process their awareness of political agendas becomes heightened.

Buchanan and Badham (1999a) offered an idealized picture of trends through time which highlighted current preoccupations and perceived priorities, and located the topic of power and politics historically (table 24.9). The authors were careful to stress that this comparison of the 1960s with the 1990s was 'an exaggerated portrayal' of trends, that it was potentially an artefact of bias in the published literature, and that it was empirically untestable. It could be read as representing either a real shift or a shift in perceptions of organizational trends. Thompson and Davidson (1995) argued that the contemporary theme of 'turbulent times' was a creation of the 'pop management' literature [**link**, chapter 16, organization strategy and design].

Cynthia Hardy (1995) believes that the academic literature about power is diverse and confusing because it includes research from sociology, psychology, anthropology, economics and, not least, political science. This leads to different aspects of power and politics being studied in different ways, for different reasons, by different people. The study of power has coalesced around two unequal approaches, the rationalist and the political, which were discussed earlier. The mainstream perspective is the rationalist one (table 24.7). It distinguishes power from authority, with the latter being defined as the right to guide or direct the actions of others and extract from them responses that are appropriate to the attainment of an organization's goals. Authority is held to be a legitimate, normal and inevitable aspect of the formal design of organizations; managerial authority

Table 24.9: Has the ground moved?

	1960s–1970s It was all so simple then	1980s–1990s Uncertainty rules
Context factors	Job redesign, local technology and shop floor-level change	Organizational transformation, multiple levels of change
	Local implementation, with predictable ripples	Systemic, with many unpredictable ripple effects
	Recruit organization members	Redesign the whole activity chain
	Apparent system stability	Apparent system instability
	Narrowly defined gains—gimme productivity	Broad and rapid gains—gimme speed
Technique factors	Unambiguous paradigm	Competing versions of 'teamwork'
	Clear exemplars	Contradictory exemplars (e.g. Japanese and Scandinavian)
	'Dry', unfashionable management theory	Heathrow organization theory is 'HOT'
	Few competing fads and techniques (what's BPR?)	Guru worship (what's next?)
Moral factors	Management licence, operating behind closed doors	Management visible, open to scrutiny and challenge
	Managing 'the voiceless'	Managing a 'culture of complaint'
	Quality of working life	Competitive advantage
	Managerial humanism	Moral relativism
	Premium on involvement	Premium on exclusion
	Social responsibility, ethical clarity	Change politically charged; post-modern uncertainty and confusion

From David Buchanan and Richard Badham, *Power, Politics and Organizational Change*, Sage, London, 1999, p.216.

is seen as being embedded in structural and technological aspects of the formal organization. Authority is considered to be apolitical, taken-for-granted and 'functional', in the sense of contributing to the achievement of organizational goals. This rational perspective is also referred to as *managerialist*.

Having translated power into authority, the managerialist perspective then proceeds to exclude it from analysis and research. Instead, it concentrates on what it labels 'illegitimate' power. This is defined as any power which falls outside the legitimate authority that is embedded in organizational structures. Non-authority power and any associated politics are thus considered illegitimate from this point of view. Writers such as Drory and Romm (1990), Gandz and Murray (1980) and Mayes and Allen (1977) all reflect this managerialist–functionalist perspective, seeing any power that is exercised by any non-managers as illegitimate behaviour which is designed to promote their own self-interest rather than the achievement of organizational goals.

The management perspective criticizes those who seek to challenge the smooth operation of the enterprise. When used by non-managers, power is seen as a political tool intended to disrupt operations. When managers use power, however, it is considered to be in self-defence, to counter such attacks. The perspective sees power as a useful and flexible resource, good when used by managers but 'bad' when used against them. Historically, studies of managerial power have been conducted from this perspective. They have ignored questions of how power becomes embedded in an organization's structure, culture, practices, rules and regulations. Hardy believed that the functionalist perspective concentrated only on the surface aspects of power, advocating the status quo, hiding the way in which powerful groups in the organization maintained their dominance, and generally neglecting the way power operated to shape the lives of both employees and managers.

An alternative, albeit much less influential, approach to power views it as a means of domination and sees resistance to power as an emancipatory tool. This political perspective is also referred to as the 'critical' or 'sociological' perspective. Originally, it examined power from the standpoint of decisions and asked who made them. Then researchers asked if the interests and grievances of certain groups were not being recognized and if they were being excluded from the decision-making arena. Power was being exercised by excluding them in favour of safe decisions. This process was termed 'non-decision making' and emphasized the ability of powerful players to determine outcomes behind the scenes (Bachrach and Baratz, 1962). Next, it focused on power and non-observable conflict, noting that power holders could prevent conflict arising at all by shaping the perceptions, cognitions and preferences of the powerless. They used their power to get them to accept their positions as natural and unchangeable, and thus prevented them raising their grievances. More recently, labour process theory has studied how seemingly neutral, legitimate working arrangements—the choice of technology, the culture of the company, the shape of its formal structure—all mask the means by which workers are dominated in the organization.

Much of the current debate on power and politics in organizations focuses on the work of Michel Foucault described earlier. Mary Jo Hatch (1997) argued that discussions of the political model of organization provide the beginnings of the post-modernist view emerging in organization behaviour and theory. She quotes a section from Pfeffer's *Power in Organizations* (Pfeffer, 1981, p.14) where he raised the question of whether considering management and organization was itself a political act. She saw his comment as foreshadowing the post-modern turn towards critical and self-reflective thinking. Pfeffer wrote:

The argument, then, is that the very literature of management and organization behaviour ... is itself political ... and causes support to be generated and oppo-

Jeffrey Pfeffer

sition to be reduced as various conceptions of organizations are created and maintained in part through their very repetition.

The managerial writers, in contrast, ignore such issues, considering the formal organizational arrangements to be natural, logical and functional. Their chosen technologies, cultures and structures are treated as apolitical tools and are thus considered as neither power nor domination. To the critical writers, this represents a surface approach that misrepresents the true balance of power. It attributes too much power to subordinate groups, who are castigated for using what little power they have, while hiding the way in which senior managerial power holders use the power they have, behind the scenes, to further their own positions by shaping legitimacy, values, technology and information. The functionalist managerialist perspective essentially de-politicizes organizational life.

The overwhelming dominance of this approach in the managerial literature has, for a long time, been largely successful in eliminating the discussion of power and politics within organizations. As noted earlier, the power embedded in organizational structures and technology is not seen as power. For many years, research studies of the powerless in organizations have ceased to be fashionable [**link**, chapter 23, conflict]. However, in Britain, since the accession of the Labour government, there has been a renewed interest in what has been labelled 'social exclusion', in particular in persons who are excluded from social services, local government and internet access. Thus academics who wish to study 'exclusion' are more likely to be supported now than in the past. In addition, there has been publicity for the poor (as well as the powerless) who are not being paid the minimum wage, an election pledge which the Labour Party has implemented.

The history of the study of the topic of power and politics in Britain reflects changing priorities and interests. During the 1970s, there was a concern about poor working conditions, and the effect of this on health and safety issues, the exploitation of individual workers, and industrial relations (Beynon, 1975). As working conditions improved, interest shifted to the question of whether the 'working class' had become 'middle class' and the 'privatized, instrumental worker (Goldthorpe *et al.*, 1968). During the 1980s, Thatcherism in Britain increased competition, and globalization in the 1990s swept aside both trade union rights and resistance on the one hand, and Dickensian working conditions (for many workers) on the other. One might argue that, as physical working conditions and to some extent financial rewards have generally (not universally) improved during the late twentieth century, so interest in management–employee conflict, once a major media and public concern, has waned. It is certainly the case that the literature on many management topics (total quality management, business process re-engineering, the new leadership, empowerment, teamworking) either implies or in some cases explicitly espouses the old unitarist ('we are all on the same side facing the same enemy') perspective.

Recap

1. *Appreciate the importance of power and politics in organizational life.*
   - Whether real or perceived, greater turbulence in the context of organization has created increased fluidity, uncertainty, ambiguity and discontinuity, providing the ideal conditions in which power and politics can be exercised.

2. *Compare and contrast different perspectives on power.*
   - Power can be considered from the 'power-as-property' a 'faces-of-power' and a 'disciplinary power' viewpoint.
   - The 'power-as-property' viewpoint offers three perspectives, seeing power as a property of individuals, of relationships or as an embedded property of structures.
   - The 'faces-of-power' viewpoint offers three dimensions, seeing power as overt and observable, as covert and unobservable and as internalized by employees.
   - Disciplinary power reduces subordinates' ability to dissent by creating and managing meanings for them.

3. *Distinguish different bases of power.*
   - The five bases of power are reward, coercion, referent, legitimate and expert.

4. *Identify organizational factors which enhance the power of departments.*
   - Factors enhancing the power of departments are dependency creation, financial resources, centrality, non-substitutability and uncertainty reduction.

5. *Differentiate between power tactics and influencing strategies.*
   - Power tactics can be classified under the headings of image building, selective information, scapegoating, formal alliances, networking, compromise, rule manipulation and covert 'dirty tricks' methods.
   - Influencing strategies include reason, friendliness, coalition, bargaining; sanctions, assertiveness and higher authority.

6. *Distinguish between the rational and political models of organization.*
   - Whereas the rational model of organizations sees behaviour in organizations as guided by clear goals and choices made on the basis of reason, the political model of organization sees no such logical behaviour but sees organizations as made up of groups possessing their own interests, goals and values, and in which power and influence are needed in order to reach decisions.

7. *Identify the characteristics of individuals most likely to engage in political behaviour.*
   - Persons most likely to engage in political behaviour have a high need for power (*n*Pow), a high Mach score, an internal locus of control and risk-seeking propensity.

8. *Explain why politics is a feature of organizational life.*
   - The effects of differentiation, interdependence, differing goals, differing members' assumptions, differing implementation beliefs and scarcity of resources all create the possibility of conflict between individuals, groups and departments within an organization.
   - If, in addition, the issue in dispute is important to those involved, and power is distributed unevenly within the organization, the chances of individuals engaging in political behaviour is maximized.

Revision

1. Why should every employee and manager take an interest in power and politics within their organization?

2. How can someone low in the organization hierarchy obtain power?

3. Are organizations rational or political entities?

4. 'Power is most potent when it is appears to be absent'. What does this statement mean? Do you agree with it? Give reasons and examples to support your view.

5. Why are some departments, units or groups more powerful than others?

Springboard

Buchanan, D. and Badham, R., 1999, *Power, Politics and Organizational Change*, Sage, London.

Considers power and politics from a change management perspective, arguing that those who lead change in organizations ('change agents') also need to act as 'political entrepreneurs' if they are to succeed.

Clegg, S.R., 1989, *Frameworks of Power*, Sage, London.

A classic text written by one of Britain's leading experts on the subject. It has provided the basis for much subsequent theory and research.

Hardy, C. (ed.), 1995, *Power and Politics in Organizations*, Dartmouth Publishing, Aldershot.

Collection of contemporary contributions on different aspects of the topic.

Horrocks, C., 1997, *Beginner's Guide to Foucault*, Icon Books, London.

All of Foucaults's writings are challenging for the introductory reader, while the 'edited highlights' and the secondary literature not much easier. Horrocks's graphic novel therefore provides a basic starting point.

Huczynski, A.A. 1996, *Influencing Within Organizations*, Prentice Hall, Hemel Hempstead.

The book considers power and politics from an individual, careerist perspective, using theoretical and empirical research. It offers a 'survival guide' for graduates entering the world of work, highlighting what to look out for, what to avoid and what to do.

Johnson, P. and Gill, J., 1993, *Management Control and Organizational Behaviour*, Paul Chapman/Sage, London.

Within its central themes of organizational structure, culture and power, the book considers the interaction of formally designed administrative control systems with social and self-control.

Knights, D. and Willmott, H., 1999, *Management Lives*, Sage, London.

Subtitled, 'Power and Identity in Work Organizations', this is an innovative text which uses novels to explore power and politics in various organizational contexts.

Mintzberg, H., 1983, *Power In and Around Organizations*, Prentice Hall, Englewood Cliffs, NJ.

A major contribution from a North American perspective.

Pfeffer, J., 1992, *Managing With Power: Politics and Influence in Organizations*, Harvard Business School Press, Boston (first edition 1981).

A discussion of power and politics for a management audience by one of the leading US academic researchers and authors.

Home viewing

In the film *One Flew Over The Cuckoo's Nest* (1975, directed by Milos Forman), R.P. McMurphy (played by Jack Nicholson) is serving time at a penal farm. He pretends to be insane so that he can be transferred to a mental institution, where he believes life will be easier. He is assigned to a ward supervised by Nurse Ratched 'Big Nurse' (played by Louise Fletcher). Life in the ward is far from easy. Nurse Ratched uses tight discipline, a tough group of orderlies and a stern and unyielding exercise of authority to eliminate any resistance or rebellion from her patients. Most of the patients are there 'voluntarily' and make no effort to assert themselves until McMurphy arrives on the scene. The struggle between Big Nurse, a symbol of the establishment, and McMurphy, a symbol of the oppressed, is the theme of both the original book by Ken Kesey and the film based upon it.

What examples of power, influencing and political behaviour can you identify? Who does them, when, and how successful are they?

OB in literature

Michael Crichton, *Disclosure*, HarperCollins, 1995.

This novel (also a film) describes office politics, with female harassment and rape instead of male. What political tactics are used against the victimized male, and what tactics does he employ in response?

Chapter exercises

1: The Machiavellian personality

Objectives

1. To assess your level of Machiavellianism.

2. To allow you to identify which approach to others you typically use.

Procedure

Read each of the following 20 statements carefully, and tick the number at the point on the scale which most closely represents your own attitude.

Statement	Strongly agree	Agree	Neutral	Disagree	Strongly disagree
1. The best way to handle people is to tell them what they want to hear.	5	4	3	2	1
2. When you ask someone to do something for you, it is best to give the real reasons for wanting it rather than giving reasons which might carry more weight.	1	2	3	4	5
3. Anyone who completely trusts anyone else is asking for trouble.	5	4	3	2	1
4. It is hard to get ahead without cutting corners here and there.	5	4	3	2	1
5. Honesty is the best policy in all cases.	1	2	3	4	5
6. It is safest to assume that all people have a vicious streak and it will come out when given a chance.	5	4	3	2	1
7. Never tell anyone the real reason you did something unless it is useful to do so.	5	4	3	2	1
8. One should take action only when sure it is morally right.	1	2	3	4	5
9. It is wise to flatter important people.	5	4	3	2	1
10. All in all, it is better to be humble and honest than important and dishonest.	1	2	3	4	5
11. Barnum was very wrong when he said there's a sucker born every minute.	1	2	3	4	5
12. People suffering from incurable diseases should have the choice of being put painlessly to death.	5	4	3	2	1
13. It is possible to be good in all respects.	1	2	3	4	5
14. Most people are basically good and kind.	1	2	3	4	5
15. There is no excuse for lying to someone else.	1	2	3	4	5
16. Most people forget more easily the death of their father than the loss of their property.	1	2	3	4	5
17. Most people who get ahead in the world lead clean, moral lives.	1	2	3	4	5

18. Generally speaking, people won't work hard unless they are forced to do so.	1	2	3	4	5
19. The biggest difference between criminals and other people is that criminals are stupid enough to get caught.	1	2	3	4	5
20. Most people are brave.	1	2	3	4	5

Calculate your score by simply adding the numbers beside the boxes that you ticked. Note your score here:

Analysis

This personality inventory (known as 'Mach IV') measures how Machiavellian you are in relation to others. You score will lie between 20 and 100.

A moderate score is around 60.

Consider yourself a Low Mach if you have a score of 45 or lower.

Consider yourself a High Mach if you have a score of 75 or higher.

The inventory was developed by Richard Christie and Florence Geiss and appears in their book (Christie and Geiss, 1970). They claim that scores are a good predictor of how we behave with other people—whether we become emotionally involved, or whether we simply use others to suit our own ends.

Questions

1. Some people regard the label 'Machiavellian' as a serious insult. How do you feel about this?

2. How do you feel about your score? Do you think it is an accurate reflection of your personality?

3. Would you like to be more or less Machiavellian than you currently are? Why?

2: Who has power?

Objectives

1. To distinguish French and Raven power bases.

2. To assess the power possessed by the 'powerful' and the 'powerless'.

Procedures

Below are listed eight sets of pairs of individuals who are frequently in interaction with each other. Complete the table below. For each set, indicate

(a) What type(s) of power each individual in the pair has over the other.

(b) Which individual in the pair, on balance, has more overall power.

(c) Which type of power is most significant in each set.

(d) Instances in which one type of power is equally divided between the two.

Set Pairs	Power				
	Reward	Coercive	Referent	Legitimate	Expert
1 Professor → Student Student → Professor					
2 Supermarket manager → Checkout operator Checkout operator → Supermarket manager					
3 Prime Minister/ President → Citizens Citizens → Prime Minister/President					
4 Executive → Secretary Secretary → Executive					
5 Car salesperson → Customer Customer → Car salesperson					
6 Parent → Child Child → Parent					
7 Team captain → Team player Team player → Team captain					
8 Doctor → Patient Patient → Doctor					

From Ricky W. Griffin and Thomas C. Head, *Practising Management*, Houghton Mifflin, Boston, second edition, 1987.

References

Ackroyd, S. and Thompson, P., 1999, *Organizational Misbehaviour,* Sage Publications, London.

Adams, J.S., 1963, 'Toward an understanding of inequity', *Journal of Abnormal and Social Psychology*, vol.67, no.4, pp.422–36.

Adams, J.S., 1965, 'Inequity in social exchange', in L. Berkowitz (ed.), *Advances in Experimental Social Psychology*, Academic Press, New York, pp.267–99.

Adams, R., 1973, *Watership Down*, Puffin Books, London.

Adcroft, A. and Willis, R., 2000, 'Innovation or optimization: facing up to the challenge of the global economy', in J. Barry, J. Chandler, H. Clark, R. Johnson and D. Needle (eds), *Organization and Management: A Critical Text*, Business Press, Thomson Learning, London, pp.171–91.

Adler, P.S. 1993a, 'Time-and-motion regained', *Harvard Business Review*, vol.71, no.1, January–February, pp.97–108.

Adler, P.S., 1993b, 'The learning bureaucracy: New United Motors Manufacturing, Inc.', in B.M. Staw and L.L. Cummings (eds), *Research in Organizational Behaviour: Volume 15'*, JAI Press, Greenwich, CT, pp.111–94.

Adler, P.S., 1999, 'The emancipatory significance of Taylorism', in M.P.E. Cunha and C.A. Marques (eds), *Readings in Organization Science—Organizational Change in a Changing Context*, Instituto Superior de Psicologia Aplicada, Lisbon, pp.7–14.

Adler, N.J., 1999, *International Dimensions of Organizational Behaviour*, International Thomson, London (third edition).

Adler, P.S. and Cole, R.E., 1993, 'Designed for learning: a tale of two plants', *Sloan Management Review*, vol.34, no.3, pp.85–94.

Alderfer, C., 1972, *Human Needs in Organizational Settings*, Free Press, New York.

Allen, R.W., Madison, D.L., Porter, L.W., Renwick, P.A. and Mayes, B.T., 1979, 'Organizational politics: tactics and characteristics of actors, *California Management Review*, vol.22, no.1, pp.77–83.

Allison, G.T., 1971, *Essence of Decision*, Little, Brown & Co., Boston.

Allport, F.H., 1920, 'The influences of the group upon association and thought', *Journal of Experimental Psychology*, vol.3, pp.159–82.

Allport, G.W., 1937, *Personality*, Holt, New York.

Allport, G.W. and Odbert, H.S., 1936, 'Trait-names, a psycholexical study', *Psychological Monographs*, vol.47, no.1, whole issue.

Alvesson, M., 1990, 'Organization: from substance to image', *Organization Studies*, vol.11, no.3, pp.373–94.

Alvesson, M. and Deetz, S., 1999, *Doing Critical Management Research*, Sage Publications, London.

Analoui, F. and Kalkabadse, A.P., 1991, *Sabotage—How to Recognize and Manage Employee Defiance,* Mercury, London.

Anand, J., 1999, 'How many matches are made in heaven?' *Financial Times*, Mastering Strategy Part 5, 25 October, pp.6–7.

Ancona, D.G. and Caldwell, D., 1990, 'Improving the performance of new product teams', *Research Technology Management*, vol. 33, no.2, pp.25–9.

Anderson, A., 1999, 'Nice CV, shame about the aura', *The Times*, 'Crème de la Crème' supplement, 14 April, p.3.

Anderson, N. and Shackleton, V., 1993, *Successful Selection Interviewing*, Blackwell, Oxford.

Ansoff, I., 1997, 'Measuring and managing for environmental turbulence: the Ansoff Associates approach', in Alexander Watson Hiam (ed.), *The Portable Conference on Change Management*, HRD Press Inc., pp.67–83.

Anthony, P.D., 1994, *Managing Culture*, Open University Press, Milton Keynes.

Appignanesi, R. and Garratt, C., 1995, *Postmodernism for Beginners*, Icon Books, Cambridge.

Applebaum, E. and Batt, R. 1994, *The New American Workplace*, ILR Press, Ithaca, NY.

Argyris, C., 1960, *Understanding Organizational Behaviour*, Dorsey Press, Homewood, IL.

Argyris, C., 1972, *The Applicability of Organizational Sociology*, Cambridge University Press, London.

Argyris, C., 1982, *Reasoning, Learning, and Action*, Jossey-Bass, San Francisco.

Argyris, C. and Schon, D., 1974, *Theory in Practice*, Jossey-Bass, San Francisco.

Argyris, C. and Schon, D. (eds), 1978, *Organizational Learning*, Addison-Wesley, Cambridge, MA.

Aronson, E., Wilson, T.D. and Akert, R.M, 1994, *Social Psychology*, HarperCollins, New York.

Arroba, T. and James, K., 1988, 'Are politics palatable to women managers? How women can make wise moves at work', *Women in Management Review*, vol.3, no.3, pp.123–30.

Asch, S.E., 1951, 'Effects of group pressure upon the modification and distortion of judgements', in H. Guetzkow (ed.), *Groups, Leadership and Men*, Carnegie Press, Pittsburgh, PA, pp.177–90.

Asch, S.E., 1952, *Social Psychology*, Prentice Hall, Englewood Cliffs, NJ.

Asch, S.E., 1956, 'Studies of independence and conformity: a minority of one against a unanimous majority', *Psychological Monographs: General and Applied*, vol.70, no.9, pp.1–70.

Astley, W.G. and Sachdeva, P.S., 1984, 'Structural sources of intra-organizational power: a theoretical synthesis', *Academy of Management Review*, vol.9. no.1, pp.104–13.

Atkinson, J., 1985, 'The changing corporation', in D. Clutterbuck (ed.), *New Patterns of Work*, Gower, Aldershot, pp.13–24.

Augustine, N. and Adelman, K., 1999, *Shakespeare in Charge: The Bard's Guide to Leading and Succeeding on the Business Stage*, Hyperion Books.

Averett, S. and Korenman, S., 1993, 'The economic reality of the beauty myth', NBER working paper no. 4521.

Bach, S. and Sisson, K. (eds), 2000, *Personnel Management: A Comprehensive Guide to Theory and Practice*, Blackwell Business, Oxford (third edition).

Bach, S. and Sisson, K., 2000, 'Personnel management in perspective', in S. Bach and K. Sisson (eds), *Personnel Management: A Comprehensive Guide to Theory and Practice*, Blackwell Business, Oxford (third edition), pp.3–42.

Bacharach, S.B. and Lawler, E.J., 1981, *Power and Politics in Organizations: The Social Psychology of Conflict, Coalitions and Bargaining*, Jossey-Bass, San Francisco.

Bachrach, P. and Baratz, M.S., 1962, 'The two faces of power', *American Political Science Review*, vol.56, pp.947–52.

Baldridge, J.V., 1971, *Power and Conflict in the University*, John Wiley, New York.

Bales, R.F., 1950a, *Interaction Process Analysis*, Addison-Wesley, Reading, MA.

Bales, R.F., 1950b, 'A set of categories for the analysis of small group interaction', *American Sociological Review*, vol.15, no.2, pp.257–63.

Bales, R.F., 1953, 'The equilibrium problem in small groups', in T. Parsons, R.F. Bales and E.A. Shils (eds), *Working Papers in the Theory of Action*, Free Press, New York, pp.111–61 (reissued 1967).

Ballard, J.G., 1996, *Cocaine Nights*, Flamingo/HarperCollins, London, 1996.

Bandler, R. and Grinder, J., 1975, *The Structure of Magic*, Science and Behavior Books, Palo Alto, CA.

Bandler, R. and Grinder, J., 1979, *Frogs into Princes*, Real People Press, Utah.

Bandura, A., 1977, *Social Learning Theory*, Prentice Hall, Englewood Cliffs, NJ.

Bandura, A., 1986, *Social Foundations of Thought and Action: A Social Cognitive Theory*, Prentice Hall, Englewood Cliffs, NJ.

Banks, I., 1999, *The Business*, Little, Brown & Co., London.

Barbour, M., 1999, 'British fat cats take the cream', *The Times*, 29 March, p.48.

Barley, S. 1983, 'Semiotics and the study of occupational and organization cultures', *Administrative Science Quarterly*, vol.28, no.3, pp.393–414.

Barley, S., 1996, *The New World of Work*, British–North American Committee, London.

Barnard, C., 1938, *The Functions of the Executive*, Harvard University Press, Cambridge, MA.

Baron, R.A. and Greenberg, J, 1990, *Behaviour in Organizations*, Allyn & Bacon, Upper Saddle River, NJ (third edition).

Baron, R.S., 1986, 'Distraction–conflict theory: progress and problems', in L. Berkowitz (ed.), *Advances in Experimental Social Psychology*, vol.20, pp.1–40, Academic Press, New York.

Bass, B.M., 1985a, *Bass and Stogdill's Handbook of Leadership: Theory, Research and Managerial Applications*, Free Press, New York (third edition).

Bass, B.M., 1985b, *Leadership and Performance Beyond Expectations*, Free Press, New York.

Bass, B.M. and Avolio, B.J. 1990, 'The implications of transactional and transformational leadership for individual, team and organizational development', *Research and Organizational Change and Development*, vol.4., pp.321–72.

Bass, B.M. and Avolio, B.J., 1994, *Improving Organizational Effectiveness through Transformational Leadership*, Sage, Thousand Oaks, CA.

Bavelas, A. and Barrett, D., 1951, 'An experimental approach to organizational communication', *Personnel*, vol.27, March, pp.367–71.

Bavelas, A., 1968, 'Communication patterns in task-orientated groups', in D. Cartwright and A. Zander (eds), *Group Dynamics: Research and Theory*, Tavistock, London (third edition), pp.503–26.

Bazerman, M.H., 1994, *Judgement in Managerial Decision Making*, Wiley, New York (third edition).

Beardwell, I. and Holden, L., 1997, *Human Resource Management: A Contemporary Perspective*, Pitman, London (second edition).

Becker, G. 1964, *Human Capital*, National Bureau of Economic Research, New York.

Becker, H, 1982, 'Culture: a sociological view', *Yale Review*, vol.71, pp.513–27.

Beckhard, R., 1969, *Organization Development: Strategies and Models*, Addison-Wesley, Reading, MA.

Bedeian, A.G., 1980, *Organization Theory and Analysis*, Dryden Press, IL.

Bedeian, A.G., 1986, *Management*, CBS International, New York.

Bedeian, A.G. and Zammuto, R.F., 1991, *Organizations: Theory and Design*, Dryden Press, London.

Beeman, D.R. and Sharkey, T.W., 1987, 'The use and abuse of corporate politics', *Business Horizons*, vol.30, no.2, March–April, pp.26–31.

Beer, M., Spector, B., Lawrence, P.R., Quinn Mills, D. and Walton, R.E., 1984, *Managing Human Assets*, Free Press, New York.

Beer, M., Lawrence, P.R., Quinn Mills, D. and Walton, R.E., 1985, *Human Resource Management: A General Manager's Perspective*, Free Press, Glencoe, IL.

Beer, M. and Spector, B., 1985, 'Corporate wide transformations in human resource management', in R.E. Walton and E.R. Lawrence (eds), *Human Resource Management Trends and Challenges*, Harvard Business School Press, Boston.

Behar, R., 1989, 'Joe's bad trip', *Time*, 24 July, pp.54–9.

Belbin, R.M., 1981, *Management Teams: Why They Succeed or Fail*, Heinemann, London.

Belbin, R.M, 1993a, *Team Roles at Work*, Butterworth-Heinemann, Oxford.

Belbin, R.M., 1993b, 'A psychometric assessment of the Belbin Team-Role Self-Perception Inventory—comment', *Journal of Occupational and Organizational Psychology*, vol.66, no.3, pp.389–405.

Belbin, R.M., 1996, *The Coming Shape of Organizations*, Butterworth-Heinemann, London.

Belbin, R.M., 2000, *Beyond the Team*, Butterworth-Heinemann, Oxford.

Bell, D., 1999, *The Coming of Post Industrial Society*, Basic Books, New York (reprinted with a new introduction; first published in 1976).

Benders, J. and Van Hootegem, G., 2000, 'How the Japanese got teams', in S. Procter and F. Mueller (eds), *Teamworking*, Macmillan, London, pp.43–59.

Benders, J. and Van Hootegem, G., 1999, 'Teams and their context: moving the team discussion beyond existing dichotomies', *Journal of Management Studies*, vol.36, no.5, pp.609–28.

Benders, J., Doorewaard, H. and Poutsma, E., 2000, 'Modern Sociotechnology', in M. Beyerlin (ed.), *Work Teams: Past, Present and Future*, Kluwer Academic Publishers, Boston.

Benders, J., Huijgem, F., Pekruhl, U. and O'Kelly, K., 1999, *Useful but Unused: Findings from the EPOC Survey*, European Foundation for the Improvement of Living and Working Conditions, Loughlinstown, Co. Dublin.

Benfari, R.C., Wilkinson, H.E., and Orth, C.D., 1986, 'The effective use of power', *Business Horizons*, vol.29, May–June, pp.12–16.

Benne, K.D. and Sheats, P., 1948, 'Functional roles of group members', *Journal of Social Issues*, vol.4, pp.41–9.

Bennis, W.G. and Nanus, B., 1985, *Leaders: The Strategies for Taking Charge*, HarperCollins, New York.

Bennis, W.G., 1969, *Organization Development: Its Nature, Origins and Prospects*, Addison-Wesley, Reading, MA.

Berger, M., 1964, *The Arab World Today*, Doubleday & Co., Garden City, New York.

Berger, P. and Luckmann, T., 1966, *The Social Construction of Reality*, Penguin Books, Harmondsworth.

Berggren, C., 1993a, *Alternatives to Lean Production*, Macmillan, Basingstoke.

Berggren, C., 1993b, 'The Volvo Uddevalla plant: why the decision to close it is mistaken', *Journal of Industry Studies*, vol.1, no.1, October, pp.75–87.

Berggren, C., 1995, 'The fate of the branch plants—performance versus power', in A. Sandberg (ed.), *Enriching Production: Perspectives on Volvo's Uddevalla Plant as an Alternative to Lean Production*, Avebury, Aldershot, pp.105–26.

Berggren, C., Bjorkman, T. and Hollander, E., 1991, 'Are they unbeatable?', Centre for Corporate Change paper 012, Australian Graduate School of Management, University of New South Wales, Kensington.

Bessant, J., 1983, 'Management and manufacturing innovation: the case of information technology', in G. Winch (ed.), *Information Technology in Manufacturing Processes*, Rossendale, London, pp.14–30.

Beynon, H., 1995, *Working for Ford*, Penguin, Harmondsworth.

Blake, R.R. and McCanse, A.A., 1991, *Leadership Dilemmas: Grid Solutions*, Gulf Publishing, Houston, TX.

Blake, R.R. and Mouton, J.S., 1964, *The Managerial Grid*, Gulf Publishing, Houston, TX.

Blake, R.R. and Mouton, J.S., 1968, *Corporate Excellence Through Grid Organization Development: A Systems Approach*, Gulf Publishing, Houston, TX.

Blake, R.R. and Mouton, J.S., 1969, *Building a Dynamic Corporation Through Grid Organization Development*, Addison-Wesley, Reading, MA.

Blau, P. M., 1966, *The Dynamics of Bureaucracy*, University of Chicago Press, Chicago (second edition).

Blauner, R., 1964, *Alienation and Freedom: The Factory Worker and his Industry*, The University of Chicago Press, Chicago.

Blinkhorn, S., 1988, 'The hazards of occupational testing', *The Listener*, 14 January, p.9.

Blyton, P. and Bacon, N., 1997, 'Recasting the occupational culture in steel: some implications of changing from crews to teams in the UK steel industry', *Sociological Review*, vol.45, no.1, pp.79–101.

Boddy, D. and Gunson, N., 1997, *Organizations in the Network Age*, Routledge, London.

Boje, D.M. and Winsor, R.D., 1993, 'The resurrection of Taylorism: total quality management's hidden agenda', *Journal of Organizational Change Management*, vol.6, no.4, pp.57–70.

Bolman, L. and Deal, T., 1991, *Re-framing Organizations*, Jossey-Bass, San Francisco.

Bolman, L.G. and Deal, T.E., 1999, *Reframing in Action,* Jossey-Bass, San Francisco.

Bond, C.F., 1982, 'Social facilitation: a self-presentational view', *Journal of Personality and Social Psychology*, vol.42, pp.1042–50.

Bouchard, T., Barsaloux, J. and Drauden, G. 1974, 'Brainstorming procedure, group size and sex as determinants of problem solving effectiveness of groups and individuals', *Journal of Applied Psychology*, vol.59, pp.135–8.

Braverman, H., 1974, *Labor and Monopoly Capital: The Degradation of Work in the Twentieth Century*, Monthly Review Press, New York.

Bray, P., 1999, 'Falling under the psychologist's spell', *The Sunday Times*, 'The Restless Customer' supplement, 13 June, p.9.

Brayfield, C., 1999, 'Big wheels don't drive Fiestas', *The Times*, 18 March, p.22.

Bredin, A., 1996, *The Virtual Office Survival Handbook: What Telecommuters and Entrepreneurs Need to Succeed in Today's Nontraditional Workplace*, John Wiley, New York.

Bresnahan, T.F., 1999, 'Computerization and wage dispersion: an analytical reinterpretation', *Economic Journal*, vol.109, no.456, pp.390–415.

Briskin, J., 1983, *The Onyx*, Grafton Books. London.

Broucek, W.G. and Randell, G., 1996, 'An assessment of the construct validity of the

Belbin Self-Perception Inventory and Observer's Assessment from the perspective of the five-factor model', *Journal of Occupational and Organizational Psychology*, vol.69, no.4, pp.389–405.

Broussine, M. and Vince, R., 1996, 'Working with metaphor towards organizational change', in C. Oswick and D. Grant (eds), *Organization Development: Metaphorical Explorations*, Pitman, London, pp.57–72.

Brown, M., 1998, *Richard Branson*, Michael Joseph, London.

Bryant, S. and Kearns, J., 1982, '"Workers brains as well as their bodies": quality circles in a federal facility', *Public Administration Review*, vol.42, no.2, pp.144–50.

Bryman, A., 1986, *Leadership and Organizations*, Routledge & Kegan Paul, London.

Bryman, A. (ed.), 1988, *Doing Research in Organizations*, Routledge, London.

Bryman, A., 1989, *Research Methods and Organization Studies*, Routledge, London.

Bryman, A., 1996, 'Leadership in organizations', in S.R. Clegg, C. Hardy and W.R. Nord (eds), *Handbook of Organization Studies*, Sage, London, pp.276–92.

Buchanan, D.A., 1979, *The Development of Job Design Theories and Techniques*, Saxon House, Aldershot.

Buchanan, D.A., 1994, 'Cellular manufacture and the role of teams', in J. Storey (ed.), *New Wave Manufacturing Strategies: Organizational and Human Resource Management Dimensions*, Paul Chapman, London, pp.204–225.

Buchanan, D.A., 1994, 'Principles and practice in work design', in K. Sisson (ed.), *Personnel Management*, Blackwell Publishers, Oxford, pp.85–116.

Buchanan, D.A., 1996, 'The limitations and opportunities of business process re-engineering in a politicized organizational climate', *Human Relations*, vol.50, no.1, pp.51–72.

Buchanan, D.A., 2000, 'An eager and enduring embrace: the ongoing rediscovery of teamworking as a management idea', in S. Procter and F. Mueller (eds), *Teamworking*, Macmillan Business, Houndmills and London, pp.25–42.

Buchanan, D. and Badham, R., 1999a, *Power, Politics, and Organizational Change: Winning the Turf Game*, Sage, London.

Buchanan, D. and Badham, R., 1999b, 'Politics and organizational change: the lived experience', *Human Relations*, vol.52, no.5, pp.609–29.

Buchanan, D.A. and Boddy, D., 1982, 'Advanced technology and the quality of working life: the effects of word processing on video typists', *Journal of Occupational Psychology*, vol.55, no.1, pp.1–11.

Buchanan, D.A. and Boddy, D., 1983a, *Organizations in the Computer Age: Technological Imperatives and Strategic Choice*, Gower, Aldershot.

Buchanan, D.A. and Boddy, D., 1983b, 'Advanced technology and the quality of working life: the effects of computerized controls on biscuit-making operators', *Journal of Occupational Psychology*, vol.56, no.2, pp.109–19.

Buchanan, D.A. and Boddy, D., 1992, *The Expertise of the Change Agent: Public Performance and Backstage Activity*, Prentice Hall, Hemel Hempstead.

Buchanan, D.A. and McCalman, J., 1989, *High Performance Work Systems: The Digital Experience*, Routledge, London.

Buchanan, D. and Preston, D., 1992, 'Life in the cell: supervision and teamwork in a "manufacturing systems engineering" environment', *Human Resource Management Journal*, vol.2, no.4, pp.55–76.

Buchanan, D. and Wilson, B., 1996a, 'Next patient please: the operating theatres problem at Leicester General Hospital NHS Trust', in J. Storey (ed.), *Cases in Human Resource and Change Management*, Blackwell Business, Oxford, pp.190–205.

Buchanan, D. and Wilson, B., 1996b, 'Re-engineering operating theatres: the perspective assessed', *Journal of Management in Medicine*, vol.10, no.4, pp.57–74.

Buchanan, D., Claydon, T. and Doyle, M., 1999, 'Organization development and change: the legacy of the nineties', *Human Resource Management Journal*, vol.9, no.2, pp.20–37.

Buono, A.F., Bowditch, J.L. and Lewis, J.W., 1985, 'When cultures collide: the anatomy of a merger', *Human Relations*, vol.38, no.5, pp.477–500.

Burawoy, M., 1979, *Manufacturing Consent*, University of Chicago Press, Chicago.

Burke, K., 1999, 'It's good to talk', *Personnel Today*, 21 January, pp.23–5.

Burke, W.W., 1980, 'Organization development and bureaucracy in the 1980s', *Journal of Applied Behavioral Science*, vol.16, no.3, pp.423–37.

Burke, W.W., 1987, *Organization Development: A Normative View*, Addison-Wesley, Reading, MA.

Burne, J. and Aldridge, S., 1996, 'Who do you think you are?' *Focus Extra*, April, pp.1–8.

Burnes, B., 2000, *Managing Change: A Strategic Approach to Organizational Dynamics*, Financial Times Prentice Hall, Harlow, Essex (third edition).

Burnett, A., 2000, 'Virtual organizations and virtuality, working paper, Department of Management Studies, University of Glasgow.

Burnett, A. and Warhurst, C., 1999, 'All that's solid melts into air?: virtual organizations and scientific management', presented to the 17th Annual International Labour Process Conference, Royal Holloway College, University of London, March.

Burns, J.M., 1978, *Leadership*, Harper & Row, New York.

Burns, T. and Stalker, G.M., 1961, *The Management of Innovation*, Tavistock, London.

Burns, P. and Jewhurst, J. (eds), 1996, *Small Business and Entrepreneurship*, Macmillan Business, Houndmills, Basingstoke.

Burrell, G., 1998, *Pandemonium: Towards a Retro-Theory of Organization*, Sage, London.

Burrell, G. and Morgan, G., 1979, *Sociological Paradigms and Organizational Analysis*, Heinemann, London.

Butcher, D. and Harvey, P., 1999, 'Be upstanding', *People Management*, vol.5, no.13, pp.37–42.

Butler, T. and Waldroop, J., 1999, 'Job sculpting: the art of retaining your best people', *Harvard Business Review*, vol.77, no.5, pp.144–52.

Cairncross, F., 1995, 'The death of distance: a survey of telecommunications', *The Economist*, 30 September, special supplement.

Carr, N., 1999, 'Being virtual: character and the new economy', *Harvard Business Review*, vol.77, no.3, pp.181–90.

Carroll, P., 1994, *Big Blues: The Unmaking of IBM*, Orion Books, London.

Cartwright, D. and Zander, A. (eds), 1968, *Group Dynamics: Research and Theory*, Tavistock, London (third edition).

Carver, C.S. and Scheier, M.F., 1981, *Attention and Self-regulation: A Control Theory Approach to Human Behaviour*, Springer-Verlag, New York.

Cattell, R., 1951, 'New concepts for measuring leadership in terms of group syntality', *Human Relations*, vol.4, pp.161–8.

Chandler, A.D., 1962, *Strategy and Structure*, MIT Press, Boston.

Chandler, A.D., 1988, 'Origins of the organization chart', *Harvard Business Review*, vol.66, no.2, pp.156–7.

Chandler, A.D., 1990, *Scale and Scope: The Dynamics of Industrial Capitalism*, Harvard University Press, Cambridge, MA.

Chandler, A.D., Hastrom, P. and Solvell, O. (eds), 1999, *Dynamic Firm: The Role of Regions, Technology, Strategy and Organization*, Oxford University Press, Oxford.

Chanlat, J.-F., 1997, 'Conflict and politics', in A. Sorge and M. Warner (eds), *Handbook of Organization Behaviour*, International Thomson Business Press, London, pp.472–80.

Charm, R. and Colvin, G., 1999, 'Why CEOs fail', *Fortune*, vol.139, no.12, 21 June, pp.69–78.

Child, J., 1969, *British Management Thought: A Critical Analysis*, George Allen & Unwin, London.

Child, J., 1972, 'Organizational structure, environment and performance: the role of strategic choice', *Sociology*, vol.6, no.1, pp.1–22.

Child, J., 1984, *Organization: A Guide to Problems and Practice*, Harper & Row, London (second edition).

Child, J., 1985, 'Managerial strategies, new technology and the labour process', in D. Knights, H. Willmott and D. Collinson (eds), *Job Redesign*, Gower, Aldershot, pp.107–41.

Child, J., 1997, 'Strategic choice in the analysis of action, structure, organizations and environments: retrospect and prospect', *Organization Studies*, vol.18, no.1, pp.43–76.

Child, C. and Faulkner, D., 1998, 'Networks and virtuality', in C. Child and D. Faulkner (eds), *Strategies of Co-operation: Managing Alliances, Networks and Joint Ventures*, Oxford University Press, Oxford, pp.113–42.

Christie, R. and Geis, F.L. 1970, *Studies in Machiavellianism*, Academic Press, New York.

Cialdini, R.B., 1988, *Influence: Science and Practice*, HarperCollins, London.

Ciminero, S.M., 1997, 'Anglian Water: customer service transformation', Harvard Business School case N9–897–093, April.

Clark, J., 1995, *Managing Innovation and Change: People, Technology and Strategy*, Sage, London.

Clarke, A., 1999, 'Employees under surveillance', *The Times*, 6 April, p.35.

Clarke, D., 1989, *Stress Management*, National Extension College, Cambridge.

Clarry, T., 1999, 'Premium Bonding', *People Management*, vol.5, no.17, 2 September, pp.34–9.

Clegg, S., 1989, *Frameworks of Power*, Sage, London.

Clegg, S., 1990, *Modern Organizations: Organization Studies in the Postmodern World*, Sage, London.

Clegg, S. and Dunkerley, D., 1980, *Organization, Class and Control*, Routledge & Kegan Paul, London.

Clegg, S. and Hardy, C., 1996, 'Organizations, organization and organizing', in S. Clegg, C. Hardy and W.R. Nord (eds), *Handbook of Organization Studies*, Sage, London, pp.1–28.

Clegg, S.R. and Hardy, C., 1996, 'Conclusion: representations', in S.R. Clegg, C. Hardy and W.R. Nord (eds), *Handbook of Organization Studies*, Sage, London, pp.676–708.

Clegg, S.R., Hardy, C. and Nord, W.R., 1996, *Handbook of Organization Studies*, Sage, London.

Coch, L. and French, J.R.P., 1948, 'Overcoming resistance to change', *Human Relations*, vol.1, pp.512–32.

Cohen, A.R. and Bradford, D.L., 1989, 'Influence without authority: the use of alliances, reciprocity and exchange to accomplish work', *Organizational Dynamics*, Winter, pp.4–17.

Cohen, A.R. and Bradford, D.L. 1991, *Influence Without Authority*, John Wiley, New York.

Cohen, A.R., Fink, S.L., Gadon, H. and Willits, R.D., 1988, *Effective Behaviour in Organizations*, Irwin, Chicago (fourth edition), (sixth edition, 1995).

Cohen, M.D., March, J. and Olsen, J, 1972, 'A garbage can model of organization choice', *Administrative Science Quarterly*, vol.17, no.1, pp.1–25.

Cohen, S., Ledford, G. and Spreitzer, G., 1996, 'A predictive model of self-managing work team effectiveness', *Human Relations*, vol.49, no.5, pp.643–76.

Colebatch, H. and Lamour, P., 1993, *Market, Bureaucracy and Community*, Pluto Press, London.

Coles, M., 1998, 'Unlock the power of knowledge', *The Sunday Times*, 20 September, p.7.28.

Collier, P. and Horowitz, D., 1987, *The Fords: An American Epic*, Futura/Collins, London.

Colling, T., 1995, 'Experiencing turbulence: competition, strategic choice and the management of human resources in British Airways', *Human Resource Management Journal*, vol.5, no.5, pp.18–33.

Collins, D., 1998, *Organizational Change: Sociological Perspectives*, Routledge, London.

Collins, D., 2000, *Management Fads and Buzzwords*, Routledge, London.

Collinson, D.L. ,1988, 'Engineering humour: masculinity, joking and conflict in shop floor relations', *Organization Studies*, vol.9, no.2, pp.181–99.

Comer, D.R., 1995, 'A model of social loafing in real work groups', *Human Relations*, vol.48, no.6, pp.647–67.

Constantino, C.A. and Merchant, C.S., 1996, *Designing Management Systems: A Guide to Creating Productive and Healthy Organizations*, Jossey-Bass, San Francisco.

Conti, R.F. and Warner, M., 1993, 'Taylorism, new technology and just-in-time systems in Japanese manufacturing', *New Technology, Work and Employment*, vol.8, no.1, pp.31–42.

Cooper, C., 2000, 'Management blasted at nuclear plant', *People Management*, vol.6, no.6, 19 March, pp.16–17.

Cooper, C., Liukkonen, P. and Cartwright, S., 1996, *Stress Prevention in the Workplace: Assessing the Costs and Benefits to Organizations*, European Foundation for the Improvement of Living and Working Conditions, Dublin.

Corrigan, P., 1999, *Shakespeare on Management: Leadership Lessons for Today's Managers*, Kogan Page, London.

Cosier, R.A. and Schwenck, C.R., 1990, 'Agreement and thinking alike: ingredients for poor decisions', *Academy of Management Executive*, vol.4, no.1, pp.69–74.

Costa, P. and McCrae, R.R., 1992, *NEO PI-R: Professional Manual*, Psychological Assessment Resources, Odessa, Florida.

Cottrell, N.B., Wack, K.L., Sekerak, G.J. and Rittle, R., 1968, 'Social facilitation in dominant responses by presence of an audience and the mere presence of others', *Journal of Personality and Social Psychology*, vol.9, pp.245–50.

Crichton, A., 1968, *Personnel Management in Context*, B.T. Batsford, London.

Crichton, M., 1992, *Rising Sun*, Century Arrow, London.

Crichton, M., 1995, *Disclosure*, HarperCollins, London.

Crichton, M., 1997, *Airframe*, Arrow Books, London.

Critchley, W. and Casey, D., 1984, 'Second thoughts on team building', *Management Education and Development*, vol.15, no.2, pp.163–75.

Cully, M., O'Reilly, A., Millward, N., Forth, J., Woodland, S., Dix, G. and Bryson, A., 1998, *The 1998 Workplace Employee Relations Survey: First Findings*, Department of Trade and Industry, London.

Cummings, T.G. and Worley, C.G., 1993, *Organization Development and Change*, West Publishing, Minneapolis/St Paul (fifth edition).

Cyert, R. and March, J.G., 1992, *A Behavioral Theory of the Firm*, Prentice Hall, Englewood Cliffs, NJ (second edition; first edition 1963).

Czarniawska-Joerges, B. and de Monthoux, P.G. (eds), 1994, *Good Novels, Better Management: Reading Organizational Realities in Fiction*, Harwood Academic Publishers, Reading.

Dalton, M., 1959, *Men Who Manage*, Wiley, New York.

Dalton, R. and Lynn, M., 1999, 'Companies lead university revolution', *The Sunday Times*, 7 February, p.3.4.

Damasio, A.R., 2000, *The Feeling of What Happened*, Heinemann, London.

Danford, A., 1998, 'Team working and labour regulation in the autocomponents industry, *Work, Employment and Society*, vol.12, no.3, pp.403–31.

Darbourne, B., 1993, *Lessons from Change at South Somerset District Council*, a South Somerset District Council Publication, August.

Davenport, T., H., 1993, *Process Innovation: Re-engineering Work Through Information Technology*, Harvard Business School Press, Boston.

Davidow, W. and Malone, M., 1992, *The Virtual Corporation*, HarperCollins, New York.

Davidson, M.J. and Burke, R.J., 2000, *Women in Management: Current Research Issues Volume II*, Sage, London.

Davidson, M.J. and Cooper, C.L., 1992, *Shattering the Glass Ceiling: The Woman Manager*, Paul Chapman, London.

Davis, D., Millburn, P., Murphy, T. and Woodhouse, M., 1992, *Successful Team Building: How To Create Teams That Really Work*, Kogan Page, London.

Davis, L.E. and Taylor, J.C., 1975, 'Technology effects on job, work, and organizational structure: a contingency view', in L.E. Davis and A.B. Cherns (eds), *The Quality of Working Life: Problems, Prospects and the State of the Art*, Free Press, New York, pp.220–41.

Davis, L.E. and Taylor, J.C., 1976, 'Technology, organization and job structure', in R. Dubin (ed.), *Handbook of Work, Organization and Society*, Rand McNally, Chicago, pp.379–419.

Davis, L.E. and Wacker, G.J., 1987, 'Job design', in G. Salvendy (ed.), *Handbook of Human Factors*, New York, Wiley, pp.431–52.

Davis, S.M. and Lawrence, P.R., 1978, 'Problems of matrix organizations', *Harvard Business Review*, vol.56, no.3, pp.131–42.

Dawson, P., 1994, *Organizational Change: A Processual Approach*, Paul Chapman, London.

Dawson, P., 1996, *Technology and Quality: Change in the Workplace*, International Thomson Business Press, London.

Deal, T.E. and Kennedy, A.A., 1982, *Organization Cultures: The Rites and Rituals of Organization Life*, Addison-Wesley, Reading, MA.

Dean, A., Carlisle, Y. and Baden-Fuller, C., 1999, 'Punctuated and continuous change: the UK water industry', *British Journal of Management*, vol.10, special conference issue, pp.3–18.

de Bernières, L., 1994, *Captain Corelli's Mandolin*, Secker & Warburg/Vintage, London, 1994.

de Board, R., 1978, *The Psychoanalysis of Organizations*, Tavistock, London.

Denison, D.R., Hart, S.L. and Kahn, J.A., 1996, 'From chimneys to cross-functional teams: developing and validating a diagnostic model', *Academy of Management Journal*, vol.39, no.4, pp.1005–23.

Dennis, A.R. and Valacich, J.S., 1993, 'Computer brainstorms: more heads are better than one'', *Journal of Applied Psychology*, vol.78, no.4, pp.531–37.

Denzin, N.K. and Lincoln, Y.S. (eds), 1994, *Handbook of Qualitative Research*, Sage, Thousand Oaks, CA.

Department of Trade and Industry, 1999, *Working for the Future: The Changing Face of Work Practices*, HMSO, London.

de Sitter, L.U., 1994, *Synergetisch Produceren* (Producing Synergistically), van Gorcum, Assen, the Netherlands.

de Sitter, L.U., den Hertog, J.F. and Dankbaar, B., 1997, 'From complex organizations with simple jobs to simple organizations with complex jobs', *Human Relations*, vol.50, no.5, pp.497–534.

Diehl, M. and Stroebe, W., 1987, 'Productivity loss in brainstorming groups: toward the solution of a riddle', *Journal of Personality and Social Psychology*, vol.53, no.3, pp.447–509.

Diehl, M., and Stroebe, W., 1991, 'Productivity loss in idea generating groups: tracking down the blocking effect', *Journal of Personality and Social Psychology*, vol.61, no.3, pp.392–403.

Diener, E., 1979, 'Deindividuation, self awareness and disinhibition', *Journal of Personality and Social Psychology*, vol.37, no.7, pp.1160–71.

Diener, E., 1980, 'Deindividuation: the absence of self-awareness and self-regulation in group members', in H.B. Paulus (ed.), *The Psychology of Group Influence*, Lawrence Erlbaum, Hillsdale, NJ, pp.209–42.

Dimmick, S., 1995, *Successful Communication Through NLP: A Trainer's Guide*, Gower, Aldershot.

Dixon, N.F., 1994, *On The Psychology of Military Incompetence*, Pimlico, London.

Dixon, N.M., 1999, *The Organizational Learning Cycle: How We Can Learn Collectively*, Gower, Aldershot (second edition).

Dodd-McCue, D., 1991, 'Led like sheep: an exercise for linking group decision making to different types of tasks', *Journal of Management Education*, vol.15, no.3, pp.335–9.

Doherty, N. and Tyson, S., 1998, *Mental Well Being in the Workplace: A Resource Pack for Management Training and Development*, Health and Safety Executive, London.

Doms, M. and van Avermaet, E., 1981, 'The conformity effect: a timeless phenomenon?' *Bulletin of the British Psychological Society*, vol.36, pp.180–8.

Drory, A., 1993, 'Perceived political climate and job attitudes', *Organization Studies*, vol.14, no.2, pp.59–71.

Drory, A. and Romm, T., 1990, 'The definition of organizational politics: a review', *Human Relations*, vol.43, no.11, pp.1134–54.

Drucker, P.F., 1955, *The Practice of Management*, Heinemann, London.

Drucker, P.F. 1989, *The New Realities*, Heinemann, London.

Drummond. G., 1994, 'Irresistible science of the super-sellers', *Focus*, November, pp.24 and 26.

DuBrin, A.J., 1994, *Applying Psychology: Individual and Organizational Effectiveness*, Prentice Hall, Englewood Cliffs, NJ.

Dulewicz, S.V., 1995, 'A validation of Belbin's team roles from 16PF and OPQ using bosses' ratings of competence', *Journal of Occupational and Organizational Psychology*, vol.68, no.2, pp.81–99.

Dumaine, B., 1990, 'Who needs a boss?' *Fortune*, 7 May, pp.10 and 40–7.

Duncan, R.B., 1972, 'Characteristics of perceived environments and perceived environmental uncertainty', *Administrative Science Quarterly*, vol.17, no.3, pp.313–27.

Duncan, R.B., 1973, 'Multiple decision making structures in adapting to environmental uncertainty: the impact of organizational effectiveness', *Human Relations*, vol.26, pp.273–91.

Duncan, R.B., 1974, 'Modifications in decision making structures in adapting to the environment: some implications for organizational learning', *Decision Sciences*, vol.5, pp.704–25.

Duncan, R.B., 1979, 'What is the right organization structure?: decision tree analysis provides the answer', *Organizational Dynamics*, Winter, pp.59–80.

Dunphy, D., 1981, *Organizational Change by Choice*, McGraw-Hill, Sydney (reprinted 1993).

Dunphy, D.C. and Stace, D.A., 1990, *Under New Management: Australian Organizations in Transition*, McGraw-Hill, Sydney.

Earley, P.C., 1989, 'Social loafing and collectivism: a comparison of the United States and the People's Republic of China', *Administrative Science Quarterly*, vol.34, no.4, December, pp.565–81.

Earley, P.C., 1993, 'East meets West meets Mideast: further explorations of collectivist and individualistic work groups', *Academy of Management Journal*, vol.36, no.2, April, pp.319–48.

Easterby-Smith, M. and Araujo, L., 1999, 'Organizational learning: current debates and opportunities', in M. Easterby-Smith, L. Araujo and J. Burgoyne (eds), *Organizational Learning and the Learning Organization: Developments in Theory and Practice*, Sage, London, pp.1–21.

Easterby-Smith, M., Burgoyne, J. and Araujo, L. (eds), 1999, *Organizational Learning and the Learning Organization: Developments in Theory and Practice*, Sage, London.

Ebers, M. (ed.), 1999, *The Formation of Inter-Organizational Networks*, Oxford University Press, Oxford.

Eccles, T., 1994, *Succeeding With Change: Implementing Action-Driven Strategies*, McGraw-Hill, London.

The Economist, 1993, 'Jury science', 8 July, p.86.

The Economist, 1994, 'The Selling out of America', 17 December, pp.71–2.

The Economist, 1994, 'Just deserts', January, p.77.

The Economist, 1995, 'Heightism: short guys finish last', December 23, pp.21–6.

The Economist, 1996, 'Not clever enough', 18 May, p.105.

The Economist, 1998, 'Compaq goes after Big Blue', 31 January, pp.78–9.

The Economist, 1998, 'The science of alliance', 4 April, p.91.

The Economist, 1998, 'Service with a smile', 25 April, pp.85–6.

The Economist, 1998, 'After the PC', 12 September, pp.93–5.

The Economist, 1999, 'The Exxon Valdez: stains that remain', 20 March, p.63.

The Economist, 1999, 'The end of privacy: the surveillance society', 1 May, pp.105–7.

The Economist, 1999, 'A price on the priceless', 12 June, pp.94 and 98.

The Economist, 1999, 'Rethinking thinking', 18 December, pp.77–9.

The Economist, 2000, 'In search of the new Japanese dream', 19 February, pp.69–71.

Edwards, R.C., 1979, *Contested Terrain: The Transformation of Industry in the Twentieth Century*, Heinemann, London.

Egan, G., 1994, *Working the Shadow Side: A Guide to Positive Behind-the-Scenes Management*, Jossey-Bass, San Francisco.

Einsiedel, A.A., 1983, 'Decision making and problem solving skills: the rational versus the garbage can model of decision making', *Project Management Quarterly*, vol.14, no.4, pp.52–7.

Eisenhardt, K.M. and Bourgeois, L.J., 1988, 'Politics of strategic decision making in high-velocity environments: towards a mid-range theory', *Academy of Management Journal*, vol.31, no.4, pp.737–70.

Ellis, B.E., 1991, *American Psycho*, Random House/Pan Books, New York/London, 1991.

Emery, R.E. and Trist, E.L., 1960, 'Socio-technical systems', in C.W. Churchman and M. Verhulst (eds), *Management Science, Models and Techniques*, Pergamon Press, London, vol.2, pp.83–97.

Emery, R.E. and Trist, E.L., 1965, 'Causal texture of organizational environments', *Human Relations*, February, pp.21–32.

Eysenck, H.J., 1970, *The Structure of Human Personality*, Methuen, London (third edition).

Eysenck, H.J., 1990, 'Biological dimensions of personality', in L.A. Pervin (ed.), *Handbook of Personality, Theory and Research*, Guilford Press, New York, pp.244–76.

Farnham, D., 1999, *Managing in a Business Context*, Institute of Personnel and Development, London.

Farrell, D. and Petersen, J.C., 1982, 'Patterns of political behaviour in organizations, *Academy of Management Review*, vol.7, no.3, pp.403–12.

Faulkner, D.O., 1996, 'Thoughts on the virtual corporation', working paper presented to the British Academy of Management Conference, Aston University, September.

Feldman, D.C. 1984, 'The development and enforcement of group norms', *Academy of Management Review*, vol.9, no.1, pp.47–53.

Feldman, M., 1991, 'The meanings of ambiguity: learning from stories and metaphors', in P. Frost, L. Moore, M. Louis, C. Lundberg and J. Martin (eds), *Reframing Organization Culture*, Sage, Newbury Park, CA, pp.145–56.

Feldman, D. and Klitch, N., 1991, 'Impression management and career strategies', in K. Giacalone and P. Rosenfeld (eds), *Applied Impression Management: How Image Making Affects Managerial Decisions*, Sage, London, pp.67–80.

Ferraro, G.P., 1990, *The Cultural Dimension of International Business*, Prentice Hall, Englewood Cliffs, NJ.

Ferster, C.S. and Skinner, B.F., 1957, *Schedules of Reinforcement*, Appleton-Century-Crofts, New York.

Festinger, L., Pepitone, A. and Newcomb, T., 1952, 'Some consequences of deindividuation in a group', *Journal of Abnormal and Social Psychology*, vol.47, pp.382–89.

Fiedler, F.E., 1967, *A Theory of Leadership Effectiveness*, McGraw-Hill, New York.

Fiedler, F.E. and Chemers, M.M., 1974, *Leadership and Effective Management*, Scott, Foresman, Glenview, IL.

Fiedler, F.E. and Chemers, M.M., 1984, *Improving Leadership Effectiveness: The Leaders Match Concept*, John Wiley, New York (second edition).

Fincham, R. and Rhodes, P.S., 1998, *The Individual, Work and Organization*, Oxford University Press, Oxford (third edition).

Fineman, S., 1995, 'Stress, emotion and intervention', in T. Newton, J. Handy and S. Fineman, *Managing Stress: Emotions and Power at Work*, Sage, London, chapter 6.

Finney, M. and von Glinow, M.A., 1990, 'Integrating academic and organizational approaches to developing the international manager', *Journal of Management Development*, vol.7, no.2, pp.16–27.

Fischbacher, M., 1999, 'Purchasing in markets and networks: the relationship between general practitioners and National Health Service Trusts', unpublished PhD thesis, University of Glasgow.

Fischbacher, M. and Francis, A., 1998, 'Purchaser–provider relationships and innovation: a case study of GP purchasing in Glasgow', *Financial Accountability and Management*, vol.14, no.4, pp.281–98.

Fisher, R., Ury, W. and Patton, B., 1997, *Getting to Yes: Negotiating Agreement Without Giving In*, Arrow Books/Random House, London.

Fisher, S.G. and Macrosson, W.K.D., 1995, 'Early influences on management team roles', *Journal of Managerial Psychology*, vol.10, no.7, pp.8–15.

Fisher, S.G., Hunter, T.A. and Macrosson, W.K.D., 1997, 'Team or group: managers' perceptions of the differences', *Journal of Managerial Psychology*, vol.12, no.4, pp.232–42.

Fisher, S.G., Hunter, T.A. and Macrosson, W.K.D., 1998, 'The structure of Belbin's team roles', *Journal of Occupational and Organizational Psychology*, vol.71, no.3, pp.283–8.

Fisher, S.G., Macrosson, W.K.D. and Sharp, G., 1996, 'Further evidence concerning the Belbin team role self-perception inventory', *Personnel Review*, vol.25, no.2, pp.61–7.

Fleishman, E.A., 1953a, 'The description of supervisory behaviour', *Journal of Applied Psychology*, vol.37, no.1, pp.1–6.

Fleishman, E.A., 1953b, 'The measurement of leadership attitudes in industry', *Journal of Applied Psychology*, vol.37, no.3, pp.153–8.

Fleishman, E.A. and Harris, E.F., 1962, 'Patterns of leadership behaviour related to employee grievances and turnover', *Personnel Psychology*, vol.15, pp.43–56.

Fombrun, C.J. 1984, 'Organization culture and competitive strategy', in C.J. Fombrun, N.M. Tichy and M.A. Devanna (eds), *Strategic Human Resource Management*, Wiley, New York, pp.203–16.

Fombrun, C.J., Tichy, N.M. and Devanna, M.A. (eds), 1984, *Strategic Human Resource Management*, John Wiley, New York.

Ford, H. and Crowther, S., 1924, *My Life and Work*, William Heinemann, London.

Ford, R.N., 1969, *Motivation Through the Work Itself*, American Management Association, New York.

Foreman, J. and Thatchenkery, T.J., 1996, 'Filmic representations for organizational analysis: the characterization of a transplant organization in the film Rising Sun', *Journal of Organizational Change Management*, vol.9, no.3, pp.44–61.

Foucault, M. 1979, *Discipline and Punish*, Penguin Books, Harmondsworth.

Fourboul, C.V. and Bournois, F., 1999, 'Strategic communication with employees in large European companies: a typology', *European Management Journal*, vol.17, no.2, pp.204–17.

Fowler, A., 1994, 'Rediscovering humanity in the workplace', *Personnel Management*, vol.26, no.13, pp.23–6.

Fox, A., 1966, *Industrial Sociology and Industrial Relations,* research paper no. 3, Royal Commission on Trade Unions and Employers Associations, HMSO, London.

Fox, A., 1973, 'Industrial relations: a social critique of pluralist ideology', in J. Child (ed.), *Man and Organization*, Allen & Unwin, London, pp.185–233.

Fox, A., 1974, *Man Mismanagement*, Hutchinson, London.

French, W.L. and Bell, C.H., 1995, *Organization Development: Behavioural Science Interventions for Organizational Improvement*, Prentice Hall International, Englewood Cliffs, NJ (fifth edition).

French, J. and Raven, B., 1958, 'The bases of social power', in D. Cartwright (ed.), *Studies in Social Power*, Institute for Social Research, Ann Arbor, MI.

Friedman, A., 1977a, *Industry and Labour: Class Struggle at Work and Monopoly Capitalism*, Macmillan, London.

Friedman, A., 1977b, 'Responsibly autonomy versus direct control over the labour process', *Capital and Class*, vol.1, Spring, pp.43–57.

Friedman, A., 1990, 'Managerial activities, techniques and technology: towards a complex theory of the labour process', in D. Knights and H. Willmott (eds), *Labour Process Theory*, Macmillan, London, pp.177–208.

Friedman, K., 1998, 'Cities in the information age: a Scandinavian perspective', in M. Igbaria and M. Tan (eds), *The Virtual Workplace*, Idea Publishing, Hershey, 1998, pp.144–76.

Friedman, M. and Rosenman, R.F., 1974, *Type A Behaviour and your Heart*, Knopf, New York.

Friedmann, G., 1955, *The Industrial Society: The Emergence of Human Problems of Automation*, Free Press, Glencoe, IL.

Fuchs, V., 1968, *The Service Economy*, Basic Books, New York.

Furnham, A., 1997, *The Psychology of Behaviour at Work*, Psychology Press/Taylor & Francis, Hove, Sussex.

Furnham, A., 1999, 'Gesture politics', *People Management*, 25 March, vol.5, no.6, pp.50–3.

Furnham, A. and Gunter, B., 1993, 'Corporate culture: definition, diagnosis and change', in C.L. Cooper and I.T. Robertson (eds), *International Review of Industrial and Organizational Psychology*, vol.8, chapter 7, pp.233–61.

Furnham, A., Steele, H. and Pendleton, D., 1993a, 'A psychometric assessment of the Belbin Team-Role Self-Perception Inventory', *Journal of Occupational and Organizational Psychology*, vol.66, no.3, pp.245–57.

Furnham, A., Steele, H. and Pendeton, D., 1993b, 'A response to Dr Belbin's reply', *Journal of Occupational and Organizational Psychology*, vol.66, no.3, p.261.

Furnsten, S., 1999, *Popular Management Books*, Routledge, London.

Gallie, D., 1991, 'Patterns of skill change; upskilling, deskilling or the polarization of skills?' *Work, Employment and Society*, vol.5, no.3, pp.319–51.

Gallie, D., White, M., Cheng, Y. and Tomlinson, M., 1998, *Restructuring the Employment Relationship*, Clarendon Press, Oxford.

Gallupe, R.B., Dennis, A.R., Cooper, W.H., Valacich, J.S., Bastianutti, L.M. and Nunamaker, J.F., 1992, 'Electronic brainstorming and group size', *Academy of Management Journal*, vol.35, no.2, pp.350–69.

Gandz, J. and Murray, V.V., 1980, 'The experience of workplace politics, *Academy of Management Journal*, vol.23, no.2, pp.237–51.

Gantt, H., 1919, *Organizing for Work*, Harcourt, Brace and Hove, New York.

Gardner, W.L., 1992, 'Lessons in organizational dramaturgy: the art of impression management', *Organizational Dynamics*, vol.21, no.1, pp.33–46.

Garrahan, P. and Stewart, P., 1992, *The Nissan Enigma: Flexibility at Work in a Local Economy*, Mansell Publishing, London.

Gartman, D., 1979, 'Origins of the assembly line and capitalist control of work at Ford', in A.S. Zimbalist (ed.), *Case Studies on the Labour Process*, Monthly Review Press, London, pp.193–205.

Geary, J.F., 1993, 'Workgroups and participation', *P+: European Participation Monitor*, no.5, pp.8–11.

Geary, J.F., 1996, 'Working at teamwork: lessons from Europe', *P+: European Participation Monitor*, no.12, pp.18–24.

Geller, E.S., 1983, 'Rewarding safety belt usage at an industrial setting: tests of treatment generality and response maintenance', *Journal of Applied Behavior Analysis*, vol.16, no.2, Summer, pp.189–202.

George, J.M., 1992, 'Extrinsic and intrinsic origins of perceived social loafing in organizations', *Academy of Management Journal*, vol.35, no.1, pp.191–202.

Gherardi, S., 1997, 'Organizational learning', in A. Sorge and M. Warner (eds), *The Handbook of Organizational Behaviour*, International Thomson Business Press, London, pp.542–51.

Gibb, J.R., 1961, 'Defensive communication', *Journal of Communication*, vol.11, September, pp.41–9.

Gibson, W., 1984, *Neuromancer*, Victor Gollancz, London.

Giddens, A., 1990, *The Consequences of Modernity*, Polity Press and Blackwell, Cambridge and Oxford.

Gilbreth, F.B. and Gilbreth, L., 1916, *Fatigue Study*, Sturgis and Walton, New York.

Gillespie, R., 1991, *Manufacturing Knowledge: A History of the Hawthorne Experiments*, Cambridge University Press, Cambridge.

Ginnett, R.C., 1993, 'Crews as groups: their formation and leadership', in E.L. Wierner, B.G. Kanki and R.L. Helmreich (eds), *Cockpit Resource Management*, Academic Press, San Diego, pp.71–98.

Glass, N., 1996, 'Chaos, non-linear systems and day-to-day management', *European Management Journal*, vol.14, no.1, pp.98–106.

Goffman, E., 1959, *The Presentation of Self in Everyday Life*, Doubleday Anchor, New York.

Golding, W., 1954, *Lord of the Flies*, Faber & Faber, London.

Goldratt, E. and Cox, J., 1993, *The Goal*, Gower, Aldershot (second edition).

Goldstein, E., 1998, *Sensation and Perception*, Brooks Cole, San Francisco.

Goldthorpe, J.H., Lockwood, D., Bechhofer, F. and Platt, J., 1968, *The Affluent Worker: Industrial Attitudes and Behaviour*, Cambridge University Press, Cambridge.

Goleman, D., 1995, *Emotional Intelligence: Why It Can Matter More Than IQ*, Bloomsbury Publishing, London.

Goleman, D., 1998, *Working with Emotional Intelligence*, Bloomsbury Publishing, London.

Goleman, D., 2000, 'Leadership that gets results', *Harvard Business Review*, vol.78, no.2, March–April, pp.78–90.

Golzen, G., 1989, 'Maestro, learn the company score', *The Sunday Times*, 25 June, Appointments section.

Goodman, P.S. and Wilson, J.M., 1998, 'New forms of work groups: exocentric teams, paper presented at Negotiations and Change: From the Workplace to Society Conference, 30–31 October, MIT, Boston.

Goodrich, C.L., 1975, *The Frontier of Control*, Pluto Press, London.

Gordon, J., 1992, 'Work teams—how far have they come?' *Training*, vol.29, no.10, pp.59–65.

Gordon, J., 1993, *A Diagnostic Approach to Organizational behaviour*, Allyn & Bacon, Boston.

Gouldner, A.W., 1954, *Patterns of Industrial Bureaucracy*, Free Press, New York.

Gouldner, A.W., 1957, 'Cosmopolitans and locals: towards an analysis of latent roles', *Administrative Science Quarterly*, vol.1, pp.281–306.

Grant, R.M., 1998, *Contemporary Strategy Analysis*, Blackwell, Oxford.

Graves, D., 1986, *Corporate Culture: Diagnosis and Change*, St Martin's Press, New York.

Gray, J.L. and Starke, F.A., 1984, *Organizational Behaviour: Concepts and Applications*, Merrill Publishing, Columbus, Ohio (third edition).

Green, G., 1975, *Twenty-one Stories*, Penguin Books, Harmondsworth.

Greenberg, J., 1976, 'The role of seating position in group interaction: a review with applications for group trainers', *Group and Organizational Studies*, vol.1, no.3, pp.310–27.

Greenberg, J. and Baron. R.A., 1997, *Behaviour in Organization*, Prentice Hall, Englewood Cliffs, NJ (sixth edition).

Gregory, K.L., 1983, 'Native view paradigms: multiple cultures and culture conflicts in organizations', *Administrative Science Quarterly*, vol.28, no.3, pp.359–76.

Griffiths, D., 1988, 'When man can't keep up with the machines of war', *Business Week*, 12 September, p.28.

Grisham, J., 1993, *The Firm*, Arrow Books, London.

Grisham, J., 1998, *The Street Lawyer*, Century Random House, London.

Groth, L., 1999, *Future Organizational Design*, Wiley, Chichester.

Grottola, M., 1994, 'Teaching the social geometry of management with literary narrative', *Journal of Management Education*, vol.18, no.1, pp.125–8.

Guest, D., 1984, 'Social psychology and organizational change', in M. Gruneberg and T. Wall (eds), *Social Psychology and Organizational Behaviour*, John Wiley, Chichester, pp.183–225.

Guest, D., 1989, 'Personnel and HRM: can you tell the difference?' *Personnel Management*, January, pp.48–51.

Guest, D., 1990, 'Human resource management and the American dream', *Journal of Management Studies*, vol.27, no.4, pp.377–97.

Guest, D., 1997, 'Human resource management and performance: a review and research agenda', *The International Journal of Human Resource Management*, vol.8, no.3, pp.263–76.

Guest, D., 1998, 'Is the psychological contract worth taking seriously?' *Journal of Organizational Behaviour*, vol.19, pp.649–64.

Guirdham, M., 1995, *Interpersonal Skills at Work*, Prentice Hall, Hemel Hempstead (second edition).

Gulowsen, J., 1979, 'A measure of work-group autonomy', in L.E. Davies and J.C. Taylor (eds), *Design of Jobs*, Goodyear, Santa Monica (second edition), pp.206–18.

Guzzo, R.A., 1996, 'Fundamental considerations about work groups', in M.A. West (ed.), *Handbook of Work Group Psychology*, Wiley, Chichester, pp.3–24.

Guzzo, R.A. and Dickson, M.W., 1998, 'Teams in organizations: recent research on performance and effectiveness, *Annual Review of Psychology*, vol.49, pp.307–38.

Gyllenhammar, P., 1977, *People at Work*, Addison-Wesley, Reading, MA.

Hackman, J.R., 1983, *A Normative Model of Work Team Effectiveness*, technical report no. 2, Research Program on Group Effectiveness, Yale School of Organization and Management.

Hackman, J.R., 1987, 'The design of work teams', in J.W. Lorsch (ed.), *Handbook of Organizational Behavior*, Prentice Hall, Englewood Cliffs, NJ, pp.315–42.

Hackman, J.R., 1990, *Groups That Work and Those That Don't*, Jossey-Bass, San Francisco.

Hackman, J.R. and Oldham, G.R., 1974, 'The job diagnostic survey: an instrument for the diagnosis of jobs and the evaluation of job redesign projects', technical report no. 4, Department of Administrative Sciences, Yale University.

Hackman, J.R., Oldham, G. and Purdy, K., 1975, 'A new strategy for job enrichment', *California Management Review*, vol.17, no.4, pp.57–71.

Hales, C., 1993, *Managing Through Organisation*, Routledge, London.

Hall, E.T., 1976, *Beyond Culture*, Doubleday/Currency, New York.

Hall, E.T., 1989, *Understanding Cultural Differences*, Intercultural Press, Yarmouth, ME.

Hamermesh, D. and Biddle, J., 1993, 'Beauty and the labour market', NBER Working Paper Series, no. 4518, National Bureau of Economic Research, Cambridge, MA.

Hamel, G. and Prahalad, C.K., 1996, 'Competing in the new economy: managing out of bounds', *Strategic Management Journal*, vol.17, no.3, pp.237–42.

Hamilton, A., 1999, 'The pay's the thing for business Bard', *The Times*, 7 April, p.9.

Hammarstrom, O. and Lansbury, R.D., 1991, 'The art of building a car: the Swedish experience re-examined', *New Technology, Work and Employment*, vol.6, no.2, pp.85–90.

Hammer, M., 1990, 'Reengineering work: don't automate, obliterate', *Harvard Business Review*, vol.68, no.4, July–August, pp.104–12.

Hammer, M., 1994, 'Hammer defends re-engineering', *The Economist*, 5 November, p.96.

Hammer, M. and Champy, J., 1993, *Reengineering the Corporation: A Manifesto for Business Revolution*, Nicholas Brealey Publishing, London.

Hammer, M. and Stanton, S.A., 1995, *The Reengineering Revolution—A Handbook*, HarperCollins, New York.

Hammond, D., 2000, 'Unit set up to take action on council's race problem', *Personnel Today*, 11 April, p.10.

Hampton, M.M., 1999, 'Work groups', in Y. Gabriel (ed.), *Organizations in Depth*, Sage, London, pp.112–38.

Handy, C., 1976, 1984, *The Future of Work*, Blackwell, Oxford.

Handy, C., 1993, *Understanding Organizations*, Penguin Books, Harmondsworth.

Handy, C., 1995, 'Trust and the virtual organization', *Harvard Business Review*, vol.73, no.3, pp.4–50.

Hardy, C., (ed.), 1995, *Power and Politics in Organizations*, Dartmouth Publishing, Aldershot.

Hardy, C. and Clegg, S.R., 1996, 'Some dare call it power', in S.R. Clegg, C. Hardy and W.R. Nord (eds), *Handbook of Organization Studies*, Sage, London, pp.622–41.

Hardy, C. and Palmer, I., 1999, 'Pedagogical practice and postmodern idea', *Journal of Management Education*, vol.23, no.4, pp.377–95.

Hare, A.P., 1992, *Groups, Teams and Social Interactions*, Praeger, New York.

Harrington, J., 1991, *Organization Structure and Information Technology*, Prentice Hall, Hemel Hempstead.

Harris, C., 1992, 'NLP: a pathway to personal effectiveness', *Personnel Management*, July, pp.44–7.

Harris, M. 1998, 'Re-thinking the virtual organization', in P.J. Jackson and J.M. van der Wielen (eds), *Teleworking: International Perspectives*, Routledge, London, pp.74–92.

Harrison, R., 1972, 'Understanding your organization's character', *Harvard Business Review*, vol.50, no.3, pp.119–28.

Harvey-Jones, J., 1993, *Managing to Survive: A Guide to Management Through the 1990s*, Heinemann, London.

Haspeslagh, P. 1999, 'Managing the mating dance in equal mergers', *Financial Times*, Mastering Strategy Part 5, 25 October, pp.6–7.

Hassard, J. and Holliday, R. (eds), 1998, *Organization-Representation: Work and Organizations in Popular Culture*, Sage, London.

Hatch, M.J., 1997, *Organization Theory: Modern, Symbolic and Postmodern Perspectives*, Oxford University Press, Oxford.

Hatchett, A., 2000, 'Ringing true', *People Management*, vol.6, no.2, 20 January, pp.40–1.

Hayes, N., 1997, *Successful Team Management*, Thomson Business Press, London.

Heider, F., 1958, *The Psychology of Interpersonal Relationships*, John Wiley, New York.

Heizer, J., 1998, 'Determining responsibility for the moving assembly line', *Journal of Management History*, vol.4, no.2, pp.94–103.

Heller, F., 1997, 'Leadership', in Arndt Sorge and Malcolm Warner (eds), *The Handbook of Organizational Behaviour*, International Thomson, London, pp.340–9.

Heller, J., 1955, *Catch 22*, Jonathan Cape, London.

Hellriegel, D. and Slocum, J.W., 1978, *Management: Contingency Approaches*, Addison-Wesley, Reading, MA.

Hendry, C., Pettigrew, A.M. and Sparrow, P.R., 1989, 'Linking strategic change, competitive performance and human resource management: results of a UK empirical study', in R. Mansfield (ed.), *Frontiers of Management Research*, Routledge, London.

Hendry, C. and Pettigrew, A.M., 1990, 'Human resource management: an agenda for the 1990s', *International Journal of Human Resource Management*, vol.1, no.1, pp.17–43.

Herbst, P.G., 1962, *Autonomous Group Functioning*, Tavistock, London.

Hersey, P. and Blanchard, K.H., 1988, *Management of Organizational Behavior: Utilizing Human Resources*, Prentice Hall International, Englewood Cliffs, NJ.

Herzberg, F., 1966, *Work and the Nature of Man*, Staples Press, New York.

Herzberg, F., 1968, 'One more time: how do you motivate employees?' *Harvard Business Review*, vol.46, no.1, pp.53–62.

Herzberg, F., 1987, 'Workers' needs the same around the world', *Industry Week*, 21 September, pp.29–30 and 32.

Hickman, G.R., 1998, *Leading Organizations: Perspectives for a New Era*, Sage, Thousand Oaks, Calif.

Hickson, D.J. and McMillan, C.J., 1981, *Organization and Nation, The Aston Programme IV*, Gower, Farnborough.

Hickson, D.J., Hinings, C.R., Lee, C.A., Schneck, R.E. and Pennings, J.M., 1971, 'A strategic contingencies theory of inter-organization power', *Administrative Science Quarterly*, vol.16, no.2, pp.216–29.

Hiley, D.R., 1987, 'Power and values in corporate life', *Journal of Business Ethics*, vol.6, no.5, pp.343–53.

Hill, G.W., 1982, 'Group versus individual performance: are N + 1 heads better than one?' *Psychological Bulletin*, vol.91, no.3, pp.517–39.

Hill, S., 1991, 'Why quality circles failed but total quality management might succeed', *British Journal of Industrial Relations*, vol.29, no.4, pp.541–68.

Hinterhuber, H.H. and Levin, B.M., 1994, 'Strategic networks—the organization of the future', *Long Range Planning*, vol.27, no.3, pp.43–53.

Hinton, P.R., 1993, *The Psychology of Interpersonal Perception*, Routledge, London.

Hite, S., 2000, *Sex and Business*, Financial Times Prentice Hall, Harlow.

Hoerr, J., 1989, 'The payoff from teamwork', *Business Week*, 10 July, pp.56–62.

Hoerr, J., Pollock, M.A. and Whiteside, D.E., 1986, 'Management discovers the human side of automation', *Business Week*, 29 September, pp.60–5.

Hofstede, G., 1984, *Culture's Consequences: International Differences in Work-related Values*, Sage Publications, Beverley Hills, CA.

Hofstede, G. 1986, 'Editorial: the usefulness of the concept of organization culture', *Journal of Management Studies*, vol.23, no.3, pp.253–7.

Hofstede, G., 1991, *Cultures and Organizations*, McGraw-Hill, London.

Hofstede, G., 1994, *Uncommon Sense About Organizations*, Sage, London.

Hofstede, G. and Bond, M., 1988, 'The Confucian connection: from cultural roots to economic growth', *Organizational Dynamics*, vol.16, no.4, pp.4–21.

Hogg, M., Turner, J.C. and Davidson, B., 1990, 'Polarized teams and social frames of reference: a test of self-categorization theory of group polarization', *Basic and Applied Social Psychology*, vol.11, pp.77–100.

Holden, L., 1997, 'Human resource management and Europe', in I. Beardwell and L. Holden (eds), *Human Resource Management: A Contemporary Perspective*, Pitman, London (second edition), pp.720–48.

Homans, G.C., 1951, *The Human Group*, Routledge & Kegan Paul, London.

House, R.J., 1988, 'Power and personality in complex organizations', in B.M. Staw and L.L. Cummings (eds), *Research in Organizational Behaviour: Volume 10*, JAI Press, Greenwich, CT, pp.305–57.

Howard, P.J. and Howard, J.M., 1993, *The Big Five Workbook: A Roadmap for Individual and Team Interpretation of Scores on the Five-Factor Model of Personality*, Center for Applied Cognitive Studies, Charlotte, NC.

Howard, P.J., Medina, P.L. and Howard, J.K., 1996, 'The big five locator: a quick assessment tool for consultants and trainers', *The 1996 Annual: Volume 1 Training*, Pfeiffer & Co., San Diego, pp.107–22.

Huczynski, A.A., 1993, *Management Gurus: What Makes Them and How to Become One*, Routledge, London.

Huczynski, A., 1996, *Influencing Within Organizations: Getting In, Rising Up and Moving On*, Prentice Hall, London.

Huczynski, A.A., 2001, *Encyclopedia of Development Methods*, Gower, Aldershot.

Hughes, R.L., Ginnett, R.C. and Curphy, G.J., 1996, *Leadership: Enhancing the Lessons of Experience*, Irwin, Chicago.

Huselid, M.A., 1995, 'The impact of human resource management practices on turnover, productivity, and corporate financial performance', *Academy of Management Journal*, vol.38, no.3, pp.635–72.

Hussey, D., 1998, *Managing Change*, Kogan Page, London.

Hutchins, E. 1990, 'The technology of team navigation', in J. Galegher, R.E. Kraut and

C. Egido (eds), *Intellectual Teamwork; Social and Technological Foundations of Co-operative Work*, Lawrence Erlbaum, Hillsdale, NJ, pp.191–220.

Hutton, D.W., 1994, *The Change Agents Handbook: A Survival Guide for Quality Improvement Champions*, ASQC Quality Press, Milwaukee, WI.

Huxley, A., 1932, *Brave New World*, Chatto & Windus (Penguin Books, Harmondsworth, 1955).

Huxley, A., 1994, *The Doors of Perception/Heaven and Hell*, Flamingo (first published in 1954 by Chatto & Windus, London).

Huysman, M., 1999, 'Balancing biases: a critical review of the literature on organizational learning', in M. Easterby-Smith, L. Araujo and J. Burgoyne (eds), *Organizational Learning and the Learning Organization*, Sage, London, pp.59–74.

Ilgen, D.R. and Knowlton, W.A. 1980, 'Performance attributional effects on feedback from superiors', *Organizational Behaviour and Human Performance*, vol.25, no.3, pp.441–56.

Incomes Data Services, 1999, *Pay and Conditions in Call Centres 1999*, Incomes Data Services, London.

Industrial Society, 1995, *Self-managed Teams*, London.

Ingham, A.G., Levinger, G., Graves, J. and Peckham, V., 1974, 'The Ringelmann effect: studies of group size and group performance', *Journal of Experimental Social Psychology*, vol.10, no. 4, pp.371–84.

Institute of Personnel and Development, 1997, *Key Facts: Psychological Testing*, IPD, London, August.

Institute of Personnel and Development, 1998, *Key Facts: Stress at Work*, IPD, London, October.

Institute of Personnel and Development, 1998, *Call Centres*, Information Note 17, IPD, London.

Ireland, D., 1971, *The Unknown Industrial Prisoner*, Angus and Robertson/Vintage, Sydney.

Ireland, D., 1997, *The Chosen*, Random House Australia, Sydney.

IRS Employment Review, 1996, 'Turn on, tune in, churn out: a survey of teleworking', June, no.609, pp.6–15.

Isenberg, D.J., 1986, 'Group polarization: a critical review and meta-analysis', *Journal of Personality and Social Psychology*, vol.50, no.6, pp.1141–51.

Ishiguro, K., 1989, *The Remains of the Day*, Faber & Faber.

Jacobs, J.H., 1945, 'The application of sociometry to industry', *Sociometry*, vol.8, pp.181–98.

Janis, I.L., 1982, *Victims of Groupthink*, Houghton Mifflin, Boston (second edition).

Jaques, E., 1952, *The Changing Culture of a Factory*, Tavistock, London.

Jaques, E., 1956, *The Measurement of Responsibility*, Tavistock, London.

Jaques, E., 1976, *A General Theory of Bureaucracy*, Heinemann, London.

Jaques, E., 1982, *The Form of Time*, Crane Russak, New York.

Jaques, E., 1989, *The Requisite Organization*, Gower, Aldershot.

Jaques, E., 1990, 'In praise of hierarchy', *Harvard Business Review*, vol.68, no.1, pp.127–33.

Jay, A., 1970, *Management and Machiavelli*, Penguin Books, Harmondsworth.

Jenkins, A., 1994, 'Teams: from ideology to analysis', *Organization Studies*, vol.15, no.6, pp.849–60.

Jenkins, R., 1999, '£47,000 for teacher made sick by stress', *The Times*, 1 October, p.11.

Jermier, J.M., Knights, D. and Nord, W.R. (eds), 1994, *Resistance and Power in Organizations*, Routledge, London.

Johnson, D.W. and Johnson, F.P., 1991, *Joining Together: Group Theory and Group Skills*, Prentice Hall, Englewood Cliffs, NJ.

Johnson, G. and Scholes, K., 1999, *Exploring Corporate Strategy*, Prentice Hall, Hemel Hempstead (fourth edition).

Johnson, P. and Gill, J., 1993, *Management Control and Organizational Behaviour*, Paul Chapman/Sage, London.

Johnson, R., 2000, 'Ascent of woman', *People Management*, vol.6, no.1, January, pp.26–32.

Johnston, R., 2000, 'Hidden Capital', in J. Barry, J. Chandler, H. Clark, R. Johnston and D.

Needle (eds), *Organization and Management: A Critical Text*, International Thomson Business Press, London, pp.16–35.

Jones, J.E., 1973, 'Model of group development', *The 1973 Annual Handbook for Group Facilitators*, Pfeiffer/Jossey-Bass, San Francisco, pp.127–9.

Jones, O., 1997, 'Changing the balance?: Taylorism, TQM and work organisation', *New Technology, Work and Employment*, vol.12, no.1, pp.13–24.

Jones, S., 1992, *The Human Factor: Maximizing Team Efficiency Through Collaborative Leadership*, Kogan Page, London.

Joseph, M., 1989, *Sociology for Business*, Basil Blackwell, Oxford.

Jung, C.G., 1953, *Collected Works*, Bollingen Series/Pantheon, New York

Jung, C.G., 1971, *Psychological Types (The Collected Works of C.G. Jung, Volume 6)*, Princeton University Press, Princeton, NJ (first published in 1923).

Kafka, F., 1926, *The Castle*, first published as *Das Schloss*, Wolff, Munich, subsequently by Penguin Books, Harmondsworth, 1957, trans. Willa and Edwin Muir.

Kahneman, D. and Tversky, A., 1972, 'Subjective probability: a judgment of representativeness', *Cognitive Psychology*, vol.3, no.3, pp.430–54.

Kahneman, D. and Tversky, A., 1973, 'On the psychology of prediction', *Psychological Review*, vol.80, no.4, pp.237–51.

Kahneman, D. and Tversky, A., 1979, 'Prospect theory: an analysis of decision under risk', *Econometrica*, vol.47, no.2, pp.263–92.

Kahneman, D. and Tversky, A., 1984, 'Choices, values and frames', *American Psychologist*, vol.39, no.4, pp.341–50.

Kakabadse, A., 1983, *The Politics of Management*, Gower, Aldershot.

Kamoche, K., 1994, A critique and a proposed reformulation of strategic human resource management', *Human Resource Management Journal*, vol.4, no.4, pp.29–47.

Kamp, D., 1999, *The 21st Century Manager: Future-Focused Skills for the Next Millennium*, Kogan Page, London.

Kanigel, R., 1997, *The One Best Way: Frederick Winslow Taylor and the Enigma of Efficiency*, Little, Brown, London.

Kanter, R.M., 1977, *Men and Women of the Corporation*, Basic Books, New York.

Kanter, R.M., 1979, 'Power failure in management circuits', *Harvard Business Review*, vol.57, no.4, pp.65–75.

Kanter, R.M., 1983, *The Change Masters: Corporate Entrepreneurs at Work*, George Allen & Unwin, London.

Kanter, R.M., 1989, *When Giants Learn to Dance: Mastering the Challenge of Strategy, Management and Careers in the 1990s*, Simon & Schuster, London.

Kaplan, E.M. and Cowen, E.L., 1981, 'Interpersonal helping behaviour of industrial foremen', *Journal of Applied Psychology*, vol.66, no.5, pp.633–8.

Karasek, R.A., 1979, 'Job demands, job decision latitudes, and mental strain: implications for job redesign', *Administrative Science Quarterly*, vol.24, no.2, pp.285–308.

Karau, S.J. and Williams, K.D., 1993, 'Social loafing: a meta-analytic review and theoretical integration', *Journal of Personality and Social Psychology*, vol.65, no.4, October, pp.681–706.

Katz, D., Maccoby, N. and Morse, N.C., 1950, *Productivity, Supervision, and Morale in an Office Situation*, University of Michigan Institute for Social Research, Ann Arbor, MI.

Katzenbach, J.R. and Smith, D.K., 1993, *The Wisdom of Teams: Creating the High Performance Organization*, Harvard Business School Press, Boston.

Katzenbach, J.R.., Beckett, F., Dichter, S., Feigen, M., Gagnon, C., Hope, Q. and Ling, T., 1997, *Real Change Leaders: How Do You Create Growth and High Performance at Your Company*, Nicholas Brealey Publishing, London.

Kay, J., 1999, 'Strategy and the delusion of grand designs', *Financial Times*, Mastering Strategy Part 1, 27 September, pp.2–4.

Keenoy, T., 1990, 'Human resource management: rhetoric, reality and contradiction', *International Journal of Human Resource Management*, vol.1, no.3, pp.363–84.

Kelley, H.H., 1971, *Attribution: Perceiving the Causes of Behaviour*, General Learning Press, New York.

Kemske, F., 1996, *Human Resources: A Business Novel*, Nicholas Brealey Publishing, London.

Keneally, T., 1991, *Flying Hero Class*, Hodder & Stoughton/Sceptre, London.

Kennedy, T., 1989, 'Personnel management 20 years on', *Personnel Management*, vol.21, no.5, pp.30–41.

Kenney, M. and Florida, R., 1993, *Beyond Mass Production: The Japanese System and its Transfer to the U.S.*, Oxford University Press, Oxford.

Kidder, T., 1997, *The Soul of a New Machine*, Random House, New York.

Kiely, M., 1993, 'When "no" means "yes"', *Marketing*, October 1993, pp.7–9.

Kilmann, R.H., Saxton, M.J. and Serpa, R., 1986, 'Introduction: five key issues in understanding and managing culture', in R.H. Kilmann, M.J. Saxton and R. Serpa (eds), *Gaining Control of the Organization Culture*, Jossey-Bass, San Francisco, pp.1–16.

Kipnis, D., Schmidt, S.M., Swaffin-Smith, C. and Wilkinson, I., 1984, 'Patterns of managerial influence: shotgun managers, tacticians and bystanders', *Organizational Dynamics*, Winter, pp.58–67.

Knights, D. and Willmott, H., 1985, 'Power and identity in theory and practice', *Sociological Review*, vol.33, no.1, pp.22–46.

Knights, D. and Willmott, H., 1999, *Management Lives: Power and Identity in Work Organizations*, Sage, London.

Knights, D. and Willmott, H. (eds), 2000, *The Reengineering Revolution: Critical Studies of Corporate Change*, Sage, London.

Kohn, A., 1993, 'Why incentive plans cannot work', *Harvard Business Review*, vol.71, no.5, pp.54–63.

Koontz, H., 1966, 'Making theory operational', *Journal of Management Studies*, vol.3, no.3, pp.229–43.

Kornhauser, A., 1965, *Mental Health of the Industrial Worker*, John Wiley, New York.

Kotter, J.P., 1982, *The General Managers*, Free Press, New York.

Kotter, J.P., 1985, *Power and Influence*, Free Press, New York.

Kotter, J.P., 1990, *A Force for Change: How Leadership Differs from Management*, Free Press, New York.

Kotter, J.P., 1995a, 'Leading change: why transformation efforts fail', *Harvard Business Review*, vol.73, no.2, pp.59–67.

Kotter, J.P., 1995b, *The New Rules: How to Succeed in Today's Post-Corporate World*, Free Press, New York.

Kotter, J.P., 1996, 'Kill complacency', *Fortune*, 5 August, pp.122–4.

Kotter, J.P., 1999, 'What effective general managers really do', *Harvard Business Review*, vol.77, no.2, pp.145–59.

Kotter, J. and Heskett, J., 1992, *Organization Culture and Performance*, Free Press, New York.

Kotter, J.P. and Schlesinger, L.A., 1979, 'Choosing strategies for change', *Harvard Business Review*, vol.57, no.2, pp.106–14.

Kouzes, J.M. and Posner, B.Z., 1987, *The Leadership Challenge: How to Get Extraordinary Things Done in Organizations*, Jossey-Bass, San Francisco.

Koza, M.P. and Lewin, A.Y., 1999, 'Putting the S-word back in alliances', *Financial Times*, Mastering Strategy Part 6, 1 November, pp.12–13.

Kravitz, D.A. and Martin, B., 1986, 'Ringelmann re-discovered: the original article', *Journal of Personality and Social Psychology*, vol.50, no.5, May, pp.936–41.

Kretch, D., Crutchfield, R.S. and Ballachey, E.L., 1962, *The Individual in Society*, McGraw-Hill, New York.

Kubler-Ross, E., 1969, *On Death and Dying*, Macmillan, Toronto.

Lamb, J., 1999, 'Face value gains credence in "unwritten" HR policies', *People Management*, vol.5, no.23, 25 November, pp.14–15.

Lamm, H. and Trommsdorf, G., 1973, 'Group versus individual performance on tasks requiring ideational proficiency (brainstorming): a review', *European Journal of Social Psychology*, vol.3, no.4, pp.361–88.

Langley, A., 1989, 'In search of rationality: the purposes behind the use of formal analysis in organizations', *Administrative Science Quarterly*, vol.34, pp.598–631.

Latane, B., Williams, K. and Harkins, S., 1979, 'Many hands make light work: the causes and consequences of social loafing', *Journal of Personality and Social Psychology*, vol.37, no.6, June, pp.822–32.

Latham, G.P. and Yukl, G.A., 1975, 'A review of research on the application of goal setting in organizations', *Academy of Management Journal*, vol.18, pp.824–45.

Laughlin, P. and Johnson, H., 1966, 'Group and individual performance on a complementary task as a function of initial entry level', *Journal of Experimental Psychology*, vol.2, no.4, pp.407–14.

Laurent, A., 1983, 'The cultural diversity of Western conceptions of management', *International Studies of Management and Organization*, vol.13, nos 1–2 (whole issue).

Laurent, A. 1989, 'A cultural view of organization change', in P. Evans, Y. Doz and A. Laurent (eds), *Human Resource Management in International Firms*, Macmillan, Basingstoke, pp.83–94.

Laville, S., 1999, 'Male workers get lessons in how to cope with women', *Daily Telegraph*, 29 March, p.10.

Lawler, E.E., 1973, *Motivation in Work Organizations*, Brooks Cole Publishing, New York.

Lawler, E.E., 1986, *High Involvment Management: Participative Strategies for Improving Organizational Performance*, Jossey-Bass, San Francisco.

Lawler, E.E., 1995, *The Ultimate Advantage: Creating the High Involvement Organization*, Maxwell Macmillan, New York.

Lawler, E.E., 1996, *From the Ground Up: Six Principles for Building the New Logic Corporation*, Jossey-Bass, San Francisco.

Lawler, E.E., Mohrman, S.A. and Ledford, G.E., 1998, *Strategies for High Performance Organizations*, Jossey-Bass, San Francisco.

Lawrence, P.R. and Lorsch, J.W., 1967, *Organization and Environment*, Addison-Wesley, Boston.

Leavitt, H.J., 1975, 'Suppose we took groups seriously', in E.L. Cass and F.G. Zimmer (eds), *Man and Work in Society*, Van Nostrand Reinhold, London, pp.67–77.

Legge, K., 1978, *Power, Inovation, and Problem Solving in Personnel Management*, McGraw-Hill, London.

Legge, K., 1995, *Human Resource Management: Rhetorics and Realities*, Macmillan Business, Houndmills, Basingstoke.

Leidner, R., 1993, *Fast Food, Fast Talk: Service Work and the Routinization of Everyday Life*, University of California Press, Berkeley.

Leigh, A. and Walters, M., 1998, *Effective Change: Twenty Ways to Make it Happen*, Institute of Personnel and Development, London.

Leshner, M. and Brown, A., 1993, 'Increasing efficiency through cross-training', *Best's Review*, vol.94, no.8, pp.39–40.

Levine, R.V., 1990, 'The pace of life', *American Scientist*, September–October, pp.450–9.

Lewin, K., 1951, *Field Theory in Social Science*, Harper & Row, New York.

Li, A.Y.L., 1992, 'Team concept in apparel manufacturing: Hong Kong experience', *The Hong Kong Manager*, November–December, pp.18–21.

Likert, R., 1961, *New Patterns of Management*, McGraw-Hill, New York.

Likert, R., 1967, *The Human Organization*, McGraw-Hill, New York.

Lindblom, C., 1959, 'The science of muddling through', *Public Administration Review*, vol.34, no.4, pp.79–88.

Littlefield, D., 1999, 'One in a millennium', *People Management*, vol.5, no.24, pp.38–9.

Littlepage, G.E., 1991, 'Effects of group size and task characteristics on group performance: a test of Steiner's model', *Personality and Social Psychology Bulletin*, vol.17, pp.449–56.

Littler, C.R., 1982, *The Development of the Labour Process in Capitalist Societies*, Heinemann, London.

Littler, C. and Salaman, G., 1982, 'Bravermania and beyond: recent theories and labour process', *Sociology*, vol.16, no.2, pp.251–69.

Locke, E.A., 1968, 'Towards a theory of task performance and incentives', *Organizational Behaviour and Human Performance*, vol.3, no.2, pp.157–89.

Locke, E.A., 1975, 'Personnel attitudes and motivation', *Annual Review of Psychology*, vol.26, pp.457–80.

Locke, E.A. and Latham, G.P., 1990, *A Theory of Goal Setting and Task Performance*, Prentice Hall, Englewood Cliffs, NJ.

Lodge, D., 1989, *Nice Work*, Penguin Books, Harmondsworth.

Lorenz, A. and Smith, D., 1998, 'Britain fails to close the competitiveness gap', *The Sunday Times*, 11 October, pp.3.10–11.

Lukes, S., 1974, *Power: A Radical View*, Macmillan, London.

Lunn, T., 1988, 'How to pick the winners', *The Sunday Times*, May 1, p.E1.

Luthans, F. and Davis, T.R.V., 1979, 'Behavioural self-management: the missing link in managerial effectiveness', *Organizational Dynamics*, vol.18, pp.42–60.

Luthans, F. and Kreitner, R., 1985, *Organizational Behaviour Modification and Beyond*, Scott, Foresman, Glenview, IL (second edition).

Luthans, F., Stajkovic, A., Luthans, B.C. and Luthans, K.W., 1998, 'Applying behavioural management in Eastern Europe', *European Management Journal*, vol.16, no.4, pp.466–74.

McCauley, C., 1989, 'The nature of social influence in groupthink: compliance and internalization', *Journal of Personality and Social Psychology*, vol.57, no.2, pp.250–60.

McClelland, D.C., 1961, *The Achieving Society*, Van Nostrand, Princeton, NJ.

McClelland, D.C. and Boyatzis, R.E., 1982, 'Leadership motive pattern and long-term success in management', *Journal of Applied Psychology*, vol.67, no.6, pp.737–43.

McClelland, D.C. and Burnham, D.H., 1995, 'Power is the great motivator', *Harvard Business Review*, vol.73. no.1, pp.126–39 (first published in 1976).

McClelland, D.C., Atkinson, J.W., Clark, R.A. and Lowell, E.L., 1976, *The Achievement Motive*, Irvington, New York (second edition).

MacDonald, S., 1999, 'Femininity rules, OK', *The Times*, First Executive supplement, 30 September, p.2.

MacDuffie, J.P., 1988, 'The Japanese auto transplants: challenges to conventional wisdom', *ILR Report*, vol. xxvi, no.1, Fall, pp.12–18.

McGrath, J.E., 1964, *Social Psychology*, Holt, Rinehart & Winston, New York.

McGregor, D.M., 1960, *The Human Side of Enterprise*, McGraw-Hill, New York.

McKenna, E.P., 1997, *When Work Doesn't Work Anymore: Women, Work and Identity*, Hodder & Stoughton, New York.

McKinlay, A. and Taylor, P., 2000, *Inside the Factory of the Future: Work, Power and Authority in Microelectronics*, Routledge, London.

McLoughlin, I., 1999, *Creative Technological Change: The Shaping of Technology and Organizations*, Routledge, London.

McLoughlin, I. and Clark, J., 1994, *Technological Change at Work*, Open University Press, Buckingham (second edition).

McNabb, R. and Whitfield, K., 1999, 'The distribution of employee participation schemes at the workplace', *International Journal of Human Resource Management*, vol.10, no.1, pp.122–36.

McNeill, D., 2000, *The Face*, Penguin Books, London.

McRae, R.R. (ed.), 1992, 'The five-factor model: issues and applications', *Journal of Personality*, vol.60, no.2 (special issue).

Machiavelli, N., 1961, *The Prince*, Penguin Books, Harmondsworth, (trans. G. Bull).

Macy, B.A. and Izumi, H., 1993, 'Organizational change, design and work innovation: a meta analysis of 131 North American field studies: 1961–91', *Research in Organizational Change and Design: Vol. 7*, JAI Press, Greenwich, CT.

Madison, D.L., Allen, R.W., Porter, L.W., Renwick, P.A. and Mayes, B.T., 1980, 'Organizational politics: an exploration of managers' perceptions', *Human Relations*, vol.33, no.2, pp.79–100.

Mandela, N., 1994, *The Long Road to Freedom*, Little, Brown, London.

Mangham, I., 1979, *The Politics of Organizational Change*, Greenwood Press, Westport, CT.

Mann, S., 1995, 'Politics and power in organizations: why women lose out', *Leadership and Organization Development Journal*, vol.16, no.2, pp.9–15.

Manning, T., 1997, 'Team work, team roles and personality', *QWL News and Abstracts*, no. 129, Advisory, Conciliation and Arbitration Service (ACAS), pp.4–9.

March, J.G., 1962, 'The business firm as a political coalition', *Journal of Politics*, vol.24, no.4, November, pp.662–78.

March, J.G., 1988, *Decisions and Organizations*, Blackwell, London.

March, J.G. and Olsen, J.P., 1976, *Ambiguity and Choice in Organizations*, Universitetsforlaget, Oslo.

March, J.G. and Simon, H.A., 1958, *Organizations*, Wiley, New York.

Marchington, M., 1992, *Managing the Team: A Guide to Successful Employee Involvement*, Blackwell, Oxford.

Marcic, D., 1992, *Organizational Behavior: Experiences and Cases*, West Publishing, St Paul, MN (third edition).

Margerison, C. and McCann, D., 1990, *Team Management*, W.H. Allen, London.

Martel, L. and Biller, H., 1987, *Stature and Stigma*, D.C. Heath.

Martin, J., 1985, 'Can organization culture be managed?' in P.J. Frost, L.F. Moore and M.R. Louis (eds), *Organization Culture*, Sage, Beverley Hills, CA, pp.95–8.

Martin, J., 1992, *Cultures in Organizations: Three Perspectives*, Oxford University Press, Oxford.

Maslow, A., 1943, 'A theory of human motivation', *Psychological Review*, vol.50, no.4, pp.370–96.

Maslow, A., 1954, *Motivation and Personality*, Harper & Row, New York.

Maslow, A., 1971, *The Farther Reaches of Human Nature*, Penguin Books, Harmondsworth.

Maurer, S.D., Sue-Chan, C. and Latham, G.P., 1999, 'The situational interview', in R.W. Eder and M.M. Harris (eds), *The Employment Interview Handbook*, Sage, Thousand Oaks, CA, pp.159–77.

Mayes, B.T. and Allen, R.W., 1977, 'Toward a definition of organizational politics', *Academy of Management Review*, vol.2, pp.672–78.

Mayo, E., 1933, *The Human Problems of an Industrial Civilization*, Macmillan, New York.

Mayo, E., 1945, *The Social Problems of an Industrial Civilization*, Harvard University Press, Cambridge, MA.

Mead, G.H., 1934, *Mind, Self and Society*, University of Chicago Press, Chicago.

Meek, V.L., 1988, 'Organization culture: origins and weaknesses', *Organization Studies*, vol.9, no.4, pp.453–73.

Merkle. J., 1980, *Management and Ideology*, University of California Press, Berkeley.

Merton, R.K., 1940, 'Bureaucratic structure and personality', *Social Forces*, vol.18, pp.560–68.

Meyerson, D. and Martin, J., 1987, Culture change: an integration of three different views, *Journal of Management Studies*, vol.24, no.6, pp.623–47.

Micklethwait, J. and Wooldridge, A., 1996, *The Witch Doctors*, Heinemann, London.

Miles, R.E. and Snow, C.C., 1986, 'Organizations: new concepts for new forms', *California Management Review*, vol.28, no.3, pp.62–73.

Milgram, S., 1974, *Obedience to Authority*, Tavistock, London.

Milkman, R., 1998, 'The new American workplace: high road or low road?' in P. Thompson and C. Warhurst (eds), *Workplaces of the Future*, Macmillan, Basingstoke, pp.25–39.

Miller, E.J. and Rice, A.K., 1967, *Systems of Organization: The Control of Task and Sentient Boundaries*, Tavistock, London.

Mintzberg, H., 1973, *The Nature of Managerial Work*, HarperCollins, London.

Mintzberg, H., 1977, 'The manager's job: folklore and fact', *Harvard Business Review*, vol.55, no.4, July–August, pp.49–61.

Mintzberg, H., 1979, *The Structure of Organizations*, Prentice Hall, Englewood Cliffs, NJ.

Mintzberg, H., 1983a, *Power In and Around Organizations*, Prentice Hall, Englewood Cliffs, NJ.

Mintzberg, H., 1983b, *Structure in Fives: Designing Effective Organizations*, Prentice Hall, Englewoood Cliffs, NJ.

Mintzberg, H., 1989, *Mintzberg on Management: Inside Our Strange World of Organizations*, Free Press, New York.

Mintzberg, 1994, 'That's not "turbulence", Chicken Little, it's really opportunity', *Planning Review*, vol.22, no.6, pp.7–9.

Mintzberg, H.J., Raisinghani, D. and Theoret, A., 1976, 'The structure of "unstructured" decision processes', *Administrative Science Quarterly*, vol.21, no.2, June, pp.246–75.

Mitchell, W., 1999, 'Alliances: achieving long term value and short term goals', *Financial Times*, Mastering Strategy Part 4, 18 October, pp.6–7.

Mohrman, S.A., Cohen, S.G. and Mohrman, A.M., 1995, *Designing Team-Based Organizations*, Jossey-Bass, San Francisco.

Moreno, J.L., 1953, *Who Shall Survive?* Beacon Press, New York (second edition).

Morgan, G., 1989, *Creative Organization Theory*, Sage, London.

Morgan, G., 1997, *Images of Organization*, Sage, London (second edition; first edition 1986).

Morgan, G., Frost, J. and Pondy, L., 1983, 'Organization symbolism', in L. Pondy, P. Frost,

G. Morgan and T. Dandridge (eds) *Organization Symbolism*, JAI Press, Greenwich, CT, pp.55–65.

Morris, S., 1999, 'An Eastern art of healing that is heading West', *The Times*, 26 October, p.47.

Morton, C., 1998, *Beyond World Class*, Macmillan Business, Houndmills, Basingstoke.

Moscovici, S., 1980, 'Towards a theory of conversion behaviour', in L. Berkowitz (ed.), *Advances in Experimental Social Psychology*, vol.13, Academic Press, New York, pp.209–39.

Moscovici, S., 1984, 'The phenomenon of social representations', in R.M. Farr and S. Moscovici (eds), *Social Representations*, Cambridge University Press, Cambridge.

Mowshowitz, A., 1994, 'Virtual organization: a vision of management in the information age', *The Information Society*, vol.10, no.4, pp.267–94.

Mullins, L., 1999, *Management and Organizational Behaviour*, Pitman Financial Times, London (fifth edition).

Mumford, E. and Hendricks, R., 1996, 'Business process re-engineering RIP', *People Management*, 2 May, pp.22–7.

Murakami, T., 1997, 'The autonomy of teams in the car industry: a cross-national comparison', *Work, Employment and Society*, vol.11, no.4, pp.749–58.

Murphy, M., 1996, *Small Business Management*, Pitman, London.

Myers, D.G., 1990, *Social Psychology*, McGraw-Hill, New York (third edition; fourth edition 1993).

Myers, D.G. and Lamm, H., 1976, 'The group polarization phenomenon', *Psychological Bulletin*, vol.83, no.4, pp.602–27.

Myers, I.B., 1962, *The Myers–Briggs Type Indicator Manual*, Educational Testing Service, Princeton, NJ.

Myers, I.B., 1976, *Introduction to Type*, Centre for Applications of Psychological Type, Gainesville, FL, second edition.

Myers, I.B. and McCaulley, M.H., 1985, *Manual: A Guide to the Development and Use of the Myers-Briggs Type Indicator*, Consulting Psychologists Press, Palo Alto, CA.

Narayanan, V.K. and Rath, R.N., 1993, *Organization Theory: A Strategic Approach*, Richard D. Irwin, Homewood, IL.

Needle, D., 2000, 'Culture at the level of the firm: organizational and corporate perspectives', in J. Barry, J. Chandler, H. Clark, R. Johnson and D. Needle (eds), *Organization and Management: A Critical Text*, Business Press, Thomson Learning, London, pp.101–18.

Neider, L., 1980, 'An experimental field investigation utilizing an expectancy theory view of participation', *Organizational Behaviour and Human Performance*, vol.26, no.3, pp.425–42.

Nelson-Jones, R., 2000, *Introduction to Counselling Skills: Text and Actitivies*, Sage, London.

Nemeth, C., 1986, 'Differential contributions of majority and minority influence', *Psychological Review*, vol. 93, no.1, pp.23–32.

Nevis, E., 1983, 'Using an American perspective in understanding another culture: toward a hierarchy of needs for the People's Republic of China, *Journal of Applied Behavioral Science*, vol.19, no.3, pp.249–64.

Nohria, N., 1992, 'Is a network perspective a useful way of studying organizations?' in N. Nohria and R.G. Eccles (eds), *Networks and Organizations*, Harvard Business School Press, Boston, pp.1–22.

Nonaka, I. and Takeuchi, H., 1995, *The Knowledge Creating Company*, Oxford University Press, New York.

Nonaka. I., Umemoto, K. and Sasaki, K., 1999, 'Three tales of knowledge-creating companies', in G. von Krogh, J. Roos and D. Kleine (eds), *Knowing in Firms: Understanding, Managing and Measuring Knowledge*, Sage, London, pp.146–72.

Noon, M., 1992, 'HRM: a map, model or theory?' in P. Blyton and P. Turnbull (eds), *Reassessing Human Resource Management*, Sage, London, pp.16–32.

Noon, M. and Blyton, P., 1997, *The Realities of Work*, Macmillan Business, London.

Norstedt, J.P. and Aguren, S., 1973, *Saab-Scania Report*, Swedish Employers' Confedertion, Stockholm.

Nota, B., 1988, 'The socialization process at high-commitment organizations', *Personnel*, vol.65, no.8, pp.20–3.

Nuttall, N., 1999, 'ICI heads list of worst polluters', *The Times*, 22 March, p.7.

OECD, 1994, *Jobs Study: Evidence and Explanations Parts 1 and 2*, OECD, Paris.

Ogburn, W.F., 1922, *Social Change: With Respect to Culture and Original Nature*, B.W. Huebsch, New York.

O'Leary-Kelly, A.M., Griffin, R.W. and Glew, D.J., 1996, 'Organization-motivated aggression: a research framework', *Academy of Management Review*, vol.21, no.1, pp.225–53.

Oliver, N., Delbridge, R., Jones, D. and Lowe, J., 1994, 'World class manufacturing: further evidence in the lean production debate', *British Journal of Management*, vol.5, special edition, June, pp.53–63.

Orasanu, J.M., 1993, 'Decision making in the cockpit', in E.L. Wiener, B.G. Kanki and R.L. Helmreich, (eds), *Cockpit Resource Management*, Jossey-Bass, San Francisco, pp.137–72.

Organ, D.W., 1986, 'Review: *Management and the Worker*', by F.J. Roethlisberger and W.J. Dickson, Wiley, Science Editions, New York, 1964, *Academy of Management Review*, vol.11, no.2, pp.459–64.

Ouchi, W., 1981, *Theory Z*, Addison-Wesley, Reading, MA.

Ouchi, W.G. and Johnson, A.M., 1978, 'Type Z organizations: stability in the midst of mobility', *Academy of Management Review*, vol.3, no.2, April, pp.305–14.

Parker, G.M., 1990, *Team Players and Teamwork: The New Competitive Business Strategy*, Jossey-Bass, Oxford.

Parker, M., 2000, *Organizational Culture and Identity*, Sage, London.

Parker, M. and Slaughter, J., 1988, *Choosing Sides: Unions and the Team Concept*, South End Press, Boston.

Parkinson, M., 1999, *Using Psychology in Business*, Gower, Aldershot.

Parsons, M.B., Schepis, M.M., Reid, D.H., McCarn, J.E. and Green, C.W., 1987, 'Expanding the impact of behavioural staff management: a large-scale, long-term application in schools serving severely handicapped', *Journal of Applied Behaviour Analysis*, vol.20, no.2, Summer, pp.139–50.

Pascale, R.T, 1985, 'The paradox of corporate culture: reconciling ourselves to socialization', *California Management Review*, vol.27, no.2, pp.26–41.

Pascale, R.T. and Athos, A.G., 1982, *The Art of Japanese Management*, Penguin Books, Harmondsworth.

Pascale, R.T., Millemann, M. and Gioja, L., 1997, 'Changing the way we change', *Harvard Business Review*, November–December, pp.127–39.

Pasmore, W. and Friedlander, F., 1982, 'An action research programme to increase employee involvement in problem solving', *Administrative Science Quarterly*, vol.27, no.3, pp.343–62.

Patten, S., 1999, 'Incentives prove key method of keeping staff', *The Times*, 12 October, p.38.

Patterson, M.G., West, M.A., Lawthom, R. and Nickell, S., 1997, *Impact of People Management Practices on Business Performance*, Institute of Personnel and Development, London.

Paul, W.J. and Robertson, K.B., 1970, *Job Enrichment and Employee Motivation*, Gower, Aldershot.

Payne, R., 1990, 'Madness in our method: a comment on Jackofsky and Slocum's paper "A longitudinal study of climates"', *Journal of Organizational Behavior*, vol.11, no.1, January, pp.77–81.

Payne, R., 1996, 'The characteristics of organizations', in P. Warr (ed.), *Psychology at Work*, Penguin, Harmondsworth, pp.383–407.

Pease, A., 1985, *Body Language: How to Read Others' Thoughts by their Gestures*, Camel Publishing, Avalon Beach, NSW, Australia (third edition, 1997, Sheldon Press, London).

Pedler, M., Burgoyne, J. and Boydell, T., 1997, *The Learning Company: A Strategy for Sustainable Development*, McGraw-Hill, London (second edition).

Peixoto, J.C. and Schumacher, U., 1997, 'AutoEuropa: the team concept', *P+ European Participation Monitor*, no.13, pp.20–5.

Perlman, E., 1998, *Three Dollars*, Picador/Pan Macmillan, Sydney.

Perrow, C., 1970, *Organizational Analysis: A Sociological View*, Wadsworth, Belmont, CA.

Perrow, C., 1973, 'The short and glorious history of organizational theory', *Organizational Dynamics*, Summer.

Personnel Today, 1999, 'BAE Systems grapples with merger bias fears', 14 December, p.4.

Personnel Today, 2000, 'Management commitment to partnership deals fading', 1 February, p.7.

Peters, T., 1987, *Thriving on Chaos: Handbook for a Management Revolution*, Macmillan, London.

Peters, T.J. and Waterman, R.H., 1982, *In Search of Excellence*, Harper & Row, New York.

Pettigrew, A.M., 1973, *The Politics of Organizational Decision-Making*, Tavistock, London.

Pettigrew, A.M., 1977, 'Strategy formulation as a political process', *International Studies of Management and Organization*, vol.7, no.2, pp.78–87.

Pettigrew, A.M., 1985, *The Awakening Giant: Continuity and Change in ICI*, Basil Blackwell, Oxford.

Pettigrew, A.M, 1987, 'Context and action in the transformation of the firm', *Journal of Management Studies*, vol.24, no.6, pp.649–70.

Pettigrew, A.M. (ed.), 1988, *The Management of Strategic Change*, Basil Blackwell, Oxford.

Pettigrew, A., 1998, 'Success and failure in corporate transformation initiatives', in R.D. Galliers and W.R.J. Baets (eds), *Information Technology and Organizational Transformation*, Wiley, Chichester, pp.271–89.

Pettigrew, A., 1999, 'Organizing to improve company performance', *Hot Topics*, vol.1, no.5, February, Warwick Business School, Warwick University.

Pettigrew, A. and Fenton, E. (eds), 2000, *Process and Practice in New Forms of Organizing*, Sage, London.

Pettigrew, A.M. and McMulty, T. 1995, 'Power and influence in and around the boardroom', *Human Relations*, vol.48, no.8, pp.845–73.

Pfeffer, J., 1981, *Power in Organizations*, HarperCollins, London (second edition, 1992).

Pfeffer, J., 1992a, 'Understanding power in organizations', *California Management Review*, vol.34, no.2, pp.29–50.

Pfeffer, J., 1992b, *Managing With Power: Politics and Influence in Organizations*, Harvard Business School Press, Boston.

Pfeffer, J., 1996, *Competitive Advantage Through People: Unleashing the Power of the Work Force*, Harvard Business School Press, Boston.

Pfeffer, J., 1998, *The Human Equation: Building Profits by Putting People First*, Harvard Business School Press, Boston.

Pfeffer, J. and Salancik, G.R. 1978, *The External Control of Organizations: A Resource Dependence Perspective*, Harper & Row, New York.

Pickard, J., 1993, 'The real meaning of empowerment', *Personnel Management*, November, pp.28–33.

Pickard, J., 1999, 'Sense and sensitivity', *People Management*, vol.5, no.21, 28 October, pp.48–56.

Pinker, S., 1997, *How the Mind Works*, Penguin Books, London.

Piore, M. and Sabel, C., 1984, *The Second Industrial Divide*, Basic Books, New York.

Pollert, A., 1996, '"Teamwork" on the assembly line: contradiction and the dynamics of union resilience', in P. Ackers, C. Smith and P. Smith (eds), *The New Workplace and Trade Unionism*, Routledge, London, pp.178–209.

Porter, L.W. and Lawler, E.E., 1968, *Managerial Attitudes and Performance*, Irwin, Homewood, IL.

Powell, W.W., 1987, 'Hybrid organizational arrangements: new form or transitional development?' *California Management Review*, vol.30, no.1, pp.67–87.

Powell, W.W., 1990, 'Neither market nor hierarchy: network forms of organization', *Research in Organizational Behaviour*, JAI Press, Greenwich, CT, vol.12, pp.295–336.

Preece, D., 1995, *Organizations and Technical Change: Strategy, Objectives and Involvement*, Routledge, London.

Preece, D., Steven, G. and Steven, V., 1999, *Work, Change and Competition: Managing for Bass*, Routledge, London.

Procter, S. and Mueller, F. (eds), 2000, *Teamworking*, Macmillan, Houndmills, Basingstoke.

Procter, S. and Mueller, F., 2000, 'Teamworking, strategy, structure, systems and culture', in S. Procter and F. Mueller (eds), *Teamworking*, Macmillan, Houndmills, Basingstoke, pp.3–24.

Pruitt, S. and Barrett, T., 1991, 'Corporate virtual workspace', in M. Benedikt (ed.), *Cyberspace: First Steps*, MIT Press, Boston, pp.383–409.

Puffer, S.M., 1991, *Managerial Insights from Literature*, PWS, Kent.

Pugh, D.S. (ed.), 1971, *Organization Theory: Selected Readings*, Penguin Books, Harmondsworth.

Pugh, D.S. and Hickson, D.J., 1976, *Organizational Structure in its Context: The Aston Programme I*, Gower, Farnborough.

Pugh, D.S. and Hinings, D.J., 1976, *Organizational Structure Extensions and Replications: The Aston Programme II*, Gower, Farnborough.

Pugh, D.S. and Payne, R.L. 1977, *Organizational Structure in its Context: The Aston Programme III*, Gower, Farnborough.

Purcell, J., 1995, 'Corporate strategy and its link with human resource management strategy', in J. Storey (ed.), *Human Resource Management: A Critical Text*, Routledge, London, pp.63–86.

Puzo, M., 1998, *The Godfather*, Arrow Books, London.

Quah, D.T., 1997, 'Weightless economy packs a heavy punch', *Independent on Sunday*, 18 May, p.4.

Rajan, A., Lank, E. and Chapple, K., 1999, *Good Practices in Knowledge Creation and Exchange*, Focus/London Training and Enterprise Council, London.

Rakos, R.F. and Grodek, M.V., 1984, 'An empirical evaluation of a behavioural self-management course in a college setting', *Teaching of Psychology*, October, pp.157–62.

Ray, C.A., 1986, 'Corporate culture; the last frontier of control?', *Journal of Management Studies*, vol.23, no.3, pp.287–97.

Reeves, T.K., Turner, B.A. and Woodward, J., 1970, 'Technology and organizational behaviour', in J. Woodward (ed.), *Industrial Organization: Behaviour and Control*, Oxford University Press, London, pp.3–18.

Reich, R., 1993, *The Work of Nations*, Simon & Schuster, London.

Reuer, J., 1999, 'Collaborative strategy: the logic of alliances', *Financial Times*, Mastering Strategy Part 2, 4 October, pp.12–13.

Richards, T., 1997, *Star Trek in Myth and Legend*, Orion Books, London.

Richardson, R. and Thompson, M., 1999, *The Impact of People Management Practices on Business Performance: A Literature Review*, Institute of Personnel and Development, London.

Riley, P., 1983, 'A structuralist account of political cultures', *Administrative Science Quarterly*, vol.28, no.3, pp.414–37.

Ritchie, S. and Martin, P., 1999, *Motivation Management*, Gower, Aldershot.

Ritzer, G., 1993, *The McDonaldization of Society: An Investigation into the Changing Character of Contemporary Social Life*, Pine Forge Press, Thousand Oaks, CA London.

Ritzer, G., 1997, *The McDonaldization Thesis: Explorations and Extensions*, Sage, London.

Robertson, I.T., 1994, 'Personality and personnel selection', in C.L. Cooper and D.M. Rousseau (eds), *Trends in Organizational Behaviour*, John Wiley, London.

Robbins, S.P., 1990, *Organization Theory*, Prentice Hall, Englewood Cliffs, NJ.

Robbins, S.P., 1997, *Managing Organizational Conflict: A Non-traditional Approach*, Prentice Hall, Englewood Cliffs, NJ.

Robbins, S.P., 1998, *Organizational Behavior: Concepts, Controversies and Applications*, Prentice Hall, Englewood Cliffs, NJ (eighth edition).

Robinson, J., 1999, 'BP Amoco in £370m HR outsourcing deal', *Personnel Today*, 14 December, p.1.

Robinson, S.L. and Rousseau, D.M., 1994, 'Violating the psychological contract: not the exception but the norm', *Journal of Organizational Behavior*, vol.15, pp.245–59.

Roethlisberger, F.J., 1977, *The Elusive Phenomenon: An Autobiographical Account of my Work in the Field of Organizational Behaviour at the Harvard Business School*, Harvard University Press, Boston.

Roethlisberger, F.J. and Dickson, W.J., 1939, *Management and the Worker*, Harvard University Press, Cambridge, MA.

Rogelberg, S.G., Barnes-Farrell, J.L. and Lowe, C.A., 1992, 'The stepladder technique: an alternative group structure facilitating effective group decision making', *Journal of Applied Psychology*, vol.77, no.5, pp.337–58.

Rogers, A., 1999, 'Personality transplant tames the boss', *The Sunday Times*, 13 June, p.7.19.

Rollinson, D., Broadfield, A. and Edwards, D.J., 1998, *Organisational Behaviour and Analysis: An Integrated Approach*, Addison Wesley Longman, Harlow, Essex.

Rosenfeld, P., Giacalone, R.A. and Riordan, C.A., 1995, *Impression Management in Organizations: Theory, Measurement, Practice*, Routledge, London.

Rosenthal, R., 1973, *On the Social Psychology of the Self-fulfilling Prophecy: Further Evidence for Pygmalion Effects and their Mediating Mechanisms*, MSS Modular Publication, Ann Arbor, MI., vol.53, pp.1–28.

Rosenthal, R. and Jacobson, L., 1968, *Pygmalion in the Classroom*, Holt, Rinehart & Winston, New York.

Rost, J.C., 1991, *Leadership for the Twenty-First Century*, Praeger/Greenwood Publishing, Westport, CT.

Rotter, J.B., 1966, 'Generalized expectations for internal v. external control of reinforcement', *Psychological Monographs*, vol.80, whole issue no.609, pp.1–28.

Rousseau, D.M., 1990, 'New hire perceptions of their own and their employers' obligations: a study of psychological contracts', *Journal of Organizational Behavior*, vol.11, pp.389–400.

Rousseau, D.M., 1995, *Psychological Contracts in Organizations: Understanding Written and Unwritten Agreements*, Sage, London.

Rousseau, D.M., 1999, 'Why workers still identify with organizations', *Journal of Organizational Behavior*, vol.19, no.3, pp.217–33.

Rowe, H., 2000, 'Half of all NHS ethnic staff face racial harassment', *Personnel Today*, 11 April, p.8.

Roy, D., 1952, 'Quota restriction and goldbricking in a machine ship', *American Journal of Sociology*, vol.57, no.5, pp.427–42.

Roy, D., 1958, 'Efficiency and "the fix": informal intergroup relations in a piecework machine shop', *American Journal of Sociology*, vol.66, no.3, pp.255–66.

Roy, D., 1960, 'Banana time: job satisfaction and informal interaction', *Human Organization*, vol.18, pp.312–24.

Ruigrok, W., Pettigrew, A., Peck, S. and Whittington, R., 1999, 'Corporate restructuring and new forms of organizing in Europe', *Management International Review*, vol.39, no.2, pp.41–64.

Ryan, R.M. and Connell, J.P., 1989, 'Perceived locus of causality and internalization', *Journal of Personality and Social Psychology*, vol.57, no.5, pp.749–61.

Sabel, C., 1991, 'Möbius-strip organizations and open labour markets: some consequences of the reintegration of conception and execution in a volatile economy', in P. Bourdieu and D.S. Coleman (eds), *Social Theory for a Changing Society*, Sage, London, pp.23–61.

Sackman, S.A. (ed.), 1997, *Cultural Complexity in Organizations*, Sage, London.

Saffold, G., 1988, 'Culture traits, strength, and organizational performance: moving beyond the "strong" culture', *Academy of Management Review*, vol.13, no.4, pp.546–58.

Salancik, G.R. and Pfeffer, J., 1974, 'The bases and use of power in organizational decision-making: the case of the university', *Administrative Science Quarterly*, vol.19, no.4, pp.453–73.

Salancik, G.R. and Pfeffer, J., 1977, 'Who gets power—and how they hold on to it: a strategic contingency model of power', *Organizational Dynamics*, Winter, pp.3–21.

Salovey, P. and Mayer, J.D., 1990, 'Emotional intelligence', *Imagination, Cognition and Personality*, vol.9, pp.185–211.

Sandberg, A. (ed.), 1995, *Enriching Production: Perspectives on Volvo's Uddevalla Plant as an Alternative to Lean Production*, Avebury, Aldershot.

Savage, G.T., Blair, J.D. and Soreson, R.L., 1989, 'Consider both relationships and substance when negotiating strategy', *Academy of Management Executive*, vol.3, no.1, pp.37–48.

Scarbrough, H., 1999, 'System error', *People Management*, 8 April, pp.68–74.

Schaffer, R.H. and Thomson, H.A., 1992, 'Successful change programs begin with results', *Harvard Business Review*, January–February, pp.80–9.

Schein, E.H., 1969, *Process Consultation: Its Role in Organizational Development*, Addison-Wesley, Reading.

Schein, E.H., 1983, 'The role of the founder in creating organizational culture', *Organizational Dynamics*, vol.12, no.1, Summer, pp.13–28.

Schein, E.H., 1984, 'Coming to a new awareness of organizational culture', *Sloan Management Review*, vol.25, no.2, Winter, pp.3–16.

Schein, E.H., 1985, *Organizational Culture and Leadership*, Jossey-Bass, San Francisco.

Schein, E.H., 1988, *Organizational Psychology*, Prentice Hall, Englewood Cliffs, NJ (third edition).

Schilt, W.K., 1986, 'An examination of individual differences as moderators of upward influence activity in strategic decisions', *Human Relations*, vol.39, no.10, pp.933–53.

Scholz, C., 1987, 'Organization culture and strategy—the problem of strategy fit', *Long Range Planning*, vol.20, no.4, pp.78–87.

Schmitt, N. and Chan, D., 1998, *Personnel Selection: A Theoretical Approach*, Sage, Thousand Oaks, CA.

Schon, D.A., 1983, *The Reflective Practitioner*, Basic Books, New York.

Schuler, R.S. and Jackson, S.E., 1987, 'Linking competitive strategies with human resource management practices', *Academy of Management Executive*, vol.9, no.3, pp.207–19.

Schuler, R.S. and Jackson, S.E., 1996, *Human Resource Management: Positioning for the 21st Century*, West Publishing Co., Minneapolis/St Paul.

Schuler, R.S. and Jackson, S.E. (eds), 1999, *Strategic Human Resource Management*, Blackwell Business, Oxford.

Schultz, M., 1995, *Studying Organizational Cultures: Diagnosis and Understanding*, W. De Gruyter, Berlin.

Scott, A., 1994, *Willing Slaves: British Workers Under Human Resource Management*, Cambridge University Press, Cambridge.

Scully, J.A., Sims, H.P., Olian, J.D., Schnell, E.R. and Smith, K.A., 1996, 'Tough times make tough bosses: a meso analysis of CEO leader behaviour', *Irish Business and Administrative Research*, vol.17, no.1, pp.71–102.

Semler, R., 1993, *Maverick*, Century, London.

Senge, P., 1990, *The Fifth Discipline: The Art and Practice of the Learning Organization*, Doubleday Currency, New York.

Senge, P., Kleiner, A., Roberts, C., Ross, R., Roth, G. and Smith, B., 1999, *The Dance of Change: The Challenges of Sustaining Momentum in Learning Organizations*, Nicholas Brealey Publishing, London.

Senior, B., 1997a, *Organizational Change*, Pitman, London.

Senior, B., 1997b, 'Team roles and team performance: is there "really" a link?' *Journal of Occupational and Organizational Psychology*, vol.70, no.3, September, pp.241–58.

Sennett, R., 1998, *The Corrosion of Character: The Personal Consequences of Work in the New Capitalism*, W.W. Norton, New York.

Sewell, G. and Wilkinson, B., 1992, 'Someone to watch over me: surveillance, discipline and just-in-time labour process', *Sociology*, vol.26, no.2, pp.271–91.

Shannon, C.E. and Weaver, W., 1949, *The Mathematical Theory of Communication*, University of Illinois Press, Urbana.

Shapiro, E.C., 1996, *Fad Surfing in the Boardroom*, Capstone, Oxford.

Shaw, M.E., 1971, *Group Dynamics*, McGraw-Hill, New York.

Shaw, M.E., 1978, 'Communication networks fourteen years later', in L. Berkowitz (ed.), *Group Processes*, Academic Press, New York, pp.351–61.

Sheldon, W., 1942, *The Varieties of Temperament: A Psychology of Constitutional Differences*, Harper, New York.

Sheldrake, M., 1995, *Management Theory*, International Thomson Business Press, London.

Sherif, M., 1936, *The Psychology of Group Norms*, Harper & Row, New York.

Simmons, D., 1990, *Hyperion*, Headline Books, London.

Simon, H., 1957, *Administrative Behaviour*, Macmillan, New York (second edition).

Simon, H., 1960, *The New Science of Management Decision*, Harper, New York.

Simon, H., 1986, 'Rationality in psychology and economics', *Journal of Business*, October, pp.209–26.

Simpson, P., 1999, 'Blurred boundaries', *Personnel Today*, 16 November, p.31.

Sims, D., Fineman, S. and Gabriel, Y., 1993, *Organizing and Organizations: An Introduction*, Sage, London.

Sims, H.P. and Lorenzi, P., 1992, *The New Leadership Paradigm*, Sage, Newbury Park, CA.

Sinclair, A, 1992, 'The tyranny of team ideology, *Organization Studies*, vol.13, no.4, pp.611–26.

Sisson, K., 1994, 'Personnel management: paradigms, practice and prospects', in K. Sisson (ed.), *Personnel Management*, Blackwell, Oxford, pp.3–50.

Sitkin, S.B. and Pablo, A.L., 1992, 'Reconceptualizing the determinants of risk behavior', *Academy of Management Review*, vol.17, no.1, pp.9–38.

Skinner, B.F., 1948, *Walden II*, Macmillan, London.

Skinner, W., 1981, 'Big hat, no cattle: managing human resources', *Harvard Business Review*, vol.59, no.5, pp.106–14.

Slovic, P. and Lichtenstein, S., 1971, 'Comparison of Bayesian and regression approaches in the study of information processing in judgment', *Organizational Behavior and Human Decision Processes*, vol.6, no.6, November, pp.649–744.

Smart, B. (ed.), 1999, *Resisting McDonaldization*, Sage, London.

Smircich, L., 1983, 'Concepts of culture and organization analysis', *Administrative Science Quarterly*, vol.28, no.3, pp.339–58.

Smircich, L. and Morgan, G., 1982, 'Leadership: the management of meaning', *Journal of Applied Behavioral Science*, vol.18, no.2, pp.257–73.

Smith, W.P., 1987, 'Conflict and negotiation: trends and emerging Issues', *Journal of Applied Social Psychology*, vol.17, no.7, pp.631–77.

Smither, R.D., 1988, *The Psychology of Work and Human Performance*, Harper & Row, New York.

Snow, C.C., Miles, R.E. and Coleman, H.J., 1992, 'Managing 21st century network organizations', *Organizational Dynamics*, vol.20, no.3, pp.5–20.

Sonnenfeld, J.A., 1985, 'Shedding light on the Hawthorne studies', *Journal of Occupational Behaviour*, vol.6, no.2, pp.111–30.

Sorge, A. and Warner, M. (eds), 1997, *The Handbook of Organizational Behaviour*, International Thomson Business Press, London.

Sparrow, P., 1998, *Human Resource Management: The New Agenda*, Financial Times Pitman, London.

Sparrow, P. and Hiltrop, J.-M., 1994, *European Human Resource Management in Transition*, Prentice Hall, Hemel Hempstead.

Spencer, J. and Pruss, A., 1992, *Managing Your Team*, Piatkus, London.

Stace, D.A., 1996, 'Transitions and transformations: four case studies in business-focused change', in J. Storey (ed.), *Cases in Human Resource and Change Management*, Blackwell Business, Oxford, pp.43–72.

Steiner, I.D., 1972, *Group Process and Productivity*, Academic Press, New York.

Steiner, I.D. and Rajaratnam, N.A., 1961, 'A model for the comparison of individual and group performance scores', *Behavioural Science*, vol.6, no.2, April, pp.142–7.

Steiner, R., 1999, 'Pinstripes put Roddick on the right scent', *The Sunday Times*, 24 October, p.3.15.

Sternberg, R.J., 1988, *The Triarchic Mind: A New Theory of Human Intelligence*, Viking, New York.

Sternberg, R., 1999, 'Survival of the fit test', *People Management*, vol.4, no.24, 10 December, pp.29–31.

Sternberg, R.J. and Soriano, L.J., 1984, 'Styles of conflict resolution', *Journal of Personality and Social Psychology*, vol.47, no.1, July, pp.115–26.

Stewart, R., 1963, *The Reality of Management*, Pan/Heinemann Books, London.

Stiles, P., Gratton, L., Truss, C., Hope-Hailey, V. and McGovern, P., 1997, 'Performance management and the psychological contract', *Human Resource Management Journal*, vol. 7, no.1, pp.57–66.

Stogdill, R.M., 1948, 'Personal factors associated with leadership', *Journal of Psychology*, vol.25, pp.35–71.

Stogdill, R.M., 1950, 'Leadership, membership and organization', *Psychological Bulletin*, vol.47, pp.1–14.

Stogdill, R.M., 1974, *Handbook of Leadership: A Survey of Theory and Research*, Free Press, New York.

Stogdill, R.M. and Coons, A.E. (eds), 1951, *Leader Behaviour: Its Description and Measurement*, Research Monograph no. 88, Ohio State University Bureau of Business Research, Columbus, Ohio.

Stoner, J.A.F., 1961, 'A comparison of individual and group decisions involving risk', unpublished masters degree thesis, Massachusetts Institute of Technology, Boston, cited in D.G. Marquis, 'Individual responsibility and group decisions involving risk', *Industrial Management Review*, 1962, vol.3, pp.8–23.

Storey, J., 1989, *New Perspectives on Human Resource Management*, Routledge & Kegan Paul, London.

Storey, J., 1992, *Developments in the Management of Human Resources: An Analytical Review*, Blackwell Business, Oxford.

Storey, J. (ed.), 1995, *Human Resource Management: A Critical Text*, Routledge, London.

Strasser, G. and Titus, W., 1985, 'Pooling of unshared information in group decision-making: biased information sampling during discussion', *Journal of Personality and Social Psychology*, vol.48, no.6, pp.1467–78.

Stredwick, J. and Ellis, S., 1998, *Flexible Working Practices: Techniques and Innovations*, Institute of Personnel and Development, London.

Stuttaford, T., 1999, 'Addicted to risk?: it's your novelty gene', *The Times*, 14 October, p.38.

Sundstrom, E. and Altman, I., 1989, 'Physical environments and work group effectiveness', in L.L. Cummings and B. Staw (eds), *Research in Organizational Behavior: Volume 11*, JAI Press, Greenwich, CT, pp.175–209.

Sundstrom, E., de Meuse, K.P. and Futrell, D., 1990, 'Work teams: applications and effectiveness', *American Psychologist*, vol.45, no.2, February, pp.120–33.

Sutton, R.I. and Hargadon, A., 1996, 'Brainstorming groups in context: effectiveness in a product design firm', *Administrative Science Quarterly*, vol.41, no.4, pp.685–718.

Sweeney, P.D., McFarlin, D.B. and Inderrieden, E.J., 1990, 'Using relative deprivation theory to explain satisfaction with income and pay level: a multistudy examination', *Academy of Management Journal*, vol.33, pp.423–36.

Syrett, M., 1988, 'Giving job interviews a situational bite', *The Sunday Times*, 7 February, p.E1.

Taffinder, P., 1998, 'Conflict is not always a bad thing', *Personnel Today*, 10 September, p.19.

Taggert, W.M. and. Silbey, V., 1986, *Informational Systems: People and Computers in Organizations*, Allyn & Bacon, Boston.

Tailby, S. and Winchester, D., 2000, 'Management and trade unions: towards a social partnership', in S. Bach and K. Sisson (eds), *Personnel Management*, Blackwell Business, pp.365–88 (third edition).

Tajfel, H. and Fraser, C., 1990, *Introducing Social Psychology*, Penguin Books, Harmondsworth.

Tajfel, H. and Turner, J.C., 1986, 'The social identity theory of inter-group behaviour', in S. Worchel and W.G. Austin (eds), *Psychology of Inter-group Relations*, Nelson-Hall, Chicago (second edition).

Talbott, F. (ed.), 1994, *Shakespeare on Leadership: Timeless Wisdom for Daily Challenges*, T. Nelson, Nashville, Tenn.

Tannen, D., 1990, *You Just Don't Understand: Women and Men in Conversation*, William Morrow, New York.

Tannen, D., 1995, 'The power of talk: who gets heard and why', *Harvard Business Review*, vol.73, no.5, pp.138–48.

Tannenbaum, R. and Schmidt, W.H., 1958, 'How to choose a leadership pattern', *Harvard Business Review*, vol.37, March–April, pp.95–102 (reprinted in the May–June issue of 1973).

Taylor, D., Berry, P.C. and Bloch, C.H., 1958, 'Does group participation when using brainstorming techniques facilitate or inhibit creative thinking?' *Administrative Science Quarterly*, vol.3, no.1, pp.23–47.

Taylor, F.W., 1911, *Principles of Scientific Management*, Harper, New York.

Taylor, P. and Bain, P., 1999, 'An assembly line in the head: work and employee relations in a call centre', *Industrial Relations Journal*, vol.30, no.2, pp.101–17.

Thatcher, M., 1996, 'Allowing everyone to have their say', *People Management*, 21 March, pp.28–30.

Thomas, A.B., 1993, *Controversies in Management*, Routledge, London.

Thomas, H., 1974, 'Finding a better way', *Guardian*, 17 January, p.12.

Thomas, K.W., 1976, 'Conflict and conflict management', in M.D. Dunnette (ed.), *Handbook of Industrial and Organizational Psychology*, Rand McNally, Chicago, pp.889–935.

Thomas, K.W., 1977, 'Towards multi-dimensional values in teaching: the example of conflict behaviors', *Academy of Management Review*, vol.2, no.3, July, pp.484–528.

Thomas, M., 1994, 'What you need to know about: business process re-engineering', *Personnel Management*, January, pp.28–31.

Thompson, G., Francis, J., Levacic, R. and Mitchell, J. (eds), 1991, *Markets, Hierarchies and Networks: The Co-ordination of Social Life*, Sage/Open University Press, London.

Thompson, J.D., 1967, *Organizations in Action*, McGraw-Hill, New York.

Thompson, J. and McGivern, J., 1996, 'Parody, process and practice', *Management Learning*, vol.27, no.1, pp.21–35.

Thompson, J. and Tuden, A., 1959, 'Strategies, structures and processes of organizational decisions', in J.D. Thompson, P.B. Hammond, R.W. Hawkes, B.H. Junker and A. Tuden (eds), *Comparative Studies in Administration*, University of Pittsburgh Press, Pittsburgh, PA, pp.195–216.

Thompson, P. and Ackroyd, S., 1995, 'All quiet on the workplace front?: a critique of recent trends in British industrial sociology', *Sociology*, vol.29, no.4, pp.610–33.

Thompson, P. and Davidson, J.O., 1995, 'The continuity of discontinuity: managerial rhetoric in turbulent times', *Personnel Review*, vol.24, no.4, pp.17–33.

Thompson, P. and McHugh, D., 1995, *Work Organization: A Critical Introduction*, Macmillan, London (second edition).

Thompson, P. and Warhurst, C. (eds), 1998, *Workplaces of the Future*, Macmillan, Houndmills, Basingstoke.

Tichy, N.M. and Devanna, M.A., 1986, *The Transformational Leader*, Wiley, New York.

Tiefenbrun, I., 1993, 'Manufacturing in the future', *RSA Journal*, vol.CLXI, no.5441, July, pp.549–57.

The Times Magazine, 1999, 'Someone is watching you—and it could be your boss', 6 November 1999, pp.26–30.

Toffler, A., 1970, *Future Shock*, Pan Books, London.

Torrington, J., 1996, *The Devil's Carousel*, Martin Secker & Warburg/Minerva, London.

Townley, B., 1994, 'Communicating with employees', in K. Sisson (ed.), *Personnel Management: A Comprehensive Guide to Theory and Practice in Britain*, Blackwell Business, Oxford, pp.595–633.

Trice, H.M. and Beyer, J.M., 1984, 'Studying cultures through rites and organizational ceremonies', *Academy of Management Review*, vol.9, no.4, pp.653–69.

Trice, H.M. and Beyer, J.M., 1993, *The Cultures of Work Organizations*, Prentice Hall, Englewood Cliffs, NJ.

Triplett, N., 1898, 'The dynamogenic factors in pacemaking and competition', *American Journal of Psychology*, vol.9, pp.507–33.

Trist, E.L. and Bamforth, K.W., 1951, 'Some social and psychological consequences of the longwall method of coal-getting', *Human Relations*, vol.4, no.1, pp.3–38.

Trist, E.L., Higgin, G.W., Murray, H. and Pollock, A.B., 1963, *Organizational Choice*, Tavistock, London.

Trompenaars, F., 1994, *Riding the Waves of Culture*, Irwin, Burr Ridge, IL.

Tuckman, B.C., 1965, 'Development sequence in small groups', *Psychological Bulletin*, vol.63, no.6, pp. 384–99.

Tuckman, B.C. and Jensen, M.A.C., 1977, 'Stages of small group development revisited', *Group and Organization Studies*, vol.2, no.4, pp.419–27.

Turner, A.N. and Lawrence, P.R., 1965, *Industrial Jobs and the Worker: An Investigation of Response to Task Attributes*, Division of Research, Harvard Business School, Boston.

Tversky, A. and Kahneman, D., 1971, 'Belief in the law of numbers', *Psychological Bulletin*, vol.76, no.2, pp.105–10.

Tversky, A. and Kahneman, D., 1973, 'Availability: a heuristic for judging frequency and probability', *Cognitive Psychology*, vol.5, no.2, pp.207–32.

Tversky, A. and Kahneman, D., 1974, 'Judgement under uncertainty: heuristics and biases', *Science*, vol.185, no.4157, pp.1124–31.

Tversky, A. and Kahneman, D., 1981, 'The framing of decisions and the psychology of choice', *Science*, vol.211, no.4481, pp.453–58.

Tversky, A. and Kahneman, D., 1983, 'Extensional versus intuitive reasoning: the conjunction fallacy in probability judgement', *Psychological Review*, vol.90, no.4, pp.293–315.

Tversky, A. and Kahneman, D., 1992, 'Advances in prospect theory: cumulative representation of uncertainty', *Journal of Risk and Uncertainty*, vol.5, no.4, pp.297–323.

Ulrich, D., 1997, 'Measuring human resources: an overview of practice and a prescription for results', *Human Resource Management*, vol.36, no.3, pp.303–20.

Ulrich, D., 1998, 'A new mandate for human resources', *Harvard Business Review*, vol.76, no.1, pp.124–34.

Ury, W., 1991, *Getting Past No: Negotiating With Difficult People*, Bantam Books, New York.

Ury, W. and Patton, B., 1997, *Getting to Yes: Negotiating An Agreement Without Giving In*, Arrow Books, London (second edition).

Vaill, P.B., 1982, 'The purposing of high-performing systems', *Organizational Dynamics*, Autumn, pp.23–39.

van Eijnatten, F.M. 1993, *The Paradigm that Changed the Workplace*, van Gorcum, Assen the Netherlands.

van Fleet, D.D. and Griffin, R.W., 1989, 'Quality circles: a review and suggested future directions', in C.L. Cooper and I.T. Robertson (eds), *International Review of Industrial and Organizational Psychology 1989: Volume 4*, Wiley, Chichester, pp.213–33.

van Maanen, J., 1991, 'The smile factory: work at Disneyland', in P. Frost, L. Moore, M. Louis, C. Lundberg and J. Martin, (eds), *Reframing Organizational Culture*, Sage, Newbury Park, CA, pp.31–54.

van Maanen, J. and Schein, E.H. 1979, 'Toward a theory of organization socialization', *Research in Organizational Behavior Vol. 1*, JAI Press, Greenwich, CT, pp.209–64.

van Maanen, J. and Barley, S., 1984, 'Occupational communities: culture and control in organizations', in B. Staw and L. Cummings (eds), *Research in Organization Behaviour, Vol. 6*, JAI Press, Greenwich, CT, pp.287–366.

Venkatraman, N. and Henderson, J.C., 1998, 'Real strategies for virtual organizing', *Sloan Management Review*, vol.40, no.1, pp.33–48.

Vernon, H.M., Wyatt, S. and Ogden, A.D., 1924, *On the Extent and Effects of Variety in Repetitive Work*, Medical Research Council Industrial Fatigue Research Board, report no. 26, HMSO, London.

Vickerstaff, S. (ed.), 1992, *Human Resource Management in Europe: Text and Cases*, Chapman & Hall, London.

Vinnicombe, S., 2000, 'The position of women in management in Europe', in M.J. Davidson and and R.J. Burke (eds), *Women in Management: Current Research Issues Volume II*, Sage, London, pp.9–25.

Viteles, M.S., 1950, 'Man and machine relationship: the problem of boredom', in R.B. Ross (ed.), *Proceedings of the Annual Fall Conference of the Society for Advancement of Management*, New York, pp.129–38.

Voss, F., 1991, *Goodstone*, Bloodaxe Books, Newcastle upon Tyne.

Vroom, V.H., 1964, *Work and Motivation*, John Wiley, New York.

Vroom, V.H. and Yetton, P.W., 1973, *Leadership and Decision Making*, University of Pittsburgh Press, Pittsburgh, PA.

Vroom, V.H. and Jago, A.G., 1988, *The New Leadership: Managing Participation in Organizations*, Prentice Hall, Englewood Cliffs, NJ.

Walker, C.R., 1950, 'The problem of the repetitive job', *Harvard Business Review*, vol.28, no.3, pp.54–8.

Walker, C.R. and Guest, R.H., 1952, *The Man on the Assembly Line*, Harvard University Press, Cambridge, MA.

Wallach, M.A., Kogan, N. and Bem, D.J., 1962, 'Group influences on individual risk taking', *Journal of Abnormal and Social Psychology*, vol.65, no.2, pp.75–86.

Wallach, M.A., Kogan, N. and Bem, D.J., 1964, 'Diffusion of responsibility and level of risk taking in groups', *Journal of Abnormal and Social Psychology*, vol.68, no.3, pp.263–74.

Walsh, D., 1999, 'Corporate profile: Bass', *The Times*, 8 March, p.44.

Walsh, D. and Davies, P., 1999, 'All aboard with takeover travel', *The Times*, 1 May, pp.30–1.

Walters, C.C. and Grusec, J.E., 1977, *Punishment*, W.H. Freeman, San Francisco.

Walther, G.R., 1993, *Say What You Mean and Get What You Want*, Piatkus, London.

Walton, R.E. and McKersie, R.B., 1965, *A Behavioural Theory of Labour Relations*, McGraw-Hill, New York.

Walton, R.E. and Susman, G.I., 1987, 'People policies for the new machines', *Harvard Business Review,* March–April, no.2, pp.98–106.

Waples, J. and Coffer, A., 1999, 'Which of Britain's bosses give best value for pay?' *The Sunday Times*, 31 October, pp.3.10–3.11.

Warhurst, C. and Thompson, P., 1998, 'Hands, hearts and minds: changing work and workers at the end of the century', in P. Thompson and C. Warhurst (eds), *Workplaces of the Future*, Macmillan Business, London, pp.1–24.

Warrick, D.D., 1984, *MODMAN: Managing Organizational Change and Development*, Science Research Associates Inc., New York.

Waterson, P.E., Clegg, C., Bolden, R., Pepper, K., Warr, P. and Wall, T., 1997, *The Use and Effectiveness of Modern Manufacturing Practices in the United Kingdom*, Institute of Work Psychology, Sheffield.

Watson, T.J., 1977, *The Personnel Managers*, Routledge & Kegan Paul, London.

Watson, T., 1994, *In Search of Management: Culture, Chaos and Control in Management Work*, Routledge, London.

Weber, M., 1947, *The Theory of Social and Economic Organization*, translated by A.M. Henderson and T. Parsons, Oxford University Press, Oxford.

Weber, C.E., 1984, 'Strategic thinking—dealing with uncertainty', *Long Range Planning*, vol.17, no.5, October, pp.60–70.

Weick, K. 1977, 'Organizational design: organizations as self-organizing systems', *Organizational Dynamics*, Autumn, pp.31–67.

Weick, K., 1979, *The Social Psychology of Organizing*, Addison-Wesley, Boston.

Weick, K.E. and Westley, F., 1996, 'Organizational learning: affirming an oxymoron', in S.R. Clegg, C. Hardy and W.R. Nord (eds), *Handbook of Organization Studies*, Sage, London, pp.440–58.

Weiner, E.L., Kanki, B.G. and Helmreich, R.L. (eds.), 1993, *Cockpit Resource Management*, Academic Press, New York.

Weick, K., 1979, *The Social Psychology of Organizing*, Addison-Wesley, Reading, MA (second edition).

Weick, K.E., 1995, *Sensemaking in Organizations*, Sage, London.

Weldon, E. and Weingart, L.R, 1993, 'Group goals and group performance', *British Journal of Social Psychology*, vol.32, no.4, pp.307–34.

West, M.A., Borrill, C.S. and Unsworth, K.L., 1998, 'Team effectiveness in organizations', in C.L. Cooper and I.T. Robertson (eds), *International Review of Industrial and Organizational Psychology 1998: Volume 13*, Wiley, Chichester, pp.1–48.

Whetton, D., Cameron, K. and Woods, M., 1994, *Developing Management Skills for Europe*, Harper Collins, London.

White, R.W., 1959, 'Motivation reconsidered: the concept of competence', *Psychological Review*, vol.66, pp.297–333.

White, R. and Lippitt, R., 1960, *Autocracy and Democracy*, Harper & Row, New York.

Whitehead, M., 1999, 'Watch your workloads', *People Management*, vol.5, no.14, 15 July, pp.12–13.

Whitehead, T.N., 1938, *The Industrial Worker*, Harvard University Press, Cambridge, MA.

Whittell, G., 1999, 'Exxon challenges payout a decade after Valdez spill', *The Times*, 25 March, p.20.

Whittington, R., Pettigrew, A., Peck, S., Fenton, E. and Conyon, M., 1999a, 'Change and complementarities in the new competitive landscape: a European panel study, 1992–1996', *Organization Science*, vol.10, no.5. pp.583–600.

Whittington, R., Pettigrew, A. and Ruigrok, W., 1999b, 'New notions of organizational fit', *Financial Times*, Mastering Strategy Part 10, 29 November, pp.8 and 10.

Whyte, W.F., 1948, *Human Relations in the Restaurant Industry*, McGraw-Hill, New York.

Whyte, W.H., 1955, *The Organization Man*, Penguin Books, Harmondsworth.

Wickens, P., 1993, 'Steering the middle road to car production', *Personnel Management*, June, pp.34–8.

Wickens, P., 1995, *The Ascendent Organization Combining Commitment and Control for Long Term Sustainable Business Success*, Macmillan, Basingstoke.

Wickens, P., 1999, 'Values added', *People Management*, vol.5, no.10, 20 May, pp.33–7.

Wiener, N., 1954, *The Human Use of Human Beings: Cybernetics and Society*, Avon Books, New York.

Wiener, E.L., Kanki, B.G. and Helmreich, R.L. (eds.), 1993, *Cockpit Resource Management*, Academic Press, San Diego.

Williams, A., Donson, P. and Walters, M., 1989, *Changing Culture: New Organizational Approaches*, Institute of Personnel Management, London.

Williamson, O.E., 1975, *Markets and Hierarchies: Analysis and Antitrust Implications, A Study in the Economics of Internal Organizations*, Macmillan, London.

Willmott, H., 1993, 'Strength is ignorance, slavery is freedom: managing culture in modern organizations', *Journal of Management Studies*, vol.30, no.4, pp.515–52.

Wilson, F., 1999, *Organizational Behaviour: A Critical Introduction*, Oxford University Press, Oxford.

Wilson, J.M., 1995, 'Henry Ford: a just-in-time pioneer', *Production and Inventory Management Journal*, vol.37, no.2, pp.26–31.

Winner, L., 1977, *Autonomous Technology: Technics-Out-Of-Control as a Theme in Political Thought*, MIT Press, Cambridge, MA.

Wolfinger, R.E., 1971, 'Nondecisions and the study of local politics', *American Political Science Review*, vol.65, pp.1063–80.

Womack, J., Jones, D. and Roos, D., 1990, *The Machine That Changed the World*, Rawson Associates, New York.

Wood, J., 1995, 'Mastering management: organizational behaviour', *Financial Times*, supplement (part 2 of 20).

Woodcock, M., 1989, *Team Development Manual*, Gower, Aldershot.

Woodward, J., 1965, *Industrial Organization: Theory and Practice*, Oxford University Press, Oxford.

Wooldridge, A., 1999, 'The world in your pocket: a survey of telecommunications', *The Economist*, 9 October, pp.33–4.

Wren, D.S., 1979, *The Evolution of Management Thought*, Wiley, New York (latest edition 1994).

Wright, C. and Lund, J., 1996, 'Best practice Taylorism: Yankee speed-up in Australian grocery distribution', *Journal of Industrial Relations*, vol.38, no.2, pp.196–212.

Wright, P. and Taylor, D., 1984, *Improving Leadership Performance*, Prentice Hall, Hemel Hempstead.

Wyatt, S., Fraser, J.A. and Stocks, F.G.L. 1928, *The Comparative Effects of Variety and Uniformity in Work*, Medical Research Council Industrial Fatigue Research Board, report no. 52, HMSO, London.

Yamashita, H., 1998, *Competitiveness and Corporate Culture*, Ashgate, Aldershot.

Yates, S., 1985, *The Politics of Management*, Jossey-Bass, San Francisco.

Yerkes, R.M. and Dodson, J.D., 1908, 'The relationship of strength of stimulus to rapidity of habit formation', *Journal of Comparative Neurology and Psychology*, vol.18, pp.459–82.

York, P., 1999, 'The gender agenda', *Management Today*, October, pp.56–63.

Zajonc, R.B., 1965, 'Social facilitation', *Science*, vol.149, no.3681, pp.269–74.

Zajonc, R.B., 1980, 'Compresence', in P.B. Paulus (ed.), *Psychology of Group Influence*, Laurence Erlbaum, Hillsdale, NJ, pp.35–60.

Zaleznik, A., 1977, 'Managers and leaders: are they different?' *Harvard Business Review*, vol.15, no.3, pp.67–84.

Zaleznik, A., 1993, 'The mythological structure of organization and its impact', in L. Hirschhorn and C.K. Barnett (eds), *The Psychodynamics of Organizations*, Temple University Press, Philadelphia.

Zaleznik, A. and Kets de Vries, M., 1975, *Power and the Corporate Mind*, Houghton Mifflin, Boston.

Zalkind, S.S. and Costello, T.W., 1962, 'Perception: some recent research and implications for administration', *Administrative Science Quarterly*, vol.7, pp.218–35.

Zeleny, L.D., 1947, 'Selection of compatible flying partners', *American Journal of Sociology*, vol.5, pp.424–31.

Zimbardo, P.G. *et al.*, 1973, 'A Pirandellian prison', *The New York Times Magazine*, 8 April.

Zuboff, S., 1988, *In the Age of the Smart Machine: The Future of Work and Power*, Heinemann Professional Publishing, Oxford.

Glossary

Accountability: an obligation placed on a subordinate to report back on their discharge of the responsibilities which they have undertaken.

Action: the term given to the things that people do and the reasons that they have for doing them; action is thus also defined as *meaningful behaviour*, prompting us to ask the question 'why?' as well as 'what?' and 'how?'

Action research: a model of organization development consulting that involves the feedback of findings from interventions, or actions, to help in the design and implementation of further action and improvements to organizational effectiveness.

Action team: a type of team that executes brief performances which are repeated under new conditions. Its members are technically specialized, and the team has a high need to co-ordinate its output with that of other work units.

Acquisition: a situation in which one firm buys the equity stake or assets of another. A major control acquisition is called a 'takeover' and may be friendly or hostile.

Activities: in George Homans' theory, these are the physical movements, and verbal or non-verbal behaviours, that are engaged in by group members.

Adaptive decision: a type of decision that requires human judgement based on clarified criteria and which is made using basic quantitative decision tools.

Additive task: a type of task whose accomplishment depends on the sum of all group members' efforts.

Adhocracy: a type of organization design which is temporary, adaptive, creative, in contrast to bureaucracy, which tends to be permanent, rule-driven and inflexible. *Adhocracy* is similar to the concepts of *organic* and *integrative* organizational styles, while bureaucracy equates with *mechanistic* and *segmentalist* approaches.

Advice team: a type of team created primarily to provide a flow of information to management for use in its decision making.

Affiliation power: the ability of a leader to exert influence based on the belief of followers that the leader has a close association with other powerful figures on whose authority they are able to act.

Aggregate: a collection of unrelated people who happen to be in close physical proximity for a short period of time.

Anchor-and-adjustment heuristic: a predisposition to make a judgement by starting from an initial value or 'anchor' and then making adjustments from that point, before making a final decision.

Arbitration: a process in which a third party to a conflict has the authority to impose an agreement that is binding on the parties in conflict.

Attribution: the process by which we make sense of our environment through our perceptions of causality. An *attribution*, therefore, is a *belief* about the cause or causes of an event or an action.

Authority: the right to guide or direct the actions of others and extract from them responses that are appropriate to the attainment of an organization's goals.

Autonomous teamworking: a process whereby management gives formal groups the right to make decisions on how their work is performed on a group basis without reference to management.

Autonomous work group: a team of workers allocated to a significant segment of the workflow, with discretion concerning how the work will be carried out, and how tasks and responsibilities will be allocated, shared and rotated.

Availability heuristic: a predisposition to base a judgement of probability on the basis of information that is readily available.

Balanced scorecard: an approach to organizational effectiveness which uses a predetermined range of quantitative and qualitative measures to guide management decision making and to assess organizational performance.

Basic assumptions: in Edgar Schein's model of organization culture, these are the invisible, preconscious and 'taken-for-granted' understandings held by individuals with respect to aspects of human behaviour, the nature of reality and the organization's relationship to its environment.

Behaviour: the term given to the things that people do that can be directly observed.

Behaviour modification: a technique for encouraging desired behaviours and discouraging unwanted behaviours using *operant conditioning*.

Behavioural self-management: a technique for changing one's own behaviour by systematically manipulating cues, cognitive processes and contingent consequences.

Behavioural theory of decision making: a theory which recognizes that bounded rationality limits the making of optimal decisions.

Behaviourism: a psychological perspective which focuses on the study of observable behaviour, arguing that it is pointless to explain behaviour in terms of unobservable factors, such as needs, drives, thought processes, attitudes or motives.

Behaviourist or stimulus–response psychology: a perspective on the psychology of learning which argues that what we learn are chains of muscle movements. As brain or mental processes are not directly observable, they are not considered valid issues for study.

Biases: prejudiced predispositions or systematic distortions caused by the application of heuristics.

Big five: broad trait clusters that appear from research consistently to capture the traits that we use to describe ourselves and other people: openness, conscientiousness, extroversion, agreeableness and neuroticism ('OCEAN') (see **type** and **trait**).

Bounded instability: a state in which there is a mixture of order and disorder, many unpredictable events and changes, and in which an organization's behaviour has an irregular pattern.

Bounded rationality: the tendency of individuals to make decisions by constructing simplified models that extract the essential features from problems without capturing all their complexity.

Brainstorming: a technique in which all group members are encouraged to propose ideas spontaneously, without critiquing or censoring others' ideas. The alternative ideas so generated are not evaluated until all have been listed.

Bureaucracy: corresponds to the legal type of authority. It is a form of organization structure that is characterized by a specialization of labour, a specific authority hierarchy, a formal set of rules, and rigid promotion and selection criteria.

Business process re-engineering: the radical rethinking and redesign of organizational processes to achieve dramatic improvements in critical measures of performance, such as cost, quality, service and time.

Certainty: a condition in which individuals possess full knowledge of alternatives and a high probability of these alternatives being available; they can calculate the costs and benefits of each alternative and have high predictability of outcomes.

Centralization: the concentration of authority and responsibility for decision making in the hands of managers at the top of an organization's hierarchy.

Chain (or line) of command: the unbroken line of authority that extends from the top of the organization to the bottom and clarifies who reports to whom.

Change agent: any member of an organization seeking to promote, further, support, sponsor, initiate, implement or deliver change. Change agents are not necessarily senior managers and do not necessarily hold formal 'change management' job titles and positions.

Characteristics of mass production:	features of large-volume manufacturing work such as mechanical pacing, no choice of tools or methods, repetitiveness, minute subdivision of production, minimum skill requirements, and surface mental attention.
Charisma:	see **referent power.**
Charismatic authority:	the belief that the ruler had some special unique virtue, either religious or heroic. Religious prophets, charismatic politicians and pop and film stars all wield this type of power.
Classical decision theory:	a theory which assumes that decision makers are objective, have complete information and consider all possible alternatives and their consequences before selecting the optimal solution.
Coding:	the stage in the interpersonal communication process in which the transmitter chooses how to articulate and express that message for transmission to someone else.
Coercive power:	the ability of a leader to exert influence based on the belief of followers that the leader can administer penalties or sanctions that are considered to be unwelcome.
Cognitive psychology:	a perspective which accepts as legitimate the study of internal mental states and processes, and which seeks to develop explanations of human behaviour based on the study of these factors, even though they are not directly observable.
Cognitive or information-processing psychology:	a perspective on the psychology of learning which argues that what we learn are mental structures, and that mental processes are both important and are amenable to study, even though they cannot be directly observed.
Communication climate:	the prevailing organizational atmosphere in which ideas and information are exchanged; an *open* climate promotes collaborative working, which is discouraged by a *closed* communication climate.
Communication network analysis:	a technique that uses analysis of documents and data transmission to determine the source, direction and quantity of verbal and written communication between the dispersed members of a group.
Communication network chart:	a chart that indicates the source, direction and quantity of verbal and written communication between the dispersed members of a group.
Communication pattern analysis:	technique that uses direct observation to determine the source, direction and quantity of a verbal communication between congregated members of a group.
Communication process:	the transmission of information, and the exchange of meaning, between at least two people.
Communigram:	a chart that indicates the source, direction and quantity of verbal communication between the congregated members of a group.
Compensatory mechanisms:	processes that delay or deflect the replacement effects of new technology on jobs, and which can lead to the creation of new products and services, new organizations, new sectors and new jobs through technological innovation.
Complementarities:	the potential for mutually reinforcing effects when one or more business practices are operated in parallel or simultaneously. Practices are said to be complementary when doing more of one increases the returns for doing more of another.
Compliance:	a majority's influencing of a minority.
Concurrent feedback:	in a learning context, information which arrives during our behaviour and which can be used to control behaviour as it unfolds (see **delayed feedback**).
Conflict:	a process which begins when one party perceives that another party has negatively affected, or is about to negatively affect, something the first party cares about.
Conflict resolution:	a process which has as its objective the ending of the conflict between the disagreeing parties.
Conflict stimulation:	a process of engendering conflict between parties where none existed before, or escalating the current conflict level if it is too low.

Conjunctive task: a task whose accomplishment depends on the performance of the group's least talented member.

Consideration: a pattern of leadership behaviour that demonstrates sensitivity to relationships and to the social needs of employees (see **initiating structure**).

Consolidation: the process through which company ownership in a sector becomes concentrated in a smaller number of much larger and sometimes global enterprises.

Contingency theory of leadership: a perspective which argues that leaders, to be effective, must adjust their style in a manner consistent with aspects of the context, such as attributes of followers and the nature of the work being done.

Contingency theory of organization structure: a perspective which argues that an organization, to be effective, must adjust its structure in a manner consistent with the type of environment in which it operates, the technology it uses and other contextual factors.

Control concept: the process of imposing a pattern on previously haphazard activities, such as the operation of machinery, the interaction of machinery with people or the interactions between individuals.

Controlled performance: the process of setting performance standards, measuring actual performance, comparing actual with standard, and taking corrective action when necessary.

Conversion: a minority's influence of a majority.

Coping cycle: a human response to trauma and significant loss, suggesting that the individual typically (but not always) passes through a series of emotional stages including denial, anger, bargaining, depression and acceptance.

Cross-functional team: a team composed of employees from about the same hierarchical level but from different work areas or functions in the organization, who are brought together to complete a particular task.

Cybernetic analogy: a perspective which seeks to explain the learning process with reference to the components and operation of a feedback control system.

Death of distance: the observation that geographical separation no longer determines the costs or difficulties of global person-to-person communication.

Decentralization: the downward dispersion of authority and responsibility for decision making to operating units, branches and lower-level managers.

Decision making: a process of making choices from among several options.

Decoding: the stage in the interpersonal communication process in which the recipient interprets a message transmitted to them by someone else.

Deconstruction: within the perspective of *postmodernism*, the process of (1) identifying the assumptions underpinning arguments and claims about 'truth' and 'reality'; (2) challenging and/or rejecting those assumptions; and (3) asking whose interests are served by representing 'the truth' in that manner in the first place.

Deindividuation: an increased state of anonymity that loosens normal constraints on individuals' behaviour, reduces their sense of responsibility and leads to an increase in impulsive and antisocial acts.

Delayed feedback: in a learning context, information which is received after a task is completed, and which can be used to influence future performance (see **concurrent feedback**).

Departmental-ization: a process of grouping together employees who share a common supervisor and resources, who are jointly responsible for performance and who tend to identify and collaborate with each other.

Dependent variable: the factor or variable in a research investigation whose behaviour is to be explained; in a study of how variations in pay affect individual work output, output is the dependent variable (because it is thought to *depend* on level of pay) (see **independent variable**).

Descriptive models of decision making:	models of decision making which investigate how individuals actually make decisions.
Differentiation:	the degree to which the tasks and the work of individuals, groups and units are divided up within an organization.
Differentiation perspective:	a view in organization culture theory which regards an organization as consisting of sub-cultures. Each sub-culture represents a fenced-in island of localized consensus, beyond which ambiguity reigns.
Disjunctive task:	a task whose accomplishment depends on the performance of the group's most talented member.
Distributive bargaining:	a negotiating strategy in which a fixed sum of resources is divided up. It leads to a win–lose situation between the parties.
Double-loop learning:	the ability not only to maintain performance at a predetermined standard but also to challenge and redefine the assumptions underlying that standard to improve performance significantly (see **single-loop learning**).
Drives:	innate biological determinants of human behaviour activated by deprivation.
Dysfunctional conflict:	a form of conflict which does not support organization goals and hinders organizational performance.
Employment cycle:	the sequence of stages through which all employees pass in each working position they hold, from recruitment and selection, to termination; the stages of the employment cycle define the activities of the personnel function (see **personnel management**).
Empowerment:	the term given to organizational arrangements that allow employees more autonomy, discretion and unsupervised decision-making responsibility.
Enacted environment:	the parts of an environment perceived by an organization's managers.
Encounter stage of socialization:	a period of learning in the process of socialization during which the new recruit learns about organizational expectations.
Environment:	issues, trends, events and other factors outside the boundaries of an organization but which can influence internal decisions and behaviours.
Environmental complexity:	the range of external factors—customers, suppliers, regulatory agencies, competitors—relevant to the activities of the organization; the more factors, the higher the complexity (see **environmental uncertainty**).
Environmental determinism:	a perspective which claims that internal organizational responses are wholly or mainly shaped, influenced or determined by external environmental factors.
Environmental dynamism:	the pace of change in relevant factors external to the organization; the greater the pace of change, the more dynamic the environment (see **environmental uncertainty**).
Environmental scanning:	the term for a number of techniques for identifying and predicting the potential impact of external trends and developments on the internal functioning of an organization.
Environmental uncertainty:	the degree of unpredictable turbulence and change in the external political, economic, social, technological, legislative and ecological context in which an organization operates; the more the dimensions of the external context are interrelated, the higher the environmental uncertainty (see **environmental complexity** and **environmental dynamism**).
Equity theory:	a process theory of motivation which argues that the perception of unfairness in a social or organizational setting leads to tension, which in turn motivates the individual to act to resolve that unfairness.
Expectancy:	the individual's perceived likelihood that effort will result in good performance. As a subjective probability, expectancy can be measured on a scale from 0 (no chance) to 1 (certainty) (see **expectancy theory** of motivation).
Expectancy theory:	a process theory of motivation which argues that the strength or 'force' of an individual's motivation to perform well is expressed as the product of the *valence* of the outcome from

that behaviour, the *expectancy* that effort will lead to good performance and the *instrumentality* of good performance in leading to valued outcomes (see **valence**, **instrumentality** and **expectancy**).

Expert power: the ability of a leader to exert influence based on the belief of followers that the leader has superior knowledge relevant to the situation and the task in hand.

Explanatory models of decision making: models of decision making which seek to account for decisions made by individuals, groups and organizations.

Explicit knowledge: knowledge and understanding which is codified, expressed and available to anyone (see **tacit knowledge**).

Explosive instability: a state in which there is no order or pattern.

External work team differentiation: the degree to which a work team stands out from its organizational context, in terms of its membership, temporal scope and territory.

External work team integration: the degree to which a work team is linked with the larger organization of which it is a part. It is measured in terms of how its goals and activities are co-ordinated and synchronized with those of other managers, peers, customers and suppliers.

Extinction: in behavioural psychology, the attempt to eliminate or to weaken undesirable behaviours by attaching no consequences, positive or negative. Indifference and silence thus follow the undesired behaviour (see **punishment**).

Extrinsic feedback: in a learning context, information which comes from our environment, such as the visual and aural information needed to drive a car (see **intrinsic feedback**).

Extrinsic motivation: a form of motivation that stresses valued outcomes or benefits provided by others such as promotion, pay increases, a bigger office desk, praise and recognition.

Extrinsic rewards: valued outcomes or benefits provided by others, such as promotion, pay increases, a bigger office desk, praise and recognition (see **intrinsic rewards**).

Feedback: in the context of interpersonal communication, mechanisms through which the transmitter of a message in interpersonal communication can detect whether and how a message has been received and decoded.

Feedback: in the context of learning, information concerning the outcomes of our behaviour.

Field experiment: a research design which approximates in a work organization setting the structure of a laboratory experiment, with a 'control' group and a 'treatment' group whose responses to an intervention (e.g. new payment system, job redesign, change of layout) can be compared in order to isolate the effects of that intervention.

Force-field analysis: a technique for assessing the factors that encourage and the factors that resist movement towards a desired target situation, thus allowing an assessment of the viability of the change and suggesting action to alter the balance of forces, if necessary.

Fordism: the application of scientific management principles to workers' jobs, the installation of single-purpose machine tools to manufacture standardized parts and the introduction of the mechanized assembly line.

Formal group: a group which has been consciously created to accomplish a defined part of an organization's collective purpose. The formal group's functions are the tasks which are assigned to it, and for which it is officially held responsible.

Formal organization: a collection of work groups that have been consciously designed by senior management to maximize efficiency and achieve organizational goals.

Formal status: a collection of rights and obligations associated with a position, as distinct from the person who may occupy that position.

Formalization: the degree to which formal procedures and rules exist and are used within an organization.

Fragmentation (conflict) perspective:	a view in organization culture theory which regards an organization as consisting of a loosely structured and incompletely shared system that emerges dynamically as cultural members experience each other, events and the organization's contextual features.
Functional conflict:	a form of conflict which supports organization goals and improves performance.
Functional foremanship:	an approach devised by Frederick Taylor in which the job of the general foreman was divided into its constituent parts. Each of the main parts was given to a different individual, who would oversee and be responsible for that aspect of a worker's job.
Functional relationship:	a situation where staff department specialists have the authority to insist that line managers implement their instructions concerning a particular issue.
Future shock:	the stress and disorientation suffered by people when they are subjected to excessive change. Alvin Toffler called *future shock* 'the disease of change'.
Generalized other:	what we understand other people expect of us, in terms of our attitudes, values, beliefs and behaviour.
Globalization:	the intensification of worldwide social relations which link distant localities in such a way that local happenings are shaped by events occurring many miles away, and vice versa.
Goal setting:	a process theory of motivation and a motivational technique, based on the argument that work performance can be explained with reference to characteristics of the objectives being pursued, such as goal difficulty, goal specificity and knowledge of results.
Great man theory:	a historical perspective based on the premise that the fate of societies, and organizations, is in the hands of key, powerful, idiosyncratic (male) individuals who by force of personality reach positions of influence from which they can direct and dominate the lives of others.
Grid organization development:	an organization-wide, structured approach to organization development, based on a diagnostic approach to developing an effective management style, and on a comprehensive six-phase organizational change model.
Groupthink:	a mode of thinking that people engage in when they are deeply involved in a cohesive in-group, when the members' strivings for unanimity override their motivation to appraise realistically the alternative courses of action.
Group cohesion:	the number and strength of mutual positive attitudes towards group members.
Group leadership:	the performance of those acts which help the group to achieve its objectives.
Group norms:	expected modes of behaviour and beliefs that are established either formally or informally by a group. Norms guide behaviour and facilitate interaction by specifying the kinds of reactions expected or acceptable in a particular situation.
Group polarization:	the process in which individuals in a group begin by taking a moderate stance on an issue related to a common value and, after having discussed it, end up taking a more extreme decision than the average of members' decisions. The extremes could be more risky or more safe.
Group power:	the ability of a leader to exert influence based on the belief of followers that the leader has collective support from a team or group.
Group process:	the patterns of interactions between the members of a group.
Group relations:	the interactions within and between groups, and to the stable arrangements that result from them.
Group sanction:	both the punishments and rewards that are given by members to others in a group in the process of enforcing group norms. Punishments are a negative sanction and rewards are a positive sanction.
Group socialization:	the process whereby members learn the values, symbols and expected behaviours of the groups to which they belong.

Group structure: the relatively stable pattern of relationships between different group members. There is no single group structure, and the concept can be expressed in several and overlapping ways.

Group self-organization: the tendency of groups to form interests, develop autonomy and establish identities.

Growth need strength: a measure of the readiness and capability of an individual to respond positively to job enrichment.

Habituation: the decrease in our perceptual response to stimuli once they have become familiar.

Halo effect: a judgement based on a single striking characteristic, such as an aspect of dress, speech, posture or nationality. Halos can be positive or negative.

Hard HRM: a human resource management perspective which emphasizes the full utilization of employees in a formal, rational and dispassionate manner, similar to the way that any other resources available to the organization are used (see **soft HRM**).

Hawthorne effect: the tendency of people being observed, as part of a research effort, to behave differently than they otherwise would.

Heuristics: simple and approximate rules, guiding procedures, shortcuts or strategies that are used to solve problems.

Hierarchy: the number of levels of authority to be found in an organization.

High-context culture: a culture in which people tend to rely heavily on a range of social and non-verbal clues when communicating with others and interpreting their messages (see **low-context culture**).

High-performance work system: a form of organization that operates at levels of excellence far beyond those of comparable systems.

Human-centred manufacturing: the design of production technologies in a way that complements human skills and abilities, rather than distances or replaces them.

Human relations approach: a school of management thought based on the research findings of Elton Mayo which emphasizes the importance of social processes at work.

Human resource management: a managerial perspective, with theoretical and prescriptive dimensions, which argues for the need to establish an integrated series of personnel policies consistent with organization strategy, thus ensuring quality of working life, high commitment and performance from employees, and organizational effectiveness and competitive advantage (see **personnel management**).

Hygiene factors: aspects of work which remove job dissatisfaction but which do not contribute to motivation and performance; they include pay, company policy, supervisory style, status, security and working conditions; also known as *context factors* (see also **motivator factors**).

Identification: the incorporation of the thoughts, feelings and actions of others into one's self-esteem or reducing the threat from powerful others. Typically, it takes the form of 'I want'.

Idiographic: an approach to the study of personality which emphasizes the uniqueness of the individual, challenging the assumption that we can all be measured and compared on the same dimensions (see **nomothetic**).

Impression management: the process whereby people seek to control the image others have of them.

Independent variable: the factor or variable in a research investigation which is deliberately manipulated by the researcher to discover what effect this has on another factor or variable; in a study of how variations in pay affect individual work output, pay is manipulated and is the independent variable (see **dependent variable**).

Individualism –collectivism: the tendency to take care of oneself and one's family versus the tendency to work together for the collective good.

Influencing: the ability to affect another's attitudes, beliefs or behaviours—seen only in its effect—without using coercion or formal position, and in such a way that influencees believe that they are acting in their own best interests.

Informal group:	a collection of individuals who become a group when members develop interdependencies, influence one another's behaviour and contribute to mutual need satisfaction.
Informal organization:	the network of relationships that spontaneously establish themselves between members of an organization on the basis of their common interests and friendships.
Information power:	the ability of a leader to exert influence based on the belief of followers that the leader has privileged access to information that is not public knowledge.
Initiating structure:	a pattern of leadership behaviour that emphasizes performance of the work in hand and the achievement of product and service goals (see **consideration**).
Initiative and incentive system:	a form of job design practice in which workers are given a task to perform by management, which also provides them with a financial incentive. Workers are then left to use their own initiative as to how to complete the task and which tools to use.
Innovative decisions:	decisions which address novel problems, lack pre-specified courses of action and are made by senior managers.
Instrumentality:	the individual's perceived likelihood that good performance will lead to valued rewards. As a subjective probability, instrumentality can be measured on a scale from 0 (no chance) to 1 (certainty) (see **expectancy theory** of motivation).
Interactions:	in George Homans' theory, these refer to the two-way communications between group members.
Interaction process analysis:	a technique used to categorize the content of speech.
Interactionist frame of reference:	a perspective on conflict which sees it as a positive and necessary force within organizations that is essential for their effective performance.
Integration:	the required level to which units in an organization are linked together, and their respective degree of independence. Integrative mechanisms include rules and procedures and direct managerial control.
Integration (or unitary) perspective:	a view of organization culture which regards it as monolithic, characterized by consistency, organization-wide consensus and clarity. It holds that these integrating features will lead to improved organizational effectiveness through greater employee commitment and employee control, as measured by productivity and profitability.
Integrative bargaining:	a negotiation strategy that seeks to increase the total amount of resources. It creates a win–win situation between the parties.
Intensive technology:	a technology that is applied to tasks that are performed in no predetermined order.
Intergroup development:	an organization development intervention which seeks to change the perceptions and attitudes that different groups in an organization hold with respect to each other, and to improve their interaction and collaboration. Variants of this technique are also known as *intergroup confrontation* and *peacemaking*.
Intermittent reinforcement:	the procedure whereby a reward is provided only occasionally following correct responses, and not for every correct response.
Internal work team differentiation:	the degree to which a team's members possess different skills and knowledge that contribute towards the achievement of the team's objective.
Intrinsic feedback:	in a learning context, information which comes from within our bodies, from the muscles, joints, skin and other internal mechanisms such as that concerned with maintaining balance when walking (and is also called 'proprioception') (see **extrinsic feedback**).
Intrinsic motivation:	a form of motivation that stresses valued outcomes or benefits that come from within the individual, such as feelings of satisfaction, competence, self-esteem and accomplishment.
Intrinsic rewards:	valued outcomes or benefits which come from within the individual, such as feelings of satisfaction, competence, self-esteem and accomplishment (see **extrinsic rewards**).

Introjection: a formerly external regulation or value that has been 'taken in' by an individual, and is now enforced through internal pressures such as guilt, anxiety or related self-esteem dynamics.

Job definition: determining the task requirements of each job in the organization. It is the first decision in the process of organizing.

Job description (or post profile): a summary statement of what an individual should do on the job.

Job Diagnostic Survey (JDS): an opinion questionnaire designed to evaluate the motivating potential of jobs by measuring the five core job dimensions of skill variety, task identity, task significance, autonomy and feedback (see **motivating potential score**).

Job enrichment: a technique for broadening the experience of work to enhance employee need satisfaction and to improve work motivation and performance.

Job enlargement: a work design method in which tasks are recombined to widen the scope of a job.

Job rotation: a work design method in which employees are switched from task to task at regular intervals.

Just-in-time systems: managing inventory (stock) in which items are delivered when they are needed in the production process, instead of being stored by the manufacturer.

Joint venture: an arrangement in which two or more companies remain independent but establish a new organization that they jointly own and manage.

Knowledge management: the conversion of tacit knowledge into explicit knowledge so that it can be shared with others, turning individual learning into organizational learning (see **learning organization**).

Leadership: the process of establishing goals and influencing the behaviour of others in the pursuit of effective goal achievement.

Lean production: an approach to manufacturing which combines conventional machine pacing, standardized work methods, just-in-time materials flow, continuous improvement or *kaizen*, problem-solving teams, instant problem rectification, and powerful first-line supervision.

Learning: the process of acquiring knowledge through experience which leads to an enduring change in behaviour.

Learning organization: a form of organization that enables the learning of its members in such a way that it creates positively valued outcomes, such as innovation, efficiency, better alignment with the environment and competitive advantage; also described as a *learning company*.

Least preferred coworker score: an assessment of the kind of person with whom a leader feels they could not work effectively.

Legitimate authority: a form of power based on formal, written rules which have the force of law. The authority of present-day presidents, chief executive officers and cardinals is based on the position that they hold.

Legitimate power: the ability of a leader to exert influence based on the belief of followers that the leader has authority to issue orders, which they in turn have an obligation to accept; also referred to as *position power*, as this depends on the leader's formal organizational position and title.

Line employees: those workers who are directly responsible for manufacturing goods or providing a service.

Locus of control: an individual's generalized belief about internal (self-control) versus external control (control by the situation or by others).

Long-linked technology: a technology that is applied to a series of programmed tasks performed in a predetermined order.

Long-term– short-term orientation:	the ability to pursue long-term and general goals versus short-term gain and advantage.
Low-context culture:	a culture in which people tend to focus on the written and spoken word when communicating with others and interpreting their messages (see **high-context culture**).
McDonaldization:	an approach to work organization based on efficiency, calculability, predictability and control, using sophisticated technology to enhance these objectives by limiting employee discretion and creativity.
Machiavellianism:	a personality trait or style of behaviour towards others which is characterized by (1) the use of guile and deceit in interpersonal relations; (2) a cynical view of the nature of other people; and (3) a lack of concern with conventional morality.
Machine bureaucracy:	a type of organization structure that possesses all the bureaucratic characteristics. The important decisions are made at the top, while at the bottom, standardized procedures are used to exercise control.
Managerial enactment:	the active modification of perceived and selected parts of the organization's environment by managers.
Masculinity– femininity:	the extent to which highly assertive masculine values predominate (acquisition of money at the expense of others) versus showing sensitivity and concern for others' welfare and the quality of life.
Material technology:	technology—apparatus—that can be seen, touched and heard.
Matrix structure:	a type of organization design that combines two different, traditional types of structure, usually a functional structure and a project structure, which results in an employee being part of both a functional department and a project team, and in consequence, having two reporting relationships.
Maximizing:	a decision-making approach where all alternatives are compared and evaluated in order to find the best solution to a problem.
Mechanistic structure:	a type of organization structure possessing a high degree of task specialization, many rules, tight specification of individual responsibility and authority, and one in which decision making is centralized.
Mediating technology:	a technology that links independent but standardized tasks.
Mediation:	a process in which a neutral third party to the conflict assists in the achievement of a negotiated solution by using reason, persuasion and the presentation of alternatives.
Merger:	a situation in which two companies voluntarily join together, pool the ownership interests of the two sets of shareholders, who come to own the new combined entity.
Metamorphosis stage of socialization:	the period in socialization during which the new employee adjusts to their organization's values, attitudes, motives, norms and required behaviours.
Motivating potential score:	a measure of how motivating a job is likely to be for an individual, taking into account the core job dimensions of skill variety, task identity, task significance, autonomy and feedback (see **Job Diagnostic Survey**).
Motivation:	the cognitive decision-making process through which goal-directed behaviour is initiated, energized and directed and maintained (see **motives**).
Motivator factors:	aspects of work which lead to high levels of job satisfaction, motivation and performance, and include achievement, recognition, responsibility, advancement, growth and the work itself; also know as *content factors* (see **hygiene factors**).
Motive:	socially acquired needs activated by a desire for their fulfilment (see **motivation**).

Need for achievement (nAch):	a general concern with meeting standards of excellence, the desire to be successful in competition and the motivation to excel in an activity significant to the individual.
Need for power (*n*Pow):	the desire to make an impact on others, change people or events, and make a difference in life.
Negative reinforcement:	in behavioural psychology, the attempt to encourage desirable behaviours by *withdrawing negative consequences* when the desired behaviour occurs. The desired behaviour thus leads to the withdrawal of negative consequences (see **positive reinforcement**).
Network organization:	a collection of essentially equal agents or agencies that are in informal relationships with each other based on affiliation.
New leader:	an indispensable and inspirational visionary, a coach, a facilitator concerned with building a shared sense of purpose and mission, with creating a culture which ensures that everyone is aligned with the organization's goals and is skilled and empowered to go and achieve them.
Noise:	factors extraneous to the interpersonal communication process, but which interfere with or distract attention from the transmission and reception of the intended meaning. Noise is 'anything that gets in the way'.
Nomothetic:	an approach to the study of personality which emphasizes the identification of universal personality traits and looks for systematic relationships between different aspects of personality (see **idiographic**).
Non-verbal communication:	the process of coding meaning through behaviours such as facial expressions, limb gestures and body postures that do not involve the use of words.
Norms:	expected modes of behaviour.
Open system:	a system that interacts, in a purposive way, with its external environment in order to survive.
Operational definition:	the definition of a term or variable that is the method used to measure the incidence of that variable in practice.
Organic structure:	a type of organization structure possessing little task specialization, few rules, a high degree of individual responsibility and authority, and one in which decision making is delegated.
Organization:	a social arrangement for achieving controlled performance in pursuit of collective goals.
Organization chart:	a pictorial record which shows the formal relations which the company intends should prevail within it.
Organization culture:	a collection of relatively uniform and enduring values, beliefs, customs, traditions and practices that are shared by an organization's members, learned by new recruits and transmitted from one generation of employees to the next.
Organization development:	an effort (1) planned, (2) organization-wide and (3) managed from the top to (4) increase organization development and health through (5) planned interventions in the organization's 'process', using behavioural science knowledge.
Organization development intervention:	a specific methodology or technique used to effect change in the target organization or section of the organization, to improve organizational effectiveness (however defined).
Organization structure:	the formal system of task and reporting relationships that controls, co-ordinates and motivates employees so that they work together to achieve organizational goals.
Organization values:	those things that have personal or organizational worth or meaning to the founders or senior management. Values are typically based on moral, societal or religious precepts that are learned in childhood and modified through experience.
Organizational behaviour:	the study of the structure, functioning and performance of organizations, and the behaviour of groups and individuals within them.

Organizational choice:	the argument that work and organization design are not uniquely determined by technology, that the technical system does not determine the social system.
Organizational dilemma:	the perennial question of how to reconcile the potential inconsistency between individual needs and aspirations on the one hand, and the collective purpose of the organization on the other.
Organizational effectiveness:	a multidimensional concept defined differently by different stakeholders and stakeholder groups, using a wide range of quantitative and qualitative measures; there is no common agreed definition of this term.
Organizational misbehaviour:	anything that workers do in the workplace which they are not supposed to do, as defined by management
Organizational socialization:	the process through which an individual's pattern of behaviour, and their values, attitudes and motives, are influenced to conform with those seen as desirable in a particular organization.
Pavlovian conditioning:	also known as *classical* and as *respondent conditioning,* is a technique for associating an established response (a dog salivating at the sight of food, for example) with a new stimulus (say, the sound of a bell) (see **Skinnerian conditioning**).
Perception:	the dynamic psychological process responsible for attending to, organizing and interpreting sensory data.
Perceptual filters:	characteristics of the individual that interfere with the effective transmission and receipt of messages, such as predispositions to hear, or not to hear, particular types of information, or preoccupations which divert attention elsewhere.
Perceptual organization:	the process through which incoming stimuli are organized or patterned in systematic and meaningful ways.
Perceptual set:	an individual's predisposition to respond to events in a particular manner. A perceptual set is also known as a *mental set.* As we tend to perceive what we expect to perceive, this can also be called our *perceptual expectations.*
Perceptual world:	the individual's personal internal image, map or picture of their social, physical and organizational environment.
Peripheral norms:	socially defined standards relating to behaviour and beliefs which are important but not crucial to a group's objective and survival.
Personalized power:	a form of power that is self-serving and used for personal gain, influence and advancement.
Personality:	the psychological qualities that influence an individual's characteristic behaviour patterns in a distinctive and consistent manner, across different situations and over time.
Personnel management:	the specialist management function responsible for determining and implementing the policies and procedures which determine the stages of the employment cycle, in a manner that contributes both to the well-being of individual employees and to organizational effectiveness (see **employment cycle** and **human resource management**).
PESTLE analysis:	the identification of the Political, Economic, Social, Technological, Legal and Ecological factors affecting an organization.
Phenomenology:	a broad social scientific perspective which claims that the social world has no external, objective, observable truth but instead that our reality is *socially constructed*; the social science task is not to gather facts and measurements but to study patterns of meanings and interpretations, to discover how experience is understood.
Pivotal norms:	socially defined standards relating to behaviour and beliefs which are central to a group's objective and survival.
Pluralist frame of reference:	a perspective on conflict which sees organizations as consisting of different natural interest groups, each with their own potentially constructive, legitimate interests, which make conflict between them inevitable.

Political model of organization: a perspective that holds that organizations are made up of groups that have separate interests, goals and values, and in which power and influence are needed in order to reach decisions.

Politics: activities undertaken within an organization to acquire, develop and use power and other resources to obtain one's preferred outcomes in a situation in which there is uncertainty or an absence of consensus about choices.

Positive reinforcement: in behavioural psychology, the attempt to encourage desirable behaviours by introducing *positive consequences* when the desired behaviour occurs. The desired behaviour thus leads to positive consequences (see **negative reinforcement**).

Positivism: a broad social scientific perspective which assumes that the social world and its properties can be studied using objective methods, and not through the use of subjective inference; the organization in this perspective possesses an objective reality or truth that exists independently of anyone's attitudes towards or interpretations of it.

Position power: see **legitimate power**.

Postmodernism: a mode of thinking, an epistemology, which focuses on the way in which language is used symbolically and selectively to construct versions of 'truth' and 'reality' to serve the interests of particular social groupings; postmodernism consequently rejects the positivistic approach which underlies modern science (natural and social) as a way of developing our understanding of the world.

Post-modern organization: an idealized concept—is a networked, information-rich, delayered, downsized, lean, boundaryless, high-commitment, organization employing highly skilled, well-paid autonomous knowledge workers.

Power: the capacity of individuals to overcome resistance on the part of others, to exert their will and to produce results consistent with their interests and objectives.

Power distance: the extent to which an unequal distribution of power is accepted by members of a society.

Pre-arrival stage of socialization: the period of learning in the process of socialization that occurs before an applicant joins an organization.

Predictive validity: the extent to which scores on a test or assessment can accurately predict performance or behaviour on other measures.

Prescriptive models of decision making: models which recommend how individuals should behave in order to achieve a desired outcome.

Process consultation: an organization development intervention in which an external consultant acts in a facilitating, supporting, advisory and catalytic capacity to enhance the diagnostic, conceptual and action-planning skills of managers in the organization.

Processual/contextual theory: a theoretical perspective which argues that, to understand organizational change fully, it is necessary to consider how the substance, the context and the process of change interact with each other. In this perspective, the 'unit of analysis' that is to be understood is 'the process of change in context'.

Production team: a stable number of individuals in a relationship involving shared and recognized production goals, with work status defined through a system of social roles and behavioural norms supported by a set of incentives and sanctions.

Project team: a collection of employees from different work areas in an organization brought together to accomplish a specific task within a finite time.

Professional bureaucracy: a type of organization which possesses all the bureaucratic characteristics. In addition, there are few levels between the strategic apex and the operating staff, control of which is achieved through professional indoctrination.

Projective test: a form of personality assessment based on abstract or ambiguous images, which the person being assessed is asked to interpret, in a manner which reveals their inner feelings, preoccupations and motives, as these are 'projected' into their interpretations of the images presented (see **thematic apperception test**).

Psychological contract:	an implicit set of obligations and expectations concerning what the individual and the organization expect to give to and receive from each other.
Psychological group:	two or more people, in face-to-face interaction, each aware of his or her membership in the group, each aware of the others who belong to the group, and each aware of their positive interdependence as they strive to achieve mutual goals.
Psychometrics:	an area of psychology concerned with the systematic testing, measurement and assessment of intelligence, aptitudes and personality.
Punishment:	in behavioural psychology, the attempt to eliminate or to weaken undesirable behaviours through the application of negative consequences, or by withholding a positive consequence, following undesired behaviour. Punishment thus follows the undesired behaviour (see **extinction**).
Quality circles:	shop-floor employees from the same department, who meet for a few hours each week to discuss ways of improving their work environment.
Radical frame of reference:	a perspective on conflict which sees it as an inevitable consequence of exploitative employment relations in a capitalist economy.
Rationalism:	a theory that reason is the foundation of certainty in knowledge.
Rationality:	the use of scientific reasoning, empiricism and positivism; and with the use of decision criteria of evidence, logical argument and reasoning.
Rational decisions:	refer to choices based on rationality, that is, on a rational mode of thinking.
Rational economic model:	assumes that decision making is and should be a rational process consisting of a sequence of steps that enhance the probability of attaining a desired outcome.
Rational model of organizations:	is a perspective that holds that behaviour within organizations is not random; but that goals are clear, and choices are made on the basis of reason in a logical way. In making decisions, the objective is defined, alternatives are identified, and the option with the greatest chance of achieving the objective is selected.
Readiness for change:	a predisposition, perhaps even an impatience, to welcome and embrace change. Where readiness is high, management may be able to implement change without too many problems. Where readiness is low, however, some preparatory work may be required to increase readiness among those affected.
Referent power:	the ability of a leader to exert influence based on the belief of followers that the leader has desirable abilities and personality traits that can and should be copied, also referred to as *charisma*.
Reliability:	the degree to which an assessment or test produces consistent results when the assessment is repeated or when it is conducted in comparable ways.
Replacement mechanisms:	processes through which intelligent machines are used to substitute for people in work organizations, leading to unemployment.
Representative heuristic:	a predisposition to base a judgement of probability on the basis of things which are familiar.
Resistance:	a more or less covert behaviour which counteracts and restricts management attempts to exercise power and control in the workplace.
Resistance to change:	an inability, or an unwillingness, to discuss or to accept organizational changes that are perceived in some way to be damaging or threatening to the individual.
Risk-seeking propensity:	the willingness of an individual to choose options which entail risks.
Responsibility:	an obligation placed on a person who occupies a certain position in the organization structure to perform a task, function or assignment.
Reward power:	the ability of a leader to exert influence based on the belief of followers that the leader has access to valued rewards which will be dispensed in return for compliance with instructions.

Risk: a condition in which managers have a high knowledge of alternatives, know the probability of these being available, can calculate the costs and know the benefits of each alternative and have a medium predictability of outcomes.

Risky-shift phenomenon: the tendency of a group to make decisions that are riskier than those that the members of the group would previously have recommended individually.

Role: the pattern of behaviour expected by others from a person occupying a certain position in an organization hierarchy.

Role conflict: the simultaneous existence of two or more sets of role expectations on a focal person in such a way that compliance with one makes it difficult to comply with the others.

Role set: the collection of persons most immediately affected by the focal person's role performance, who depend upon the focal person for their own role performance, and who therefore have a stake in it.

Routine decision: decision that is made according to established procedures and rules.

Rules: procedures or obligations explicitly stated and written down in organization manuals.

Satisficing: a decision-making approach where the first solution that is judged to be 'good enough' (i.e. satisfactory and sufficient) is selected, and the search is then ended.

Scenario building: the development of one or more likely pictures of the dimensions and characteristics of the future for the organization, based on environmental scanning, and with an attempt to identify the most probable future scenario as a basis for current planning and action.

Schedule of reinforcement: in behavioural psychology, establishes the pattern and frequency of rewards contingent on the display of desirable behaviour.

Scientific management: a form of job design theory and practice which stresses short, repetitive work cycles; detailed, prescribed task sequences; a separation of task conception from task execution; and motivation based on economic rewards.

Selective attention: the ability, often exercised unconsciously, to choose from the stream of sensory data, to concentrate on particular elements and to ignore others.

Self-actualization: the desire for personal fulfilment, to develop one's potential, to become everything that one is capable of becoming.

Self-concept: the way in which we view ourselves, the set of perceptions that we have about ourselves.

Self-esteem: the part of the self which is concerned with how we evaluate ourselves.

Self-fulfilling prophecy: is an expectation that leads to a certain pattern of behaviour whose consequences confirm the expectation.

Sensitivity training: a technique for enhancing individual self-awareness and self-perceptions, and for changing behaviour, through unstructured group discussion.

Sentiments: in George Homans' theory, these refer to the feelings, attitudes and beliefs held by group members.

Shaping: the selective reinforcement of chosen behaviours in a manner that progressively establishes a desired behaviour or pattern of behaviours.

Shared frame of reference: a set of assumptions that are held in common by group members, which shape their thinking, decisions, actions and interactions, while being constantly defined and reinforced through those interactions.

Single-loop learning: the ability to use feedback to make continuous adjustments and adaptations, to maintain performance (individual, group, organizational) at a predetermined standard (see **double-loop learning**).

Situational leadership: an approach to determining the most effective style of influencing, taking into account the amounts of direction and support the leader gives, and the readiness and maturity of followers to perform a particular task.

Skinnerian conditioning: also known as *instrumental* and as *operant conditioning,* is a technique for associating a response or a behaviour (a rat in a box nudges a lever) with its consequence (when the lever is nudged, food is delivered). If the consequence is desirable, the frequency of the behaviour is likely to increase (see **Pavlovian conditioning**).

Social construction of reality: a perspective which, like *phenomenology,* argues that our social and organizational surroundings possess no ultimate truth or reality but are instead determined by the way in which we experience and understand those worlds which we construct and reconstruct for ourselves in interaction with others.

Social facilitation: the strengthening of the dominant (prevalent or likely) responses due to the presence of others.

Social identity: that part of the self-concept which comes from our membership of groups. It contributes to our self-esteem.

Social influence: the process where attitudes and behaviour are influenced by the real or implied presence of others.

Social loafing: the tendency for individuals to exert less effort when working as part of a group than when working alone.

Social representations: refer to the beliefs, ideas, values, objects, people and events that are constructed by current group members, and which are transmitted to its new members.

Social role: the set of expectations that others hold of an occupant of a position.

Social status: the relative ranking that a person holds and the value of that person as measured by a group.

Social technology: the technology which seeks to order the behaviour and relationships of people in systematic, purposive ways through structures of co-ordination, control, motivation and reward.

Socialization: the process through which an individual's pattern of behaviour, and their values, attitudes and motives, are influenced to conform with those seen as desirable in a particular organization, society or sub-culture.

Socialized power: a form of power that is used for the common good, on behalf of the whole organization.

Sociogram: a chart that shows the liking (social attraction) relationships between individual members of a group.

Sociometry: the study of interpersonal feelings and relationships within groups.

Socio-technical system: a system which possesses both a material technology (apparatus) and a social organization (job specifications, management structure).

Soft HRM: a human resource management perspective which emphasizes the need to develop the potential and resourcefulness of employees in order to encourage commitment and high performance in pursuit of organizational goals (see **hard HRM**).

Stable equilibrium: a state in which the elements are always in, or quickly return to, a state of balance.

Span of control: the number of subordinates who report directly to a single manager or supervisor.

Stakeholder: anyone likely to be affected, directly or indirectly, by an organizational change or programme of changes.

Staff employees: workers who are in advisory positions and who use their specialized expertise to support the efforts of line employees (see **line employees**).

Stereotype: a category, or personality type, to which we consign people on the basis of their membership of some known group.

Strategic alliance: an arrangement in which two firms agree to co-operate to achieve specific commercial objectives.

Strategic change: a term used to describe organizational redesign or refocusing that is major, radical, 'frame-breaking' or 'mould-breaking' or 'paradigmatic' in its nature and implications. The term 'strategic' denotes scale, magnitude or depth. Deciding whether change is strategic or not depends on specific organizational circumstances.

Strategic choice: the view that holds that the environments, markets and technology of an organization are the result of senior management decisions.

Strategic contingencies: events and activities, both inside and outside an organization, that are essential for it to attain its goals.

Structured task: a task with clear goals, few correct or satisfactory solutions and outcomes, few ways of performing it, and clear criteria of success (see **unstructured task**).

Superleader: a leader who is able to develop leadership capacity in others, developing and empowering them, reducing their dependence on formal leaders, stimulating their motivation, commitment and creativity.

Surface manifestations of culture: in Edgar Schein's model of organization culture, these are the most visible and most accessible forms of culture, which are the visible and audible behaviour patterns and objects.

Survey feedback: an organization development intervention in which the results of an opinion survey are fed back to respondents in the organization in a manner that triggers problem solving with respect to the issues highlighted by the survey findings.

Synergy: the positive or negative result of the interaction of two or more components, producing an outcome that is different from the sum of the individual components.

System: something that functions by virtue of the interdependence of its component parts.

Systems concept: a management perspective which emphasizes the interdependence between the various parts of an organization, and also between the organization and its environment.

Systematic soldiering: the conscious and deliberate restriction of output by operators.

Tacit knowledge: personal knowledge and understanding, specific to the individual, difficult to articulate or to communicate to others because it derives from accumulated experience and includes insights, intuition, hunches and judgements (see **explicit knowledge**).

Task analysability: the degree to which standardized solutions are available to solve problems that arise.

Task variety: the number of new and different demands that a task places on an individual or a function.

Team autonomy: the extent to which a team experiences freedom, independence and discretion in decisions in the performance of its tasks.

Team building: an organization development intervention which seeks to improve team performance by helping members to understand their own team roles more clearly, and to improve their interaction and collaboration.

Team performance: externally focused concerns meeting the needs and expectations of outsiders such as customers, company colleagues or fans. It is assessed using measures such as quantity, quality and time.

Team role: an individual's tendency to behave in particular preferred ways which contribute to and interrelate with other members in a team.

Team viability: the social dimension which is internally focused and concerns the enhancement of the group's capability to perform effectively in the future. It is assessed using measures such as group cohesion and mutual liking.

Technical complexity: the degree of predictability about and control over the final product permitted by the technology used; it is usually related to the level of mechanization used in the production process.

Technological determinism: the argument that technology can be used to explain the nature of jobs, work groupings, hierarchy, skills, values and attitudes in organizational settings.

Technological interdependence: the extent to which the work tasks performed in an organization by one department or team member affect the task performance of other departments or team members. It can be high or low.

Thematic apperception test:	a type of 'projective' assessment in which the individual is shown ambiguous pictures and is invited to create stories of what may be happening in these pictures, projecting their own interests and preoccupations into their accounts, which are scored in terms of their achievement, affiliation or power imagery (see **projective test**).
Time-and-motion studies:	measurement and recording techniques which attempt to make operations more efficient.
Time span of responsibility:	the time period for which an individual's decisions can commit an organization.
Total quality management:	a philosophy of management that is driven by customer needs and expectations, and which is committed to continuous improvement.
Traditional authority:	the belief that the ruler had a natural right to rule. This right is either God-given or by descent. The authority enjoyed by kings and queens would be of this type.
Trait:	a relatively stable quality or attribute of an individual's personality, influencing behaviour in a particular direction. Examples of traits include shyness, excitability, reliability and moodiness (see **type**).
Transactional leader:	a leader who treats relationships with followers in terms of an exchange, giving followers what they want in return for what the leader desires, following prescribed tasks to pursue established goals (see **transformational leader**).
Transformational leader:	a leader who treats relationships with followers in terms of motivation and commitment, influencing and inspiring followers to give more than mechanical compliance to orders and to change organizational performance radically (see **transactional leader**).
Trigger of change:	any 'disorganizing pressure', arising outside or inside the organization, indicating that current arrangements, systems, procedures, rules and other aspects of organization structure and process are no longer effective.
Type:	a descriptive label for a distinct pattern of personality characteristics. Examples of personality types include extrovert, neurotic, conscientious and agreeable (see **trait**).
Type A personality:	a behaviour syndrome which concerns a combination of emotions and behaviours characterized by ambition, hostility, impatience and a sense of constant time pressure. If you have a Type A personality, you are more likely to suffer stress-related disorders and coronary disease (see **type** and **Type B personality**).
Type B personality:	a behaviour syndrome which concerns a combination of emotions and behaviours characterized by relaxation, calm, lack of preoccupation with achievement and an ability to take time to enjoy leisure. If you have a Type B personality, you are less likely to suffer stress-related disorders and coronary disease (see **type** and **Type A personality**).
Uncertainty:	a condition in which managers have a low knowledge of alternatives, a low knowledge of the probability of these being available, can to some degree calculate the costs and benefits of each alternative, but have no predictability of outcomes.
Uncertainty avoidance:	the extent to which members of a society feel threatened by ambiguous situations and have created beliefs and institutions which try to avoid these.
Unilateral agreement:	a co-operative arrangement in which one firm provides another with a service, on a fairly intimate basis, in exchange for money.
Unitarist frame of reference:	a perspective on conflict which sees management and employee interests as coincident and which thus regards (organizational) conflict as harmful and to be avoided.
Unstructured task:	a task with ambiguous goals, many correct solutions and satisfactory outcomes, many ways of achieving acceptable outcomes, and vague criteria of success (see **structured task**).
Valence:	the perceived value or degree of preference that an individual has for a particular outcome. As one may either seek or avoid certain outcomes, or be ambivalent about them, valence can be positive, negative or neutral (see **expectancy theory** of motivation).
Vertical integration:	a situation where one company buys another in order to make the latter's output its own input, thereby securing that source of supply through ownership.

Vertical loading factors: methods for enriching work content and improving motivation, through removing controls, increasing accountability, creating natural work units, providing direct feedback, introducing new tasks, allocating special assignments and granting additional authority (see **job enrichment** and **content factors**).

Virtual organization: (1) several conventional companies working very closely together (even fronting the market as one organization) with electronic channels or even common systems of communication; (2) an organization where a large number of the organization members use electronic channels as their main (or even only) medium of contact with each other, and with the rest of the organization.

Yerkes–Dodson law: a psychology hypothesis which states that task performance increases as our state of arousal increases, and that beyond some 'optimal' point, we become overwhelmed by the level of stimulation or pressure and performance starts to fall.

Subject Index

Note: Page references in *italics* refer to figures; those in **bold** refer to Tables

Name Index